W9-CUA-789

THE LAW OF ARMED CONFLICT
International Humanitarian Law in War

The Law of Armed Conflict: International Humanitarian Law in War introduces law students, undergraduates, and other interested readers to the law of war in an age of terrorism. What law of armed conflict (LOAC) or its civilian counterpart, international humanitarian law (IHL), applies in a particular armed conflict? Are terrorists legally bound to abide by that law? What is the status of the participants in an armed conflict? What constitutes a war crime? What (or who) is a lawful target and how are targeting decisions made? What are "rules of engagement" and who formulates them? Which weapons are unlawful and what renders them such? How can an autonomous weapon system be bound by the law of armed conflict? What is the status of land mines, cluster munitions, and white phosphorus in LOAC, in international law, and in American law? Is a cyberattack a war crime? Why were Guantánamo military commissions a failure? This book takes the student through these LOAC/IHL questions and more, employing real-world examples, moving from the basics to the finer points of battlefield law. The book is a United States–weighted text that incorporates lessons and legal opinions from jurisdictions worldwide. From Nuremberg to 9/11, from courts-martial to the U.S. Supreme Court, from the nineteenth to the twenty-first centuries, the law of war is explained, interpreted, and applied.

Gary D. Solis is a retired Professor of Law of the United States Military Academy, where he taught the law of armed conflict and directed West Point's Law of War program for six years. He was a 2007 Library of Congress scholar in residence. He also is a retired U.S. Marine Corps lieutenant colonel, having twice served in Vietnam, where he was a company commander. He holds law degrees from the University of California at Davis and George Washington University. He has a doctorate in the law of war from the London School of Economics and Political Science. He is a member of the American Law Institute and, as an adjunct professor, teaches the law of war at Georgetown University Law Center. His books include *Marines and Military Law in Vietnam* (1989) and *Son Thang: An American War Crime* (1997).

The Law of Armed Conflict

INTERNATIONAL HUMANITARIAN LAW IN WAR

Second Edition

Gary D. Solis
United States Military Academy (Retired)

CAMBRIDGE
UNIVERSITY PRESS

CAMBRIDGE
UNIVERSITY PRESS

32 Avenue of the Americas, New York NY 10013

Cambridge University Press is part of the University of Cambridge.

It furthers the University's mission by disseminating knowledge in the pursuit of education, learning, and research at the highest international levels of excellence.

www.cambridge.org
Information on this title: www.cambridge.org/9781107135604

© Gary D. Solis 2016

First published 2010
Second edition 2016

Printed in the United States of America by Sheridan Books, Inc.

A catalog record for this publication is available from the British Library.

Contents

LAW OF ARMED CONFLICT AND INTERNATIONAL
HUMANITARIAN LAW: A FRAMEWORK

**LAW OF ARMED CONFLICT AND INTERNATIONAL
HUMANITARIAN LAW: BATTLEFIELD ISSUES**

Contents

DEALING WITH VIOLATIONS OF CUSTOMS AND USAGES
OF WARFARE

Foreword

It gives me great pleasure to contribute the Foreword to this second edition of *The Law of Armed Conflict*. I have had the good fortune of working with the author, Dr. Gary Solis, for fifteen years. He is a gifted teacher, and a mentor to America's military and civilian youth. For years prior to our meeting, I knew of him by virtue of his stellar reputation in military legal circles. We finally met when serving together on the faculty of the Department of Law at the United States Military Academy, at West Point.

Dr. Solis is one of the nation's leading scholars of the law of armed conflict, with a deep and wide-ranging expertise. Significantly, he also is a retired U.S. Marine Corps officer with twenty-six years active service. His combat experience as an armor officer and troop commander gives him personal experience with many of the topics about which he writes.

While at the United States Military Academy, Dr. Solis created and taught a Law of Armed Conflict program, which included the first modern West Point elective on the subject. In 2006, he received the prestigious Apgar Award as the Military Academy's outstanding professor, military or civilian, for excellence in teaching. At West Point, Dr. Solis laid the foundation for this outstanding book. Over the years he continued to teach the law of war at West Point, then at Georgetown University, George Washington University, and the University of California, Davis, continually refining the book's instructional value.

I have taught the Law of Armed Conflict at West Point for nine years, using this textbook since it was first published. Every term, cadets praise it as thought provoking, practical, and easy to read: high praise from a knowledgeable audience. Having taught the law of war to graduate students, undergraduates, and American and international military students, I can say that this book is an essential resource for students and professors alike. It addresses basic issues relevant to modern armed conflicts involving nonstate actors who recognize no law and covers armed conflict topics that were unanticipated just a few years ago.

For law schools, military educational institutions, undergraduate courses, and practitioners, *The Law of Armed Conflict* is a textbook that I recommend enthusiastically. It does not matter whether the reader has military experience or not. The book is jargon-free and replete with interesting clarifying examples and cases, recent and historical. My cadets are drawn into the material, riveted by those features. "Sidebars," in shaded boxes throughout the text, provide colorful brief accounts that bring the law of armed conflict to life. I know of no one associated with this discipline who does not have a copy of *The Law of Armed Conflict* on his or her bookshelf. Not surprisingly, the first edition was awarded the American Society of International Law's 2011 Certificate of Merit, as the year's best "Contribution to a Specialized Field of International Law."

This edition only improves on the first. Besides updating first edition topics, it adds five new chapters. I cannot overstate the importance of the new chapter on cyber warfare, which gives clarity to the application of the law of war to the cyber domain. Likewise, the new chapter on Guantánamo's military commissions adds depth and understanding to that controversial subject. The second edition also explores emerging legal issues raised by U.S. forces crossing national boundaries to pursue and confront terrorist groups that attack and then retreat into neighboring "safe harbor" states. Dr. Solis defines the law of war issues and points the direction in which the law seems to be headed, at the same time interweaving his views, as well as other perspectives in agreement and disagreement. These new topics and perspectives will add to the value of any classroom discussion.

I applaud the supplementing of first edition chapters, including the growing influence of human rights law in warfare. Dr. Solis correctly notes the strong past U.S. resistance to the European incorporation of greater human rights in armed conflict, as well as the United States' current softening of that resistance. Human rights law is particularly relevant to regulating noninternational armed conflicts, in which the law of war is not as well developed as it is in international armed conflicts.

The subchapter on continuous combat function is expanded in the second edition: again, a welcome addition. The United States, in interpreting the concept of direct participation in hostilities by civilians, has embraced continuous combat function status as a basis for targeting terrorists. In addressing these issues Dr. Solis is in the forefront of the development of the law of armed conflict.

The modern battlefield is increasingly complex and uncertain. Only through a greater understanding of the intersection of law and warfare can we strike an appropriate balance between military operations and humanitarian concerns. This book's contributions to the understanding of the law of armed conflict will benefit another generation of students, teachers, and practitioners. I am honored to write its Foreword.

David Wallace
Colonel, United States Army
Professor and Head, Department of Law
United States Military Academy
West Point, New York

Preface and Acknowledgments

> It used to be a simple thing to fight a battle. . . . In a perfect world, a general would get up and say, "Follow me, men," and everybody would say, "Aye, sir" and would run off. But that's not the world anymore. . . . [Now] you have to have a lawyer or a dozen.
>
> General James L. Jones, U.S. Marine Corps, while Supreme Allied Commander, Europe

Since the initial publication of this text, only a few years ago, armed conflicts have changed dramatically. Combatant operations are more sophisticated, more technical, more "wired," and more lethal. Certainly the law of armed conflict (LOAC) still applies but, like every system of laws, it continues to evolve and mature. Today, state practice can become customary law with dizzying speed. Yesterday's settled law becomes today's debatable hypothesis. But LOAC still applies, even if sometimes murky at the edges.

This is a textbook for law students and upper-division undergraduates. A military background is not required. The text takes the reader from the essentials of LOAC to an awareness of some of the finer points of battlefield law. It refers to hundreds of cases, including American courts-martial. Many are dealt with in detail, most only in passing, but all contribute to an understanding of LOAC or, as civilians refer to it, international humanitarian law (IHL). The text concentrates exclusively on *jus in bello* – law on the battlefield – to the exclusion of *jus ad bellum*, the lawfulness of the resort to force. It does not include law of war at sea, or law of air warfare.

This is not a national security law text nor a history book, nor an ethics study. Elements of those subjects are inextricably included, particularly history, but they are not the book's main focus. The text is liberally footnoted so that readers will have a broad reference base if they wish to study an issue more deeply. Appellate opinions and legal materials are included to illustrate how *jus in bello* concepts have been applied.

The book was born in the classrooms of West Point and largely shaped in Georgetown University Law Center seminars. At West Point, knowing that my cadet students would soon put these lessons into practice in combat gave particular focus and immediacy to the book's content. Discussing and arguing LOAC/IHL issues with soldiers and Marines fresh from duty in Iraq, Afghanistan, Kosovo, and Africa, honed its arguments and conclusions. My own twenty-six-year Marine Corps career provided insights, as well.

Some will disagree with interpretations included here. Occasionally, conclusions are drawn when international consensus is not yet fully formed – little in public international law is clearly black or clearly white. That is not to suggest that I form conclusions merely for the sake of dispelling ambiguity, but where the weight of authority, in my view, indicates a nascent conclusion in an unsettled area, that conclusion is stated.

LOAC/IHL is not particularly arcane or complex, but, contrary to the expectations of some, neither is it merely instinctive. One cannot "know" the law of war through a presumption of what sounds morally right or wrong. It is not that easy. Still, in its general outlines, LOAC/IHL is a relatively narrow aspect of public international law, not especially arduous or opaque.

In a world where combat is broadcast worldwide in real time, war fighters are expected to meet a high standard of conduct and judgment. In unclear situations, when death is the rule and violence the norm, how do young combatants decide, instantly and under fire, what is right and what is wrong – not only morally, but legally? A knowledge of LOAC/IHL provides some of the answers.

The text is heavily United States weighted, but it is more than a statement solely of American positions. It incorporates lessons from the British, Dutch, Israelis, and others. Cases from around the world are included. My hope is that this textbook, and particularly this second edition, will contribute to the betterment of armed forces everywhere and to the intellectual understanding of students, civilian and military, who read it.

I thank Colonel Dave Wallace, a wonderful teacher and the Head of West Point's Department of Law. He steadfastly supports my writing, and my teaching at the Military Academy. Colonel Fred Borch, himself a fine writer and a military historian of impressive breadth, continues to be similarly supportive. Fred and Dave are the best of brothers. Colonel Hays Parks, a passionate LOAC scholar, a prolific writer, a shooter of anything with a trigger, and a friend of more than forty years, remains in a class of one.

Institutions that have supported me and encouraged the broader teaching of law of armed conflict include the United States Military Academy, which understands the critical need to teach young officers the law of war, and the Army's Judge Advocate General's Center and School, which provides a teaching platform for me. The International Committee of the Red Cross has always generously supported my teaching efforts and those of many others who seek to get the IHL word out. Thank you all.

In writing this text I could not have had a better guide and adviser than John Berger, Cambridge University Press Senior Editor. He is a friend to treasure. And to Andrea, always patient, ever helpful and supportive, "thank you" will never be enough.

I do not have a research assistant. Any mistakes in this text are mine alone.

Semper Fidelis
GDS

Table of Cases

U.S. Domestic Cases Involving LOAC/IHL-Related Charges

U.S. Military Cases Involving LOAC/IHL-Related Charges

International Criminal Tribunal for the Former Yugoslavia Cases

Table of Treaties

Law of Armed Conflict: International Humanitarian Law in War

1 Rules of War, Laws of War

1.0 Introduction

The study of the law of armed conflict (LOAC), or international humanitarian law (IHL), is not unlike building a house. First, one lays the foundation for the structure. Then a framework is erected that is tied to the foundation. Finally, outer walls and interior rooms are constructed, with the framework and foundation providing their support. The study of LOAC and IHL is much the same.

We begin by answering two foundational questions. We determine what LOAC applies in the conflict under consideration; that is, what is the conflict status? This requires that we know what LOAC and IHL are: what our building materials consist of and some of their history.

Our second foundational question is, what are the statuses of the various participants in our armed conflict? What individual statuses are possible? When do those statuses apply, how are they determined, and who assigns them? With answers to these two questions, conflict status and individual status, a basic foundation is laid.

Next, a LOAC/IHL framework is erected. What constitutes LOAC and IHL? What are their guiding principles and core values? The framework is essential for all that follows – for the many individual issues, large and small, that make up the innumerable "rooms" of our LOAC/IHL house.

We develop these questions in this chapter and in succeeding chapters. Not all armed conflict law is considered in this single volume. However, the basics are here. In this chapter, we examine the rich history of LOAC. Where did it arise, and when? Who was involved? Why was it considered necessary?

1.1 The Law of War: A Thumbnail History

If Cicero (106–43 B.C.) actually said, *"inter arma leges silent"* – in time of war the laws are silent – in a sense, he was correct. If laws were initially absent, however, there were *rules* attempting to limit armed combat virtually from the time men began to fight in organized groups. Theodor Meron notes that "even when followed, ancient humanitarian rules were soft and malleable and offered little if any expectation of compliance."[1] Still, as John Keegan writes, "War may have got worse with the passage of time, but the

---

[1] Theodor Meron, *Bloody Constraint: War and Chivalry in Shakespeare* (New York: Oxford University Press, 1998), 49.

ethic of restraint has rarely been wholly absent from its practice. . . . Even in the age of total warfare when, as in Cicero's day, war was considered a normal condition, and the inherent right of sovereign States presided, there remained taboos, enshrined in law and thankfully widely observed."[2]

When did men begin to fight in groups? Cave art of the New Stone Age, ten thousand years ago, depicts bowmen apparently in conflict.[3] Since that time, there have been few periods in human history when there has not been an armed conflict someplace.[4] Keegan tells us that Mesopotamia developed a military system of defense as early as 3000 B.C. In approximately 2700 B.C. Gilgamesh, who ruled the city of Uruk, apparently undertook one of history's first offensive military campaigns.[5] Thus, warfare entered the world at least five thousand years ago. Limitations on its conduct were close behind and, we are told, "during the five thousand six hundred years of written history, fourteen thousand six hundred wars have been recorded."[6]

No written early Roman military code survives, although it is known that within the Roman army's ranks, many of today's military criminal offenses were recognized.[7] In the early days of the empire, few rules applied to combat against non-Romans. Those that did apply were based largely on natural law. "The conduct of [Roman] war was essentially unrestrained. Prisoners could be enslaved or massacred; plunder was general; and no distinction was recognized between combatants and noncombatants."[8]

With time, that changed. Around 1400 B.C., Egypt had agreements with Sumeria and other states regarding the treatment of prisoners.[9] In about 200 B.C., in Asia, a variety of Hindu texts describe numerous rules of war. The *Mahabharata*, an epic Sanskrit poem (200 B.C.–200 A.D.), reflected Hindu beliefs. It required that "a King should never do such an injury to his foe as would rankle the latter's heart."[10] It decreed that one should cease fighting when an opponent becomes disabled; that wounded men and persons who surrender should not be killed; that noncombatants should not be engaged in combat; and that places of public worship should not be molested.[11] The Hindu Code of Manu directs that treacherous weapons, such as barbed or poisoned arrows, are forbidden and that an enemy attempting to surrender, or one badly wounded, should not be killed.[12]

In the sixth century B.C., Sun Tzu counseled limitations on armed conflict as well. "In chariot battles when chariots are captured, then ten-chariot unit commanders will

---

[2] John Keegan, *War and Our World* (New York: Vintage Books, 2001), 26.

[3] John Keegan, *A History of Warfare* (New York: Knopf, 1993), 119.

[4] A brief period from 100 to 200 A.D. is perhaps the only time the world has enjoyed peace. That period resulted from the Roman Empire's military ascendancy over all opposition.

[5] Keegan, *War and Our World*, supra, note 3, at 29.

[6] James Hillman, *A Terrible Love of War* (New York: Penguin Books, 2004), 17.

[7] Col. William Winthrop, *Military Law and Precedents*, 2d ed. (Washington: GPO, 1920), 17.

[8] Robert C. Stacey, "The Age of Chivalry," in Michael Howard, George J. Andreopoulos, and Mark R. Shulman, eds., *The Laws of War* (New Haven, CT: Yale University Press, 1994), 27.

[9] Jean Pictet, *Development and Principles of International Humanitarian Law* (Leiden: Kluwer, 1985), 7–8.

[10] Cited in Leslie C. Green, *The Contemporary Law of Armed Conflict*, 2d ed. (Manchester: Manchester University Press, 2000), 21.

[11] Suurya P. Subedi, "The Concept in Hinduism of 'Just War,'" 8-2 *J. of Conflict & Security L.* (Oct. 2003), 339, 355–6.

[12] K. P. Jayaswal, *Manu and Yâjñavalkya, A Comparison and A Contrast: A Treatise on the Basic Hindu Law* (Calcutta: Butterworth, 1930), 106.

reward the first to capture them and will switch battle standards and flags, their chariots are mixed with ours and driven, their soldiers are treated kindly when given care."[13] Sun Tzu did not suggest that his humanitarian admonitions constituted laws, or even rules of war. They were simply an effective means of waging war.

The Roman emperor Maurice, in the late sixth century A.D., published his *Strategica*. It directed, among other things, that a soldier who injured a civilian should make every effort to repair the injury, or pay twofold damages.[14]

In 621, at Aqaba, Muhammad's followers who committed to a jihad for Islam were bound to satisfy a number of conditions in its conduct. "If he has killed he must not mutilate," for example.[15] (Yet, Abyssinian victors often cut off the right hands and left feet of vanquished foes.)[16]

Under Innocent II, use of the crossbow was forbidden as "deadly and odious to God" by the Catholic Second Lateran Council in 1139, and the Third Lateran Council prescribed humane treatment of prisoners of war.[17]

During the feudal period, in the twelfth and thirteenth centuries, knights observed rules of chivalry, a major historical basis for LOAC. "Chivalry meant the duty to act honorably, even in war. The humane and noble ideals of chivalry included justice and loyalty, courage, honour and mercy, the obligations not to kill or otherwise take advantage of the vanquished enemy, and to keep one's word. ... Seldom if ever realized in full ... while humanizing warfare, chivalry also contributed to the legitimizing of war."[18] No authority was recognized that laid down universal rules of war during this period. "The 'special law' of knights was the law of arms, and it was founded in the canon and civil laws. ... These special laws were extensions of the two great written laws (just as they in turn were extensions of the natural law and the *jus jentium*), adding particular rules binding only on persons of a particular class."[19] Settling disputes of honor was left to the opinions of heralds and more experienced knights. Formal disputes over matters such as ransoms and prisoners were decided by "persons [who] had been appointed to try just that kind of matter. ... knights,

---

[13] J. H. Huang trans., *Sun Tzu: The New Translation* (New York: Quill, 1933), 46.

[14] C. E. Brand, *Roman Military Law* (Austin: University of Texas, 1968), 195–6. Also see: Timothy L. H. McCormack, "From Sun Tzu to the Sixth Committee: The Evolution of an International Criminal Law Regime," in Timothy L. H. McCormack and Gerry J. Simpson, eds., *The Law of War Crimes: National and International Approaches* (The Hague: Kluwer, 1997), 31–63, 35.

[15] Majid Khadduri, *War and Peace in the Law of Islam* (Baltimore: Johns Hopkins University Press, 1955), 87.

[16] Gerrit W. Gong, *The Standard of "Civilization" in International Society* (Oxford: Clarendon Press, 1984), 122–3.

[17] G.I.A.D. Draper, "The Interaction of Christianity and Chivalry in the Historical Development of the Laws of War," 5–3 *Int'l Rev. of Red Cross* (1965). The earliest crossbows date to 400 B.C. and the Chinese army. European crossbows date to about 1200, introduced from the East during the Crusades. Military effectiveness superseded theological concerns, for crossbows were widely employed until the seventeenth century. Still, Canon 29 of the Second Lateran Council held, "We forbid under penalty of anathema that that deadly and God-detested art of stingers and archers be in the future exercised against Christians and Catholics." Gregory M. Reichberg, Henrik Syse, and Endre Begby, eds., *The Ethics of War* (Malden, MA: Blackwell Publishing, 2006), 97.

[18] Meron, *Bloody Constraint*, supra, note 1, at 4–5.

[19] M. H. Keen, *The Laws of War in the Late Middle Ages* (London: Routledge & Keegan Paul, 1965), 15. In legal theory, *jus gentium* refers to that law established for all men by natural reason, as distinguished from *jus civile*, the law particular to one state or people.

men who would understand just what difficulties [the individual] was in and what his arguments meant."[20] To today's war fighter, chivalry may seem an idealistically romantic notion.

Nevertheless, as a catalogue of virtues and values, it remains an enviable model for honourable conduct in peace and in war. Commands to spare the enemy who asks for mercy, to aid women in distress, to keep one's promise, to act charitably and to be magnanimous transcend any one particular historical period or sociological context. . . . The idea that chivalry requires soldiers to act in a civilized manner is one of its most enduring legacies.[21]

Doubters argue that "chivalric rules actually served to protect the lives and property of privileged knights and nobles, entitling them to plunder and kill peasant soldiers, non-Christian enemies, and civilians,"[22] but that seems a harsh view. It is true that chivalry's code only applied among Christians and knights. The Scottish nationalist Sir William Wallace – "Braveheart" – was no knight. He was executed in 1305, after being convicted by an English court of atrocities in war, "sparing neither age nor sex, monk nor nun."[23] His conviction followed 1279's Statute of Westminster, which authorized the Crown to punish "soldiers" for violations of "the law and customs of the realm."[24] In 1386, Richard II's *Ordinance for the Government of the Army* decreed death for acts of violence against women and priests, the burning of houses, and the desecration of churches.[25] Henry V's ordinances of war, promulgated in 1419, further codified rules protecting women and clergy.

At Agincourt, in 1415, England's Henry V defeated the French in the Hundred Years' War and conquered much of France. Henry's longbow men made obsolete many methods of warring in the age of chivalry. Shakespeare tells us that, at Agincourt, King Harry, believing that the battle was lost and that his French prisoners would soon join with the approaching French soldiers, gave a fateful order:

> King Harry: The French have reinforced their scattered men. Then every soldier kill his prisoners. (*The soldiers kill their prisoners.*)[26]
>
> Fluellen: Kill the poys and the luggage! 'Tis expressly against the laws of arms. 'Tis as arrant a piece of knavery, mark you now, as can be offert. In your conscience now, is it not?
>
> Gower: 'Tis certain there's not a boy left alive. And the cowardly rascals that ran from the battle ha' done this slaughter. Besides, they have burned and carried away all that was in the King's tent; wherefore the King most worthily hath caused every soldier to cut his prisoner's throat. O 'tis a gallant king.[27]

Was Henry's order a war crime? Shakespeare's Fluellen and Gower plainly thought so. Nevertheless, chivalry remains a valuable, if distant, precursor to today's LOAC.

---

[20] Id., at 26.   [21] Id., at 108, 118.

[22] Chris af Jochnick and Roger Normand, "The Legitimation of Violence: A Critical History of the Laws of War," 35–1 *Harvard Int'l L. J.* (1994), 49, 61.

[23] Georg Schwarzenberger, "Judgment of Nuremberg," 21 *Tulsa L. Rev.* (1947), 330.

[24] Joseph W. Bishop Jr., *Justice under Fire: A Study of Military Law* (New York: Charterhouse, 1974), 4.

[25] Georg Schwarzenberger, *International Law: As Applied by International Courts and Tribunals*, Vol. II (London: Stevens & Sons, 1968), 15–16.

[26] William Shakespeare, *Henry V*, IV.vi.35–8.   [27] Id., vii.1–10

1.1.1 *The First International War Crime Prosecution?*

The trial of Peter von Hagenbach in Breisach, Austria, in 1474 is often cited as the first international war crime prosecution.[28] He was tried by an ad hoc tribunal of twenty-eight judges from Austria and its allied states of the Hanseatic cities for murder, rape, and other crimes. Hagenbach's defense was one still heard today: He was only following orders. His defense met the same response it usually receives today: He was convicted and hanged. Hagenbach's offenses did not actually transpire during a time of war and thus were not war crimes, strictly speaking. It also may be asked whether the prosecuting allied states at von Hagenbach's trial constituted an "international" body.[29] The event is nevertheless significant in representing one of the earliest trials resulting in personal criminal responsibility for the violation of international criminal norms.

1.1.2 *The Emergence of Battlefield Codes*

Meanwhile, battlefield rules and laws continued to sprout. In Europe, in 1590, the Free Netherlands adopted Articles of War and, in 1621, Sweden's Gustavus Adolphus published his *Articles of Military Lawwes to Be Observed in the Warres*, which were to become the basis for England's later Articles of War. Those English Articles in turn became the basis for the fledgling United States' first Articles of War. The Treaty of Westphalia, in 1648, was the first treaty between warring states to require the return, without ransom, of captured soldiers. Such early European codes, dissimilar and geographically scattered as they were, are significant.[30] They established precedents for other states and raised enforcement models for battlefield offenses – courts-martial, in the case of the British Articles of War. In the second half of the nineteenth century, the previously common battlefield practices and restrictions – customary law of war – began to coalesce into generalized rules, becoming codified and extended by treaties and domestic laws. Manuals on the subject, such as the 1884 British *Manual of Military Law*, were published.

By the mid-nineteenth century, states began writing codes that incorporated humanitarian ideals for their soldiers – the violation of which called for punishments: in other words, military laws. At the same time, there were few multinational treaties that imposed accepted limitations on battlefield conduct, with penalties for their violation. That would have to wait until the Hague Regulation IV of 1907. Even then, battlefield laws would lack norms of personal accountability for crimes in combat.

1.2 Why Regulate Battlefield Conduct?

All's fair in love and war? Hardly! Any divorce lawyer will attest that "all" is decidedly not fair in love. Just as surely, all is not fair in war. There are good reasons why warfare

---

[28] Schwarzenberger, supra, note 23, at 462–6.

[29] For a lengthier examination of von Hagenbach's case, see "Cases and Materials," this chapter. Further discussion, and the early development of the law of war, are in McCormack, "From Sun Tzu to the Sixth Committee," in McCormack and Simpson, *Law of War Crimes*, supra, note 14, at 37–9.

[30] Written European military codes were many. In the fifth century, the Frankish Salians had a military code, as did the Goths, the Lombards, the Burgundians, and the Bavarians. The first French military law code dated from 1378, the first German code from 1487, the first Free Netherlands code from 1590. A Russian military code appeared in 1715. See Winthrop, supra, note 7, at 17–8.

needs to be regulated. Simple humanitarian concerns should limit battlefield conduct. War is not a contest to see who can most effectively injure one's opponent. War cannot be simple blood sport. Indeed, modern LOAC has been largely driven by humanitarian concerns.

There are concrete, valid reasons to regulate battlefield conduct. LOAC differentiates war from riot, piracy, and generalized insurrection. It allows a moral acceptance of the sometimes-repugnant acts necessarily done on battlefields, and it lends dignity, even honor, to the sacrifices of a nation's soldiers. "War is distinguishable from murder and massacre only when restrictions are established on the reach of battle."[31] The idea of war as indiscriminate violence suggests violence as an end in itself, and that is antithetical to the fact that war is a goal-oriented activity directed to attaining political objectives. Even the view that all necessary means to achieving victory are permissible – a short step away from "all's fair in love and war" – implicitly recognizes that hostilities are limited to the means considered "necessary," further implying that violence superfluous to obtaining a military objective is *unnecessary* and thus may be proscribed.

An armed conflict might be compared to a stoplight at a busy intersection. Through the day, thousands of vehicles pass, stop, and turn at the intersection's constantly changing light, all without incident. Eventually, however, there will be an incident resulting in death or damage or both. So it is on a battlefield, where combatants, civilians, and unprivileged belligerents intersect a thousand times a day. Eventually, there will be a law of war incident. As it pertains to individuals, LOAC, perhaps more than any other branch of law, is likely to fail. In a sense, its goal is virtually impossible: to introduce moderation and restraint into an activity uniquely contrary to those qualities. At the best of times, LOAC is "never more than imperfectly observed, and at the worst of times is very poorly observed indeed."[32] In fact, one must admit that LOAC really does not "work" well at all. However, Geoffrey Best writes, "We should perhaps not so much complain that the law of war does not work well, as marvel that it works at all."[33]

It may seem paradoxical that war, the ultimate breakdown of law, should be conducted in accordance with laws. But so it is. Why would a state fighting for survival allow itself to be hobbled by legal restrictions? In fact, nations of the eighteenth and nineteenth centuries, when LOAC was in its formative stages, did not regard themselves as fighting for survival. Territory, not ideology, was the usual basis for war. Defeat meant the realignment of national boundaries, not the subjugation of the defeated population nor the dissolution of the vanquished state. "Analysis of war prior to nineteenth-century industrialization and Napoleonic enthusiasm indicates that wars were less violent and less significant and were subject to cultural restraints."[34] War will always constitute suffering and personal tragedy, but rules of warfare are intended to prevent *unnecessary* suffering that yields little or no military advantage. Critics argue that, in war, states will always put their own interests above all else, and any battlefield law that clashes with those interests will be disregarded. As we shall see, LOAC has been created by states that have their own interests,

---

[31] Michael Walzer, *Just and Unjust Wars*, 3d ed. (New York: Basic Books, 2000), 42.
[32] Geoffrey Best, *Humanity in Warfare* (London: Weidenfeld & Nicolson, 1980), 11.   [33] Id., 12.
[34] Hillman, *A Terrible Love of War*, supra, note 6, at 168.

particularly the interests of their own armed forces, in mind. LOAC is hardly an imposition on states by faceless external authorities.[35]

In modern times, despite Clausewitz's assertion that the laws of war are "almost imperceptible and hardly worth mentioning,"[36] they remain the best answer to the opposing tensions of the necessities of war and the requirements of civilization. "It is the function of the rules of warfare to impose some limits, however ineffective, to a complete reversion to anarchy by the establishment of minimum standards on the conduct of war."[37] The temporary advantages of breaching LOAC are far outweighed by the ultimate disadvantages. A basic reason to comply with LOAC is reciprocity.

> Reciprocity, a natural consequence of a system of states equal to one another, was one of the main justifications for the existence and the development of the law of war. . . . In a world of armies, each agrees to follow the law for one overriding reason: the expectation that your enemies will follow the same law and give you the same protection that you afford them. Derived from the medieval tradition of chivalry, this version of legality guaranteed a modicum of fair play even during war.[38]

"Unnecessary killing and devastation should be prohibited if only on military grounds. It merely increases hostility and hampers the willingness to surrender."[39] An example was World War II in the Pacific. After an early series of false surrenders and prisoner atrocities, Pacific island combat was marked by an unwillingness of either side to surrender, and a savagery of the worst kind by both sides resulted.[40] Eugene Sledge, author of an iconic World War II memoir, *With the Old Breed*, wrote, "You became more callous. . . . You developed an attitude of no mercy because they had no mercy on us. It was a no-quarter, savage kind of thing. . . . I've seen guys shoot Japanese wounded when it really was not necessary . . . . It was so savage. We were savages."[41] On Iwo Jima, of 21,000–23,000 Japanese combatants, 20,703 were killed. When the island was declared secure, only 212 Japanese surrendered[42] – less than 2 percent – because Marines and soldiers fearing that they would be murdered or mistreated if they surrendered simply put surrender out of mind and fought on, thereby increasing casualties to both sides. After the 1943 battle for Tarawa, of the defending Japanese force of roughly 5,000 combatants,

---

[35] Adam Roberts and Richard Guelff, *Documents on the Law of War*, 3d ed. (Oxford: Oxford University Press, 2000), 31.

[36] Carl von Clausewitz, *On War*, A. Rapoport, ed. (London: Penguin Books, 1982), 101. However, Clausewitz also wrote, "Therefore, if we find that civilized nations do not put their prisoners to death, do not devastate towns and countries, this is because their intelligence . . . taught them more effectual means of applying force than these rude acts of mere instinct." Id., at 103.

[37] Schwarzenberger, supra, note 23, at 10.

[38] Theoodor Meron, *The Making of International Criminal Justice* (Oxford: Oxford University Press, 2011), 54.

[39] Bert V. A. Röling, "Are Grotius' Ideas Obsolete in an Expanded World?" in Hedley Bull, Benedict Kingsbury, and Adam Roberts, eds., *Hugo Grotius and International Relations* (Oxford: Clarendon Press, 1990), 287.

[40] See Eugene Sledge, *With the Old Breed at Peleliu and Okinawa* (Novato, CA: Presidio Press, 1981) for examples of savagery in the Pacific theater. Paul Fussell, *Wartime: Understanding and Behavior in the Second World War* (New York: Oxford University Press, 1989), relates similar accounts from the European theater.

[41] Sledge, *With the Old Breed*, id.

[42] Stephen J. Lofgren, ed., "Diary of First Lieutenant Sugihara Kinryû: Iwo Jima, January – February 1945," 59–97. J. *Military History* (Jan. 1995).

a mere 146 prisoners were taken, all but 17 of those being Korean laborers. Of the military defenders, 99.4 percent were killed.[43] "Violations . . . can also result in a breakdown of troop discipline, command control and force security; subject troops to reciprocal violations on the battlefield or [in] P.W. camps; and cause the defeat of an entire army in a guerrilla or other war through alignment of neutrals on the side of the enemy and hostile public opinion."[44]

The rapacious conduct of World War II Nazis as they crossed Russia toward Moscow and Stalingrad exacerbated a hatred in the Russian civilian population that led to thousands of German deaths at the hands of partisans. Michael Walzer notes, "The best soldiers, the best fighting men, do not loot and . . . rape, do not wantonly kill civilians."[45] Strategically, battlefield crimes may lessen the prospect of an eventual cease-fire. War, then, must be conducted in the interest of peace.

Does LOAC end, or even lessen, the frequency of battlefield crimes? Was Thucydides correct in noting, "The strong do what they can and the weak suffer what they must"? Can we really expect laws to deter violations of IHL? Idi Amin, who robbed and raped Uganda into misery and poverty, ordered the deaths of 300,000 of his countrymen, and admitted having eaten human flesh, died in palatial comfort in Saudi Arabian exile, never called to account for the butchery he ordered during his country's internal warfare. Josef Mengele, the World War II Nazi doctor at the Auschwitz extermination camp – the "Angel of Death" who conducted horrific "medical" experiments on prisoners – escaped to a long and comfortable life in Paraguay and accidentally drowned while enjoying a day at the beach with his family in 1979. He was never tried for his war crimes.

No law will deter the lawless. No criminal code can account for every violator. No municipal or federal law puts an end to civilian criminality. Should we expect more from LOAC? Geoffrey Best writes, "If international law is, in some ways, at the vanishing point of law, the law of war is, perhaps even more conspicuously, at the vanishing point of international law,"[46] but that is no license to surrender to criminality.

Battlefield violations have always occurred, continue to occur, and will occur in the future. Despite training and close discipline, as long as nations give guns to young soldiers, war crimes are going to happen. Recognizing that unpleasant truth is not cynicism so much as an acceptance of reality. Why bother with confining rules in combat, then? The answer: for reasons similar to those that dictate rules in football games – some violence is expected, but not all violence is permitted. Are rules and laws that are frequently violated worthless for their violation? Are speed limits without value because they are commonly exceeded? In the Western world, are the Ten Command- ments, which are commonly disregarded, therefore, of no worth? There always will be limits on acceptable conduct, including conduct on the battlefield. We obey LOAC because we cannot allow ourselves to become what we are fighting and because we cannot be heard to say that we fight for the right while we are seen to commit wrongs. "Military professionals also have desires for law. For starters, they also turn to law to limit

---

[43] Matthew Hughes, "War without Mercy? American Armed Forces and the Deaths of Civilians during the Battle for Saipan, 1944," 75–1 *J. of Military History*, 93, 96 (Jan. 2011).

[44] Jordan J. Paust, letter, 25 *Naval War College Rev.* (Jan.–Feb. 1973), 105.

[45] Michael Walzer, "Two Kinds of Military Responsibility," in Lloyd J. Matthews and Dale E. Brown, eds., *The Parameters of Military Ethics* (VA: Pergamon-Brassey's, 1989), 69.

[46] Best, *Humanity in Warfare*, supra, note 32, at 12.

the violence of warfare, to ensure some safety, some decency, among professionals on different sides of the conflict."[47] We obey the law of war if for no other reason than that reciprocity tells us that what goes around comes around; if we abuse our prisoners today, tomorrow we will be the abused prisoners. We obey the law of war because it is the law and because it is the honorable path for a nation that holds itself up as a protector of oppressed peoples. We obey the law of war because it is the right thing to do. "When principle is involved, be deaf to expediency."[48]

In the calm of a college seminar room, it is easy to denounce the actions of others acting in a combat zone – soldiers, Marines, sailors, and airmen who did not have the luxury of discussion, or opportunity to study a treaty, or time for reflection before they acted. However, no armed service member is likely to be prosecuted for a single law of war violation hastily committed without thought in the heat of combat. When the battle is over, when the combatant is seen to have considered his/her actions before acting wrongly, when the action taken was patently contrary to the law of war, or when the violation was of a repeated nature, then it is reasonable to invoke LOAC.

1.2.1 *Difficult Issues*

Twenty-first-century armed conflicts often have no battlefield in the traditional sense. "Less and less do we see opposing armies take to the field while the Geneva Convention shields civilians on the sidelines. Television journalists show us every day the new characteristic engagement: brutal, neighbor-on-neighbor killing."[49] Armed conflicts have become *intra-*, rather than *interstate* affairs. Thugs seize national power; stateless terrorists attack national infrastructures; children are dragooned into "liberation" armies.

In a perceptive 2007 interview, retired the British general Sir Rupert Smith, who commanded troops in Northern Ireland, Bosnia-Herzegovina, Kosovo, and the Gulf War, noted that

> instead of a world in which peace is understood to be an absence of war and where we move in a linear process of peace-crisis-war-resolution-peace, we are in a world of continuous confrontation. . . . The new wars take place amongst the people as opposed to "between blocks of people", as occurred for instance in the Second World War . . . [in which] there was a clear division as to which side everybody belonged to and whether they were in uniform or not. This is not the case in "wars amongst the people". [Today] the people are part of the terrain of your battlefield . . . the event known as "war" is nowadays especially directed against non-combatants. . . . War as a massive deciding event in a dispute in international affairs, such wars no longer exist. Take the example of the United States, a state with the largest and best-equipped military forces in the world, which is unable to dictate the desired outcome [in Iraq] as it did in the two world wars. . . . The ends to which wars are conducted have changed from the hard, simple, destructive objectives of "industrial war" to the softer and more malleable objectives of changing intentions, to deter, or to establish a safe and secure environment. . . . The objective *is* the will of the people. Tactically the opponent often

[47] David Kennedy, *Of War and Law* (Princeton NJ: Princeton University Press, 2006), 32.
[48] Attributed to Cmdr. Matthew Fontaine Maury, USN (1806–73), a groundbreaking oceanographer.
[49] Capt. Larry Seaquist, USN, "Community War," U.S. Naval Institute's *Proceedings* (Aug. 2000), 56.

operates according to the tenets of the guerrilla . . . seeks to provoke an over-reaction so as to paint the opponent in the colours of the tyrant and oppressor. . . . Your objective is to capture the population's intentions, and the more you treat all the people as your enemy, the more all the people will be your enemy. . . . If you operate so that your measures during conflict are treating all these people as enemies . . . you are acting on behalf of your enemy; you are even co-operating with him, because that is what your opponent is aiming at with his strategy.[50]

How is LOAC to be applied and enforced in these circumstances, on nonbattlefields where the very aim of war has changed? Warfare is no longer as simple as in the mid-twentieth century. But Professor David Kennedy goes too far when he writes, "The - twentieth-century model of war, interstate diplomacy, and international law are all unraveling in the face of low-intensity conflict and the war on terror."[51] The law of war still applies and still can be applied. It still "works," but only through patient, intelligent, and resolute effort by states willing to live by the rule of law.

Why should our side observe LOAC when our opponents disregard it, or are even unaware that such laws exist? One writer points out, "There was once a legal notion, now archaic and never entirely accepted, that less-civilized opponents in effect waived the rules of war by their conduct, permitting the use of more brutal methods against them. That notion will never pass muster in the 21st century. There may be a temptation to think that a barbarous enemy deserves a like response, but this is an invitation to legal, moral, and political disaster."[52] Because there are criminals at large should we pursue them by becoming criminals? If terrorists film themselves beheading captives, shall we therefore behead our captives? We cannot allow ourselves to become that which we fight. Walzer writes, "They can try to kill me, and I can try to kill them. But it is wrong to cut the throats of their wounded or to shoot them down when they are trying to surrender. These judgments are clear enough, I think, and they suggest that war is still, somehow, a rule-governed activity, a world of permissions and prohibitions – a moral world, therefore, in the midst of hell."[53]

The former American secretary of defense Donald Rumsfeld was very wrong when he said, "There's something about the body politic in the United States that they can accept the enemy killing innocent men, women and children and cutting off people's heads, but have zero tolerance for some soldier who does something he shouldn't do."[54] Americans do not "accept" enemy war crimes; rather, we understand we are powerless to stop them when they are happening. We hope our soldiers and Marines and sailors and airmen will meet the killers in another time and place or that we may eventually capture and try the enemy for his crimes. And we rightfully expect our own combatants to meet high standards on the battlefield. As a nation we must be intolerant of lesser conduct.

---

[50] Toni Pfanner, "Interview with General Sir Rupert Smith," 864 *Int'l Rev. of the Red Cross* (Dec. 2006), 720. Emphasis in original.

[51] Kennedy, *Of War and Law*, supra, note 47, at 12.

[52] Michael H. Hoffman, "Rescuing the Law of War: A Way Forward in an Era of Global Terrorism," *Parameters* (Summer 2005), 18, 34.

[53] Walzer, *Just and Unjust Wars*, supra, note 31, at 36.

[54] Bob Woodward, *State of Denial* (New York: Simon & Schuster, 2006), 486.

1.3 Sources of the Law of Armed Conflict

Armed conflict has changed in the twenty-first century, but LOAC remains important, even inviolate, for states that respect the rule of law. Initially, battlefield rules were born of a simple desire to conduct oneself honorably. Self-interest dictates an avoidance of needless cruelty lest that same cruelty be visited upon us. So, from where are battlefield rules drawn? What are the sources of LOAC?

The Statute – the establishing decree – of the International Court of Justice (ICJ) relates the sources of international law that the Court applies. The ICJ, reads its Statute, first looks to international conventions, and then to international custom. Next, the Court will consider "general principles of law recognized by civilized nations," then to judicial decisions, and, finally, to "the teachings of the most highly qualified publicists of the various nations . . . "[55] International conventions – treaties – and custom are the ICJ's primary sources of law.[56]

The LOAC manual used by American armed forces until superseded by a new version in late 2015, Field Manual (FM) 27-10, *The Law of Land Warfare*, taking its cue from the ICJ's Statute, notes that "the law of war is derived from two principle sources . . . Treaties (or conventions, such as the Hague and Geneva Conventions [and] Custom. . . . This body of unwritten or customary law is firmly established by the custom of nations and well defined by recognized authorities on international law."[57]

1.3.1 *Custom*

Custom is one of the two primary bases of the law of war. Customary international law is binding on all states.[58] "At the outset, it is admitted that the quest for custom is not a matter of exact science. There is, unfortunately, no mathematical formula that allows one to derive . . . a customary rule from a specific quantity of practice in combination with a fixed degree of *opino juris*."[59] Summarily stated, "the formation of customary law requires consistent and recurring action . . . by states, coupled with a general recognition by states that such action . . . is required . . . by international law."[60]

Customary law is the "general practice of states which is accepted and observed as law, i.e. from a sense of legal obligation."[61] It arises when state practice is extensive and virtually uniform. A prerequisite for an internationally binding custom is that "the

---

[55] Statute of the International Court of Justice, Article 38.1 (June 26, 1945).

[56] Article 38 is actually an instruction to ICJ judges. International lawyers and tribunals do employ other sources, such as *jus cogens*, equity, and even natural law, to determine the existence of customary law.

[57] Dept. of the Army, FM 27–10: *The Law of Land Warfare*, w/change 1 (DC: GPO, 1956), para. 4.

[58] Exceptions are states that consistently and unequivocally refuse to accept a custom during the process of its formation. Often referred to as "persistent objection," the principle remains a live, if not particularly strong, tenet of international law. Because customary law is based on general patterns of expectation and practice, rather than consent, it is unlikely that a state could persistently object to a customary law. A failure of such an attempt occurred after World War II, at the Nuremberg IMT, when the tribunal upheld provisions of 1907 Hague Regulation IV as having been customary international law by 1939, despite Germany's having persistently objected to the convention as a whole.

[59] Tom Ruys, *"Armed Attack" and Article 51 of the UN Charter* (Cambridge: Cambridge University Press, 2010), 30.

[60] Roberts and Guelff, *Documents*, supra, note 35, at 7.

[61] Theodor Meron, *Human Rights and Humanitarian Norms as Customary Law* (Oxford: Clarendon Press, 1989), 3.

provision concerned should ... be of a fundamentally norm-creating character such as could be regarded as forming the basis of a general rule of law."[62] In other words, a practice begins, and then spreads to other states. The widening practice eventually is accepted by states not as an option but as a requirement, finally maturing into customary law. "Customary international law is widely recognized as a fundamental source of international law."[63] There is no bright line time element for a practice to develop into binding custom, but there must be a "constant and uniform usage" practiced by states.[64] Article 38 of the Statute of the ICJ defines international custom as evidence of a general practice that is extensive and virtually uniform, coupled with a subjective belief by states that such behavior is required by law. Today, the time element is less important than it once was, and custom can now arise in a very short time.[65]

Take, for example, the practice of ships' use of running lights. In the eighteenth century, to reduce the risk of collision, ships based in European ports began to show colored lights when under way at night. To help other ships judge the distance and direction of oncoming ships' lights, a red light was shown on a ship's port side, a green light to starboard. Over time, this maritime safety measure became common, regardless of the ship's flag. Common usage in turn became an accepted custom, and the custom spread throughout the sailing world. The custom, with its clear utility, eventually became a rule, first formulated for British mariners, for instance, in 1862. Finally, the rules for ships' underway lights at night were the basis of the 1889 International Regulations for Preventing Collisions at Sea, adopted by virtually all maritime states. After that, ships no longer showed running lights merely because they recognized it as a wise practice that enhanced the safety of all mariners; now it was required by binding regulation. Usage begat custom begat customary international law begat treaty. So it is with the law of war. Bombing becomes more accurate with the use of laser-designated targets and global-position-satellite (GPS)-guided munitions, and collateral damage is dramatically reduced. Eventually, laser target designation and GPS munitions guidance will likely become not a targeting choice but an armed combat requirement of customary international law and, in time, the subject of treaty-made law.

SIDEBAR. General George Washington was well aware of the customary law of war. "In 1776, American leaders believed that it was not enough to win the war. They also had to win in a way that was consistent with the values of their society and the principles of their cause.... In the critical period of 1776 and 1777, leaders of both the Continental army and the Congress adopted the policy of humanity... Every report of wounded soldiers refused quarter, of starving captives mistreated in the prison hulls at New York, and of the plunder and rapine in New Jersey persuaded leaders in Congress and the army to go a different way, as an act of principle and enlightened self-interest.... Washington ordered that Hessian captives would be treated as human beings with the same rights of humanity for which Americans were striving.... After the battle of Princeton, Washington ordered one of his most trusted officers, Lieutenant Colonel Samuel Blachley Webb, to look after [British prisoners]: 'You are to take charge of [211]

---

[62] *North Sea Continental Shelf* Cases, ICJ Rep. 1969, 41–2.
[63] Pierre-Hugues Verdier and Erik Voeten, "Precedent, Compliance, and Change in Customary International Law: An Explanatory Theory," 108–3 *AJIL* 389 (July 2014).
[64] *Asylum* Case, ICJ Rep. 1959, 276–7.   [65] *North Sea Continental Shelf* Cases, supra, note 62, at para. 74.

> privates of the British Army.... Treat them with humanity, and Let them have no
> reason to Complain of our Copying the brutal example of the British Army....' They
> [American leaders] set a high example, and we have much to learn from them."[66]

A crucial issue in the formation of customary international law is part and parcel of international law itself: Who is to say when "custom" shades into "requirement"? Who decides when running lights are not just a good idea, but are required? That tipping point, known as *opino juris*, is often a matter of disagreement and dissent, driven, on one hand, by those wishing to force new levels of conduct or performance favoring them and, on the other hand, those wishing to retain maximum freedom of action. "*Opino juris* is thus critical for the transformation of treaties into general law. To be sure, it is difficult to demonstrate such *opino juris*, but this poses a question of proof rather than of principle."[67] Again, there is no bright line test, no predictable point where custom becomes law.

Formative issues aside, custom remains the basis of much of the law of war. In ancient times, custom arose, then was eventually considered a binding precept cum international customary law. In many instances, it was made law in the form of multinational treaties that dictated penalties for its violation. But customary international law, even when undocumented in treaty form, is no less binding on nations.

Custom and treaties may be discussed as if they were discrete entities, but in practice the two are interrelated in complex ways. Custom is often memorialized in treaty form; treaties may give rise to rules of customary law. In contrast, treaties may be defeated by contrary state practice. The shifting interrelation of the two gives rise, of course, to conflicts, sometimes resolved in international courtrooms, sometimes on battlefields. For our purposes it is sufficient to understand that custom and treaties constitute the two primary bases of LOAC and, like many international legal concepts, they are subject to disagreements and conflicting interpretation.

1.3.2 *Treaties*

Of the two primary sources of LOAC, custom and treaties, treaties are the easier to describe. Particularly since World War II, the binding quality of such pacts has increased. Among the first treaties bearing on battlefield conduct – *jus in bello* – was the 1785 Treaty of Amity and Commerce, between Prussia and the United States. It provided, inter alia, basic rules regarding prisoners of war and noncombatant immunity, should the parties war against each other. Roberts and Guelff note that "multilateral treaties on the laws of war have been variously designated 'convention', 'declaration', 'protocol', 'procès-verbal'

---

[66] David Hackett Fischer, *Washington's Crossing* (Oxford: Oxford University Press, 2004), 375, 376, 378, 379. Samuel Eliot Morison writes of John Paul Jones, while he was captain of the *Ranger*, sending a press gang ashore at St. Mary's Isle, England. Finding no suitable prospects, Jones allowed his sailors to loot the mansion of an English count, taking, among other things, a large silver service. Jones wrote a regretful letter, to which the count replied, "In your letter you profess yourself a Citizen of the World, and that you have drawn your sword in support of the Rights of Man.... I doubt the laws of war and of nations would be very favorable to you as a citizen of the World." Jones purchased the silver service with his own funds and, after the war, returned it intact to the count. Morison, *John Paul Jones: A Sailor's Biography* (Boston: Atlantic-Little Brown, 1959), 143–55.

[67] Theodor Meron, "The Geneva Conventions as Customary Law," 81–2 *AJIL* (April 1987), 348, 367. Footnotes deleted.

or 'statute'.... [T]he 1969 Vienna Convention on the Law of Treaties defines the term 'treaty' as 'an international agreement concluded between States in written form and governed by international law.'"[68]

There is no agreement as to what treaties constitute the body of *jus in bello*. In some cases, signed treaties are never ratified, or lengthy periods pass between signing and ratification. The 1925 Geneva Gas Protocol,[69] signed by the United States in 1925, was not ratified by the United States until 1975. The 1969 Vienna Convention on Treaties is signed by the United States but remains unratified, as do 1977 Additional Protocols I and II. Generally, a signed treaty that has not been ratified still imposes an obligation on the party not to defeat the object and purpose of the treaty. To escape even that obligation, the United States took the unique step of "un-signing" the 1998 Rome Statute of the International Criminal Court (ICC). A few significant LOAC-related multinational treaties (e.g., the 1923 Hague Rules of Aerial Warfare and the 1997 Ottawa Convention Prohibiting Anti-Personnel Mines) have never been signed by the United States.

In time of war the laws are silent? Perhaps in Cicero's time, but not today. The many multinational treaties bearing on battlefield conduct and the protection of the victims of armed conflict demonstrate that there is a large and growing body of positive law, IHL, bearing on armed conflict.

In American practice, the Constitution's Article VI mandates that "this Constitution, and the laws of the United States ... and all Treaties made, or which shall be made, under the authority of the United States, shall be the supreme Law of the Land." Treaties ratified by the U.S. Senate, such as the 1949 Geneva Conventions and many others, not only bind America's armed forces, but are also "the supreme Law of the Land."

1.3.3 *Legislation and Domestic Law*

The 1949 Geneva Conventions were among the first multinational treaties that required ratifying states to enact domestic legislation to enforce their mandates by penalizing or criminalizing certain violations. (See Chapter 3, Section 3.8.2.) International treaties, in and of themselves, have no inherent enforcement powers, but states that ratify such pacts have jurisdiction over their citizen treaty offenders. Those states may enact national legislation in furtherance of the ratified treaty, promulgating administrative or criminal enforcement provisions in their domestic law. Today, the requirements for such ratifying-state enforcement measures are routinely written into multinational treaties. For example, the 1984 Convention against Torture (the CAT), in Article 2.1, directs that "each State Party shall take effective legislative, administrative, judicial or other measures to prevent acts of torture in any territory under its jurisdiction."[70] The United States ratified the CAT in 1994. In compliance with Article 2.1, the United States has passed federal legislation prohibiting torture.[71] Domestically, this legislation becomes a source of human rights and a LOAC and IHL guideline.

---

[68] Roberts and Guelff, *Documents*, supra, note 35, at 5.

[69] 1925 Geneva Protocol for the Prohibition of the Use in War of Asphyxiating, Poisonous or Other Gases, and of Bacteriological Methods of Warfare.

[70] Convention against Torture and Other Cruel, Inhuman or Degrading Treatment or Punishment (1984).

[71] See 28 U.S.C. §§ 1350, 2340(1) and 2340A. Also, the Armed Forces have issued DoD Directive 3115.09, dated 11 Oct. 2012, "DoD Intelligence Interrogations, Detainee Debriefings, and Tactical Questioning," as well as 2007's Field Manual 2–22.3, *Human Intelligence Collection Operations*, both containing torture prohibitions.

1.3.4 *Judicial Decisions*

In LOAC, "case law" refers to decisions of domestic courts, military tribunals, and international courts that relate to IHL and LOAC. Prior to 1945, other than a few unsatisfactory trials that followed World War I (Chapter 3, section 3.2.1), there was virtually no case law to interpret and flesh out the customary law of war, or to give life to its gray areas. The conclusion of World War II saw the initial efforts to remedy that lack.

The Nuremberg and Tokyo International Military Tribunals produced lengthy judgments and valuable case law. Those opinions are still studied. The judgments of the so-called Subsequent Trials, also held in Nuremberg after the war, remain significant case law. Several thousand military commissions were conducted after World War II. The United States conducted roughly one thousand such commissions, and our Allied nations conducted their own military tribunals. As with the Nuremberg judgments, military commission decisions remain significant today, but those cases, judgments, and opinions still represented a relatively small body of case law. "The body of law that governed the enforcement of IHL in the mid 1990s was very rudimentary. The substantive law ... did not benefit from well-developed jurisprudence."[72]

The International Criminal Tribunal for the former Yugoslavia (ICTY) and the International Criminal Tribunal for Rwanda (ICTR) have provided important interpretations of LOAC/IHL and the customs and usages of war. The international scope of the tribunals, with their generally well-qualified judges, and their reasoned, nuanced judgments and appellate opinions, provide essential direction for students of LOAC/IHL. However, the tribunals are international criminal courts in which elements of common law and civil law systems must be reconciled. For instance, in the common law tradition, the concept of *mens rea* is embodied in intention, recklessness, and criminal negligence. In the civil law tradition, "negligence, however gross, does not carry criminal responsibility unless a particular crime provides for its punishment."[73] Instead, civil law jurisprudence speaks of *dolus directus*, which bears a similarity to the common law's mens rea. "Notwithstanding the different architecture of the criminal systems and the ensuing differences between the operative concepts, it can be asserted that for the question of *mens rea* there is substantial overlap of the notions.... It may be concluded that the differences between the two systems in our context are real, but more conceptual than substantive."[74] The two systems' differing approaches to the mental state required for conviction illustrates one significant difference between ICTY and LOAC jurisprudence.

There is no system of precedent in international law or in LOAC.[75] (See *Prosecutor v. Kupreškić et al.*, Cases and Materials, this chapter.) "Trial chambers of the ICTY are

---

[72] Louise Arbour, "Legal Professionalism and International Criminal Proceedings," 4–4 *J. of Int'l Crim. Justice* (Sept. 2006), 674, 675.

[73] Kunt Dörmann, *Elements of War Crimes* (Cambridge: ICRC/Cambridge University Press, 2003), 491.

[74] Id., at 492–3. For a more complete discussion of the ICTY, ICTR, and ICC treatments of *mens rea*, see William A. Schabas, *An Introduction to the International Criminal Court* (Cambridge: Cambridge University Press, 2001), 292–6.

[75] Art. 38(1)(d) of the Statute of the ICJ provides that judicial decisions are a "subsidiary means for the determination of rules of law," subject to Art. 59, which holds, "The decision of the Court has no binding force except between the parties and in respect of that particular case."

bound to follow the *ratio decidendi* of the judgments of the Appeals Chamber [of the ICTY].... [This avoids] a chaotic structure in which each of the chambers could develop its own construction of the law."[76] But that practice applies only within the Court. Opinions of the ICTY, ICTR, and ICC bind only the litigants before the court, not U.S. courts or the domestic courts of any state. That U.S. position was recently made clear by Supreme Court Chief Justice Roberts: "Submitting to [the] jurisdiction [of an international court] and agreeing to be bound are two different things,"[77] but neither are the opinions of international courts simply ignored. The judgments and opinions of earlier specialized international courts and tribunals influence the judgments of later international and state courts considering similar issues.

1.3.5 *Publicists*

Custom and treaties are the primary sources of LOAC, with growing bodies of state legislation and international and domestic case law to interpret both. Publicists are another, lesser LOAC source, as the ICJ indicates in its Statute. Scholars and writers on the subject – "publicists" – discuss and write about LOAC – examining, molding, and reshaping international legal opinion, their views sometimes forming the bases of eventual state practice. If sufficiently widespread, state practice becomes custom, and so on. Publicists do not write LOAC, or influence it in a direct way, but their writings sometimes lend a cumulative intellectual and moral force to emerging LOAC/IHL concepts and practices. "The writings of ... legal scholars provide a helpful tool to put into perspective the customary practice, but one of only subsidiary nature."[78] Because of their influence, particularly when the law of war was in its formative stages, a few publicists have been deeply influential in forming today's battlefield norms.

Francisco de Victoria was such an early publicist. Also known as Franciscus de Vitoria (c. 1486–1546), he was a Spanish jurist and theologian when Spain was at the height of its international power, and he was one of the first of several prominent sixteenth-century law of war theorists. Victoria's lectures at the University of Salamanca reflected the Spanish experience in warring against Peruvian Indians in the New World. His lectures were collected in his text *Reflectiones Teologicae* (1557). His writings constituted an outline of the law of nations of the day, early building blocks for the regulation of war.

Pierino Belli (1502–75), born of a noble Italian family, was both a soldier and a jurist, a military judge in the armies of Charles V and Phillip II. In 1563, after holding diplomatic posts and serving as commander in-chief of the Holy Roman Empire's army in Piedmont, Belli wrote *De re Militari et de Bello Tractatus*. Almost seventy years before Grotius's seminal work, Belli offered a systematic treatment of the rules of war of his day.

Another early publicist was Balthazar Ayala (1548–84), a Belgo-Spanish military judge and political theorist who wrote *De Jure de Officiis Bellicis et Disciplina Militari*, three

---

[76] Alphons M. M. Orie, "*Stare decisis* in the ICTY Appeal System?" 10–3 *J. Int'l Crim. J.* 635, 640 (July 2012).

[77] *Medellin v. Texas*, 128 S Ct. 1346 (2008), at 1358. As Professor Mary Ellen O'Connell writes, however, "the majority in *Medellin* should have looked at the full range of international and foreign court and tribunal decisions that national courts regularly enforce either directly or under the terms of an enforcement treaty." *The Power & Purpose of International Law* (New York: Oxford University Press, 2008), 348.

[78] Ruys, "*Armed Attack*" *and Article 51 of the UN Charter*, supra, note 59, at 52.

volumes concerned with military discipline, the lawful causes of war, and just and unjust wars. Ayala was an officer and legal adviser to Phillip II's army in Flanders.

The most celebrated law of war publicist is the Dutch jurist and scholar Hugo Grotius (1585–1645), sometimes called the father of international law.[79] Grotius's picaresque life could be the subject of novels. At age eleven he was enrolled in Leiden University and at fifteen began the study of law at Orléans. Prolific in philology, theology, and poetry, Grotius was appointed attorney general of the province of Holland, but later was imprisoned for his religious views. After almost three years' imprisonment, he escaped by hiding in a book chest. In exile in Paris, he eventually became the Swedish ambassador to France, a noteworthy appointment for a Dutch fugitive. He earned such recognition through his writings, which were greatly admired by the Swedish king, Gustavus Adolphus.[80] Grotius's 1625 three-volume masterwork, *De Jure Belli ac Pacis* (*On the Law of War and Peace*), was published to international acclaim and is still cited as the first definitive international law text. He sought to limit war by interposing "just war" doctrine, with its stringent limitations on the initial resort to war, *jus ad bellum*, and by seeking humane limitations on the means by which war was waged, *jus in bello*.[81] "The plea made by earlier writers, including Gentili, but endorsed and fortified by Grotius, namely that limitations on warfare must be observed irrespective of the 'just' or 'unjust' nature of the initial resort to war...was and is a major contribution in legal ideas and forms part of the Grotian tradition."[82]

Through concepts of state sovereignty, the equality of sovereign states, "just war" theory, and stress on the self-defeating character of war, Grotius's text laid foundations of modern international law upon which later writers built. Although his just war doctrine was not accepted until long after his death, the concept persisted.[83] Grotius died in 1645, when shipwrecked on the Pomeranian coast.

Francisco Suárez, a sixteenth-century theologian and law of war scholar, was the author of *De Legibus ac Deo Legislatore*, in 1612. His moral and political philosophy stressed universal human custom in natural law, and its importance in warfare. He joined other law of war publicist adherents of natural law. "The teachings of Suárez show a manifest and unusually modern interest in the safeguarding and promotion of human rights. Freedom, justice ... and peace lack a solid basis ... unless the dignity and the equal and inalienable rights of the universal family are recognized."[84]

The Italian Alberico Gentili (1552–1608) was a jurist and professor of civil law at Oxford. He was counsel in England to the king of Spain. In his 1598 book *De Jure Belli Libri Tres*, Gentili found historical and legal precedents for battlefield constraints in

---

[79] The beginnings of international law arguably were in the interstate system of Italian city–states and, particularly, the writings of two Italian lawyers, Bartolo da Sassoferrato (1314–57) and Baldo degli Ubaldi (1327–1400). As influential as Grotius was, no single individual can fairly be called the father of international law.

[80] Adolphus was sufficiently impressed with Grotius's *De Jure Belli ac Pacis* that he is said to have slept with a copy under his pillow while fighting in Germany and to have ordered that Grotius be employed in the service of Sweden. Grotius served as Sweden's ambassador to France from 1635 until his death. Amos S. Hershey, "History of International Law Since the Peace of Westphalia," 6 *AJIL* (1912) 31, fn. 2.

[81] G.I.A.D. Draper, "Development of the Law of War," in Michael A. Meyer and Hilaire McCoubrey, eds., *Reflections on Law and Armed Conflict* (The Hague: Kluwer Law International, 1998), 49.

[82] Id., at 51.   [83] Id.

[84] Sergio M. Villa, "The Philosophy of International Law: Suárez, Grotius and Epigones," 320 *Int'l. Rev. of the Red Cross* (Oct. 1997), 324.

natural law and, as did Suárez, related them to just war theory. Gentili was an intellectual bridge from medieval views of international law and the more modern views of Grotius to and Kant.

A later prominent law of war publicist was the Swiss jurist Emmerich de Vattel (1714–67), who published *Le Droit de Gens ou Principes de la Loi Naturelle* in 1758. His two-volume work was instrumental in modernizing international law, transforming it from a largely theoretical study to actual practice. He continued the line of publicists advocating natural law, his influence persisting into the nineteenth century. "At the time of the American Revolution the work of Vattel was the latest and most popular if not the most authoritative of the Continental writers."[85] The U.S. Supreme Court, in *The Prize Cases*, cites Vattel, paraphrasing him in saying there are "common laws of war," which are "maxims of humanity, moderation and honor [which] ought to be observed by both parties."[86]

These and other sixteenth- and seventeenth-century scholars and publicists set the doctrinal basis for the regulation of war by interpreting and generalizing the practices of centuries. "Scholarly opinion still constitutes a subsidiary source of law. In other words, the majority view is not automatically the correct one: the crucial test is whether the customary practice of States confirms one view or the other."[87] Lassa Oppenheim, a British international law professor of the twentieth century, is a modern example of a law of war publicist who influenced national policy that led to customary international law.

In 1906, in a major shift from previous practice, Oppenheim postulated that a common defense to charges of violating the law of war, obedience to superior orders, constituted a complete and absolute defense to such charges. Anchoring his formulation on an interpretation of then-traditional concepts of international law, he held that there could be no personal responsibility in subordinates when superiors ordered criminal acts on the battlefield. Later, Oppenheim wrote Great Britain's 1912 handbook on the rules of land warfare. The new text incorporated Oppenheim's dicta that, for subordinates, obedience to orders constituted a complete defense to charges of violation of the law of war. In 1914, looking to Great Britain's example, America published its first manual on the law of war.[88] In treating defenses to law of war violations, the new American manual followed Oppenheim's lead: "Individuals of the armed forces," it read, "will not be punished for these offenses in case they are committed under the orders or sanction of their government or commanders."[89] This approach contradicted American military and civilian case law. Nevertheless, the defense prevailed in the U.S. military through World War I and into the interwar period, into a new 1934 edition of the *Rules of Land Warfare* manual, and into World War II. Even in that war, in yet another *Rules* edition of 1940, Oppenheim's formulation continued to govern, but, in 1942, the Allies announced that they would prosecute German and Japanese soldiers for obeying unlawful battlefield orders and would deny them the superior orders

---

[85] Brian Richardson, "The Use of Vattel in the American Law of Nations," 106–3 *AJIL* 547, 548 (July 2012).

[86] 67 U.S. (2 Black) 635, 667, 17 L.Ed. 459 (1863).

[87] Ruys, *"Armed Attack" and Article 51 of the UN Charter*, supra, note 59, at 327.

[88] Donald A. Wells, *The Laws of Land Warfare: A Guide to the U.S. Army Manuals* (Westport, CT: Greenwood Press, 1992), 5.

[89] War Dept., *Rules of Land Warfare*, 1914 (Washington: GPO, 1914), para. 366.

defense. Such a stance clearly required a reevaluation of the American policy reflected in its field manual. The United States could hardly continue to sponsor for its own soldiers the defense it intended to deny the vanquished enemy.

In April 1944, in a complete about-face, the United Kingdom revised its law of war manual and rejected superior orders as a defense to war crimes charges. "Seven months later, on November 15, 1944, the United States similarly reversed and revised its field manual."[90] The United States returned to its pre-1914 position – obedience to orders was *not* a perfect defense – and Oppenheim's writing of thirty-eight years before was rejected – a rarity for so notable a scholar. The practice of Great Britain and the United States, altered by a leading publicist and adhered to through two world wars, had not been generally adopted, however, so it never approached customary international law. Oppenheim remains, however, an example of the authority exercised by law of war publicists.

The International Committee of the Red Cross (ICRC) – through its *Commentaries* to the 1949 Geneva Conventions and the 1977 Additional Protocols; its journal, *International Review of the Red Cross*; its wide-ranging Web site; and its excellent occasional pamphlets and books – has become a respected corporate publicist. Its 2005 three-volume *Customary Law Study* should not be overlooked.[91] Although the *Study* has received criticism[92] and has been rejected by some governments,[93] it has much to offer scholars and readers.

Modern publicists continue to theorize, write, and advance international law and LOAC. Their scholarly and sometimes groundbreaking work will be judged by history for inclusion in the ranks of their publicist predecessors.

1.4 The Language of the Law of Armed Conflict

As most disciplines do, LOAC employs some unique terms. Although they are few in number, it is important that such terms be understood, for "semantics are

---

[90] Gary Solis, "Obedience of Orders and the Law of War: Judicial Application in American Forums," 15 *American U. Int'l L. R.* (2003), 481, 510.

[91] Jean-Marie Henckaerts and Louise Doswald-Beck, eds., *Customary International Humanitarian Law* (Cambridge: Cambridge University Press, 2005).

[92] For example, Maj. J. Jeremy Marsh, "Lex Lata or Lex Ferenda? Rule 45 of the ICRC Study on Customary International Humanitarian Law," 198 *Military L. Rev.* (Winter 2008), 116. " [M]ethodological flaws led its authors to declare as rules of CIL [customary international law] what can only be described as *lex ferenda* (what the law should be) as opposed to *lex lata* (what the law is) . . . elevating aspiration over empirical proof of actual state practice . . . seem to conclude that if there is enough mention of the 'rule' in military manuals and other questionable sources of verbal practice, then the *opino juris* prong of CIL is met . . . paid insufficient heed to two important CIL doctrines, specially affected states and persistent objection, in developing its rules" at 117–20; and David Turns, "Weapons in the ICRC Study on Customary International Humanitarian Law," 11–2 *J. of Conflict & Security L.* (Summer, 2006), 201, 203: "Sometimes, conclusions are reached on the basis of official statements unsupported by actual 'battlefield practice'."

[93] For example, U.S. Dept. of State, "Initial response of U.S. to ICRC study on Customary International Humanitarian Law with Illustrative Comments (Nov. 3, 2006)," available at http://www.state.gov/s/l/2006/98860.htm: "Places too much emphasis on written materials, such as military manuals and other guidelines published by States, as opposed to actual operational practice by States during armed conflict . . . gives undue weight to statements of non-governmental organizations and the ICRC itself . . . often fails to pay due regard to the practice of specially affected States . . . tends to regard as equivalent the practice of States that have relatively little history of participation in armed conflict."

important and perhaps nowhere more so than in the study of the law, whether domestic or international."[94]

1.4.1 *"The Law of War" or "the Law of Armed Conflict"?*

We use the terms "law of war" and "law of armed conflict." Do the two phrases represent the same discipline? If not, how do they differ? If they do represent the same discipline, why do two similar terms describe the same circumstance?

Rules of war are not the same as laws of war. A law is a form of rule that, within a particular sphere or jurisdiction, must be obeyed, subject to sanctions or legal consequences. A rule does not necessarily involve either sanctions or legal consequences. There have been *rules* for the battlefield for thousands of years, but, with significant exceptions, there have been *laws* for the battlefield – LOAC – only in the past hundred years or so. LOAC is a relatively recent phenomenon.

What is "war"? Wars on drugs, on poverty, and on illiteracy are laudable political constructs but are not literally wars, of course. A state of war has wide-ranging repercussions in contracts,[95] insurance, constitutional issues,[96] neutrality, and governmental wartime emergency powers, not to mention the life and death issues played out on the battlefield.[97] The "War on Terrorism" is not a war in the sense of Geneva Convention common Article 2,[98] although that view would not be shared by the widow or husband of a soldier killed in Iraq or Afghanistan. Still, the ICRC and LOAC publicists point out its nonwar character. (See Chapter 6, Section 6.5.2.) In international law there is no accepted and binding definition of "war." The world has passed beyond Clausewitz's description of war as "an act of force to compel our enemy to do our will."[99] The U.S. Army's judge advocate general posits four required elements: a contention (one) between at least two nation-states (two) wherein armed force is employed with (three) an intent to overwhelm (four).[100]

Since World War II, there have been many intrastate armed conflicts not amounting to "wars." Were the events in Korea a war or a police action (whatever that is)? Was the Vietnam conflict a war? Sometimes it is difficult even to distinguish between intra- and interstate conflicts, for example, the dissolution of Yugoslavia in the late twentieth century. What was initially a civil war evolved into a multistate conflict, with the original state, Yugoslavia, fragmenting into several new states. Was that conflict an intrastate war or a interstate war? An international or noninternational armed conflict? Or both? Is this

---

[94] Charles H. B. Garraway, "'Combatants' – Substance or Semantics?" in Michael Schmitt and Jelena Pejic, eds., *International Law and Armed Conflict: Exploring the Faultlines* (Leiden: Martinus Nijhoff, 2007), 316–34, 316.

[95] See, e.g., *Navios Corporation v. The Ulysses II*, 161 F. Supp. 932 (D. Md. 1958), in which contractual liability under a ship's charter depended upon the interpretation of a contractual clause providing that a declared war enabled the ship's owners to cancel the charter. In question was the character of the 1956 seizure of the Suez Canal from Egypt by France and the United Kingdom.

[96] Consider *Korematsu v. U.S.*, 323 U.S. 214 (1944) and its address of civil rights.

[97] Ingrid Detter, *The Law of War*, 2d ed. (Cambridge: Cambridge University Press, 2000), discusses (pp. 18–20) many international legal issues applying to LOAC.

[98] Common Article 2 requires an armed conflict between "two or more of the high Contracting Parties."

[99] Carl von Clausewitz, *Vom Kriege*, 18th ed. (Bonn, 1972), Bk. 1, Ch. 1, 75.

[100] Judge Advocate General's Legal Center & School, Int'l & Operational Law Dept., in *Law of War Handbook* (Charlottesville, VA: JAG School, 1997), 1–2.

distinction any longer all that significant? Nor is the conflict always between the armed forces of two states, as in World War II, when some Allied states declared war against Germany, yet shots in anger were never fired between the two. Do nonstate actors engage in warfare or criminal activity? "The centuries-old term 'war' is still in everyday use but has tended to disappear from legal language over the past decades, for 'war' has gradually been outlawed, even though resort to force, be it called 'war' or not, continues to exist. Thus, it is at present more correct to use the term 'armed conflict', as its very vagueness may be considered an advantage."[101] As the ICRC notes, "It is possible to argue almost endlessly about the legal definition of 'war'...The expression 'armed conflict' makes such arguments less easy."[102]

So, not all armed conflicts are wars, but all wars are armed conflicts. "War" has become more a descriptive term than a term of legal art. This text generally uses the term "law of armed conflict," recognizing that the matters discussed are also applicable where the faded term "war" may not strictly apply. "The term 'international law of armed conflict' has come to be used to describe this body of law. However, the older term 'laws of war' is also widely used and understood."[103]

A few scholars argue that both "law of war" and "law of armed conflict" are passé terms, replaced in the eyes of some internationalists by "international humanitarian law." The ICRC, for example, promotes the term "international humanitarian law," passing over the irony of how a body of law defining how noncombatants may lawfully be killed (i.e., collateral damage) is "humanitarian."[104]

In this text we examine only *jus in bello*, the rules and laws governing the conduct of armed conflict – battlefield law – as opposed to *jus ad bellum*, the rules and laws that govern the lawfulness of the resort to armed conflict.[105] This reflects "the cardinal principle that *jus in bello* applies in cases of armed conflict whether or not the inception of the conflict is lawful under *jus ad bellum*."[106] Emphasizing the point, the 1949 Geneva Conventions specify that LOAC "shall apply in all cases of declared war *or of any other armed conflict* which may arise."[107] In sum, what was once commonly referred to as the law of war is today more correctly termed the law of armed conflict, although long usage and acceptance render both terms acceptable.[108]

1.4.2 *The Law of Armed Conflict and Human Rights Law*

LOAC encompasses other similar and potentially confusing terms. Since the drafting of the 1949 Geneva Conventions, human rights and humanitarian goals have become

---

[101] Stanislaw E. Nahlik, "A Brief Outline of International Humanitarian Law," *Int'l Rev. of the Red Cross* (July-Aug., 1984), 7.

[102] Jean S. Pictet, ed., *Commentary, IV Geneva Convention, 1949* (Geneva: ICRC, 1958), 20.

[103] Roberts and Guelff, supra, note 35, at 2. Footnote omitted.

[104] One writer notes that "the ICRC is making a surreptitious contribution to peace by so restricting the parties in the conduct of war [through use of language] as to make war impossible as a viable means of state policy." D. Forsythe, *Humanitarian Politics: The ICRC* (Baltimore: Johns Hopkins University Press, 1977), 122.

[105] *Jus* is pronounced "use," as in "make use of a weapon."   [106] Roberts and Guelff, supra, note 35, at 1.

[107] 1949 Geneva Conventions, common Art. 2. Emphasis supplied.

[108] The 1998 Rome Statute of the ICC refers to "international law of armed conflict" (Arts. 8(2)(e) and 21(1)(b).) "International humanitarian law" is the term used in the 1993 ICTY (Art. 1) and 1994 ICTR (Art. 1) statutes.

common elements on the battlefield, encouraged by opinions of the International Court of Justice and other human rights tribunals.[109] What are the differences among LOAC, humanitarian law, IHL, international human rights law, and human rights law?

"Humanitarian law" refers to international rules that attempt to "mitigate the human suffering caused by war."[110] It is an umbrella term for laws that aim to humanize armed conflict that, taken together, form the corpus of IHL and international human rights law. "It is hardly possible to find documentary evidence of when and where the first legal rules of a humanitarian nature emerged.... For everywhere that [armed] confrontation ... did not result in a fight to the finish, rules arose ... for the purpose of limiting the effects of the violence."[111] Humanitarian law, as such, does not frequently arise when considering *jus in bello* issues. Still, "there is today no question that human rights law comes to complement humanitarian law in situations of armed conflict."[112]

IHL is the body of international legislation that applies in situations of armed conflict. As does its fraternal twin, LOAC, IHL refers to the body of treaty-based and customary international law aimed at protecting the individual in time of international or noninternational armed conflict; treaties, for example, such as 1949 Geneva Convention IV for the protection of civilians. IHL is confined to armed conflict, both international and non-international.[113] It is intended to limit the violence of armed conflicts by protecting those taking no active part in hostilities, by protecting property not considered military objectives, and by restricting the combatants' right to use any methods of warfare they choose. Until the end of World War II, IHL was an unknown term. "The term international humanitarian law is ... probably a bit more opaque than the previous term – the law of war – which has roots that are centuries old.... The change in terminology is an important one, because it not only represents the unification of Hague Law and Geneva Law, but also – and most importantly – the profound influence of human rights."[114]

Today, although the 1949 Geneva Conventions (and most military references) employ the term "law of armed conflict," IHL's invocation is widespread and growing, particularly in civilian and academic circles. "The purpose of international humanitarian law is not to prevent war. More prosaically, it seeks to preserve an oasis of humanity in battle until resort to armed force ... is no longer a means of settling differences between States."[115] "Law of armed conflict" and "international humanitarian law" have the same

---

[109] See, e.g., *Legal Consequences of the Construction of a Wall in the Occupied Palestine Territory* (The Wall Advisory Opinion), [July 2004] I.C.J. Rep. 136; and, *Advisory Opinion on the Legality of the Threat or Use of Nuclear Weapons* (The Nuclear Weapons Advisory Opinion), [1996] ICJ Rep. 226; and, *Issa v. Turkey*, 2004 Eur. Ct. H.R. 71.

[110] Frits Kalshoven and Liesbeth Zegveld, *Constraints on the Waging of War: An Introduction to International Humanitarian Law* (Geneva: ICRC, 2001), 12.

[111] Hans-Peter Gasser, *International Humanitarian Law: An Introduction* (Berne: Paul Haupt, 1993), 6.

[112] Cordula Droege, "Elective Affinities? Human Rights and Humanitarian Law," 871 *Int'l Rev. of the Red Cross* 501(Sept. 2008).

[113] ICRC, "International Humanitarian Law and the Challenges of Contemporary Armed Conflicts," 867 *Int'l Rev. of the Red Cross* (Sept. 2007), 719, 722.

[114] Meron, *The Making of International Criminal Justice*, supra, note 38, at 43. "Geneva Law" refers to the body of humanitarian law governing the treatment and protection of those who are hors de combat, civilians and prisoners; "Hague Law" pertains to the conduct of military operations in armed conflicts. Today, the two branches have effectively merged.

[115] Christophe Girod, draft, *Storm in the Desert: The International Committee of the Red Cross and the Gulf War 1990–1991* (Geneva: ICRC, 2003), 26–7.

meaning, particularly with the influential ICRC – a group that would ideally see a narrowed range of options for combatants, a worthy goal. An Australian academic clearly thinks "IHL," rather than "LOAC," when she writes, "Written by the military, for the military, about the military, international humanitarian law treaties, particularly the universally ratified *Geneva Conventions* . . . relate to bare survival during the most horrific condition humans can manufacture – armed conflict."[116] The same thought could be applied to LOAC.

The melding of battlefield laws and humanitarian goals is not without its critics. Jean Pictet, editor of the Geneva Convention *Commentaries*, wrote that IHL has been "contaminated" by ethics and idealism,[117] appearing to combine concepts of different characters, one legal, the other moral.[118]

> A possible disadvantage of the term [IHL] is that it could be thought to exclude some parts of the laws of war (such as the law on neutrality) whose primary purpose is not humanitarian. Indeed, the term "international humanitarian law" could be seen as implying that the laws of war have an exclusively humanitarian purpose, when their evolution has in fact reflected various practical concerns of states and their armed forces on grounds other than those which may be considered humanitarian.[119]

The conflation of LOAC/IHL terminology reflects a desire of humanitarian-oriented groups and nongovernmental organizations to avoid phrases like "law of *war*" in favor of more pacific terms, perhaps in the hope that battlefield actions may someday follow that description. This is in keeping with recent efforts to circumscribe the means of armed conflict – treaties banning or restricting use of antipersonnel land mines, cluster munitions, and blinding lasers come to mind.[120] The ICJ has weighed in with its own slightly different take on IHL. "These two branches of the law applicable in armed conflict ["Hague Law" and "Geneva Law"] have become so closely interrelated that they are considered to have gradually formed one single complex system, known today as international humanitarian law."[121] Actually, "a true convergence of the Hague law and the Geneva law came about only in 1977 [with the two Additional Protocols]."[122]

1.4.3 *Human Rights Law on the Battlefield*

Another related term, "human rights law" (HRL), applies in time of peace and, most commentators contend, in armed conflict as well. The American (and Israeli)[123]

---

[116] Helen Durham, "International Humanitarian Law and the Gods of War: The Story of Athena Versus Ares," 8–2 *Melbourne J. of Int'l L.* 248, 253 (2007).

[117] Jean S. Pictet, *International Humanitarian Law*, (Geneva: ICRC, 1985), 3.

[118] Jean S. Pictet, *Humanitarian Law and the Protections of War Victims* (Leyden: ICRC, 1975), 11.

[119] Roberts and Guelff, supra, note 35, at 2.

[120] See Robert J. Mathews and Timothy L. H. McCormack, "The Influence of Humanitarian Principles in the Negotiation of Arms Control Treaties," 834 *Int'l R. of the Red Cross* 331 (June 1999).

[121] *The Nuclear Weapons Advisory Opinion*, 1996 I.C.J. 35 I.L.M. 809, 827, at para. 75.

[122] Christian Tomuschat, *Human Rights: Between Idealism and Realism* (Oxford: Oxford University Press, 2003), 247.

[123] Françoise J. Hampson, "The Relationship between International Humanitarian Law and Human Rights Law from the Perspective of a Human Rights Treaty Body," 871 *Int'l Rev. of the Red Cross* 549,550 (Sept. 2008).

positions have long been that HRL does not, or *should* not, apply in the *jus in bello*. Many disagree,[124] particularly Europeans, the ICRC,[125] the International Court of Justice,[126] and human rights activists.[127] "Traditionally, human rights law and LOW [law of war] have been viewed as separate systems of protection."[128] The two have different subject matters and different roots but they overlap, at points. In the American view of past years, in cases of overlap, LOAC, the *lex specialis* of the battlefield, trumps human rights law. Again, the European position is contrary. Human rights law, European scholars and publicists hold, *always* applies, hand in hand with LOAC on the battlefield.[129] In agreement, the European professor Frits Kalshoven argues, "Half a century ago, Jean Pictet, famous top lawyer of the ICRC, defended the separate existance of the two bodies of law.... And since those early days, the awareness has grown that ... human rights organs can contribute a great deal.... To the U.S. Government, on the other hand, to pass from humanitarian law to human rights law appears to present an insurmountable hurdle. It is a cause of serious regret."[130]

"This branch of international law did not really come into its own until after World War I.... International human rights law, as we know it today, begins with the Charter of the United Nations [Articles 1, 30, 55, and 56]."[131] "While there has been a constant tension between the world of human rights and the world of war, over the past century the pendulum has swung firmly towards human rights."[132] HRL and its multinational version, international human rights law, seek to guarantee the fundamental rights of persons vis-à-vis their own governments and to protect them against actors in the international community that might violate those rights.[133] The United Nations Charter was indeed the first authoritative expression of the modern human rights movement through conventions such as the Universal Declaration of Human Rights (1948), and particularly, the 1966 International Covenant on Civil and Political Rights (ICCPR), which includes provisions on lethal targeting, detention, and a nonderogable prohibition on the arbitrary deprivation of life. The U.N. provided an institutional spur for

---

[124] Louise Doswald-Beck and Sylvain Vité, "International Humanitarian Law and Human Rights Law," 293 *Int'l. Rev. of the Red Cross* (April 1993), 94, 94; Gerd Oberleitner, *Human Rights in Armed Conflict: Law, Practice, Policy* (Cambridge: Cambridge University Press, 2015), 93–5, 148–52.

[125] Henckaerts and Doswald-Beck, *Customary International Humanitarian Law*, supra, note 91, at 299–300. "Human rights law applies at all times."

[126] *The Legality of the Threat or Use of Nuclear Weapons* (Nuclear Weapons Advisory Opinion) (1996), at para. 25.

[127] Yoram Dinstein proposes six variations of "wartime human rights" application, in which they apply, or not, according to situational factors. "Human Rights in Armed Conflict," in Meron, *Human Rights in International Law*, supra, note 61, at 345–68.

[128] Maj. Marie Anderson and Emily Zukauskas, eds., *Operational Law Handbook*, 2008 (Charlottesville VA: Judge Advocate General's Legal Center and School, 2008), 40.

[129] An excellent recitation of the European view is: Peter Rowe, *The Impact of Human Rights Law on Armed Forces* (New York: Cambridge University Press, 2006), reviewed at 101–1 *AJIL* 252 (Jan. 2007).

[130] Frits Kalshoven, *Reflections on the Law of War* (Leiden: Martinus Nijhoff, 2007), 925.

[131] Thomas Buergenthal, "The Evolving International Human Rights System," 100–4 *AJIL* (Oct. 2006), 783, 785.

[132] Meron, *The Making of International Criminal Justice*, supra, note 38, at 42.

[133] Steven R. Ratner and Jason S. Abrams, *Accountability for Human Rights Atrocities in International Law: Beyond the Nuremberg Legacy*, 2d ed. (Oxford: Oxford University Press, 2001), 10.

continuing developments in the field.[134] HRL applies in time of armed conflict, as it does in peace, the ICJ has held.[135]

Clearly, HRL applies in noninternational armed conflicts where, as we shall see, LOAC/IHL, in large part, does *not* apply. "Due to an increase in the number of non-international armed conflicts and the rise of situations of prolonged belligerent occupation, these branches of public international law have been progressively brought together."[136] The 1949 Geneva Convention IV, for example, dealing with civilians and with occupation, incorporates provisions reflecting HRL, as does 1977 Additional Protocol, I Articles 72 and 75, and Article 6 of Additional Protocol II. Those provisions are largely drawn from the ICCPR, a basic HRL document. Nevertheless, as Theodor Meron notes, there are differences between HRL and LOAC:

> It has become common in some quarters to conflate human rights and the law of war/international humanitarian law. Nevertheless ... significant differences remain. Unlike human rights law, the law of war allows ... the killing and wounding of innocent human beings not directly participating in an armed conflict, such as civilian victims of lawful collateral damage. ... As long as rules of the game are observed, it is permissible [in armed conflict] to cause suffering, deprivation of freedom, and death.[137]

Areas of significant conflict between HRL and LOAC include the use of force, requirements for self-defense, the detention and internment of prisoners, and security restrictions imposed on civilians. The war crime of torture is an example. The 1984 Convention Against Torture and Other Cruel, Inhuman or Degrading Treatment or Punishment (the C.A.T.) is a human rights–based treaty, while the ICTY is an IHL-based trial forum at which international crimes and war crimes are tried. The ICTY's jurisprudence has been "mindful to not confound ... international human rights with international humanitarian law,"[138] and in ICTY judgments there is a significant departure from the C.A.T.'s definition of torture.[139]

The U.S. view has been that LOAC is the *lex specialis* on the battlefield, to the exclusion of HRL. The European view is that the two are coequal on the battlefield. U.S. hesitance to apply human rights law on the battlefield has apparently been based on two concerns. First, "the United States is particularly critical of what they consider an unacceptably progressive jurisprudence of human rights bodies with regard to human rights in armed conflict," writes a European academic. He continues, "Such arguments ignore, however, that in light of the overwhelming support for the application of

---

[134] Henry J. Steiner and Philip Alston, *International Human Rights in Context,* 2d ed. (Oxford: Oxford University Press, 2000), 67.

[135] *Legal Consequences of the Construction of A Wall in the Occupied Palestinian Territory,* supra, note 109, at para. 106: "The Court considers that the protection offered by human rights conventions does not cease in case of armed conflict."

[136] Robert Kolb and Richard Hyde, *An Introduction to the International Law of Armed Conflicts* (Oxford: Hart, 2008), 269.

[137] Theodor Meron, "The Humanization of Humanitarian Law, 94 AJIL 239, 240 (2000).

[138] Christoph Burchard, "Torture in the Jurisprudence of the Ad Hoc Tribunals," 6–2 *J. of Int'l Crim. Justice* (May 2008), 159, 166.

[139] See, e.g., *Prosecutor v. Kunarac, et al.,* IT-96–23 & 23/1-T (22 Feb. 2001), para. 465–71; and *Kunarac,* IT-96-23 & 231-A (20 June 2002), para. 147, in which both chambers decline to apply the C.A.T.'s torture requirement that the act be inflicted by or at the instigation of a public official.

international human rights law in armed conflict, the United States is increasingly isolated; some would even refer to its position as 'anachronistic.'"[140]

Second, and more significantly, the United States has steadfastly argued that the obligations of the primary human rights document, the ICCPR, and of other human rights treaties to which it is a state party do not apply extraterritorially. Article 2 of the ICCPR reads, "Each State Party to the present Covenant undertakes to respect and to ensure to all individuals within its territory and subject to its jurisdiction the rights recognized in the present Covenant." A plain reading of "within its jurisdiction" and "subject to its jurisdiction," the United States contends, clearly excludes extraterritorial application of the covenant.

In 2005, the United States stated its position before the U.N.'s Human Rights Committee: "The United States recalls its longstanding position . . . that the obligations assumed by the United States under the [ICCPR] apply only within the territory of the United States. . . . The United States also notes the legal status and treatment of [of persons detained at Guantanánamo Bay, Iraq, and other places of detention outside U.S. borders] is governed by the law of war [rather than human rights law]."[141] That often publicly stated position is unlikely to change:

> Military action by any of the 162 states parties [to the ICCPR] anywhere in the world, including actions taken in exercise of the inherent right of self-defence . . . would bring all those affected by such operations (including enemy combatants) within the scope of the protections provided by the Covenant. . . . It would also appear to include liability for any lack of vigilance by the state in preventing violations of human rights and international humanitarian law by other actors present in areas under military occupation, including rebel groups acting on their own account.[142]

At this point, the consequences of changing the U.S. position would involve issues beyond merely announcing a new official viewpoint.

Yet, it appears that the U.S. position has, without announcement, softened perceptibly. Consider the 2011 Report of the United States, the "fifth Periodic Report" before the U.N.'s Human Rights Committee:

> Under the doctrine of *lex specialis*, the applicable rules for the protection of individuals and conduct of hostilities in armed conflict are typically found in [LOAC]. . . . [IHRL] and [LOAC] are in many respects complementary and mutually reinforcing [and] contain many similar protections. . . . Determining the international law rule that applies to a particular action taken by a government in the context of an armed conflict is a fact-specific determination, which cannot be easily generalized, and raises especially complex issues in the context of non-international armed conflicts occurring within a State's own territory.[143]

---

[140] Oberleitner, *Human Rights in Armed Conflict*, supra, note 124, at 94. Citations omitted.

[141] U.S. Dept. of State, U.N. Human Rights Committee, *Third Periodic Report – United States* (26 Nov. 2005), para. 130.

[142] Michael J. Dennis and Andre M. Surena, "Application of the International Covenant on Civil and Political Rights in Times of Armed Conflict and Military Occupation: The Gap Between Legal Theory and State Practice," 6 *European H.R. L. Rev.* (2008), 719, 724–5.

[143] U.S. Dept. of State, U.N. Human Rights Committee, *Fourth Periodic Report – United States*, (30 Dec. 2011), para. 507.

The tone seems less adamant, almost mollifying, compared to the last periodic report, six years earlier. The 2011 Report Went on to acknowledge that the ICJ[144] and other state parties held views on the application of IHRL in armed conflict contrary to the U.S. view. Indeed, the report's later acknowledgment of concurrent application of HRL and LOAC was a dramatic shift from the former U.S. insistence that LOAC displaces HRL in times of armed conflict.[145] "Some commentators see the U.S. acknowledgement of the international community's pervasive viewpoint of extraterritoriality ... as a subtle sign of a shifting policy toward U.S. recognition of international human rights obligations outside of its territorial boundaries."[146]

The 2014 *Operational Law Handbook*, published by the army's Judge Advocate General's Legal Center and School, continues to be less dogmatic in its approach to IHRL: "In situations of armed conflict ... where LOAC is silent or its guidance inadequate, specific provisions of applicable human rights law may supplement LOAC."[147] Further evidence of the U.S. acceptance of IHRL was a 2012 announcement by the U.S. Marine Corps that it had created three "law enforcement support battalions" within its three expeditionary forces.[148] Moving the Marines from LOAC doctrine, in which the use of deadly force may be the first resort, to IHRL doctrine, in which deadly force is the *last* resort, could give old-line Marines pause.

Another demonstration of change in direction is found in a 2011 letter from the commanding general of the NATO International Security Assistance Force (ISAF), in Kabul, Afghanistan, to all subordinate troops, the great preponderance of whom were American. In his letter, Marine General John R. Allen wrote: "**Respect for Human Rights.** A significant component of our campaign is championing the respect for human rights and supporting GIRoA's [the Government of the Islamic Republic of Afghanistan's] development of institutional protections of every citizen's human rights in accordance with LOAC, international law, and the laws of Afghanistan."[149] It is true that ISAF was a NATO command, but the command was largely a U.S. force.

The recent inclusion of HRL usually is unnoticed in a combat zone, for example, the collection of evidence for potential use in courts-martial or war crime trials. During the later stages of the U.S. conflict in Afghanistan, infantry personnel were routinely tasked with seizing evidence for criminal prosecutions from sites over which they had, minutes before, been fighting the enemy. An army field manual provided instruction:

> Successful prosecution of individuals depends on gathering and evaluating evidence, both testimonial and physical.... Physical evidence, such as weapons and fingerprints, is obtained by site exploitation (SE) operations. Further evidence comes from exploiting any leads discovered by SE operations and developing information obtained.... The

---

[144] *Threat or Use of Nuclear Weapons*, supra, note 109, at para. 25; *Legal Consequences of the Construction of a Wall in the Occupied Palestinian Territory*, supra, note 109, at para. 106.

[145] Major Jerrod Fussnecker, "The Effects of International Human Rights Law on the Legal Interoperability of Multinational Military Operations," *The Army Lawyer* (May 2014), 7, 15.

[146] Id.

[147] LTC William Johnson and LCDR David Lee, eds., *Operational Law Handbook 2014* (Charlottesville, VA: Army Judge Advocate General's Legal Center & School, 2014), 53.

[148] Gidget Fuentes, "Opportunity Knocks," *Marine Corps Times* (Feb. 21, 2011), 18; and Julie Watson, "Marine Corps Creates Law Enforcement Battalions," Associated Press (July 22, 2012).

[149] Letter from General John R. Allen, Commanding General, ISAF/US Forces-Afghanistan (Nov. 30, 2011). Emphasis in original. (on file with author).

evidence must withstand intense scrutiny and be admissible in court. This requires systematic procedures for collecting, handling, and documenting evidence.[150]

Evidence, fingerprints, and prosecutions are human rights–related activities, until recently the responsibility of military specialists, military policemen, and judge advocates, not the duty of troops in contact with the enemy.

The U.S. position on human rights in foreign combat zones aside, there are significant differences between HRL and LOAC. HRL is premised on the principle that citizens hold individual *rights* that their state is bound to respect; LOAC imposes *obligations* on the individual. HRL largely consists of *general* principles; LOAC is a series of *specific* provisions. HRL enunciates *state* responsibilities; LOAC specifies *individual* responsibilities as well as state responsibilities. In HRL, rights are given to *all*; LOAC links many of its protections to nationality or specific statuses, such as combatants. HRL allows for state derogation; LOAC does not.

Finally, we may say that the terms used to describe the bodies of law applicable on the battlefield boil down to three: the "law of war" and its successor term, the "law of armed conflict," which in popular usage has become synonymous with "international humanitarian law." The term "law of armed conflict" is favored in the 1949 Geneva Conventions but to use any of the three in relation to the topics in this text would not be incorrect.

1.5 Summary

For as long as armies have met in battle, there have been limits on soldiers' conduct in combat. Initially grounded in practices based on the code of chivalry, those practices became the custom, and custom evolved into rules and, in some armies, were incorporated in military codes – military law – with penalties for their violation. Such rules and laws have been based not only on national interests but on sound tactical and strategic considerations, not the least of which is the danger of reciprocal violations of similar nature. "Gratuitous violence wastes resources, provokes retaliation, invites moral condemnation, and impedes post-war relations with the enemy nation."[151] World War II Nazi war crimes and predations in Russia remain a prime example of an army's counterproductive unlawful behavior. Today, most commanders understand that if they mistreat enemy prisoners, soon their soldiers will be subjected to the same mistreatment. Moreover, well-disciplined troops simply do not commit war crimes, for indiscipline in one aspect of soldiering may inevitably represent a general indiscipline.

Battlefield violations will never be entirely eliminated. In fact, upon close inspection, LOAC does not work very well. The passions of war and the adrenaline rush of combat, combined with powerful weapons in the hands of young men and women, are a mix that assures occasional offenses. Former general Colin Powell writes, "The kill-or-be-killed nature of combat tends to dull fine perceptions of right and wrong."[152] The historian and combat veteran Paul Fussell adds, "You're going to learn that one of the most brutal

---

[150] Dept. of the Army, ATTP 3-90.15 (FM 3-90.15), *Site Exploitation Operations* (July 2010), Appendix B, para. B-1.

[151] Chris af Jochnick and Roger Normand, "The Legitimation of Violence: A Critical History of the Laws of War," 35–1 *Harvard Int'l L. J.* (Winter 1994), 49, 54.

[152] Colin L. Powell, *A Soldier's Way: An Autobiography* (London: Hutchinson, 1995), 144.

things in the world is your average nineteen-year-old American boy."[153] Still, an armed force well trained and disciplined in LOAC, led by responsible and educated noncommissioned and commissioned officers, is the best assurance of limiting violations.

Like all international law, LOAC is based on agreements between nations and on the practice of states. Publicists and scholars moderate the debate and shape arguments that eventually settle into state practice and multilateral treaties. That interrelated mix ideally results in a framework that a combatant can understand. Whether it is called the law of war, IHL, or LOAC, the goal is to confine fighting as closely as possible to combatants and to spare noncombatants; to target those things having a military need for destruction and sparing property not necessary to achieve the military ends of the conflict. These aspirations are lofty, but they are goals worthy of civilized and caring peoples.

CASES AND MATERIALS

HELLENICA, BOOK II, BY XENOPHON

Introduction. *In ancient Greece, the Peloponnesian War was fought between the two great powers of the time, Athens and Sparta. This brief extract is from a book written in 380 B.C., by Xenophon, who completed the work of Thucydides, who died before his history of the Peloponnesian War was complete.*

In 405 B.C., in the war's twenty-sixth year, the conflict reached an unanticipated climax on the shores of the Hellespont. Lysander, the great Lacedaemonian (Spartan) admiral, sailed from his base in Rhodes, entered the Hellespont, and captured Lamsacus, a city allied to Athens. Upon learning of the fall of Lamsacus, 180 Athenian ships immediately set sail, intent on recapturing Lamsacus and defeating Lysander's force. Instead, when the Athenians reached the Hellespont and beached their ships, Lysander's force fell upon them and captured their ships and most of the embarked soldiers.

Having decisively defeated the Athenians, Lysander considered what further action he should take.

As for Lysander, he took his prizes and prisoners and everything else back to Lampsacus, the prisoners including Philocles, Adeimantus, and some of the other generals.... After this Lysander gathered together the allies and bade them deliberate regarding the disposition to be made of the prisoners. Thereupon many charges began to be urged against the Athenians, not only touching the outrages they had already committed and what they had voted to do if they were victorious in the battle, – namely, to cut off the right hand of every man taken alive, – but also the fact that after capturing two triremes, one a Corinthian and the other an Andrian, they had thrown the crews overboard to a man. And it was Philocles, one of the Athenian generals, who had thus made away with

---

[153] Paul Fussell, *Doing Battle: The Making of a Skeptic* (Boston: Little, Brown, 1996), 124.

these men. Many other stories were told, and it was finally resolved to put to death all of the prisoners who were Athenians, with the exception of Adeimantus, because he was the one man who in the Athenian Assembly had opposed the decree in regard to cutting off the hands of captives.... As to Philocles, who threw overboard the Andrians and Corinthians, Lysander first asked him what he deserved to suffer for having begun outrageous practices towards Greeks, and then had his throat cut.[154]

Conclusion. Do we discern in these events the rough outlines of proceedings that were to occur 2,000 years later? Although he led the coalition of forces against the enemy, upon achieving victory Lysander took no action on his own. Instead, he gathered his allies in the victorious campaign against Athens. They publicly debated the disposition of the defeated enemy. Allegations that the Athenians had violated customs of war were raised and discussed. Specific charges were alleged against particular officers of the enemy forces, and individuals "testified." At the conclusion of the testimony a decision was resolved, or reached, and a sentence decided upon by the allies. All but one of the accused were determined to be guilty, and, but for that one, death was decided as the appropriate punishment. The sentence was promptly carried out, in one case personally by the victorious commander, Lysander.

Two thousand years later, the procedure at Lampsacus finds faint echoes in the post–World War II Nuremberg IMT, in the courtrooms of the ICTY, and in other international tribunals.[155]

THE 1474 BREISACH TRIAL

Introduction. What makes a tribunal an "international" tribunal? Have war crimes always been defined in terms similar to those of today? What were defenses to war crime charges before the Nuremberg IMT? These and other questions are raised by a trial held in Europe more than 500 years ago.

"The trial in 1474 of Peter von Hagenbach deserves to be considered as a forerunner of contemporary international war crimes trials. It is all the more relevant because the oral proceedings at this trial centered on one of the most controversial issues of post-1945 war crimes trials: the defense of superior orders."[156]

Duke Charles of Burgundy had raised his country to international power through fierce armed struggles with territorial sovereigns. Charles's friends called him Charles the Bold, whereas his enemies knew him as Charles the Terrible. His 1472 massacre of the inhabitants of Nesle had surely earned him the latter title.

In 1469, financial difficulties forced the Archduke of Austria to pledge to Charles his possessions on the Upper Rhine, including the fortified town of Breisach, a city in what is today southwest Germany. Charles installed Peter von Hagenbach as his Governor.

---

[154] Xenophon, *Hellenica*, Books I–V, Carlton L. Brownson, trans. (London: William Heinemann, 1918), 101, 107.

[155] This idea derives from a 1951 speech by the Greek professor Georges S. Maridakis (1890–1979), republished in 4–4 J. *Int'l Crim. Justice* (Sept. 2006), 847.

[156] Schwarzenberger, *International Law: As Applied by International Courts and Tribunals*, supra, note 25, at 462. Except where indicated, this account is a paraphrasing of Professor Schwarzenberger's description of the trial, his footnotes omitted.

As long as Charles held the pledged territories he was entitled under the agreement to exercise territorial jurisdiction, although he could not impair the liberties of their citizens. Actually, Charles had no intention of ever returning the pledged territories to the Archduke of Austria, intending instead to incorporate them into his Burgundian empire.

In forcing the citizens of Breisach to submit to Charles's rule, Governor von Hagenbach said he merely carried out his master's directions, but the brutality with which he acted was his personal contribution to Burgundian policy. His regime was one of arbitrariness and terror, extending to murder, rape, illegal taxation, and the confiscation of private property. The victims of his depredations included the inhabitants of neighboring territories, as well as Swiss merchants on their way to and from the Frankfurt fair.

Charles's ill-concealed ambition, to transform Burgundy into a kingdom and use it as a springboard to the Imperial Crown, made him powerful enemies. Yet, von Hagenbach's outrages, remarkable even by lax fifteenth-century standards, contributed to forging what had previously been considered impossible, alliances against Burgundy by her Holy Roman Empire neighbors, Austria, Berne, France, and the towns and knights of the Upper Rhine.

To strengthen their case against him, the Allies of the Holy Roman Empire authorized the Archduke of Austria to offer full repayment of his debt to Charles. On flimsy pretexts, Charles refused to accept repayment, but a subsequent revolt by the citizens, and by Hagenbach's German mercenaries at Breisach, enabled the Allies to seize Hagenbach and put him on trial. (This was before the Allies' later war with Burgundy, in which Charles was defeated and killed in the 1477 battle of Nancy.)

The Archduke of Austria, in whose territory Hagenbach had been captured, ordered his trial. Whereas an ordinary trial would have taken place in a local court, the Allies agreed on an ad hoc tribunal, consisting of twenty-eight judges from the Holy Roman Empire towns. Eight of these judges were nominated by Breisach, and two by each of the other allied Alsatian and Upper Rhenanian towns, Berne, a member of the Swiss Confederation, and Solothurn, allied with Berne. As Breisach's sovereign, Austria provided the presiding judge.

In the trial's early inquisitorial stages leading to his formal accusation, Hagenbach was subjected to severe torture. Given the clarity of his crimes, this was pointless, for it produced the predictable confessions which, just as predictably, Hagenbach recanted at trial.

At the public portion of the trial, the Archduke was represented by a spokesman, Heinrich Iselin. Iselin argued on the Archduke's behalf that Hagenbach had "trampled under foot the laws of God and man." On a less secular level, Hagenbach was charged with murder, rape, perjury, and ordering mercenaries to kill the men in the houses in which they were quartered, so that the women and children would be at their mercy.

Hagenbach, defended by Hans Irmy, relied on the defense of superior orders: "Sir Peter von Hagenbach does not recognize any other judge and master but the Duke of Burgundy from whom he had received his commission and his orders. He had no right to question the orders which he was charged to carry out, and it was his duty to obey. Is it not known that soldiers owe absolute obedience to their superiors?. . . Had not the Duke by his presence subsequently confirmed and ratified all that had been done in his name?"

In his personal address to the tribunal, Hagenbach repeated that defense and asked for an adjournment to obtain confirmation of his assertions from his master. The tribunal refused the request on the grounds that to accept Hagenbach's defense would be contrary to the law of God, and that his crimes were established beyond doubt. With that, the tribunal found him guilty, stripped him of his knighthood, and condemned him to death. The executioner of Colmar was selected from among eight contenders. Finally, the marshal of the tribunal gave his order to the executioner, "Let justice be done."

Hagenbach's crimes were committed before the outbreak of open war between Burgundy and its enemies. Strictly speaking, then, they were not war crimes, although the borderline between peace and war in those times was more fluid than today. Nevertheless, the administration of Breisach and the Upper Rhine, in open breach of the treaty obligations of Charles of Burgundy, made the occupation more akin to a wartime rather than a peacetime occupation, and the trial was probably "the first genuinely international trial for the perpetration of atrocities."[157] The Breisach trial may be thought of as an experiment in medieval international justice, soon subsumed by the sanctity of state sovereignty as embodied in the 1648 Treaty of Westphalia. It remains a notable initial effort. In broad post–World War terms, Hagenbach's crimes would be termed crimes against humanity and war crimes.[158]

Conclusion. *Hagenbach's 1474 trial represents the first known interposition of the defense of obedience to orders. One hundred thirty years later, the guard commander at the execution of Charles I, Captain Axtell, raised the defense of superior orders as his defense to charges of traitorous conduct, with the same result as Hagenbach's.[159] Then, as now, from Hagenbach to Calley, it is a defense that rarely succeeds, yet remains the most frequently employed defense to war crime charges.*

UNITED STATES V. PLENTY HORSES[160]

Federal District Court, Sioux Falls, South Dakota (1891, not reported)

Introduction. *When does LOAC apply? What is a "war," and what are the legal implications of a finding of war? Who, and in what legal forums, are such issues decided? By the end of the twentieth century, these questions were largely settled, but a hundred years ago the answers were less clear. A U.S. federal case, Plenty Horses, offers guidelines to answers to these questions. The case is little noted because an appellate opinion, used to study the legal issues raised at trial, was not produced.*

In January 1891, the American Civil War had been over for twenty-six years, but the U.S. Army was still fighting Plains Indians in the country's rugged west and north.[161] The fighting was drawing to a close as the bonds of civilization were confining Indians to reservations. In the two-year-old state of South Dakota, word of a December 29, 1890 massacre at

---

[157] Schabas, *An Introduction to the International Criminal Court*, supra, note 74, at 1.

[158] Meyer and McCoubrey, *Reflections*, supra, note 81, at 3.

[159] *Roger L. DiSilvestro, A Report of Divers Cases in Pleas to the Crown*, 84 Eng. Rep. 1055, 1066 (K.B. 1708). In the Shadow of Wounded Knee, Copyright © 2005, Walker & Company, quoted with permission.

[160] The research assistance of the Office of the Sioux Falls, SD, U.S. District Clerk of Court in locating the case record is appreciated,

[161] This account is taken from: Roger L. DiSilvestro, *In the Shadow of Wounded Knee* (New York: Walker, 2005), and, Robert M. Utley, "The Ordeal of Plenty Horses," 26–1 *American Heritage* (Dec. 1974), 15.

Wounded Knee Creek reached the Sioux Rosebud Reservation, twenty miles to the east of Wounded Knee. Ostensibly fearing an attack by soldiers similar to that at Wounded Knee, the Reservation's Brulé Sioux rebelled and took up defensive positions in the northwestern portion of the nearby Pine Ridge Reservation. The Sioux feared the worst for their own band and they formed small bands of young men to fight the U.S. soldiers.

One of the Sioux fighters was twenty-two-year-old Senika-Wakan-Ota, or Plenty Horses, as he was known to English speakers.[162] Among the Sioux, Plenty Horses was viewed with some suspicion. He had five years of schooling, forced upon him by the U.S. government, from age thirteen to eighteen, at the Indian boarding school at Carlisle Barracks, Pennsylvania. He had returned to the reservation burdened with the white man's ways and language, no longer considered fully an Indian, but clearly not a white man. "I was an outcast.... I was no longer an Indian," Plenty Horses said.[163]

First Lieutenant Edward W. "Ned" Casey, West Point class of 1873,[164] had almost twenty years of Army service, including four years as a tactics instructor at the Military Academy. His father, Brevet Major General Silas Casey, was an author of the Army's infantry tactics manual, and his brother, Brigadier General Thomas L. Casey, was Chief of the Army Corps of Engineers.[165] A capable and popular officer of proven bravery in the Sioux campaigns of 1877, Ned Casey's lengthy time in grade as a lieutenant was a reflection of the Army's promotion-by-seniority system, rather than any lack of soldierly skills.

On the morning of January 7, Lieutenant Casey and two Cheyenne scouts approached the Brulé and Oglala camp at No Water, South Dakota. Casey intended to parley with the chiefs and see if a peaceful settlement of the Wounded Knee uprising could be achieved. At White Water Creek, Casey and his scouts were met by a band of approximately forty Brulé Sioux, including Plenty Horses. Handshakes were exchanged and Casey explained his desire to meet with their chiefs. He conversed briefly with Plenty Horses, whose English had deteriorated since his return from the Carlisle boarding school, years before. An emissary from the chiefs rode out and said that Casey should not go further because younger Indians in the camp remained agitated over Wounded Knee and, besides, the chiefs planned to confer with Casey's superior, General Nelson Miles, the next day. Casey turned his horse to depart. "Plenty Horses took his Winchester from under his blanket, calmly raised it to his shoulder, and fired one shot. The bullet tore into the back of Casey's head and came out just under the right eye. The horse reared and pitched its rider from the saddle. Casey crashed to the ground on his face, dead."[166]

Unrelated to Casey's death, eight days later, on January 15, 1891, the Sioux leaders surrendered to General Miles and the last Plains Indian campaign was over. Miles, who would be promoted to full general twelve years later, had not forgotten Lieutenant Casey, however. He ordered Colonel William Shafter to arrest Plenty Horses for Casey's murder. The arrest was made and, in the civilian community, a Deadwood South Dakota grand jury indicted Plenty Horses for murder. He was released by military authorities for trial in the federal district court at Sioux Falls. The trial opened in late April, housed in the Sioux Falls Masonic Temple, where the court sat when it came to town.

---

[162] Some sources record his name as Tasunka Ota, and his age as twenty-one. Court records indicate otherwise.

[163] Id., DiSilvestro, at 3.   [164] 2002 *Bicentennial Register of Graduates* (USMA: AOG, 2002), 4–57.

[165] MG Silas Casey, USMA class of 1826; BG Thomas Casey, first in the class of 1852. Id., at 4–14 and 4–38.

[166] Utley, "The Ordeal of Plenty Horses," supra, note 161.

From the outset, Plenty Horse's two lawyers, George Nock and David Powers, both working pro bono, made clear the defense strategy: the U.S. Army and the Sioux Indians viewed themselves as opposing belligerents in a state of war, they said. Under customary law of war, combatants of opposing belligerent armed forces are entitled to kill each other without criminal penalty – the combatant's privilege. The trial began. Evidence adduced over the first three days of trial made clear that Plenty Horses had killed Lieutenant Casey and that the Indians in No Water camp thought themselves at war with all U.S. soldiers. When Plenty Horses took the witness stand to testify, the two judges, Alonzo Edgerton, a former Army brigadier general, and Oliver Shiras, a Civil War veteran like Edgerton, would not allow him an interpreter. Angrily, Plenty Horse's lawyers closed the defense case then and there. Closing arguments followed, and Judge Shiras instructed the jury:

> Although the Sioux did not constitute an independent nation with legal authority to declare war, he said, they still had the power to go to war. If the jurors felt that a state of war existed in actual if not in legal fact, they should acquit the defendant. If they judged a war not to be in progress and Plenty Horses to have shot Casey with malice and deliberation, they should find him guilty of murder. If in the second circumstance the killing had occurred without premeditation and in a condition of great mental excitement, the verdict should be manslaughter.[167]

The jury, mostly local farmers, deliberated through the night and into the next day. Shortly before noon they informed the judges that after twenty-three ballots they remained deadlocked, six for murder, six for manslaughter. The judges declared a mistrial. Leaving the courtroom, Plenty Horses said in halting English, "I thought last night that they would hang me sure, but now I feel it will not be so."[168]

Days later, on May 23, 1891, the second trial of Plenty Horses opened with essentially the same participants. The testimony, too, was much the same as in the first trial and the concept of the combatant's privilege was again the central issue. The prosecutor, William Sterling, had called on General Miles at his headquarters in Chicago, asking him to testify that the Army had not been in a state of war with the Sioux. Instead, Miles sent an officer from his staff, Captain Frank D. Baldwin, to Sioux Falls to testify not for the government but for the defense! Newspapers reported that General Miles advised the prosecutor, "My boy, it was a war." He added, "You do not suppose that I am going to reduce my campaign to a dress-parade affair?"[169] After all, Miles pointed out, until handed over to federal marshals for trial, Plenty Horses was held at Fort Meade as a prisoner of war;[170] the Army's report of Lieutenant Casey's death indicated that he had been scouting a hostile camp; a written order from General Miles indicated that Plenty Horses was a "war prisoner." After meeting with General Miles, Prosecutor Sterling was powerless to stop the train bearing down on his case.

Miles's emissary, Captain Baldwin, had been awarded not one but two Medals of Honor. He had been a close friend of Lieutenant Casey's, and he testified in the defense case as General Miles predicted.[171] Baldwin also proffered Army documents proving who

---

[167] Id.   [168] Id.   [169] Id.
[170] National Archives and Records Administration, record group 73, items 1183, 1260, and 1264.
[171] Paul Drew Stevens, ed., *The Congressional Medal of Honor: The Names, the Deeds* (Forest Ranch, CA: Sharp & Dunnigan, 1984), 712.

Lieutenant Casey's killer was, and additionally indicating the state of hostilities between the Army and the Sioux. Following Captain Baldwin's testimony, defense attorney Nock announced that the defense case was concluded. He turned to deliver his closing argument to the jury.

Judge Shiras raised his hand. "Wait a moment, gentlemen...If you have both concluded the presentation of testimony, I have something to say to the jury.... It clearly appears that on the day when Lieutenant Casey met his death there existed in and about the Pine Ridge Agency a condition of actual warfare between the Army of the United States there assembled under the command of Major General Nelson Miles and the Indian troops occupying the camp on No Water and in its vicinity."[172] The judge went on to note that the trial turned on this question of war, which, he then opined, had been shown to exist beyond a reasonable doubt. He went on to say that Casey unquestionably was a combatant. Although the manner in which Plenty Horses killed him merited severe condemnation, Casey was engaged in legitimate warfare against the Sioux and, the judge said, with equal legitimacy, Casey could be killed by the enemy against whom he was fighting. If the attack on Wounded Knee was not a wartime event, Shiras reminded the court, then the soldiers who had participated should all be charged with murder.[173] If Lieutenant Casey were to have killed Plenty Horses while reconnoitering the Indian camp at No Water, the judge continued, surely he would not have been charged with murder. The killing of Casey could only be viewed as an act of war. Shiras directed the jury to so find, which they promptly did. The two trials of Plenty Horses were over.

During the trial, prosecutor Sterling had not asked witnesses why, if Plenty Horses was at war, he had immediately opened fire upon encountering the Casey group, or why he shot only Lieutenant Casey and not the scouts who accompanied him. Or why the scouts had not returned his fire. Or why the parties had engaged in conversation before the killing of Casey. Nor did Sterling point out that prior U.S. treaties with the Sioux and other Indians referred to them as "tribes," rather than "nations." Now those points were moot, as was the question of whether General Miles dispatched Captain Baldwin to testify for the defense to insure that no soldier could be charged for actions at Wounded Knee. The day's leading interpreter of military law, William Winthrop, wrote of Plenty Horses, "the laws of war justify the killing or disabling of members of the one army by those of the other in battle or hostile operations. In such operations would be included, with us, Indian hostilities."[174]

Following his acquittal, Plenty Horses, a lawful combatant by decision of a U.S. District Court, returned to South Dakota's now peaceful Rosebud Reservation. He eventually married and had a son, Charles. His return to obscurity was interrupted only by a personal appearance at the South Dakota exhibit of the Chicago World's Fair, in 1893. Never fully accepted by the Sioux and only tolerated by the white man, Plenty Horses died on June 15, 1933, a year after the deaths of his wife and son.

---

[172] DiSilvestro, *In the Shadow of Wounded Knee*, supra, note 161, at 192, citing the *New York World*, May 29, 1891.

[173] There might also have been questions regarding the twenty Medals of Honor awarded for actions at Wounded Knee. Even in a day when the criteria for the award were relaxed, it seems a generous number.

[174] Winthrop, *Military Law and Precedents*, supra, note 7, at 778.

IN RE GÖRING AND OTHERS

Judgment of the International Military Tribunal (IMT)
at Nuremberg (October 1, 1946)[175]

Introduction. *What is the nature of war? There is no settled answer but, fifty-five years after the Plenty Horses opinion, and its "seat-of-the-pants" decision by two judges seeking to do the right thing under the law as they understood it, four judges of the post–World War II IMT at Nuremberg discussed the nature of aggressive warfare with a deeper reference to international law. From this tribunal's Judgment:*

Crimes against Peace

(1) *War of Aggression as a Crime. The Principle of Retroactivity.* "The charges in the Indictment that the defendants planned and waged aggressive wars are charges of the utmost gravity. War is essentially an evil thing. Its consequences are not confined to the belligerent states alone, but affect the whole world. To initiate a war of aggression, therefore, is not only an international crime; it is the supreme international crime, differing only from other war crimes in that it contains within itself the accumulated evil of the whole. The first acts of aggression referred to in the Indictment are the seizure of Austria and Czechoslovakia, and the first war of aggression charged in the Indictment is the war against Poland begun on the 1st September 1939. Before examining that charge it is necessary to look more closely at some of the events which preceded these acts of aggression. The war against Poland did not come suddenly out of an otherwise clear sky; the evidence has made it plain that this war of aggression, as well as the seizure of Austria and Czechoslovakia, was premeditated and carefully prepared, and was not undertaken until the moment was thought opportune for it to be carried through as a definite part of the preordained scheme and plan. For the aggressive designs of the Nazi Government were not accidents arising out of the immediate political situation in Europe and the world; they were a deliberate and essential part of Nazi foreign policy.

"To assert that it is unjust to punish those who in defiance of treaties and assurances have attacked neighboring states without warning is obviously untrue, for in such circumstances the attacker must know that he is doing wrong, and so far from it being unjust to punish him, it would be unjust if his wrong were allowed to go unpunished. Occupying the positions they did in the government of Germany, the defendants, or at least some of them, must have known of the treaties signed by Germany, outlawing recourse to war for the settlement of international disputes; they must have known that they were acting in defiance of all international law when in complete deliberation they carried out their designs of invasion and aggression....

(2) *General Treaty for the Renunciation of War of 1928 (Kellogg-Briand Pact).* "In the opinion of the Tribunal this Pact was violated by Germany in all the cases of aggressive war charged in the Indictment. It is to be noted that on the 26th January, 1930, Germany signed a Declaration for the Maintenance of Permanent Peace with Poland, which was

---

[175] H. Lauterpacht, ed., *Annual Digest and Reports of Public International Law Cases – 1946* (London: Butterworth & Co., 1951), 203, 207–10, 212. Footnotes omitted.

explicitly based on the Pact of Paris [the Kellogg-Briand Pact], and in which the use of force was outlawed for a period of ten years....

"The question is, what was the legal effect of this Pact? The nations who signed the Pact or adhered to it unconditionally condemned recourse to war for the future as an instrument of policy, and expressly renounced it. After the signing of the Pact, any nation resorting to war as an instrument of national policy breaks the Pact. In the opinion of the Tribunal, the solemn renunciation of war as an instrument of national policy necessarily involves the proposition that such a war is illegal in international law; and that those who plan and wage such a war, with its inevitable and terrible consequences, are committing a crime in so doing. War for the solution of international controversies undertaken as an instrument of national policy certainly includes a war of aggression, and such a war is therefore outlawed by the Pact....

"In the opinion of the Tribunal, those who wage aggressive war are doing that which is equally illegal, and of much greater moment than a breach of one of the rules of the [1907] Hague Convention. In interpreting the words of the Pact, it must be remembered that international law is not the product of an international legislature, and that such international agreements as the Pact of Paris have to deal with the general principles of law, and not with administrative matters of procedure. The law of war is to be found not only in treaties, but in the customs and practices of states which gradually obtained universal recognition, and from the general principles of justice applied by jurists and practiced by military courts. This law is not static, but by continual adaptation follows the needs of a changing world. Indeed, in many cases treaties do no more than express and define for more accurate reference the principles of law already existing....

"All these expressions of opinion, and others that could be cited, so solemnly made, reinforce the construction which the Tribunal placed upon the Pact of Paris, that resort to a war of aggression is not merely illegal, but is criminal."

(3) *Aggression as a Method. Invasion of Austria and Poland.* "In the opinion of the Tribunal, the events of the days immediately preceding the 1st September, 1939, demonstrate the determination of Hitler and his associates to carry out the declared intention of invading Poland at all costs, despite appeals from every quarter. With the ever increasing evidence before him that this intention would lead to war with Great Britain and France as well, Hitler was resolved not to depart from the course he had set for himself. The Tribunal is fully satisfied by the evidence that the war initiated by Germany against Poland on the 1st September, 1939, was most plainly an aggressive war, which was to develop in due course into a war which embraced almost the whole world, and resulted in the commission of countless crimes, both against the laws and customs of war and against humanity."

Conclusion. *The Judgment goes on to discuss the element of premeditation involved in the Nazi invasions of Norway, Denmark, Belgium, the Netherlands, Luxemburg, Greece, Yugoslavia, and Russia, as well as the subject of crimes against humanity, slave labor, the plunder of public and private property, hostages, and other war crimes and crimes against humanity, including the persecution of Jews. The Judgment concludes by finding Hermann Göring and sixteen of his coaccused guilty of various crimes, including crimes against peace, crimes against humanity, and war crimes. Göring and eleven others were sentenced to death by hanging. The death sentences were quickly carried out for all but Göring, who, with the unwitting assistance of an American military police officer, committed suicide hours before his execution date.*

PROSECUTOR V. KUPREŠKIĆ, ET AL.

IT-95–16-T (14 January 2000), footnotes omitted

Introduction. *The International Criminal Tribunal for the Former Yugoslavia, in a 2000 Trial Chamber Judgment, addressed the significance of case law to the Tribunal's findings. In doing so, it discusses the sources of international criminal law, the value and place of precedent and stare decisis in the Tribunal's jurisprudence, and the relation of national (domestic) law to the Tribunal's judgments.*

537. The Tribunal's need to draw upon judicial decisions is only to be expected, due to the fact that both substantive and procedural criminal law is still at a rudimentary stage in international law. In particular, there exist relatively few treaty provisions on the matter. By contrast, especially after World War II, a copious amount of case law has developed on international crimes.... [I]t was difficult for international law makers to reconcile very diverse and often conflicting national traditions in the area of criminal law and procedure by adopting general rules capable of duly taking into account those traditions. By contrast, general principles may gradually crystallise through their incorporation and elaboration in a series of judicial decisions delivered by either international or national courts dealing with specific cases. This being so, it is only logical that international courts should rely heavily on such jurisprudence. What judicial value should be assigned to this *corpus*?

538. The value to be assigned to judicial precedents to a very large extent depends on and is closely bound up with the legal nature of the Tribunal, i.e. on whether or not the Tribunal is an international court proper....

539. Indisputably, the ICTY is an international court, (i) because this was the intent of the Security Council, as expressed in the resolution establishing the Tribunal, (ii) because of the structure and functioning of this Tribunal ... and (iii) because it is called upon to apply international law to establish whether serious violations of IHL have been committed in the territory of the former Yugoslavia. Thus, the normative *corpus* to be applied by the Tribunal *principaliter*, i.e. to decide upon the principle issues submitted to it, is international law. True, the Tribunal may be well advised to draw upon national law to fill possible *lacunae* in the Statute or in customary international law....

540. Being international in nature and applying international law principaliter, the Tribunal cannot but rely upon the well-established sources of international law and, within this framework, upon judicial decisions. What value should be given to such decisions? The Trial Chamber holds the view that they should only be used as a "subsidiary means for the determination of rules of law" (to use the expression in Article 38 (1)(d) of the Statute of the International Court of Justice...). Hence, generally speaking ... the International Tribunal cannot uphold the doctrine of binding precedent (*stare decisis*) adhered to in common law countries. Indeed, this doctrine among other things presupposes to a certain degree a hierarchical judicial system. Such a hierarchical system is lacking in the international community. Clearly, judicial precedent is not a distinct source of law in international criminal adjudication. The Tribunal is not bound by precedents established by other international criminal courts such as the Nuremberg or Tokyo Tribunals, let alone by cases brought before national courts adjudicating international crimes. Similarly, the Tribunal cannot rely on a set of cases, let alone on

a single precedent, as sufficient to establish a principle of law.... [P]rior judicial decisions may persuade the court that they took the correct approach, but they do not compel this conclusion by the sheer force of their precedential weight....

541. As noted above, judicial decisions may prove to be of invaluable importance for the determination of existing law. Here again attention should however be drawn to the need to distinguish between the various categories of decisions and consequently to the weight they may be given for the purpose of finding an international rule or principle. It cannot be gainsaid that great value ought to be attached to decisions of such international criminal courts as the international tribunals of Nuremberg or Tokyo, or to national courts operating by virtue, and on the strength, of Control Council Law no. 10, a legislative act jointly passed in 1945 by the four Occupying Powers and thus reflecting international agreement among the Great Powers on the law applicable to international crimes and the jurisdiction of the courts called upon to rule on those crimes. These courts operated under international instruments laying down provisions that were either declaratory of existing law or which had been gradually transformed into customary international law.... Conversely, depending upon the circumstances of each case, generally speaking decisions of national courts on war crimes or crimes against humanity delivered on the basis of national legislation would carry relatively less weight.

542. In sum, international criminal courts such as the International Tribunal [for the former Yugoslavia] must always carefully appraise decisions of other courts before relying on their persuasive authority as to existing law. Moreover, they should apply a stricter level of scrutiny to national decisions than to international judgments, as the latter are at least based on the same *corpus* of law as that applied by international courts, whereas the former tend to apply national law, or primarily that law, or else interpret international rules through the prism of national legislation.

Conclusion. *The Trial Chamber confirms that there is no* stare decisis *in international courts, and clarifies why the judgments of domestic courts have little impact on those of international courts, whereas those of other international forums enjoy greater weight. The informative and instructive remarks of the Tribunal are themselves dicta – observations in a judicial opinion not necessary for a decision in the case. Although they are probably representative, these remarks represent the views of but one of several ICTY Trial Chambers.*

2   Codes, Conventions, Declarations, and Regulations

2.0 Introduction

The first of two foundational questions in the study of the law of armed conflict (LOAC) and international humanitarian law (IHL) is, What is the conflict status? What law of war applies to the armed conflict being examined? In this chapter, we examine the beginnings of the modern laws of war, an understanding of which is necessary to answer this first foundational question. Where and when did LOAC, as we know it today, arise? Who was instrumental in its founding? What documentary history may we look to?

2.1 A Basic Rule of Warfare

The most basic rule of warfare is stated in the Armed Forces' guide to conduct in war, *The Law of Land Warfare*: "The right of belligerents to adopt means of injuring the enemy is not unlimited."[1] That an army has the means to defeat an adversary does not necessarily indicate that it may use that weapon or means to do so. The British law of war manual adds, "There are compelling dictates of humanity, morality, and civilization to be taken into account."[2] Accordingly, poison gas is outlawed as a means of warfare, despite its battlefield effectiveness. Blinding lasers, biological weapons, and hollow-point bullets are prohibited. They may be effective in a military sense, but their effects are so horrific that their use in combat is prohibited. They increase suffering without conferring military advantage. This basic rule for combatants was first articulated in Article 22 of 1907 Hague Regulation, Convention IV, which was itself taken from 1899 Hague Regulation, Convention II; both are examined in this chapter. The simple statement that the means of injuring and killing the enemy are not unlimited is a part of the customary law of war and an unspoken tenet of one of the principal documents on the law of war, the 1863 Lieber Code.

---

[1] Department of the Army, Field Manual (FM) 27–10, *The Law of Land Warfare* (Washington, DC: GPO, 1956), para. 33; also, *Department of Defense Law of War Manual*, para 2.6.2.1 (June 2015).

[2] United Kingdom Ministry of Defense, *The Manual of the Law of Armed Conflict* (Oxford: Oxford University Press, 2004), 102.

2.2 Francis Lieber

"The roots of the modern law of war lie in the 1860s."[3] During that decade, the first Geneva Convention was concluded, the first multilateral treaty banning a particular weapon was signed,[4] and the Lieber Code was adopted.

Francis Lieber was born either in 1798 or in 1800 (sources differ because Lieber was given to "amending" his age to place himself at the battle of Waterloo) in Berlin, Germany, where, as a young boy in 1806, he saw Napoleon's French occupation troops arrive. At the age of fifteen, with a hatred of Napoleon, Lieber enlisted in the Prussian Army's Colberg regiment. In 1815, still little more than a child, he was severely wounded at Namur while fighting the French. After a long convalescence, he returned to Berlin. Discharged from the army, he studied at several German universities, eventually earning a doctorate at Jena. As a young man, Lieber harbored a deep idealism that took him to Greece to fight the Turks. After that conflict, he traveled to Italy to study further, after which he returned to Germany. His travels and his anti-authoritarian streak aroused government suspicions, and he was arrested, not for the first time. Charged with sedition and imprisoned for several months, Lieber was penniless when released. Not yet thirty, he had already fought in two conflicts, earned a doctorate, and developed a distrust for authority. He opted to leave his native Germany and, in 1826, emigrated to London.[5]

The next year, with a teaching offer in hand, he left England for Boston. Once in the United States, Lieber took a variety of writing jobs in addition to teaching to maintain his growing family. One such endeavor involved the translation of the thirteen-volume Brockhaus *Conversations Lexicon*, which later became the foundation of the first edition of the *Encyclopedia Americana*, which Lieber edited. Searching for greater financial security than occasional writing jobs offered, he became a professor of history and political economy at South Carolina College, now the University of South Carolina. While there, he published his 1853 two-volume *On Civil Liberty and Self-Government*, still considered the first systematic work on political science to appear in America. He wrote several other scholarly books, all to critical praise.

Never comfortable in the southern United States and actively opposed to slavery, in 1856, Lieber moved again, this time to Columbia College, in New York City, where he was professor of history and political economy. By the outbreak of the Civil War, he was a somewhat prominent (and highly conceited, some said)[6] political philosopher and a frequent consultant to the Union government owing to his influential writings and lectures on military law.

This is all review of Lincoln's Code.

---

[3] Burris M. Carnahan, "Lincoln, Lieber and the Laws of War: The Origins and Limits of the Principle of Military Necessity," 92–2 AJIL (April 1998), 213–31, 213.

[4] *Declaration Renouncing the Use, in Time of War, of Explosive Projectiles Under 400 Grammes Weight* (Dec. 1868).

[5] Col. James R. Miles, "Francis Lieber and the Law of War," XXIX-1–2 *Revue de Droit Militaire et de Droit de la Guerre* (1990), 256.

[6] Karma Nabulsi, *Traditions of War: Occupation, Resistance, and the Law* (Oxford: Oxford University Press, 1999), 166.

2.3 Writing the Lieber Code

In 1861, with the Civil War looming, Lieber lectured at Columbia on the customs and usages of war, among other subjects. General Henry W. Halleck (adopted son of Baron Frederic von Steuben) appointed general-in-chief of the Union forces in 1862, heard of Lieber's lectures and asked him for copies. Taking advantage of Halleck's interest, Lieber urged that he be allowed to write a pamphlet on guerrillas as a guide to Union officers, who, even at the outbreak of the Civil War, were plagued by "irregulars." The Union government's acceptance of that twenty-two-page work, *Guerrilla Parties considered with reference to the Law and Usages of War,* led to Lieber's next suggestion that he be assigned to write a compilation of the customary rules of warfare. In December 1862, the War Department agreed and appointed a board of senior officers, including Lieber, to propose "a Code of Regulations for the government of armies in the field."[7] Whereas the military officers for the most part worked on a revision of the Articles of War, Lieber, drawing on his wide knowledge of battlefield law and on personal experience, wrote the code that bears his name.

Lieber was a deeply moral and religious man and a "just war" traditionalist. Writing and publishing a law of war code while a civil war was ongoing was a significant accomplishment. "The full significance of the [Code] becomes apparent only when the Code is considered in light of the paucity of existing legal materials regarding the law of war."[8] By 1863, all armies had acknowledged some limitations on battlefield conduct. The welfare of civilians and prisoners had long been recognized, although precise limitations were not agreed. Napoleon's recent Peninsular Wars in Spain and Portugal had blurred traditional concepts of combatant and civilian. "Lieber in his 1862 pamphlet on guerrilla warfare deplored the Spanish experience. He emphasized that combatants should be commanded, disciplined, follow the rules of war and distinguish themselves from civilians before they were entitled to be prisoners of war."[9] This perspective is found in Lieber's code, reflecting the customary practices of armies of that period – practices that had evolved over hundreds of years of warfare. "This work was prepared to meet the needs of the large numbers of commanders and staff officers in the Federal Forces, whose experience in the field was limited."[10]

> It could not yet be clear, when he [wrote his code], that the war would be a long one and that unprecedented masses of men would have to be raised to fight it, but from the start it was clear that most of the American professional officers were going to be on the Confederate side and that the generally less experienced men in charge of

---

[7] R. R. Baxter, "The First Modern Codification of the Law of War," part I, 25 *Int'l. Rev. of the Red Cross* (April 1963), 171, 183. The other members of the board were Major General Ethan Allen Hitchcock, president; Major General George L. Hartsuff; Brigadier General John H. Martindale; and Major General George Cadwalader, a lawyer in civilian life. General Martindale retired and left the board before its work was completed.

[8] Id., 186. In 1847, Lieutenant General Winfield Scott, also a lawyer in civilian life, had published General Order 20, as "a supplemental code" to the "rules and articles of war," but they were far less complete in their coverage than Lieber's Code.

[9] Miles, *Francis Lieber,* supra, note 5, at 260.

[10] G.I.A.D. Draper, "The Development of International Humanitarian Law," in Michael A. Meyer and Hilaire McCoubrey, eds., *Reflections on Law and Armed Conflicts* (The Hague: Kluwer Law, 1998), 70–1.

the Union's militias and volunteers would need all of the instruction they could get about how to fight.[11]

Impressed by the final 157-article code, and with the Halleck board's endorsement of it, President Lincoln directed that Lieber's work be incorporated into the Union Army's General Orders, and in 1863 it became "General Order 100."[12] (It is sometimes erroneously referred to as "General Orders 100." Imagine a binder containing all general orders; it would be titled "General Orders." The one-hundredth order, however, would not take on the plural of the binder's title but would simply be General Order 100.)

Francis Lieber, then, was the first to promulgate a codification of the law of war for soldiers. "The Instructions, which were to be read primarily by commanders in the field, fulfilled a dual purpose: They were at once a short text on the law of war and a set of rules."[13] Lieber colorfully described his code as "short but pregnant and weighty like some stumpy Dutch woman when in the family way with coming twins."[14] He wrote little in the code that was original, and it is not particularly well organized. The code's genius lay in the gathering – in one accessible document – of the gist of the writings of publicists and the customs of armed forces of the day: customs and usages of war that Lieber had not only studied, but experienced.[15]

Written for the Union forces, it was a military order rather than a law of general application – a significant distinction. Binding only on Union soldiers, its application went no further. But Lieber's Code was widely read and its value recognized far beyond the Union Army. Although the Confederacy initially denounced it as "confused ... undiscriminating" and "obsolete," it later adopted the code for the instruction of its own soldiers and commanders.[16] Lieber's Code became the basis of similar codes issued by Great Britain, France, Prussia, Spain, Russia, Serbia, Argentina, and the Netherlands.[17] Thus, a code written for a civil war ironically became a code for international armed conflicts. Today's United Kingdom *Manual of the Law of Armed Conflict* pays respect to Lieber, saying, "The most important early codification of the customs and usages of war generally was the Lieber Code issued by President Lincoln."[18]

---

[11] Geoffrey Best, *War and Law Since 1945* (Oxford: Oxford University Press, 1994), 41.

[12] Lieber had three sons, all of whom fought in the Civil War. Two of them, Hamilton and Guido, fought for the Union, Hamilton losing an arm in the battle of Fort Donelson. Lieber's other son, Oscar, was a geologist, eventually appointed state geologist of Mississippi. At the outbreak of the war, Oscar joined the Confederate army and was killed at the battle of Williamsburg. Before the war, Guido, sometimes known by his middle name, Norman, graduated from Harvard Law School. After fighting in the war as an infantry officer, he remained in the army, serving as the head of the Department of Law at West Point from 1878 to 1882, eventually rising to be the brigadier general judge advocate general of the U.S. Army.

[13] R. R. Baxter, "The First Modern Codification of the Law of War," part II, 26 *Int'l. Rev. of the Red Cross* (May 1963), 234, 235.

[14] Richard S. Hartigan, *Lieber's Code and the Law of War* (Chicago: Precedent, 1983), 1.

[15] In Article 13 of the code, e.g., Lieber wrote, "Military jurisdiction ... is derived from the common law of war."

[16] Sec. of War James Seddon to Col. Robert Ould, CSA (24 June 1863), reprinted in Hartigan, *Lieber's Code*, supra, note 14, at 120. Seddon also wrote that the code was biased, condoning "a barbarous system of warfare under the pretext of military necessity."

[17] Thomas E. Holland, *The Laws of War on Land (Written and Unwritten)* (Oxford: Clarendon Press, 1908), 72–3.

[18] United Kingdom, *The Manual of the Law of Armed Conflict*, supra, note 2, at 7.

2.3.1 *The Combatant's Privilege*

The combatant's privilege has always been an important customary element of the law of war. In his landmark 1625 work, Grotius writes, "According to the law of nations, anyone who is an enemy may be attacked anywhere. As Euripides says: 'The laws permit to harm a foe where'er he may be found.'"[19]

To this day, the combatant's privilege remains basic to the fighting of armed conflicts. Lieber recorded the privilege in Article 57 of his Code: "So soon as a man is armed by a sovereign government and takes the soldier's oath of fidelity, he is a belligerent; his killing, wounding, or other warlike acts are not individual crimes or offenses." As recently as 2002, an inter-American human rights body noted, "The combatant's privilege ... is in essence a license to kill or wound enemy combatants and destroy other enemy military objectives."[20] "The [1907] Hague Regulations expressed [the combatant's privilege] in attributing the 'rights and duties of war'. ... All members of the armed forces ... can participate directly in hostilities, i.e., attack and be attacked."[21] One hundred years after the Lieber Code's promulgation, Brigadier General Telford Taylor, Nuremberg chief prosecutor, wrote: "War consists largely of acts that would be criminal if performed in time of peace. ... Such conduct is not regarded as criminal if it takes place in the course of war, because the state of war lays a blanket of immunity over the warriors. But the area of immunity is not unlimited, and its boundaries are marked by the laws of war."[22]

Combatants are privileged in the law of war to kill and wound without penalty. Presuming this privilege is not abused by an unlawful battlefield act, the privilege accrues to all lawful combatants. Captured soldiers who have engaged in combat and killed the enemy by lawful means are not held captive by that enemy for committing criminal acts because their killings and other warlike acts, in Lieber's words, "are not individual crimes or offenses." They are prisoners of war, held not to be punished, but solely to prevent their return to the fight. In contrast, fighters who are not lawful combatants are not privileged to exercise this exemption.

2.3.2 *Parsing the Lieber Code*

Lieber adopted and expanded the core military concept of military necessity, perhaps the most significant aspect of the code. He believed wars should be as brief as possible, although understanding that sharp wars call for more intense fighting and greater destruction. "Military necessity admits of all direct destruction of life and limb of armed enemies, and of other persons whose destruction is incidentally unavoidable ... it allows all destruction of property ... and of all withholding of sustenance or means of life from

---

[19] Hugo Grotius, *The Law of War and Peace* (Buffalo, NY: Hein reprint of Kelsey translation, 1995), book III, chapter IV, VIII.

[20] Inter-American Commission on Human Rights, Report on Terrorism and Human Rights, OEA/Ser.L/-V/ II.116 Doc. 5 rev. 1 corr., 22 Oct. 2002, para. 68, cited in Knut Dörmann, "The Legal Situation of 'Unlawful/Unprivileged Combatants,'" 85 *Int'l Rev. of the Red Cross*, 45 (March 2003).

[21] Yves Sandoz, Christophe Swinarski, Bruno Zimmermann, eds., *Commentary on the Additional Protocols of 8 June 1977* (Geneva: Martinus Nijhoff, 1987), 515. (Hereinafter *Protocols Commentary*). 1977 Additional Protocol I, Art. 43.2, essentially repeats the Hague Regulation formulation.

[22] Telford Taylor, *Nuremberg and Vietnam: An American Tragedy* (Chicago: Quadrangle Books, 1970), 19.

the enemy."[23] (Notice Lieber's reference to "incidentally unavoidable" destruction, describing in 1863 what today is called "collateral damage.") Although the specifics of military necessity were far from settled when the Lieber Code was written, the mere use of the term was significant, for it suggested limitations on what was permissible in warfare. Still, by endorsing military necessity with only the vaguest suggestion of what those limitations were, the code essentially required only that belligerents act in their military self-interest. Military necessity, which remains a concept largely free of objective limits, would achieve greater recognition a few years later, in the St. Petersburg Declaration of 1868, which applied the code and renounced the use of explosive projectiles in warfare.

Some point to the Union Army general William T. Sherman and his three-hundred-mile march to the sea, from Atlanta to Savannah, as a violation of military necessity and contrary to General Order 100. Lieber, however, would have viewed the "destruction of property . . . and of all withholding of sustenance or means of life from the enemy" as "incidentally unavoidable." Article 29 of the Lieber Code says that "the more vigorous wars are pursued, the better it is for humanity. Sharp wars are brief." Lieber did not object to starvation of the enemy, civilian, and soldier. "War is not carried on by arms alone," he wrote in Article 17. "It is lawful to starve the hostile belligerent, armed or unarmed, so that it leads to the speedier subjection of the enemy." → necessity

How could Lieber, a religious moralist, justify the starving of noncombatants? He answers in Article 21: "The citizen or native of a hostile country is thus an enemy . . . and as such is subjected to the hardships of war."[24] Although that was the customary law of the period, Lieber ameliorates this harsh view, adding in Article 22, "Nevertheless . . . [civilization recognizes] the distinction between the private individual belonging to a hostile country and . . . its men in arms. . . . The unarmed citizen is to be spared in person, property, and honor as much as the exigencies of war will admit"; and in Article 25, "Protection of the inoffensive citizen of the hostile country is the rule."[25] Significantly, Lieber notes in Article 15, "Men who take up arms against one another in public war do not cease on this account to be moral beings, responsible to one another and to God."

Lieber by no means gave license to a soldier's cruelty or criminality, as he makes clear in Article 44:

> All wanton violence committed against persons in the invaded country, all destruction of property not commanded by the authorized officer, all robbery . . . all rape, wounding, maiming, or killing of such inhabitants, are prohibited under the penalty of death. . . . A soldier, officer or private, in the act of committing such violence,

---

[23] Lieber Code, Article 15.

[24] The same formulation is repeated in *The Law of Land Warfare*: "Under the law of the United States, one of the consequences of the existence of a condition of war between two States is that every national of the one State becomes an enemy of every national of the other." FM 27–10, *The Law of Land Warfare*, supra, note 1, at para. 26.

[25] Even in his march to the sea, Union General Sherman ordered that private homes were to be left unmolested. His Field Order of November 14, 1864, directed that "soldiers must not enter the dwellings of the inhabitants, or commit any trespass; but, during a halt or camp, they may be permitted to gather turnips, potatoes, and other vegetables." Burke Davis, *Sherman's March* (New York: Vintage Books, 1988), 31. Little was done to enforce the order's prohibitions, however.

and disobeying a superior ordering him to abstain from it, may be lawfully killed on the spot by such superior.

Today, the summary execution of an enemy soldier, never mind a soldier of one's own army, is anathema, clearly prohibited by LOAC. Lieber's guidance in Article 69 is open to discussion and disagreement, as well: "Outposts, sentinels, or pickets are not to be fired upon, except to drive them in," suggesting that individual enemy soldiers not actively engaged in combat should not be targeted. This interpretation of the law of war is more stringent than that asserted in the modern era.

Another departure from modern LOAC is the code's assertion that "a commander is permitted to direct his troops give no quarter, in great straits, when his own salvation makes it *impossible* to cumber himself with prisoners."[26] To give no quarter means, of course, that surrender is not accepted; every enemy will be put to the sword. True, this language is preceded in the same article by a general rule to the contrary, "It is against the usage of modern war to resolve ... to give no quarter." Today's LOAC is clear that quarter may never be denied, no matter how great the straits.[27] (The giving of quarter, or not, involves the initial acceptance of enemy surrender. The killing of prisoners already in one's control is another strictly prohibited act.)

In late 2001, President George W. Bush said of Osama bin Laden, "I want him – hell, I want – I want justice, and there's an old poster out west ... 'Wanted: Dead or Alive.'"[28] That presidential statement is a departure from U.S. military policy[29] and is contrary to Article 148 of the Lieber Code: "The law of war does not allow proclaiming either an individual belonging to the hostile army, or a citizen, or a subject of the hostile government, an outlaw, who may be slain without trial by any captor." War is made on opposing states, not on individuals. This does not mean that specific individuals are not targeted in the course of an armed conflict, such as individual enemy commanders. But they are targeted as commanders, or specialist combatants, or simply as enemy combatants or enemy fighters. In other words, the individual filling the special position or unique status is the target, not the person, per se. To target an individual because of his/her billet is lawful. To issue battlefield wanted posters exceeds the military's combat mission to "close with and destroy the enemy," transforming it into "close with and kill this particular individual."

In keeping with then-prevailing customary law of war (and U.S. Supreme Court decisions),[30] the code allows the destruction of noncombatant property that might later be used by the enemy (Article 38). A variation of that view is repeated in today's Geneva Convention IV: "Any destruction ... of real or personal property belonging ... to private persons ... is prohibited, except where such destruction is rendered absolutely necessary by military operations."[31]

---

[26] Instructions for the Government of Armies of the United States in the Field (Army General Order 100 of 24 April 1863), Art. 60. Emphasis in original.

[27] 1977 Additional Protocol I, Art. 40; 1913 *Oxford Manual of Naval War*, Art. 17(3); 1907 Hague Convention IV Respecting the Laws and Customs of War on Land, Art. 23(d); and 1899 Hague Convention II Respecting the Laws and Customs of War on Land, Art. 23(d), for examples.

[28] CNN Newsroom, 21 Dec. 2001, http://transcripts.cnn.com/TRANSCRIPTS/0112/21/nr.00.html

[29] FM 27–10, *The Law of Land Warfare*, supra, note 1, at para. 31.

[30] *Brown v. United States*, 12 U.S. 110, 122–3 (1814). "That war gives to the sovereign full right to take the persons and confiscate the property of the enemy wherever found, is conceded." Marshall, C.J.

[31] Geneva Convention IV, Relative to the Protection of Civilian Persons in Time of War of August 12, 1949, Art. 53.

The same article of the Lieber Code permits the seizure of civilian property, if needed by the military: "Private property ... can be seized only by way of military necessity, for the support or other benefit of the army or of the United States. ... The commanding officer will cause receipts to be given." This provision, repeated in later Hague regulations,[32] was tested in 2004, during the war in Iraq. In separate courts-martial, Army First Lieutenant Bradley J. Pavlik and Sergeant First Class James Williams were convicted of offenses related to Sergeant Williams's seizure of civilian property, an Iraqi-owned personal vehicle.

> Early in the war, soldiers were allowed to commandeer vehicles belonging to civilians for military purposes. They were instructed to leave a receipt so the vehicle could be returned to the owner or money could be paid to him. Sergeant Williams said Lieutenant Pavlik was angry that his own vehicle had broken down and told squad leaders to find him another. The vehicle was taken without force, but no receipt was left. The army later paid the owner thirty-two thousand dollars.[33]

The members (military jury) sentenced the lieutenant to one month's confinement and dismissal from the army. The sergeant was reduced to the grade of private and received a bad conduct discharge. The Lieber Code's vitality was demonstrated 140 years after its publication.

Through several provisions quite similar to the Geneva Convention protecting prisoners of war, the Code required humane treatment of prisoners.[34]

Anticipating "unlawful combatants" by nearly a century, the Code provided that

> Men, or squads of men, who commit hostilities ... without being part and portion of the organized hostile army ... who do so with intermitting returns to their homes and avocations, or with the occasional assumption of the semblance of peaceful pursuits, divesting themselves of the character or appearance of soldiers ... are not entitled to the privileges of prisoners of war, but shall be treated summarily as highway robbers or pirates.[35]

This 1863 description neatly fits the Vietnam War's Viet Cong, Iraq's insurgents, and other modern-day enemy fighters around the world.

Interestingly, the code did not address the issue of obedience of orders. Lieber did write on the subject elsewhere, saying that obedience is essential in any armed force but that obedience to unlawful orders cannot be mandated, and such obedience would not negate personal responsibility.[36] Professor L. C. Green considers that

> the most significant feature of the Lieber Code and its importance for the development of the law is in Article 71, which may well be regarded as the forerunner of what is today accepted as universal jurisdiction over those guilty of committing war crimes:

---

[32] Hague Convention IV Respecting the Laws and Customs of War on Land, 1907, Art. 23(g): "It is especially forbidden ... to destroy or seize the enemy's property, unless such destruction or seizure be imperatively demanded by the necessities of war."

[33] Associated Press, "Jury Calls for Officer's Ouster Over S.U.V.," NY *Times*, 14 Aug. 2004, A7. The trial counsel (prosecutor) in the lieutenant's case was Capt. Howard H. Hoege III, the 1994 West Point first captain.

[34] Arts. 55–7, 67, 72–80.

[35] Art. 82. See Chapters 6.4.3. 6.5, 15.6.2, and 15.6.3 for discussions of "unlawful combatants."

[36] Miles, "Francis Lieber," supra, note 5, at 272.

"Whoever intentionally inflicts additional wounds on an enemy already wholly disabled, or kills such an enemy, or who orders or encourages soldiers to do so, shall suffer death, if duly convicted, *whether he belongs to the Army of the United States, or is an enemy captured after having committed his misdeed.*"[37]

Praise for the code has not been universal, of course. The offenses it specifies were already crimes in most national penal codes. "Lieber ... liked to spell out the reasons for everything,"[38] making the code overly detailed. "It makes no reference to the need to ensure that members of the U.S. armed forces are made aware of what they may and may not do,"[39] a reference to an absence of a requirement that the code be disseminated to the members of the military. One scholar opined that it lacked the clarity that a more militarily experienced writer might have provided.[40] Compared to the significance of its contributions, however, these are cavils that little detract from the international import-ance of the Lieber Code.

2.4 Lieber's Legacy

After the Civil War, and after his tenure at the War Department ended, Lieber returned to Columbia University. He was appointed by Secretary of State Edwin Stanton as archivist of records of the Confederate government. Lieber's son Norman, still an army officer, was briefly appointed his assistant. Lieber never retired. Fluent in two languages, he continued to pursue his interests in penology, the jury system, and political ethics and published a volume of poetry, as well. In 1872, Francis Lieber died in New York City, aged seventy-two.

"[The code] was many years ahead of its time."[41] "Lieber's Code has long since been formally superseded by more elaborate (and sometimes not quite so clear) rules and regulations. ... It had, though, a remarkably long run, remaining virtually unchanged until 1949."[42] It continued to be America's law of war guide through the 1898 war with Spain, and through the Philippine insurrection. It was not until 1914, on the eve of World War I, that the United States published a new law of land warfare manual. Its opening reads: "It will be found that everything vital contained in G.O. 100 [the Lieber Code] ... has been incorporated in this manual."[43] Until then, the code remained in effect as an Army General Order. Its impact in the United States and internationally was great and long-lasting as the first codification for soldiers in the field of customary rules of battlefield conduct. Much of LOAC that has followed – the Hague Regulations of 1899 and 1907, the first Geneva Convention in 1864, even the 1949 Geneva Conventions – owes a substantial debt to Francis Lieber and his 1863 code.

---

[37] Leslie C. Green, *Essays on the Modern Law of War*, 2d ed. (Ardsley, NY: Transnational, 1999), 63. Emphasis in original, although not in Professor Green's source, Art. 71.

[38] Geoffrey Best, *Humanity in Warfare* (London: Weidenfeld & Nicolson, 1980), 170.   [39] Id., at 231.

[40] Percy Bordwell, *The Law of War between Belligerents: A Commentary* (Chicago: Callaghan, 1908), 74.

[41] Dieter Fleck, ed., *The Handbook of Humanitarian Law in Armed Conflicts* (Oxford: Oxford University Press, 1995), para. 116.

[42] Richard Shelly Hartigan, *Lieber's Code and the Law of War* (Bethesda, MD: Legal Classics Library, 1995), 24.

[43] War Department, *Rules of Land Warfare* (Washington, DC: GPO, 1914), 7.

2.5 A First Geneva Convention

The 1859 Battle of Solferino was a significant battle in an insignificant war, the war of Austria against Piedmont (later the Kingdom of Sardinia) and France. Some historical accounts refer to it as the Second Italian War of Independence. The war lasted from March to July 1859, a mere four months, but most nineteenth-century wars were brief, fought perhaps to realign a national border or gain access to a seaport. "Warfare involved governments and armies, arousing surprisingly little interest in the majority of the population, who often did not notice a change in rulers that resulted from battles won or lost."[44] Citizens living in the countryside were sometimes unaware that their nation was even at war. "Analysis of war prior to nineteenth-century industrialism and Napoleonic enthusiasm indicates that wars were less violent and less significant and were subject to cultural restraints."[45] Not so, the War of Austria against Piedmont and France. The objective of Piedmont/France was to end Austria's occupation of Sardinia and gain northern Italian independence. King Victor Emmanuel II of Italy fought (with French support from Napoleon III, who personally led a French army allied with the Italians) for Italian unification and independence from Austria.

Austria invaded Piedmont and, on June 24, 1859, the Battle of Solferino was fought alongside the Mincio River, in Lombardy, not far from Milan and Verona. In a battle involving more than 200,000 troops, the Piedmont/French force, commanded by Napoleon, defeated the Austrian force, led by the youthful Emperor Franz-Josef. Although numbers differ from account to account, there were roughly 17,200 French casualties and 22,000 Austrian – more dead and wounded than in any European battle since Waterloo. It was a costly victory for the French and for Piedmont.

As was the military practice of the time, the wounded who were unable to keep up with their departing army, or who had no comrades to assist them in keeping pace, were left to their fates on the field of battle where they had fallen. A civilian observer of the battle was thirty-one-year-old Henry Jean Dunant, a well-to-do Swiss businessman who was horrified at the sight of the untended wounded and their pitiful cries. In Italy on business, Dunant delayed his departure to spend the next week helping to police the battlefield of wounded soldiers of both sides and to assist in their care. "The French forces had four vets for every thousand horses, but only one doctor for every thousand men. A week before the battle, one surgeon had reported that he had no instruments for amputations."[46] In such circumstances, Dunant did what little he could to alleviate the suffering of the wounded.

> **SIDEBAR.** U.S. Army Major General Philip Kearny fought at Solferino with Napoleon's Cavalry Division of the Imperial Guard. Kearny, who earlier lost his left arm in the Mexican-American War (1846–8), was a major, medically retired, and living in Paris when the war broke out. He appealed to Napoleon personally to join the French forces. Fighting in his U.S. Army uniform, Major Kearny so distinguished himself at Solferino that he was the first American ever awarded the cross of the Legion

[44] John A. Nagl, *Learning to Eat Soup with a Knife* (Chicago: University of Chicago, 2002), 16.

[45] James Hillman, *A Terrible Love of War* (New York: Penguin, 2004), 168.

[46] Caroline Moorehead, *Dunant's Dream* (New York: Carroll & Graf, 1999), 3. Also see, Pierre Boissier, *Henry Dunant* (Geneva: Henry Dunant Institute, 1974).

d'Honneur, France's highest award for valor. Returned to active duty in the U.S. Army when the American Civil War broke out, Major General Kearny was killed at the Battle of Chantilly, three years later.[47]

2.5.1 A Memory of Solferino *and the International Committee of the Red Cross*

Three years after the battle, unable to forget the horror of that week, Dunant wrote a passionate book, *A Memory of Solferino*, describing what he had witnessed. Despite serious business reversals, Dunant paid for its publication with his own funds. The slim volume quickly became the *Gone with the Wind* of its day. Dunant's somewhat lurid descriptions of the battle and its aftermath shocked much of Europe, including kings, queens, and heads of state:

> Here is a hand-to-hand struggle in all its horror and frightfulness; Austrians and allies trampling each other under foot, killing one another on piles of bleeding corpses, felling their enemies with their rifle butts, crushing skulls, ripping bellies open with saber and bayonet. No quarter is given; it is a sheer butchery; a struggle between savage beasts, maddened with blood and fury. Even the wounded fight to the last gasp. When they have no weapon left, they seize their enemies by the throat and tear them with their teeth.[48]

His description of the care given the wounded who survived to receive hospital care was no less disturbing. "The operating surgeon had removed his coat. ... With one knee on the ground and the terrible knife in his hand, he threw his arm round the soldier's thigh, and with a single movement cut the skin round the limb. A piercing cry rang through the hospital."[49]

A worldwide political arousal followed the publication of Dunant's book, the last few pages of which contain the seed of an idea for the formation of neutral relief committees in time of peace, to train volunteers who would treat the wounded in time of war, with an international agreement to recognize and protect those committees. There was a consensus that something had to be done.

In Geneva, three years and eight months later, in February 1863, Dunant and four others of the Geneva aristocracy, members of the Geneva Public Welfare Society, formed the International Committee for Relief to the Wounded, a politically neutral body to translate Dunant's ideas for the care of wounded soldiers into practice.[50] The Swiss government agreed to sponsor a diplomatic conference, and, in August 1864, delegates from sixteen countries gathered in Geneva to lay down the basic principles for the fledgling body. Groups of medical volunteers would be organized by societies in each subscribing country to give aid to the wounded, regardless of their nationality. Similar branches soon formed all over Europe. In 1864, the International Committee became the International Committee of the Red Cross (ICRC), with their identifying emblem, the flag of Switzerland with colors reversed. (Contrary to 1949 Geneva

---

[47] John Watts DePeyster, *Personal and Military History of Philip Kearny* (New York: Rice & Gage, 1869), 167–83.

[48] Henry Dunant, *A Memory of Solferino* (Geneva: ICRC reprint, 1986), 19.   [49] Id., at 90–1.

[50] François Bugnion, *The Emblem of the Red Cross* (Geneva: ICRC, 1977), 6; and, "From the Battle of Solferino to the Eve of the First World War," ICRC (28–12–2004), www.icrc.org/web/eng/siteengo.nsf/html/57JNVP

Convention I,[51] there is no contemporary record confirming that the delegates to the 1863 meeting who adopted the ICRC's symbol actually had the Swiss flag in mind.)[52]

2.5.2 *The 1864 Geneva Convention*

In August 1864, the first ICRC Convention met in Geneva, a year after America's adoption of the Lieber Code. At the meeting, the ICRC dedicated itself to establishing guidelines for the protection and care of the wounded, which it did through its first written convention of ten brief articles. "The Convention also was an expression of the European tradition of natural law that had started to emerge in the sixteenth century, under which legal experts strove to overcome the particularity of laws and practices and replace them with universally applicable principles."[53] Of the sixteen nations present, twelve (Baden, Belgium, Britain, France, Hesse, Italy, the Netherlands, Portugal, Prussia, Spain, Switzerland, and Wurttenberg) signed the convention.[54] A U.S. representative was present but did not sign. America was still a young nation, wary of foreign entanglements, even humanitarian ones. In 1882, eighteen years later, the United States did ratify the first Geneva Convention.

For his efforts, his dedication, and his vision, in 1901 Henry Dunant shared the first Nobel Prize in peace.[55] He died in October 1910.

2.6 The 1868 St. Petersburg Declaration

There are many treaties, compacts, declarations, and protocols – some more significant than others – relating to the law of war. The St. Petersburg Declaration is among the more important.

For centuries, there have been efforts, largely unsuccessful, to ban particular weapons. "In ancient times, the Laws of Manu … prohibited Hindus from using poisoned arrows; and the Greeks and Romans customarily observed a prohibition against using poison or poisoned weapons. During the Middle Ages the Lateran Council of 1132 declared that the crossbow and arbalest were 'unchristian' weapons."[56] The subject of the 1868 St. Petersburg Declaration was a type of bullet that exploded on contact with any hard surface. Such a bullet had been developed for the Russian Imperial Army's use in blowing up enemy ammunition wagons. An 1867 modification allowed the bullet to explode and shatter even on contact with soft targets – soldiers, for example. It was no more effective than an ordinary bullet; it wounded or killed only one soldier, but because of its explosive character the bullet caused particularly severe wounds. The Russians came to consider it an inhumane round, improper for use against troops in any

---

[51] Art. 38: "As a compliment to Switzerland, the heraldic emblem of the red cross on a white ground, formed by reversing the Federal colours, is retained as the emblem and distinctive sign of the Medical Service of armed forces."

[52] Bugnion, *The Emblem of the Red Cross*, supra, note 50, at 12–13.

[53] Daniel Thürer, "Dunant's Pyramid: Thoughts on the 'Humanitarian Space'," 865 *Int'l Rev. of the Red Cross*, 47, 50 (March 2007).

[54] Moorehead, *Dunant's Dream*, supra, note 46, at 44–5.

[55] The Norwegian Nobel Institute records Dunant's name as "Jean Henry Dunant."

[56] Adam Roberts and Richard Guellf, *Documents on the Laws of War*, 3d ed. (Oxford: Oxford University Press, 2000), 53.

circumstances. Despite having developed it, they strictly controlled its distribution, and Russia's war minister urged the czar to renounce its use entirely. In response, Czar Alexander II invited states to attend an international military commission to St. Petersburg to discuss the matter. Seventeen states attended, and all but one (Persia) signed the declaration.[57] The United States did not participate.[58]

The states that ratified the St. Petersburg Declaration Renouncing the Use in War of Certain Explosive Projectiles agreed not to use explosive bullets weighing less than 400 g (400 g equals 14.11 ounces, somewhat larger than a modern .50 caliber bullet and smaller than a 22 mm bullet.) Explosive bullets should not be confused with "tracer" bullets, which allow the shooter to see the "trace" of his shot, or with dum-dum bullets, which expand upon contact rather than explode. Following the lead of the 1868 declaration, dum-dums were the subject of their own international agreement at the 1899 Hague Peace Conference.

The St. Petersburg Declaration was the first international agreement in which the use of a weapon developed through advances in technology was banned on humanitarian grounds. A century later, Georg Schwarzenberger wrote, "It is the function of the rules of warfare to impose some limits, however ineffective, to a complete reversion to anarchy by the establishment of minimum standards on the conduct of war."[59] The St. Petersburg ban on explosive bullets was such a minimum standard.

The declaration is also noteworthy because of its preamble. In fact, "the significance of the Declaration does not lie in its actual provisions which are no longer of any practical import,"[60] but in its preamble, which enunciated two of the basic concepts of warfare, unnecessary suffering and military necessity:

> That the only legitimate object which States should endeavor to accomplish during war is to weaken the military forces of the enemy; That for this purpose it is sufficient to disable the greatest possible number of men; That this object would be exceeded by the employment of arms which uselessly aggravate the sufferings of disabled men, or render their death inevitable; That the employment of such arms would, therefore, be contrary to the laws of humanity.

For the first time, the core concept of unnecessary suffering – "the employment of arms which uselessly aggravate the sufferings of disabled men, or render their death inevitable [is] contrary to the laws of humanity" – was embodied in an international agreement.

---

[57] The seventeen states at the St. Petersburg Commission were Austria-Hungary, Bavaria, Belgium, Denmark, France, Great Britain, Greece, Italy, the Netherlands, Persia, Portugal, Prussia and the North German Confederation, Russia, Sweden, Switzerland, Turkey, and Wurttemberg.

[58] The United States still has not ratified the declaration, although it agrees that "bullets designed specifically to explode in the human body clearly are illegal." The U.S. recognition of illegality does not extend, however, to high-explosive projectiles "designed primarily for anti-matériel purposes ... which may be employed for anti-matériel *and* anti-personnel purposes." John B. Bellinger III and William J. Haynes II, "A US Government Response to the International Committee of the Red Cross Study of Customary International Humanitarian Law," 866 *Int'l Rev. of the Red Cross* (June 2007), 443, 460–1. Emphasis supplied.

[59] Georg Schwarzenberger, *International Law: As Applied by International Courts and Tribunals.* Vol. II. *The Law of Armed Conflict* (London: Stevens, 1968), 10.

[60] Judith Gardam, *Necessity, Proportionality and the Use of Force by States* (Cambridge: Cambridge University Press, 2004), 50.

The object of armed conflict is to defeat the enemy force, not simply to kill as many of the enemy as possible or to inflict the greatest possible wounds.

Similarly, the preamble enunciates the core concept of military necessity: "The only legitimate object ... during war is to weaken the military forces of the enemy." If the object of military action is other than to weaken opposing military forces, it is illegitimate. Military necessity had been enunciated in prior documents – the Lieber Code, for example – but it was emphasized in this declaration, reinforcing the point that there are limits to what is permitted on the battlefield. LOAC is about those limits.*

The St. Petersburg Declaration led to other declarations renouncing specific means of warfare at the 1899 and 1907 Hague Peace Conferences. Although one searches in vain for an example, other than the declaration's exploding bullets, of a weapon actually withdrawn from use because it violated the declaration, or because it caused unnecessary suffering, "the St. Petersburg Declaration remains a significant influence upon the modern law of war – not as a precedent for the prohibition of a specific weapon, but as a statement of fundamental principles. These principles have helped shape the modern law [of armed conflict] and retain still the potential to affect the future of that law."[61]

2.7 The 1899 and 1907 Hague Peace Conferences

In the nineteenth century, the European world, along with the United States, developed a confidence in modern progress that extended to a hope that the abolition of war was possible. A popular belief arose that the establishment of a permanent international court would be a major step toward the abolition of war. The work of Clara Barton, Florence Nightingale, and Henry Dunant had captured the world public's attention. A peace movement arose, most strongly in Europe. "It was the carnage of the Napoleonic war that gave rise to the simultaneous outburst of peace societies to be signaled in Britain, the Continent and the United States alike from 1815 onwards."[62] The movement was a significant force for political action aimed at the abolition, or at least control, of war in part because warfare had changed so dramatically in the nineteenth century, making it more horrific than ever. Combat moved from muzzle-loading flintlock muskets to repeating rifles; from wooden sailing ships to steel dreadnought steamships. The machine gun was born. The Industrial Revolution led to greater interaction among states through investment and trade, allowing arms industries to flourish. It also enhanced states' ability to wage war by allowing the mass production of the new weapons, and the creation of the means to transport them in large volume.

---

* The limits defined at St. Petersburg have not been applied to aerial warfare, unknown in 1868, of course. Today, aircraft lawfully use high-explosive rounds weighing less than four hundred grams against enemy aircraft and other nonhuman targets. There is no body of international law specific to aerial warfare, but well-known customary limitations regarding targeting apply in aerial combat as in land warfare.

[61] George H. Aldrich, "From the St. Petersburg Declaration to the Modern Law of War," in Nicolas Borsinger, ed., *125th Anniversary of the 1868 Declaration of St. Petersburg* (Geneva: ICRC, 1994), 50–1.

[62] Arthur Eyffinger, *The Peace Palace: Residence for Justice – Domicile of Learning* (The Hague: Carnegie Foundation, 1988), 14.

2.7.1 *The First Hague Peace Conference*

The 1899 Peace Conference, held at The Hague, in the Netherlands, was an international effort to move beyond the ad hoc international arbitration that had been the recent model and to advance toward a permanent international court for the settlement of national disputes. Today, arbitration is not the first consideration when seeking a means to end armed conflict. In the eighteenth and nineteenth centuries, however, it was successfully employed, for example, in the Jay Treaty of 1794 between America and Great Britain, and the *Alabama*–United States–Great Britain case, in 1871–2. America, too, became an advocate for the establishment of a permanent court of arbitration.

An August 1898 circular was issued by the Russian czar Nicholas II, proposing a conference of governments having diplomatic representatives at the Russian Imperial Court. The proposal set disarmament, and the peaceful settlement of disputes, as the issues for discussion: not dispute resolution but the avoidance of war. "The present moment would be very favorable for seeking, by means of international discussion, the most effective means of ensuring to all peoples the benefits of a real and lasting peace, and, above all, of limiting the progressive development of existing armaments."[63]

An unspoken impetus for the czar's call for a conference was his sense that Russia's economy could not bear the burgeoning costs of new weapons, particularly rifled artillery.[*] His circular proposing the peace conference heavily stressed the financial burdens of warfare: "The ever-increasing financial charges strike and paralyze public prosperity at its source . . . hundreds of millions are spent in acquiring terrible engines of destruction . . . economic progress, and the production of wealth are either paralyzed or perverted in their development."[64]

> The first to put in an official answer was the United States. The event actually constitutes a landmark in America's foreign policy, for it was on this occasion that the United States first abandoned its policy of splendid isolation. Admittedly, the armaments and navy built up by the [United States] were not yet of any real impact on world politics. Still, the increasing capitalism and rapidly expanding international trade had opened the eyes of United States politicians and captains of industry to the world markets and had already resulted in conflict with the Spanish over Cuba and the Philippines.[65]

The first peace conference was held at The Hague from May through July 1899, attended by representatives of twenty-eight nations. One of the six American delegates to the 1899 conference was the naval warfare theorist U.S. Navy Captain Alfred Thayer Mahan. Also participating was a Russian delegate, Fyodor F. Martens, about whom more would be heard. There were three conference "commissions," one concerned with the primary issue, the creation of a permanent international court of arbitration; another with armaments; and the third with the laws of war.[66]

---

[63] James Brown Scott, ed., *The Hague Conventions and Declarations of 1899 and 1907* (New York: Oxford University Press, 1918), v, citing the Russian note.

[*] Austria had developed a rapid-firing field gun with a rate of fire six times that of any Russian artillery. The gun was already in use by the French and Germans, and its use showed that Russia could not match their expenditures. An international peace conference seemed a prudent alternative.

[64] Id., xv.   [65] Eyffinger, *The Peace Palace*, supra, note 62, at 11.

[66] See, generally, "Symposium: The Hague Peace Conferences," 94–1 *AJIL* 1–98 (Jan. 2000).

From the outset, arms limitation was a conference dead letter. Even before the conference convened, delegates of the major powers had been instructed to reject any attempt at weapons regulation.[67] One author has written, "One hundred years later, the legacy of the 1899 conference continues most obviously in the institution it created, the Permanent Court of Arbitration."[68] Indeed, a court of arbitration was raised, after a fashion, but in reality it was a phantom, in that only a secretariat was established. It would be eighty years before this weak beginning became the basis for the Permanent Court of Arbitration. At the time, however, the sentiment of the German delegation was prevalent: "The German delegation declares that it cannot adhere to any of the projects which tend to establish universal obligatory arbitration. ... Certain controversies ... must necessarily be withdrawn from arbitration. They are those which concern honor, independence, and vital interests of States"[69] (in other words, those matters often giving rise to war, which the peace conference had hoped to consign to obligatory arbitration).

A more fruitful result of the 1899 conference was Declaration (IV, 2) Concerning Asphyxiating Gases, which declared, in part, "inspired by the sentiments which found expression in the Declaration of St. Petersburg [in its preamble] ... the contracting Powers agree to abstain from the use of projectiles the sole object of which is the diffusion of asphyxiating or deleterious gases." Among the states that ratified the declaration were Austria-Hungary, France, Germany, and Great Britain, all of which would employ poison gases less than fifteen years later in World War I.

Included in the 1899 Preamble to Convention II on land war was what came to be known as the Martens Clause, named for its Russian author, the conference organizer, diplomat, and humanist who, in 1902, received the ICRC's Distinguished Service Award.[70] The Martens Clause read:

> Until a more complete code of the laws of war is issued, the high contracting Parties think it right to declare that in cases not included in the Regulations adopted by them, populations and belligerents remain under the protection and empire of the principles on international law, as they result from the usages established between civilized nations, from the laws of humanity, and the requirements of the public conscience.[71]

A common article in each of the four 1949 Geneva Conventions repeats the Martens Clause, and it is found in most LOAC/IHL treaties. The significance of this reference to humanitarian principles is indicated by its continuing relevance and citation in cases adjudicating law of war issues.[72] Judge Theodor Maron writes that "conceptually, the most important part of the 1899 and 1907 Conventions was the ... Martins Clause, which states that all people, regardless of any specific provisions in treaties or laws, must be

---

[67] U.S. Dept. of State, Instructions to the American Delegates to the Hague Conference of 1899, cited in James B. Scott, ed., *The Proceedings of the Hague Peace Conference* (Whitefish, MT: Kessinger Publishing Reprint, 2007), 6–7.

[68] David D. Caron, "War and International Adjudication: Reflections on the 1899 Peace Conference," 94–4 *AJIL* 4 (2000).

[69] Cited in Shabtai Rosenne, ed., *The Hague Peace Conference of 1899 and 1907: Reports and Documents* (The Hague, Asser Press, 2001), 294.

[70] Vladimir V. Pustogarov, "Fyodor Fyodorovich Martens (1845–1909) – a Humanist of Modern Times," 312 *Int'l Rev. of the Red Cross* (1966), 300–14.

[71] Scott, *The Hague Conventions*, supra, note 63, at 101–2.

[72] See, e.g., *The Corfu Channel Case* (Merits), [1949] *ICJ Rpt.* 4, 260.

protected by the principles of humanity and the dictates of public conscience. . . . Thus, matters not regulated are not simply left to the discretion of the military commander.[73]

The 1899 Peace Conference notwithstanding, peace remained as elusive as ever. Between the 1899 and 1907 conferences, there was war between Britain and the Boers, Russia and Japan, and the United States and the Philippines.

2.7.2 *The Second Hague Peace Conference*

In 1904, U.S. President Teddy Roosevelt called for a second conference, which was formally proposed on behalf of the czar. The conference again convened in The Hague from June to mid-October 1907; this time forty-four of the world's fifty-seven states participated. The U.S. delegation included Brigadier General George B. Davis, judge advocate general of the army, and Rear Admiral Charles H. Sperry, former president of the Naval War College. As in the first peace conference, no African state was represented. Once again, the primary matter of concern was the establishment of a permanent international court of arbitration to settle disputes among states that might otherwise lead to war, rather than a juridical body to be convened only in specific cases. Again, the effort ultimately failed, sunk on the shoals of judicial selection; each country feared exclusion and distrusted the proposed systems of choosing judges. Arms limitations were not mentioned in the czar's conference proposal; his recent defeat in the 1905 Russo-Japanese War required Russia's massive rearmament.

The conference met with greater success in considering weapons and rules of war, a result unforeseen by the czar. "Before 1899, treaties relating to the laws of land warfare had only addressed specialized areas of the law (such as the wounded, and explosive projectiles)."[74] In 1907, the three conventions agreed on at the 1899 conference were revised and ten new conventions and one declaration were adopted. The 1899 conference included an attachment to Convention II: a listing of rules for land warfare. In 1907, that listing was repeated as "Convention IV Respecting the Laws and Customs of War on Land," and Convention IV's annex of the same title listed those laws and customs as they were observed in 1907.[75] Although Annex IV, today usually referred to as "Hague Regulation IV," contains few provisions for the protection of civilians, those laws and customs formed the basis for much of the 1949 Geneva Conventions.

2.7.3 *Parsing 1907 Hague Regulation IV*

Hague Regulation IV continued the "modern" codification of customary battlefield law that began with the Lieber Code.[76] Long-established law of war practices that had

---

[73] Theodor Meron, *The Making of International Criminal Justice: A View from the Bench* (Oxford: Oxford University Press, 2011), 48.

[74] Roberts and Guelff, *Documents on the Laws of War*, supra, note 56, at 67.

[75] Col. G.I.A.D. Draper notes, "The Hague Regulations of 1907 have been seen, perhaps erroneously, as an instrument governing the conduct of hostilities on land. In fact, they also dealt with the protection of prisoners of war, spies, pacific relations between belligerents and military authority in occupied territory. Thus the isolation of Hague Convention IV from the main stream of the development of humanitarian law is erroneous." Draper, "The Development of International Humanitarian Law," in Meyer and McCoubrey, *Reflections on Law and Armed Conflicts*, supra, note 10, at 74.

[76] Geoffrey Best, *War and Law since 1945*, supra, note 11, at 41.

matured into custom were, practice by practice, becoming embodied in written codes and multinational treaties – were becoming positive international law of war.

Notably, there is a penalty clause in Article 3 of 1907 Hague Convention (IV) Respecting the Laws and Customs of War on Land convention: "A belligerent party which violates the provision of the said Regulations shall ... be liable to pay compensation [to the injured belligerent party]." Accepting that "compensation" constitutes a form of penalty, this was the first time a penalty provision was found in a multinational treaty involving the regulation of battlefield conduct, the first time, one might argue, that rules of war became laws of war, in that Hague Regulation IV specifies conduct that is unlawful, and Hague Convention (IV) assesses a penalty for violation: monetary compensation. "However, the Convention did not provide for the prosecution of individuals who violated the Regulations. Trials of those persons were conducted," if at all, "by national tribunals applying customary international law, the Hague Regulations, or, in the case of their own personnel, the national military or criminal code."[77] The words "crime" and "breach" do not appear in the convention. Instead, as is common in international law, the penalty for any breach is imposed on the state of the offending individual. It had to wait until the post–World War II Nuremberg International Military Tribunal for *individual* punishment to be imposed,[78] but it was a beginning. Although the 1907 convention contains no enforcement clause, other than the solemn promises of the signatories, Hague Convention (IV) and Regulation IV were an initial effort to fix responsibility and levy a penalty for battlefield misconduct.

Drawing from historical precedent, such as the 1874 Brussels Declaration concerning the Laws and Customs of War, and the 1880 Oxford Manual, *The Laws of War on Land*, the 1899 and 1907 Hague regulations specify the criteria for entitlement to combatant and prisoner of war status, laying out the four preconditions to be met by volunteer fighters and resistance movements that remain familiar to today's LOAC/IHL students.

For the first time in a multinational treaty, Hague Regulation IV addresses the status of spies. Contrary to the opinion of many soldiers of the twentieth century (and today?), an enemy captured behind his opponent's lines in wartime is not automatically a spy. The state representatives at The Hague defined a spy as a person "acting clandestinely or on false pretenses [who] obtains or endeavors to obtain information ... with the intention of communicating it to the hostile party."[79] So, commando raiders in uniform, escaping prisoners of war, and soldiers who have broken through enemy lines who are captured behind those enemy lines are not necessarily spies but are lawful combatants entitled to prisoner of war protections. Of course, the simple recitation of the formulation was not the end of international dissension on the topic. Forty years later, after World War II, spies were again the subject of discussion and argument as 1949 Geneva Convention IV was hammered out. Spies were only one of many customary battlefield practices codified in Hague Regulation IV.

---

[77] United Kingdom, *The Manual of the Law of Armed Conflict*, supra, note 2, at para. 1.25.3 (references deleted).

[78] George P. Fletcher and Jens David Ohlin, *Defending Humanity* (New York: Oxford University Press, 2008), 187.

[79] Art. 29, Hague Regulation IV.

2.7.4 *Parsing 1899 Hague Declaration 3*

Hague Declaration 3, Concerning Expanding Bullets, is another annex to the 1899 Hague Regulations. It was written with dum-dum bullets in mind. "Expanding bullets" are described in the declaration as "bullets which expand or flatten easily in the human body, such as bullets with a hard envelope which does not entirely cover the core or is pierced with incisions." Dum-dum bullets, a form of expanding bullet, were named for bullets first manufactured at the British Indian arsenal at Dum-Dum, near Calcutta.[80] They were bullets whose hard jackets did not cover their core, or whose tips were scored, both causing a mushrooming of the bullet on impact, producing wounds of much greater severity than similar wounds involving unscored and fully jacketed rounds. "The contracting Parties agree to abstain from the use of bullets which expand or flatten easily in the human body, such as bullets with a hard envelope which does not entirely cover the core or is pierced with incisions." Both Britain and the United States objected to the 1899 prohibition. Britain, the manufacturer of the bullets, used them in its African colonial wars and argued that they were needed to disable the "savages."[81] Britain and the United States were overruled, and the provision was left in Declaration 3.[82] In 1907, Britain finally signed and ratified the declaration. The United States never has. Regardless, the prohibition of dum-dums became customary law long ago, binding all states regardless of their ratification or nonratification of the 1907 declaration.[83]

Some experts suggest that today's high-velocity combat rifle ammunition, said to tumble end over end on striking its target, is essentially the same as a dum-dum bullet. This argument was advanced by several European states, particularly Switzerland, with regard to the bullet fired by the M-16 rifle during its initial adoption as the standard U.S. infantry weapon. There is no prohibition of the use of high-velocity ammunition against human targets, all such bullets tending to yaw or tumble to one degree or another. The argument persisted that, by analogy to dum-dums, the M-16's 5.56×45 mm round was prohibited. Other countries, the United States obviously included, contest that analogy, pointing out the difference between a bullet tumbling (arguably unlawful) and a bullet yawing (arguably lawful). No consensus has been reached, and the issue remains controversial. The United States is firm in contending that the M-16 round presents no LOAC violation in fact or spirit.[84]

The 1956 U.S. manual on the law of land warfare only mentions the illegality (established through "usage") of the scoring or filing the ends from bullets.[85] Meanwhile, the International Criminal Court's list of war crimes criminalizes the use of "bullets which expand or flatten easily in the human body, such as bullets with a hard envelope which does not entirely cover the core or is pierced with incisions."[86]

---

[80] Lassa Oppenheim, *International Law: A Treatise.* Vol. II. *Disputes, War and Neutrality*, 7th ed., H. Lauterpacht, ed. (London: Longman, 1952), 341.

[81] Scott, *Proceedings*, supra, note 67, at 343.

[82] Britain also objected to the prohibition believing the rounds did not produce wounds of exceptional cruelty. The United States objected for several reasons, including the belief that dum-dums were not inhumane. Roberts and Guelff, *Documents on the Laws of War*, supra, note 56, at 63.

[83] Ratifications by accession have continued since 1907. The last state to ratify was Ukraine, in 2015.

[84] For a review of the arguments from the U.S. viewpoint, see W. Hays Parks, "Annual Report on International Efforts to Prohibit Military Small Arms" address (2002), http://www.dtic.mil/ndia/2001smallarms/parks1.pdf

[85] FM 27–10, *The Law of Land Warfare*, supra, note 1, at para. 34.b.

[86] Rome Statute of the International Criminal Court, War Crimes, Art. 8.2 (b) xix.

2.7.5 *The Peace Conferences' Legacy*

The peace conference did not restrict the development or use of a single weapon or tactic but was nevertheless generally judged a significant accomplishment. "Not unlike its predecessor, this Second Conference was hailed as a success and condemned as an utter failure. . . . Mr. Elihu Root, the American Secretary of State . . . concluded, 'The work of the Second Hague Conference presents the greatest advance ever made at any single time toward the reasonable and peaceful regulation of international conduct.'"[87]

A hundred years on, many Hague Regulation IV mandates remain binding. Not all of the Hague regulations and declarations have stood the test of time, some articles being superseded by the 1949 Geneva Conventions. Many, however, have become unquestioned elements of customary international law,[88] cited as such by, for example, the 1946 Nuremberg and 1948 Far East International Military Tribunals.[89] As the International Military Tribunal at Nuremberg held, "The rules of land warfare expressed in the Convention [IV] undoubtedly represented an advance over existing international law at the time of their adoption. By . . . 1939 these rules laid down by the Convention were recognized by all civilized nations, and were regarded as being declaratory of the laws and customs of war."[90] In the 2006 U.S. Supreme Court decision *Hamdan v. Rumsfeld*, the Court cites 1907 Hague Convention IV, nearly a hundred years old, as authoritative and relevant law.[91] Along with other tribunals, the International Criminal Tribunal for the Former Yugoslavia, from its earliest to its final opinions, cited Hague Convention IV as binding law, the violation of which still constitutes punishable offenses.[92]

Perhaps the most enduring aspect of the 1899 and 1907 Hague conferences is found in Article 22 of 1907 Convention IV: "The right of belligerents to adopt means of injuring the enemy is not unlimited." That humanitarian admonition, read in conjunction with the Preamble's Martens Clause, serves as a moral reference point for considering new weapons, unknown at the time of the Conferences. Just because you can does not mean you should.

At the conclusion of the second conference, although establishment of a permanent court of arbitration was defeated, the delegates began planning for a third conference, when another effort to form a court would be initiated. World War I derailed that conference.

The work of the Hague peace conferences was, in no small part, the basis not only for the 1949 Geneva Conventions, but for the creation of the Permanent Court of International Justice (PCIJ), the League of Nations' adjudicatory body. The PCIJ, in turn,

---

[87] Eyffinger, *The Peace Palace*, supra, note 62, at 91.

[88] FM 27–10, *Law of Land Warfare*, supra, note 1, at para. 6; and Yoram Dinstein, *The Conduct of Hostilities under the Law of International Armed Conflict* (Cambridge: Cambridge University Press, 2004), 10.

[89] *Trial of German Major War Criminals* (Nuremberg, 1947), Vol. 1, at 254; *In re Hirota*, 15 Ann. Dig. (1948), 356, 366.

[90] International Military Tribunal, Nuremberg, Judgment and Sentences, 1946, 41 *AJIL* 172, 248–9 (1947).

[91] *Hamdan v. Rumsfeld*, 548 U.S. 557 (2006), at 603 and 604.

[92] E.g., *Trial of Albert Wagner*, French Military Tribunal, XIII *LRTWC* 118, 119 (1946); *Prosecutor v. Duško Tadić*, IT-94-1-A, appeals sentencing judgment (15 July 1999), para. 98, fn. 117; *Prosecutor v. Tihomir Blaškić*, IT-95-14-A, appeals sentencing judgment (29 July 2004), para. 147; and *Prosecutor v. Naser Orić*, IT-03-68-T, trial sentencing judgment (30 July 2006), para. 252.

became today's International Court of Justice, the United Nations' adjudicatory body. In 1976, the Permanent Court of Arbitration was revived, and it remains a working body.

The law of war is a young and evolving body of law, essentially having been initiated only in 1899, with the Hague conventions of that year.

2.8 Summary

The second half of the nineteenth century was a LOAC watershed. For hundreds of years there were rules of war, and battlefield regulations, and codes imposed by this or that king, commander, or marshal. In the 1863 Lieber Code this polyglot mass was assembled in a single government-sponsored document. For the first time, customary battlefield law was made accessible to the ordinary soldier in the field. The utility of the code was clear and led to similar codes throughout Europe, further rationalizing the law of war on an international basis. On the Continent, only months behind Lieber, a simmering public concern over the inhumanity of warfare was given voice by a Swiss businessman, and the ICRC issued its first convention. The Red Cross movement rapidly spread around the world, and a new wave of humanitarian concern for wounded combatants was amplified in the United States by the work of Florence Nightingale, Mary Walker, and Clara Barton. In St. Petersburg, in 1868, there was another first: a multinational treaty limiting the weaponry of war, along the way referring to military necessity and unnecessary suffering as limiting factors on the battlefield. These advances were capped by the 1899 and 1907 Hague peace conferences, a lasting result of which is Hague Regulation IV, still good law and arguably the first true *law* of war. The stage was set for finding personal responsibility for violation of laws of war that were on the international legal horizon.

CASES AND MATERIALS

THE TRIAL OF CAPTAIN HENRY WIRZ

A Military Commission Convened at Washington, D.C.,
August 23–October 24, 1865

Introduction. *The exact number of Union prisoners of war who died at Andersonville prisoner-of-war camp will never be known.*[93] *At Andersonville National Cemetery the number given is 12,914. Overcrowding and lack of proper food, water, and shelter at Camp Sumter, the camp's actual name, all contributed to the deaths of the prisoners. Considering that the camp existed for slightly less than fourteen months, the death rate was appalling.*

---

[93] The account of the trial is from John D. Lawson, ed., *American State Trials*, Vol. VIII (St. Louis: F. H. Thomas Law Book, 1916), 666.

At the war's outbreak, neither side was prepared to handle prisoners of war. Initially, captured soldiers were simply exchanged at the conclusion of the battle. Then a formal exchange system was accepted by both sides. That system collapsed over procedural disagreements and racial issues. Permanent confinement facilities were constructed. Camp Sumter, approximately sixty miles south of Macon, Georgia, was the largest prisoner of war camp. At sixteen and one half acres, it was designed to hold 6,000 enlisted Union soldiers. It eventually held 45,000.

At war's end, while unburied Union prisoners lay dead of starvation and exposure at Andersonville, tons of supplies were found at Confederate commissaries less than twenty miles away.

> *The Confederacy's inept bureaucracy and inadequate, often corruptly operated railroads kept those supplies from reaching [Andersonville]. . . . Almost one-third . . . of the men who entered its gates rest in its cemetery. Thousands more died from the effects of staying at Camp Sumter after they had been released. . . . In August [1864] . . . the death count rose to 2,992 men for the month.[94]*

Confederate Captain Henry Wirz, a Swiss-born doctor, was in charge of the stockade interior. His superior officer was Brigadier General W. Sidney Winder. Winder died two months before the war ended. Wirz, arrested at the camp after the war ended, was brought to Washington, D.C. for trial before a military commission.[95] The nine-officer commission consisted of four Union major generals, three brigadier generals, a colonel, and a lieutenant colonel. The senior member was Major General Lew Wallace, later the author of the novel, Ben Hur. *The judge advocate (prosecutor) was Colonel N. P. Chipman, assisted by Major A. A. Hosmer. Wirz's counsel were civilians James Hughes, James W. Denver, Charles F. Peck, and Louis Schade. The commission was conducted in the Court of Claims room of the Capitol, in Washington.*

In media presentations, Henry Wirz is often presented as a sympathetic figure, unfairly persecuted by a vengeful Union military commission. The record of the trial reveals a far different depiction of Wirz. His defense, like that of Peter von Hagenbach, three hundred ninety years before, was that he was only following orders and that he did the best he could with what he had. Although not the first time the defense had been raised by an American officer,[96] Wirz's case is the most well known. Tried and convicted, Wirz was sentenced to death and executed, hanged on gallows specially erected in front of the U.S. Capitol building. He was the only Civil War soldier on either side to be convicted of war crimes.

Extracts from the Record of Wirz's Military Commission

The specification of Charge 1 against Captain Wirz was that he maliciously, wilfully and traitorously, and in aid of the armed rebellion against the United States of America, on or

[94] Robert S. Davis, "Escape from Andersonville: A Study in Isolation and Imprisonment," 67–4 J. *of Military History* (Oct. 2003), 1065, 1067, 1069.

[95] Michael A. Marsh, *Andersonville: The Story behind the Scenery* (Las Vegas: KC, 2000), 4–29.

[96] That distinction goes to Navy Captain George Little, in *Little v. Barreme*, 6. U.S. (2 Cranch) 170 (1804). See Chapter 9.1.

before 1 March 1864, and on diverse other days until 10 April 1865, conspiring with John H. Winder, Richard B. Winder, W. S. Winder, Joseph White, R. R. Stevenson and unknown others, to injure the health and destroy the lives of United States soldiers being prisoners of war, to the end that the armies of the United States might be weakened and impaired, in violation of the laws and customs of war.

The first specification of Charge 2: Captain Wirz, on or about 8 July 1864, as commandant of a prison by authority of the so-called Confederate States for the confinement of prisoners of war from the armies of the United States, feloniously, wilfully and of his malice aforethought, did make an assault with a loaded revolver upon an unknown soldier of the United States, a prisoner of war in his custody, inflicting a mortal wound upon the said soldier.

The fifth specification of Charge 2: Captain Wirz, on or about 20 August 1864, feloniously, and with malice aforethought, did confine and bind within an instrument of torture called "the stocks," an unknown soldier of the United States, a prisoner of war in his custody, in consequence of which said cruel treatment, maliciously and murderously inflicted, the said soldier, soon thereafter, died. [*]

Witnesses for the Government

Dr. John C. Bates: "was a contract surgeon at Andersonville prison ... saw men lying partially naked, dirty and lousy in the sand; others were crowded together in small tents ... The men would gather around me and ask for a bone. [97] Clothing we had none; the living were supplied with the clothing of those who had died. Of vermin and lice there was a prolific crop. ... Sat down and made a report on the condition of things I found at the hospital; for some of the things I said I received a written reprimand. ... My attention was called to a patient who was only sixteen years; he would ask me to bring him a potato, bread or biscuit, which I did. ... He had the scurvy and gangrene ... he became more and more emaciated, his sores gangrened, and for want of food and from lice he died. ... Saw but little shelter excepting what ingenuity had devised; found them suffering with scurvy, dropsy, diarrhoea, gangrene, pneumonia and other diseases ... if persons whose systems were reduced by inanition should perchance stump a toe or scratch the hand, the next report to me was gangrene ... 50 or 75 per cent of those who died might have been saved. ... There was much stealing among them. All lived each for himself. ...

"The rations were less than 2 ounces in 24 hours. Think a man would starve to death on it. Sometimes the meat was good, and sometimes it was bad. ... The amputations and re-amputations, owing to gangrenous wounds, were numerous ... [men] hobbled along on crutches; others crawled on the ground with tin cups in their mouths, because they could carry these articles in no other way. ... I made several reports as to conditions, but none of them were heeded."

James Mahan: "Was in the Confederate army, and on duty at Andersonville, took 13 men to the blacksmith shop to have iron collars and chains fastened on them; received the order from Capt. Wirz; one of the men called Frenchy made his escape; Capt. Wirz

---

[*] There were thirteen specifications of Charge 2. The three specifications repeated here are paraphrased.

[97] Witness accounts recorded before the military commission, and Wirz's statement and that of the judge advocate, are from Leon Friedman, ed., *The Law of War: A Documentary History*, Vol. I (New York: Random House, 1972), 785–98.

said, when he heard of it, That d – d Frenchy has escaped again, and he sent for the dogs, which got on the trail of the man, who was captured near the stream; Wirz got off his horse and went alongside of the dogs and fired his pistol at the man; the man's trousers were torn by the dogs; do not know whether the flesh was injured; have heard Wirz remark that he wished all the prisoners were in hell, and himself with them."

Abner A. Kellog: "Am of the 40th Ohio. When we were at Andersonville we were robbed of blankets, canteens and watches, which were removed to Capt. Wirz's head-quarters; they were never returned. A crazy man having been shot, the sentry was asked why he did so; he replied he was acting under orders of Capt. Wirz. The latter, on being asked by a prisoner whether he expected the men to live with such usage and unwhole-some food as was shown to him replied, it is good enough for you – Yankees. In August, 1864, saw a sick man at the gate for 24 hours with a sore on him as large as the crown of my hat, filled with maggots, fly-blown; the sergeant asked Capt. Wirz to have the man carried to the hospital; No, said Wirz; let him stay there and die. The man was afterward carried out a corpse."

Grottfeld Brunner: "Am of the 14th Connecticut. Prisoners were treated well until Capt. Wirz assumed command. Wirz used to come into the stockade every morning, and if one man was missing, the whole detachment would be deprived of food until he was accounted for. Being sick one day, I was not at morning roll-call; Wirz came into my tent and called me a Yankee –, drew his revolver and threatened to kill me on the spot; I replied it would be better if Wirz would kill me, whereupon he kicked me out of bed. ... "

Sidney Smith: "Am of the 14th Connecticut. Saw Wirz knock a man down with his revolver; another man, who was sick, received a severe bayonet wound; almost every time a sentry shot a man he was relieved on thirty days furlough.

The Prisoner Wirz's Written Statement

"In this closing scene of a trial which must have wearied the patience of this honorable commission, and which has all but exhausted the little vitality left me, I appear to put on record my answer to the charges on which I am arraigned, and to protest and vindicate my innocence. I know how hard it is for one, helpless and unfriended as I am, to contend against the prejudices produced by popular clamor and long-continued misrepresenta-tion, but I have great faith in the power of the truth. ... "

"Of the one hundred and sixty witnesses who have testified, no one ever heard a syllable, or saw an act indicative of his knowledge of the existence of such a hellish plot [of conspiracy with John H. Winder and others]; nor was there the least scrap of paper found in his office, or a word in the archives of the Confederacy to show that such a conspiracy existed ... and if there was guilt anywhere, it certainly lay more deep and damning on the souls of those who held high positions than on him who was a mere subaltern officer. ... Furthermore, if he, as a subaltern officer, simply obeyed the legal orders of his superiors in the discharge of his official duties, he could not be held responsible for the motive that dictated such orders. And if he overstepped them and violated the laws of war, and outraged humanity, he should be tried and punished according to the measure of his offense."

"From his position at Andersonville, he should not be held responsible for the crowded condition of the stockade, the unwholesome food, etc., ... he was not responsible for the location ... that he did not assume command until March 1864 ... that Colonel Parsons' testimony fully exonerated him (Wirz) from complicity in the selection of the location, overcrowding the stockade, or failure to provide proper shelter for the prisoners. ... "

"As to the third charge, that of murder ... the specifications accused him of no less than thirteen distinct crimes of the grade of murder; yet in no instance were the name, date, regiment or circumstances stated."

The Judge Advocate's Argument

"May it please the Court. ... Before advancing further in the argument, let me define briefly the laws of war, which, it is alleged by the government in its indictment against this prisoner and his co-conspirators, have been inhumanely and atrociously violated. ... Whatever the peculiar forms or rights of this or that government, its subjects require no control or power other than is sanctioned by the great tribunal of nations. We turn, then, to the code international. ... "

"Grotius derived the *jus gentium* from the practice of nations. ... He, in Books three and four, insists that all acts of violence, which have no tendency to obtain justice or determinate the war, are at variance both with the duty of the Christian and with humanity itself. ... "

"Whatever the form of government may have been to which the leaders of the Confederacy so-called aspired ... the moment they asked a place among nations they were bound to recognize and obey those laws international, which are, and of necessity must be, applicable alike to all. ... "

"Thus far we have not pretended to enter with any particularity into the questions of the cruel treatment of prisoners. ... There was another mode of punishment instituted at that prison and carried on under the direction of this prisoner which we must notice; and that is the stocks."

"These implements of torture were of two kinds: in the one the prisoner was lashed to a wooden frame-work, his arms extended at right angles from his body, and his feet closely fastened; and in this condition, unable to move either hand or foot, he was compelled to stand erect, or, as was sometimes the case, to lie upon the ground with his face turned upwards, exposed to the heat of the sun and to the rain; in the other the prisoner's feet were fastened in a wooden frame, and so much elevated above the center of gravity that it was difficult for him to sit, and he was therefore compelled to lie on his back with his face exposed to the sun. ... "

"I know that it is urged that during all this time he [Wirz] was acting under General Winder's orders, and for the purposes of argument I will concede that he was so acting. A superior officer cannot order a subordinate to do an illegal act, and if a subordinate obeys such an order and disastrous consequences result, both the superior and the subordinate must answer for it. General Winder could no more command the prisoner to violate the laws of war than could the prisoner do so without orders. The conclusion is plain, that where such orders exist both are guilty, and *a fortiori* where the prisoner at the bar acted upon his own motion he was guilty.

"We now come to notice charge second, alleging 'murder in violation of the laws of war,' under which there are laid numerous specifications, alleging, with all the particularity that was possible, the circumstances in each case. ... The various cases of death which are justly to be laid to the charge of this prisoner as murders, may be considered under four heads:

1. The cases of death resulting from mutilation by the hounds.
2. The instances of death resulting from confinement in the stocks and the chain-gang.
3. The cases of killing of prisoners by the guards, pursuant to the direct order of the accused given at the time; and
4. The cases of killing by the prisoner's own hand.

"This classification does not embrace those very numerous cases (which it is not deemed necessary to recount in detail) where prisoners at or near the dead-line were shot by the guards when the accused was not present. . . . "

"May it please the court, I have hastily analyzed and presented the evidence under Charge Second. . . . Mortal man has never been called to answer before a legal tribunal to a catalogue of crime like this. One shudders at the fact, and almost doubts the age we live in. I would not harrow up your minds by dwelling farther upon this woeful record. The obligation you have taken constitutes you the sole judge of both law and fact. I pray you administer the one and decide the other."

Verdict and Sentence

October 24.

Today the Court announced its decision as follows:

It finds the accused, Henry Wirz, of Charge I, "Guilty," viz.: that he did combine, confederate and conspire with John H. Winder, Richard B. Winder, W. S. Winder, R. Stevenson, and others, names unknown, engaged in armed rebellion against the United States, against the laws of war, to impair and injure the health, and to destroy the lives of large numbers of Federal prisoners, to-wit: 45,000 at Andersonville.

> Of Specification first to Charge II, "Guilty."
> Of Specification second to Charge II, "Guilty."
> Of Specification third to Charge II, "Guilty."
> Of Specification four to Charge II, "Not Guilty."
> Of Specification five to Charge II, "Guilty."
> Of Specification six to Charge II, "Guilty."
> Of Specification seven to Charge II, "Guilty."
> Of Specification eight and nine to Charge II, "Guilty."
> Of Specification ten to Charge II, "Not Guilty."
> Of Specification eleven to Charge II, "Guilty."
> Of Specification twelve to Charge II, "Guilty."
> Of Specification thirteen to Charge II, "Not Guilty."

And the Commission does therefore sentence him, the said Henry Wirz, "to be hanged by the neck until he be dead, at such time and place as the President of the United States may direct, two-thirds of the court concurring therein."

November 3, 1865.

The proceedings, findings, and sentence of the court in the within case are approved, and it is ordered that the sentence be carried into execution by the officer commanding the Department of Washington on Friday, the 10th day of November, 1865, between the hours of 6 o'clock a.m., and 12 o'clock noon.

Andrew Johnson, President.

Conclusion. Captain Wirz's case, a century and a half ago, illustrates elements of war crime trials that have been repeated virtually unchanged through World Wars I and II, the conflict in the former Yugoslavia, and in Iraq. The law of war concerning the torture and mistreatment of prisoners, the giving of unlawful orders, and obeying unlawful orders, is little changed. That law has been adjudicated in courts-martial, military commissions, ad hoc international tribunals, and in domestic courts. As in Wirz's case, arguments as to the fairness of the proceedings continue long after judgment: Did Wirz realistically have a choice in the provisions and shelter he provided prisoners? Were the circumstances in Andersonville inevitable, given the subordinate position of Wirz? What should, or could, he have done? Did the Union Army have options other than convening a military commission?

UNITED STATES V. MAJOR JOHN HENRY GEE

A Military Commission Convened at Washington, D.C.
by Special Order No. 35, of 8 Feb. 1866

Introduction. Andersonville and the trial of Henry Wirz is well-known. That of John Gee, however, is virtually unknown even though, in its own way, Gee's case is as remarkable as that of Wirz's. Major Gee's and Wirz's cases are two of the first recorded trials for war crimes. The entire account that follows is taken from the excellent article written by Prof. Guénaël Mettraux, of the University of Amsterdam.[98]

John Gee was a medical doctor who served in both the Seminole and Mexican wars before volunteering to serve in the Confederate Army. In August 1864 he took command of the Salisbury Confederate prison camp, the conditions of which were terrible even before he arrived. "Diseases were rampant, food insufficient and the water unclean or infected. ... Thousands of Union prisoners died of malnutrition and diseases. Others were killed as they tried to escape."[99]

At his military commission, Gee was charged with two counts of violating the laws and customs of war – cruel and inhuman treatment of prisoners, and the murder of numerous prisoners. His pretrial motion, that the terms of the Confederacy's surrender provided for the paroling of crimes committed during the war, was denied on the ground that the terms of the surrender did not apply to acts committed in violation of the laws and customs of war. A similar motion had also been denied by Wirz's military commission.

In Gee's military commission, prosecution witnesses testified to the terrible conditions that prevailed within the camp, although none tied Gee, personally, to the commission of any of the crimes charged. "The defense case was as simple as the prosecution position had been straightforward: conditions were terrible at the time and prisoners died in numbers, but Major Gee was neither responsible for these conditions nor for the deaths

---

[98] Guénaël Mettraux, "A Little-Known Case from the American Civil War," 8–4 *J. of Int'l Crim. J.* (Sept. 2010), 1059–1068.

[99] Id., at 1060.

of the prisoners. Instead, he did all that was within his power to try to improve their lot."[100] After fifty-seven days, the military commission closed. Later on the same day, the commission returned its verdict. Gee was found not guilty of all charges. The military commission specifically noted that higher Confederate authorities ("the Rebel Government") were to blame for the circumstances in Salisbury prison camp.

> What is perhaps most remarkable about these proceedings is the extraordinary fairness with which they were conducted. ... How two cases, those of Wirz and Gee, which in factual terms were so similar, could have been treated in such different ways and resulted in diametrically opposed findings remains somewhat of a mystery. ... The defense of "a good man in a bad situation" that was advanced by Gee's counsel on his behalf is not unusual in war crimes cases. What is unusual, however, is that in Gee's case it succeeded.[101]

Author Mettraux concludes that the Gee military commission illustrates "the principle already laid down in *Wirz* that an individual could be made accountable for his acts directly as a result of international law. Long before the [1946] Nuremberg proceedings, individual criminal responsibility was therefore recognized as forming part of the arsenal of international law."[102]

Conclusion. *One might offer that the difference between the Wirz and Gee military commissions was that, in Wirz's case, the testimony of numerous prosecution witnesses firmly tied Wirz to the personal commission of the criminal acts of which he was convicted, while no witness did so in Gee's case.*

THE COURT-MARTIAL OF GENERAL JACOB H. SMITH

Manila, Philippine Islands, April 1902

In the nineteenth and early twentieth centuries, courts-martial were far more common (and far less fatal to one's military career) than in today's armed forces. Still, some courts-martial were notable for their offenses, unusual outcomes, or their accused. The court-martial of a general officer has always been of special note because of its rarity. The 1902 general court-martial of General Smith remains not only interesting, but relevant.

In 1901, Army Brigadier General Jacob Smith commanded Army and Marine Corps troops on the Philippine island of Samar, during the 1899–1902 U.S.-Philippine War. Samar had proven a difficult area to subdue, the *insurrectos* a battle-hardened lot not given to observing the law of war, such as it was. Smith, "a short, wizened 62-year-old who had earned the nickname 'Hell-Roarin' Jake,"[103] had been seriously wounded in the Civil War battle of Shiloh. He had also spent twenty-seven years in grade as a captain, a dishearteningly long time between promotions but not unheard of in a day when Army advancement was based strictly on seniority.

General Smith was determined to succeed where his predecessors had failed and quell all enemy resistance. Smith summoned one of his more aggressive subordinates, Marine Major Littleton W. T. Waller, who was about to initiate a patrol against the *insurrectos*.

---

[100] Id., at 1064.   [101] Id., at 1066.   [102] Id., at 1068.
[103] Max Boot, *The Savage Wars of Peace* (New York: Basic Books, 2002), 120.

According to his court-martial charge sheet, before witnesses General Smith told Waller, "I want no prisoners. I wish you to kill and burn. The more you kill and burn, the better you will please me. The interior of Samar must be made a howling wilderness." He added that he wanted all persons killed who were capable of bearing arms, anyone ten years of age or older.[104]

Referred to a general court-martial when his statements became public, Smith already had a record marred by, not one, but two prior general court-martial convictions. Five years earlier, he had been saved from dismissal from the Army pursuant to a court-martial sentence only by the intervention of President Grover Cleveland, who granted clemency on the understanding that, after such a close call, Smith would retire. Smith confounded both President Cleveland and his Army superiors (who were eager to end the service of such a continually troublesome officer) by remaining on active duty.

At his court-martial, General Smith admitted that he instructed Major Waller "not to burden himself with prisoners, of which he, General Smith, already had so many that the efficiency of his command was impaired."[105] In mitigation of his unlawful instructions to Waller, the cruel nature of the enemy was repeated by court-martial witnesses:

> The [American] dead were mutilated. This is shown in the evidence of Major Combe, surgeon of volunteers, who accompanied the relief expedition to Balangiga, and who found a smoldering fire still burning about the head and face of Captain Connell. A deep wound across the face of Lieutenant Bumpas had been filled with jam, and one of the enlisted men "had his abdomen cut open and codfish and flour had been put in the wound. . . . " No prisoners were taken [by the *insurrectos*].[106]

Nevertheless, there was testimony from several officers, including Major Waller, that *insurrectos* who attempted to surrender were indeed taken prisoner. The same witnesses expressed doubt that, despite his clear directions, General Smith actually meant to instruct subordinate officers that no quarter be given. Major Waller testified, "Always when prisoners came in and gave themselves up, they were saved, they were not killed – not slaughtered at that time. But in the field, whenever they opposed us, we fought until there was nothing else to fight."[107]

General Smith was convicted of a single charge and specification of "conduct to the prejudice of good order and military discipline," and he was sentenced merely to be admonished.[108] The very lenient sentence no doubt reflected the court's deference to his many years of Army service, which included being twice seriously wounded in the Civil War and once in the Cuban-American War. But, after his third general court-martial conviction, he was still a brigadier general and he was still on active duty.

A court-martial sentence is not final until it has been reviewed and approved by the officer or individual who ordered the court convened. In the early twentieth century, the President of the United States was the convening authority for general officer courts-martial, unusual as they were. In his July 1902 court-martial review, President Theodore

---

[104] S. Doc. No. 213, 57th Cong., 2nd Sess. (1903), at pp. 5–17.
[105] Id., at 804, quoting from the posttrial review by Judge Advocate General of the Army BGen. George B. Davis.
[106] Id.   [107] Id., at 811.
[108] National Archives and Records Administration, record group 94, file 309120.

Roosevelt, aware of continuing public concern over accounts of cruelties in the war by U.S. forces, as well as by the enemy, wrote:

> The findings and sentence of the court are approved. I am well aware of the danger and great difficulty of the task our Army has had in the Philippine Islands and of the well-nigh intolerable provocations it has received from the cruelty, treachery, and total disregard of the rules and customs of civilized warfare on the part of its foes. I also heartily approve the employment of the sternest measures necessary to put a stop to such atrocities, and to bring the war to a close. ... But the very fact that warfare is of such character as to afford infinite provocation for the commission of acts of cruelty by junior officers and the enlisted men, must make the officers in high and responsible position peculiarly careful in their bearing and conduct so as to keep a moral check over any acts of an improper character by their subordinates. Almost universally the higher officers have so borne themselves. ... But there have been exceptions; there have been instances of the use of torture and of improper heartlessness in warfare on the part of individuals or small detachments. ... It is impossible to tell exactly how much influence language like that used by General Smith may have had in preparing the minds of those under him for the commission of the deeds which we regret. Loose and violent talk by an officer of high rank is always likely to excite to wrongdoing those among his subordinates whose wills are weak or whose passions are strong. ...
>
> [I]t is deeply to be regretted that [General Smith] should have so acted in this instance as to interfere with his further usefulness in the Army. I hereby direct that he be retired from the active list.[109]

Hell-Roarin' Jake Smith's forty-one years of active military service were ended by order of President Roosevelt, who was himself a former Army brigadier general, and a Medal of Honor holder, as well.

Note that Smith was found guilty "despite the absence of evidence that his orders had led to the commission of any actual crime ... one of the first illustrations of the principle that the fact that an order is not obeyed does not preclude the criminal responsibility of the superior who issued it if he knew it to be illegal."[110]

UNITED STATES V. PVT. MICHAEL A. SCHWARZ

45 cmr 852 (ncmr, 1971)

Introduction. In June 1970, at DaNang, Republic of South Vietnam, the first of four related general courts-martial began. The accused, U.S. Marine Corps Private Michael Schwarz, was charged with sixteen specifications (counts) of premeditated murder committed in the course of a patrol in contested territory. One of the issues considered by the court was the briefing given the patrol by a superior officer. Was the briefing inciting and

---

[109] Friedman, *The Law of War*, supra, note 97, at 799–800.

[110] Guénaël Mettraux, "US Courts-Martial and the Armed Conflict in the Philippines (1899–1902): Their Contribution to National Case Law on War Crimes," 1–1 *J. of Int'l Crim. Justice* (April 2003), 135, 142. The same result was seen in post–World War II military commissions in the *High Command Trial*, the *Hostages Trial*, and other cases. UN War Crimes Comm., *Law Reports of Trials of War Criminals*, Vol. XV (London: UNWCC, 1949), 133.

reminiscent of General Smith's briefing of Major Waller, sixty-eight years earlier, or was it no more than encouragement to be aggressive and careful?

It was the fifth year of the Vietnam War. Schwarz's unit, B Company, had been on patrol for several days, "in the bush" looking for Viet Cong (VC), and often under fire. The unit operated in a highly contested area where enemy contact was constant. In the past five months, B Company had suffered fourteen killed in action and eighty-five wounded in action. On February 19, B Company bivouacked for the night. As they were settling into their nighttime perimeter, a VC booby-trap killed a Marine, Private First Class Whitmore. Later, the company commander, twenty-three-year-old 1st Lieutenant A_____, directed that a defensive patrol be sent out. A patrol leader was designated, Lance Corporal H_____, and a five-checkpoint route assigned that would take several hours to traverse. Before the patrol left, Lieutenant A_____ spoke to the five men. At Schwarz's later court-martial, Lieutenant A_____ testified about his briefing:

Q: Now, what sort of briefing did you give this team before it went out?

A. I gave them a pep talk, sir.

Q. Would you briefly relate to the court exactly the contents – what you remember of that pep talk?

A. I was talking to H_____ [the patrol leader]. I told him, I went over it very, very in detail. I didn't want any casualties. I wanted him to keep his people spread out. I didn't want any booby-trap incident. Since they [the patrol] were out there alone, there wouldn't be much I could do. And I emphasized the fact to him not to take any chances, to shoot first and ask questions later. I reminded him of the nine people that we had killed on the 12th of February, and I reminded him of Whitmore, who had died that day. I said, "Don't let them get us any more. I want you to pay these little bastards back." That's about it.[111]

Shortly after nightfall, the patrol left Hill 50. At their first checkpoint, a small hamlet named Son Thang (4) on U.S. maps, the patrol forced Vietnamese noncombatants from three "hooches" in turn. One of the patrol members later testified that at the first hooch,

A. H_____ [the patrol leader] gave the order to kill the . . . people, and I told him not to do it. . . . Then he says, "Well, I have orders to do this by the company commander, and I want it done," and he said it again, "I want these people killed!" And I turned to PFC Boyd, and I said to PFC Boyd, "Is he crazy, or what?" And Boyd said, "I don't know, he must be."

Q. And what happened then?

A. And then everybody started opening up on the people and by the time it was all over, all the people were on the ground.[112]

Conclusion. *The same scenario was repeated at two more hooches: Vietnamese forced outside, H____'s orders to open fire, victims left where they fell. In all, sixteen women and children (no adult males) were killed.*

---

[111] *U.S. v. Schwarz*, record of trial, p. 348.   [112] Id., at 287.

At Schwarz's trial, the primary issues were Lance Corporal H_____'s repeated orders to fire on noncombatants, the legality of those orders, and whether they should have been obeyed. Lieutenant A_____'s briefing was properly a secondary issue. The briefing nevertheless recalls President Theodore Roosevelt's admonition in General Smith's case: "It is impossible to tell exactly how much influence language like that . . . may have had in preparing the minds of those under him for the commission of the deeds which we regret. Loose and violent talk by an officer of high rank is always likely to excite to wrongdoing those among his subordinates whose wills are weak or whose passions are strong. . . . "

Should the Lieutenant have been charged? If so, with what offense? What would the probability of conviction have been? Does the probability of conviction matter in considering offenses that might have been charged?[*]

UNITED STATES V. MAJOR EDWIN F. GLENN

Samar, Philippine Islands, April 1902

Introduction. *During the 1899–1901 Philippine insurrection, at least eight U.S. Army and Marine Corps officers were court-martialed for acts constituting war crimes, in most instances for subjecting prisoners to the "water cure," a variation on today's "waterboarding." Among the most notorious of the convicted officers was Army Captain Edwin Glenn, a "completely unprincipled" officer.*[113] *Besides torturing prisoners, Glenn was alleged to have burned to the ground the pueblo (town) of Igbarras while it was still occupied by its 10,000 inhabitants. Ironically, although not a lawyer, Glenn was the judge advocate of the island of Panay,*[114] *even while committing the war crime of which he was convicted.*[115] *During Glenn's assignment to the Philippine Islands, "the most notorious method of interrogation was the 'water cure,' described by one witness thus: 'The victim is laid flat on his back and held down by his tormentors. Then a bamboo tube is thrust into his mouth and some dirty water, the filthier the better, is poured down his unwilling throat.'. . . Some intelligence officers, such as Edwin F. Glenn, were eager practitioners."*[116] *The water cure causes a frantic, panic-inducing sense*

---

[*] "The actions of the Company Commander, 1st Lieutenant A_____, a well-respected and effective young combat officer, were formally investigated. After lengthy consideration, it was decided to impose nonjudicial punishment, rather than impose a trial by court-martial. Lieutenant A_____ received a letter of reprimand from the Commanding General of the 1st Marine Division, and forfeitures of half a month's pay ($250) for two months. It was, at that time, the maximum punishment imposable at nonjudicial punishment." Gary D. Solis, *Marines and Military Law in Vietnam* (Washington, DC: GPO, 1989), 183.

[113] Brian M. Linn, *The Philippine War: 1899–1902* (Lawrence: University of Kansas Press, 2000), 253.

[114] U.S. War Department, *The Military Laws of the United States*, 1915, 5th ed. (Washington, DC: GPO, 1917), 194. "469. Acting judge-advocates . . . shall be detailed from officers of the grades of captain or first lieutenant of the line of the Army, who, while so serving, shall continue to hold their commissions in the arm of the service to which they permanently belong. Upon completion of a tour of duty, not exceeding four years, they shall be returned to the arm in which commissioned." The author and military law expert Army Col. Winthrop describes the duties of a judge advocate of that day: "The designation of 'judge advocate' is now [1896], strictly, almost meaningless; the judge advocate in our procedure being neither a judge, nor, properly speaking, an advocate, but a prosecuting officer with the added duty of legal adviser to the court, and a recorder." William Winthrop, *Military Law and Precedents*, 2d ed. (Washington, DC: GPO, 1920), 179.

[115] Moorfield Storey and Julian Codman, *Secretary Root's Record: "Marked Severities" in Philippine Warfare* (Boston: Ellis Co., 1902), 62.

[116] Linn, *The Philippine War*, supra, note 113, at 223.

of suffocating and drowning, the cure repeated until the desired result, information, true or false, is obtained. It has the added diabolical advantage of leaving no mark on the victim, who is soon mobile and apparently physically unscathed.

As you read this century-old report of the trial, see how often you are reminded of events and legal arguments regarding the conduct of operations in the recent conflict in Iraq.

From the July 18, 1902, Judge Advocate General's report on the verbatim record of trial of Major Glenn:[117]

The Secretary of War:

> Sir: I beg leave to submit the following report. ... Major Glenn was tried on the following charge and specification.

Charge

Conduct to the prejudice of good order and military discipline, in violation of the sixty-second article of war.

Specification

In that Maj. Edwin F. Glenn, Fifth U.S. Infantry (promoted from captain, Twenty-fifth U.S. Infantry), being on duty commanding the United States troops while at the pueblo of Igbarras, province of Iloilo, island of Panay, Philippine Islands, and having in his charge one Tobeniano Ealdama, presidente of the town of Igbarras aforesaid, did unlawfully order, direct, and by his presence and authority, cause an officer and soldiers, subject to his the said Glenn's command, to execute upon him, the said Tobeniano Ealdama, a method of punishment commonly known in the Philippine Islands as the "water cure"; that is, did cause water to be introduced into the mouth and stomach of the said Ealdama against his will.

This at Igbarras, Panay, on or about the 27th day of November, 1900.

The accused pleaded "Not guilty" to the charge and specification, but submitted the following [written] statement, in the nature of an admission of fact, in connection with his arraignment.

The defendant is prepared to admit that he is Maj. Edwin F. Glenn ... and had in his charge one Tobeniano Ealdama, presidente of the town of Igbarras; that he did order and direct, and by his presence and authority did cause an officer and soldiers subject to his command to execute upon the same Tobeniano Ealdama a method of punishment commonly known in the Philippine Islands as the "water cure. ... "

I would like to state to the court, in explanation of this plea, the facts and circumstances that brought it about. ... [A] short time since the commanding general of the Division of the Philippines called me into his office and said that he has just received a cablegram from the United States informing him that two enlisted men, now citizens, but formerly of the Twenty-sixth U.S. Volunteer Infantry, had testified before the United States Senate committee that I, while in command at Igbarras, Panay, of a detachment of United States troops had caused the water cure, so called, to be given to the presidente of that town. And the general added that his orders were to prefer charges against me and bring me to trial ... I stated to him that I thought it would be an injustice to me to send me to the town of San Francisco, in the United States, to be tried there for an alleged offense committed in the Philippine Islands, for two reasons:

---

[117] Friedman, ed., *The Law of War*, supra, note 97, at 814–29.

First. Because of the then high state of excitement in the United States upon the subject of the so-called water cure and the consequent misunderstanding of what was meant by that term, and for the additional reason that any court organized in the United States from the officers there would be absolutely unprepared to pass upon any question involving so important a point as the action of officers in the field in the Philippine Islands.

This he told me was fair and he would ask for a court here.

The question came up as to whether these two men should be brought out, and my remarks to him were, in substance, that I was bitterly opposed to having these men come out on a pleasure jaunt at the expense of the United States Government; that I did not propose to avoid responsibility for anything I had done, and that I would admit, as I have admitted here, the facts, but I reserved the right to bring before the court all the facts by witnesses, so that they might pass on this question intelligibly.

Subsequently this question came up between myself and the judge-advocate, and it was insisted that I should admit the word "water cure," and I have admitted it. My only reason for objection was that the word "water cure" is not a fixed term in its meaning. . . .

Tobeniano Ealdama, the native who was subjected to the water cure by Major Glenn's order, was called as a witness for the prosecution and testified (in Spanish) that . . . Major Glenn arrived in Igbarras in command of a detachment of United States troops, established his headquarters at the convent, and sent for witness (Ealdama). The witness was asked where [the *inserrecto*] General Delgado was, and replied that he was not in the town of Igbarras. He was then asked:

> What did they do to you then? A: They told me if I did not tell I would be punished. They told me to take my shirt off, and they tied my arms. The captain and doctor and lieutenant sat at the table and there were some soldiers in the hall way. They laid me on my back and had some water with a faucet, and held my arms tight and proceeded to open my mouth. After they gave me some water for a little while the doctor told them to stop, and then asked me whereabouts of General Delgado. I told them that I did not know where the general was, and they proceeded again with the water. They gave me water, some through the nose and some through the mouth. I had shortness of breath and pain in the stomach.

Q: Did it have any other effect on you? A: My throat also hurt me on account of so much water put through it.

Q: How much water did you take in? A: Four bottles, about four bottles, as best I know . . .

Q: Did you retain this water on your stomach? A: Yes, sir; I did vomit some.

Q: What did they do with you then? A: They asked me quite a number of questions and I did not know the answer to them, and the Major said, "All right, let him up."

Q: What did they do to you then? A: I went to the table and sat down and waited, and they administered water to the school-teacher while I was waiting. . . .

Q: What did they do to you there? A: They asked me if I was in communication with the insurrectos. I said that I was not.

Q: What did they do to you then? A: They said, "You are a liar. Take off your clothes."

Q: Well, go on. A: Then I was sleeping. (The interpreter said that he thought the witness meant that he was in a recumbent position.) They brought a kind of syringe.

Q: What did they do with it? A: Open my mouth and put water in my mouth.
Q: What kind? A: Salty.
Q: How much did they put in? A: About one bottle.
Q: What effect did that have? A: It was very bitter.
Q: Did it have any other effect? A: My stomach and throat pained me, and also the
     nose where they passed the salt water through.

It is proper to say that subsequent to the occurrences above testified to, the witness
(Tobeniano Ealdama), was tried by a military commission ... under the charge of "being
a war traitor," the specification alleging holding intercourse with the enemy by means of
letters, contributing money, and food to the insurrectionary forces, and directing others,
members of said forces, to collect contributions. He was also charged with "violating the laws
of war" by joining and becoming a captain in the insurrectionary forces and recruiting and
swearing into the Insurgent service the members of the local police force of Igbarras. He was
found guilty of the offenses charged and sentenced to confinement at hard labor for ten years.
He was released from confinement to enable him to testify as a witness in this case.

The accused admitted the facts in connection with the administration of the water
cure, but undertook to show, in defense, that his act was not unlawful; that is, it was
justified by military necessity and was warranted as a legitimate exercise of force by the
laws of war. ...

The law governing the case is set forth in paragraph 16, General Order, No. 100
[the Lieber Code], which provides that –

> Military necessity does not admit of cruelty, that is, the infliction of suffering for the sake
> of suffering or for revenge, nor of maiming or wounding, except in fight, nor of torture
> to extort confessions.

The offense of the accused consisted in a resort to torture with a view to extort a confession.
The question is, did an emergency exist, so instant and important to justify the disobedience
of the plain requirements of General Order, No. 100? I think not. A rare or isolated case can
be conceived of in which the movement of an army or a military operation of importance
may depend upon obtaining the unwilling service of an inhabitant of the enemy's
country. ... In such a case a similar resort to force may be justified as a measure of
emergency, but no such case existed in the vicinity of Igbarras at the date of the specifications.

It must be remembered also that the resort to torture is attempted to be justified, not as
an exceptional occurrence, but as the habitual method of obtaining information from
individual insurgents. The accused took considerable pains to establish the fact that
torture was the usual practice of the Spaniards; that it was practiced by the insurgents. ...
If this be admitted, the accused was attempting to justify his conduct, not as an act
dictated by military necessity, but as a method of conducting operations.

When looked at from this point of view the defense falls completely, inasmuch as it is
attempted to establish the principle that a belligerent who is at war with a savage or
semicivilized enemy may conduct his operations in violations of the rules of civilized
war. This no modern State will admit for an instant; nor was it the rules in the Philippine
Islands. It is proper to observe that the several general officers who have exercised chief
command in the Philippine Islands have, all of them, expressly forbidden practices like
that of which the accused is here charged. Their principle subordinates have given
similar instructions forbidding a resort to cruelty in the most positive terms. ...

The rules respecting the treatment of guerrillas contemplate the existence of large armies which are annoyed in their operations by the presence of small guerrilla bands. ... This was not the case in the Philippine Islands, generally, where there were no large armies operating against each other as organized bodies. The [U.S.] troops were operating in detachments against isolated bands or bodies of insurgents, all of which were acting as guerrillas and were conducting their operations in flagrant disregard of the rules of civilized war. The situation thus presented was difficult and to the last degree exasperating, but it did not relieve the officers and men of the occupying forces of their obligation to adhere to the rules of war. ...

The accused was found guilty upon both charge and specification, and the following sentence was imposed:

> To be suspended from command for the period of one month, and to forfeit the sum of $50 for the same period. The court is thus lenient on account of the circumstances as shown in the evidence.

Although the accused was tried for but a single administration of the water-cure – not for habitually resorting to it in the conduct of operations against the insurrectionary forces – the sentence imposed, in my opinion, was inadequate to the offense established by the testimony of the witnesses and the admission of the accused. The sympathy of the court seems to have been with the accused throughout the trial; the feeling of the [jury] members in that respect is also indicated by qualifying words which are added to the sentence, and by the unanimous recommendation to clemency which is appended to the record.

I am of the opinion that the court upon reconsideration[118] would adhere to the sentence originally imposed, and it is therefore recommended that the sentence be confirmed and carried into effect.

Very respectfully,
George B. Davis*
Judge-Advocate-General

---

[118] Strange as it sounds today, in the United States, until enactment of the Uniform Code of Military Justice in 1950, under both the Army's Articles of War and the Navy's Articles for the Government of the Navy, court-martial results that dissatisfied the convening authority – the officer who made the court-martial happen – could be returned to the trial court for revision – euphemistically referred to as "reconsideration." In practice, reconsideration meant the convening authority expected either that "not guilty" findings should be changed to "guilty," or that there be an upward revision of the sentence, or both. During World War I, fully one-third of all army court-martial acquittals were "revised" to findings of guilty in reconsideration sessions. William T. Generous, Jr., *Swords and Scales* (New York: Kennikat Press, 1973), 12–13. Also see: Articles of War 1920 (as amended Dec. 15, 1942) Article 50 ½. For an account of proceedings in revision provided for in Regulations of the Navy, 1870, see Winthrop, *Military Law and Precedents*, supra, note 114, at 454–9. The U.S. Supreme Court approved the practice in Ex Parte *Reed*, 100 U.S. 13 (1879).

* Brigadier General Davis's ire was not that of an armchair warrior. General Davis enlisted in the cavalry at age sixteen. After participating in seventeen Civil War battles as an enlisted cavalryman, he attended West Point, graduating in 1871. As an officer, he fought Indians on the western frontier for five years, served two tours as a West Point professor, and, as a major, was transferred to Washington, D.C., and the Judge Advocate General's Department. While in Washington he earned two law degrees at what is now George Washington University, then returned to West Point for a third time. Promoted to brigadier general in 1901, he served as judge advocate general of the army for ten years, during which he represented the United States at the 1907 Hague Peace Conference. He was promoted to major general upon his retirement in 1911. Dept. of the Army, *The Army Lawyer: A History of the Judge Advocate General's Corps, 1775–1975* (Washington, DC: GPO, 1975), 101–2.

Conclusion. As Major General Davis suggests, Glenn's risible sentence, a mere fifty dollars,[119] and a month off, appears woefully inadequate to the offense of which he was convicted and illustrates the members' – the military jury's – permissive view of the water cure. The torture technique is at least as old as the Inquisition, during which its use is documented.

Edwin Glenn, who was promoted from the grade of captain to that of major while his charges were pending, continued his military career and retired a brigadier general.

Is military necessity a defense to charges of torture? If not, should it be? Does Article 2.2 of the 1984 Convention Against Torture, ratified by the United States in 1994, provide guidance?

---

[119] One critic noted that the fifty-dollar fine was "one-half the fine that may be imposed for spitting in a street-car in Boston." Storey and Codman, *Secretary Root's Record: "Marked Severities" in Philippine Warfare,* supra, note 115, at 66.

3 Two World Wars and Their Law of Armed Conflict Results

3.0 Introduction

The 1863 Lieber Code and 1907 Hague Regulation IV are the foundations of much of today's law of war. In this chapter we examine the fruit of those initial efforts, the *jus in bello*, the battlefield law, which is in effect today, along with some of the efforts to give clearer definitions of Lieber and the Hague outcomes. What took us from the 1863 Lieber Code to the 1949 Geneva Conventions? What are the Geneva Conventions and, in our study of law of armed conflict/international humanitarian law (LOAC/IHL), how should we navigate them?

3.1. The 1906 Geneva Convention

The passage of time generated calls for the revision of the first Geneva Convention for protection of the wounded. In 1868, several articles were added to the 1864 convention and, in 1906, thirty-five states, including the United States, met in Geneva, and a revised version of the 1864 convention, now containing thirty-three articles, was adopted.

The revised convention, again addressing care of the wounded, added provisions for the transfer of information by the warring states regarding wounded prisoners.[1] These informational provisions evolved into today's Central Prisoners of War Information Agency, and the Central Information Agency for protected persons.[2] First envisioned by Hague Regulation IV,[3] the two agencies collect information on prisoners of war (POWs) and protected persons and transmit it to their states of origin or residence, informing not only the state but the families of the status and whereabouts of loved ones held by the opposing side.

3.2 World War I (1914–1918)

In the world's first large-scale industrialized armed conflict, the War to End All Wars, 65 million troops were mobilized worldwide. The concept of total war was born.

---

[1] George B. Davis, "The Geneva Convention of 1906," 1–2 *AJIL* (April 1907), 409.
[2] 1949 Geneva Convention III, Art. 123, and Convention IV, Art. 140, respectively.
[3] 1907 Hague Reg. IV, Art. 14: "An inquiry office for prisoners of war is instituted . . . to reply to all inquiries about the prisoners."

"Warfare at the beginning of the First World War . . . differed little from that practiced in the eighteenth century. By 1917 . . . a new way of warfare was developed, where industrial mobilization, technological improvements in military methods, and the emergence of new weapons played a crucial role in changing the character of war."[4] By war's end, the Allies had suffered 5.4 million dead and 7 million wounded. The enemy suffered 4 million dead and 8.3 million wounded. It was a war of unparalleled ferocity in which modern weaponry was widely employed for the first time. The machine gun, rifled artillery, submarines, poisonous gas, and aircraft first made their contributions. At the Battle of Ypres, in a single attack, the British gained one hundred yards at a cost of thirteen thousand men in three hours. On the first day of the Battle of the Somme, British forces suffered sixty thousand casualties in one assault. Other battles yielded casualties nearly as numerous.

Peace eventually recurred, as it always does. With the recent Hague Peace Conferences in mind, there was international concern that war crimes be punished. The French government issued a notice that "acts so contrary to International Law, and to the very principles of human civilisation, should not go unpunished," and "There must be punishment and it must be swift."[5] That concern, shared by all the Allies, was reflected in the treaty ending the war, the 1919 Treaty of Versailles.[6]

Article 227 of the treaty "publicly arraigns" William II (Kaiser Wilhelm), the former emperor of Germany, "for a supreme offense against international morality and the sanctity of treaties. A special tribunal will be constituted to try the accused." The treaty did not charge the kaiser with a specific war crime, but "for the first time, a treaty thus addressed the individual responsibility of a head of state for initiating and conducting what we now call a crime of aggression or crime against peace."[7] The kaiser was never tried, however. On the day before the armistice, he fled to the Netherlands, the country of The Hague Peace Conferences. The Dutch government granted him asylum and refused to hand him over for trial. (The Dutch monarch, Queen Wilhelmina, was Wilhelm's cousin.) Holland argued that there was no international law defining the offenses charged against Wilhelm. "In fact, the [Allies] probably never intended to prosecute the Kaiser. The British . . . were not eager to prosecute a crowned head, particularly when the family lineage of that crowned head was related to their own monarchy."[8] The kaiser's "public arraignment" ultimately came to nothing, but it was indicative of a turning of international opinion regarding war crimes.

---

[4] Andrew N. Liaropoulos, "Revolutions in Warfare: Theoretical Paradigms and Historical Evidence – the Napoleonic and First World War Revolutions in Military Affairs," 70–2 *J. of Military History* (April 2006), 363, 377.

[5] Claud Mullins, *The Leipzig Trials* (London: Witherby, 1921), 5.

[6] The United States, in a minority position, was "unalterably opposed" to the prosecution of heads of state, believing the law in that regard was uncertain, that their own countries should be the authorities to try them, and that their trial would represent ex post facto prosecution. The United States also opposed the creation of an international criminal court for the trial of accused German war criminals. United Nations, *Historical Survey of the Question of International Criminal Jurisdiction* (Lake Success, NY: U.N.G.A., 1949), 57–9.

[7] Theodor Meron, "Reflections on the Prosecution of War Crimes by International Tribunals," 100–3 *AJIL* (July 2007), 551, 557.

[8] M. Cherif Bassiouni, "Justice and Peace: The Importance of Choosing Accountability over Realpolitik," 35–2 *Case Western Reserve J. of Int'l L.* (Spring 2003), 191, 193.

The kaiser's nonprosecution aside, the Treaty of Versailles, in Articles 227, 228, and 229, was the first to include provisions applying individual criminal responsibility for violations of the law of war. The 1920 Treaty of Sèvres was one of the several treaties ending World War I, this one between the Allied Powers and the Ottoman Empire. It provided for war crimes trials for atrocities committed in Armenia, but the Kemal Atatürk–led Turkish nationalist movement prevented implementation of the treaty, which was supplanted by the 1923 Treaty of Lausanne preventing any prosecutions.[9] Neither the Treaty of Sèvres nor the Treaty of Versailles obligated the Allies to try their own for any alleged violations.

3.2.1 *The Leipzig Trials (1921)*

After World War I, even before the fighting concluded, the Allies formed a commission to report on enemy violations of the law of war. The commission's report caused Articles 228–230, calling for military tribunals to try alleged enemy war criminals, to be inserted into the Treaty of Versailles, signed shortly after the commission's report was issued.[10] An initial proposal that an international criminal court be established to try those charged was rejected as a result of objections by the United States and Japan. If war crimes were to be punished, another route to trial would have to be found.

Lists of accused war criminals were prepared by the Allies, finally totaling 895 named suspects. A sampling of 45 names was given to the Germans, along with a demand for their production. Disregarding their treaty agreement, the Germans refused to deliver the individuals.

> The German Government represented, and their representations were accepted ... that if they attempted to arrest many of those whose names figured upon the list, it would bring the Government – none too stable – to the ground. They made a counter proposition that they should have the evidence submitted to them, and try before the Supreme Court of Leipzig those against whom the charges were made. ... The Allies tentatively accepted this proposal and presented a list of forty-five cases to be tried by way of experiment.[11]

The Allies, already worried that trials might weaken the German government and give rise to militarists or Bolsheviks, did not press the issue. The Allies did retain the right to repudiate any German trials and demand full execution of Treaty Article 228, providing for trial of accused war criminals by the Allies. The treaty was silent as to the means of trial, however, leaving the door open for the prosecution of enemy war criminals by the enemy's own courts. "Gradually, the Allies lost interest in prosecution. ... In fact, they were ready to let bygones be bygones. However, in Europe, particularly in France, an influential group ... continued to press for prosecution. In response, the Allies pacified advocates of accountability by requesting

---

[9] Erik Goldstein, *Wars and Peace Treaties: 1816–1991* (London: Routledge, 1992), 49, 52.

[10] Art. 228. "The German Government recognizes the right of the Allied and Associated Powers to bring before military tribunals persons accused of having committed acts in violation of the laws and customs of war. ... The German Government shall hand over to the Allied and Associated Powers ... all persons accused of having committed an act in violation of the laws and customs of war ... "

[11] Mullins, *Leipzig Trials*, supra, note 5, at 8–9.

that Germany take on the responsibility of prosecutions."[12] The defeated enemy's entreaties to conduct the trials prevailed.

The Germans pointed out, however, that the war was over and participant soldiers had scattered. Many of the forty-five accused war criminals on the Allies' list could not be located, they insisted. Eventually, twelve of the charged individuals were found and tried by the German high court at Leipzig. Of the twelve, six were acquitted. As to the six who were convicted, the German court "coupled stern and solemn judgments with very light sentences that also were subject to post-trial, nonjudicial modification. German authorities simply allowed convicts to 'escape' after their trials."[13] The maximum sentence of the six who were convicted was four years confinement. Three of the six were sentenced to less than one year. The Allied mission to Leipzig withdrew in protest, genuine or feigned, and the two convicted Germans with the longest sentences escaped their house of detention – not a prison – under suspicious circumstances. "Many characterized these proceedings as little more than a form of political theater held by the Germans to appease the Anglo-French firebrands who sought stern, draconian justice upon all responsible parties of the former German Empire implicated in the war."[14]

> The Leipzig trials are principally remembered for the opportunity they gave the German military to expound its views upon such concepts as "military necessity" and "defense of superior orders. ... " London pronounced itself satisfied with the verdicts and promptly suspended further investigations, but the blatantly political nature of the proceedings in Leipzig was too much for the French and Belgians, who abandoned the trials and pledged to pursue matters through their own courts. The unedifying spectacle, played out over the remainder of the decade, of German officers being found guilty, in absentia, in Belgium and France, only to have their behavior triumphantly exonerated by the German Reichsgericht, merely prolonged and exacerbated the resentment and bitterness felt by all sides.[15]

In the next few years, the French did prosecute some twelve hundred Germans charged with war crimes, and the Belgians about eighty more. The other Allies declined any attempt to pursue their treaty right to try other accused war criminals. The lesson learned by the Allies (who had themselves been less than aggressive, if not outright complicit in the failed effort) was that "entrusting trials of alleged war criminals entirely to the courts of the criminals' own countries would not produce real justice. Instead, an international tribunal was required."[16] Leipzig would be remembered twenty-five years later, at tribunals in Nuremberg and Tokyo.[17]

In condemning the results of the Leipzig trials, it should not be forgotten that, however ill conceived and poorly executed, the trials were a first stumbling step toward imposing

---

[12] Bassiouni, "Justice and Peace," supra, note 8. This telling differs dramatically from that of an historian of the day, Claud Mullins, supra, note 5, but it would explain the Allies' general lassitude in the matter.

[13] Peter Maguire, *Law and War: An American Story* (New York: Columbia University Press, 2000), 10.

[14] John C. Watkins, Jr., and John P. Weber, *War Crimes and War Crime Trials: From Leipzig to the ICC and Beyond* (Durham, NC: Carolina Academic Press, 2006), 6–7.

[15] Neville Wylie, "The 1929 Prisoner of War Convention and the Building of the Inter-War Prisoner of War Regime," in Sibylle Scheipers, ed., *Prisoners in War* (Oxford: Oxford University Press, 2010), 91, 93.

[16] Meron, "Reflections," supra, note 7, at 559.

[17] As to French and Belgian cases tried, see Nina H. B. Jørgensen, *The Responsibility of States for International Crimes* (Oxford: Oxford University Press, 2000), 9.

personal criminal responsibility for battlefield war crimes. "Great principles are often established by minor events. The Leipzig Trials undoubtedly established the principle that individual atrocities committed during a war may be punished when the war is over."[18]

3.3 The League of Nations

In a war-weary world, a search for assured peace continued. The Covenant of the League of Nations, based on the concept of collective security against criminal threats of war, was drafted in 1919. Although the league was strongly promoted in the United States by President Woodrow Wilson, the treaty failed ratification and the United States was never a member of the league. Still wary of foreign entanglements, America objected to Article 16 of the charter, which required all members to preserve the territorial independence of all other members.

Sixty-three nations were league members at one time or another. Article 16 of the covenant provided for sanctions against any state party resorting to aggressive war in violation of the articles. Seeking personal responsibility for violations was not among the sanctions, but the League of Nations was another tentative step in that direction. The league achieved minor success in preserving peace, settling disputes between Finland and Sweden and between Greece and Bulgaria. Finally, however, it was a failure, in part because the covenant's Article 16 did not reflect international law of that day. Despite the league, France occupied the Ruhr and Italy occupied Corfu. The German Nazi government withdrew from the league in 1933, as did Japan's. "The League's failure to halt Japan's annexation of Manchuria in 1931–3 . . . was by every test a grave, almost fatal blow, not only to the League and Covenant, but to the whole idea of the enforcement of peace by collective action."[19] In 1932, the league failed to prevent war between Bolivia and Paraguay and to stop the Italian conquest of Ethiopia in 1935. The Soviet Union was expelled after its 1939 attack on Finland. Finally, in 1946 the league voted its own dissolution. Still, "the League of Nations itself was a brave, almost quixotic act of defiance against man's inhumanity to himself."[20]

3.4 The 1928 Kellogg–Briand Pact

The peace movement that animated the 1899 and 1907 Hague Peace Conferences remained vital, if utopian, through the early years of the twentieth century. A triumph in its day was the Kellogg–Briand Pact, also known as the Treaty of Paris. (Its actual title was the General Treaty for the Renunciation of War.) The U.S. secretary of state, Frank B. Kellogg, and the French foreign minister, Aristide Briand, both Nobel Prize in peace winners, are credited as the eponymous driving forces of the agreement.

Representatives of sixty-three states met in Paris and agreed that "the High Contracting Parties solemnly declare . . . that they condemn recourse to war for the solution of international controversies and renounce it as an instrument of national policy in their relations with one another."[21] The pact did not purport to abolish war, however.

---

[18] Mullins, *Leipzig Trials*, supra, note 5, at 224.
[19] F. S. Northedge, *The League of Nations* (Leicester: Leicester University Press, 1986), 161.   [20] Id., at 186.
[21] Art. 1, General Treaty for the Renunciation of War (1928).

According to its terms, it remained lawful for parties to take up arms in self-defense, and to take armed action against other parties that resorted to war in contravention of the pact. The treaty "made no provision for determining whether [the pact] had been violated ... or for enforcement action by the parties to the pact against a state guilty of violation."[22] Sanctions, national or personal, were not included, and the treaty came to be seen as a statement of intent, rather than an enforceable prohibition in international law.

Having no provisions for lapse or renunciation, the Kellogg–Briand Pact is technically still in force. "The treaty was of almost universal obligation since only four states in international society as it existed before the Second World War were not bound by its provisions. Nor did the treaty remain in isolation. It had considerable effects on state practice. In the years that followed numerous treaties were concluded which reaffirmed the obligations of the Kellogg-Briand Pact."[23]

"The General Treaty for the Renunciation of War at present stands together with the United Nations Charter as one of the two major sources of the norm limiting resort to force by states."[24] For the law of war, the pact's significance was that the post–World War II Nuremberg and Tokyo International Military Tribunals heavily relied upon it in contending that, since the pact's formation, aggressive war is a crime in international law, allowing personal accountability for violations. (It is unfortunate that the World War II declarations of war by the United States, Great Britain, and France failed to mention the pact in this regard.) The pact also led to the prohibition of the use of force found in Article 2(4) of the United Nations Charter. Although usually viewed as having been ineffective, the Kellogg–Briand Pact was the initial international effort to ban aggressive war. Like the Leipzig trials and the League of Nations, it was imperfect progress toward outlawing criminality in armed conflict and the assessment of personal liability for violators.

3.5 The 1929 Geneva Conventions

The international Red Cross movement continued to add national representative bodies to its committee, and diplomatic conferences continued to be held in Geneva. World War I highlighted the need to strengthen protections accorded POWs, an unprecedented number of whom had been captured during the war, revealing gaps, deficiencies, and imprecision in the 1907 Hague regulations regarding prisoners. Thus, in their 1929 conference, the International Committee of the Red Cross (ICRC) delegates adopted the first convention for the protection of POWs, to join the original convention protecting the wounded. The first Geneva POW convention supplemented, rather than replaced, the POW protections contained in 1907 Hague Regulation IV.[25] Reprisals were largely prohibited by the 1929 convention, as were collective penalties. Provisions for the repatriation of seriously wounded and sick prisoners were added, and protections for medical aircraft, few as they were in 1929, were initiated. The new POW convention was

---

[22] Morris Greenspan, *The Modern Law of Land Warfare* (Berkeley: University of California Press, 1959), 518.

[23] Ian Brownlie, *International Law and the Use of Force by States* (Oxford: Clarendon Press, 1963), 75.

[24] Id., at 91.

[25] Adam Roberts and Richard Guelff, *Documents on the Laws of War*, 3d ed. (Oxford: Oxford University Press, 2000), 243.

signed by forty-seven states, including the United States. Russia and Japan did not sign or ratify, foreshadowing difficult POW issues in World War II.[26]

At the same time, the 1906 Convention for the Amelioration of the Condition of the Wounded and Sick was amended and strengthened. In 1929, for the first time, two Geneva Conventions were in effect.

In July 1939, the POW convention was amended by incorporating Articles 1, 2, and 3 of 1907 Hague Regulation IV. Article 1, which was to be repeated in the 1949 Geneva convention on POWs, specifies that "militia and volunteer corps" that fulfill four conditions, commanded by one responsible for subordinates, have a fixed distinctive sign recognizable at a distance, carry arms openly, and conduct operations in accordance with the laws and customs of war, were also entitled to POW status.

3.6 The Spanish Civil War (1936–1939)

The Spanish Civil War neither was a solely Spanish conflict; nor was it civil. The war in Spain was the training ground for the Second World War. Spanish Republican forces fought against Spain's Nationalist military caste, landowners, and fascism. The rebelling Spanish Republicans controlled sufficient territory that they could carry out sustained and concerted military operations. They were supported by passionate antifascist fighters from fifty-five countries (the International Brigades), including several thousand American volunteers who formed the "Abraham Lincoln Brigade," one member of whom was the writer George Orwell, wounded in combat,[27] and the Sacco and Vanzetti *centuria*, a multinational force with many American members. The Republicans also received aircraft, pilots, tanks, and advisers, not to mention political direction, from Joseph Stalin's Soviet Union.

The opposing Spanish Nationalists, commanded by the Spanish army's former chief of staff, General Francisco Franco, fought Marxism, labor unions, and land reform movements. The Nationalists were supported by an Irish brigade and an entire air force, including thousands of pilots, provided by Adolf Hitler (the "Condor Legion"), as well as seventy-five thousand Italian troops sent by Mussolini.

---

[26] Japan did not sign because becoming a prisoner was contrary to Bushido. "The Japanese believed that . . . in practice only Japan would have to assume the obligations of the treaty. Japan would have to provide food and housing for prisoners, while other countries were spared this obligation since there would be no Japanese prisoners." National Defense Intelligence College, *Interrogation: World War II, Vietnam, and Iraq* (Washington, DC: NDIC Press, 2008), 51. In 1942, Japan nevertheless gave a qualified promise to abide by the convention. In 1941, Russia announced that it would follow the terms of the 1907 Hague Conventions, which did not provide for the exchange of prisoners' names, POW correspondence, or neutral inspection of camps. After World War II, in "The High Command Case," a principal issue was whether the 1929 POW convention bound Germany vis-à-vis the Soviet Union. The court found that, despite not having ratified the convention, Germany was bound. "They were binding insofar as they were in substance an expression of international law as accepted by the civilized nations of the world, and this Tribunal adopts this viewpoint." *U.S. v. von Leeb* ("The High Command Case"), *XI Trials of War Criminals* (Washington, DC: GPO, 1951), 534.

[27] Peter N. Carroll, *The Odyssey of the Abraham Lincoln Brigade* (Stanford, CA: Stanford University Press, 1994), 77, 88. A less enthusiastic view of the Lincoln Brigade is offered in Cecil D. Eby, *Comrades and Commissars: The Lincoln Battalion in the Spanish Civil War* (University Park: Pennsylvania State University Press, 2007).

More than half a century later, wars in Afghanistan and Iraq saw a similar infusion of foreign volunteer fighters – mujahidin and jihadists. The Spanish Civil War, in both its internal and international aspects, was particularly savage, leading diplomats and military officers to begin conceptualizing what would eventually become Geneva Convention common Article 3.[28] For the first time, undefended cities, such as Guernica and Durango, were set aflame by air raids. Civilians were openly calculated targets. "The wanton killing of opponents and suspects, the execution of prisoners and a rising tide of reprisals became common place on both sides. . . . The war remained marked to the end by extreme brutality."[29]

The war ended badly for the Republican forces, and Franco remained Spain's dictator until 1975. For its gross disregard for the principle of distinction, and the tremendous loss of civilian life and property, the Spanish Civil War remains significant. It is also notable because it was an internal armed conflict in which domestic law, rather than the 1929 Geneva Conventions, applied. "The Spanish Civil War represents a turning point in the international regulation of civil wars in many respects."[30] Its well-publicized atrocities by both sides led to an international call for civil conflicts to be made more humane, largely through the efforts of the ICRC. The killing of so many civilians demonstrated the need to impose limitations on the means and methods of warfare in internal armed conflicts, and the concerns raised in the war were significant factors in framing the 1949 Geneva Conventions.

3.7 World War II (1939–1945)

World War II is history's largest war in terms of geographic span, state involvement, and casualties. It also was "a watershed for the law of armed conflict."[31] Deaths exceeded 55 million, almost two-thirds of them civilians. To say that law of war violations by both sides were frequent does not impart the brutality of the conflict. POWs suffered terribly. The Nazis murdered millions of Soviet POWs, many directly, many more through starvation and maltreatment. Some 200,000 handicapped or mentally ill Germans were killed, as were a large portion of Europe's Gypsies. At the hands of the German state, millions of European Jews went from discrimination and persecution to deportation and death. The roster of victim groups was lengthy. Hundreds of thousands of civilians perished in the U.S. firebombing of Japan and in the area bombing of Germany by the British and, to a lesser degree, Americans. "The atrocities of World War II gave birth to the human rights movement, . . . to the insistence on individual criminal responsibility, to the judgment of the Nuremberg Tribunal and to the promulgation of the Universal Declaration of Human Rights (1948)."[32]

Michael Walzer writes, "War is so awful that it makes us cynical about the possibility of restraint, and then it is so much worse that it makes us indignant at the absence of

---

[28] Lt.Col. Yair M. Lootsteen, "The Concept of Belligerency in International Law," 166 *Military L. Rev.* (Dec. 2000), 109.

[29] François Bugnion, *The International Committee of the Red Cross and the Protection of War Victims* (Oxford: Macmillan/ICRC, 2003), 268.

[30] Eve La Haye, *War Crimes in Internal Armed Conflicts* (Cambridge: Cambridge University Press, 2008), 38.

[31] United Kingdom Ministry of Defense, *The Manual of the Law of Armed Conflict* (Oxford: Oxford University Press, 2004), para. 1.28.

[32] Theodor Meron, *The Humanization of International Law* (Boston: Martinus Nijhoff, 2006), 6.

restraint."[33] Clearly, if they were to have continuing relevance, the two existing Geneva Conventions required protections for civilians and strengthening of POW coverage. The result of these and other concerns was the 1949 Geneva Conventions.

In 1914, the U.S. Army published the first version of *Rules of Land Warfare*, "for the information and government of the armed land forces of the United States."[34] The manual was heavily influenced by the 1863 Lieber Code. Redesignated Field Manual (FM) 27–10, it was republished without substantial change in 1934 and 1940. With some accuracy, it can be said that America entered World War II with battlefield legal guidelines dating from the Civil War. It was time for a change.

Would new conventions make a difference? "You may say, 'Yes, how admirable, but will any belligerent take any notice of these restraints?' One may reply that one may only disregard these prohibitions in the Conventions by a clear and manifest resort to criminality before the whole world. States do not willingly brand themselves as criminal agencies."[35] Given the near-universal abhorrence of the enemy's war crimes committed during World War II, and the unanimity of desire for strengthening battlefield law, few nations would be willing to contravene new regulations. Taking advantage of this unique international opportunity, the new conventions did not merely revise the 1929 conventions; in some instances they fundamentally rewrote battlefield law.

> **SIDEBAR.** The 1956 version of FM 27–10, *The Law of Land Warfare*, was drafted by the former U.S. Army colonel Richard R. Baxter, while he was a Harvard Law School professor. He went on to become the editor in chief of the *American Journal of International Law* and, eventually, a judge on the International Court of Justice. Judge Baxter, then America's leading LOAC expert, died in 1980. The long-gestating complete revision of the 1956 version of FM 27–10 became available in mid-2015. Its writing was a lengthy and difficult collaborative effort led by W. Hays Parks, a retired U.S. Marine Corps colonel and Vietnam combat veteran, and foremost LOAC expert. Bureaucratic conflicts between Department of State efforts to inject more human rights law into U.S. war fighting practice and Department of Defense resistance delayed publication of the new manual for years.

3.8 The 1949 Geneva Conventions

In 2002, Alberto Gonzales, then-counsel to the president and, later, attorney general of the United States, wrote of the 1949 Geneva Convention for the Protection of Prisoners of War: "In my judgment, this new paradigm [the war against terrorism] renders obsolete Geneva's strict limitations on questioning of enemy prisoners and renders quaint some of its provisions requiring that captured enemy be afforded such things as commissary

---

[33] Michael Walzer, *Just and Unjust Wars*, 3d ed. (New York: Basic Books, 1997), 46.

[34] War Department, *Rules of Land Warfare – 1914* (Washington, DC: GPO, 1914), 3. The army has long had primary responsibility among U.S. Armed Forces for law of war matters. Manuals such as this one, although published by the army, apply to all U.S. Armed Forces.

[35] G. I. A. D. Draper, "The Historical Background and General Principles of the Geneva Conventions of 1949," in Michael A. Meyer and Hilaire McCoubrey, eds., *Reflections on Law and Armed Conflict* (The Hague: Kluwer Law International, 1998), 60.

privileges, scrip (i.e., advances of monthly pay), athletic uniforms, and scientific instruments."[36] The POW convention allows, but does not require, athletic uniforms and musical instruments, but the thought behind the counsel's statement is worrisome, suggesting a U.S. retreat from one of the most significant multinational treaties in existence: a treaty born in no small measure of the suffering of American prisoners and of those of other nations. In 2007, the Dutch legal adviser to the Ministry of Foreign Affairs said, "It has been suggested that the rules of international humanitarian law, which would have been sufficient for dealing with past conflicts, are inadequate in the case of terrorism. This suggestion ... leads to the suggestion that the existing but – supposedly – inadequate rules need not be applied. This ... is a dangerous line of thinking."[37]

Ambassador George H. Aldrich has noted that "the history of development of this branch of international law is largely one of reaction to bad experience. After each major war, the survivors negotiate rules for the next war that they would, in retrospect, like to have seen in force during the last war. The 1929 *and 1949 Geneva Conventions* attest to this pattern."[38] The 1949 conventions, Counsel Gonzales's opinion notwithstanding, have proven more lasting and resilient than their predecessors.

The four 1949 Geneva Conventions are the cornerstone of LOAC. They are the most ratified treaties in the history of the world. As of August 2006, with the signing and ratification by the Republic of Montenegro, all of the world's nations have ratified the conventions. New states will arise in the future and, as with Montenegro, the 1949 Geneva Conventions will be among the first treaties they ratify and join by accession. If for some reason a new state were not to join the conventions by accession, in many respects it nevertheless will be bound by the conventions because many of their provisions, particularly those addressing basic human rights, are by now customary law, accepted by and binding on every state. The fact that all states have ratified the conventions goes far in suggesting that they are customary law, although numbers alone are not determinative of customary status.[39] "Customary rules have the advantage of being applicable to all parties to an armed conflict – State and non-State – independent of any formal ratification process. ... However ... [customary] rules or contents are frequently challenged owing to its mostly non-written form."[40] A 1993 report of the U.N. secretary-general to the Security Council states that "the part of conventional

---

[36] Alberto R. Gonzales, Memorandum for the President; Subject: Decision re Application of the Geneva Convention on Prisoners of War to the Conflict with al Qaeda and the Taliban; dated 1/25/2002.

[37] Liesbeth Lijnzaad, "Developments in International Humanitarian Law Since 1977," in *Protecting Human Dignity in Armed Conflict* (The Hague: Netherlands Red Cross, 2008), 17.

[38] George H. Aldrich, "Some Reflections on the Origins of the 1977 Geneva Protocols," in Christophe Swinarski, ed., *Studies and Essays on International Humanitarian Law and Red Cross Principles, in Honour of Jean Pictet* (Geneva: ICRC, 1984), 129. Footnote omitted, emphasis in original.

[39] See Theodor Maron, "The Geneva Conventions as Customary Law," 81–2 *AJIL* (April 1987), 348. "Many provisions of Conventions I, II, and II are based on earlier Geneva Conventions, and thus have a claim to customary law status. Geneva Convention No. IV, in contrast, was the first Geneva Convention ever to be addressed to the protection of civilian persons." The passage of more than twenty years since Professor Maron's article was written, and universal ratification that has transpired since it was written, clarify the customary status of all four 1949 Conventions.

[40] ICRC, "International Humanitarian Law and the Challenges of Contemporary Armed Conflicts," 867 *Int'l Rev. of the Red Cross* (Sept. 2007), 719–57, 742.

international humanitarian law which has beyond doubt become part of international customary law" includes the four 1949 Geneva Conventions.[41]

That many articles of the conventions enjoy customary law status is significant. Should a state consider withdrawing from the conventions, it could not terminate its customary law obligations, making withdrawal largely pointless.[42] Additionally, "reservations to the Conventions may not affect the obligations of the parties under provisions reflecting customary law to which they would be subject independently of the Conventions."[43] As the International Court of Justice (ICJ) notes in the *Nicaragua* judgment, "an obligation [to respect the conventions] does not derive from the Conventions themselves, but from the general principles of humanitarian law to which the Conventions merely give specific expression."[44]

"Calamitous events and atrocities have repeatedly driven the development of international humanitarian law. The more offensive or painful the suffering, the greater the pressure for accommodating humanitarian restraints."[45] The treatment of wounded captives by both former enemy states demonstrated a need for the strengthening of the 1929 convention regarding protection of the wounded; the unacceptable treatment of POWs, including medical experimentation, mandated a stronger regime of protections for POWs; the grievous loss of civilian lives and property demonstrated a need for a new convention that protected civilians.

From their inception in 1864, the purpose of the Geneva Conventions has been to protect the victims of armed conflict – the sick and wounded, POWs, and civilians. The means of waging war – the lawfulness of weapons, the legitimacy of tactics, protection of cultural objects, and neutrality – are issues left to what was formerly referred to as "Hague law." Thus, one finds no mention in the Geneva Conventions of such significant matters as command responsibility, obedience to orders, distinction, or military necessity. These topics were left to Hague treaties such as 1907 Hague Regulation IV, and to the 1868 St. Petersburg Declaration, as well as to customary law of war, which had not yet been reduced to multinational pacts. The 1949 conventions maintained this somewhat artificial "Hague law"/ "Geneva law" distinction. Although the distinction largely faded with the adoption of the two 1977 "Protocols Additional to the 1949 Geneva Conventions," it is still sometimes referenced. By now, however, Hague law has so fully mixed with Geneva law that it is pointless to maintain the distinction.

With the 1949 conventions, the ICRC secured its place as the principal protector and enunciator of IHL. "The ICRC may be, and has been, accused of acting like a peace or disarmament organization and exceeding its primary mandate to protect and assist victims."[46] The ICRC's role is essential, however, and, along with other nongovernmental organizations, it provides an essential public oversight of military actions.

[41] Report of the Secretary-General Pursuant to Paragraph 2 of Security Council Resolution 808 (1993), U.N. doc. S/25704 of 3 May 1993, p. 9.
[42] Common Article 63/62/142/158, provides for denunciation of the Conventions.
[43] Meron, "The Geneva Conventions," supra, note 39, at 349.
[44] *Case concerning Military and Paramilitary Activities in and against Nicaragua (Nicaragua v. United States)*, Merits, (27 June 1986), 114. ICJ Rpts 14, ¶ 220.
[45] Meron, "Humanization of Humanitarian Law," supra, note 32, at 243.
[46] Toni Pfanner, "Editorial," 859 *Int'l Rev. of the Red Cross* (Sept. 2005), 413, 416.

3.8.1 *A Geneva Conventions Roadmap*

There are four 1949 conventions. The first is entitled Geneva Convention for the Amelioration of the Condition of the Wounded and Sick in Armed Forces in the Field of August 12, 1949. This first convention is a derivative and an expansion of the 1929 convention on the same subject. The Convention for the Wounded and Sick is also referred to as "GC I" and, occasionally, as "GCW."

The second 1949 convention is the Geneva Convention for the Amelioration of the Condition of Wounded, Sick and Shipwrecked Members of the Armed Forces at Sea. (The formal titles of all four conventions end with the date of their adoption, August 12, 1949.) There is considerable duplication within the four conventions. It can especially be argued that the first and second conventions could have been combined into one, but having two conventions for the wounded and sick, one relating to land forces, the other to forces at sea, reflects the historical distinction of rules and laws especially applicable to seaborne forces. Similar to the first convention, this second convention is also referred to as "GC II" or sometimes as "GCWSea."

The third convention, the Geneva Convention Relative to the Treatment of Prisoners of War, is also descended and expanded from the 1929 convention of the same subject. It is often referred to as "GC III" or "GPW."

The fourth convention is the Geneva Convention Relative to the Protection of Civilian Persons in Time of War, "GC IV," or confusingly, "GC." This was the first multinational treaty devoted solely to the protection of civilians in wartime. In the nineteenth century, the law of war was only marginally concerned with the protection of civilians. They were thought to be outside the war and not in need of regulation. Since the First World War, civilians have been the most numerous victims of war, and a vehicle for their protection was badly needed. "The undertaking was an arduous one, however. The legal field in question was completely new. Until then the Geneva Conventions had only applied to the armed forces, a well-defined category of persons. ... It was now necessary to include an unorganized mass of civilians scattered over the whole of the countries concerned."[47] The fourth convention "was largely the result of the policies pursued by the Germans during the occupation of Europe and particularly relating to the Holocaust."[48]

> Now civilians, whenever they are in the hands of the enemy power, have a detailed protection that can be supervised by the Protecting Power and the International Committee of the Red Cross, and enforced by direct penal action against those, whether they be private individuals or officials, who violate that protection in a grave manner. This Civilian's Convention was called into being by the civilized States of the community of nations as a direct result of the experience of the Second World War.[49]

Those "civilized States of the community of nations" still search for some means of encouraging nonstate actors to observe the conventions.

GC IV, Article 123, mandates a continuation of ICRC identification of civilian prisoners like the system formalized in the 1929 POW convention. The Central Information Agency for protected persons continues to be a significant element of the

---

[47] Jean Pictet, ed., *Commentary, IV Geneva Convention* (Geneva: ICRC, 1958), 5.

[48] L. C. Green, "'Grave Breaches' or Crimes against Humanity," 8 *J. of Legal Studies* (1997–8), 19, 21.

[49] Draper, "Historical Background and General Principles of the Geneva Conventions," *supra*, note 35, at 58.

conventions' protections, nearly identical to the Information Agency provided for POWs since 1870.[50] The agency (GC IV, Article 140) continues to collect information on civilians' location and condition and transmits it to the country of origin or residence of the person concerned, providing important information that is relayed to relatives of the individual.

The reference to the fourth convention, the civilian's convention, as "GC" can be confusing, as the 1949 Geneva Conventions as a whole are sometimes referred to as the "GCs." The context of the reference usually makes clear which is intended. Today, when "the GCs," or "the Geneva Conventions," are spoken of, it is the 1949 conventions to which they refer.

3.8.1.1 Common Articles

The 1949 conventions contain roughly twenty articles known as "common articles." As the term implies, these are articles that are common to all four of the 1949 conventions. The common articles reflect matters that the drafters considered significant enough to merit emphasis through repetition – issues applicable across LOAC board, not limited to a single convention. In three instances, these common articles are found in precisely the same place in all four conventions. That is, in all four 1949 conventions Article 1 reads exactly the same; it is not only common to all four conventions, it is found in the same place in all four conventions. Common Articles 1, 2, and 3 are identical in content and, within their respective conventions, identical in location. Other common articles read substantially but not precisely alike and are in differing locations within the conventions. Throughout the study of LOAC, there will be frequent references to "common Article 2" and to "common Article 3," both of which are important foundations for other LOAC issues.[*]

3.8.2 Enact Domestic Penal Legislation for Grave Breaches

The 1949 conventions introduced four significant innovations to the law of war: first, a requirement that ratifying states enact domestic legislation to prosecute those having committed grave breaches of the conventions; second, agreement by ratifying states to seek out and try those who have committed grave breaches; third, the concept of "grave breaches" itself; and fourth, common Article 3 protections. As Professor Colonel G. I. A. D. Draper wrote, "They establish clearly that the Geneva Conventions are not the starry-eyed wishful thinking of 'do-gooders'. They are a body of practical legal rules, pragmatic and enforceable by criminal prosecution."[51] Alas, he might have added, if the ratifying state party has the political courage and the will to do so.

---

[50] See GC III, Art. 123. The Central Prisoners of War Information Agency was created by the ICRC during the 1870 Franco-German War and was reflected in Art. 79 of the 1929 Geneva Convention on POWs. Its purpose, like that of the later 1949 GC IV agency, is to collect and forward information on POWs to prisoners' governments.

[*] Other common articles that read substantially alike are common Art. 6/6/6/7, common Art. 7/7/7/8, common Art. 8/8/8/9, common Art. 9/9/9/10, common Art. 10/10/10/11, common Art. 11/11/11/12, common Art. 12/12/13/16, and common Art. 49/50/129/146. There are numerous others. Common Articles relating to implementation of the conventions are found in the "Final Provisions" chapters of the four conventions, as well.

[51] Draper, "Historical Background and General Principles of the Geneva Conventions," supra, note 35, at 61.

The first of the four 1949 innovations, enactment of domestic legislation to punish grave breaches, is required by common Article 49/50/129/146. This common article "lays the foundations of the system adopted for suppressing breaches of the Convention. The system is based on three fundamental obligations ... to enact special legislation ... to search for any person accused of violation ... and the obligation to try such persons."[52] As related earlier, there have been battlefield rules and laws for hundreds of years. Enforcement and punishment of violations had always been another matter. The 1863 Lieber Code, for instance, recites numerous prohibitions but offers no means of punishing persons who violate them. The 1907 Hague Regulation IV imposes monetary fines on the state of the soldier-violator; the state can punish, or not, the actual violator. The 1864, 1906, and 1929 Geneva Conventions are silent on the matter of violations and their punishment.[*] The post–World War II International Military Tribunals (IMTs) at Nuremberg and Tokyo raised a new standard that imposed personal criminal responsibility on individuals found guilty of serious violations of the law of war. Post–World War II military commissions held by Allied nations joined in the imposition of personal criminal responsibility for violations committed by the Japanese, the Nazis, and their allies. Mindful of these advances, and the many violations that occurred during World War II, the framers of the 1949 conventions realized that, to impose the requirements and prohibitions of the conventions effectively, there had to be a vehicle by which penalties could be imposed for violations – penalties of a criminal nature levied against the offending individuals.

The framers' solution was common Article 49/50/129/146. It reads, "The High Contracting Parties undertake to enact any penal legislation necessary to provide effective penal sanctions for persons committing, or ordering to be committed, any of the grave breaches of the present Convention defined in the following Article." And the subsequent article specifies the grave breaches to be punished.

This ingenious provision requires each state that ratifies the conventions to enact within two years domestic criminal provisions by which violators may be tried and punished. Today, domestic enforcement provisions are common to multinational treaties, but half a century ago they were novel.

The *Commentary* to GC I notes that "the proceedings before the courts should, moreover, be uniform in character, whatever the nationality of the accused. Nationals, friends and enemies should all be subject to the same rules of procedure, and should be judged by the same courts. The creation of special tribunals to try war criminals of enemy nationality is thus excluded."[53] The last sentence, written after World War II's military commissions were completed, raises interesting issues regarding the use of military commissions to try enemy personnel and nonstate actors charged with committing grave breaches.

A notable absence from the enforcement provision is that "there is no reference to the responsibility of those who fail to intervene, in order to prevent or suppress an infraction. ... In view of the silence of the Convention it must be assumed that the matter is one which must be settled by national legislation, either by express provision or

---

[52] Jean Pictet, ed., *Commentary, I Geneva Convention* (Geneva: ICRC, 1952), 362.

[*] Article 28 of the 1906 convention does provide for repression of cases of pillage and ill treatment of the wounded, and abuse of the Red Cross flag or armlet.

[53] Id. (Pictet), at 366.

by applying the general provisions contained in the country's penal code."[54] This issue would arise years later, in the context of the U.S.–Iraq war.

3.8.2.1 Charging One's Own Soldiers: The Uniform Code of Military Justice

Most high contracting parties comply with the common article's domestic legislation requirement through their military justice systems. (The military penal codes of Switzerland, Romania, the Soviet Union, and Cuba specifically provided for the punishment of certain law of war violations even before the 1949 conventions.)[55] In the United States, the Uniform Code of Military Justice (UCMJ) is the federal law enacting a criminal code to which personnel of all U.S. armed services are subject. Crimes under the UCMJ include, inter alia, murder, maiming, rape, aggravated assault, and abuse of a prisoner, all of which may be grave breaches of the Geneva Conventions, as well as violations of U.S. military law. A U.S. soldier suspected of committing a grave breach would be charged with the corresponding UCMJ violation, no reference to the law of war being necessary.[*] The UCMJ was not enacted with enforcement of the Geneva Conventions in mind but, as to American combatants, the UCMJ's 1951 implementation neatly met the conventions' requirements. The *Manual for Courts-Martial* is the text that implements the UCMJ, lays out rules of evidence and procedure, and instructs judge advocates in pretrial, trial, and posttrial processes. The first two sentences of the *Manual for Courts-Martial* read: "The sources of military jurisdiction include the Constitution and international law. International law includes the law of war." Article 18 of the UCMJ reads in pertinent part, "General courts-martial also have jurisdiction to try any person who by the law of war is subject to trial by a military tribunal and may adjudge any punishment by the law of war."

An advantage of military courts is that "jurisdiction is, of course, easy when the accused is a member of the armed forces of the nation whose courts are involved."[56] Nor is the verdict of the court-martial merely the expression of one nation's military law. "The military court, by punishing the acts, executes international law even if it applies ... its own military law."[57]

---

[54] Id., at 364.   [55] Id., at 356.

[*] In U.S. military practice it is possible, although procedurally difficult, to charge grave breaches as war crimes. See UCMJ Articles 18 and 21, and *Discussion*, Rule of Court-Martial 307 (c) (2). Also, Maj. Martin N. White, "Charging War Crimes: A Primer for the Practitioner," *Army Lawyer* (Feb. 2006), 1–11; and Maj. Mynda Ohman, "Integrating Title 18 War Crimes into Title 10: A Proposal to Amend the UCMJ," 57 *Air Force L. Rev.* (2005), 1. Only two actual instances of such charging have been located. Two My Lai accused, Capt. Eugene Kotouc and 1st Lt. Thomas Willingham, were charged with war crimes qua war crimes. Kotouc went to trial and was acquitted; Willingham's charges were then dropped prior to trial. [U.S. Army, *Report of the Dept. of the Army Review of the Preliminary Investigation Into the My Lai Incident*, vol. 2, book 16 (Pentagon: Dept. of the Army, n.d.), testimony of Capt. Kotouc, designated by the code letters "BX," [n.p.]. Directly charging violations of the law of war is common in other forums, such as the ICTY. See *Prosecutor v. Delalić* (IT-96-21-T), Judgment (16 Nov. 1998).

[56] Leslie C. Green, "Aftermath of Vietnam: War Law and the Soldier," in Richard A. Falk, ed., *The Vietnam War and International Law*, Vol. 4 (Princeton, NJ: Princeton University Press, 1976), 147, 149.

[57] Hans Kelsen, *Peace through Law* (Chapel Hill: University of North Carolina Press, 1944), 77. For a contrary view, see R. R. Baxter, "The Municipal and International Law Basis of Jurisdiction over War Crimes," 28 BYIL (1951), 382.

If U.S. service personnel charged with violations of the law of war are tried by U.S. courts-martial, what legislation provides for the trial of enemy violators? Historically, military commissions have been the trial forum for the enemy. That is true not only for the United States but for many states.

3.8.2.2 Charging Civilians I: The 1996 War Crimes Act

In the United States, domestic legislation enacted to prosecute civilians criminally includes the War Crimes Act of 1996[58] and the Military Extraterritorial Jurisdiction Act (MEJA).[59] The War Crimes Act was a long time coming, forty-two years after U.S. ratification of the conventions. Initially, it did not occur to American legislators that civilians – noncombatants – might commit grave breaches of the law of war. Conflicts like those in Vietnam and the former Yugoslavia starkly demonstrated that possibility, and legislation was undertaken.

The Vietnam War's My Lai massacre of hundreds of South Vietnamese noncombatants remains a stain on the reputation of American fighting forces. Eventually, only four officers and two enlisted soldiers were court-martialed for the events in My Lai-4 and their subsequent cover-up. First Lieutenant William L. Calley Jr. was the sole individual convicted. The event occurred on March 16, 1968, but, because of the cover-up orchestrated by participants and their senior officers, My Lai-4 did not attract public attention until mid-1969. In the intervening fifteen months, a number of soldiers suspected of My Lai-4 war crimes were discharged from the army – as many as twenty-two, according to one federal court.[60] In that era, court-martial jurisdiction did not survive discharge from active military duty,[61] and, in 1969, there was no U.S. domestic court with jurisdiction over foreign shore grave breaches, leaving former soldiers suspected of war crimes free of possible prosecution. (Trial in Vietnam, the site of the crimes, was a theoretical option but a practical impossibility.) This lacuna in the law – soldier criminals discharged into jurisdictional freedom – was corrected by the War Crimes Act, which, as amended in 1997, and by the Military Commissions Act of 2006, prohibits "grave breaches" of common Article 3, when those offenses are committed either by or against members of the U.S. Armed Forces or U.S. nationals. "Grave breaches" of common Article 3 are defined to include torture, cruel or inhuman treatment, biological experiments, murder of individuals not taking part in hostilities, mutilation or maiming, intentionally causing serious bodily injury, rape, sexual assault or abuse, and hostage taking. The act has both domestic and extraterritorial application. Oddly, "the United States has apparently never prosecuted a person under the War Crimes Act. Perhaps as a result, there is some question concerning the Act's scope."[62] One suspects that few U.S. attorneys are eager to undertake the expensive prosecution of an alleged grave breach with a foreign locus, with witnesses to transport and house, for a questionable outcome. Also, the prosecutor

---

[58] 18 U.S. Code § 2441.   [59] MEJA, 18 U.S. Code §§ 3261–7.

[60] *Calley v. Callaway*, 519 F.2d 184, 191 fn. 6 (1975). This figure is exaggerated, as there were only twenty-five men in Lieutenant Calley's 1st platoon, C Company, on the day of the massacre. [Lt. Gen. William R. Peers, *The My Lai Inquiry* (New York: Norton, 1979), 173.] The number might include suspects from Lt. Steven K. Brooks's 2nd platoon, adjacent to Lt. Calley's platoon in the My Lai operation.

[61] *Toth v. Quarles*, 350 U.S. 11 (1955).

[62] Michael John Garcia, *The War Crimes Act: Current Issues*, (Washington, DC: Congressional Research Service, Sept. 15, 2006).

could be required to prove a "war" was in progress at the time of the alleged crime – a potential political minefield for politically appointed U.S. attorneys.

Perhaps with this practical limitation in mind, in 2006 the UCMJ was amended to provide court-martial jurisdiction over former armed service personnel – in other words, civilians – newly suspected of having committed a serious criminal act prior to military discharge.[63] In 2006, the UCMJ was amended to provide court-martial jurisdiction over certain other civilians, as well.[64] Any conviction based on expanded UCMJ jurisdiction will likely be appealed on constitutional grounds, for civilian appellate courts are traditionally reluctant to extend military jurisdiction to civilians.[65]

Civilians have long been subject to military trial, however. Nearly a century ago, the 1916 Articles of War, Article 2, "Persons subject to military law," read in subsection (d), "All retainers to the camp and all persons accompanying or serving with the armies of the United States without the territorial jurisdiction of the United States, and in time of war all such retainers and persons accompanying or serving with the armies ... in the field, both within and without the territorial jurisdiction of the United States."

That provision continued essentially unchanged in the UCMJ and, during the U.S.–North Vietnam War, in Vietnam the U.S. Marine Corps tried at least four American civilians.[66] (The army argued against such trials, urging that U.S. civilians should be tried in Vietnamese courts. Several were.)[67] In 1969 and 1970, the United States Court of Military Appeals, the military's highest appellate court, and a U.S. federal district court reversed two Vietnam-sited civilian court-martial convictions.[68]

Exercise of expanded UCMJ jurisdiction is limited to former service members who have not completed their full service commitment. That is, most active duty enlistments are followed by a contractual period of active reserve duty, Individual Ready Reserve (IRR) duty, or a combination of both. IRR duty is actually *no* duty; the service member merely "serves" the remaining period of his contract as a civilian, subject to recall to active duty only in extraordinary circumstances. Recall for purposes of court-martial is an extraordinary circumstance.

Under the UCMJ's expanded jurisdiction, the first court-martial conviction of a civilian since the Vietnam era was in June 2008. An Iraqi-Canadian civilian translator employed by the U.S. Army in Iraq, Alaa "Alex" Mohammad Ali, was convicted at court-martial of stabbing another civilian translator with a knife that Ali stole from a U.S. soldier. With a pretrial agreement, Ali pleaded guilty to wrongful appropriation of the knife, obstruction of justice for wrongfully disposing of the knife, and making a false

---

[63] UCMJ, Art. 3(a).

[64] 2006 UCMJ amendments of Art. 2(10), (11), and (12) extend court-martial jurisdiction to "persons serving with or accompanying an armed force in the field;" and "persons serving with or employed by, or accompanying an armed force in the field outside the United States"; and "persons within an area leased by or otherwise reserved or acquired for use of the United States ... outside the United States." The phrase "in the field" means serving "in an area of actual fighting" at or near the battlefront where "actual hostilities are under way" (*Reid v. Covert*, 354 U.S. 1, 35).

[65] See *Reid v. Covert* and its progeny, *Kinsella v. U.S.* ex rel. *Singleton*, 361 U.S. 234 (1960), *Grisham v. Hagan*, 361 U.S. 278 (1960), and *McElroy v. Guagliardo*, 361 U.S. 281 (1960).

[66] Maj. Gen. George S. Prugh, *Law at War: Vietnam 1964–1973* (Washington, DC: Dept. of the Army, 1975), 109.

[67] Lt. Col. Gary D. Solis, *Marines and Military Law in Vietnam* (Washington, DC: GPO, 1989), 99–100.

[68] *U.S. v. Latney*, Navy Court-Martial #68–1965 and its civilian court appeal, *Latney v. Ignatius*, 416 F.2d 821 (1969); and *U.S. v. Averette*, 19 USCMA 363 (1970).

statement to investigators. He was sentenced to five months confinement.[69] Further courts-martial of civilians serving with the military are sure to follow.

One of the first exercises, if not the first exercise, of expanded UCMJ jurisdiction over former service members occurred in 2009. The case involved a former Marine who had not completed the IRR portion of his enlistment contract and was charged with the 2004 murder of four Iraqi prisoners in the midst of the battle for Fallujah II, one of the Marine Corps' hardest-fought Iraq battles. Although he went to trial as a civilian, in trial he was a uniformed service member. His court-martial resulted in acquittal.[70]

3.8.2.3 Charging Civilians II: The Military Extraterritorial Jurisdiction Act

The Military Extraterritorial Jurisdiction Act (MEJA) took effect in 2005.[71] It is another means by which the United States complies with its responsibility to enact domestic legislation criminalizing the commission of grave breaches of the Geneva Conventions. MEJA establishes federal, non–court-martial jurisdiction for any crime, not just war crimes, committed by civilians employed by the armed forces, as well as crimes by former members of the military who are discharged from active duty before a military prosecution can be initiated. For MEJA jurisdiction to attach to a former member of the military, he or she probably will have completed his or her entire service obligation, including IRR time. (If not, he or she would have been tried by court-martial under the expanded UCMJ jurisdiction.)

> Persons "[e]mployed by the armed forces" is defined to include civilian employees of the Department of Defense (DOD) as well as DOD contractors and their employees (including subcontractors at any tier), and civilian contractors and employees from other federal agencies ... to the extent that their employment is related to the support of the DOD mission overseas. It does not appear to cover civilian and contract employees or agencies engaged in their own operations overseas.[72]

Such legislation had been sought by the military since the 1950s to fill the jurisdictional gap created by the line of Supreme Court decisions starting with *Reid v. Covert*,[73] restricting the military's ability to try civilians, including discharged soldiers, by court-martial. A 2000 court of appeals case in which an apparently guilty accused individual went free for lack of jurisdiction finally provided the impetus for Congress to act.[74]

---

[69] John R. Crook, ed., "Contemporary Practice of the United States Relating to International Law," 102–4 *AJIL* (Oct. 2008), 860, 898. Also see: Multinational Corps-Iraq press release 20080623–01, "Civilian Contractor Convicted at Court-Martial (23 June 2008)," http://www.mnf-iraq.com. Because the sentence did not extend to confinement for a year or more, there was no review of the case by a military appellate court. See UCMJ, Art. 66.

[70] *U.S. v. Sgt. Ryan G. Weemer*, Camp Pendleton, CA (April 9, 2009), acquitted.

[71] 18 U.S.C. §3261. Also, see DoD Instruction 5525.11, *Criminal Jurisdiction over Civilians Employed by or Accompanying the Armed Forces outside the United States, Certain Service Members, and Former Service Members* (March 3, 2005), which implements MEJA policies and procedures.

[72] Jennifer K. Elsea and Nina M. Serafino, *Private Security Contractors in Iraq: Background, Legal Status, and Other Issues*, updated (Washington, DC: Congressional Research Service, July 11, 2007), 19. Footnote omitted.

[73] 354 U.S. 1 (1957).

[74] *U.S. v. Gatlin*, 216 F.3d 207 (2d Cir. 2000), in which a civilian on a U.S. base in Darmstadt, Germany, charged with sexually abusing a minor was released for lack of jurisdiction.

For whatever reasons, the 1996 War Crimes Act had proven ineffective in closing that gap. The criminal actions of civilian contractors in Iraq and Afghanistan, conflicts including grave breaches of LOAC, also were spurs to MEJA's enactment.

MEJA extends Title 18 of the U. S. Code, granting federal jurisdiction over offenses committed outside the United States by persons employed by or accompanying the armed forces, as well as former service members, if such offenses would be punishable by imprisonment for more than one year, if committed in the United States.

As to former service members, MEJA could be invoked in a My Lai–like situation in which a service member's crime is discovered only after her discharge from all military duty, including her IRR obligation. MEJA jurisdiction may also apply to active duty personnel, if a codefendant no longer subject to military jurisdiction is charged in a U.S. court.[75]

A significant limitation of both UCMJ and MEJA jurisdictional grants is that, in both cases, the grants specify that the civilian to be tried must be a member of, or be accompanying, the armed forces. Crimes allegedly committed by American private security contractors during U.S. involvement in the Iraq insurgency revealed that most private security contractors accompany a U.S. agency or corporation, the State Department or Halliburton, for example, not the armed forces or the Department of Defense. Although the distinction initially seems inconsequential, it is sufficient to defeat UCMJ and MEJA jurisdiction.

Although it represents a broad potential for prosecutions, there have been few trials under MEJA. "This legislation is not a perfect solution to the jurisdictional gap faced by the government, and it poses challenges of both implementation and application. ... It does not obligate the Department of Justice to prosecute; nor does it otherwise affect the discretion that rests with both with federal prosecutors and with the foreign country regarding whether to prosecute a specific case."[76]

The first MEJA case of a military veteran charged with war crimes involved a coaccused of the marine described earlier in this chapter. Both of them, and a third marine, were charged with the 2004 murder of four Iraqi prisoners during the second battle for Fallujah. The accused former Marine had served his entire enlistment, including his IRR obligation, and was no longer subject to military jurisdiction. The U.S. attorney for the Central District of California, where the former marine was now a police officer, undaunted by the expense involved, brought the case under MEJA, charging four counts of voluntary manslaughter, assault with a deadly weapon, and use of a firearm in committing a violent crime. The civilian jury, as did their military counterparts, acquitted the accused of all charges.[77] Subsequently, there have been other MEJA-based prosecutions.[78]

---

[75] MEJA, supra, note 59, at § 3261(d)(2).

[76] Mark J. Yost and Douglas S. Anderson, "The Military Extraterritorial Jurisdiction Act of 2000: Closing the Gap," 95–2 *AJIL* (April 2001), 446, 447.

[77] Gidget Fuentes, "Not Guilty," *Marine Corps Times* (Sept. 8, 2008), 8; and A.P., "Ex-Marine Is Cleared in Killing of Unarmed Iraqi Detainees," *NY Times*, Aug. 29, 2008, A9.

[78] A civilian South African citizen employed by DynCorp in Kandahar, Afghanistan, in 2010 stabbed another DynCorp employee. Tried in the Eastern District of Virginia, he pleaded guilty to aggravated assault and was sentenced to forty-two months confinement. Appeal denied. *U.S. v. Sean Theodore Brehm*, No. 11–4755, 4th USCA (Aug. 11, 2012). Available online.

Still, MEJA, along with the War Crimes Act and the UCMJ, are examples of U.S. compliance with the Geneva Conventions' mandate to enact domestic legislation to provide penal sanctions for those persons, be they military or civilian, committing grave breaches.

3.8.2.4 Charging Civilians III: Another Route

There is another rarely employed route to prosecution of civilians suspected of committing grave breaches. A section of the USA Patriot Act,[79] codified under provisions concerning the special maritime and territorial jurisdiction of the United States, provides jurisdiction over crimes committed by or against a U.S. national on lands or facilities designated for use by the U.S. government, which includes overseas military bases. Only one exercise of this jurisdiction involving war crimes is known.[80]

3.8.3 *Search Out and Try Grave Breaches*: Aut Dedere aut Judicare

In late 2007, the U.S. Department of Justice announced, "Federal Court Revokes Citizenship of Former Nazi Policeman Who Shot Jews." The former Nazi policeman entered the United States in 1949, lying in his visa application about his World War II activities. He became a U.S. citizen in 1955.[81] A 2007 *New York Times* headline read, "Nazi Suspect to Be Deported."[82] The eighty-five-year-old man, who had lived in Georgia for fifty-two years, was discovered to have been a guard in World War II death camps. He was deported to Germany to face war crimes charges there.

In 2009, an eighty-three-year-old Austrian, an immigrant to the United States in 1956 and a citizen since 1964, was arrested by immigration authorities at his home in Wisconsin. He admitted having been a World War II Nazi death camp guard and having participated in the 1943 murder of eight thousand Jewish prisoners at the Trawniki death camp in Poland. After six years of appeals, he was deported to Austria.[83]

Common Article 49/50/129/146, the same common article requiring enactment of domestic legislation to criminalize grave breaches, further obligates states ratifying the conventions "to search for persons alleged to have committed, or to have ordered to be committed, such grave breaches, and shall bring such persons, regardless of their nationality, before its own courts. In lieu of prosecution, it may also ... hand such persons over for trial to another High Contracting Party." The requirement is an expression of the universality of war crimes jurisdiction. Although the realities of

---

[79] Public Law 107–56, of 26 Oct. 2001. Section 804 of the act has been codified as 18 U.S.C. § 7(9). Also see 18 U.S.C. § 113(a).

[80] In August 2006, under the jurisdiction of the Patriot Act, the CIA contract employee David A. Passaro was convicted of assault, having initially been charged with the 2003 beating death of an Afghan detainee. *U.S. v. David A. Passaro*, case # 5:04-CR-211-1-BO (E.D. N.C. 2006). See 100–4 *AJIL* 959 (Oct. 2006).

[81] Department of Justice press release, March 30, 2007, www.usdoj.gov/opa/pr/2007/March/07_crm_203 .html

[82] Brenda Goodman, "Nazi Suspect to Be Deported," *NY Times*, Oct. 2, 2007, A17.

[83] National Brief, "Wisconsin: Nazi Guard Is Deported," *NY Times* (March 20, 2009), A14. Because Austria's statute of limitations for such crimes had run out in 1965, he was freed by Austria. Austrian authorities had made this known to U.S. authorities beforehand, raising the question of whether his extradition was really for purposes of trial.

international politics make the exercise of universal jurisdiction rare, the conventions make the possibility explicit.[84] In fact, there have been grave breach convictions based on universal jurisdiction.[85] "The relevant provisions [of the *aut dedere aut judicare* requirement] represented a momentous departure from customary law. . . . It is probable that the exceedingly bold character of this [universal jurisdiction] regulation contributed to its remaining ineffective for many years."[86]

This convention requirement, *aut dedere aut judicare*, transfer or try, is one of long standing. "The *aut dedere aut judicare* doctrine is derived from the legal work of Hugo Grotius, *De Jure Belli ac Pacis* (1624), and is recognized as a general principle of international law. The principle has been the most important and effective element in the struggle against acts and offences contrary to international law, in particular war crimes and terrorism."[87] The principle is also found in the Genocide Convention (Article 7), 1977 Additional Protocol I (Article 88), the 1984 Convention Against Torture (Article 7), and several treaties and conventions of less broad application. *Aut dedere aut judicare* is central to international terrorism treaties.

In practice, just as soldiers suspected of grave breaches are charged under UCMJ provisions without explicit reference to war crimes, the transfer of a suspected war criminal to a second state may be effected through an ordinary extradition treaty, without mention of the Geneva Conventions.[88] The death camp guard from Georgia, for example, was extradited to his native Germany for trial. That was done because, at the time of his alleged offenses, World War II, there was no U.S. statute criminalizing his actions. "The United States approach to alleged Second World War criminals has been to denaturalize and deport for the most part, and to extradite in a few cases. . . . There is . . . no legislative basis under US law to prosecute such alleged World War Two war criminals."[89]

The case of John Demjanjuk, thought to be a notoriously brutal Nazi death camp guard, "Ivan the Terrible," is such a case. Immigrating to the United States from Germany after World War II on the basis of fraudulent immigration forms, Demjanjuk for decades was an Ohio autoworker. He became a U.S. citizen in 1958 and was first charged with war crimes in 1977. He fought deportation and lost several court challenges. He was finally deported to Israel and, in 1988, convicted of crimes against

---

[84] See Sonja Boelaert-Suominen, "Grave Breaches, Universal Jurisdiction and Internal Armed Conflict: Is Customary Law Moving towards a Uniform Enforcement Mechanism for All Armed Conflicts?" 5–1 *J. Conflict & Security L.* (June 2000), 63, 71.

[85] For example, *Niyonteze v. Public Prosecutor*, Tribunal *militaire de cassation* (Switzerland), discussion at 96–1 *AJIL* 231 (Jan. 2002): "The conviction in Niyonteze . . . for war crimes committed in an internal armed conflict is the first by a municipal court exercising universal jurisdiction under the 1949 Geneva Conventions and Additional Protocol II."

[86] Antonio Cassese, *International Criminal Law* (Oxford: Oxford University Press, 2003), 41.

[87] Adel Maged, "International Legal Cooperation: An Essential Tool in the War against Terrorism," in Wybo P. Heere, ed., *Terrorism and the Military* (The Hague: T. M. C. Asser Press, 2003), 157, 164–5.

[88] E.g., in May 2012, a former Bosnian-Serb police commander, Dejan Radojkovic, accused of rounding up Bosnian Muslims, who were killed at Srebrenica in July 1995, was deported to Bosnia-Herzegovina. John Crook, ed., "Contemporary Practice of the U.S. Relating to International Law," 106–4 *AJIL* (Oct. 2012), 881.

[89] Sharon A. Williams, "Laudable Principles Lacking Application: The Prosecution of War Criminals in Canada," in Timothy L. H. McCormack and Gerry J. Simpson, eds., *The Law of War Crimes* (The Hague: Kluwer Law International, 1997), 151, 157.

humanity and sentenced to death. Shortly before his execution, World War II documents discovered in East German archives when the Berlin Wall fell revealed that he indeed had been a Nazi death camp guard, but *not* the guard known as Ivan the Terrible. His conviction was reversed and he was released in 1993 and returned to the United States. His U.S. citizenship was again revoked in 2004 on the basis of lies in immigration forms regarding his history as a guard at Sobibor, another Nazi death camp, where he had served as a guard. His appeals failed and, in 2009, at age eighty-nine, Demjanjuk was deported again, this time to Germany for trial for alleged World War II crimes.[90] Reflecting a change in German legal policy whereby it would prosecute alleged World War II war criminals from other states (Demjanjuk was originally a Ukrainian), in 2011 Demjanjuk was convicted of 27,900 counts of accessory to murder, the number of Jewish prisoners killed at Sobibor while Demjanjuk was a guard there. He was sentenced to five years confinement. Released pending appeal of his conviction, Demjanjuk died in 2012 in a German nursing home before his appeal was heard. He was ninety-one.[91]

In the United States, the denaturalization and extradition of suspected World War II war criminals were the responsibility of the Office of Special Investigations (OSI), a small division (eight prosecutors, ten investigative historians) of the Criminal Division of the U.S. Department of Justice (DOJ), created in 1979. As late as 2006, OSI's director could say, "Despite the lateness of the date, OSI's World War II–era caseload remains a relatively heavy one."[92] In 2010, the OSI was incorporated into a new office, the Human Rights and Special Prosecutions Section, within the DOJ's Criminal Division.

A scholar writes, "This regime has not … been successful at apprehending and trying war criminals since 1949. Many states have implemented the Geneva Conventions internally but have felt under no compulsion to arrest, extradite or try suspected war criminals."[93] There have been numerous apprehensions and even trials, but it is true that relatively few war criminals, now settled in new countries with new identities, are discovered and tried.[94] Persons who committed heinous crimes in World War II are very old now. Most were lower in the hierarchy, and few witnesses survive, making prosecutions difficult. Should such elderly former low-ranking soldiers, often no longer mentally alert, be tried at all? Ask the families of their victims.

---

[90] Demjanjuk's citizenship- and extradition-related cases, bracketing his Israeli conviction and reversal, are: *Demjanjuk v. Petrovsky*, 776 F. 2d 571 (6th Cir. 1985) and 10 F. 3d 338 (6th Cir. 1993). After return to the United States from Israel, his citizenship was revoked for a second time: *United States v. Demjanjuk*, 367 F.3d 623 (6th Cir. 2004), petition for review denied at: *Demjanjuk v. Mulkasey* No. 07–3022 (Jan. 30, 2007).

[91] Robert D. McFadden, "John Demjanjuk, 91, Dogged by Charges of Atrocities as Nazi Camp Guard, Dies," *NY Times* (March 17, 2012), A1.

[92] Eli M. Rosenbaum, "An Introduction to the Work of the Office of Special Investigations," 54–1 *United States Attorneys' Bulletin* (Jan. 2006), 1.

[93] La Haye, *War Crimes in Internal Armed Conflicts*, supra, note 30, at 108.

[94] In 2008, Norway convicted Misrad Repak, a Bosnian, of war crimes and crimes against humanity, in 1992 in the former Yugoslavia, sentencing him to five years confinement. In 2010, the Norwegian Supreme Court reversed the conviction. Norway's criminal code amendment regarding crimes against humanity and war crimes took effect in 2008, making the crime of which Repak was convicted an unconstitutional retroactive application of the law. "National Implementation of International Humanitarian Law," 93–881 *Int'l Rev. of the Red Cross* (March 2011), 227, 234.

3.8.4 "Grave Breaches"

The 1949 Geneva Conventions, in common Article 50/51/130/147, raise another unique element in LOAC, and that is the term "grave breaches" itself. The phrase was unknown before the 1949 conventions. It is not "war crimes" for which states must enact domestic criminalizing legislation; it is not those who commit war crimes that states must seek out and try; it is "grave breaches" that must be criminalized and tried.

Grave breaches are the most serious breaches of the law of war – a technical term formulated by a committee of government experts at the ICRC Diplomatic Conference of 1949[95] and used in the 1949 Conventions and in 1977 Additional Protocol I. Grave breaches are traditionally applicable only in common Article 2 international armed conflicts. (See Chapter 3, Section 3.8.7, however.) Think of the criminal law dichotomy of misdemeanors and felonies; grave breaches might be thought of as the "felonies" of the law of war. Virtually all acts physically harmful to prisoners or protected persons will be grave breaches. The *Commentary* to GC I recites the origin of the term.

> The actual expression "grave breaches" was discussed at considerable length. The USSR Delegation would have preferred the expression "grave crimes" or "war crimes." The reason why the conference preferred the words "grave breaches" was that it felt that, though such acts were described as crimes in the penal laws of almost all countries, it was nevertheless true that the word "crimes" had different legal meanings in different countries.[96]

Grave breaches are a closed category.[97] If the offense is not specified in common Article 50/51/130/147, no matter how heinous the act, it is not a grave breach (although 1977 Additional Protocol I [Chapter 4, Section 4.2.1.1.] in Articles 11.4, 85.3, and 85.4 raises several additional grave breaches). Mutilating a dead body? Cannibalism? They are not named as grave breaches and, heinous as such acts may be, they are not grave breaches.[98] Such offenses are left to military commissions or courts-martial, or to the domestic criminal codes of the states involved, to be tried as simple war crimes.

Grave breach offenses that are specified in all four of the 1949 conventions are willful killing, torture or inhuman treatment, and willfully causing great suffering or serious

---

[95] The Joint Committee was assembled by the ICRC specifically to write the common article penal provisions. Committee members were the United Kingdom's Professor Hersh Lauterpacht; the Dutch naval captain and Supreme Court judge Martinus Mouton; the British colonel Henry Phillmore; a former Nuremberg prosecutor, Professor Jean Graven of Geneva University; and the ICRC chairman Max Huber, a former judge on the PCIJ.

[96] Pictet, *Commentary, I Geneva Convention*, supra, note 52, at 371.

[97] Id. However, Pictet writes, at 371, "As regards the list of 'grave breaches' itself ... it is not to be taken as exhaustive." Yet, at 370, he suggests otherwise, writing, "The idea of including a definition of 'grave breaches' in the actual text of the Convention came from the experts called in by the [ICRC]. ... It was thought necessary to establish what these grave breaches were." In any event, in the more than five decades since Pictet's writing, state practice has established that grave breaches include only those listed in the common article, and new grave breaches in 1977 Additional Protocol I, Articles 11.4 and 85.3-.4.

[98] Id., at 367. Pictet refers to the pre-1949 convention cases *Trial of Max Schmid*, U.S. General Military Government Court, Dachau Germany (1947) in U.N.W.C.C., *Law Reports of Trial of War Criminals*, vol. XIII (London: U.N., 1949), 151–2, and trial of eight Japanese soldiers before a 1946 U.S. military commission on Guam. See Chester Hearn, *Sorties into Hell: The Hidden War on Chichi Jima* (Westport, CT: Praeger, 2003), 189.

injury. Each of the four conventions includes several additional grave breaches appropriate to the category of protected individual in that particular convention.

Not every violation of the law of war is a grave breach. As the third paragraph of common Article 49/50/129/146 – not the grave breach article – implies, there are simple breaches of the law of war that do not rise to grave breaches: "Each High Contracting Party shall take measures necessary for the suppression of all acts contrary to the provisions of the present Convention other than the grave breaches defined in the following Article." The *Commentary* for Article 49 adds, "the primary purpose of the [third] paragraph is the *repression* of infractions other than 'grave breaches'" for which administrative action may be taken.[99] These lesser breaches of the law of war are still tried, of course,[100] but they are tried as disciplinary offenses, rather than under the mandatory provisions of the grave breaches provisions of common Article 50/51/130/147.

The conventions do not contain an exhaustive listing of what constitutes war crimes other than grave breaches. Nor do they mention punishments to be imposed for violations. If a grave breach is tried as a violation of the UCMJ, or of domestic law, the UCMJ or domestic penalties that attach to the charged offense apply. If tried by U.S. military authorities as war crimes qua war crimes, under the authority of UCMJ Articles 18 and 21, the maximum punishment would be that mandated by the customary law of war, and the customary penalty may be harsh. "The death penalty may be imposed for grave breaches of the law of war."[101]

3.8.4.1 Crimes, War Crimes, and Grave Breaches

Since the 1949 Geneva Conventions, then, the law of war recognizes crimes, war crimes, and grave breaches. We know that a crime is a positive or negative act in violation of some penal law. A crime is not necessarily associated with warfare but it may be. For example, while deployed in Iraq and assigned to a combat outpost, Sergeant Able becomes drunk on duty and strikes Private Baker. Able has violated UCMJ Articles 112, drunk on duty, and 128, assault – simple military crimes for which he may be court-martialed.

Change the scenario. While deployed to an Iraq combat outpost, Sergeant Able becomes drunk on duty and strikes an unresisting Iraqi detainee suspected of being an insurgent. Now Able has breached Geneva Convention IV, Articles 27 and 32, which prohibit corporal punishment and violence toward prisoners – violations of LOAC and war crimes. Able may be court-martialed for assault of a prisoner, because court-martial is the means the United States employs to enforce its Geneva Convention obligations involving service members.

However, if Sergeant Able becomes drunk on duty and willfully shoots and kills the same unresisting Iraqi prisoner, Able has committed a grave breach of Article 147 of Convention IV, for which, again, he may be court-martialed.* Note that, although Able is

---

[99] Pictet, *Commentary, I Geneva Convention*, supra, note 52, at 367.

[100] For example, *Prosecutor v. Tadić*, IT-94–1, Judgment in Sentencing appeals (26 Jan. 2000), para. 5; *Prosecutor v. Martić* IT-95–11-T, (12 June 2007), para. 39; and *Slobodan Milosevic* (IT-02–54), Charge in 1st Amended Indictment (23 Oct. 2002).

[101] Dept. of the Army, FM 27–10, *The Law of Land Warfare* (Washington, DC: GPO, 1956), para. 508.
  * Sergeant Able's act is a grave breach of GC IV, because his victim was a civilian prisoner protected by GC IV.

in a combat zone, the combatant's privilege (Chapter 2, Section 2.3.1) does not apply; neither Able nor the prisoner is engaged in combat, and Able's shooting of the prisoner was not a lawful combatant's act. Murder can be committed in a combat zone. "It is important to emphasise that not all war crimes are in fact grave breaches. ... War crimes cover both 'grave breaches' and other serious violations of the laws and customs applicable in armed conflict – be that conflict international or non-international."[102]

When considering unwarranted *jus in bello* violence, keep in mind this three-tiered distinction of wrongful acts that can be committed on the battlefield and ask yourself whether the event is a crime, a war crime, or a grave breach.

3.8.5 *Genocide, Crimes against Humanity, and Crimes against Peace*

Neither genocide nor crimes against humanity are grave breaches or war crimes.[103] Nor are crimes against peace. All three are crimes under international criminal law. Professor L. C. Green writes of genocide, "Since genocide may be committed in both peace and war, and since it constitutes the most grievous crime against humanity and against international humanitarian law, the silence of the Geneva Law in this respect is a matter of regret."[104] Not that civilians are unprotected. "However, these crimes – which can also be committed in peacetime – transcend the compass of LOIAC [the law of international armed conflict]."[105] The Statute of the International Criminal Tribunal for the former Yugoslavia (ICTY) does require that crimes against humanity be committed in armed conflict. Armed conflict "is not an element of that crime in customary law, but merely a jurisdictional requirement specific to the ICTY."[106]

Crimes against humanity, first recognized in the Charter of the post–World War II Nuremberg IMT, and again in the Statute of the ICTY, initially required a nexus with an armed conflict. "It is now widely recognized that 'crimes against humanity are no longer linked to the laws of war but rather to human rights law.'"[107]

Crimes against peace also were defined in the Nuremberg IMT Charter as "planning, preparation, initiation or waging a war of aggression," an offense that was restricted to "high ranking military personnel and high state officials."[108] Although the Statute of the International Criminal Court (ICC) confers jurisdiction over the offense of "aggression," that crime remains undefined by the Court. There have been no prosecutions for crimes

---

[102] Knut Dörmann, *Elements of War Crimes under the Rome Statute of the International Criminal Court* (Cambridge: Cambridge University Press, 2003), 128.

[103] *Prosecutor v Tadić*, IT-94-1-T, Decision on Defense Motion on Jurisdiction (10 Aug. 1995), at para. 81. "This view that crimes against humanity are autonomous is confirmed by ... Oppenheim's International Law, where special reference is made to the fact that crimes against humanity 'are now generally regarded as a self-contained category, without any formal link with war crimes. '" Citation omitted.

[104] Green, "'Grave Breaches' or Crimes against Humanity," supra, note 48, at 21.

[105] Yoram Dinstein, *The Conduct of Hostilities under the Law of International Armed Conflict* (Cambridge: Cambridge University Press, 2004), 233.

[106] Guénaël Mettraux, *International Crimes and the Ad Hoc Tribunals* (Oxford: Oxford University Press, 2005), 321. An ICTR case and appeal involving genocide: *Prosecutor v. Kalimanzira*, ICTR-05-88-A (20 Oct. 2010).

[107] Payam Akhavan, "Reconciling Crimes against Humanity with the Law of War," 6–1 *J. of Int'l Crim. Justice* (March 2008), 21–37, 26. Footnote omitted.

[108] Hans-Heinrich Jescheck, "The General Principles of International Criminal Law Set Out in Nuremberg, as Mirrored in the ICC Statute," 2–1 *J. of Int'l Crim. Justice* (March 2004), 38, 49.

against peace since the Nuremberg IMT, where sixteen of the accused were charged and twelve were convicted of the offense. There have been no prosecutions since Nuremberg, and it is considered "somewhat of a dead letter."[109]

Although genocide and crimes against humanity are not violations of the law of war, commanders nevertheless have an affirmative duty to take measures within their power to control troops under their command and stop them from acts sounding in genocide or crimes against humanity.[110]

3.8.6 Common Article 3

Perhaps the most significant innovation of the 1949 Geneva Conventions is common Article 3. Since the 1648 Peace of Westphalia recognized the territorial sovereignty of nations, with the resultant rise of the city–state, acts of sovereign leaders within their own state's borders were considered beyond international concern. The act of state doctrine arose. "This is to the effect that the courts of one state do not, as a rule, question the validity or legality of the official acts of another sovereign state or of the official or officially avowed acts of its agents, at any rate insofar as those acts involve the exercise of the state's public authority, purport to take effect within the sphere of the latter's own jurisdiction and are not in themselves contrary to international law."[111] In 1897, the U.S. Supreme Court concurred that "every sovereign state is bound to respect the independence of every other sovereign, and the courts of one country will not sit in judgment on the acts of another government done within its own territory."[112] In effect, dictators and despots were free to do as they would to their own peoples within their own borders, with no other state to interfere. Not until World War II, and formation of the United Nations, the Nuremberg IMT, and the Nuremberg Principles,[113] did the act of state doctrine lose vitality.

The framers of the 1949 conventions determined that there must be some minimal international humanitarian protections for the victims of internal armed conflicts – conflicts occurring within one state's borders, not involving a second nation. World War II revealed the stark absence of protections for civilians in wartime. To raise new protections would involve a departure from Geneva's previously uninterrupted fixation on conflicts between states and a certain disregard of the long-entrenched act of state doctrine. The international community was unanimous, however, that it could not stand by while depredations such as those committed by the Nazis took place in future conflicts, internal or not. Not even in the United Nations Charter is there a similar effort to regulate intrastate armed force.

There are significant problems in imposing an external regulatory regime, however cursory, on any state. Not the least is that common Article 3 has no enforcement or supervisory mechanism. Also, many governments, particularly those of developing nations, view any attempted international regulation of their internal conflicts as excuses for foreign intervention and intrusions on sovereignty. The typically chaotic conditions of

---

[109] Roy Gutman and David Rieff, eds., *Crimes of War* (New York: Norton, 1999), 109.

[110] See *In re Yamashita*, 327 U.S. 1, 14 (1946).

[111] Lassa Oppenheim, *International Law: A Treatise.* Vol. I. *Peace* (London: Longmans Green, 1967), 365–6.

[112] *Underhill v. Hernandez*, 168 U.S. 250 (1897).

[113] U.N., *Yearbook of the International Law Commission*, 1950, Vol. II, 374.

internal conflicts are among the worst possible situations for the effective rule of law. In internal armed conflicts, at least one of the parties may have never accepted international regulation or possess the political ability to enforce it. Nor is there effective international machinery to control internal armed conflicts.[114] Still, the framers were determined to make an effort. Common Article 3 is the result.

Common Article 3 is the sole article in all the Geneva Conventions that deals with internal armed conflicts – armed uprisings, sustained insurrections, civil wars. Because common Article 3 contains, in abbreviated form, a range of basic humanitarian norms it is often referred to as a Geneva convention in miniature.[115] "It has the merit of being simple and clear ... [and] the additional advantage of being applicable automatically, without any condition of reciprocity. Its observance does not depend on preliminary discussions as to the nature of the conflict. ... It is true that it merely provides for the application of the *principles* of the Convention and not for the application of specific provisions, but it defines those principles."[116] Common Article 3 provides:

> In the case of armed conflict not of an international character occurring in the territory of one of the High Contracting Parties, each Party to the conflict shall be bound to apply, at a minimum, the following provisions:
>
> (1) Persons taking no active part in the hostilities, including members of armed forces who have laid down their arms and those placed *hors de combat* by sickness, wounds, detention, or any other cause, shall in all circumstances be treated humanely.

There follows a brief list of prohibitions, acknowledged to be incomplete: violence to life and person, in particular murder, mutilation, cruel treatment, and torture; taking of hostages; humiliating and degrading treatment; and passing of sentences without previous judgments from regularly constituted courts.

What common Article 3 requires is humane treatment. It is "pointless and even dangerous to try to enumerate things with which a human being must be provided [to constitute humane treatment] ... or to lay down in detail the manner in which one must behave towards him in order to show that one is treating him 'humanely'. ... The details of such treatment may, moreover, vary according to circumstances ... and to what is feasible."[117] It is easier to enumerate that which is incompatible with humane treatment, and that is the approach taken by the conventions. The ICRC's study of customary international law provides generalized guidance as to what constitutes humane treatment:

> The actual meaning of "humane treatment" is not spelled out. ... The requirement ... is an overarching concept. It is generally understood that the detailed rules found in international humanitarian law and human rights law give expression to the meaning of "humane treatment." ... However, these rules do not necessarily express the full

---

[114] Michael J. Matheson, "The Law of Internal Armed Conflict," 97–2 *AJIL* [book review: Lindsay Moir, *The Law of Internal Armed Conflict* (April 2003)], 466, 467.

[115] For example, *Prosecutor v. Kayishema and Ruzindana*, ICTR-96-1-A, Trial judgment (1 June 2001), para. 165. Also, Pictet, *Commentary, IV Geneva Convention*, supra, note 47, at 34.

[116] Pictet, *Commentary I*, supra, note 52, at 48. Emphasis supplied.   [117] Id., at 53.

meaning of what is meant by humane treatment, as this notion develops over time under the influence of changes in society.[118]

Common Article 3 simply requires that, in noninternational armed conflicts, basic humanitarian norms be afforded those who are hors de combat – out of the fight. That is a major advance.

3.8.6.1 Does Common Article 3 Apply?

The sometimes difficult key to common Article 3 is recognizing the situations in which its application is appropriate. Its opening sentence says it applies in armed conflicts not of an international character. It originally applied only in cases of "internal" armed conflicts. Today, it is clear that common Article 3, and its requirement of humane treatment for all those who fall under its protection, applies in all armed conflicts, regardless of their characterization. It does not apply in internal instances of riot, disorder, or mere banditry, however.

By its terms, common Article 3 applies only to noninternational armed conflicts. However, so basic are its humanitarian norms that, today, common Article 3's application is said to extend to international armed conflicts, as well, its norms subsumed in the humanitarian norms of any armed conflict. As was first said in the ICJ's *Nicaragua* case,[119] "Common Article 3 may thus be considered as the 'minimum yardstick' of rules of international humanitarian law ... applicable to both internal and international conflicts."[120] Common Article 3 applies across the spectrum of armed conflict.

The second point to remember, and a bit of a challenge to grasp, is that, when common Article 3 applies, *no other part of the 1949 Geneva Conventions applies*. In a noninternational armed conflict there are no POW protections in common Article 3,[121] because POW protections are contained in Geneva Convention IV, not in common Article 3, and when common Article 3 applies no other portion of the 1949 conventions apply.[122] Traditionally, in a noninternational armed conflict there are no grave breaches and no war crimes – because there is no war; there is only an internal armed conflict.[123] There are no protected persons, per se, because "protected person" is a status found in Geneva Convention IV, not in common Article 3. Of course, the domestic law of the state in which the armed conflict exists continues in effect, and rioters, bandits, and insurrectionists may be prosecuted for any warlike act they commit that violates the state's domestic law.

3.8.7 War Crimes in Noninternational Armed Conflicts

"This law [of war] is not static, but by continual adaptation follows the needs of a changing world."[124] Illustrating the continuing growth and evolution of LOAC, it is no

---

[118] Jean-Marie Henckaerts and Louise Doswald-Beck, eds., *Customary International Humanitarian Law*. Vol. I. *Rules* (Cambridge: Cambridge University Press, 2005), Rule 87, at 307–8.

[119] *Nicaragua v. United States*, Merits, supra, note 44, at, ¶114.

[120] *Prosecutor v. Delalić, et al.* IT-96–21-A (Feb. 20, 2001), para. 143, footnote omitted.

[121] The parties to a common Article 3 conflict may stipulate that each other's captives will be accorded POW status, however. See penultimate paragraph of common Article 3.

[122] ICRC, "International Humanitarian Law," supra, note 40, at 728.

[123] L. C. Green, *The Contemporary Law of Armed Conflict*, 2d ed. (Yonkers, NY: Juris, 2000), 319.

[124] *Trial of the Major War Criminals before the International Military Tribunal*, Vol. I (Nuremberg, 1947), Judgment, at 221.

longer correct (as it only recently was) to assert that there are no war crimes in common Article 3 noninternational armed conflicts.

Within the last decade there has been an international recognition that the concept of war crimes and grave breaches is applicable in internal, as well as international, armed conflicts. In 2000, a scholar wrote of war crimes in noninternational conflicts, "Gradually, states are chipping away at the [international conflict and non-international conflict] two-legged edifice of the laws of armed conflict."[125] A decade later, that edifice has crumbled.

The ICTY Appeals Chamber initiated the change in the 1995 *Tadić* case. In an appellate opinion, the chamber first took the traditional position, holding that "[we] must conclude that, in the present state of development of the law, Article 2 of the [ICTY] Statute ['Grave breaches of the Geneva Conventions of 1949'] only applies to offenses committed within the context of international armed conflicts."[126] In doing so, the Appeals Chamber reversed the Trial Chamber's pioneering position on the matter. Then, later in the same appellate decision, in *dictum*, the Appeals Chamber opened the door for later change, writing, "We have no doubt that they [violations of rules of warfare in international law] entail individual criminal responsibility, regardless of whether they are committed in internal or international armed conflicts. Principles and rules of humanitarian law reflect 'elementary considerations of humanity' widely recognized as the mandatory minimum for conduct in armed conflicts of any kind."[127]

In a separate opinion on the same decision, a second judge reinforced the Appeals Chamber's view, writing, "One of the merits of the [Trial Chamber's] Decision is that by finding that 'graves breaches' are subsumed in the 'serious violations of the laws or customs of war' it resituated the Statute firmly within the modern trend recognizing the essential identity of the legal regime of violations of the two strands [international and non-international] of the *jus in bello*."[128]

Six years later, the Appeals Chamber in the *Čelebići* case took the tribunal through the door opened by *Tadić* and ruled that "to maintain a legal distinction between the two legal regimes and their criminal consequences in respect of similarly egregious acts because of the differences in the nature of conflicts would ignore the very purpose of the Geneva Conventions."[129] Clearly, "the acknowledgement by the *ad hoc* [ICTY and ICTR] Tribunals that much of the law of international armed conflicts would apply in the context of internal armed conflicts may be one of their most significant jurisprudential achievements as far as war crimes are concerned."[130] Theodor Meron adds that "there is no moral justification, and no truly persuasive

---

[125] Boelaert-Suominen, "Grave Breaches, Universal Jurisdiction and Internal Armed Conflict, supra, note 81, at 102.

[126] *Prosecutor v. Tadić*, Defense Motion for Interlocutory Appeal, supra, note 103, at para. 84.

[127] Id., at para. 129. The Appeals Chamber adds (para. 126) that the migration of war crimes from international armed conflicts to noninternational cannot take place "in the form of a full and mechanical transplant of those rules to internal conflicts [but instead] the general essence of those rules, and not the detailed regulation they may contain, has become applicable to internal conflicts."

[128] Id., (Abi-Saab, J., concurring).   [129] *Delalić*, supra, note 120, para. 172, footnote omitted.

[130] Mettraux, *International Crimes and the* Ad Hoc *Tribunals*, supra, note 106, at 132.

legal reason, for treating perpetrators of atrocities in internal conflicts more leniently than those engaged in international wars."[131]

The former view, that war crimes could arise only in international armed conflicts, prevailing since implementation of the 1949 Geneva Conventions, is still held by very few commentators. William Schabas, in his *Commentary* on the International Criminal Court, notes "the antiquated view that war crimes were confined to international armed conflicts."[132] Recent international and domestic court opinions and international legislation make denial of war crimes in noninternational conflicts a difficult position to maintain. "The very serious character of the violations of the laws of war committed during internal armed conflicts coupled with the ineffectiveness of domestic jurisdictions to deal with these crimes, call for the application of the concept of war crimes in internal armed conflicts. It is not only desirable, but also crucial to curb the phenomenon of impunity attached to serious violations of the laws of war in internal armed conflicts."[133]

The Rome Statute of the ICC adds force to the view that there are war crimes and grave breaches in noninternational conflicts. The statute, in *Article 8, War crimes,* subparagraphs 8.2.(c) and (e), specifies sixteen "serious violations," all but one of them war crimes or grave breaches that may occur in common Article 3 armed conflicts – in noninternational conflicts. The domestic legislation of fifty-four states criminalizes serious violations of LOAC in internal armed conflicts.[134] The United Kingdom's *Manual of the Law of Armed Conflict* urges that war crimes in noninternational armed conflicts have risen to customary law status: "Although the treaties governing internal armed conflicts contain no grave breach provisions, customary law recognizes that serious violations of those treaties can amount to punishable war crimes. It is now recognized that there is a growing area of conduct that is criminal in both international and internal armed conflict."[135] The ICTY and the International Criminal Tribunal for Rwanda (ICTR) have convicted individuals of committing war crimes in noninternational conflicts.[136] Taken together, this compelling evidence confirms that war crimes can indeed be committed in noninternational common Article 3 armed conflicts.

---

[131] Theodor Meron, "International Criminalization of Internal Atrocities," 89–3 *AJIL* (July 1995), 554–77, 561.

[132] William A. Schabas, *The International Criminal Court: A Commentary on the Rome Statute* (Oxford: Oxford University Press, 2010), 197–98.

[133] La Haye, *War Crimes in Internal Armed Conflicts*, supra, note 30, at 121.

[134] La Haye, *War Crimes in Internal Armed Conflicts*, supra, note 30, at 170.

[135] United Kingdom, *Manual of the Law of Armed Conflict*, supra, note 31, paras. 15.32, 15.32.1, at 397.

[136] Those cases include *Prosecutor v. Tadić*, IT-94-1-T (May 7, 1997); *Delalić*, IT-96-21-T (Nov. 16, 1998); *Jelisić*, IT-95-10-T (Dec. 14, 1999); *Kupreškić*, IT-95-16-T (Jan. 14, 2000); *Furundžija*, IT-95-17/1-A (July 21, 2000); *Krstić*, IT-98-33-T (Aug. 2, 2001); *Krnojelac*, IT-97-25-T (March 15, 2002); *Kunarac*, IT-96-23/1-A (June 12, 2002); *Pavel, Struger, Miodrag, et al.,* IT-01-42-AR72, Decision on Interlocutory Appeal (Nov. 22, 2002); *Vasiljević*, IT-98-32-T (29 Nov. 2002); *Kvočka*, IT-98-03/1-A (Feb. 28, 2003); *Stakić*, IT-97-24-T (July 31, 2003); *Krnojelac*, IT-97-25-A (Sept. 17, 2003); *Galić*, IT-98-29-T (Dec. 5, 2003); *Blagojević et Jokić*, IT-02-60-T (Jan. 17, 2005); *Strugar*, IT-01-42-T (Jan. 31, 2005); *Hadžihasanović*, IT-01-47-T (March 15, 2006); and *Orić*, IT-03-68-T (June 30, 2006); and ICTR opinions, *Prosecutor v. Semanza*, ICTR-97-20-T (May 15, 2003) and *Rutaganda*, ICTR-96-3-A (May 26, 2003). See La Haye, *War Crimes in Internal Armed Conflicts*, supra, note 30, at 175, fns. 406–16 and 426 for specific paragraphs at which the Tribunals announce conviction.

SIDEBAR. The 2006 Military Commissions Act (MCA)[137] offers its own definition of "grave breaches" of common Article 3.[138]

The act's creation of "Grave Breaches ... " is both novel and unfounded. "Grave breaches" of the Geneva Conventions are exhaustively defined, [and] do not include common Article 3. ... Conversely, common Article 3 is an autonomous "convention within a convention", containing what the International Court of Justice has described as "elementary considerations of humanity", that apply in conflicts of either international or non-international character. There is no precedent for their amalgamation.[139]

Prior to the MCA, the War Crimes Act established personal criminal liability for U.S. personnel who violated common Article 3 without distinguishing between its provisions. The MCA also limits the scope of liability for torture under common Article 3(1) (a).

U.S. legislation altering these aspects of the Geneva Conventions has effect in U.S. jurisdictions but does not affect either the conventions themselves or U.S. international obligations under the unaltered conventions. The eventual impact of the MCA's purported addition of grave breaches to common Article 3 offenses remains to be seen.

One may argue that common Article 3 makes no provision for either war crimes or grave breaches,[140] that the international community is not bound by ICTY or ICTR opinions or decisions, that the domestic legislation of foreign states is of no significance beyond those states' borders, or that U.N. resolutions urging criminalization of war crimes in internal conflicts have no binding effect. In the face of a broad corpus of contrary state and international practice, however, those seem unpersuasive arguments. No system of laws is static and, if change increases the protection of victims of armed conflict, impedes impunity in internal conflicts, and is not contrary to other LOAC provisions, contrary arguments are weak at best. Arguably, it is not yet customary law, but it is clear that there can be both war crimes and grave breaches in internal armed conflicts.

There clearly are war crimes in noninternational armed conflicts, but the same cannot be said of grave breaches. There is basis for arguing that "the definition of grave breaches in the 1949 Geneva Conventions has passed into customary international law. Whether the same can be said about all the grave breaches under Additional Protocol I, however, requires further research into state practice."[141] Even though the International Law Commission of the United Nations has accepted that grave breaches, as well as war crimes, apply in noninternational armed conflicts,[142] that position has not been fully

---

[137] Pub. L., No. 109–366, 120 Stat. 2600 (2006).   [138] MCA § 6(a).

[139] James G. Stewart, "The Military Commissions Act's Inconsistency with the Geneva Conventions," 5–1 *J. of Int'l Crim. Justice* (March 2007), 26, 33.

[140] Harmen van der Wilt, "Genocide v. War Crimes in the *Van Anraat* Appeal," 6–3 *J. of Int'l. Crim. Justice* (July 2008), 557, 559.

[141] Jean-Marie Henckaerts, "The Grave Breaches Regime as Customary International Law," 7–4 *J. of Int'l Crim. Justice* (Sept. 2009), 683, 691.

[142] See the definition of war crimes, Art. 20(f), U.N. Doc. A/51/10 (1996), at 55.

embraced. "Clear state practice and *opino juris* in support of the applicability of grave breaches to internal armed conflict remains relatively limited."[143]

"So what?" one may ask. What does it matter whether you charge a LOAC/IHL violation as a grave breach or as a simple violation of the law of armed conflict? It does matter. Grave breaches initiate ratifying states' responsibility to comply with Geneva Convention common Article 49/50/129/146 to search for those alleged to have committed, or ordered committed, grave breaches, and to take them before the states' courts, or to transfer them to another ratifying state that *will* prosecute. Such cases are expensive in monetary terms, manpower expenditures, and, often, loss of political capital, should prosecution fail to proceed. A simple war crime prosecution seldom has the same baggage.

One should also note that, since prisoner of war status derives in principle from the lawfulness of combatancy (GC III, Article 4.A (2)), "there is no POW status in non-international armed conflicts."[144] How does one refer to prisoners held in noninternational armed conflicts? As detainees or, simply, prisoners. That there are no POWs in internal conflicts is a position unlikely to change in the foreseeable future.

3.8.8 *Deciding When Common Article 3 Applies*

Who decides whether and when common Article 3 applies? Common Article 3 does not define what is meant by "noninternational conflict"; nor does it mention enforcement. Who says an "uprising" within a country is (or is not) actually a criminal band seeking political cover for their illegal acts? What international agency rules that a "revolution" is in progress?

Here is the weakness of international law generally, and common Article 3 in particular: the lack of a supranational enforcement or judicial arm. "The object of the [Geneva] Conventions was to provide for their immediate and automatic application in cases of internal conflict, and not leave the question of application up to the parties to the conflict."[145] State practice falls short of that objective.

The issue becomes, who decides? Who decides, international conflict or internal conflict; uprising or criminality; revolutionaries or criminals?[146] Often, the ruling government simply announces that the insurgents are merely bandits, to be dealt with by the government's paramilitary forces or national police. Pictet writes, "In a civil war the lawful Government, or that which so styles itself, tends to regard its adversaries as common criminals."[147] The insurgents, if insurgents they be, rarely have a public voice to rally international recognition of their cause. No nation is eager to announce that it cannot control violence within its own borders among its own citizenry. So the application of common Article 3 is infrequent. "If the state remains in control and domestic

---

[143] Lindsay Moir, "Grave Breaches and Internal Armed Conflicts," 7–4 *J. of Int'l Crim. Justice* (Sept. 2009), 763, 773–74.

[144] Giulia Pinzauti, "Protecting Prisoners of War," 8–1 *J. of Int'l Crim. Justice* 199, 203 (March 2010).

[145] Lindsay Moir, *The Law of Internal Armed Conflict* (Cambridge: Cambridge University Press, 2002), 27, citing the twenty-third and twenty-fourth meetings of the Special Committee, *Final Record II-B*, 76–9.

[146] Burt Neuborne, "Spheres of Justice: Who Decides?" 74–5/6 *George Washington L. R.* (Aug. 2006), 1090, examines the "who decides" issue in a context of U.S. domestic politics.

[147] Pictet, *Commentary I*, supra, note 52, at 39.

law continues to be enforced through the courts, there may be a case for arguing that it is not an armed conflict at all but an internal security problem. It is when, owing to internal violence, that control has ceased in a significant part of the state or when the normal apparatus of domestic law has broken down that an armed conflict may be said to exist."[148] In its *Commentary* to the Geneva Conventions, the ICRC suggests four nonbinding conditions that should make common Article 3 applicable:

(1) That the party in revolt ... possesses an organized military force, an authority responsible for its acts, acting within a determinate territory and having the means of respecting and ensuring respect for the Conventions.

(2) That the legal government is obliged to have recourse to the regular military forces against insurgents organized as military and in possession of a part of the national territory.

(3) (a) That the *de jure* Government has recognized the insurgents as belligerents. ...
(d) That the dispute has been admitted to the agenda of the Security Council or the General Assembly of the United Nations as being a threat to international peace. ...

(4) (a) That the insurgents have an organization purporting to have the characteristics of a State.
(b) That the insurgent civil authority exercises de facto authority over persons within a determinate territory.[149]

In their totality, these criteria are rarely met. The multiplicity of hurdles reflects the difficult multinational negotiations and compromises that produced common Article 3. Still, they provide guidelines for determining when common Article 3 might be applicable. Given the need for the protection of noncombatants in such situations, it should be applied as widely as possible.

In deciding when an armed conflict arises, the ICTY applies a lower threshold than does the *Commentary*: "**An armed conflict exists whenever there is a resort to armed force between States or protracted armed violence between governmental authorities and organized armed groups. ... International humanitarian law applies from the initiation of such conflicts**."[150] (The terms "protracted" and "organized" are described, if not precisely defined, in ICTY case law.)[151]

> No requirements that the insurgents exercise territorial control or meet their obligations under common Article 3 were included, and it was also felt to be unnecessary that the government be forced to employ its armed forces (or even that the government be a party to the conflict at all), or that the insurgents be recognized as belligerents. ... The requirement that violence must be protracted hints that it must have reached a certain level of intensity, although expressed in terms of the duration rather than the scale of the violence.[152]

---

[148] Maj Gen A. V. P. Rogers, *Law on the Battlefield*, 2d ed. (Huntington, NY: Juris, 2004), 216.

[149] Pictet, *Commentary I*, supra, note 52, at 49–50.

[150] *Tadić*, Decision on Motion for Interlocutory Appeal on Jurisdiction, supra, note 103, at para. 70.

[151] For descriptions of "protracted," and "organization," see *Prosecutor v. Boškoski and Tarčulovski*, IT-04–82-T (10 July 2008), paras. 190 and 196 respectively. Organization is also discussed in *Prosecutor v. Limaj*, IT-03–66-T (30 Nov. 2005), paras. 89 and 190.

[152] Moir, *The Law of Internal Armed Conflict*, supra, note 145, at 43, footnote omitted.

If the fighting does not meet the requirements for a noninternational armed conflict, it is banditry, or an unorganized or short-lived insurrection, or terrorist activity, to which LOAC/IHL do not apply. (See Cases and Materials, this chapter, for factors indicating a noninternational conflict.)

Although the ICRC standard enjoys greater acceptance, in practice, there is no "correct" or binding standard. Rather, it depends on who decides. Although that is hardly a definitive or reassuring answer, it reflects the sometimes-uncertain state of LOAC.

For U.S. Armed Forces, with little fear of an internal armed conflict, questions of application are simplified. "The U.S. considers Common Article 3 applicable to either internal OR international conflicts. This view is based on the 1986 International Court of Justice opinion [*Nicaragua v. U.S.*] holding that this Article is a 'minimum yardstick of protections to be afforded to all civilians in any type of conflict.' The U.S. applies the type of protections across the entire operational spectrum (war, conflict, and peace)."[153]

Overall, common Article 3 has not been particularly successful. "The practical application of common Article 3 is widely perceived as having been disappointing. ... One scholar, writing in 1978, even claimed that it had never been applied in any situation to date, despite numerous civil wars exceeding the minimum threshold."[154]

3.8.9 *Are the Geneva Conventions "Quaint" and "Obsolete," Requiring Change?*

As all regulatory frameworks do, the Geneva Conventions require periodic updating and reinterpretation to meet evolving battlefield realities and international imperatives. Their "modernizations" in 1906 and 1929, not to mention 1949, are evidence of that need, as are 1977 Additional Protocols I and II, discussed in the next chapter. In an era of increased acts of terrorism, do the conventions remain effective and adequate to their purpose? In 1970, a prominent LOAC publicist, the British colonel G. I. A. D. Draper, said, "The Geneva Conventions of 1949 are excellent instruments of humanitarian law but they were unfortunately backwards-looking to the experience of World War II. They are already failing to respond and meet post 1949 conditions of combat and organizations of combatants."[155] Music to White House Council Gonzales's ears, perhaps, supporting his dismissive view of the conventions, but Colonel Draper's assessment has proven darker than warranted. The 1949 conventions have shown themselves to be remarkably resilient and adaptable to emerging warfare modalities hardly perfect, but equal to unforeseeable circumstances and needs.

There are a few convention articles, it must be admitted, that could confirm Council Gonzales's "quaint/obsolete" label, although not the articles he specified. Anachronistic convention provisions – every legal and regulatory system has them – merely reflect a mid-twentieth-century vision of a better world that the Geneva delegates hoped for; a more restrained future battlefield that the international community wished for, even if sometimes naively.

---

[153] Cdr. Mark E. Newcomb, ed., *Law of War Workshop Deskbook* (Charlottesville, VA: The Judge Advocate General's School, 1997), 6–13. Emphasis in original.

[154] Moir, *Law of Internal Armed Conflict*, supra, note 145, at 67.

[155] Draper, "The Legal Classification of Belligerent Individuals," in Meyer and McCoubrey, *Reflections on Law and Armed Conflict*, supra, note 35, at 199–200.

An example of a Geneva Convention rule sometimes viewed as outdated is Article 17 of Convention III: "Prisoners of war who refuse to answer [interrogation questions] may not be ... exposed to any unpleasant or disadvantageous treatment of any kind."

No unpleasantness for POWs? On a first reading, Article 17 appears to require a laughable sensitivity to the feelings of an enemy, a restraint suitable for gentlemanly conflict on European battlefields of another age. But does it?

> During the Second World War, certain categories of prisoners were placed in special camps, known as "interrogation camps" before being sent to a normal prisoner-of-war camp. In order to try to secure information, great hardship was inflicted on them. Such camps were outside the control of ... the ICRC, which in most cases had no knowledge of their existence. ... The holding of prisoners incommunicado, which was practiced by certain Detaining Powers in "interrogation camps" during the last war, is also implicitly forbidden by this paragraph.[156]

Although Article 17's "unpleasant treatment" sounds like rather tender care, the article is included in the POW convention for reasons all too clear in recent history. How many World War II POWs were beaten, tortured, experimented on, or murdered? How many Korean War prisoners were "brainwashed"? How many Vietnam War prisoners were tortured, some to death? POWs are not prisoners because they are criminals, to be questioned until they "break." They are held only to prevent them from returning to the fight. Although a POW's circumstances are inevitably "unpleasant," a gross violation of Article 17 could constitute a grave breach, calling for criminal prosecution. History repeatedly proves that the potential for the most serious of breaches is present when the treatment of POWs is unrestrained. Indeed, the majority of post–World War II military commission trials of German and Japanese soldiers were for crimes related to the mistreatment of POWs. Hence Article 17.

Another provision of Geneva Convention III, Article 44, mandates, "In order to insure service in officers' [POW] camps, other ranks ... shall be assigned in sufficient numbers. ... Such orderlies shall not be required to perform any other work."

Enlisted orderlies – "batmen" in British military parlance – for officers in POW camps? Until recently, in some European states, military regulations and custom relieved officers of personal fatigue duties, this work being assigned to enlisted men and women. It was not illogical that the convention should recognize this practice. Still, this is one of the odder articles in the 1949 conventions. (It is repeated verbatim in the U.S. military's 1956 FM 27–10, *The Law of Land Warfare*, at paragraph 120.) Article 44 probably owes its existence to its predecessor, Article 22 of the 1929 POW convention. By 1949, however, it could have expired and gone the way of treaties restricting the use of armed balloons. Its presence, however, does no material harm. Its violation would be contrary to that provision of the conventions, an administrative violation, constituting no war crime.

Arguments for amending the 1949 conventions do not rest on articles like these, but on national and international limitations and frustrations raised in fighting an enemy unwilling to recognize or abide by basic humanitarian norms. The so-called war on

---

[156] Jean de Preux, *Commentary: III Geneva Convention Relative to the Treatment of Prisoners of War* (Geneva: ICRC, 1960), 163.

terrorism presents the United States and its allies with a nonstate enemy that employs tactics like those of guerrillas and insurgents through the ages. Nonstate actors, not eligible to become parties to Geneva conventions, are often willing to ignore elementary humanitarian norms in pursuit of their goals. Traditionally, the law of war was effective, in part, because of

> the concentration of weapons in the hands of territorial elites who were subject to the dynamic of reciprocity and retaliation that underlies international law. That dynamic does not operate for non-state actors, for they are neither beneficiaries of nor hostages to the territorial system. As long as non-state actors did not amass significant arsenals, their indifference or even hostility to world public order was inconsequential. . . . The United States, on the morning of September 11, 2001, awoke to a new reality.[157]

America's "new reality" is old business for Great Britain, France, Spain, Egypt, Jordan, Israel, and other countries that have dealt with domestic terrorism for many years. "There will be no surrender or peace treaty with terrorists. The war against them will go on, just as the war against crime in America continues in perpetuity."[158]

In the "war on terrorism," the Geneva Conventions are not an entirely comfortable fit. During the brief 2001 U.S. war in Afghanistan, the application of customary LOAC and the relevance of the 1949 Conventions were never questioned. In Iraq, however, the combatant/noncombatant distinction has been blurred by both the United States and insurgents. When is a civilian taking an active part in hostilities, making him a lawful target? Insurgents, who are neither soldiers nor civilians under the conventions, are referred to as "unlawful enemy combatants," a term unknown in the conventions. If insurgents are enemy combatants, why does the combatant's privilege not apply to them? The United States is rightfully unwilling to afford POW status to captured insurgents, but are hearings to determine their status unnecessary? May coercive interrogation methods that many consider torture be employed against insurgents who are, others argue, not covered by the conventions? May "detainees," like POWs, be held until the termination of hostilities? Are we at war, at peace, or somewhere in between? The "war on terror" does not comport with the conventions' description of an armed conflict. The difficult questions raised by armed conflict with nonstate actors have raised calls for revisions of the laws of war, or at least their reinterpretation.[159] The MCA of 2006 goes so far as to permit the U.S. president to reinterpret common Article 3, a power George W. Bush exercised with regard to Central Intelligence Agency interrogation techniques.[160]

---

[157] W. Michael Reisman, "Assessing Claims to Revise the Laws of War," 97–1 *AJIL* (Jan. 2003), 82, 86.

[158] Joel Rosenthal, "New Rules For War?" Vol. LVII, No. 3/4, *Naval War College Rev.* (2004), 91, 97.

[159] In a Feb. 7, 2002, memorandum, President George W. Bush wrote, "The war against terrorism ushers in a new paradigm. . . . Our nation recognizes that this new paradigm . . . requires new thinking in the law of war." The former secretary of defense James Schlesinger, in a report on Abu Ghraib offenses, wrote: "The United States needs to redefine its approach to customary and treaty international humanitarian law, which must be adapted to the realities of the nature of conflict in the 21st Century." *Final Report of the Independent Panel to Review DoD Detention Operations* (Aug. 2004), at 80–1 and 91, available online. In a newspaper, the Harvard Law professor Alan Dershowitz writes that "the Geneva Conventions are so outdated . . . that they have become a sword used by terrorists to kill civilians," *Jewish World*, May 28, 2004.

[160] "Executive Order: Interpretation of the Geneva Conventions Common Article 3 as Applied to a Program of Detention and Interrogation Operated by the Central Intelligence Agency," (July 20, 2007), available online. In an editorial, the executive order was attacked by General P. X. Kelley, former commandant of the Marine Corps, and a cowriter: "It is clear to us that the language in the executive order cannot even

Terrorism is hardly a new tactic; nor is its control a wilderness of untested options. Certainly modern weaponry gives al Qaeda the firepower that few terrorist groups previously possessed. Nevertheless, states need be wary of endorsing quick-fix antiterrorism measures at the expense of tested counterterrorism measures arrived at through years of military effort and by painstaking international negotiation and agreement. Sometimes, issues asserted to be intractable are already addressed by LOAC. Geneva Convention IV regarding civilian protections, for example, is applicable throughout periods of occupation. It addresses the treatment of "unlawful combatants" in Articles 4, 27, and 49; terrorism is prohibited in Article 33; violations of the law of war committed by civilians are briefly addressed in Article 70; the trial of civilians who breach the law of war during periods of occupation is covered in Articles 71–5. Periods of occupation aside, "while states are the subjects of international law, 'non-state actors' are governed instead by national law. In respect of 'terrorists' and 'terrorist organizations' . . . the principle source of applicable law is national law. . . . The responsibility of individuals for established crimes under international law – such as . . . war crimes – arises irrespective of whether the perpetrator was a state official or a non-state actor."[161] A multiplicity of multinational antiterror conventions is also among the legal resources available to prosecutors combating terrorists and their unlawful activities.

A U.S. Army officer wrote in 2005, "Because the law of war in its current form is more than adequate to face the new GWOT [Global War on Terror] challenges, it does not warrant revision. Should a party to an armed conflict like the GWOT continue to apply 20th Century standards of conduct in an environment where the enemy refuses to reciprocate? . . . Yes, and even though the author acknowledges the cost of such a decision has been, and will always be, extremely high, he firmly believes the alternative is unacceptable."[162] The writer continues, "The disciplined application of the law of war at the expense of military necessity has proven challenging, but . . . if ever an element of national policy existed that demands unwavering conviction aimed at avoiding situational ethics at all costs, this is it."[163] The army's then-chief of staff, General Peter Schoomaker, concurred, saying, "Our values are sacrosanct . . . everything else is on the table."[164] Professor Jordan Paust writes:

> The pretense that "new" forms of social violence exist and that new laws of war are needed might be claimed by some in an effort to avoid responsibility for misinterpretation or misapplication of present laws of war, but the laws of war do not need to be changed because of September 11th. . . . Indeed, claimed changes in the status of war, thresholds for the application of the laws of war, and "combatant" status could have serious consequences for the United States, other countries, [and] U.S. military personnel. . . . Mean-spirited denials of international legal protections would

---

arguably be reconciled with America's clear duty under Common Article 3 to treat all detainees humanely and to avoid any acts of violence against their person." P. X. Kelley and Robert F. Turner, "War Crimes and the White House," *Wash. Post* (July 26, 2007), A21.

[161] Helen Duffy, *The 'War on Terror' and the Framework of International Law* (Cambridge: Cambridge University Press, 2005), 61, 62.

[162] LTC David P. Cavaleri, *"The Law of War: Can 20th-Century Standards Apply to the Global War on Terrorism?"* (Fort Leavenworth, KS: Combat Studies Institute Press, 2005), 2–3.

[163] Ibid., at 101–2.

[164] R. L. Brownlee and Gen. Peter J. Schoomaker, *Serving a Nation at War* (Washington, DC: Army Strategic Communications, 2004), foreword.

not only be unlawful, but would also disserve a free people. Such denials have no legitimate claim to any role during our nation's responses to terrorism.[165]

Any state considering unilateral changes to LOAC, or to the Geneva Conventions, would do well to remember the principle of unintended consequences, as the United States found in its Iraq and Afghanistan conflicts. Nevertheless, important changes in the law of war tend to emerge unexpectedly. For example, a multinational treaty will emerge, banning antipersonnel land mines. Or terrorists will unexpectedly be deemed to have a "continuous combat function," permitting them to be killed lawfully merely upon being identified. State practice will show that war crimes do occur in noninternational armed conflicts. Or one will find "that the distinction between internal and international conflicts is being greatly reduced."[166]

3.9 Summary

World War I was followed by a strengthening of the 1906 Geneva Convention, as well as the unsatisfactory Leipzig trials. The postwar period saw both promise (the League of Nations and Kellogg–Briand) and disappointment (wars in Spain, Manchuria, and elsewhere) in both customary and treaty-based law of war. World War II produced the cornerstone of law of war, the four 1949 Geneva Conventions. "The adoption of the Geneva Conventions in 1949 . . . marked a radical departure from old concepts and generated a new universe with regard to the law of war. Their importance as a break-through of new perspectives, substantive rules and systematic coordinates wŞas epochal."[167] Along with 1907 Hague Regulation IV, and the large body of case law represented by the postwar military commissions held by all the Allied nations after World War II, battlefield law was maturing. After 1949, "law of war" broadened to include noninternational conflicts and became "the law of armed conflict."

The continuing significance of common Article 3, a "Geneva convention in mini-ature," cannot be overlooked. Recent conflicts have predominantly been noninterna-tional in character, and the basic humanitarian norms of common Article 3 have become particularly important. It should be remembered that ICTY case law has found "that the principles and rules embodied in common Article 3 now apply to any sort of armed conflict, regardless of its characterization."[168] Despite the plain language of its first sentence, common Article 3 should not be thought of as applicable only in noninterna-tional armed conflicts.

Nonstate terrorism tests the limits of the Geneva Conventions as no previous armed conflict has, raising objections that the conventions are no longer adequate. Such appraisals are incorrect. No law will deter the lawless. "You do not expect terrorists to obey the law: their whole purpose is to do the opposite, to overturn the law, so you would

---

[165] Jordan J. Paust, "There Is No Need to Revise the Laws of War in Light of September 11th," ASIL Task Force on Terrorism (2004), www.asil.org/taskforce/paust.pdf.

[166] Meron, "Reflections," supra, note 7, at 49.

[167] Robert Kolb, "Main Epochs of Modern International Humanitarian Law Since 1864," in Kjetil Larsen, Camilla G. Cooper, and Gro Nystuen, *Searching for a "Principle of Humanity"* (Cambridge: Cambridge University Press, 2013), 45.

[168] Mettraux, *International Crimes and the* Ad Hoc *Tribunals*, supra, note 106, at 135.

not expect members of al Qaeda, for example, to follow the kinds of norms we have been discussing. ... The purpose of codes, charters and ultimately international law is precisely to single out and make clear what constitutes unacceptable behavior and illegal acts. The players define themselves by their behavior."[169]

To laud the concepts of grave breaches, mandatory prosecution, and the creation of common Article 3 is not to say that the 1949 conventions perfected LOAC. Prosecutors and other hard-eyed realists appreciate, for example, that war criminals and the evidence against them are not often located within the same state, making charging difficult; for political reasons some nations decline to hand over accused persons within their borders; states holding evidence may decline to transmit it to a prosecuting state, or the prosecuting state may refuse to hand over the accused person to the state holding the evidence. For that matter, the conventions themselves contain no enforcement measures whatsoever. "It is somewhat trite to note that neither the 1949 Geneva Conventions nor the Additional Protocols are 'perfect' documents. They reflect the compromise of negotiations inherent in the treaty making process."[170]

Even with their admitted imperfections, the 1949 Geneva Conventions remain a historic step toward regulating battlefield conduct, and the best answer to impunity and uncontrolled violence. "Generally speaking, it is doubtful that there is any multilateral convention on the same scale that has achieved ... a better overall success rate in terms of actual respect and performance."[171] Even in an age of transnational terrorism, the 1949 conventions remain both relevant and applicable.

There is a contrary view, of course. In a best-selling 2007 book, Marcus Luttrell, a U.S. Navy SEAL veteran of Afghanistan combat who earned the Navy Cross, second only to the Medal of Honor, fairly seethes when he writes:

These terrorists/insurgents know the rules. ... They're not their rules. They're *our* rules, the rules of the Western countries, the civilized side of the world. And every terrorist knows how to manipulate them in their own favor. ... They know we are probably scared to shoot them, because we might get charged with murder. ... The truth is, in this kind of terrorist/insurgent warfare, no one can tell who's a civilian and who's not. So what's the point of framing rules that cannot be comprehensively carried out by anyone? Rules that are unworkable, because half the time no one knows who the goddamned enemy is, and by the time you find out, it might be too late to save your own life. ... Never mind there's no shooting across the border [into] Pakistan, the illegality of the Taliban army, the Geneva Convention, yada, yada, yada. ... The truth is, any government that thinks war is somehow fair and subject to rules like a baseball game probably should not get into one. Because nothing's fair in war, and occasionally the wrong people do get killed. It's been happening for about a million years. Faced with the murderous cutthroats of the Taliban, we are not fighting under the rules of Geneva IV Article 4. We are fighting under the rules of Article 223.556 mm – that's the caliber and bullet gauge of our M4 rifle.[172]

[169] "Means of Warfare: Interview with Terance Taylor," 859 *Int'l. Rev. of the Red Cross* (Sept. 2005), 419, 425.
[170] BGen. Kenneth Watkin, "21st Century Conflict and International Humanitarian Law: Status Quo or Change?" in Michael N. Schmitt and Jelena Pejic, eds., *International Law and Armed Conflict: Exploring the Faultlines* (Leiden: Martinus Nijhoff, 2007), 264–96, 292.
[171] Yoram Dinstein, "Comments on Protocol I," 320 *Int'l Rev. of the Red Cross* (Oct. 1997), 515.
[172] Marcus Luttrell with Patrick Robinson, *Lone Survivor* (New York: Little, Brown, 2007), 168–70.

He adds, "By the way, if anyone should dare to utter the words *Geneva Convention* ... I might more or less lose control."[173] His is not an isolated view of LOAC, particularly among armed forces members who have seen firsthand the enemy's disregard of LOAC. Nevertheless, one suspects that if an enemy fighter were to surrender to Luttrell, he would accept the surrender without harming him – in fact, in his book he relates having done so; if confronted with insurgents firing from a crowd of noncombatants, he would either aim for the shooters or not fire at all; and, upon encountering a wounded and incapacitated enemy who was recently fighting him, he would treat the enemy's wounds, rather than kill him.

However, if a U.S. combatant is suspected of purposely killing an enemy attempting to surrender, firing indiscriminately into noncombatant groups, or executing the wounded, there will be consequences. No one can make a soldier (or SEAL) believe that there is enforceable LOAC, but that soldier should always know for what he will be court-martialed.

CASES AND MATERIALS

THE TRIALS OF LIEUTENANT-GENERAL KARL STENGER AND MAJOR BENNO CRUSIUS

A War Criminal Trial before the Criminal Senate of the Imperial Court of Justice Sitting in Leipzig, Germany (1921)

Introduction. *"The [Leipzig] trials resulted in six convictions and six acquittals."[174] The trial of German General Stenger, pressed by the French government, was the last of the twelve trials.[175] Stenger's co-accused, rarely noted in accounts of the Leipzig trials, was his subordinate, Major Crusius. Stenger was acquitted, his subordinate convicted.*

General Stenger was charged with issuing, on August 21 and 26, 1914, unlawful orders to the effect that all enemy prisoners and all enemy wounded be summarily executed; specifically, that "No prisoners are to be taken from today onwards; all prisoners, wounded or not, are to be killed," and "all prisoners are to be killed; the wounded, armed or not, are to be killed; men captured in large organized units are to be killed. No enemy must remain alive behind us." "Major Crusius was charged with having passed on General Stenger's order, and with having thereby caused the killing of several French wounded. He was further charged with having on separate occasions himself intentionally killed several (seven at least) French prisoners or wounded, and with having induced his subordinates to do the same."[176]

---

[173] Id., at 367. Emphasis in original.
[174] Dept. of the Army, *International Law*, Vol. II (Washington, DC: GPO, 1962), 221–2.
[175] Charges, descriptions, and accounts are from reports of the Leipzig Court, unless otherwise noted.
[176] Mullins, *The Leipzig Trials*, supra, note 5, at 152.

Consider whether the Court's pronouncements sound reasonable and fair, or not. Can a Court's opinion be written in such a way as to make the outrageous sound reasonable? If so, how is one to know? The following is from the court's report of the cases.

According to Major Crusius, on 21st August the brigade was standing in order of battle near the chapel at the eastern exit from the Saarburg drill ground. ... General Stenger gathered the officers of the 1st Battalion of the 112th Regiment around him and gave the order that all wounded left on the battlefield were to be shot. ... Crusius unhesitatingly construed these instructions as a brigade order. ... [The wounded] were shot soon after, as he concluded was the case from shots from the front lines which were not necessitated by the state of the battle. ...

As far as he [Stenger] could remember, he did not say anything at all which could in any way have been understood or interpreted in the sense imputed by Crusius. He said nothing about the shooting of wounded. Moreover, in the state of affairs at that time there was nothing to induce him to do so. ...

The commanders of the two regiments belonging to the 58th Brigade, Neubauer and Ackermann, declared that the promulgation of an order, such as Crusius insists he heard from General Stenger's lips during the halt near the chapel, was quite impossible. They did not hear such an order, and, had it been issued, they must have heard it. ...

The witness Heinrich, Lieutenant in the Reserve, at the time orderly officer to the 58th Brigade, was, according to the evidence, present within hearing at the time of the conversation near the chapel ... [and] declared emphatically that the order which Major Crusius maintains was given ... was not given. ... Heinrich has added that General Stenger always dictated to him the brigade orders intended for the troops.

The witness Albansröder heard, from a little distance off, a conversation between General Stenger and five or six officers about the method of fighting adopted by the French at Saarburg, namely the shooting from the rear by wounded men. He said that General Stenger expressed his opinion about this excitedly and angrily, and said words to the effect that no quarter should be given to the French who did such things, but they should simply be shot. ...

The witness Kaupp confirmed the handing of the "order" as stated by Major Crusius, after the conversation of the officers near the chapel. ...

The witness Ernst stated that immediately after the conversation an order was passed along the 3rd Company to the effect that no prisoners were to be taken. Colour-Sergeant Flörchinger doubted the accuracy of the order and made further inquiry as to its source. The answer was: "Brigade order." While going across the parade ground, the witness heard that Major Müller, in the immediate neighbourhood of Major Crusius, gave the order to shoot the French lying in a hollow. One of these Frenchmen is reported to have been killed.

Dr. Döhner ... was in the firing line with the 1st Battalion, where dead and wounded were lying. There he saw Major Crusius, with flushed face and bulging eyes, his revolver in hand, run across the square, and heard him shout loudly: "Will you not carry out the brigade order?" One of the men told the witness, "We are to shoot the Frenchmen lying there." The witness declared that he would not do it. The other men refused also, as they could not shoot defenceless men. ...

One of the men, named Jägler, about ten minutes after this order was issued, shot dead a wounded Frenchman, who lay, without a rifle, with his back against a sheaf of corn, and who raised his hands begging for mercy. The witness reproached Jägler for doing this, but only received the answer, "That's no concern of yours; it is an order." Farther back more shots were heard, and his comrades told the witness later that the French wounded were shot down *en masse*. . . .

Findings of the Court

The accusations made [against General Stenger] are refuted. None of the officers who were in the immediate neighbourhood of General Stenger, and to whom such an order must have been addressed, heard anything at all about it. . . . An order of the nature maintained by the accused Crusius would have been in absolute contradiction to the character of the accused Stenger. . . .

It has been established that the accused Crusius caused the death of an undetermined number of men at Saarburg in Lorraine on the 21st August, 1914, through negligence. . . . Crusius acted in the mistaken idea that General Stenger . . . had issued the order to shoot the wounded. He was not conscious of the illegality of such an order, and therefore considered that he might pass on the supposed order to his company, and indeed must do so.

So pronounced a misconception of the real facts seems only comprehensible in view of the mental condition of the accused. Already on the 21st August he was intensely excited and suffered from nervous complaints. The medical experts have convincingly stated that these complaints did not preclude the free exercise of his will, but were, nevertheless, likely to affect his powers of comprehension and judgment. But this merely explains the error of the accused; it does not excuse it. . . . Had he applied the attention which was to be expected from him . . . [it] would not have escaped him, namely, that the indiscriminate killing of all wounded was a monstrous war measure, in no way to be justified.

Having found General Stenger not guilty because an order to kill the wounded would have been "in absolute contradiction" to his character, the Court found Major Crusius guilty of killing through negligence.

The Court then considered the charge that, on August 25, at Sainte Barbe wood, near Thiaville, France, Stenger, in writing, had ordered, with regard to surrendering French troops, that no quarter be given – that no prisoners be taken but that they should be killed. Again, the accuser was General Stenger's co-accused, Major Crusius. The testimony of witnesses conflicted, with the majority denying knowledge of such an order. The defense case was aided by the fact that, on the day in question and while General Stenger was present, numerous French prisoners were in fact taken alive.

The Court again acquitted the general. The Court also found that Major Crusius had "passed on" an order of no quarter, then discussed whether Crusius could be found guilty of the charge:

> At the moment when the alleged brigade order was passed on in the afternoon of the 26th August (not merely at the time when it was executed), the accused was suffering from a morbid derangement of his mental faculties which rendered impossible the exercise of his free volition. . . .

According to the evidence it was only in the late afternoon of the 26th August that a complete mental collapse, a state of complete mental derangement excluding beyond any doubt all criminal responsibility, can with certainty be said to have occurred. . . .

As in accordance with practice, reasonable doubt as to the volition of the guilty party does not allow of a pronouncement of guilt, no sentence can be passed against Crusius as regards the 26th of August. In respect of this part of the indictment the accused Crusius must be acquitted. . . .

The accused Crusius is sentenced [for his previous shooting of enemy wounded] for homicide caused by negligence to two years' imprisonment and to deprivation of the right to wear officer's uniform. He is acquitted in respect of all other charges. The period during which he has been detained on remand is to be deducted from the sentence.

Conclusion. *Thus, General Stenger was acquitted of all charges. Major Crusius was found guilty of significantly reduced charges and received a minimal sentence. "All the defendants received what were considered, among the Allied States, at least, to be lenient sentences."*[177] *A contemporary historian who was present at the trials wrote, "it is very difficult to suppress an underlying suspicion that some words were used by General Stenger which could reasonably have been interpreted as an order to kill the prisoners and wounded."*[178] *Indeed.*

"THE HIGH COMMAND CASE," UNITED STATES V. WILHELM VON LEEB, ET AL.

Nuernberg Military Tribunal V, Case 12[179]

Introduction. *Perhaps the most significant post–World War II war crimes trials were those held in Nuremberg under Control Council Law # 10. The trials are referred to as "the Subsequent Proceedings." These twelve military tribunals, which overlapped the Nuremberg International Military Tribunal, were that conflict's high-water mark for war crimes trials, in terms of efforts to achieve fairness and equity for all parties. Perhaps the most significant Subsequent Proceeding was "The High Command Case." The accused were fourteen high ranking Nazi military officers (including the Judge Advocate General of the OKW, the High Command of the German Armed Forces). The trial ran from December 1947 through October 1948. Many significant LOAC issues were argued. This extract from the record of trial illustrates an unusual instance of an American military tribunal trying a German officer for war crimes committed against Russian prisoners. The issue relates to the inhumane treatment of Russian prisoners by their German captors. This extract from Nazi General Georg Reinhardt's defense counsel's closing argument highlights the work that POWs may lawfully be compelled to do. It also highlights the infrequently encountered war crime defense of* tu quoque *(you also). From the tribunal's judgment:*

I shall now turn to the legal question as to whether or not the employment of Russian prisoners of war, especially the employment for the construction of field fortifications in the rear area outside the combat zone, can be objected to from the point of view of international law.

---

[177] Timothy L. H. McCormack, "From Sun Tzu to the Sixth Committee: The Evolution of an International Criminal Law Regime," in McCormack and Simpson, *The Law of War Crimes, supra,* note 89, at 31, 50.

[178] Mullins, *Leipzig Trials, supra,* note 5, at 168.

[179] United Nations War Crimes Commission, *Law Reports of Trials of War Criminals,* Vol. XI (Wahington, DC: GPO, 1950), 408–11. Footnotes omitted.

I. According to the view held by the prosecution ... the employment of prisoners of war for labor is considered a war crime and crime against humanity, if such work is involved as is expressly prohibited according to the "Geneva Convention of 1929, concerning the treatment of prisoners of war." The first vital question then is: Was the Geneva Convention applicable at all in the relationship between Germany and Russia? This question can be answered only with a clear "no." For –

1. The Soviet Union has not ratified the "Geneva Convention of 1929 concerning the treatment of prisoners of war."
2. From the very beginning of the last World War the Soviet Union did not abide by the rules of the Geneva Convention.
3. The Soviet Union has not observed the rules of the "Geneva Convention of 1929 concerning the improvement of the lot of the wounded," which she signed and ratified under the title of the U.S.S.R.
4. In its verdict of 30 September 1946 the IMT has stated that the "Geneva Convention concerning prisoners of war" was not valid as far as Germany and Russia were concerned.

In the face of these incontestable facts, the document presented in this connection by the prosecution in rebuttal loses any significance. ... If, however, the Geneva Convention was not applicable, then the employment of the prisoners of war for labor was more or less permitted in as far as it did not violate the most elementary human rights of prisoners of war. It cannot be alleged that the construction of fortifications outside the combat zone constituted a violation of the most elementary human rights of the prisoners of war. This did not involve the employment of prisoners of war in "war operations against their own country," nor did this work expose the prisoner to greater danger than any other work that prisoners of war have to perform in wartime. The idea will never occur to anyone to consider the employment of prisoners of war for farm labor in the Reich illegal, although these persons were exposed to much greater danger in view of the enormous numbers of low flying Allied planes which, in the course of their operations, used to fire with all their weapons even on civilians who were peacefully working in their fields.

II. But even assuming for a moment that the Geneva Convention is directly applicable in the judgment of the legality of such an employment, one cannot arrive at any other conclusion. According to chapter 3, Article 31, of the Geneva Convention – only the use of prisoners of war for the "production and transportation of material designed for the fighting troops" is expressly prohibited.

Article 32 prohibits the use of prisoners of war for "unbearable or dangerous work." The construction of field fortifications outside of the combat zone is not included in this Article on the list of expressly prohibited work. ...

How can one try, in view of this state of facts, to indict a German general as a war criminal because he did not attain during the war the conception of law which was maintained by a minority [of Geneva delegates], and which the prosecution tries to set up today, so to speak in a dictatorial manner, as solely valid and solely justified?

How many German prisoners of war were employed in England during the war for the construction of air fields from which later on the bombers took off? Nobody would think of considering this employment as being in direct connection with the operations of war (Geneva Agreement, Article 31). How then, can one do so with respect to the employment of prisoners of war for the construction of field fortifications if these field fortifications were in many cases constructed 100 km. and more behind the combat zone and many of them were not even used later on.

III. If one goes still further and assumes that the Geneva Convention not only applied, but that it even had the meaning alleged by the prosecution, and consequently also prohibited the employment of prisoners of war for the construction of field fortifications outside the combat zone, the charge made against General Reinhardt is nevertheless still unfounded. For, in this case, the legal principle of *"tu quoque"* must be applied, which has approximately the following meaning:

> A state cannot blame another state for having violated the law by an action which it commits itself.

Probably not a single German who participated in the fighting against the Soviet Union will have the slightest doubt that the Soviet Union employed her German prisoners of war to a much larger extent for the construction of field fortifications, particularly even for the construction of field fortifications within the combat zone. I may in this connection be allowed to remind the Tribunal of how General Reinhardt described on the witness stand so impressively how he personally observed in the foremost front line, through his field glasses, that on the other side the Russians employed German prisoners of war in the foremost position, within the range of our own fire, for the construction of field fortifications. . . .

If, then, this is a fact, this circumstance – even if the Geneva Convention applies and its provisions are interpreted in a most narrow, literal way – must benefit General Reinhardt. Especially with regard to the legal principle of *"tu quoque"* the IMT made a fundamental decision in the case of Admiral of the Fleet Döenitz by recognizing the application of this principle as a legal excuse. The IMT indeed found that Admiral Döenitz had violated international law on this point, but nevertheless it did not convict him because of this violation, because the same breaches of international law had been committed by the enemy.

The application of the same principle to the case of General Reinhardt must result in his acquittal, even if the validity of the Geneva Convention is affirmed and its interpretation by the prosecution is accepted as binding. For the Soviet Union not only committed the same violation, but went much further by employing prisoners of war even within the range of enemy fire for the construction of field fortifications. . . .

At a time in which the Soviet Union . . . compels German citizens to perform slave labor on a large scale in the true meaning of the word beyond the borders of Germany, it is difficult, especially for a German, to keep faith in international law. . . .

Conclusion. *Actually, the Nuremberg IMT did convict Grand Admiral Döenitz of ordering German submarines to conduct unrestricted submarine warfare and to not pick up survivors of sunken ships. But, on the basis of the* tu quoque *defense, Döenitz received no sentence for that charge, but ten years for other charges of which he was convicted. [D]efense attorneys at Nuremberg invoked the tu quoque principle several times pointing to the bombing of Dresden, for example, as evidence that the Allies had not come to*

Nuremberg with clean hands. The most successful use of this argument occurred in the case of Admiral Döenitz who argued, with some justification, that the "crime" of failing to pick up enemy survivors of submarine attacks was in fact the policy of U.S. Forces in the Pacific under the command of General [sic] Nimitz.[180]

Unlike Admiral Döenitz, however, General Reinhardt did not have an affidavit from Fleet Admiral Chester Nimitz, and the British Admiralty, confirming that the United States and United Kingdom had engaged in the same conduct.[181] *Nor did he have such confirmation from any Soviet officer regarding his charge. Reinhardt was convicted of this and other charges and was sentenced to fifteen years' confinement.*

Former Nuremberg Chief Prosecutor Telford Taylor notes that, Döenitz's case notwithstanding, the tu quoque *defense is no defense. "In general criminal law, if a defendant has committed a particular crime, the fact that others have also, even if the others are the accusers, is no defense."*[182] *"The High Command Case" judgment held as much. Half a century later, the ICTY confirmed that, "the* tu quoque *defence has no place in contemporary international humanitarian law . . . Indeed, there is in fact no support either in State practice or in the opinions of publicists for the validity of such a defense."*[183]

THE TRIAL OF HEINZ HAGENDORF[184]

United States Intermediate Military Government Court at Dachau, Germany, August 8–9, 1946

Introduction. *Is the offense charged in the following record of trial a crime, a war crime, or a grave breach? How do you decide? Why does it matter? The Hagendorf case suggests answers to these questions.*

Improper Use of Red Cross Insignia

A *Outline of the Proceedings*

1 The Charge

The accused, Heinz Hagendorf, a German soldier, was tried . . . being charged with having "wrongfully used the Red Cross emblem in a combat zone by firing a weapon at American soldiers from an enemy ambulance displaying such emblem."

---

[180] Gerry J. Simpson, "War Crimes: A Critical Introduction," in McCormack and Simpson, *The Law of War Crimes,*" supra, note 89, at 5.

[181] Adm. Karl Doenitz, *Memoirs: Ten Years and Twenty Days* (New York: DeCapo Press, 1977), 256; E. B. Potter, *Nimitz* (Annapolis, MD: Naval Institute Press, 1976), 422–3; and Telford Taylor, *The Anatomy of the Nuremberg Trials* (New York: Knopf, 1992), 408–9.

[182] Id., Taylor, *Anatomy of the Nuremberg Trials,* at 400.

[183] *Prosecutor v. Kupreškić,* supra, note 136, at paras. 511, 516.

[184] United Nations War Crimes Commission, *Law Reports of Trials of War Criminals,* Vol. XIII (London: H. M. Stationery Office, 1949), 146–8. Footnotes omitted.

2 The Evidence

The evidence before the court showed the following:

> On 15th January, 1945, at about 2 p.m., an American unit, the 3rd Platoon, Company "G," 329th Infantry, was located in the little hamlet of Henyelez, in Belgium. A German ambulance, bearing Red Cross insignia, approached the road intersection at a high speed. It was first noticed by an American captain, by the name of Bates. The vehicle passed Captain Bates rapidly, and shots were fired from it through windows and doors. It then continued through the village and was next seen by two American privates. Here again shots were fired from the ambulance at the two soldiers. The latter took cover in nearby houses, while a third U.S. private hit the ambulance with a shot from a bazooka. The vehicle stopped and two German soldiers got out of it and began to run toward one of the houses. Both were fired upon by American soldiers. One was killed, and the other, accused Hagendorf, was captured.

It was established that the ambulance was driven by the German killed, and that the accused was the sole passenger. The accused pleaded not guilty, alleging that he had not fired any shots from the ambulance, but that it was the latter that received fire from the Americans.

3. Findings and Sentence

The defense plea was rejected on the grounds of the evidence proving the facts as stated above. The accused was found guilty of the charge and sentenced to 6 months' imprisonment.

B Nature of the Offence

Liability for improper use of Red Cross insignia is covered by an express provision of The [1907] Hague Regulations respecting the Laws and Customs of War on Land ... Article 23(f) of the Hague Regulations provides that "it is particularly forbidden" to "make improper use of a flag of truce, of the national flag, or of the military insignia, and uniform of the enemy, as well as of the distinctive signs of the Geneva Convention." ... The effect of these rules is that no person wearing the Red Cross sign may be treated as a combatant, or his equipment taken as a military objective or target.

The above-mentioned protection was, however, made subject to a general condition. According to Article 7 of the 1929 Convention, the protection ceases to exist if medical formations or establishments "are made use of to commit acts harmful to the enemy." This comprises the general prohibition for the medical personnel to use arms or serve as combatants. According to Article 8 the use of arms by medical personnel is permitted only in one exceptional type of case: if they have used arms in their own defence or in that of the sick and wounded in their charge. ...

In the case tried it was the rule concerning the use of arms in self-defence which was implicated. In his plea the accused had contended that his ambulance had been machine-gunned by the Americans while driving in order to collect wounded Germans at Henyelez. When considering the accused's allegations the court established, among other facts, that the evidence was clearly that shots were fired from the German ambulance at American military personnel. In face of the same evidence the court at the same time rejected as untrue the allegation that, prior to that, the ambulance had been fired upon by the Americans. This apparently was done as a result of inconsistencies in the accused's defence. He had contended that he was in the back of the ambulance at the time of the alleged crime, and that the vehicle was of a right-hand drive type. This, in view of the position of the vehicle on the spot of the incident, was meant to show that the accused could not have fired the shots charged. This allegation was disproved by photographic evidence taken immediately after the accused's capture, which showed that the vehicle was of a left-hand drive type, and that, by admitting that he was not driving, as was corroborated by the evidence, the accused must have sat on the side from which the shots were fired, that is, the right-hand side. . . .

As previously stressed, misuse of the Red Cross emblem is a specific violation of the terms of The Hague and Geneva Conventions. It is hard to conceive of a more flagrant misuse than the firing of a weapon from an ambulance by personnel who were themselves protected by such emblems and by the Conventions, in the absence of attack upon them. This constituted unlawful belligerency, and a criminal course of action.

It should be observed that not *every* violation of the Conventions concerning the use of the Red Cross insignia would of necessity constitute a punishable act. The need for maintaining a distinction between mere violations of rules of warfare, on the one hand, and war crimes on the other – the latter being the only ones to entail penal responsibility and sanctions – is urged by authoritative writers, such as Professor Lauterpacht. In the opinion of the learned author war crimes are violations of the laws of war and are criminal in the ordinary and accepted sense of fundamental rules of warfare and of general principles of criminal law by reason of their heinousness, their brutality, their ruthless disregard of the sanctity of human life and personality, or their wanton interference with rights of property unrelated to reasonably conceived requirements of military necessity. Violations not falling within this description would remain outside the sphere of war crimes and consequently of acts liable to penal proceedings.

The Court's findings in the trial under review were limited to the specific case of unlawful use of arms under the cover of the Red Cross emblem. It would therefore be unjustified and at any rate premature to conclude from the Court's implementation of the Geneva Convention, that any other violation of the latter's rules is of necessity a war crime.

Conclusion. *Hagendorf's offense clearly was not a grave breach even under the 1929 Geneva Conventions, but just as clearly it was a violation of the law of war. Its commission resulted in death, which is always serious. In terms of war crimes, however, Hagendorf's offense would be considered a disciplinary, or administrative offense, as reflected by the relatively light sentence imposed by the military court.*

The misuse of marked ambulances was not restricted to World War II, of course. In a book about the 2004 war in Iraq and the second Battle of Fallujah, No True Glory, Bing West recounts how Marine Corps infantrymen and snipers, using thermal scopes on their weapons, killed insurgents in nighttime darkness. "Every day," West writes, "Red Crescent ambulances drove up to the lines to remove the corpses. During the first week in April [2004], Marines shot the drivers of two ambulances carrying armed fighters. After that the ambulances stayed out of the fight and conducted only humanitarian missions."[185]

---

[185] Bing West, *No True Glory* (New York: Bantam, 2006), 175–6.

In some circumstances, firing on an ambulance may constitute no crime. In 2007, an Italian Military Tribunal acquitted two Italian soldiers who, in Nassiriyah, Iraq, in darkness, fired on an approaching Iraqi ambulance, killing four noncombatants, including three women, one of whom was pregnant. The tribunal accepted the soldiers' defense of a version of military necessity – that they fired "based on the need to ensure the security of an emplacement or military position."[186]

In 2008, Columbian soldiers, posing as members of a nongovernmental aid organization, rescued and airlifted out of the Columbian jungle fifteen hostages held for years by Fuerzaj Aruadas Revolucionarias de Colombia (F.A.R.C.) rebels. One of the rescuers wore a bib over his Kevlar vest that bore a large red cross. After concerned ICRC officials met with governmental officials, the ICRC accepted the government's explanation that the rescuer acted "mistakenly and contrary to orders."[187] *No further action was taken. (See Chapter 11, Section 11.1, for an examination of this event.)*

---

[186] Antonio Cassese, "Under What Conditions May Belligerents Be Acquitted of the Crime of Attacking an Ambulance?" 6–2 *J. of Int'l Crim Justice* (May 2008), 385–9, citing the case of *Corporal X and others* (Rome Military Tribunal, 2007), unpublished.

[187] Associated Press, "Columbian Soldier Wore Red Cross Logo in Hostage Rescue," NY *Times*, July 17, 2008, A12. Also see: "Columbia: ICRC Underlines Importance of Respect for Red Cross Emblem," available on-line at ICRC 16-07-2008 News Release 08/129.

4 Protocols and Politics

4.0 Introduction

This chapter completes the description of essential laws of armed conflict that are in effect today with discussion of Additional Protocols I, II, and III. There are other multinational treaties, Security Council pronouncements, domestic laws, appellate opinions, and military orders and regulations that bear on conduct in armed conflict, but, with an awareness of 1907 Hague Regulation IV, the 1949 Geneva Conventions, and the 1977 Additional Protocols, one has the essential basics of today's *jus in bello*. This, in turn, allows one to determine what law applies on any battlefield.

4.1 Why New Law of Armed Conflict?

The law of armed conflict (LOAC) is young; only a hundred years have passed since modern LOAC was "formalized" in 1907 Hague Regulation IV. Whereas customary law of war finds its roots in antiquity, treaty-based battlefield law, *jus in bello*, is a historical youngster. As any youthful entity does, it continues to grow and mature.

Soon after the 1949 Geneva Conventions began to gather ratifications (the United States ratified in August 1955, after the U.S.–North Korean conflict ended), the international community recognized that the character of armed conflict was changing. World War II–type conflicts, large armies fighting large-scale battles involving thousands, even hundreds of thousands of troops, were giving way to guerrilla-type internal armed conflicts and revolutionary movements. Wars involving two or more states were seen less frequently, whereas noninternational armed conflicts grew in number and ferocity. The British general Rupert Smith writes, "War no longer exists ... war as battle in a field between men and machinery, war as a massive deciding event in a dispute in international affairs."[1]

Human rights law (HRL), unknown until the end of World War II, was expanding across the international spectrum. Although it was (and is) concerned with the relationship of states and their own nationals in times of peace, any new LOAC would inevitably be influenced by the impact of human rights laws.[2] Insurgencies were challenging the Geneva Conventions. Combatant status, not addressed by the 1949 conventions, became

---

[1] Gen. Rupert Smith, *The Utility of Force: The Art of War in the Modern World* (New York: Knopf, 2007), 3.

[2] Adam Roberts and Richard Guelff, *Documents on the Laws of War*, 3d ed. (Oxford: Oxford University Press, 2000), 420.

an important issue because of guerrilla actions. New attention focused on the law of occupation. "The Geneva Conventions did not cover all aspects of human suffering in armed conflict. ... In addition, the law of The Hague, which is concerned with developing rules on hostilities and the use of weapons, had not undergone any significant revision since 1907."[3] By the late 1960s, LOAC was ripe for updating, and the United States led the way in pressing for the negotiation of new rules.

4.2 The 1977 Additional Protocols

In 1971 and 1972, government experts from more than a hundred states conferred in Geneva, sponsored by the International Committee of the Red Cross (ICRC), to review draft protocols modernizing the 1949 conventions. Not all LOAC areas were on the table. "The Conference settled into the view ... that it ought not to get into the matter of naval warfare and the protection of civilian persons and property at sea."[4] Broad change was in the air, however. Among the U.S. representatives to Geneva was the Harvard Law School professor Richard R. Baxter, formerly a colonel in the U.S. Army. Further conference sessions were held in 1974, 1975, 1976, and, finally, in 1977.

> In order to ensure broad participation, the Conference invited certain national liberation movements to participate fully in the deliberations, although only states were to be entitled to vote. In fact, in recognition of the particular importance of achieving universality of acceptance in addressing the laws of war, for most of the time the Conference used the procedure of making decisions by consensus. Various international organizations were represented in an observer status.[5]

The participation of national liberation groups in the drafting process was not welcomed by the major Western powers. The interests of the Palestine Liberation Organization, the Irish Republican Army, the African National Congress, and Algeria's FLN (Front de Libération Nationale), to name but four groups present, did not neatly coincide with those of, for example, the United States, the United Kingdom, or France. Although national liberation groups did not have a vote, they had significant influence over states sympathetic to their goals. In 1977, those goals often involved scaling back and constricting the power and influence of the major powers. The potency of revolutionary movements acting in concert with state sponsors was particularly felt because, attempts at consensus aside, each state present was entitled to one vote. The vote of Vanuatu was equal to that of France; the vote of Kiribati equal to that of Great Britain.[6] No delegates were antagonistic toward a democratic process, but not every state participated in, for example, United Nations peace enforcing operations. Not all nations present were involved in regional defense pacts or were expected to go to the aid of countries in humanitarian crises. Yet, nations that did not have deployable armies could join in imposing on more powerful states their views of how the Geneva Conventions should be amended. The voting failed "to pay due regard to the practice of specially affected

---

[3] Yves Sandoz, Christophe Swinarski, and Bruno Zimmermann, eds., *Commentary on the Additional Protocols of 8 June 1977 to the Geneva Conventions of 12 August 1949* (Geneva: ICRC, 1987), xxix.

[4] R. R. Baxter, "Modernizing the Law of War," 78 *Military L. R.* (1978), 165, 168. Footnote omitted.

[5] Roberts and Guelff, *Documents on the Laws of War*, supra, note 2, at 419.

[6] Neither Vanuatu nor Kiribati was an independent nation during the period when the 1977 Additional Protocols were drafted.

States ... [and the voting] tends to regard as equivalent the practice of States that have relatively little history of participation in armed conflict and the practice of States that have had a greater extent and depth of experience or that have otherwise had significant opportunities to develop a carefully considered military doctrine."[7]

The concerns of some of the major powers were realized in the final versions of the two Protocols Additional to the Geneva Conventions, usually referred to simply as "Additional Protocol I," and "Additional Protocol II." (A "protocol" is merely another term to describe a treaty or pact.) Many of the protocols' provisions represented customary law, but some new provisions, in the understated words of the *Commentary*, "introduce fairly bold innovations."[8] The bold innovations were, for the most part, firmly resisted by the United States and, initially at least, by its major allies. After long and sometimes heated negotiations, however, the majority of states accepted the changes, despite objections of the Western community.[9]

The two protocols supplement the 1949 conventions, rather than replace any portion of them. They supplement the conventions "by extending the scope of their application, the categories of protected persons and objects and the protection conferred."[10] Today, the 1949 Geneva Conventions cannot be considered without also considering their interrelated 1977 protocols.

4.2.1 1977 *Additional Protocol I*

The full title, "1977 Geneva Protocol I Additional to the Geneva Conventions of 12 August 1949, and Relating to the Protection of Victims of International Armed Conflicts," informs us that the ninety-one substantive articles of Additional Protocol I are concerned with *international* armed conflicts – conflicts involving two or more states. Additional Protocol I is subject to more ratifying state reservations and declarations than any other LOAC agreement. Internal, noninternational armed conflicts are dealt with in Additional Protocol II.

4.2.1.1 New Grave Breaches in Additional Protocol I

We know that grave breaches of the Geneva Conventions are a closed category, limited to the offenses listed in the four 1949 conventions. Additional Protocol I, Article 11.4, taking a tack not applauded by all,[11] adds to the conventions' roster of grave breaches, making attacks on certain individuals or objects in specified circumstances grave breaches. Attacking an individual who is hors de combat is made a grave breach in Article 85.3. Also made grave breaches in that article are apartheid, delayed prisoner of war (POW) repatriation, attacking some protected objects, transfers or deportations of certain people to or from occupied territory, and depriving protected persons of a fair and regular trial. A question is whether these new grave breaches have validity with regard to

---

[7] This statement is not contemporary to the formation of the Additional Protocols. It is taken from the November 2006 U.S. response to the ICRC's 2005 three-volume study, *Customary International Humanitarian Law*. The U.S. response to the study is at 101–3 *AJIL* (July 2007), 640.

[8] Sandoz, *Commentary on the Additional Protocols*, supra, note 3, at xxxiv.

[9] For a discussion of the negotiations: id., at 39–56.   [10] Id., at 1085.

[11] G. I. A. D. Draper, "War Criminality," in Michael A. Meyer and Hilaire McCoubrey, eds., *Reflections on Law and Armed Conflicts* (The Hague: Kluwer Law International, 1998), 169–70.

states that have not ratified the additional protocols or are customary international law, binding even absent ratification?

4.2.1.2 Advances in Additional Protocol I

With Additional Protocol I, the preponderance of the customary law of war has become formalized. With the notable exception of military necessity, customary *jus in bello* is almost completely reduced to a stronger multinational treaty form, with states explicitly bound by agreements specifically recognizing LOAC.

Additional Protocol I contains significant advances in LOAC. The core LOAC concepts of distinction, unnecessary suffering, and proportionality, formerly found only in customary law, are codified and described in Additional Protocol I, if only in broad terms.[12] Command responsibility, the accountability of military leaders for the offenses of their troops that they are aware of, is laid out in Articles 86.2 and 87.1. "Beyond the general principles, Additional Protocol I extends special protection to specified objects, most notably medical establishments, cultural objects, places of worship, objects indispensable to the civilian population ... and works and installations containing dangerous forces."[13] Area bombing, widely practiced by both sides during World War II, is forbidden in Articles 51.2 and 51.5, providing new protections for civilian populations. After the Vietnam experience, the United States saw Article 24, giving new protections to medical aircraft, as a positive addition to LOAC. In contrast, the Vietnam experience, which included the use of herbicides such as Agent Orange by U.S. forces, led other nations to include Article 35.3, prohibiting attacks on the natural environment.

Article 87.1, dealing with the duties of commanders, states that not to report a violation of the conventions is itself a LOAC violation. Article 42 specifies that persons parachuting from an "aircraft in distress" (as opposed to paratroopers) may not be attacked during descent.* (See Chapter 14.5.)

Article 82 requires that legal advisers be available to advise commanders and instruct troops on LOAC issues. "As a result ... judge advocates now play a key role in training troops and commanders, before deployment or between deployments. They also give continuing on-the-ground advice to troops and commanders on a range of legal matters, including the appropriate limits on the use of force."[14]

A particular failure of Additional Protocol I is its lack of restrictions on the use of either conventional or nuclear weapons. Sweden's leading effort to create conventional weapon restrictions was opposed by the USSR and its allies. The United States took no hard stand regarding conventional weapons – unlike its position opposing any

---

[12] Distinction is described in Art. 48; unnecessary suffering in Art. 35.2; proportionality in Arts. 51.5(b), and 57(2)(b). The proportionality definition, never easy to apply in concrete cases, "is little more than a cautionary rule, requiring the commander to stop and think before he orders a bombardment." Baxter, "Modernizing the Law of War," supra, note 4, at 179.

[13] Michael N. Schmitt, "War, Technology and the Law of Armed Conflict," in Anthony M. Helm, ed., *International Law Studies*. Vol. 82. *The Law of War in the 21st Century: Weaponry and the Use of Force* (Newport, RI: Naval War College, 2006), 137, 141.

    * Art. 42 was resisted by some Arab states that, in past conflicts, had shot down Israeli aircraft, only to have the pilots parachute back into Israel to rejoin the attack.

[14] Laura A. Dickinson, "Military Lawyers on the Battlefield: An Emperical Account of International Law Compliance," 104–1 *AJIL* (Jan. 2010), 1, 11.

restriction on the use of nuclear weapons, which was vigorously and successfully contested by the United States and other nuclear powers.

4.2.1.3 Objections to Additional Protocol I

There are significant objections to Additional Protocol I, particularly by the United States. Sir Adam Roberts and Professor Richard Guellf describe a controversial innovation that the United States continues to resist:

> First, the Protocol spells out in unprecedentedly detailed rules relating to discrimination in the conduct of military attacks. These are mainly in [Articles 48–67] dealing with the general protection of the civilian population. ... Some of these provisions caused concern in certain states because of fears that commanders might be subject to accusations of war crimes not based on an understanding of the fact that in war commanders have to take action on the basis of imperfect information.[15]

Second, through several articles, Additional Protocol I largely prohibits reprisals, raising concerns about what can lawfully be done immediately to deter enemy states that violate provisions of LOAC.

Third, under Article 47 of Additional Protocol I, mercenaries may be considered neither POWs nor lawful combatants. Although mercenaries retain fundamental humanitarian protections under Article 75, the United States believes that no combatant should be denied a battlefield status. "But many of the newly independent states had fought against mercenaries in their wars of independence and they saw little reason to protect such combatants."[16] (If mercenaries are not POWs or lawful combatants, what is their individual status?)[17]

4.2.1.3.1 "CARs"

The objections of many Western powers center on two other Protocol I provisions. A fourth objection relates to Additional Protocol I's first article. Article 1.1.3 notes that the protocol supplements the 1949 Geneva Conventions and applies in situations of international armed conflict. So far so good, but Article 1.4 goes on to expand the definition of what constitutes an international armed conflict, declaring that "the situations referred to in the preceding paragraph" – international armed conflicts – "include armed conflicts in which peoples are fighting against colonial domination and alien occupation and against racist régimes in the exercise of their right of self-determination."

This provision, then, applies all of the 1949 conventions, and all of Additional Protocol I, not only to international armed conflicts as they are commonly understood, but also to situations in which insurgents profess to be fighting colonialism, in which guerrillas allege they are conducting armed resistance to a force or government occupying their country, and in which rebels say they are fighting their racist government. This was

---

[15] Roberts and Guelff, *Documents on the Laws of War*, supra, note 2, at 420.

[16] Philip Sutter, "The Continuing Role for Belligerent Reprisals," 13–1 *J. of Conflict & Security L.* (Spring 2008), 93, 112.

[17] Because they are not members of the armed forces of a party to the conflict, they are civilians. Because they directly participate in hostilities, they are unprivileged belligerents – unlawful combatants – subject to prosecution for the acts they committed that make them unlawful belligerents.

indeed a "fairly bold innovation." Commonly referred to as the "CARs" provision (*colonial* domination, *alien* occupation, *racist* regime) it was hotly contested in Geneva's conference rooms.

Some established states saw the CARs provision as providing rebels – in their view, troublemakers, brigands, and armed criminal groups – with the full panoply of Geneva Convention protections. A Central American government, perhaps beset by internal political division and civilian unrest, would not be eager to extend Geneva protections to individuals seen by the government as no more than outlaws.

National liberation movements, along with their sponsoring states, primarily the USSR and its allies, saw matters differently, however, and had the numbers to make their view prevail. The CARs article "was steamrollered through the first session of the Conference."[18]

> The concept of the right of self-determination ... which was proclaimed by the French Revolution, and was subsequently often denied, has from the outset constantly come up against the legal order; this did not prevent it from being applied with increasing frequency and from growing in strength. ...
>
> The Charter of the United Nations therefore consisted of turning this principle of self-determination of peoples into a right established in an instrument of universal application. ...
>
> The General Assembly recognized the legitimacy of the struggle of colonial peoples against colonial domination in the exercise of their right to self-determination.[19]

Additional Protocol I followed suit. The ICRC's *Commentary* says, "In our opinion, it must be concluded that the list [CARs] is exhaustive and complete: it certainly covers all cases in which a people, in order to exercise its right of self-determination, must resort to the use of armed force against the interference of another people, or against a racist régime."[20]

Some established powers, including the United States, were unmoved. They would have preferred a continuation of armed authority limited to the state, with a LOAC that protected traditional combatants. CARs, they argue, blurs national and international conflicts, making the applicability of Additional Protocol I, and therefore the 1949 conventions, turn on the asserted motive of a rebel force. Meanwhile, those considering themselves as oppressed saw a resort to arms – with international protections through the Geneva Conventions and Additional Protocol I – as a precondition to freedom.

> Historically, nations that view themselves as likely victims of aggression and enemy occupation have argued that guerrillas, partisans and members of resistance movements should be regarded as patriots and privileged combatants, while major military powers have argued that only regular, uniformed and disciplined combatants who distinguish themselves clearly from the civilian population should have the right to participate in hostilities.[21]

"The post World War II process of decolonization – sometimes peaceful, sometimes violent – created among most newly independent countries strong support for wars of

---

[18] Baxter, "Modernizing the Law of War," supra, note 4, at 172.

[19] Sandoz, *Commentary on the Additional Protocols*, supra, note 8, at 41–3. Footnotes omitted.

[20] Id., at 54–5.

[21] Waldemar Solf, "A Response to Douglas J. Feith's Law in the Service of Terror – the Strange Case of the Additional Protocol," 20 *Akron L. Rev.* (1986), 261, 269.

national liberation against the colonial powers."[22] Energized by the Vietnam War, at Geneva those countries sought new LOAC provisions that legitimized guerrilla tactics.

To a significant extent, the passage of time has rendered CARs a less important issue than it was in 1977. "The fight against the remnants of colonialism is no longer an issue today."[23] Japan was stripped of its colonies after World War II. Most states that had colonial holdings, such as Portugal and Belgium in Africa (the Belgian Congo), Portugal and the United Kingdom in China (Macao and Hong Kong), and the United Kingdom in South America (Guyana), have relinquished their overseas holdings. The Philippines gained independence from the United States long before the Additional Protocols took force. France maintains its colonial presence in South America in French Guiana, and New Zealand retains a small colonial holding in the Pacific, Tokelau.[24] Colonies are largely a relic of history.

"Alien occupation" was already governed by 1907 Hague Regulation IV, Articles 42 through 56, and by 1949 Geneva Convention IV. In Additional Protocol I the term was presumably "inserted to catch the votes of the Arab States"[25] involved in one of the few continuing instances of alien occupation: the Israeli occupation of the West Bank. American support of Israel precludes the United States' accepting that Hamas or the PLO might be covered by the Geneva Conventions.

What constitutes a "racist regime" is arguable, but cases such as Bosnians in Kosovo and Saddam Hussein–controlled Iraqi dominance of Kurds have ended. Rhodesia threw off its racist rule in 1980, becoming Zimbabwe. The prototypical racist regime, South Africa, officially ended apartheid in 1994.

Despite the retreat of situations involving colonial domination, alien occupation, and racist regimes, CARs remains a U.S. objection to Additional Protocol I.

4.2.1.3.2 *Modification of POW qualifications*

A continuing and significant objection held by many states is Protocol I's alteration of traditional views of combatants who may be considered lawful belligerents.

A century and a half ago, Francis Lieber summarized the customary law of war when he wrote, "Men, or squads of men, who commit hostilities ... without being part and portion of the organized hostile army ... with the occasional assumption of the semblance of peaceful pursuits, divesting themselves of the character or appearance of soldiers ... are not entitled to the privileges of prisoners of war, but shall be treated summarily as highway robbers or pirates."[26] Building on the Lieber Code, the first article of 1907 Hague Regulation IV holds that, to benefit from the laws of war – to enjoy the

---

[22] George H. Aldrich, "Some Reflections on the Origins of the 1977 Geneva Protocols," in Christophe Swinarski, ed., *Studies and Essays on International Humanitarian Law and Red Cross Principles, in Honour of Jean Pictet* (Geneva: ICRC, 1984), 135.

[23] Hans-Peter Gasser, "Acts of Terror, 'Terrorism' and International Humanitarian Law," 847 *Int'l Rev. of the Red Cross* (Sept. 2002), 547, 549.

[24] In February 2007, the people of Tokelau, a group of three small atolls between New Zealand and Hawaii, with a population of fourteen hundred, voted to reject independence and continue as a colony of New Zealand.

[25] Baxter, "Modernizing the Law of War," supra, note 4, at 173.

[26] Instructions for the Government of Armies of the United States in the Field (Army General Order 100 of April 24, 1863), Art. 82.

combatant's privilege or to be a POW upon capture, for instance – combatants, including partisans, guerrillas, and insurgents, are obliged to meet four preconditions.

The laws, rights, and duties of war apply not only to armies, but also to militia and volunteer corps fulfilling the following conditions:

1. To be commanded by a person responsible for his subordinates;
2. To have a fixed distinctive emblem recognizable at a distance;
3. To carry arms openly; and
4. To conduct their operations in accordance with the laws and customs of war.

More than fifty years later, those words of Article 1, 1907 Hague Regulation IV, Respecting the Laws and Customs of War on Land, are repeated almost verbatim in Article 4.A.(2) of Geneva Convention III, concerning the right of "volunteer corps, including those of organized resistance movements," to POW status.

Additional Protocol I alters that customary law formulation, significantly broadening it to embrace as POWs individuals previously subject to trial as unprivileged belligerents/ unlawful combatants. Unprivileged belligerents have been defined as "persons who are not entitled to treatment either as peaceful civilians or as prisoners of war by reason of the fact that they have engaged in hostile conduct without meeting the qualifications established by Article 4 of the Geneva Prisoners of War Convention of 1949."[27]

In altering the customary formulation, Article 43.1 repeats Hague Regulation IV and Geneva III's first and fourth requirements that armed forces, groups, and units must be under a command responsible for the conduct of subordinates, and that they must enforce compliance with the rules of armed conflict. (The requirement of "responsible command" does *not* mean there necessarily must be a hierarchal chain of command similar to that in national armed forces.)[28]

Article 44.3, however, modifies the traditional second requirement that lawful combatants wear a distinctive sign or emblem recognizable at a distance, to "distinguish themselves from the civilian population *while they are engaged in an attack or in a military operation preparatory to an attack.*" What constitutes "a military operation preparatory to an attack" is not detailed.[29] The same article alters the traditional third requirement, that lawful combatants must carry their arms openly, to a requirement that they carry their arms openly *during* "military engagement," *and* "*during such time as he is visible to the adversary while he is engaged in a military deployment preceding the launching of an attack.*" Once again, it is unclear just when arms must openly be carried.

Worse was to come, in the eyes of the United States and other major military powers. Article 44.4 provides that a "combatant who falls into the power of an adverse Party while failing to meet the requirements [of distinction] shall forfeit his right to be a prisoner of war, *but he shall, nevertheless, be given protections equivalent in all respects to those accorded to prisoners of war*" (emphasis supplied). This article "effectively erases the distinction between lawful and unlawful combatants and gives prisoner of war protection

---

[27] Richard R. Baxter, "So-Called 'Unprivileged Belligerency': Spies, Guerrillas, and Saboteurs," 28 *Brit. Y.B. Int'l L.* (1951), 323, 328.

[28] *Prosecutor v. Musema*, ICTR-96–13-A, Trial Judgment (Jan. 27, 2000), para. 257.

[29] For an interpretation of Art. 44.3's ambiguous language, see: Maj. William H. Ferrell III, "No Shirt, No Shoes, No Status: Uniforms, Distinction, and Special Operations in International Armed Conflict," 178 *Military L. R.* (Winter 2003), 94, 108.

to all combatants regardless of their conduct in respect to the law of war."[30] Armed resistance groups are essentially granted one of the most significant benefits of LOAC, POW status upon capture, without fulfilling its requirements.[31]

Shortly after the protocols were opened for signature, Major General George Prugh of the U.S. Army, one of the U.S. representatives to the protocols' negotiations, put the best face possible on Article 44: "A long-range patrol, operating in the adversary's rear area, would fit the situation permitting the patrol to retain the status of combatant merely by carrying arms openly during each military engagement and while engaged in the preceding deployment. ... As understood by the U.S. delegation ... the Article did not authorize soldiers to conduct military operations while disguised as civilians."[32] (The last sentence apparently indicates the expectation that, prior to actual engagement, the patrol would revert to wearing a uniform, or other fixed distinctive sign.)

Nevertheless, it is primarily this issue that makes Additional Protocol I "implacably objected to by the United States."[33] The United States believes that the traditional criteria for POW status are not only adequate but necessary to ensure that civilians not be allowed, for example, to conceal their arms as they pass a combatant patrol and then, appearing to be innocent and no danger, and showing no sign or symbol of enemy allegiance, suddenly fire on the patrol at close range, as from ambush. That, the United States contends, is a violation of the requirement that combatants distinguish themselves from noncombatants and is antithetical to law of war arrived at through hundreds of years of battlefield practice and custom. "Declaration of belligerent status is essential to the protection of the civilian population. If ... a combatant can disguise himself as a civilian and be immune from the use of force against him until he opens fire, this will prejudice the legal protection of all citizens. Unless a clear line can be drawn between combatants, who fight openly, and civilians, who are to be protected, all civilians will be put at peril."[34]

In the U.S. view, Additional Protocol I is objectionable not only because it loosens the preconditions for POW status; to allow insurgents to shelter under the umbrella of Geneva Conventions by simply declaring that they are fighting against colonial domination, alien occupation, or a racist regime politicizes the conventions, introducing subjective elements into LOAC. Application of the Geneva Conventions was previously based on the equality of application to all belligerents. Politics should play no part in the protections afforded by LOAC.

An insurgent might respond that no doubt the four requirements for lawful combatancy and POW status suit established governments very well, but they are a blueprint for guerrilla suicide. How long would any revolutionary group survive, wearing its colors on shoulder patches to be seen by any passing policeman or soldier? Or, in countries where it is not the custom, if guerrilla forces went about with their weapons in view? As the

---

[30] Sutter, "Continuing Role for Belligerent Reprisals," supra, note 16, at 111. The 1863 Lieber Code's Article 53 provided that chaplains and doctors, "retainees" in modern LOAC, may be treated as prisoners of war, but they were not unprivileged belligerents.

[31] A. D. Sofaer, "Agora: The U.S. Decision Not to Ratify Protocol I to the Geneva Convention," 82 *AJIL* (1988), 784, 785–6.

[32] Maj. Gen. George S. Prugh, "*Armed Forces and Development of the Law of War, Recueils de la Société Internationale de Droit Pénal Militaire et de Droit de la Guerre* (1982), 277, 285.

[33] Yoram Dinstein, *The Conduct of Hostilities under the Law of International Armed Conflict* (Cambridge: Cambridge University Press, 2004), 11. Footnote omitted.

[34] Baxter, "Modernizing the Law of War," supra, note 4, at 174.

British publicist Colonel G. I. A. D. Draper wrote, "any resistance fighters in occupied territory that seek to meet the 'open' nature that these conditions require of them would cease to be effective very quickly."[35] In the 1770s, did American colonists wear a sign or symbol recognizable at a distance or carry their arms openly while deploying? Has *any* guerrilla group ever complied with the four requirements?

There are valid reasons why insurgencies are resisted by established governments; reasons relate to political stability, security of the citizenry, and the continued welfare of the nation. In some states the rule of law is sometimes abused in the name of national security, yet far more frequently peace, stability, and progress are fostered by established governmental systems. Who determines when an established government is so corrupted and repressive that violent resistance is justified? Article 44.3 is an effort to protect those who would engage in armed resistance. The United States believes it goes too far in doing so, and that it is contrary to long-respected LOAC. And,

> Article 44 constitutes a considerable relaxation, for at least one side to a conflict, of the historic requirement ... This change was not accomplished inadvertently. Some of those pressing for it in the law-making process simply wished to favor the so-called national liberation combatants – to help them win – without regard to the consequences for noncombatants. Others rationalized the change in the hope that, in return for the relaxation of the uniform and open-arms requirement, irregular forces would have an incentive to comply with other parts of the law of war. The rationalization was of doubtful logic and morality ... and any future adversary could now – lawfully – fight without uniforms and without bearing arms openly. ... It was of doubtful morality because even if the rationalization proved to be correct ... that gain would be purchased with the lives of noncombatants.[36]

SIDEBAR. Under Additional Protocol I, the invocation of Geneva Convention protections – and obligations – requires only a simple declaration by a national liberation movement not a party to the Geneva Conventions. Article 96.3 requires that "the authority representing a people engaged against a High Contracting Party in a [CARs] armed conflict ... may undertake to apply the Conventions and this Protocol to that conflict by means of a unilateral declaration addressed to the depositary [the Swiss government]," but it is not quite as simple as that. The *Commentary* to the protocols explains that "the status recognized to liberation movements indeed gives them ... the right to choose whether or not to submit to international humanitarian law (IHL), insofar as it goes beyond customary law. In this respect they are in a fundamentally different legal position from insurgents in a non-international armed conflict."[37] The head of the U.S. Diplomatic Delegation to the Protocol negotiations scoffs, regarding CARs and Article 96.3:

> The political phraseology of [the CARs] text was chosen because it was understood by its sponsors to be self-limiting to wars against Western powers by oppressed peoples

---

[35] Draper, "The Legal Classification of Belligerent Individuals," in Meyer and McCoubrey, *Reflections on Law and Armed Conflicts*, supra, note 11, at 200.

[36] W. Michael Reisman, "Editorial Comment: Holding the Center of the Law of Armed Conflict," 100–4 *AJIL* (Oct. 2006), 852, 858.

[37] Sandoz, *Commentary on the Additional Protocols*, supra, note 8, at 1089–90.

> and would not apply to wars within newly independent States. No matter that most liberation movements could not hope to comply with the obligations of the Protocol and the Geneva Conventions and therefore will probably not ask to have it applied or that the [CARs] text was written in such insulting terms that no government fighting rebels would ever be prepared to admit that the provision applied to it.[38]
>
> Professor Yoram Dinstein concurs, calling Article 96 "one of the more preposterous innovations of the Protocol," because, although a liberation group's leadership may make an Article 96.3 declaration, the terrorists themselves will inevitably fail to observe LOAC.[39]
>
> No national liberation movement has ever made serious application under Article 96.3.[40]

The *Commentary* to Additional Protocol I notes that "the text of Article 44 is a compromise. . . . It is aimed at increasing the legal protection of guerrilla fighters as far as possible, and thereby encouraging them to comply with the applicable rules of armed conflict, without at the same time reducing the protection of the civilian population."[41] The *Commentary* continues, "The visible carrying of arms and distinguishing signs may either have no significance (for example, in sabotage or in an ambush), or they may really be incompatible with the practicalities of the action. . . . Because of this, refusing to allow specific procedures [foregoing a visible sign and concealing weapons] would be to refuse guerrilla warfare."[42] At the end of the day, it is telling that no party to any armed conflict has ever invoked either the CARs provisions or the expanded combatant status of Article 44.[43] Has the sound and the fury been about nothing?

It is ironic that Article 44.3 allows the feigning of civilian noncombatant status, while Article 37 prohibits perfidy and provides a specific example, "feigning of civilian, non-combatant status." The incompatibility of those two Additional Protocol I provisions, both of which reasonably envision engaging in combat in civilian garb, illustrates the compromises that the drafters felt necessary to incorporate, hoping to induce liberation movements to recognize and conform to LOAC.

4.3 1977 Additional Protocol II

Additional Protocol II has raised relatively few problems for the international community. As Additional Protocol I does, Additional Protocol II supplements the 1949 Geneva Conventions; it does not amend or replace any part of them. Also like Additional Protocol I, Additional Protocol II cannot yet be said to be customary law, but many of its provisions are.[44] "Because there are doubts as to which of its provisions are now

---

[38] Aldrich, "Some Reflections," supra, note 22, at 135–6.

[39] Yoram Dinstein, "Comments on Protocol I," 320 *Int'l Rev. of the Red Cross* (Oct. 1997), 515.

[40] In 1980, the African National Congress made what it called a "Declaration" to the ICRC, via a letter to the U.N. secretary-general, limited to announcing an intent to respect the "general principles of humanitarian law applicable in armed conflicts." The declaration did not refer to either Art. 96.3 or Art. 1.4. U.N. Doc. A/35/710 (1980).

[41] Sandoz, *Commentary on the Additional Protocols*, supra, note 8, at 522.   [42] Id., at 529–30, fn. 40.

[43] Gasser, "Acts of Terror, 'Terrorism' and International Humanitarian Law," supra, note 23, at 563.

[44] *Prosecutor v. Tadić*, IT-94–1, Appeals Chamber Decision on Jurisdiction (2 Oct. 1995), para. 117.

part of customary international law, and because its fundamental guarantees largely overlap with common Article 3 (which undoubtedly is part of customary law), common Article 3 has almost systematically been preferred as a basis to bring criminal charges [at ad hoc tribunals]."[45]

Additional Protocol II is an effort to "broaden the scope of application of basic humanitarian rules [as] experience demonstrated the inadequacy of the common Article [3]."[46] Additional Protocol II develops and supplements common Article 3 and applies in noninternational armed conflicts, its mere eighteen substantive provisions largely repeating humanitarian norms that are mandated in other treaties. However, "the provisions are so general and incomplete that they cannot be regarded as an adequate guide for the conduct of belligerents."[47] It is not helpful that the drafters had in mind two varieties of internal armed conflicts: one involving major civil war, like that in Spain in the 1930s, and another more like the "contained" civil wars of Nigeria and the Congo, in the 1970s. "Through this definition two levels of internal armed conflicts were created, even as to parties to both the Conventions of 1949 and Protocol II – the lower level, governed by Article 3, and the higher level, governed by Protocol II. Such nice legal distinctions do not make the correct application of the law any easier."[48] Indeed, today the distinction is forgotten and common Article 3, rather than Additional Protocol II, has become the protection invoked in noninternational armed conflicts of every variety.

Nevertheless, Additional Protocol II is a part of today's *jus in bello*. Who is protected by it? Victims of internal or civil armed conflicts. Additional Protocol II Article 4.1, with echoes of common Article 3, specifies that "all persons who do not take a direct part or who have ceased to take part in hostilities" are protected and "shall in all circumstances be treated humanely."

Article 1.2 attempts to make clear when Additional Protocol II does *not* apply: "This Protocol shall not apply to situations of internal disturbances and tensions, such as riots, isolated and sporadic acts of violence and other acts of a similar nature, as not being armed conflict." The same problems of application encountered with common Article 3 apply to Additional Protocol II, however. Who decides whether and when Additional Protocol II becomes operative? When do "sporadic acts of violence" rise to a rebellion or civil war constituting a noninternational conflict?

The International Criminal Tribunal for Rwanda offers guidance in applying Additional Protocol II, writing that an armed conflict may be distinguished from an internal disturbance by the intensity of the fighting and the degree of organization of the parties involved.[49] But what government willingly announces that it is host to an internal revolution so serious as to constitute a noninternational armed conflict? Entrenched authority is more likely to contend that, regardless of the level or breadth of internal violence, the government is in control, the violence is less than sporadic, and it will be contained by the national police or units of the army. "The governmental authorities against which the rebellious forces are engaged, even though these forces may claim to be engaged in efforts to achieve self-determination, describe such opponents as 'terrorists' and refuse to acknowledge that they possess any rights under the law of armed conflict."[50]

---

[45] Guénaël Mettraux, *International Crimes and the Ad Hoc Tribunals* (Oxford: Oxford University Press, 2005), 140.

[46] Roberts and Guelff, supra, note 2, at 481.   [47] Id., at 482.

[48] Baxter, "Modernizing the Law of War," supra, note 4, at 172.

[49] *Prosecutor v. Akayesu*, ICTR-96-4-T, Trial judgment (Sept. 2, 1998), para. 625.

[50] L. C. Green, "'Grave Breaches' or Crimes against Humanity?" 8 *J. of Legal Studies* (1997–8), 19, 20.

Nor should supporters of insurgents be allowed to take refuge behind the tired bromide that "one man's terrorist is another man's freedom fighter." "On this view, there is nothing for theorists and philosophers to do but choose sides, and there is no theory or principle that can guide their choice. But this is an impossible position, for it holds that we cannot recognize, condemn, and actively oppose the murder of innocent people."[51]

4.3.1 Advances in Additional Protocol II

Although Additional Protocol II largely recapitulates noncombatant protections already specified in customary law, or contained in common Article 3, there are provisions worthy of note. The protocol does develop the humanitarian protections of common Article 3. It includes specific provisions for the protection of civilians from attack, as well as adding protection for objects indispensable to the survival of the civilian population. Article 4.3 provides requirements for the care of children, including education, and a ban on the recruitment or participation in hostilities of persons less than age fifteen. The requirement of fair trials of persons charged with offenses, contained in common Article 3, is expanded on by Article 6. The starvation of civilians as a method of combat, allowed in the Lieber Code's Article XVII, is prohibited in Article 14.

4.3.2 Objections to Additional Protocol II

LOAC has always been state-oriented, although that tradition is tested by Additional Protocol I. "The strongly positivist basis of international law, certainly since the 19th century, has focused on the state as the source of legal obligation,"[52] and the source of legal authority and power, as well. Several states, with little concern that they might face internal rebellions, contend (in a turnabout favoring revolutionary groups) that Additional Protocol II is effectively neutered by its implementing requirement: Article 1.1 mandates that Additional Protocol II is applicable only in armed conflicts between the armed forces of a ratifying state "and dissident armed forces or other organized armed groups which ... exercise such control over a part of its territory as to enable them to carry out sustained and concerted military operations and to implement this Protocol." One writer notes that "the provisions in art. 1 of Additional Protocol II, including the requirement of 'territorial administration', exclude the activities of the Irish Republican Army in Ireland, the Basque Separatists in Spain, and the Shining Path in Peru. By confusing the application of Additional Protocol II in this way, states have ensured that international legitimacy is not given to groups that fight within their borders."[53]

Controlling sufficient territory from which to launch military operations is a difficult threshold for a revolutionary group to surmount, one seldom met since the Royalist forces of General Francisco Franco during the Spanish Civil War, in the 1930s. Conflicts in Colombia, El Salvador, Guatemala, Liberia, Rwanda, Sierra Leone, and the former

---

[51] Michael Walzer, *Arguing about War* (New Haven, CT: Yale University Press, 2004), 13.

[52] BGen. Kenneth Watkin, "21st Century Conflict and International Humanitarian Law: Status Quo or Change?" in Michael Schmitt and Jelena Pejic, eds., *International Law and Armed Conflict: Exploring the Faultlines* (Leiden: Martinus Nijhoff, 2007), 265, 272.

[53] Alison Duxbury, "Drawing Lines in the Sand – Characterising Conflicts for the Purposes of Teaching International Humanitarian Law," 8–2 *Melbourne J. of Int'l L.* (2007), 258–72, 269. Footnote omitted.

Yugoslavia, for instance, "have raised questions regarding the extent to which 1977 Geneva Protocol II may be effective in practice."[54] The ICRC responds:

> the three criteria that were finally adopted on the side of the insurgents i.e. – a responsible command, such control over part of the territory as to enable them to carry out sustained and concerted military operations, and the ability to implement the Protocol – restrict the applicability of the Protocol to conflicts of a certain degree of intensity. This means that not all cases of non-international armed conflict are covered, as in the case in common Article 3.[55]

In practice, the three criteria have meant that Additional Protocol II has seldom played a role in noninternational armed conflicts. Examples of its apparent application are Colombia's 1999 ceding of approximately 160,000 square miles of south-central Colombian territory – about the size of Switzerland – to the Fuerzas Armadas Revolucionarias de Colombia (FARC) and Ejército de Liberación Nacional (ELN) terrorist movements,[56] and Pakistan's 2009 conceding the Swat valley to the Taliban.[57] "Practice since 1977 shows that in the instances where Protocol II could be deemed to apply, legitimate governments had had a tendency not to recognize its applicability."[58] The result has been the continued suffering of civilians in Chechnya, Yemen, El Salvador, and Ethiopia, among other states.

4.4 1977 Additional Protocols I and II in U.S. Practice

Shortly after the Geneva conferences formulating the Additional Protocols concluded, the Harvard Law professor R. R. Baxter, a member of the U.S. Delegation, wrote, "The two new Protocols will now have to be submitted to the Senate for its advice and consent prior to ratification. This procedure will probably move quickly, and before long the two new Protocols will be in force for the United States."[59] It was not to be.

The protocols were opened for signature in December 1977, the United States signing both on the first day they were opened. More than thirty years later, America has ratified neither. The United States signed believing that reservations and statements of understanding, common to most international agreements, could cure America's problems with Additional Protocol I. In 1997, Ambassador George Aldrich, head of the U.S. Delegation, wrote, "Looking back ... I deeply regret ... I did not press, within the executive branch of my government, for prompt submission of the Protocols to the Senate. ... I failed to realize that, with the passage of time, those in both [the U.S. State and Defense] Departments who had negotiated and supported the Protocols would be replaced by skeptics and individuals with a different political agenda."[60]

---

[54] Roberts and Guelff, supra, note 2, at 482.

[55] Sandoz, *Commentary on the Additional Protocols*, supra, note 8, at 1349.

[56] Geoff Demarest, "In Colombia – a Terrorist Sanctuary?" *Military Review*, (March–April 2002), n.p.

[57] Jane Perlez, "Pakistan Makes a Taliban Truce, Creating a Haven," NY *Times*, Feb. 17, 2009, A1. "The government announced Monday that it would accept a system of Islamic law in the Swat valley and agreed to a truce, effectively conceding the area as a Taliban sanctuary. ... With the accord, 'the government is ceding a great deal of space' to the militants. ... "

[58] Eve La Haye, *War Crimes in Internal Armed Conflicts* (Cambridge: Cambridge University Press, 2008), 46.

[59] Baxter, "Modernizing the Law of War," supra, note 4, at 182.

[60] George H. Aldrich, "Comments on the Geneva Protocols," 320 *Int'l R. of the Red Cross* (Oct. 31, 1997), n.p. Hays Parks argues that throughout protocol negotiations, the American delegation did not well

Indeed, the Department of State did take aim at Additional Protocol I: "The Protocol grants irregulars a legal status which is at times superior to that accorded regular forces. ... No distinction has ever previously been made under the law of war based on the cause for which one of the parties claims to be fighting. ... Liberation groups can enjoy many of the benefits of the law of war without fulfilling its duties."[61] Additional Protocol II, largely seen as a recapitulation of common Article 3, drew little fire from either the Department of State or Defense.

After nine years of U.S. consideration and debate, on January 29, 1987, President Ronald Reagan recommended to the Senate that it ratify Additional Protocol II.[62] In the transmitting letter he also concluded that the United States could not ratify Additional Protocol I, calling it "fundamentally and irreconcilably flawed."[63] No action was taken by the Senate on either protocol; Additional Protocol II had become too closely associated with Additional Protocol I, and its ratification was not advised.

Between the 1977 conclusion of the protocols' negotiations and 1987, the United States had changed from a proponent of LOAC change to a vocal opponent. "Protocol [I] encroached upon two politically sensitive topics"[64] – CARs and POW status. Initially, the objections of the Department of Defense to Additional Protocol I were not as vociferous as is generally believed. Certainly Defense has consistently held strong objection to Additional Protocol I's broadening of POW status availability, but, Ambassador Aldrich noted, "the Department of Defense was involved at every step of the way in the negotiation of the Protocol, [and] the Joint Chiefs of Staff approved every one of our position papers."[65] As time went on, though, Department of Defense objections hardened.

Political administrations change and new viewpoints dominate. The Additional Protocol negotiations were conducted throughout President Gerald Ford's tenure (1974–7); the resulting Additional Protocols were initially considered during President Jimmy Carter's term (1977–81); their unacceptability was decided in President Reagan's presidency (1981–9).[66] In a period of nine years, the protocols' turnabout, from support to opposition, was complete.

represent the United States Moreover, he writes, "the delegation members prepared their position papers with little or no consultation with the military service staffs, the Office of the Secretary of Defense, or the JCS, and then submitted their position papers to the JCS for approval. ... [There was a] lack of military cognizance over the actions of the U.S. delegation." W. Hays Parks, "Air War and the Law of War," 32–1 *Air Force L. Rev.* (1990), 1, 143.

[61] Judge Abraham D. Sofaer, Legal Adviser, Dept. of State, "Agora: The Rationale for the United States Decision," 82 *AJIL* (1988), 784, 785–6.

[62] Letter of Transmittal from President Ronald Reagan, Protocol II Additional to the 1949 Geneva Conventions, and Relating to the Protection of Victims of Non-International Armed Conflicts, S. Treaty Doc. No. 2, 100th Cong., 1st Sess., at III (1987), reprinted at 81–4 *AJIL* (Oct. 1987), 912, and Cases and Materials, this chapter.

[63] Id.

[64] Theodor Meron, "The Time Has Come for the United States to Ratify Geneva Protocol I," 88 *AJIL* (1994), 678, 679.

Two U.S. representatives to the conferences were Maj. Gen. George S. Prugh, recently retired from active duty as the Judge Advocate General of the Army, and Maj. Gen. Walter D. Reed, on active duty as Assistant Judge Advocate General of the Air Force, soon to become the Judge Advocate General.

[65] George H. Aldrich, "Prospects for United States Ratification of Additional Protocol I to the 1949 Geneva Conventions," 85 *AJIL* (1991), 1, 11.

[66] Several years after Additional Protocol II's failure of ratification, Ambassador Aldrich bitterly noted that "one polemicist, Douglas J. Feith, then [1985] a Deputy Assistant Secretary of Defense, even described the

In late 1987, Hans-Peter Gasser, ICRC legal adviser, commented on the U.S. decision not to seek ratification of Additional Protocol I.

> Failure by the United States to ratify Protocol I would not render that treaty inoperational, because 68 states from different parts of the world are already bound by it. In addition, many other administrations are preparing to ratify it. . . .
>
> Failure to ratify by a major power such as the United States would deprive the world of a common framework for the humanitarian rules governing armed conflicts. It would hinder the development and acceptance of universal standards in a field where they are particularly needed: armed conflict. . . .
>
> Representations by a nonparty to Protocol I regarding violations . . . might have less impact than if they came from a state that had itself formally undertaken to respect those rules.
>
> I trust that the United States will eventually ratify not only Protocol II but also Protocol I, as this is truly "law in the service of mankind."[67]

"The controversial strictures of Protocol I preclude any chance of its achieving universal acceptance."[68] Nevertheless, a broad international acceptance of both protocols approaching universal acceptance has been achieved. As of this writing, 174 states have ratified Additional Protocol I. Additional Protocol II has been ratified by 168. (Currently, 192 states are represented in the U.N. General Assembly.)[69] Year by year, the number of states ratifying the protocols increases, along with the births of new states that quickly become new accessions.

In 1987, adding pressure on America to accept Protocol I, a U.S. Department of State Deputy legal adviser announced that the United States affirmed that it considers fifty-nine of Additional Protocol I's ninety-one substantive Articles to be customary international law. When those fifty-nine articles are involved, all nations are bound whether or not they have ratified the Additional Protocol.[70] Twenty years after the protocol's rejection by the president, the United States considered itself bound by 65 percent of the Protocol.[71] In January 2001, the Persian Gulf War, Operations Desert Storm, and Desert

---

negotiations as a 'sinister and sad tale' and a 'prostitution of the law.'" Id., at 4. At the time of the 9/11 attacks on America, Mr. Feith was the under secretary of defense for policy, and a leading advocate for the invasion of Iraq. Thomas E. Ricks, *Fiasco* (New York: Penguin, 2006), 31, 55. Feith boasts, "I helped counter an effort by terrorist groups and their state supporters to co-opt the Geneva Conventions. . . . The arguments I used in the mid-1980s to defend the Conventions resurfaced after 9/11, and helped shape President Bush's decision on the legal status of enemies captured in the war on terrorism." Douglas J. Feith, *War and Decision* (New York: Harper, 2008), 38.

[67] Hans-Peter Gasser, "An Appeal for Ratification by the United States," 81 *AJIL* (Oct. 1987), 912, 924–5.

[68] Dinstein, "Comments on Protocol I," supra, note 39, n.p.

[69] The United Nations Web site lists 193 G.A. members, as of July 2015, (www.un.org/members/list.shtmo). The ICRC Web site lists 196 member states, including the Holy See and the Cook Islands, neither of which is a U.N. member (www.icrc.org/IHL.nsf/(SPF)/party_main_treaties).

[70] Mike Matheson, "Additional Protocol I as Expressions of Customary International Law," 2–2 *Am. U. J. Int'l L. & Policy* (Fall 1987), 415, 425. The Articles confirmed as customary law, in the U.S. view, are Article 5 (subject to refusal by the state in question), Articles 10 through 35, Article 37, 38, 40, 42, 51 (except the prohibition of reprisals in this and subsequent Articles), 52, and 54, Articles 57 through 60, and Articles 62, 63, and 70, and Articles 73 through 90. Notably, the Matheson confirmation has not been repeated in further, or later, official government statements.

[71] The Matheson announcement, made in his official capacity as a State Department Deputy Legal Adviser and indicating the U.S., rather than a personal, position, has been called "overbroad" (2005 *Operational Law Handbook* [Charlottesville, VA: Int'l and Operational Law Dept., 2005], errata sheet), and "personal

Shield commenced. The Allied coalition included British, Canadian, Egyptian, and French forces, as well as Gulf Cooperation Council forces (Saudi Arabia, Bahrain, Qatar, the United Arab Emirates [UAE], Oman, and Kuwait), along with medical support from Japan, Poland, and Hungary, and basing rights in Saudi Arabia, Italy, Spain, Germany, Greece, and Turkey.[72] Most of that coalition had already ratified Additional Protocol I and followed most of its provisions. To a large extent the United States did so, as well, because of the need to coordinate command and control issues, air operations, and rules of engagement within the coalition. As the Defense Department's report on the war observes, the United States followed Protocol I because numerous provisions are "generally regarded as a codification of the customary practice of nations, and therefore [as] binding on all."[73]

In other words, historical experience is that when the United States is engaged in coalition warfare with Protocol I–ratifying states as allies, America is also effectively bound, despite not having ratified. Because every U.S. ally, save Israel and Turkey,[*] has ratified, virtually any combat operation involving an ally will effectively bind the United States to follow its basic provisions. America can disregard Protocol I only when engaged in armed conflict on its own and without allies – and then it can disregard only those provisions that are contended not to be customary law.

In 1994, Theodor Meron urged that "international reality and a fresh view of U.S. interests have compelled rethinking of U.S. attitudes" and "power implies responsibility and invites leadership. By ratifying the Protocol, we would be recognizing the former and accepting the latter."[74]

Prospects for U.S. ratification of Additional Protocol I remain distinctly dim, but it hardly matters. U.S. armed forces are, in many respects, already effectively bound.

Is American resistance to Additional Protocol I principled and idealistic, or is it foolish and self-defeating, or a bit of all of those things? In a scathing review of the protocol that captured the frustrations of many Protocol opponents, Hays Parks wrote:

> The ICRC is unqualified to draft provisions regarding the regulation of modern war. And while some of the "experts" who attended its preparatory conferences in 1971 and 1972 may have known something about the law of war, their knowledge of modern warfighting was weak. The draft provisions bring to mind John Galsworthy's statement that, "Idealism increases in direct proportion to one's distance from the problem.". . . . The ICRC's composition (as a private organization of private citizens in a neutral nation) betrayed it, through lack of knowledge of modern warfighting, and through

---

opinion" (W. Hays Parks, "'Special Forces' Wear of Non-Standard Uniforms," 4 *Chicago J. of Int'l L.* (2003), 519, fn. 55), and "no longer considered 'authoritative'" (Charles Garraway, "'England Does Not Love Coalitions': Does Anything Change?" in Anthony M. Helm, ed., *International Law Studies*, Vol. 82. *The Law of War in the 21st Century: Weaponry and the Use of Force* [Newport, RI: Naval War College, 2006], 234, 238). None of the authors cited, however, provides a basis for his assertions that the Matheson statement is not authoritative. No retreat from or disavowal of the Matheson announcement has ever been issued by any branch of the U.S. government. (Nor has it been repeated, however.)

[72] U.S. Dept. of Defense, *Conduct of the Persian Gulf War: Final Report to Congress* (Washington, DC: GPO, 1992), 21–2.

[73] Meron, "Time Has Come for the United States to Ratify," supra, note 64, at 681, citing the Dept. of Defense Final Report to Congress regarding the Persian Gulf War.

[*] Should Turkey gain admittance to the European Union, it must ratify the Additional Protocols as a membership requirement.

[74] Meron, "Time Has Come for the United States to Ratify," supra, note 64, at 680, 686.

the ICRC's alliance throughout the drafting and negotiating process with the governments (though not the military) of Switzerland and Sweden. ... Finally, the ICRC undertook a major and commendable step – though a calculated risk – to introduce the law of war to the Third World. Its effort failed miserably, for instead of requiring the nations of the Third World to rise to certain minimum standards of conduct in combat, the law of war succumbed to the tyranny of the majority. ... The new law of war contained in Protocols I and II regrettably takes a step back by reverting to concepts regarding the justness of one's cause that were expressly rejected by the 1949 Geneva Conventions.[75]

Over time, much of the world, rather than rejecting the protocols, has learned to live with them and, in some respects, appreciate them. In 2004, the Canadian brigadier general Kenneth Watkin, a friend of America, and judge advocate general of the Canadian Armed Forces from 2006 to 2010, wrote:

The United States has not ratified Additional Protocol I. As that Protocol was drafted specifically to deal with the changing nature of conflict associated with guerrilla warfare and national liberation movements ... the unwillingness to adjust the law to meet the realities of those conflicts demonstrates a preference for the mid-[twentieth] century legal status quo. Such resistance to change, particularly by dominant nation states, has been a regular feature in the development of international humanitarian law.[76]

Perhaps. Should captured al Qaeda fighters be granted POW-like status? Should the Taliban be protected by the Geneva Conventions? A British military writer notes, "The existence of the Protocol cannot be ignored, nor the fact that the majority of the United States' traditional allies are parties to it. ... We need to know what the United States position is and uncertainty simply undermines the trust that is vital for coalition operations."[77]

Politics has always played a role in LOAC. In 1977 Additional Protocols I and II, its role has been particularly significant.

The status of Protocol I's Article 75, which grants a wide range of human rights ("Fundamental guarantees") to military and civilian prisoners in international armed conflicts, is of particular importance. In his 1987 address at American University's school of law, Mike Matheson, the U.S. Department of State deputy legal adviser, seemed to confirm that the United States views Article 75 as customary international law.[78] In 2006, a plurality of the Supreme Court, in *Hamdan*, concluded that the trial protections set forth in Article 75 are customary law.[79] "The Obama administration announced in 2011 that the United States would apply Article 75 out of a 'sense of legal obligation' in international armed conflicts, but the administration neither stated that Article 75 is

---

[75] Parks, "Air War and the Law of War," supra, note 60, at 219.

[76] Watkin, "21st Century Conflict and International Humanitarian Law," supra, note 52, at 282.

[77] Garraway, "'England Does Not Love Coalitions,'" in Helm, ed., *International Law Studies*, Vol. 82, supra, note 71, at 238.

[78] Mr. Matheson's words were that the guarantees in Art. 75 were among those parts of Additional Protocol I that the United States believed "should be observed and in due course recognized as customary law." John B. Bellinger and Vijay M. Padmanabhan, "Detention Operations in Contemporary Conflicts: Four Challenges for the Geneva Conventions and Other Existing Law," 105–2 *AJIL* (April 2011), 201, 207.

[79] *Hamdan v. Rumsfeld*, 548 U.S. 557, 633 (2006).

customary international law nor agreed to apply Article 75 in non-international armed conflicts."[80] The administration did not *deny* Article 75's customary status, even in noninternational armed conflicts, however.

4.5 2005 Additional Protocol III

At the end of Additional Protocol I, Annex I identifies persons and objects protected by the 1949 Geneva Conventions and Protocol I. Article 4 of Annex I of Protocol I pictures three emblems protecting, inter alia, medical and religious personnel. The protective symbol agreed upon was, of course, a red cross. It is universally known that a red cross on a white field, worn on a helmet, brassard, motor vehicle, aircraft, or ship, identifies a medic (in the U.S. Army), corpsman (in the U.S. Marine Corps and Navy), medical worker, or medical transport or ship. The symbol indicates that the wearer or object is not a lawful target and should not be fired on.

The Red Cross protective emblem was adopted at an October 1863 meeting of the International Standing Committee for Aid to Wounded Soldiers. The minutes of the meeting give no reason for selecting that symbol, although there certainly is no suggestion that it was religiously inspired.[81] The participants sought "a single simple sign, recognizable from a distance, known to all and identical for friend and foe: a sign of the respect due to the wounded and to the medical personnel: a sign which would have the backing of the law."[82] Article 7 of the first 1864 Geneva Convention mandated the red cross on a white background as that sign.

During the Russo-Turkish War (1876–8), Turkey attributed a religious significance to the red cross and, in a fait accompli, informed the Swiss depository of the first Geneva convention that, although Turkey would respect the red cross, its own forces would use a red crescent as the protective sign. This was the first of many divisive suggestions for additional protective signs. The ICRC, possessed only of moral authority, could only argue (and hope) for no further unilateral derogations.

By the time of the 1907 Hague Peace Conference, the ICRC had reached a modus vivendi with the Turks' use of the red crescent, essentially agreeing to their use of a differing sign but urging there be no others. The next dissent arose at the peace conference itself. Persia opted to employ the lion and red sun in place of the red cross, leading to employment of a third protective sign. It, along with the red crescent, was finally officially recognized in the 1929 Geneva Convention for the Amelioration of the Condition of the Wounded and Sick.

At a 1949 diplomatic conference in Geneva, the new State of Israel sought recognition of the red shield of David, the familiar six-point star, already used by the Israelis in the 1948 war with Palestine, as a fourth protective emblem. Israel's effort was rebuffed. At the same conference, Iran, the successor state to Persia, agreed to give up its special emblem, the lion and red sun.

At subsequent international conferences, Israel continued to seek authority to use the red shield of David, resisted by Arab states that considered the six-point star a religious symbol. The disagreement prevented Israel, unlikely to adopt a cross or crescent as an

---

[80] Bellinger and Padmanabhan, "Detention Operations in Contemporary Conflicts," supra, note 78.

[81] François Bugnion, *The Emblem of the Red Cross: A Brief History* (Geneva: ICRC, 1977), 11–12.

[82] Id., at 7.

emblem, from joining the International Federation of Red Cross and Red Crescent Societies, which enjoyed near-universal membership. Meanwhile, Israel employed the red shield of David protective sign in its armed conflicts.

Over the years, other emerging states proposed their own new protective emblems: Afghanistan proposed a red archway; India, a red wheel; Lebanon, a red cedar tree; a red rhinoceros was proposed by Sudan; Syria, a red palm; Zaire, a red lamb; and, in a short-lived effort, Sri Lanka sought a red swastika.

Finally, in December 2005, Switzerland convened a diplomatic conference at which Additional Protocol III was adopted, adding a new, third, neutrality emblem, "the red crystal." The red crystal is a red, four-sided, diamond-shaped sign with thick borders.[83] A state opting to adopt the red crystal may add its own smaller emblem to the interior of the open diamond. Israel will add the red shield of David's six-pointed star. Indicative of the politics involved in Additional Protocol III's adoption,

> Syria ... mounted efforts to block the protocol. ... Adoption of the emblem removes a long-standing barrier to full membership [in the Red Cross/Red Crescent movement] of the Magen David Adom (MDA), Israel's national [Red Cross] society ... and removes a major irritant in relations between the nongovernmental American Red Cross and the International Red Cross and Red Crescent Movement. (The American Red Cross has ... withheld more than $35 million in dues from the International Federation of Red Cross and Red Crescent Societies to protest the failure to resolve the issue.)[84]

Upon adoption of the red crystal the *New York Times* huffed, "About time."[85] The ICRC warned, "The danger of proliferation [of neutrality emblems] therefore cannot be ignored. The ICRC for its part will not endorse a solution allowing every State and every National Society to use the emblem of its choice."[86] There will be no new emblems approved in the near future. Additional Protocol III entered into force in early 2007 and quickly began gathering ratifications and accessions. The United States became a state party in March 2007.

4.6 Summary

All three Additional Protocols are weighted with international and domestic political freight. Agree with them or not, Additional Protocols I, II, and III must be taken into account.

Additional Protocol I remains contested. "To its supporters [CARs] was an acknowledgement of the failure of traditional international law to address the needs of colonized peoples. Critics of national liberation movements point to the illegality of the whole strategy of guerrilla warfare, the blurring of the combatant/non-combatant distinction and the resultant impossible burden on their opponents."[87] This is not an argument that either side will win.

---

[83] The emblem may be seen at www.icrc.org/eng. The ICRC *Commentary* to Additional Protocol III is found at 865 *Int'l Rev. of the Red Cross* (March 2007), 178–207.

[84] John R. Crook, ed. "Contemporary Practice of the United States, 100–1 *AJIL* (2006), 244. Footnote omitted.

[85] "Message to Red Cross: About Time," NY *Times*, Dec. 9, 2005, A36.

[86] François Bugnion, *Red Cross, Red Crescent, Red Crystal* (Geneva: ICRC, 2007), 31.

[87] Luc Reydams, "'A la Guerre Comme à la Guerre': Patterns of Armed Conflict, Humanitarian Law Responses and New Challenges," 864 *Int'l Rev. of the Red Cross* (Dec. 2006), 729, 743.

The United States, frequently called on to provide combatant forces to keep or enforce peace in the world's far corners, to protect humanitarian missions, and to end armed incidents in violent places, has reason to object to Additional Protocol I, most particularly with regard to the protocol's relaxing the criteria for POW status. States with lesser stakes in the realities of *jus in bello* can more easily accept Protocol I's "fairly bold innovations" and object to the U.S. position. Still, influential voices within the United States urge ratification of the 1977 protocols, with understandings and reservations, as originally envisioned, and as many U.S. allies have done.

The United States remains unlikely to ratify Protocol I, but that is not as significant as it once was. "The Reagan administration won a battle in rejecting the Protocol I amendments to the Geneva Conventions in 1987. But it lost the war, for by 2001 almost all of our allies had ratified Protocol I."[88] Having once accepted that 65 percent of the protocol is customary international law, and necessarily forced to comply with the remaining portion of the protocol when operating in combat coalitions in which all of our allies have ratified, United States in its rejection of Additional Protocol I nears irrelevance. Additional Protocol I "is thoroughly represented in U.S. military doctrine, practice and rules of engagement."[89] The army's school for military lawyers notes in its 2008 *Operational Law Handbook,* "This difference in obligation has not proven to be a hindrance to U.S. allied or coalition operations."[90] The same *Handbook* adds, regarding targeting restrictions in Additional Protocol I, "These rules are not United States law but should be *considered* because of the pervasive international acceptance of AP I and II."[91]

Additional Protocol II, as did Additional Protocol I, saw its first opportunity for adjudication in the International Criminal Tribunals for the Former Yugoslavia and Rwanda. Additional Protocol I has provided a rich body of appellate case law. Not so, Additional Protocol II, however.

> The *ad hoc* Tribunals have produced very little jurisprudence related to Additional Protocol II ... and no accused has been convicted for a violation of the Protocol. ... The limited categories of armed conflicts to which Additional Protocol II may be said to apply and doubts as to the extent to which it is now part of customary international law have deterred the Prosecution ... from entering the realm of Additional Protocol II with much enthusiasm, preferring instead to rely on common Article 3.[92]

Even the head of the U.S. Delegation to the Protocol negotiations could find little good to say: "Protocol II ... affords very limited protections and has escape clauses designed to make its applicability easily deniable. In the end, the only useful result of Protocol II may

---

[88] Jack Goldsmith, *The Terror Presidency* (New York: Norton, 2007), 117.

[89] Maj. Jefferson D. Reynolds, "Collateral Damage on the 21st Century Battlefield: Enemy Exploitation of the Law of Armed Conflict and the Struggle for a Moral High Ground," 56 *Air Force L. Rev.* (Jan. 2005), 23–4. Language in several joint armed service publications says as much. In Joint Publication 3–63, *Detainee Operations* (13 Nov. 2014), pp. i-ii, for example: "Commanders of forces operating as part of a multinational (alliance or coalition) military command should follow multinational doctrine and proced-ures ratified by the United States. For doctrine and procedures not ratified by the United States, commanders should evaluate and follow the multinational command's doctrine and procedures, where applicable and consistent with U.S. law, regulations, and doctrine."

[90] Maj. Marie Anderson and Emily Zukauskas, eds., *Operational Law Handbook*, 2008 (Charlottesville, VA: Int'l and Operational Law Dept., The Judge Advocate General's Legal Center and School, 2008), 15.

[91] Id., at 22. Emphasis in original.   [92] Mettraux, *International Crimes*, supra, note 45, at 144.

be to make it somewhat more likely that [common] Article 3 . . . may be found applicable in lieu of Protocol II."[93]

Overall, "neither the 1949 Geneva Conventions nor the Additional Protocols are 'perfect' documents. They reflect the compromise of negotiation inherent in the treaty making process."[94] If not ideal, however, they remain guides to which the international community can look.

The effect of Additional Protocol III's adding a red crystal (with an additional interior symbol permitted) to the red cross and red crescent protective signs remains to be seen. Perhaps we will see a red rhinoceros, after all. For some combatant forces, protective signs are becoming a moot point for medical personnel. Israel directs its uniformed medical personnel not to wear any identifying protective sign in combat. On Iraqi and Afghan battlefields, many U.S. corpsmen and medics forgo red cross markings on armbands and helmets because the enemy specially targets medical personnel. In the era of transnational terror, ununiformed insurgency, and frequent disregard for LOAC, the red crystal, like the red cross, may become merely a convenient aiming point.

Finally, an Australian law professor provides a real-world perspective: "I will continue to discuss the importance of the legal characterisation of an armed conflict, the legal distinction between international and non-international armed conflict, and the recognition of an internationalized armed conflict. But . . . these are just that – legal distinctions – and do not define the suffering of peoples who are affected by violence and conflict . . . "[95]

CASES AND MATERIALS

THE UNITED KINGDOM'S MANUAL OF THE LAW OF ARMED CONFLICT

Introduction. In considering what LOAC applies, when is an armed conflict "international" and when is it "noninternational"? The distinction is not always clear. The United Kingdom's 2004 Manual of the Law of Armed Conflict[96] provides excellent guidance to recognizing a noninternational armed conflict and, by implication, an international armed conflict. Also note paragraph 15.32, relating the United Kingdom's view of war crimes and grave breaches in internal armed conflicts.

1.33.3. International law has historically regulated relations between states. A state's internal affairs, including responsibility for the maintenance of law and order and the

---

[93] Aldrich, "Some Reflections on the Origins of the 1977 Geneva Protocols," supra, note 22, at 136.

[94] Watkin, "21st Century Conflict and International Humanitarian Law," in Schmitt and Pejic, *International Law and Armed Conflict,* supra, note 52, at 292.

[95] Duxbury, "Drawing Lines in the Sand," supra, note 53, at 272.

[96] United Kingdom Ministry of Defence, *The Manual of the Law of Armed Conflict* (Oxford: Oxford University Press, 2004), footnotes omitted.

defence of territorial integrity against domestic insurgents, were largely regarded as the exclusive business of the state concerned. The notion of international law regulating a conflict occurring within a state would generally have been regarded as being at variance with this approach. However, it was possible for insurgents in an internal armed conflict to be recognized as belligerents and for the law of armed conflict to apply.

1.33.4. The internal use of force against criminal and terrorist activity is not regulated by the law of armed conflict unless the activity is of such a nature as to amount to armed conflict. However, human rights law would apply. Sometimes, as a matter of policy, governments and armed forces have applied basic principles drawn from the law of armed conflict, in such matters as the treatment and interrogation of detainees, even in situations in which the law of armed conflict did not formally apply.

1.33.6. In practice, many armed conflicts have at the same time certain aspects which have the character of an internal armed conflict, while other aspects are clearly international. For example, an internal conflict may become internationalized, with the armed forces of outside states actively involved. Different parts of the law of armed conflict may, therefore, apply to different phases or aspects of the conflict. There is thus a spectrum of violence ranging from internal disturbances through to full international armed conflict with different legal regimes applicable at the various levels of that spectrum. It is often necessary for an impartial organization, such as the International Committee of the Red Cross, to seek agreement between the factions as to the rules to be applied.

3.4.1. Conflicts of this nature [in which peoples are fighting against colonial domination, alien occupation, or racist regimes] within the territory of a state had hitherto been regarded as internal. Under the Protocol [I], such conflicts are treated as if they were international armed conflicts.

3.6.1. The point at which situations of internal disturbances and tensions develop into an armed conflict is open to interpretation. Although common Article 3 specifically provides that its application does not affect the legal status of the parties to a conflict, states have often been reluctant to admit to such a development. Traditional factors that might be used to indicate the existence of an armed conflict, such as recognition of a status of insurgency by third parties ... have lessened in importance. ... Whilst states may not be willing to admit to the application of common Article 3 as a matter of law, its provisions are frequently applied in fact.

3.9. The application of the law of armed conflict to internal hostilities thus depends on a number of factors. In the first place, it does not apply at all unless an armed conflict exists. If an armed conflict exists, the provisions of common Article 3 apply. Should the dissidents achieve a degree of success and exercise the necessary control over a part of the territory, the provisions of Additional Protocol II come into force. Finally, if the conflict is recognized as a conflict falling within Additional Protocol I, Article 1(4) [colonial domination, alien occupation, racist regimes], it becomes subject to the Geneva Conventions and Protocol I.

15.1.1. In practice many conflicts since 1945 have had the characteristics of both international and non-international armed conflicts. For example, in many cases, outside states have become involved in support of the rival parties in what may have originated as an internal conflict. In such cases, the more fully developed rules applicable in international armed conflict may be applied. ...

15.2.1. 'Situations of internal disturbances and tension, such as riots, isolated and sporadic acts of violence and other acts of a similar nature' do not amount to armed conflict. These situations are covered mainly by the municipal laws of states. The main body of international law applicable to these situations is human rights law, including the law relating to crimes against humanity and genocide, but in addition, as a matter of policy, states have sometimes taken the view that, even if a particular situation is not an armed conflict under international law, the relevant principles and rules of the law of armed conflict will be applied.

15.3. Once the level of violence has reached the intensity of an armed conflict, the provisions of common Article 3 to the Geneva Conventions apply.

15.3.1. The point at which internal disturbances and tensions develop into an armed conflict is open to interpretation. Attempts to define the term 'armed conflict' have proved unsuccessful and although common Article 3 specifically provides that its application does not affect the legal status of the parties to a conflict, states have been, and always will be, reluctant to admit that a state of armed conflict exists. Factors that may determine whether an internal armed conflict exists include whether the rebels possess organized armed forces, control territory, and ensure respect for the law of armed conflict. ... The terms of common Article 3 are really no more than 'rules which were already recognized as essential in all civilized countries, and embodied in the national legislation of the States in question, long before the Convention was signed'. It follows that whilst states may not be willing to admit to the application of common Article 3 as a matter of law, its provisions are frequently applied in practice.

15.4.1. These provisions do not preclude the application of the relevant national law – except to the extent that a particular rule of national law directly conflicts with any of the provisions of common Article 3. Thus captured insurgents, whether nationals of the state or not, may be tried for offenses they have committed, provided that the basic requirements of the law of armed conflict for humane treatment and judicial guarantees are observed. Captured insurgents are not legally entitled to be treated as prisoners of war. Common Article 3 does, however, state that the parties should 'further endeavour to bring into force, by means of special agreements, all or part' of the main provisions of the Conventions. Thus there is nothing to prevent greater application of the Conventions, for example, the conferring of status akin to that of prisoners of war, where agreed and appropriate.

15.5.5. There has been no consensus between states as to the extent to which rules of the law of armed conflict other than those specifically laid down in treaties apply to internal armed conflicts. The jurisprudence of the International Criminal Tribunal for the former Yugoslavia suggests that some of those rules do apply and the Rome Statute of the International Criminal Court ... lists a series of acts which, if committed in internal armed conflicts, are considered war crimes. While it is not always easy to determine the exact content of the customary international law applicable in non-international armed conflicts, guidance can be derived from the basic principles of military necessity, humanity, distinction, and proportionality. ...

15.32. Although the treaties governing internal armed conflicts contain no grave breach provisions, customary law recognizes that serious violations of those treaties can amount to punishable war crimes.

PROSECUTOR V. TADIĆ

(IT-94–1-A) Defense Motion for Interlocutory Appeal on Jurisdiction
(2 October 2, 1995)

Introduction. *Case law, one of the primary sources of LOAC, is helpful in interpreting its provisions. The ICTY is a rich source of modern LOAC case law even though binding only the parties before the court. Early in the long-running Tadić case, the ICTY's Appeals Chamber addressed the question of when an armed conflict arises, but provided little guidance in differentiating between international and non-international armed conflicts. From the tribunal's order:*

> We find that an armed conflict exists whenever there is a resort to armed force between States or protracted armed violence between governmental authorities and organized armed groups within a State. International humanitarian law applies from the initiation of such armed conflicts and extends beyond the cessation of hostilities until a general conclusion of peace is reached; or, in the case of internal conflicts, a peaceful settlement is achieved. Until that moment, international humanitarian law continues to apply in the whole territory of the warring States or, in the case of internal conflicts, the whole territory under the control of a party, whether or not actual combat takes place there.[97]

Two years later, the Tadić Trial Chamber was more helpful:

> The test applied [for] the existence of an armed conflict for the purposes of the rules contained in common Article 3 [a non-international armed conflict] focuses on two aspects of a conflict; the intensity of the conflict and the organization of the parties to the conflict. In an armed conflict of an internal or mixed character, these closely related criteria are used solely for the purpose, at a minimum, of distinguishing an armed conflict from banditry, unorganized and short-lived insurrections, or terrorist activities, which are not subject to international humanitarian law.[98]

Conclusion. For a fuller discussion of the Tadić court's findings on this issue, see Chapter 5, Cases and Materials.

Commentary to 1949 Geneva Convention I: For the Amelioration of the Condition of the Wounded and Sick in Armed Forces in the Field

Introduction. *The* Commentary *to Convention I provides a brief but instructive discussion of the distinction between international and noninternational armed conflicts.* [99]

What is meant by "armed conflict not of an international character"? That was the burning question which arose again and again at the Diplomatic Conference. The expression was so general, so vague, that many of the delegations feared that it might be taken to cover any act committed by force of arms – any form of anarchy, rebellion, or even plain banditry. ... These different conditions, although in no way obligatory, constitute convenient criteria ... they are as follows:

---

[97] *Prosecutor v. Tadić*, supra, note 44, at para. 70.
[98] *Prosecutor v. Tadić*, IT-94–1-T, Judgment (May 7, 1997), para. 562. Footnotes omitted.
[99] Jean S. Pictet, ed., *Commentary, I Geneva Convention* (Geneva: ICRC, 1952), Art. 3.1, at 49–50.

(1) That the party in revolt against the *de jure* Government possesses an organized military force, an authority responsible for its acts, acting within a determinate territory and having the means of respecting and ensuring respect for the Convention.

(2) The legal Government is obliged to have recourse to the regular military forces against insurgents organized as military and in possession of a part of the national territory.

(3) (a) That the *de jure* Government has recognized the insurgents as belligerents; or (b) that it has claimed for itself the rights of a belligerent; or (c) that it has accorded the insurgents recognition as belligerents for the purposes only of the present Convention; or (d) that the dispute has been admitted to the agenda of the Security Council or the General Assembly of the United Nations as being a threat to international peace, a breach of the peace, or an act of aggression.

(4) (a) That the insurgents have an organization purporting to have the characteristics of a State.
(b) That the insurgent civil authority exercises *de facto* authority over persons within a determinate territory.
(c) That the armed forces act under the direction of the organized civil authority and are prepared to observe the ordinary laws of war.
(d) That the insurgent civil authority agrees to be bound by the provisions of the Convention.

That above criteria are useful as a means of distinguishing a genuine armed conflict from a mere act of banditry or an unorganized and short-lived insurrection.

Does this mean that Article 3 is not applicable in cases where armed strife breaks out in a country, but does not fulfil any of the above conditions (which are not obligatory and are only mentioned as an indication)? We do not subscribe to this view. We think, on the contrary, that the Article should be applied as widely as possible. ... No Government can object to respecting, in its dealings with internal enemies, whatever the nature of the conflict between it and them, a few essential rules which it in fact respects daily, under its own laws, even when dealing with common criminals.

Conclusion. *For a thoughtful argument that Pictet's criteria for the finding of internal armed conflict are too broad, allowing its invocation in situations not intended by the drafters, see: Lindsay Moir,* The Law of International Armed Conflict *(Cambridge: Cambridge University Press, 2002), 34–42.*

LETTER OF TRANSMITTAL: 1977 ADDITIONAL PROTOCOL II

Introduction. *Moving beyond the question of when a conflict within a single state constitutes an armed conflict within the meaning of common Article 3, recall that the United States has signed, but not ratified, the two 1977 Additional Protocols to the 1949 Geneva Conventions. Could U.S. objections to the Protocols be satisfied through reservations and statements of understanding, as have the objections of many U.S. allies? Are U.S. objections little more than domestic politics, or are they grounded in principled objections to significant issues? Does President Ronald Reagan's letter to the Senate*

*requesting the required advice and consent for the ratification of Additional Protocol II
shed light on these questions?*

The White House, January 29, 1987
   To the Senate of the United States:

   I transmit herewith, for the advice and consent of the Senate to ratification, Protocol II
   Additional to the Geneva Conventions of 12 August 1949, concluded at Geneva on June
   10, 1977. I also enclose for the information of the Senate the report of the Department of
   State on the Protocol.

The United States has traditionally been in the forefront of efforts to codify and
improve the international rules of humanitarian law in armed conflict, with the
objective of giving the greatest possible protection to victims of such conflicts, consistent with legitimate military requirements. The agreement that I am transmitting today
is, with certain exceptions, a positive step toward this goal. Its ratification by the United
States will assist us in continuing to exercise leadership in the international community
in these matters.
   The Protocol is described in detail in the attached report of the Department of State.
Protocol II to the 1949 Geneva Conventions is essentially an expansion of the fundamental humanitarian provisions contained in the 1949 Geneva Conventions with respect to
non-international armed conflicts, including humane treatment and basic due process
for detained persons, protection of the wounded, sick and medical units, and protection
of noncombatants from attack and deliberate starvation. If these fundamental rules were
observed, many of the worst human tragedies of current internal armed conflicts could be
avoided. In particular, among other things, the mass murder of civilians is made illegal,
even if such killings would not amount to genocide because they lacked racial or
religious motives. ... This Protocol makes clear that any deliberate killing of a noncombatant in the course of a non-international armed conflict is a violation of the laws of
war and a crime against humanity, and is therefore also punishable as murder.
   While I recommend that the Senate grant advice and consent to this agreement, I have
at the same time concluded that the United States cannot ratify a second agreement on
the law of armed conflict negotiated during the same period. I am referring to Protocol
I additional to the 1949 Geneva Conventions, which would revise the rules applicable to
international armed conflicts. Like all other efforts associated with the International
Committee of the Red Cross, this agreement has certain meritorious elements. But
Protocol I is fundamentally and irreconcilably flawed. It contains provisions that would
undermine humanitarian law and endanger civilians in war. One of its provisions, for
example, would automatically treat as an international conflict any so-called "war of
national liberation." Whether such wars are international or non-international should
turn exclusively on objective reality, not on one's view of the moral qualities of each
conflict. To rest on such subjective distinctions based on a war's alleged purposes would
politicize humanitarian law and eliminate the distinction between international and
non-international conflicts. It would give special status to "wars of national liberation,"
an ill-defined concept expressed in vague, subjective, politicized terminology. Another
provision would grant combatant status to irregular forces even if they do not satisfy the
traditional requirements to distinguish themselves from the civilian population and
otherwise comply with the laws of war. This would endanger civilians among whom

terrorists and other irregulars attempt to conceal themselves. These problems are so fundamental in character that they cannot be remedied through reservations, and I therefore have decided not to submit the Protocol to the Senate in any form, and I would invite an expression of the sense of the Senate that it shares this view. Finally, the Joint Chiefs of Staff have also concluded that a number of the provisions of the Protocol are militarily unacceptable.

It is unfortunate that Protocol I must be rejected. We would have preferred to ratify such a convention, which as I said contains certain sound elements. But we cannot allow other nations of the world, however numerous, to impose upon us and our allies and friends an unacceptable and thoroughly distasteful price for joining a convention drawn to advance the laws of war. In fact, we must not, and need not, give recognition and protection to terrorist groups as a price for progress in humanitarian law.

The time has come for us to devise a solution for this problem, with which the United States is from time to time confronted. In this case, for example, we can reject Protocol I as a reference for humanitarian law, and at the same time devise an alternative reference for the positive provisions of Protocol I that could be of real humanitarian benefit if generally observed by parties to international armed conflicts. We are therefore in the process of consulting with our allies to develop appropriate methods for incorporating these positive provisions into the rules that govern our military operations, and as customary international law. I will advise the Senate of the results of this initiative as soon as it is possible to do so.

I believe that these actions are a significant step in defense of traditional humanitarian law and in opposition to the intense efforts of terrorist organizations and their supporters to promote the legitimacy of their aims and practices. The repudiation of Protocol I is one additional step, at the ideological level so important to terrorist organizations, to deny these groups legitimacy as international actors.

Therefore I request that the Senate act promptly to give advice and consent to the ratification of the agreement I am transmitting today, subject to the understandings and reservations that are described more fully in the attached report. I would also invite an expression of the sense of the Senate that it shares the view that the United States should not ratify Protocol I, thereby reaffirming its support for traditional humanitarian law, and its opposition to the politicization of that law by groups that employ terrorist practices.

Ronald Reagan

Conclusion. *The Seanate did not provide advice and consent regarding Additional Protocol II, of course. On 7 March 2011, President Obama again submitted Protocol II to the Senate for its advice and consent.*[100] *Years later, no action has been taken.*

---

[100] White House Fact Sheet: New Actions on Guantánamo and Detention Policy (March 7, 2011), available online.

Law of Armed Conflict and International Humanitarian Law: A Framework

5 Conflict Status

5.0 Introduction

On a most basic level, essentials of the law of armed conflict/international humanitarian law (LOAC/IHL) are 1907 Hague Regulation IV, the four 1949 Geneva Conventions, and 1977 Additional Protocols I and II. In what circumstances do they apply, and how do they interact? In a given case, do they all apply, do they apply only in part, or do they apply at all?

Now we can resolve those questions, as well as the first of the two questions a law of war student should always be prepared to answer: What is the conflict status? (The second foundational question, addressed in the next chapter, is, What is the status of the individuals involved in the conflict?) In determining conflict status, one asks what law of war, if any, applies in the armed conflict under consideration.

It is not always an obvious determination. "The problem is that the Geneva Conventions do not provide an authoritative definition of 'armed conflict.' Substantial evidence suggests, in fact, that the drafters of the Conventions purposely avoided any rigid formulation that might limit the applicability of the treaties."[1] As in many matters of law, there is no "bright line test," no formula to determine whether there is an armed conflict in progress, let alone what LOAC/IHL may apply. With an understanding of the basics, and a modest tolerance for ambiguity, one can make a sound assessment.

5.1 Determining Conflict Status

The judge advocate general of the Canadian Armed Forces writes: "The application of the law of war is dependent upon the categorization of conflict. ... Law and order is ultimately dependent upon the drawing of jurisdictional lines."[2] Why does the characterization of a conflict matter? Prior to the 1949 Geneva Conventions, when customary law and treaty rules applied without reference to conflict characterization, it mattered little. That is no longer true. Today, "in view of the fact that an international conflict is subject to the law of war, while this is not so with a non-international conflict, the issue of

---

[1] Derek Jinks, "The Applicability of the Geneva Conventions to the 'Global War on Terrorism,'" 46–1 *Virginia J. of Int'l L.* (2006), 1, 20–1.

[2] BGen. Kenneth Watkin, "Chemical Agents and Expanding Bullets: Limited Law Enforcement Exceptions or Unwarranted Handcuffs?" in Anthony M. Helm, ed., *International Law Studies. Vol. 82. The Law of War in the 21st Century: Weaponry and the Use of Force* (Newport, RI: Naval War College, 2006), 193, 199.

classification becomes of major significance, particularly in so far as the law concerning 'atrocities' and other 'breaches' is concerned."[3]

What conflict characterizations – what statuses – are possible? "The classification of an armed conflict presents few difficulties in the case of a declared war between two states. Such a conflict would clearly qualify as an international armed conflict to which the Geneva Conventions would apply in their entirety. Such conflicts have also become rare."[4]

If two or more Geneva Convention high contracting parties are fighting, it may be a common Article 2 interstate conflict, in which all of the 1949 Geneva Conventions and Additional Protocol I apply. Depending on whether they are fighting each other or both are fighting an armed opposition group, it could be a common Article 3 intrastate conflict – a noninternational conflict in which common Article 3 and, perhaps, Additional Protocol II apply. It may be a noninternational armed conflict in which domestic law applies, and (other than common Article 3) the Geneva Conventions and the Protocols do not figure at all. If a nonstate armed opposition group is fighting a high contracting party, the situation may be more difficult to unravel. As Yoram Dinstein says, "Drawing the line of demarcation between inter-State and intra-State armed conflicts may be a complicated task."[5] There are guidelines, however.

5.1.1 Common Article 2 International Armed Conflicts

In 1949 Geneva Convention common Article 2, one category of armed conflict is defined: "The present Convention shall apply to all cases of declared war or of any other armed conflict which may arise between two or more of the High Contracting Parties, even if the state of war is not recognized by one of them." (Because all states – countries – have ratified the 1949 conventions, all states are "High Contracting Parties.")

In a common Article 2 conflict – an international armed conflict – two or more states are engaged in armed conflict against each other. All four of the 1949 Geneva Conventions apply, plus, for states that have ratified it, 1977 Additional Protocol I. World War II, Korea, Vietnam, the U.S. invasion of Afghanistan – in each case at least two states were fighting each other, so they were common Article 2 conflicts. Why does Additional Protocol I also apply? Because, as Protocol I, Article 1.3, notes, "This Protocol ... *supplements* the Geneva Conventions" and "shall apply in the situations referred to in Article 2 common to those Conventions."

Also, recall that Protocol I, Article 1.4, specifies that the situations referred to in Geneva Convention common Article 2 *include* armed conflicts in which peoples are fighting against colonial domination and alien occupation and against racist régimes" (CARs) Thus, any declared CARs conflict implicates the same LOAC: the Geneva Conventions *and* Protocol I.

---

[3] L. C. Green, *The Contemporary Law of Armed Conflict*, 2d ed. (Manchester: Juris Manchester University Press, 2000), 65–6.

[4] Jennifer Elsea, *Treatment of "Battlefield Detainees" in the War on Terrorism* (Congressional Research Service, Rpt. for Congress, Jan. 13, 2005), 12.

[5] Yoram Dinstein, *The Conduct of Hostilities under the Law of International Armed Conflict* (Cambridge: Cambridge University Press, 2004), 14.

A declaration of war is not required for a common Article 2 international armed conflict to exist. If the armed conflict is between two states, how the conflict is characterized by the parties is irrelevant. The last declaration of war was on August 8, 1945, when, one day before Nagasaki was atom-bombed, Russia declared war on Japan. Given the U.N. Charter, we are unlikely to see another formal declaration of war. Call it a war, a police action, or a conflict: If it is an armed conflict between two or more states, it is a common Article 2 conflict in which all four Geneva Conventions and Additional Protocol I apply.

labels don't matter as long as it is an armed conflict nonetheless.

5.1.2 *Armed Conflicts Short of War*

Confusing the issue, there sometimes are armed conflicts involving two or more states that fall short of what might be called "war." There is a long history of such events. From 1798 to 1801, American naval operations against France were violent and protracted. America and France seized each other's vessels as prizes, others were sunk, and U.S. citizens were captured and imprisoned. Yet, although an 1801 convention ended the dispute, "the French and United States governments did not consider that a war existed between them and the American legislation [ratifying the convention] referred only to 'the existing differences.'"[6]

The British officially called their 1827 naval battle at Navarino with the Turkish fleet, in which sixty Turkish ships were sunk and four thousand men perished, an "accident." The 1900–1 Boxer Rebellion involved armed forces from a host of states fighting Chinese militias. U.S. forces involved in the Boxer Rebellion received combat pay, and the level of fighting is indicated by the fifty-nine medals of honor awarded U.S. combatants. Except France, no government involved chose to describe the conflict as a war, however.[7] And a U.S. federal court held that the Boxer Rebellion was not a war.[8] The early twentieth century saw a flurry of American armed forays in Mexico and Central America, none of which was denominated a war. The United States saw brief but heavy fighting in Vera Cruz, Mexico, in 1914. A short time later, in 1916, the United States launched an abortive expedition into Mexico led by Brigadier General John Pershing to capture Villa. ("Explanations of an agreement between the United States and Mexico concerning mutual border crossings for 'hot pursuit' swayed [resisting Mexican military officers] not at all.")[9] Between 1917 and 1941, U.S. Marines landed and fought nonwars in Siberia, Cuba, Haiti, Santo Domingo, and Nicaragua (twice).[10] None of these events was considered or was referred to as a "war."

Common Article 2 conflicts are usually easily recognized, one country engaged in armed conflict against another, but sometimes it is not clear. If an Indian soldier on sentry duty on the India–Pakistan border, bored and without orders, were to fire at and kill a Pakistani sentry several hundred meters away, is that "an international armed conflict"? What if several Pakistani sentries return fire and wound the Indian shooter?

---

[6] Ian Brownlie, *International Law and the Use of Force by States* (Oxford: Oxford University Press, 1963), 29.
[7] Id., at 31.   [8] *Hamilton v. McClaughry*, 136 F. 445, 450 (C.C.D. Kan. 1900).
[9] Frank E. Vandiver, *Black Jack: The Life and Times of John J. Pershing*, Vol. II (College Station: Texas A & M University Press, 1977), 610.
[10] Edwin Howard Simmons, *The United States Marines: A History*, 4th ed. (Annapolis: Naval Institute Press, 2003), 107–17.

Is *that* an armed conflict between two states? What if a young Indian lieutenant, alarmed at the sudden volume of fire his sentry post is receiving, calls for artillery support and the Pakistani position receives preregistered 155 mm artillery fire, killing several Pakistani soldiers? Is *that* an international armed conflict? Two states are clearly involved, and obviously there is conflict in progress that involves arms.

In LOAC, such a situation would be viewed as a border "incident," falling short of an armed conflict. A key *indicium* is whether the incident is protracted. The longer an incident continues, the more difficult it is to describe it as merely an incident.

> Incidents involving the use of force without reaching the threshold of war occur quite often. . . . Border patrols of neighboring countries may exchange fire; naval units may torpedo vessels flying another flag; interceptor planes may shoot down aircraft belonging to another State; and so forth. . . . In large measure, the classification of a military action as either war or a closed incident ("short of war") depends on the way in which the two antagonists appraise the situation. As long as both parties choose to consider what transpired as a mere incident, and provided that the incident is rapidly closed, it is hard to gainsay that view. Once, however, one of the parties elects to engage in war, the other side is incapable of preventing the development.[11]

An international armed conflict is characterized by the specific intention of one state to engage in armed conflict against another specific state. In the border incident just described, if India *intended* to initiate an armed conflict, it would be a different situation. If somewhere in the escalating violence, Pakistan formed the view that an armed conflict was necessary to its self-defense and *intended* to engage in a state-on-state armed conflict, it would be a different situation.

Generally speaking, an armed *incident*, even when between two states, is not sufficient to constitute an armed conflict in the sense of common Article 2; however, when one of the parties decides to engage in an armed conflict, the other party cannot prevent that development.[12] "[A] number of isolated or sporadic inter-state uses of armed force that have been described as "border incursions', 'naval incidents', 'clashes' and other 'armed provocations' do not qualify as [international armed conflicts] because of the low intensity of violence involved, as a result of which states did not explicitly designate them as such."[13] The United Kingdom's *Manual of the Law of Armed Conflict* adds, "Whether any particular intervention crosses the threshold so as to become an armed conflict will depend on all the surrounding circumstances."[14] The way in which the two states choose to characterize the action (incident or war) can make the difference. Armed conflict "classification in practice is often a subjective matter for the participants rather than an objective analysis of facts and law."[15]

---

[11] Yoram Dinstein, *War, Aggression and Self-Defence*, 4th ed. (Cambridge: Cambridge University Press, 2005), 11.

[12] Id.

[13] ICRC, *International Humanitarian Law and the Challenges of Contemporary Armed Conflicts: Report to the 31st Conference of the Red Cross and Red Crescent, Geneva, 28 Nov.–1 Dec. 2011* (ICRC: Geneva, 2011) 7.

[14] U.K. Ministry of Defence, *The Manual of the Law of Armed Conflict* (Oxford: Oxford University Press, 2004), para. 3.3.1., at 29.

[15] Elizabeth Wilmshurst, "Conclusions," in Wilmshurst, ed., *International Law and the Classification of Conflicts* (Oxford: Oxford University Press, 2012), 478, 499.

5.1.3 *Common Article 3 Non-international Armed Conflicts*

Common Article 3, examined in Chapter 3, Section 3.8.6, describes another category of conflict: "armed conflict not of an international character occurring in the territory of one of the High Contracting Parties." A common Article 3 noninternational conflict arises in cases of "internal" armed conflicts. In other words, if there is armed conflict within a state and the government's opponents are not combatants of another state's armed force, it is a common Article 3 noninternational conflict. At some point, the conflict may be formally recognized as a belligerency. Recognition of belligerency indicates that the parties are entitled to exercise belligerent rights, thus accepting that the rebel group possesses sufficient international personality to support the possession of such rights and duties. Recognition of belligerency, which applies the laws and customs of war to the parties in an internal armed conflict, can be by the government fighting the rebels or, more often, by another state. "The government was therefore putting the belligerents under an obligation to respect the customs of war against its own forces, and at the same time freeing itself from any responsibility for acts committed by the recognised belligerents."[16] Today, formal recognition of belligerency has fallen into disuse. Whether or not there is a recognition of belligerency, and usually there is not, one should keep in mind that, **in a noninternational armed conflict, common Article 3 and, perhaps, Additional Protocol II, apply, along with customary international law. No other portion of the Geneva Conventions applies**.

When does Additional Protocol II also apply? As Article 1.1 of Protocol II states, it applies when an organized armed group exercises sufficient control over territory to enable them to carry out sustained and concerted military operations, and to implement the additional protocol. If the conflict does not clear that rather high bar, Additional Protocol II does not come into play.

Geneva Convention Article 3 in its first sentence indicates that it applies "in the case of armed conflict not of an international character *occurring in the territory* of one of the High Contracting Parties" (emphasis supplied). That sentence, indicating that a noninternational armed conflict must take place within the borders of a single state, was written before nonstate transnational armed opposition groups were foreseeable.

The plain meaning of the phrase "occurring in the territory of one" state has come to be disregarded in state practice. "In view of the recognition by the ICJ [International Court of Justice] that the provisions of Article 3 emanate from general principles of law, namely 'elementary considerations of humanity', the territorial requirement of Article 3 can be regarded as obsolete."[17] The ICRC takes the same view, albeit on a different basis: "Common Article 3 may nowadays be evolutively interpreted as a matter of treaty law to apply not only to non-international armed conflicts occurring wholly within the territory of a state but also to armed conflicts involving state and non-state parties initially *arising*

---

[16] Eve La Haye, *War Crimes in Internal Armed Conflicts* (Cambridge: Cambridge University Press, 2008), 35.

[17] Andreas Paulus and Mindia Vashakmadze, "Asymmetrical War and the Notion of Armed Conflict – a Tentative Conceptualization," 91/873 *Int'l Rev. of the Red Cross* (March 2009), 95, 17, citing *Prosecutor v Tadić*, Decision on Defence Motion for Interlocutory Appeal, ¶¶ 67 and 70; and, *Armed Activities on the Territory of the Congo* (*Dem. Rep. Congo v. Uganda*), Separate Opinion of Judge Sima, ICJ Rpts. 19 Dec. 2005, ¶ 23.

in the territory of a state. ... [A] NIAC will be governed by Common Article 3 as long as there is a 'hook' to a national territory."[18]

Examples of common Article 3 noninternational armed conflicts were those in Iraq and Afghanistan, in which the governments of two states, Iraq and the United States in the first case, Afghanistan and the United States in the second case, are opposing armed opposition groups. They were not opposing lawful combatants of the armed force of a second state. (Recall the more detailed discussion of common Article 3's application in Chapter 3, Section 3.8.6.1.)

Riot, disorder, and banditry do not rise to common Article 3 conflict status. For example, in the 1970s, in California's San Francisco Bay area, a group of disaffected individuals formed the Symbionese Liberation Army (SLA), a radical leftist group. The SLA declared themselves revolutionaries and financed their violent operation through kidnapping, bank robbery, and murder. One of their number, Sara Jane Moore, attempted to assassinate President Gerald Ford.[19] Another was captured only in 2001.[20] Patricia Hearst, heiress to the Hearst newspaper fortune, was kidnapped and briefly converted to the SLA's cause, famously posing before the SLA flag while brandishing an automatic weapon. Revolution? Armed conflict? Was this a common Article 3 armed conflict, then? No, it was not. Despite their rhetoric of "revolution," the SLA was no more than a criminal conspiracy to be dealt with by local police and domestic law.[21] (In May 1974, most of the SLA membership were killed in a police shootout in Oakland, California.)

The International Criminal Tribunal for the Former Yugoslavia (ICTY) has articulated a basis for differentiating common Article 3 armed conflicts from other forms of internal violence:

> The test applied by the Appeals Chamber to the existence of an armed conflict for the purposes of the rules contained in Common Article 3 focuses on two aspects of a conflict; the **intensity** of the conflict and the organization of the **parties** to the conflict. In an armed conflict of an internal ... character, these closely related criteria are used solely for the purpose, as a minimum, of distinguishing an armed conflict from banditry, unorganized and short-lived insurrections, or terrorist activities, which are not subject to international humanitarian law.[22]

(See Cases and Material, this chapter, for a detailed list of factors indicating the existence, or absence, of a noninternational armed conflict.)

LOAC has little direct application in a common Article 3 conflict. "Legally ... the Parties to the conflict are bound to observe Article 3 and may ignore all other Articles [of the Geneva Conventions]."[23] To an ever-greater degree, however, IHL and other elements of LOAC are making their way into common Article 3 conflicts. Generally

---

[18] Jelena Pejic, "The Protective Scope of Common Article 3: More than Meets the Eye," 93–881 *Int'l Rev. of the Red Cross*, 189, 204–5 (March 2011). Emphasis in original.

[19] Randal C. Archibald, "One of Ford's Would-Be Assassins Is Paroled," *NY Times*, Jan. 1, 2008, A15.

[20] Associated Press, "Former '70s Radical Is Back in Custody after a Parole Error," *NY Times*, March 23, 2008, A14.

[21] "The Fascist Insect Bites Back," *Economist*, Jan. 26, 2002, 31.

[22] *Prosecutor v Tadić*, IT-94-1-T, Judgment (May 7, 1997), para. 562. Emphasis supplied.

[23] Jean S. Pictet, ed., *Commentary, IV Geneva Convention* (Geneva: ICRC, 1958), 42.

speaking, though, the domestic law of the state involved, along with common Article 3 and human rights law, apply in noninternational armed conflicts.

5.1.4 *"Transformers": Common Article 3 Conflict, to Common Article 2, and Back*

A common Article 2 conflict can become a common Article 3 conflict. On March 19, 2003, the United States invaded Iraq, opening a common Article 2 armed conflict. On May 1, aboard the USS *Abraham Lincoln*, President Bush announced an end of major combat operations in the Iraq conflict. On or about that date, a U.S. occupation of Iraq began, during which all of the Geneva Conventions remained applicable.[24] The U.S. occupation lasted until Iraq regained its sovereignty on June 28, 2004, when Ambassador Paul Bremmer, head of the Coalition Provisional Authority, passed control of the country to the new interim Iraqi government. In terms of LOAC, at that point the continuing conflict in Iraq became one between insurgents operating in Iraq and the new government of Iraq – a common Article 3 noninternational conflict. The United States remains present in Iraq ostensibly to aid and assist Iraq in its fight against its insurgents – a common Article 3 conflict in which Iraqi domestic law is paramount; aside from common Article 3, the Geneva Conventions and Protocol I no longer apply.

In other words, "consider an armed conflict to remain internal where a foreign state intervenes on behalf of a legitimate government to put down an insurgency, whereas foreign intervention on behalf of a rebel movement would 'internationalize' the armed conflict."[25]

This illustrates a wrinkle in LOAC. If Redland is fighting rebels within its own borders, it is a common Article 3 noninternational armed conflict. If Redland seeks and receives assistance from another state, Blueland, then the subsequent presence of Blueland's armed forces in Redland to provide assistance such as training and logistical help for Redland does not alter the character of the conflict; it continues to be a common Article 3 conflict.[26] That remains true even if Blueland forces engage the rebels in combat, Redland continues to combat its rebels, aided by Blueland. The ICTY has held:

> It is indisputable that an armed conflict is international if it takes place between two or more States. In addition, in case of an internal armed conflict breaking out on the territory of a State, it may become international (or, depending upon the circumstances, be international in character alongside an internal armed conflict) if (i) another State intervenes in that conflict through its troops, or alternatively if (ii) some of the participants in the internal armed conflict act on behalf of that other State.[27]

---

[24] Common Article 2: "The Convention shall also apply to all cases of partial or total occupation of the territory of a High Contracting Party." For those of the Allied coalition who had ratified Additional Protocol I, it, too, applied throughout the occupation.

[25] Elsea, *Treatment of "Battlefield Detainees*," supra, note 4, at 13, citing John Embry Parkerson, Jr., "United States Compliance with Humanitarian Law Respecting Civilians during Operation Just Cause," 133 *Mil. L. Rev.* (1991), 31, 41–2. Elsea's full quote indicates that she is not necessarily among those accepting such a status transformation.

[26] In disagreement, one ICTY trial chamber held that the significant and continuous intervention of Croatian armed forces in support of Bosnian Croats against its rebels transformed the Bosnian internal armed conflict into an international armed conflict. *Prosecutor v. Rajić*, IT-95-12, Review of Indictment (Sept. 13, 1996), at para. 21.

[27] *Prosecutor v Tadić*, IT-94-1-A (July 15, 1999), para. 84.

Foreign financial assistance or logistical support for a rebel movement will not internationalize the conflict unless the foreign state also has overall control of the rebel group. "In practice, many armed conflicts have at the same time certain aspects which have the character of an internal armed conflict, while other aspects are clearly international. For example, an internal conflict may become internationalized, with the armed forces of outside states actively involved."[28] If the Redlandian rebels, rather than the Redlandian government, seek and receive assistance from Blueland, LOAC situation changes. Now Redland is fighting Redlandian rebels *and* Blueland armed forces – two high contracting parties, Redland and Blueland (plus Redlandian rebels), are engaged in combat. This defines a common Article 2 international armed conflict.

A continuing question is the degree of intervention required to bring about a circumstance of armed conflict. The mere supply of arms to rebels does not appear to qualify. "But there comes a point – for instance, when the weapons are accompanied by instructors training the rebels – at which the foreign country is deemed to be waging warfare."[29]

Both the International Court of Justice (ICJ) and the ICTY have ruled on the level of a state's involvement in an armed conflict that moves that state into the conflict as a party. This is a significant issue in the so-called war on terrorism. Books have been written on this narrow issue, but suffice it to say that the ICTY employs an "overall control" test,[30] whereas the ICJ uses a more strict "sending by or on behalf of" test.[31]

> The general principle that States can technically commit an armed attack through association with non-State actions ... remains intact. What appears to have changed is the level of support that suffices. It would seem that in the era of transnational terrorism, very little State support is necessary to amount to an armed attack; at least in this one case [the post-9/11 U.S. attack of Afghanistan] merely harboring a terrorist group was enough. This is a far cry from *Nicaragua*'s "sending by or on behalf" or *Tadic*'s "overall control."[32]

Appropriately, normative interpretations are changing – or have changed – in response to changed circumstances.

---

[28] UK Ministry of Defence, *The Manual of the Law of Armed Conflict* (Oxford: Oxford University Press, 2004), para. 1.33.6., at 16. The ICJ examined such a circumstance in the 1986 *Nicaragua* case and arrived at a contrary conclusion. Nicaragua was fighting Nicaraguan rebels (*contras*), who were aided by the United States. The ICJ held that "the conflict between the *contras*' forces and those of the Government of Nicaragua is an armed conflict which is 'not of an international character'. The acts of the *contras* toward the Nicaraguan Government are therefore governed by the law applicable to conflicts of that character; whereas the actions of the United States in and against Nicaragua fall under the legal rules relating to international conflicts." The court chose to consider as separate conflicts that of the *contras* versus Nicaragua, and that of their supporters, the United States versus Nicaragua. That approach is not customary. *Case Concerning Military and Paramilitary Activities in and against Nicaragua* (Merits), (1986) *ICJ Rpt.* 14, at para. 114.

[29] Yoram Dinstein, *War Aggression and Self-Defence*, 5th ed. (Cambridge: Cambridge University Press, 2011), 10.

[30] *Prosecutor v. Tadić*, Judgment, supra, note 27, at paras. 585–608.

[31] *Military and Paramilitary Activities in and against Nicaragua*, supra, note 28, at paras. 109, 219.

[32] Michael N. Schmitt, "Responding to Transnational Terrorism under the Jus ad Bellum: A Normative Framework," in Michael Schmitt and Jelena Pejic, eds., *International Law and Armed Conflict: Exploring the Faultlines* (Leiden: Martinus Nijhoff, 2007), 157–95, at 187.

5.1.5 *Dual Status Armed Conflicts*

A mixed category of armed conflict, what might be called a dual status conflict, is one in which both international and internal conflicts are occurring *at the same time within the same state.* In northern Afghanistan in 2001, the Taliban government was fighting the rebel Northern Alliance – a common Article 3 noninternational armed conflict. In October 2001, while Afghanistan's Taliban government continued to fight its rebels in the north, the U.S.-led coalition invasion of Afghanistan commenced – one high contracting party invading a second high contracting party, that is, a common Article 2 international armed conflict in the south, occurring simultaneously with the continuing common Article 3 armed conflict in the north. "The fact that a belligerent State is beset by enemies from both inside and outside its territory does not mean that the international and the internal armed conflicts necessarily merge."[33]

Common Article 2, common Article 3, transforming, and dual status armed conflicts: It can be confusing. Witness the December 1997 report of a Belgian appellate review of a court-martial acquittal:

> The military Court upheld a verdict of acquittal in the case of two Belgian soldiers, members of the UNOSOM II operation in Somalia in 1993. The soldiers had been accused of causing bodily harm with intent and of threatening a Somali child. The Court refused to proceed under the 1993 Law on the repression of grave breaches of humanitarian law [the Belgian law implementing the Geneva Conventions] as the Geneva Conventions were not applicable in this particular case. According to the Court, there was no [common Article 2] international conflict at that time in Somalia, as the UN troops were "peace troops" which were neither party to the conflict nor an occupying power. The Court also stated that there was no [common Article 3] non-international conflict in the sense of common Article 3 as the fighting involved irregular, anarchic armed groups with no responsible command.[34]

The acquittal of the soldiers was based not on insufficient evidence, but on the prosecutor's procedural error in charging; the court-martial was forced to acquit the soldiers on the basis of the charges before it, which incorrectly alleged the offenses as occurring in the course of an armed conflict. As the appellate report notes, a U.N. peacekeeping mission is neither a common Article 2 nor a common Article 3 conflict; it is, uniquely, a peacekeeping mission. Because armed conflict was an element to be proved by the prosecution, which could not do so because of the facts of the conflict, the charge was fatally defective. (One suspects that after acquittal the soldiers were recharged, alleging the same offenses, absent the element that they occurred during armed conflict, reducing the maximum possible punishment.) Such cases lend weight to Sir Adam Roberts's suggestion that when a conflict has elements of both common Article 2 and common Article 3, perhaps one should not attempt to categorize it as either.

Conflict status matters because it determines what law applies in the armed conflict under discussion. What are the rights and duties, the privileges and prohibitions, applicable to the parties to the conflict, whether they be states or armed opposition

---

[33] Dinstein, *Conduct of Hostilities*, at 14.
[34] Military Court, Dec. 17, 1997 (*Ministère public and Centre pour l'égalitè des chances et la lutte contre le racisme v. C ... et B ...*), *Journal des Tribunaux* (April 4, 1998), 286–9. Unofficial French translation, available on-line.

groups? What are individuals, whether combatant or civilian, permitted to do and prohibited from doing? Are there prisoners of war in the conflict? Are there grave breaches? In an international armed conflict, are the parties to the conflict obligated to search out and try those who committed or ordered grave breaches, or are they free of that considerable obligation? These and other significant issues are determined by conflict status.

5.2 Nonstate Actors and Armed Opposition Groups Are Bound by LOAC/IHL

What LOAC applies when nonstate actors such as al Qaeda, not controlled by any state, are the opposing "armed force" in an armed conflict? "The application of the laws of war in counter-terrorist operations has always been particularly problematical."[35]

Terrorist groups are a variety of armed opposition group (until they defeat the government forces and *become* the government). They are not states and therefore may not be parties to the Geneva Conventions, the additional protocols, or any *multinational* treaty. Terrorist attacks, if the terrorists have a sufficient organization and if the attacks are sufficiently intense, may rise to noninternational common Article 3 conflicts. If they are not sufficiently organized, and if the attacks are not sufficiently intense in nature, they are simply criminal events.

Terrorist attacks, no matter how organized the group, and how violent or intense the fighting, cannot be considered an international armed conflict for the same reason that terrorist groups cannot be parties to the Geneva Conventions: Terrorist attacks are conducted by nonstates.[36] More than a half-century ago, Professor Oppenheim expressed the traditional law of war view: "To be war, the contention must be *between States*."[37] When engaged in armed combat, terrorists and other armed opposition group members in a common Article 3 conflict enjoy no combatant's privilege (Chapter 2, Section 2.3.1) and upon capture they may be prosecuted for their illegal combatant-like acts prior to capture. (Chapter 6, Section 6.5, discusses the status of Taliban and al Qaeda fighters, for example, and their individual status in LOAC.) Rebels, terrorists, and insurgents, including nonstate actors, may be held accountable not only for their violations of the domestic law of the state in which they act but, if their attacks rise to a common Article 3 noninternational armed conflict, for any violations of common Article 3 and Additional Protocol II.

"While the practice concerning criminalization of individual members of rebel groups under international law is now well-established (with regards to, *inter alia*, war crimes and crimes against humanity), the question of whether the groups *as such* can be said to have violated international criminal law remains, however, under explored."[38] Under-explored perhaps, but not undetermined. "The obligations created by international

---

[35] Adam Roberts, "The Laws of War in the War on Terror," in Wybo P. Heere, ed., *Terrorism and the Military: International Legal Implications* (The Hague: Asser Press, 2003), 65.

[36] Terrorists and their attacks can be state sponsored, of course – a subject beyond the scope of this chapter.

[37] Lassa Oppenheim, *International Law: A Treatise*. Vol. II. *Disputes, War and Neutrality*, 7th ed. H. Lauterpacht, ed. (London: Longman, 1952), 203. Emphasis in original.

[38] Andrew Clapham, "Extending International Criminal Law beyond the Individuals to Corporations and Armed Opposition Groups," 6–5 *J. of Int'l Crim. Justice* (Nov. 2008), 899, 920. A footnote suggesting a lack of unanimity among commentators regarding the criminalization of individual members of nonstate armed opposition groups is omitted.

humanitarian law apply not just to states but to individuals and non-state actors such as a rebel faction or secessionist movement in a civil war."[39]

"It is generally accepted that [IHL] is binding on organized armed groups – that is, those armed groups that are sufficiently organized to render them a party to an armed conflict. Both conventional and customary IHL make it abundantly clear that IHL applies to each party to a non-international armed conflict."[40] With some modification, that includes issues of command responsibility within such groups.[41]

Several international law approaches bind armed opposition groups to LOAC/IHL. The most frequently cited explanation is the doctrine of legislative jurisdiction: The group's "parent" state accepted a particular LOAC/IHL rule and the state had the capacity to legislate for all of its nationals, including the state's right to impose obligations on its citizens that arise from international law, even if some of those citizens should later take up arms against the state. The rebelling group need not have consented to LOAC/IHL rules involved to be bound by them.[42] "The fact that certain individuals group together and challenge the authority of the state does not impact upon the binding nature of the rules upon them."[43]

Another approach is that the long-recognized binding force of the law of war on individuals – those who are prosecuted for war crimes they commit – makes it clear that individuals, whether they are combatants, civilians, or unprivileged belligerent civilians, bear the duties that flow directly from the law of war.[44] Unlike the doctrine of legislative jurisdiction, which seeks to bind the armed group as a whole, this approach binds individual members of the group.

An additional approach is that an armed opposition group that exercises de facto governmental functions will be held to the standards of conduct required of a government. "If the responsible authority at their head exercises effective sovereignty, it is bound by the very fact that it claims to represent the country, or part of the country."[45]

Thus, even if a member of an armed opposition group can claim that he cannot read and has never heard of the Geneva Conventions, he may be prosecuted for his or her violations of the laws and customs of war.

If armed groups are to be held to LOAC/IHL standards, determining *which* armed groups may be accountable is an issue. To be accountable "they must have a minimum degree of organization, but the exact degree is not settled in law."[46] In common Article 3,

---

[39] Christopher Greenwood, "Scope of Application of Humanitarian Law," in Dieter Fleck, ed., *The Handbook of Humanitarian Law in Armed Conflict*, 2d ed. (Oxford: Oxford University Press, 2007), 45, 76. In the first edition of the *Handbook*, Greenwood writes at p. 48, "Both common Art. 3 and the [second 1977] Protocol apply with equal force to all parties to an armed conflict, government and rebels alike."

[40] Jann K. Kleffner, "The Applicability of International Humanitarian Law to Organized Armed Groups," 93/882 *Int'l Rev. of the Red Cross* (June 2011), 443–4.

[41] Sandesh Sivakumaran, "Command Responsibility in Irregular Groups," 10–5 *J. of Int'l Ctim. Justice* (Dec. 2012), 1129.

[42] Kleffner, "Applicability of International Humanitarian Law to Organized Armed Groups" supra, note 40, at 445–6.

[43] Sandesh Sivakumaran, *The Law of Non-International Armed Conflict* (Oxford: Oxford University Press, 2012), 241.

[44] Id., at 449–51.   [45] Pictet, *Commentary, IV Geneva Convention*, supra, note 23, at 37.

[46] Marco Sassòli, "The Implementation of International Humanitarian Law: Current and Inherent Challenges," in Timothy L. H. McCormack, ed., *Yearbook of International Humanitarian Law* (The Hague: Asser Press, 2009), 45, 56.

the words of application mandating that *"each party* to the conflict shall be bound to apply" (emphasis supplied) indicate that both sides of a noninternational armed conflict shall be bound.

Viewed on an imaginary "armed group" continuum, at one end there are revolutionary groups that are loosely organized, if at all, committing only intermittent acts of armed violence. These groups are outlaws, criminals, to be dealt with by the state's domestic criminal law. At the other end of the armed group continuum there are organizations such as the Taliban, with something akin to a military chain of command (or an actual chain of command) and with an ability to plan and carry out acts of armed violence. Groups at this end of the continuum, with an organization and a certain level of territorial control, are armed opposition groups to which the international community assigns the responsibility of respecting LOAC/IHL and imposes sanctions on the group's membership for their violations. Of course, "an armed group whose aim constitutes per se a flagrant violation of international humanitarian law, such as a group that pursues a policy of ethnic cleansing, is unlikely to be concerned about sanctions."[47] Nevertheless, "international practice confirms ... that armed opposition groups are bound by Common Article 3 and Protocol II, and that they are so [bound] as a group."[48] It was once believed that no customary international law applied to noninternational armed conflicts, but today it is apparent that customary rules concerning the protection of civilians in hostilities also apply to armed opposition groups in non-international armed conflicts.[49]

There have been cases in which armed groups (none of them nonstate groups, however) have attempted to declare their adherence to the 1949 Geneva Conventions. Traditionally it is not possible for both the government of the state in which the armed group operates and the armed group itself to claim to represent the government of that state, and such efforts have been rebuffed.[50]

> As armed opposition groups cannot become parties to the Geneva Conventions or Additional Protocols, and are not required to declare themselves bound by the relevant norms, they derive their rights and obligations contained in Common Article 3 and Protocol II through the state on whose territory they operate. Once the territorial state has ratified the Geneva Conventions and Protocol II, armed opposition groups operating on its territory become automatically bound by the relevant norms laid down therein.[51]

The obligations of armed opposition groups, including nonstate actors and groups of nonstate actors such as al Qaeda and the Taliban, are essentially to respect the basic humanitarian norms of common Article 3, not to kill outside combat, and not to attack

---

[47] Anne-Marie LaRosa and Carolin Wuerzner, "Armed Groups, Sanctions and the Implementation of International Humanitarian Law," 870 *Int'l Rev. of the Red Cross* (June 2008), 327, 331.

[48] Liesbeth Zegveld, *The Accountability of Armed Opposition Groups in International Law* (Cambridge: Cambridge University Press, 2002), 10.

[49] *Prosecutor v Tadić*, Interlocutory Appeal on Jurisdiction, supra, note 17, at para. 127: "It cannot be denied that customary rules have developed to govern internal strife. These rules ... cover such areas as protection of civilians from hostilities, in particular from indiscriminate attacks ... protection of all those who do not (or no longer) take active part in hostilities ... and ban of certain methods of conducting hostilities."

[50] Zegveld, *Accountability of Armed Opposition Groups*, supra, note 48, at 14–15, citing the Provisional Revolutionary Government of Algeria when it was considered a part of France, the breakaway Smith government of Rhodesia, and the Kosovo Liberation Army in the former Yugoslavia.

[51] Id., at 15. Footnote omitted.

civilians or civilian objects. "Or, in other words, international bodies have focused on what armed opposition groups must *not* do. Examples of practice according *rights* to armed opposition groups have been exceptional."[52]

5.2.1 *Cross-Border Terrorist Attacks by Non-state Armed Opposition Groups*

"Is it lawful for a state to invade its neighbor if that neighbor fails to prevent its territory from being used to launch attacks across the common border? Are illegal attacks across a border by insurgents to be attributed to the state from which they are launched? There may be a growing inclination to answer that question in the affirmative."[53] This is an emergent category of armed conflict relating to terrorism, to nonstate actors, and to a state's right of self-defense.[54]

In 1916, U.S. forces crossing into Mexico after Villa called their cross-border foray a "punitive expedition."[55] Today such events are sometimes referred to as "cross-border non-international armed conflicts,"[56] or, to use Professor Yoram Dinstein's term, "extra-territorial law enforcement." Theodor Meron warns, "Deliberate terrorist attacks on civilians, accompanied by complete disregard of international law, diminish the incentives for other parties to comply with the principles of international humanitarian law and increase pressure for deconstruction and revision of the law, or simply disregard of the rules."[57] Cross-border attacks in self-defense against continuing attacks by nonstate actors who then take refuge in a neighboring state that cannot or will not control the unlawful activity of the nonstate group that harbors within its borders may be seen as such a revision of the law. "Use of force on necessity grounds may be permitted," one scholar argues, "as an extraordinary remedy, to the extent that this is indispensable to safeguard an essential interest of the acting state against a grave and imminent peril."[58] Two ICJ cases, *Nicaragua*[59] and *the Congo*,[60] address cross-border activities. "While both decisions appear to imply that the provision of sanctuary and support for a cross-border insurgency might potentially rise to the level of an armed attack, justifying a military response, neither offers a principled rule by which that threshold may be determined in subsequent disputes."[61] It may be argued that subsequent state practice has provided such a rule. Although not all commentators agree, state practice in conflicts in Afghanistan,

---

[52] Id., at 92. Emphasis in original.

[53] Thomas M. Franck, "On Proportionality of Countermeasures in International Law," 102–4 AJIL (Oct. 2008), 715, 764.

[54] Tom Ruys, *"Armed Attack" and Article 51 of the UN Charter* (Cambridge: Cambridge University Press, 2010), at 442–53 offers recent examples of cross-border attacks and responses from European and Pacific states.

[55] Brig. Gen. John J. Pershing, "Report of the Punitive Expedition to June 30, 1916," (Oct. 7, 1916), cited in Vandiver, *Black Jack*, supra, note 9, at 605, fn. 34.

[56] Pejic, "Protective Scope of Common Article 3," supra, note 18, at 204–5 (March 2011). In accord: ICRC, 31st International Conference: *challenges of contemporary armed conflicts* , supra, note 13, at 9–10.

[57] Theodor Meron, *The Humanization of International Law* (Leiden: Martinus Nijhoff, 2006), 86.

[58] Tarcisio Gazzini, "A Response to Amos Guiora: Pre-Emptive Self-Defence against Non-State Actors?" 13–1 *J. of Conflict & Security L.* (Spring 2008), 25, 28.

[59] *Case Concerning Military and Paramilitary Activities against Nicaragua* (Merits), supra, note 28. See *Nicaragua*, paras. 199, 211, Cases and Materials, this chapter.

[60] *Armed Activities on the Territory of the Congo (Dem. Rep. Congo v. Uganda)*, ICJ, 19 Dec. 2005, http://www.icj-cij.org.

[61] Franck, "On Proportionality of Countermeasures in International Law," supra, note 53, at 722.

Pakistan, Yemen, and Somalia, among other states, appears to have moved cross-border attacks based upon self-defense far toward international acceptance.

In July 2006, an armed unit of the Lebanese terrorist organization Hezbollah crossed into Israel from Lebanon and attacked an Israeli Defense Force patrol. Several soldiers were killed and two Israelis were captured by the Hezbollah force. There was, of course, a long and highly charged background to these events, each side blaming the other for provoking the incident. Israeli forces responded and entered Lebanon. Their efforts to rescue the Hezbollah-held prisoners resulted in further casualties. The fighting escalated into a thirty-three-day armed conflict involving thousands of Israeli air strikes and artillery fire missions and, on Hezbollah's part, thousands of rockets fired into Israel.[62] Ultimately, 159 Israelis and 1,084 Lebanese, including approximately 650 Hezbollah fighters, were reportedly killed.[63] Israel's 2006 cross-border attack of Hezbollah in Lebanon may be considered an example of extraterritorial law enforcement. Central LOAC/IHL issues were Hezbollah's indiscriminate rocket attacks on Israeli civilian areas and, with regard to Israel's response, proportionality both in the sense of Israel's decision to resort to cross-border armed force – *jus ad bellum* – and in the sense of Israel's response viewed against the backdrop of noncombatants killed and civilian objects destroyed – *jus in bello*.[64]

In terms of *jus ad bellum*, Hezbollah's firing of rockets incapable of precise targeting into civilian areas was a LOAC/IHL violation. Was the armed Israeli reaction proportionate to the Hezbollah incitements? The culminating cross-border raid by Hezbollah was only one in a series of incursions, including hundreds of rockets fired into Israeli cities and villages over an extended period. Hezbollah, in contrast, might argue that Israeli's control of Lebanese border-crossing points, depriving civilians of basic necessities, constituted an unlawful punishment of the civilian population, justifying Hezbollah's actions and depriving Israel of a lawful right to initiate a cross-border action.

In terms of *jus ad bellum*, was Israel's decision to attack Lebanon proportional to Hezbollah's incitement? In terms of *jus in bello*, when the decision to attack was made, was Israel's military reaction, spearheaded by infantry, tanks, and air strikes, proportionate, or was it excessive in relation to the concrete and direct military advantage anticipated?

> We are referring here to necessity and proportionality. ... Necessity in the context of self-defense is closely related to the existence of an ongoing armed attack and/or the credible threat of (renewed) attack within the immediate future. ... With respect to proportionality within the context of self-defense, we are dealing with the overall scale of

---

[62] U.N. Report of the Commission of Inquiry on Lebanon Pursuant to Human Rights Council Resolution S-2/1 (27 Nov. 2006), available online.

[63] Col. Reuven Erlich, "Hezbollah's Use of Lebanese Civilians as Human Shields," Part 1, paras. 44–5, at 55, available online.

[64] E.g., Enzo Cannizzaro, "Contextualizing Proportionality: Jus ad Bellum and Jus in Bello in the Lebanese War," 864 *Int'l Rev. of the Red Cross* (Dec. 2006), 779, in which the author, at 792, chides Israel: "[A] state cannot freely determine the standard of security for its own population if the achievement of that standard entails excessive prejudicial consequences for civilians of the attacked state. Even if the destruction of rocket bases and the eradication of paramilitary units ... were proved to be the only means by which Israel might prevent further attacks, these objectives cannot be attained if they entail, as a side effect, a disproportionate humanitarian cost."

the measures taken in self-defense. The response must be roughly equivalent in scale and effects to the attack and the nature of the threat posed by the attacker.[65]

One writer objects, "Localized border encounters between small infantry units, even those involving the loss of life, do not constitute an armed attack. ... It follows that minor violations ... falling below the threshold of the notion of armed attack do not justify a corresponding minor use of force as self-defense."[66] Support for that viewpoint is found in ICJ rulings.[67] On the other hand, Mary Ellen O'Connell notes that "a series of [such] acts amounts to armed attack justifying armed force in self-defense either against a foreign state or against a group within the state."[68] Rosalyn Higgins, before she was appointed an ICJ judge, wrote: "Proportionality here cannot be in relation to any specific prior injury – it has to be in relation to the overall legitimate objective, of ending the aggression or reversing the invasion. And *that*, of course, may mean that a use of force is proportionate, even though it is a more severe use of force than any single prior incident might have seemed to have warranted."[69] Professor O'Connell adds, "If terrorists have conducted a series of significant attacks, planned future ones, and their identities and whereabouts are known to the defending State, the conditions of lawful self-defense may be met, as long as the defense is necessary and proportional."[70] Proportionality is not a matter of tit-for-tat response, mandating a reaction weighted similar to only the last assault.

What of the fact that, in the eyes of Israel and others, the aggressor was Hezbollah, a Muslim extremist group and nonstate actor? Does LOAC/IHL allow for an exercise of armed cross-border defensive action by a victim state, Israel in this case, against a grouping of nonstate actors entrenched in another state, Lebanon in this case? What of the Lebanese government that hosts or harbors (or endures) the terrorist nonstate actors? What of the host state's sovereignty and right of self-defense against a responding victim state whose armed forces cross its border? "The question arises whether recourse to unilateral (individual or collective) measures can be made as a reaction to acts of terrorism, in exercise of the right of self-defense under Article 51 [of the U.N. Charter]."[71] Michael Schmitt suggests:

> The only sensible balancing of the territorial integrity and self-defense rights is one that allows the State exercising self-defense to conduct counter-terrorist operations in the State where the terrorists are located *if* that State is either unwilling or incapable of policing its own territory. A demand for compliance should precede the action and the State should be permitted an opportunity to comply with its duty to ensure its territory is not being used to the detriment of others. If it does not, any subsequent nonconsensual counter-terrorist operations into the country should be strictly limited to the purpose of

---

[65] Terry D. Gill, "The Eleventh of September and the Right of Self-Defense," in Heere, *Terrorism and the Military*, supra, note 35, at 23, 32–3.

[66] Cannizzaro, "Contextualizing Proportionality," supra, note 64, at 782.

[67] *Case Concerning Military and Paramilitary Activities against Nicaragua*, supra, note 28, at paras. 195, 230, holding that a mere cross-border flow of arms and supplies does not constitute a violation of the prohibition against use of force justifying a use of armed force in response.

[68] Mary Ellen O'Connell, *The Power and Purpose of International Law* (New York: Oxford University Press, 2008), 182.

[69] Rosalyn Higgins, *Problems and Process* (Oxford: Oxford University Press, 1994), 232.

[70] O'Connell, *Power and Purpose of International Law*, supra, note 68, at 187.

[71] Yoram Dinstein, "*Ius ad Bellum* Aspects of the 'War on Terrorism,'" in Heere, *Terrorism and the Military*, supra, note 35, at 13, 16.

eradicating the terrorist activity . . . and the intruding force must withdraw immediately upon accomplishment of its mission."[72]

It was not contended that Lebanon controlled Hezbollah. To the contrary, Lebanon was seen as unable to exert either political or police control over the nonstate group that makes its base within Lebanon's borders. Judge Higgins writes: "It must be remembered that the Charter does indeed have its own procedures for dealing with international threats to peace. . . . At the same time, in a nuclear age, common sense cannot require one to interpret an ambiguous provision in a text in a way that requires a state passively to accept its fate before it can defend itself."[73] Ruth Wedgwood, more direct in her assessment, adds, "If a host country permits the use of its territory as a staging area for terrorist attacks when it could shut those operations down, and refuses requests to take action, the host government cannot expect to insulate its territory against measures of self-defense."[74] Nor is an ineffective government a defense:

> If the Government of Arcadia does not condone the operations of armed bands of terrorists emanating from within its territory against Utopia, but it is too weak (militarily, politically or otherwise) to prevent these operations, Arcadian responsibility *vis-à-vis* Utopia (if engaged at all) may be nominal. Nevertheless, it does not follow that Utopia must patiently endure painful blows, only because no sovereign State is to blame for the turn of events.[75]

Professor Dinstein addresses the issue of nonstate actor cross-border aggression using the United States and al Qaeda as examples: "If Al Qaeda terrorists find a haven in a country which . . . declines to lend them any support, but all the same is too weak to expel or eliminate them, the USA would be entitled (invoking the right of self-defense) to use force against the terrorists within the country of the reluctant host State."[76] Dinstein refers to this as extraterritorial law enforcement.[77] Others call it a cross-border form of a noninternational armed conflict. By either name, it is an assertion of the right to self-defense in the age of terrorism: **If a nonstate terrorist group attacks a state from a safe haven in another host state that will not or cannot take action against the nonstate armed group, the attacked state may employ armed force against the terrorist group within the borders of the host state. Extraterritorial law enforcement is not an attack on the host state, but on its parasitical terrorist group.**

A state's cross-border attack in self-defense against terrorist strongholds is a common Article 3 noninternational armed conflict because it is not between two high contracting parties and the harboring state does not sponsor or actively support the terrorist group.[78] Given that the

---

[72] Michael N. Schmitt, "Targeting and Humanitarian Law: Current Issues," 33 *Israel Yearbook on Human Rights* (2003), 59, 88–9.

[73] Higgins, *Problems and Process*, supra, note 69, at 242. On the Court, Judge Higgins has maintained her position. See her Separate Opinion, *Legal Consequences of the Construction of a Wall in the Occupied Palestinian Territory*, Advisory Opinion (9 July 2004), para. 33.

[74] Ruth Wedgwood, "Responding to Terrorism: The Strikes against bin Laden," 24 *Yale J. of Int'l L.* (1999), 559, 565.

[75] Dinstein, *War, Aggression and Self-Defence*, supra, note 11, at 245.

[76] Dinstein, "*Ius ad Bellum* Aspects of the 'War on Terrorism,'" supra, note 71, at 21.

[77] Dinstein, *War, Aggression and Self-Defence*, supra, note 30, at 247.

[78] Sivakumaran, *Law of Non-International Armed Conflict*, supra, note 43, at 229. Notably, Professor Dinstein disagrees, holding that "the notion that a NIAC may be a cross-border affair is simply not cogent. Naturally, a NIAC in one state may have a spillover impact on a neighboring state . . . that may trigger a parallel

fighting in the Israel–Lebanon example – the armed conflict – does not directly involve the state of Lebanon or its armed forces, or those of any second state, it is reasonable to view the conflict as a common Article 3 conflict. "Modern conflict often does not appear to fit nicely into the strict traditional legal concepts of what constitutes international and non-international 'armed conflict.'"[79]

If a cross-border response to terrorist attacks is considered lawful, before exercising self-defense in the form of a nonconsensual violation of a terrorist-host state's sovereignty, an attacked state must allow the host state a reasonable opportunity to take action against the terrorist group. If an incursion by the attacked state follows, care must be taken that only objects connected to the terrorists be targeted. Of course, if the terrorist group is merely a surrogate, acting for the state within which it is harbored, or if the host state is capable of effectively acting against the group but refuses to do so, the host state itself may be open to attack.[80]

What law does extraterritorial law enforcement enforce? It enforces customary international law of self-defense, described in Article 51 of the U.N. Charter. The Security Council has repeatedly characterized international terrorism as a threat to international peace and security,[81] most notably after the attacks of September 11, 2001, on the United States.[82] "In Resolution 1368, the Council affirmed 'the inherent right of individual or collective self-defense in accordance with the Charter,' an important recognition of the applicability of the right of self-defense in response to terrorist attacks."[83] Professor Schmitt writes, "Although traditionally viewed as a matter for law enforcement, States and inter-governmental organizations now style terrorism as justifying, within certain conditions, the use of military force pursuant to the jus ad bellum. It is not so much that the law has changed as it is that existing law is being applied in a nascent context."[84] He adds, "With 9/11, international law became unequivocal vis-à-vis the propriety of using armed force to counter transnational terrorism. The military has been added as yet another arrow in the quiver of international counter-terrorism strategy."[85]

NIAC ... and/or even an IAC." Yoram Dinstein, reviewing Sivakumaran's *Law of Non-International Armed Conflict*, 107–1 AJIL 270, 272 (Jan. 2013).

[79] Brig. Gen. Kenneth Watkin, "21st Century Conflict and International Humanitarian Law: Status Quo or Change?" in Schmitt and Pejic, *International Law and Armed Conflict*, supra, note 33, at 273.

[80] James Crawford, *The International Law Commission's Articles on State Responsibility* (Cambridge: Cambridge University Press, 2002), 110. Discussing Article 8, Conduct directed or controlled by a state: "The attribution to the State of conduct in fact authorized by it is widely accepted in international jurisprudence. ... More complex issues arise in determining whether conduct was carried out 'under the direction or control' of a State."

[81] E.g., in regard to Bali (SC Res. 1438 [Oct. 14, 2002]); in regard to Moscow (SC Res. 1440 [Oct. 24, 2002]); in re Kenya (SC Res. 1450 [Dec. 13, 2002]); in re Bogatá (SC Res. 1465 [Feb. 13, 2003]); in re Istanbul (SC Res. 1516 [Nov. 20, 2003]); in re Madrid (SC Res. 1530 [March 11, 2004]); in re London (SC Res. 1611 [July 7, 2005]); and in re Iraq (SC Res. 1618 [Aug. 4, 2005]).

[82] SC Res. 1368 (Sept. 12, 2001), reaffirmed by SC Res. 1373 (Sept. 28, 2001). In subsequent resolutions, neither the Security Council nor the General Assembly has considered U.S. operations in Afghanistan a violation of the charter.

[83] Jane Stromseth, David Wippman, and Rosa Brooks, *Can Might Make Rights?* (New York: Cambridge University Press, 2006), 40–1, citing S.C. Res. 1368 (2001), operative para. 1.

[84] Schmitt, "Responding to Transnational Terrorism" in Schmitt and Pejic, *International Law and Armed Conflict*, supra, note 32, at 159.

[85] Id., at 167. Another professor agrees, "Hence, all these [U.N.] resolutions provided legitimacy for the resort to force against terrorist bases on the territory of states that are unable or unwilling to prevent terrorist

The possibility of abuse of extraterritorial law enforcement is evident: How strong must the evidence be to allow a state to act in self-defense? Whatever the answer, the right to self-defense cannot be ignored. If "a State suffers a series of successive and different acts of armed attack from another State, the requirements of proportionality will certainly not mean that the victim State is not free to undertake a single armed action on a much larger scale in order to put an end to this escalating succession of attacks."[86]

There are limitations on a state's right to self-defense against terrorist attacks, as Israel, widely criticized for violating *jus in bello* proportionality, has repeatedly found. Those limitations are immediacy, necessity, and, most significant, proportionality. Israel was widely criticized for its "excessive, indiscriminate and disproportionate"[87] response to the July 2006 attack by Hezbollah. "But proportionate to what? To the casualties inflicted by Hezbollah's July 12 raid? Or to the whole panorama of hostilities that Israel has endured ... from Lebanese territory?"[88] Professor Schmitt writes:

> Proportionality does not require any equivalency between the attacker's actions and defender's response. Such a requirement would eviscerate the right of self-defence, particularly in the terrorist context. ... Instead, proportionality limits defensive force to that required to repel the attack. This may be less or more than used in the armed attack that actuated the right to self-defence; in essence, the determination is an operational one. ... To the extent that law enforcement is likely to prevent follow-on attacks, the acceptability of large-scale military operations drops accordingly.[89]

"In short, there is no barrier in international law of either a customary or conventional nature to the applicability of the right of self-defense to acts of terrorism which are comparable in their scale and effects to an armed attack carried out by more conventional means. This is particularly the case when there is a close relationship between a host or supporting State and a terrorist organization."[90]

Instances of state action alleged to have been self-defense in response to cross-border terrorist attacks are many. They include the 1837 British incursion into U.S. territory to end American waterborne shipments of men and materiel to Britain's enemies – the *Caroline* incident; America's already-mentioned 1916 punitive expedition into Mexico against "Pancho" Villa; Israel's invasion of Lebanon in 1982 in response to Palestinian Liberation Organization (PLO) attacks; the 1985 Israeli bombardment of PLO headquarters in Tunisia; the U.S. bombardment of an alleged chemical weapons factory in response to al Qaeda attacks on American embassies in Kenya and Tanzania in 1999; the 1986 U.S. bombing of Libyan targets in response to a terrorist attack on a Berlin discothèque; and Israel's invasions of Lebanon in 2006 and Gaza in 2009. Virtually

---

actions." Muge Kinacioglu, "A Response to Amos Guiora: Reassessing the Parameters of Use of Force in the Age of Terrorism," 13–1 *J. of Conflict & Security L.* (Spring 2008), 33, 41.

[86] Robert Ago, International Law Commission rapporteur in: Addendum – Eighth Report on State Responsibility, para. 121, UN Doc. A/CN.4/318/Adds.5–7, reprinted in 2 Y.B. *Int'l Comm.*, pt. 1, at 13, 69–70 (1980), UN Doc. A/CN.4/SER.A/1980/Add. 1 (Part 1).

[87] Implementation of United Nations General Assembly Resolution 60/251, "Human Rights Council" Report of Commission of Inquiry on Lebanon (March 15, 2006).

[88] Franck, "On Proportionality of Countermeasures in International Law," supra, note 53, at 733.

[89] Schmitt, "Responding to Transnational Terrorism" in Schmitt and Pejic, *International Law and Armed Conflict*, supra, note 32, at 172.

[90] Gill, "The Eleventh of September and the Right of Self-Defense," in Heere, *Terrorism and the Military*, supra, note 65, at 28.

all of the modern-day actions have been decried by the international community as violations of proportionality.

Cross-border attacks by victim states in noninternational armed conflicts cannot be said to have achieved customary law status, and the concept is hardly objection-free. There have been few objections to its recent invocation, however. "Post-September 11, Security Council resolutions have in effect extended the definition of armed attack to include acts undertaken by non-state actors operating from the territory of a state that is unable or unwilling to prevent terrorist acts. The extension of the right to self-defence as such has largely remained controversy free."[91]

(See Chapter 15.10 for a more complete examination of LOAC/IHL involved in cross-border attacks in response to a terrorist group's initial attack.)

5.3 Criminal Justice Model or Military Model?

The traditional approach to combating terrorism, internationally and within the United States, is to employ the criminal justice model: Investigate, arrest, and try terrorists for their criminal acts that violate domestic law.[92] The British and the Spanish have employed the criminal justice model in the face of repeated terrorist bombings of civilians and civilian objects, even within the capital cities of London and Madrid.[93] Until the 9/11 attacks, the United States usually looked to the criminal justice model, as well.

After 9/11 the United States took a different approach: Maintaining the "war on terrorism" theme, it turned to the military model. The Taliban and al Qaeda represent "a different dimension of crime, a higher, more dangerous version of crime, a kind of super-crime incorporating some of the characteristics of warfare. . . . They are criminals who are also enemies."[94] Although the United States has, for the most part, adopted the military model in fighting transnational terrorism, government officials continue to use law enforcement–related language like "punishment," "justice," "evidence," and "perpetrators." Without examining the lawfulness of going to war – *jus ad bellum* – there are arguments that terrorist acts, including those perpetrated by al Qaeda, should be met with a criminal justice response, rather than with military force. However, a criminal justice model in many situations would be unworkable against many, if not most, armed opposition groups – in tribal areas of Pakistan, for example. In such circumstances, when the state's domestic police lack the training and weaponry to meet that of an armed opposition group, the involvement of the state's military force is common.

---

[91] Muge Kinacioglu, "A Response to Amos Guiora," supra, note 85, at 39.

[92] Steven R. Ratner, "Predator and Prey: Seizing and Killing Suspected Terrorists Abroad," 15–3 *J. of Pol. Philosophy* (2007), 251, in which the author, at 254, points out U.S. use of the criminal justice model in terrorist incidents including the 1988 bombing of Pan Am flight 103 and the 1993 World Trade Center bombing; and, at 255, examples of the military model, including the 1986 bombing of Libya, and the cruise missile attacks against al Qaeda targets in Sudan and Afghanistan, after 1998 U.S. embassy bombings.

[93] Clive Walker, "Clamping Down on Terrorism in the United Kingdom," 4–5 *J. of Int'l Crim. Justice* (Nov. 2006), 1137, 1145.

[94] George P. Fletcher, "The Indefinable Concept of Terrorism," 4–5 *J. of Int'l Crim. Justice* (Nov. 2006), 894, 899. Douglas Feith, under secretary of defense for policy (2001–5), agrees. "[T]e magnitude of 9/11, and the danger of more terrorist attacks, had driven home the inadequacy of treating terrorism as a law enforcement matter. . . . No police force is organized and equipped to stop a campaign of sophisticated, internationally supported terrorist attacks." Douglas J. Feith, *War and Decision* (New York: Harper, 2008), 9.

The military is there "to regulate situations where the threat surpasses the capacities of ordinary police forces, especially when the intensity of the violence or its territorial extensions are of such a nature that the police is not equipped to fight it.[95]

The military model does not necessarily lead to a common Article 2 or Article 3 armed conflict. Oppenheim writes, "A contention may, of course, arise between armed forces of a State and a body of armed individuals, but this is not war."[96] Another writer adds, "While acts of violence against military objectives in internal armed conflicts remain subject to domestic criminal law, the tendency to designate them a 'terrorist' completely undermines whatever incentive armed groups have to respect international law."[97]

In the "war against terrorism," the U.S. admixture of military and criminal justice models, particularly as to detention practices, has resulted in confusion[98] and litigation. The 9/11 attacks obviously were an armed attack meriting a military, rather than a police response.[99] Indeed, "all lingering doubts on this issue have been dispelled as a result of the response of the international community to the shocking events of 9 September 2001 ... that these acts amounted to an armed attack."[100] Still, the Geneva-based International Commission of Jurists charged:

> The United States ... has adopted a war paradigm in the expectation that this provides a legal justification for setting aside criminal law and human rights law safeguards, to be replaced by the extraordinary powers that are supposedly conferred under international humanitarian law. ... Conflating acts of terrorism with acts of war, is legally flawed and sets a dangerous precedent. ... Where terrorist acts trigger or occur during an armed conflict, such acts may well constitute war crimes, and they are governed by international humanitarian law. ... The US's war paradigm has created fundamental problems. Among the most serious is that the US has applied war rules to persons not involved in situations of armed conflict, and in genuine situations of warfare, it has distorted, selectively applied and ignored otherwise binding rules.[101]

Employing the military model as the U.S. choice for combating terrorism, military directives require that, as a matter of policy, if not law, "Members of the DOD

---

[95] Constantin von der Groeben, "The Conflict in Columbia and the Relationship between Humanitarian Law and Human Rights Law in Practice,"16–1 *J. of Conflict & Security L.* (Spring 2011), 141, 154.

[96] Oppenheim, *International Law*, supra, note 37, at 203.

[97] Jelena Pejic, "Terrorist Acts and Groups: A Role for International Law?" 75 BYIL (2004), 71, 75. Also, Marco Sassòli, "The Status of Persons Held in Guantanamo under International Humanitarian Law," 2–1 *J. of Int'l Crim. Justice* (March 2004), 96.

[98] Major Richard V. Meyer, "When a Rose Is Not a Rose: Military Commissions v. Courts-Martial," 5–1 *J. of Int'l Crim. Justice* (March 2007), 48.

[99] Sean D. Murphy, "Terrorism and the Concept of 'Armed Attack' in Article 51 of the U.N. Charter," 43 *Harvard Int'l L. J.* (2002), 41, 47–50. Professor "Murphy gives six reasons for concluding that the attacks of September 11 were an 'armed attack': the scale of the incidents was akin to that of a military attack; the United States immediately perceived the incidents as akin to military attack; the U.S. interpretation was largely accepted by other nations; the incidents could properly be viewed as both a criminal act and an armed attack; there was prior state practice supporting the view that terrorist bombings could constitute an armed attack; and 'the fact that the incidents were not undertaken directly by a foreign government cannot be viewed as disqualifying them from constituting an armed attack.'" 98–1 AJIL (Jan. 2004), 3, fn. 11.

[100] Dinstein, *War, Aggression and Self-Defence*, supra, note 11, at 206–7.

[101] International Commission of Jurists, *Report of the Eminent Jurists Panel on Terrorism, Counter-Terrorism and Human Rights*, Executive Summary (Geneva, July 22, 2009), available online.

Components comply with the law of war during all armed conflicts, however such conflicts are characterized, and in all other military operations."[102]

Whatever response to terrorism a nation takes, "states neither need, nor should be allowed, to 'pick and choose' different legal frameworks concerning the conduct of hostilities or law enforcement, depending on which gives them more room to manoeuvre."[103]

5.4 U.S. Military Practice

U.S. practice, mandated by Department of Defense (DOD) directive, is to apply LOAC in all conflicts. Military commanders are required to "ensure that the members of their Components comply with the law of war during all conflicts, *however such conflicts are characterized*, and with the principles and spirit of the law of war during all operations."[104]

The war on terrorism does not meet the criteria for common Article 2 armed conflicts, but the fact of armed conflict is clear.[105] DOD Directive 5100.77 removes any doubt that U.S. forces are required to comply with the principles and spirit of the law of war in fighting the Taliban, al Qaeda, or any other terrorist or insurgent armed opposition group. The same directive requires that commanders implement programs to prevent LOAC violations.[106]

When it is said that LOAC will apply "in all conflicts," that does not mean that every article of Hague Regulation IV, of each Geneva convention, and of each additional protocol will automatically apply. That would negate, for example, distinctions between international and noninternational conflicts, and differences between lawful combatants and unprivileged belligerents. Rather, it means that the basic protections and the humanitarian spirit of LOAC/IHL apply in every conflict, no matter how it is characterized.

5.5 Summary

In studying any LOAC issue, the first question is, What law of war provisions apply to this conflict? What LOAC/IHL applies in an armed conflict between two or more high contracting parties – two states? This circumstance describes a common Article 2 conflict ("between two or more high contracting parties"), in which the 1949 Geneva Conventions apply, en toto, along with 1977 Additional Protocol I, for those states that have ratified it. Customary international law, sometimes referred to as "customary law of war," also applies. A "declared war" is not required, only armed conflict, even if one of the parties does not recognize it as such.

What LOAC applies in an internal armed conflict – an insurrection, rebellion, or civil war – that rises to a common Article 3 conflict? Common Article 3, and no other part of the Geneva Conventions, applies. Additional Protocol II *may* also apply, if the rebels

---

[102] Chairman of the Joint Chiefs of Staff Instruction 5810, "Implementation of the DOD Law of War Program,"30 April 2010, Policy, para. 4.a.

[103] Pejic, "Terrorist Acts and Groups: A Role for International Law?" supra, note 97, at 91.

[104] DoD Directive 5100.77, "DoD Law of War Program," Dec. 9, 1998, para. 5.3.1. Emphasis supplied.

[105] Geoffrey S. Corn, "'Snipers in the Minaret – What Is the Rule?' The Law of War and the Protection of Cultural Property: A Complex Equation," *The Army Lawyer* (July 2005), 28–40, 31, fn. 27.

[106] Directive 5100.77, supra, note 104.

control sufficient territory from which to launch concerted military operations. Because applicable LOAC/IHL is so sparse in noninternational conflicts, it is important to remember that customary international law also applies – some provisions of Additional Protocol I customary law. When the provision is customary law, despite the lack of U.S. ratification of Protocol I, that customary law provision of Protocol I, written for international armed conflicts, binds the United States in any noninternational armed conflict in which it is engaged, by virtue of its being customary law.

When is an "internal armed conflict" indicated? When there is protracted armed violence between governmental authorities and an organized group, or between such organized groups, within a single state.[107] In deciding whether an internal armed conflict exists, consider, among other factors, the degree of rebel organization,[108] the territory they control, the duration and intensity of the fighting, and the seriousness and recurrence of the rebel attacks and whether they have spread.[109] The ICTY's *Prosecutor v. Limaj* opinion provides guidance in distinguishing a common Article 3 conflict,[110] as does the aggregate list of factors, included along with a *Limaj* extract in this chapter's Cases and Materials.

In so-called CARs conflicts, which are described in Article 1.4 of Additional Protocol I, what LOAC applies? All four Geneva Conventions apply, en toto, along with 1977 Additional Protocol I, just as in a common Article 2 conflict. (Lack of conformance with Protocol I Article 96.3, the CARs registration requirement, has not been tested or adjudicated, so the result of a failure to register is unknown.) When a CARs conflict is initiated, and to date none has been, it is treated as an international armed conflict.

When does 1977 Additional Protocol I apply? Anytime the 1949 conventions apply – whenever there is armed conflict between two or more high contracting parties – a common Article 2 conflict. Protocol I never applies alone; it always goes hand in hand with the four 1949 conventions.

When does Protocol II, alone, apply? In any noninternational armed conflict, and in common Article 3 conflicts in which the rebels control sufficient territory from which to launch concerted military operations. Protocol II does not apply in cases of criminality or mere banditry, and it does not apply if the rebels do not hold sufficient territory.

In cases of mere criminality and banditry, what LOAC applies? No LOAC applies, not even common Article 3. Nor does customary international law apply. Domestic law, which includes human rights law, applies.

What LOAC applies if State A is combating an internal insurgency and asks for assistance from State B, and State B sends trainers from its army to assist State A in its armed conflict? Because the conflict remains between State A and its insurgents, and not between State B's trainers and the insurgents, it continues to be a common Article 3 internal armed conflict.

---

[107] *Prosecutor v. Tadić*, Decision on Interlocutory Appeal, supra, note 17, at para. 70.

[108] *Prosecutor v. Mrkšić, et al.*, IT-95-13/1-T (27 Sept. 2007), para. 407: "Some degree of organization" by the parties will suffice to establish the existence of an armed conflict, citing *Tadić*, supra, note 17, at para. 562: "The test applied ... to the existence of an armed conflict for the purposes of the rules contained in Common Article 3 focuses on two aspects of a conflict; the intensity of the conflict and the organization of the parties to the conflict."

[109] *Tadić*, Opinion and Judgment, supra, note 23, at paras. 566–8; *Prosecutor v. Kordić and Čerkez*, IT-95–14, (Feb. 26, 2001), para. 29–30; *Prosecutor v. Delalić* (aka Mucić/"Čelebici"), IT-96–21-T (16 Nov. 1998), paras. 190–2.

[110] *Prosecutor v. Limaj*, IT-03-66-T (Nov. 30, 2005), paras. 167–70. See Cases and Materials, this chapter.

What LOAC applies if State A is combating an internal insurgency and the insurgents ask for assistance from State B, and State B sends the insurgents trainers from its army to assist the insurgents in their armed conflict against State A? Now the conflict is between the insurgents *and* armed forces from State B, both engaged in armed conflict against State A. It has become a common Article 2 international armed conflict.[111]

Additionally, case law makes clear that common Article 3, despite its wording apparently limiting it to noninternational conflicts, applies in all armed conflicts – international, noninternational, peace keeping, or peace-enforcing operations, et cetera.[112]

Whether viewed as a common Article 2 or 3 conflict, responsive cross-border attacks in self-defense of attacks by terrorists who then retreat and harbor in states abutting an active battlefield, sometimes called "extraterritorial law enforcement," though not universally embraced, is becoming an accepted if arguable concept of international law. When a state is attacked by a terrorist group, whether or not the terrorists make physical entry into the victim state, and the attack is sufficient to raise a *jus ad bellum* right to self-defense, and the terrorist group is based in or harbored in another state that will not or cannot act to control the terrorist group, the victim state has the right to cross the other state's borders to enforce the international law of self-defense and attack the terrorist group. Such an attack may not target the harboring state, however.

Finally, if all this is less than crystal clear, do not be discouraged. It is sometimes challenging to classify armed conflicts. Difficult examples include the long-running British–Irish Republican Army (IRA) conflict in Northern Ireland, and the December 1989 U.S. invasion of Panama (Operation Just Cause). In The Hague, "the ICTY Prosecutor maintained Article 2 charges and successfully established the international nature of the armed conflict in only seven cases out of eighteen. In the other eleven cases, the Prosecutor only established the existence of an armed conflict."[113] American jurists can find it difficult to determine the status of an armed conflict. For example, the U.S. conflict in Afghanistan, the status of which is blithely decided in these pages as a noninternational armed conflict, has trod a twisted trail in American courts:

> These three [U.S. court] decisions offer three separate opinions on the way in which the conflict in Afghanistan with al Qaeda should be classified: ... [The trial court decided it was] an international armed conflict within the *Geneva Conventions*;[114] the Court of Appeals also characterized it as an international conflict (but one that was outside the scope of the *Geneva Conventions*);[115] and the Supreme Court decided (at the very least) that the protections afforded in non-international armed conflicts should be applied.[116] The *Hamdan* cases demonstrate the painstaking and sometimes frustrating discussions that take place in applying (or misapplying) the law of armed conflict to a situation that may not easily be characterized as either an internal or international armed conflict. ... The different rulings

---

[111] *Prosecutor v. Tadić*, supra, note 27, at para. 84.

[112] *Prosecutor v. Delalić, et al.*, (IT-96–21-A). Appeal Judgment (Feb. 20, 2001), para. 143, footnote omitted.

[113] La Haye, *War Crimes in Internal Armed Conflicts*, supra, note 16, at 322.

[114] *Salim Ahmed Hamdan v. Donald H. Rumsfeld, Secretary of Defense*, 344 F Supp.2d 152, 161 (2004).

[115] *Salim Ahmed Hamdan v. Donald H. Rumsfeld, Secretary of Defense*, 415 F.3d 33, 41–2 (2005).

[116] *Hamdan v. Rumsfeld*, 548 U.S. 557 (2006).

encapsulate ... the difficulties in utilizing these definitions in a system that lacks a formal mechanism for classifying conflicts.[117]

We are not alone in our occasional confusion. The passage of time has yielded case law and writings of commentators that make the decision easier.

CASES AND MATERIALS

FACTORS INDICATING A NON-INTERNATIONAL ARMED CONFLICT

Introduction. The characterization of an international armed conflict is clear; World War II (1939–45), for example, was obviously a common Article 2 international armed conflict, states versus states. But was the conflict in the former Yugoslavia (1991–2001) national or noninternational? Or was it both, changing at some point from one to the other? Or was it a series of wars of both characterizations? What if a "border incident" escalates and becomes protracted and eventually involves heavy weapons? If the Texas Free State declares its independence from the United States, backing its declaration with small arms and threats to kill federal agents or military troops who approach their "state," is that a common Article 3 noninternational armed conflict? The criteria for a noninternational armed conflict that follow have been culled from ICTY case law and authoritative writing on the subject.

The "Parties" Requirement

"Common Article 3 expressly refers to 'each Party to the conflict' thereby implying that a precondition for its application is the existence of at least two **'parties.'**"[118]
Factors indicating the existence of a party include:

1. An ability to implement LOAC;[119]
2. The existence of a headquarters;[120]
3. Disciplinary rules and mechanisms;[121]
4. Ability to plan, coordinate, and carry out military operations, including troop movements and logistics;[122]
5. Designated zones of operation;[123]
6. The ability to procure, transport, and distribute arms;[124]
7. An ability to negotiate and conclude agreements, such as ceasefire or peace accords.[125]

---

[117] Alison Duxbury, "Drawing Lines in the Sand – Characterising Conflicts for the Purposes of Teaching International Humanitarian Law," 8–2 *Melbourne J. of Int'l L.* (2007), 259, 263. Footnotes as in original.
[118] Pejic," Protective Scope of Common Article 3," supra, note 18, at 191.   [119] Id., at 192
[120] *Prosecutor v. Limaj, et al.*, IT-03-66-T, ICTY Judgment, para. 90 (Nov. 30, 2005). Footnotes omitted
[121] Pejic, "Protective Scope of Common Article 3," supra, note 18, at 192.   [122] Id.
[123] *Limaj*, supra, note 110.   [124] Id.
[125] Pejic, "Protective Scope of Common Article 3," supra, note 18, at 192.

The "Intensity" Requirement for a NIAC

Factors indicating the requisite level of intensity include:

1. The number, **duration,** and **intensity** of individual confrontations;[126]
2. The seriousness of attacks and whether there has been an increase in armed attacks;[127]
3. The spread of clashes over territory and over a period of time;[128]
4. Any increase in the number of government forces and mobilization and the distribution of weapons among both parties to the conflict;[129]
5. The type of weapons and other military equipment;[130]
6. The number and caliber of munitions fired;[131]
7. The number of persons and types of forces partaking in the fighting;[132]
8. The number of casualties and extant of material destruction;[133]
9. The number of civilians fleeing the combat zones;[134]
10. Whether the conflict has attracted the attention of the United Nations Security Council, and, whether any resolutions on the matter have been passed.[135]
11. Whether the engagement of the armed forces is required.[136]

Conclusion. No international armed conflict is likely to exhibit all of these indicia. Nor are the indicia unvarying or fixed. Neither are they law. Every case is unique and requires the application of informed judgment.

DETERMINING CONFLICT STATUS: AN EXERCISE

Upon reading of an armed conflict in a newspaper, magazine, or blog, or seeing a televised or online account of one, it usually is not difficult to determine the conflict status, the first question a student of LOAC/IHL should answer. Most conflicts will reveal their nature with a little informed thought. For example, what conflict status does this scenario suggest?

Scenario

On the night of November 26, 2008, ten individuals of Pakistani origin landed by boat in the Indian port city of Mumbai. The ten young men, members of the radical Muslim Lashkar-e-Taiba group, were led by a twenty-five-year-old Pakistani. They had received prior military-like training in Pakistan over an extended period, allegedly from the Pakistani army. Armed with automatic rifles, handguns, hand grenades, and explosives, the ten men had departed from Karachi, Pakistan, by sea, in a small boat. They commandeered a fishing boat, murdered the crew, and, at about 2030, landed in Mumbai. Well rehearsed, they split into two-man teams and proceeded to five targets. Directed by GPS devices, they maintained communication via cell phones with each other and with others still in Pakistan. One team of attackers struck Mumbai's crowded train station, another team fired on a popular tourist restaurant, and a third team attacked a Jewish center. Two other teams entered two luxury hotels. Each team fired at random targets of opportunity as they progressed. The small band of attackers reunited and took

---

[126] Id.   [127] *Limaj*, supra, note 110.   [128] Id.   [129] Id.
[130] Pejic, "Protective Scope of Common Article 3," supra, note 18, at 192.   [131] Id.   [132] Id.   [133] Id.
[134] Id.   [135] *Limaj*, supra, note 110.
[136] *Prosecutor v. Boškoski, Johan Tarčulovski*, IT-04-82-T, ICTY Judgment, para. 190 (July 10, 2008).

over the two popular tourist hotels, killing occupants as they went room to room, receiving instructions and advice by cell phone from handlers in Pakistan: "At the Oberoi [hotel], an attacker asked whether to spare women ('Kill them,' came the terse reply)."[137]

The next day, Indian commandos rappelled from helicopters onto the roofs of the two hotels, one of which had been set afire by the attackers. For the next two days, Indian army and navy troops, along with National Security Guard commandos, cleared the two hotels, room by room. At the train station, the restaurant, the Jewish center, and the hotels, Indian police and armed forces eventually killed nine of the raiders and captured the remaining attacker. Before they were killed or captured, the attackers killed 163 noncombatants and 18 Indian security force members. Additionally, they wounded 293 civilians.

Question: Was this a common Article 2 international armed conflict, a common Article 3 noninternational armed conflict, or a domestic law enforcement event?

Answer: A basic question is whether the event was an armed conflict at all. An armed robbery of a bank by a gang of well-trained criminals is simple criminality not constituting "armed conflict" in the sense of LOAC/IHL. A simple exchange of shots between border guards of two unfriendly states on a contested national boundary approaches armed conflict between two states but is unlikely to be considered more than a border incident. There is no internationally accepted definition of "armed conflict" because the circumstances that might or might not constitute an armed conflict are numerous and nuanced. A commonsense assessment of the facts of a given situation will usually indicate whether an event constitutes an armed conflict. It is settled, however, that a terrorist attack, or series of terrorist attacks, such as al Qaeda's 9/11 attacks on the United States, may give rise to an attacked state's resort to armed force in self-defense. Pictet writes, "Any difference arising *between two States* and leading to the intervention of armed forces is an armed conflict within the meaning of Article 2."[138]

The situation described in the scenario evolved over a period of days and involved police, security, and military forces, as well as the deaths of nearly two hundred people. Violence of this duration and intensity, involving military units and a well-organized armed group, could be viewed as an armed conflict, but in examining situations in which the conflict status is not obvious, like this scenario, the prudent student should examine the two possible armed conflict statuses before deciding whether the event was armed conflict or something less, such as a domestic law enforcement problem.

First consider the most significant LOAC/IHL possibility: Was the situation a common Article 2 international armed conflict? What facts and circumstances suggest satisfaction of the requirements of common Article 2? "The present Convention shall apply to all cases of declared war or of any other armed conflict which may arise *between two or more High Contracting Parties.*"

In the scenario, the attackers were trained in Pakistan, presumably by Pakistanis, and provided with Pakistani weaponry. They initiated their attack in Pakistan and landed in India; they were from one state and they acted in another state. The victims were from several states.

---

[137] Somini Sengupta, "In Mumbai Transcripts, an Attack Directed from Afar," NY *Times*, Jan. 7, 2009, A5.
[138] Jean S. Pictet, ed., *Commentary, I Geneva Convention* (Geneva: ICRC, 1952), 32, footnote omitted, emphasis supplied.

Presuming for the sake of analysis that there was armed conflict, was it armed conflict *between two or more high contracting parties*, as required by common Article 2? Clearly it was not. Although two or more states had roles in the attack, and although Pakistani attackers acted in India, this does not appear to be a case of one state (high contracting party) acting against a second state. It was a case of *individuals* from one state acting against *individuals* from other states. One could even argue that it was individuals from one state acting against another state, per se, but it does not appear to be one *state* acting against another *state*. Nor does it appear to be one state dispatching foreign or nonstate surrogates to attack another state. It was not a common Article 2 armed conflict.

It may be argued that there was sufficient Pakistani governmental involvement and control to consider the attack an act of Pakistan.[139] Additional facts may surface over time supporting or confirming that view, but, as of this writing, the argument is weak and insufficient to confirm that position. Rather, the reported evidence indicates that the terrorist attackers were controlled by religious extremists located in Pakistan.

If not a common Article 2 conflict, next look at the remaining conflict status possibilities. Consider the two remaining possibilities jointly. What facts in the scenario suggest it was either a common Article 3 noninternational armed conflict or a domestic law enforcement event?

What circumstances suggest satisfaction of the requirements of common Article 3? Was the incident an "armed conflict not of an international character occurring in the territory of one of the High Contracting Parties"? The attack obviously occurred in the territory of a high contracting party, India. (The event should be considered a single attack, even though the attackers had multiple objectives.) Might the attack have been a domestic law enforcement event, rather than a common Article 3 armed conflict? Making a determination between the two choices requires review of the factors bearing on conflict status classification. What are the scenario's indicia of a noninternational armed conflict, as opposed to a domestic criminal event, and vice versa?

For a finding of common Article 3 conflict status, there are two primary determining considerations: first, the level, intensity, and duration of violence that occurred; and second, the organization of the terrorist attackers who were involved. There are other considerations: Were the armed forces of the state required to meet the attackers' violence? Was territory controlled by the attackers? If so, how much territory and for how long? Were other assaults mounted by the attackers, or was it a one-time event?

There is no bright-line guide to the relative significance to be given these factors, other than that the first two are usually given greater weight than the others. A student should consider each of the two possibilities and make an assessment based on the totality of the circumstances that the event was either a common Article 3 armed conflict or a

---

[139] The U.N.'s 2001 *International Law Commission's Draft Articles on Responsibility of States for Internationally Wrongful Acts*, http://www.ilsa.org/jessup/jessup06/basicmats2/DAS, in its *Commentary* to Article 8, reads in pertinent part: "(1) As a general principle, the conduct of private persons or entities is not attributable to the State under international law. Circumstances may arise, however, where such conduct is nevertheless attributable to the State because there exists a specific factual relationship between the person or entity engaging in the conduct and the State. Article 8 deals with two such circumstances. The first involves private persons acting on the instructions of the State in carrying out the wrongful conduct. The second deals with a more general situation where private persons act under the State's direction or control." The *Commentary* goes on to discuss the standards for finding state control as found in the ICJ's *Nicaragua* case and the ICTY's *Tadić* case.

terrorist attack to be dealt with by domestic law enforcement, even if it involves the armed forces.

In the scenario, the armed violence was brief and, with due respect to those innocents killed and wounded, not particularly intense. (Media coverage does not necessarily correlate to level and intensity of violence.) The attackers were well rehearsed but only ten in number, making their organization a less significant issue. Indian armed forces were employed, but that does not necessarily indicate a common Article 3 conflict. In the United States, the national guard is called on to curb rioters, control posthurricane looters, and manage resisters of federal laws. Those situations are not considered armed conflicts. The scenario's attackers controlled no territory in their one-time attack. As Article 1.2 of 1977 Additional Protocol II notes, "This Protocol shall not apply in situations of internal disturbances ... such as riots, isolated and sporadic acts of violence ... as not being armed conflicts." Considering the totality of these circumstances, the November 26–9, 2008, attack on Mumbai was not a common Article 3 armed conflict and, in fact, was not an armed conflict as that term is used in LOAC/IHL. Contrary indicators may be cited and arguments raised in favor of common Article 3 but, all factors considered, the attack on Mumbai constituted a sporadic act of violence to be resolved by India's domestic law enforcement system.

Could one consider the attack an exercise of armed force short of war? No, two states were not involved. More significantly, this was not a case of a state attacked by an armed opposition group retaliating by crossing the group's host state border.

With this suggested guidance in mind, what was the conflict status of al Qaeda's 9/11 attacks on the United States?

PROSECUTOR V. FATMIR LIMAJ

IT-03–66-T (November 30, 2005). Footnotes omitted.

Introduction. When does an "armed conflict" arise? What factors indicate an armed conflict? The ICTY's Limaj *case offers answers to these sometimes-difficult questions.*

168. The Defence submit that a series of regionally disparate and temporally sporadic attacks carried out over a broad and contested geographic area should not be held to amount to an armed conflict. In the Chamber's view, the acts of violence that took place in Kosovo from the end of May 1998 at least until 26 July 1998 are not accurately described as temporally sporadic or geographically disperse. As discussed in the preceding paragraphs, periodic armed clashes occurred virtually continuously at intervals averaging three to seven days over a widespread and expanding geographic area.

169. The Defence further submit that a purely one-sided use of force cannot constitute protracted armed violence which will found the beginning of an armed conflict. In the Chamber's view, this proposition is not supported by the facts established in this case. While the evidence indicates that the KLA [Kosovo Liberation Army] forces were less numerous than the Serbian forces, less organized and less prepared, and were not as well trained or armed, the evidence does not suggest that the conflict was purely one-sided. KLA attacks were carried out against a variety of Serbian military, community and commercial targets over a widespread and expanding area of Kosovo. Further, KLA forces were able to offer strong and often effective

resistance to Serbian forces undertaking military and police operations. While very large numbers of Serbian forces, well equipped, were deployed in the relevant areas of Kosovo during the period relevant to the indictment, the KLA enjoyed a significant level of overall military success, tying up the Serbian forces by what were usually very effective guerrilla-type tactics.

170. Finally, the Defence submit that the strength of the Serbian forces does not indicate that their purpose was to defeat the KLA, but to ethnically cleanse Kosovo. While it is true that civilians were driven out of their homes and forced to leave Kosovo as a result of military operations, the evidence discloses this to be true for both sides. Undoubtedly civilians fled as their homes and villages were ravaged and in some cases armed units of both sides set about ensuring this. It is not apparent to the chamber, however, that the immediate purpose of the military apparatus of each side during the relevant period, was not directed to the defeat of the opposing party, even if some further or ultimate objective may also have existed. The two forces were substantially engaged in their mutual military struggle. While the Serbian forces were far more numerous and better trained and equipped, it appears they were ill-prepared to deal effectively with small guerrilla type forces that would not engage them in prolonged fixed engagements. Serbian military intelligence may also have overestimated the strength and capability of the KLA at the time so that the Serbian forces were arraigned in greater number and with greater military resources than was warranted by the actual KLA forces. In this respect, as revealed by the evidence, many combat operations were carried out in the area of Drenica where the KLA developed earlier and was probably best organised. But, most importantly in the Chamber's view, the determination of the existence of an armed conflict is based solely on two criteria: the intensity of the conflict and organization of the parties, the purpose of the armed forces to engage in acts of violence or also achieve some further objective is, therefore, irrelevant.

(iii) Conclusion

171. The Chamber is satisfied that before the end of May 1998 an armed conflict existed in Kosovo between the Serbian forces and the KLA. By that time the KLA had a General Staff, which appointed zone commanders, gave directions to the various units formed or in the process of being formed, and issued public statements on behalf of the organization. Unit commanders gave combat orders, and subordinate units and soldiers generally acted in accordance with these orders. Steps have been established to introduce disciplinary rules and military police, as well as to recruit, train, and equip new members. Although generally inferior to the VJ [Army of Yugoslavia] and MUP's [forces of the Ministry of Interior of the Republic of Serbia] equipment, the KLA soldiers had weapons, which included artillery mortars and rocket launchers. By July 1998 the KLA had gained acceptance as a necessary and valid participant in negotiations with international governments and bodies to determine a solution for the Kosovo crisis, and to lay down conditions in these negotiations for refraining from military action.

172. Further, by the end of May 1998 KLA units were constantly engaged in armed clashes with substantial Serbian forces. ... The ability of the KLA to engage in such varied operations is a further indicator of its level of organization. Heavily armed special forces of the Serbian MUP and VJ forces were committed to the conflict on the Serbian side and their efforts were directed to the control and quelling of the KLA forces.

Civilians, both Serbian and Kosovo Albanian, had been forced by the military actions to leave their homes, villages and towns and the number of casualties was growing.

173. In view of the above the Chamber is persuaded and finds that an internal armed conflict existed in Kosovo before the end of May 1998. This continued until long after 26 July 1998.

Conclusion. The difference between the facts in this case and those in the ten-man attack in the preceding scenario is evident. Here, in a case fraught with potential jurisdictional problems, the chamber was careful to recite the facts in support of its finding of a common Article 3 conflict.

PROSECUTOR V. DUSKO TADIĆ

(IT-94-1-A) Defense Motion for Interlocutory Appeal on Jurisdiction
(October 2, 1995)

Introduction. In the seminal Tadić case, the ICTY Appeals Chamber examines the character of international and non-international conflicts involving a bewildering array of combatant forces. The opinion wrestles with the question of the nature of the conflict: Is it an armed conflict at all? If so, what is its nature, international or internal (non-international), and what factors make it so? The opinion reflects the difficulty of applying seemingly clear-cut rules defining the nature of a conflict.

Rulings of the ICTY are not binding on U.S. courts. On issues of LOAC/IHL they are, however, persuasive.

(Lieutenant Colonel Brenda Hollis, a U.S. Air Force judge advocate, and U.S. Marine Corps Major Michael Keegan, also a judge advocate, were both assigned temporary duty with the ICTY and were on the five-member Tadić prosecution team.)

66. Appellant [Dusko Tadić] now asserts the new position that there did not exist a legally cognizable armed conflict – either internal or international – at the time and place that the alleged offenses were committed. Appellant's argument is based on a concept of armed conflict covering only the precise time and place of actual hostilities. Appellant claims that the conflict in the Prijedor region (where the alleged crimes are said to have taken place) was limited to a political assumption of power by the Bosnian Serbs and did not involve armed combat (though movements of tanks are admitted). This argument presents a preliminary issue to which we turn first.

67. International humanitarian law governs the conduct of both internal and international armed conflicts. Appellant correctly points out that for there to be a violation of this body of law, there must be an armed conflict. The definition of "armed conflict" varies depending on whether the hostilities are international or internal but, contrary to Appellant's contention, the temporal and geographical scope of both internal and international armed conflicts extends beyond the exact time and place of hostilities. With respect to the temporal frame of reference of international armed conflicts, each of the four Geneva Conventions contains language intimating that their application may extend beyond the cessation of fighting. For example, both Conventions I and II apply until protected persons who have fallen into the power of the enemy have been released and repatriated. . . .

68. Although the Geneva Conventions are silent as to the geographical scope of international "armed conflicts," the provisions suggest that at least some of the provisions

of the Conventions apply to the entire territory of the Parties to the conflict, not just to the vicinity of actual hostilities. Certainly, some of the provisions are clearly bound up with the hostilities and the geographical scope of those provisions should be so limited. Others, particularly those relating to the protection of prisoners of war and civilians, are not so limited. With respect to prisoners of war, the Convention applies to combatants in the power of the enemy; it makes no difference whether they are kept in the vicinity of hostilities. In the same vein, Geneva Convention IV protects civilians anywhere in the territory of the Parties. . . .

69. The geographical and temporal frame of reference for internal armed conflicts is similarly broad. This conception is reflected in the fact that beneficiaries of common Article 3 of the Geneva Conventions are those taking no active part (or no longer taking active part) in the hostilities. This indicates that the rules contained in Article 3 also apply outside the narrow geographical context of the actual theater of combat operations. . . .

70. On the basis of the foregoing, we find that an armed conflict exists whenever there is a resort to armed force between States or protracted armed violence between governmental authorities and organized armed groups or between such groups within a State. International humanitarian law applies from the initiation of such armed conflicts and extends beyond the cessation of hostilities until a general conclusion of peace is reached; or, in the case of internal conflicts, a peaceful settlement is achieved. Until that moment, international humanitarian law continues to apply in the whole territory under the control of a party, whether or not actual combat takes place there. Applying the foregoing concept of armed conflicts to this case, we hold that the alleged crimes were committed in the context of an armed conflict. Fighting among the various entities within the former Yugoslavia began in 1991, continued through the summer of 1992 when the alleged crimes are said to have been committed, and persists to this day. Notwithstanding the various temporary cease-fire agreements, no general conclusion of peace has brought military operations in the region to a close. These hostilities exceed the intensity requirements applicable to both international and internal armed conflicts. There has been protracted, large-scale violence between the armed forces of different States and between governmental forces and organized insurgent groups. Even if substantial clashes were not occurring in the Prijedor region at the time and place the crimes allegedly were committed – a factual issue on which the Appeals Chamber does not pronounce – international humanitarian law applies. It is sufficient that the alleged crimes were closely related to the hostilities occurring in other parts of the territories controlled by the parties to the conflict. There is no doubt that the allegations at issue here bear the required relationship. The indictment states that in 1992 Bosnian Serbs took control of the Opstina of Prijedor and established a prison camp in Omarska. It further alleges that crimes were committed against civilians inside and outside the Omarska prison camp as part of the Bosnian Serb take-over and consolidation of power in the Prijedor region, which was, in turn, part of the larger Bosnian Serb military campaign to obtain control over Bosnian territory. Appellant offers no contrary evidence. . . . In light of the foregoing, we conclude that, for the purposes of applying international humanitarian law, the crimes alleged were committed in the context of an armed conflict. . . .

72. In adopting resolution 827, the Security Council established the International Tribunal with the stated purpose of bringing to justice persons responsible for serious

violations of international humanitarian law in the former Yugoslavia, thereby deterring future violations and contributing to the re-establishment of peace and security in the region. The context in which the Security Council acted indicates that it intended to achieve this purpose without reference to whether the conflicts in the former Yugoslavia were internal or international.

As the members of the Security Council well knew, in 1993, when the Statute [of the ICTY] was drafted, the conflicts in the former Yugoslavia could have been characterized as both internal and international, or alternatively, as an internal conflict alongside an international one, or as an international conflict that had subsequently been replaced by one or more internal conflicts, or some combination thereof. The conflict in the former Yugoslavia had been rendered international by the involvement of the Croatian Army in Bosnia-Herzegovina and by the involvement of the Yugoslav National Army ("JNA") in hostilities in Croatia, as well as in Bosnia-Herzegovina at least until its formal withdrawal on 19 May 1992. To the extent that the conflicts had been limited to clashes between Bosnian Government forces and Bosnian Serb rebel forces in Bosnia-Herzegovina, as well as between the Croatian Government and Croatian Serb rebel forces in Krajina (Croatia), they had been internal. ... It is notable that the parties to this case also agree that the conflicts in the former Yugoslavia since 1991 have had both internal and international aspects. ...

73. The varying nature of the conflicts is evidenced by the agreements reached by the various parties to abide by certain rules of humanitarian law. Reflecting the international aspects of the conflicts ... representatives of the Federal Republic of Yugoslavia, the Yugoslavia People's Army, the Republic of Croatia, and the Republic of Serbia entered into an agreement on the implementation of the Geneva Conventions of 1949 and the 1977 Additional Protocol I. ... Significantly, the parties refrained from making any mention of common Article 3 ... concerning non-international armed conflicts.

By contrast, an agreement ... between the various factions of the conflict within the Republic of Bosnia and Herzegovina reflects the internal aspects of the conflicts. The agreement was based on common Article 3 ... which, in addition to setting forth rules governing internal conflicts, provides ... that the parties to such conflicts may agree to bring into force provisions of the Geneva Conventions that are generally applicable only in international armed conflicts. In the Agreement, representatives of [Bosnia and Herzegovina, Serbia, and Croatia] committed the parties to abide by the substantive rules of internal armed conflict contained in common Article 3 and in addition agreed, on the strength of common Article 3, paragraph 3, to apply certain provisions of the Geneva Conventions concerning international conflicts. ... Clearly, this Agreement shows that the parties concerned regarded the armed conflicts in which they were involved as internal but, in view of their magnitude, they agreed to extend to them the application of some provisions of the Geneva Conventions that are normally applicable to international armed conflicts only. ...

Taken together, the agreements reached between the various parties to the conflict(s) ... bear out the proposition that, when the Security Council adopted the Statute [of the ICTY], it did so with reference to situations that the parties themselves considered at different times and places as either internal or international armed conflicts, or as a mixed internal-international conflict.

74. The Security Council's many statements leading up to the establishment of the [ICTY] reflect an awareness of the mixed character of the conflicts. ... The Prosecutor

makes much of the Security Council's repeated reference to the grave breaches provisions of the Geneva Conventions, which are generally deemed applicable only to international armed conflicts. This argument ignores, however, that ... it has also referred generally to "other violations of international humanitarian law," an expression which covers the law applicable in internal armed conflicts as well. ...

77. On the basis of the foregoing, we conclude that the conflicts in the former Yugoslavia have both internal and international aspects, that the members of the Security Council ... and that they intended to empower the [ICTY] to adjudicate violations of humanitarian law that occurred in either context.

CASE CONCERNING MILITARY AND PARAMILITARY ACTIVITIES IN AND AGAINST NICARAGUA

Judgment (Merits) of 27 June 1986 (ICJ Rep. 14). Footnotes and case citations omitted.

Introduction. This ICJ judgment demonstrates some of the considerations involved in determining conflict status. The opinion concerns collective self-defense and non-intervention in another state's government, and the U.N. Charter's interpretation of those subjects. It also focuses on the elements of control necessary for a foreign state to be said to control forces, including insurgents, of another state. In the 275-page opinion, customary law is frequently mentioned, the Geneva Conventions seldom spoken of. Conflict status is mentioned only briefly, although it is an underlying issue throughout. "By absolving the government of Nicaragua of responsibility for 'any flow of arms' to the Salvadorian insurrection 'at either period,' [para. 160] the Court essentially accepted the truth of the affidavit of the Nicaraguan foreign minister. To what should have been the profound embarrassment of the Court, it subsequently was proved that the affidavit of the Nicaraguan foreign minister was false and that the Sandanista government of Nicaragua grossly misled the Court."[140]

As you read these excerpts going to conflict status ask yourself what that status was. Do you agree with the Court's assessment in paragraph 219?

19. The attitude of the United States Government to the "democratic coalition government" was at first favorable; and a programme of economic aid to Nicaragua was adopted. However, by 1981 this attitude had changed. ... According to the United States, the reason for this change of attitude was reports of involvement of the government of Nicaragua in logistical support, including provision of arms, for guerrillas in El Salvador. ... In September 1981, according to testimony called by Nicaragua, it was decided [by the U.S.] to plan and undertake activities directed against Nicaragua.

20. The armed opposition to the new Government in Nicaragua, which originally comprised various movements, subsequently became organized into two main groups: the Fuerza Democrática Nicaragüense (FDN) and the Alianza Revolucionaria Democrática (ARDE). ... However, after an initial period in which the "covert" operations of

---

[140] Stephen M. Schwebel, "Editorial Comment: Celebrating a Fraud on the Court," 106–1 *AJIL* (Jan. 2012), 102, 103.

United States personnel ... were kept from becoming public knowledge, it was made clear ... that the United States Government had been giving support to the *contras*, a term employed to describe those fighting against the present Nicaraguan Government. ... It is contended by Nicaragua that the united States Government is effectively in control of the contras ... and that the purpose of that Government was, from the beginning, to overthrow the Government of Nicaragua. ...

75. ... The Court will first deal with events which, in the submission of Nicaragua, involve the responsibility of the United States in a more direct manner. These are the mining of Nicaraguan ports or waters in early 1984; and certain attacks on, in particular, Nicaraguan port and oil installations. ... It is the contention of Nicaragua that these were not acts committed by members of the *contras* ... but either United States military personnel or persons of the nationality of unidentified Latin American countries, paid by, and acting on the direct instructions of, United States military or intelligence personnel. ...

92. ... Nicaragua claims that the United States has on a number of occasions carried out military maneuvers jointly with Honduras; it alleges that much of the military equipment flown in to Honduras for the joint maneuvers was turned over to the *contras* when the maneuvers ended. ...

100. In the affidavit of the former FDN leader, Mr. Chamorro ... he gives considerable detail as to the assistance given to the FDN. The Court does not however possess any comparable direct evidence as to support for the ARDE. ...

101. According to Mr. Chamorro, training was at the outset provided by Argentine military officers, paid by the CIA, gradually replaced by CIA personnel. The training was given in "guerrilla warfare, sabotage, demolitions, and in the use of a variety of weapons.". ...

106. In light of the evidence and material available to it, the court is not satisfied that all the operations launched by the contra force, at every stage of the conflict, reflected strategy and tactics wholly devised by the United States. ...

107. To sum up ... at least initially, the financial support given by the Government of the United States to the military and paramilitary activities of the *contras* in Nicaragua is a fully established fact. ...

114. According to Nicaragua, the *contras* are no more than bands of mercenaries which have been recruited, organized, paid and commanded by the Government of the United States. This would mean that they have no real autonomy in relation to that Government. Consequently, any offenses which they have committed would be imputable to the Government of the United States, like those of any other forces placed under the latter's command. ...

164. The Court, while not as fully informed on the question as it would wish to be, therefore considers as established the fact that certain trans-border military incursions into the territory of Honduras and Costa Rica are imputable to the Government of Nicaragua. ...

172. The Court now has to turn its attention to the question of the law applicable to the present dispute. ...

199. At all events, the Court finds that in customary international law ... there is no rule permitting the exercise of collective self-defence in the absence of a request by the State which regards itself as the victim of an armed attack. ...

211. For one State to use force against another, on the ground that the State has committed a wrongful act of force against a third State, is regarded as lawful, by way of exception, only when the wrongful act provoking the response was an armed attack. ...

States do not have a right of "collective" armed response to acts which do not constitute an "armed attack.". ...

218. ... Article 3 which is common to all four Geneva Conventions of 12 August 1949 defines certain rules to be applied in the armed conflicts of a non-international character. There is no doubt that, in the event of international armed conflicts, these rules also constitute a minimum yardstick, in addition to the more elaborate rules which are also to apply to international conflicts; and they are rules which, in the Court's opinion, reflect what the Court in 1949 called "elementary considerations of humanity.". ...

219. The conflict between the *contras*' forces and those of the Government of Nicaragua is an armed conflict which is "not of an international character". The acts of the *contras* towards the Nicaraguan Government are therefore governed by the law applicable to conflicts of that character; whereas the actions of the United States in and against Nicaragua fall under the legal rules relating to international conflicts. ...

241. The Court however does not consider it necessary to seek to establish whether the intention of the United States to secure a change of government policies in Nicaragua went so far as to be equated with an endeavor to overthrow the Nicaraguan Government. It appears to the Court to be clearly established first, that the United States intended, by its support of the *contras*, to coerce the Government of Nicaragua in respect of matters in which each State is permitted, by the principle of State sovereignty, to decide freely ... and secondly that the intention of the *contras* themselves was to overthrow the present Government of Nicaragua. ... Even if it be accepted, for the sake of argument, that the objective of the United States in assisting the *contras* was solely to interdict the supply of arms to the armed opposition in El Salvador, it strains belief to suppose that a body formed in armed opposition to the Government of Nicaragua, and calling itself the "Nicaraguan Democratic Force", intended only to check Nicaraguan interference in El Salvador and did not intend to achieve violent change of government in Nicaragua.

Conclusion. In its decision, the ICJ rejected the U.S. justification of collective self-defense for its activities against Nicaragua, found that the United States had wrongfully intervened in the affairs of Nicaragua and had employed armed force against Nicaragua in breach of customary international law, and decided that the United States owed reparations to Nicaragua. The amount of reparations was later fixed at seventeen billion dollars. The check is not in the mail.

For our purposes, the most interesting conclusion of the Court was the conflict's status: a dual status conflict.

HAMDAN V. RUMSFELD

548 U.S. 557 (2006), at 630–631; 126 S. Ct. 2749, 2795–2796 (2006)[*]

Introduction. In 2006, a plurality of the Supreme Court of the United States had its own difficulties characterizing the conflict with al Qaeda. The Court had little doubt, however, as to whether common Article 2 or common Article 3 applied, and what protections therefore applied to "detainees" held by the United States. In this extract from the plurality opinion, the Court discusses whether the appellant, Hamdan, an accused member of al

---

[*] Citations and footnotes omitted.

*Qaeda confined at Guantanamo, Cuba, awaiting trial before a military commission, is
protected by common Article 3, with its requirement that "those placed hors de combat
by ... detention" be tried by a regularly constituted court.*

*The Court several times refers to Geneva Convention High Contracting Parties as "signa-
tories." In fact, High Contracting Parties are ratifiers, not merely signatories of the Conventions.*

The Court of Appeals thought, and the Government asserts, that Common Article 3 does
not apply to Hamdan because the conflict with al Qaeda, being "international in scope,"
does not qualify as a "conflict not of an international character." That reasoning is
erroneous. The term "conflict not of an international character" is used here in contradis-
tinction to a conflict between nations. ... Common Article 2 provides that "the present
Convention shall apply to all cases of declared war or of any other armed conflict which
may arise between two or more of the High Contracting Parties." High Contracting Parties
(signatories) also must abide by all terms of the Conventions vis-à-vis one another even if
one party to the conflict is a nonsignatory "Power," and must so abide vis-à-vis the
nonsignatory if "the latter accepts and applies those terms. Common Article 3, by contrast,
affords some minimal protection, falling short of full protection under the Conventions, to
individuals associated with neither a signatory nor even a nonsignatory "Power" who are
involved in a conflict "in the territory of" a signatory. The latter kind of conflict is
distinguishable from the conflict described in Common Article 2 chiefly because it does
not involve a clash between nations (whether signatories or not). In context, then, the
phrase "not of an international character" bears its literal meaning. ...

Although the official commentaries accompanying Common Article 3 indicate that an
important purpose of the provision was to furnish minimal protection to rebels involved
in one kind of "conflict not of an international character," *i.e.*, a civil war, the commentaries also make clear "that the scope of the Article must be as wide as possible." In fact,
limiting language that would have rendered Common Article 3 applicable "especially
[to] cases of civil war, colonial conflicts, or wars of religion," was omitted from the final
version of the Article, which coupled broader scope of application with a narrower range
of rights than did earlier proposed iterations.

Common Article 3, then, is applicable here and ... requires that Hamdan be tried by a
"regularly constituted court affording all the judicial guarantees which are recognized as
indispensable by civilized peoples."

Conclusion. *The Court goes on to find that "the [military commission] procedures adopted to
try Hamdan ... fail to afford the requisite guarantees," required by common Article 3, and
remands the case to a lower court for further proceedings. The opinion is significant because it
settles that, in the "war on terrorism," accused members of al Qaeda and, presumably, captured
members of any nonstate sponsored insurgency, fall under the protection of common Article 3.*

OSIRAK: ARMED CONFLICT?

Introduction. *More than thirty years ago, Israel attacked a nuclear facility inside Iraq,
much as they did in 2007, in Syria.*[141] *As you read this brief account of the 1979 attack, look*

---

[141] "Syria: Uranium Traces Found at Bombed Site, Diplomats Say," *NY Times*, Nov. 11, 2008, A11.

for indicia of conflict status. Could it be considered an instance of extraterritorial law enforcement? Or armed conflict short of war? Brief as the engagement was, what kind of conflict was it and what LOAC applied, if any?

The OPEC oil embargo of 1973–4 had recently ended, but the Western world still shuddered at the thought of losing Middle-Eastern oil, a considerable portion of which is held by Iraq. At about that time, France, dependent on Iraq for much of its oil, agreed to build a nuclear reactor for Iraq, at al-Tuwaitha, near the Tigris River. The original name of the facility was Osiris, the Egyptian god of the underworld. Ironically, several of the French contractors who worked on the Osiris project had also secretly built Israel's Dimona nuclear reactor in the 1960s. Italian firms provided critical chemical-reprocessing equipment. A second, smaller reactor, Isis, was to be built alongside Osiris and it was in the early stages of construction. France also agreed to provide Iraq with weapons-grade enriched uranium, U-235, as start-up fuel. U-235 can be converted to use in atomic weapons.

As Osiris neared completion, Saddam Hussein renamed the reactor Osirak, incorporating his nation's name in the reactor's designation. In May 1977, Israeli intelligence officers came into possession of photos of the rapidly rising structures at al-Tuwaitha. Laboratories, a reprocessing unit, administration buildings, and a thirty-foot high aluminum-domed nuclear reactor were already in place. As an oil-rich nation, Iraq had little need for nuclear power. Despite Israeli efforts to have the United States exert pressure on France to halt the project, the French carried on. They considered the financial aspects of the agreement with Iraq too lucrative to abandon. Osirak would apparently be fueled with radioactive uranium within three or four years of the construction start-up. It was estimated that the facility could produce enriched uranium to annually build several Hiroshima-sized nuclear bombs. Israel, Iraq's traditional enemy, was extremely concerned.

The United States and U.K. also expressed concern, but European heads of state, recalling the recent oil embargo, had no desire for a confrontation with oil-rich Iraq. Believing that it had to act, Israel began plans to destroy the facility at Osirak. Initially, Israeli intelligence opposed a military raid, considering any military effort to shut down the reactor a risky undertaking tantamount to an act of war. Besides, should the timing of any raid be off, even by only a few days, and the reactor activated, it could be "hot" and its destruction might release radiation that could kill thousands of civilians as far away as Baghdad. Nevertheless, Israeli Prime Minister Menachem Begin ordered contingency plans for a military operation to target Osirak.

In April 1979, at La Seyne-sur-Mer, France, heavily guarded French trucks carrying the two nuclear reactor cores to port for shipment to Iraq were bombed by Israeli agents. At a rest stop, the Israelis created a diversionary car accident while other Israelis placed plastic explosives at critical points on the huge reactor shipping containers. Although the explosives would not destroy the heavy metal cores, they would damage them. After the bombing it was determined that it would take two years to remanufacture replacement cores. Iraq insisted the damaged cores be repaired, instead. They were willing to accept the French reactor cores with hairline cracks. Despite the Israeli sabotage, and the mysterious deaths of two critical Iraqi engineers who were visiting France, work at Osirak continued.

In Israel, military planning proceeded. An Entebbe-like mission was not feasible because of the complex logistics involved in the ingress and egress of combatant troops. Tall earthen embankments surrounding Osirak, topped by electrified fencing and antiaircraft gun towers, made a commando-style raid unlikely. An air attack seemed the only alternative. Israel had recently purchased from the United States eight F-16 fighters originally intended for the Iranian Air Force. The Shah's fall had voided the sale. Now, a search was mounted for the best pilots in the Israeli Air Force. In Israel's view, time was growing short. Israeli intelligence, aided significantly by U.S. KH-11 reconnaissance satellite photos, predicted that Osirak would be operational within six months. Operation Babylon was no longer a contingency plan.

In October 1980, Prime Minister Begin ordered the attack. F-16s, flying 600 miles nonstop and without midair refueling, would strike Osirak just before sundown on a Sunday, minimizing civilian casualties while at the same time providing necessary light for bombing. The Israelis were concerned that as few French scientists and civilians as possible be killed. The handpicked Israeli pilots began training for a long-range, low-level mission.

The question of munitions was considered. "Smart" bombs externally mounted on the F-16s were not an option. Their weight and drag would increase fuel use, which was already a critical factor. The six-hundred-mile round-trip was forty miles beyond the F-16's maximum range. Instead, each F-16 would carry two 2,000-pound "dumb" bombs to penetrate Osirak's dome and destroy the reactor inside.

The Israeli pilots, used to flying only seconds before they engaged enemy targets in adjacent enemy countries, would have to fly for hours at treetop level, violating Jordanian airspace on the way in and out of Iraq. Nearing the target, pairs of F-16s would pop up to 5,000 feet and approach the reactor at high speed as they dove at a steep angle while under Iraqi antiaircraft fire. Aiming visually, they would release their bombs and then seek high altitude beyond surface-to-air missile range. While in training, two of the twelve pilots collided in midair and died. A third pilot died in another training mishap. (Another Israeli pilot on the Osirak mission, Ilan Ramon, later was selected as an astronaut in the American space flight program. He died when Columbia exploded on reentry, in February 2003.)

At 1601 on Sunday, June 7, 1981, eight F-16s took off from the Israeli Air Force base at Etzion in the northern Sinai. Israel estimated that Osirak would be operational within weeks. French technicians installing the reactor later said it was scheduled to be operational only by the end of 1981. Regardless, on June 7, as the F-16s took off, six F-15s were already airborne to shadow the eight attackers and keep any Baghdad-based MiGs off their backs. At a modest speed of 360 knots to minimize fuel consumption, they flew toward Iraq in radio silence. Although the setting sun would be behind them, they were on their own in evading shoulder-fired SA-7 antiaircraft missiles, and the far deadlier SAM-6s.

An hour and a half after takeoff, the attackers crossed their initial point, a lake just west of Osirak. Moving into tight formation, the F-16s prepared to attack in pairs at thirty-second intervals. Amazingly, there was no antiaircraft fire. Surprise was complete. Flying on full military power, in four seconds the F-16s popped up to 5,000 feet, rolled belly-up for a few moments to maintain positive Gs until the diving 480-knot bomb run commenced. In a deep dive, the F-16s released their bombs at 3,400 feet, pulled left, dumped chaff, and climbed for altitude and safety from Iraqi SAMs and MiGs. The final two F-16 pairs flew through a storm of antiaircraft fire and SA-7s – but no SAMs. Later it was learned that half an hour before the Israelis arrived, Iraqi soldiers manning the SAM batteries had left for chow, shutting down their radars as they left.

As the final pair of F-16s released their ordnance, the Osirak dome exploded in a fireball. In little more than two minutes, years of French and Iraqi work was destroyed.

Fourteen of the sixteen bombs had been on target. The first two delay-fused bombs penetrated the dome, opening a gaping hole for twelve succeeding bombs. Isis and the Italian laboratories remained intact, but the crucial nuclear reactor was gone, destroyed without casualties among the attackers.[142]

International repercussions were immediate. Israel asserted that its attack was a matter of anticipatory self-defense, and some scholars agreed.[143] Israel said that it acted to remove a nuclear threat to its existence, claiming "pre-emptive self-defense for the strike on the basis that a nuclear-armed Iraq would constitute an unacceptable threat, given Saddam Hussein's overt hostility towards the Jewish state. Israel also claimed to have met the requirement of proportionality, having bombed the construction site on a Sunday in order to lessen the risk to foreign workers."[144] But U.N. Security Council Resolution 487, unanimously passed, denounced the attack as being "in clear violation of the Charter . . . and the norms of international conduct."[145] Prior to the U.N. vote on a resolution to denounce Israel, Canada "argued that the General Assembly should not use the term 'acts of aggression'; it was a matter for the Security Council to make such determinations."[146] The United States, which might have been expected to abstain, voted to condemn Israel. The international community's reaction was damning.

> Assuming for purposes of legal analysis that the government of Israel perceived an imminent danger in the Iraqi nuclear program . . . it is clear that it undertook at most very limited peaceful procedures or diplomatic measures to deal with the threat. . . . In evaluating the Israeli claim of actual necessity, it is decisive that the community of states has rejected the Israeli claim. So far as is known, not one single state has accepted its validity.[147]

Was the Israeli bombing successful in ending the Iraqi nuclear threat? "Israeli intelligence . . . was convinced that their strike in 1981 on the Osirak nuclear reactor about 10 miles outside Baghdad had ended Saddam's program. Instead [it initiated] covert funding for a nuclear program code-named 'PC3' involving 5,000 people testing and building ingredients for a nuclear bomb."[148]

Conclusion. The U.N., of course, considered the issue of the Osirak bombing. "However, when dealing with the Osiraq raid, one ought not to lose sight of the distinctive features of the particular case. Indeed, what Israel was doing was not so much responding to a prior armed attack as originally envisioned under Article 51 U.N. Charter, but rather relying on a broad

---

[142] See Rodger W. Claire, *Raid on the Sun* (New York: Broadway Books, 2004), for a full account of the raid on Osirak.

[143] See, e.g., Stanimar A. Alexandrov, *Self-Defense against the Use of Force in International Law* (The Hague: Kluwer, 1996); and Timothy L. H. McCormack, *Self-Defense in International Law: The Israeli Raid on the Iraqi Nuclear Reactor* (New York: St. Martin's Press, 1996).

[144] Michael Byers, *War Law* (New York: Grove Press, 2005), 72. Although Israeli intelligence was convinced that the strike had ended Saddam's nuclear program, "Saddam was [still] on a crash program to build and detonate a crude nuclear weapon in the desert." Bob Woodward, *State of Denial* (New York: Simon & Schuster, 2006), 215.

[145] U.N. Security Council Resolution 487, June 19, 1981.

[146] Christine Gray, *International Law and the Use of Force* (Oxford: Oxford University Press, 2000), 13.

[147] W. Thomas Mallison, "The Disturbing Questions," 63 *Freedom at Issue* (Nov.–Dec. 1981), 9, 10, 11 cited in John Norton Moore et al., *National Security Law* (Durham, NC: Carolina Academic Press, 1990), 154–5.

[148] Bob Woodward, *State of Denial* (New York: Simon & Schuster, 2006), 215.

reading of self-defence allowing for 'pre-emptive' or even 'preventive self-defence."[149] During the debate, a range of viewpoints were put forward, including the following exchange:

SECURITY COUNCIL CONSIDERATION OF A COMPLAINT BY IRAQ

36 U.N. S.C.O.R., 2280–2288 (1981)

Ambassador Yehuda Blum (Israel):

57. On Sunday, 7 June 1981, the Israeli Air Force carried out an operation against the Iraqi atomic reactor called "Osirak".

58. In destroying Osirak, Israel performed an elementary act of self-preservation, both morally and legally. In so doing, Israel was exercising its inherent right of self-defense as understood in general international law and as preserved in Article 51 of the Charter of the United Nations.

59. A threat of nuclear obliteration was being developed against Israel by Iraq, one of Israel's most implacable enemies. Israel tried to have the threat halted by diplomatic means. Our efforts bore no fruit. Ultimately, we were left with no choice. We were obliged to remove that mortal danger. . . .

97. The Government of Israel, like any other Government, has the elementary duty to protect the lives of its citizens. In destroying Osirak last Sunday, Israel was exercising its inherent and natural right to self-defense. . . .

99. In a similar vein, Professor Morton Kaplan and Nicholas de B. Katzenbach wrote in their book, *The Political Foundations of International Law:*

> Must a state wait until it is too late before it may defend itself? Must it permit another the advantages of military build-up, surprise attack, and total offense, against which there may be no defense? It would be unreasonable to expect any State to permit this – particularly when given the possibility that a surprise nuclear blow might bring about the total destruction, or at least total subjugation, unless the attack were forestalled.

102. We sought to act in a manner which would minimize the danger to all concerned, including a large segment of Iraq's population . . . Our Air Force was only called in when . . . we learned on the basis of completely reliable information that there was less than a month to go before Osirak might have become critical.

Ambassador Anthony Parsons (United Kingdom):

Mrs. Thatcher was asked about the fact that, whereas Iraq has signed the nuclear Non-Proliferation Treaty and . . . Israel has not. She replied:

> A tragedy of this case was that Iraq was a signatory to the Agreement and had been inspected, but neither of these facts protected her. It was n unprovoked attack, which we must condemn. Just because a country is trying to manufacture energy from nuclear sources, it must not be believed that she is doing something totally wrong.

151. **The President** ... : "I shall now put to the vote the draft resolution. . . .

A vote was taken by show of hands. The draft resolution condemning Israel's action was unanimously adopted.

---

[149] Ruys, *"Armed Attack" and Article 51 of the UN Charter,* supra, note 54, at 97.

Ambassador Jeane Kirkpatrick (United States of America):

156. Like other members of the Council, the United States does not regard the resolution just adopted as a perfect one.

157. In addition, our judgment that Israeli actions violated the Charter of the United Nations is based solely on the conviction that Israel failed to exhaust peaceful means for the resolution of this dispute.

158. Nothing in this resolution will effect my Government's commitment to Israel's security.

Conclusion: On June 19, 1981, Security Council Resolution 487 condemned Israel's military attack on Osirak.

What conflict status is indicated by the Osirak raid? Two states were involved. Unlike the 2007 Israeli bombing of a Syrian nuclear facility that was under construction[150] and the 1979 Israeli bombing of nuclear reactor storage sites in France,[151] there was a heavy volume of enemy fire, indicating armed conflict. Was this a common Article 2 "armed conflict ... between two or more of the High Contracting Parties" or was it essentially a border incident writ large? Neither state chose to call it an outbreak of war or armed conflict. Was it a case of armed conflict short of war, then?

In terms of conflict status, how does the Osirak raid compare with the 1986 U.S. bombing raid of Libya?[152] How does it compare with the 1967 Israeli attack on the USS Liberty, a U.S. Navy combatant ship? In international waters, Israelis killed 34 U.S. personnel and wounded 172 others aboard the Liberty. The day-long armed conflict between the two well-organized forces was between two states, and the level of combat was heavy. For his actions in the fighting, the Liberty's captain, Commander William L. McGonagle, was awarded the Medal of Honor. The Executive Officer was awarded a posthumous Navy Cross.[153] The words "war," or "armed conflict" were never uttered by either government in regard to the Liberty incident.

The Osirak incident, and responses to it within the U.N., illustrates that some events involving armed conflict allow their being "assigned" a status, but an unthinking application of what appears to be a conflict status rule does not always lead to the correct LOAC result. As pointed out earlier, Dinstein writes, "In large measure, the classification of a military action as either war or a closed incident ... depends on the way in which the two antagonists appraise the situation. As long as both parties choose to consider what has transpired as a mere incident, and provided that the incident is rapidly closed, it is hard to gainsay that view."[154] In this instance, Iraq chose to not respond militarily to Israel's incursion, and Israel chose to not further militarily attack Iraq. The bombing of the Osirak nuclear power plant might be characterized merely as an "incident" – armed conflict short of war.

---

[150] David E. Sanger and Mark Mazzetti, "Analysts Find Israel Struck a Syrian Nuclear Project," NY *Times*, Oct. 14, 2007, A1; David E. Sanger, "Bush Administration Releases Images to Bolster Its Claims about Syrian Reactor," NY *Times*, April 25, 2008, A5.

[151] Loch K. Johnson, "On Drawing a Bright Line for Covert Operations," 86–2 *AJIL* (April 1992), 284, 292.

[152] See, Anthony D'Amato, "Editorial Comment," 84–3 *AJIL* (July 1990), 705.

[153] Lt.Cmdr. Walter L. Jacobsen, "A Juridical Examination of the Israeli Attack on the U.S.S. *Liberty*," 36 *Naval L. Rev.* (Winter 1986), 1; David C. Walsh, "Friendless Fire," *U.S. Naval Institute Proceedings* (June 2003), 58; James Bamford, *Body of Secrets* (New York: Doubleday, 2001), 187–239. For a contrary view: A. Jay Cristol, *The Liberty Incident* (New York: Brassey's, 2002).

[154] Dinstein, *War, Aggression and Self-Defence*, supra, note 29, at 11.

6   Individual Battlefield Status

6.0 Introduction

We have resolved, more or less, the first foundational question that a LOAC/IHL (law of armed conflict/international humanitarian law) student should answer regarding any armed conflict: What is the conflict status – what law of war, if any, applies in the armed conflict under examination? Now the second foundational question: What are the statuses of the participants in that conflict? For example, are all of them, or some of them, combatants, or are they unprivileged belligerents? Some of them or all of them? Are they civilians or insurgents? Prisoners of war (POWs) or retained personnel? A *levée en masse* or protected persons?

The first foundational question, status conflict, is critical because it determines if domestic law, limited LOAC or the entire spectrum of LOAC is in play. It is the difference between a criminal trial for murder in a domestic court and POW status with the protection of the combatant's privilege.

The second foundational question, the individual status of those on the battlefield, is just as significant. Individual status determines the rights and protections afforded a fighter, if captured, as well as the prohibitions that may apply to his/her conduct. If you are the officer-in-charge of a military unit ordered to parachute into, say, an African country that has requested U.S. training assistance, and several U.S. Army trainers have already been kidnapped and murdered by a splinter rebel group in the course of an internal rebellion, you know that you probably are going into a common Article 3 armed conflict in which Additional Protocol II probably does not apply – you know LOAC that will apply on your battlefield.

You also want to know if you are going to jump as part of a uniformed airborne unit, in civilian clothes, or disguised as a local resident or as a soldier from a neighboring country. Different statuses are involved, each dictating how you should conduct yourself and how you should be treated, if captured. True, if you are captured by insurgents, it probably will not matter what Geneva calls for – you are in for a hard day; however, one does not observe or disregard LOAC according to the enemy's conduct. We know and respect LOAC because, as a nation, we have pledged to do so through our ratification of particular LOAC-related treaties. We respect LOAC and customary law because they are the law, and because it is the right and honorable thing to do.

6.1 Individual Status

In American law schools there are 1-Ls and 3-Ls. There are West Point firsties and West Point plebes. There are Navy ensigns and Navy captains. There are assembly line workers, shop stewards, and foremen; Broadway stagehands, understudies, and stars; assistant professors, professors, and deans. Each has a different status in the educational, military, employment, or career system within which the person functions. Status can dictate one's autonomy, authority, salary, office location, vacation length, parking space – in a sense, one's way of life. On the battlefield, individual status may determine your life in a literal sense. It determines if you are a lawful target or not; a POW or a spy, a combatant or a noncombatant.

On the battlefield, no one is without some status and an accompanying level of humanitarian protection.

> In short,…[there is] a general principle which is embodied in all four Geneva Conventions of 1949. Every person in enemy hands must have some status under international law: he is either a prisoner of war and, as such, covered by the Third Convention, a civilian covered by the Fourth Convention, or again, a member of the medical personnel of the armed forces who is covered by the First Convention. There is no intermediate status; nobody in enemy hands can be outside the law.[1]

There are many possible battlefield individual statuses. We examine several that, combined, represent the bulk of those individuals encountered on the battlefield in common Article 2 and 3 armed conflicts, as well as in combat operations against nonstate actors, such as terrorists and insurgents.

6.2 Lawful Combatants/Prisoners of War

In his 1863 Code, Francis Lieber writes in Article 155, "All enemies in regular war are divided into two general classes – that is to say, into combatants and noncombatants…" Modern warfare has complicated Lieber's recitation of nineteenth-century customary law of war, but in broad terms it remains true that on any common Article 2 battlefield there are combatants and there are others.

Combatants fall into two categories: members of the armed forces of a party to a conflict (other than medical and religious personnel), and any others who take a direct part in hostilities.[2] **The defining distinction of the lawful combatant's status is that upon capture he or she is entitled to the protections of a POW,** "one of the most valuable rights of combatants under the Law of War."[3] "Entitlement to the status of a prisoner of war – on being captured by the enemy – is vouchsafed to every combatant, subject to the *conditio sine qua non* that he is a lawful combatant."[4]

Article 43.2 of 1977 Additional Protocol I defines combatants in common Article 2 conflicts: **"Members of the armed forces of a Party to a conflict (other than medical personnel and chaplains…) are combatants, that is to say, they have the right to participate directly in hostilities."** Members of the armed forces involved in the conflict including, in the case of U.S. armed forces, Reserve forces, and National Guard units,

[1] Jean Pictet, ed., *Commentary, IV Geneva Convention* (Geneva: ICRC, 1958), 51.
[2] Yoram Dinstein, *The Conduct of Hostilities under the Law of International Armed Conflict* (New York: Cambridge University Press, 2004), 27.
[3] Col. G. I. A. D. Draper, "Personnel and Issues of Status," in Michael A. Meyer and Hilaire McCoubrey, eds., *Reflections on Law and Armed Conflicts* (The Hague: Kluwer Law International, 1998), 194, 197.
[4] Dinstein, *The Conduct of Hostilities*, supra, note 2, at 29.

and, excepting medical personnel and chaplains, are combatants who may engage in hostilities. They may attack and be attacked; they may kill and be killed.

Many categories of soldiers, sailors, Marines, airmen, and Coast Guardsmen contribute to the combat effort in ways that have little to do with actually firing weapons – cooks, administrative personnel, graves registration teams, musicians, and so on. They are nevertheless combatants, for they are *entitled* to fight.[5] There no longer are statuses of "quasi-combatant"[6] or "semi-civilian."[7] The status of combatant is not conduct-based;[8] while assigned as an army cook (conduct) you remain a combatant (status) authorized to fight. "[A] combatant is a person who fights...[T]he combatant is a person who is authorized by international law to fight in accordance with international law applicable in international armed conflict."[9] The consideration of combatant status occupies much of LOAC study because in traditional warfare combatants are the most numerous battlefield players, with an entire Geneva Convention devoted to their treatment upon capture.

"Combatants may be attacked at any time until they surrender or are otherwise hors de combat, and not only when actually threatening the enemy."[10] A combatant remains a combatant when he/she is not actually fighting. When a soldier is bivouacked and sleeping she remains a combatant and so remains a legitimate target. While sleeping, she may be lawfully killed by an opposing lawful combatant. If a combatant is targeted far behind the front lines, no matter how unlikely such targeting may be, she continues to be a legitimate target for opposing lawful combatants. Taken an unrealistic step further, if a combatant is home on leave and in uniform, far from the combat zone, and is somehow targeted by an opposing combatant, she remains a legitimate target and may be killed – just as the opposing combatant, if discovered outside the combat zone, may be killed by *his* enemy. That illustrates the downside of combatancy: A lawful combatant enjoys the combatant's privilege, but also is a continuing lawful target.

Common Article 2 combatants are not combatants forever, however. They "can withdraw from hostilities not only by retiring [or demobilizing] and turning into civilians, but also by becoming *hors de combat* [i.e., out of the fight]. This can happen either by choice through a lying down of arms and surrendering, or by force of circumstance as a result of getting wounded, sick or shipwrecked. A combatant who is *hors de combat* and falls into the hands of the enemy is in principle entitled to the privileges of a prisoner of war."[11]

Consider this possibility: in World War II, a pilot in a British "Eagle Squadron" was a U.S. citizen. Was he a lawful combatant? If not, what was his individual

---

[5] Yves Sandoz, Christophe Swinarski, and Bruno Zimmerman, eds., *Commentary on the Additional Protocols* (Geneva: ICRC/Martinus Nijhoff, 1987), 515.

[6] Maj. Gen. A. P. V. Rogers, *Law on the Battlefield*, 2d ed. (Huntington, NY: Juris, 2004), 9.

[7] Sandoz, *Commentary on the Additional Protocols*, supra, note 5, at 515.

[8] See, e.g., Charles H. B. Garraway, "'Combatants' – Substance or Semantics?" in Michael N. Schmitt and Jelena Pejic, eds., *International Law and Armed Conflict: Exploring the Faultlines* (Leiden: Martinus Nijhoff, 2007), 317. Status often *is* conduct-based, but combatant status is not.

[9] Dieter Fleck, ed., *The Handbook of Humanitarian Law in Armed Conflicts* (Oxford: Oxford University Press, 1995), para. 301, at 67.

[10] Marco Sassòli and Laura M. Olson, "The Relationship Between International Humanitarian and Human Rights Law Where it Matters: Admissible Killing and Internment of Fighters in Non-international Armed Conflicts," 871 *Int'l Rev. of the Red Cross* (Sept. 2008), 599, 605–6.

[11] Dinstein, *Conduct of Hostilities*, supra, note 2, at 28.

[handwritten annotation: Citizenship and armed forces membership do not have to be the same. ie. Romanian fighting for Germany] 203

status? How about a Romanian citizen in a World War I German infantry unit? A lawful combatant or not? What if a U.S. Marine retired from active military service and returned to his native state of Redland, where he joined the Redlandian army, which then engaged in a common Article 2 armed conflict with the United States. If captured by U.S. forces, what is the retired Marine's status? In all three cases, the individuals are uniformed members of the armed forces of a party to the conflict and therefore all three are lawful combatants. Citizenship is not the point of lawful combatancy; membership in an army of a party to the conflict is the issue.

In December 2003, Iraq's Saddam Hussein was captured by U.S. forces. What was his individual status? The common Article 2 phase of the conflict had ended the previous May, and the United States was occupying Iraq. Common Article 2 makes clear, however, that all of the Geneva Conventions continue to apply during "cases of partial or total occupation." Saddam commanded the Iraqi army, often wore a military uniform, and frequently went about armed. He was a combatant. Captured in civilian attire, was he a *lawful* combatant? In World War II, if British Field Marshal Bernard Montgomery had been captured by German forces, would he have been a lawful combatant and a POW? Of course. As members of the armed forces of a party to the conflict, Saddam and Montgomery, even when not engaged in combat, remained lawful combatants.

But Iraqi soldiers often violated the law of war, the fourth requirement for lawful combatancy. (See Chapter 6, section 6.3.1.) Does that bear on Saddam's status? Certain members of the Iraqi armed forces did violate the law of war, but law of war violations committed by individuals may not be ascribed to every member of the violator's armed force. Saddam was presumed to be a POW, and that is the status eventually accorded him.[12]

In 2007, a former U.S. police officer was hired by a U.S. armed security contractor to provide security for American diplomatic officials in Iraq. Being a man of action, the ex-policeman longed to participate in an operational U.S. Army convoy in the Baghdad area, where he was posted. After a period of wheedling and cajoling his new-found Army buddies, the former policeman was finally allowed to surreptitiously participate in a resupply run as the top-side machine-gunner on a humvee. If captured while on the resupply mission by an enemy who observed the Geneva Conventions, what was his individual status?[13]

SIDEBAR. During World War II, in April 1943, Admiral Isoroku Yamamoto, Commander-in-Chief of the Japanese Combined Fleet, was on an inspection tour hundreds of miles behind the front lines. Having broken the Japanese navy's message code, U.S. forces knew his flight itinerary and sent sixteen Army Air Force P-38

---

[12] U.S. Dept. of Defense, Armed Forces Press Service, "Red Cross Visits Saddam Hussein," (Feb. 21, 2004), http://www.defenselink.mil/news/newsArticle.aspx?id=27283. A question is why other captured members of the Iraqi armed forces were not accorded POW status.

[13] In fact, while on the resupply run, the former policeman was killed by an Improvised Explosive Device (IED). Does that make a difference to his status? No. Does it make a difference that he was not a member of the army of a party to the conflict? Yes. See section 6.4 for his individual status.

> Lightning fighter aircraft to intercept him.[*] Near Bougainville, in the northern Solomons, the U.S. fighter pilots shot down their target, a Betty bomber, killing all on board, including Admiral Yamamoto. Yamamoto's status was that of a combatant in a common Article 2 armed conflict, and he was killed by opposing combatants. "There is nothing treacherous in singling out an individual enemy combatant (usually, a senior officer) as a target for a lethal attack conducted by combatants distinguishing themselves as such....even in an air strike."[14] The fact that Yamamoto was targeted far away from the front lines is immaterial. Combatants may be targeted wherever found, armed or unarmed, on a front line or a mile or a hundred miles behind the lines, "whether in the zone of hostilities, occupied territory, or elsewhere."[15]

In a common Article 2 international conflict, captured combatants are entitled to POW status, with its Geneva Convention III rights and protections. As Lieber points out, "A prisoner of war is subject to no punishment...nor is any revenge wreaked upon him by the intentional infliction of any suffering, or disgrace, by cruel imprisonment...death, or any other barbarity....Prisoners of war are subject to confinement or imprisonment such as may be deemed necessary on account of safety, but they are to be subjected to no other intentional suffering or indignity."[16] A century ago, the 1914 edition of the U.S. Army's *Rules of Land Warfare* similarly noted, "Prisoners of war must not be regarded as criminals or convicts. They are guarded as a measure of security and not of punishment."[17] While they may be tried for any unlawful precapture acts they may have committed, and for unlawful acts they commit while in captivity,[18] POWs are confined only to keep them from returning to further fighting. Captured fighters who are not entitled to POW status, such as unlawful combatants (unprivileged belligerents), do not enjoy the same consideration or treatment.

<u>Nowhere is it *required*</u> that captured unlawful combatants be denied POW status. "Indeed, U.S. practice has been to accord POW status generously to irregulars, to support such status for irregular forces at times, and to raise objections whenever an adversary has sought to deny U.S. personnel POW status based on a general accusation that the U.S. forces were not in compliance with some aspect of the law of war."[19] More often, captives are treated as if they were POWs while not actually being accorded POW status – a subtle but significant difference. During the Spanish Civil War (1936–9), there was a special agreement between the two sides, the Madrid Government of Spain and the

---

[*] One of the Navy code breakers was Navy Lieutenant John Paul Stevens, later Associate Justice of the Supreme Court of the United States. Jeffrey Rosen, "The Dissenter," *New York Times Magazine*, Sept. 23, 2007, 50.

[14] Dinstein, *Conduct of Hostilities*, supra, note 2, at 200.

[15] FM 27–10, *The Law of Land Warfare* (Washington, DC: GPO, 1956), para. 31.

[16] *Instructions for the Government of Armies of the United States in the Field* (April 24, 1863), Arts. 56, 75. Hereafter: the Lieber Code.

[17] War Department, *Rules of Land Warfare – 1914* (Washington, DC: GPO, 1914), para. 60, at 27.

[18] E.g., *Rex v. Perzenowski, et al.*, Canada, Supreme Ct. of Alberta (App. Div.), Oct. 1946, in H. Lauterpacht, ed., *1946 Annual Digest and Reports of Public International Law Cases* (London: Butterworth, 1951), 300. Perzenowski, a German POW held in Medicine Hat, Alberta, conspired with others and killed a fellow German POW they believed to be a communist.

[19] Jennifer Elsea, *Treatment of "Battlefield Detainees" in the War on Terrorism*, Congressional Research Service, Rpt. for Congress (Jan. 13, 2005), at CRS-8.

Burgos Junta, that certain prisoners would have a status equivalent to POWs. During the U.S.-Vietnam conflict, "[t]he MACV [U.S. Military Advisory Command-Vietnam] policy was that all combatants captured...were to be accorded prisoner of war status, irrespective of the type of unit to which they belonged."[20] There has been no such accommodation for captured Taliban or al Qaeda fighters, however.

What about common Article 3 non-international armed conflicts? The traditional view is that, just as there are no POWs in non-international armed conflicts, there are no "combatants," lawful or otherwise, in common Article 3 conflicts. There may be combat in the literal sense, but in terms of LOAC there are fighters, rebels, insurgents, or guerrillas who engage in armed conflict, and there are government forces, and perhaps armed forces allied to the government forces. There are no combatants as that term is used in customary law of war, however. Upon capture such fighters are simply prisoners of the detaining government; they are criminals to be prosecuted for their unlawful acts, either by a military court or under the domestic law of the capturing state.

I feel like this assumes the State actor is in the right.... we know this isn't always the case.

6.2.1 Retainees

Retainees occupy a unique place in the law of war. Upon capture they are not POWs, although they receive the same treatment as POWs. They are "retained personnel," described in Article 28 of Geneva Convention I. More than one hundred forty years ago, Lieber wrote, "The enemy's chaplains, officers of the medical staff, apothecaries, hospital nurses and servants, if they fall into the hands of the American Army, are not prisoners of war, unless the commander has reasons to retain them. In this latter case, or if, at their own desire, they are allowed to remain with their captured companions, they are treated as prisoners of war, and may be exchanged if the commander sees fit." LOAC remains much the same today.

Medical personnel and chaplains, although members of the armed forces, are not combatants – they are the only members of the armed forces of a state who are noncombatants. "The term noncombatant as used in the present connection to describe certain elements [medical personnel and chaplains] within the armed forces is, of course, to be distinguished from the term noncombatant as applied to the general population of a belligerent, that is, those who do not belong to its armed forces."[21] So, the presence of noncombatant members of the armed forces at a military objective does not require an attacking enemy to take any special precautionary measures, as would the presence of civilians. Medical personnel and chaplains are subject to capture by the enemy, but they do not hold POW status. Although they are POWs to all outward appearances, their status is "retained personnel," or retainees. Retainees include dentists, surgeons, and other medical doctors, but not medical orderlies or chaplains' assistants.[22] The distinction is based on the fact that orderlies and chaplains assistants, formally titled "Religious

---

[20] MG George S. Prugh, *Law at War: Vietnam 1964–1973* (Washington, DC: Dept. of the Army, 1975), 66.

[21] Morris Greenspan, *The Modern Law of Land Warfare* (Berkeley: University of California Press, 1959), 57.

[22] 1949 Geneva Convention for the Amelioration of the Condition of the Wounded and Sick in Armed Forces in the Field, Arts. 25, 29. Hereafter: Geneva Convention I. In accordance with these Articles, "hospital orderlies, nurses, or auxiliary stretcher-bearers ... shall be prisoners of war," rather than retained personnel. FM 27–10, *Law of Land Warfare*, supra, note 15, para. 68, at 29. The British take a broader view of who is a retained person: "The term [medical personnel] embraces not only doctors and nurses but also a wide range of specialists, technicians, maintenance staff, drivers, cooks, and administrators." UK Ministry

Program Specialists," or "RPs," are not considered "permanent staff"[23] in medical or pastoral terms. Orderlies and chaplains' assistants are armed and may lawfully directly participate in hostilities.

Captured medical personnel and chaplains are "retained by the detaining power with a view to providing medical care or religious ministration to prisoners of war...and they are to be given treatment not less favorable than that given prisoners of war."[24] Retainees may not lawfully be compelled to do work other than their medical or pastoral work. When there no longer is a need for their services (no pun intended, Chaplain) they are to be returned to their own lines – repatriated.[25] Although there were a number of prisoner exchanges throughout World War II,[26] repatriation of retained personnel is a requirement seldom observed since then, because as long as there are POWs, the retainee's unique skills will likely be needed.

In combat, medics and corpsmen traditionally wore brassards – armbands – bearing "the distinctive sign," a red cross on a white background, to mark the wearers as noncombatants and not lawful targets.[27] (In U.S. practice, the Army refers to field medical personnel as "medics," whereas the Marine Corps and Navy call them "corpsmen.") Since World War II, the grim reality of combat has caused medics and corpsmen to frequently discard their distinctive red cross insignia, which too often becomes an enemy aiming point rather than a protective emblem. Additionally, they have usually armed themselves with light individual weapons, which is in accord with LOAC, as long as the weapons are only used for self-defense or the defense of the wounded in their charge.[28] "The expression 'light individual weapons', in both Article 13(2) and Article 65(3), denotes 'weapons which are generally carried and used by a single individual', including sub-machine guns..."[29] During World War II, in the 1945 battle for Okinawa, Navy Corpsman Robert E. Bush, in the words of his Medal of Honor citation,

> was advancing to administer blood plasma to a marine officer lying wounded on the skyline when the Japanese launched a savage counterattack...[H]e resolutely maintained the flow of lifegiving plasma. With the bottle held high in 1 [sic] hand, Bush drew his pistol with the other and fired into the enemy's ranks until his ammunition was expended. Quickly seizing a discarded carbine, he trained his fire on the Japanese charging pointblank over the hill, accounting for 6 of the enemy despite his own serious wounds and the loss of one eye suffered during the desperate battle in defense of the helpless man...

---

of Defence, *The Manual of the Law of Armed Conflict* (Oxford: Oxford University Press, 2004), para. 7.11.1., at 126.

[23] Jean Pictet, ed., *Commentary, I Geneva Convention* (Geneva: ICRC, 1952), 221.

[24] *Manual of the Law of Armed Conflict*, supra, note 22, at para. 8–8, at 146. Also see: Geneva Convention I, Art. 32.

[25] Id., *Manual*, para. 8.58, at 165. Also see: Geneva Convention I, Arts. 28 and 30 and 1949 Geneva Convention Relative to the Treatment of Prisoners of War, Arts. 33 and 35. Hereafter: Geneva Convention III.

[26] See: David Miller, *Mercy Ships* (London: Continuum, 2008). Miller documents U.S.-German exchanges of POWs, female nurses, diplomatic internees, and others, as well as U.S.–Japanese, U.K.–German, and U.S./U.K./German–Swiss exchanges.

[27] Geneva Convention I, Arts. 41, 25.   [28] Id., Art. 22(1); 1977 Additional Protocol I, Art. 13.2(a).

[29] Dinstein, *The Conduct of Hostilities*, supra, note 2, at 151, citing Sandoz, *Commentary on the Additional Protocols*, supra, note 5, at 178.

Corpsman Bush employed light individual weapons in self-defense and in defense of the wounded Marine in his charge, textbook compliance with the Convention then in effect, the 1929 Geneva Convention for the Amelioration of the Condition of the Sick and Wounded in Armies in the Field, Article 8.1, which reads essentially the same as 1949 Geneva Convention I, Article 22(1).

In 2008, in Iraq, the U.S. Marine Corps, concerned about reports of its Navy corpsmen directly participating in hostilities, issued written instructions to "knock it off":

> 1. *Situation.* U.S. Navy Hospital Corpsmen are being assigned to duties unrelated to their medical service...and may be jeopardizing the special protections and status they are afforded as noncombatants...
>
> 3. a. *Commander's Intent.*...Corpsmen may perform only those duties related to their medical service...Corpsmen may be armed only for the limited purpose of self-defense and/or defense of their patients and abstain from any form of participation in hostile acts.
>
> 3. c.(2). *Prohibited Duties.*...Corpsmen may not be assigned as a gunner in a turret of a tactical vehicle. •...Corpsmen may not set down suppressive fire for a Marine unit in order to allow maneuver. • Corpsmen may not man defensive positions or checkpoint/control points...• Corpsmen may not be utilized as members of an ambush/sniper team....[30]

This instruction may have had the desired effect in the short term but probably was ignored in the long term. A year later, it was revealed that a Navy doctor, on patrol with a joint American and Afghan unit, had been awarded the Navy Cross, second only to the Medal of Honor, for his combat valor in firefights with al Qaeda and Taliban forces.[31]

Chaplains, by reason of their noncombatancy,[32] are prohibited by U.S. service regulations from carrying or using any weapon.[33] Their enlisted "RPs," (often referred to as "chaplains' assistants"), are tasked with protecting their chaplains in combat situations. In ancient times, "not only were all clerics exempt from military service, but their presence on the battlefield frequently resulted in a temporary cessation of hostilities, just as conflict ceased on saints' days and religious holidays."[34] Times, and battlefield customs, change. Today, fighting does not abate for the presence of clerics.

---

[30] USMC, Multi National Force – West, II Marine Expeditionary Force (Forward); Policy Letter 16–07, Oct. 8 2007, on file with author.

[31] Andrew Scutro, "Mystery Medical Officer Earned a Navy Cross He Can't Display," *Marine Corps Times*, Nov. 10, 2008, 24. The doctor's 2003 award details, including his name, were secret because the action occurred in Pakistan at a time when U.S. forces were not permitted to be there. The citation for the Navy's second highest combat award reveals that the doctor returned enemy fire and led a "fighting retreat" when his unit was caught in an ambush. His identity, Lt. Mark L. Donald, and additional Silver Star, Bronze Star, and Purple Heart medals, were made public in 2009. Mark Donald, *Battle Ready* (New York: St.Martins Press, 2013).

[32] 1977 Additional Protocol I, relating to international armed conflicts, Art. 43.2 Hereafter, Additional Protocol I.

[33] National Guard Recruiting, "Will I Carry a Gun?" www.nh.ngb.army.mil/Recruiting/Chaplain.htm.

[34] L. C. Green, *The Contemporary Law of Armed Conflict*, 2d ed. (Manchester: Juris/Manchester University Press, 2000), 103, footnote omitted. A modern instance of a holiday cessation of hostilities was the World War I "Christmas truce" of 1914. On Christmas day troops spontaneously, albeit cautiously, emerged from their opposing trench lines, then greeted one another, traded cigarettes, buried their dead, and sang Christmas carols together, and briefly even played soccer in fields of mud and barbed wire. AP, "Alfred Anderson, 109, Last Man from 'Christmas Truce' of 1914," *NY Times* obituary, Nov. 22, 2005, B9. Also: "Though [the Christmas truce] was to become so widespread as to impact much of the front, no one was

On rare occasions American chaplains in Iraq have disregarded the weapons prohibition. In April 2003, a U.S. Army chaplain was with a unit in the initial push into Baghdad, which involved intense close combat:

> As he surveyed the melee around him, he was afraid the U.S. troops would be overrun. Army chaplains were under instructions not to bear arms. In the most extreme circumstances, where their lives were at stake, chaplains could declare an exception. It was called the "moment of decision" and was a judgment each chaplain had to make for himself, but one the Army Chaplain Corps discouraged. [The chaplain] decided it was time to fight. He picked up a weapon and started firing at the enemy.... "I picked up a weapon and I was firing, and I have no problem with that in my conscience."[35]

There is no *written* authority for chaplains to "declare an exception." The Baghdad chaplain was hardly the first man of the cloth to engage in combat, however. During the U.S. Civil War, Union Chaplain Milton L. Haney also took up arms. His brief Medal of Honor citation reads: "Voluntarily carried a musket in the ranks of his regiment and rendered heroic service in retaking the Federal works which had been captured by the enemy."

Today, any chaplain or medical person who takes a direct part in hostilities becomes a combatant, forfeits noncombatant immunity, and becomes a lawful target. If captured by an opposing force that abides by LOAC, they still would be retained persons, but would be subject to trial for their unlawful precapture combatant acts,[36] just as lawful combatant POWs would be subject to trial for their unlawful precapture acts.[37]

6.3 Others Whose Status upon Capture is POW

Recall that POW status arises only in common Article 2 international armed conflicts, and in such conflicts the 1949 Geneva Conventions apply *in toto*, along with 1977 Additional Protocol I.

---

ever certain where or how it had begun." Commanders, fearing the will to fight would be lost, ordered an immediate resumption of fighting. On both sides many soldiers complied by firing harmlessly into the air. Stanley Weintraub, *Silent Night* (New York: Free Press, 2001), 21. In a World War II incident in the Huertgen Forest, during a Nov. 7, 1944 local truce at the Kall River Gorge, American and German doctors and corpsmen converged to retrieve and evacuate their own, and each other's, wounded. Charles B. MacDonald, *United States Army in World War II: The European Theater of Operations; The Siegfried Line Campaign* (Washington, DC: Center of Military History, 2001), 371–2. John Keegan discusses similar nonholiday truces in *The Face of Battle* (London: Barrie & Jenkins, 1988), 239. Briefer, less dramatic truces are not unknown to the battlefield. An example was a Sept. 24, 1944, two-hour British–German truce during Operation Market Garden's battle of Nijmegen, during which both sides held fire while the British collected their wounded. Cornelius Ryan, *A Bridge Too Far* (New York: Simon & Schuster, 1974), 556–9.

[35] Michael R. Gordon and Lt.Gen. Bernard E. Trainor, *Cobra II* (New York: Pantheon Books, 2006), 405–6.

[36] Geneva Convention III, Art. 85.

[37] E.g., *Trial of Max Schmid*, U.S. General Military Government Court at Dachau, Germany, 19 May, 1947. LRTWC, Vol. XIII (London: UNWCC, 1949), 151. In the dispensary he commanded, Schmid, a medical doctor, beheaded the dead body of a U.S. airman. He boiled it, removed the skin, bleached the skull and kept it on his office desk. He was convicted and sentenced to ten years confinement.

In common Article 2 conflicts, a combatant is a member of the armed forces of a party to the conflict, wearing a uniform or other distinguishing sign. Although lawful combatants make up the greater number of POWs, by far, the 1949 POW Convention specifies six other groups that are also entitled to those protections.[38]

6.3.1 *Members of Other Militias and Members of Other Volunteer Corps*

Here is the age-old issue of partisans, guerrillas, and POW status. Geneva Convention III, Article 4A also encompasses a state's auxiliary and reserve armed forces, as well as partisans. The term, "reserve armed forces," does not refer to organized military reserve units that have been incorporated into a nation's armed forces. Rather, it refers to a reserve force that, for whatever reason, has not been integrated into the armed forces but nevertheless actively participates in hostilities – an unusual circumstance today.

As noted in Chapter 4, for partisans (or reserve armed forces just described) to gain POW status the Convention has four special requirements.

> Members of other militias and members of other volunteer corps, including those of organized resistance movements, belonging to a Party to the conflict and operating in or outside their own territory, even if the territory is occupied, provided that such militias or volunteer corps, including such organized resistance movements, fulfill the following conditions:
>
> (a) that of being commanded by a person responsible for his subordinates;
> (b) that of having a fixed distinctive sign recognizable at a distance;
> (c) that of carrying arms openly;
> (d) that of conducting their operations in accordance with the laws and customs of war.[39]

Special requirements (b) and (c) are modified by 1977 Additional Protocol I, Article 44.3, which requires that combatants distinguish themselves ("a fixed distinctive sign") only while in an attack or preparatory to an attack and, if they cannot do that because of the nature of the situation, they still must carry their arms openly during that period. (Chapter 4, section 4.2.1.3.) What does this modification mean for members of "other militias" and "other volunteer corps" or for rebels and insurgents? The International Committee of the Red Cross (ICRC) points out, "if resistance movements are to benefit by the Convention, they must respect the four special conditions. . ."[40] If they fail to do so they are unlawful combatants.

The first of the four special conditions is clear. In an international armed conflict, the partisan, guerrilla, or rebel group, however designated, must have a leader, civilian or military, who is responsible for their conduct. This requirement is not for a hierarchical "chain of command" that is familiar to military units[41] – although there often is such a chain of authority in resistance movements. The requirement is merely intended to exclude individuals acting on their own who, in effect, initiate private wars. Such unaffiliated fighters always have been forbidden by LOAC.

---

[38] 1949 Geneva Convention III, Art. 4A.(2)–(6).   [39] Id.
[40] Jean Pictet, *Commentary, III Geneva Convention* (Geneva: ICRC, 1960), 59.
[41] *Prosecutor v. Musema*, ICTR-95-13-T (27 Jan. 2000), para. 257.

(2) The second special condition: a distinctive sign. The distinctive sign of a state's armed forces usually is a uniform. For partisans, a distinctive sign may be any emblem recognizable at a reasonable distance, in daylight, with unenhanced vision. A distinctive sash, coat, shirt, badge, or emblem, even just a distinctive armband will do, but it must be the same distinctive sign for everyone in the partisan group and it must be used only by them. A white shirt, for example, may not be "the distinctive sign" because a white shirt is not distinctive. A distinctive cap or hat, like the beret of the World War II French *Maquis* resistance fighters, is not adequate because it may easily be removed or put on, too easily defeating the requirement for distinction.* A uniform, per se, is not required for irregular forces. A uniform is obviously distinctive, but a uniform is not required for a combatant to be distinctive; any distinctive sign is permitted. Nor is camouflage outlawed. "The issue is not whether combatants can be seen, but the lack of desire on their part to create the <u>false impression that they are civilians</u>."[42] In 1999, during armed conflict in Kosovo, press and television depicted members of a paramilitary group, the Kosovo Liberation Army (KLA), wearing camouflage uniforms with the KLA patch at their shoulder.[43] Although they were not members of an army of a party to the conflict, the KLA did take pains to distinguish themselves from noncombatants.

[margin note: They clearly aren't doing this by wearing camo.]

(3) The third requirement, carrying arms openly, has always been difficult.[44] "Carrying arms openly" <u>does not mean one's weapon must be carried *visibly*.</u> How can a weapon be carried openly, yet not visibly? A good question. What is required is that the fighter carry his weapon openly "during such time as he is visible to the adversary while he is engaged in a military deployment preceding the launching of an attack in which he is to participate."[45] A U.S. Air Force reference cited in the ICRC's study of customary law says that this requirement is not met "by carrying arms concealed about the person or if the individuals hide their weapons on the approach of the enemy."[46] A handgun or grenade may be carried in a pocket or holster, however. "[W]hat counts is not the ambiguous language [of the requirement] but the nucleus of the condition. A lawful combatant must abstain from creating the false impression that he is an innocent civilian...He must carry his arms openly in a reasonable way, depending on the nature of the weapon and the prevailing circumstances."[47]

[margin note: very ambiguous!]

(4) The final special condition, that the laws and customs of war be complied with, is essential, and is inherent in the three other requirements. Although "the laws and customs of war" is a somewhat vague locution, it reasonably informs the partisan or insurgent of LOAC's requirements. "Unless a combatant is willing himself to respect [LOAC/IHL], he is estopped from relying on that body of law when desirous of enjoying its benefits."[48]

---

* The *Commentary* is ambiguous on this point, saying, "It may be a cap (although this may frequently be taken off and does not seem fully adequate) ... " Pictet, *Commentary, III Geneva Convention*, supra, note 40, at 60. Indeed a cap does not seem adequate.

[42] Dinstein, *The Conduct of Hostilities*, supra, note 2, at 38.

[43] Rogers, *Law on the Battlefield*, supra, note 6, at 37.

[44] W. Hays Parks, "Air War and the Law of War," 32–1 *Air Force L. R.* (1990), 1, 84.

[45] 1977 Additional Protocol I, Art. 44.3.

[46] Jean-Marie Henckaerts and Louise Doswald-Beck, eds., *Customary International Humanitarian Law.* Vol. I. *Rules* (Cambridge: Cambridge University Press, 2005), Rule 106, at 386.

[47] Dinstein, *The Conduct of Hostilities*, supra, note 2, at 39.   [48] Id.

6.3.1.1 Additional Conditions for POW Status?

Some commentators contend that there are additional requirements for POW status for members of militias and other volunteer groups. An additional three that are sometimes proposed: hierarchical organization; belonging to a party to the conflict; and nonallegiance to the detaining power.

The first of these asserted additional requirements, hierarchical organization, requires that "[l]awful combatants must act within a hierarchic framework, embedded in discipline, and subject to supervision by upper echelons of what is being done by subordinate units in the field."[49] This additional requirement would task irregulars with having a military-style chain of command. Even if complying with the traditional four conditions for POW status, bands of combatants cannot operate "free style," on their own. They must have a leader and, this additional requirement would add, a command structure including senior leaders to oversee their operations. This requirement is not cited as a precondition for POW status in most texts. The ICRC study of customary law specifies the number of preconditions when it says, "members of militias and volunteer corps are required to comply with *four* conditions..."[50] Nowhere are further preconditions mentioned.

The second asserted additional requirement, belonging to a party to the conflict, stipulates that irregulars be affiliated with one side or the other. Such a requirement is not new. In a common Article 2 conflict, an individual may not form an independent group of fighters to fight for their own cause or goals, unassociated with either of the states opposing each other in the conflict. Private citizens and independent armed groups have always been excluded from entitlement to the combatant's privilege and POW status. This requirement of state affiliation is seen in the *Kassem* case, in this chapter's Cases and Materials.

The third asserted additional requirement is nonallegiance to the detaining power. To oversimplify, POWs cannot be nationals of the nation holding them. For example, during the U.S.–Vietnam conflict, if a U.S. national of Vietnamese extraction returned to North Vietnam, enlisted in the North Vietnamese army, and was then captured by U.S. forces, as a U.S. national that individual would not be entitled to POW status while held by U.S. forces. Although he would retain the combatant's privilege, he would be subject to trial, conviction, and imprisonment under U.S. law for having enlisted in a foreign service.[51] This asserted additional requirement is illustrated in a 1967 U.K. case decided by the U.K.'s Privy Council.[52] Like the first additional requirement, nonallegiance is not cited in texts as a precondition for POW status.

The careful student will know Geneva Convention III's four customary requirements for POW status for irregulars, guerrillas, and insurgents, but be aware that some authorities urge these three additional requirements, the first and third of which are not state practice. The second has always been an unspoken requirement.

[49] Id.
[50] Henckaerts and Doswald-Beck, *Customary International Humanitarian Law*, Vol. I, supra, note 46, Rule 106, at 385. Emphasis added.
[51] 18 U.S. Code, § 959, Enlistment in Foreign Service.
[52] *Public Prosecutor v. Koi et al.* (1967), [1968] AC 829.

6.3.2 *Regular Armed Forces Professing Allegiance to an Unrecognized Authority*

This group of potential POWs is unlikely to be encountered today. The provision reads, "Members of regular armed forces who profess allegiance to a government or an authority not recognized by the Detaining Power [are prisoners of war]."[53] It was added to the Convention to remedy a specific circumstance of World War II.

After Germany occupied France, "Free French" forces under General Charles de Gaulle continued armed resistance in France against the Nazis. The Germans did not recognize de Gaulle's Free French government in exile. An Article of the 1942 French–German armistice stipulated that, because the Free French were, the Germans said, fighting unlawfully, they would not be protected under the law of war and would not be accorded POW status if captured. General de Gaulle's Free French forces were considered by the Allies as France's lawful regular armed force; an armed force that professed allegiance to a French government not recognized by Germany, their detaining power if captured. A similar situation arose in 1943, when Germany refused to recognize Italy's government in exile, or its forces fighting in Italy under Marshal Pietro Bagdoglio.

To ensure that such attempts to put combatants beyond the protections of the Conventions would not arise in the future, Geneva's Conference of Government Experts added this provision.[54] (See the *Kassem* case, Cases and Materials, this chapter.)

6.3.3 *Persons Who Accompany the Armed Forces without Being Members Thereof*

The POW convention provides protection for groups other than combatants. In October 2007, for the first time, the U.S. Marine Corps based a squadron of MV-22B Osprey tiltrotor transport aircraft in Iraq. The mechanically novel part-helicopter, part-turboprop aircraft was twenty-four years and twenty-two billion dollars in development. Its two wingtip-mounted engines, which rotate in flight from helicopter mode to aircraft mode, are complex to operate and maintain. Three civilian technical representatives from the plane's manufacturer, Boeing-Bell, and one civilian from the engine-maker Rolls-Royce, deployed to Iraq with the squadron[55]. If these four civilians were to be captured by an enemy force that recognized and complied with LOAC, what would their status be?

The answer is found in Article 4A.(4): "Persons who accompany the armed forces without actually being members thereof, such as. . .war correspondents, supply contractors, members of labour units or of services responsible for the welfare of the armed forces, provided that they have received authorization from the armed forces which they accompany, who shall provide them. . .with an identity card. . ."

In 1863, Lieber wrote, "Moreover, citizens who accompany an army for whatever purpose, such as sutlers, editors, or reporters of journals, or contractors, if captured, may be made prisoners of war, and be detained as such. . . ."[56] Although the purposes for which individuals may accompany the armed forces are limited, Lieber's recitation of then-customary law remains much the same today.

---

[53] 1949 Geneva Convention III, Art. 4A.(3).
[54] Pictet, *Commentary, III Geneva Convention*, supra, note 40, at 61–4.
[55] Richard Whittle, "A Test, Not a Final Exam," U.S. Naval Institute *Proceedings* (Feb. 2008), 20, 21.
[56] The Lieber Code, supra, note 16, at Art. 50.

The Osprey "tech reps" accompany the armed forces, but they are not members of the armed forces. Their status upon capture is POW. If a CNN reporter, cameraman, and sound technician are captured? POWs. If a Red Cross worker, USO show cast member, or civilian mess hall worker were captured, all three would be POWs.

Should they be captured, are employees of an American-based armed private security contractor POWs? In 2007, in Iraq, such a company, Blackwater Worldwide, was prominent in news stories involving the deaths of noncombatants. Logic and Black-water's military-like armament suggested that they would be POWs if captured, but they would not be. Their contracts were with the U.S. Department of State, not the Department of Defense (DoD).[57] Blackwater accompanies not the armed forces, but the State Department. That unsatisfying explanation is why, if captured, their status would be that of "protected persons," with far fewer protections than a POW. (Protected persons are discussed in Chapter 6, section 6.10.)

6.3.4 *Merchant Marine and Civilian Aircraft Crews*

Upon capture in a common Article 2 international armed conflict, the crews of merchant marine vessels and civilian aircraft of a party to the conflict are entitled to POW status. The merchant seamen and women who crew government-contracted civilian vessels transporting supplies to the combat zone are often armed. Civilian aircraft manned by unarmed civilians often transport troops to and from the combat zone. In the event of capture they, too, merit POW status. Not included in this category are civilians who are aboard ship or aircraft not as crew, but passengers – Department of State civilians or technical representatives returning home on leave or having completed their contractual obligation, for instance. Medical aircraft are exempt from capture, as are (oddly) fishing boats.[58]

The capture of civilian crew members is unusual, but it happens. In 1965, during the U.S.–Vietnam conflict, Ernest C. Brace, a civilian pilot flying U.S. Agency for International Development (USAID) supply missions, was captured in Laos by North Vietnamese Army troops. He was held prisoner for seven years and ten months, longer than any other civilian in that conflict. A former U.S. Marine, Brace received the civilian Medal for Distinguished Service for his conduct as a POW.[59] Of the 771 Americans and allies captured during the conflict in Vietnam, fifty-one were civilians – tech reps, construction workers, teachers, interpreters, U.S. and British government employees, nurses and missionaries, as well as civilian air crew like Brace. No merchant seamen were captured. Civilians usually received the same poor treatment as captured military pilots.[60] "[T]he Hanoi government stated that it would treat captured American fliers humanely, but it would not accord them prisoner of war status as they

[57] U.S. Dept. of State, Secretary Condoleezza Rice, "Interview with the New York Post Editorial Board," (Oct. 1, 2007), http://www.state.gov/secretary/rm/2007/10/93046.htm.

[58] Louise Doswald-Beck, ed., *San Remo Manual on International Law Applicable to Armed Conflicts at Sea* (Cambridge: Cambridge University Press, 1995), 36, para. 142(a) regarding medical aircraft; and 1907 Hague Convention XI, Art. 3, as to fishing boats.

[59] Ernest C. Brace, *A Code to Keep* (New York: St. Martin's Press, 1988), 261.

[60] Stuart I. Rochester and Frederick Kiley, *Honor Bound* (Washington, DC: Historical Office, Office of the Secretary of Defense, 1998), 58, 64, 253, 283, 450, and 452.

were 'pirates' engaged in unprovoked attacks on North Vietnam."[61] The treatment of all captives held by the North Vietnamese was far short of humane.

6.3.5 Levée en Masse

On December 24, 1941, two weeks after Pearl Harbor, U.S.-held Wake Island fell to invading Japanese forces. More than eleven hundred American civilian construction workers were among the island's population. "More than sixty civilians are known to have taken part in the ground fighting, and their valor – if not their combat skills – equaled that of the servicemen."[62] One hundred twenty-four Americans died before Wake Island was forced to surrender. Seventy-five of the dead were civilians who manned shore batteries and heavy machine guns, held defensive positions and, when Japanese infantry landed, fought in counterattacks.[63]

What was the status of the approximately 1,118 civilians who were captured on Wake Island by Japanese forces?

Traditionally, wrote Lieber, "the people of that portion of an invaded country which is not yet occupied by the enemy...at the approach of a hostile army, [may] rise...*en masse* to resist the invader...and, if captured, are prisoners of war."[64] The Wake Island civilians are what Lieber described – inhabitants of nonoccupied U.S. territory who, on the approach of the enemy, spontaneously took up arms to resist the invading Japanese force without having had time to form themselves into regular armed units, carrying their arms openly and respecting the laws and customs of war. They were a *levée en masse*, a gathering entitled to POW status upon capture.[65]

In the Wars of the French Revolution (1792–1800), at the 1793 Battle of Wattignies, French *levées en masse* beat back invading Austrian troops. In the U.S. Civil War, in May 1864, upon the approach of Union forces, 257 cadets of Virginia Military Institute took up arms and fought at the Battle of New Market. Ten were killed and forty-five wounded. Seven months later, at Tulifinny, South Carolina, a battalion of cadets from The Citadel, along with South Carolina home guard and militia units, were called out to stop Union forces marching toward Charleston.[66] The cadet units were *levées en masse*.

During World War II, in August 1941, the still-undefeated German army attacked Tallinn, the capital of Estonia. Tallinn's hastily erected defenses, manned by naval personnel, were no match for the battle-hardened Nazi *Wehrmacht*. "By nightfall the Nazis pushed into the lovely beach community of Pirita, and...the last reserves of the command had been assembled – the cadets of the Frunze Naval Academy."[67] The cadets, some still in their teens, none yet members of the active armed forces, were

---

[61] Prugh, *Law at War: Vietnam*, supra, note 20, at 63.

[62] Gregory J. W. Urwin, *Facing Fearful Odds* (Lincoln: University of Nebraska Press, 1997), 528.

[63] Lt.Col. Frank O. Hough, Maj. Verle E. Ludwig, and Henry I. Shaw, *History of Marine Corps Operations in World War II. Vol. I. Pearl Harbor to Guadalcanal* (Washington, DC: GPO, 1958), 132–43.

[64] The Lieber Code, supra, note 16, at Art. 51.   [65] 1949 Geneva Convention III, Art. 4A.(6).

[66] Gary R. Baker, *Cadets in Gray* (Lexington, SC: Palmetto Bookworks, 1990), 134–52; and, Rod Andrew, Jr., *Long Gray Lines: The Southern Military School Tradition, 1839–1915* (Chapel Hill: University of North Carolina Press, 2007), 30–1.

[67] Harrison E. Salisbury, *The 900 Days: The Siege of Leningrad* (Cambridge MA: De Cappo Press, 1969), 227.

formed into a *levée en masse*. "That night, the Germans overran the thin line of sailors. . .Almost all perished in the hand-to-hand battle."[68]

In the 2011 Libyan civil war, dozens of teenagers travelled to the "front" to fight along with rebel fighters to bring down the Qaddafi regime.[69] Three years later, when Russian-sponsored fighters invaded the Ukraine in 2014, Ukranians flocked to the combat zone to oppose the invaders. "The sergeant. . .who repairs shoes in civilian life, said his comrades in the unit defending the airport were working class men like him. 'One was a tea boy on the trains, another transported cash for banks, a third was a car mechanic,' he said. We can manage."[70] The *levée en masse* is not an historical relic.

"The law of war has had to evolve an uneasy. . .compromise between the legitimate defence of regular belligerent forces and the demands of patriotism. . . .The protected position afforded the members of the *levée en masse* is a monument to these sentiments. . ."[71] The International Criminal Tribunal for the Former Yugoslavia (ICTY) has defined a *levée en masse* as "inhabitants of a non-occupied territory who, on the approach of the enemy, spontaneously took up arms to resist the invading forces, without having had time to form themselves into regular armed units, and at all times they carried arms openly and respected the laws and customs of war."[72]

"The conditions [for a *levée en masse*] are those of emergency and a form of last-ditch defence of a country when time permits of no other means."[73] Partisans, rebels, guerillas, and insurgents are not a *levée en masse*, for they are not a last-ditch defense of a country. Because of the character of a *levée en masse*, its members are allowed to dispense with the otherwise required commander responsible for subordinates and the wearing of a fixed distinctive sign – the only time that the four customary requirements for POW status are eased. But, "In the absence of any distinctive sign, the requirement of carrying arms 'openly' is of special significance. . .[T]his requirement is in the interest of combatants themselves who must be recognizable in order to qualify for treatment as prisoners of war. They must therefore carry arms visibly."[74]

Finally, a *levée en masse* can lawfully exist only during the actual period of invasion – a common Article 2 conflict. Resistance beyond the period of the actual invasion must be conducted by regular forces, or the *levée* members must be incorporated into regular forces. Armed resistance by civilian combatants that continues into an occupation renders the fighters unlawful combatants unprivileged belligerents.

Despite its history, and although it is recognized in Geneva Convention III, the *levée en masse* is uncommon in modern times. Since World War II, "[t]his situation has hardly ever arisen in actual practice. . ."[75] and is "extremely rare and limited. . ."[76] Still, in

---

[68] Id.

[69] Kareem Fahim, "In Libya Revolt, Youth Will Serve, or at Least Try, *NY Times*, March12, 2011, A1.

[70] Carlotta Gall, "Ukraine's Neglected and Battered Army Inspires Citizens to Pitch In," *NY Times*, Sept. 23, 2014, A4.

[71] Major Richard R. Baxter, "So-Called 'Unprivileged Belligerency': Spies, Guerrillas, and Saboteurs," 28 *BYIL* (1951), 335.

[72] *Prosecutor v. Delalić*, IT-96–21-T (16 Nov. 1998), para. 268.

[73] Draper, "Personnel and Issues of Status," supra, note 3, at 198.

[74] Pictet, *Commentary, III Geneva Convention*, supra, note 40, at 67.

[75] Pictet, *Commentary, IV Geneva Convention*, supra, note 1, at 51.

[76] Draper, "The Legal Classification of Belligerent Individuals," in Meyer and McCoubrey, *Reflections on Law and Armed Conflicts*, supra, note 3, at 202.

August 2008, Russian troops invaded the South Ossetia region of neighboring Georgia and, overcoming resistance of the Georgian army, pushed on, into Georgia itself.[77]

> As swaths of the country fell before Russian troops, it was not only the army that rose in its defense but also regular citizens...[Two young Georgian men] hoped to join the fight...despite the fact that neither had served in the military...part of a group of a dozen civilians, some in camouflage and some wearing bullet-proof vests, who said they were there to defend the city from Russian attack. "Many of them now think it is the last chance to defend their homeland," Ms. Lagidze said. "It comes from the knowledge that the army is not enough and every man is valuable.[78]

Levées en masse are not as improbable on today's battlefields as believed.

6.3.6 *Demobilized Military Personnel and Military Internees in Neutral Countries*

An often overlooked provision of Geneva Convention III, Article 4, is subparagraph B, again included as a direct result of World War II experience. In occupied territories, the Nazis often arrested and shot retired or demobilized military personnel, often ex-officers who refused to comply with internment orders or attempted to rejoin their former units. To prevent such acts in future conflicts, this provision of Article 4 requires that such detained individuals receive POW protection.[79]

The internment of military personnel in neutral countries was a significant World War II issue, particularly for the United States. For British-based American bomber crews, Switzerland was not far from many German targets. U.S. bombers too badly damaged over Germany to return to their distant English bases often opted to land in Switzerland, rather than risk crash-landing in Axis territory. As required by Article 57 of 1899 Hague Regulation II, Switzerland, a neutral state, interned the American air crews as "troops belonging to the belligerent armies..."[80] One thousand, seven hundred forty American officers and enlisted air crew, and 13,500 other foreign military personnel, primarily German, British, and Russian,[81] were interned in Switzerland during the war. The crews were held in approximately a hundred camps across the country, all with armed Swiss guards. The interned former combatants were guarded at night and forbidden to attempt escape, but during the day were allowed outside the camps, often passing time in the small towns near their internment facilities. Article 4B of Geneva Convention III clarifies the status, treatment, and repatriation of such belligerents who are detained by a neutral state.

---

[77] Michael Schwirtz and Andrew E. Kramer, "Russian Forces Capture Military Base in Georgia," *NY Times*, Aug. 12, 2008, A8.

[78] Nicholas Kulish and Michael Schwirtz, "Sons Missing in Action, If Indeed They Found It," *NY Times*, Aug. 12, 2008, A10. Both young men described in the media account were swiftly captured, harshly treated, forced to clean up debris left from the fighting, and released nineteen days later, after all fighting ended. They never held a weapon, never fought the enemy. Michael Schwirtz, "2 Georgians Went to War but Never Got to Fight," *NY Times*, Sept. 2, 2008, A8.

[79] Pictet, *Commentary, IV Geneva Convention*, supra, note 1, at 68–9.

[80] 1899 Hague Convention II Respecting the Laws and Customs of War on Land. 1899 H.C. II was the analogue of 1907 H.R. IV and most of its Articles were the basis for similar Articles in 1907 H.R. IV. Article 57 is an exception, with no similar Article in 1907 H.R. IV. Although the United States, Germany, Italy, and Japan ratified 1899 H.C. II, Switzerland did not, in keeping with her long-standing neutral stance.

[81] Cathryn J. Prince, *Shot from the Sky: American POWs in Switzerland* (Annapolis, MD: Naval Institute Press, 2003), 21–43.

6.4 Direct Participation in Hostilities

With rare exception, such as France's 1793 Declaration of the Rights of Man, which conferred the people's "sacred right" to rise up against an oppressive government, armed rebellion has been considered a serious offense against the state and an illegitimate avenue of protest. "In theory, states have a monopoly on the use of force and the members of their armed forces are the only ones empowered to wield it. It is always the state that determines who the enemy is and...no entity other than the state has the right to resort to force."[82] Today, civilians who employ armed force in an armed conflict are said to "directly participate in hostilities."

Giving definitional substance to the phrase "direct participation in hostilities" has vexed LOAC/IHL students and practitioners since it was included in the 1977 Additional Protocol I. Article 51.3 of Protocol I reads: "Civilians shall enjoy the protection afforded by this Section, [General Protection Against Effects of Hostilities], unless and for such time as they take a direct part in hostilities." Additional Protocol II, Article 13.3, applicable in non-international armed conflicts, reads the same. Publicists, practitioners, and scholars have debated the meaning of "for such time" and "direct part" since the publication of the Protocol.

Direct participation in hostilities is a concept that applies only to civilians. The hostilities may be either international or non-international. In an international armed conflict, civilians are "persons who are neither members of the armed forces of a party to the conflict nor participants in a *levée en masse*..."[83] In a non-international armed conflict, the term, "civilian" takes its usual meaning, a person not associated with the military. Civilians who take a direct part in hostilities, if captured, "do not have the right to prisoner-of-war status."[84]

But what constitutes a civilian taking "a direct part in hostilities"? Direct participation must refer to specific hostile acts, and it clearly suspends a civilian's noncombatant protection. The *Commentary* to Protocol I provides some clarification: direct participation means "acts of war which by their nature or purpose are likely to cause actual harm to the personnel and equipment of the enemy armed forces."[85] Direct participation "implies a direct causal relationship between the activity engaged in and the harm done to the enemy at the time and the place where the activity takes place."[86] These two statements are helpful, but can be difficult to apply to real-world situations. Few legal phrases of significance can be perfectly or comprehensively defined in a few paragraphs, but in this case, more comprehensive guidance was needed. It is provided in a 2009 report issued jointly by the ICRC and the Asser Institute that reflects a five-year study of the phrase by panels of experts.[87] The then-President of the ICRC said of the study, "Without changing existing law, the ICRC's Interpretive Guidance document provides our recommendations on how IHL relating to the notion of direct participation in hostilities should

---

[82] Vincent Bernard, "Editorial: Understanding Armed Groups and the Law," 93/882 *Int'l Rev. of the Red Cross* (June 2011), 261, 265.

[83] Civilians are defined in Additional Protocol I, Art. 50.

[84] Henckaerts and Doswald-Beck, *Customary International Humanitarian Law*, supra, note 46, Rule 106, at 384.

[85] *Commentary*, Additional Protocols, supra, note 5, para. 1679, at 516.   [86] Id., para. 1944, at 619.

[87] ICRC, "Interpretive Guidance on the Notion of Direct Participation in Hostilities under International Humanitarian Law," reprinted in 90/872 *Int'l Rev. of the Red Cross* (Dec. 2008), 991–1047, 995. Although the date of the journal is 2008, the guidance was not released until mid-2009.

be interpreted in contemporary armed conflict. It constitutes much more than an academic exercise. The aim is that these recommendations will enjoy practical application where it matters, in the midst of armed conflict."[88] Although not perfect, the *Interpretive Guidance* provides a clarity previously absent.

6.4.1 *Criteria for Direct Participation in Hostilities*

According to the ICRC report, in a common Article 2 international armed conflict, three criteria must be met for a civilian to be considered directly participating in hostilities. All three criteria must be met to constitute direct participation.

First, **the civilian's act must be likely to adversely affect the military operations of a party to the conflict or, alternatively, be likely to inflict death, injury or destruction of persons or objects protected against direct attack**. This is the "threshold of harm requirement." That the harm actually occur is not required, only that there is an objective *likelihood* that it will occur. Attempts, for example, meet this criterion. Sabotage or other unarmed activities qualify, if they restrict or disturb logistics or communications of an opposing party to the conflict. Clearing mines, guarding captured military personnel, even computer attacks, meet this qualification. Violent acts specifically directed against civilians or civilian objects, such as sniper attacks or the bombardment of civilian residential areas, satisfy this requirement.[89]

Second, **there must be a direct causal link between the act and the harm likely to result**. This is a requirement of "direct causation" that goes beyond the actual conduct of armed hostilities. Direct causal links include war-sustaining acts that objectively contribute in a direct way to the defeat of an opposing armed force.

A frequent classroom example of such a link is a civilian volunteer driving a military ammunition truck to operationally engaged fighters. The driver's act is a direct causal link to a likely adverse affect on the military operations of the opposing party to the conflict. The civilian is taking a direct part in hostilities and forfeits his civilian protection.

Moving ammunition from the factory where it is manufactured to a port for shipment to a warehouse in the conflict zone is *not* a direct causal link, however. Political, economic, and media activities, such as propaganda dissemination, and supportive financial transactions, although war-sustaining, are too indirect to result in a civilian's loss of protection.[90] The design, production, assembly, or shipment of weapons and military equipment and the construction or repair of roads or bridges are all part of the general war effort but, according to the ICRC *Guidance*, do not constitute a sufficiently *direct* causal link likely to adversely affect the military operations of an opposing party. This should not be confused with the planting or detonation of bombs, mines, booby-traps, or improvised explosive devices – acts that *do* have a direct link and result in a loss of the civilian's targeting protection. The *Interpretive Guidance* holds that, in a combat zone, assembling an IED is not direct participation, an opinion with which many commentators disagree. Identifying and marking targets and transmission of tactical intelligence also are direct causal links. The *Guidance* cautiously holds that

---

[88] Jakob Kellenberger, "Sixty Years of the Geneva Conventions: Learning from the Past to Better Face the Future, 91/875 *Int'l Rev. of the Red Cross* (Sept. 2009), 613, 615.

[89] ICRC, "Interpretive Guidance on the Notion of Direct Participation," supra, note 87, at 1016–19.

[90] Id., at 1020.

"[w]here civilians voluntarily and deliberately position themselves to create a physical obstacle to military operations of a party to the conflict, they *could* directly cross the threshold of harm required for a qualification as direct participation."[91] While the possible death or wounding of civilians, including voluntary human shields, always figures in proportionality calculations, opposing commanders are likely to take a harsher view of such civilian volunteers.

A civilian's provision to an armed <u>terrorist group</u> of <u>financial contributions</u> or construction materials or supplies, alone, is too attenuated to rise to the direct causal link required to constitute direct participation. The same may be said of scientific research and design of weapons and equipment. The recruitment and general training of personnel "may be indispensable, but [is] not directly causal, to the subsequent infliction of harm."[92] Cooks and housekeepers provide no direct causal relation.

Not only must the civilian's act objectively be likely to adversely affect the military operations of a party to the conflict, or be likely to inflict death, injury, or destruction of persons or objects protected against direct attack and have a direct link between the act and the harm likely to result, it must, third, **specifically be designed to directly cause the required threshold of harm in support of a party to the conflict and to the detriment of another**. In other words, there must be a "belligerent nexus" between the civilian's act and the resultant harm. An example is an exchange of gunfire between police and hostage takers during a bank robbery. There is no connection between that brief shooting and an armed conflict. It is a matter for resolution by domestic law enforcement and domestic courts. Additionally, "although the use of force by civilians to defend themselves against unlawful attack or looting, rape, and murder by marauding soldiers may cause the required threshold of harm, its purpose clearly is not to support a party to the conflict against another."[93] In such an instance, civilians employing armed force against rogue soldiers would not constitute direct participation in hostilities because the force is not employed to support any party to the conflict.

The three criteria include a civilian's actions preparatory to acts of direct participation. That is, direct participation in hostilities includes deployment to and return from the location of the direct participation. It includes the preparatory collection of tactical intelligence, the transport of personnel, the transport and positioning of weapons and equipment, as well as the loading of explosives in, for example, a suicide vehicle – although not, without more, the hiding or smuggling of weapons; not financial or political support of armed individuals.

> Applied in conjunction, the three requirements of *threshold of harm*, *direct causation* and *belligerent nexus* permit a reliable distinction between activities amounting to direct participation in hostilities and activities which, although occurring in the context of an armed conflict, are not part of the conduct of hostilities and, therefore, do not entail loss of protection against direct attack.[94]

These three criteria constitute a reasonably broad description of direct participation; one that, in an armed conflict against an enemy without uniforms or insignia, who moves

---

[91] Id., at 1024. Emphasis supplied. The human shield, voluntary or otherwise, is never the targeted object. That which they attempt to shield is the military object. A commander's proportionality question is whether the military object remains a proper target despite the presence of the human shield.
[92] Id., at 1022.   [93] Id., at 1028.   [94] Id., at 1030–1. Emphasis in original.

among and depends on civilians for concealment, gives the unlawful combatant's opponent guidance that offers significant targeting latitude.

Further discussion of continuous combat function is found in chapter 15.6.3 and in chapter 15 Cases and Materials.

6.4.2 Armed Opposition Groups

In a common Article 2 armed conflict, unlawful combatants/unprivileged belligerents are usually an exception rather than the norm, and they are identified by their armed activities. However, in a common Article 3 non-international conflict, the unlawful combatant is the norm. Armed opposition groups are described as identifiable entities, with political objectives, that they pursue by violent means, possessing an organized military force and an authority responsible for its acts.[95] As previously noted (Ch. 5.2), armed opposition groups are bound by LOAC/IHL.

In an armed conflict between a state and an organized armed group, such as al Qaeda or the Taliban, the organized armed opposition group does not enjoy the combatant's privilege but, the ICRC report notes, it is in fact "the armed forces of a non-State party to the conflict."[96] Just as the *Légion étrangère*, the Foreign Legion, is an armed force of France, or just as the U.S. Army is an armed force of the United States, organized armed Taliban fighters are the armed force of that Sunni Muslim fundamentalist movement. Of course, not every Sunni Muslim fundamentalist is a terrorist or Taliban fighter. Not all Taliban are unlawful combatants taking a direct part in hostilities. Who among the Taliban and al Qaeda, then, are "the armed forces" of those nonstate parties to conflicts in Afghanistan and Iraq and how are they recognized?

In a non-international armed conflict, "both State and non-State parties to the conflict have armed forces distinct from the civilian population."[97] An armed opposition group, if present, is the armed force of the non-state party to the conflict. That implies that the group belongs to a party to the conflict – that it has a *de facto* relationship with a party to the conflict and that there is an articulable criterion for membership in such an armed force. Accepting that the armed forces of a non-state party to a non-international conflict is comprised of individuals whose function is to take a direct part in hostilities, **the defining criterion for such individuals is that they have a continuous combat function.**

6.4.3 Continuous Combat Function

The term "continuous combat function" arose in 2008, after multi-year meetings of international experts under the auspices of the ICRC. (See Cases and Materials, Ch. 14) There was significant dissention among some of the experts involved as to several aspects of the ICRC's final report (the "Interpretive Guidance"). The report's basic concept of continuous combat function was nevertheless seen by many commentators in the U.S. and other states fighting armed opposition groups in the middle east as a reasonable

---

[95] Pictet, *Commentary, I Geneva Convention* , supra, note 23, at 49, referring to the two criteria of possessing an organized military force and an authority responsible for its acts among several others, which can serve to indicate the existence of a non-international armed conflict in the sense of Common Article 3.

[96] ICRC, "Interpretive Guidance on the Notion of Direct Participation," supra, note 87, at 995.

[97] Id., at 995.

solution, within the bounds of LOAC/IHL, to the difficult issue of "revolving door" individual status raised by Additional Protocol I's Article 51.3. That is, civilians who directly participate in hostilities lose their protection as civilians and may be targeted and killed, but only "for so long as" they are actually directly participating in hostilities. Article 51.3 thus limits the time and circumstances when unlawful and potentially deadly civilian acts may be countered. It also creates a virtual revolving door that would allow unlawful civilian fighters to abruptly cease their direct participation, become protected civilians again and then, when convenient to their purposes, once again take up arms and directly participate in the hostilities. Such on-again, off-again conduct made lawful counter-measure by combatants they victimized difficult and dangerous. Continuous combat function is an important evolution in interpreting the law of war.

The term, "continuous combat function," and its definition, were necessitated by the twentieth-century reinvigoration of terrorism, combined with twenty-first century weaponry. The term illustrates the evolution and continuing relevance of the 1949 Geneva Conventions and the ongoing interpretation of its terms through informed debate and eventual international consensus.

Although the term is not found in the Conventions, the phrase, "armed forces" in Geneva Convention common Article 3(1), by clear implication, includes the armed forces of nonstate parties – organized armed groups. The armed forces of the nonstate party (i.e., the organized armed group belonging to the nonstate party to the conflict) "refers exclusively to the armed or military wing of [the] non-state party; its armed forces in a functional sense."[98] Membership in armed opposition groups is not evidenced by uniform or ID card, but by function.

> [M]embership must depend on whether the continuous function assumed by an individual corresponds to that collectively exercised by the group as a whole, namely the conduct of hostilities on behalf of a non-State party to the conflict...[T]he decisive criterion for individual membership in an organized group is whether a person assumes a continuous function for the group involving his or her direct participation in hostilities..."continuous combat function"...[which] requires lasting integration into an organized armed group acting as the armed forces of a non-State party to an armed conflict...A continuous combat function may be...for example, where a person has repeatedly directly participated in hostilities in support of an organized armed group in circumstances indicating that such conduct constitutes a continuous function rather than a spontaneous, sporadic, or temporary role...[99]

Thus, a civilian's unorganized or occasional hostile act does not constitute membership in an organized armed group or represent continuous combat function. (Naturally, in any armed attack by armed civilians, an opposing combatant's right to self-defense is unconstrained, even if the individual's attack is unorganized or sporadic in nature.)

This description of continuous combat function goes far to erase the significance of the phrase in Article 51.3 that was formerly subjected to minute parsing: "...unless and for such time as..." The *Interpretive Guidance's* description clarifies that an al Qaeda leader does not regain civilian protection against direct attack merely because he temporarily stores his weapon to visit his family in government-controlled territory. A Taliban fighter who plants improvised antipersonnel mines remains a lawful target

[98] Id., at 1006.   [99] Id., at 1007, 1008.

when he puts down his tools and walks home for lunch with his family. A senior terrorist insurgent may be targeted when he is asleep. An insurgent commander remains a lawful target whenever he may be located and whatever he may be doing. Proportionality always remains an issue, but his targeting is not precluded because the organized armed group member who has a continuous combat function is not actually fighting at the moment of his targeting.

Continuous combat function cannot be recognized by an opposing combatant in a firefight. The enemy fighter wears no sign announcing his status. How, then, does the on-the-ground combatant know? She doesn't. In a firefight she may return fire and may target and kill the enemy fighter on the basis of self-defense, without knowing her target had a continuous combat function. Her senior officers, however, through communicar-tions intercepts and human intelligence sources, know who has a continuous combat function. Upon confirmed identification of the individual's status they may target him with artillery fire, attack by aviation assets, by armed drone, even by sniper. After positive identification as having continuous combat function, the enemy fighter is a lawful target.

6.5 Unlawful Combatants/Unprivileged Belligerents

The terms "unlawful combatant" and "unprivileged belligerent," which describe the same individuals, do not appear in the Geneva Conventions, the Additional Protocols, or any other LOAC treaty, convention, or protocol. Nevertheless, **"unlawful combatant,"** a term frequently employed by the United States,[100] is a *de facto* individual status.

"[T]he term 'combatant,' as well as its colloquial derivations, 'unlawful combatant,' 'enemy combatant,' and 'unprivileged combatant,' are germane only to common Article 2 international armed conflict."[101] A characteristic of unlawful combatants is that upon capture they are *not* entitled to POW status. Despite the fact that these terms are properly applicable only to international armed conflicts, they are commonly used in non-international armed conflicts. No harm is done in using them in the colloquial sense; indeed, their use connotes actions, and a status, that most individuals will, without explanation, immediately understand. In that sense the terms, incorrect as they may be, have real utility. Students of LOAC/IHL, however, should understand that the correct term for such enemy fighters, in both international or non-international conflicts, is unprivileged belligerents.

"Unlawful combatant" has been described by an ICRC legal advisor "as describing all **persons taking a direct part in hostilities without being entitled to do so and who**

---

[100] Professor Kalshoven derides recent American use of the term to legitimize prisoner treatment. "In American jurisprudence, 'unlawful combatant' is a magic term: combatants so qualified are beyond the pale and ... they should not expect any protection from the U.S. courts." Frits Kalshoven, *Reflections on the Law of War* (Leiden: Martinus Nijhoff, 2007), 924. Professor George Fletcher and Dr. Jens Ohlin agree: "The Bush administration has pointed to the concept [of unlawful combatant] to explain its posture of nonreciprocal warfare. When combatants are unlawful, the argument goes, they are subject to the burdens of combatancy (they can be killed), but they have no reciprocal rights ... The phrase unlawful combatant as used today combines the aspect of unlawful from the law of crime and the concept of combatant from the law of war. For those thus labeled, it is the worst of all possible worlds." George P. Fletcher and Jens David Ohlen, *Defending Humanity* (New York: Oxford University Press, 2008), 183.

[101] Jelena Pejic, "'Unlawful/ Enemy Combatants:' Interpretations and Consequences," in Schmitt and Pejic, *International Law and Armed Conflict*, supra, note 8, at 335.

therefore cannot be classified as prisoners of war on falling into the power of the enemy."[102] (One should add to that definition that the persons taking a direct part must be civilians.) Some contend that there is no such status as unlawful combatant in the law of war and, in fact, the term does not occur in the Geneva Conventions, the Additional Protocols, or the 1907 Hague Regulations. There is a body of scholarship and state practice that delineates and defines the status, however.[103] "There is a long record of certain people coming into the category of unlawful combatants – pirates, spies, saboteurs, and so on. It has been absurd that there should have been a debate about whether or not that category exists."[104]

Recall that there are only two categories of individual on the battlefield: combatants and civilians. Unlawful combatants/unprivileged belligerents are *not* a third battlefield category. "'[U]nlawful combatant' is a shorthand expression useful for describing those civilians who take up arms without being authorized to do so by international law. It has an exclusively *descriptive* character. It may not be used as proving or corroborating the existence of a third category of persons…"[105] Just as guerrillas and militias may be a subset of "combatant," unlawful combatants are a subset of "civilian."[106]

---

[102] Knut Dörmann, "The Legal Situation of 'Unlawful/Unprivileged Combatants,'" 849 *Int'l Rev. of Red Cross* (2003), 45. In U.S. domestic law, an unlawful combatant is defined as a person who has engaged in, or purposefully and materially supported another in engaging in, hostilities against the United States and its allies, and who does not qualify as a lawful combatant, or an individual who has been deemed an unlawful enemy combatant by a Combatant Status Review Tribunal or any other competent tribunal. *Military Commissions Act of 2006*, 10 USC 47(A), § 948a(1).

[103] Judge Aharon Barak, retired President of Israel's Supreme Court, correctly wrote, "It is difficult for us to see how a third category [unlawful combatants] can be recognized in the framework of the Hague and Geneva Conventions. It does not appear to us that we were presented with data sufficient to allow us to say, at the present time, that such a third category has been recognized in customary international law." *The Public Committee against Torture in Israel v. the Government of Israel* [The Targeted Killing Case] (2006) HCJ 769/02, para. 28, available on-line. Yoram Dinstein, Georg Schwarzenberger, BGen. Kenneth Watkin, and Dieter Fleck, among others, describe unlawful combatants not as a third battlefield category but as a subcategory of civilian. See Dinstein, *The Conduct of Hostilities*, supra, note 2, at 29–33: "The distinction between lawful and unlawful combatants is a corollary of the fundamental distinction between combatants and civilians"; Georg Schwarzenberger, *International Law*. Vol. II. *The Law of Armed Conflict* (London: Stevens & Sons, 1968), 116–17: "By the introduction of the additional distinction between lawful and unlawful combatants … it becomes possible to give far-reaching protection to the overwhelming majority of the civilian population of occupied territories and captured members of enemy forces."; Green, *Contemporary Law of Armed Conflict*, supra, note 34, at 104; Kenneth Watkin, "21st Century Conflict and International Humanitarian Law: Status Quo or Change?" in Schmitt and Pejic, *International Law and Armed Conflict*, supra, note 8, at 285: "[T]here is no universal agreement … that persons who take a direct part in hostilities have civilian status. One approach has been to categorize such participants as 'unlawful combatants' … "; and Fleck, *Handbook of Humanitarian Law*, supra, note 9, at 68: "[P]ersons who take a direct part in the hostilities without being entitled to do so (unlawful combatants) face penal consequences."

[104] Sir Adam Roberts, in John Bellinger III and Vijay M. Padmanabhan, "Detention Operations in Contemporary Conflicts," 105–2 *AJIL* (April 2011), 201, 217 at fn. 80.

[105] Antonio Cassese, expert opinion, "On Whether Israel's Targeted Killings of Palestinian Terrorists Is Consonant with International Humanitarian Law," (2006), http://www.stoptorture.org.il. Emphasis in original.

[106] *A and B v. State of Israel*, Supreme Court of Israel, sitting as the Court of Criminal Appeals, No. 6659/06 (11 June 2008), available on-line, para. 12, citing *Israel v. The State of Israel* ("The Five Techniques case") (HCJ 5111/94), 1999: "[T]he term 'unlawful combatants' does not constitute a separate category but is a sub-category of 'civilians' recognized by international law."

The origin of the term "unprivileged belligerents" is usually ascribed to a 1951 Richard Baxter article.[107]

> The...civilians who carry out belligerent acts that might well be conducted lawfully by combatants [are unlawful belligerents]....Civilians who engage in combat lose their protected status and may become lawful targets for so long as they continue to fight. They do not enjoy immunity under the law of war for their violent conduct and can be tried and punished under civil law for their belligerent acts. However, they do not lose their protection as civilians under the Geneva Convention if they are captured.[108]

Unlawful combatants sometimes band together to form unlawful combatant organizations; that is, armed opposition groups. During the U.S.–Vietnam War, an often-heard phrase regarding the Viet Cong, a Vietnamese civilian group of clandestine fighters, was, "Farmer by day, fighter by night." (When did he sleep?) "A person who engages in military raids by night, while purporting to be an innocent civilian by day, is an unlawful combatant. He is a combatant in the sense that he can be lawfully targeted by the enemy, but he cannot claim the privileges appertaining to lawful combatancy. Nor does he enjoy the benefits of civilian status...."[109] This characterization does not suggest that an unlawful combatant is outside LOAC/IHL. At a minimum, captured unlawful combatants are entitled to the basic humanitarian protections of common Article 3, and Article 75 of Additional Protocol I.[110] Although the U.S. has not ratified Additional Protocol I, its Article 75 is considered customary law – although the U.S., in 2011, announced that it considers Article 75 applicable "to any individual it detains in an *international* armed conflict..."[111] (Emphasis supplied.) The import of this U.S. position, contrary to most states' views of Article 75's universal application, has not been explained.

In an international conflict, a civilian who fires an infrequent shot at Afghan government forces and a Taliban fighter are both unlawful combatants. Their difference is that the Taliban fighter may have a continuous combat function and may be targeted and killed whenever he can be positively identified. The civilian shooter may only be targeted for such time as he is actually engaged in his unlawful combatancy.

Alexander the Great, in his central Asian operations (329–327 B.C.) battled Sogdianan guerrillas. Throughout France's invasion of Spain during the Peninsular War (1807–8), Napoleon Bonaparte's invading army was beset by local insurgents, the term "guerrilla" originating here. In the mid-nineteenth century, the insurgent fighter, Giuseppe Garibaldi, was admired throughout Europe.[112] In 1863, however, Lieber wrote of insurgents:

---

[107] Baxter, "So-Called 'Unprivileged Belligerency,'" supra, note 71, at 323. In his article, Baxter uses the term "unlawful combatancy."

[108] Elsea, *Treatment of "Battlefield Detainees,"* supra, note 19, at 22.

[109] Dinstein, *The Conduct of Hostilities*, supra, note 2, at 29.

[110] Pejic, "'Unlawful/Enemy Combatants," supra, note 101, at 340; FM 27–10, *Law of Land Warfare*, supra, note 15, at para. 31; UK MOD, *Manual of the Law of Armed Conflict*, supra, note 22, at para. 9.18.1, at 225; and, *Prosecutor v. Delalic*, supra, note 72, at para. 271.

[111] The White House, "Fact Sheet: New Actions on Guantánamo and Detainee Policy" (March 7, 2011). Executive Order 13567, "Periodic Review of Individuals Detained at Guantánamo Bay Naval Station ... " to which the Fact Sheet pertains, makes no mention of Article 75. The Fact Sheet likely anticipates attacks on conditions of confinement of Guantánamo detainees.

[112] Tim Parks, "The Insurgent," *The New Yorker*, July 9 and 16, 2007, 92–7.

Lieber

Men, or squads of men, who commit hostilities, whether by fighting. . .or by raids of any kind, without commission, without being part and portion of the organized hostile army, and without sharing continuously in the war, but who do so with intermitting returns to their homes and avocations, or with the occasional assumption of the semblance of peaceful pursuits, divesting themselves of the character or appearance of soldiers – such men, or squads of men. . .if captured, are not entitled to the privileges of prisoners of war, but shall be treated summarily as highway robbers or pirates.[113]

We no longer summarily execute unlawful combatants, but the point remains that unlawful combatants are as old as warfare, even if the title is not.

Unlawful combatants, including those with a continuous combat function, are not entitled to the privileges and protections of POW status but, as mentioned, a state may accord POW status or, in the words of Additional Protocol I, Article 44.4, "protections equivalent in all respects to those accorded prisoners of war," to dissidents in an internal armed conflict, even to unlawful combatants in an international armed conflict. The United States has given limited POW status to enemy captives in the Civil War, the Philippine War, and the Vietnam War.[114]

The wrongfulness of the unlawful combatant is reflected in Additional Protocol I, Article 48. "In order to ensure respect for and protection of the civilian population. . .the Parties to the conflict shall at all times distinguish between the civilian population and combatants. . . ." Unlawful combatants, fighters without uniform or distinguishing insignia, violate the bedrock concept of distinction. (Aircraft can violate the concept of distinction, as well.[115]) When the distinction requirement is disregarded, opposing combatants cannot discern fighters from civilians, opposing shooters from friendly shooters, good guys from bad guys,* eroding the lawful combatant's presumption that civilians he encounters are non-combatants who present no danger. "If combatants were free to melt away amid the civilian population, every civilian would suffer the results of being suspected as a masked combatant. . . .It follows that a sanction. . .must be imposed on whoever is seeking to abuse the standing of a civilian while in fact he is a disguised combatant."[116]

---

[113] The Lieber Code, supra, note 16, at Art. 82. Also see Art. 85, describing "war rebels."

[114] Elsea, *Treatment of "Battlefield Detainees*," supra, note 19, at 27. Elsea mentions only Philippine POWs.

[115] Draft Rules of Air Warfare Drafted by A Commission of Jurists at The Hague, December, 1922–February 1923, Art. 3. "A military aircraft shall bear an external mark indicating its nationality and military character." The Draft Hague Rules of Air Warfare were never adopted or embodied in an international convention but are instructive. See J. M. Spaight, *Air Power and War Rights*, 3d ed. (London: Longmans Green, 1947), 42. During the abortive April 1980 U.S. rescue of hostages held in the American embassy in Tehran, Iran (Operation Eagle Claw), all U.S. aircraft participating in the rescue effort carried false Iranian markings. Some carried the markings of several additional countries, to be applied over U.S. markings in case the aircraft had to be abandoned.

* In Sept. 1944, Charles A. Lindbergh, first man to fly the Atlantic nonstop, apparently engaged in aerial action that rendered him an unlawful combatant. His offer to enlist having been refused by the Army Air Corps, Lindbergh traveled to Marine Corps airfields in the Pacific as a civilian consultant for Chance Vought Aircraft to instruct pilots in the advanced operation of the F-4U Corsair fighter. While on Roi Namur, he flew a Corsair on a bombing mission to Wotje island, a Japanese base. See: Col. E. Gerald Tremblay, "Charles Lindbergh Saved My Life," *Marine Corps Gazette*, May 1990, 89–90. Lindbergh reportedly flew a total of fifty fighter combat missions and shot down at least one Japanese plane. Mark M. Boatner, *Biographical Dictionary of World War II* (Novato, CA: Presidio Press, 1996), 320.

[116] Yoram Dinstein, "The Distinction between Unlawful Combatants and War Criminals," in Yoram Dinstein, ed., *International Law at a Time of Perplexity* (Dordrecht: Nijhoff, 1989), 103, 105.

Irregulars...do not merely breach the formal reciprocal rules of fair play, their tactics and camouflage and disguise take advantage of the very code they breach. Irregulars are...free riders on the prohibitions civilized nations adhere to. Furthermore, by acquiring a hybrid identity of combatant-civilian, they also blur the more basic moral distinction between those who may and those who may not be targeted in wartime. Thus, the more fundamental vice of irregular combatants is not merely their formal lawlessness, or even unfairness, but rather the threat they pose to "civilized" conduct of war and the protections it affords to an identifiable defenseless civilian population.[117]

U.S. Navy SEAL Marcus Luttrell, describing conflict in Afghanistan, takes a pessimistic view of the requirement for distinction: "The truth is, in this kind of terrorist/insurgent warfare, no one can tell who's a civilian and who's not. So what's the point of framing rules that cannot be comprehensively carried out by anyone? Rules that are unworkable, because half the time no one knows who the goddamned enemy is, and by the time you find out, it might be too late to save your own life."[118] Without the rules Petty Officer Luttrell derides, however, a combat zone would spiral into chaos, an old west Dodge City without a sheriff, where one can shoot first and ask no questions at all.

The *Commentary* to Additional Protocol I discusses what constitutes unlawful combatancy:

> In general the immunity afforded civilians is subject to a very stringent condition: that they do not participate directly in hostilities, i.e., that they do not become combatants, on pain of losing their protection. Thus, "direct" participation means acts of war which by their nature or purpose are likely to cause actual harm to the personnel and equipment of the enemy armed forces.[119]

The *Commentary* further notes, "Direct participation in hostilities implies a direct causal relationship between the activity engaged in and the harm done to the enemy at the time and place where the activity takes place."[120] It is this direct causal relationship that is explained in the 2009 ICRC report on direct participation in hostilities.

What privilege is it that the unprivileged belligerent does not have? The very significant combatant's privilege and the privilege of POW status, if captured. It is not a violation of LOAC/IHL to be an unprivileged belligerent, but what an individual *does* that makes him or her an unprivileged belligerent is a violation. If the enemy fighter – an unprivileged belligerent – kills, wounds, or destroys, he or she has violated LOAC/IHL and may be tried. Judicial proceedings may be conducted before either military or domestic courts.[121] Spain, for example, employed its domestic courts to try the 2004 Madrid train-bombing suspects,[122] as did the United Kingdom, after the 2005 London bombings.[123] The Madrid and London

---

[117] Tamar Meisels, "Combatants – Lawful and Unlawful," 26–1 *L. & Phil.* (2007), 31, 55–6.

[118] Marcus Luttrell, *Lone Survivor* (New York: Little, Brown, 2007), 169.

[119] Sandoz, *Commentary on the Additional Protocols*, supra, note 5, at 619. Emphasis in original, bolding supplied.

[120] Id., at 516. This description of "direct participation" is also cited in Michael J. Dennis, "Current Developments: Newly Adopted Protocols to the Convention on the Rights of the Child," 94–4 *AJIL* (Oct. 2000), 789, 792.

[121] Dinstein, *The Conduct of Hostilities*, supra, note 2, at 31. In accord: Sandoz, *Commentary on the Additional Protocols*, supra, note 5, ¶ 1670, at 510.

[122] Victoria Burnett, "Detainees Plotted Bombing in Spain, Judge Says," *NY Times*, Jan. 24, 2008, A6.

[123] "Britain: Prison for 5 Who Helped Failed London Bombers," *NY Times*, Feb. 5, 2008, A6.

bombings were not considered armed conflicts by the victim governments, but the point that captured terrorists may be tried in domestic courts was validated in those cases.

A problem in the U.S. conflicts in Iraq and Afghanistan was that "the sheer numbers of 'unprivileged belligerents'...makes it impossible to deal with the problem by way of criminal proceedings."[124] Issues such as questionable jurisdiction, chain of custody problems, and coerced statements also make trials of unlawful combatants in U.S. domestic courts and military commissions difficult, if not impossible.

6.5.1 *The Status of Armed Opposition Group Fighters*

What was the individual status of an al Qaeda, or Taliban, or any terrorist armed opposition group fighter? Initially, decide the first question when considering any conflict: What is the conflict status? What LOAC, if any, was applicable to the U.S. conflict in Afghanistan, the location of most Taliban fighters? On October 7, 2001, the United States invaded Afghanistan,[125] initiating an armed conflict between two state parties to the 1949 Geneva Conventions, a common Article 2 international armed conflict. LOAC/IHL that applied was the 1949 Geneva Conventions in their entirety and, for states that had ratified it, 1977 Additional Protocol I, and customary international law

At the same time, in northern Afghanistan, there was an ongoing conflict between Afghanistan's Taliban government and the United Islamic Front for the Salvation of Afghanistan – the Northern Alliance, made up of various Afghan groups. That was a common Article 3 non-international armed conflict – an internal conflict. LOAC/IHL that applied to that fighting was common Article 3, customary international law and, possibly, 1977 Additional Protocol II. The common Article 2 conflict soon ended and a brief U.S. occupation of Afghanistan followed, with continuing U.S. combat operations against the Taliban. The Geneva Conventions and Additional Protocol I continue to apply during periods of occupation.[126]

The U.S.-backed Afghan Interim Authority assumed power on December 22, 2001 and formed a new Afghan government in January 2004.[127] At that point the U.S. occupation ended, although armed conflict within Afghanistan did not. When the new government assumed power, continuing American involvement became an armed presence bolstering Afghanistan's fight against the Taliban insurgents; a common Article 3 non-international conflict. Where the insurgents were from was irrelevant.

Accepting that the Taliban did not then exercise such control over any part of Afghanistan as to enable them to carry out sustained and concerted military operations, a point open to argument, Additional Protocol II did not apply. Accordingly, after the formation of the new Afghan government, common Article 3 and customary international law, and no other part of the Geneva Conventions applied.

If we consider that the Taliban *did* control sufficient territory to carry out sustained and concerted military operations, Additional Protocol II also applied. That would bring added nuance to common Article 3 protections, but no new protections of note.

---

[124] Garraway, "'Combatants' – Substance or Semantics?" supra, note 8, at 331.

[125] U.S. Department of State, "Key Events in Afghanistan's Political and Economic Reconstruction (Jan. 26, 2006)," available on-line.

[126] 1949 Geneva Convention I, Art. 2.   [127] Department of State, "Key Events," supra, note 125.

Next, answer the second question relevant to any armed conflict: What is the individual status of Taliban fighters *after* the new Afghan government was established and common Article 3 became applicable? Recall that there are no combatants, lawful or otherwise, in a common Article 3 conflict.[128] There are government forces and enemy fighters. In approaching the question of individual status we need not consider whether black turbans constitute a distinctive sign, or whether the Taliban carry their arms openly, for those issues are not encountered in common Article 3 conflicts. Whether they obey the law of war *is* considered, for war crimes, may be committed in non-international armed conflicts.

In a common Article 3 non-international armed conflict, Taliban fighters are terrorists, in violation of domestic law. If they commonly engage in combat, they may have a continuous combat function and may be targeted at any time by opposing forces. They are also criminals who, upon capture, enjoy common Article 3 and Additional Protocol I, Article 75 protections. They may be tried in domestic or military courts for unlawful acts that they committed before capture.

If captured, they are not POWs, for there are no POWs in a common Article 3 conflict. They have no combatant immunity. The U.S. position was that captured Taliban were "unlawful enemy combatants," or simply, "detainees."

What was the Taliban's status during the brief period of the U.S.–Afghan common Article 2 conflict? Were the Taliban the army of a party to the conflict? Additional Protocol I defines an army: "[A]ll organized armed forces, groups and units which are under a command responsible to that Party for the conduct of its subordinates, even if that Party is represented by a government or an authority not recognized by an adverse party. Such armed forces shall be subject to an internal disciplinary system which, *inter alia*, shall enforce compliance with the rules of international law applicable in armed conflict."[129] Considering that definition, the Taliban might appear to qualify as the army of Afghanistan in a common Article 2 conflict, entitled to POW status upon capture.[130]

Or, were the Taliban akin to the post–World War I *Freikorps* in defeated Germany? Private paramilitary groups, ultraconservative and highly nationalistic, *Freikorps* proliferated throughout Germany in 1919, one eventually becoming the National Socialist Workers' Party – the Nazi party. But in 1920 the Nazis were just another *Freikorps* competing for a role in a new German government they talked of forming, with allegiance not to any German government but to their own *Freikorps*.[131]

There is an argument that Afghanistan's armed forces ceased to exist after the fall of the Communist government, in September 1996, and the Afghan armed forces were then supplanted by a variety of *Freikorps*-like "armies," the Taliban one of the more powerful. The argument continues that there is no showing that the Taliban became the armed force of Afghanistan, professing allegiance to the government of

---

[128] See Marco Sassòli, "Terrorism and War, in 4–5 *J. of Int'l Crim. Justice* (Nov. 2006), 958, 970; and: Marko Milanovic, "Lessons for Human Rights and Humanitarian Law in the War on Terror: Comparing Hamdan and the Israeli Targeted Killing Case," 866 *Int'l Rev. of the Red Cross* (June 2007), 373, 388.

[129] 1977 Additional Protocol I, Art. 43.1.; 1949 Geneva Convention I, Art. 13(1).

[130] Marco Sassòli, "Query: Is There a Status of 'Unlawful Combatant?'" in Richard B. Jaques, ed., *International Law Studies: Issues in International Law and Military Operations*, Vol. 80 (Newport, RI: Naval War College, 2006), 57–67, 61.

[131] William L. Shirer, *The Rise and Fall of the Third Reich* (New York: Simon & Schuster, 1960), 33–4, 42–3.

that state.[132] Rather, the argument goes, they were merely the armed group in control of Afghanistan and its government.

The better view is that, during the common Article 2 phase of the U.S.–Afghanistan conflict, the Taliban were indeed the armed force of Afghanistan. The International Law Commission (ILC) has developed guidelines to state responsibility. Article 8 of the ILC's 2001 reporting document, *Responsibility of States for Internationally Wrongful Acts*, reads: "The conduct of a person or group of persons shall be considered an act of a State under international law if the person or group of persons is in fact acting on the instructions of, or under the direction or control of, that State in carrying out the conduct."[133] That guidance, combined with Additional Protocol I's Article 43.1, lead to the conclusion that the Taliban was the armed force of Afghanistan.

During the period of the common Article 2 conflict with American forces, did captured Taliban fighters therefore merit POW protection as members of "the armed forces of a Party to the conflict…"?[134] Applying the four conditions for lawful combatancy and POW status upon capture, the answer is no: Although they were the armed force of Afghanistan, the Taliban did not wear uniforms or other distinctive fixed sign. Black turbans, common to many males in the region, do not suffice. "Since the [four] conditions are cumulative, members of the Taliban forces failed to qualify as prisoners of war under the customary law of war criteria. These criteria admit no exception, not even in the unusual circumstances of…the Taliban regime. To say that '[t]he Taliban do not wear uniforms in the traditional western sense' is quite misleading, for the Taliban forces did not wear any uniform in any sense at all…"[135] Throughout the common Article 2 phase of the U.S.–Afghanistan conflict, the Taliban failed to distinguish themselves and were not entitled to POW status.[136] Although there are reasoned views in disagreement,[137] the Taliban captured during the common Article 2 U.S. invasion were not entitled to POW status.

[132] John B. Bellinger, Legal Advisor, U.S. Dept. of State, "Armed Conflict with Al Qaeda?" *Opino Juris* blog (Jan. 15, 2007), available on-line.

[133] Available on-line. Art. 10 adds, "The conduct of an insurrectional movement which becomes the new Government of a State shall be considered an act of that State under international law." Finally, Art. 11 reads, "Conduct which is not attributable to a State under the preceding Articles shall nevertheless be considered an act of that State under international law if and to the extent that the State acknowledges and adopts the conduct in question as its own." These three Articles surely encompass the Taliban's relation to the State of Afghanistan.

[134] 1949 Geneva Convention III, Art. 4A.(1).

[135] Dinstein, *The Conduct of Hostilities*, supra, note 2, at 48. Footnote omitted.

[136] Professor Marco Sassòli writes, "This allegation may astonish those who remember that during Operation Enduring Freedom, the United States stressed that it attacked Taliban command and control centers and did not complain that it was impossible to distinguish the Taliban from civilians." Sassòli, "Query: Is There a Status of "Unlawful combatant?"" supra, note 130, at 61.

[137] Elsea, *Treatment of "Battlefield Detainees,"* supra, note 19, at 7. " … Taliban, whose members would arguably seem to be eligible for POW status as members of the armed forces of Afghanistan under a plain reading of GPW Art. 4A(1) … " Also: Robert K. Goldman and Brian D. Tittemore, "Unprivileged Combatants and the Hostilities in Afghanistan: Their Status and Rights under International Humanitarian Law and Human Rights Law," ASIL Task Force on Terrorism report (Dec. 2002), at 23–31; and George H. Aldrich, "The Taliban, al Qaeda, and the Determination of Illegal Combatants, 96–4 *AJIL* (Oct. 2002), 891, 894: "I find it quite difficult to understand the reasons for President Bush's decision that all Taliban soldiers lack entitlement to POW status."

In a common Article 2 international armed conflict, Taliban who directly participate in hostilities are unprivileged belligerents/unlawful combatants with a continuous combat function who may be targeted. If captured, they are criminals and protected persons[138] entitled to common Article 3 and Protocol I Article 75 protections. They may be interned and may be tried in domestic or military courts for acts they committed that rendered them unlawful combatants.

(In a common Article 2 conflict, should a captured Taliban fighter be a national of the capturing state – an Afghan citizen captured by Afghani armed forces, for example – they are not Geneva Convention IV, Article 4 protected persons. They remain protected, however, by common Article 3 and Additional Protocol I, Article 75.)

The U.S. position was that captured Taliban were "unlawful enemy combatants," or simply, "detainees." It would have been wise to have competent tribunals determine the status of Taliban fighters captured during the international phase of the conflict because their presumptive individual status upon capture was POW.[139] Such tribunals are called for in cases of doubt regarding the captive's status. Was there doubt as to their status?[140] The Congressional Research Service specifies several *illegitimate* reasons for not granting POW status:

> The Administration has argued that granting [al Qaeda or Taliban] detainees POW status would interfere with efforts to interrogate them, which would in turn hamper its efforts to thwart further attacks. Denying POW status may allow the Army to retain more stringent security measures...The Administration also argued that the detainees, if granted POW status, would have to be repatriated when hostilities in Afghanistan cease, freeing them to commit more terrorist acts.[141]

The U.S. position toward captured Taliban and al Qaeda status was initially based on such flawed reasoning.

Acts of terrorism are prohibited by Geneva law, including the 1977 Protocols,[142] but status determinations were needlessly complicated by the inexplicable U.S. position that the conflicts with Taliban and al Qaeda were armed conflicts, yet were neither common Article 2 nor common Article 3 conflicts.[143] Despite warnings from the Secretary of

---

[138] FM 27–10, *Law of Land Warfare*, supra, note 15, para. 73, at 31: "If a person is determined . . . not to fall within any of the categories listed [for POW status], he is not entitled to be treated as a prisoner of war. He is, however, a 'protected person' . . . "

[139] 1949 Geneva Convention III, Art. 5. Also, 1977 Additional Protocol I, Art. 45.1. Professor Thomas Franck writes, "Without doubt, the most difficult element to defend of the decisions made . . . with respect to the prisoners taken in Afghanistan is the blanket nature of the decision to deny POW status to the Taliban prisoners. By one sweeping determination, the president ruled that not a single Taliban soldier, presumably not even the army commander, could qualify for POW status under the Geneva Convention." Thomas M. Franck, "The Taliban, al Qaeda, and the Determination of Illegal Combatants," 96–4 *AJIL* (Oct. 2002), 891, 897.

[140] 1949 Geneva Convention III, Art. 5.

[141] Elsea, *Treatment of "Battlefield Detainees,"* supra, note 19, at 7.

[142] 1949 Geneva Convention IV, Art. 33; 1977 Additional Protocol I, Art. 51(2); Additional Protocol II, Arts. 4 (2)(d), and 13(2).

[143] Memorandum for William J. Haynes II, General Council, Department of Defense; From: John Yoo, Deputy Assistant Attorney General; Subject: Application of Treaties and Laws to al Qaeda and Taliban Detainees (Jan. 9, 2002) (Hereafter: Yoo Memorandum). " . . . Common Article 2 . . . is limited only to cases of declared war or armed conflict 'between two or more of the High Contracting Parties.' Al Qaeda is not a High Contracting Party. . . . Al Qaeda is not covered by common Article 3, because the current

State[144] and the Department of State's Legal Advisor,[145] the United States initially held that captured Taliban and al Qaeda fighters were unprotected by the Geneva Conventions,[146] including common Article 3.[147] "Incredibly, [the Bush administration] also argued that even if the Geneva Conventions do not apply, the United States could prosecute members of the Taliban for war crimes, including, illogically, 'grave violations of…basic humanitarian duties under the Geneva Conventions.'"[148] (The view that captured Taliban and al Qaeda were outside the protections of common Article 3 was rejected by the Supreme Court in the 2006 *Hamdan* decision.[149] The Bush administration later reaffirmed its initial view,[150] but subsequently softened that position.) The U.S. view was that human rights law, as well, did not apply to the Taliban or al

---

conflict is not covered by the Geneva Conventions … Article 3 … shows that the Geneva Conventions were intended to cover either: a) traditional wars between Nation States … or non-international civil wars. … Our conflict with al Qaeda does not fit into either category." The same conclusion applied to the Taliban: "Article 2 states that the Convention shall apply to all cases of declared war or other armed conflict between the High Contracting Parties. But there was no war or armed conflict between the United States and Afghanistan … if Afghanistan was stateless at that time. Nor, of course, is there a state of war or armed conflict between the United States and Afghanistan *now*." And, "Even if Afghanistan under the Taliban were not deemed to have been a failed State, the President could still regard the Geneva Conventions as temporarily suspended during the current military action." Memorandum reprinted in Karen J. Greenberg and Joshua L. Dratel, *The Torture Papers* (New York: Cambridge University Press, 2005), 38.

[144] Memorandum to Council to the President and Assistant to the President for National Security Affairs; From: Colin L. Powell, Secretary of State; Subject: Draft Decision Memorandum for the President on the Applicability of the Geneva Conventions to the Conflict in Afghanistan (26 Jan. 2002). Id., at 122.

[145] Memorandum to Counsel to the President; From William H. Taft, IV; Subject: Comments on Your Paper on the Geneva Convention (Feb. 2, 2002). Id., at 129.

[146] Yoo Memorandum, supra, note 143. "The weight of informed opinion strongly supports the conclusion that … Afghanistan was a 'failed State' whose territory had been largely overrun and held by violence by a militia or faction rather than by a government. Accordingly, Afghanistan was without the attributes of statehood necessary to continue as a party to the Geneva Conventions, and the Taliban militia, like al Qaeda, is therefore not entitled to the protections of the Geneva Conventions."

[147] Memorandum for Alberto R. Gonzales, Counsel to the President and William J. Haynes II, General Counsel of the Department of Defense; From: U.S. Department of Justice, Office of Legal Counsel; Subject: Application of Treaties and Laws to al Qaeda and Taliban Detainees (22 Jan. 2002). "Further, common Article 3 addresses only non-international conflicts that occur within the territory of a single state party, again, like a civil war. This provision would not reach an armed conflict in which one of the parties operated from multiple bases in several different states." Reprinted in Greenberg and Dratel, *Torture Papers*, supra, note 143, at 81.

[148] Jordan J. Paust, *Beyond the Law* (New York: Cambridge University Press, 2007), 10, citing John Yoo, Robert J. Delahunty, Memorandum for William J. Haynes II, General Counsel, Department of Defense, Application of Treaties and Laws to al Qaeda and Taliban Detainees (Jan. 9, 2002). Also see Yoo Memorandum, supra, note 133: "The President has the legal and constitutional authority to subject both al Qaeda and Taliban to the laws of war, and to try their members before military courts or commissions. … This is so because the extension of the common laws of war to the present conflicts is, in essence, a *military* measure that the President can order as Commander-in-Chief." Emphasis in original.

[149] *Hamdan v. Rumsfeld*, 548 U. S. 557 (2006).

[150] Executive Order 13440, "Interpretation of the Geneva Conventions, Common Article 3 as Applied to a Program of Detention and Interrogation Operated by the Central Intelligence Agency (July 2007). " … On February 7, 2002, I determined for the United States that members of al Qaeda, the Taliban, and associated forces are unlawful enemy combatants who are not entitled to the protections that the Third Geneva Convention provides to prisoners of war. I hereby reaffirm that determination. … " Cited at 101–4 *AJIL* (Oct. 2007), 866.

Qaeda because human rights law is not applicable in time of war and, in any event, is inapplicable extraterritorially – that is, outside U.S. borders.[151] That view, too, changed.

If not covered by the Geneva Conventions and beyond the protections of common Article 3 and human rights law, what was the individual status of captured Taliban and al Qaeda members in the view of the United States, and what treatment were they to be accorded? The murky answer was provided three months after 9/11 by Secretary of Defense Donald Rumsfeld: "The Combatant Commanders shall, in detaining al Qaeda and Taliban individuals under the control of the Department of Defense, treat them humanely and, to the extent appropriate and consistent with military necessity, in a manner consistent with the principles of the Geneva Conventions of 1949."[152] No individual status was specified. A former senior Assistant U.S. Attorney General writes, "This formulation sounded good. But it was very vague, it was not effectively operationalized into concrete standards of conduct, and it left all of the hard issues about 'humane' and 'appropriate' treatment to the discretion of unknown officials."[153] Nor was it consistent with LOAC/IHL.

6.5.2 The Status of al Qaeda Fighters

What of al Qaeda fighters in Iraq and elsewhere? What was their individual status? Was it different than that of the Taliban? No, it was not. The amended 2006 Military Commissions Act summarily states that al Qaeda members were unlawful enemy combatants.[154] A closer examination of that questionably ascribed status is called for.

Can there be an armed force without a state? "All too easily, if the history of the horse peoples of the Central Asian steppe is taken into account....In the thirteenth century...a thitherto unknown horse people, Genghis Khan's Mongols, emerged from the great Central Asian sea of grass to fall on settled civilisation in the greatest campaign of conquest ever known."[155] Terrorist armed opposition groups like al Qaeda and the Taliban are modern-day armed opposition groups without a state.

Al Qaeda do not observe LOAC/IHL. Are they protected by it? If nonstate actors do not observe LOAC, may their enemies disregard LOAC in their armed conflicts against them, as well? Of course not. "[T]here is no textual or historical evidence suggesting that the Conventions embrace this understanding of reciprocity."[156] As common Article 2 of the 1949 Geneva Conventions reads, "Although one of the Powers in conflict may not be a party to the present Convention, the Powers who are parties thereto shall remain bound by it in their mutual relations." The Geneva Conventions are not a matter of, "we will if

---

[151] Milanovic, "Lessons for Human Rights," supra, note 128, at 386–7. The author, Law Clerk to ICJ Judge Thomas Berganthal, cites as authority: opening remarks by John Bellinger, Legal Advisor, U.S. Department of State, before the U.N. Committee against Torture, May 5, 2006, http://www.us-mission .ch/Press2006/0505BellingerOpenCAT.html; and, opening Statement of Mathew Waxman, Head, U.S. Delegation before U.N. Human Rights Committee, July 17, 2006, http://geneva.usmission.gov/ 0717Waxman.html. Those two sources provide very weak confirmation, however.

[152] Memorandum for Chairman of the Joint Chiefs of Staff; from the Secretary of Defense; Subject: Status of Taliban and Al Qaeda (Jan. 19, 2002). Reprinted in Greenberg and Dratel, Torture Papers, supra, note 143, at 80.

[153] Jack Goldsmith, The Terror Presidency (New York: Norton, 2007), 121.   [154] 10 U.S.C. §§ 948a(1)(i).

[155] John Keegan, War and Our World (New York: Vintage, 1998), 36–7.

[156] Derek Jinks, "The Applicability of the Geneva Conventions to the 'Global War on Terrorism,'" 46–1 Virginia J. of Int'l L. (2006), 1, 15.

you will." Having been ratified by a state, they constitute an obligation that the state owes its own citizens, as well as all victims of war.

In 2001, shortly after the invasion of Afghanistan, the U.S. Under Secretary of Defense for Policy noted:

> [A] major issue was the legal status of these prisoners...Early interagency discussions among lawyers clarified that the 1949 Geneva Conventions...applied to conflicts between "High Contracting Parties"...and al Qaeda was *not* such a party. I heard no one argue that the Conventions, as a matter of law, applied to...al Qaeda, or that they governed U.S. detention of the al Qaeda prisoners taken in Afghanistan or anywhere else....[S]ome lawyers at the Justice Department, White House, and Pentagon believed that the United States should not apply the Conventions to its conflict with the Taliban.[157]

In the tumultuous days following 9/11, senior U.S. government lawyers were apparently blithely unaware of common Article 3's application, or Geneva Convention IV's provisions for protected persons. Or chose to ignore them. The Under Secretary continues, "The Pentagon's leadership appreciated the importance of honoring the Geneva Conventions, but issues arose time and again that required the very difficult balancing of weighty but competing interests...."[158] *In LOAC and IHL there are no "competing interests" that render the Geneva Conventions inapplicable.* Yet, in a 2002 memorandum, the President wrote, "Pursuant to my authority as Commander-in-Chief and Chief Executive of the United States...I hereby determine...none of the provisions of Geneva apply to our conflict with al Qaeda in Afghanistan or elsewhere throughout the world...."[159]

Lieutenant General Ricardo Sanchez, a former commander of all coalition troops in Iraq, writes, "This presidential memorandum constituted a watershed event in U.S. military history. Essentially, it set aside all of the legal constraints, training guidelines, and rules for interrogation that formed the U.S. Army's foundation for the treatment of prisoners on the battlefield..."[160]

What was the individual status of al Qaeda fighters? Again, answer the usual first question: Characterization of the U.S.–al Qaeda conflict as a "Global War on Terrorism" does not mean that an actual war is in progress.[161]

"Much of the debate on this issue has been clouded by the decision to categorize the campaign against transnational terrorism as a 'war' with consequent confusion over the appropriate legal regime to apply."[162] The Legal Advisor to the U.S. Secretary of State concluded that the war on terrorism is not a war.[163] "While the notion of 'war'

---

[157] Douglas J. Feith, *War and Decision* (New York: Harper, 2008), 160–1.   [158] Id., at 165.

[159] Reprinted in Greenberg and Dratel, *Torture Papers*, supra, note 143, at 134.

[160] Lt.Gen. Ricardo S. Sanchez, *Wiser in Battle* (New York: Harpers, 2008), 144.

[161] "[A]n armed conflict exists whenever there is a resort to armed force between States or protracted armed violence between governmental authorities and organized armed groups or between such groups within a State." *Prosecutor v Tadić*, IT-94-1-A, Decision on Defence Motion for Interlocutory Appeal on Jurisdiction (Oct. 2, 1995), para. 70.

[162] Garraway, "'Combatants' – Substance or Semantics?" supra, note 8, at 334.

[163] "The phrase 'the global war on terror' to which some have objected – is not intended to be a legal statement. The United States does not believe that it is engaged in a legal state of armed conflict at all times with every terrorist group in the world ... When we state that there is a 'global war on terror,' we primarily mean that the scourge of terrorism is a global problem that the international community must recognize and work together to eliminate." Bellinger, "Armed Conflict with Al Qaeda?" supra, note 132.

against terrorism is a political slogan – comparable to the 'war' against poverty or the 'war' against AIDS – the attack on a third country transforms such a [anti-terrorist] campaign into an armed conflict...,"[164] but not an armed conflict between two states, required to engage the full coverage of the Geneva Conventions, Additional Protocol I, and customary international law.

It was not a war but it was an armed conflict. To suggest that the war on terrorism was not a war is no slight to the armed forces that have fought and died in Iraq, Afghanistan, and other battlefields. It is a conclusion driven by LOAC. To be a "war" in the sense of Geneva Convention common Article 2, it must be an armed conflict between two states. There is no second option.[165] "Terrorist movements themselves generally have a non-state character. Therefore military operations between a State and such a movement, even if they involve the State's armed forces acting outside its own territory, are not necessarily such as to bring them within the scope of application of the full range of provisions regarding international armed conflict..."[166] Even considering all the worldwide acts of terrorism, they remain separate criminal acts, not parts of one and the same conflict.[167]

The component parts of the "war on terrorism," however, can be examined and LOAC applied to them. In the armed conflict in Iraq, the initial U.S. invasion ended quickly. In that brief common Article 2 phase in which U.S. forces opposed Iraqi Army units, al Qaeda members were not an army of a party to the conflict. Any al Qaeda members who directly participated in the hostilities were, in addition to members of a criminal grouping, unlawful combatants.

U.S. combat operations in Iraq commenced on March 20, 2003.[168] President Bush's May 1, 2003 "mission accomplished" speech aboard a U.S. aircraft carrier is a logical termination date for the common Article 2 conflict.[169] U.S. occupation of Iraq commenced at the same time. The occupation ended and Iraqi sovereignty was reassumed by an appointed Iraqi government on June 28, 2004, fifteen months after the invasion.[170]

---

[164] Hans-Peter Gasser, "Acts of Terror, 'Terrorism' and International Humanitarian Law," 847 *Int'l Rev. of the Red Cross* (Sept. 2002), 547, 549–50.

[165] A March 16, 2004 ICRC Statement, http://www.icrc.org/Web/eng/siteengo.nsf/html/5XCMNJ, says, "The phrase 'war on terror' is a rhetorical device having no legal significance. There is no more logic to automatic application of the laws of armed conflict to the 'war on terror' than there is to the 'war on drugs', 'war on poverty' or 'war on cancer'." Professor George H. Aldrich scolds, "[I have] limited tolerance for any purported legal concept of a war against terrorism or of a 'global war against terror'. ... One can speak of a war only emotively, as when one speaks of a war against crime or a war against drugs." 100–2 *AJIL* (April 2006), 496; finally, the ICRC's Jelena Pejic writes in, "Terrorist Acts and Groups: A Role for International Law," 75 *BYIL* (2004), 71, 88, "Terrorist acts ... are as a matter of law properly characterized as criminal acts that should ... be dealt with by the application of domestic and international human rights law, as well as international criminal law." For discussion of the status of the conflict in Iraq, see: Jinks, "Applicability of the Geneva Conventions," supra, note 156.

[166] Adam Roberts, "The Laws of War in the War on Terror," in Wybo P. Heere, ed., *Terrorism and the Military: International Legal Implications* (The Hague: Asser Press, 2003), 65, 69.

[167] ICRC, "International Humanitarian Law and the Challenges of Contemporary Armed Conflicts," 867 *Int'l Rev. of the Red Cross* (Sept. 2007), 719, 725.

[168] Thomas E. Ricks, *Fiasco* (New York: Penguin Press, 2006), 116.

[169] Id., at 135: "[I]n the view of [Commanding General Tommy] Franks and other military commanders, the assigned job had been completed ... When President Bush landed on that carrier with the 'Mission Accomplished' banner, it was right: The mission, as defined for the military as getting rid of the regime, had indeed been accomplished.'"

[170] Kenneth Katzman, *Iraq: Reconciliation and Benchmarks* (Washington, DC: Congressional Research Service, 12 May 2008), 1. "After about one year of occupation, the United States handed sovereignty to

During the occupation, the Geneva Conventions applied in their entirety, as did 1977 Additional Protocol I, for states that ratified that treaty.

If the U.S.–Iraq conflict no longer constituted a common Article 2 armed conflict, what must it have been? As the time, al Qaeda did not control sufficient territory from which to launch sustained and concerted military operations, so the threshold for application of Additional Protocol II was not met.[171] As to the United States, it could not be an internal armed conflict because the conflict was not geographically sited on U.S. territory. As in Afghanistan, the conflict in Iraq was an insurgency, a common Article 3 non-international armed conflict pitting al Qaeda against the Iraqi government, assisted by armed forces of the United States and other coalition states.[172]

"No group conducting attacks in such an egregious fashion [as the 9/11 attacks] can claim for its fighters prisoners of war status. Whatever lingering doubt which may exist with respect to the entitlement of Taliban forces to prisoners of war status, there is – and there can be – none as regards Al Qaeda terrorists."[173]

Although agreement is not universal,[174] in a common Article 2 international armed conflict, al Qaeda fighters who directly participated in hostilities were unlawful belligerents with a continuous combat function who could be targeted as combatants. If captured, they were criminals, not entitled to POW status. They were protected persons entitled to common Article 3 protections. They could be interned and could be tried in domestic or military courts for acts they committed that rendered them unlawful combatants. In a common Article 3 non-international armed conflict, they were criminals who, upon capture, enjoyed common Article 3 and Additional Protocol I, Article 75 protections. They could be tried in domestic or military courts for unlawful acts they committed before capture.

As in the case of captured Taliban, in a common Article 2 conflict, should captured al Qaeda fighters be nationals of the capturing state – Iraqi citizens captured by Iraqi armed forces, for instance – they were not Geneva Convention IV, Article 4 protected persons. They remained protected, however, by Additional Protocol I, Article 75.

6.6 World War II Allied Resistance Fighters: Historical Aside or Modern Preview?

Guerrilla warfare came into its own in World War II, when countries occupied by the Axis Powers were able to continue the fight only through guerrillas and resistance

---

an appointed Iraqi government on June 28, 2004. A government and a constitution were voted on thereafter, in line with a March 8, 2004, 'Transitional Administrative Law'. ... " The U.N. cites 30 June as the end of the period of occupation. UN SC Res. 1546 (2004).

[171] 1977 Additional Protocol II, Art. 1.1.

[172] Geoffrey S. Corn, "'Snipers in the Minaret – What Is the Rule?' The Law of War and the Protection of Cultural Property: A Complex Equation," *The Army Lawyer* (July 2005), 28, 29; and Sanchez, *Wiser in Battle*, supra, note 160, at 231. "By mid-July ... we were facing an insurgency. There was just no other way to describe it ... "

[173] Dinstein, *The Conduct of Hostilities*, supra, note 2, at 49.

[174] E.g., Jordan J. Paust, "Detention and Due Process Under International Law," in Heere, *Terrorism and the Military*, supra, note 166, 180–96, at 188. Professor Paust argues that al Qaeda fighters with the Afghan Taliban during the common Article 2 phase of the U.S.-Afghan conflict, were lawful combatants. Also Franck, "The Taliban, al Qaeda, and the Determination of Illegal Combatants," supra, note 139, at 897; and John Yoo, "Enemy Combatants and the Problem of Judicial Competence," in Peter Berkowitz, ed., *Terrorism, the Laws of War, and the Constitution* (Stanford, CA: Hoover Institution Press, 2005), 69, 74.

fighters, who might be called "insurgents" today. "The Soviet Union...regarded its guerrilla forces as an integral part of its armed forces....The Germans and Japanese took a contrary view and denied that international law protected guerrillas. Their common practice was to summarily shoot captured guerrillas."[175] Field Marshal Wilhelm Keitel "repeated Hitler's belief that the [1929] Geneva Conventions and 'soldierly chivalry' did not apply in the war against the partisans and sent the following instructions: No disciplinary action can be taken against a German engaged in anti-band [guerrilla] warfare, nor can he be called to account before a court-martial for his conduct in fighting the bands and their helpers."[176] For this and similar orders, the Nuremberg International Military Tribunal sentenced Keitel to hang.[177]

Although no Allied nation other than the Soviet Union regarded non-uniformed resistance fighters as units of their regular forces, after the war the United States and its Allies aggressively tried former enemies who had disregarded the battlefield rights of partisans. Allied concern for the just treatment of friendly guerrillas was not always as keenly applied by them to enemy soldiers who were captured out of uniform and without distinctive sign. In 1942, eight Nazi saboteurs were captured in New York and Chicago.[178] Nine days later, they were tried in secret before a military commission, despite the civilian courts being open. The 3,000-page record of trial was considered and approved by President Roosevelt, and the saboteurs' death sentences carried out within five days of the verdicts. The Supreme Court's opinion affirming the trial results was written months after the executions.[179] Discussion of the case continues to this day, one reason being that we still send soldiers behind enemy lines disguised as civilians – just as the 1942 Nazi saboteurs were disguised. The mixed record of World War II resistance fighters raises a modern LOAC/IHL issue: What is a fighter's status if captured without uniform or other distinguishing sign?

6.6.1 Out of Uniform, Out of Status?

Article 4A.(2) of Geneva Convention III, relative to POWs, specifies that, to gain POW status, members of organized resistance movements must meet the familiar four conditions – a responsible individual in charge, a fixed distinctive sign, carry arms openly, and observe the law of war. The same four conditions apply to members of the army of a party to the conflict, although that is not explicitly stated in the Convention. "The delegates to the 1949 Diplomatic Conference," the *Commentary* reports, "were...justified in considering that there was no need to specify for such armed forces the requirements stated

---

[175] Greenspan, *Modern Law of Land Warfare*, supra, note 21, at 54.
[176] I. P. Trainin, "Questions of Guerrilla Warfare in the Law of War, 40–3 AJIL (July 1946), 534–62, 561–2.
[177] *Trial of the Major War Criminals* (Nuremberg: International Military Tribunal, 1947), 366. The Nuremberg IMT's judgment notes, "On 7 December 1941 ... the so-called "*Nacht und Nebel*" Decree, over Keitel's signature, provided that in occupied territories civilians who had been accused of crimes of resistance against the army of occupation would be tried only if a death sentence was likely; otherwise they would be handed to the Gestapo for transportation to Germany. ... Keitel does not deny his connection with these acts. Rather, his defense relies on the fact that he is a soldier, and on the doctrine of 'superior orders', prohibited by Article 8 of the Charter as a defense. There is nothing in mitigation. Superior orders, even to a soldier, cannot be considered in mitigation where crimes as shocking and extensive have been committed consciously, ruthlessly, and without military excuse or justification.", at 290–1.
[178] *Ex parte Quirin*, 317 U.S. 1 (1942).
[179] David J. Danelski, "The Saboteur's Case," 1 *J. of S.Ct. History* (1996), 61.

in [Article 4A.(2)]. . ."[180] That suggests that, should a member of the armed forces of a party to a conflict engage in combat without a uniform, or other distinctive sign, it would potentially be an act of perfidy. (See Chapter 11, section 11.1.) Even absent perfidy, upon capture such a prisoner, although a member of the army of a party, would not have complied with the "fixed distinctive sign" requirement and he would not be entitled to POW status.

As to uniforms, the removal of one's uniform or other fixed distinctive sign in favor of civilian garb is not a war crime, but, in an international armed conflict, if an otherwise lawful combatant engages in combat without a uniform or fixed distinctive sign he becomes an unlawful combatant/unprivileged belligerent and, if captured, is not entitled to POW status.

As to precapture LOAC violations, the 1914 edition of U.S. *Rules of Land Warfare* says, "A prisoner of war remains answerable for his crimes committed against the captor's army or people, committed before he was captured, and for which he has not been punished by his own army."[181] Loss of POW status is not mentioned for unlawful precapture acts, such as fighting without uniform or distinctive sign. As a matter of fact, Geneva Convention III, Article 85, reads, "Prisoners of war prosecuted under the laws of the Detaining Power for acts committed prior to capture shall retain, even if convicted, the benefits of the present [prisoner of war] Convention." The *Commentary* confirms that, "the Conference agreed – that prisoners of war should continue to enjoy those benefits [of POW status] even after they had been judged."[182] How does one reconcile the Convention III provisions that, even if convicted of precapture LOAC violations an individual retains POW status (Article 85), with the provision that if a prisoner fought without uniform or other fixed sign he is denied POW status (Article 4A.2)?

Press coverage of the early stages of the conflicts in Afghanistan and Iraq detailed instances in which American combatants, Army Delta and Special Forces soldiers, wore civilian clothing in the combat zone – jeans, tee shirt, and baseball cap; in Afghanistan, they occasionally wore the flowing *abah* of local males. They were U.S. "soldiers, special operators from the units that had been at the forefront of the war in Afghanistan. . .dressed in civilian clothes and [they also] wore their hair longer than most American soldiers are allowed. All sported the beards that were ubiquitous among American special operators and intelligence operatives in Afghanistan."[183] If one of those American soldiers were captured (and if the capturing force observed LOAC), would he be entitled to POW status because he was a member "of the armed forces of a Party to the conflict," even though he had committed an unlawful precapture act, per Article 85? Or, because of his lack of uniform or distinguishing sign while engaged in combat, would he be denied such status, per Article 4A.(2)?

The issue is LOAC core concept of distinction: the ability to see and distinguish a warfighter from a noncombatant. (See Chapter 7, section 7.1.) Customary law of war did not forbid the wearing of nondistinguishing clothing, or even wearing of the enemy's

---

[180] Pictet, *Commentary, III Geneva Convention*, supra, note 40, at 63.

[181] War Department, *Rules of Land Warfare – 1914*, supra, note 17, para. 71.

[182] Pictet, *Commentary, III Geneva Convention*, supra, note 40, at 415.

[183] Sean Taylor, *Not a Good Day to Die* (New York: Berkley Books, 2005), 9.

[Handwritten marginal note: I don't understand. this is contradictory.]

uniform, but it did prohibit *engaging in combat* while doing so.[184] "[M]embers of the military who merely wear civilian clothes do not violate the law of armed conflict. Rather, they lose combatant status because they lack the prerequisites thereof. . ."[185] However, if a soldier *fights* in nondistinguishing clothing, or in the enemy's uniform, and kills, wounds, or captures an enemy in that circumstance, that constitutes perfidy, a LOAC violation.[186]

The wearing of enemy uniforms was central to the World War II case of SS *Obersturmbannführer* (Lieutenant Colonel) Otto Skorzeny. During the December 1944 "Battle of the Bulge," Skorzeny led an understrength Nazi brigade in operations behind U.S. lines. In planning the operation, "Skorzeny had been worried that any of his men captured while wearing U.S. uniforms might be treated as spies, but [he was advised] that the practice was within the rules as long as the men did not actually participate in combat."[187] When his mission failed and some of his men were captured, eighteen of them who were found in U.S. uniforms were indeed executed as spies. Skorzeny escaped, but was arrested and brought to trial after the war, in 1947, along with nine co-accused. In its opinion, Skorzeny's Military Court held, "When contemplating whether the wearing of enemy uniforms is or is not a legal ruse of war, one must distinguish between the use of enemy uniforms in actual fighting and such use during operations other than actual fighting." All ten accused were acquitted. The opinion does not explain the basis of acquittal. "Popular speculation," Colonel Hays Parks writes, "has been that the court accepted Skorzeny's claim that his men did not fight in US uniforms."[188] Indeed, his instruction to his men was that they not do so.

Today, however, the *Skorzeny* case is only of historical interest. In 1977, Additional Protocol I altered customary law and superseded the *Skorzeny* holding. Under the Protocol, wearing an enemy uniform is prohibited in essentially any circumstance.[189] Today, if a soldier is captured in civilian clothing, as opposed to an enemy uniform, with no showing that he engaged in combat while wearing civilian clothing (an unlikely but possible scenario), it would not be a LOAC violation. Without additional facts, a charge of spying also would not be warranted.[190] If captured in an enemy uniform with no

---

[184] FM 27–10, *Law of Land Warfare*, supra, note 15, at para. 54: "In practice, it has been authorized to make use of national flags, insignia, and uniforms as a ruse. . . . It is certainly forbidden to employ them during combat, but their use at other times is not forbidden."

[185] Michael N. Schmitt, "War, Technology and the Law of Armed Conflict," in International Law Studies. Vol. 82. *The Law of War in the 21st Century: Weaponry and the Use of Force* (Newport, RI: Naval War College, 2006), 151.

[186] *Trial of Otto Skorzeny and Others*, General Military Government Court of the U.S. Zone of Germany (18 Aug. 1947), IX *LRTWC* 90, 92 (London: UNWCC, 1949).

[187] Donald M. Goldstein, Katherine V. Dillon, and J. Michael Wenger, *Nuts!: The Battle of the Bulge* (Washington, DC: Brassey's, 1994), 85.

[188] W. Hays Parks, "'Special Forces' Wear of Non-Standard Uniforms," 4–2 *Chicago J. of Int'l. L.* (Fall, 2003), 493, 545 fn. 133. In agreement, Rogers, *Law on the Battlefield*, supra, note 6, at 41.

[189] 1977 Additional Protocol I, Arts. 39.1 and 39.2: "1. It is prohibited to make use in an armed conflict of the . . . uniforms of neutral or other States not Parties to the conflict," and, "2. It is prohibited to make use of . . . uniforms of adverse Parties while engaging in attacks or in order to shield, favor, protect or impede military operations." On today's battlefield it is difficult to conceive of any situation in which wearing the enemy's uniform would not be a LOAC violation.

[190] Rogers, *Law on the Battlefield*, supra, note 6, at 43, discussing the inappropriateness of spying charges against soldiers.

showing that he engaged in combat while so dressed, it would be a violation of Additional Protocol I, and a minor LOAC violation, but if the soldier is captured while directly participating in hostilities while wearing an enemy uniform, the wearer has committed perfidy and forfeits POW status.[191]

U.S. Army Field Manual 27–10, *The Law of Land Warfare*, (1956) clarified the issue of uniforms and POW status:

> Members of the armed forces of a party to the conflict. . .lose their right to be treated as prisoners of war whenever they deliberately conceal their status in order to pass behind the military lines of the enemy for the purpose of gathering military information or for the purpose of waging war by destruction of life or property. Putting on civilian clothes or the uniform of the enemy are examples of concealment of the status of a member of the armed forces.[192]

The ICRC, in its customary law study, repeats the Field Manual's position: "Rule 106: Combatants must distinguish themselves from the civilian population while they are engaged in an attack or in a military operation preparatory to an attack. If they fail to do so, they do not have the right to prisoner-of-war status."[193] The position of the United Kingdom is similar.[194]

". . .[R]egular forces are not absolved from meeting the cumulative conditions binding irregular forces.. . .[A] regular soldier committing an act of sabotage when not in uniform loses his entitlement to a prisoner of war status."[195] This does not conflict with Convention III, Article 85 ("Prisoners of war prosecuted. . .for acts committed prior to capture shall retain. . .benefits of the Convention.") because the captured soldier, due to his lack of uniform or distinguishing sign, never achieved a POW status to retain.

Colonel Hays Parks encapsulates arguments for wearing or not wearing a uniform or distinguishing sign in combat:

> The standard military field uniform should be worn absent compelling military necessity for wear of a non-standard uniform or civilian clothing. *Military convenience* should not be mistaken for *military necessity*. That military personnel may be at greater risk in wearing a uniform is not in and of itself sufficient basis to justify wearing civilian clothing. "Force protection" is not a legitimate basis for wearing a non-standard uniform or civilian attire. Risk is an inherent part of military missions, and does not constitute military necessity for wear of civilian attire.[196]

[handwritten annotation: Colonel Hays Parks doesn't see how this is ever justified]

[191] Parks, "Special Forces' Wear of Non-Standard Uniforms," supra, note 188, at 545–6: "[S]tate practice in international armed conflicts has tended *not* to treat wear of civilian attire, non-standard uniforms, and/or enemy uniforms by regular military forces as a war crime." Emphasis supplied.

[192] FM 27–10, *Law of Land Warfare*, supra, note 15, at para. 74.

[193] Henckaerts and Doswald-Beck, *Customary International Humanitarian Law*, supra, note 46, Rule 106, at 384.

[194] UK MOD, *Manual of the Law of Armed Conflict*, supra, note 22, at 43–4, para. 46. Interestingly, the British Manual also says, "Members of the armed forces who do not wear uniform, combat gear, or an adequate distinctive sign and whose sole arm is a concealed weapon, or who hide their arms on the approach of the enemy, will be considered to have lost their combatant status." Para. 4.4.3., at 42. Accordingly, they lose POW entitlement, if captured.

[195] Dinstein, *The Conduct of Hostilities*, supra, note 2, at 37. Citations omitted. Dinstein looks to two U.K. Privy Council cases, *Mohamed Ali et al. v. Public Prosecutor* (1968), [1969] AC 430, 449, and *Public Prosecutor v. Koi et al.* (1967), [1968] AC 829, in support.

[196] Parks, "Special Forces' Wear of Non-Standard Uniforms," supra, note 188, at 543. Emphasis in original.

The law of war as to captured spies, as opposed to captured lawful combatants, is the same.[197] Spies, including spies who may be members of the armed forces of a party to the conflict, who are captured in civilian clothing behind enemy lines may be denied POW status, and are subject to trial for espionage under the domestic law of the capturing state.

Regardless of the prohibition against engaging in combat in nondistinguishing clothing or in enemy uniform, armies have always sent combatants behind enemy lines disguised as civilians. In World War I, British Lieutenant Colonel Thomas E. Lawrence fought in white Arab robes and became famous as Lawrence of Arabia.[198] In World War II, Office of Strategic Services (OSS) teams in Europe almost always wore civilian clothing. In China, U.S. officers working with Chinese guerrilla forces wore Chinese uniforms, enemy uniforms, and civilian attire.[199] Throughout history such examples are many. LOAC will not alter that practice. Commanders will continue to order subordinate combatants behind enemy lines to fight without uniform or distinctive sign and, knowing the risk, subordinate combatants will willingly comply. The United States makes no secret of having issued such orders in Afghanistan.[200]

> [E]ach belligerent party is at liberty to factor in a cost/benefit calculus...If members of Special Forces units are fighting behind enemy lines, and if the enemy has a demonstrably poor track record in...the protection of *hors de combat* enemy military personnel, the conclusion may be arrived at that on the whole it is well worth assuming the risks of (potential) loss of prisoner of war status upon capture while benefiting from the (actual) advantages of disguise.[201]

Petty Officer Marcus Luttrell, a SEAL operator in Afghanistan, confirms that Navy combatants dressed as civilians: "Each one of us had grown a beard in order to look more like Afghan fighters. It was important for us to appear nonmilitary, to not stand out in a crowd."[202] Although contrary to LOAC, the practice of fighting without distinguishing oneself is not going to end, but there is a potentially high price for doing so.

6.7 Detainee, Enemy Combatant, and Unlawful Enemy Combatant

The war on terrorism brought new variations to individual status. The terms "detainee," "enemy combatant," and "unlawful enemy combatant" do not appear in 1907 Hague Regulation IV, in any Geneva Convention, or in the 1977 Additional Protocols. There is no internationally agreed upon definition of any of the three terms, yet they are commonly used in the war on terrorism. Each suggests a variation on unlawful combatant status and, upon capture, each may determine the treatment of an individual so labeled.

---

[197] 1907 Annex to Hague Convention IV Respecting the Laws and Customs of War on Land, Art. 29. "A person can only be considered a spy when, acting clandestinely or on false pretenses, he obtains or endeavors to obtain information in the zone of operations of a belligerent, with the intention of communicating it to the hostile party. Thus soldiers not wearing a disguise who have penetrated into the zone of operations of the hostile army for the purpose of obtaining information are not considered spies."

[198] Lowell Thomas, *With Lawrence in Arabia* (London: Hutchison, 1927).

[199] Parks, "Special Forces' Wear of Non-Standard Uniforms," supra, note 188, at 504, fn. 20.

[200] Id., at 498.

[201] Yoram Dinstein, "*Jus in Bello* Issues Arising in the Hostilities in Iraq in 2003," in Jaques, *International Law Studies*, supra, note 130, at 45.

[202] Luttrell, *Lone Survivor*, supra, note 118, at 15.

6.7.1 Detainee

In the U.S.–Vietnam conflict, "detainee" referred to a recently captured individual on his way to a POW camp or holding facility, where his actual status would be determined. In 1993 U.S. operations in Somalia, and in Haiti in February 2004, captured persons were referred to as "detainees," and during Operation Just Cause in Panama, in December 1989-January 1990, members of the Panamanian armed forces were also referred to as "detainees" although they were reportedly treated as prisoners of war.

In the war on terrorism, and in U.S. usage, "detainees" are described in joint forces doctrine applicable to all U.S. Armed Forces as "any person captured or otherwise detained by an armed force."[203] Any individual captured on the battlefield, the circumstances of whose capture do not immediately indicate a status, is a detainee. Additionally, any civilian suspected of being an insurgent, or aiding the insurgency, who is seized by U.S. forces is a detainee.

Confusingly, a 2006 DoD Directive, also applicable to U.S. Armed Forces personnel for much of the conflicts in Iraq and Afghanistan, provided a different, lengthy, and confusing definition of "detainee".[204] Demonstrating that the Armed Forces can learn from past mistakes, the definition in a later version of the Directive was simplified: "Detainee. Any individual captured by, or transferred to the custody or control of, DoD personnel pursuant to the law of war. This does not include persons being held solely for law enforcement purposes, except where the United States is the occupying power. Detainees who are U.S. citizens or U.S. resident aliens will continue to enjoy all applicable rights and privileges under U.S. law and DoD regulations."[205]

6.7.2 "Enemy Combatant"

In U.S. practice there also were several definitions of "enemy combatant," none agreed to be controlling, and some apparently generated only for detention and targeting purposes.

The phrase "enemy combatant" first appeared in the muddled World War II Nazi saboteur case, Ex parte Quirin.[206] (See chapter 21.4.) U.S. Supreme Court Chief Justice Stone wrote, "[A spy or] an enemy combatant who without uniform comes secretly through the lines for the purpose of waging war by destruction of life or property, are familiar examples of belligerents who are generally deemed not to be entitled to the status of prisoners of war, but to be offenders against the law of war subject to trial and punishment by military tribunals."[207] Contrary to the court's implication, spying is not, and was not in 1942, a LOAC violation. It was, and is, is a domestic law violation.

The ICRC, employing the traditional definition, says "an 'enemy combatant' is a person who, either lawfully or unlawfully, engages in hostilities for the opposing side in an international armed conflict."[208]

---

[203] Joint Publication 3–36, *Detainee Operations*, (February 6, 2008), at GL-3.
[204] DoD Directive 2310.01E, "The Department of Defense Detainee Program," Sept. 5, 2006, at Enclosure 2, Definitions.
[205] DoD Directive 2310.01E, "The Department of Defense Detainee Program," Aug. 19, 2014, at Enclosure 2, Part II, Definitions.
[206] *Ex parte Quirin*, supra, note 178.   [207] Id. at 31.
[208] ICRC, "Official Statement: The Relevance of IHL in the Context of Terrorism," available on-line.

"Traditionally, the term 'enemy combatant' refers to legitimate combatants who are entitled to prisoner of war status. It is a new usage to describe those who are deemed to be unlawful belligerents as such. What term is left for those legitimate combatants belonging to enemy armed forces?"[209] Because "a combatant, by definition, enjoys a 'privilege of belligerency', the term 'lawful combatant', is redundant, and thus, the term 'unlawful combatant' is an oxymoron."[210] The United States did not join in that view.

A definition of "enemy combatant" was found in the same 2006 DoD Directive that unsatisfactorily defined "detainee": "*Enemy combatant.* In general, a person engaged in hostilities against the United States or its coalition partners during an armed conflict. The term 'enemy combatant' included both 'lawful enemy combatants' and 'unlawful enemy combatants.'"[211] The term does not appear in the 2014 version of the DoD Directive.

In a 2004 case, *Hamdi v. Rumsfeld*,[212] the government offered yet another definition of "enemy combatant."[213]

Guantanamo's Combatant Status Review Tribunals employed yet another.[214]

Definitional confusion abated somewhat when, in March 2009, in multiple pending habeas corpus cases, the U.S. indicated it would no longer characterize detained al Qaeda or Taliban members or supporters as "enemy combatants." This was followed by an October 2011 revision of the 2009 Military Commissions Act directing that "[t]he revised MCA applies to 'alien unprivileged belligerents,' in lieu of "alien unlawful combatants" covered by the previous statute."[215] Finally (for those who had not already lost interest in the definitional confusion), enemy fighters would no longer have reference to the word "combatant" in their description, with that word's implication of a combatant's privilege.

And most observers and commentators continued to call them "enemy combatants," as they had from the beginning.

6.7.3 *Unlawful Enemy Combatant*

In common Article 2 armed conflicts it is redundant to refer to an unlawful combatant as an "unlawful *enemy* combatant," yet the term was pervasively applied to captured Taliban and al Qaeda fighters.

The 2006 DoD Directive defined unlawful enemy combatants as "...persons not entitled to combatant immunity, who engage in acts against the United States or its coalition partners in violation of the laws and customs of war during an armed conflict. For purposes of the war on terrorism, the term Unlawful Enemy Combatant is defined to include, but is

---

[209] Garraway, "'Combatants' – Substance or Semantics?" supra, note 8, at 327.

[210] Gabor Rona, "An Appraisal of US Practice Relating to 'Enemy Combatants,'" in Timothy L. H. McCormack, ed., *Yearbook of I.H.L.* Vol. 10. 2007. (The Hague: Asser Press, 2009), 232, 240.

[211] Directive 2310.01E, "Department of Defense Detainee Program," supra, note 195. Underlining in original.

[212] 542 U.S. 507 (2004).

[213] Ryan Goodman, "Editorial Comment: The Detention of Civilians in Armed Conflict," 103–1 *AJIL* (Jan. 2009), 48, 61. Emphasis in original.

[214] "An individual who was part of or supporting the Taliban or al Qaeda forces, or associated forces that are engaged in hostilities against the United States or its coalition partners. This includes any person who committed a belligerent act or has directly supported hostilities in aid of enemy armed forces."

[215] Nat'l Defense Auth. Act of 2010: Pub. L. No. 111–84, 123 Stat. 2190 (2009), § 948a (7).

not limited to, an individual who is or was part of or supporting Taliban or al Qaeda forces or associated forces that are engaged in hostilities against the United States or its coalition partners."[216] The term does not appear in the 2014 version of the Dod Instruction.

In August 2007, fourteen "high-value detainees" previously held in foreign locations in secret CIA prisons were transferred to the U.S. detention facility at Guantánamo Bay, Cuba. One of the transferees was Khalid Sheik Mohammed, the alleged 9/11 master planner. He and the other thirteen were designated "enemy combatants."[217] Why were they not *unlawful* enemy combatants? Or unprivileged belligerents? Or detainees? The designation of the fourteen illustrates the ad hoc subjective nature of labeling captured terrorists.

And most observers and commentators continued to call them "enemy combatants," as they had from the beginning.

Canadian Brigadier Kenneth Watkin suggests, "it may be time for humanitarian law advocates to concentrate more on detailed common standards of treatment for all detainees, rather than focusing on the status of participants."[218]

6.8 Article 5 "Competent Tribunals"

"Competent tribunals" have been mentioned. What is a competent tribunal, what is its purpose, how is one constituted, and when is one required?

The basic rule is that members of the armed forces of a party to the conflict have POW status upon capture. Article 5 is not evolved from the 1929 POW Convention or the 1907 Hague Regulations; it is new to the 1949 Convention.

Article 5 of Geneva Convention III raises a *presumption* that individuals who might be POWs *shall* have the POW Convention applied to them. "Presumption" and "shall" are powerful words in any legal context. A captured combatant is entitled to POW status, but, "[i]n addition, there are certain non-combatants who are entitled to this status."[219] Article 5 is the vehicle by which that entitlement is determined. An identical presumption and competent tribunal requirement is in Article 45.1, Additional Protocol I.

There is no requirement in Additional Protocol II for competent tribunals in non-international armed conflicts, although it may be argued that the 1949 Geneva Conventions, by virtue of their universal ratification, are customary law applicable in Armed conflicts of any description. Article 5 tribunals *may* be held in non-international conflicts, even if not considered mentioned in Additional Protocol II. Why would a tribunal not required by LOAC/IHL be held? To demonstrate to allies and the international community generally, that although not mandatory, when there was the merest possibility of POW status, as in a non-international conflict, the detaining power was scrupulous in observing its LOAC/IHL obligations and, out of a sense of legal caution, provided status tribunals for captured enemy fighters, even though a tribunal finding of POW status would be rare. In most instances that was not the course taken by the U.S. in the Iraq or Afghan armed conflicts, although there were some such

---

[216] Directive 2310.01E, "Department of Defense Detainee Program," supra, note 205.

[217] Josh White, "Detainees Ruled Enemy Combatants," NY *Times*, Aug. 10, 2007, A2.

[218] Watkin, "21st Century Conflict," in Schmitt and Pejic, *International Law and Armed Conflict*, supra, note 8, at 291.

[219] UK MOD, *Manual of the Law of Armed Conflict*, supra, note 22, at 143, para. 8.3. Footnotes omitted.

tribunals. The not unreasonable U.S. view was that to conduct hundreds of tribunals in a non-international armed conflict, when not required, and when the status of the detainee was clear from the moment of capture, would be a waste of combatant time and manpower.

Article 5 tribunals respond to the sometimes difficult question facing commanders: "On the common Article 2 battlefield, how do I know who merits POW status and who does not?" Article 5 instructs, "Should any doubt arise as to whether persons, having committed a belligerent act and having fallen into the hands of the enemy, belong to any of the categories enumerated in Article 4, such persons shall enjoy the protection of the present Convention until such time as their status has been determined by a competent tribunal."[220]

The words "competent tribunal" are used so that tribunals other than military tribunals are not precluded. Unlike most of the POW Convention, Article 5 is directed to irregular fighters who might have complied with the four requirements for POW status, as well as regular troops and civilians traveling with the armed forces in the field. Article 5 applies to the person who says she was accompanying the armed forces but was not a soldier, to the enemy deserter who has lost his identifying Geneva Convention card, and to the fighter who swears he was a member of a *levée en masse*. If there is a chance their story is true – "any doubt" – they *shall* be presumed to be POWs until it is determined that their status is something else.

Note that a "competent tribunal" need be employed only when there is doubt regarding a prisoner's status. When a uniformed enemy soldier is captured in the course of a common Article 2 armed conflict, there seldom is doubt that he is a POW, and no tribunal is called for. When an Afghan insurgent in civilian clothing is seized, dazed and bleeding, after a final assault on the mountain house where he and his fellow insurgents were firing on U.S. forces, there is no doubt that he is a criminal fighter and no tribunal is necessary.

Not all cases are so clear. In an international armed conflict, imagine that a Dutch patrol has detained an individual dressed in civilian clothes, carrying an AK-47 assault rifle and, in his backpack, three magazines of ammunition for the AK, a fragmentation hand grenade, and ten feet of detonation cord.* The individual was seized at a site from which the Dutch patrol had received rifle fire an hour before. Many local civilian males lawfully carry AK-47s, however. The detainee says he found the grenade, and says he uses the "det cord" in his father's construction business. Shall the presumption of POW status continue in the face of possession of such suspicious armament? A competent tribunal should be held. The tribunal should hear his story, assess the circumstances of his apprehension, and judge his veracity. Until the tribunal's determination is made, the presumption of POW status continues.

When several individuals have been captured as a group, there may be "doubt" as to one of the detainees' status. The circumstances or place of his capture may raise doubt, or the detainee himself may raise the required doubt simply by claiming POW status.[221] Once a captive persuades his captors that he is a member of the enemy armed forces,

---

[220] 1949 Geneva Convention III, Art. 5.   * A high-speed fuse commonly used for detonating explosives.
[221] *Public Prosecutor v. Ooi Hee Koi* [1968] A.C. 829, an opinion of the U.K.'s Privy Council. Also, Elsea, *Treatment of "Battlefield Detainees" in the War on Terrorism*, supra, note 19, at CRS-35.

the burden of proof that he is anything else is on the capturing force.[222] As tedious as it may initially seem, when a detainee argues that he is a POW or that he is an innocent civilian, a competent tribunal is called for.

In U.S. practice, these tribunals are commonly referred to as "Article 5 hearings." They first were instituted by the United States in the Vietnam War, in 1966,[223] although not by that name. The Vietnam conflict pitted the U.S. and South Vietnam against North Vietnam, which had been an independent state since 1945 – an international armed conflict. The United States did not initially consider captured Viet Cong (VC) as entitled to POW status. A 1966 Military Assistance Command, Vietnam, (MACV) Directive changed that – as a matter of grace, rather than a matter of law. "The MACV policy was that all combatants captured during military operations were to be accorded prisoner of war status, irrespective of the type of unit [VC Local Force, VC Main Force, or North Vietnamese Army] to which they belonged."[224] This directive was in hopes that VC holding U.S. soldiers and civilians would reciprocate and grant American prisoners they held POW status. For U.S.-captured VC/North Vietnamese Army, postcapture processing included questioning and classification at a combined U.S.-Vietnamese interrogation center – essentially, Article 5 hearings.[225]

Today, Article 5 hearings are well-established proceedings. In the first Gulf War (1990), the United States held 1,196 Article 5 hearings. "As a result, 310 persons were granted EPW [enemy prisoner of war] status; the others were determined to be displaced civilians and were treated as refugees."[226] In the war on terrorism, hundreds of Article 5 hearings have been conducted in Afghanistan and Iraq.

"As the Third Geneva Convention is silent on the procedures to be followed, procedural issues fall within the purview of the Detaining Power...[I]t is fairly clear that [the tribunals] were not envisaged as judicial bodies obliged to comply with fair trial guarantees."[227]

For U.S. combatants, there is a regulation applicable to all branches of the armed forces that specifies the constitution of Article 5 tribunals and the procedures to be followed.[228] Several U.S. orders relating to tribunals conducted by subordinate commands are available. (See Cases and Materials, this chapter, for one such order.)

The U.S. regulation specifies that three officers and an interpreter, if necessary, are necessary for an Article 5 hearing: one officer, a judge advocate, if available, acts as both recorder and the presenter of evidence, plus two other officers. The three constitute the "tribunal." The senior tribunal member is a major, or higher rank. The tribunal can order the appearance of U.S. military witnesses and can request the presence of others,

---

[222] Yoram Dinstein, "Unlawful Combatancy," in Fred L. Borch and Paul S. Wilson, eds., *International Law Studies*. Vol. 79. *International Law and the War on Terror* (Newport, RI: Naval War College, 2003), 151–74, 164.

[223] MACV Directive 20–5, "Inspections and Investigations: Prisoner of War Determinations of Status," dtd 17 May 1966. A later version, Directive 20–4, dtd May 18, 1968, is at Prugh, *Law at War*, supra, note 20, at 136.

[224] Prugh, *Law at War*, supra, note 20, at 66.   [225] Id.

[226] DoD, *Conduct of the Persian Gulf War* (Washington, DC: GPO, 1992), App. L, at 578.

[227] Pejic, "'Unlawful/Enemy Combatants," in Schmitt and Pejic, *International Law and Armed Conflict*, supra, note 8, at 336.

[228] Army Regulation 190–8/OPNAVINST 3461.c/AFJI 31–304/MCO 3461.1, Enemy Prisoners of War, Retained Personnel, Civilian Internees and Other Detainees (1 Oct. 1997), ¶ 1–6, a half-page in length. Available on-line.

all of whom testify under oath. With the detainee present and his rights to present evidence and examine witnesses having been explained, the tribunal hears the evidence and the witnesses, and then makes its determination. It is a fact-finding procedure, rather than an adversarial proceeding and hearsay evidence may be considered. Unless it is established by a preponderance of the evidence that the detainee is *not* entitled to POW status, upon majority vote of the tribunal he is granted that status. Hearings may be as brief as a half hour. The written hearing summaries in which detainees are denied POW status are examined by a senior judge advocate for legal sufficiency.[229]

Shortly after 9/11, the President and his advisors, apparently thinking the Geneva Conventions were irrelevant to the war on terrorism,[230] and believing there was no doubt as to the individual status of the few Taliban captured in Afghanistan, determined that Article 5 hearings in the cases of all captured Taliban and al Qaeda fighters were unwarranted.[231] "[T]he President could reasonably interpret GPW [Geneva Prisoner of War Convention] in such a manner that none of the Taliban forces fall within the legal definition of POWs," Assistant Attorney General Jay S. Bybee advised the White House. "A presidential determination of this nature," Bybee continued, "would eliminate any legal 'doubt' as to the prisoners' status, as a matter of domestic law, and would therefore obviate the need for Article 5 tribunals."[232]

Internationally and domestically, this was seen by many as a needless disregard of the Geneva Conventions, particularly given the brief and uncomplicated nature of Article 5 hearings. A former Assistant U.S. Attorney General and head of the Office of Legal Counsel wrote, "If the administration had simply followed the Geneva requirement to hold an informal 'competent tribunal,' or had gone to Congress for support on their detention program in the summer of 2004, it probably would have avoided the more burdensome procedural and judicial requirements that became practically necessary under the pressure of subsequent judicial review."[233] Not all agreed with that view. The Congressional Research Service, for example, notes:

> If there is no uncertainty that none of the detainees qualifies as POWs and their treatment would not change…then holding tribunals to determine each detainee's status would be largely symbolic and therefore a waste of resources. Critics of the

[229] Army Judge Advocate General's School, *Law of War Workshop Deskbook* (Charlottesville, VA: JAG School, 1997), at 5F-10–13, citing Appendix "A" of U.S. Central Command Regulation 27–13, "Captured Persons, Determination of Eligibility for enemy Prisoner of War Status," dtd 7 Feb. 1995. The procedures related in Appendix "A" are more detailed than summarized here.

[230] John Yoo, *War by Other Means* (New York: Atlantic Monthly Press, 2006), 22. "To pretend that rules written at the end of World War II, before terrorist organizations and the proliferation of know-how about weapons of mass destruction, are perfectly suitable for this new environment refuses to confront new realities."

[231] Yoo Memorandum, supra, note 143. "Therefore, neither the Geneva conventions nor the WCA [War Crimes Act] regulate the detention of al Qaeda prisoners captured during the Afghanistan conflict"; and, Memorandum for Alberto Gonzales and William Haynes; from Department of Justice, Office of Legal Counsel; Subject: Application of Treaties and Laws to al Qaeda and Taliban Detainees (22 Jan. 2002), supra, note 137. " . . . [W]e conclude that the President has more than ample grounds to find that our treaty obligations under Geneva III toward Afghanistan were suspended during the period of the conflict."

[232] Memorandum for Alberto R. Gonzales, Counsel to the President; From: Office of Legal Counsel, U.S. Department of Justice (7 Feb. 2002). Reprinted in Greenberg and Dratel, *Torture Papers*, supra, note 143, at 136, 142.

[233] Goldsmith, *The Terror Presidency*, supra, note 153, at 140.

policy respond that the U.S.' position regarding the inapplicability of the Geneva Conventions could be invoked as precedent to defend the poor human rights practices of other regimes, and it could lead to harsh treatment of U.S. service members who fall into enemy hands during this or any future conflict.[234]

In 2004, Salim Hamdan was a Guantánamo detainee scheduled for trial by military commission, after having been found to be an "enemy combatant" by a Guantánamo Combatant Status Review Board. Hamdan had never been heard by an Article 5 tribunal, however. He petitioned the U.S. District Court in Washington D.C., the court designated to hear Guantánamo cases. The court held, "This provision [Geneva Convention III, Article 5] has been implemented and confirmed by Army Regulation 190–8. . .Hamdan has asserted his entitlement to POW status, and the Army's regulations provide that whenever a detainee makes such a claim his status is in doubt [the trigger for Article 5 tribunals]. . . .There is nothing in this record to suggest that a competent tribunal has determined that Hamdan is not a prisoner-of-war. . .The government must convene a competent tribunal. . . ."[235] The court did not address the issue of the conflict's status.

On the government's appeal, the appellate court ruled that "the 1949 Geneva Convention does not confer upon Hamdan a right to enforce its provision in court. . ."[236] The court, after mis-reading in several respects the law of war it was ruling on, went on to correctly note that the conflict against al Qaeda was a non-international armed conflict and Convention III was not applicable. On the issue of Hamdan's right to an Article 5 competent tribunal the court held, "One subsection [of Army Regulation 190–8] requires that prisoners receive the protections of the [Geneva III] Convention 'until some other legal status is determined by competent authority.'. . .Hamdan claims that AR 190–8 entitles him to have a 'competent tribunal' determine his status." Missing the legal point of an Article 5 tribunal entirely, the appellate court continued, "But we believe the military commission is such a tribunal. . .We therefore see no reason why Hamdan could not assert his claim to prisoner of war status before the military commission at the time of his trial and thereby receive the judgment of a "competent tribunal" within the meaning of Army Regulation 190–8."[237]

By that uninformed logic a Guantánamo detainee could wait for (as of this writing) thirteen and-a-half years for a determination of his right to POW status and Geneva Convention III protections.

6.8.1 U.S. Military Practice

A 2014 DoD directive applicable to all U.S. Armed Forces, and in all conflicts no matter how characterized, sets a policy that "all persons subject to this directive will, without regard to a detainee's legal status, at a minimum apply: (1) The standards established in common Article 3 to [the 1949 Geneva Conventions]. (2) The principles in Articles 4–6 of [Additional Protocol II] during non-international armed conflict. (3) The principles in Article 75 of [Additional Protocol I] during international armed conflict and

---

[234] Elsea, *Treatment of "Battlefield Detainees,"* supra, note 19, at CRS-38. Also, John C. Dehn, "Why Article 5 Status Determinations are not 'Required' at Guantanamo," 6–2 *J. of Int'l Crim. Justice* (May 2008), 371.

[235] *Hamdan v. Rumsfeld*, 344 F. Supp. 2d 152, 161–2 (D.D.C. 2004).

[236] *Hamdan v. Rumsfeld*, 415 F. 3d 33, 45 (D.D.C. 2005)   [237] *Id.*, at 19.

occupation."[238] The same DoD Directive repeats the requirement of Geneva Convention III, Article 5, that, "During international armed conflict, should any doubt arise as to whether a detainee [is a POW] and as such is entitled to the protections and privileges afforded POWs, such detainees shall enjoy treatment as POWs until a tribunal convened in accordance with Article 5 of [Convention III] determines whether the detainee is entitled to such status or treatment."[239] During the war on terrorism, the Directive was often disregarded.

6.9 Civilians

An individual status encountered on every battlefield, particularly non-international conflict battlefields, is the civilian – the noncombatant. The ICTY notes, "The protection of civilians in time of armed conflict, whether international or internal, is the bedrock of modern humanitarian law...Indeed, it is now a universally recognized principle...that deliberate attack on civilians or civilian objects are absolutely prohibited by international humanitarian law."[240] Civilians may never be purposely targeted. "In the context of modern-day conflicts, it is the deliberate targeting of civilians, rather than the incidental loss of civilian life...that have placed the...responsibilities of armed groups so prominently on the international agenda."[241]

Article 50.1, Additional Protocol I, requires that, "[i]n case of doubt whether a person is a civilian, that person shall be considered to be a civilian." Although this defines "civilian" in the negative, essentially, a civilian is anyone not a member of the armed forces.[242]

The sometimes problematic civilian example is the worker in an enemy munitions factory. If civilians may never purposely be attacked, how can LOAC/IHL allow civilian armament workers to be attacked? This question arose along with the first long-range bomber aircraft. In 1930, air power proponent J. M. Spaight argued:

> There can be no shadow of a doubt that...all persons employed...in the metal works, aircraft and engine factories, petrol refineries, etc.,...are subject to attack. The case for attacking workers of these categories is overwhelming and it is idle to seek to resist it...The person who makes the killing machine is more dangerous than the soldier or sailor who uses it...Such workers, though civilians, cannot be regarded as noncombatants while actually at work.[243]

In the intervening eighty years a different view has come to prevail. "By 1939 higher-level military schools such as the Army War College were teaching America's senior leaders that despite European acceptance of wanton air attacks on defenseless civilians as inevitable, such tactics were considered 'butchery in the eyes of a trained soldier'..."[244]

---

[238] DoD Directive 2310.01E, "Department of Defense Detainee Program," supra, note 204, at para. 3.a., 3.b.

[239] Id., at para. 3.h.   [240] *Prosecutor v. Kupreškić et al.*, IT-95-16-T, Trial Judgment (Jan. 14, 2000), para. 521.

[241] Howard M. Hensel, ed., *The Law of Armed Conflict* (Aldershot, UK: Ashgate, 2005), 172.

[242] Id. Article 50.1 further reads: "any person who does not belong to one of the categories of persons referred to in Article 4A(1) [a member of the armed forces of a Party to the conflict]; (2) [a member of other volunteer corps, including those of organized resistance movements], (3) [regular armed forces who profess allegiance to a government not recognized by the Detaining Power] and (6) [a *levée en mass*] of the Third Convention and in Article 43 [again, the armed forces of a Party to the conflict] of this Protocol ... " is a civilian.

[243] J. M. Spaight, *Air Power and the Cities* (London: Longmans & Green, 1930), 150–2.

[244] Conrad C. Crane, *Bombs, Cities, and Civilians* (Lawrence: University Press of Kansas, 1993), 23.

Although this statement idealizes American interwar thought, it is correct that in World War II the United States pursued precision bombing rather than area bombing and, to the degree possible, avoided civilian casualties.* Granted, the bombing technology of World War II, despite the laudatory publicity of the Norden bombsight, was rudimentary, but every effort was made by the U.S. Army Air Corps to minimize civilian casualties in the European Theater. Among other objectives was the targeting by American bombers of enemy munitions plants and weapons-manufacturing factories. Civilians were known to be working in the targeted plants and factories, but civilians were not the targets. The factories were the targets. The incidental injury and death of civilians is addressed through the principle of proportionality.[245] (See Chapter 7.4.)

"Did indiscriminate bombing occur during World War II? Of course, and each major participant was guilty of it at one time or another."[246] But contrary to Spaight's 1930 prediction, civilian armorers and workers were not targeted. The World War II exception is Japan, where civilian cities were purposely targeted, fire-bombed and atom-bombed by the U.S.[247] An approach emphasizing distinction and proportionality is easier to maintain with the advent of laser-designated targeting and precision-guided munitions.

"It is essential for the conduct of civilized warfare that a firm line be drawn between the armed forces and the rest of the population, so that the enemy soldier will know who can kill and wound him and therefore be subject to the like treatment; and which elements of the population have the rights and obligations of civilians, that is, not to be intentionally killed or wounded and, therefore, not to kill and wound."[248] Care must always be taken when attacking legitimate targets "that civilians are not needlessly injured through carelessness."[249] This basic premise is affirmed by war crime tribunal convictions. The ICTY, for instance, has held that when the civilian population is the primary object of the attack, such targeting may constitute a crime against humanity.[250]

In an insurgency, as in Iraq and Afghanistan, LOAC/IHL requirement to distinguish civilians from combatants is easier stated than done. Yet, civilians are critical actors on the insurgency battlefield, and their safety must be an important operational and LOAC/IHL consideration.

Terrorists are not true civilians,[251] they are well-armed, but which civilians are terrorists? Additional Protocol I, Article 45.3, without specifically referring to them, notes that

---

* There were notable exceptions, such as the American bombing of Hamburg and Dresden. The United States also took a far different approach in the Pacific Theater of Operations, where more than a score of Japanese cities were fire-bombed, and atom bombs targeted city centers.

[245] UK MOD, *Manual of the Law of Armed Conflict*, supra, note 22, para. 2.5.2., at 24.

[246] Parks, "Air War and the Law of War," supra, note 44.

[247] See, e.g., J. Samuel Walker, *Prompt and Utter Destruction: Truman and the Use of Atomic Bombs against Japan* (Chapel Hill: University of North Carolina Press, 1997; Tami Davis Biddle, *Rhetoric and Reality in Air Warfare* (Princeton, NJ: Princeton University Press, 2002); and Kenneth P. Werrell, *Blankets of Fire: U.S. Bombers over Japan during World War II* (Washington DC: Smithsonian Institution Press, 1996).

[248] Greenspan, *The Modern Law of Land Warfare*, supra, note 21, at 55.

[249] *Prosecutor v. Kupreškić*, supra, note 240, at para. 524.

[250] *Prosecutor v. Naletilic*, IT-98–34-T, (31 March 2003), para. 235; and *Prosecutor v. Kunarac*, IT-96–23 & 23-T (22 Feb. 2001), para. 421.

[251] Roberts, "The Laws of War in the War on Terror – Discussion," in Heere, *Terrorism and the Military*, supra, note 166, at 107. However, former Senator Max Cleland, who lost three limbs in Vietnam combat, says of civilians, "This objective of 'hearts and minds?' Well, *hello*! You didn't know which heart and mind was going to blow you up!" Matt Bai, "The McCain Doctrines," NY *Times Magazine*, May 18, 2008, 42.

terrorists are persons taking part in hostilities who are not military persons but who are entitled to the fundamental protections of Article 75, suggesting a unique status. As Professor Dinstein writes, "You are either a combatant or a civilian, you cannot be both."[252]

Should civilian casualties occur, they are not necessarily criminal. What LOAC forbids is making civilians the object of attack. "Collateral damages are a part of almost every military operation and are regarded as acceptable to the extent that precautions are taken so that the civilian casualties are not disproportionate to the anticipated military advantage."[253] To constitute a LOAC/IHL violation – murder or manslaughter, rather than a collateral death – the act must involve a course of criminal conduct, rather than being an isolated incident.

6.10 Protected Persons

An important individual status in an insurgency, be it politically-based or terrorist inspired, is that of "protected person." A protected person enjoys the benefits (and responsibilities) of Geneva Convention IV. Absent that status, a civilian is protected only by common Article 3 and Articles 13–26 of Convention IV, and Article 75 of Additional Protocol I. Those protections are considerable, but fall far short of Convention IV's protections. Protected person status is possible only in a common Article 2 international armed conflict. In a common Article 3 conflict, because only that common Article applies, there are no protected persons, although common Article 3 confirms protections akin to protected person status. Additionally, the term, "protected person" is often heard in discussing non-international armed conflicts because, although the status is not found in common Article 3 conflicts, the term communicates many of the roughly similar protections due civilians in non-international armed conflicts through common Article 3, Articles 13–26 of Convention IV, and Article 75 of Additional Protocol I.

Article 4 of Geneva Convention IV, the civilians' Convention, describes protected persons as, "**Persons protected by the Convention are those who, at a given moment and in any manner whatsoever, find themselves, in case of a conflict or occupation, in the hands of a Party to the conflict or Occupying Power of which they are not nationals.**" This definition is followed by several qualifying phrases.

More simply put, **a protected person is a noncombatant who finds him/herself in the hands of the other side**. Civilian inhabitants of occupied territory are protected persons with specific rights, including humane treatment. Additional Protocol II, Article 2.1, provides similar protections for civilians in internal conflicts, without suggesting they have any special status. Several ICTY opinions promote an expanded view of who may be considered a protected person, one Trial Chamber writing that the "protections should be applied to as broad a category of persons as possible."[254]

Imagine that, in the midst of a conflict in which Redland has invaded Blueland, a common Article 2 conflict, a senior civilian diplomat of Blueland is detained by invading Redland. The Blueland diplomat is not a POW. Nor is he an unlawful combatant. He is a civilian who finds himself in the hands of a party to the conflict of which he is not a

---

[252] Yoram Dinstein, "Discussion," in Heere, *Terrorism and the Military*, supra, note 166, at 109.

[253] Guénaël Mettraux, *International Crimes and the Ad Hoc Tribunals* (Oxford: Oxford University Press, 2005), 159.

[254] *Prosecutor v. Delalić*, supra, note 72, at para. 263.

national/citizen – a citizen of one side in the hands of the other side. He is the Article 4 definition of a protected person.

Change that scenario: During the Redland invasion, a Blueland civilian is captured while engaged in a firefight with Redland forces. Is she still a civilian, is she part of a *levée en masse*, or is she an unlawful combatant with a continuous combat function? In any of those cases she is in the hands of the other side and is a protected person. Her presumed POW status was negated by the fact that she is a civilian who took a direct part in hostilities. There being no doubt as to her unlawful combatant status, she need not be given an Article 5 hearing...unless she might have been part of a *levée en masse*.

Change the scenario again: The Redland invasion has defeated Blueland armed forces, and Redland forces occupy all of Blueland. A Blueland civilian has been detained on suspicion of supporting an insurgency that has arisen. He is not part of a *levée en masse*, not a POW, and not shown to be an unlawful combatant. He is suspected of violation of Blueland domestic law, which is still operative. There is no doubt as to his status, so an Article 5 hearing is unnecessary. Under Article 4, he is a protected person.[255]

Change the situation: Blueland is beset by an armed internal rebellion. The rebel group, *Unido Azul* (UA), has strongholds around the country but does not actually control any portion of Blueland. UA's leader, Commander Macho, has been captured by Blueland soldiers. What is his status? Initially one might consider Macho a protected person. But this is a common Article 3 non-international internal armed conflict. The sole applicable portion of the Geneva Conventions is common Article 3 itself. No other portion of the Conventions applies. Protected persons are a construct of Convention IV. Blueland domestic law and human rights law apply. Commander Macho is a prisoner of Blueland authorities, a detainee, or simply, a prisoner, to be charged and tried under Blueland's domestic criminal laws or, perhaps, a military commission if Commander Macho has committed a war crime, or if he is charged with a war crime on the basis of command responsibility. (See Ch. 10.3.)

POWs are *not* protected persons, strange as that may at first sound. In a common Article 2 international armed conflict, POWs are considerably more than protected persons, having the entire panoply of rights and protections of Convention III, which go far beyond the protections of a protected person. "But, if for some reason, prisoner of war status...were denied to them, they would become protected persons under the present [fourth] Convention."[256] U.S. air crews shot down and captured in North Vietnam, who were denied POW status under Convention III, were, and should have been treated as, protected persons under Convention IV. It bears repeating that "[e]very person in enemy hands must have some status under international law...*There is no intermediate status; nobody in enemy hands can be outside the law*."[257]

There are limitations on the application of Convention IV's Article 4. Protected person status does not attach to nationals of a state that has not ratified the Geneva Conventions. There is no such state today, but in the future a new state could be recognized and it could decline to ratify the Conventions. Although significant portions of the Conventions are customary law – arguably all but the administrative Articles – that would bind

---

[255] FM 27–10, *The Law of Land Warfare*, supra, note 15, at 98, para. 247.b. "[T]hose protected by the Geneva Conventions also include all persons who have engaged in hostile or belligerent conduct but who are not entitled to treatment as prisoners of war."

[256] Pictet, *Commentary, IV Geneva Convention*, supra, note 1, at 50.   [257] Id., at 51. Emphasis in original.

the new state regardless of nonratification, the nationals of such a state would not be covered by Article 4.

There is another limitation on the application of Article 4. During a common Article 2 international armed conflict, Article 4 applies to all detained persons of a foreign nationality and to persons without any nationality. In other words, protected person status applies to detained persons whose nationality is different than that of their captors. This is the "nationality requirement" of Article 4. The Conventions' framers, concerned that they not interfere with a state and its citizens, considered that fellow nationals of the detaining state, neutrals, and co-belligerents, could resolve their detention problems through the available diplomatic offices of the detainee's own state.[258] The nationality requirement was included in Article 4 to ensure that non-interference.

Again, LOAC/IHL may be evolving, portending change in the nationality requirement. "[T]imes have changed since the Geneva Conventions were adopted in 1949, the [ICTY] Appeals Chamber has said, and Article 4...'may [now] be given a wider construction so that a person may be accorded protected status, notwithstanding the fact that he is of the same nationality as his captors.'"[259] Given repeated ICTY holdings that an individual's protected status should not depend on a strict interpretation of Article 4, domestic laws regarding nationality may not necessarily be determinative.[260] Not in ICTY cases, at least. The ICTY's protected person opinions have been in relation to the confusing issue of nationality in the former Yugoslavian conflict, and not all authorities agree with the Tribunal. Time will tell if the tribunal's view will become state practice. For now, the ICTY's position remains a minority view, authoritative but not binding other courts or tribunals.

Accepting the traditional view that a prisoner must be of a different nationality than the detaining state, what if the prisoner is *not* of a different nationality? In the U.S.-Iraqi conflict, what if an insurgent is captured by Iraqi forces while she is directly participating in hostilities and she turns out to be an Iraqi citizen, just as her captors? She is not a POW, not a combatant, and (ICTY jurisprudence aside) not a protected person because she does not meet the nationality requirement. Such individuals are simply prisoners, or detainees with common Article 3 protection, subject to trial under Iraqi domestic law or military commission for their unlawful combatant-like acts they may have committed.

A third limitation on protected person status is uncontested. Article 4 does not apply to nationals of a neutral or a co-belligerent state, as long as that state has normal diplomatic relations in the state in whose territory they are. In other words, if a detained person is a national of a state that is neutral in the conflict, or if the detained person is an ally of the detaining state – a co-belligerent – and if the state of which the detainee is a national has diplomatic relations with the detaining state, the detainee is not a protected person.

---

[258] Id., at 48–9.
[259] Mettraux, *International Crimes*, supra, note 253, at 68, quoting *Prosecutor v. Aleksovski*, IT-95–14/1-A, (March 24, 2000), para. 151; and *Prosecutor v. Delalić*, supra, note 72, at, para. 58; and *Prosecutor v. Tadić*, IT-94–1-A (July 15, 1999), paras. 164 and 169.
[260] Id., Mettraux, at 68.

> **SIDEBAR.** During the U.S.–Vietnam conflict, South Vietnam was a co-belligerent of the United States. Accordingly, the South Vietnamese inhabitants of My Lai (4) were allies of the United States. As co-belligerents, they were not protected persons. It is ironic that, on March 16, 1968, when at least 350 inhabitants of My Lai were murdered by U.S. Army troops under Lieutenant William Calley's command, the victims were U.S. allies not covered by Geneva Convention IV's Article 4. Although the satisfaction their survivors might have obtained through South Vietnamese diplomatic offices is questionable, such are the terms of Geneva Convention IV, Article 4. The Army Court of Military Review's later appellate opinion in the Calley court-martial incorrectly held, "Although all charges could have been laid as war crimes, they were prosecuted under the Uniform Code of Military Justice." (*U.S. v Calley*, 46 CMR 1131, 1138 (ACMR, 1973).) Because the victims were allies, My Lai represents not a war crime, but a case of multiple murder, rape, aggravated assault, and maiming, triable as such concurrently under the domestic law of South Vietnam's then-functioning courts, or under the American Uniform Code of Military Justice.

Applying protected person status to individuals is not a sop to critics of IHL. "The Fourth Convention has not been drafted by professional do-gooders or professors, but by experienced diplomats and military leaders fully taking into account the security needs of a state confronted with dangerous people."[261] The U'S. conflict in Iraq illustrated why protected person status, although often violated, remains important.

6.11 Minimum *Jus in Bello* Protections Due Captured Individuals

In a common Article 2 international armed conflict, captured combatants are protected by all of 1949 Geneva Convention III, the POW convention. Similarly protected are captured medical personnel and chaplains, as well as persons who accompany the armed forces without being members thereof, merchant marine and civilian aircraft crews, and members of *levées en masse*.

In a common Article 2 conflict, protected persons are due the protections of 1977 Additional Protocol I and Geneva Convention common Article 3. Although a plain reading of common Article 3 indicates it is applicable only in non-international armed conflicts, today common Article 3 is considered customary international law applicable in all armed conflicts, regardless of their nature.

In either common Article 2 or common Article 3 armed conflicts, civilians are also protected by a variety of human rights treaties and by customary international law. For the United States these include the U.N. International Covenant on Civil and Political Rights, and the U.N. Convention Against Torture and Cruel, Inhuman or Degrading Treatment or Punishment.[262]

Under LOAC and IHL, in a common Article 2 international armed conflict, what are the minimal protections to which captured unlawful combatants/unprivileged belligerents are entitled? "The minimum guarantees applicable to all persons in the power of a

---

[261] Marco Sassòli, "The Status of Persons Held in Guantànamo under International Humanitarian Law," 2–1 *J. of Int'l Crim Justice* (March 2004), 96, 104.

[262] Elsea, *Treatment of "Battlefield Detainees,"* supra, note 19, at CRS-12–13.

party to conflict are defined nowadays in Article 75 of AP I [Additional Protocol I]."[263]
Those guarantees, along with the humane treatment requirements of common Article 3,
are basic rights which are due every prisoner, detainee, unlawful combatant, enemy
combatant, unlawful enemy combatant, and high value detainee. That is not to say that
the Geneva Conventions or Additional Protocol I in their entireties are always applicable
to each of those categories, but the guarantees in Article 75 of Additional Protocol I, and
common Article 3, both customary international law, are the minimum protections
applicable to them. (The U.S. holds that Article 75 of Protocol I is customary law in
international armed conflicts, but not in non-international conflicts.)

What constitutes common Article 3's "humane treatment"? The *Commentary* to
Geneva Convention I says:

> Lengthy definition of expressions such as "humane treatment" or "to treat humanely" is
> unnecessary, as they have entered sufficiently into current parlance to be understood.
> It would therefore be pointless and even dangerous to try to enumerate things with
> which a human being must be provided for his normal maintenance. . .or to lay down in
> detail the manner in which one must behave towards him. . .The details of such
> treatment may, moreover, vary according to circumstances. . .and to what is <u>feasible</u>.[264]

[handwritten margin note: left open should be common sense?]

One hopes the *Commentary* is correct in saying that a definition of humane treatment is
unnecessary.

6.12 Summary

Individual status is the second of the two critical questions to be answered when
examining any armed conflict. We see that, as in any question of law, there are gray
areas and unresolved issues.

An individual's status is very significant. Whether one is a combatant or a civilian (or a subset
of either), individual status determines what one may lawfully do, and what one is prohibited
from doing, in armed conflict and, if captured by an enemy who respects LOAC/IHL, how
one will be treated. In a conflict against terrorists showing no inclination to such observance,
jus in bello individual status becomes all the more important to U.S. and coalition forces who
do respect it. The international community rightly focuses on the treatment accorded captured
terrorists and insurgents as a measure of the holding state's commitment to law.

Combatants, lawful or otherwise, are creatures of common Article 2 international
armed conflicts; that status does not apply in common Article 3 non-international
conflicts. Similarly, POWs and protected persons are aspects of common Article 2 conflicts only. Unlawful combatants/unprivileged belligerents are civilians in an international armed conflict who take a direct part in hostilities. They lose their civilian
immunity and become lawful targets without POW entitlement.

Terrorists are criminals. In a common Article 2 international armed conflict, they are
not entitled to POW status. Terrorists are criminals who directly engage in armed conflict,
to be captured and tried under domestic law or military commission for their unlawful acts.

In a common Article 3 non-international armed conflict terrorists are no more than well-
armed criminals. As in common Article 2 conflicts, terrorists are unprivileged belligerents
to be captured and tried under domestic law or military commission for their unlawful acts.

---

[263] Dörmann, "The Legal Situation of 'Unlawful/Unprivileged Combatants,'" supra, note 102, at 67.
[264] Pictet, *Commentary, I Geneva Convention*, supra, note 23, at 53.

When there is doubt as to a captive's status, his default status in an international armed conflict is POW. The question of his status, if any, is resolved through an Article 5 hearing. Such hearings are not called for when the captive's status is apparent or obvious, only when there is doubt. Even those determined by an Article 5 hearing to be terrorists, insurgents, or unlawful combatants are protected by LOAC/IHL, of course.

In terms of LOAC, the "war on terrorism" is not a war nor, since the post-Saddam and post-Taliban governments of Iraq and Afghanistan were established, is it an international armed conflict. Neither the Taliban nor al Qaeda constitute states, and only states can be parties to a conflict in which the laws and customs of war apply. Nor do Taliban or al Qaeda fighters qualify as combatants under 1977 Additional Protocol I, including its CARs provisions. They and their opponents, the United States, Iraq, Afghanistan, and coalition forces, are engaged in common Article 3 non-international armed conflicts. Taliban and al Qaeda fighters are not combatants, lawful or unlawful. They are civilian criminals who, if they have committed violations of LOAC/IHL, upon capture are subject to trial and punishment under the domestic law of the capturing state or by military commission.

The war on terrorism's uneasy blend of military and law enforcement models – soldiers and other government forces fighting enemy fighters who, if captured, may be prosecuted in domestic courts and military tribunals – presents unique battlefield issues. Today, combating terrorism involves a mix of LOAC/IHL with a heavy injection of human rights law, overlaid with domestic criminal law.

The Geneva Conventions, and even the 1977 Additional Protocols, do not seamlessly fit this new blend. The Conventions and Protocols are like the expensive suit you bought several years ago. The suit is no longer comfortable, confining across the shoulders and a bit tight all over, but it is the only suit you have, so you have to wear it. If you could manage to acquire another suit of similar quality and workmanship you would do so, but, given your current situation, that is not a realistic option. So, wear it, use it, make it work. It is still a good suit with outstanding qualities. The most you can do is seek some tailoring here and there; arrange multinational treaties to alter it a little here, a little there. There's a lot of life left in this suit.

CASES AND MATERIALS

IN RE BUCK AND OTHERS[265]

Wuppertal, Germany, British Military Court, May 10, 1946

Introduction. *After World War II, when the 1929 Geneva Convention regarding POWs was in effect, a British military commission considered the rights of POWs and resistance fighters to a trial before punishment, as well as the lawfulness of Hitler's Commando Order. The law of war that a common soldier may reasonably be expected to know is also discussed in this brief extract:*

---

[265] H. Lauterpacht, ed., *Annual Digest and Reports of Public International Law Cases: Year 1946* (London: Butterworth, 1951), 293. Footnotes omitted.

The Facts: The accused Buck was in charge of a German prisoner of war camp. The other accused were subordinate members of the staff. They were charged with executing without trial, in May 1944, ten British and United States prisoners of war and four French nationals.

The accused pleaded that an Order of Hitler of October 18, 1942, provided that enemy airmen who landed by parachute behind the German front line were not to be treated as prisoners of war but were to be executed without trial. It was contended by the defence that the British prisoners of war belonged to the Special Air Service whose function it was to organize and support the French resistance movement, that all of the prisoners had been in possession of sabotage equipment and instructions on demolition, and that some of them were spies.

In his summing up, the Judge Advocate advised the Court that Article 2 of the Geneva Convention relative to the treatment of Prisoners of War of 1929 applied to the British and United States prisoners of war and that the French nationals, although not prisoners of war, were also protected by the laws and usages of war. He pointed out that under the Hague Regulations even spies were entitled to a trial; there seemed to him to be no evidence that the executed persons were tried before a Court. He said: "What did each of these accused know about the rights of a prisoner of war? That is a matter of fact upon which the Court has to make up its mind. The Court may well think that men are not lawyers: they may not have heard either of the Hague Convention or the Geneva Convention; they may not have seen any book of military law upon the subject; but the Court has to consider whether men who are serving either as soldiers or in proximity to soldiers know as a matter of the general facts of military life whether a prisoner of war has certain rights and whether one of those rights is not, when captured, to security for his person....The position under international law is that it is contrary to rules of international law to murder a prisoner, and if this Court took the view that the shooting of these four French nationals was a murder of a prisoner held by the Germans and under the control of these accused, the Court would be entitled to convict these accused of the violation of the rules of international law." The Judge Advocate pointed out that in principle superior orders afforded no defence to a criminal charge...He expressed the view that a person would be guilty if he committed a war crime in pursuance of an order: if the order was obviously unlawful, if the accused knew that the order was unlawful, or if he ought to have known it to be unlawful had he considered the circumstances in which it was given.

Held: That Buck and nine other accused were guilty. One accused was acquitted. Buck and four other accused were sentenced to death. Five accused were sentenced to terms of imprisonment.

Conclusion. The differences between a post–World War II military commission and military commissions related to the war on terrorism are apparent. Military commissions were initially held at or near the field of battle, their procedure based on familiar court-martial practice, charging familiar offenses, although with relaxed rules of procedure and evidence. The difficulties of implementing a new trial system, with new trial procedure, new rules of evidence, and new and novel offenses, are apparent in Guantanamo's military commissions.

MILITARY PROSECUTOR V. OMAR MAHMUD KASSEM AND OTHERS

Israel, Military Court sitting in Ramallah. April 13, 1969

Introduction. *Before 1977 Additional Protocol I, the requirements to be a combatant and, upon capture, a POW, were well-known and clear. As we know, the various criteria for POW status are contained in 1949 Geneva Convention III, Article 4A (1) through (6). The Kassem trial illustrates that seemingly clear LOAC is not always so. Were this case tried in 1979, after the formation of the 1977 Additional Protocols, instead of 1969, would the result have been different? Of what legal impact is it that Israel has not ratified the Additional Protocols?*

The following is the judgment of the Court:

The first of the accused pleaded that he was a prisoner of war, and similar pleas were made by the remaining defendants....

The second defendant...was prepared to testify on oath...He claimed that he belonged to the "Organization of the Popular Front for the Liberation of Palestine" and when captured was wearing military dress and had in his possession a military pass issued to him on behalf of the Popular Front, bearing the letters J.T.F. [Popular Front for the Liberation of Palestine], my name and my serial number."....

[W]e hold that we are competent to examine and consider whether the defendants are entitled to prisoner-of-war status, and if we so decide, we shall then cease to deal with the charge....

We shall now inquire into the kinds of combatants to whom the status of prisoners of war is accorded upon capture....

The principles of the subject were finally formulated in the Geneva Convention [III] of 12 August 1949....We proceed on the assumption that it applies to the State of Israel and its armed forces; Israel in fact acceded to the Convention on 6 July 1951, Jordan did so on 29 May 1951.

Article 4A of this Convention defines all those categories of person who, having fallen into enemy hands, are regarded as prisoners of war....

Without a shadow of a doubt, the defendants are not, in the words of paragraph (1), "Members of the armed forces of a Party to the conflict" or "members of militias or volunteer corps forming part of such armed forces"....

...[T]he Convention applies to relations between States and not between a State and bodies which are not States and do not represent States. It is therefore the Kingdom of Jordan that is a party to the armed conflict that exists between us and not the Organization that calls itself the Front for the Liberation of Palestine, which is neither a State nor a Government and does not bear allegiance to the regime which existed in the West Bank before the occupation and which exists now within the borders of the Kingdom of Jordan. In so saying, we have in fact excluded the said Organization from the application of the provisions of paragraph (3) of Article 4 [of Geneva Convention III, regarding members of the armed forces with allegiance to an authority not recognized by the Detaining Power].

Paragraph (6) of Article 4 [*leveés en masse*] is also not pertinent, since the defendants are not inhabitants of a non-occupied territory who, on the approach of the enemy, spontaneously take up arms to resist the invading forces without having had time to form themselves into regular armed forces....

Another category of persons mentioned in the Convention are irregular forces, i.e., militia and volunteer forces not forming part of the regular national army, but set up for the duration of the war or only for a particular assignment and including resistance movements belonging to a party to the armed conflict, which operates within or outside their own country, even if it is occupied. To be recognized as lawful combatants, such irregulars must, however, fulfil the following four conditions: (a) they must be under the command of a person responsible for his subordinates; (b) they must wear a fixed distinctive badge recognizable at a distance; (c) they must carry arms openly; (d) they must conduct their operations in accordance with the laws and customs of war.

Let us now examine whether these provisions of Article 4A, paragraph (2) [militias, other volunteer corps, and organized resistance movements], are applicable to the defendants and their Organization.

First, it must be said that, to be entitled to treatment as a prisoner of war, a member of an underground organization on capture by enemy forces must clearly fulfil all the four above mentioned conditions and that the absence of any of them is sufficient to attach to him the character of a combatant not entitled to be regarded as a prisoner of war....

For some reason, however, the literature on the subject overlooks the most basic condition of the right of combatants to be considered upon capture as prisoners of war, namely, the condition that the irregular forces must belong to a belligerent party. If they do not belong to the Government or State for which they fight, then it seems to us that, from the outset, under current International Law they do not possess the right to enjoy the status of prisoners of war upon capture....

...If International Law indeed renders the conduct of war subject to binding rules, then infringement of these rules are offenses, the most serious of which are war crimes. It is the implementation of the rules of war that confers both rights and duties, and consequently an opposite party must exist to bear responsibility for the acts of its forces, regular and irregular. We agree that the Convention applies to military forces (in the wide sense of the term) which, as regards responsibility under International Law, belong to a State engaged in armed conflict with another State, but it excludes those forces – even regular armed units – which do not yield to the authority of the State and its organs of government. The Convention does not apply to those at all. They are to be regarded as combatants not protected by the International Law dealing with prisoners of war, and the occupying Power may consider them as criminals for all purposes.

The importance of allegiance of irregular troops to a central Government made it necessary during the Second World War for States and Governments-in-exile to issue declarations as to the relationship between them and popular resistance forces (see, e.g., the Dutch Royal Emergency Decree of September 1944). In fact, the matter of allegiance of irregular combatants first arose in connection with the Geneva Convention. The Hague Convention of 18 October 1907 did not mention such allegiance, perhaps because of the unimportance of the matter, little use being made of combat units known as irregular forces, guerrillas, etc., at the beginning of the century. In view, however, of the experience of two World Wars, the nations of the world found it necessary to add the fundamental requirement of the total responsibility of Governments for the operations of irregular corps and thus ensure that there was someone to hold accountable if they did not act in accordance with the laws and customs of war.

In the present case, the picture is otherwise. No Government with which we are in a state of war accepts responsibility for the acts of the Popular Front for the

Liberation of Palestine. The organization itself, so far as we know, is not prepared to take orders from the Jordan Government, witness the fact that it is illegal in Jordan and has been repeatedly harassed by the Jordan authorities. The measures that Jordan has adopted against it have included the use of arms. This type of underground activity is unknown in the international community, and for this reason, as has been pointed out, we have found no direct reference in the relevant available literature to irregular forces being treated as illegal by the authorities to whom by the nature of things they should be subject. If these authorities look upon a body such as the Popular Front for the Liberation of Palestine as an illegal organization, why must we have to regard it as a body to which international rules relating to lawful bodies are applicable?....

Not every combatant is entitled to the treatment which, by a succession of increasingly humane conventions, have ameliorated the position of wounded members of armed forces. Civilians who do not comply with the rules governing *"levée en masse"* and have taken an active part in fighting are in the same position as spies. Similarly, combatants who are members of the armed forces, but do not comply with the minimum qualifications of belligerents or are proven to have broken other rules of warfare, are war criminals and as such are liable to any treatment and punishment that is compatible with the claim of a captor State to be civilised.

By the introduction of additional distinctions between lawful and unlawful combatants, and combined application of the test of combatant and non-combatant character and of civilian and military status, it becomes possible to give far-reaching protection to the overwhelming majority of the civilian population of occupied territories and captured members of the armed forces.

Within narrower limits even those categories of prisoners who are excluded from such privileged treatment enjoy the benefits of the standard of civilization. At least they are entitled to have the decisive facts relating to their character as non-privileged prisoners established in...judicial proceedings. Moreover, any punishment inflicted on them must keep within the bounds of the standard of civilization.

From all the foregoing, it is not difficult to answer the submission of counsel for the defence that a handful of persons operating alone and themselves fulfilling the conditions of Article 4A(2) of the Convention may also be accorded the status of prisoners of war. Our answer does not follow the line of reasoning of learned counsel.

...[A] person or body of persons not fulfilling the conditions of Article 4A(2) of the Convention can never be regarded as lawful combatants even if they proclaim their readiness to fight in accordance with its terms. He who adorns himself with peacock's feathers does not therefore become a peacock.

What is the legal status of these unlawful combatants under international law? The reply...If an armed band operates against the forces of an occupant in disregard of the accepted laws of war...then common sense and logic should counsel the retention of its illegal status. If an armed band operates in search of loot rather than on behalf of the legitimate sovereign of the occupied territory, then no combatant or prisoner of war rights can be or should be claimed by its members.

If we now consider the facts we have found on the evidence of the witnesses for the prosecution...we see that the body which calls itself the Popular Front for the Liberation of Palestine acts in complete disregard of customary International Law accepted by civilized nations.

The attack upon civilian objectives and the murder of civilians in Mahne Yehuda Market, Jerusalem, the Night of the Grenades in Jerusalem, the placing of grenades and destructive charges in Tel Aviv Central Bus Station, etc., were all wanton acts of terrorism aimed at men, women and children who were certainly not lawful military objectives.... Immunity of non-combatants from direct attack is one of the basic rules of the international law of war.

The presence of civilian clothes among the effects of the defendants is, in the absence of any reasonable explanation, indicative of their intent to switch from the role of unprotected combatants to that of common criminals. Acts involving the murder of innocent people, such as the attack on the aircraft at Athens and Zurich airports, are abundant testimony of this.

International Law is not designed to protect and grant rights to saboteurs and criminals. The defendants have no right except to stand trial in court and to be tried in accordance with the law and with the facts established by the evidence, in proceedings consonant with the requirements of ethics and International Law.

We therefore reject the plea of the defendants as to their right to be treated as prisoners of war and hold that we are competent to hear the case in accordance with the charge-sheet....

Conclusion. *Do you agree with the court's holding that a prisoner must belong to a party to the conflict to merit POW status? In answering, consider Geneva Convention III, Article 4A(2).*

"THE ĈELEBIĆI CASE," PROSECUTOR V. DELALIĆ, ET AL.

IT-96–21-T (16 November 1998). Footnotes omitted.

Introduction. *Thirty years after the Kassem decision, the ICTY also examined the criteria for several varieties of POW status. The Tribunal systematically examines the possible categories of POW in determining if any of the victims of the accused were other than civilians. Might their victims have been eligible for POW status?*

267. Article 4(A) of the Third Geneva Convention sets the rather stringent requirements for the achievement of prisoner of war status. Once again, this provision was drafted in light of the experience of the Second World War and reflects the conception of an international armed conflict current at that time. Thus, the various categories of persons who may be considered prisoners of war are narrowly framed.

268. In the present case, it does not appear to be contended that the victims of the acts alleged were members of the regular armed forces of one of the parties to the conflict, as defined in sub-paragraph 1 of the Article. Neither, clearly, are sub-paragraphs 3, 4 or 5 applicable. Attention must, therefore, be focused on whether they were members of militias or volunteer corps belonging to a party which: (a) were commanded by a person responsible for his subordinates; (b) had a fixed distinctive sign recognizable at a distance; (c) carried arms openly; and (d) conducted their operations in accordance with the laws and customs of war. Alternatively, they could have constituted a *levée en masse,* that is, being inhabitants of a non-occupied territory who, on the approach of the enemy, spontaneously took up arms to resist the invading forces, without having had time to form themselves into regular armed units, and at all times they carried arms openly and respected the laws and customs of war.

269. The Prosecution seeks to invoke the provisions of Additional Protocol I to interpret and clarify those of Article 4(A) (2) and wishes to take a liberal approach to the detailed requirements that the sub-paragraph contains. Even should this be accepted, and despite the discussion above of the need to take a broad and flexible approach to the interpretation of the Geneva Conventions, the Trial Chamber finds it difficult, on the evidence presented to it, to conclude that any of the victims of the acts alleged in the Indictment satisfied these requirements. While it is apparent that some of the persons detained in the Ĉelebići prison-camp had been in possession of weapons and may be considered to have participated in some degree in 'hostilities', this is not sufficient to render them entitled to prisoner of war status. There was clearly a Military Investigating Commission established in Konjic, tasked with categorising the Ĉelebići detainees, but this can be regarded as related to the question of exactly what activities each detainee had been engaged in prior to arrest and whether they posed a particular threat to the security of the Bosnian authorities. Having reached this conclusion, it is not even necessary to discuss the issue of whether the Bosnian Serbs detained in Ĉelebići "belonged" to the forces of one of the parties to the conflict.

270. Similarly, the Trial Chamber is not convinced that the Bosnian Serb detainees constituted a *levée en masse*. This concept refers to a situation where territory has not yet been occupied, but is being invaded by an external force, and the local inhabitants of the areas in the line of this invasion take up arms to resist and defend their homes. It is difficult to fit the circumstances of the present case...into this categorisation. The authorities in the Konjic municipality were clearly not an invading force from which the residents of certain towns and villages were compelled to resist and defend themselves. In addition, the evidence provided to the Trial Chamber does not indicate that the Bosnian Serbs who were detained were, as a group, at all times carrying their arms openly and observing the laws and customs of war. Article 4(A) (6) undoubtedly places a somewhat high burden on local populations to behave as if they were professional soldiers and the Trial Chamber, therefore, considers it more appropriate to treat all such persons in the present case as civilians.

271. It is important, however, to note that this finding is predicated on the view that there is no gap between the Third and the Fourth Geneva Conventions. If an individual is not entitled to the protections of the Third Convention as a prisoner of war (or of the First or Second Conventions) he or she necessarily falls within the ambit of Convention IV, provided that its Article 4 [protected person] requirements are satisfied....

273. The Prosecution has further argued that Article 5 of the Third Geneva Convention required that, where there was some doubt about the status of the Ĉelebići detainees, they had to be granted the protections of the Convention until that status was determined by a competent tribunal. On this basis they were "protected persons" and subject to the grave breaches provisions of the Third Convention. While there may, on the basis of this Article, have been a duty upon the Bosnian forces controlling the Ĉelebići prison-camp to treat some of the detainees as protected by the Third Geneva Convention until their status was properly determined and thus treat them with appropriate humanity, the Trial Chamber has found that they were not, in fact, prisoners of war. They were, instead, all protected civilians under the Fourth Geneva Convention and the Trial Chamber thus bases its consideration of the existence of "grave breaches of the Geneva Conventions" on this latter Convention....

Conclusion. The accused Delalić was acquitted of all charges. His three co-accused were convicted of various violations of the ICTY Statute and sentenced to seven, twenty, and fifteen years confinement, respectively.

Theodor Meron writes, "The literal application of Article 4 in the Yugoslav context was unacceptably legalistic. This would also be true of other cases involving conflicts among contesting ethnic or religious groups. In many contemporary conflicts, the disintegration of States and the quest to establish new ones make nationality too impractical a concept on which to base the application of international humanitarian law. In light of the protective goals of the Geneva Conventions, in situations like the one in the former Yugoslavia, Article 4's requirement of different nationality should be construed as referring to persons in the hands of an adversary...In the Čelebići case, an ICTY Trial Chamber moved in this direction."[266] Do you agree that there should be a relaxation of Article 4A's requirements in some cases? Can you say why?

ENEMY PRISONERS OF WAR, RETAINED PERSONNEL, CIVILIAN INTERNEES, AND OTHER DETAINEES

Army Regulation 190–8/ OPNAVINST 3461.6/ AFJI 31-304/ MCO 3461.1,

1 October 1997

Introduction. The U.S. direction to its armed forces regarding how a Geneva Convention III, Article 5, "competent tribunal" should be conducted is notably brief, leaving much of its interpretation to the combatant commander in the field, aided by his judge advocate legal advisor (required by Additional Protocol I, Article 82).

1–6. Tribunals

a. In accordance with Article 5, GPW, if any doubt arises as to whether a person, having committed a belligerent act and been taken into custody by the US Armed Forces, belongs to any of the categories enumerated in Article 4, GPW, such persons shall enjoy the protection of the present Convention until such time as their status has been determined by a competent tribunal.

b. A competent tribunal shall determine the status of any person not appearing to be entitled to prisoner of war status who has committed a belligerent act or has engaged in hostile activities in aid of enemy armed forces, and who asserts that he or she is entitled to treatment as a prisoner of war, or concerning whom any doubt of a like nature exists.

c. A competent tribunal shall be composed of three commissioned officers, one of whom must be of a field grade. The senior officer shall serve as President of the Tribunal. Another non-voting officer, preferably an officer in the Judge Advocate General Corps, shall serve as the recorder.

d. The convening authority shall be a commander exercising general courts-martial convening authority.

---

[266] Theodor Meron, *The Humanization of International Law* (Leiden: Martinus Nijhoff, 2006), 34–5.

e. Procedures.
   (1) Members of the Tribunal and the recorder shall be sworn. The recorder shall be sworn first by the President of the Tribunal. The recorder will then administer the oath to all voting members of the Tribunal to include the President.
   (2) A written record shall be made of proceedings.
   (3) Proceedings shall be open except for deliberation and voting by the members and testimony or other matters which would com-promise security if held in the open.
   (4) Persons whose status is to be determined shall be advised of their rights at the beginning of their hearings.
   (5) Persons whose status is to be determined shall be allowed to attend all open sessions and will be provided with an interpreter if necessary.
   (6) Persons whose status is to be determined shall be allowed to call witnesses if reasonably available, and to question those wit-nesses called by the Tribunal. Witnesses shall not be considered reasonably available if, as determined by their commanders, their presence at a hearing would affect combat or support operations. In these cases, written statements, preferably sworn, may be submitted and considered as evidence.
   (7) Persons whose status is to be determined have a right to testify or otherwise address the Tribunal.
   (8) Persons whose status is to be determined may not be compelled to testify before the Tribunal.
   (9) Following the hearing of testimony and the review of documents and other evidence, the Tribunal shall determine the status of the subject of the proceeding in closed session by majority vote. Preponderance of evidence shall be the standard used in reaching this determination.
   (10) A written report of the tribunal decision is completed in each case. Possible board determinations are:
      (a) EPW.
      (b) Recommended RP, entitled to EPW protections, who should be considered for certification as a medical, religious, or volunteer aid society RP.
      (c) Innocent civilian who should be immediately returned to his home or released.
      (d) Civilian Internee who for reasons of operational security, or probable cause incident to criminal investigation, should be detained.
f. The recorder shall prepare the record of the Tribunal within three work days of the announcement of the tribunal's decision. The record will then be forwarded to the first Staff Judge Advocate in the internment facility's chain of command.
g. Persons who have been determined by a competent tribunal not to be entitled to prisoner of war status may not be executed, imprisoned, or otherwise penalized without further proceedings to determine what acts they have committed and what penalty should be imposed. The record of every Tribunal proceeding resulting in a determination denying EPW status shall be reviewed for legal sufficiency when the record is received at the office of the Staff Judge Advocate for the convening authority.

Conclusion. *Brief as this "competent tribunal" guidance is, it seems sufficient for its purpose. Compare the Regulation's skeletal direction with the lengthier order, below,* *written by the commander of a unified command (i.e., one composed of units from different armed force branches) for use in the conflict in Afghanistan.*

GENEVA CONVENTION III, ARTICLE 5 HEARING: A GUIDE[267]

Introduction. *The Commentary to Geneva Convention III is silent on how to conduct a "competent tribunal." Until 1997, and the directive re-printed above, there was no guidance for U.S. Armed Forces conducting Article 5 hearings. Although more than 1,000 Article 5 hearings were conducted during the first Gulf War, virtually all by the Army, their procedure was left to the headquarters of the major Army units that captured individuals whose status was often in doubt. In its entirety, this is the guidance provided by Central Command Headquarters:*

R 27–13
UNITED STATES CENTRAL COMMAND
7115 South Boundary Boulevard
MacDill Air Force Base, Florida 33621–5101
REGULATION
07 FEB 1995
NUMBER 27–13
Legal Services
CAPTURED PERSONS. DETERMINATION OF ELIGIBILITY
FOR ENEMY PRISONER OF WAR STATUS

1. PURPOSE. This regulation prescribes policies and procedures for determining whether persons who have committed belligerent acts and come into the power of the United States Forces are entitled to enemy prisoner of war (EPW) status under the Geneva Convention Relative to the Treatment of Prisoners of War, 12 August 1949 (GPW).
2. APPLICABILITY. This regulation is applicable to all members of United States Forces deployed to or operating in support of operations in the US CENTCOM AOR.
3. REFERENCES.
   a. Geneva Convention Relative to the Treatment of Prisoners of War, 12 August 1949.
   b. DA Pamphlet 27–1, Treaties Governing Land Warfare, December 19956.
   c. FM 27–10, the Law of Land Warfare, July 1956.
   d. J. Pictet, Commentary on the Geneva Convention Relative to the Treatment of Prisoners of War of 12 August 1949, International Committee of the Red Cross.
4. GENERAL.
   a. Persons who have committed belligerent acts and are captured or otherwise come into the power of the United States Forces shall be treated as EPWs if they fall into any of the classes of persons described in Article 4 of the GPW (Annex A).
   b. Should any doubt arise as to whether a person who has committed a belligerent act falls into one of the classes of persons entitled to EPW status under GPW

---

[267] https://www.mpf.usmc.mil/TermApp/SJA/Topics/20051102113719/LOWW%20Master%20Document.pdf.

Article 4, he shall be treated as an EPW until such time as his status has been determined by a Tribunal convened under this regulation.

c. No person whose status is in doubt shall be transferred from the power of the United States to another detaining power until his status has been determined by a Tribunal convened under GPW Article 5 and this regulation.

5. DEFINITIONS.

a. Belligerent Act. Bearing arms against or engaging in other conduct hostile to United States' persons or property or to the persons or property of other nations participating as Friendly Forces in operations in the USCENTCOM AOR....

b. Detainee. A person, not a member of the US Forces, in the custody of the United States Forces who is not free to voluntarily terminate that custody.

c. Enemy Prisoner of War (EPW). A detainee who has committed a belligerent act and falls within one of the classes of persons described in GPW Article 4....

d. Person Whose Status is in Doubt. A detainee who has committed a belligerent act, but whose entitlement to status as an EPW under GPW Article 4 is in doubt.

e. President of the Tribunal. The senior Voting member of each Tribunal. The President shall be a commissioned officer serving in the grade of 04 [major] or above.

f. Recorder. A commissioned officer detailed to obtain and present evidence to a Tribunal convened under this regulation and to make a record of the proceedings thereof....

g. Screening officer. Any US military or civilian employee of the Department of Defense who conducts an initial screening or interrogation of persons coming into the power of the United States Forces.

h. Tribunal. A panel of three commissioned officers, at least one of whom must be a judge advocate, convened to make determinations of fact pursuant to GPW Article 5 and this regulation.

6. BACKGROUND.

a. The United States is a state party to the four Geneva Conventions of 12 August 1949. One of these conventions is the Geneva Convention Relative to the Treatment of Prisoners of War. The text of this convention may be found in DA Pamphlet 27–1.

b. By its terms, the GPW would apply to an armed conflict between the United States and any country.

c. The GPW provides that any person who has committed a belligerent act and thereafter comes into the power of the enemy will be treated as an EPW unless a competent Tribunal determines that the person does not fall within a class of persons described in GPW Article 4.

d. Some detainees are obviously entitled to EPW status, and their cases should not be referred to a Tribunal. These include personnel of enemy armed forces taken into custody on the battlefield....

e. When a competent Tribunal determines that a detained person has committed a belligerent act as defined in this regulation, but the person does not fall into one of the classes of persons described in GPW Article 4, that person will be delivered to the Provost Marshal for disposition as follows:

    (1) If captured in enemy territory. In accordance with the rights and obligations of an occupying power under the Law of Armed Conflict (see references at paragraph 3).

    (2) If captured in territory of another friendly state. For delivery to the civil authorities unless otherwise directed by competent US authority.

7. **RESPONSIBILITIES.**

  a. All US military and civilian personnel of the Department of Defense (DoD) who take or have custody of a detainee will:

    (1) Treat each detainee humanely and with respect.

    (2) Apply the protections of the GPW to each EPW and to each detainee whose status has not yet been determined by a Tribunal convened under this regulation.

  b. Any US military or civilian employee of the Department of Defense who fails to treat any detainee humanely, respectfully or otherwise in accordance with the GPW, may be subject to punishment under the UCMJ or as otherwise directed by competent authority.

  c. Commanders will:

    (1) Ensure that personnel of their commands know and comply with the responsibilities set forth above.

    (2) Ensure that all detainees in the custody of their forces are promptly evacuated, processed, and accounted for.

    (3) Ensure that all sick or wounded detainees are provided prompt medical care. Only urgent medical reasons will determine the priority in the order of medical treatment to be administered.

    (4) Ensure that detainees determined not to be entitled to EPW status are segregated from EPWs prior to any transfer to other authorities.

  d. The Screening Officer will:

    (1) Determine whether or not each detainee has committed a belligerent act as defined in this regulation.

    (2) Refer the cases of detainees who have committed a belligerent act and who may not fall within one of the classes of persons entitled to EPW status under GPW Article 4 to a Tribunal convened under this regulation.

    (3) Refer the cases of detainees who have not committed a belligerent act, but who may have committed an ordinary crime, to the Provost Marshal.

    (4) Seek the advice of the unit's servicing judge advocate when needed.

    (5) Ensure that all detainees are delivered to the appropriate US authority, e.g. Provost Marshal, for evacuation, transfer or release as appropriate.

  e. The USCENTCOM SJA will:

    (1) Provide legal guidance, as required, to subordinate units concerning the conduct of Article 5 Tribunals.

    (2) Provide judge advocates to serve on Article 5 Tribunals as required.

    (3) Determine the legal sufficiency of each hearing in which a detainee who committed a belligerent act was not granted EPW status. Where a Tribunal's decision is determined not to be legally sufficient, a new hearing will be ordered.

    (4) Retain the records of all Article 5 Tribunals conducted. Promulgate a Tribunal Appointment Order IAW Annex B of this regulation.

    f. Tribunals will:

      (1) Following substantially the procedures set forth at Annex C of this regulation, determine whether each detainee referred to that Tribunal:

        (a) did or did not commit a belligerent act as defined in this regulation and, if so, whether the detainee

        (b) Falls or does not fall within one of the classes of persons entitled to EPW status under Article 4 of the GPW.

      (2) Promptly report their decision to the convening authority in writing.

    g. The servicing judge advocate for each unit capturing or otherwise coming into possession of new detainees will provide legal guidance to Screening Officers and others concerning the determination of EPW status as required.

8. PROPONENT. The proponent of this regulation is the Office of the Staff Judge Advocate, CCJA. Users are invited to send comments and suggested improvements on DA Form 2028 (Recommended Changes to Publications and Blank Forms) directly to United States Central Command, CCJA, 7115 South Boundary Boulevard, MacDill Air Force Bas, Florida 33621–5101.

FOR THE COMMANDER IN CHIEF
    OFFICIAL: R. I. NEAL
          LtGen, USMC
          Deputy Commander in Chief
   /s/
ROBERT L. Henderson
LTC, USA
Adjutant General
DISTRIBUTION:
A (1 ea)

Conclusion. *Compared to detainee-related procedures employed after 9/11, this regulation appears simplistic. It is also clear, concise, effective, and in compliance with the requirements of LOAC/IHL. It leaves little doubt as to what is required of U.S. combatant forces. During and after Operation Desert Shield/Desert Storm, when this regulation was in effect, there were virtually no complaints raised, domestically, internationally, or in the media, regarding the handling or treatment of enemy prisoners in the field, most of whom were initially anticipated to be POWs.*

Granted, most of those captured post-9/11 were Taliban and al Qaeda members or adherents whose capture presented issues greatly more complex than the Iraqi combatants captured during and after the brief period of armed conflict in Kuwait and Iraq. Still, the straightforward approach taken by Central Command, giving clear guidance to subordinate combatants in the field and leaving matters of interrogation and intelligence gathering to those traditionally tasked with those matters, has much to recommend it.

4 core concepts:
- *distinction*
- *military necessity*
- *unnecessary suffering*
- *proportionality*

7 Law of Armed Conflict's Core Principles

7.0 Introduction

The two foundational questions in examining any armed conflict have been addressed. The first is, What is the conflict status? What law of armed conflict/international humanitarian law (LOAC/IHL), if any, applies to the conflict being considered? That question is not always as easily or as cleanly resolved as one might wish. The second question: What are the individual statuses of those involved in the conflict? What can they lawfully do, what may they not do, and to what rights and protections are they entitled, should they be captured? Although the second question is usually easier to resolve, it, too, has gray areas, particularly in a "war on terrorism." Ambiguity and lack of complete clarity are features of all varieties of law, however, not just LOAC/IHL.

We know what constitutes LOAC/IHL. We also know, as much as it can be known, in what circumstances they apply, and do not apply. There is one more matter critical to LOAC framework: LOAC's core concepts. Just as every conflict has a status, and every battlefield player has an individual status, every battlefield incident may be examined for compliance with LOAC's four core concepts.

As this almost formulaic examination of LOAC/IHL suggests, we are studying the construction of an LOAC/IHL matrix: conflict, individual, and event. We examine the conflict for its applicable law then look at the participants to determine their place in the conflict. Finally, we look at a specific event involving the participants. The event can be a suspected war crime, or the use of a questionable weapon, or an attack on a place or group not to be attacked. The matrix is simple. The application of LOAC/IHL may be less so.

When a common Article 2 international armed conflict arises, there are basic principles that any army, regardless of its nationality, no matter its political credo, must apply in its combat operations. These prescripts, four in number, case law and many commentators agree are the core LOAC/IHL principles that bind every armed force. "Despite the codification of much customary law into treaty form during the last one hundred years, four fundamental principles still underlie the law of armed conflict."[1] They are distinction, military necessity, unnecessary suffering, and proportionality. Other sources may suggest two or three other, or additional, core principles that are as "battlefield appropriate" as these four. There is no treaty or case that specifies an "official" list of core

---

[1] United Kingdom Ministry of Defence (MOD), *The Manual of the Law of Armed Conflict* (Oxford: Oxford University Press, 2004), para. 2.1, at 21.

principles. Distinction, military necessity, unnecessary suffering, and proportionality are an excellent point from which to start, however.

In examining common Article 2 battlefield events, such as the bombing of a village, the attack of a defended position, the use of a particular munition, the targeting of a specific combatant, each of those events – and any other – may be examined in terms of the core concepts. Did the targeted killing of Sheik X comply with the concept of distinction? Did the bombing of objective Y raise an issue of military necessity? Did the use of white phosphorus artillery cause unnecessary suffering? Were proportionality issues raised in attacking that enemy-held village? Many, if not most, *jus in bello* decisions above the individual combatant's level may be examined in light of the core concepts, the four of which are closely intertwined. That examination, in turn, often can indicate whether LOAC/IHL has been observed.

Some suggest other names for one or two of the core concepts, but, by any name, their observance remains a duty of every commander and every soldier.

7.1 Distinction

Distinction, sometimes referred to as discrimination, is the most significant battlefield concept a combatant must observe.

The two-volume study by the International Committee of the Red Cross (ICRC), *Customary International Humanitarian Law*, begins: "Rule 1. The parties to the conflict must at all times distinguish between civilians and combatants. Attacks may only be directed against combatants. Attacks must not be directed against civilians."[2] That is the core LOAC concept of distinction.

A corollary rule, relating to objects, rather than persons, is "The parties to the conflict must at all times distinguish between civilian objects and military objectives. Attacks may only be directed against military objectives. Attacks must not be directed against civilian objects."[3] Additional Protocol I combines the two rules.

So, distinction has two aspects, one relating to individuals, the other relating to objects. First, combatants must distinguish themselves as such – wear a uniform or a distinctive sign that is recognizable at a distance so that, unlike civilians, they may be seen to be combatants and the lawful targets of opposing combatants. Second, combatants must target only military objectives – distinguish between military objectives and civilian objects, sparing civilian objects.

For centuries, wars were waged not only against states and their armies, but against the inhabitants of the enemy states, as well. Civilians of a defeated state were at the mercy of the conquering army, and were often murdered or enslaved. "The notion that war is waged between soldiers and that the population should remain outside hostilities was introduced in the sixteenth century and became established by the eighteenth century. The customs of war acquired a more humanitarian character through the process of civilization and as a result of the influence of thinkers and jurists."[4]

---

[2] Jean-Marie Henckaerts and Louise Doswald-Beck, *Customary International Humanitarian Law. Vol. I. Rules* (Oxford: Oxford University Press, 2005), 3.

[3] Id., at 25.

[4] Yves Sandoz, Christophe Swinarski, and Bruno Zimmermann, eds., *Commentary on the Additional Protocols* (Geneva: Martinus Nijhoff, 1987), 585. Hereafter: "Protocols *Commentary*."

As most LOAC/IHL concepts did, distinction grew from this *jus in bello* practice that eventually matured into customary law. Early glimpses of distinction are seen in the preamble of the 1868 St. Petersburg Declaration, which specifies "that the only legitimate object which states should endeavor to accomplish during war is to weaken the military force of the enemy," not civilians who support the enemy, or their property (objects), but the enemy's military force. "Civilian objects" are undefined, but military necessity requires that attacks be limited to military objectives. "Thus attacks on the following are prohibited unless they are being used for military purposes: civilian dwellings, shops, schools, and other places of nonmilitary business, places of recreation and worship, means of transportation, cultural property, hospitals, and medical establishments and units."[5]

The 1863 Lieber Code, Article XXII, invokes distinction when it documents the turn from warring on noncombatants: "As civilization has advanced during the last centuries, so has likewise steadily advanced, especially in war on land, the distinction between the private individual belonging to a hostile country and the hostile country itself, with its men in arms. The principle has been more and more acknowledged that the unarmed citizen is to be spared in person, property, and honor as much as the exigencies of war will admit."

The principle of distinction "had been hardening in the minds of decent warriors for several centuries and was no doubt customary law before it received positive formulation in the 1860s."[6] The "positive formulation," the Lieber Code, and the first Geneva convention, in 1864, ascribed neutrality to sick and wounded soldiers – a form of distinction. Still, no multinational convention explicitly extended similar protection to civilians until 1949 Geneva Convention IV.

Before the First World War there was little need for statement of the rule because the civilian population and its objects suffered relatively little from the combatant's use of weapons, unless civilians were actually in the combat zone. World War I changed that situation, however, with the arrival of long-range artillery, aerial bombardment, and reprisals that were directed at towns and their civilian inhabitants. World War II only increased the suffering and death of noncombatants and the destruction of noncombatant objects – "objects" meaning civilian houses, buildings, vehicles, art, industrial works, and so on, unrelated to the war.[7]

Although it was customary law, the principle of distinction, per se, was not mentioned in conventions and treatises until 1977, when it was explicitly stated in Additional Protocol I, Article 48: **"In order to ensure respect for and protection of the civilian population and civilian objects, the Parties to the conflict shall at all times distinguish between the civilian population and combatants and between civilian objects and military objectives and accordingly shall direct their operations only against military objectives."** Additional Protocol II, Article 13.1 approaches distinction obliquely by providing that "the civilian population and individual civilians shall enjoy general

---

[5] United Kingdom MOD, *Manual of the Law of Armed Conflict*, supra, note 1, para 15.16.1. at 391.

[6] Geoffrey Best, "The Restraint of War in Historical and Philosophic Perspective," in Astrid J. M. Delissen and Gerard J. Tanja, eds., *Humanitarian Law of Armed Conflict Challenges Ahead* (Dordrecht: Martinus Nijhoff, 1991), 17.

[7] Protocols *Commentary*, supra, note 4, at 600: "Civilian objects are all objects which are not military objectives as defined in paragraph 2 of [Article 52].

protection against the dangers arising from military operations." The ICRC writes of Additional Protocol I, Article 48:

> It is the foundation on which the codification of the laws and customs of war rests: the civilian population and civilian objects must be respected and protected in armed conflict, and for this purpose they must be distinguished from combatants and military objectives. The entire system established in The Hague in 1899 and 1907 [where the Hague Regulations of those years were laid down] and in Geneva [Conventions] from 1864 to 1977 is founded on this rule of customary law.[8]

Moreover, "under no circumstances would military necessity justify any encroachment upon that general prohibition against attacks on civilians and civilian objects."[9]

What about those civilian workers in the enemy defense factory? This is a mixture of distinction's two aspects, individuals (civilian workers) and objects (the factory). In a common Article 2 international armed conflict, we target the factory, knowing that civilian workers will inevitably be killed. Nevertheless, that is not a violation of distinction. Any civilians killed or wounded are collateral to the attack on the legitimate target, the factory. The intent of the bombing was not to kill or injure civilians. To hold otherwise, that no objective is a lawful target if civilians might be killed within that objective, would preclude virtually all military targeting. Not a bad thing, perhaps, but the end of military targeting in armed conflicts is unlikely.

Can enemy civilians be targeted because they are contributing to their state's war effort by, say, working in a defense department office as contract officers for the armed forces? Although this anticipates the discussion of targeting (Chapters 13 and 15), the answer is no. Such a civilian is not a lawful target. To target her purposely would violate distinction and be a grave breach, as well.[10] The defense department office in which she works is a lawful target, but she is not.

SIDEBAR. In 1932, a well-to-do young American originally from La Jolla, California, Peter Ortiz, joined the French Foreign Legion and became a paratrooper. For five years Ortiz fought Berbers in the Moroccan desert and rose to the grade of sergeant. His enlistment completed, he returned to California, but, when World War II broke out in Europe, he returned to the Foreign Legion. He rose to the grade of lieutenant and fought the Nazis for two years, once being severely wounded. He was captured, as well, but escaped. When America entered the war, Ortiz returned to the United States and enlisted in the U.S. Marine Corps. Soon commissioned, he was seconded to the Office of Strategic Services (OSS) and several times parachuted into France to lead OSS teams. He was once captured by American soldiers, who at first refused to believe his U.S. identity. Ortiz knew the requirement of distinction. On his missions in occupied

---

[8] Id., at 598. Distinction should not be confused with discrimination. 1949 Geneva Convention IV, Article 13, for example, prohibits actions based on "adverse *distinction* based ... on race, nationality, religion or political opinion." Emphasis supplied.

[9] Guénaël Mettraux, *International Crimes and the Ad Hoc Tribunals* (Oxford: Oxford University Press, 2005), 120, citing *Prosecutor v. Galić*, IT-98-29-T (Dec. 5, 2003).

[10] Additional Protocol I, Article 85.3: "In addition to the grave breaches defined in Article 11, the following acts shall be regarded as grave breaches of this Protocol, when committed wilfully ... (a) making the civilian population or individual civilians the object of attack."

France, he usually wore a full Marine Corps uniform, including khaki shirt, tie, and blouse complete with U.S. insignia, under an overcoat, even while in combat against the Nazis. "Ortiz, who knew not fear, did not hesitate to wear his U.S. Marine Captain's uniform in town and country alike; this cheered the French but alerted the Germans, and the mission was constantly on the move."[11] Eventually, Major Ortiz was awarded two Navy Crosses, two Purple Hearts, the British Order of the British Empire, and numerous French decorations. He left active service as a colonel. The 1947 movie 13 *Rue Madeleine*, was a fictionalized account of his OSS activities in France.[12]

The combatant's task of distinction is no easier today than it was before Additional Protocol I raised the concept from customary law to treaty law. Early in the common Article 2 international conflict phase of the united States–Iraq war, a U.S. Army major defending a motorized convoy was heard to say, "The first day that I had seen the enemy and I realized we were fighting a different force. They weren't in uniform. They were civilian individuals that were running around with weapons, people dressed as civilians that were engaging our forces from that site."[13] The United States had seen unlawful combatants before, but, in Iraq and Afghanistan, terrorist fighters made their disregard of distinction a hallmark of the conflicts.

> The traditional laws of war rely on the ability and willingness of the contending parties to distinguish between civilian and combatants, and between military and non-military targets. During internal armed conflict, however, such clear distinctions may be impossible. Insurgents, often bereft of the military hardware and manpower available to government forces, frequently feel compelled to resort to guerrilla warfare and indiscriminate attacks.[14]

Despite frequent disregard of the concept by insurgents and other nonstate actors, distinction is embedded in virtually all aspects of LOAC and IHL. It applies in all types of conflicts, including guerrilla warfare and insurgencies.[15] Also inherent in distinction "is a duty to take reasonable steps to determine whether or not a person or object is a legitimate target."[16]

Distinction, as described in Protocol I's Article 48, is related to Protocol I's Article 44.3 (discussed in Chapter 4, Section 4.2.1.3.2). As Article 48 does, Article 44.3 requires combatants to distinguish themselves from the civilian population by wearing a uniform or distinguishing sign: "In order to promote the protection of the civilian population from the effects of hostilities, combatants are obliged to distinguish themselves from the civilian population." The difference between the two articles is that Article 48 is the basic rule of distinction, whereas the admonition of Article 44.3 is a minimalist interpretation, *sub silentio* directed to irregular forces who may be granted prisoner of war

---

[11] Capt. M. R. D. Foote, *SOE in France* (London: HMSO, 1966), 357. This text is the official history of the Special Operations Executive's missions in France during World War II.

[12] Ortiz file, Marine Corps History Division, Research Branch, Marine Corps Base, Quantico, VA.

[13] Michael R. Gordon and Gen. Bernard E. Trainor, *Cobra II* (New York: Pantheon, 2006), 208.

[14] Lindsay Moir, *The Law of Internal Armed Conflict* (New York: Cambridge University Press, 2002), 2–3.

[15] H. P. Glasser, "Prohibition of Terrorist Acts in International Humanitarian Law," *Int'l Rev. of the Red Cross* (1986), 200.

[16] Christopher Greenwood, "Customary Law Status of the 1977 Geneva Protocols," in Delissen and Tanja, *Humanitarian Law of Armed Conflict Challenges Ahead*, supra, note 6, at 109.

(POW) status. Article 48 is an outward-looking obligation – combatants are admonished to take care not to harm noncombatants – whereas Article 44.3 is an inward-looking responsibility – irregular combatants are admonished to differentiate themselves so they may be seen to be combatants. Both are intended to protect noncombatants.

> A classic example of the need to carry this principle [of distinction] over to the MOOTW [military operations other than war] environment was Somalia [1993]. Faced with a hostile force that was virtually indistinguishable from the local civilian population, United States forces continued to attempt to make distinctions between lawful and unlawful targets based on the distinguishing factors available, which often amounted to little more than identifying a hostile act directed towards United States forces. . . . Even if the conflict had amounted to an international armed conflict triggering the full body of the law of war, these adversaries would never have technically qualified for prisoner of war status upon capture. . . . The United States forces, however, did not use this fact to reject the imperative of attempting to make the critical distinction between "combatant" and "non-combatant." This is the essence of the principle of distinction, a principle that must always form the foundation of the war-fighter's decision-making process.[17]

One Somalia operation involved an effort to capture top lieutenants of a Somali warlord who was disrupting efforts to provide humanitarian assistance to Somali civilians. When two U.S. Army helicopters involved in the operation were shot down, a rescue effort into central Mogadishu became a two-day running battle with ununiformed Somalis. The failure of distinction was the rule, not the exception. The book *Black Hawk Down* describes the event:

> Closer to the wrecked helicopter, a woman kept running out into the alley, screaming and pointing toward the house . . . where many of the [U.S.] wounded had been moved. No one shot at her. She was unarmed. But every time she stepped back behind cover a wicked torrent of fire would be unleashed where she pointed. After she'd done this twice, one of the D-boys [U.S. Delta Force soldiers] said, "If that bitch comes back, I'm going to shoot her." Captain Coultrop nodded his approval. She did, and the D-boy shot her down in the street.[18]

In another instance, "A woman in a flowing purple robe darted past on the driver's side of the truck. Maddox had his pistol resting on his left arm. . . . 'Don't shoot,' Spalding shouted. 'She's got a kid!' The woman abruptly turned. Holding the baby in one arm, she raised a pistol with her free hand. Spalding shot her where she stood. He shot four more rounds into her before she fell. He hoped he hadn't hit the baby."

[handwritten margin note: not violations]

Presuming the accuracy of these accounts, were they violations of distinction? Were they grave breaches? No, they were not. Additional Protocol I, Article 51.3, states, "Civilians shall enjoy the protection afforded by this Section, unless and for such time as they take a direct part in hostilities." Acting as a spotter for enemy combatants, and aiming a weapon at an opposing combatant, are clear instances of taking "a direct part in hostilities." Tragedy often surrounds the breakdown of distinction. An Israeli soldier speaks:

> Maybe I'll tell you a story. A car came towards us, in the middle of the [Lebanese] war, without a white flag. Five minutes before another car had come, and there were four

---

[17] Major Geoffrey Corn, "International and Operational Law Notes; Principle 2: Distinction," *Army Lawyer* (Aug. 1998), 35, 38.
[18] Mark Bowden, *Black Hawk Down* (New York: Atlantic Monthly Press, 1999), 217.

Palestinians with RPGs [rocket-propelled grenades] in it – killed three of my friends. So this new Peugeot comes toward us, and we shoot. And there was a family there – three children. And I cried, but I couldn't take the chance. It's a real problem ... children, father, mother. All the family was killed, but we couldn't take the chance.[19]

Was this a violation of distinction and a grave breach, or was it a reasonable mistake in the exercise of lawful self-defense? If you were the Israeli soldier's commanding officer, would you have brought charges against him?

On today's battlefields, combatants must sometimes make hard decisions instantaneously. Their decisions do not always cut against distinction and noncombatants. In 2002, in an operation in Afghanistan's high mountains, during the common Article 2 phase of the U.S.–Afghan conflict, a U.S. soldier in a vital hidden observation post was approached by an Afghan goat herder. If the civilian saw the soldier he would surely communicate the soldier's presence to the nearby Taliban. "His mind raced through his options if the goatherd stumbled upon him. He couldn't think of many. There was no way he would shoot an unarmed civilian, and if he took the man prisoner, his family would probably come looking for him within twenty-four hours. [His] only course of action would be to let the man go and immediately call back ... the news that his team had been compromised."[20] Ultimately, the soldier was not seen and his observation post remained intact and effective. Had the approaching Afghan been an enemy fighter, the soldier would have killed him. Distinguishing the unarmed civilian from a combatant despite his lack of distinguishing sign enabled the Afghan to live and the soldier to carry out his mission.

The concept of distinction is related to Protocol I, Article 51.2, which prohibits terror attacks, such as World War II "area bombing" that was employed by both sides, including the Japanese.[21] The victims were predominantly civilian. Article 51.2 reads: "The civilian population as such, as well as individual civilians, shall not be the object of attack. Acts or threats of violence the primary purpose of which is to spread terror among the civilian population are prohibited." The ICRC notes that "Article 51 is one of the most important articles in the Protocol. It explicitly confirms the customary rule that innocent civilians must be kept outside hostilities as far as possible."[22] They are kept outside hostilities through the exercise of distinction.

The Army Air Force general Curtis LeMay, commander of the World War II Pacific theater bombers that fire-bombed Japanese cities, reportedly said, "I suppose if I had lost the war, I would have been tried as a war criminal."[23] Brigadier General Telford Taylor, deputy chief counsel at the Nuremberg International Military Tribunal, and later a

---

[19] Lt. Col. Dave Grossman, *On Killing* (Boston: Little, Brown, 1995), 199, citing Gwynne Dyer, *War* (London: Guild, 1985).

[20] Sean Naylor, *Not a Good Day to Die* (New York: Berkley Books, 2005), 168.

[21] "The Japanese pioneered the strategy of war against a civilian populace that came to be used by all nations in the Second World War. ... [They] used the powerful new weapon of air power, as in the sustained saturation bombing of Chungking." I. C. B. Dear, ed., *The Oxford Companion to the Second World War* (Oxford: Oxford University Press, 1995), 212. The Japanese also sent thousands of wind-borne antipersonnel bombs tethered to 29.5 foot diameter balloons from the home islands across the Pacific to the United States, resulting in the deaths of six U.S. noncombatants. Robert C. Mikesh, *Japan's World War II Balloon Bomb Attacks on North America* (Washington, DC: Smithsonian Institution Press, 1972).

[22] Protocols *Commentary*, supra, note 4, at 615.

[23] Victor Davis Hanson, "The Right Man," in Robert Cowley, ed., *No End Save Victory* (New York: Putnam, 2001), 638, 647.

Columbia Law School professor, wrote, "The great air raids of the war – Hamburg, Berlin, Dresden, Tokyo, Hiroshima, and Nagasaki – had been conducted by the British and the United States, which made it most unlikely that the [Nuremberg] prosecution would make a big thing out of the German's earlier raids which, destructive as they were, paled by comparison."[24] A British general writes of World War II, "The paradigm of interstate industrial war took the people as its target. This was not war amongst the people of later times – this was war against the people. From the Holocaust, which declared a group of civilians as a target, to the Blitz, to the strategic bombing of Germany and Japan, and finally the atomic bomb, the Second World War removed forever the sanctity of the non-combatant."[25] Ideally it did not. Since World War II, IHL has emerged and LOAC continues to mature. The choices and imperatives for combatants are more humane, and more difficult, than in World War II. Strategic leaders in that war sometimes disregarded distinction. Today, that is not a combatant's option.

7.1.1 *The Al Firdos Bunker*

In Gulf War I, Desert Storm/Desert Shield (1991), the bombing of the Al Firdos bunker raised issues of distinction. The city-block-square bunker, sometimes referred to as the Amariyah, or Al-'Amariyah shelter, was located in the Amariyah suburb of southwest Baghdad. It was built in the early 1980s by Finnish contractors and was renovated in 1985. During the Iran–Iraq War (1980–6), it was used as a civilian air raid shelter, but by 1991 the multilevel bunker was camouflaged, guarded, surrounded by barbed wire, and, according to a spy who was an official in Saddam Hussein's government, one level of the bunker was used by the Mukhabarat, the Ba'ath Party's secret police, and another level as a military command and control center.[26] On February 5, signals intelligence revealed command and control radio traffic emanating from the bunker, beside which military vehicles were regularly parked. The Al Firdos bunker was added to the U.S. Air Force's Master Attack Plan.

Although 3,263 reconnaissance sorties were flown during the war and its run-up, including daylight satellite coverage of the bunker, it was not detected that, each night, the wives and children of the secret police sheltered from U.S. air raids in the bunker's basement.[27] On the night of February 12–13, 1991, at 0430 local, two F-117s each dropped a two-thousand-pound GBU-27 laser-guided delay-fused bomb, each bomb slicing through the ten-foot-thick hardened roof of the Al Firdos bunker.

The next morning, CNN televised rescuers as they removed 204 bodies, most of them civilians, many of them children, from the ruins of the shelter. "Without doubt U.S. intelligence erred, grievously, in failing to detect the presence of so many civilians. ... The horrific scenes from Amariyah, televised around the world, provided Saddam with an immense propaganda victory."[28] In future months, any air strike proposed for

---

[24] Telford Taylor, *The Anatomy of the Nuremberg Trials* (New York: Knopf, 1992), 326.

[25] Gen. Rupert Smith, *The Utility of Force* (New York: Knopf, 2007), 142.

[26] U.S. Dept. of Defense, *Conduct of the Persian Gulf War* (Washington, DC: GPO, 1992), Appendix O, at 615.

[27] Michael W. Lewis, "The Law of Aerial Bombardment in the 1991 Gulf War," 97–3 *AJIL* (July 2003), 481, 502–4; and Rick Atkinson, *Crusade* (Boston: Houghton Mifflin, 1993), 275–7, 285–6.

[28] Id., Atkinson, *Crusade*, at 287, 288.

Baghdad – and they dwindled dramatically in number – was personally reviewed and approved both by the chairman of the Joint Chiefs, General Colin Powell, and, in Riyadh, by General Norman Schwarzkopf, the Allied coalition's commander.

Was the bombing of the Al Firdos bunker a violation of distinction, or was it a lawful military objective? Were civilians targeted? Were the victims effectively human shields? Was the United States reckless in its targeting? If a party to a conflict places its citizens in positions of danger through failure to separate military and civilian activities, does that party bear responsibility for the consequences?

The International Criminal Tribunal for the Former Yugoslavia (ICTY) has held that, to constitute a violation of distinction, the act must have been committed willfully, "intentionally in the knowledge ... that civilians or civilian property were being targeted."[29] The term "willfully" incorporates recklessness, but excludes simple negligence. Thus, an accused who recklessly attacks civilians or civilian objects acts willfully,[30] and the presence of individual combatants in the midst of a civilian population does not change the civilian character of that population.[31]

Still, distinction is not an absolute. "Civilians may be put at risk by attacks on military targets, as by attacks on terrorist targets, but the risk must be kept to a minimum, even at some cost to the attackers."[32] The bombing of the Al Firdos bunker was not a war crime.

Nuclear weapons are not specifically addressed by the Geneva Conventions of the Additional Protocols. Nor are they considered in the ICRC's study of *Customary International Humanitarian Law*. Would the use of nuclear weapons be a violation of LOAC/IHL? A response, although not a dispositive answer, to that question is found in a 1997 writing by the Principal deputy legal adviser of the U.S. Department of State. The edited article is found in this chapter's Cases and Materials.

7.2 Military Necessity

Francis Lieber, in what some consider his "greatest theoretical contribution to the modern law of war,"[33] defined military necessity in Article 14 of his 1863 code. Drawing upon his knowledge of *jus in bello* principles and his own battlefield experience, Lieber wrote, "Military necessity, as understood by modern civilized nations, consists in the necessity of those measures which are indispensable for securing the ends of the war, and which are lawful according to the modern law and usages of war."[34] No more force or greater violence should be used to carry out a military operation than is necessary in the circumstances.[35] "IHL is a compromise between humanity and military necessity, a compromise which cannot always satisfy humanitarian agendas, but which has the immense advantage that it has been accepted by states as law that can be respected, even in war."[36]

---

[29] *Prosecutor v. Blaškić*, IT-95-14-T (3 March 2000), at para. 180.   [30] *Galić*, supra, note 9, at para. 54.

[31] Id., at para. 50.

[32] Michael Walzer, *Arguing about War* (New Haven, CT: Yale University Press, 2004), 61.

[33] Burris M. Carnahan, "Lincoln, Lieber and the Laws of War: The Origins and Limits of the Principle of Military Necessity," 2 AJIL (1998), 213.

[34] U.S. War Department, General Orders No. 100, Apr. 24, 1863. Hereafter, "Lieber Code."

[35] Frederic de Mulinen, *Handbook of the Law of War for Armed Forces* (Geneva: ICRC, 1987), para. 352.

[36] Marco Sassòli, "The Implementation of International Humanitarian Law: Current and Inherent Challenges," in Timothy L. H. McCormack, ed., *Y.B. of Int'l Humanitarian L.* (The Hague: Asser Press, 2009), 45, 50.

Military necessity is not codified in the 1949 Geneva conventions or in Additional Protocol I. It does appear in 1907 Hague Regulation IV, Article 23(g), and it may be the basis of an International Criminal Court (ICC) war crime charge.[37] Its status as customary law is indicated by the International Law Commission's statement that it is one of the "obligations arising out of a peremptory norm of international law, i.e., a norm from which no derogation is permitted."[38]

The United States follows Lieber's lead in describing the concept: "**Military necessity … has been defined as that principle which justifies those measures not forbidden by international law which are indispensable for securing the complete submission of the enemy as soon as possible**," cautioning, "Military necessity has been generally rejected as a defense for acts forbidden by the customary and conventional laws of war."[39] Napoleon reportedly said, "My great maxim has always been, in politics and war alike, that every injury done to the enemy, even though permitted by the rules, is excusable only so far as it is absolutely necessary; everything beyond that is criminal."[40] His words articulate military necessity.

The international law concept of necessity should not be confused with military necessity. In international law, "necessity" is usually applicable when action is necessary for the security or safety of the state – a form of self-preservation.[41]

The post–World War II "*Hostage case*," in which senior Nazi officers were tried, summarized military necessity in the context of belligerent occupation:

> Military necessity permits a belligerent, subject to the laws of war, to apply any amount and kind of force to compel the complete submission of the enemy with the least possible expenditure of time, life and money. In general, it sanctions measures by an occupant necessary to protect the safety of his forces and to facilitate the success of his operations. It permits the destruction of life of armed enemies and other persons whose destruction is incidentally unavoidable by the armed conflicts of the war … but it does not permit the killing of innocent inhabitants for purposes of revenge or the satisfaction of a lust to kill. The destruction of property to be lawful must be imperatively demanded by the necessities of war. Destruction as an end in itself is a violation of international law. There must be some reasonable connection between the destruction of property and the overcoming of the enemy forces. It is lawful to destroy railways, lines of communication, or any other property that might be utilized by the enemy. Private homes and churches may even be destroyed if necessary for military operations.[42]

In practice, military necessity is inextricably linked to two other core principles, unnecessary suffering and proportionality. It is, then, a broad formulation, what the law professor Alan Dershowitz has called, "the most lawless of legal doctrines."[43] A state may do

---

[37] International Criminal Court (ICC) Statute, Art. 8(2) (b) (xiii) – Destroying or seizing the enemy's property unless such destruction or seizure be imperatively demanded by the necessities of war.

[38] Protocols *Commentary*, supra, note 4, at 392, citing *Y.B. Int'l L. Comm'n* (1980), Vol. II, part two, p. 50, para. 37.

[39] Dept. of the Army, Field Manual 27–10, *The Law of Land Warfare* (Washington, DC: GPO, 1956), para. 3. a., at 4. Bolding supplied.

[40] Geoffrey F. A. Best, *War and Law since 1945* (Oxford: Clarendon Press, 1994), 242, citing 7 Max Huber, *Zeitschrift für Volkerrecht* (1913), 353.

[41] Ian Brownlie, *International Law and the Use of Force by States* (Oxford: Clarendon Press, 1963), 42.

[42] *United States v. Wilhelm List, et al.* ("The Hostage Case") (1948), XI TWC 1253–54.

[43] Alan M. Dershowitz, *Shouting Fire* (New York: Little, Brown, 2002), 473.

anything that is not unlawful to defeat the enemy. "In its broad sense, military necessity means 'doing what is necessary to achieve a war aim'. . . . [It] acknowledges the potential for unavoidable civilian death and injury ancillary to the conduct of legitimate military operations. However, as noted in *The Hostage Case* judgment, this principle requires that destroying a particular military objective will provide some type of advantage in weakening the enemy military forces."[44] The ICRC warns, however, that "military necessity covers only measures that are lawful in accordance with the laws and customs of war."[45] Military necessity does not mean doing "whatever it takes," because "whatever it takes" could easily include unlawful actions in the name of, for example, successfully accomplishing a mission, or capturing a prisoner, or retrieving a comrade held prisoner. A military mind-set of "whatever it takes" can give entrée to actions unrestrained by either law or wisdom. "If military necessity were to prevail completely, no limitation of any kind would have been imposed on the freedom of action of belligerent States. . . . Conversely, if benevolent humanitarianism were the only beacon to guide the path of armed forces, war would have entailed no bloodshed, no destruction and no human suffering . . . In actuality, [LOAC] takes a middle road."[46] Military necessity, although mentioned in all four 1949 Geneva conventions, as well as both 1977 additional protocols,[47] is undefined in those foundational treaties. The concept is uncodified customary law, but is no less enforceable for its customary nature. The ICC specifically provides for prosecution of violations of military necessity, as does the ICTY.[48]

In his code, Lieber illustrates the principle. "Military necessity admits of all direct destruction of life or limb of armed enemies, and of other persons whose destruction is incidentally unavoidable. . . . it allows of all destruction of property . . . and of all withholding of sustenance of means of life from the enemy."[49] Noting the impermissible, Lieber continues, "Military necessity does not admit of cruelty . . . nor of maiming or wounding except in fight, nor of torture to extort confessions . . . and, in general, military necessity does not include any act of hostility which makes the return to peace unnecessarily difficult."[50] Military necessity is an attempt to realize the purpose of armed conflict, gaining military advantage, while minimizing human suffering and physical destruction; it is battlefield violence counterbalanced by humanitarian considerations.

It was not always so. Versions of what might be called military necessity existed before General Order 100, but were not codified or clearly articulated. In the seventeenth century, Grotius wrote, "All engagements, which are of no use for obtaining a right or putting an end to war, but have as their purpose a mere display of strength . . .

---

[44] *Galić*, supra, note 9, at fn. 76.

[45] Knut Dörmann, *Elements of War Crimes under the Rome Statute of the International Criminal Court* (Cambridge: ICRC/Cambridge University Press, 2003), 81.

[46] Yoram Dinstein, *The Conduct of Hostilities under the Law of International Armed Conflict* (New York: Cambridge University Press, 2004), 16–17.

[47] Military necessity is mentioned in GCI Arts. 8, 30, 33, 34, and 50; GC II Arts. 8, 28, and 51; GC III Arts. 8, 76, 126, and 130; GC IV Arts. 9, 49, 53, 55, 108, 112, 143, and 147; Protocol I Arts. 54, 62, 67, and 71; Protocol II Art. 17; and 1907 HR IV, Art. 23(g).

[48] Statute of the Court, Arts. 8 (2) (a) (iv), Intentionally launching an attack knowing it will cause excessive death and damage; and, Art. 8 (2) (b) (xiii), Destroying or seizing enemy property.

[49] Lieber Code, supra, note 34, at Art. 15.   [50] Id., Art. 16.

are incompatible both with the duty of a Christian and with humanity itself."[51] In the Middle Ages, "though a captor might ... have obligations to pay shares on a ransom to others, his right to payment [of ransom] from the prisoner was as absolute as a right to such property as a fief."[52] As late as 1814, Chief Justice John Marshall noted, "That war gives to the sovereign full rights to take the persons and confiscate the property of the enemy wherever found, is conceded."[53] "That the property might have no military significance was irrelevant. Military necessity was not a legal prerequisite to visiting indiscriminate destruction on the unarmed subjects of an enemy state. ... The unfettered discretion to enjoy enemy property, and to 'take' noncombatant enemy nationals, was put to rest by Lieber's doctrine of military necessity."[54]

Lieber's embrace of the then-nebulous concept raised military necessity to a general legal principle and a commander's requirement. When it was implicitly embodied in the 1868 St. Petersburg Declaration banning small-caliber explosive bullets because they caused unnecessary suffering without military necessity, it attained international recognition.[55] Lieber's code influenced the 1899 and 1907 Hague Peace Conferences and Hague Regulation IV,[56] still in effect as a LOAC/IHL foundation.

Before the 1949 conventions, on October 18, 1942, Adolf Hitler secretly issued what is referred to as the *Kommando Befehl*, or Commando Order. It directed that captured Allied commandos be refused quarter and be summarily executed.[57] The greater part of this flagrantly unlawful order "was devoted to a lengthy demonstration of how necessary the policy was from a military point of view: sabotage bands were apt to cause great damage ... the only effective method of fighting the bands was to slaughter them. ... The suggestion of 'banditry' ... merely served, internally, to salve the consciences of those who would be charged with execution of the directive."[58] The postwar tribunal that tried senior Nazi officers who enforced the Commando Order wrote:

> It has been the viewpoint of many German writers and to a certain extent has been contended in this case that military necessity includes the right to do anything that contributes to the winning of a war. We content ourselves on this subject with stating that such a view would eliminate all humanity and decency and all law from the

---

[51] Hugo Grotius, *De Jure Belli Ac Pacis*, Vol. 2, Francis W. Kelsey, trans. (Buffalo, NY: William Hein reprint, 1995), book III, chapter XI, XIX, at 743–4.

[52] M. H. Keen, *The Laws of War in the Middle Ages* (London: Routledge & Kegan Paul, 1965), 159.

[53] *Brown v. United States*, 12 U.S. (8 Cranch) 110, 122–3 (1814).

[54] Carnahan, "Lincoln, Lieber and the Laws of War," supra, note 33, at 217.

[55] *Declaration Renouncing the Use, in Time of War, of Explosive Projectiles under 400 Grammes Weight*, Nov. 29/Dec. 11, 1868. The declaration adopts military necessity when it notes, "The only legitimate object which states should endeavor to accomplish during war is to weaken the military forces of the enemy."

[56] Hague Convention No. IV, Respecting the Laws and Customs of War on Land, 18 Oct., 1907, Art. 22, reads in part, "The right of belligerents to adopt means of injuring the enemy is not unlimited."

[57] From the Commando Order: "3. From now on all enemies on so-called commando missions in Europe or Africa challenged by German troops, even if they are to all appearance soldiers in uniform or demolition troops, whether armed or unarmed, in battle or in flight, are to be slaughtered to the last man. ... Even if these individuals, when found, should apparently be prepared to give themselves up, no pardon is to be granted them on principle." *United States v. von Leeb*, "The High Command Case" XI *TWC* (Washington, DC: GPO, 1950), 526.

[58] Frits Kalshoven, *Belligerent Reprisals*, 2d ed. (Leiden: Martinus Nijhoff, 2005), 192–3.

conduct of war and it is a contention which this Tribunal repudiates as contrary to the accepted usages of civilized nations.[59]

To suggest that in combat "anything goes" has long been an uninformed belief. Even in cases of potential self-preservation, military necessity may not be invoked to commit a grave breach of the law of war.[60]

The sixth-century Abbey of Monte Cassino was the cradle of the Benedictine monastic order. It stood on Cassino Ridge, overlooking Italy's Liri Valley. In World War II, in February 1944, the fortified town below the abbey, Cassino, was a key part of the Nazi's Gustav Line, barring the U.S. lieutenant general Mark Clark's 5th Army from advancing to Rome. Indian troops of Lieutenant General Bernard Freyberg's New Zealand Corps were directed to attack the town of Cassino. Fearing that German troops were observing from the abbey, and would direct artillery fire on them, they requested that the abbey be bombed. The abbey had been stormed by the Lombards in 589, the Saracens in 884, the Normans in 1030, and the French in 1799, but it still stood. Its architecture was historic. General Clark resisted ordering bombing, not because of the abbey's history, or its religious importance, but because he knew that if bombed, its ruins would make it an ideal Nazi defensive position. In fact, the Nazis had promised the Vatican that they would not use the abbey, and they did not. Clark's hand was forced, however, by Freyberg, who was supported by the British general Harold Alexander, Clark's superior.

The abbey, occupied only by monks and civilians, was bombed to rubble. Not a single Nazi soldier was killed, as none was in or near the abbey. Pope Pius XII's secretary of state, Cardinal Luigi Maglione, called the bombing "a piece of gross stupidity."[61] As General Clark foresaw, the abbey's remains were occupied by German forces, who put them to expert use as a defensive position.[62] The Germans beat back all Allied attacks until, after more than three months and thirty-five hundred Allied casualties, they withdrew of their own accord.

Was the bombing of this historic religious site a violation of military necessity? Of distinction? Of proportionality? Of all three? Was it only a commander's mistaken tactical judgment,[63] or was it "one of the most inexcusable bombings of the war"?[64] As will be explained, had General Freyberg been tried by a neutral tribunal, he likely would have been acquitted.

During the U.S. Civil War, Confederate cotton crops were destroyed, not because of their direct military value to the enemy but because, in an area with little manufacturing capability, the sale of cotton financed the Confederate purchase of arms and other war materiel. As much on the basis of political considerations as military, the Union viewed it

[59] "High Command Case," supra, note 57, at 541.
[60] FM 27–10, *Law of Land Warfare*, supra, note 39, at para. 85: "It is likewise unlawful for a commander to kill his prisoners on grounds of self-preservation, even in the case of airborne or commando operations, although the . . . operation may make necessary rigorous supervision of and restraint upon the movement of prisoners of war." The British LOAC manual is in agreement. United Kingdom MOD, *Manual of the Law of Armed Conflict*, supra, note 1, para. 8.32.1, at 156.
[61] David Hapgood and David Richardson, *Monte Cassino* (New York: Congdon & Weed, 1984), 227.
[62] Correlli Barnett, ed., *Hitler's Generals* (London: Weidenfeld & Nicolson, 1989), 248.
[63] Maj. Gen. A. V. P. Rogers, *Law on the Battlefield*, 2d ed. (Manchester: Juris, 2004), 93–4, suggesting that the abbey was a legitimate military objective.
[64] Williamson Murray and Allan R. Millett, *A War to Be Won* (Cambridge, MA: Belknap Press of Harvard University Press, 2000), 383.

as a military necessity to attack the enemy's economic infrastructure. Seventy-five years later, the implications of that view were seen in strategic bombing.

In the Korean War (1950–3), North Korean irrigation dams initially were restricted bombing targets. When truce negotiations stalled, however, it was then considered a military necessity to target dams whose destruction would cut communication lines – and encourage a resumption of truce talks. The political aspect of this strategic decision is apparent. In the United States–Vietnam War (1965–73), bombing targets in and near Hanoi were restricted until 1972, when peace talks stalled. The United States decided that military necessity called for reconsideration, and targets in Hanoi and Haiphong were bombed,[65] forwarding U.S. political objectives, as well as achieving tactical goals.

In the French–Algerian War (1954–62), terrorist attacks were met with France's *guerre revolutionnaire* – effective, but ruthlessly brutal. General Jacques Massu remains notorious for his victory in Algiers, gained through the use of torture, murder, and disappearances. General Paul Aussaresses, Massu's intelligence chief, was convicted of minor offenses in French civil court in 2002, the statute of limitations having run for the murder and torture that he freely admitted in a book. "Sometimes I captured high-ranking FLN (National Liberation Front) guys and I said to myself: 'That one's dangerous; he has to be killed.' And I did it":[66] military necessity as interpreted by one officer.

Enemy oil wells are usually legitimate targets. In 1991, during the Gulf War, retreating Iraqi forces set ablaze more than six hundred Kuwaiti oil wells that remained afire for months, creating serious environmental damage, but little tactical impediment.[67] Because the wells were located in an occupied country being evacuated by the defeated Iraqis, "their systematic destruction – which could not possibly affect the progress of the war – did not offer a definite military advantage"[68] and there was no military necessity for sabotaging the wells.

Military necessity is relevant to the development of weaponry. Depleted uranium, 1.7 times as dense as lead, is used primarily in an antiarmor role. Although only mildly radioactive, at impact depleted uranium burns off in a fine spray of dust, with potentially grave health effects on both combatants and noncombatants in the vicinity of the spent round (e.g., children, who may play inside a tank destroyed by a depleted uranium round). A legal review of the munition conducted for compliance with Geneva requirements found "that any hazards that do exist are far outweighed by the military usefulness of the substance."[69] Military necessity trumps the modest health risks to civilians. This outcome also illustrates the relationship of military necessity to unnecessary suffering and proportionality.

Military necessity also bears on force protection and rules of engagement, in that force protection is often considered a military necessity. Well before the U.S. armed conflicts in Afghanistan and Iraq, the then-major, now-professor Geoffrey Corn wrote:

---

[65] Carnahan, "Lincoln, Lieber and the Laws of War," supra, note 33, at 224–5.

[66] Lara Marlowe, "French Generals Admit Hand in Algeria Killings," *Irish Times*, Nov. 23, 2000, 1.

[67] Adam Roberts, "Environmental Issues in International Armed Conflict: The Experiences of the 1991 Gulf War," 69 *Int'l. L. Studies* (1996), 222, 247.

[68] Dinstein, *Conduct of Hostilities*, supra, note 46, at 192.

[69] Judith Gardam, *Necessity, Proportionality and the Use of Force by States* (New York: Cambridge University Press, 2004), 71–2.

Military necessity does not justify all actions that arguably enhance force protection. The customary international law prohibitions against state practiced murder; torture; cruel, inhumane, or degrading treatment; and prolonged arbitrary detention serve as limitations to what military necessity may justify. ... To illustrate, the need to extract information from a local civilian for the military necessity of protecting the force does not justify subjecting that individual to torture as a means of obtaining the information. Thus, even without an "enemy" in the classic sense, the principle of military necessity remains relevant."[70]

Such admonitions regarding arbitrary detention and torture find echoes in the war against terrorism.

Can military necessity, the need to save one's own life or the lives of one's troops, be invoked to permit, say, the killing of prisoners? The 1956 U.S. Army manual on the law of land warfare makes clear that it cannot.[71] "A commander may not put his prisoners to death because their presence retards his movements or diminishes his power of resistance by necessitating a large guard, or by reason of their consuming supplies. ... It is likewise unlawful for a commander to kill his prisoners on grounds of self-preservation, even in the case of airborne or commando operations."[72]

In contrast, although the murder of prisoners is never justified, "application of humanitarian principles does not override the needs of practical realism. Idealism and a belief in humanitarianism must not result in an automatic rejection of military needs."[73] LOAC protects the civilian population, yet permits bombardment of a military objective containing civilians if there is reasonable evidence that the objective is sufficiently important to justify the bombing, despite the danger to civilians. "It should not be assumed, however, that humanitarian law and military requirements will necessarily be opposed to one another. On the contrary, most rules of humanitarian law reflect good military practice."[74]

The legal issue is determining what constitutes "military necessity." Sometimes, military necessity is invoked when military convenience is closer to truth. Determining what constitutes military necessity is a duty of the battlefield commander. As a starting point, the law presumes good faith on the part of the commander; that, given the information available to her at the time she made her decision, military necessity reasonably required that she take the action she did.[75] Case law clarifies that this "test" is not entirely subjective. The Supreme Court justice Robert Jackson, in his

---

[70] Major Geoffrey Corn, "International and Operational Law Note," *Army Lawyer* (July 1998), 73.

[71] There has been disagreement. Telford Taylor, *Nuremberg and Vietnam: An American Tragedy* (Chicago: Quadrangle, 1970), 36: "Small detachments on special missions, or accidentally cut off ... may take prisoners under such circumstances that men cannot be spared to guard them ... and that to take them along would greatly endanger the success of the mission or the safety of the unit. The prisoners will be killed by operation of the principle of military necessity." It is difficult to square this very surprising declaration by the former Nuremberg chief prosecutor, which is so clearly contrary to LOAC/IHL, with the principles of the judgment of the Nuremberg IMT that he was instrumental in writing.

[72] FM 27–10, *Law of Land Warfare*, supra, note 39, at para. 85. Also see Additional Protocol I, Art. 41.3, in this regard.

[73] Leslie C. Green, *The Contemporary Law of Armed Conflict*, 2d ed. (Manchester: Manchester/Juris, 2000), 353.

[74] Dieter Fleck, ed., *The Handbook of Humanitarian Law in Armed Conflicts* (Oxford: Oxford University Press, 1999), 33.

[75] Lt. Col. William J. Fenrick, Canadian Forces, "The Rule of Proportionality and Protocol I in Conventional Warfare," *Military L. Rev.* 98 (Fall 1982), 91, 126.

1944 dissenting opinion in *Korematsu v. United States*, described the difficulty of applying judicial oversight to decisions taken in combat:

> The very essence of the military job is to marshal physical force, to remove every obstacle to its effectiveness, to give it every strategic advantage. Defense measures will not, and often should not, be held within the limits that bind civil authority in peace. ... The limitation under which courts always will labor in examining the necessity for a military order are illustrated by this case. How does the Court know that these orders have a reasonable basis in necessity? ... And thus it will always be when courts try to look into the reasonableness of a military order. In the very nature of things, military decisions are not susceptible of intelligent judicial appraisal. They do not pretend to rest on evidence, but are made on information that often would not be admissible and on assumptions that could not be proved."[76]

Despite Justice Jackson's hesitancy to judge either military necessity or a commander's reasonableness in assessing it (within a year Jackson became the U.S. chief prosecutor at the Nuremberg International Military Tribunal), reasonableness does have an objective element and it again reflects the close links among the four core principles: Did the commander take reasonable steps to gather information to determine, for example, the legitimacy of the target, and that incidental damage would not be disproportionate? Did the commander act reasonably in light of the information gathered? In other words, would a reasonably prudent commander acting in conformance with LOAC/IHL, knowing what the suspect commander knew, have acted similarly in similar circumstances?

Looking to a specific illustrative situation, an ICTY opinion holds that civilian property inside enemy territory, as opposed to that in occupied territory, is not protected by the conventions and its unwarranted destruction is not subject to violation of military necessity charges.[77] Additionally, "in order to be held criminally responsible for this offense, the perpetrator ... must apparently have acted with intent to destroy the property in question or in reckless disregard for the likelihood of its destruction. It would be insufficient to establish that the destruction is accidental or the result of mere negligence."[78] Although it is an application of twenty-first-century case law to a twentieth-century event, this may explain why General Freyberg, who ordered the bombing of the Monte Cassino Abbey, would likely have been acquitted, if even tried; the abbey was in enemy territory, and his intent was to destroy an enemy position, rather than a religious site.

Latitude should also be allowed for the stresses under which commanders must sometimes act in military operations.[79] "Now, the moral point of view derives its legitimacy from the perspective of the actor. When we make moral judgments, we try to recapture that perspective."[80]

A "challenge in conflicts with nonstate actors is to identify the humanitarian limits on military necessity."[81] Military necessity makes it necessary to confine such nonstate enemy fighters to prevent them from returning to the fight, but LOAC/IHL and human

---

[76] *Korematsu v. United States*, 323 U.S. 214, 244–5 (1944). (Jackson, J., dissenting).

[77] *Prosecutor v. Kordić and Čerkez*, IT-95–14 (Feb. 26, 2001), at para. 337.

[78] Mettraux, *International Crimes and the* Ad Hoc *Tribunals*, supra, note 9, at 93.

[79] Morris Greenspan, *The Modern Law of Land Warfare* (Berkeley: University of California Press, 1959), 279.

[80] Michael Walzer, *Just and Unjust Wars*, 3d ed. (New York: Basic Books, 2000), 8.

[81] John B. Bellinger and Vijay M. Padmanabhan, "Detention Operations in Contemporary Conflicts: Four Challenges for the Geneva Conventions and Other Existing Law," 105–2 *AJIL* 201, 214 (April 2011).

rights documents pertaining to non-international armed conflict provide little guidance to the requirements and prohibitions involved in confining them. (Chapter 22 details this problem.)

In October 1944, Generaloberst Lothar Rendulic was armed forces commander North, a responsibility that included command of Nazi forces in Norway. (Between World Wars I and II, Rendulic had practiced law in his native Austria.) After World War II, he was prosecuted for, among other charges, issuing an order "for the complete destruction of all shelter and means of existence in, and the total evacuation of the entire civilian population of the northern Norwegian province of Finmark."[82] Entire villages were destroyed, bridges and highways bombed, and port installations wrecked. Tried by an American military commission, Rendulic offered a defense of military necessity. He presented evidence that the Norwegian population would not voluntarily evacuate and that rapidly approaching Russian forces would use existing housing as shelter and exploit the local population's knowledge of the area to the detriment of retreating German forces. The tribunal acquitted Rendulic of the charge, finding reasonable his belief that military necessity mandated his orders.[83] His case offers one of the few adjudicated views of what constitutes military necessity. (See Cases and Materials, this chapter.)

More recently, the ICTY has decided cases in which military necessity was a factor. In the 2006 *Rajić* case, the accused, a captain (first class) in the former Yugoslavian People's Army and prior to the war "an exemplary professional soldier,"[84] planned and ordered an attack on the lightly defended village of Stupni Do, in Bosnia-Herzegovina. "The [trial] chamber found that the evidence indicated that the village had been destroyed, that its destruction had not been necessary to fulfill any legitimate objectives, that the civilian population was the target of the attack, and that the offense appeared to have been planned in advance . . . all of which were unjustified by military necessity."[85] Thirty-seven civilians were murdered, as well. Although the absence of military necessity was only one aspect of the case, pursuant to his guilty plea, Rajić was sentenced to twelve years' confinement.

7.2.1 *Kriegsraison*

The Lieber Code, with its provisions for military necessity, was adopted by several European states, including, in 1870, Prussia. In that militaristic society, however, military necessity had already evolved into the doctrine of *Kriegsraison geht vor Kriegsrecht* – military necessity in war overrides the law of war.

Kriegsraison first appeared in late-eighteenth-century German literature. *Kriegsmanier* was the conduct of war according to the customs and laws of war; *kriegsraison*, its opposite, was the nonobservance of those customs and laws. "*Kriegsraison*' took precedence over '*Kriegsrecht*'"[86] and was endorsed by German theorists.[87] It was

---

[82] *United States v. List*, "Hostage Case," supra, note 42, at 1113.

[83] For a persuasive deconstruction of Rendulic's defense, see: Best, *War and Law since 1945*, supra, note 40, at 328–30.

[84] *Prosecutor v. Rajić*, IT-95–12-T (8 May 2006), at para. 159.

[85] Bernard H. Oxman, "International Decisions," 91–3 *AJIL* (July 1997), 518, 529.

[86] Jean Pascal Zanders, "International Norms against Chemical and Biological Warfare: An Ambiguous Legacy," 8–2 *J. of Conflict & Security L.* (Oct. 2003), 391, 401.

[87] The German professor Carl Lueder's development of the concept in the late nineteenth century is discussed in Lassa Oppenheim, ed., *The Collected Papers of John Westlake on Public International Law*

employed by a minority of German politicians and military officers from 1871 through World War II.[88] "However, it is probable that the resort to this doctrine was above all based on contempt for the law."[89] A 1915 book proposed:

> If therefore, in the following work the expression "the law of war" is used, it must be understood that by it is meant not a lex scripta introduced by international agreements, but only a reciprocity of mutual agreement. ... The danger that, in this way, [the German officer] will arrive at false views about the essential character of war must not be lost sight of. ... By steeping himself in military history an officer will be able to guard himself against excessive humanitarian notions, it will teach him that certain severities are indispensable to war, nay more, that the only true humanity very often lies in a ruthless application of them ... [and] teach him whether the governing usages of war are justified or not, whether they are to be modified or whether they are to be observed.[90]

Kriegsraison holds that military necessity overrides and renders inoperative ordinary law and the customs and usages of war; in extreme circumstances of danger, one may abandon humanitarian law in order to meet the danger.[91] "Necessity might permit a commander to ignore the laws of war when it was essential to do so to avoid defeat, to escape from extreme danger, or for the realization of the purpose of the war."[92] *Kriegsraison* grants belligerents, even individual combatants, the right to do whatever is required to prevail in armed conflict; to do whatever *they* believe is required to win. *Kriegsraison*, then, is the unlimited application of military necessity.

In disagreement, the American ethicist Michael Walzer writes, "Belligerent armies are entitled to try to win their wars, but they are not entitled to do anything that is or seems to them necessary to win. They are subject to a set of restrictions that rest in part on the agreements of states but that also have an independent foundation in moral principle."[93] Among the "agreements of states" Walzer refers to are LOAC and IHL. "Otherwise, the concept of military necessity would reduce the entire body of the laws of war to a code of military convenience."[94] Lieber, a proponent of sharp but short wars, agreed that "men who take up arms against one another in public war do not cease on this account to be moral beings, responsible to one another and to God."[95]

Necessity cannot overrule the law of war, and the phrase frequently heard in relation to the war on terror, "whatever it takes," if defined literally, is an expression of *kriegsraison* and potential unlawful overreaching. "The doctrine [of *kriegsraison*] practically is that if a belligerent deems it necessary for the success of its military operations to violate a rule of

---

(Cambridge: Cambridge University Press, 1914), 244–6. Also see T. J. Lawrence, *The Society of Nations* (New York: Oxford University Press, 1919), 104–7; and Jesse S. Reeves, "The Neutralization of Belgium and the Doctrine of Kriegsraison," XIII, No. 3 *Michigan L. Rev.* (1914–15), 179–84.

[88] William H. Downey, "The Law of War and Military Necessity," 47–2 *AJIL* (April 1953), 251, 253.

[89] Protocols *Commentary*, supra, note 4, at 391.

[90] J. H. Morgan, trans., *The German War Book* (London: John Murray, 1915), 53–5, cited in: *United States v. List*, "Hostage Case," supra, note 42, at 1255.

[91] Louise Doswald-Beck, "International Humanitarian Law and the Advisory Opinion of the International Court of Justice on the Legality of the Threat or Use of Nuclear Weapons," 316 *Int'l Rev. of the Red Cross* 33 (1997).

[92] United Kingdom MOD, *Manual of the Law of Armed Conflict*, supra, note 1, para 2.3. at 23.

[93] Walzer, *Just and Unjust Wars*, supra, note 80, at 131.

[94] Green, *Contemporary Law of Armed Conflict*, supra, note 73, at 123.

[95] Francis Lieber, *Lieber Code*, supra, note 34, at Art. 15.

international law, the violation is permissible. As the belligerent is to be the sole judge of the necessity, the doctrine is really that a belligerent may violate the law or repudiate it or ignore it whenever that is deemed to be for its military advantage."[96]

Not all Allied military commanders subscribed to the idea of limiting actions in warfare to those necessary to defeat the enemy. General George Patton wrote, "War is not a contest with gloves. It is resorted to only when laws (which are rules) have failed."[97] The World War I era British admiral John A. "Jackie" Fisher, referring to the 1907 Hague Conventions, said, "The humanizing of war! You might as well talk of the humanizing of Hell. When a silly ass got up at The Hague and talked about the amenities of civilized warfare ... as if war could be civilized. If I'm in command when war breaks out I shall issue my order – The essence of war is violence. Moderation in war is imbecility.'"[98] One doubts, however, that First Sea Lord Fisher would consider moderation to include the abrogation of the law of war.

An example of *kriegsraison* did involve World War I at sea and the killing in the water of survivors by the submarine that had torpedoed their ship. The thinking went "If we don't kill the survivors, they will be picked up soon and report our presence and recent position." At the post–World War I Leipzig trials, such a case involved two German U-boat officers, First Lieutenants Ludwig Dithmar and John Bolt. They were charged with using the German submarine U-86's deck gun to sink the lifeboats of the *Llandovery Castle*, a marked British hospital ship carrying Canadian sick and wounded sunk by the U-86. (The sub's captain had taken refuge in Danzig, then an independent state, and could not be found for trial.) A defense witness, Vice-Admiral Adolf von Trotha, former chief of staff of the German High Seas Fleet, testified that "submarine commanders were convinced that no feelings of humanity must be allowed to check their efforts."[99] Not even the tame German court would accept their assertion of *kriegsraison*. The court ruled:

> It is certainly to be urged in favor of the military subordinates, that they are under no obligation to question the order of their superior officer, and they can count upon its legality. But, no such confidence can be held to exist, if such an order is universally known to everybody, including also the accused, to be without any doubt whatever against the law. This happens only in rare and exceptional cases. But this case was precisely one of them. For in the present instance, it was perfectly clear to the accused that killing defenseless people in the lifeboats could be nothing else but a breach of law. ... They should, therefore, have refused to obey. As they did not do so they must be punished.[100]

Dithmar and Bolt were convicted and sentenced to a notably light four years confinement.

[96] Downey, "The Law of War and Military Necessity," supra, note 88, at 253.
[97] Maj. George S. Patton Jr., "The Effect of Weapons on War," *Cavalry Journal* (Nov. 1930), http://www.pattonhq.com/textfiles/effect.html.
[98] Adm. Sir R. H. Bacon, *The Life of Lord Fisher of Kilverstone – Admiral of the Fleet*, Vol. I (London: Hodder & Stoughton, 1929), 120–1.
[99] Claud Mullins, *The Leipzig Trials* (London: Witherby, 1921), 123.
[100] Quoted in *United States v. Ohlendorf and 23 others* ("The Einsatzgruppen Case"), *Trials of War Criminals before the Nuernberg Military Tribunals*, Vol. IV (Washington, DC: GPO, 1950), 484.

After World War II, a similar result was seen in 1944, when the German submarine U-852, commanded by Kapitänleutnant Heinz Eck, torpedoed and sank the Greek steamer S.S. *Peleus,* after which the sub surfaced and, despite objections by a leading noncommissioned officer, for five hours methodically machine-gunned and grenaded survivors. At his 1948 British military trial, Eck defended his actions as being an operational necessity – *kriegsraison* – to protect his boat and crew.[101] "His defence is emergency and necessity," said Eck's defense counsel.[102] Eck and two of his officers were convicted and executed by firing squad.

What is LOAC/IHL regarding survivors in the water? The Geneva Convention requires that "at all times, and particularly after an engagement, Parties to the conflict shall, without delay, take all possible measures to search for and collect the wounded and sick."[103] "Parties to conflict are under an obligation to search for the dead ... it is also affirmed with regard to the wounded and sick. ... Persons who die as a result of armed conflict often remain unaccounted for because their death is not recorded."[104]

When a submarine sinks an enemy ship, be it a merchant ship or ship of war, is that submarine required to surface and collect survivors before beginning its escape from the site of the sinking – which may have been communicated by the sinking ship? The Convention I Article reads that Parties to the conflict shall "take all possible measures." The same article continues, "Whenever circumstances permit." What measures are possible? When do circumstances permit?

A submarine is not configured to carry passengers, not equipped to treat numerous wounds of noncrew members, and not able to feed or "house" many more than its assigned crew. No submarine commander or crew member has been prosecuted for not picking up survivors in the water. They *may* do so, but are not required to do so by LOAC/IHL.

What a submarine crew clearly may not do is fire on or otherwise attack survivors in the water, under any circumstances.[105] The submarine may only depart the scene of the sinking. Is that not leaving the survivors possibly to drown? To die of thirst or hunger? To be attacked by sharks? The harsh reality is that survivors of a sinking may ultimately die in the sea. Making all the difference in the eyes of the law of war, however, the submarine's crew did not kill them. No more than a medical doctor passing the scene of a traffic accident with injured victims visible on the roadway kills those survivors of the crash. Yes, some jurisdictions have "good samaritan" laws requiring medical doctors to stop and render aid. Other jurisdictions do not. There is no good samaritan law in the law of war, particularly in the age of instant communications that can pinpoint a submarine's location for antiship missiles fired from over the horizon. There is a military necessity for the submarine to depart the scene of the sinking quickly.

---

[101] *Trial of Kapitänleutnant Heinz Eck and Four Others* ("The Peleus Trial") I *LRTWC* (London: U.N. War Crimes Commission, 1947), 1, 4.

[102] David M. Fyfe, ed., *War Crimes Trials. Vol. I. The Peleus Trial* (London: William Hodge, 1948), 102.

[103] Geneva Convention I, Art. 15. Convention II, Art. 3(2) specifically mentions those "shipwrecked"; Convention IV, Art. 16; and Protocol II, Art. 8 are to the same effect.

[104] Anna Petrig, "The War Dead and Their Gravesites," 91–874 *Int'l Rev. of the Red Cross* (June 2009), 341, 346.

[105] United Kingdom. Ministry of Defence, *Manual of the Law of Armed Conflict,* supra, note 1, para. 13.129, at 373.

Depending on the circumstances, surface ships may have differing military necessities and differing legal obligations. When circumstances permit, all possible measures must be taken to collect survivors in the water. "The wounded, sick, and shipwrecked are to be respected and protected. ... They must be treated humanely. They must be provided with medical care. ... Priority of treatment is dictated by medical reasons only. Women must be treated with respect, with due regard for their sex and no less favorably than men ... [and] protect [all survivors] against pillage and ill-treatment.[106]

In one of the post–World War II Nuremberg subsequent trials, *The Krupp Case*, the military tribunal held, "The defense has argued that the acts complained of were justified by the great emergency in which the German war economy found itself. ... The contention that the rules and customs of warfare can be violated if either party is hard pressed in war must be rejected on other grounds. War is by definition a risky and hazardous business. ... Rules and customs of warfare are designed specifically for all phases of war ... To claim they can be wantonly – and at the sole discretion of any one belligerent – disregarded when he considers his own situation to be critical, means nothing more or less than to abrogate the laws and customs of war entirely."[107]

LOAC is aware that, sometimes, military exigencies may force combatants to take actions otherwise considered violations of *jus in bello*. Examples of LOAC explicitly taking military necessity into account are numerous. In a military occupation, the destruction of private or state property is prohibited – "except where such destruction is rendered absolutely necessary by military operations."[108] An occupying force may totally evacuate an area and its occupants if "imperative military reasons so demand."[109] Military necessity may allow shipments to internees of food, clothing, and medical supplies to be limited, along with the activities of relief[110] and civil defense personnel,[111] including visits by ICRC representatives to POWs and protected persons.[112] The property of aid societies may be requisitioned by belligerents "in case of urgent necessity."[113] POW and internee correspondence may be temporarily prohibited.[114] The return of retained personnel, doctors, and chaplains to their own lines may be delayed by military requirements.[115] Hospitals, civil defense buildings, and ships' sick bays may be diverted from their medical and sheltering purposes in cases of military necessity, as long as the wounded and sick continue to receive care.[116] Military necessity even allows the destruction of things indispensable to the survival of the civilian population.[117] These allowances in the name of military necessity demonstrate that LOAC remains cognizant that military necessity sometimes requires extreme measures. In these allowances, terms like "if possible," "as far as possible," and "if urgent" introduce elements of uncertainty and risks of arbitrary conduct. Without these concessions, which take reality into account, the allowances could not have been formulated and approved in the first place.[118]

"The [*kriegsraison*] argument, first internationally criticized after the Franco-Prussian War (1870–71), is clearly obsolete. Modern LOAC takes full account of military necessity.

[106] Id.   [107] *United States v. Krupp*, IX TWC (1949), 1347.   [108] 1949 Geneva Convention IV, Art. 53.

[109] Id., Arts. 5, 49; 1977 Additional Protocol II, Art. 17.

[110] Geneva Convention IV, Art. 108; 1977 Additional Protocol I, Art. 71.3.

[111] 1977 Additional Protocol I, Art. 62.1.

[112] Geneva Conventions III and IV, Arts. 126 and 143, respectively.   [113] Geneva Convention I, Art. 34.

[114] Geneva Conventions III and IV, Arts. 76 and 112, respectively.   [115] Geneva Convention I, Art. 30.

[116] Id., Art. 33; 1977 Additional Protocol I, Art. 67.4; and GC II, Art. 28.

[117] 1977 Additional Protocol I, Art. 54.5.   [118] Protocols *Commentary*, supra, note 4, at 394.

Necessity cannot be used to justify actions prohibited by law. The means to achieve military victory are not unlimited."[119]

Consider, however, the words of the International Court of Justice. In its 1996 advisory opinion regarding nuclear weapons, it wrote:

> The threat or use of nuclear weapons would generally be contrary to the rules of international law applicable in armed conflict ... ; however, in view of the current state of international law ... the Court cannot conclude definitively whether the threat or use of nuclear weapons would be lawful or unlawful in an extreme circumstance of self-defence, in which the very survival of a State would be at stake.[120]

Professor Dinstein writes, "The last sentence is most troublesome. The linkage between the use of nuclear weapons and 'extreme circumstances ...' is hard to digest: it appears to be utterly inconsistent with the basic tenet that [LOAC] applies equally to all belligerent States, irrespective of the merits of their cause."[121] Might *kriegsraison*, in the guise of state necessity, survive when "the very survival of a state" is in the balance? As Dinstein concludes, "The Court should have come to grips with the exceptional circumstances in which recourse to nuclear weapons is legitimate. That it did not do."[122]

Like the term "state survival," the phrase "I did it to save American lives" is sometimes heard. Too often those words are raised to explain or excuse unlawful acts, including torture, wrongly seen as somehow necessary to mission accomplishment. "*Military convenience* should not be mistaken for *military necessity*."[123] Combatants cannot claim a military necessity to do "whatever it takes," either to accomplish the mission or to save American lives. *Kriegsraison* is rejected for good reason, and neither it nor military necessity is a defense to law of war violations.

7.3 Unnecessary Suffering

The core LOAC concept of unnecessary suffering, a concept applicable to combatants, rather than civilians, is codified in Additional Protocol I, Article 35.2: "**It is prohibited to employ weapons, projectiles and material and methods of warfare of a nature to cause superfluous injury or unnecessary suffering.**"[124]

What does "of a nature" mean? In warfare, what is meant by "superfluous injury"? In a battlefield context, define "unnecessary suffering." Attempts to parse such words and terms often yield only further inscrutable terms. Over the past century, however, in the experience of wars and the written opinions of difficult cases that followed them, "unnecessary suffering" has come to have a meaning that soldiers and citizens can apply.

Unnecessary suffering is mentioned by inference in the epic Sanskrit poem *Mahabharatha*, in the Code of Manu, and by Sun Tzu.[125] It finds its earliest *jus in bello*

---

[119] United Kingdom MOD, *Manual*, supra, note 1, at 23. Footnote omitted.
[120] Advisory Opinion on the *Legality of the Threat or Use of Nuclear Weapons*, [1996] *ICJ Rep.* 226.
[121] Dinstein, *Conduct of Hostilities*, supra, note 46, at 78.   [122] Id., 79.
[123] W. Hays Parks, "Special Forces' Wear of Non-Standard Uniforms," 4–2 *Chicago J of Int'l L* (Fall 2003), 493, 543. Emphasis in original.
[124] Emphasis supplied. A slightly different form of prohibition on unnecessary suffering is contained in 1969 U.N.G.A. Resolution 2444 (XXIII).
[125] Leslie C. Green, *Essays on the Modern Law of War*, 2d ed. (Ardsley, NY: Transnational, 1999), 330.

incarnation in the preamble of the 1868 St. Petersburg Declaration regarding explosive bullets. After the Brussels Conference of 1874, a declaration pertaining to the rules and customs of war was agreed.[126] The Brussels declaration was a basis of the 1899 Hague Peace Conference regulations and, in turn, 1907 Hague Regulation IV. Article 23 reads, "In addition to the prohibitions provided by special Conventions, it is especially forbidden – (e.) To employ arms, projectiles, or material calculated to cause unnecessary suffering." French is a primary language of LOAC. In the French translation of the Brussels Declaration, the term *maux superflus* is used – an expression of a sense of moral and physical suffering, lending a somewhat broader meaning to the term than "unnecessary" suffering. The French-influenced term, "superfluous injury," is a formulation sometimes encountered instead of "unnecessary suffering."

The principle of unnecessary suffering, the obverse of military necessity, is intended to constrain the suffering inflicted on opposing combatants, rather than civilians. "Warfare ... justifies subjecting an enemy to massive and decisive force, and the suffering that it brings. Military necessity justifies the infliction of suffering upon an enemy combatant. ... However ... military necessity only justifies the infliction of as much suffering as is necessary to bring about the submission of an enemy."[127] Military necessity is the balance between destruction of the enemy and humanity. But "what pain is superfluous? What pain is necessary? By what yardstick should one measure whether or not the suffering is justified?"[128] These are difficult questions for a commander.

"Destruction of the enemy" implies weapons, and it is in the area of weaponry that issues of unnecessary suffering most often arise. "[A] weapon is not banned on the ground of 'superfluous injury or unnecessary suffering' merely because it causes 'great' or even 'horrendous' suffering or injury. The effects of ... certain weapons may be repulsive, but this is not, in and of itself, enough to render these weapons illegal."[129] Banned weapons include explosive bullets, glass-filled projectiles, "dum-dum" bullets, poison and poisoned weapons, asphyxiating gases, bayonets with serrated edges – all of which increase suffering without increasing military advantage. "Perhaps one of the most significant developments with regard to actual suppression of weapons ... with a view to the reduction of unnecessary suffering, is to be found in the 1980 Convention on Prohibition or Restrictions on the Use of Certain Conventional Weapons Which May be Deemed to be Excessively Injurious or to Have Indiscriminate Effects"[130] (more usually called "the Conventional Weapons Convention," it is examined in Chapter 16).

1907 Hague Regulation IV, Article 23 (e), holds that it is especially forbidden "to employ arms, projectiles, or material calculated to cause unnecessary suffering"; 1977 Additional Protocol I, Article 36, "changed the general obligation of treaty adherence [to Hague Regulation IV] to a specific one through codification."[131] Article 36

---

[126] Henri Meyrowitz, "The Principle of Superfluous Injury or Unnecessary Suffering," 299 *Int'l Rev. of the Red Cross* (March-April 1994), 98, 100–1.

[127] Major Geoffrey Corn, "International and Operational Law Note: Principle 4: Preventing Unnecessary Suffering," *Army Lawyer* (Nov. 1998), 50.

[128] Antonio Cassese, *Violence and Law in the Modern Age*, S. J. K. Greenleaves, trans. (Princeton, NJ: Princeton University Press, 1988), 15.

[129] Dinstein, *The Conduct of Hostilities*, supra, note 46, at 59. Citations omitted.

[130] Green, *Essays on the Modern Law of War*, supra, note 125, at 365.

[131] W. Hays Parks, "Conventional Weapons and Weapons Reviews," *YIHL* (2005), 55, 57.

requires that "in the study, development, acquisition or adoption of a new weapon ... a High Contracting Party is under an obligation to determine whether its employment would ... be prohibited by this Protocol." In other words, states ratifying Protocol I are required to test and ensure that new weapons comply with the protocol's prohibition of unnecessary suffering. "This obligation applies to countries manufacturing weapons, as well as those purchasing them."[132] Nuclear weapons are not included in this requirement,[133] presumably because they could not comply with such a test. ← HELLO!

U.S. compliance with Article 36 is guided by army regulation, *Review of Legality of Weapons under International Law*.[134] Language in the army's review of the combat shotgun is instructive:

> The Combat Shotgun raises two issues with regard to legality. First, does a weapon capable of inflicting multiple wounds upon a single enemy combatant cause superfluous injury. ... Second, does the No. oo buckshot projectile ... expand or flatten easily, in violation of the Hague Declaration Concerning Expanding Bullets of 29 July 1899? ... In determining whether a weapon causes *superfluous injury*, a balancing test is applied between the force dictated by military necessity to achieve a legitimate objective vis-à-vis injury that may be considered superfluous to the achievement of the ... objective (in other words, whether the suffering caused is out of proportion to the military advantage to be gained). ... The degree of "superfluous" injury must be clearly disproportionate to the intended objective(s) for the development of the weapon (that is, the suffering must outweigh substantially the military necessity for the weapon).[135]

The test for unnecessary suffering, which reflects the consensus of many states,[136] is clearly delineated, including the intertwining of unnecessary suffering with military necessity. The description of the U.S. review process for the combat shotgun is applicable to any new weapon or ammunition. (The review goes on to find that both the shotgun and its double-aught ammunition meet the standards of Additional Protocol I.) The International Court of Justice offers that unnecessary suffering means "a harm greater than that avoidable to achieve legitimate military objectives."[137]

The language used in the review of the combat shotgun is an excellent guide, but there is no objective test, no black letter rule, to apply in determining what constitutes unnecessary suffering. Relevant factors include the inevitability of serious permanent disability and the inevitability of death.[138] Logic is not always a reliable guide: The ICRC notes "that none of the rules explicitly protects combatants from incendiary weapons such as flamethrowers or napalm. However ... these weapons should not be used in such a way that they will cause unnecessary suffering, which means in particular they should not be used against individuals without cover."[139] Individual napalm or flame-thrower targets will be killed, cover or no cover, but that does not constitute unnecessary suffering.

---

[132] Protocols *Commentary*, supra, note 4, at 426.   [133] Id., at 427.

[134] Army Regulation (AR) 27–53, *Review of Legality of Weapons under International Law*, dated Jan. 1, 1979. The AR is in compliance with DoD Instruction 5500.15, of the same title, dtd Oct. 16, 1974.

[135] W. Hays Parks, "Joint Service Combat Shotgun Program," *Army Lawyer* (Oct. 1997), 16, 18. Emphasis in original.

[136] Henckaerts and Doswald-Beck, *Customary International Humanitarian Law*, supra, note 2, at 240.

[137] Advisory Opinion on the *Legality of the Threat or Use of Nuclear Weapons*, supra, note 120, at para. 78.

[138] Henckaerts and Doswald-Beck, *Customary International Humanitarian Law*, supra, note 2, at 241.

[139] Protocols *Commentary*, supra, note 4, at 406. Citation omitted.

Unnecessary suffering cannot be measured or determined by medical means. It is impossible "to objectively define suffering or to give absolute values permitting comparisons between human individuals. Pain, for instance, which is but one of many components of suffering, is subject to enormous individual variations. . . . Likewise, general effects caused by a local injury are subject to many variables and make comparison between different individuals difficult."[140]

Determining the level of force or deciding what weapons package may be applied to an enemy unit or objective is a controversial and subjective proposition. At what point does armed force segue into unnecessary force, and who is to review a commander's determination of that issue? "But no right in war is without limit. . . . What is certain is that if applicable, the standard [employed for combatants] must be more permissive than the standard used to protect non-combatants."[141] The concept of unnecessary suffering is that standard for combatants; it is "the principle that forbids destructive acts unnecessary to secure a military advantage."[142]

Finally, there is a certain resistance to increased protections for enemy combatants. Reflecting what Best calls the "militarization of humanitarianism,"[143] weapons that have proven effective on the battlefield tend to withstand or evade humanitarian scrutiny, even if they are often harmful to noncombatants as well as combatants.[144] Flame-throwers, white phosphorus, and napalm, for example, remain lawful. Great suffering is not the measurement by which a weapon is banned; the question is whether the suffering caused is substantially disproportional to the military advantage gained.

7.4 Proportionality

In the fictional cold war–era movie *Dr. Strangelove*, the air force general Buck Turgidson urges the president of the United States to initiate a nuclear first strike against Russia. The president hesitates, saying, "'But even if we struck first we would still suffer horrible civilian casualties.' 'Well now,' Turgidson said, 'I'm not saying we wouldn't get our hair mussed, Mister President, but I do say not more than ten to twenty million dead, depending on the breaks'."[145] In real life, Professor Dinstein writes:

> The current disproportion of the civilian/combatant ration of casualties is totally unacceptable. Anyone even mildly interested in international humanitarian law must strive to bring about a better world in which civilian losses in war are minimized. Nevertheless, the realistic goal is to minimize civilian casualties, not to eliminate them altogether. There is no way to eliminate civilian deaths and injuries due to collateral damage, mistake, accident and just sheer bad luck.[146]

---

[140] Id., at 408.   [141] Id., at 52.

[142] Michael N. Schmitt, "War and the Environment: Fault Lines in the Prescriptive Landscape," in Jay E. Austin and Carl E. Bruch, eds., *The Environmental Consequences of War: Legal, Economic and Scientific Perspectives* (New York: Cambridge University Press, 2000), 101.

[143] Geoffrey Best, *Humanity in Warfare* (London: Weidenfeld and Nicolson, 1980), 172.

[144] Gardam, *Necessity, Proportionality and the Use of Force by States*, supra, note 69, at 75.

[145] Peter George, *Dr. Strangelove or: How I Learned to Stop Worrying and Love the Bomb* (New York: Barnes & Noble, 1998), 52.

[146] Yoram Dinstein, "Discussion: Reasonable Military Commanders and Reasonable Civilians," in Andru E. Wall, ed., *International Law Studies*. Vol. 78. *Legal and Ethical Lessons of NATO's Kosovo Campaign* (Newport, RI: Naval War College, 2002), 173, 219.

On the battlefield, how is a commander to balance human life against the destruction of an enemy target? How can human lives be compared to "things"? That is the terrible and impossible problem of proportionality. Hays Parks correctly writes, "by American domestic law standards, the concept of proportionality ... would be constitutionally void for vagueness."[147] The concept, originating in chivalry, is voiced in Article 22 of 1907 Hague Regulation IV: "The right of belligerents to adopt means of injuring the enemy is not unlimited." Combatants may not make war without regard to civilians and their objects.

Additional Protocol I of 1977 defines proportionality in two articles. Article 51.5(b) describes a proportionality violation as "**an attack which may be expected to cause incidental loss of civilian life, injury to civilians, damage to civilian objects, or a combination thereof, which would be excessive in relation to the concrete and direct military advantage anticipated.**" Article 57.2(b) directs that "an attack shall be cancelled or suspended if it becomes apparent that the objective is not a military one or ... that the attack may be expected to cause incidental loss of civilian life, injury to civilians, damage to civilian objects, or a combination thereof, which would be excessive in relation to the concrete and direct military advantage anticipated."

Article 51.5(b) relates to the protection of civilians generally, whereas 57.2(b) relates to precautions necessary in the attack of a military objective. The imprecise wording of the prohibition – what constitutes "excessive," for example – reflects the compromise necessary for Geneva delegates to reach a consensus on a controversial limitation on military action. "Putting these provisions into practice ... will require complete good faith on the part of the belligerents."[148]

Article 57.2(b) reflects the delegates' fear that the general prohibition of 51.5(b) was insufficiently precise and that, if a commander were to be tried for the grave breach of an indiscriminate attack, or targeting civilians, his legal exposure would be excessive.[149] "Those who favored a greater degree of precision argued that in the field of penal law it is necessary to be precise, so that anyone violating the provisions would know that he was committing a grave breach."[150] The result is two protocol articles addressing proportionality.

The ICRC's study of customary IHL defines proportionality essentially as a combination of the two protocol articles.[151] The U.S. Army 1956 *Law of Land Warfare* field manual expresses it most simply: "**Loss of life and damage to property incidental to attacks must not be excessive in relation to the concrete and direct military advantage expected to be gained.**"[152]

---

[147] W. Hays Parks, "Air War and the Law of War," 32–1 *Air Force L. Rev.* (1990), 1, 173.

[148] Protocols *Commentary*, supra, note 4, at 625.

[149] Recall that Additional Protocol I creates new grave breaches; in this instance, Art. 85.3.

[150] Protocols *Commentary*, supra, note 4, at 679.

[151] Henckaerts and Doswald-Beck, *Customary International Humanitarian Law*, supra, note 2, at 46. However, in its commentary to Rule 156, proportionality, the ICRC Study adds (at 576) the modifying word "clearly," making the requirement for violation, in the study's view, the launch of an attack that is clearly excessive in relation to the military advantage. "The commentary to the rule does not explain the addition of this term, which ... simply raises the threshold and introduces greater uncertainty into the law in this area." Robert Cryer, "Of Custom, Treaties, Scholars and the Gavel: The Influence of the International Criminal Tribunals on the ICRC Customary Law Study," 11–2 *J. of Conflict & Security L.* (Summer 2006), 239–63, 259–60.

[152] FM 27–10, *Law of Land Warfare*, supra, note 39, at para. 41, Change No. 1.

Proportionality is a necessary consideration in attacks on civilians, not on combatants. Combatants seek to maximize the death of combatant enemies and maximize the destruction of enemy military objects, quite the reverse of their goal in regard to civilians and their objects. As the rule indicates, however, proportionality is not a *total* prohibition. What constitutes "excessive" loss of life? "As attacks directed at the civilian population are already prohibited by [Additional Protocol I] Article 51(2), it is clear that attacks directed in theory against military objectives which cause such injury to civilians as to make it obvious that the attack was in fact directed against them would be 'excessive', but how much higher the standard is to be drawn is unclear."[153] Like the meaning of the legal term "reasonable," what constitutes "excessive" is left to the interpretation of legal forums. "Proportion is an elastic concept, but not indefinitely elastic."[154] What is clear is that to violate proportionality, the discrepancy between loss of civilian life and destruction of civilian objects must be *clearly* disproportionate to the direct military advantage anticipated.[155] "Close" issues do not rise to a violation.

The *Commentary* to the protocols says of proportionality:

> The armed forces and their installations are objectives that may be attacked wherever they are, except when the attack could incidentally result in loss of human life among the civilian population, injuries to civilians, and damage to civilian objects which would be excessive in relation to the expected direct and specific military advantage. In combat areas it often happens that purely civilian buildings or installations are occupied or used by the armed forces and such objectives may be attacked, provided that this does not result in excessive losses among the civilian population. . . . Outside the combat area the military character of objectives that are to be attacked must be clearly established and verified.[156]

Indiscriminate weapons such as cluster bombs in populated areas, even aerial bombardment by "dumb" bombs, raise proportionality issues. "Additionally, the bombing accuracy resulting from the development of [precision-guided munitions] has brought with it a significant reduction in collateral damage. As a result, while the law of armed conflict has not changed – there is no legal requirement to use PGMs . . . – planners and operators choosing between laser-guided ordnance or 'dumb' bombs now more than ever must consider collateral damage."[157] Precision-guided munitions are not a LOAC/IHL requirement, but a failure, or inability, to discriminate may be inherently disproportional. Thus, proportionality must be assessed from several perspectives.

First, proportionality is a factor in the selection of the target. If civilian losses are inevitable, because of either the intermingling of civilian and military targets or the dual character of the target itself, these must be balanced against the military advantage.

---

[153] Fenrick, "Rule of Proportionality and Protocol I," supra, note 75, at 102. This article provides an excellent history of the formation of the protocol articles relating to proportionality.

[154] Oliver O'Donovan, *The Just War Revisited* (Cambridge: Cambridge University Press, 2003), 62.

[155] See: ICC Statute, Art. 8 (2) (b) (iv).   [156] Protocols *Commentary*, supra, note 4, at 620–1.

[157] Col. Frederic L. Borch, "Targeting after Kosovo," *Naval War College Rev.* (Spring 2003), 64, 67. Underscoring a basic misunderstanding of targeting and weapons capabilities, in 2008 a U.S. under secretary of defense for policy wrote, "Until the late twentieth century, the major problem with any bombing campaign was accuracy. By the time of Afghanistan, however, that problem was largely solved." Douglas J. Feith, *War and Decision* (New York: Harper, 2008), 96. That was true only when precision-guided munitions (PGMs) were employed. Few states possessed the technical and monetary resources to build and employ PGMs.

Second, the means and methods of attack must be assessed. Some weapons are more likely to involve indiscriminate damage than others. ... Finally, even if these requirements are met, the conduct of the attack itself must not be negligent and involve unnecessary civilian casualties.[158]

There is no reference to proportionality in Additional Protocol II, relative to non-international armed conflicts. The ICRC argues that proportionality is inherent in the concept of humanity, which is applicable in Protocol II, "and that, as a result, the principle of proportionality cannot be ignored in" internal armed conflicts.[159] Several national courts have found proportionality to be customary law, as has the ICTY.[160]

Defenders, as well as attackers, have a responsibility to minimize the potential for proportionality problems. Additional Protocol I, Article 58, requires defenders to "endeavor to remove the civilian population ... and civilian objects ... from the vicinity of military objectives," and to "avoid locating military objectives within or near densely populated areas," and to take other precautions to protect the civilian population. Proportionality is a requirement that most often falls on the attacker, however.

During the first Gulf War (1991–2), "actions were taken by the government of Iraq to use cultural property to protect legitimate targets from attack; a classic example was the positioning of two fighter aircraft adjacent to the ancient temple of Ur ... on the theory that Coalition respect for the protection of cultural property would preclude the attack of those aircraft."[161] Although LOAC permitted an attack on the fighters, with Iraq responsible for any damage to the temple, U.S. commanders decided not to attack. Their decision was aided by noting that there was no servicing equipment for the planes, nor a nearby runway from which they could take off.

Proportionality often involves what is euphemistically referred to as "collateral damage," a term first encountered in the 1991 Gulf War.[162] Grotius writes, "One must take care, so far as is possible, to prevent the death of innocent persons, even by accident."[163] Lieber likewise counsels, "Commanders, whenever admissible, inform the enemy of their intention to bombard a place, so that the noncombatants, and especially the women and children, may be removed before the bombardment commences."[164] Collateral damage is "the damage to surrounding human and non-human resources, either military or non-military, as the result of action or strikes directed specifically against enemy forces or military facilities."[165] Targeting mistakes that kill civilians and are not associated with strikes against an enemy force, are not collateral damage; they are simply mistakes.[166] Most often, however, "collateral damage" refers to noncombatants who are incidentally killed in attacking a lawful military objective.

---

[158] Judith Gail Gardam, "Proportionality and Force in International Law," 87–3 *AJIL* (July 1993), 391, 407.

[159] Henckaerts and Doswald-Beck, *Customary International Humanitarian Law*, supra, note 2, at 48.

[160] *Prosecutor v. Kupreškić and Others*, IT-95–16-T (Jan. 14, 2000), para. 524.

[161] Department of Defense, *Conduct of the Persian Gulf War*, supra, note 26, Appendix O, at 615.

[162] Sahr Conway-Lanz, *Collateral Damage* (New York: Routledge, 2006), 221.

[163] Grotius, *De Jure Belli Ac Pacis*, supra, note 51, book III, chapter XI, VIII, at 733.

[164] Lieber Code, supra, note 34, at Article XIX.

[165] William Safire, *Safire's New Political Dictionary* (New York: Random House, 1993), 682–3.

[166] Carlotta Gall, "U.S. Killed 90 in Afghan Village, Including 60 Children, U.N. Finds," *NY Times*, Aug. 27, 2008, A5. In Washington, military officers disputed initial accounts that the civilian deaths, suffered in air strikes, were not associated with combat with Taliban forces. Eric Schmitt, "U.S. Officials Describe Afghan Airstrike," *NY Times*, Aug. 28, 2008, A9.

During World War II, in the Philippines, in February 1945, U.S. forces were fighting to enter the heavily defended city of Manila. Subordinates of the U.S. commander, General Douglas MacArthur, repeatedly asked permission to bomb enemy positions in the city. General MacArthur refused, saying, "You would probably kill off the Japanese all right, but there are several thousand Filipino civilians in there who would be killed too. The world would hold up its hands in horror if we did anything like that."[167] Proportionality was respected, and Manila was taken without aerial bombardment, although with exceptionally heavy losses on both sides.

> The presence of civilians will not render a target immune from attack. ... An attacker must exercise reasonable precautions to minimize incidental or collateral injury to the civilian population or damage to civilian objects, consistent with mission accomplishment and allowable risk to the attacking forces. The defending party must exercise reasonable precautions to separate the civilian population and civilian objects from military objectives, and avoid placing military objectives in the midst of the civilian population. ... [A] defender is expressly prohibited from using the civilian population or civilian objects ... to shield legitimate targets from attack.[168]

Once again, the close relationship of the core concepts of proportionality and military necessity is apparent. Distinction and proportionality are closely related, as well. "Discrimination [i.e., distinction] requires combatants to differentiate between enemy combatants, who represent a threat, and noncombatants, who do not. ... This restriction means that combatants cannot intend to harm noncombatants, though proportionality permits them to act, knowing some noncombatants may be harmed."[169] Soldiers faced with constant violations of distinction, as in Iraq, may feel justified in disregarding proportionality themselves.[170] When noncombatants become victims, the intent of the shooters is all-important. In 2006, in response to indiscriminate rocketing by Hezbollah fighters located in Lebanon, Israeli forces entered and bombed Lebanon, raising mixed issues of distinction and proportionality on both sides:

> "The scale of killings in the region, and their predictability, could engage personal criminal responsibility of those involved, particularly those in a position of command and control," said Louise Arbour, the [U.N.'s] high commissioner for human rights. ... "Indiscriminate shelling of cities constitutes a foreseeable and unacceptable targeting of civilians," she said. ... The Swiss-based International Red Cross ... said Wednesday that Israel had violated the principle of proportionality.[171]

If an enemy sniper is spotted in a remote and isolated desert hiding spot, he could lawfully be targeted and killed with a two-thousand-pound bomb, or a B-52 bomber's load of two-thousand-pound bombs. It would be a gross waste of munitions, but there would be no proportionality issue because there are no civilians or civilian objects with which to be concerned. To kill a sniper in a crowded orphanage with a mere hand grenade could

---

[167] D. Clayton James, *The Years of MacArthur: Triumph and Disaster 1945–1964*, Vol. 3 (Wilmington, MA: Houghton Mifflin, 1970), 635.

[168] Department of Defense, *Conduct of the Persian Gulf War*, supra, note 26, at 615.

[169] U.S. Army/Marine Corps, *Counterinsurgency Field Manual* (Chicago: University of Chicago Press, 2007), para. 7–34, at 248.

[170] Robin GeiÔ, "Asymmetric Conflict Structures," 864 *Int'l Rev. of Red Cross* (Dec. 2006), 757, 766.

[171] Warren Hoge, "Attacks Qualify as War Crimes, Officials Say," *NY Times*, July 20, 2006, A11.

easily be a violation of proportionality, however, because of the close presence of so many civilians.

On the other hand, "even extensive civilian casualties may be acceptable if they are not excessive in light of the concrete and direct military advantage anticipated. The bombing of an important army or naval installation (like a naval shipyard) where there are hundreds or even thousands of civilian employees need not be abandoned merely because of the risk to those civilians. ... Much depends on the factual situation."[172] In the 2004 first battle of Fallujah, Iraq, for instance, the United States was determined to root out hardcore Sunni insurgents who effectively controlled the city and harbored the killers who had recently mutilated and put on display the bodies of four civilian contractors. Urban combat is always harsh business, however. Lieutenant General Ricardo Sanchez, commander of the marines who were assigned the mission, wrote that "the Fallujah offensive was going to be a pretty ugly operation, with a lot of collateral damage – in both infrastructure and the inevitable civilian casualties."[173] Nevertheless, the direct military advantage of securing Fallujah was considered sufficiently important to attack the city and the insurgents harbored there.

In practice, issues of proportionality can sometimes confound even generals. During the U.S. invasion of Iraq (March 20–May 1, 2003), estimates of civilian casualties from U.S. air strikes were determined by using a software program nicknamed "bug splat."[174] The commanding general of the invasion was the army general Tommy Franks. "Franks also indicated that he would not hesitate to propose attacks that put civilians at risk if high-priority targets were identified. 'High collateral damage targeting will occur,' he said. ... It was vital to shock the [Iraqi] regime and to do so as rapidly as possible. Under existing procedures, however, any attack that was estimated to result in the death of thirty or more civilians had to be approved by [Secretary of Defense] Rumsfeld."[175]

Proportionality can also be difficult for junior officers. What if the pilot of a fighter aircraft in an attack against a railway bridge, a legitimate military target, begins his bombing run and sees a passenger train just starting across the bridge? Should he break off his attack or carry out the mission? There is no matrix, no order, no formula that resolves that dilemma.

A different problem arose during heavy fighting in Afghanistan in 2007, pitting U.S. forces against Taliban fighters cornered in a mountain village, including a particular house:

When [army captain Daniel] Kearney's moment of decision came, two of [his] 2nd Platoon's sergeants ... had been shot, and the fight was still going on. Kearney could see a woman and child in the house. "We saw people moving weapons around," Kearney told me. "I tried everything. I fired mortars to the back side to get the kids to run out the front. I shot to the left, to the right. The Apache" – an attack helicopter – "got shot at and left. I kept asking for a bomb drop, but no one wanted to sign off on the collateral damage of dropping a bomb on a house." Finally, he said, "We shot a Javelin and a TOW" – both armor-piercing missiles. "I didn't get shot at from there for two months," Kearney said. "I ended up killing that woman and that kid."[176]

---

[172] Dinstein, *Conduct of Hostilities*, supra, note 46, at 121.
[173] Lt.Gen. Ricardo S. Sanchez, *Wiser in Battle* (New York: Harper, 2008), 333.
[174] Gordon and Trainor, *Cobra II*, supra, note 13, at 110.   [175] Id., at 89.
[176] Elizabeth Rubin, "Battle Company Is Out There," NY *Times Magazine*, Feb. 24, 2008, 41.

Taking fire from the house and sustaining casualties, the captain had the right and the duty to exercise self-defense. He had little choice but to neutralize the house, but that makes the decision to fire no easier.

"Application of the principle of proportionality is more easily stated than applied in practice. . . . The law is not clear as to the degree of care required of the attacker and the degree of risk that he must be prepared to take. . . . There may be occasions when a commander will have to accept a higher level of risk to his own forces in order to avoid or reduce collateral damage to the enemy's civil population."[177]

New technology attempts to minimize, but cannot eliminate, collateral damage. In 2007, a new five-hundred-pound bomb was first used in Iraq by U.S. forces. Containing less explosive mass, it produces "a reduced fragmentation pattern and blast radius . . . for use in situations where friendly forces or civilians are close to the target."[178]

How is proportionality to be measured? Who decides whether munitions factory Y is "worth" X civilian lives? "It is, of course, impossible to measure human lives against a military advantage to be gained. However, as long as wars are fought, and if there is to be compliance with the law of war, some such approximation must be made."[179]

"Although the decision as to proportionality tends to be subjective, it must be made in good faith and may in fact be measured and held excessive in a subsequent war crimes trial. In deciding whether the principle of proportionality is being respected, the standard of measurement is always the contribution to the military purpose of the . . . operation as a whole, as compared with other consequences of that action, such as the effect upon civilians or civilian objects."[180]

In the U.S. invasion of Iraq, how many noncombatant lives would be acceptable forfeit for the targeting and killing of Saddam Hussein and his two sons, the three of whom were legitimate military targets? Would the anticipated direct military advantage gained by their deaths, while the international armed conflict was still in progress, mitigate the deaths of ten civilians? Twenty? A hundred? The answer was at least twelve. In April 2003, reliable information was received that Hussein and his sons were in or near a particular Baghdad restaurant. "Less than 45 minutes later, a B-1 bomber obliterated the site with four satellite-guided bombs, leaving a deep crater and at least a dozen dead."[181] Saddam Hussein and sons were not among them. Did that alter the proportionality equation?

In World War II, during July 1944, an even more difficult balancing of lives against military objective was made by Lieutenant General (later General of the Army) Omar Bradley. He commanded the U.S. 1st Army in the cross-channel Normandy landings. His advance was blocked by Nazi holdouts in the so-called Falaise Gap. Bradley turned to Army Air Force heavy bombers to "carpet bomb" the location of the German resistance, an area of five square miles, including the French city of St.-Lô, to open the way to Caen, the 1st Army's critical seaport objective. General Bradley briefed reporters on the coming

---

[177] A. V. P. Rogers, "Zero-Casualty Warfare," 837 *Int'l Rev. of the Red Cross* (March 2000), 165, 169.

[178] Cmdr. Jan C. Jacobs, "U.S. Naval Aviation and Weapon Development in Review," U.S. Naval Institute *Proceedings* (May 2008), 68, 74, describing the BLU-126/B bomb.

[179] Howard S. Levie, *The Code of International Armed Conflict*, Vol. 1 (New York: Oceana, 1986), 85.

[180] Green, *Contemporary Law of Armed Conflict*, supra, note 73, at 351.

[181] Bob Drogin, "German Spies Aided U.S. Attempt to Kill Hussein In Aerial Attack," *L.A. Times*, Jan. 12, 2006, A1.

attack. Bradley recalled, "one of the newsmen asked if we would forewarn the French living within the bounds of the carpet. I shook my head . . . no. If we were to tip our hand to the French, we would also show it to the Germans. The enemy might then move out, leaving us to bomb vacant fields while he collected reserves for a counterattack. . . . It was essential we have surprise even if it meant the slaughter of innocents as well."[182] Professor Michael Walzer comments:

> Even if a large number of civilians lived in those five square miles . . . and even if all of them were likely to die, it would seem a small price to pay for a breakout that might well signal the end of the war . . . Perhaps the attack could have been redirected through some less populated area (even at great risk to the soldiers involved). Perhaps the planes, flying low, could have aimed at specific enemy targets, or artillery could have been used instead (since shells could then be aimed more precisely than bombs), or paratroops dropped or patrols sent forward to seize important positions in advance of the main attack. . . . For the bombs missed the carpet and killed or wounded several hundred American soldiers. How many French civilians were killed or wounded Bradley does not say.[183]

How much care is required of a commander? What degree of risk to his own troops' lives must a leader accept before risking the lives of noncombatants? In the case of St.-Lô, it is reasonable to estimate that hundreds of French civilians were killed. Raising the deadly price even higher, Lieutenant General Leslie J. McNair, a longtime critic of U.S. air support,[184] was among the 126 Americans killed and 621 wounded by the misdirected bombs.[185] Although McNair was a combatant and therefore does not figure in the proportionality calculus, he remains the most senior American officer killed in World War II. General Bradley wrote, "We buried him secretly two days later with only senior officers in attendance. The news was suppressed by censorship until a successor could be picked and rushed over to take McNair's place"[186] There were no news reports regarding the French civilians killed, either.

Was General Bradley's decision an abuse of proportionality and a violation of the law of war? Absent a trial, no one can conclusively say, but, as Professor Walzer notes, the deaths of the French civilians were probably not excessive in light of the direct military advantage anticipated, which was great.

Such calculations are one of the burdens of high military command. As one academic too-harshly views it, "The key to the dilemma is the subjective nature of assessing proportionality. It requires balancing between two opposing goals: the swift achievement of the military goal with the minimum losses of one's own combatants and the protection of the other party's civilian population. The military are extremely unwilling to see the balance shift from the emphasis on the former."[187] More accurately, "the most important reason why the proportionality standard is so difficult to handle is its inherently

---

[182] General of the Army Omar N. Bradley, A Soldier's Story (New York: Henry Holt, 1951), 345–6.

[183] Walzer, Just and Unjust Wars, supra, note 80, at 318–19.

[184] Russell F. Weigley, Eisenhower's Lieutenants (Bloomington: Indiana University Press, 1981), 164.

[185] Killed in action/wounded in action figures from U.S. bombing on two successive days are from Martin Blumenson, The Battle of the Generals (New York: William Morrow, 1993), 134–41. Blumenson provides a detailed account of the debacle.

[186] Bradley, Soldier's Story, supra, note 182, at 349.

[187] Gardam, "Proportionality and Force in International Law," supra, note 158, at 409.

contextual nature. Indeed, a magical template applicable to all instances . . . simply does not exist, since so much resides in the contingencies of the situation."[188]

7.4.1 *What Proportionality Is Not*

For a term so frequently used in LOAC/IHL discussions, proportionality is often misunderstood:

> The issue of collateral damage to civilians is tied in with that of proportionality. . . . Protocol I does not mention proportionality at all. The only expression used there is "excessive." The question is whether the injury to civilians or damage to civilian objects is excessive compared to the military advantage anticipated. Many people tend to confuse excessive with extensive. However, injury/damage to non-combatants can be exceedingly extensive without being excessive, simply because the military advantage anticipated is of paramount importance.[189]

A British text discusses the 1982 Falklands War between the United Kingdom and Argentina. "In that conflict the sinking of the Argentine cruiser *General Belgrano* by the British submarine *HMS Conqueror* has been widely criticized," the author writes. "The large loss of life – 368 Argentine seamen died as a result of the action, making this the most costly single incident in the whole of the war – seems out of all proportion to the threat posed by the ship at the time of the attack. . . . Was this an instance of an excessive or disproportionate use of force?"[190]

The author frames the issue incorrectly. Even had the sunken ship not been a ship of war, proportionality is not a question of equal proportions, civilian deaths versus anticipated military advantage. The Argentine warship was a legitimate military target engaged in a common Article 2 armed conflict, sunk by an opposing combatant. Because it was a warship, there was in the first place no issue of distinction. Its sinking by lawful means contributed to the defeat of the enemy and thus was in keeping with military necessity, and it was accomplished without apparent unnecessary suffering. The overriding point is that there was no civilian loss of life or property, so the question of proportionality simply does not arise. It was a lamentable loss of life, but lost lives in armed conflict are not the measure of possible violations of LOAC/IHL.

After World War II, in the trial of the Nazi field marshal Wilhelm List and eleven other high-ranking Nazi officers, the prosecution noted in its opening statement, "On 9 October 1941, [Lieutenant General Franz] Boehme informed List of 'an execution by shooting of about 2,000 Communists and Jews in reprisal for 22 murdered men of the 2d Battalion of the 521st Army Signal Communications Regiment.'"[191] Innocent civilians in starkly disproportionate numbers were killed with little military advantage reasonably anticipated. This was not, however, a violation of proportionality, or even distinction. It was not even an act of warfare. The victims were not killed in an attack ill planned by military commanders or during the defense of a military objective within a civilian

---

[188] Tom Ruys, *"Armed Attack" and Article 51 of the UN Charter* (Cambridge: Cambridge University Press, 2010), 111.

[189] Dinstein, "Reasonable Military Commanders," in Wall, *Legal and Ethical Lessons of NATO's Kosovo Campaign*, supra, note 145, at 177.

[190] A. J. Coates, *The Ethics of War* (Manchester: Manchester University Press, 1997), 209–10.

[191] *United States v. List*, "Hostage Case," supra, note 42, at 805.

complex. The killings were murders committed by uniformed individuals who were not engaged in armed conflict. The killers and their commanders enjoyed no combatant's privilege for such homicides outside combat. It is true that reprisals were lawful in World War II, but in such starkly disproportionate numbers they clearly were law of war violations, regardless.

Proportionality employs a different standard in a civilian law enforcement context, where human rights law prevails, rather than LOAC/IHL. In armed conflict, lethal force is often the first recourse. In civilian law enforcement, when "a state agent uses force against an individual ... the effect on the individual is balanced with the aim of protecting a person against unlawful violence. The action is only proportionate if the smallest amount of force necessary is used. Lethal force is only permissible in very narrow circumstances."[192] This interpretation of proportionality is contrary to that in LOAC/IHL. "While law enforcement standards provide that the use of force must be proportional to the 'legitimate objective to be achieved', international humanitarian law permits direct attacks against military objectives, including combatants and other persons taking a direct part in hostilities, which are not governed by proportionality. Proportionality under international humanitarian law is the balancing test that must be employed."[193] Civilian law enforcement considerations give proportionality a meaning quite different from its meaning in a *jus in bello* context. In short, under the law of war, deadly force may be the lawful *first* resort; under human rights law, deadly force is the *last* resort.

International law also employs the term "proportionality" somewhat differently than LOAC/IHL. "The customary right of self-defence involved the assumption that the force used must be proportionate to the threat."[194] This description refers to the uncontroversial requirement of proportionate defense when a state is attacked, or anticipates attack. The term "proportionality" in this sense usually refers to high command considerations of constraint in the use of force. In 1987 and 1988, the United States attacked Iranian oil platforms in the Persian Gulf in response to Iranian attacks on U.S. and other vessels with missiles and mines. The Untied States contended that the oil platforms were staging points for Iranian attackers. The International Court of Justice held that the oil platform attacks, combined with the sinking of two Iranian frigates and other naval vessels, and the destruction of Iranian aircraft, were disproportionate uses of force in a self-defense response.[195] This use of the term "proportionality" is correct, but it is one that is infrequently encountered on the battlefield.

During the 1991 Gulf War, in operation Desert Shield/Desert Storm, between Iraq and a coalition of forces led by the United States, the hundred-hour war stopped by virtue of a cease-fire declared by President Bush. Two days later, on March 2, near the Rumaila oil fields, the army major general Barry McCaffrey's 24th Infantry Division received small arms fire from a band of retreating Iraqi soldiers of the Hamurabi Armored Division and other regular forces. In the ensuing U.S. counterattack, reportedly begun two hours after the initial exchange of fire,[196] a five-mile-long Iraqi column was attacked with the full

---

[192] Heike Krieger, "A Conflict of Norms: The Relationship between Humanitarian Law and Human Rights Law in the ICRC Customary Law Study," 11–2 *J. of Conflict & Security L.* (Summer 2006), 265, 280–1.

[193] Jelena Pejic, "Terrorist Acts and Groups: A Role for International Law," 75 *BYIL* (2004), 71, 88.

[194] Brownlie, *International Law and the Use of Force*, supra, note 41, at 261.

[195] *Iran v. United States* (Oil Platforms Case) 42 *ILM* 1334 (2003), para. 78.

[196] Seymour M. Hersh, "Overwhelming Force," *New Yorker*, May 22, 2000, 62–3.

might of American arms, including three tank task forces and five artillery battalions. General McCaffrey later reported having destroyed 34 tanks, 224 trucks, 41 armored personnel carriers, 43 artillery pieces, and 319 antitank guns, with an estimated four hundred enemy killed. No U.S. soldiers were killed.[197] The media called the battle site "The Highway of Death."

The author Seymour Hersh wrote, "Many of the generals interviewed [about Rumaila] . . . believe that McCaffrey's attack went too far, and violated one of the most fundamental military doctrines: that a commander must respond in proportion to the threat."[198] Was Rumaila a case of "piling on"? Was it a slaughter of the defenseless and a violation of proportionality? One U.S. soldier–participant, Lieutenant Colonel (and later the commander of all Army troops in Iraq) Ricardo Sanchez, considered it a controversially disproportionate victory.[199] The 24th Division's official history of the war calls it "one of the most dramatic lopsided victories in U.S. Army history."[200]

Whereas other generals might have taken different approaches, General McCaffrey's overwhelming response did not constitute a violation of proportionality. In a common Article 2 armed conflict, soldiers were under fire from a retreating enemy, however ineffective that fire. A commander is not required to take enemy fire without countering; he need not weigh the volume or effectiveness of incoming fire and finely tune his response to that particular situation. There were no civilians or civilian objects on the battlefield. Tacitly invoking human rights principles that limit armed violence, a respected scholar objects that "combatants are legitimate objects of attack, but only as long as they are capable of fighting, willing to fight or resist capture. Once incapable in this sense, and so *hors de combat*, they are immune from attack, but may be taken prisoner. . . . The principle of humanity regulates the degree of permitted violence, forbidding action which is unnecessary or excessive for the achievement of victory."[201] "But this is a misconception . . . " Professor Dinstein responds; "the fleeing soldiers of today are likely to regroup tomorrow as viable military units."[202] It is true that, in the seventh century B.C., a Chinese code of chivalry held it to be unchivalrous to

---

[197] 24th Mechanized Infantry Division Combat Team, *Historical Reference Book: A Collection of Historical Letters, Briefings, Orders, and Other Miscellaneous Documents Pertaining to the Defense of Saudi Arabia and the Attack to Free Kuwait* (Fort Stewart, GA, 1991), Vol. 1, n.p., Section V, Operation Desert Storm, Post-Battle Operations, Tab. 70, CG's End-of-Campaign Message, item 10, available in the library of the U.S. Army Judge Advocate General's School and Training Center, Charlottesville, Virginia.

[198] Hersh, "Overwhelming Force," supra, note 196, at 52.

[199] Sanchez, *Wiser in Battle*, supra, note 173, at 80.

[200] Major Jason K. Kamiya, *A History of the 24th Mechanized Infantry Division Combat Team during Operation Desert Storm* (Fort Stewart, GA, 1991), 37. Sanchez, a lieutenant colonel when he participated in the fight at Rumaila, believed that it was a U.S. "lopsided victory" but agreed with the decision to attack. Sanchez, *Wiser in Battle*, supra, note 173 at 80.

[201] Green, *Contemporary Law of Armed Conflict*, supra, note 73, at 124–6. The classic human rights case involving the right to life in armed conflict is *Abella v. Argentina (Tablada)*, Inter-American Commission on Human Rights, Case #11.137, Report #55/97 (18 Nov. 1997), para. 178: "Civilians . . . who attacked the Tablada base . . . whether singly or as a member of a group thereby . . . are subject to direct individualized attack to the same extent as combatants and lose the benefit of the proportionality principle and of precautionary measures."

[202] Dinstein, "Legitimate Military Objectives under the Current Jus In Bello," in Wall, *International Law Studies*. Vol. 78. *Legal and Ethical Lessons*, supra, note 146, at 153.

take advantage of a retreating enemy whose chariot had broken down,[203] but today, when it is combatants who have not surrendered who are involved, the humanity objection is unwarranted and it is not the law. (See Chapter 7.5 and Chapter 15.2.1.)

Exemplifying a divergence of IHL and LOAC, in an ongoing battle there is not a point at which, seeing that the enemy is being overcome, the other side must cease fire, or stop to ascertain the current combat capability of the opponent. If the enemy is no longer capable of resisting he may indicate a desire to cease resisting – by surrendering and becoming *hors de combat*. The stronger opponent is not tasked with divining when that point is reached. The principle of humanity *may*, at some point, suggest a situation in which an enemy is so unable to defend himself that the attacker *may* cease firing and initiate surrender negotiations, but that is not a LOAC/IHL requirement.

History suggests that course may sometimes be unwise, as well. In December 1944, during the Battle of the Bulge, the Nazi General der Panzertruppe Heinrich von Lüttwitz offered to accept the surrender of the badly battered U.S. 101st Airborne Division, at Bastogne,[204] but von Lüttwitz misjudged the combat capabilities of his opponent. The Americans did not surrender; von Lüttwitz was later defeated and ended the war as an American prisoner. It is not the attacker's task to stop himself; it is the defender's task to stop him.

Clearly, it is unlawful to announce that no quarter will be given.[205] In support of Professor Green's objection, it is a basic rule of warfare that the right of belligerents to adopt means of injuring the enemy is not unlimited. There are compelling dictates of humanity, morality, and civilization to be taken into account.[206] Although these phrases are usually applied to the use of restricted weapons, it may be argued that they apply equally to the killing of enemy troops no longer effective in battle. That argument is more humanitarian in nature than most commanders would be willing to accept, when engaged in combat with an enemy in retreat but not evidencing a desire to surrender.

If civilians are present on the battlefield, attacks that violate proportionality *are* possible. The legal standard is whether "a reasonably well-informed person in the circumstances of the actual perpetrator, making reasonable use of the information available to him or her, could have expected excessive civilian casualties to result from the attack."[207] If so, the attacking commander may be obliged to stop, reroute, or moderate his forces' attack.

"The main problem with the principle of proportionality is not whether or not it exists but what it means and how it is to be applied. . . . Unfortunately, most applications of the principle . . . are not quite so clear cut. . . . One cannot easily assess the value of innocent human lives as opposed to capturing a particular military objective."[208] Difficult or not, combatants must try.

---

[203] M. Cherif Bassiouni, *The Legislative History of the International Criminal Court*, Vol. 1 (Ardsley, NY: Transnational, 2005), 4.

[204] John W. Chambers II, et al., eds., *The Oxford Companion to American Military History* (Oxford: Oxford University Press, 1999), 93–4; and Donald Goldstein, Katherine Dillon, and J. Michael. Wenger, *Nuts! The Battle of the Bulge* (Washington, DC: Brassey's, 1994), 113–14.

[205] 1907 Hague Resolution IV, Art. 23 (d); 1977 Additional Protocol I, Article 40; Additional Protocol II, Art. 4.1.

[206] United Kingdom MOD, *Manual of the Law of Armed Conflict*, supra, note 1, para 6.1.1., at 102.

[207] *Prosecutor v. Galić*, supra, note 9, at para. 58.

[208] ICTY, "Final Report to the Prosecutor by the Committee Established to Review the NATO Bombing Campaign against the Federal Republic of Yugoslavia," n.d., available on-line.

7.4.2 Proportionality and Force Protection

In January 2009, in response to incursions into Israel, the kidnapping of Israeli troops by terrorist Hamas fighters, and continued rocket attacks on its civilian villages and towns, Israel launched a three-week cross-border attack into the Gaza Strip against Hamas. With overwhelming force, including artillery, air, and tank support, the Israelis made short work of any enemy they encountered, but were heavily criticized, accused of significant violations of proportionality.

In one incident, Israeli commanders said that, yes, civilian houses had been destroyed, but only if weapons caches were found inside. One destroyed house was examined by a nongovernmental organization (NGO) weapons expert, however, and no evidence of explosives or secondary blasts was found. Asked why the house had been destroyed, the Israeli commander, identified only as "Y," replied: "'We had advance intelligence that there were bombs inside the house,' Captain Y said. 'We looked inside from the doorway and saw things that made us suspicious. I didn't want to risk the lives of my men. We ordered the house destroyed.' That seemed to be the guiding principle for a number of the operations in El Atatra: avoid Israeli casualties at all costs."[209]

Casualty aversion, often referred to as "force protection," has become an oft-stated goal of commanders in the armed forces of many nations, including the United States. Force protection is defined as "preventive measures taken to mitigate hostile actions against Department of Defense personnel (to include family members), resources, facilities, and critical information. Force protection does not include actions to defeat the enemy."[210] Yet, on rare occasion, military commanders have mistakenly viewed force protection as a secondary military mission.[211] Referring to U.S. military operations, an American commentator wrote, "During peace operations of the 1990s, force protection effectively became part of the mission, privileging the Soldier over the civilian. Because the civilian is fundamental to the COIN [counterinsurgency] mission, force protection must now give way."[212] LOAC/IHL requires that, where proportionality would be violated, force protection give way in all military missions.

Preventing friendly casualties is clearly a foremost goal of every military commander, as it should be. Force protection is a legitimate consideration of every commander. If a combatant ship might be at risk, with its large crew and strategic value, even greater latitude in force protection measures should be granted its commander. Force prevention is neither a ship's purpose nor an infantry unit's mission, however. The infantry's mission is to close with and destroy the enemy. Von Clausewitz wrote, "The destruction of the enemy's force underlies all military actions; all plans are ultimately based on it."[213] He added, "Avoidance of bloodshed, then, should not be taken as an act of policy if

---

[209] Ethan Bronner and Sabrina Tavernise, "In Shattered Gaza Town, Roots of Seething Split," NY Times, Feb. 4, 2009, A1.

[210] Dept. of Defense, Joint Publication 1–02, Department of Defense Dictionary of Military and Associated Terms (Washington, DC: GPO, 2001, amended through Oct. 17, 2008).

[211] Id. Mission is defined as "2. In common usage, especially when applied to lower military units, a duty assigned to an individual or unit, a task."

[212] Sarah Sewall, "Introduction to the University of Chicago Press Edition," Counterinsurgency Field Manual, supra, note 169, at xxix.

[213] Carl von Clausewitz, On War, Michael Howard and Peter Paret, eds. and trans. (New York: Knopf, Everyman's Library, 1993), 111.

our main concern is to preserve our forces. On the contrary, if such a policy did not suit the particular situation it would lead our forces to disaster. A great many generals have failed through this mistaken assumption."[214] Von Clausewitz's words are no less true today. That does not imply that commanders should ever disregard friendly casualties. LOAC/IHL problem with force protection as an overriding consideration is illustrated in Captain Y's actions, raising international criticism of his armed force and his country for his violation, whether actual or perceived, of proportionality.

Force protection, for example, is the use of remotely delivered weapons in heavily defended airspace, rather that risking a human pilot, or a commander's allowing his military personnel to wear civilian clothing in noncontested areas of a foreign state to prevent recognition.[215] The exercise of armed force in the service of self-protection, however, should not be confused with the casual use of excessive precautionary armed force. Modern firepower should not be used "just in case." A U.S. field manual makes the harsh point that "combat requires commanders to be prepared to take some risk, especially at the tactical level. . . . Closing with the enemy and sustaining casualties day in and day out requires resolve and mental toughness in commanders and units."[216] As a marine commander writes, "self-protection is not the reason that soldiers, sailors, airmen, and Marines deploy into war zones."[217]

Force protection does not supersede the requirements of proportionality. Nor is a proportionality exception granted because an attacker's casualties are heavier than anticipated, or because a defender disregards Article 58's mandate to minimize potential proportionality problems. Nor does enemy incitement or prior LOAC violation relieve a combatant of his responsibility to observe proportionality. "Sometimes a method of attack that would minimize the risk to civilians may involve increased risk to the attacking forces. The law is not clear as to the degree of risk that the attacker must accept. . . . The attacker may have to accept the increased risk as being the only way of pursuing an attack in a proportionate way."[218]

Force protection is not a concrete and direct military advantage that allows proportionality to be slighted. Were it otherwise, an attacker with superior arms would be free to annihilate all opposition with overwhelming firepower and call any civilian casualties collateral. "An armed force perceived as ultra-protective of its own personnel, but willing to risk the lives of civilians as well as the adversary's soldiers, is liable to be viewed with suspicion and even hatred. Force protection is no cure-all.[219] Finally, a combatant commander's observance of proportionality at the cost of force protection should not be mistaken for the principle of humanity.

7.5 Humanity: A Core Principle?

"There is no dispositive treaty definition of these [core] principles; even the terminology used in reference to them varies from source to source: core, fundamental,

---

[214] Id., at 113.   [215] Parks, "Special Forces' Wear of Non-Standard Uniforms," supra, note 123, at 493.

[216] Army/Marine Corps, *Counterinsurgency Field Manual*, supra, note 169, paras. 7–13, 7–14, at 241.

[217] Lt. Col. Michael D. Grice, "Force Protection and the Death of Common Sense," *Marine Corps Gazette* (Aug. 2009), 8.

[218] United Kingdom MOD, *Manual of the Law of Armed Conflict*, supra, note 1, para. 2.7.1. at 25–6.

[219] Adam Roberts, "The Equal Application of the Laws of War: A Principle under Pressure," 872 *Int'l. Rev. of the Red Cross* (Dec. 2008), 931, 959.

foundational. ... However, while definitions may vary slightly at the fringe, there is virtually no dispute that these principles provide the foundation for the regulation of hostilities."[220]

Recognizing that there is no agreed upon international basis for inclusion or exclusion of a particular principle as a "core" principle, there is reason to consider the concept of "humanity" as a fundamental, or core, principle of LOAC/IHL. The United Kingdom's *Manual of the Law of Armed Conflict* describes the principle of humanity as **forbidding "the infliction of suffering, injury, or destruction not actually necessary for the accomplishment of legitimate military purposes.**"[221] "It has also been suggested that the principle of humanity 'enjoins that capture is to be preferred to wounding, and wounding to killing'. ... While as a moral principle this may be correct, it is not a legal principle or rule of IHL."[222] (This erroneous suggestion is also applied in the ICRC's 2009 *Interpretive Guidance on the Notion of Direct Participation in Hostilities*, discussed in Chapter 15.2.1.)

So, there also is a basis for viewing the concept of humanity as an admirable hope, rather than a legal requirement in armed conflict.

> When discussing humanity, references to morality are often very close by. How this relationship between laws and morals is viewed may differ depending on whether one comes from a positivistic background or not. ... Someone representing a positivist view may argue that law and morality are separated. ... Persons with a non-positivistic view, however, may be inclined to argue that there are moral requirements that affect the content of positive law. Moral requirements are considered to be external factors, i.e., outside positive law, which are still legally relevant.[223]

This text takes a positivist outlook. If LOAC/IHL addresses, for example, the lawfulness of targeting and killing civilians who directly participate in armed conflict and indicates that such civilians may be killed for so long as they are so participating, the issue is clear. Those who urge "capture rather than wounds, and wounds rather than death"[224] go beyond the requirements of the law.

As with many significant issues in international law, there is no supranational body to decide with finality what is a "core principle" and what is not.[225] Indeed, the core principles of LOAC are hardly agreed upon unanimously. The United Kingdom's

---

[220] Geoffrey Corn, Victor Hansen, Richard B. Jackson, Chris Jenks, Eric Talbot. Jensen, and James A Schoettler Jr., *The Law of Armed Conflict: An Operational Approach* (New York: Wolters Kluwer, 2012), 110. Professor Corn, et al., consider humanity to be a major principle of LOAC/IHL, at 112.

[221] United Kingdom MOD, *Manual of the Law of Armed Conflict*, supra, note 1, para. 2.4, at 23. Emphasis supplied.

[222] Ian Henderson, *The Contemporary Law of Targeting* (Leiden: Martinus Nijhoff, 2009), 87, citing ICRC Conference of Government Experts on the Reaffirmation and Development of IHL Applicable in Armed Conflicts. Vol. I. Report on the Work of the Conference (1972), "above n. 25 (Chapter I), 131, where a draft rule that some experts considered might be interpreted as an obligation to capture was considered unacceptable."

[223] Sigrid R. Johansen, "The Occupied and the Occupier: The Case of Norway," in Kjetil Larsen, Camilla G. Cooper and Gro Nystuen, eds., *Searching for a 'Principle of Humanity' in International Humanitarian Law* (Cambridge: Cambridge University Press, 2013), 206, 213–14.

[224] Jean Pictet, *Humanitarian Law and the Protection of War Victims* (Leyden, Netherlands: Henry Dunant Institute,1975), 32.

[225] The four "cardinal" principles are examined in the ICJ's 1996 *Nuclear Weapons Advisory Opinion*, supra, note 120: distinction at paras. 78, 92 and 95; military necessity at paras. 30, 32, 43 and 48; unnecessary

Manual of the Law of Armed Conflict lists them as "military necessity, humanity, distinction, and proportionality."[226]

The United Kingdom's view as to humanity is widely shared. The law of war is rife with references to the concept of humanity. The 1863 Lieber Code, in Article 4, admonishes occupying forces to be "guided by the *principles* of justice, honor, and *humanity. . . .* " The 1868 St. Petersburg Declaration refers to "the laws of *humanity*," as do the preambles to the 1899 and 1907 Hague Convention IV, Respecting the Laws and Customs of War on Land. The 1949 Geneva convention common Article 63/62/142/158 refers to "the laws of humanity." Humanity is referred to in the Preambles to 1977 Additional Protocol II, and the 1980 Convention on Certain Conventional Weapons. The International Criminal Tribunal for the Former Yugoslavia refers to "the principles of humanity" in the *Kupreskić* case.[227] A leading contemporary European scholar writes:

> The principle permeates the whole body of modern IHL. . . . This originally moral principle, inspired by mercy, compassion and solidarity, has been inserted into the positive law of armed conflicts by express provisions of the Geneva Conventions, namely common article 3 for [noninternational armed conflicts] ("shall in all circumstances be treated humanely") and in articles 12/12/13/27 of Geneva Conventions I–IV ("shall be treated humanely"; "shall at all times shall be treated humanely").[228]

The European professor Daniel Thürer suggests that "the principle of humanity, which underlies international humanitarian law . . . embraces, besides the classic set of human rights . . . the idea of public obligations and mutual responsibility. . . . The idea of humanity . . . was, in a way, a forerunner for the development of modern human rights."[229]

A question, however, is, Does the principle of humanity exist with legal impact as an independent and binding LOAC norm? Have international prosecutions been based on humanity, as have distinction, military necessity, unnecessary suffering, and proportionality?

Knowledgeable publicists, commentators, and academics sometimes advance important LOAC principles as core principles. "Precaution," for example, based upon 1977 Additional Protocol I, Article 57, mandates precautions in military operations for the protection of civilians who might be injured or killed.[230] Precaution has been cited as a core principle. But without the support of an international court judgment, or a multinational treaty commemorating it, is it any more significant than, say, individual

---

suffering at paras. 77–8 and 95; proportionality at paras. 41–4 and 46. Humanity is discussed at paras. 1, 78–9, 92 and 95, but not as a law of war principle.

[226] United Kingdom MOD, *Manual of the Law of Armed Conflict*, supra, note 1, para. 2.1, at 21, citing the Martens Clause in the Preamble to 1907 Hague Convention IV, as its source.

[227] *Prosecutor v. Kupreskić*, Trial Judgment, supra, note 160, at para. 525.

[228] Robert Kolb, *Advanced Introduction to International Humanitarian Law* (Cheltenham, UK: Edward Elgar, 2014), 79.

[229] Daniel Thürer, *International Humanitarian Law: Theory, Practice, Context* (The Hague: Hague Academy of International Law, 2011), 197.

[230] Cordula Droege, "Get Off My Cloud: Cyber Warfare, International Humanitarian Law, and the Protection of Civilians," 94/886 *Int'l. Rev. of the Red Cross* (Summer, 2012), 533, 553: "D] the core rules of IHL on the conduct of hostilities – that is, the principles of distinction, proportionality, and precaution – only apply to operations that constitute attacks?" One of the author Droege's fellow ICRC legal advisers, however, refers to the following "The classic *rule* on precautions against the effects of attacks . . . perhaps remains somewhat rudimentary." Jean-François Quéguiner, "Precautions under the Law Governing the Conduct of Hostilities," 88/864 *Int'l Rev. of the Red Cross* (Dec. 2006), 793, 817 (emphasis supplied).

responsibility (Geneva Convention II, Article 33), or protection of children (Additional Protocol I, Article 77), neither of which is urged as a core principle? Arguing against humanity as a core principle, "the [European Court of Human Rights] has never expressly referred to a 'principle of humanity' in any form."[231] But is that dispositive of its legal force?

Other principles advanced as "general principles of law," rather than core principles, are sometimes offered. The principle of limitation, for example, "negates the admissibility of total war, where a belligerent could do everything it sees fit in order to overpower the enemy."[232]

Might humanity, if not a core principle, be a general principle? Should humanity even be considered "a 'principle' in the same sense as other general principles in IHL? When references are made to core principles, such as the principle of distinction, the principle of proportionality, or the principle of unnecessary suffering, the use of the term 'principle' implies a particular legal impact of the specified concept. Does the 'principle of humanity' have a similar legal impact?"[233] Professor Yoram Dinstein thinks not:

> The principles of humanity should be viewed not as legal norms but as extra-legal considerations. ... The difference between principles and considerations (or requirements) transcends semantics and goes into substance. Humanity is not an obligation (or a set of obligations) incorporated *per se* in positive IHL. There is no overarching, binding, norm of humanity that tells us what we must do (or not do) in wartime. What we actually encounter are humanitarian considerations, which pave the road to the creation of legal norms. ... These considerations do not by themselves amount to law. ... Considerations of humanity are inspiring and instrumental, yet they are no more than considerations. ... If benevolent humanitarianism were the only factor to be weighed in hostilities, war would have entailed no bloodshed, no human suffering and no destruction of property; in short, war would not be war. IHL must be predicated on a subtle balance – and compromise – between conflicting considerations of humanity, on the one hand, and the demands of military necessity, on the other.[234]

Professor Kjetil Larsen, of Oslo's Norwegian Centre of Human Rights, agrees:

> Norms which provide protection of the individual under HRL [human rights law], such as the right to life, are detailed and clear, whereas a "principle of humanity" would be vague and uncertain; HRL is undoubtedly legally binding on certain conditions, whereas a "principle of humanity" has little (if any) legal effect; HRL is also perceived as legally binding by the states, whereas a "principle of humanity" can, at best, be perceived as moral obligation.[235]

Is there a core LOAC principle of humanity, then? It is argued that there is not. Is there a *principle* of humanity, core or otherwise? "If by principle one means a legal norm, legally binding as such, it seems safe to conclude that such a principle of humanity does not exist, and there are limited grounds for even arguing that such a principle is

---

[231] Kjetil M. Larsen, "A 'Principle of Humanity' or a 'Principle of Human-rightism'?" in Larsen, Cooper and Nystuen, *Searching for a 'Principle of Humanity'*, supra, note 223, at 132.

[232] Kolb, *International Humanitarian Law*, supra, note 228, at 80.

[233] Kjetil M. Larsen, Camilla G. Cooper, and Gro Nystuen, "Introduction by the editors," in Larsen, Cooper and Nystuen, *Searching for a 'Principle of Humanity'* supra, note 223, at 1.

[234] Id., Yoram Dinstein, "Principle of Proportionality," at 73.

[235] Id., Larsen, "'Principle of Humanity' or a 'Principle of Human-rightism'?," at143.

emerging."[236] One might ask those who believe humanity is a core principle to offer a definition or description of the principle and enumerate its specific law of war prohibitions and requirements.

On the other hand, humanity is widely thought to be an important LOAC/IHL principle. Is there anything wrong with considering humanity to be a general or even a core principle to be honored in armed conflict? As long as it is understood that there is no basis for the prosecution of combatants based solely on an asserted violation of humanity, there is no harm.

7.6 Summary

Distinction, military necessity, unnecessary suffering, and proportionality are referred to as "core principles" for good reason. They indeed constitute the core of LOAC. Virtually any LOAC issue or event can be examined through the lens of the core principles. The four are not merely related; they are inextricably intertwined. Any military action that is unnecessary (i.e., lacking a military necessity) will yield unnecessary suffering, and resulting civilian deaths will probably be disproportional. A disproportional attack can hardly help but violate distinction. A violation of one of the four core principles raises a violation of another, usually two, and sometimes three.

One should not be dismayed by the sometimes indistinct outlines of the four concepts or that the word "reasonable," vague as it is, appears so often in describing them. The politics of Geneva are little different from those of most bureaucracies. Besides having strongly held and honorable views of LOAC and IHL, state delegations to Geneva sometimes have divergent goals and agendas. "The need to achieve a consensus has led those drafting these provisions to formulate them in a way that is sometimes ambiguous. Several delegates remarked on this when the article [AP I, Article 51 relating to proportionality] was adopted."[237] When many lives might hang in the balance, a slightly ambiguous protective provision is preferable to none. No rule can foresee every potential application. Flexibility is no vice, and "reasonable" is the language of the law, not just LOAC. Nevertheless, some hold a darker view:

> [Proportionality] leaves the belligerents plenty of room to act as they feel the military situation requires. Would it be fair to say that in proclaiming the two principles [proportionality and distinction] states were being entirely hypocritical, pretending to accept bans that are not bans because they can be eluded at every step? ... The Great Powers, without whose consent these principles would never have become legal precepts, had every reason to leave them as loose as possible. ... Yet, since they are not very effective, they can be applied only in exceptional circumstances when their relevance is undeniable. In other words ... they become effective in highly pathological and "dramatic" situations, when the disproportion between what they "impose" and how one or more of the belligerents behaves, is gigantic.[238]

There is no denying that the four core concepts are "loose." Were they tightly constricting, however, would they not make many, if not most, commanders potential accuseds?

---

[236] Id., Larsen and Cooper, "Conclusion," in Larsen, Cooper and Nystuen, *Searching for a 'Principle of Humanity'*, at 349, 355.

[237] Protocols *Commentary*, supra, note 4, at 620.

[238] Cassese, *Violence and Law in the Modern Age*, supra, note 128, at 17.

The core principles attempt to find a balance between impunity and inaction. To see international duplicity in such an effort is wrong.

CASES AND MATERIALS

THE UNITED STATES V. WILHELM LIST, ET AL.

"The Hostage Case" Trials of War Criminals before the Nuernberg Military Tribunals, vol. XI, 757 (1948)[239]

Introduction. *The case of Generaloberst (General) Lothar Rendulic is briefly discussed in this chapter's text. In 1944, he was commander in chief of German armed forces in Norway. Following the war's conclusion, Rendulic was one of the accused in* The Hostage Case. *His trial is one of the few that consider a commander's actions in relation to the concept of military necessity.*

"Obviously, it is especially difficult to render convincing second opinions when assessing, after the fact, the necessity and economy of battlefield tactical decisions. Nevertheless, the very fact that military and civilian tacticians have been accountable to second opinions – for example, to the 'reasonable commander' test – must have some restraining effect on the choice of measures employed in battle."[240]

These extracts are from the record of Rendulic's trial.

From Count two of the group indictment:

9.a. On or about 10 October 1944, the Commander in Chief of the 20th Mountain Army, the defendant Rendulic, issued an order to troops under his command and jurisdiction, for the complete destruction of all shelter and means of existence in, and the total evacuation of the entire civilian population of, the northern Norwegian province of Finmark. During the months of October and November 1944, this order was effectively and ruthlessly carried out. For no compelling military reasons, and in literal execution of instructions to show no sympathy to the civilian population, the evacuated residents were made to witness the burning of their homes and possessions and the destruction of churches, public buildings, food supplies, barns, livestock, bridges, transport facilities, and natural resources of an area in which they and their families had lived for generations. Relatives and friends were separated, many of the evacuees became ill from cold and disease, hundreds died from exposure or perished at sea in the small boats and fishing smacks used in the evacuation, while still others were summarily shot for refusing to leave their homeland – in all, the thoroughness and brutality of this evacuation left some 61,000 men, women, and children homeless, starving and destitute.

---

[239] *United States v. List*, supra, note 42, at 770, 836–9, 889, 1113, 1131–6, 1162, 1253–4, and 1295–7.
[240] Thomas M. Franck, "On Proportionality of Countermeasures in International Law," 102–4 *AJIL* 715, 765 (Oct. 2008).

From the opening statement of the Chief Prosecutor, Brigadier General Telford Taylor:

Late in October 1944, the German High Command ... issued the following order to Rendulic. ...

> "Because of the unwillingness of the northern Norwegian population to voluntarily evacuate, the Fuehrer has ... ordered that the entire Norwegian population east of the fiord Lyngen be evacuated by force in the interest of their own security and that all homes are to be burned down or destroyed.
>
> "[Rendulic] is responsible that the Fuehrer's order is carried out without consideration. Only by this method can it be prevented that the Russians with strong forces, and aided by these homes and the people familiar with the terrain, follow our withdrawal operations. ... This is not the place for sympathy for the civilian population.
>
> "It must be made clear to the troops engaged in this action that the Norwegians will be thankful in a few months that they were saved from bolshevism. ... "

[handwritten: direct order]

.... This ruthless and in large part unnecessary decision was carried out by Rendulic's forces according to plan. Northern Norway, from Kirkenes nearly to Tromso, was turned into an Arctic desert.

From the opening statement of Dr. Hans Laternser, one of the accuseds' defense counsel:

In the case of the measures with which the defendants here are being charged the principle of military necessity plays an important role. This principle, which formed the basis of all German military measures, was formulated in paragraph 4 of the American "Rules of Land Warfare"[241] as the highest general principle of warfare and recognized to a very far-reaching degree.

This principle, however, must not be scrutinized in an abstract manner, but must be considered in connection with the conditions with which the accused were confronted and under which they had to discharge their task. ... Nothing of what forms the subject of this trial can be understood if considered apart from the fundamentals, as is done by the prosecution.

From the testimony of the accused justifying the destruction carried out at his order, that portion offered here being only a small portion of his testimony:

Everybody [in the German forces] was aware of the difficulty of the position. From censorship of soldiers' mail we learned that the morale of the soldiers sometimes bordered on panic. ... There was a very dangerous crisis among the [German] soldiers especially with regard to confidence in their leaders which could have led to catastrophe. ... At first sight one might suppose that marching [pursuing Russian] troops would only need the localities along the march route for quarters, but that is not the case. ... The villages along the march route were never sufficient for the accommodation of the marching troops.

[handwritten: Rendulic's testimony (?)]

Instead, these troops also had to use those places which were a good distance away from the march route ... when it was necessary to quarter them in houses, etc., and that would have undoubtedly been necessary at that time in Finmark because of the climate. ...

---

[241] FM 27–10, Rules of Land Warfare (Oct. 1, 1940), para. 4. **"Basic Principles**. ... a. The *principle of military necessity*, under which, subject to the principles of humanity and chivalry, a belligerent is justified in applying any amount and any kind of force to compel the complete submission of the enemy with the least possible expenditure of time, life, and money."

testimony cont'd.

The inhabited localities along the coast and along the fjords were of the same significance. ... It further has to be considered that an army does not only march; it also has to live, especially when it is supposed to prepare an attack. Then the army is apt to spread over the whole country. Not only do the troops have to be accommodated but there are also many installations to be taken care of such as work shops, hospitals, depots, installations for supply; and for all these installations everything that was there concerning houses, etc., was necessary to accommodate all these operations and that was the military significance of the apparently far distant inhabited localities. ...

... You must not think that we destroyed wantonly or senselessly. Everything we did was dictated by the needs of the enemy. That was its necessity. ...

... I did not think it was absolutely necessary to transfer the population to other areas but I could not close my eyes to Hitler's reasons of military necessity. I could not deny that they were justified.

Finally, I had to tell myself that it would possibly be better for the population to be transferred to other areas rather than to spend the hard winter in the destroyed country. I participated in both winter battles in Russia. Therefore, I know what flight from cold means. I had to realize that the Russians, if they followed us ... it was certain that they would not spare the population. Therefore, in the final analysis it was the best thing for the population that they were removed. ...

... I attached the greatest importance to good relations between myself and the Norwegian population. For this reason alone I insisted that the evacuation should not give any cause for misgivings among the population. You may also rest assured that if any kind of excesses had become known to me, any unnecessary harshness or any inconsideration, I would have taken countermeasures immediately. ...

From the closing arguments of Mr. Walter Rapp, Associate Prosecution Counsel:

The argument of the defense of military necessity is unconvincing here for several reasons. In the first place ... the plea of military necessity can never be used as a defense for the taking of an unarmed civilian's life. ...

In the second place, it is inconsistent to attempt to defend the same action by the plea of superior orders and also by that of military necessity because the two are mutually exclusive. If an act was committed solely because of superior orders, then presumably there was no military necessity for doing it; whereas if it was done because of military necessity, it would have been done anyhow regardless of the existence or nonexistence of superior orders.

In the third place, the defense of military necessity flies into the teeth of all the available evidence here. ...

From the Tribunal's opinion[242]:

Military necessity has been invoked by the defendants as justifying ... the destruction of villages and towns in the occupied territory. ... The destruction of property to be lawful must be imperatively demanded by the necessities of war. ... There must be some reasonable connection between the destruction of property and the overcoming of the enemy forces. It is lawful to destroy railways, lines of communication, or any other property that might be utilized by the enemy. Private homes and churches even

---

[242] *United States v. List*, supra, note 42, at 1,296.

may be destroyed if necessary for military operations. It does not admit the wanton devastation of a district or the willful infliction of suffering upon its inhabitants for the sake of suffering alone. . . .

The evidence shows that the Russians had very excellent troops in pursuit of the Germans. Two or three land routes were open to them as well as landings by sea behind the German lines. . . . The information obtained concerning the intentions of the Russians was limited. . . . It was with this situation confronting him that he carried out the "scorched earth" policy in the Norwegian province of Finmark. . . . The destruction was as complete as an efficient army could do it. . . .

There is evidence in the record that there was no military necessity for this destruction and devastation. An examination of the facts in retrospect can well sustain this conclusion. But we are obliged to judge the situation as it appeared to the defendant at the time. If the facts were such as would justify the action by the exercise of judgment, after giving consideration to all the factors and existing possibilities, even though the conclusion reached may have been faulty, it cannot be said to be criminal. After giving careful consideration to all the evidence on the subject, we are convinced that the defendant cannot be held criminally responsible although when viewed in retrospect, the danger did not actually exist. . . .

. . . We are not called upon to determine whether urgent military necessity for the devastation and destruction in the province of Finmark actually existed. We are concerned with the question whether the defendant at the time of its occurrence acted within the limits of honest judgment on the basis of the conditions prevailing at the time. The course of a military operation by the enemy is loaded with uncertainties. . . . It is our considered opinion that the conditions, as they appeared to the defendant at the time, were sufficient upon which he could honestly conclude that urgent military necessity warranted the decision made. This being true, the defendant may have erred in the exercise of his judgment but he was guilty of no criminal act. We find the defendant not guilty of the charge.

Conclusion. Renduli's testimony that the actions he ordered were actually for the benefit of the Norwegian populace, and that they would eventually be grateful that they were forced from their homes in wintertime and – if they managed to survive – were displaced to locations hundreds of miles away, is absurd, of course. As the opinion makes clear, however, the standard of guilt or innocence is the facts as they appeared to the accused at the time, given the circumstances at the time.

Although acquitted of the charge under Count two, Rendulic was found guilty of charges under Counts one, three, and four, relating to the murders of hostages. He was sentenced to twenty years imprisonment, with credit for seventeen months served awaiting trial and judgment. He actually served a few days less than three years.

The Rendulic standard remains unchanged. Fifty-four years later, in 2003, the ICTY wrote, "In determining whether an attack was proportionate it is necessary to examine whether a reasonably well-informed person in the circumstances of the actual perpetrator, making reasonable use of the information available to him or her, could have expected excessive civilian casualties to result from the attack."[243]

---

[243] *Prosecutor v. Galić*, supra, note 9, at para. 58.

THE OPINIONS OF THE INTERNATIONAL COURT OF JUSTICE ON THE THREAT OR USE OF NUCLEAR WEAPONS

By Michael J. Matheson, 91-3 *American Journal of International Law* 417-35 (July 1997)

Introduction: *To offer the essential aspects of the nineteen-page source article in a concise form, this brief extract is stripped of significant nuance and detail. A full understanding of the author's legal views (from an American perspective, admittedly) requires that the full article be read. Better yet, consult the Court's forty-five-page opinion. This extract, however, fairly condenses the author's main points relative to the law of armed conflict.*

I. Introduction

I do not believe that the Court's opinions suggest a need for any change in the nuclear posture and policy of the United States or the North Atlantic Treaty Organization (NATO) alliance. . . . First, the request [to the ICC for an advisory opinion] did not arise from any specific situation or operational problem but, rather, presented a wholly hypothetical question. . . . Second, the [United Nations General Assembly] request did not present a specific question about the interpretation of a particular agreement or instrument but, rather, a very abstract and vague question about international law in general. . . . The Court agreed [to offer an advisory opinion]. . . .

III. Applicability of Peacetime Law

First, it was argued [to the Court] that the use of nuclear weapons would violate the "right to life" guaranteed by Article 6 of the International Covenant on Civil and Political Rights and certain other human rights instruments. The United States and others responded that [Article 6] was only a protection against "arbitrary" deprivation of life, which obviously could not be absolute in time of armed conflict.

Second, some [of the parties] argued that the use of nuclear weapons violated various principles of environmental law [and] these principles were not suspended in wartime. [Those opposing] this view argued that there was no absolute prohibition on weapons causing serious environmental damage but, rather, a balancing of such damage against the military advantage served by the method of warfare. Once again, the Court agreed with the latter approach.

IV. Application of the Law Relating to the Use of Armed Force

. . . The use of any nuclear weapon, whatever its size or effects, would certainly carry with it "profound risks" . . . and, under the requirement of proportionality, weighed against the magnitude and consequences of the armed attack that the use of nuclear weapons is designed to defeat. Of course, this statement provides little concrete guidance in judging when a particular use of nuclear weapons would in fact be proportionate. . . . Such a judgment simply cannot be made in the abstract for all possible uses of nuclear weapons. . . .

Next, it was argued that the use of nuclear weapons was made unlawful by the various instruments of LOAC that prohibit the use of poisoned weapons ... "asphyxiating, poisonous or other gases and of all analogous liquids, materials or devices. ... It was argued that nuclear weapons fall within these prohibitions because they create radioactive by-products. ... [Opponents of this view] responded that these prohibitions were designed to apply to weapons whose primary purpose is to kill or injure by toxic effects – such as chemical weapons. They were not intended to apply to weapons that may produce toxic by-products but are primarily designed to kill or injure by blast, fragmentation or thermal effects. ... The Court agreed with the latter view. ...

No international agreement expressly prohibits all use of nuclear weapons. On the other hand, several agreements place restrictions of various kinds on nuclear weapons, including prohibitions or restrictions on their testing, prohibitions on their acquisition by non-nuclear weapon states, prohibitions on their possession or use in certain geographical areas, limits on testing or deployment of systems for their delivery, and measures to reduce the risk of a nuclear exchange.

Some argued that these provision, taken together, amounted to a general prohibition of all use of nuclear weapons. The Court rejected this argument. ...

The Court then considered whether a prohibition on the use of nuclear weapons had become a part of customary international law since 1945. The United States and others pointed out that ... the fact that nuclear weapons have not actually been used since World War II results not from an *opino juris* that their use is totally prohibited but from other military, political and humanitarian considerations.

The Court agreed that there was no such *opino juris*. ...

Next it was argued that the illegality of the use of nuclear weapons had been established by the adoption of a series of UNGA resolutions beginning in 1961, which (over the opposition of many states) had declared such use to be contrary to international law. The United States and others responded that these UNGA resolutions cannot create international law, but can only constitute evidence of preexisting customary law if generally accepted by states, which was not true here.

The Court agreed with the latter view. ...

Some argued that any use of nuclear weapons would violate the principle of distinguishing between civilian and military targets. ... This principle does not address the problem of collateral injury but, rather, prohibits the directing of attacks against non-military targets and the use of weapons that cannot be directed against specific targets. ... Good examples of weapons prohibited by this principle are the German V-1 and V-2 missiles of World War II. ...

Collateral damage and injury ... are dealt with by the rule of proportionality. ... This rule necessarily requires a case-by-case assessment of the specific circumstances of the particular situation, and it is not possible to in the abstract to conclude that all uses of a weapon will violate the principle. ... A persistent and serious flaw in much of the analysis of nuclear opponents on this point is the apparent assumption that all uses of nuclear weapons would necessarily involve the destruction of population centers and the infliction of hundreds of thousands of civilian casualties, which is clearly not the case.

Some argued that any uses of nuclear weapons would violate the rule against weapons whose nature is to cause unnecessary suffering, because of the extreme thermal and radiation effects of nuclear weapons. ... This rule was intended to preclude weapons designed to increase suffering beyond that necessary to accomplish any legitimate military objective. ...

In any event, the Court did not reach a conclusion as to whether all uses of nuclear weapons would be prohibited by these various principles, but did indicate that it had serious concerns because of the severe effects of nuclear weapons. ...

Accordingly, the Court's overall finding on this point ... was a qualified one; ... "The threat or use of nuclear weapons would *generally* be contrary to the rules of international law applicable in armed conflict, and in particular the principles and rules of humanitarian law." The Court's use of the term, "generally" was clearly intended to as a means of avoiding the assertion that all uses of nuclear weapons would be illegal, though it is not clear what types of uses it believed would or would not be prohibited. ... The Court went on to conclude:

> However, in view of the current state of international law, and the elements of fact at its disposal, the Court cannot conclude definitively whether the threat or use of nuclear weapons would be lawful or unlawful in an extreme circumstance of self-defence, in which the very survival of a State would be at stake.

What the Court meant by the "very survival of a State" is not clear; for example, whether it refers to the political survival of the government of a state, the survival of the state as an independent entity, or the physical survival of the population. ...

During World Wars I and II, the "very survival" of states was threatened and some did not in fact survive. In the course of the Korean War and the Persian Gulf war, and arguably in several phases of other recent conflicts, the "very survival" of states was seriously threatened. ...

Precisely what the Court's conclusion (or lack of one) on this category was based on is not clear. Is it that the use of nuclear weapons violates IHL but that a threat to the survival of a state may justify such a violation? As some pointed out, this would be surprising, since it has never been supposed that a state that is losing a war has the right to disregard the rules of armed conflict to the extent necessary to avoid defeat, and such a notion could produce results that would be fundamentally at odds with the purpose of humanitarian law.

Or did the Court mean that the rules of IHL themselves – particularly the rule of proportionality – allow the weighing of the importance of preserving a state against the very severe damage, injury and suffering that may result? This interpretation, in my view, would clearly be more consistent with the logic of the rules of armed conflict. ...

... In my view, the legality of any use of nuclear weapons would have to be judged on the basis of the specific circumstances of their use. ...

The "policy of deterrence." The Court stated that it "does not intend to pronounce here upon the practice known as the 'policy of deterrence'. ... This is a very significant point. The main purpose of nuclear arsenals is to deter enemy attack. ... Yet a policy of deterrence necessarily presumes that actual use is possible and lawful if such an attack occurs – or else the policy would be hollow and lack credibility.

The question of deterrent policy is related to the question of the legality of a threat to use nuclear weapons, as distinguished from actual use. The Court did not go very far into this question. ...

Significantly, the opinions of at least six judges ... seem to take the view that there are indeed circumstances in which the use of nuclear weapons would not be unlawful, and the opinions of several others do not give a clear indication of their view on this question. Only three judges clearly expressed the contrary conclusion that all uses of nuclear weapons would be unlawful. Thus, whether one looks at the votes themselves or at the content of the various judges' statements, the conclusion is that the Court is uncertain and divided on whether and in what circumstances the use of nuclear weapons is prohibited, and only a minority appears to have taken the position that all uses are prohibited. ...

In making this request for an advisory opinion, the General Assembly had put the Court in a difficult position. It had asked a question that could not effectively be answered in the abstract, and that was replete with serious political implications and pitfalls. Although the Court could not bring itself to refuse the General Assembly's request, it is to the Court's credit that it found a way to avoid giving an incorrect categorical answer to the question posed without appearing to be indifferent to the potential horrors of nuclear war.

Conclusion. *The legal complexity of the many issues bearing on nuclear weapons is emphasized by the fact that, besides the opinion of the Court as a whole, fourteen of the Court's fifteen judges wrote separate opinions.*

The moral questions attending the use, or threat of use, of nuclear weapons may be beyond the scope of the law of armed conflict, or any law.

SHIMODA, ET AL. V. STATE[244]

Tokyo District Court, December 7, 1963

355 Hanrei Jiho [Decisions Bulletin] 17
8 *Japanese Annual of Int'l L.* 231 (1964) (Citations to expert witnesses omitted.)

Introduction. *"The rule against inflicting 'superfluous' casualties leaves unilluminated whether it is permissible to kill large numbers of civilians to achieve a necessary military objective (destroying enemy forces deliberately dispersed in a civilian neighborhood) or to bring a costly war to a speedier end (the nuclear bombing of Hiroshima and Nagasaki)."[245] A 1963 trial discussed the outlines of these questions.*

The Shimoda case is the sole attempt by a court to assess the legality of the use of atomic weapons. Prior claims by survivors for monetary relief had been rejected by the city of Hiroshima although, under Japan's Atomic Survivor's Support Law, survivors are eligible for government-provided health care, up to $1,260 per month in reparations, and funeral expenses.

The plaintiffs in this civil suit were Ryuichi Shimoda and four others, residents of Hiroshima or Nagasaki who had been injured in the atomic bombings of their cities. They sued Japan in lieu of the United States for their injuries, alleging that the bombings were unlawful and that Japan had wrongfully waived the claims for compensation of her citizens. The Japanese government defended that the bombings were not unlawful, stressing that, although many noncombatants were killed and injured, the bombings brought about the surrender of Japan, preventing many other casualties on both sides.

The Court found for the defendant, Japan, on other grounds. It did rule that the bombings were unlawful, however, focusing on whether there were appropriate military objectives in

---

[244] http://www.icrc.org/ihl-nat.nsf/46707c419d6bdfa24125673e00508145/aa559087dbcflaf5c1256a1c0029f14d?
OpenDocument

[245] Franck, "On Proportionality of Countermeasures in International Law," supra, note 240, at 766.

Hiroshima and Nagasaki that justified the noncombatant deaths and injuries. As you read this extract from the Court's opinion, note the references to all four core LOAC principles.

2 International Law Aspects

(1) There is no doubt that, whether or not an atomic bomb having such a character and effect is a weapon which is permitted in international law as a so-called nuclear weapon, is an important and very difficult question in international law. In this case, however, the point at issue is whether the acts of atomic bombing of Hiroshima and Nagasaki by the United States are regarded as illegal by positive international law at that time. . . .

(3) . . . The defendant State alleges that the question of violation of positive international law does not arise, since there was neither international customary law nor treaty law prohibiting the use of atomic bombs at that time, and the use is not prohibited clearly by positive international law. Of course, it is right that the use of a new weapon is legal, as long as international law does not prohibit it. However . . . from the interpretation and analogical application of existing international laws and regulations . . . the prohibition includes also the case where . . . the use of a new weapon is admitted to be contrary to the principles [of international law].

(4) . . . It is right and proper that any weapon contrary to the custom of civilized countries and to the principles of international law, should be prohibited even if there is no express provision in the laws and regulations. . . . Although there are always many objections in every field against the invention and use of new weapons. They are soon regarded as advanced weapons, and the prohibition of the use of such weapons becomes altogether nonsensical. With the progress of civilization, a new weapon comes to be rather an efficient means of injuring the enemy. This is shown in history, and the atomic bomb is not an exception. . . . This, however, is not always true. This will be clear from the recollection of the existence of the above-mentioned treaties prohibiting the use of dum-dum bullets and poisonous gases. Therefore, we cannot regard a weapon as legal only because it is a new weapon, and it is still right that a new weapon must be exposed to the examination of positive international law.

(5) . . . Against the defended city and place, indiscriminate bombardment is permitted, while in the case of an undefended city and place, bombardment is permitted only against combatant and military installations (military objectives) and bombardment is not permitted against non-combatant and non-military installations (non-military objectives). Any contrary bombardment is necessarily regarded as an illegal act of hostility. . . .

(6) With regard to air warfare, there are "Draft Rules of Air Warfare." Article 24 of the Draft Rules provides that: "(1) Aerial bombardment is legitimate only when directed at a military objective, that is to say, an object of which the destruction or injury would constitute a distinct military advantage to the belligerent. (2) Such bombardment is legitimate only when directed exclusively at the following objectives: military forces; military works; military establishments or depots; factories constituting important and well-known centers engaged in the manufacture of arms, ammunition, or distinctively military supplies; lines of communication or transportation used for military purposes. (3) The bombardment of cities, towns, villages, dwellings, or buildings not in the immediate neighborhood of the operations of land forces is prohibited. In cases where

the objectives specified in paragraph (2) are so situated that they cannot be bombarded without the indiscriminate bombardment of the civilian population, the aircraft must abstain from bombardment. (4) In the immediate neighborhood of the operations of land forces, the bombardment of cities, towns, villages, dwellings, or buildings is legitimate, provided there exists a reasonable presumption that the military concentration is sufficiently important to justify such bombardment, having regard to the danger thus caused to the civilian population. . . . Further, Article 22 provides that "aerial bombardment for the purpose of terrorizing the civilian population, of destroying or damaging private property not of military character, or of injuring non-combatants, is prohibited." In other words, these Draft Rules of Air Warfare prohibit useless aerial bombardment and provide for the principle of military objective first of all. . . . The Draft Rules of Air Warfare cannot directly be called positive law, since they have not yet become effective as a treaty. However, international jurists regard the Draft Rules as authoritative with regard to air warfare. . . . Therefore, we can safely say that the prohibition of indiscriminate aerial bombardment on an undefended city and the principle of military objective, which are provided for by the Draft Rules, are international customary law. . . .

(7) Then, what is the distinction between a defended city and an undefended city? Generally speaking, a defended city is a city resisting any possible occupation attempt by land forces. A city which is far distant from the battlefield, and is not in pressing danger of the enemy's occupation, even if there exists defensive installations or armed forces, cannot be said to be a defended city, since there is no military necessity of indiscriminate bombardment. . . . On the contrary, against a city resisting a possible occupation attempt by the enemy, indiscriminate bombardment is permitted out of military necessity, since an attack made upon the distinction between military objective and non-military objective has little military effect and cannot accomplish the expected purposes. Thus, we can say that it is a long-standing, generally recognized principle in international law respecting air raids, that indiscriminate aerial bombardment is not permitted on an undefended city and that only aerial bombardment on military objectives is permitted. Of course, it is naturally anticipated that the aerial bombardment of a military objective is attended with the destruction of non-military objectives or casualty of non-combatants; and this is not illegal if it is an inevitable result accompanying the aerial bombardment of a military objective. However, it necessarily follows that in an undefended city, an aerial bombardment directed at a non-military objective, and an aerial bombardment without distinction between military objectives and non-military objectives (the so-called blind aerial bombardment) is not permitted in light of the above-mentioned principle. . . .

(8) It is a well-known fact that Hiroshima and Nagasaki were not cities resisting a possible occupation attempt by land forces at that time. Further, it is clear as stated above that both cities did not come within the purview of the defended city, since they were not in the pressing danger of an enemy's occupation, even if both cities were defended with anti-aircraft guns, etc. against air raids and had military installations. Also, it is clear that some 330,000 civilians in Hiroshima and some 270,000 civilians in Nagasaki maintained homes there, even though there were so-called military objectives such as armed forces, military installations, and munitions factories in both cities. Therefore, since an aerial bombardment with an atomic bomb brings the same result as a blind aerial bombardment from the tremendous power of destruction, even if the aerial bombardment has only a military objective as the target of its attack, it is proper to understand that an aerial bombardment with an atomic bomb on both cities of

Hiroshima and Nagasaki was an illegal act of hostility as the indiscriminate aerial bombardment of undefended cities.

(9) Against the above conclusion, there is a counter-argument that the war of the day was the so-called total war, in which it was difficult to distinguish between combatant and non-combatant, and between military objective and non-military objective, and that the principle of military objective was not necessarily carried through during World War II. ... However, we cannot say that the distinction between military objective and non-military objective has gone out of existence. For example, schools, churches, temples, shrines, hospitals and private houses cannot be military objectives, however total the war may be. If we understand the concept of total war to mean that all people who belong to a belligerent are more or less combatant, and all production means production injuring the enemy, there arises the necessity to destroy the whole people and all the property of the enemy; and it becomes nonsensical to distinguish between military objective and non-military objective. ... The concept of total war is not advocated in such a vague meaning as stated above, and there was no actual example of such situation. Accordingly, it is wrong to say that the distinction between military objective and non-military objective has gone out of existence because of total war.

(10) During World War II, aerial bombardment was once made on the whole place where military objectives were concentrated, because it was impossible to confirm an individual military objective and attack it where munitions factories and military installations were concentrated in comparatively narrow places, and where defensive installations against air raids were very strong and solid; and there is an opinion regarding this as legal. ... However, the legal principle of the aerial bombardment on an objective zone cannot apply to the city of Hiroshima and the city of Nagasaki, since it is clear that both cities could not be said to be places where such military objectives concentrate.

(11) Besides, the atomic bombing on both cities of Hiroshima and Nagasaki is regarded as contrary to the principles of international law that the means which give unnecessary pain in war and inhumane means are prohibited as means of injuring the enemy. In the argument of this point, it goes without saying that such an easy analogy that the atomic bomb is necessarily prohibited since it has characteristics different from former weapons in the inhumanity of its efficiency, is not admitted. For international law respecting war is not formed only by humane feelings, but it has as its basis both military necessity and efficiency and humane feelings, and is formed by weighing these two factors. ... On the other hand, however great the inhumane result of the use of a weapon may be, the use of the weapon is not prohibited by international law, if it has a great military efficiency. The issues in this sense are whether atomic bombing comes within the purview of "the employment of poison or poisonous weapons" prohibited by article 23(a) of the [1907] Hague Regulations respecting war on land. ... With regard to this point, there is not an established theory among international jurists in connection with the difference of poison, poison-gas, bacterium, etc. from atomic bombs. However, judging from the fact that the St. Petersburg Declaration declares that "considering that the use of a weapon which increases uselessly the pain of people who are already placed out of battle and causes their deaths necessarily is beyond the scope of this purpose, and considering that the use of such a weapon is thus contrary to humanity" and that article 23(e) of the Hague Regulations respecting war on land prohibits "the employment of such arms, projectiles, and material as cause unnecessary

injury," we can safely see that besides poison, poison-gas and bacterium the use of the means of injuring the enemy which causes at least the same or more injury is prohibited by international law. The destructive power of the atomic bomb is tremendous, but it is doubtful whether atomic bombing really had an appropriate military effect at that time and whether it was necessary. ... In this sense, it is not too much to say that the pain brought by the atomic bombs is severer than that from poison and poison-gas, and we can say that the act of dropping such a cruel bomb is contrary to the fundamental principle of the laws of war that unnecessary pain must not be given.

4 Claims for Damages of the Sufferers

(4) The plaintiffs allege that an individual has a claim in international law, since the right of the individual is exercised by the home government. However, if the purport is that the state exercise the right in international law in the citizen's name as his agent for his sake, there is no such example in international law and there is no reason in international law to recognize this. ...

(5) As understood from the above, there is no general way open to an individual who suffers damages from an illegal act of hostility in international law, to claim damages. ...

5 Waiver of Claims

(2) Article 19(a) of the Peace Treaty between the Allied Powers and Japan ... provides that: "Japan waives all claims of Japan and its nationals against the Allied Powers and their nationals arising out of the war or out of actions taken because of the existence of a state of war. ... Accordingly, claims for compensation for damages caused to Japan by illegal acts of hostility, for example, are necessarily included. ...

(7) Conclusion

For the above reasons, the plaintiffs' claims in this suit are ruled improper ... and we can only dismiss the plaintiffs' claims on the merits. ...

Conclusion. *Reading the Court's opinion, one is reminded of American author Paul Fussell, author of* The Great War and Modern Memory (1975). *In World War II, he was badly wounded in European combat and, upon recovery, was scheduled to participate in the invasion of Japan. The atom bombs cancelled those plans. Fussell quotes a friend who said, "Those for whom the use of the A-bomb was 'wrong' seem to be implying 'that it would have been better to allow thousands on thousands of American and Japanese infantrymen to die in honest hand-to-hand combat on the beaches than to drop those two bombs.' People holding such views, he notes, 'do not come from the ranks of society that produce infantrymen or pilots'."[246] Fussell also addresses the purported imminent Japanese surrender: "But at that time, with no indication that surrender was on the way, the kamikazes were sinking American vessels ... and Allied casualties were running to over 7,000 per week. ... Two weeks more means 14,000 more killed and wounded, three weeks*

[246] Paul Fussell, *Thank God for the Atom Bomb and Other Essays* (New York: Summit Books, 1988), 14–15.

more, 21,000. *Those weeks mean the world if you're one of those thousands or related to one of them. ... In general, the principle is, the farther from the scene of horror, the easier the talk."*[247]

Fussell's viewpoint is not that of Geneva. Students of the law, however sympathetic, sometimes must take a longer, less personal view of jus in bello *issues. As human beings, we also remember that armed conflict is more than rules and court cases.*

If Japan, with its World War II record of law of war violations, had the atomic bomb, would she have used it on the United States? When examining the lawfulness of its use by the United States, does Japan's law of war record matter? Would employment of the hydrogen bomb against an enemy raise and exacerbate the same issues? The atom bombing of Hiroshima and Nagasaki remains not only a significant LOAC/IHL issue, but an emotional and moral issue not likely to be settled soon.

Today, there still is no multinational treaty banning the use of nuclear weapons.

KUPREŠKIĆ AND OTHERS

IT-95–16-T (14 January 2000). Citations omitted.

Introduction. *The ICTY sometimes provides LOAC/IHL tutorial dicta, as in this account of distinction. The Trial Chamber's opinion sheds welcome light on issues related to distinction, such as the loss of civilian immunity and civilian objects' immunity.*

521. The protection of civilians in time of armed conflict, whether international or internal, is the bedrock of modern humanitarian law. In 1938, the Assembly of the League of Nations, echoing an important statement made, with reference to Spain, in the House of Commons by the British Prime Minister Neville Chamberlain, adopted a Resolution concerning the protection of civilian populations against bombing from the air, in which it stated that "the international bombing of [the] civilian population is illegal". Indeed, it is now a universally recognised principle, recently restated by the International Court of Justice, that deliberate attacks on civilians or civilian objects are absolutely prohibited by international humanitarian law.

522. The protection of civilians and civilian objects provided by modern international law may cease entirely or be reduced or suspended in three exceptional circumstances: (i) when civilians abuse their rights; (ii) when, although the object of a military attack is comprised of military objectives, belligerents cannot avoid causing so-called collateral damage to civilians; and (iii) at least according to some authorities, when civilians may legitimately be the object of reprisals.

523. In the case of clear abuse of their rights by civilians, international rules operate to lift that protection which would otherwise be owed to them. Thus, for instance, under Article 19 of the Fourth Geneva Convention, the special protection against attacks granted to civilian hospitals shall cease, subject to certain conditions if the hospital "[is used] to commit, outside [its] humanitarian duties, acts harmful to the enemy", for example if an artillery post is set up on top of the hospital. Similarly, if a group of civilians takes up arms in an occupied territory and engages in fighting against the enemy

---

[247] Id., 18–19.

belligerent, they may be legitimately attacked by the enemy belligerent whether or not they meet the requirements laid down in Article 4(A) (2) of the Third Geneva Convention of 1949.

524. In the case of attacks on military objectives causing damage to civilians, international law contains a general principle prescribing that reasonable care must be taken in attacking military objectives so that civilians are not needlessly injured through carelessness. This principle ... has always been applied in conjunction with the principle of proportionality, whereby any incidental (and unintentional) damage to civilians must not be out of proportion to the direct military advantage gained by the military attack. In addition, attacks, even when they are directed against legitimate military targets, are unlawful if conducted using indiscriminate means or methods of warfare, or in such a way as to cause indiscriminate damage to civilians. These principles have to some extent been spelled out in Articles 57 and 58 of the First Additional Protocol of 1977. Such provisions, it would seem, are now part of customary international law, not only because they specify and flesh out general pre-existing norms, but also because they do not appear to be contested by any State, including those which have not ratified the Protocol. Admittedly, even these two provisions leave a wide margin of discretion to belligerents by using language that might be regarded as leaving the last word to the attacking party. Nevertheless, this is an area where the "elementary considerations of humanity" rightly emphasised by the International Court of Justice in the *Corfu Channel*, *Nicaragua* and *Legality of the Threat or Use of Nuclear Weapons* cases should be fully used when interpreting and applying loose international rules, on the basis that they are illustrative of a general principle of international law.

525. More specifically, recourse might be had to the celebrated Martens Clause which, in the authoritative view of the International Court of Justice, has by now become part of customary international law. True, this Clause may not be taken to mean that the "principles of humanity" and the "dictates of public conscience" have been elevated to the rank of independent sources of international law, for this conclusion is belied by international practice. ...

526. As an example of the way in which the Martens Clause may be utilised, regard might be had to considerations such as the cumulative effect of attacks on military objectives causing incidental damage to civilians. In other words, it may happen that single attacks on military objectives causing incidental damage to civilians, although they may raise doubts as to their lawfulness, nevertheless do not appear on their face to fall foul per se of the loose prescriptions of Articles 57 and 58 (or of the corresponding customary rules). However, in case of repeated attacks, all or most of them falling within the grey area between indisputable legality and unlawfulness, it might be warranted to conclude that the cumulative effect of such acts entails that they may not be in keeping with international law. Indeed, this pattern of military conduct may turn out to jeopardize excessively the lives and assets of civilians, contrary to the demands of humanity.

Conclusion. *As basic and long-standing as the concept of distinction is, international tribunals and domestic courts regularly deal with its violation. This opinion relates distinction to the Martens Clause (Chapter 2, Sections 2.7.1 and 2.7.5), as well as to customary law.*

PROSECUTOR V. KUNARAC, ET AL.

IT-96–23 & 23/1-T (February 22, 2001) Citations omitted

Introduction. In the Kunarac *opinion, the ICTY Trial Chamber examines the core concepts of distinction and proportionality through an examination of an attack on a civilian town, and determines what acts must be committed to constitute the grave breach of attacking a civilian population. (Additional Protocol I, Article 85.3.) The Trial Chamber's opinion confirms that such an attack may be a grave breach and a crime against humanity, as well.*

3. The attack must be "directed against any civilian population" [to constitute the offense].

421. The expression "directed against" specifies that in the context of a crime against humanity the civilian population is the primary object of the attack.

422. The desire to exclude isolated or random acts from the scope of crimes against humanity led to the inclusion [in the International Law Commission's 1991 report, *Systematic or Mass Violations of Human Rights*] of the requirement that the acts be directed against a civilian "population". In the words of the Trial Chamber in the *Tadic* case, the expression "directed against any civilian population" ensures that generally, the attack will not consist of one particular act but of a course of conduct.

423. The protection of Article 5 [of the ICTY Statute] extends to "any" civilian population including, if a state takes part in the attack, that state's population. It is therefore unnecessary to demonstrate that the victims are linked to any particular side of the conflict.

424. The expression "population" does not mean that the *entire* population of the geographical entity in which the attack is taking place (a state, a municipality or another circumscribed area) must be subject to the attack.

425. The "civilian population" comprises . . . all persons who are civilians as opposed to members of the armed forces and other legitimate combatants. The targeted population must be of a predominantly civilian nature. However, the presence of certain non-civilians in its midst does not change the character of the population.

426. Individually, a person shall be considered to be a civilian for as long as there is a doubt to his or her status. As a group, the civilian population shall never be attacked as such. Additionally, customary international law obliges parties to the conflict to distinguish at all times between the civilian population and combatants, and obliges them not to attack a military objective if the attack is likely to cause civilian casualties or damage which would be excessive in relation to the military advantage anticipated.

427. The attack must be either "widespread" or "systematic", thereby excluding isolated and random acts.

428. The adjective "widespread" connotes the large-scale nature of the attack and the number of its victims. . . .

429. The adjective "systematic" signifies the organized nature of the acts of violence and the improbability of their random occurrence. Patterns of crimes – that is the non-accidental repetition of similar criminal conduct on a regular basis – are a common expression of such systematic occurrence.

430. The widespread or systematic nature of the attack is essentially a relative notion. The Trial Chamber must first identify the population which is the object of the attack

and, in light of the means, methods, resources and result of the attack upon the population, ascertain whether the attack was indeed widespread or systematic.

431. Only the attack, not the individual acts of the accused, must be "widespread" or "systematic". A single act could therefore be regarded as a crime against humanity if it takes place in the relevant context:

> For example, the act of denouncing a Jewish neighbor to the Nazi authorities – if committed against a background of widespread persecution – has been regarded as amounting to a crime against humanity. An *isolated act*, however – i.e. an atrocity which did not occur within such a context – cannot.

4. The mental element: the perpetrator knows of the broader criminal context in which his acts occur

433. The Appeals Chamber in the *Tadic* case made it clear that the motives of the accused for taking part in the attack are irrelevant and that a crime against humanity may be committed for purely personal reasons.

434. In addition to the intent to commit the underlying offence, the perpetrator needs to know that there is an attack on the civilian population and that his acts comprise part of the attack, or at least to take the risk that his act is part of the attack. This, however, does not entail knowledge of the details of the attack.

435. Finally ... Article 5 of the statute protects civilians as opposed to members of the armed forces and other legitimate combatants, but the Prosecution does not need to prove that the accused chose his victims for their civilian status. However, and as a minimum, the perpetrator must have known or considered the possibility that the victim of his crime was a civilian. The Trial Chamber stresses that, in case of doubt as to whether a person is a civilian, that person shall be considered to be a civilian. The Prosecution must show that the perpetrator could not reasonably have believed that the victim was a member of the armed forces.

The judgment is admirable for the clarity with which it enunciates the elements necessary to constitute the war crime and crime against humanity, in ICTY jurisprudence, of attacking civilians, a basic violation of the core concept of distinction.

PROSECUTOR V. GALIĆ

IT-98–29-T (December 5, 2003). Citations omitted.

Introduction. *The ICTY's Galić opinion also offers a clear explanation of the grave breach and crime against humanity of disregarding distinction in attacking civilians, going into finer detail than previous cases, and including discussion of disproportionate attacks, and their required mental elements.*

42. The constitutive elements of the offence of attack on civilians have not yet been the subject of a definitive statement of the Appeals Chamber. ... In the *Blaskić* case the Trial Chamber observed in relation to the *actus reus* that "the attack must have caused deaths and/or serious bodily injury within the civilian population or damage to civilian property. ... Targeting civilians or civilian property is an offense when not justified by military necessity." On the *mens rea* it found that "such an attack must have been conducted intentionally in the knowledge ... that civilians or civilian property were

being targeted not through military necessity." The Trial Chamber in the *Kordić and Cerkez* case held that "prohibited attacks are those launched deliberately against civilians or civilian objects in the course of an armed conflict and are not justified by military necessity. They must have caused deaths and/or serious bodily injuries."

43. .... The question remains whether attacks resulting in non-serious civilian casualties, or in no casualties at all, may also entail the individual criminal responsibility of the perpetrator . . . even though they do not amount to grave breaches of Additional Protocol I.

44. The Trial Chamber does not however subscribe to the view that the prohibited conduct set out in the first part of Article 51(2) of Additional Protocol I is adequately described [in the *Blaskić* and *Kordić* cases] as "targeting civilians when not justified by military necessity" ... [Article 51(2)] does not mention any exceptions. In particular it does not contemplate derogating from this rule by invoking military necessity.

45. The Trial Chamber recalls that the provision in question explicitly confirms the customary rule that civilians must enjoy general protection against the danger arising from hostilities. The prohibition against attacking civilians stems from a fundamental principle of international humanitarian law, the principle of distinction, which obliges warring parties to distinguish *at all times* between the civilian population and combatants. ...

47. .... Article 51(2) of Additional Protocol I proscribes making the civilian population as such, or individual civilians, the object of attack. According to Article 50 ... "a civilian is any person who does not belong to one of the categories of persons referred to in Article 4(A)(1), (2), (3) and (6) of the Third Geneva Convention and in Article 43 of Additional Protocol I." ... The term "civilian" is defined negatively as anyone who is not a member of the armed forces or of an organized military group belonging to a party to the conflict. It is a matter of evidence in each particular case to determine whether an individual has the status of civilian.

48. The protection from attack afforded to individual civilians by Article 51 ... is suspended when and for such time as they directly participate in hostilities. To take a "direct" part in hostilities means acts of war which by their nature or purpose are likely to cause actual harm to the personnel or matériel of the enemy armed forces. .... Combatants and other individuals directly engaged in hostilities are considered to be legitimate military targets.

50. The presence of individual combatants within the population does not change its civilian character. In order to promote the protection of civilians, combatants are under the obligation to distinguish themselves at all times from the civilian population; the generally accepted practice is that they do so by wearing uniforms, or at least a distinctive sign, and by carrying their weapons openly. In certain situations it may be difficult to ascertain the status of particular persons in the population. The clothing, activity, age, or sex of a person are among the factors which may be considered in deciding whether he or she is a civilian. A person shall be considered to be a civilian for as long as there is a doubt as to his or her real status. ...

51. ... [I]n accordance with the principles of distinction and protection of the civilian population, only military objectives may be lawfully attacked. A widely accepted definition of military objectives is given by Article 52 of Additional Protocol I as "those objects which by their nature, location, purpose or use make an effective contribution to military action and whose total or partial destruction, capture or neutralization, in the circumstances ruling at the time, offers a definite military advantage". In case of doubt as to whether an object which is normally dedicated to

civilian purposes is being used to make an effective contribution to military action, it shall be presumed not to be so used. . . .

54. The Trial Chamber will now consider the mental element of the offense on civilians . . . Article 85 of Additional Protocol I explains the intent required for the application of the first part of Article 51(2). It expressly qualifies as a grave breach the act of *wilfully* "making the civilian population or individual civilians the object of attack". The Commentary to Article 85 [at para. 3474] of Additional Protocol I explains the term [wilfully]. . . . The Trial Chamber accepts this explanation, according to which the notion of "wilfully" incorporates the concept of recklessness, whilst excluding mere negligence. The perpetrator who recklessly attacks civilians acts "wilfully".

55. For the *mens rea* recognized by Additional Protocol I to be proven, the Prosecution must show that the perpetrator was aware or should have been aware of the civilian status of the persons attacked. In case of doubt as to the status of a person, that person shall be considered to be a civilian. However, in such cases, the Prosecution must show that in the given circumstances a reasonable person could not have believed that the individual he or she attacked was a combatant.

57. . . . Indiscriminate attacks, that is to say, attacks which strike civilians or civilian objects and military objectives without distinction, may qualify as direct attacks against civilians. It notes that indiscriminate attacks are expressly prohibited by Additional Protocol I. This prohibition reflects a well-established rule of customary law applicable in all armed conflicts.

58. One type of indiscriminate attack violates the principle of proportionality. The practical application of the principle of distinction requires that those who plan or launch an attack will take all feasible precautions to verify that the objectives attacked are neither civilians nor civilian objects, so as to spare civilians as much as possible. Once the military character of a target has been ascertained, commanders must consider whether striking this target is "expected to cause incidental loss of life, injury to civilians, damage to civilian objectives or a combination thereof, which would be excessive in relation to the concrete and direct military advantage anticipated." If such casualties are expected to result, the attack should not be pursued. The basic obligation to spare civilians and civilian objects as much as possible must guide the attacking party when considering the proportionality of an attack. In determining whether an attack was proportionate it is necessary to examine whether a reasonably well-informed person in the circumstances of the actual perpetrator, making reasonable use of the information available to him or her, could have expected excessive civilian casualties to result from the attack.

59. To establish the *mens rea* of a disproportionate attack the Prosecution must prove, instead of the above-mentioned *mens rea* requirement, that the attack was launched wilfully and in knowledge of circumstances giving rise to the expectation of excessive civilian casualties.

60. The Trial Chamber considers that certain apparently disproportionate attacks may give rise to the inference that civilians were actually the object of attack. This is to be determined on a case-by-case basis in light of the available evidence.

61. . . . The parties to a conflict are under an obligation to remove civilians, to the maximum extent feasible from the vicinity of military objectives and to avoid locating military objectives within or near densely populated areas. However, the failure of a party to abide by this obligation does not relieve the attacking side of its duty to abide by the principles of distinction when launching an attack.

8 What Is a "War Crime"?

8.0 Introduction

The foundation having been laid and the framework erected, we may examine specific law of armed conflict/international humanitarian law (LOAC/IHL) issues. Initially, what is a war crime? This is a basic question for, if there is law on the battlefield, then violations of that law are possible. What constitutes a war crime, and who may be charged with a violation?

During World War II, teenaged George MacDonald Fraser, who later became a popular writer of military fiction, was an enlisted infantryman in the British army, fighting in the ferocious campaign against the Japanese in Burma. He wrote of learning that Japanese prisoners had been murdered the night before by his fellow soldiers:

> That is not to say that I condone major war crimes, or would take any but a short way with those who commit them. I know that the killing (or murder, which is what it was) of those Japanese was well beyond the civilized borderline. But being of my generation, in the year 1945, towards the end of a war of a peculiarly vicious, close-quarter kind, against an enemy who wouldn't have known the Geneva Convention if it fell on him, I never gave it a second thought.[1]

Would the same view prevail today? Is the nature of the enemy, or the period of the conflict, an excuse for grave breaches? Less-disciplined units might color the facts in such a way but, of course, they are neither legal nor moral excuses. While there are always unfortunate exceptions, the training of today's combatant forces, particularly of officers and noncommissioned officers, will not condone grave breaches. The battlefield omnipresence of personal electronic devices with integrated cameras only reinforces the likelihood of prosecutions. But, alas, as long as there are wars, there will be war crimes.

There are four requirements for an act to constitute a war crime. First, an armed conflict must be in progress at the time of the charged act; second, the charged offense must be incorporated in an applicable criminal or prosecutorial code; third, there must be a nexus between the charged act and the armed conflict; and forth, presuming the prosecuting tribunal is a law of war military commission (see Chapter 20.4.1.), the charged offense must constitute a violation of the laws and customs of war.

---

[1] George MacDonald Fraser, *Quartered Safe Out Here* (New York: Skyhorse Publishing, 2001), 191.

8.1 Defining War Crimes

"First, there must be an armed conflict."[2] An armed conflict, international or noninternational, or involving an armed opposition group, in progress at the time of the charged act, is a prerequisite to war crimes and grave breaches. Whereas armed conflict is easily discernable in a common Article 2 context, it is not always so in a noninternational situation. One commonly employed test for determining the existence of an armed conflict is set out in the *Tadić* jurisdiction decision:

> An armed conflict exists whenever there is a resort to armed force between States or protracted armed violence between governmental authorities and organized armed groups within a State. ... International humanitarian law continues to apply in the whole territory of the warring States or, in the case of internal conflicts, the whole territory under the control of a party, whether or not actual combat takes place there.[3]

In armed conflict there are crimes – simple violations of a domestic code, such as the state's criminal or military codes – and there are war crimes – violations of LOAC; and there are grave breaches – the more serious violations of LOAC/IHL, specified in the Geneva conventions and Additional Protocol I. Genocide, crimes against humanity, and crimes against peace are offenses under international criminal law but not included in LOAC/IHL.

The United Nations War Crimes Commission describes the laws and customs of war as the "rules of international law with which belligerents have customarily, or by special conventions, agreed to comply in case of war."[4] A war crime is defined, in turn, as "a serious violation of the laws or customs of war which entails individual criminal responsibility under international law."[5] The 1956 U.S. field manual, *Law of Land Warfare*, defines a war crime as "the technical expression for a violation of the law of war by any person or persons, military or civilian. *Every* violation of the law of war is a war crime."[6] The last sentence, however, is an overbroad statement, and "such an assertion has never been supported in actual State practice."[7] The British law of war manual employs the more specific definition from the London Charter, which established the Nuremberg International Military Tribunal: "**Violations of the laws or customs of war. Such violations shall include, but not be limited to, murder, ill-treatment or deportation to slave labour or for any other purpose of civilian population of or in occupied territory, murder or ill-treatment of prisoners of war or persons on the seas,**

---

[2] *Prosecutor v. Haradinaj, et al.*, IT-04–84-T (April 3, 2008), para. 36. *Haradinaj*, offers numerous examples of situations that rise to armed conflicts, well illustrating the test involved.

[3] *Prosecutor v Tadić*, IT-94–1-A, Decision on Defense Motion for Interlocutory Appeal on Jurisdiction (Oct. 2, 1995), at para. 70.

[4] United Nations War Crimes Commission (UNWCC), *History of the United Nations War Crimes Commission and the Development of the Laws of War* (London: His Majesty's Stationery Office, 1948), 24.

[5] Id.

[6] FM 27–10, *The Law of Land Warfare* (Washington, DC: GPO, 1956), para. 499, at 178. Emphasis supplied.

[7] Yoram Dinstein, *The Conduct of Hostilities under the Law of International Armed Conflict* (New York: Cambridge University Press, 2004), 229. "As pointed out by H. Lauterpacht, 'textbook writers and, occasionally, military manuals and official pronouncements have erred on the side of comprehensiveness' in making 'no attempt to distinguish between violations of the rules of warfare and war crimes.'" Footnote omitted.

killing of hostages, plunder of public or private property, wanton destruction of cities, towns or villages, or devastation not justified by military necessity."[8]

Article 8(2) of the 1998 Statute of the International Criminal Court (ICC) contains the most detailed definition, listing four categories of war crimes: "grave breaches"; "other serious violations of the laws and customs applicable in international armed conflict"; "serious violations of article 3 common to the four Geneva Conventions" committed in armed conflicts not of an international character; and "other serious violations of the laws and customs applicable in armed conflicts not of an international character."

The International Committee of the Red Cross (ICRC) study of customary law simply says, "Serious violations of international humanitarian law constitutes war crimes."[9] In a formal written objection to the ICRC's study, the United States notes, "The national legislation cited in the commentary to [the ICRC's definition] employs a variety of definitions of 'war crimes,' only a few of which closely parallel the definition apparently employed by the *Study*, and none matches it exactly."[10] As the study's commentary confirms, there is no single binding definition of "war crime."

✴   Despite the broad range of acceptable definitions, courts still occasionally mistake what constitutes a war crime. In 2008, the Italian Court of Cassation, in an unreported case, initiated a criminal case against an American soldier (who was not present in court) over a 2005 incident at a Baghdad checkpoint. The soldier fired on a speeding approaching vehicle, killing a senior Italian intelligence officer, wounding the driver (another intelligence officer), and wounding a recently freed Iraqi insurgent kidnap victim, a female Italian reporter. The soldier was charged under Italian criminal law with voluntary murder and voluntary attempted murder.

At trial, the soldier's defense counsel urged jurisdictional immunity because he was acting in an official capacity as a state agent. The prosecution countered that if his act was a war crime, the soldier would not enjoy such immunity. That led the court to describe war crimes as "odious and inhuman" acts, not isolated and individual acts, and acts that are intentional. Although the court's actual description of a war crime was lengthier, the elements it highlighted were erroneous. Not all war crimes are odious or inhuman acts: Misuse of the Red Cross emblem or appropriation of private property, for instance. Individual acts clearly may constitute war crimes, and intent is not indispensable to prosecution. If it were, intent would have to be established in each grave breach prosecution, and that is not the case. Recklessness, as well as intent, is a sufficient prosecutorial basis.

Finding the soldier's act not to have been a war crime, the court ruled that he was fulfilling official duties and enjoyed immunity; the Italian court lacked jurisdiction.[11]

---

[8] UK Ministry of Defence, *The Manual of the Law of Armed Conflict* (Oxford: Oxford University Press, 2004), para. 16.21 at 422. Emphasis suplied.

[9] Jean-Marie Henckaerts and Louise Doswald-Beck, eds., *Customary International Humanitarian Law. Vol. II. Practice*, Part 1 (Cambridge: Cambridge University Press, 2005), Rule 156, at 568. This definition is followed by six pages of discussion of the meaning of the nine-word definition.

[10] John B. Bellinger III and William J. Haynes II, "A US Government Response to the International Committee of the Red Cross Study Customary International Humanitarian Law," 866 *Int'l Rev. of the Red Cross* (June 2007), 443, 467.

[11] Antonio Cassese, "The Italian Court of Cassation Misapprehends the Notion of War Crimes," 6–3 *J. of Int'l. Crim. Justice* (Nov. 2008), 1077.

War crimes are not subject to a statute of limitations.[12] "Once a war criminal, always a war criminal."[13] (Interestingly, the statutes of the International Criminal Tribunal for the Former Yugoslavia, the ICC, and the Nuremberg and Tokyo International Military Tribunals all omit mention of a statute of limitations, or its absence.)[14]

8.2 War Crimes in Recent History

There are breaches of the law of war that do not constitute grave breaches.[15] Such offenses are nevertheless violations of the laws and customs of war. A U.S. Marine Corps reference directs, "However, [war crimes] investigators should primarily concern themselves with violations that are serious in nature ... and that have a nexus to armed conflict."[16] Disciplinary or administrative offenses against LOAC do not have penal significance or trigger the mandatory actions that grave breach offenses require.

> For example, would a third state have the right to prosecute a foreign army officer for failure to comply with Article 94 of the Third Geneva Convention, which requires notification on recapture of an escaped prisoner of war? Or with Article 96, which requires that a record of disciplinary punishment be kept by the camp commander? I think not. ... These technical breaches are not recognized by the community of nations as of universal concern.[17]

An example of a disciplinary war crime is *The Trial of Heinz Hagendorf* (Cases and Materials, Chapter 3), a 1946 military commission involving the misuse of the Red Cross emblem.[18] Another example is the *Trial of Christian Baus*, a 1947 post–World War II French military tribunal, in which the accused, Baus, was a German civilian transport contractor. As a land superintendent *(Bauerfuehrer)* in occupied France, he managed six French farms. Late in the war, during Germany's retreat from France, Baus stole a household of furniture and belongings from the owners of two farms he oversaw. Convicted of theft, pillage, and "abuse of confidence," Baus was sentenced to two years' confinement.[19] The theft and abuse charges were based on the French penal code, but, under the French law establishing jurisdiction in military tribunals (the Ordinance of 28th August 1944), military courts could incorporate such civil offenses. "The Court had taken the view that misappropriation by abuse of confidence was in itself a war crime, and ... a further illustration of war crimes against property, and of the laws and customs of war as understood by one country."[20]

In another 1947 French military tribunal, *Trial of Gustav Becker, Wilhelm Weber and 18 Others*,[21] twenty German officers, noncommissioned officers, and men of the Customs

---

[12] 1968 U.N. Convention on the Non-Applicability of Statutory Limitations to War Crimes and Crimes against Humanity, *UN Juridical Y.B.* (1968), 160–1.

[13] Dinstein, *Conduct of Hostilities*, supra, note 7, at 234.

[14] Antonio Cassese, ed., *The Oxford Companion to International Criminal Justice* (Oxford: Oxford University Press, 2009), 522.

[15] 1949 Geneva Conventions common Article 49/50/129/146.

[16] Marine Corps Reference Publication (MCRP) 4–11.8B, *War Crimes* (Sept. 6, 2005), 3.

[17] Theodor Meron, "International Criminalization of Internal Atrocities," 89–3 *AJIL* (July 1995), 554, 570–1.

[18] UNWCC, *Law Reports of Trials of War Criminals*, Vol. XIII (London: H.M. Stationary Office, 1949), 146–8. (Footnotes omitted.)

[19] Id., Vol. IX, at 68–71.   [20] Id., from "Notes on the Nature of the Case," at 70.

[21] Id., Vol. VII, at 67–73. (Footnotes omitted.)

Commissariat in French Savoy arrested French civilians, badly mistreating some. Three victims later died in German captivity. The twenty officers were charged with the war crimes of illegal arrest and ill treatment. Are those war crimes? "Illegal arrest or detention does not appear in the list of war crimes drawn up by the 1919 Commission on Responsibilities [that sought to assign responsibility for beginning World War I]. Neither is it explicitly mentioned in the Hague Regulations respecting the Laws and Customs of War on Land, 1907. It has, however, emerged as a clear case of war crime . . . under the impact of the criminal activities of the Nazis and their satellites, during the second world war."[22] Once again, under French military commission law, the acts were war crimes. One of the *Becker* accused was acquitted for lack of evidence. The others were convicted of illegal arrest and ill treatment, two were sentenced to two and three years' imprisonment, and seventeen others were sentenced to twenty years' confinement at hard labor.

Were these civil offenses really war crimes? A civilian stealing furniture from a civilian farm in occupied territory? Illegal arrests by combatant officers? Yes, they were. As will be seen (Chapter 21.4.1), there are three types of military commission, each with its own jurisdictional basis. Military government commissions, the type of military commission employed in the French cases described, "may try ordinary crimes – e.g., manslaughter or robbery – and violations of military orders committed by soldiers or civilians in territories under . . . military government."[23] More familiar are law of war military commissions that, as the name implies, may solely try violations of the laws and customs of war. America's Guantánamo military commissions had such a jurisdictional basis. The third variety, martial law military commissions, has an even more narrow jurisdiction. Depending on its jurisdictional grant, ordinary domestic crimes may be tried by a military commission, as they were in the French cases.

"War crimes" is an elastic rubric, and necessarily so. No list of war crimes or grave breaches could embrace all possible violations. Cannibalism, for example, was never envisioned as a potential crime of war. Yet, after World War II at least nine Japanese combatants were convicted of cannibalism as a war crime.[24] Other undefined delicts are addressed by customary rules and national codes, like those in the French tribunals. "Customary rules have the advantage of being applicable to all parties to an armed conflict – State and non-State – independent of any formal ratification process. In substance, they fill certain gaps and regulate some issues that are not sufficiently addressed in treaty law."[25] Grave breach offenses are another matter.

8.3 Grave Breaches and Universal Jurisdiction

Grave breaches are defined in the 1949 conventions and the 1977 additional protocols. Universal jurisdiction is a significant aspect of grave breaches. The convention "lays the

---

[22] Id., from "Notes on the Case," at 68.

[23] *Ali Hamza Ahmad Suliman al Bahlul v. United States*,____F.2d____(D.C. Circuit., July 15, 2014).

[24] Judgment, Tokyo International Military Tribunal, cited in Leon Freidman, ed., *The Law of War: A Documentary History* (New York: Random House, 1972), 1029–183, 1088: "This horrible practice was indulged in from choice and not of necessity." Also, Chester Hearn, *Sorties into Hell* (Westport, CT: Praeger, 2003), 181–92, relating two 1946 Guam military commission sentences; and "Japanese Officer's Cannibalism," *London Times*, Dec. 3, 1945, http://forum.axishistory.com/viewtopic.php?t=21498.

[25] ICRC, "International Humanitarian Law and the Challenges of Contemporary Armed Conflicts," 867 *Int'l Rev. of the Red Cross* (Sept. 2007), 719, 742.

foundation of the system adopted for suppressing breaches of the Convention[s]. The system is based on three fundamental obligations, which are laid on each Contracting Party – namely the obligation to enact special legislation ... the obligation to search for any person accused of violation ... and the obligation to try such persons or, if the Contracting Party prefers, to hand them over for trial to another State concerned."[26] States ratifying the Geneva Conventions are obliged to enact criminal legislation that extends not only to their own nationals, but to any person who has committed a grave breach, including its enemies.[27]

> When charges are preferred against a war criminal, the overriding consideration in the matter of jurisdiction is that the crimes at issue are defined by international law itself. The governing principle is then universality: all States are empowered to try and punish war criminals. The upshot is that a belligerent State is allowed to institute penal proceedings against an enemy war criminal, irrespective of the territory where the crime was committed or the nationality of the victim. In all likelihood, a neutral State (despite the fact that it does not take part in the hostilities) can also prosecute war criminals.[28]

That is a statement of universal jurisdiction. The 1949 conventions envisioned that grave breaches could be committed only in an international armed conflict, and, until recently, that was the traditional view. However, under emergent state practice, bolstered by International Criminal Tribunal for the Former Yugoslavia (ICTY) opinions, grave breaches may be committed in noninternational armed conflicts, as well.[29] (See Chapter 3, Section 3.8.7.) ICTY opinions, buttressed by inconsistent state practice, however, do not rise to the extensive or uniform practice required to constitute customary international law. One International Court of Justice (ICJ) separate opinion finds that *absolute* universal jurisdiction – jurisdiction asserted over an offense committed elsewhere by an individual not present in the forum state and having no connection to the forum state – is not reflected in any current state legislation.[30]

Still, grave breaches are ostensibly subject to imposition of universal jurisdiction. Universal jurisdiction, usually seen as a supplementary or optional jurisdictional basis, negates the need for a link, such as nationality, between the accused and the state in which he is tried. The essence of universal jurisdiction is that some customary international law offenses – piracy,[31] slave trade, traffic in children and

---

[26] Jean S. Pictet, *Commentary: I Geneva Convention for the Amelioration of the Condition of the Wounded and Sick in Armed Forces in the Field* (Geneva: ICRC, 1952), 362. Hereafter, *Commentary*, Geneva Convention I.

[27] Jean de Preux, *Commentary: III Geneva Convention Relative to the Treatment of Prisoners of War* (Geneva: ICRC, 1960), 623. Hereafter, *Commentary*, Geneva Convention III.

[28] Dinstein, *Conduct of Hostilities*, supra, note 7, at 236.

[29] Eve La Haye, *War Crimes in Internal Armed Conflicts* (New York: Cambridge University Press, 2008), 229. "European states and newly independent republics of Eastern Europe ... have included war crimes committed in *internal* armed conflicts in their criminal codes and have also extended universal jurisdiction over such offenses. These countries include ... Colombia, Costa Rica ... Denmark ... France, Finland ... the Netherlands ... Norway, Portugal, the Republic of Congo, Sweden ... Spain, Switzerland." Footnotes omitted, emphasis supplied.

[30] *Arrest Warrant of 11 April 2000 (Democratic Republic of Congo v. Belgium)*, judgment [2002], ICJ Rpts 3, joint separate opinion of Judges Higgins, Kooijmans, and Burgenthal, para. 20–1.

[31] *Republic of Korea v. Araye*, No. 2011 Do 12927, Supreme Court of Republic of Korea (Dec. 22, 2011), a case upholding universal jurisdiction over Somali pirates who hijacked a Korean vessel in the Indian Ocean. Case digest at 106–3 *AJIL* (July 2012), 630.

women, grave breaches – are so heinous that every state is considered to have an interest in their prosecution.[*]

Universal jurisdiction is not a universally shared goal. Henry Kissinger has written, "It has spread with extraordinary speed and has not been subjected to systematic debate. ... To be sure, human rights violations, war crimes, genocide, and torture have so disgraced the modern age ... that the effort to interpose legal norms to prevent or punish such outrages does credit to its advocates. The danger lies in pushing the effort to extremes that risk substituting the tyranny of judges for that of governments."[32] More immediately, "the exercise of jurisdiction by one state on the basis of the universality principle may intrude upon the sovereignty of other states. For that reason it is generally assumed that states must have consented to the exercise of universal jurisdiction in a particular treaty, or that such exercise must follow from customary international law over a particular category of crimes."[33] Examples of cases involving universal jurisdiction are the 1962 *Adolf Eichmann*, 1981 *John Demjanjuk*, and, less constructively, 1998–9 *Augusto Pinochet* cases.[34]

Although there have been numerous worldwide prosecutions for grave breaches, prosecutions based on absolute universal jurisdiction are few. States are averse to the possible exercise of such jurisdiction against their citizens, seeing it as a threat to sovereignty, or they argue that the suspect can be adequately dealt with by their own domestic law, civil or military.[35] States rarely initiate a criminal proceeding on the basis of universal jurisdiction unless the suspect is present in the state – although, if the suspect is present, then the prosecution is not an *absolute* universal jurisdiction prosecution, but a *permissive* universal jurisdiction prosecution.[36]

In U.S. practice, the War Crimes Act of 1996 does not provide for universal jurisdiction.[37] Other countries – particularly Denmark, Germany, the Netherlands, Spain, and Switzerland – have vigorous universal jurisdiction laws.[38] Spain applied pure universal jurisdiction when, in February 2008, it issued an indictment charging forty current and former Rwandan military officials, who were not present in Spain, with war crimes, terrorism, crimes against humanity, and genocide. "The Indictment cites ... the [Spanish] Organic Law on the Judiciary to find that Spanish courts may exercise universal jurisdiction without any connection between the crimes and the *forum* state.

[margin annotation: unsurprisingly]

---

[*] Today, universal jurisdiction has been extended by treaty to a wide range of offenses, including aircraft hijacking, hostage taking, apartheid, torture, mercenaries, counterfeiting, and theft of nuclear material. In each case, however, the presence of the accused in the territory of the charging state is required.

[32] Henry A. Kissinger, "The Pitfalls of Universal Jurisdiction," *Foreign Affairs* (July/August 2001).

[33] Sonja Boelaert-Suominen, "Grave Breaches, Universal Jurisdiction and Internal Armed Conflict: Is Customary Law Moving towards a Uniform Enforcement Mechanism for All Armed Conflicts?" 5–1 J. *Conflict & Security L.* (June 2000), 63, 71–2.

[34] *Eichmann v. Attorney General of Israel*, 136 ILR 277 (1962); and United Kingdom House of Lords: *Regina v. Bartle and the Commissioner of Police for the Metropolitan District and Others, ex Parte Pinochet* (Nov. 25, 1998 and March 24, 1999). Demjanjuk's conviction (and sentence to death) was overturned by the Israeli Supreme Court: *Demjanjuk v. Attorney General of Israel* (July 29, 1993).

[35] Jaques Verhaegen, "Legal Obstacles to Prosecution of Breaches of Humanitarian Law," 261 *Int'l Rev. of the Red Cross* 607 (Nov.–Dec. 1987).

[36] See: La Haye, *War Crimes in Internal Armed Conflicts*, supra, note 29, chapter 5, for a discussion of universal jurisdiction and war crimes.

[37] 18 USC Part I, Chapter 118, §2441. *U.S. v. Ramzi Yousef and Others*, 327 F. 3rd 56 (2nd Cir., 2003), held that the crime of terrorism was not subject to universal jurisdiction.

[38] Luc Reydams, *Universal Jurisdiction* (Oxford: Oxford University Press, 2003), 157, 191, 201.

This assertion of 'unconditional' or 'absolute' universal jurisdiction is in line with the most recent jurisprudence of Spanish courts."[39] (In mid-2009, the Spanish legislature limited the court's universal jurisdiction authority.) German case law, under the Code of Crimes against International Law, has also embraced pure universal jurisdiction.[40]

Territorial jurisdiction remains the preferred jurisdictional basis for trial, but many, including Louise Arbour, see an expanding role for the prosecution of war crimes under universal jurisdiction.[41] Others disagree,[42] pointing to Belgium's ignominious retreat, under U.S. pressure, from its universal jurisdiction statute.[43]

The first domestic prosecution based on the grave breaches universal jurisdiction provisions of the Geneva Conventions did not occur until 1994, forty-five years after their enactment in the 1949 conventions.[44] It remains to be seen whether universal jurisdiction, absolute or permissive, will become a force in the prosecution of war crimes and grave breaches.

8.3.1 *Prosecuting War Crimes: Codification and the Required Nexus*

Defining war crimes or grave breaches is a **first step** in assessing individual criminal responsibility for LOAC/IHL breaches. Committing a well-defined grave breach, alone, is not sufficient. "It is not enough to sign a treaty. States also have to take positive steps to enact domestic law or otherwise ensure that the provisions of the international treaties are put into effect."[45] To allow prosecution, the war crime must be incorporated into a criminal code, a prosecutorial vehicle – the **second requirement** for war crimes. That vehicle may be the military code of the state, such as the U.S. Uniform Code of Military Justice, or it may be a domestic civil or criminal code, such as the U.S. War Crimes Act. It may be the code of an ad hoc international tribunal, such as the statute of the ICTY, or that of a standing international court, such as the statute of the ICC.

Including war crimes and grave breaches in a criminal code is not the last consideration. "A great many crimes are committed in armed conflicts that do not constitute war crimes."[46] If a war crime or grave breach is charged, "the necessity of the connection between the conduct in question and the ongoing conflict – often called the nexus – is crucial in order to determine if one faces a violation of domestic law or a war crime."[47]

---

[39] Commentator, "The Spanish Indictment of High-Ranking Rwandan Officials," 6–5 *J. of Int'l Crim. Justice* (Nov. 2008), 1003, 1006.

[40] 2002 *Bundesgesetzblatt, Teil I*, at 2254, cited at id., 1007.

[41] Louise Arbour, "Will the ICC Have an Impact on Universal Jurisdiction?" 1–3 *J. of Int'l Crim. Justice* (Dec. 2003), 585–8.

[42] George P. Fletcher, "Against Universal Jurisdiction," 1–3 *J. of Int'l Crim. Justice* (Dec. 2003), 580–84; and Georges Abi-Saab, "The Proper Role of Universal Jurisdiction," 1–3 *J. of Int'l Crim. Justice* (Dec. 2003), 596–602.

[43] Luc Reydams, "Belgium Reneges on Universality," 1–3 *J. of Int'l Crim. Justice* (Dec. 2003), 679.

[44] *The Prosecution v. Refiik Saric*, unpublished (Denmark High Ct., 1994), referenced in *Prosecutor v Tadić*, Defense Motion on Jurisdiction, supra, note 3, at para. 83.

[45] Brigadier General Kenneth Watkin, "21st Century Conflict and International Humanitarian Law: Status Quo or Change?" in Michael N. Schmitt and Jelena Pejic, eds., *International Law and Armed Conflict: Exploring the Faultlines* (Leiden: Martinus Nijhoff, 2007), 264–96, 283.

[46] Guénaël Mettraux, *International Crimes and the Ad Hoc Tribunals* (Oxford: Oxford University Press, 2005), 38.

[47] La Haye, *War Crimes in Internal Armed Conflicts*, supra, note 29, at 110.

This is the <u>third requirement</u> for a war crime. As in the post–World War II *Baus* case, involving furniture theft, and in the *Becker* illegal arrest case, acts not usually thought of as war crimes in a given context may be such. "In the judgments rendered so far, the ad hoc Tribunals [the ICTY and the International Criminal Tribunal for Rwanda (ICTR)] have used an objective test to determine the existence and character of an armed conflict, as well as the nexus to the conflict."[48]

> If, for instance, a civilian merely takes advantage of the general atmosphere of lawlessness created by the armed conflict to kill a hated neighbor or to steal his property without his acts being otherwise closely connected to the armed conflict, such conduct would not generally constitute a war crime. ... There should be no presumption ... that, because a crime is committed in time of war, it therefore automatically constitutes a war crime.[49]

Sometimes the determination is easily made. On a September 1966 night during the United States–Vietnam War, a nine-man patrol entered the Vietnamese hamlet of Xuan Gnoc (2). Led by Private First Class John Potter, U.S. Marine Corps, the nine went on a criminal rampage. They raped two women and shot and killed the husband, sister, and child of one of the rape victims; the sister's child; and another villager. Found out by a suspicious company commander who did not believe their patrol report, the patrol members received courts-martial. Potter was convicted of five counts of premeditated murder, rape, and attempted rape. He was sentenced to confinement at hard labor for life.[50] Were his acts war crimes, and what facts indicate the answer?

The crimes of the Potter patrol were grave breaches. They were committed in the midst of the conflict. The Marines were combatants, and the victims were noncombatants. Potter and his coaccuseds would not have been at the scene but for the patrol they were carrying out in furtherance of their military command's mission. The armed conflict played a substantial role in the perpetrators' ability to commit their crimes. All of these factors make clear that the crimes of the Potter patrol were war crimes and grave breaches.

SIDEBAR. In 1969, in South Vietnam, Army Sergeant Roy Bumgarner was charged with the premeditated murder of three Vietnamese civilian men. Bumgarner admitted the killings but urged that he had killed the three in combat. He was convicted at court-martial of the lesser offense of unpremeditated murder, times three, and was sentenced to reduction in rank to private, and forfeiture of ninety-seven dollars pay per month for twenty-four months. Shockingly, after convicting Bumgarner of three murders, the military jury imposed no punitive discharge and no confinement. Upon appellate review, error was found and the sentence was reduced to a reduction to private and loss of ninety-seven dollars pay per month for six months. Private Bumgarner was then reenlisted for further military duty. The case says much about the attitude that was sometimes taken toward Vietnamese crime victims.[51] Was this a war crime?

---

[48] Knut Dörmann, *Elements of War Crimes* (Cambridge: ICRC/Cambridge University Press, 2003), 27.
[49] Mettraux, *International Crimes and the* Ad Hoc *Tribunals*, supra, note 46, at 42.
[50] *U.S. v. John D. Potter*, 39 CMR 791 (NBR, 1968).
[51] *U.S. v. Plt. Sgt. Roy E. Bumgarner* (43 C.M.R. 559, ACMR, 1970).

The "Kosovo War" (1996–9) pitted Serbia and Yugoslavia against the Kosovo Liberation Army. That conflict was immediately followed by that of Yugoslavia against North Atlantic Treaty Organization forces, the fighting ending in June 1999. In January 2000, in Vitina, Kosovo, a small Macedonian village, Staff Sergeant Frank Ronghi, a U.S. Army 82nd Airborne Division peacekeeper, kidnapped, raped, and murdered an eleven-year-old Kosovar girl. He was quickly apprehended, court-martialed, and sentenced to imprisonment for life without possibility of parole.[52] Were his acts war crimes? They were not. The armed conflict had ended and his acts had no relation to any ongoing conflict. The armed conflict played no role in Rongi's ability to commit his crimes. There is no hard-and-fast rule that differentiates a war crime from a domestic crime, but there are guidelines. "What distinguishes a war crime from a purely domestic crime is that a war crime is shaped by or dependent upon the environment – the armed conflict – in which it is committed."[53]

In the context of a noninternational armed conflict, a 2002 ICTY case provides indicators that the nexus requirement may have been met: "The fact that the perpetrator is a combatant; the fact that the victim is a non-combatant; the fact that the victim is a member of the opposing party; the fact that the act may be said to serve the ultimate goal of a military campaign and the fact that the crime is committed as part of or in the context of the perpetrator's official duties."[54] While such guidelines are helpful, each case is fact-specific and contextual, requiring its own assessment.

The <u>fourth requirement</u> for a war crime seems so obvious as to require no mention: The charged offense must constitute an offense within the jurisdictional grant of the tribunal involved. Recall that there are three varieties of military commission, each with its own jurisdictional basis – military government military commissions, martial law military commissions, and the more usual *law of war* military commissions. (See Chapter 21.4.1.)

If a military government military commission is the authorized trial forum, the charged act must be a violation of the domestic criminal law of the state conducting the trial, or a violation of the laws and customs of war. Prosecution in a military government military commission requires that only one prong or the other be satisfied.

If the military commission is a law of war military commission, such as those tried by the U.S. at Guantánamo Bay, Cuba, the charged offense must be an internationally recognized violation of the laws and customs of war.[55]

At Guantánamo, beginning in 2006, this war crime requirement generated international attention for its failure to be met. The U.S. Congress legislated at least four war crimes for prosecution at the Guantánamo law of war military commissions that U.S. appellate courts subsequently found were not, in fact, internationally recognized

---

[52] *U.S. v. Frank J. Ronghi*, 60 MJ 83 (CAAF, 2004), cert. den., 543 U.S. 1013 (2004).

[53] La Haye, *War Crimes in Internal Armed Conflicts*, supra, note 29, at 45. Footnote omitted.

[54] Ken Roberts, "The Contribution of the ICTY to the Grave Breaches Regime," 7–4 *J. of Int'l. Crim. J.* 743, 752 (Sept. 2009), citing *Prosecutor v. Kunarac, et al.* (IT-96-23-A), Judgment (June 12, 2002).

[55] It is within the authority of a state to pass domestic legislation making *any* act a "war crime." Unless the legislated act is internationally recognized as a violation of the customs and laws of war, however, that "war crime" may lawfully be prosecuted (subject to ex post facto doctrine) as a war crime only in the domestic courts and military tribunals of the state that made it a "war crime." Passing a domestic law that something is a war crime does not make it so, 1–3 *J. of Int'l Crim. Justice* (Dec. 2003), 596–602 in international criminal law.

violations of the laws and customs of war. The appellate courts found that material support for terrorism and conspiracy to commit terrorist acts, two of the most frequent Guantánamo charges, were not internationally recognized as war crimes. Two other charges, murder in violation of the law of war and solicitation to commit a war crime, were also found not to constitute war crimes. The appellate rejection of these charges was a serious blow to the effectiveness and credibility of U.S. military commissions, the jurisdiction of which rested solely on violations of the laws and customs of war. (See Chapter 21.7.4 for a full discussion of this issue.)

8.3.2 *Prosecuting War Crimes: Who?*

A war crime charging consideration is whether the suspect is amenable to charges. Who can commit a war crime?

Members of the armed forces of a party to the conflict, including enemy fighters/unlawful combatants in a noninternational armed conflict, obviously may be charged with LOAC violations under civil or military codes.

Civilian property can be the subject of a war crime prosecution, as well. Article 35 of the 1863 Lieber Code reminded Union soldiers that "classical works of art, libraries, scientific collections, or precious instruments, such as astronomical telescopes, as well as hospitals, must be secured against all avoidable injury." Today's roster of protected property is longer and more specific (see Chapter 18). If, during a period of occupation, a civilian vehicle, or other property belonging to civilians or civilian companies, is seized absent military necessity, or if cash, art, cultural objects, historic monuments, or spiritual objects belonging to the occupied state are taken or purposely damaged or destroyed without military necessity, a war crime has been committed.[56] The wanton extensive destruction and appropriation of property are grave breaches.[57] A too-frequent violation is, upon capture, the taking of a prisoner of war's (POW's) personal property.[58] Common sense indicates what and when civilian property may be seized, although common sense in occupied territory is sometimes in short supply. In World War II, "nearly all the men in ETO [the European Theater of Operations] participated in the looting. It was a phenomenon of war. Thousands of men who had never before in their lives taken something of value that did not belong to them began taking it for granted that whatever they wanted was theirs. ... Anything any German soldier had was fair game; looting from civilians was frowned upon, but it happened anyway."[59] Though many such breaches are disciplinary in nature, they constitute the crime of theft and subject the violator to administrative or criminal disciplinary action.

Just as civilians can be the victims of war crimes, they can commit them. In convicting the makers of poison gas used by the Nazis in their World War II extermination camps, a British tribunal ruled in 1946, "the decision of the Military Court in the present case is a clear example of ... the rule that the provisions of the laws and customs of war are

---

[56] 1907 Hague Regulation IV, Articles 23(g) and 53; 1977 Additional Protocol I, Art. 53(a), and Additional Protocol II, Art. 16.

[57] 1949 Geneva Convention common Art. 50/51/130/147.

[58] 1949 Geneva Convention III, Relative to the Treatment of Prisoners of War, Art. 18. Hereafter: "Geneva Convention III."

[59] Stephen E. Ambrose, *Band of Brothers* (New York: Simon & Schuster, 1992), 268.

addressed not only to combatants and to members of state and other public authorities, but to anybody who is in a position to assist in their violation. ... Any civilian who is an accessory to a violation of the laws and customs of war is himself also liable as a war criminal."[60] The ICTY and ICTR have convicted many civilians, including unlawful combatants, of war crimes.[61]

In a common Article 3 noninternational armed conflict, such as the U.S. "war on terrorism," can Taliban and al Qaeda members be charged with war crimes? Is it possible to charge nonstate actors with violations of the Geneva Conventions or Additional Protocol I, instruments to which they have never agreed and to which they may not become parties? Yes, although not directly. There are several approaches to prosecuting rebels – civilians who fight against their parent state.[62] Under international criminal law both organizations are criminal groups, and their members common criminals. Like any other criminals, they may be prosecuted under the criminal law of the states in which they commit terrorist acts. Any LOAC/IHL violations they commit may be tried as the corresponding criminal acts made criminal by the domestic codes of the victim states. Just as members of the armed forces who commit grave breaches are tried under their state's military code, Taliban and al Qaeda members are tried under their state's penal code, or the opposing state's military tribunals for violations of LOAC. While in military custody, even in a common Article 3 noninternational conflict, enemy fighters remain protected by common Article 3 and Article 75 of Additional Protocol I.[63]

In short, anyone can commit a war crime. Absent one of the usual exclusions for criminal responsibility, diminished responsibility and insanity, duress, mistake of fact, or mistake of law, both combatants and civilians may be charged.

8.4 Rape and Other Gender Crimes

Gender crimes, including rape and other forms of sexual violence, were long ignored in LOAC/IHL. That has changed dramatically. "The primary impetus for the new developments in redressing sex crimes was the establishment of the International Criminal Tribunal for the Former Yugoslavia ... in 1993."[64]

The 1863 Lieber Code, Articles 44 and 47, specifies rape as a war crime. Still, rape was common in all combat theaters of World War II, committed by both Axis and Allied forces. "Rape has always been considered a war crime, although it was not mentioned as such in either the Nuremberg Charter or the Geneva Conventions, which probably

---

[60] *Trial of Bruno Tesch and Two Others* ("The Zyklon B Case"), U.N. War Crimes Commission, *LRTWC*, Vol. I (London: U.N. War Crimes Comm., 1947), 93, 103.

[61] E.g., *Prosecutor v. Musema*, ICTR-96–13-A, trial judgment (Jan. 27, 2000), at paras. 12, 279.

[62] See Lindsay Moir, *The Law of Internal Armed Conflict* (New York: Cambridge University Press, 2002), 52–8; and Liesbeth Zegveld, *The Accountability of Armed Opposition Groups in International Law* (Cambridge: Cambridge University Press, 2002), 14–26.

[63] As noted in previous chapters, the United States considers Art. 75 customary international law, as do most states. The United States, however, views it as customary law only in common Art. 2 international armed conflicts. The White House, "Fact Sheet: New Actions on Guantánamo and Detainee Policy" (March 7, 2011). Executive Order 13567, "Periodic Review of Individuals Detained at Guantánamo Bay Naval Station" to which the Fact Sheet pertains, makes no mention of Article 75, however.

[64] Kelly D. Askin, "A Decade of the Development of Gender Crimes in International Courts and Tribunals: 1993 to 2003," 11–3 *Human Rights Brief* (American University Washington College of Law, Spring 2004), 16. The arc of cases described in this section is from Ms. Askin's perceptive article.

reflects the fact that it was not always prosecuted with great diligence."[65] It is not specified as a grave breach in the 1949 Geneva Conventions; nor is it mentioned in common Article 3, although it is prohibited in Geneva Convention IV, Article 27, in relation to protected persons. It was first explicitly nominated a crime against humanity after World War II, in Control Council Law No. 10, the document that authorized Nuremberg's "subsequent proceedings," but, until recently, battlefield rape was viewed with little concern. In 1991, the conflict in the former Yugoslavia changed that. "Today it is firmly established that rape and other acts of sexual violence entail individual criminal responsibility under international law,"[66] and LOAC/IHL. In 1993, Theodor Meron wrote:

> That the practice of rape has been deliberate, massive and egregious, particularly in Bosnia-Hercegovina, is amply demonstrated. ... The special rapporteur appointed by the UN Commission on Human Rights ... highlighted the role of rape both as an attack on the individual victim and as a method of "ethnic cleansing" "intended to humiliate, shame, degrade and terrify the entire ethnic group." Indescribable abuse of thousands of women in the territory of former Yugoslavia was needed to shock the international community into rethinking the prohibition of rape as a crime under the laws of war.[67]

The international community's shock led to a reinvigorated criminalization and prosecution of rape. Article 5 of the ICTY's statute, based on 1907 Hague Regulation IV, lists rape as a crime against humanity. The Rome Statute of the ICC declares it a war crime and a violation of the laws and customs of both international and noninternational armed conflict.[68] "State practice establishes this rule as a norm of customary international law applicable in both international and non-international armed conflicts."[69] In U.S. military practice, upon conviction of rape the maximum punishment (although not imposed in the last half-century) is death.[70] Forced pregnancy is criminalized in ICC Articles 8 (2) (b) (xxii), and 8 (2) (e) (vi), relating to international and noninternational armed conflicts, respectively. Domestic courts are also taking a newly invigorated stance toward gender crimes in armed conflict.[71] The U.N. Security Council, in 2008, condemned sexual violence in armed conflict, calling for prosecution and an end to its inclusion in conflict-ending amnesty provisions.[72]

---

[65] William A. Schabas, *An Introduction to the International Criminal Court* (Cambridge: Cambridge University Press, 2001), 43.

[66] Wolfgang Schomburg and Ines Peterson, "Genuine Consent to Sexual Violence under International Criminal Law," 101–1 *AJIL* (Jan. 2007), 121, 122.

[67] Theodor Meron, "Rape as a Crime under International Humanitarian Law," 87–3 *AJIL* (July 1993), 424–8, 425. Footnotes omitted.

[68] Arts. 8.2.(b)(xxii) and 8.2.(e)(vi), respectively.

[69] Jean-Marie Henckaerts and Louise Doswald-Beck, eds., *Customary International Humanitarian Law. Vol. I. Rules* (Cambridge: Cambridge University Press, 2005), Rule 93, at 323.

[70] *Manual for Courts-Martial, United States* (Washington, DC: GPO, 2008), appendix 12, Table of Maximum Punishments, Art. 120, at A12–3. For a review of U.S. armed services' involvement with rape in World War II, see J. Robert Lilly, *Taken by Force: Rape and American GIs in Europe during World War II* (New York: Palgrave Macmillan, 2007).

[71] E.g., Angela J. Edman, "Crimes of Sexual Violence in the War Crimes Chamber of the State Court of Bosnia and Herzegovina: Successes and Challenges," 16–1 *Human Rights Brief* (American University Washington College of Law, Spring 2004), 21.

[72] S.C. Resolution 1820 (June 9, 2008).

The sea change in the approach to sexual crimes as war crimes, torture, and crimes against humanity is seen in five ICTR and ICTY cases: *Akayesu*, *Delalić*, *Furundžija*, *Kunarac*, and *Kvočka*.

SIDEBAR. The leading decision confirming rape as a crime against humanity is the ICTR's *Akayesu* judgment.[73] The mayor of the Rwandan town of Taba was Jean-Paul Akayesu. His initial indictment did not charge sexual violence. "In the midst of the trial, a witness on the stand spontaneously testified about the gang rape of her 6-year-old daughter. A subsequent witness testified that she herself was raped and she witnessed or knew of other rapes. The sole female judge at the ICTR at that time, Judge Navanethem Pillay [a South African Tamil], was one of the three judges sitting on the case. Having extensive expertise in gender violence, Judge Pillay questioned the witness about these crimes. Suspecting that these were not isolated instances of rape, the judges invited the prosecution to consider ... amending the indictment to include charges for the rape crimes."[74] The prosecution did so. At the resumed trial, several other witnesses described pervasive rape and forced nudity in Akayesu's presence and with his encouragement. The trial chamber held that sexual violence was widespread and systematic in Taba, committed by Hutus to humiliate, harm, and destroy Tutsis. Akayesu was convicted of, inter alia, rape as genocide and as a crime against humanity. He was sentenced to imprisonment for life.[75]

As significant as the *Akayesu* decision is, its focus on coercion as an element of rape was reversed in subsequent jurisprudence.[76]

The Appeals Chamber in *Kunarac* [a 2002 ICTY opinion] confirmed that the correct requirement was lack of consent of the victim. ... The Elements of Crimes of the ICC Statute were drafted before the Appeals Chamber's decision in *Kunarac* and they depart from it, requiring as they do that the acts be committed by force or by threat of force or coercion, such as that caused by fear of violence, duress, detention, psychological oppression or abuse of power, against such person or persons, or another person, or by taking advantage of a coercive environment or such person's or persons' incapacity to give genuine consent. The ICC Statute thus arguably departs from customary international law.

Akayesu was followed by the ICTY's *Prosecutor v. Delalić*[77] (also called the *Čelebić* case, the name of the Bosnian prison camp where the crimes occurred). Delalić was convicted of torture for the forcible penetrations that he committed while raping his victims multiple times. (See *Delalić*, paras. 475–90, Cases and Materials, Chapter 12, for further discussion of rape as war crime.)

Delalić was followed in turn by *Furundžija*.[78] Anto Furundžija commanded the Jokers, a particularly repellent Croatian paramilitary group. He interrogated a civilian

---

[73] *Prosecutor v. Akayesu*, ICTR-96–4-T (Sept. 2, 1998).
[74] Askin, "Decade of the Development of Gender Crimes," supra, note 64, at 17.   [75] Id.
[76] Fannie Lafontaine, "Canada's Crimes against Humanity and War Crimes Act on Trial," 8–1 *J. of Int'l Crim Justice* (March 2010), 269, 279.
[77] *Prosecutor v. Delalić, et al.*, IT-96–21-T (Nov. 16, 1998).
[78] *Prosecutor v. Furundžija*, IT-95–17/1-T (Dec. 10, 1998).

woman over the course of eleven days, while a coaccused raped her multiple times before an audience of laughing soldiers. Although Furundžija was not the soldier's superior, and although he did not touch the victim, the trial chamber found that he facilitated the rapes and was as responsible as if he had himself raped her. He was convicted as a coperpetrator of rape as torture and as a war crime.

Dragoljub Kunarac commanded a reconnaissance unit of the Bosnian Serb Army. He and two coaccused took civilian women from a detention camp in Foča, sexually enslaving them for weeks or months. He was convicted of rape and enslavement as crimes against humanity.[79] In *Kunarac* the trial chamber redefined the elements of rape in ICTY jurisprudence, as well.[80]

> The Trial Chamber in *Kunarac* held that a definition of rape given in earlier judgments focused too narrowly on the element of coercion, force, or threats of force, thus failing to recognize other factors which may render an act of sexual penetration non-consensual or non-voluntary. ... The essence of rape as an international crime was therefore said to consist in the non-consensual aspect of the act, rather than the use of force or constraint.[81]

Miroslav Kvočka and four coaccused were convicted of sex crimes associated with their tenure at the notorious Omarska detention camp. *Kvočka* is significant for its holding regarding forced nudity, molestation, sexual slavery, sexual mutilation, forced prostitution,[82] forced marriage, forced abortion, forced pregnancy, and forced sterilization, all held to be international crimes of sexual violence.[83] Presuming the proper trial forum, these crimes may be tried as violations of domestic law, or international criminal law or, if there is a nexus to an armed conflict, as violations of LOAC.

Not only does rape constitute a crime against humanity but, because it involves severe pain or suffering, it also constitutes the war crime of torture.[84] Moreover, in an international criminal law context, because the offenses of rape and torture contain

---

[79] *Prosecutor v. Kunarac, et al.*, IT-96–23 and 23/1-A-T (February 22, 2001).

[80] Id., at para. 460. That definition: "The sexual penetration, however slight: (a) of the vagina or anus of the victim by the penis of the perpetrator or any other object used by the perpetrator; or (b) of the mouth of the victim by the penis of the perpetrator; where such sexual penetration occurs without the consent of the victim. Consent for this purpose must be consent given voluntarily, as a result of the victim's free will, assessed in the context of the surrounding circumstances. The *mens rea* is the intention to effect this sexual penetration, and the knowledge that it occurs without the consent of the victim. Force is merely one indicia of the victim's lack of consent. *Prosecutor v. Kunarac*, supra, note 54, at para. 125. It is not necessary for the prosecution to demonstrate that the victim consistently and genuinely resisted. This definition differs slightly from that in *Akayesu*, supra, note 74, at para. 688; see: Schomburg and Peterson, "Genuine Consent to Sexual Violence," supra, note 66, at 132. Also see *Prosecutor v. Kunarac*, supra, note 80, at paras. 127–8; and *Prosecutor v. Akayesu*, supra, note 73, at para. 686.

[81] Mettraux, *International Crimes and the* Ad Hoc *Tribunals*, supra, note 46 at 108.

[82] The offense of forced prostitution was foreshadowed by a post–World War II Dutch war crimes prosecution, *Trial of Washio Awochi*, Netherlands Temporary Court-Martial at Batavia, Oct. 25, 1946, 13 *Law Reports of Trials of War Criminals* (London: UN War Crimes Comm., 1949), 122.

[83] *Prosecutor v. Kvočka*, IT-98–30/1-T (Nov. 2, 2001). *Prosecutor v. Issa Hassan Sesay, Morris Kallon and Augustine Gbao*, The Special Court for Sierra Leone (March 2, 2009) "imposed groundbreaking convictions for the crimes against humanity of sexual slavery and forced marriage." David J. Bederman, ed., "International Decisions," 104–1 *AJIL* (Jan. 2010), 66, 74.

[84] Id., *Kvočka*, at para. 150. "Some acts establish *per se* the suffering of those upon whom they were inflicted. Rape is obviously such an act."

differing elements, an accused may be convicted of both offenses for the commission of a single act of rape.[85]

There have been numerous ICTY and ICTR[86] cases since the five mentioned that address gender war crimes, but those five established the precedents that ICTY trial chambers have followed. The Special Court for Sierra Leone, in its first trial judgment, also found forced marriage a form of sexual slavery and an inhumane act under the Statute of the Special Court.[87] "Rape has now been explicitly recognized as an instrument of genocide, a crime against humanity, and a war crime. ... Sex crimes are justiciable as war crimes regardless of whether they are committed in international or internal armed conflict."[88]

8.5 War Crimes or Not?

Grave breaches are well known and recognizable, being specified in the 1949 conventions and Protocol I. War crimes are also usually apparent in their battlefield wrongfulness, but they are not always recognized. On other occasions, acts presumed to be war crimes are not, just as acts seemingly unrelated to the conflicts in which they occur are held to be war crimes. Several examples follow that illustrate the sometimes-difficult assessments in recognizing possible LOAC violations. The majority of the illustrations involve U.S. combatants. It would be wrong to conclude, because of that, that American combatants are less respectful of LOAC/IHL than are the soldiers of other states. Because recent conflicts have often involved U.S. soldiers and Marines, and because research material involving U.S. forces is more readily available, they appear more frequently in these examples.

Are these acts war crimes? What makes them so, and how logical is the outcome? Each example (except the first) is based on events that occurred in the U.S.–Iraqi armed conflict.

8.5.1 Escaping Prisoners of War

Is it either a war crime or a grave breach for a POW camp guard to shoot and kill an unarmed escaping POW?

It is neither. Because POW status is given, a common Article 2 armed conflict is involved. As to the use of deadly force, "the use of weapons against prisoners of war, especially against those who are escaping or attempting to escape, shall constitute an extreme measure, which shall always be preceded by warnings appropriate to the circumstances."[89] The *Commentary* to Convention III explains:

> Captivity is based on force, and ... the Detaining Power has the right to resort to force in order to keep prisoners captive. ... "An extreme measure" means that fire may be opened only when there is no other means of putting an immediate stop to the attempt.

---

[85] Id., at para. 557.

[86] E.g., *Prosecutor v. Gacumbitsi*, ICTR-2001-64-T (June 17, 2004), at Chapter II.E., paras. 21, 34, 39. Mayor Sylvestre Gacumbitsi was convicted of directing and participating in the particularly heinous rape and murder of Tutsi women sheltering in a church.

[87] *Prosecutor v. Alex Tamba Brima*, SCSL-04-16-T (June 20, 2007), para. 701. Also see Neha Jain, "Forced Marriage as a Crime against Humanity," 6–5 *J. of Int'l Crim. Justice* (Nov. 2008), 1013; and David J. Bederman, ed., "International Decisions," 103–1 *AJIL* (Jan. 2009), 97, 103.

[88] Askin, "A Decade of the Development of Gender Crimes," supra, note 64, at 19.

[89] Geneva Convention III, Art. 42.

From the moment the person attempting to escape comes to a halt, he again places himself under the protection of the Detaining Power. ... Even when there is justification for opening fire, the Convention follows the international custom ... and gives prisoners of war one last chance to abandon the attempt and escape the penalty.[90]

The law of war recognizes that it would be odd indeed if the armed guards of POWs were not permitted to employ force, even deadly force, to keep them confined.[91] That permission to fire, even to kill, however, does not extend beyond the time of the discovery of the escape attempt.

In World War II, on the night of March 24–5, 1944, seventy-six British and Allied officer POWs escaped from Stalag-Luft III, located near Sagan, Germany.[92] One hundred twenty additional POWs did not make it out of the escape tunnels because of approaching daylight. (In mid-1943, U.S. Army Air Force POWs had been transferred to an adjoining camp, so no Americans were involved in the escape, although many worked on digging and concealing the four escape tunnels.) Three of the escapees successfully reached England. Seventy-three were recaptured; fifty of the seventy-three were murdered by the Gestapo. The event, popularized in a 1963 motion picture, has become known as "the Great Escape."

Hitler personally authorized the murder of the recaptured Stalag-Luft III POWs as a disincentive for future escapes. Ernst Kaltenbrunner, head of the Sicherheitsdienst, the Nazi Party security services (SD), and the Gestapo, directed that the excuse for the murders would be that the POWs were killed while attempting to escape, and that, in any event, their wearing of civilian clothes deprived them of the protection of the 1929 Geneva POW convention. The Nazi major general Fritz von Graevenitz objected to Fieldmarshal Wilhelm Keitel that escape is a soldier's duty, and the directive to murder the escapees should not be obeyed. Keitel scoffed at Graevenitz's objection. Major General Adolf Westhoff daringly lodged a formal complaint with Kaltenbrunner. He too was ignored. Selection of the fifty to be murdered was made in Berlin by Schutzstaffeln (SS) General Artur Nebe; it was based on his ideas of who was too young, or who had too many children, to die. Most of the murders were carried out by the Breslau Gestapo office, commanded by Wilhelm Scharpwinkel, who escaped to Russia after the war.

The recaptured POWs were killed in ones and twos and, in one case, in a group of ten. "Their bodies were immediately cremated, and the urns containing their ashes were returned to the camp."[93] Soon after the escape, the commandant of Stalag-Luft III,

---

[90] Preux, *Commentary: Geneva Convention III*, supra, note 27, at 246–7.

[91] In December 1944, twenty-five German POWs tunneled their way out of their holding camp near Yuma, Arizona. All were recaptured and returned to the same POW camp within weeks, most within days. Their punishment: solitary confinement and bread and water rations for the same number of days as they had been escapees. John H. Moore, *The Faustball Tunnel* (Annapolis, MD: Naval Institute Press, 1978). Near the war's end, 425,871 enemy POWs were held in camps located within the continental United States – Dept. of the Army Pamphlet 20–213, *History of Prisoner of War Utilization by the United States Army 1776–1945* (Washington, DC: GPO, 1955), 91.

[92] This account is based on the court opinion in *Trial of Max Wielen and 17 Others* (The Stalag Luft III Case), British Military Court, Hamburg, Germany (July–Sept. 1947), *LRTWC*, Vol. XI (London: UN War Crimes Comm., 1949), 31–53, supplemented by Dept. of the Army Pamphlet 27–161–2, *International Law*, Vol. II (Washington, DC: GPO, Oct. 1962), 90–1; and, Aidan Crawley, *Escape from Germany* (London: Collins, 1956).

[93] Judgment, *Trial of the Major War Criminals before the International Military Tribunal*, Vol. I (Nuremberg: IMT, 1947), 171, 229.

Lieutenant Colonel Friedrich von Lindeiner, of the Luftwaffe, was court-martialed by his Nazi superiors, along with ten other camp staff. All were convicted and sentenced to imprisonment, their sentences cut short only by the end of the war.

The murder of those recaptured was noted in the judgment of the postwar Nuremberg International Military Tribunal as a war crime for which the accused were held to answer. "It was not contended by the defendants that this was other than plain murder, in complete violation of international law."[94]

The Allied investigation of the murders, conducted by a dedicated few members of the Royal Air Force's (RAF's) Special Investigations Branch, began in 1946, after many trails had gone cold. For two years the RAF investigators covered Europe looking for the killers. Seventy-two suspects were identified, but many had been killed in wartime air raids or died after the war, never brought to justice. Others fled into Eastern Europe, including Russia.

The postwar German government tried at least three of the involved Nazis. One, Alfred Schimmel, was convicted and hanged in 1948. Another killed himself in his cell before his sentencing. A third was acquitted.

In 1947, the British brought eighteen involved Germans to trial. Fourteen were convicted and sentenced to death, although only nine were actually hanged. Two were sentenced to imprisonment for life, two of them to ten years' imprisonment. Two committed suicide, and one died of natural causes before trial. It is unclear what happened to the remaining two.

The chief of a Gestapo office involved in the murders, Fritz Schmidt, was arrested in 1967. He was tried, pleading obedience to orders as his defense. He was convicted and sentenced to two years' confinement. His was the last conviction involving the Great Escape.

In an earlier World War II incident, in 1942, captured British soldiers involved in the raid against the German heavy water plant at Telemark, Norway, were also murdered by the Nazis acting under Hitler's infamous *Kommandobfehl* (commando order) of October 1942. Prior to the raid (actually against the Norsk Hydro Hydrogen Electrolysis Plant at Vemork), a Halifax glider tug and two gliders with thirty members of the Royal Engineers aboard, crashed. The twenty-one survivors, some severely wounded in the crashes, were all executed.[95]

Reminiscent of the Great Escape, if a single enemy accused is involved in a series of incidents in which his prisoners are killed "attempting to escape," he will be the focus of prosecutorial attention. In March 1945, Major Karl Rauer, commandant of a Nazi airfield at Dreierwalde, Germany, was involved in three such incidents that resulted in the deaths of twelve Allied POWs. Shortly after the war, Rauer and six others were tried by a British military court. "It was less reasonable," the court held, "for these [accused] officers to believe after the second incident that the prisoners involved were shot while trying to escape than it was after the first, and that measures should have been taken after the first shootings to prevent a repetition." The seven were convicted. Rauer was sentenced to life imprisonment, and the others were hanged.[96]

---

[94] Id., 229.

[95] Christopher Mann, "Combined Operations, the Commandos, and Norway, 1941–1944," 73–2 *J. of Military History* (April 2009), 471, 483–7.

[96] *Trial of Major Karl Rauer and Six Others*, British Military Court, LRTWC, Vol. IV (London: UN War Crimes Comm., 1949), 113, 117.

8.5.2 *Suicide Attacks*

Westerners give little thought to the law of suicide attacks, but such attacks are addressed not only by LOAC/IHL, but by the Taliban's code of conduct, the *Layha*. The second edition of the *Layha* was published and took effect on May 29, 2010. "The Taliban's claim that they are the *mujahideen* (holy warriors) of the Islamic Emirate of Afghanistan obviously suggests that they must abide by the rules of Islamic law on the conduct of hostilities. The *Layha* [is] the code of conduct for their fighters."[97] The *Layha* makes no mention of LOAC/IHL. The Taliban assert that the *Layha* is based on Islamic law.

> The *Layha* allows suicide attacks but there are certain conditions with which the *mujahideen* should comply. First, the suicide bomber should be trained very well to execute the mission. Second, suicide attacks should be carried out against high-value targets. Third, the killing of ordinary people and damage to property should avoided as far as possible. Finally, all would-be suicide bombers must obtain permission and advice for suicide attack from the provincial authority. This rule does not apply to those *mujahideen* who are given a "special programme and permission by the higher authority". Suicide attacks were also allowed in the 2009 edition [of the *Layha*].[98]

Although the *Layha* seems even more loosely worded than Western definitions of military necessity, the point is that suicide bombings apparently comport with Islamic religious law. Non-Muslim commentators obviously disagree: "Any attack targeted against individual civilians or the civilian population as such is clearly unlawful and constitutes a war crime. Even where such attacks are targeted against military objectives, there are still issues of indiscriminate attacks, proportionality, and perfidy to be considered."[99]

Suicide bombings clearly are violations of LOAC/IHL. Precisely what violations are committed depends on the bomber's target and the circumstances of the execution of the bombing. The successful bomber cannot be prosecuted, of course, but his military commander or civilian superior may be (Chapter 10.5).

8.5.3 *Firing on Mosques*

In 2008, a combat correspondent wrote of his experience accompanying U.S. Marines in combat in Fallujah, Iraq: "From the start, the guerrillas had used the minarets: to shoot, to spot, to signal one another. When American soldiers first came into Fallujah, 6,000 of them on foot in the middle of a November night in 2004, they weren't allowed to shoot at mosques without permission. After 12 hours, they threw the rule away."[100]

Threw away the rule? Article 53 of Additional Protocol I reads, "It is prohibited: (a) to commit any acts of hostility directed against the historic monuments, works of art or places of worship which constitute the cultural or spiritual heritage of peoples." 1907 Hague Regulation IV and 1954 Hague Convention for the Protection of Cultural

---

[97] Muhammad Munir, "The Layha for the Mujahideen: An Analysis of the Code of Conduct for the Taliban Fighters under Islamic Law," 93–881 *Int'l Rev. of the Red Cross* (March 2011), 81, 101. The author, at the time of publication, was associate professor and chairman, Department of Law, Faculty of Shari'a and Law, International Islamic University, Islamabad.

[98] Id., at 98.

[99] Annyssa Bellal, Gilles Giacca, and Stuart Casey-Maslen, "International Law and Armed Non-State Actors in Afghanistan," 93–881 *Int'l Rev. of the Red Cross* (March 2011), 47, 77.

[100] Dexter Filkins, "My Long War," NY *Times Magazine*, Aug. 24, 2008, 36, 38.

Property also prohibit "acts of hostility" directed toward places of worship. The prohibition is known to members of all armed forces. Can the prohibition against firing on places of worship be disregarded, thrown away, because the enemy does not respect the sanctity of their own churches or mosques?

Yes, in some cases the rule may be disregarded. Article 53 of Additional Protocol I also reads, "It is prohibited: (b) to use such objects in support of the military effort"; Hague Regulation IV, Article 27, is clearer: "In sieges and bombardments all necessary steps must be taken to spare, as far as possible, buildings dedicated to religion ... *provided they are not being used at the time for military purposes*"[101] (emphasis supplied). This does not suggest that one may use a church steeple as a machine-gun position, as in the closing scenes of the 1999 movie *Saving Private Ryan*, or that minarets of Iraqi mosques may be targeted because they are believed to be locations of enemy snipers or artillery spotters, as in the abbey of Monte Cassino. If insurgents actually use mosques as weapons collection locations, sniper firing points, or command posts, however, as they commonly did in Iraq, it is no LOAC violation, when such use is confirmed, if the mosques are fired upon in response.

Hospitals and marked wounded collection points are also protected locations.[102] As with places of worship, they lose their protection if used for improper purposes. Additional Protocol I, Article 12, refers to military facilities: "Medical units shall be respected and protected at all times and shall not be the object of attack." In addition, "Under no circumstances shall medical units be used in an attempt to shield military objectives from attack." The protection of civilian medical facilities, such as civilian hospitals in areas of combat operations, is also addressed. Article 13.1 states: "The protection to which civilian medical units are entitled shall not cease unless they are used to commit, outside their humanitarian function, acts harmful to the enemy. Protection may, however, cease only after a warning has been given." During Operation Urgent Fury, the 1983 United States invasion of Grenada, a mental hospital located near Richmond Hill was taken under fire by U.S. forces. The hospital was incorrectly thought to be the site of an antiaircraft gun.[103] In the ensuing air strike, called in because weapons were thought to be on the hospital grounds, portions of the hospital were destroyed and twelve patients were reportedly killed.[104]

Did the attack on the Richmond Hill hospital constitute a war crime? If the soldier calling in the air strike honestly and reasonably believed that the hospital hid an antiaircraft gun, did he have the defense of mistake of fact? If so, were the twelve patients who were killed collateral damage?

The protection accorded churches and hospitals is in keeping with the purposes of LOAC/IHL. Just as a surrendering soldier who suddenly draws a weapon loses his

---

[101] Geoffery S. Corn, "'Snipers in the Minaret – What Is the Rule?' The Law of War and the Protection of Cultural Property: A Complex Equation," *Army Lawyer* (July 2005), 128, 36. Professor Corn, closely reading the Hague prohibition, notes, "While this provision reflects a general goal of protecting religious and cultural objects, it does not expressly prohibit the use of such objects for military purposes. Furthermore, the 'as far as possible' caveat suggests a 'military necessity' exception to this general prohibition."

[102] 1977 Additional Protocol I, Art. 12.

[103] Major Ronald M. Riggs, "The Grenada Intervention: A Legal Analysis," 109 *Military L. Rev.* (1985), 1.

[104] B. Drummond Ayres Jr., "U.S. Concedes Bombing Hospital in Grenada, Killing at Least 12," NY *Times*, Nov. 1, 1983, A16.

protection under LOAC/IHL, protected churches and hospitals lose their protection should they become sites of offensive activities.

8.5.4 Hostages

The taking of hostages is prohibited by LOAC/IHL, and violations of the prohibition constitute a grave breach.[105] It was not always so. In ancient times, hostages were commonly held to ensure the execution of treaties, offered up by one side to the other as a form of insurance. As late as 1948, the judgment of the U.S. tribunal in *The Hostages Case* held, "Hostages may be taken in order to guarantee the peaceful conduct of the populations of occupied territories and, when certain conditions exist and the necessary preliminaries have been taken, they may, as a last resort, be shot."[106]

The same tribunal judgment held, however, that "customary international law is not static. It must be elastic enough to meet the new conditions that natural progress brings to the world."[107] World War II and the excesses suffered by hostages taken by the Nazi regime particularly were among the "certain conditions" that produced an international consensus that hostage taking could no longer be condoned by civilized nations. "[State] practice since then shows that the prohibition of hostage-taking is now firmly entrenched in customary international law."[108] There is not a universally applicable definition.

> [Generally] speaking, hostages are nationals of a belligerent State who of their own free will or through compulsion are in the hands of the enemy and are answerable with their freedom or their life for the execution of his orders and the security of his armed forces. ... The modern form ... is the taking of hostages as a means of intimidating the population in order to weaken its spirit of resistance and to prevent breaches of the law and sabotage."[109]

Hostage taking should not be confused with reprisals, which are acts of retaliation in the form of conduct that would otherwise be unlawful, resorted to solely to compel the enemy to cease his own LOAC/IHL violations. In both international and noninternational armed conflicts, the prohibition on hostage taking is absolute.

Despite the prohibition of more than half a century's standing, hostage taking was encountered in the U.S.–Iraqi conflict. In July 2003, a brigade commander of the U.S. Army's 4th Infantry Division (ID) said that tough intelligence-gathering methods were being used by his soldiers, who had arrested the wife and daughter of a former Iraqi lieutenant general. The soldiers left a note that read, "If you want your family released,

---

[105] 1949 Geneva Convention common Art. 3(I) (a), and Convention IV, Art. 34. Convention IV, Art. 147 specifies that the taking of hostages is a grave breach. Hostage taking is prohibited by 1977 Additional Protocol I, Art. 75.2. (c) and Protocol II, Art. 4.2. (c), as well as by the Rome Statute of the ICC in both international (Art. 8(2) (a) (viii)) and noninternational (Art. 8 (2) (c) (iii)) armed conflicts. It is further prohibited by the U.N. International Convention against the Taking of Hostages (June 1979), which is ratified by the United States.

[106] *U.S. v. List, et al.* ("The Hostage Case"), XI *T.W.C. before the Nuernberg Military Tribunals under Control Council Law No. 10* (Washington, DC: GPO, 1950), judgment, 1249.

[107] Id., at 1241.

[108] Henckaerts and Doswald-Beck, *Customary International Humanitarian Law*, Vol. I, supra, note 69, Rule 96, at 334.

[109] Jean S. Pictet, *Commentary: IV Geneva Convention Relative to the Protection of Civilian Persons in Time of War* (Geneva: ICRC, 1958), 229. Hereafter, "Geneva Convention IV."

turn yourself in."[110] The colonel said that the tactics were justified because "it's an intelligence operation with detainees, and these people have info."[111] Five months later, during the search for Saddam Hussein, another brigade of the 4th ID missed Saddam Hussein but seized family members[112] and the family members of a close aide.[113] In 2006, an Iraqi female whose male relative was suspected of being a terrorist was released after being held for four months. She was one of five women who were held for the same reason. A memo reportedly written by a Defense Intelligence Agency officer said that the husband had been the target of the raid on the woman's home, but she was arrested "in order to leverage the primary target's surrender."[114] As late as 2008, female family members of wanted Iraqis were seized by U.S. Army troops of the 1st ID:

> As the U.S. military searches for tactics to break an escalating guerrilla war … few occurrences have unleashed more anger and etched deeper the cultural divide than several arrests of wanted men's relatives – particularly women. … Some villagers insist the relatives have been taken as hostages … a charge the military has denied. … "I told them they were creating enemies for themselves," the sheik said. "If they don't exist already, you'll make them exist now."[115]

It is disturbing that LOAC/IHL violations have been directed by senior military officers. Sometimes argued as being akin to law enforcement techniques in investigating serious crime ("In certain cases it becomes necessary to detain anyone 'who has knowledge of the acts of particularly nefarious people.'"),[116] no competent American police force arrests relatives of suspects for their possible knowledge of their relative's acts. Hostage taking under any guise is a grave breach, and these cases, brief as their descriptions are, meet the definition of hostage taking.[117] "At no time can Soldiers and Marines detain family members or close associates to compel suspected insurgents to surrender or provide information. This kind of hostage taking is both unethical and illegal."[118]

8.5.5 Human Shields

Is it a war crime or grave breach to employ human shields – closely related to hostages? In World War II, in 1944, U.S. Marines assaulted the Japanese-held island of Saipan and its thirty-thousand-man enemy garrison.

> Japanese soldiers used civilians as human shields in combat, making it even harder for fighting men to discriminate: "Enemy troops are using civilians as shields, retiring in

[110] Thomas E. Ricks, "U.S. Adopts Aggressive Tactics on Iraqi Fighters," *Wash. Post*, July 28, 2003, A1.
[111] Id.
[112] Eric Schmitt, "Finding Hussein Took Skill and Plenty of Legwork," *NY Times*, Dec. 16, 2003, A18.
[113] "Arrests in Iraq," *NY Times*, Dec. 16, 2003, A8.
[114] Nancy A. Youssef, "U.S. Has Detained Women in Iraq as Leverage," *Miami Herald*, Jan. 28, 2006, 1.
[115] Anthony Shadid, "U.S. Detains Relatives of Suspects in Iraq Attacks," *Wash. Post*, Nov. 6, 2008, A21.
[116] Id.
[117] The ICRC writes: "'Hostage-taking' has occurred when both of the following conditions are fulfilled: • A person has been captured and detained illegally. •A third party is being pressured, explicitly or implicitly, to do or refrain from doing something as a condition for releasing the hostage or for not taking his life or otherwise harming him physically." "ICRC Position on Hostage-Taking," 846 *Int'l Rev. of the Red Cross* (June 2002), 467.
[118] *The U.S. Army-Marine Corps Counterinsurgency Field Manual* (Chicago: University of Chicago Press, 2007), paras. 7–41, at 250.

groups with them, hiding with them in places of cover and caves. Cases have been reported of using civilians as decoys to entice our troops out in the open. There appears also to have been cases of troops restraining civilians from surrendering and even killing them to prevent this." The Japanese used civilians as cover for assault operations, as on 15–16 June at the Marine beach-head: "On the southern beaches, small groups of enemy soldiers, one spearheaded by a shield of civilians, hit once at 03.30 and again an hour later."[119]

In 1944 there was no Geneva Convention protecting civilians. Today, there are human shield prohibitions in LOAC/IHL. Article 51.7 of Additional Protocol I makes clear that "the presence ... of the civilian population or individual civilians shall not be used to render certain points or areas immune from military operations, in particular in attempts to shield military objectives from attacks. ... The Parties shall not direct the movement of the civilian population or individual civilians in order to attempt to shield military object-ives from attacks or to shield military operations." In agreement, Article 28 of Geneva Convention IV mandates that "the presence of a protected person may not be used to render certain points or areas immune from military operations." Article 23 of Convention III provides the same protection for POWs,[120] as does Article 19 of Convention I for medical units. The Statute of the ICC, Article 8(2) (b) (xxiii), recognizes the use of human shields as a war crime. "Irrefutably, this norm mirrors customary international law."[121] There is no treaty-based prohibition on the use of human shields in noninternational armed conflicts.

In 1967, during the U.S.–Vietnamese conflict, the Hanoi thermal power plant was successfully attacked by American aircraft. "Subsequently the North Vietnamese housed several U.S. prisoners of war ... in the facility as hostages to preclude its reattack. It remained off-limits from attack until confirmation was received that the POWs had been removed."[122] Then the power plant was again attacked, and it was out of service for the rest of the conflict. North Vietnam's use of human shields was an LOAC/IHL breach, but, until discontinued, was successful in achieving the enemy's aim.

If civilians are forced to act as human shields, as is most often the case, they are hostages, the use of whom constitutes a grave breach.[123]

Article 51.7 of AP I also prohibits deliberately placing a military objective in the midst of, or close to, a civilian area, "for example by positioning a piece of artillery in a school yard or a residential area."[124] If civilian casualties result from an illegal attempt to shield a legitimate military objective with a human shield, those casualties are the responsibility of the side using the human shield, not the attacking side.[125]

---

[119] Matthew Hughes, "War without Mercy? American Armed Forces and the Deaths of Civilians during the Battle for Saipan, 1944," 75–1 *J. of Military History* (Jan. 2011). 93, 112, citing D-2 [Intelligence] report, July 7–8, 1944, 2nd Marine Division D-2 Periodic Reports, p. 2.

[120] It has long been customary law that POWs may not be used as shields for enemy activity. See: *Trial of Kurt Student*, British Military Court, Luneberg, Germany (May 1946), LRTWC, Vol. IV (London: UN War Crimes Commission, 1948), 118.

[121] Dinstein, *Conduct of Hostilities*, supra, note 7, at 130.

[122] W. Hays Parks, "Righting the Rules of Engagement," U.S. Naval Institute *Proceedings* (May 1989), 83, 92.

[123] Geneva Convention IV, Art. 147.

[124] Jean-François Quéguiner, "Precautions under the Law Governing the Conduct of Hostilities," 864 *Int'l Rev. of the Red Cross* (Dec. 2006), 793, 812. Also, Stéphanie Bouchié de Belle, "Chained to Cannons or Wearing Targets on Their T-Shirts: Human Shields in IHL," 872 *Intl. Rev. of the Red Cross* (Dec. 2008), 883.

[125] W. Hays Parks, "Air War and the Law of War," 32–1 *AFLR* (1990), 1, 174.

What if the individuals making up the human shield are ~~willing participants?~~ In July 2006, Lebanese Hezbollah militants crossed into neighboring Israel and attacked an Israeli patrol, killing three soldiers and capturing two. The thirty-three-day conflict that followed illustrates a difficult human shield problem. "The [Lebanese] civilian population were seriously regarded by Israel as being involved in the conflict insofar as they provided Hezbollah with logistical support and permitted it to operate behind a shield of civilians. This is a frequent occurrence in modern conflict. ... The question is whether there is any justification for violating humanitarian law in response to the corresponding [human shield] violations by the other party."[126] Can the placement of civilians in a military objective area, a form of human shield, bar an attack by enemy forces? Virtually no military target will be completely free of a civilian presence. The principle of proportionality, then, becomes central to the human shield issue. "However ... the actual test of excessive injury to civilians must be relaxed. That is to say, the appraisal whether civilian casualties are excessive in relation to the military advantage anticipated must make allowances for the fact that – if an attempt is made to shield military objectives with civilians – civilian casualties will be higher than usual."[127]

Israel was ruthless in attacking suspected Hezbollah bases and missile sites in Lebanon, to include Lebanese residential areas from which Hezbollah fired rockets into Israel. More than twelve thousand air strikes, cluster bombs, and more than 100,000 artillery rounds were fired into Lebanon.[128] Israel estimated that 1,084 Lebanese civilians were killed.[129] International condemnation over the lack of proportionality was widespread.[130] Was it an abuse of proportionality amounting to a war crime, or should the Lebanese have suffered criticism for use of human shields?

The proportionality/human shield conundrum of military objectives surrounded by civilians, often by accident, sometimes with forethought, is not unique to Israel. American forces regularly encounter the same issue in Iraq and Afghanistan.[131]

What if the enemy employs human shields, but persons constituting the human shields are not merely willing, but are ~~volunteers?~~ What if they knowingly place themselves, or allow themselves to be placed, at locations that are legitimate military objectives? Some experts contend that acting as a voluntary human shield constitutes taking a direct part in hostilities. In March 2003, as the U.S. invasion of Iraq began, there were roughly 250 Americans and Europeans voluntarily in Iraq specifically there to act as voluntary human shields for the Iraq government to place at military

---

[126] Enzo Cannizzaro, "Contextualizing Proportionality: Jus ad Bellum and Jus in Bello in the Lebanese War," 864 *Int'l Rev. of Red Cross* (Dec. 2006), 779, 789–90.

[127] Dinstein, *Conduct of Hostilities*, supra, note 7, at 131.

[128] Uzi Rubin, "Hizballah's Rocket Campaign against Northern Israel: A Preliminary Report," Jerusalem Center for Public Affairs (Aug. 31, 2006), available on-line.

[129] Reuven Erlich, "Hezbollah's Use of Lebanese Civilians as Human Shields," part 2 (2006), 6, available online.

[130] E.g., Steven Erlanger, "With Israeli Use of Force, Debate over Proportion," NY *Times* (July 19, 2006), A1; Warren Hoge, "Attacks Qualify as War Crimes, Officials Say," NY *Times*, July 20, 2006, A11; and John Kifner, "Human Rights Group Accuses Israel of War Crimes in Lebanon, NY *Times*, Aug. 24, 2006, A6.

[131] E.g., Paul von Zielbauer, "U.S. Investigates Civilian Toll in Airstrike, but Holds Insurgents Responsible," NY *Times*, Oct. 13, 2007, A5; Carlotta Gall, "British Criticize U.S. Air Attacks in Afghan Region," NY *Times*, Aug. 9, 2007, A1.

objectives. On April 1, two buses carrying the volunteers were fired upon, reportedly wounding several.[132] Was a war crime committed?

Yes, it was a LOAC/IHL violation, but not as to the shooters. The party to the conflict who uses human shields, volunteers or not, is in violation of Article 51.7. The volunteer human shields, if killed or wounded, have no cause of action against the party who fired on them. Military objectives protected by human shields remain lawful targets despite the presence of such shields.

8.5.6 Explosive Vests and Burning Bodies

In Iraq, in July 2008, a U.S. Army Special Operations unit encountered and engaged insurgent fighters. After the firefight, an inspection of the scene of the battle revealed a number of dead enemy insurgents. Three of them were wearing explosive vests they had not detonated in the course of the firefight. The Special Operations unit did not have explosive ordnance disposal (EOD) specialists attached to the unit who could deactivate the vests; nor could EOD personnel reach the location of the firefight before the soldiers had to depart. There was a village very near the site of the engagement. How should the on-scene commander handle dead insurgents still wearing vests containing armed explosives? Any attempt to move the bodies could result in a detonation of a vest and death or injury to friendly troops. To leave the bodies where they lay would invite unfriendly Iraqis to retrieve the vests and make new deadly use of them. The effect of detonating the vests while they remained on the bodies is clear. Having a village nearby raised the possibility of noncombatant injury, and to have villagers observe the effect of detonating the vests while they remained on the bodies only complicated the commander's decision. Grotius wrote in 1625, "All agree that even public enemies are entitled to burial. Appian calls this 'a common right of wars'. . . . Says Tacitus: 'Not even enemies begrudge burial.'"[133] Grotius had not dealt with explosive vests, however. What should the commander do both to solve his problem and to avoid committing a war crime?

In a common Article 2 conflict, Article 130, Geneva Convention IV, addresses the treatment of the bodies of internees who die in custody. "The detaining authorities shall ensure that internees who die while interned are honorably buried, if possible according to the rites of the religion to which they belonged." Directions for grave sites and registering the sites follow. In a common Article 3 conflict, absent internees, the intent of the same article should be considered. Considering only common Article 3, mistreatment of enemy dead might be considered a violation of paragraph (1) (c): "outrages upon personal dignity, in particular, humiliating and degrading treatment."

In a common Article 2 conflict, Additional Protocol I, Article 34.1, directs that "the remains of persons who have died for reasons related to occupation or in detention resulting from occupation or hostilities . . . shall be respected, and the gravesites of all such persons shall be respected." These general requirements are followed by directions concerning grave sites and their registration and tending. Geneva Convention III,

---

[132] Scott Peterson, "'Human Shields' in Tug-of-War," *Christian Science Monitor*, March 17, 2003, http://www.csmonitor.com/2003/0317/p01s04-woiq.html; and Rym Brahimi, "Were Human Shields Attacked?" CNN.com./World, available online.

[133] Hugo Grotius, *The Law of War and Peace* (Buffalo, NY: Hein reprint of Kelsey translation, 1995), book II, chapter XIX, III.

Article 120, relating to deceased POWs, calls for similar respect and honorable treatment of the remains of deceased prisoners.

The dead insurgents were neither prisoners nor internees, nor in occupied territory, but the legal and moral requirements of LOAC/IHL are clear. Enemy bodies may not be ill treated. If not turned over to relatives, bodies should be buried, the location of the grave recorded and reported. Respectful treatment is the clear common theme.

The explosive vests were not in violation of LOAC/IHL. The degree of injury that detonation of the vests might inflict would not be clearly disproportionate to the intended objective, the killing of the U.S. enemy. There was not an issue of military necessity because resolution of the vest issue, no matter how decided, was not indispensable for securing the submission of the enemy as soon as possible. The sole issue was the action to be taken by the U.S. commander and its lawfulness.

When the event occurred, the commander consulted his unit's legal adviser. After considering the tactical situation, including the lack of EOD support, the proximity of potential noncombatant victims, and the need to withdraw from the area, the judge advocate made his recommendation to the commander, who agreed. The vests were detonated in place while they remained on the dead insurgents' bodies. Given the circumstances, that appears a prudent decision, and <u>not a violation of LOAC.</u>

Not all issues of enemy dead are so well considered. In Kandahar province in southern Afghanistan, in October 2005, a U.S. Army unit engaged a band of Taliban fighters. Afterward, a psychological warfare team piled the bodies of Taliban fighters killed in the engagement at the base of a hill where an Afghan village was located. Then, while being filmed by an Australian television crew, they set fire to the bodies they had soaked with gasoline. Over loudspeakers, the team taunted any Taliban in the village to avenge the burning of their comrades' corpses ("Come and fight like men.")[134] The televised event raised immediate complaints that such conduct violated Geneva Convention prohibitions on the treatment of enemy dead, and U.S. and Afghan investigations followed. The *Los Angeles Times* reported:

> U.S. investigators found that the burning of the bodies and the broadcasting of the taunts were separate incidents. Two soldiers involved in cremating the bodies and two others who took part in the psychological warfare operation received reprimands. . . . "The weather was hot, the remains were heavily damaged by gunfire, laying exposed for over 24 hours and beginning to rapidly decompose," the report said. "The unit planned to remain on that hill for 48 to 72 more hours and thus made the decision to dispose of the remains in this manner for hygiene reasons only."[135]

Unlikely assertions of hygiene notwithstanding, the burning of bodies in that manner constituted LOAC/IHL violations.

8.5.7 *Photos of POWs*

Is it a war crime to photograph an enemy prisoner? The question arises with increasing frequency when U.S. combatants routinely carry cell phones with photographic and motion-capture capabilities. Cameras and phones are linked to ubiquitous laptop

---

[134] Chuck Neubauer, "Soldiers Rebuked in Corpse Burning," *LA Times*, Nov. 27, 2005, A1.   [135] Id.

computers, making images from remote Afghanistan and Iraq available to relatives and news agencies, virtually in real time. Are such photos a LOAC/IHL violation?

The lawyerlike answer is, It depends. Italian domestic law forbids the publication of the photo of any police prisoner showing him/her to be wearing handcuffs. Geneva Convention III, Article 13, does not go that far: "Prisoners of war must at all times be humanely treated. . . . Likewise, prisoners of war must at all times be protected, particularly against acts of violence or intimidation and against insults and public curiosity." The *Commentary* adds, "The protection [due prisoners of war] extends to moral values, such as the moral independence of the prisoner (protection against acts of intimidation) and his honour (protection against insults and public curiosity)."[136]

What is the nature of the photograph? Is it a depiction of unlawful treatment, as in the infamous Abu Ghraib photos? Obviously, those photos were demeaning, pandering to the base emotions of the soldiers involved. They were degrading images, their taking contrary to Article 13.[137] Digitally obscuring the faces of the prisoners made them publishable for purposes of documenting the misconduct involved in their taking; the photos were only the final act in LOAC/IHL violations they depicted. But what if, unlike the Abu Ghraib photos, photos of prisoners are taken for use in a lawsuit against the party holding them, or as evidence to be provided to the ICRC to document prisoner abuse? Such use would be for the protection of the depicted prisoners rather than for purposes of public curiosity and, as long as they were not made public, would be no violation.

Professor Daniel Thürer argues that Article 13 "states that prisoners of war 'must at all times be protected . . . ' It follows from this that the broadcasting of such images is not lawful if the prisoners' faces can be identified."[138] He does not suggest how release of an image showing a POW's face intimidates, endangers, insults, or panders to public curiosity.

Immediately after the initiation of the 2003 United States–Iraq conflict, Iraqi television showed footage of American soldiers being captured and of other wounded U.S. captive soldiers. Could the Iraqi footage be described as intimidating, insulting, or playing to public curiosity? There were strenuous U.S. objections to the "humiliating" treatment of captured Americans.[139] As one European writer contends, however, "not all images or films of prisoners of war, even if broadcast globally, violate the protection guaranteed by Article 13. Only instances where prisoners are individually identifiable on film constitute such a violation of rights. . . . If prisoners are identifiable, the potential of satellite communications makes it possible for them to become objects of global curiosity and repeated and manifold sensationalism."[140] On the other hand, when a clearly identifiable prisoner is seen on television, the world knows that he is alive and

---

[136] Preux, *Commentary*, Geneva Convention III, supra, note 27, at 141.

[137] Julia Preston, "Officials See Risk in the Release of Photos and Videos of Iraqi Prisoners," *NY Times*, Aug. 12, 2005, A12.

[138] Daniel Thürer, *International Humanitarian Law: Theory, Practice, Context* (The Hague: Hague Academy of International Law, 2011), 359.

[139] Jack M. Beard, "The Geneva Boomerang: The Military Commissions Act of 2006 and U.S. Counterterror Operations," 101–1 *AJIL* (Jan. 2007), 56, 68.

[140] Horst Fischer, "Television Footage of Prisoners of War: From Violations to War Crimes," *Bofaxe* No. 244E (March 24, 2003).

apparently well. After the picture is seen, his captors cannot credibly deny his captivity and health, and they have reason to ensure his continued well-being.

Whether a photo constitutes a war crime may turn on the purpose for which it was taken and the use to which it is put. During the common Article 2 phase of the U.S.–Iraqi conflict, a photo of Saddam Hussein wearing only underpants was widely published in newspapers around the world. The photo was seemingly taken, and was published, to demean and humiliate Saddam Hussein, an insult in pixels. In contrast, if the picture was shown only to a seminar of judge advocates for purposes of illustrating what constitutes a violation of Convention III, Article 13, the taking of the photo remains a violation, but its publication in the judge advocates' seminar is not.

In antiterrorist actions, photographs may actually be required for purposes of possible prosecution. "Units should use photographs to connect the individual being detained to the basis for detention. These photographs can be and frequently are presented to judges at the Central Criminal Court of Iraq. ... Therefore, the more photographs that the unit takes on the objective, the better the potential case has for prosecution."[141] Photos of relevant evidence, such as weapons, money, or detonators, is encouraged. Of course, such photos are not for general publication.

The wrongfulness or innocence of a photo may depend on the audience for whom a picture is intended. Do lingering scenes of a bearded and recently captured Saddam Hussein having his widely opened mouth examined pander to public curiosity, or do they merely provide irrefutable evidence to a doubting Iraqi public that he was alive and in U.S. hands? The U.S. commander in Iraq, in charge of Saddam Hussein the prisoner, said:

> When we released a short video clip of the exam, the press immediately began speculating that the physician's assistant was checking Saddam's beard for lice and looking inside his mouth as if he were checking out a slave or an animal. That was not the case, however. He was simply checking for the cuts and bruises that Saddam had mentioned [receiving during capture]. ... Our sole intention was to convince the Iraqi people that we had, indeed, captured Saddam Hussein.[142]

The Iraqi audience for whom the general says the video clip was taken would see Saddam Hussein only as being humiliated and held up to public ridicule by the invader. Surely another portion of the clip could have been released, one not showing him being probed and prodded, one not tending toward insult or pandering to the desire to show a defeated and debased Saddam Hussein.

Should state parties be concerned with protecting the sensitivities of the Saddam Husseins of the world, per Article 13, or should the limitations of Article 13 be strictly observed? If the United States broadcasts such images, do we, in effect, waive the "right" to complain when individual U.S. prisoners are shown? When does the legitimate recording of identity shade into Article 13's pandering to public curiosity?

---

[141] Maj. Marie Anderson and Emily Zukauskas, eds., *Operational Law Handbook*, 2008 (Charlottesville VA: Judge Advocate General's Legal Center and School, 2008), 189.

[142] Lt.Gen. Ricardo S. Sanchez, *Wiser in Battle* (New York: Harpers, 2008), 299. Should the dead bodies of Saddam Hussein's sons, Uday and Qusay, killed resisting capture by U.S. forces, have been shown on television, as they were? "Because the Geneva Conventions did not allow [this], we had to take the issue all the way to Washington. ... The administration made the decision to override the Conventions." Id., at 241.

Will particular photos, even if lawful, inflame the enemy and ultimately create unnecessary friendly casualties? Such questions are outside the ambit of LOAC/IHL, but any commander must carefully consider that issue before allowing the release of even innocuous-seeming photos that picture the enemy.

The Saddam Hussein movie notwithstanding, it may be argued that there is an overblown sensitivity to showing any photos whatsoever of captives. As long as the camera does not linger on a particular captive, show him or her in humiliating poses or situations, or use the picture for propaganda purposes, the necessary *mens rea*, or culpable negligence for a criminal prosecution, is absent. Even the brief image of a prisoner's face in the context of a legitimate informational account should not lead to concern for a prisoner's protection under the Geneva Convention.

8.5.8 Burying the Enemy Alive

On February 24, 1991, U.S. and Allied forces started the "hundred-hour war" against Iraq, a common Article 2 armed conflict. On a ten-mile portion of the front – the "Saddam Line" – the U.S. 1st Infantry Division (Mechanized) faced the entrenched 110th Brigade, 26th Iraqi Infantry Division. Eight U.S. M-1A1 heavy tanks with large saw-toothed plow blades affixed to their bows were supported by Bradley Fighting Vehicles. On signal, the Abrams plows punched through the sand berms and turned to their flanks to face the enemy infantrymen in the trenches they had just crossed. Supported by 25mm fire from the supporting Bradleys, the tanks plowed forward, burying the enemy combatants where they hunkered. Many Iraqi soldiers were buried alive. Was a war crime or grave breach committed?

When, as in this case, there is no specific provision in a LOAC convention, protocol, or treaty relating to questioned conduct, how does one determine whether a war crime might have been committed, short of a trial? A reasonable indication of the lawfulness of a questioned *jus in bello* act may be determined by examining it in terms of the four core LOAC principles. In this case, there is no issue of proportionality because civilians were not involved. There is no issue of distinction because the uniformed identity of the opposing combatants was clear to both sides.

Was there a valid military necessity to employ the Abrams-mounted plows? Is the tactic employed by the Americans prohibited by LOAC/IHL? No, it is not. Was it indispensable for securing the complete submission of the enemy as soon as possible? There were a variety of tactics available to the commander of the 1st Infantry Division to overcome the enemy, such as bombing by heavy bombers, artillery bombardment, or assault by infantry. *Some* method of attack was essential, and the technique used is not prohibited, and appeared likely to overcome the enemy force quickly. There was no violation of military necessity.

Did the tactic constitute unnecessary suffering? The answer may be determined by asking whether the suffering caused was substantially outweighed by the military advantage to be gained. The answer to this key question is no; given the great military importance of quickly breaching the Saddam Line and launching the initial attack against the Iraqi enemy, the suffering caused the enemy combatants was not clearly disproportionate to the military advantage gained. The commander of the tank forces points out, "Burying people alive doesn't sound very nice, as if being burned alive in a tank does, or being bayoneted or grenaded does. ... Most people don't realize, I think, how violent ground combat is."[143] Another 1st ID officer asked, "Would it have been better if we had dismounted [from armored vehicles] and gone into the trenches with our rifles and bayonets and taken probably hundreds of American casualties?"[144] The Iraqi combatants had the opportunity to surrender upon the approach of the American tanks, and many did. Those who did not faced a battle in which they were outgunned and eventually overwhelmed. No military commander wants an equal or "fair" battle; planning to maximize the possibility of an unequal fight is a mark of good generalship and no war crime. "Military doctrine – and common sense – clearly dictated [using the tanks]. To do otherwise would have been criminally irresponsible. Was it 'fair'? The question itself is silly."[145]

In cases not covered by the laws of war, the Martens Clause requires adherence to the principles of humanity. In modern armed conflict, "humanity" can be a broadly interpreted term.

8.5.9 Pillage

In March 2003, U.S. Army Task Force 3/15, from the 2nd Brigade of the 3rd Infantry Division, fought its way into Baghdad. Two soldiers carefully picked their way through one of the numerous palaces deserted by Saddam Hussein and his family. The two soldiers discovered four locked safes, which they forced open. In the fourth safe they discovered $856,000 in large-denomination U.S. bills, along with substantial amounts of British pounds and Jordanian dinars. Bingo! Unobserved, the soldiers put the currency into Meals, Ready-to-Eat (MRE) boxes, which they then taped closed. One of the soldiers, however, unable to maintain his secret, sent thousands of dollars home in ordinary envelopes and stuffed inside teddy bear souvenirs. He was also unable to resist the lure of satellite cell phones, expensive watches, and other costly items available from Iraqi street vendors even in the midst of the combat zone. The soldier's profligate spending soon led his superiors to suspect him. The soldier later said, "All of a sudden, you come across $850 million [sic]? Do you think you're not gonna try to get some of that home to your family? How is anything wrong with that? I need somebody to explain that to me."[146] When a fellow soldier allegedly stole $54,000 from the original thief, investigation and courts-martial followed.

Pillage, often referred to as "plunder," has long been recognized as prohibited by customary LOAC. The ICTY has defined it as "the fraudulent appropriation of public or private funds belonging to the enemy or the opposing party perpetrated during an armed conflict and related thereto."[147] It has also been more simply defined as "unlawful appropriation of property in armed conflict."[148] The latter definition seems preferable as there is no customary law basis for limiting the crime to "funds."[149]

The two Baghdad thieves were charged with violation of Article 103 of the Uniform Code of Military Justice. "Any person subject to this chapter who . . . engages in looting

---

[143] Barton Gellman, "Reaction to Tactic They Invented Baffles 1st Division Members," *Wash. Post*, Sept. 13, 1991, A21.

[144] Id. [145] Harry Summers, "Bambifying War," *Wash. Times*, Sept. 19, 1991, G1.

[146] Billy Cox, "The Spoils of War," *Marine Corps Times*, July 7, 2008, 14, 15.

[147] *Prosecutor v. Jelišić*, IT-95-10-T (Dec. 14, 1999), para. 48.

[148] *Prosecutor v. Delalić*, supra, note 77, at para. 591.

[149] Mettraux, *International Crimes and the* Ad Hoc *Tribunals*, supra, note 46, at 96.

or pillaging; shall be punished as a court-martial may direct." The *Manual for Court-Martial* defines the offense as "unlawfully seizing or appropriating property which is located in enemy or occupied territory."[150] Pillaging is also addressed in Geneva Convention IV, Article 16 ("As far as military considerations allow, each Party to the conflict shall . . . assist [endangered persons and] protect them against pillage and ill-treatment"). It is covered in Geneva Convention I, Article 15; Convention II, Article 18; Convention IV, Article 33; Additional Protocol I, Article 4.2; ICC Article 8(2) (b) (xvi); and 1907 Hague Convention IV, Articles 28 and 47. Both soldiers were convicted at their April 2004 courts-martial and sentenced to one year's confinement.[151]

Did they violate LOAC and did they commit a war crime? Clearly their acts were violations of specific laws and customs of war. Just as clearly, however, their acts were not grave breaches recognized by the community of nations as of universal concern. This was a crime committed in the combat zone, arguably associated with the conflict itself. It was a violation of the laws and customs of war and therefore a war crime, *stricto sensu*, but a violation meriting no more than a disciplinary response.

8.5.10 *"Double-Tapping"*

There is no official or agreed upon definition of a practice often encountered among U.S. soldiers and marines in Afghanistan and Iraq.[152] The tactic is known as a "double-tap," or, in some Marine Corps circles, a "dead check." It is the shooting of wounded or apparently dead insurgents to ensure that they are dead.

Killing enemy wounded, or prisoners, is hardly new to warfare. On both sides in World War II it happened in the Pacific[153] and in Europe,[154] and in World War I,[155] and before.[156] Seldom has the practice been as openly acknowledged as it is today, however.

A reasonable definition of double-tapping is, during the initial transit of a military objective, *indiscriminately* to twice shoot a wounded or an apparently dead enemy to ensure he is not feigning death. A double-tap should not be confused with a "controlled double," which is the firing of two aimed shots at a lawful enemy target.

Soldiers, sailors, and marines often assault an objective such as a terrain feature, a house, or other structure. Upon taking the objective, wounded or apparently dead insurgents are sometimes encountered. Two quickly fired shots, "a double-tap," into the head or body

---

[150] *Manual for Courts-Martial, United States* (Washington, DC: GPO, 2008), iv–40.

[151] *U.S. v. PFC. Earl B. Coffey*, unreported; pet. for rev. den. June 29, 2005; and *U.S. v. John R. Getz*, unreported; pet. for rev. den. March 8, 2005. Although pillage has long been recognized as contrary to customary law of war, it has been practiced for just as long.

[152] Israeli forces have encountered the grave breach of double-tapping, as well: Haim Watzman, "When You Have to Shoot First," *Int'l Herald Tribune* (July 29, 2005), 6. "Two of the assailants were shot dead. The third was also on the ground, badly wounded but conscious. 'I went up to him and raised my rifle and switched it to automatic,' Eldad told me. 'He put up his hands as if to fend me off, or maybe beg for mercy. But I just pulled the trigger. . . . ' But you killed a wounded and disabled man, I objected . . . 'He could still use his hands, and he might have had a grenade. . . . He was going to die anyway. And he deserved it.'"

[153] E.g., E. B. Sledge, *With the Old Breed* (Novato, CA: Presidio, 1981), 34, 118, 148.

[154] E.g., Stephan E. Ambrose, *Band of Brothers* (New York: Simon & Schuster, 1992), 152, 210.

[155] E.g. Lt. Col. Dave Grossman, *On Killing* (New York: Little, Brown, 1995), 175–6. Also, Cases and Materials, following Chapter 3, *Trial of Major Benno Crusius*, convicted of murdering French wounded.

[156] John Keegan, *The Face of Battle* (London: Barrie & Jenkins, 1988), 93, 175, relating the murder of prisoners at Agincourt and Waterloo.

of those wounded or dead insurgents assures the soldier or marine that they are, in fact, dead – a "dead check." The soldier, sailor, or marine knows that when he passes a double-tapped insurgent, he will not rise to shoot him or his fellow fighters in the back.

The reasons asserted for employing a double-tap always boil down to "so the enemy won't feign death, and later shoot my soldiers in the back." Feigning death with the intent to kill or wound the unsuspecting enemy is the war crime of perfidy.

An account of an enemy encounter near Ramadi, Iraq, is typical: "Stark saw a wounded insurgent on the ground with a hand behind his back. 'Turn on your stomach!' Gilbertson, the gunner, yelled, intending to detain the man. But the insurgent hurled a grenade. ... The pin failed, and Gilbertson shot him with his machine gun. ... After that, the soldiers said, they decided to kill any wounded insurgents able to move."[157] Is that a reasonable response to such an experience? Is it a lawful response? Is it self-defense? Is it merely war?

General Jean-René Bachelet, former general inspector of the Armed Forces of the French Republic, said of a similar situation in Sarajevo, in 1995, when he was a commanding officer of troops:

> There is an exceptionally narrow dividing line between soldierly behavior, as dictated by our cultural heritage and international law, and barbaric behavior. ... In situations like that, the natural instinct is barbaric. That is where the commander plays an essential, determinative role: provided that he has the support of his men, that he ... holds sway by his strength of character, his authority and his skills, but also his inner qualities, he is the only person capable of controlling combat hysteria, which otherwise leads to barbaric behavior. That is the weight of his responsibility. ... [A]scendancy must be gained over the enemy, the upper hand must be gained over the forces of violence, the soldiers need to be the strongest. In the name of our civilization's values, however, that is not done anyhow or at any price; the principle of humanity is no less essential. Force could thus not be unbridled violence.[158]

A U.S. Marine recon officer in Iraq simply said, "An officer's job isn't only to inspire his men to action but also to rein them in when fear and adrenaline threaten to carry them away."[159]

At some level, every combatant knows that double-tapping – shooting the wounded – is contrary to LOAC/IHL. In contrast, if a wounded but still living enemy exhibits any offensive intent, he is a lawful target, no matter how grievously wounded he may be. "Any offensive intent" is sometimes open to subjective assessment, but it may not be presumed as a matter of course. If there is an *honest and reasonable belief* in the soldier's mind that the wounded enemy presents a danger to the soldier or his fellow soldiers, the fallen enemy is a lawful target. Otherwise, he is not. It is always a possibility that the enemy may feign death, then fire on the opposing force from behind. That is why any area with apparently dead enemy fighters should be secured and the "bodies" examined, or at least watched, while friendly troops remain in the area. If it is not possible to examine enemy bodies or post a security watch, and it often is not in a combat situation, the risk of a perfidious enemy does exist. That is, and always has been, a combatant's risk.

---

[157] Ann Scott Tyson, "A Deadly Clash at Donkey Island," *Wash. Post*, Aug. 19, 2007, A1.

[158] Jean-René Bachelet, "Address by General Jean-René Bachelet," 870 *Int'l Rev. of the Red Cross* (June 2008), 215, 217.

[159] Nathaniel Fick, *One Bullet Away* (New York: Houghton Mifflin, 2006), 253.

That is easy to say in the calm of a seminar classroom, but that makes it no less true in the chaos of combat. The possibility of perfidy is not an excuse to violate LOAC as a matter of course. "Members of the Armed Forces are expected to behave responsibly under adverse conditions, even when no peer supervision is present. Members of the military are expected to resist temptation – which may be considerable in battle – to deviate from what they know to be ethically proper."[160]

Indiscriminate – and "indiscriminate" is stressed – double-tapping is a grave breach of LOAC, in violation of Article 12 of Geneva Convention I: "Members of the armed forces . . . who are wounded . . . shall be respected and protected in all circumstances. . . . Any attempts upon their lives, or violence to their persons, shall be strictly prohibited; in particular, they shall not be murdered or exterminated." Double-tapping is the grave breach of murder. To double-tap a wounded enemy who appears to be reaching for a weapon is no crime, however. If a marine honestly and reasonably believed that a wounded insurgent he killed had a weapon, but the marine was mistaken, it still is no crime. The issue turns on the honesty and reasonableness of the marine's belief, and, in combat, marines and soldiers should be given every benefit of the doubt. That benefit should not be stretched to constitute license, however.

The prohibition against indiscriminate double-tapping is customary law and is at least 140 years old. The Lieber Code mandates in Article LXI that "troops . . . have no right to kill enemies already disabled on the ground, or prisoners captured by other troops." The U.S. law of war manual prohibits indiscriminate double-tapping: "It is especially forbidden . . . to declare that no quarter will be given" and "to kill or wound an enemy who, having laid down his arms, or having no longer means of defense, has surrendered at discretion."[161] Double-tapping is contrary to Additional Protocol I, Articles 40 and 41, as well. Article 40: "It is prohibited to order that there shall be no survivors, to threaten an adversary therewith or to conduct hostilities on this basis." Article 41: "1. A person who is recognized or who, in the circumstances should be recognized to be *hors de combat* shall not be made the object of attack. 2. A person is *hors de combat* if: (c) he has been rendered unconscious or is otherwise incapacitated by wounds . . . and therefore is incapable of defending himself."

Double-tapping is an easy course, however, and it continues. During the common Article 2 phase of the U.S. invasion of Iraq, in April 2003, a U.S. Army column from the 3rd Infantry Division (Mechanized) was fighting its way toward Baghdad. As the Abrams tanks and Bradley fighting vehicles drove northward, they encountered a new enemy tactic.

> They [Iraqis] would lie next to the ditches, pretending to be dead. After the tanks had passed, they would leap up, aim an RPG tube, and fire grenades at the rear of the tanks. . . . From the commander's hatch of his Bradley, [the commander] . . . spotted two Iraqi fighters in the median. One was waving a white flag. . . . They were making wild "don't shoot" gestures. [The commander] let them go. But just after he passed them, the two men picked up weapons and opened fire. . . . Over the net, other commanders were complaining about the phony dead men rising up and firing weapons. They wanted permission to make sure people who appeared to be dead really were dead. Lieutenant Colonel [in

---

[160] Th. A. van Baarda and D. E. M. Verweij, *Military Ethics: The Dutch Approach* (Leiden: Martinus Nijhoff, 2006), 12.

[161] FM 27–10, *The Law of Land Warfare*, supra, note 6, paras. 28 and 29, at 17.

charge] had heard enough. He got on the net and ordered his men to "double tap." Anything you see, he instructed, don't assume it's dead. Double tap it. Shoot it again.[162]

It is facile to criticize the conduct of those on the battlefield who sometimes must make instantaneous decisions that may mean the success or failure of an assigned mission or the death or wounding of one's own troops. Ordering or allowing the shooting of a wounded enemy should never be a commander's decision, however. "Effective leadership demands judgments which are sound from the operational *and* the ethical point of view."[163] As with police officers, soldiers and Marines cannot lawfully fire on someone who *could* pose risk; they cannot carry enough ammunition to kill everyone who *could* be a threat. They cannot double-tap a wounded insurgent because yesterday they heard of an insurgent who hid a grenade he used to kill himself and an approaching soldier. For both police officers and soldiers, it is potentially a harsh law, but the profession of arms is harsh. Nor is "I did it to save American lives" license to violate LOAC. That is *kriegsraison*, the individual's belief that he has the right to do whatever is required to prevail; to do whatever he believes is required to win. It is murder on the battlefield.

An possible alternative that is not a law of war violation is an "eye thump."

[A] Marine veteran of the wars in Iraq and Afghanistan explained: "If I would press you in the eyeball, if you're alive you're going to have a response. If you're dead you're not going to have a response. In Iraq we had a lot of people who were fake dead." So the Marines, he said, "put the muzzle of their weapon on the chest of the enemy combatant, they press down on it and then they thump them in the eye, and if there's a response, they're not dead. And then you take them as a combatant and detain them."[164]

8.6 U.S. Military Policy

"Long before U.S. troops were engaged in combat in Vietnam, the Army had included in its training programs material designed to inculcate in the troops a knowledge of the rights and obligations under the Geneva conventions of 1949."[165] During that conflict, on April 20, 1965, little more than a month after the initial major American units landed at Da Nang, South Vietnam, the first Military Advisory Command, Vietnam (MACV) directive dealing with war crimes was published. MACV Directive 20–4 ordered that it was "the responsibility of all military personnel having knowledge or receiving a report of an incident or of an act thought to be a war crime to make such incident known to his commanding officer as soon as practicable."[166] The directive applied to members of all branches of U.S. Armed Forces in South Vietnam.

From that date forward, there have been multiple orders in effect in every U.S. armed service requiring that war crimes and suspected war crimes be promptly reported. Rules

---

[162] David Zucchino, *Thunder Run* (New York: Grove Press, 2004), 32.
[163] van Baarda and Verweij, *Military Ethics*, supra, note 160, at 2. Emphasis in original.
[164] Elizabeth Bumiller, "Training for Consulate Attacks, in Case There's a Next Time," NY *Times*, Sept. 29, 2012, A15.
[165] MGen. George S. Prugh, *Law at War: Vietnam 1964–1973* (Washington, DC: Dept of the Army, 1975), 74.
[166] Id., 72, 137.

of engagement pocket cards carried by U.S. combatants usually repeat that admonition. The semiannual classes on LOAC that every U.S. armed service member is required by service order to attend, starting in basic training, repeat that war crimes are to be immediately reported. This training is in keeping with the requirements of Geneva Convention common Article 47/48/127/144 and Additional Protocol I, Article 87.1.

But, just as no domestic law is going to end domestic crime, no military order, regardless of how often repeated, can prevent all criminal conduct by armed men and women engaged in combat. The unit that perpetrated horrific grave breaches at My Lai was subject to a multiplicity of Department of Defense, Department of the Army, MACV, and division orders regarding the prevention and reporting of war crimes. Yet they had not received adequate law of war training. Lieutenant General William Peers, who conducted the most comprehensive of the My Lai investigations, wrote, "Undoubtedly part of the problem was rooted in the lackadaisical manner in which the training was handled."[167]

Still, as with most states, it is long-standing U.S. policy that all service members be trained in LOAC, receive regular refresher training, and be made aware of their obligation to report war crimes and suspected war crimes. That policy is vigorously pursued, and most war crimes that come to light are revealed as a result of reports by service members. At the same time, the perception of some younger war fighters that telling superiors of a possible crime committed by another soldier or marine is "ratting out" a buddy inhibits reporting.[168] In such cases the silent witnesses, if found out, may be (and some have been) disciplined for not reporting a war crime of which they knew.[169] We will never know how often known war crimes are not reported.

8.7 Summary

Crimes, war crimes, and grave breaches: For combatants, the first are defined in the state's military justice code – for the Untied States, the Uniform Code of Military Justice (UCMJ). While of little direct significance for LOAC and IHL, the UCMJ is important because it is the vehicle by which war crimes are usually charged, when committed by U.S. combatants.

Grave breaches are specified in Geneva Convention common Article 49/50/129/146. They are the most serious LOAC/IHL crimes, usually committed against military or civilian prisoners. States ratifying the 1949 Geneva conventions are pledged to prosecute grave breaches. Originally considered limited to international armed conflicts, today grave breaches are often prosecuted when committed in noninternational conflicts, as well.

---

[167] Lt. Gen. W. R. Peers, *The My Lai Inquiry* (New York: Norton, 1979), 230. Gen. Peers adds, "Even accepting these training deficiencies ... there were some things a soldier did not have to be told were wrong – such as rounding up women and children and then mowing them down, shooting babies out of mothers' arms, and raping." Id.

[168] An example of such thinking is found in literature and media reports. The front page of the June 9, 2008, *Marine Corps Times*, in inch-high letters, read, "Stand by Your Squad." The subhead read, "The Story of One Marine Who Refused to Snitch," referring to U.S. federal grand jury proceedings regarding alleged 2004 grave breaches in Fallujah, Iraq.

[169] Chris Amos, "6 Sailors Charged with Detainee Abuse in Iraq: 5 Others Get NJP For Failing To Report It," *Navy Times* Website, Aug. 14, 2008, http://www.navytimes.com/news/2008/08/navy_bucca_081408/

Some war crimes are sufficiently minor to be considered disciplinary in nature. There is no internationally agreed definition of war crimes, and no definition could encompass all possible war crimes any more than a municipal criminal code can enumerate all possible criminal acts. However, an authoritative listing of war crimes is found in the statute of the ICC.

A mandatory requirement of grave breaches, besides that requiring criminal provisions for their violation, is that ratifying states seek out and try those who have committed them, a form of <u>universal jurisdiction.</u> In practice, some states exercise permissive universal jurisdiction – that is, they prosecute grave breaches no matter where committed, but only if the accused is present in their state.

When it is determined that a war crime has been committed, it may be prosecuted if that offense is reflected in the state's military code or has been incorporated in the state's domestic criminal code, and if the act has a nexus, a connection, to an armed conflict. War crimes are most often committed by combatants but may be committed by civilians, as well.

By now, as grave breaches have, most lesser war crimes have been codified in treaties such as the Geneva conventions and additional protocols. Those that are not may be, and continue to be, tried as violations of the laws and customs of war.

CASES AND MATERIALS

PROSECUTOR V. DUSKO TADIĆ

(IT-94–1-T) Opinion and Judgment (May 7, 1997). Footnotes omitted.

Introduction. *The ICTY's* Tadić *case is one of the most significant in LOAC for several reasons. One reason is that it explains essential concepts that had not been decided since their incorporation in the 1949 Geneva Conventions. A concept it examines is the requirement of a nexus between the alleged wrongful acts of an accused and an armed conflict.*

572. The existence of an armed conflict or occupation and the applicability of international humanitarian law to the territory is not sufficient to create international jurisdiction over each and every serious crime committed in the territory of the former Yugoslavia. For a crime to fall within the jurisdiction of the International Tribunal, a sufficient nexus must be established between the alleged offence and the armed conflict which gives rise to the applicability of international humanitarian law.

573. In relation to the applicability of international humanitarian law to the acts alleged in the Indictment, the Appeals Chamber has held that:

Even if substantial clashes were not occurring ... at the time and place the crimes were allegedly committed ... international humanitarian law applies. It is sufficient that the alleged crimes were closely related to the hostilities occurring in other parts of the territories controlled by the parties to the conflict.

For an offence to be a violation of international humanitarian law, therefore, this Trial Chamber needs to be satisfied that each of the alleged acts was in fact closely related to the hostilities. It would be sufficient to prove that the crime was committed in the course of or as part of the hostilities in, or the occupation of, an area controlled by one of the parties. It is not, however, necessary to show that armed conflict was occurring at the exact time and place of the proscribed acts alleged to have occurred, . . . nor is it necessary that the crime alleged takes place during combat, that it be part of a policy or of a practice officially endorsed or tolerated by one of the parties to the conflict, or that the act be in actual furtherance of a policy associated with the conduct of war or in the actual interest of a party to the conflict; the obligations of individuals under international humanitarian law are independent and apply without prejudice to any questions of the responsibility of States under international law. The only question to be determined in the circumstances of each individual case, is whether the offenses were closely related to the armed conflict as a whole.

574. In any event, acts of the accused related to the armed conflict in two distinct ways. First, there is the case of the acts of the accused in the take-over of Kozarac. . . . Given the nature of the armed conflict as an ethnic war and the strategic aims of the *Republika Srpska* to create a purely Serbian State, the acts of the accused during the armed take-over and ethnic cleansing of Muslim and Croat areas . . . were directly connected with the armed conflict.

575. Secondly, there are the acts of the accused in the camps run by the authorities of the *Republika Srpska*. Those acts clearly occurred with the connivance or permission of the authorities running these camps and indicate that such acts were part of an accepted policy towards prisoners in the camps. . . . Indeed, such treatment effected the objective of the Republika Srpska to ethnically cleanse, by means of terror, killings or otherwise, the areas of the Republic of Bosnia and Herzegovina controlled by Bosnian Serb forces. Accordingly, those acts too were directly connected with the armed conflict.

Conclusion. *Having found the required nexus between Tadić's wrongful acts and the armed conflict, the Trial Chamber was satisfied that he had committed war crimes, rather than violations of the domestic law. The Chamber eventually found Tadić not guilty of several charges but convicted him of multiple counts of persecution, cruel treatment, crimes against humanity, inhumane acts, and assaults. He was sentenced to confinement for a period of ten years.*

PROSECUTOR V. KUNARAC, ET AL.

IT-96–23 & 23/1-A (June 12, 2002). Footnotes omitted.

Introduction. *Five years after the* Tadić *opinion, the nexus requirement was further clarified in the* Kunarac *opinion.*

55. There are two general conditions for the applicability of Article 3 of the [ICTY] Statute: first, there must be an armed conflict; second, the acts of the accused must be closely related to the armed conflict.

56. An "armed conflict" is said to exist "whenever there is a resort to armed force between States or protracted armed violence between governmental authorities and organized armed groups or between such groups within a State".

57. There is no necessary correlation between the area where the actual fighting is taking place and the geographical reach of the laws of war. The laws of war apply in the whole territory of the warring states or, in the case of internal armed conflicts, the whole territory under the control of a party to the conflict, whether or not actual combat takes place there, and continue to apply until a general conclusion of peace or, in the case of internal armed conflicts, until a peaceful settlement is achieved. A violation of the laws or customs of war may therefore occur at a time when and in a place where no fighting is actually taking place. . . . The requirement that the acts of the accused must be closely related to the armed conflict would not be negated if the crimes were temporarily and geographically remote from the actual fighting. It would be sufficient, for instance, for the purpose of this requirement, that the alleged crimes were closely related to hostilities occurring in other parts of the territories controlled by the parties to the conflict.

58. What ultimately distinguishes a war crime from a purely domestic offense is that a war crime is shaped by or dependent upon the environment – the armed conflict – in which it is committed. It need not have been planned or supported by some form of policy. The armed conflict need not have been causal to the commission of the crime, but the existence of an armed conflict must, at a minimum, have played a substantial part in the perpetrator's ability to commit it, his decision to commit it, the manner in which it was committed or the purpose for which it was committed. Hence, if it can be established . . . that the perpetrator acted in furtherance of or under the guise of the armed conflict, it would be sufficient to conclude that his acts were closely related to the armed conflict. . . .

59. In determining whether or not the act in question is sufficiently related to the armed conflict, the Trial Chamber may take into account, *inter alia*, the following factors: the fact that the perpetrator is a combatant; the fact that the victim is a non-combatant; the fact that the victim is a member of the opposing party; the fact that the act may be said to serve the ultimate goal of a military campaign; and the fact that the crime is committed as part of or in the context of the perpetrator's official duties.

60. The Appellant's proposition that the laws of war only prohibit those acts which are specific to actual wartime situations is not right. The laws of war may frequently encompass acts which, though they are not committed in the theater of conflict, are substantially related to it. The laws of war can apply to both types of acts. The Appeals Chamber understands the Appellant's argument to be that if an act can be prosecuted in peacetime, it cannot be prosecuted in wartime. This betrays a misconception about the relationship between the laws of war and the laws regulating a peacetime situation. The laws of war do not necessarily displace the laws regulating a peacetime situation; the former may add elements requisite to the protection which needs to be afforded to victims in a wartime situation. . . .

64. Furthermore, the Appeals Chamber considers that the Prosecutor did not have to prove that there was an armed conflict in each and every square inch of the general area. The state of armed conflict is not limited to the areas of actual military combat but exists across the entire territory under the control of the warring parties. . . .

65. . . . The Appeals Chamber does not accept the Appellant's contention that the laws of war are limited to those acts which could only be committed in actual combat. Instead, it is sufficient for an act to be shown to have been closely related to the armed conflict. . . .

Conclusion. *With this opinion, it becomes clear that, in ICTY practice, at least, short of a crime committed between and among one side's combatants, a nexus between an alleged wrongful act and an ongoing armed conflict is not difficult to establish.*

"THE ZYKLON B CASE"

Trial of Bruno Tesch and Two Others

British Military Court, Hamburg, Germany (March 1–8, 1946)[170]

Introduction. The Zyklon B Case, *conducted shortly after the conclusion of World War II, was a military tribunal that examined,* inter alia, *the liability of civilians for the commission of war crimes, although this was not a major issue in the case. (The Prosecutor was Major, later Colonel, G. I. A. D. Draper, later a prominent British law of war publicist and professor.) From the War Crimes Commission report of the commission:*

> Bruno Tesch was owner of a firm which arranged for the supply of poison gas intended for the extermination of vermin, and among the customers of the firm were the [Nazi] S.S. Karl Weinbacher was Tesch's Procurist or second-in-command. Joachim Drosihn was the firm's first gassing technician. These three were accused of having supplied poison gas used for killing allied nationals interned in concentration camps, knowing that it was so used. The Defence claimed that the accused did not know of the use to which the gas was to be put; for Drosihn it was also pleaded that the supply of gas was beyond his control. Tesch and Weinbacher were condemned to death. Drosihn was acquitted.

From the record of the British Military Court that prosecuted the three civilians:

B Notes on the Case

2 Questions of Substantive Law

(II) Civilians as War Criminals

The decision of the Military Court in the present case is a clear example of the application of the rule that the provisions of the laws and customs of war are addressed not only to combatants and to members of the state and other public authorities, but to anybody who is in a position to assist in their violation.

The activities with which the accused in the present case were charged were commercial transactions conducted by civilians. The Military Court acted on the principle that any civilian who is an accessory to a violation of the laws and customs of war is himself also liable as a war criminal.

Conclusion. *Clearly, not only soldiers can be held criminally liable for grave breaches and war crimes. In other post–World War II trials, government officials, industrialists, judges and prosecutors, and concentration camp inmates and guards were found guilty of war crimes.*

PROSECUTOR V. FURUNDŽIJA

IT-95–17/1-T (December 10, 1998). Footnotes Omitted.

Introduction. *An ICTY Trial Chamber discusses universal jurisdiction in the context of the grave breach of torture. Years before the U.S. Military Commissions Act of 2006, this*

---

[170] U.N. War Crimes Commission, *LRTWC*, Vol. I (London: UN War Crimes Comm., 1947), 93–103.

opinion deliberates the legal ineffectiveness of a state's legislative attempt to immunize those who torture, which critics charge the Military Commissions Act with doing.[171]

155. The fact that torture is prohibited by a peremptory norm of international law has other effects at the inter-state and individual levels. At the inter-state level, it serves to internationally de-legitimize any legislative, administrative or judicial act authorizing torture. . . . If such a situation were to arise, the national measures, violating the general principle and any relevant treaty provision, would . . . not be accorded international legal recognition. . . . What is even more important is that perpetrators of torture acting upon or benefiting from those national measures may nevertheless be held criminally responsible for torture, whether in a foreign State, or in their own State under a subsequent regime. In short, in spite of possible national authorization by legislative or judicial bodies to violate the principle banning torture, individuals remain bound to comply with that principle. As the International Military Tribunal at Nuremberg put it: "individuals have international duties which transcend the national obligations of obedience imposed by the individual State".

156. Furthermore, at the individual level, that is, that of criminal liability, it would seem that one of the consequences of the *jus cogens* character bestowed by the international community upon the prohibition of torture is that every State is entitled to investigate, prosecute and punish or extradite individuals accused of torture, who are present in a territory under its jurisdiction. Indeed, it would be inconsistent on the one hand to prohibit torture to such an extent as to restrict the normally unfettered treaty-making power of sovereign States, and on the other hand bar States from prosecuting and punishing those torturers who have engaged in this odious practice abroad. This legal basis for States' universal jurisdiction over torture bears out and strengthens the legal foundation for such jurisdiction found by other courts in the inherently universal character of the crime. It has been held that international crimes being universally condemned wherever they occur, every State has the right to prosecute and punish the authors of such crimes. As stated in general terms by the Supreme Court of Israel in *Eichmann*, and echoed by a USA court in *Demjanjuk*, "it is the universal character of the crimes in question [i.e., international crimes] which vests in every State the authority to try and punish those who participated in their commission."

157. It would seem that other consequences include the fact that torture may not be covered by a statute of limitations, and must not be excluded from extradition under any political offence exemption.

Conclusion. *Does this opinion, buttressed by reference to a U.S. Federal District Court opinion,*[172] *suggest anything about possible travel plans for leaders of states who sponsor legal efforts to immunize those who torture?*

IN RE AMBERGER[173]

Wuppertal, Germany, British Military Court, March 14, 1946

Introduction. *The duty of captured combatants to escape, if reasonably possible, and the duty of their captors to foil attempts to escape, are highlighted here. Amberger's was a case sadly*

---

[171] E.g., Jordan J. Paust, *Beyond the Law* (New York: Cambridge University Press, 2007), 32.

[172] *Demjanjuk v. Petrovsky*, 776 F. 2d 571 (6th Cir. 1985), cert. den., 475 U.S. 1016, 106 S.Ct. 1198 (1986), which discusses universal jurisdiction in relation to war crimes.

similar to many other post–World War II military commissions. It is notable only for the judge advocate's frank, even stark, assessment of the duties and rights of the opposing parties.

The Facts: The accused Amberger, who was a warrant officer in the German Army, was charged with the killing at Dreierwalde, on March 22, 1945, of four enemy prisoners of war. The circumstances were as follows: during a severe air raid on March 21, 1945, five Australian and British airmen were forced to bail out from their aeroplane. On landing they were made prisoners of war and taken to the near-by aerodrome of Dreierwalde. On the following evening the five prisoners were placed in charge of the accused Amberger and two German non-commissioned officers, and marched off in the direction of a railway station, ostensibly en route for a prisoner of war camp. After proceeding for a distance of about a mile and a half, the party turned along a track which led into a wood. The five prisoners of war were walking abreast and in an orderly fashion in front of the guards when, without warning, the accused Amberger and the two other guards opened fire on them. All the prisoners with the exception of one, Flight-Lieutenant Berick, were killed. The latter, although wounded, managed to escape.

In his defense the accused said that he had seen the prisoners of war talking to one another in a suspicious manner and taking their bearings from canal bridges and from the stars. Their conduct had led him to believe that they were about to make an attempt to escape. The accused asserted that in the failing light four of the prisoners had then tried to escape in various directions, while the fifth prisoner had attacked him.

In his summing up, the Judge Advocate said with regard to rules applicable to escape of prisoners of war: "It is the duty of an officer or a man if he is captured to try and escape. The corollary to that is that the Power which holds him is entitled to prevent him from escaping, and in doing so no great niceties are called for by the Power that has him in his control; by that I mean it is quite right, if it is reasonable in the circumstances, for a guard to open fire on an escaping prisoner, though he should pay great heed merely to wound him; but if he should be killed, though that is very unfortunate, it does not make a war crime. ... If the accused, Karl Amberger, did see that his prisoners were trying to escape or had reasonable grounds for thinking that they were attempting to escape, then that would not be a breach of the rules and customs of war, and therefore you would not be able to say a war crime had been committed."

Held: That the accused Amberger was guilty. The accused was sentenced to death.

"DOUBLE-TAPPING"

Introduction. *This e-mail was reportedly written by R. V., an enlisted soldier in the 2d Battalion, 327th Parachute Infantry, 101st Airborne Division, while serving in Iraq. It reflects the feelings of many soldiers and marines regarding "double-tapping" and dead checks.*

You media pansies may squeal and may squirm / But a fighting man knows that the way to confirm / That some jihadist bastard is finally dead / Is a brain-tappin' round fired into his head.

---

[173] H. Lauterpacht, ed., *Annual Digest and Reports of Public International Law Cases: Year 1946* (London: Butterworth (1951), 291.

To hell with some weenie with his journalist degree / Safe from the combat, tryin' to tell me / I should check him for breathing, examine his eyes. / Nope, I'm punchin' his ticket to Muj' paradise.

To hell with you wimps from your Ivy League schools, / Sittin' far from the war tellin' me about rules, / And preaching to me your wrong-headed contention / That I should observe the Geneva Convention.

Which doesn't apply to a terrorist scum, / So evil and cruel their own people run / From cold-blooded killers who love to behead. / Shove that mother' Geneva, I'm leavin' him dead.

You slick talking heads may preach, preen and prattle, / But you're damn well not here, in the thick of the battle. / It's chaotic, confusing, and comes at you fast, / So it's Muj' checkin' out, because I'm gonna last.

Yeah, I'll last through this fight and send his ass away / To his fat ugly virgins while I'm still in play. / If you journalist weenies think that's cold, cruel and crass, / Then pucker up sweeties; kiss a fighting man's ass.

Conclusion. *Is it possible to convince a soldier, young, articulate, and intelligent as this soldier apparently is, that he is mistaken and that he subscribes to a LOAC/IHL grave breach? It is possible only through training and supervision by noncommissioned and commissioned officers. Soldiers and their units usually take on the characteristics of their leaders, particularly at the company and battalion levels. Leadership and training remain essential to the combat performance of a command and to that of young soldiers.*

Law of Armed Conflict and International Humanitarian Law: Battlefield Issues

9 Obedience to Orders, the First Defense

9.0 Introduction[1]

"I was only following orders!" The phrase has been heard so often in so many circumstances that it is its own parody. It is a plea mouthed by the relatively innocent junior soldier and by the duplicitous battlefield murderer. Is it a legitimate defense to grave breach charges? Was it ever a legitimate defense to war crimes? In all nations, among any soldier's first catechism is that he shall obey orders. "No military force can function effectively without routine obedience, and it is the routine that is stressed. . . . But there is some ultimate humanity that cannot be broken down, the disappearance of which we will not accept. . . . Trained to obey 'without hesitation,' they remain nevertheless capable of hesitating."[2]

In 1996, in Berlin, former German Democratic Republic (GDR) border guards who killed German civilians fleeing to the West raised the defense of obedience to superior orders.[3] In Rome, also in 1996, a former S.S. captain invoked the defense,[4] as did a French National Assembly deputy, in Paris.[5] In International Criminal Tribunal for the Former Yugoslavia (ICTY) trials, Serb and Croat defendants raise the defense today.[6] In Germany, in 1999, a former Gestapo agent was tried for assisting in the murder of seventeen thousand Jews at the Nazi death camp at Maidanek, Poland, during World War II. His defense: I was only following orders.[7]

Is a soldier immune from punishment because his or her acts were carried out pursuant to the orders of a superior? It was not until World War II that the question of personal responsibility appeared resolved. In fact, World War II, Nuremberg, and the

---

[1] An early version of this chapter appeared in 15–2 *American U. Int'l L. Rev.* (1999), 481–526.

[2] Michael Walzer, *Just and Unjust Wars*, 3d ed. (New York: Basic Books, 2000), 311.

[3] *Border Guards Prosecution Case* (1996), 5 StR 370/92 [BGH] [Supreme Court] (FRG). Convicted of manslaughter, the defendants were sentenced to twenty months' probation, suspended. Five years later, "in a landmark judgment, *Streletz, Kesler and Krenz v. Germany*, the European Court of Human Rights . . . unanimously held that criminal prosecution of the leaders of the German Democratic Republic (GDR) for ordering to kill individuals attempting to flee the GDR is compatible with the principle *nullum crimen sine lege* and . . . the prohibition on retroactive criminal laws." 95–4 *AJIL* 904 (Oct. 2001).

[4] The eighty-four-year-old Priebke was eventually sentenced to life in prison.

[5] *Papon* case, unpublished transcript of Judgment Sept. 18, 1996), *Cour d'appel de Bordeaux, Chambre d'accusation Arrêt du*, no. 806.

[6] *Prosecutor v. Erdemović*, IT-96-22-T (1997).

[7] "Germany: Ex-Gestapo Agent on Trial," NY *Times*, April 28, 1999, A10.

"subsequent proceedings" materially altered the legal position of the soldier who pleaded obedience to superior orders in defense of his war crimes.

9.1 A History of the First Defense

Obedience to orders, a defense as ancient as the laws and rules of war, has been the most frequent defense raised by soldiers charged with their violation, whatever the incarnation of those laws. It rarely is a successful defense.[8] One of the first recorded instances of its use as a defense was in 1474, when Peter von Hagenbach, appointed governor of Breisach by Charles of Burgundy, unsuccessfully raised the defense to charges of murder, arson, and rape. (See Chapter 1, Cases and Materials.) Captain Axtell, the guard commander at the execution of Charles I, one hundred thirty years after von Hagenbach, raised the same defense and fared no better. In the guard commander's case the English court held, "[The captain] justified all that he did was as a soldier, by the command of his superior officer, whom he must obey or die. It was ... no excuse, for his superior was a traitor ... and where the command is traitorous, there the obedience to that command is also traitorous."[9] Both von Hagenbach and Axtell were convicted and put to death. Then as now, societies faced the dark deeds of their own, as well as those of the enemy's. Too often, those deeds arose not from passions raised in battle, but from the directions of superiors to subordinates.

In his plays, Shakespeare (1564–1616) told of the dire consequences of soldiers' obedience to illegal orders.[10] In the seventeenth century, Grotius wrote, "If the authorities issue any order that is contrary to the law of nature or to the commandments of God, the order should not be carried out."[11] Apparently no adherent of Grotius, the British Military Code of 1715, from which America's first military laws were drawn, was said to have provided that refusal to obey a military order was a capital offense, no qualification being made as to the lawfulness of the command.[12]

In early America, the defense of superior orders was first defined in nonmilitary civil and criminal cases tried in U.S. domestic courts – employers' instructions to employees and police supervisors' orders to patrolmen. Those early cases rejected the defense if the order upon which the subordinate relied was illegal in the abstract, without considering

---

[8] A May 2005 Russian Federation court-martial of several Special Forces members resulted in acquittal of murder and destruction of civilian property based "on orders from their superiors and that military discipline had compelled them to commit their actions." 87–859 *Int'l Rev. of the Red Cross* (Sept. 2005), 593.

[9] *Axtell's Case* (1661), Kelyng 13; 84 E.R. 1060.

[10] Theodor Meron, "Leaders, Courtiers and Command Responsibility in Shakespeare," in Michael Schmitt and Jelena Pejic, eds., *International Law and Armed Conflict: Exploring the Faultlines* (Leiden: Martinus Nijhoff, 2007), 403–11.

[11] Hugo Grotius, *De Jure Belli ac Pacis Libri Tres*, Francis W. Kelsey, trans. (New York: Hein reprint, 1995), book I, chap. 4, § I.3.

[12] Hersch Lauterpacht, "The Law of Nations and the Punishment of War Crimes," 21 *British Yearbook of Int'l L.* (1944), 58, 73. However, a review of Col. William Winthrop, *Military Law and Precedents*, 2d ed. (Washington, DC: GPO, 1920), reveals no British code of that date. Art. XV of the 1688 British Articles of War does provide that any disobedience shall result in "such Punishment as a Court-Martial shall think fit." There is no such disobedience provision in the British Articles of War of 1765 nor in the American Articles of War of 1775, 1776, or 1786.

the order's appearance of legality to the subordinate.[13] In an 1813 civil case involving a police officer, the court enunciated a civilian standard that has stood the test of time for combatants, as well as civilian noncombatants: Obedience to a superior's order is not a defense if the subordinate knew, or should have known, that the order was illegal.[14]

The first recorded case of an American military officer pleading the order of his superior in defense of having committed an offense grounded in international law was that of the navy captain George Little. In 1799, during the U.S. war with France, and pursuant to a federal law, Captain Little seized the Danish ship *Flying Fish*. The seizure, alas, was not in conformance with the federal law relating to seizures, although it was in keeping with President John Adams's written instructions as to how that law should be carried out by U.S. naval commanders. The owners of the Danish ship sued for damages. In the subsequent Supreme Court opinion – an opinion that could have current relevance – Chief Justice John Marshall wrote for the majority that naval commanders acted at their peril when they obeyed presidential instructions that were at variance with the law. If the instructions are not "strictly warranted by law" the commander is answerable.[15] If the instruction is illegal it may not be obeyed, and he who *would* obey is tasked with recognizing its illegality.

This military officer's burden of legal interpretation was even greater for the unschooled seaman or soldier. In those early days, however, there are no recorded cases of enlisted soldiers or sailors being charged with committing illegal acts pursuant to a superior's order. An opinion addressing that situation would wait another sixty-three years, until 1867.

In 1813, Captain Little's unsuccessful defense was raised in another federal case involving a superior's command, and it was again rejected. The junior officers of a privateer pleaded their captain's order in defense to charges of their assault and theft on board a captured ship. The court held, "No military or civil officer can command an inferior to violate the laws of his country; nor will such command excuse, much less justify the act. . . . The participation of the inferior officer, in an act he knows, or ought to know to be illegal, will not be excused by the order of his superior."[16] So the 1804 *Little* standard was made clearer: A military officer is liable for those orders that he knows, *or should know*, to be illegal.

In an 1849 case, Private Samuel Dinsman, a Marine embarked aboard the USS *Vincennes*, disobeyed the orders of the ship's captain, receiving twenty-four lashes ("stripes") and confinement as a consequence. In approving Dinsman's punishment, the high court emphasized the authority of military officers and the folly of a subordinate questioning their orders: "[An officer's] position . . . in many respects, becomes quasi judicial. . . . Especially it is proper, not only that a public officer, situated like the defendant [the ship's captain], be invested with a wide discretion, but be upheld in it. . . . It is not enough to show he committed an error in judgment, but it must have been a malicious and wilful error."[17] Early on, then, the Supreme Court's view of

---

[13] E.g., *U.S. v. Bright*, 24 F.Cas. 1232 (C.C.D. Pa., 1809).

[14] *U.S. v. Jones*, 26 F. Cas. 653 (C.C.D. Pa., 1813).

[15] *Little et al. v. Barreme et al.*, 6 U.S. (2 Cranch) 170, (1804). To the same effect, *U.S. v. Jones*, id.; and *U.S. v. Bevans*, 24 F.Cas. 1138 (C.C.D. Mass. 1816), and more recently, *Neu v. McCarthy*, 309 Mass. 17, 33 N.E.2d 570 (1941).

[16] *U.S. v. Jones*, supra, note 14.   [17] *Wilkes v. Dinsman*, 48 U.S. (7 How.) 89, 129–30, 131 (1849).

officer–enlisted relationships, based in part on British cases,[18] allowed little room for military subordinates to question a superior's orders.

Thirty-eight years after the *Little* case, in 1851, the Supreme Court decided the same issue with the same result, Chief Justice Roger Taney adding, "The [superior's] order may palliate, but it cannot justify."[19] This dictum, which has since become U.S. policy, suggested that a superior's order might extenuate an offense committed at that order, leading to a lesser punishment.[20]

Until then, the focus had been either on the officer's legal responsibility for issuing an improper order or on the subordinate's penalty for disobeying the officer's proper order. In 1867, a federal district court addressed the enlisted man's liability, not for disobeying, but for executing an *illegal* superior order. In *McCall v. McDowell*, the court declared, "Except in a plain case ... where at first blush it is apparent and palpable to the commonest understanding that the order is illegal, I cannot but think that the law should excuse the military subordinate when acting in obedience to the orders of his commander."[21]

So, after 1867, in at least one federal court district, enlisted American soldiers and sailors were essentially off the legal hook. If one were to connect Captain Little's 1804 Supreme Court opinion with McCall's 1867 federal opinion, a first implicit standard for military personnel was established: The acts of subordinates, even if illegal, were protected by the orders of their superiors, unless such orders were *clearly* illegal. The superior remained liable for any illegal act or order given.[22]

Throughout this period Great Britain took the same tack as the United States. During the Napoleonic Wars, for example, a young British ensign, at his superior's order, killed a French prisoner. A Scottish court rejected the ensign's plea of superior orders in terms an American officer of that day might have recognized: "If an officer were to command a soldier to go out to the street and to kill you or me, he would not be bound to obey. It must be a legal order. ... Every officer has a discretion to disobey orders against the known laws of the land."[23]

The Lieber Code is silent on whether superior orders could justify a violation of the rules he recorded. Lieber apparently presumed that the opinions announced by U.S. domestic courts would control the issue. Despite the code's silence, the Civil War raised another opportunity for a court to rule on the issue in the military commission that tried Major Henry Wirz, commandant of the Andersonville, Georgia, prisoner of war (POW) camp where twelve thousand Union soldiers died. (See Chapter 2, Cases and Materials.) Charged with conspiracy to maltreat federal prisoners and thirteen counts of murder, Wirz pleaded that he had only obeyed his superiors' orders. The military commission

---

[18] Several such cases are cited in *Wilkes*, id., at 131.

[19] *Mitchell v. Harmony*, 54 U.S. (13 How.) 115, 137 (1851). The *Harmony* decision was reasserted in *Dow v. Johnson*, 100 U.S. 158 (1879).

[20] Department of the Army, FM 27–10, *The Law of Land Warfare* (Washington, DC: GPO, 1956), para. 509.a.

[21] *McCall v. McDowell*, 15 Fed. Cas. 1235 (C.C.D. Cal. 1867).

[22] Nineteenth-century American courts essentially rejected the doctrine of *respondeat superior*. That era's 9th Article of War read, "The principle of conduct is, that illegal orders are not obligatory."

[23] Alan M. Wilner, "Superior Orders as a Defense to Violations of International Criminal Law," 26 *Maryland Law Review* (1966), 127, 130.

found Wirz personally responsible for the acts charged and he was hanged, the Civil War's only soldier of either side to be executed for offenses amounting to war crimes.[24]

9.1.1 *The Twentieth Century's Evolving Standard*

The Civil War ended, a new century turned, and obedience to orders continued as a valid defense not only for enlisted men,[25] but for civilians tried in civil courts, as well.[26] In Great Britain a military case, *Regina v. Smith*, reached the same conclusion: "By focusing ... on the state of mind of the actor and the surrounding circumstances, a reasonable belief in the legality of the orders would exculpate the defendant by negating the requisite *mens rea*."[27] The Second Boer War (1899–1902) provided several other British cases involving the defense, the most notorious of which involved Lieutenant Harry H. "Breaker" Morant, executed after failing in asserting a defense of superior orders.[28]

For the United States and Great Britain, the standard of the mid-nineteenth century remained fixed: An officer was criminally responsible for the issuance or execution of orders he knew, or should have known, to be illegal. Subordinates were *not* liable for illegal orders they carried out, unless the illegality of those orders was clear.

Case law was just beginning to define what "clear illegality" meant. Two civilian appellate opinions refer to illegal orders as those whose illegality was "apparent and palpable to the commonest understanding,"[29] and "so plain as not to admit of a reasonable doubt."[30] Still, a lack of legal clarity as to the meaning of "clear illegality" would persist into the twenty-first century.

In 1902, during the U.S.–Philippine War, several American officers were charged with committing or ordering war crimes,[31] including a U.S. Marine Corps major, who testified that he had been ordered by an army brigadier general to kill and burn, and told that the more he killed and burned the more it would please the general.[32] The major was acquitted. The general was tried for his order and was convicted. In 1906, however, the prominent British publicist Lassa Oppenheim wrote that obedience to superior orders constituted *a complete defense* to a criminal prosecution. "If members of the armed forces commit violations by order of their Government, they are not war criminals and cannot be punished by the enemy. ... In case members of forces commit violations ordered by their commanders, the members may not be punished, for their commanders are alone responsible."[33]

---

[24] 8 *American State Trials*, 666 ff. (1918).

[25] E.g., *Riggs v. State*, 43 Tenn. 85 (1886); *In re Fair, et al.*, 100 Fed. 149 (D.Neb. 1900).

[26] E.g., *Hately v. State*, 15 Ga. 346 (1854); *Thomas v. State*, 134 Ala. 126, 33 So. 130 (1902).

[27] *Regina v. Smith*, 17 Cape Reports 561 (S. Africa 1900), the era's leading British case that rejects the defense of obedience to orders.

[28] Kit Denton, *Closed File* (Adelaide: Rigby, 1983), a lay account reflecting a case history far different from the 1982 film *Breaker Morant*.

[29] *In re Fair*, supra, note 25, at 155.

[30] *Commonwealth ex rel. Wadsworth v. Shortall*, 206 Pa. 165, 55 A. 952 (1903).

[31] See: Guénaël Mettraux, "US Courts-Martial and the Armed Conflict in the Philippines (1899–1902): Their Contribution to National Case Law on War Crimes," 1–1 *J. of Int'l Crim. Justice* (April 2003), 134–50.

[32] *U.S. v. Maj. Littleton W. T. Waller* (General court-martial, Manila, P.I., Special Order No. 54, March 1902). Unreported.

[33] Lassa F. L. Oppenheim, *International Law*, Vol. II, 1st ed. (London: Longmans Green, 1906), 264–5.

Basing his formulation on traditional concepts of international law, Oppenheim intertwined obedience to orders with *respondeat superior* (let the superior answer) and its related act of state doctrine. In doing so, Oppenheim was instrumental in bringing about a major change to the obedience defense. Enlisted soldiers bore no personal responsibility, Oppenheim held, when superiors ordered their criminal acts. Even the clear illegality of the orders was not an issue. (Forty-two years later, in the judgment of the post–World War II "Hostage Case," the tribunal dryly noted of this change, "We think Professor Oppenheim espoused a decidedly minority view.")[34] In 1912, Oppenheim wrote Great Britain's handbook on the rules of land warfare, a revision of Britain's first 1903 manual.[35] The new handbook by Oppenheim incorporated his view that, for subordinates, obedience to orders constituted a complete defense to law of war charges.

Looking to the British example, as the United States historically did in matters of military law and, to a lesser degree, looking to France's new manual on the topic, America revised General Orders 100 and, in 1914, published its first law of war manual. *Rules of Land Warfare (1914)*, paragraph 366, "Punishment of Individuals – War Crimes," reads, "Individuals of the armed forces will not be punished for these offenses in case they are committed under the orders or sanction of their government or commanders. The commanders ordering the commission of such acts ... may be punished by the belligerent into whose hands they may fall."

With this paragraph, the United States joined Britain in making a subordinate's obedience to orders a complete legal defense, setting aside American military and civilian case law of the previous 110 years. Although the U.S. manual held that officers ordering illegal acts "may be punished," the next phrase, "by the belligerent into whose hands they may fall," suggests that, should the officer never be captured, or should he be of the ultimately victorious army, it was questionable whether there would be any punishment at all.

Curiously, imperial Germany, where obedience was popularly thought to be absolute, employed a less forgiving rule for its soldiers. Subordinates were punished if they executed an order knowing that it related to an act that obviously aimed at a crime, "even if no crime was actually committed. It is sufficient if the order aims at the commission of a crime or offense."[36] No *actus reus* required.

In the United States, the various versions of the Articles of War were the precursors of today's Uniform Code of Military Justice, setting out offenses for which soldiers could be tried and punished. Article 64 of the 1912 Articles of War was pertinent to the issue of obedience of orders. That article, willful disobedience of a superior officer, is explained in the army's 1917 *Manual for Courts-Martial* (the first such *Manual*). The *Manual's* discussion of Article 64 notes that willful *dis*obedience of "any lawful command of his superior officer" was punishable.[37] Furthermore, "an accused can not be convicted of a violation of this article if the order was in fact unlawful; but, unless the order is plainly

[34] *U.S. v. List and 10 Others* ("The Hostage Case"), *T.W.C. Before the Nuernberg Mil. Tribs.*, Vol. XI (Washington, DC: GPO, 1950), judgment, 1237.

[35] Donald A. Wells, *The Laws of Land Warfare: A Guide to the U.S. Army Manuals* (Westport, CT: Greenwood Press, 1992), 5.

[36] *U.S. v. Ohlendorf and 23 others* ("The Einsatzgruppen Case"), *T.W.C. Before the Nuernberg Mil. Tribs.*, Vol. IV (Washington, DC: GPO, 1950), 486.

[37] A *Manual for Courts-Martial, Courts of Inquiry and Other Procedure under Military Law* (Washington, DC: GPO, 1916), 208.

illegal, the disobedience of it is punishable."[38] The *Manual*'s discussion completely ignored the contrary *Rules of Land Warfare* paragraph 366 providing the accused a complete defense.

In practice, however, the two manuals did not conflict. If a soldier obeyed a superior's order, for example, to murder prisoners, the issue of disobedience did not arise, and the soldier was protected from punishment for his illegal act by the land warfare manual – superior orders were the soldier's complete defense. In contrast, if the soldier *refused* to obey the order to shoot the prisoners, he was protected from punishment by the *Manual for Courts-Martial* – the order's illegality exempting him from prosecution for disobedience.

America fought World War I with those two dueling manuals in effect, while U.S. civilian law continued its steady and separate path regarding obedience to orders, a path contrary to the new military standard.

During the Great War, the Allies considered punishing Germans who had violated the law of war, from the kaiser to the lowest conscript. At the war's conclusion, the Preliminary Peace Conference created a Commission on Responsibilities[39] to study the issue of accountability for the war. In March 1919, the conference reported, "Military authorities cannot be relieved from responsibility by the mere fact that a higher authority might have been convicted of the same offense. It will be for the court to decide whether a plea of superior orders is sufficient to acquit the person charged."[40] Although this statement of the commission related to senior government and military authorities, it was also applicable to more junior officers. Thus, contrary to the U.S., British, and French field manuals of the day, Article 228 of the Treaty of Versailles ("Bring before military tribunals persons accused of having committed acts in violation of the laws and customs of war") documented the intention of the Allies to seek individual responsibility for law of war violations and disregard any defense of superior orders. The U.S. military standard was not to be applied. An international law scholar of the period wrote, "[Article 228] appears to be the first treaty of peace in which an attempt has been made by the victorious belligerent to enforce against the defeated adversary the application of the principle of individual responsibility for criminal acts during war by members of his armed forces against ... the other party."[41]

There were Leipzig proceedings that provide a window to the German court's thinking as to the concept of obedience to orders. In a harbinger of Grand Admiral Karl Dönitz's World War II Nuremberg trial, Grand Admiral von Tirpitz, Secretary of State of the German navy from 1914 to 1916, was charged with having originated and issued orders for unrestricted submarine warfare, but the high court at Leipzig found that responsibility did not lie with him (or his coaccused successors, Admirals Von Capelle, Scheer, Hipper, and Muller). Instead, responsibility lodged in the supreme command of naval operations, the former kaiser himself. At Leipzig, no personal responsibility was to be found in the high command. Von Tirpitz and his fellow admirals were acquitted.

---

[38] Id., at 210.

[39] Officially titled "The Commission on the Responsibility of the Authors of the War and on Enforcement of Penalties."

[40] J. W. Garner, "Punishment of Defenders against the Laws and Customs of War," 14 *AJIL* 95, 117 (1920).

[41] Id., at 70–1.

Two notable Leipzig cases were defended on the basis of superior orders. Lieutenant Karl Neumann, commander of a German submarine, admitted that he had torpedoed and sunk the British hospital ship, *Dover Castle*, pleading that he did so only in obedience to orders issued by the Admiralty. The German government had asserted that Allied hospital ships were being used for military purposes, in violation of customary international law, and declared in a March 1917 order that hospital ships not complying with several German conditions would be attacked. Neumann, the court held, believed the order to be a lawful reprisal, as the order specified, and thus he was not criminally responsible for the sinking he carried out. Citing the German obedience to orders standard, §47(2) of the German Military Penal Code,[42] by which a subordinate acting in conformity with superior orders is liable to punishment only when he knows that his orders constitute a felony or misdemeanor, Neumann was acquitted.[43] The court held, "Subordinates . . . are under no obligation to question the order of their superior officer, and they can count upon its legality. But no such confidence can be held to exist, if such an order is universally known to everybody, including the accused, to be without any doubt whatever against the law."[44] Obedience to orders was a complete defense – *unless* the order was patently unlawful.

A similar case saw a different result, however, and arguably set a lasting standard. The submarine U-86, commanded by Captain Helmuth Patzig, sank a Canadian hospital ship, the *Llandovery Castle*, with the loss of hundreds of lives. At trial, the evidence revealed that, just after the sinking, Patzig and two subordinates, Lieutenants Ludwig Dithmar and Johann Boldt, conferred and decided to conceal their act by killing the survivors. Patzig and another officer machine-gunned the 234 survivors in lifeboats and in the water, assisted by Dithmar and Boldt, who spotted targets and maintained a lookout. At least two lifeboats were sunk by gunfire, and many of the 234 were killed. A precise number was unknowable because many drowned or were killed by subsequent shark attacks.

Patzig, having taken refuge in Danzig, then an independent state, was ruled beyond extradition. As Neumann had before them, Dithmar and Boldt pleaded "not guilty" on the basis of superior orders from the German naval high command. As with Neumann, Dithmar and Boldt were found not guilty of sinking the hospital ship by reason of their obedience to superior orders that were not obviously unlawful. But their machine-gunning of survivors resulted in guilty findings for aiding and abetting manslaughter. The court held, "According to the Military Penal Code, if the execution of an order . . . involves such a violation of law as is punishable, the superior officer issuing such an order is alone responsible. However, the subordinate obeying such an order is liable to punishment if it was known to him that the order . . . involved the infringement of civil or military law. This applies in the case of the accused."[45]

Even for the Leipzig judges, shooting survivors in the water was manifestly contrary to customary law of war, and, applying a test of actual knowledge, the judges found that the two accused must have known that to be so.

---

[42] German Military Penal Code, 1872, which was based upon the Prussian Military Code, 1845.
[43] The *Dover Castle* Case, 16 AJIL (1921), 704, decided under German military law.
[44] Cited in Wilner, supra, note 23, at 134.
[45] The *Llandovery Castle* Case, 16 AJIL 705 (1921), also decided under German military law.

At Leipzig, in the twentieth century's first significant effort to assess criminal responsibility for battlefield war crimes, the German court applied the strict German military code's standard, a code similar to the one from which the American victors had retreated. The familiar German formulation: Subordinates were liable for carrying out orders they knew, or should have known, to be illegal. At the commander's level, officers issuing orders they knew, or should have known, to be illegal were personally liable.

Whatever ironic justice there may have been in the convictions of Dithmar, Boldt, and Neumann dissipated when, several months after trial, all three escaped, apparently with the connivance of their jailers. And the American soldier's defense of obedience to orders remained unchanged. It was also essentially unconsidered by military courts. There was little incentive to do so. In 1920, the leading military legal scholar of the era, the army colonel William Winthrop, wrote, "That the act charged as an offense was done in obedience to the order – verbal or written – of a military superior, is, in general, a good defense at military law." However, a few lines later he added:

The order, to constitute a defense, must be a *legal* one. … It is the "lawful command of his superior officer" which by the 21st Article of war,[46] "any officer or soldier" may be punished even with death for disobeying. … Where the order is apparently regular and lawful on its face, he is not to go behind it to satisfy himself that his superior has proceeded with authority, but is to obey it … [except] orders so manifestly beyond the legal power or discretion of the commander as to admit of no rational doubt of their unlawfulness.[47]

This caveat to the standard announced in the 1914 *Rules of Land Warfare* was Winthrop's addition and was not reflected in the *Manual for Courts-Martial*. It was historically based and reflected common sense, if not official policy. There was no evaluation of the authority of Winthrop's addition at court-martial because the nation was at peace, without occasion for a war crimes trial.

Today, military law expects soldiers to presume the lawfulness of their orders.[48] Case law suggests that, even if a soldier doubts the legality of an order, but remains unsure, he will not be held liable for obeying an unlawful order.[49] As the Nuremberg International Military Tribunal (IMT) noted, it is not "incumbent upon a soldier in a subordinate position to screen the orders of superiors for questionable points of legality."[50]

Between the wars, court-martial cases centered on the offense of *disobedience*, rather than obedience. The *Rules of Land Warfare* still made superior orders a complete defense to battlefield war crimes. The common military offense of disobedience, with its prerequisite for acquittal being the illegality of the order, had little bearing on invocation of the war crime defense.

---

[46] Article 64, 1912 Articles of War.

[47] Winthrop, *Military Law and Precedents*, supra, note 12, at 296–7, emphasis in original.

[48] E.g., *Unger v. Ziemniak*, 27 M.J. 349 (C.M.A. 1989). When the defense raises the issue of lawfulness by some evidence, the prosecution has the burden to disprove lawfulness beyond a reasonable doubt. *U.S. v. Tiggs*, 40 C.M.R. 352 (A.B.R. 1968).

[49] *U.S. v. Kinder*, 14 C.M.R. (A.F.B.R., 1954), 742, 750.

[50] *U.S. v. von Leeb* ("The High Command Case") XI *TWC* (Washington, DC: GPO, 1950), 510–11.

9.1.2 *Genesis of the Current American Standard*

Prior to World War II, customary law of war was considered to apply to nations, rather than individuals. Act of state doctrine, in the context of domestic courts, held that no state could exercise jurisdiction over another state. This position was based on then-accepted principles of the sovereignty and the equality of states. Associated with this doctrine, sovereignty was regarded as attaching to individuals within a state. The sovereign was a definable person to whom allegiance was due, and, as an integral part of his or her mystique, the sovereign could not be made subject to the judicial processes of his country or any other country.[51] Vestiges of act of state doctrine survive in today's exemption from suit of certain governmental entities and persons officially acting for those entities – in American jurisprudence the *Feres* doctrine, for example.[52] In 1918, however, the Allies' postwar attempts to hold the kaiser personally and criminally responsible as an "author" of the war represented a significant assault on act of state doctrine. In the twentieth century the doctrine was dying, but in the 1920s and 1930s it was not yet moribund.

It was an aspect of act of state doctrine that allowed the United States and Great Britain to view military officers as personifications of their states. If the state – exempt from criminal process – ordered a common soldier to act, the soldier had no choice but to obey. Having no choice, the soldier must be free of liability for that obedience. Western nations were coming to recognize, however, that military officers were not credible embodiments of the state. Even kaisers, kings, and commanders were being questioned; the doctrine was in doubt. "In the extensive literature on the question of international crimes and international jurisdiction which has appeared since 1920 a considerable number of writers," Ian Brownlie reports, "have envisaged criminal responsibility of states alone." As to individual criminal responsibility, he continues, "it is nevertheless suggested that the concept has no legal value, cannot be justified in principle, and is contradicted by ... international law."[53] By the time of World War II Act of State doctrine had effectively been rejected.[54]

The numerous bilateral and multinational treaties of the interwar period were silent on the subject of superior orders, with the exception of the 1922 Washington Treaty relating, inter alia, to submarine warfare. With World War I's recent prosecutions of submarine commanders in mind, Article II of the Washington Treaty read: "Any person ... who shall violate any of these rules, whether or not such person is under orders of a governmental superior, shall be deemed to have violated the laws of war and shall be liable to trial and punishment."[55] The treaty was ratified by the future World War II combatants America, Great Britain, Italy, and Japan, although rejected by France.

As the Second World War approached, the United States and Great Britain continued to view superior orders as a complete defense. In the 1929 edition of its land warfare

---

[51] The classic case illustrating the relationship between territorial jurisdiction and sovereign immunity is *The Schooner Exchange v. McFaddon*, 11 U.S. (7 Cranch.) 116 (1812).

[52] *Feres v. U.S.*, 340 U.S. 135 (1950).

[53] Ian Brownlie, *International Law and the Use of Force by States* (Oxford: Clarendon Press, 1963), 150–2.

[54] Hans Kelsen, "Collective and Individual Responsibility in International Law with Particular Regard to the Punishment of War Criminals," 31 *Cal. L. Rev.* (1943), 530; and Oppenheim, *International Law*. Vol. II. *Disputes, War and Neutrality*, supra, note 33.

[55] *Treaties, Conventions, International Acts, Protocols, and Agreements between the United States of America and Other Powers*, Vol. III (1910–23), 67th Con., Doc. No. 348, at 3118 (1923).

manual, Great Britain held, as did the 1912 edition, "It is important, however, to note that members of the armed forces who commit such violations of the recognized rules of warfare as are ordered by their Government or by their commander are not war criminals and cannot therefore be punished by the enemy. He may punish the officials or commanders responsible for such orders if they fall into his hands."[56] The manual did not say how its prohibition on punishing British subjects might be viewed by injured states holding British prisoners accused of war crimes.

In 1934, the United States published a second edition of *Rules of Land Warfare*. Its paragraph addressing superior orders was unchanged from the original 1914 edition. The failure of the manual's index to include a "superior orders" entry suggests the degree of concern paid the issue. A soldier's law of war offenses remained fully exempt from prosecution if committed pursuant to the order of a superior. There was no qualification that the order must have been reasonable, legal, or within the authority of the superior.

9.1.3 World War II and an Old "New" Standard

In 1940, with the war already raging in Europe, the United States followed its 1934 law of war manual with yet another version. This version's paragraph 347 on superior orders replicated the 1934 and 1914 standard. By 1940, the more optimistic of the Allies began considering eventually punishing enemy leaders for their roles in the war, not only their senior leadership, but soldiers who might have committed battlefield war crimes, as well. In 1942 the Allies announced that "they intended to prosecute German and Japanese soldiers for obeying improper orders and to deny the opportunity for them to plead superior orders. But this clearly required a reassessment of our own [American] manual."[57] The results of Leipzig were not to be repeated; the Allies, not the enemy, would try enemy war crimes suspects. But we could not ourselves sponsor the defense we intended to deny the vanquished enemy.

Recall that in 1906 Oppenheim, in his text *International Law*, was instrumental in establishing the prevailing UK/U.S. military standard of liability (or its lack) for obedience to illegal superior orders. Succeeding editions of his work continued to exert their influence among international legal authorities. The 1940 sixth edition was edited by Professor Hersch Lauterpacht, in place of then-deceased Oppenheim, and Lauterpacht made a significant amendment. He urged a reversion to the pre-1906 military standard, at the same time distancing himself from the standard that his predecessor's work had been instrumental in establishing. "The fact that a rule of warfare has been violated in pursuance of an order ... of an individual belligerent commander does not deprive the act in question of its character as a war crime; neither does it, in principle, confer upon the perpetrator immunity from punishment by the injured belligerent. A different view has occasionally been adopted by writers, but it is difficult to regard it as expressing a sound legal principle."[58]

---

[56] Col. J. E. Edmonds and L. Oppenheim, *Land Warfare: An Exposition of the Laws and Usages of War on Land for the Guidance of Officers of His Majesty's Army*, ed. of 1929 (London: HMSO, 1912), ch. X, para. 443, at 95.

[57] Wells, supra, note 35, at 24.

[58] Oppenheim, *International Law*. Vol. II. *Disputes, War and Neutrality*, supra, note 33, at 264–5.

The fact that Lauterpacht's native Great Britain was engaged in mortal struggle with an enemy who would (it was hoped) face the international criminal bar surely had a bearing on this new stance. "By the sixth edition of 1940, the world looked very different ... [and Lauterpacht] must have been influenced by the experience of the first year of the war. The earlier main rule was now relegated to a footnote."[59] Lauterpacht noted the incongruity of differing civil and military standards,[60] and found that subordinate immunity was simply "at variance with the corresponding principles of English criminal and constitutional law ... It is not believed to represent a sound principle of law."[61] His altered position reflected a changing and maturing international law, as well as the withering of act of state doctrine, with the concomitant ripening of personal responsibility for wrongful battlefield acts.

In January 1944, the newly formed United Nations War Crimes Commission took up the issue of obedience to orders. The United States was squarely behind a recommendation that the defense be rejected: "The plea of superior orders shall not constitute a defense ... if the order was so manifestly contrary to the laws of war that a person of ordinary sense and understanding would know or should know ... that an order was illegal."[62] The commission could not reach agreement on the issue, however, stymied by the varied practice and laws of several member nations. Finally declaring it futile to attempt formulation of an absolute rule, the commission recommended that the validity of the plea of superior orders be left to national courts, "according to their own views of the merits and limits of the plea."[63] The stage was set for basic change in America's superior orders doctrine, and it was not long in coming.

In April 1944, in a striking development, the United Kingdom revised its law of war manual, adopting almost word for word Lauterpacht's language in his sixth edition of *International Law*. That modification was, of course, a complete about-face. Seven months later, in November 1944, the United States similarly reversed and revised FM 27–10, *Rules of Land Warfare*, affirming that not only individuals, but organizations and government officials could now be considered culpable for law of war offenses: "Individuals and organizations who violate the accepted laws and customs of war may be punished thereof. However, the fact that the acts complained of were done pursuant to order of a superior or government sanction may be taken into consideration in determining culpability, either by way of defense or in mitigation of punishment. The person giving such orders may also be punished."[64] As before 1914, obedience to a superior's orders was no longer an automatic or complete defense. That paragraph was the sole change in the new 1944 manual.

---

[59] Martti Koskenniemi, "Hersch Lauterpacht and the Development of International Criminal Law," 2–3 *J. of Int'l Crim. Justice* (Sept. 2004), 810–25, 816–17.

[60] *Neu v. McCarthy*, 33 N. E.2d 570 (1941); and *State v. Roy*, 64 S.E.2d 840 (1951) are representative of cases wherein soldiers are convicted of civil wrongs in state courts despite "superior orders" defenses. "It is an interesting gloss on the complexity of the problem that in Great Britain and in the United States the plea of superior orders is, on the whole, without decisive effect in internal criminal or constitutional law, although it is apparently treated as a full justification in relation to war crimes." Lauterpacht, "Law of Nations," supra, note 12, at 72–3.

[61] Id., Lauterpacht, at 69, fn. 2.

[62] Mark P. Osiel, *Obeying Orders* (New Brunswick, NJ: Transaction, 1999), 278.   [63] Id.

[64] Department of the Army, FM 27–10, *Field Manual: Rules of Land Warfare*, Change No. 1, 15 Nov. 1944 (Washington, DC: GPO, 1944), para. 345(1).

France, to be consistent with its allies, made a similar change to its law of war manual, as did Canada. The Soviet approach remained, as it had always been, identical to the older American/British position.[65]

Throughout World War II, Nazi Germany itself professed an opposition to the defense of superior orders, adhering to the standard rediscovered by the United States and Great Britain in 1944. Early that year, after captured Allied pilots were murdered by German civilian mobs, the Nazi propaganda minister, Joseph Goebbels, explicitly condemned the plea of superior orders as inadmissible in contemporary international law. "He did so, naturally, in regard to the Allies, and with the intention of justifying the Nazi practice of shooting captured Allied airmen."[66] In the *Deutsche Allgemeine Zeitung*, Goebbels wrote, "No international law of warfare is in existence which provides that a soldier who has committed a mean crime can escape punishment by pleading as his defense that he followed the commands of his superiors."[67] In the official Nazi newspaper, *Volkisher Beobachter*, "The [Allied] pilots cannot validly claim that as soldiers they obeyed orders . . . if these orders are in striking opposition to all human ethics, to all international customs in the conduct of war."[68]

Throughout the war, the *Wehrmacht-Untersuchungsstelle für Verletzungen des Völkerrechts*, the Bureau for the Investigation of War Crimes, was a unit of the German army. Knowing what we do about Nazi practices in Russia and other conquered territories, it is ironic that the bureau regularly gathered evidence for the court-martial of Nazi soldiers charged with war crimes; reportedly, death sentences often resulted.[69]

Nazi battlefield excesses are often recalled, and rightly so. War crimes are not committed only by the enemy, however. World War II, like all wars before and after, was violent, brutal, and often unmindful of legal restrictions. Two examples are illustrative.

A troubling event involved the U.S. Navy commander who skippered the submarine USS *Wahoo* (SS-238). During a January 1943 patrol, the commander's boat surfaced after having sunk a troop-carrying freighter. The sea was filled with Japanese survivors – probably more than a thousand. "Whatever the number, [he] was determined to kill every single one."[70] He ordered the submarine's deck guns and machine guns to fire on enemy lifeboats and survivors in the water, and his sailors did, for more than an hour. The *Wahoo*'s second in command, Richard O'Kane, later a rear admiral and Medal of Honor holder, reported, "*Wahoo*'s fire . . . was methodical, the small guns sweeping from abeam forward like fire hoses cleaning a street. . . . Some Japanese troops were undoubtedly hit during this action, but no individual was deliberately shot in the boats or in the sea. The boats were nothing more than flotsam by the time our submarine had completed [firing]."[71]

On returning to Pearl Harbor, the *Wahoo* was lauded, the boat receiving a Presidential Unit Citation and the skipper a Navy Cross. In his patrol report, the submarine

[65] Morris Greenspan, *The Modern Law of Land Warfare* (Berkeley: University of California Press, 1959), 491.
[66] U.N. War Crimes Commission, *History of the United Nations War Crimes Commission and the Development of the Laws of War* (London: HMSO, 1948), 288.
[67] Id.   [68] Cited in Greenspan, *Modern Law of Land Warfare*, supra, note 63, at 442.
[69] Alfred M. deZayas, *The Wehrmacht War Crimes Bureau, 1939–1945* (Lincoln: University of Nebraska Press, 1989), 10, 18, 20–1, 86.
[70] Clay Blair Jr., *Silent Victory* (New York: Lippincott, 1987), 384.
[71] Richard H. O'Kane, *Wahoo* (Novato, CA: Presidio Press, 1987), 153–4.

commander freely described the killing of the hundreds of survivors of the sunken transport. "To some submariners, this was cold-blooded murder and repugnant. However, no question was raised."[72] The commander's order to fire on survivors appears no different from that of the World War I sub commander Helmuth Patzig, who was sought as a war criminal by the Leipzig court. Patzig's subordinates, Dithmar and Boldt, were convicted by the Leipzig court of acts similar to those of the *Wahoo's* skipper.[73]

Excuses that "the defeat of the Axis required the use of force in a fashion that more squeamish times – when the fundamental *survival* of the West was less directly threatened – have been found repugnant,"[74] although they may have stated a popular view. Such excuses ignore the laws of war that states are obliged to observe.

By war's end, neither Nazi Germany nor imperial Japan was in a position to charge battlefield war crimes by its enemies. The United States was, and in October 1945, the United States began its first World War II war crimes trial, that of General Tomoyuki Yamashita, commander of the defeated Japanese forces in Manila. The issue of superior orders did not arise directly in the course of Yamashita's trial before a military commission of five army general officers. Later, however, the Supreme Court justice Frank Murphy, in a passionate and oft-quoted dissent from the Court's opinion involving Yamashita's conviction, noted that individual criminal responsibility lies not only in those who commit battlefield war crimes, but those who order them, as well.[75] Justice Murphy's affirmation of the 1944 *Rules of Land Warfare* standard, and the responsibility of commanders who order war crimes, differed little from Chief Justice Marshall's 1804 opinion regarding Captain George Little of the U.S. Navy and the *Flying Fish*. The Yamashita case would resonate beyond the Far East IMT,[76] even into the Vietnam War and the cases of Lieutenant William Calley and Captain Ernest Medina,[77] of My Lai infamy.

---

[72] Blair, supra, note 68, at 386. During the November 1942 naval battle of Guadalcanal, for example, the tug *Bobolink*, at the command of its skipper, similarly machine-gunned Japanese survivors in the water. Samuel Eliot Morison, *History of United States Naval Operations in World War II*, Vol. V (Boston: Little, Brown, 1966), 256.

[73] Historically, it has been forbidden to harm survivors of sunken vessels who are in the water. (See Chapter 7.2.1.) 1907 Hague Convention III for the Adaptation to Maritime Warfare of the Principles of the Geneva Convention, Art. 16: "After every engagement, the two belligerents, so far as military interests permit, shall take steps to look for the shipwrecked, sick, and wounded, and to protect them … against pillage and ill-treatment." At World War II's Nuremberg IMT, Grand Admiral Karl Dönitz was charged with, but acquitted of, ordering Nazi submarines to kill shipwreck (i.e., sinking) survivors. *Trial of the Major War Criminals*, Vol. I (Nuremberg: IMT, 1947), 313.

[74] Williamson Murray, "The Meaning of World War II," 8 *Joint Forces Quarterly* (Summer 1995), 50, 54.

[75] *In re Yamashita*, 327 U.S. 1, 38 (1945), not a decision on the merits, but a decision on an application for habeas corpus and prohibition writs.

[76] B. V. A. Röling, "Introduction" to C. Hosoya, N. Andō, Y. Ōnuma, and R. Minear, eds., *The Tokyo War Crimes Trial: An International Symposium* (New York: Harper & Row, 1986).

[77] General Yamashita was convicted of failure to control his troops, who he *knew, or should have known*, were committing war crimes, the long-established standard for a commander's liability. Medina was acquitted on the basis of his court's instruction that conviction must be based on the commander's *actual knowledge* of his troops' crimes. Medina's prosecutor acknowledged that the court's instruction (which was requested by the government) was erroneous. Col. William G. Eckhardt, "Command Criminal Responsibility: A Plea for a Workable Standard," 97 *Military L. Rev.* 1 (1982).

9.2 The Standard Applied: The Nuremberg International Military Tribunal

The Nuremberg IMT's procedural rules were a product of the London Agreement of August 1945.[78] Article 8 of the IMT charter embodied the change initiated by Professor Lauterpacht four and a half years earlier and incorporated in the U.S. *Rules of Land Warfare* less than nine months previously. Article 8 read: "The fact that the defendant acted pursuant to orders of his Government or of a superior shall not free him from responsibility, but may be considered in mitigation of punishment." The Nazis were to be held criminally responsible, personally responsible, for war crimes they committed and for war crimes they ordered. Obedience to superior orders would be no legal shield. "The fundamental principle involved: the criminal responsibility of individuals."[79] As the IMT noted in reference to war crimes, "Crimes against international law are committed by men, not by abstract entities, and only by punishing individuals who commit such crimes can the provisions of international law be enforced."[80] The Tokyo IMT charter's Article 6(b), as well as paragraph 16 of American Regulations Governing the Trial of War Criminals in the Pacific Area, were similar to Nuremberg's Article 8. As at Nuremberg, pleas of superior orders were unsuccessfully raised in Pacific Area cases, the *Jaluit Atoll Case*,[81] for example.

The American/British legal detour had lasted thirty years, but the Nuremberg IMT seemingly advanced the soldiers' legal defense full circle: A law of war violation pursuant to a superior's manifestly illegal order remained a war crime. That was the law applied at Nuremberg and, as Geoffrey Best points out, "no element of Nuremberg legislation was more single-mindedly adhered to than this one, the emphatic assertion of individual responsibility."[82]

Still, it is not entirely correct to assert that "the IMT Charter ... *eliminated* the defense of superior orders."[83] As single-mindedly as the element may have been applied as to senior officers and officials, the IMT injected an unanticipated ameliorating factor not in keeping with a strict interpretation of the charter: "The true test," the tribunal noted, "which is found in varying degrees in the criminal law of most nations, is not the existence of the [manifestly illegal] order, but whether moral choice was in fact possible."[84] "Moral choice" was not, and is not, the same as simple "manifest illegality."

The assertion that it [the "true test"] is in conformity with the law of all nations is patently false. More obscurely, it seems to add the requirement that there was no "moral choice" to the test relating to superior orders. Dinstein gives the best explanation for this. He claims that in reality the tribunal was accepting that superior orders were not, in and of themselves, a defense under the Nuremberg IMT charter,

---

[78] BGen. Telford Taylor, *Final Report to the Secretary of the Army on the Nuernberg War Crimes Trials under Control Council Law No. 10* (Washington, DC: GPO, 1949), 1.

[79] U.N., *The Charter and Judgment of the Nürnberg Tribunal: History and Analysis* (New York: UNGA, 1949), 39.

[80] Brownlie, supra, note 53, at 154, citing *Trial of German Major War Criminals* (London: HMSO, 1946), 41.

[81] *Trial of Masuda, et al.* (1945), U.S. Mil. Comm., Marshall Islands, L.R.T.W.C., I.

[82] Geoffrey Best, *War and Law since 1945* (Oxford: Clarendon Press, 1994), 190.

[83] Steven R. Ratner and Jason S. Abrams, *Accountability for Human Rights Atrocities in International Law* (Oxford: Clarendon Press, 1997), 6.

[84] The IMT is quoted in *U.S. v. Ohlendorf*, supra, note 36, at 471.

but expressing its view that the existence of superior orders was relevant to other such defenses as coercion (duress).[85]

"The superior orders defense remains very much alive wherever the criminality of the defendant's conduct cannot convincingly be categorized as immediately obvious."[86] Even after the Nuremberg tribunal, "superior orders will still operate as a defense if the subordinate had no good reason for thinking that the order concerned was unlawful."[87]

Despite the Nuremberg trials, the defense of superior orders lives. It is true that no military case is found in U.S. jurisprudence within the past sixty years in which the defense has been successful, but it cannot be said that the defense is dead.

9.2.1 *The Standard Applied: The "Subsequent Proceedings"*

Following the Nuremberg IMT, the United States initiated a series of war crimes trials in its sector of Berlin, as did the French, British, and Russians in their sectors. Referred to as "the subsequent proceedings" because they were subsequent to the IMT in purpose and method, the trials were based on a 1945 Joint Chiefs of Staff directive[88] and generally paralleled the IMT's procedures and rules. The proceedings' implementing directive was Control Council Law Number 10, a reference to the Allied Council that oversaw the governing of Berlin. In what eventually totaled twelve U.S. trials, an aggregate of 191 high-ranking military and civilian Nazis were tried in the subsequent proceedings.

There was little similarity between the IMT charter and Control Council Law Number 10,[89] except in one article. In language essentially identical to IMT charter Article 8, the subsequent proceedings' Article II.4(b) read, "The fact that any person acted pursuant to the order of . . . a superior does not free him from responsibility for a crime, but may be considered in mitigation." Brigadier General Telford Taylor, the U.S. proceedings' chief prosecutor, wrote, "The major legal significance of the [Control Council] Law No. 10 judgment lies, in my opinion, in those portions of the judgments dealing with the *area of personal responsibility* for international law crimes."[90] (Taylor had been deputy chief counsel at the Nuremberg IMT, under the chief counsel, the Supreme Court justice Robert H. Jackson.) Taylor continued, "The tribunal had to determine whether the plea of 'duress' or 'superior orders' was genuine . . . and, if the plea was found to be bona fide, to what extent it should be given weight in defense or mitigation."[91] General Taylor's questioning of the plain language of the subsequent proceeding Article ii.4(b) that repeated Article 8 of the Nuremberg IMT charter suggests the difficulty the IMT may have had in applying Article 8 as written. The subsequent

---

[85] Robert Cryer, "The Boundaries of Liability in International Criminal Law, or 'Selectivity by Stealth,'" 6–1 *Conflict & Security L.* (June 2001), 3, 12. Footnotes omitted. In accord: Hans-Heinrich Jescheck, "The General Principles of International Criminal Law Set Out in Nuremberg, as Mirrored in the ICC Statute," 2–1 *Journal of Int'l Crim. Justice* (March 2004), 38, 46. "However, the Court's view that '[t]he provisions of this article are in conformity with the laws of all nations' cannot hold. In fact, the contrary is true as regards military orders."

[86] Osiel, supra, note 62, at 97.

[87] Hilaire McCoubrey, *International Humanitarian Law: The Regulation of Armed Conflicts* (Aldershot: Dartmouth, 1990), 221.

[88] Taylor, *Final Report*, supra, note 78, at 2–10; App. C.

[89] Telford Taylor, *The Anatomy of the Nuremberg Trial* (New York: Alfred Knopf, 1992), 275.

[90] Id. at 109, emphasis in original.   [91] Id. at 110.

proceedings had many more opportunities to test the courtroom workability of the test. The "subsequent tribunals had greater difficulty. They sought to resolve the matter by treating it as an issue of intent."[92] That diluted formulation, expressed as "moral choice," is seen in the *Einsatzgruppen* (Ohlendorf) and *High Command* (Leeb) cases, two of the twelve subsequent proceedings.

The moral choice test that effectively modified the IMT's Article 8 by ameliorating its blanket rejection of superior orders as a defense also affected subsequent proceedings Article II.4(b) and led to a required showing of duress as a necessary part of a successful defense of superior orders.[93] Despite Article 8 and Article II.4(b), "in various judgments ... the tribunal nevertheless applied a limited responsibility doctrine."[94] The consideration of the "moral choice" test is apparent in the subsequent proceedings' *Flick* and *Farben* judgments,[95] while, in the *High Command* case the tribunal notes, "within certain limitations, [a soldier] has the right to assume that the orders of his superiors ... are in conformity to international law."[96] In Canada, the moral choice test is accepted by the Supreme Court even today.[97]

Still, some Nazis never did get it. In the course of the IMT's general staff prosecution, Brigadier General Taylor relates the testimony of SS General Otto Ohlendorf when asked about the legality of orders. Ohlendorf replied, "I do not understand your question; since the order was issued by the superior authorities, the question of illegality could not arise in the minds of these individuals, for they had sworn obedience to the people who had issued the orders."[98] Taylor notes, "That was carrying the defense of 'superior orders' to the absolute: *Befehl ist Befehl.*"[99] (Orders are orders.) Ohlendorf was convicted and hanged.

Although finding the presence of moral choice in several subsequent proceedings cases, Article 8 of the charter was strictly applied in other trials, for example, in the *Pelius*

---

[92] Col. Charles Garraway, "Superior Orders and the International Criminal Court: Justice Delivered or Justice Denied," 836 *Int'l Rev. of the Red Cross* (Dec. 1999), 785.

[93] Duress and superior orders are conceptually distinct and separate issues, although the same factual scenario may raise both concepts. "As obedience to superior orders may be considered merely as a factual element in determining whether duress is made out on the facts, the absence of a superior order does not mean that duress as a defense must fail. ... The fact that the Appellant obeyed an order of a superior does not go to the preceding legal question of whether duress may at all be pleaded." *Erdemović Judgment*, supra, note 6, at 25–7.

[94] Nico Keijzer, *Military Obedience* (Leiden, The Netherlands: Sijthoff, 1978), 212.

[95] In the judgment of the *Flick* case the tribunal notes, "Quotas for production were set for industry by the Reich. ... The defendants were justified in their fear that the Reich authorities would take drastic action ... might even have been sent to a concentration camp. ... Under such compulsion [the defendants] submitted to the program." The longest sentenced imposed was seven years, with credit for time served. *U.S. v. Flick*, Trials of War Criminals Before the Nuernberg Military Tribunals, Vol. VI (Washington, DC: GPO, 1952), 1197–8. In the *Farben* case, "this Tribunal is not prepared to say that these defendants did not speak the truth when they asserted that in conforming to the slave-labor program they had no other choice than to comply. ... Refusal of a Farben executive ... would have been treated as treasonous sabotage and would have resulted in prompt and drastic retaliation. ... As applied to the facts here, we do not think there can be much uncertainty as to what the words 'moral choice' mean." The longest sentence was eight years, with credit for time served. *Trials of War Criminals before the Nuernberg Military Tribunals*, Vol. VIII, pt. 2 (Washington, DC: GPO, 1952), 1175–6.

[96] *U.S. v. von Leeb*, supra, note 50, at 511.

[97] *R. v. Finta* [1994] 1 S.C.R. 701. See Cases and Materials, this chapter.

[98] Taylor, *The Anatomy of the Nuremberg Trials*, supra, note 89, at 248.   [99] Id.

Case,[100] *The Scuttled U-Boats Case*,[101] and the *Almelo*,[102] *Dostler*,[103] and *Belsen*[104] cases. In each of those trials, unlawful superior orders were held not to eliminate subordinates' personal responsibility for their war crimes.

In contrast, some tribunals in effect held that if a subordinate did not know, and could not be expected to know, that the order he carried out was illegal, mens rea was lacking and the subordinate was not guilty. This reflection of today's U.S. military standard is seen, for example, in the *Hostage* and *Einsatsgruppen* cases. "If the act done pursuant to a superior's order be murder, the production of the order will not make it any less so," the *Hostage Case* tribunal wrote. "It may mitigate but it cannot justify the crime. We are of the view, however, that if the illegality of the order was not known to the inferior, and he could not reasonably have been expected to know of its illegality, no wrongful intent necessary to the commission of the crime exists and the inferior will be protected."[105] Similar language is found in the *Einsatzgruppen Case*.[106]

9.3 What Orders Should Not Be Obeyed? Manifestly Illegal Orders

No state's armed services instruct its members in *dis*obeying orders. Moreover, members of all armed services have a right to presume the lawfulness of orders they receive. One may go through an entire military career and never encounter an illegal order. They are exceedingly rare, but they are sometimes given. My Lai and Abu Ghraib are only two prominent U.S. examples. Service members must know what an illegal order is and what to do if they receive such an order. My Lai "was not a fearful and frenzied extension of combat, but 'free' and systematic slaughter, and those men that participated in it can hardly say that they were caught in the grip of war. They can say, however, that they were following orders, caught up in the grip of the United States Army"[107] (which is no excuse, legal or moral). It should not be forgotten that at My Lai four young soldiers refused to carry out Calley's orders to fire on the unarmed, unresisting noncombatants.[108]

The issue of illegal orders is not covered in the Geneva conventions because the conventions describe the protections due victims of war, rather than addressing specific battlefield criminal issues. For U.S. combatants, *The Law of Land Warfare*, paragraph 409.a, addresses the issue and specifies the current U.S. standard:

> a. The fact that the law of war has been violated pursuant to an order of a superior authority, whether military or civil, does not deprive the act in question of its

---

[100] *Trial of Eck, et al.* ("The Peleus Trial") L.R.T.W.C., Vol. I (London: U.N.W.C.C., 1947), at 1.
[101] *Trial of Grumpelt* ("The Scuttled U-Boats Case") 1946, L.R.T.W.C., Vol. I (London: U.N.W.C.C., 1947), at 55.
[102] *Trial of Sandrock, et al.* ("The Almelo Trial") L.R.T.W.C., Vol. I (London: U.N.W.C.C., 1947), at 35.
[103] *The Dostler Case*, L.R.T.W.C., Vol. I (London: U.N.W.C.C., 1947), at 22.
[104] *Trial of Kramer, et al.* ("The Belsen Trial"), 1945, L.R.T.W.C., Vol. II (London: U.N.W.C.C., 1947), at 1.
[105] *U.S. v. List* ("The Hostage Case"), supra, note 34, at 1236.
[106] *U.S. v. Ohlendorf*, supra, note 36, at 470.   [107] Walzer, *Just and Unjust Wars*, supra, note 2, at 310.
[108] They were PFC James Dursi, Dennis Bunting, Specialist-4 Robert Maples (even as Calley's M-16 was pointed at him), and Sergeant Michael Bernhardt. Additionally, Warrant Officer Hugh Thompson, with his gunner Larry Colburn and observer Glenn Andreotti, landed his helicopter between a group of U.S. soldiers pursuing fleeing Vietnamese, and, after directing Colburn to fire on the Americans if they did not comply, ordered the soldiers, led by a lieutenant, to break off their pursuit. The moral and physical courage of these "disobedient" soldiers has never been adequately recognized.

character as a war crime, nor does it constitute a defense in the trial of an accused individual, unless he did not know and could not reasonably have been expected to know that the act ordered was unlawful. ... The fact that the individual was acting pursuant to orders may be considered in mitigation of punishment.[109]

b. In considering ... whether a superior order constitutes a valid defense, the court shall take into consideration the fact that obedience to lawful military orders is the duty of every member of the armed forces; that the latter cannot be expected, in conditions of war discipline, to weigh scrupulously the legal merits of the orders received. ... At the same time it must be borne in mind that members of the armed forces are bound to obey only lawful orders.

This paragraph clearly lays out the basic rule for U.S. military personnel: Obedience to orders is not a legal defense, per se; military law provides a reasonable exception (derived from post–World War II war crimes cases).[110] Superior orders specifically may not be considered by a court *unless* the accused did not know and could not be expected to have known the orders' illegality; and in case of a prosecution it provides triers of fact with a mitigating consideration in making a determination of guilt or innocence: mistake of law: The accused did not know and could not reasonably have been expected to know the order was unlawful.

> [A] soldier or airman is not an automaton but a "reasoning agent" who is under a duty to exercise judgment in obeying orders of a superior officer. ... Where such orders are manifestly beyond the scope of the issuing officer's authority and are so palpably illegal on their face that a man of ordinary sense and understanding would know them to be illegal, then the fact of obedience to the order of a superior officer will not protect a soldier.[111]

Exactly what constitutes an illegal order? The term denoting required disobedience is "manifestly"; manifestly illegal orders must not be obeyed. "Manifestly" is first encountered in the 1886 edition of Winthrop's *Military Law and Precedents*: "The only exceptions recognized in the rule of obedience being cases of orders so manifestly beyond the legal power or discretion of the commanders to admit of no rational doubt of their unlawfulness."[112] "Manifest illegality" gained wide recognition in a post–World War I trial. The German commander Karl Neumann, a submarine commander who freely admitted sinking a British hospital ship, the *Dover Castle*, claimed that he thought his orders to do so constituted a lawful reprisal. In a widely reviled decision, he was acquitted by the German Supreme Court at Leipzig, on the basis of superior orders. The court ruled that Neumann lacked knowledge of the manifest illegality of his "ordered" act.[113]

Manifest illegality is not a soldier's disobeying on the basis of the asserted illegality of his nation's *jus ad bellum* resort to force.[114] Nor may a service person's conscience,

---

[109] FM 27–10, *The Law of Land Warfare*, supra, note 20.   [110] For example, *U.S. v. List*, supra, note 34.

[111] *U.S. v. Kinder*, supra, note 49, at 776. This language is from the post–World War II case, *U.S. v. Ohlendorf*, supra, note 36, at 470.

[112] Winthrop, *Military Law and Precedents*, supra, note 12, at 296–7.

[113] "German War Trials: Judgment in Case of Commander Karl Neumann," 16–4 *AJIL* (Oct. 1922), 704–8; and, Jackson N. Maogoto, "The Superior Orders Defense: A Game of Musical Chairs and the Jury Is Still Out," 10 *Flinders J. of L. Reform* (2007), 1–26, 6–7.

[114] In the context of Operation Desert Storm, such an argument was held a nonjusticiable political question; the court holding that the duty to disobey an unlawful order applies only to "a positive act that constitutes a

religious beliefs, moral judgment, or personal philosophy rise to manifest illegality to justify or excuse the disobedience of an otherwise lawful order.[115]

What does constitute manifest illegality? Like the term "war crime," it cannot be defined in the abstract. The U.S. Uniform Code of Military Justice does not define it because whether a subordinate's act, or a superior's order, is manifestly illegal is usually an objective question related to a specific situation.[116] The question is, would a reasonable person recognize the wrongfulness of the act or order, even in light of a soldier's duty to obey? "In short, where wrongfulness [of an order] is clear, you must disobey, but you must resolve all genuine doubts about wrongfulness in favor of obedience."[117] In an ambivalent situation, uncertainty as to whether the conduct or order was manifestly illegal must be resolved by the courts in favor of the defendant, for "the whole point of the rule is that no 'reasoning why' is necessary to discern the wrongfulness of an order immediately displaying its criminality on its face."[118] An Israeli court offered a dramatic description:

> The distinguishing mark of a "manifestly unlawful order" should fly like a black flag above the order given. ... Not formal unlawfulness, hidden or half-hidden, nor unlawfulness discernable only to the eyes of legal experts. ... Unlawfulness appearing on the face of the order itself ... unlawfulness piercing the eye and revolting the heart, be the eye not blind nor the heart stony and corrupt, that is the measure of "manifest unlawfulness" required to release a soldier from the duty of obedience.[119]

An 1867 American civil case described a manifestly unlawful order as one "so palpably atrocious as well as illegal that one ought to instinctively feel that it ought not to be obeyed."[120] During the Korean War, the order of an Air Force lieutenant to an airman first class to "take him [a wounded Korean trespasser] out to the Bomb Dump and shoot him" was found manifestly unlawful.[121] The U.S. Court of Military Appeals found manifestly illegal an army specialist's order to a private to continue driving when the truck's brakes were not working properly.[122] In Vietnam, an army captain commanded,

---

crime [that is] so manifestly beyond the legal power or discretion of the commander as to admit of no rational doubt of their lawfulness." *U.S. v. Huet-Vaughn*, 43 M.J. (1995), 105, 107. Another such case was *Germany v. "N"* (2005), in which a Bundeswehr major refused duty associated with the U.S. invasion of Iraq, asserting "his constitutional right of freedom of conscience," 100–4 *AJIL* 911 (Oct. 2006).

[115] *Manual for Courts-Martial*, 1995, part IV, para. 14c(2)(a)(iii). See also, *U.S. v. Kabat*, 797 F.2d 580 (8th Cir. 1986).

[116] The German Military Penal Code is one of the few that attempt a definition: Illegality is manifest when contrary "to what every man's conscience would tell him anyhow." Cited in Osiel, *Obeying Orders*, supra, note 62, at 77.

[117] Id., Osiel, at 84. This discussion of manifest illegality is informed by Professor Osiel's excellent exposition on the topic in his chapter 3, at 71–89.

[118] Id., 115.   [119] *Kafr Kassen* case App. 279–83 (1958), Id., at 77, fn. 13.

[120] *McCall v. McDowell*, supra, note 21.

[121] *U.S. v. Kinder*, supra, note 49, at 754. The fate of the officer who gave the order is detailed in Chapter 10. *U.S. v. Schreiber*, 18 C.M.R. 226 (C.M.A., 1955).

[122] *U.S. v. Cherry*, 22 M.J. 284, 286 (C.M.A. 1986). Although there are several cases finding orders, for example, over broad (*U.S. v. Milldebrandt*, 25 C.M.R. 139 [C.M.A. 1958]), and *U.S. v. Wysong*, 26 C.M.R. 29 (C.M.A. 1958), or arbitrary (*U.S. v. Wilson*, 30 C.M.R. 165 [C.M.A. 1961]), and *U.S. v. Dykes*, 6 M.J. 744 (N.C.M.R. 1978), or arbitrary and unreasonable (*U.S. v. Green*, 22 M.J. 711 [A.C.M.R. 1986]), or arbitrary, incapable of being obeyed, and void for vagueness (*U.S. v. Lloyd*, General Court-Martial [U.S. Army Southern European Task Force and 5th Support Command, Vicenza, Italy, Aug. 27–30, 1985]), few orders are found manifestly illegal. Another case that does so is *U.S. v. Dykes*, earlier.

"take [the prisoner] down the hill and shoot him."[123] Can possible disciplinary action for not obeying such commands excuse the obeying of them? Recognizing the illegality of such orders requires neither superior intellect nor academic accomplishment.

There are improper orders of less clear illegality, no doubt, subtle in their wrongfulness, requiring a fine moral discernment to avoid criminality in their execution. Such orders are rare on the battlefield and are not *manifestly* unlawful. Manifest illegality requires not fine moral discernment but obviousness. Junior soldiers are not expected to parse the orders they receive or apply a lawyer's judgment to directions from those of higher grade. They are not expected to review law books or be familiar with case law. "Any uncertainty about whether the defendant's conduct was manifestly illegal must be resolved in his favor."[124] In doubtful cases, the order must be presumed lawful and it must be obeyed. Because it was an uncertain or doubtful case, it was not a manifestly unlawful order and the soldier should not face disciplinary action for obeying it.

9.4 Upon Receiving a Manifestly Illegal Order

What should a U.S. combatant do upon receiving an unlawful order? First, if she believes the order is manifestly illegal – patently and obviously unlawful – or beyond the authority of the superior issuing the order, as a threshold matter the order should not be obeyed. Second, the service member should ask for clarification of the order to ensure it was correctly understood, or correctly heard, or was not merely misspoken by the senior person. Simply asking, "Sir, do I correctly understand that your order is to murder the prisoner?" may make the senior officer realize the order's illegality – or at least prompt realization that the subordinate appreciates its illegal nature. Third, if the superior individual – officer, noncommissioned officer, or civilian authority – persists in the manifestly unlawful order, after refusing to obey, the subordinate should report the incident to a higher authority.[125] If it was higher authority who issued or condoned the order, the incident should be reported to still higher authority, or to any judge advocate – that is, any military lawyer.[126]

Receipt of a manifestly illegal order is *not* justification for a subordinate to attempt to relieve the superior of duty or, even more unwise, to take physical action, such as resorting to armed force, to stop a superior's unlawful plan. The subordinate's duty is fulfilled when he refuses to obey and reports the incident. Any subsequent action should be left to higher authority.

Whether one is a combatant or a noncombatant, upon learning of a war crime or of a suspected war crime, the service member or civilian should report it to higher military authority. Combatants are taught that obligation and are expected to understand and

---

[123] *U.S. v. Griffen*, 39 C.M.R. (ACMR, 1968), 586.   [124] Osiel, *Obeying Orders*, supra, note 62, at 109.

[125] A typical U.S. directive is Marine Corps reference publication MCRP 4–11.8B, *War Crimes* (6 Sept. 2005), at 9. "It is DOD, joint, and Department of the Navy policy that: . . . All 'reportable incidents' committed by or against members of, or persons serving with or accompanying the US Armed Forces, must be promptly reported, thoroughly investigated, and, where appropriate, remedied by corrective action." The publication notes, "A 'reportable incident' is a possible, suspected or alleged violation of the law of war."

[126] Lt.Gen. William Peers, who led the army's most thorough and complete investigation into the My Lai incident, wrote, "This left the soldier in a dilemma. A specific problem was: To whom should a soldier report a war crime when his immediate commander was personally involved in the conduct of the crime?" Lt.Gen. W. R. Peers, *The My Lai Inquiry* (New York: Norton, 1979), 33.

carry out that responsibility. The requirement for high contracting parties to train their combatants in the Geneva conventions includes such instruction.[127] "A civilian or serviceman thus instructed will not in the future be able to plead as a defense that he knew not that his conduct was prohibited by the law of war or that he thought that the order he received was lawful."[128]

Unfortunately, army studies involving army and Marine corps infantrymen indicate that, despite training, there is a significant reluctance to report fellow soldiers and Marines who injure or kill innocent noncombatants.[129]

9.5 The First Defense in Foreign and International Forums

After World War II, the Nuremberg IMT, and "subsequent proceedings," the defense of superior orders was essentially that superior orders were not a defense, per se, but that they could be relevant for other defenses, such as duress. U.S. armed forces, as instructed in FM 27–10, *Rules of Land Warfare*, carried on under that view.[130] Article 7.4 of the ICTY's 1993 statute adopted much the same position, as did Article 6 of the International Criminal Tribunal for Rwanda (ICTR) 1994 statute.[131] There were, as always, thoughtful dissenters,[132] but they were few and their voice weak.

However, the International Criminal Court (ICC), in Article 33 of its Rome Statute, adopts the strict "manifest illegality" standard of the Nuremberg charter: "Article 33.1. The fact that a crime within the jurisdiction of the Court has been committed by a person pursuant to an order of a government or of a superior, whether military or civilian, shall not relieve that person of criminal responsibility unless: ... (c) the order was manifestly unlawful." Professor Antonio Cassese writes, "Article 33 must be faulted as marking a retrogression."[133]

> The decision that was taken to adopt Article 33 represented, in the view of most, a sensible and practical solution which could be applied in all cases. In particular, it was

---

[127] The 1949 Geneva conventions common Article 47/48/127/144: "High Contracting Parties undertake, in time of peace as in time of war, to disseminate the text of the present Convention as widely as possible in their respective countries, and, in particular, to include the study thereof in their programs of military and, if possible, civil instruction."

[128] Col. G. I. A. D. Draper, "Rules Governing the Conduct of Hostilities – the Laws of War and Their Enforcement," in Michael A. Meyer and Hilaire McCoubrey, eds. *Reflections on Law and Armed Conflicts* (The Hague: Kluwer Law, 1998), 87–93, 92.

[129] Office of the Surgeon General, Multinational Force – Iraq; and, Office of the Surgeon General, United States Army Medical Command, *Mental Health Advisory Team (MHAT) IV*, *Operation Iraqi Freedom 05–07*, *FINAL REPORT* (Nov. 17, 2006), at 36. A graph documents that 40 percent of 447 Marines and 55 percent of 1,320 soldiers questioned in Iraq would report unit members for injuring or killing innocent noncombatants. Another graph shows that 87 percent of soldiers and 86 percent of Marines questioned "received training that made it clear how I should behave towards non-combatants." (This important study, once available at http://www.behavioralhealth.army.mil, is no longer at that site.)

[130] See FM 27–10, *Law of Land Warfare*, supra, note 20. The change, from superior orders constituting a complete defense, was initiated with Change I to the 1940 edition of FM 27–10, dated Nov. 15, 1944.

[131] "Article 7.4. The fact that an accused person acted pursuant to an order of a Government or of a superior shall not relieve him of criminal responsibility, but may be considered in mitigation of punishment if the International Tribunal determines that justice so requires." The ICTR's provision is identical.

[132] Cryer, "The Boundaries of Liability in International Criminal Law," supra, note 85, at 13, fn. 70.

[133] Antonio Cassese, "The Rome Statute of the International Criminal Court: Some Preliminary Reflections," 10–1 *European J. of Int'l L.* (1999), 144–71, 157.

limited to war crimes, as it was recognized that conduct that amounted to genocide or crimes against humanity would be so manifestly illegal that the defence should be denied altogether. ... It would, of course, not prevent superior orders being raised as part of another defence such as duress.[134]

Soviet law rejected and continues to reject the superior orders defense to war crimes. Today's German military law rejects them as a defense, although they are allowed as a defense under its criminal law.[135] Denmark and Norway excuse the soldier who disobeys lawful orders that he reasonably believes to be illegal.[136]

Negotiations during the formulation of the 1977 Additional Protocols illustrated that the Communist bloc and many Third World states, wishing to maximize compliance with official directives, offer their soldiers full immunity when they obey *un*lawful orders, even if they cannot demonstrate that they mistakenly believed the orders lawful.[137] Despite lengthy negotiations to draft an additional protocol provision limiting the defense of superior orders, that effort was unsuccessful as a result of objections to its limitation by African and Asian states.[138] Accordingly, there are no provisions in the 1977 protocols regarding a subordinate's obedience of orders.

ICTY trials have seen the defense raised even though the ICTY's articles specifically reject it.[139] From the outset, the tribunal has made clear that, although not a defense, obedience of orders may be a relevant and admissible defense.[140] "Most of the Nuremberg defendants attempted to plead that they were acting under superior orders. ... This is in stark contrast with the three United Nations *ad hoc* tribunals [the ICTY, ICTR, and the Special Court for Sierra Leone], where the defense of superior orders has been raised only rarely."[141]

In the ICTY's first case, Dražen Erdemović, upon his plea of guilty, was sentenced to ten years' confinement. As the *Washington Post* phrased it, "The tribunal rejected the hauntingly familiar excuse of Nazi war criminals – that Erdemović was following orders."[142] The Erdemović case, however, raised the haunting defense of duress. (See Cases and Materials, this chapter.) Similar guilty verdicts followed in other ICTY cases: The prison commander Zdravco Mucic, convicted of ordering subordinates to commit murders;[143] Major General Radislav Krstić, who directed the 1995 attack on Srebrenica,

---

[134] Garraway, "Superior Orders and the International Criminal Court," supra, note 92, at 788.

[135] UNWCC, *War Crimes*, supra, note 66, at 66–7.   [136] Keijzer, *Military Obedience*, supra, note 94, at 79.

[137] Col. Howard S. Levie, *Protection of War Victims: Protocol I to the 1949 Geneva Conventions, Supplement* (1985), 10, 15, 19, 22, 31, 37–44.

[138] Col. Howard S. Levie, "The Rise and Fall of an Internationally Codified Denial of the Defense of Superior Orders," 30 *Mil. L. & L. of War Rev.* (1991), 204.

[139] Article 7.3 of the tribunal's statute expands the concept of the senior's responsibility, or *respondeat superior*. It holds that acts committed by a subordinate do not relieve his "superior" of individual criminal responsibility. The word "superior," rather than the more frequently found "commander," allows for the prosecution of civilian as well as military leaders.

[140] *Erdemović*, supra, note 6. "While the complete defense based on moral duress and/or a state of necessity stemming from superior orders is not ruled out absolutely, its conditions of application are particularly strict."

[141] William A. Schabas, *The UN International Criminal Tribunals* (New York: Cambridge University Press, 2006), 330–1.

[142] Charles Trueheart, "Balkan War Crimes Court Imposes First Sentence," *The Wash. Post*, Nov. 30, 1996, A31.

[143] Charles Trueheart, "Croat, 2 Bosnian Muslims Convicted of Atrocities Against Serbs," *Wash. Post*, Nov. 17, 1998, A34. "The first judgment of its kind since the post–World War II tribunals in Nuremberg and Tokyo rejected the arguments of mid-level officers who claimed they were just following orders."

charged with genocide for personal involvement, as well as his command responsibility;[144] the paramilitary commander Anto Furundžija, sentenced to ten years for
failing to stop subordinates' rapes.[145] Low-ranking and high-, all pleaded the defense
of obedience of orders. (See Chapter 10, Cases and Materials, for the ICTY's Krstić
opinion.)

9.6 Summary

It should be remembered that illegal orders are rare. A combatant need not anticipate
that they will periodically arise, nor carefully examine each order's lawfulness. Yet, they
do occur, and when they do, their illegality will be clear – will be manifest.

Obedience of orders is a defense frequently raised but seldom successful. The
defense has a lengthy history not only in war crimes cases, but in civil trials, not only
in the United States, but in armed forces worldwide. Its application has not been
uniform in either U.S. or foreign courts-martial. "Obviously, universal acceptance will
be out of the question; indeed, several experts [during Additional Protocol I's early
negotiations] took pains to emphasize the need of military discipline and the difficulty
'in time of armed conflict to permit soldiers to decide whether to obey or not.'"[146]
Befehl ist befehl?

The U.S. approach – obedience is not a defense, as such, but it may be mitigating and
may be relevant in the assertion of other defenses – is widely but not universally shared by
other states. The standard of what it is that constitutes an unlawful order – manifest
illegality – is also widely shared, even if there can be no black letter definition of that
term that will meet all cases.

There is potential conflict between the U.S. view of manifest illegality and that of
other states. What will be the result if a non-American U.N. commander directs a U.S.
contingent to carry out orders that the Americans view as contrary to customary
international law?[147] If the order is manifestly unlawful, of course it should not be
obeyed, but the legal outcome of conflicting understandings of "manifest" remains to
be seen.

The defense of superior orders will be raised in the future, by generals and by enlisted
service members. Illegal orders will be issued and, given the overbearing influence of a
military force's hierarchical structure (which is felt particularly in the lower ranks, and
particularly in combat), those illegal orders will be obeyed.[148] It is a topic to be debated
for as long as armed conflicts persist.

---

[144] Steven Erlanger, "Bosnian Serb General Is Arrested by Allied Force in Genocide Case," *Wash. Post*,
Dec. 3, 1998, A1.

[145] "Bosnian War Crimes Panel Finds Commander Guilty in Rape Case," *NY Times*, Dec. 11, 1998, A1.

[146] Frits Kalshoven, "The Conference of Government Experts on the Reaffirmation and Development of
International Humanitarian Law Applicable in Armed Conflicts (Second Session), May 3–June, 2, 1972,"
in *Reflections on the Law of War: Collected Essays* (Leiden: Martinus Nijhoff, 2007), 57–99, 88.

[147] E.g., the 1995 fall of Srebrenica, and the subsequent murder of sixty-five hundred Muslim men and boys
by Bosnian Serbs have been attributed, in part, to differing objectives of the states whose soldiers were
supposed to provide a safe haven. Jan Willem Honig and Norbert Both, *Srebrenica* (New York: Penguin, 1997).

[148] Osiel, *Obeying Orders*, supra, note 62, at 241, fn. 21.

CASES AND MATERIALS

UNITED STATES V. WILLIAM L. CALLEY, JR.

United States Court of Military Appeals, 22 CMR 19 (1973)

Introduction. *Lieutenant Calley led the 1ˢᵗ platoon of Company C, a portion of the cobbled-together Task Force Barker that was tasked with assaulting the hamlet of My Lai (4). On 16 March 1968, in My Lai-4, Calley's 1ˢᵗ Platoon, at his direction and with his personal involvement, murdered at least 350 South Vietnamese civilian women, children and elderly men. They also committed horrific sexual crimes in which Calley was not personally involved. Calley was eventually convicted by a general court-martial of the premeditated murder of twenty-two infants, children, women and old men, and of assault with intent to murder a child of about two years. (U.S. v. Calley, 46 CRM 1131 (ACMR, 1973).) The court-martial, composed of combat veteran officers, sentenced Calley to dismissal from the Army, and confinement at hard labor for life.*

On appeal, Calley alleged that his conviction should be set aside on any one of four grounds: prejudicial pretrial publicity, insufficient evidence to establish guilt, prejudicial errors in the military judge's instructions to the members (the jury), and his principal defense, that he acted in execution of his company commander, Captain Ernest Medina's, order to kill everyone in My Lai (4). The following extract is from the opinion of the military's highest appellate court, the U.S. Court of Military Appeal, known today as the U.S. Court of Appeals for the Armed Forces. The appellate court quotes the trial judge at great length ("I therefore instruct you . . ."), in this extract from its opinion:

At trial, Calley's principal defense was that he acted in execution of Captain Medina's order to kill everyone in My Lai 4. Appellate defense counsel urge this defense as the most important factor in assessment of the legal sufficiency of the evidence. The argument, however, is inapplicable to whether the evidence is *legally* sufficient. Captain Medina denied that he issued any such order, either during the previous day's briefing or on the date the killings were carried out. Resolution of the conflict between his testimony and that of the accused was for the triers of the facts. . . . The general findings of guilty, with exceptions as to the number of persons killed, does not indicate whether the court members found that Captain Medina did not issue the alleged order to kill, or whether, if he did, the court members believed that the accused knew the order was illegal. For the purpose of the legal sufficiency of the evidence, the record supports the findings of guilty. . . .

Both combatants captured by and noncombatants detained by the opposing force, regardless of their loyalties, political views, or prior acts, have the right to be treated as prisoners until released, confined, or executed, in accordance with law and established procedures, by competent authority sitting in judgment of such detained or captured individuals. Summary execution of detainees or prisoners is forbidden by law. Further, it's clear under the evidence presented in this case, that hostile acts or support of the enemy North Vietnamese or Viet Cong forces by inhabitants of My Lai (4) at some time prior to 16 March 1968, would not justify the summary execution of all or a part of the occupants of My Lai (4) on 16 March, nor would hostile acts committed that day, if, following the hostility, the belligerents surrendered or were captured by our forces.

I therefore instruct you, as a matter of law, that if unresisting human beings were killed to My Lai (4) while within the effective custody and control of our military forces, their deaths cannot be considered justified, and any order to kill such people would be, as a matter of law, an illegal order. Thus, if you find that Lieutenant Calley received an order directing him to kill unresisting Vietnamese within his control or within the control of his troops, *that order would be an illegal order.*

A determination that an order is illegal does not, of itself, assign criminal responsibility to the person following the order for acts done in compliance with it. Soldiers are taught to follow orders, and special attention is given to obedience of orders on the battlefield. Military effectiveness depends upon obedience to orders. On the other hand, the obedience of a soldier is not the obedience of an automaton. A soldier is a reasoning agent, obliged to respond, not as a machine, but as a person. The law takes these factors into account in assessing criminal responsibility for acts done in compliance with illegal orders.

The acts of a subordinate done in compliance with an unlawful order given him by his superior are excused and impose no criminal liability upon him unless the superior's order is one which a man of *ordinary sense and understanding* would, under the circumstances, know to be unlawful, or if the order in question is actually known to the accused to be unlawful.

... In determining what orders, if any, Lieutenant Calley acted under, if you find him to have acted, you should consider all of the matters which he has testified reached him and which you can infer from other evidence that he saw and heard. Then, unless you find beyond a reasonable doubt that he was not acting under orders directing him in substance and effect to kill unresisting occupants of My Lai (4), you must determine whether Lieutenant Calley actually knew those orders to be unlawful. ...

In determining whether or not Lieutenant Calley had knowledge of the unlawfulness of any order found by you to have been given, you may consider all relevant facts and circumstances, including Lieutenant Calley's rank; educational background; OCS [Officer Candidate School] schooling; other training while in the Army, including basic training, and his training in Hawaii and Vietnam; his experience on prior operations involving contact with hostile and friendly Vietnamese; his age; and any other evidence tending to prove or disprove that on 16 March 1968, Lieutenant Calley knew the order was unlawful. If you find beyond a reasonable doubt, on the basis of all the evidence, that *Lieutenant Calley actually knew* the order under which he asserts he operated was unlawful, the fact that the order was given operates as no defense.

Unless you find beyond reasonable doubt that the accused acted with actual knowledge that the order was unlawful, you must proceed to determine whether, under the circumstances, *a man of ordinary sense and understanding would have known the order was unlawful. You deliberations on this question do not focus on Lieutenant Calley and the manner in which he perceived the legality of the order found to have been given him. The standard is that of a man of ordinary sense and understanding under the circumstances.*

Think back to the events of 15 and 16 March 1968. ... Then determine, in light of all the surrounding circumstances, whether the order, which to reach this point you will have found him to be operating in accordance with, is one which a man of ordinary sense and understanding would know to be unlawful. Apply this to each charged act which you have found Lieutenant Calley to have committed. Unless you are satisfied from the evidence, beyond a reasonable doubt, that a man of ordinary sense and understanding would have known the order to be unlawful, you must acquit Lieutenant Calley for committing acts done in accordance with the order.

Conclusion. *On 21 December 1973, the Court of Military Appeals denied all of Calley's appeal issues and affirmed his conviction. While his case had been on appeal, President Richard Nixon ordered that Calley be restricted to his officers' quarters, under house arrest. Prior to his appeal having been heard Calley's sentence to confinement had been reduced to twenty years by the court-martial convening authority. It was further reduced to ten years by the Secretary of the Army, as permitted by federal law. By the time the Court of Military Appeals confirmed Calley's reduced sentence he had already "served" a third of it, making him immediately eligible for parole. Calley spent three days in an Army stockade before he was put under house arrest and served a total of four and-a-half post-conviction months in the Fort Leavenworth stockade before he was paroled to civilian life on 9 November 1974, by order of Secretary of the Army Howard H. Callaway. It was not the military justice system's brightest moment.*

ATTORNEY-GENERAL OF THE GOVERNMENT OF ISRAEL V. ADOLF EICHMANN

Israel, District Court of Jerusalem, December 12, 1961

Introduction. *During World War II, SS Obersturmbannführer (Lieutenant Colonel) Adolf Eichmann led the Race and Resettlement Office of the RSHA, or Reich Security Main Office, which administered the mass extermination of European Jewry, the "Final Solution," and other "undesirables." At the end of the war, he escaped to Argentina where, working under the name Ricardo Klement for a water company, he lived with his family until kidnapped by Israeli agents in 1960. He was tried in Israel.*

Judgment of the District Court

1. Adolf Eichmann has been arraigned before this Court on charges of unsurpassed gravity – crimes against the Jewish people, crimes against humanity, and war crimes. The period of the crimes ascribed to him, and their historical background, is that of the Hitler régime in Germany and in Europe, and the counts of the indictment encompass the catastrophe which befell the Jewish people during that period – a story of bloodshed and suffering which will be remembered to the end of time. ... How could this happen in the full light of day, and why was it just the German people from whom this great evil sprang? Could the Nazis have carried out their evil designs without the help given them by other peoples in whose midst the Jews dwelt? Would it have been possible to avert the catastrophe, at least in part, if the Allies had displayed a greater will to assist the persecuted Jews? Did the Jewish people in the lands of freedom do all in their power to rally to the rescue of their brethren and to sound the alarm for help? ...

216. The accused's principal defence is that everything he did was in accordance with orders from his superiors. This he regards as full justification for all his deeds. He explains that his S.S. training inculcated in him the idea of blind obedience as the supreme

virtue, obedience based on boundless faith in the judgment of the leadership, which would always know what the good of the Reich demanded and give its orders accordingly. At the end of the trial, we heard this argument in its most extreme form from counsel for the defence, as follows:

> The basic principle of all States is loyalty to their leadership. The deed is dumb and obedience is blind. These are the qualities on which the State is founded. Do such qualities merit reward? That depends on the success of its policy. If a policy is unsuccessful the order will be considered a crime in the eyes of the victors. Fortune will not have served the one who has obeyed and he will be called to judgment for his loyalty. The gallows or a decoration – that is the question. To fail is an abominable crime. To succeed is to sanctify the deed. . . .

If in these words counsel for the defendant intended to describe a totalitarian régime based on denial of law, as was Hitler's régime in Germany, then his words are indeed apt. Such a régime seeks to turn the citizen into an obedient subject who will carry out every order coming from above, be it to commit injustice, to oppress or to murder. It is also true that under such a regime the criminal who acts in obedience to a criminal leader is not punished but on the contrary earns a reward, and only when the entire régime collapses will justice reach him. But arguments of this kind are not to be heard in any State in the world whose system of government is based on the rule of law. The attempt to turn an order for the extermination of millions of innocent people from a crime into a political act in order thus to exempt from personal criminal responsibility those who gave and those who carried out the order will not avail. And let not the counsel for the defence console us with the promise of a World Government to come when such "acts of State" will pass from the world. We do not have to wait for such a radical change in the relations between nations to bring a criminal to judgment for his personal responsibility for his deeds, which is the basis of criminal jurisdiction the world over.

We have already considered elsewhere in our judgment the defence of "act of State" in international law, and have shown that it cannot avail the accused. . . .

The personal responsibility of a government official for his acts lies at the foundation of the rule of law which we have adopted under the inspiration of the Common Law. As Dicey, *Law of the Constitution*, 10th ed., Ch. XI, p. 326, explains:

> The Minister or servant of the Crown . . . is legally responsible for the act in which he is concerned, and he cannot get rid of his liability by pleading that he acted in obedience to royal orders. Now supposing that the act done is illegal – he becomes at once liable to criminal or civil proceedings in a court of law.

220. Here we shall add that the rejection of the defence of "superior orders" as exempting completely from criminal responsibility, has now become general in all civilized countries. . . .

It should be pointed out here that even the jurists of the Third Reich did not dare to set down on paper that obedience to orders is above all else. They did not repeal Section 47(2) of the German Military Criminal Code, which provides that whoever commits an offence against the criminal law through obedience to an order of his superior is punishable as an accomplice to a criminal act if he knew that the order concerned an act which is a crime or an offence according to general or military law. This provision was applicable also to S.S. men, according to the laws of their jurisdiction.

221. It is self-evident that the accused knew well that the order for the physical extermination of the Jews was manifestly unlawful and that in carrying out this order he engaged in criminal acts on a colossal scale. . . .

Not only was the order for physical extermination manifestly unlawful, but also all the other orders for the persecution of Jews for being Jews, even though they were framed in the formal language of legislation and subsidiary legislation, since these were only a cloak for arbitrary discrimination contrary to the basic principles of law and justice. . . .

Conclusion. *Eichmann was found guilty of crimes against the Jewish people, crimes against humanity, and war crimes. He was hanged on May 31, 1962. His corpse was cremated and his ashes scattered at sea.*

"THE EINSATZGRUPPEN CASE" THE UNITED STATES V. OHLENDORF, ET AL.

Trials of War Criminals before the Nuernberg Military Tribunals, vol. IV (1948)[149]

Introduction. *SS Gruppenführer (Lieutenant General) Otto Ohlendorf commanded one of four einsatzgruppen – mobile task forces to carry out "liquidations" in occupied countries. Ohlendorf's units operated in the Ukraine and Crimea. In 1941, units he commanded were responsible for a single mass murder of more than 14,000 victims, most of them Jews. He was charged with a total of 90,000 executions. He later was also appointed a Deputy Secretary of State. Ohlendorf and twenty coaccused were tried before a military tribunal. The following is from the Tribunal's 1948 Judgment:*

Superior Orders

Those of the defendants who admit participation in the mass killings which are the subject of this trial, plead that they were under military orders and, therefore, had no will of their own. . . . It is axiomatic that a military man's first duty is to obey. If the defendants were soldiers and as soldiers responded to the command of their superiors to kill certain people, how can they be held guilty of crime? This is the question posed by the defendants. The answer is not a difficult one.

The obedience of a soldier is not the obedience of an automaton. A soldier is a reasoning agent. . . . It is a fallacy of wide-spread consumption that a soldier is required to do everything his superior officer orders him to do. . . . The fact that a soldier may not, without incurring unfavorable consequences, refuse to drill, salute, exercise, reconnoiter, and even go into battle, does not mean that he must fulfill every demand put to him. In the first place, an order to require obedience must relate to military duty. An officer may not demand of a soldier, for instance, that he steal for him. And what the superior officer may not militarily demand, the subordinate is not required to do. Even if the order refers to a military subject it must be one which the superior is authorized, under the circumstances, to give.

---

[149] *U.S. v. Ohlendorf*, "Einsatzgruppen Case," supra, note 36, at 470–1, 473–4, 480–2, 509.

The subordinate is bound only to obey the lawful orders of his superior and if he accepts a criminal order and executes it with a malice of his own, he may not plead superior orders in mitigation of his offense. If the nature of the ordered act is manifestly beyond the scope of the superior's authority, the subordinate may not plead ignorance to the criminality of the order. If one claims duress in the execution of an illegal order it must be shown that the harm caused by obeying the illegal order is not disproportionally greater than the harm which would result from not obeying the illegal order. It would not be an adequate excuse, for example, if a subordinate, under orders, killed a person known to be innocent, because by not obeying it he himself would risk a few days of confinement. Nor if one acts under duress, may he, without culpability, commit the illegal act once the duress ceases.

The [Nuremberg] International Military Tribunal, in speaking of the principle to be applied in the interpretation of criminal superior orders, declared that –

"The true test, which is found in varying degrees in the criminal law of most nations, is not the existence of the order, but whether moral choice was in fact possible."

. . .

Superior Orders Defense Must Establish Ignorance of Illegality

To plead superior orders one must show an excusable ignorance of their illegality. The sailor who voluntarily ships on a pirate craft may not be heard to answer that he was ignorant of the probability he would be called upon to help in the robbing and sinking of other vessels. He who willingly joins an illegal enterprise is charged with the natural development of that unlawful undertaking. What SS man could say that he was unaware of the attitude of Hitler toward Jewry? . . .

Some of the defendants may say they never knew of the Nazi Party extermination program or, if they did, they were not in accord with the sentiments therein expressed. But again, a man who sails under the flag of the skull and cross-bones cannot say that he never expected to fire a cannon against a merchantman.. . .

Duress Needed for Plea of Superior Orders

But it is stated that in military law even if the subordinate realizes that the act he is called upon to perform is a crime, he may not refuse its execution without incurring serious consequences, and that this, therefore, constitutes duress. Let it be said at once that there is no law which requires that an innocent man must forfeit his life or suffer serious harm in order to avoid committing a crime which he condemns. The threat, however, must be imminent, real, and inevitable. No court will punish a man who, with a loaded pistol at his head, is compelled to pull a lethal lever. Nor need the peril be that imminent in order to escape punishment. But were any of the defendants coerced into killing Jews under the threat of being killed themselves if they failed in their homicidal mission? The test to be applied is whether the subordinate acted under coercion or whether he himself approved of the principle involved in the order. If the second proposition be true, the plea of superior orders fails. The doer may not plead innocence to a criminal act ordered by his superior if he is in accord with the principle and intent of the superior. When the will of the doer merges with the will of the superior in the execution of the illegal act, the doer may not plead duress under superior orders. . . .

Superior means superior in capacity and power to force a certain act. It does not mean superiority only in rank. It could easily happen in an illegal enterprise that the captain guides the major, in which case the captain could not be heard to plead superior orders in defense of his crime.

If the cognizance of the doer has been such, prior to the receipt of the illegal order, that the order is obviously but one further logical step in the development of a program which he knows to be illegal in its very inception, he may not excuse himself from responsibility for an illegal act which could have been foreseen by the application of the simple law of cause and effect. . . .

One who embarks on a criminal enterprise of obvious magnitude is expected to anticipate what the enterprise will logically lead to.

In order to successfully plead the defense of superior orders the opposition of the doer must be constant. It is not enough that he mentally rebel at the time the order is received. If at any time after receiving the order he acquiesces in its illegal character, the defense of superior orders is closed to him.

Many of the defendants testified that they were shocked with the order [to execute all Jews in their areas of responsibility] when they first heard it. . . . But if they were shocked by the order, what did they do to oppose it? . . . The evidence indicates that there was no will or desire to deprecate its fullest intent.

[I]t is not enough for a defendant to say . . . that it was pointless to ask to be released, and, therefore, did not even try. Exculpation is not so easy as that. No one can shrug off so appalling a moral responsibility with the statement that there was no point in trying. . . .

Several of the defendants stated that it would have been useless to avoid the order by subterfuge, because had they done so, their successors would accomplish the task and thus nothing would be gained anyway. The defendants are accused here for their own individual guilt. No defendant knows what his successor would have done. . . . One defendant stated that to have disobeyed orders would have meant a betrayal of his people. Does he really mean that the German people, had they known, would have approved of this mass butchery?

That so much man-made misery should have happened in the twentieth century . . . makes the spectacle almost insupportable in its unutterable tragedy and sadness. Amid the wreckage of the six continents, amid the shattered hearts of the world, amid the sufferings of those who have borne the cross of disillusionment and despair, mankind pleads for an understanding which will prevent anything like this happening again.

Conclusion. *Defendant Ohlendorf and thirteen others were convicted of multiple crimes and sentenced to death by hanging. Two other accused were sentenced to confinement for life, another three to twenty years, and another two to ten years.*

UNITED STATES V. PRIVATE MICHAEL A. SCHWARZ

45 C.M.R. 852 (NCMR, 1971)

Introduction. *The Military Tribunal's opinion clearly articulates the nuances of the law of war associated with the defense of obedience of orders. It drew a template for subsequent courts to follow. The following case illustrates how young judge advocates in the*

*U.S.–Vietnam conflict, in a court-martial conducted in the combat zone, did their best to
follow the law of Nuremberg.*

*On February 19, 1970, not far from Da Nang, South Vietnam, Private Schwarz was
part of a five man "killer team." The patrol, led by a young Lance Corporal, received a
fiery briefing by their company commander [see Chapter 2, Cases and Materials], then
departed on their nighttime patrol. Upon reaching their first checkpoint, the small
hamlet of Son Thang-4, the patrol went to three thatch-roofed "hooches" where, in turn,
they murdered six, then four, then six more unarmed, unresisting Vietnamese women and
children. The testimony of Schwarz was that he had followed the orders of the patrol
leader to open fire on the victims at point-blank range, at all three hooches. During his
general court-martial, held in Da Nang in June 1970, Schwarz, charged with sixteen
specifications (counts) of premeditated murder, opted to testify under oath. His direct and
cross-examination reveal how one young Marine understood the defense he was raising,
obedience to orders. The following direct examination questions (by the Marine defense
counsel) and answers (by the accused, Schwarz) are from the verbatim court-martial
record.[150] At this point in the trial the accused is trying to show how thoroughly he was
conditioned to obey orders:*

Q.   During your stay at Parris Island [boot camp], what instructions, if any, were you
      given regarding obedience to orders?
A.   To do what they asked. If I'm given an order to do it, and not question.

Q.   How much of this instruction did you receive?
A.   Extensively, sir. Most every day, sir. In one way or another.

Q.   Where did you attend ITR [Infantry Training Regiment, where new marines
      receive infantry training]?
A.   Camp Geiger, north of Camp LeJeune, North Carolina.

Q.   Did you receive any instruction there, in regard to obeying orders? . . .
A.   About the same as boot camp. That if I'm given an order to obey it. All of us in
      formal classes were given this.

Q.   What if you had a question about an order?
A.   Then to go up the chain of command and question through the proper steps.

Q.   Have you ever had occasion to discuss when it would be wrong or when it would be
      right to obey an order? . . .
A.   Once at ITR I asked the sergeant or corporal about this, if there was any occasion,
      instance, when you were permitted to disobey an order, and he said there was. . . .
      He used the example, if I'm told to scrub out a toilet with my hands that I didn't
      have to do that, that I should refuse to do it, there wouldn't be any trouble. But, if
      I was going to refuse, to make sure that I was right.

Q.   Did you run into any other occasions? . . .
A.   When I was in recon [3d Reconnaissance Battalion, Schwarz's former unit] after
      I got to Vietnam, it wasn't a formal class, but we were asking about two instances.

---

[150] On file with author.

I heard about it. I asked a man who was with me about it. If it came down, you're supposed to do it. If you're ordered to do it, you have to do it. That the only time you disobey it is only when it's completely ridiculous. That there's no way that you should or could do it. . . .

Q. [In Son Thang-4, upon hearing a shot] what did you find, when you came out [of the hooch you were searching]?

A. I ran out, looked around, and I saw this one woman falling over. I thought she got – I just thought she got shot by someone. So, I got there and H____ [the patrol leader] said, "Open up, kill them all, kill all of them." . . . Me, I made up my mind I wasn't going to shoot them unless I seen someone to shoot at. He fired his '79 [M-79 grenade launcher], then he re-loaded. And, all the time he was re-loading, he was yelling, "Shoot them, kill them all, kill all of them bitches." . . .

Q. Then what happened?

A. Then someone yelled, "Cease fire," sir.

Q. What happened after that?

A. I was standing there. I heard a baby cry and H____ said, "Recon [Schwarz's nickname], go shoot the baby and shut it up." I couldn't see no baby. So, I went over there. When I found the one that was crying, it was on my left – it would be on the right side of the group. I got down. I couldn't see no baby but I could hear him crying, and something snapped in my mind. If you clapped your hands in front of a baby he's going to shut up, and that's all my concern was, to keep the baby quiet. So, I put my .45 [pistol] down and fired two rounds over the right shoulder – the left shoulder – the right shoulder.

Q. You didn't hit anybody?

A. No, sir. I know definitely I didn't hit anyone. . . .

Q. I just want to back up one moment. Why didn't you obey that order that H____ gave you?

A. I just couldn't see shooting a baby. . . .
   Cross-examination by the Marine prosecutor:

Q. When your brothers were telling you about the women and children in Vietnam, did they ever tell you it was lawful to bring women and children out of a hooch and shoot them down – unarmed women and children?

A. No, sir.

Q. They never did tell you that?

A. No, sir.

Q. Private Schwarz, you did know that there were some orders that you could refuse to obey, did you not?

A. Yes, sir.

Q. And, in fact, on that particular night you claim you did disobey some of those orders?

A. Yes, sir. But, not for the fact that I thought they were illegal orders. I just thought morally I couldn't do it.

Q.   You didn't think it was an illegal order? It was your own moral compunction?
A.   Right, sir.

Q.   You said that if you were going to disobey, you better make sure that you were right?
A.   Yes, sir.

Q.   Were you sure that you were right when you disobeyed one of the orders, by not
      shooting the child, for example?
A.   To me it was right, sir.

Q.   So, then you knew it to be the opposite of that; to shoot the child would be wrong?
A.   No, sir. Because that's what I'd been ordered. As far as I knew, these were the
      enemy. . . .

Q.   Private Schwarz, at the time that you went out on that killer team that night, were
      you aware that it was wrong and not permitted for Marines to kill unarmed
      civilians?
A.   Unarmed prisoners, yes, sir. Any civilians, you're not allowed to kill them unless he's
      putting harm toward you, sir. . . .

Q.   But [at the first hooch] you really didn't know what was going on, then?
A.   No, sir, I didn't. [At] number one, no, sir. I didn't know if we were taking fire or
      what, and I just knew that the team leader had ordered to shoot, because I wasn't
      out there, I was just going along. I thought he knew what he was doing, because he
      ordered it. . . .

*Following the government and defense cases-in-chief, and the government's case in
rebuttal, the members (military jury) were excused while the trial counsel (prosecutor, or
"TC") and defense counsel ("DC"), in the presence of the accused, discussed jury instructions with the military judge ("MJ"). (The government's case-in-chief included testimonial
evidence that a young child had been found at the scene, dead from a gunshot wound to
the head.) The following discussion is from the record of trial:*

DC   to MJ: Sir, in regard to the instruction regarding defense for obedience to
      orders . . . I would like to put in there also that the presumption of the legality of
      an order when it relates to military duties, as we have here. . . .
TC: Colonel, the government felt that the only issue here is not whether the order was
      in fact legal or illegal . . . but whether the accused believed it was, reasonably.
DC: This points out that it is presumed to be legal, and he disobeys it at his own
      peril. . . .
MJ: How about saying, or working something in, along these lines: I have here a copy
      of the *Keenan* instruction [regarding obedience to orders][151] which I propose to
      adapt and modify as applicable in this case. . . . I don't want to get into this
      business, "disobeyed at the peril of the subordinate" type thing. That's a matter
      I think you can argue.
DC: The thing I want to get before the court without arguing is that he is under this
      burden as to whether or not to obey the order. . . . He disobeys the order given at
      his own peril.

[151] Referring to *U.S. v. Keenan*, 39 CMR 108 (CMA, 1969).

MJ: Well, everyone violates the law at his own peril. We all know that.

DC: He has conflicting duties, here. One says he should and the other says he shouldn't, and I just want the court instructed as to the law regarding when he has the duty to –

MJ: I think that [the *Keenan* instruction] clearly brings to mind the principle you have in mind; that the court must find that, beyond a reasonable doubt, the illegal nature of the order known by the accused before they can convict him.

A portion of the instructions eventually agreed upon by both counsel and the accused, and given by the military judge to the members, was the Keenan *instruction, tailored to the circumstances of Schwarz's case:*

MJ: If you find beyond a reasonable doubt that the accused, under the circumstances of his age and military experience, could not have honestly believed the order issued by his team leader to be legal under the laws and usages of war, then the killing . . . was without justification. A marine is a reasoning agent, who is under a duty to exercise judgment in obeying orders. . . . Where such orders are manifestly beyond the scope of the authority of the one issuing the order, or are palpably illegal upon their face, then the act of obedience to such orders will not justify acts pursuant to such illegal orders.

Conclusion. *The members found Schwarz guilty of twelve of the sixteen specifications of premeditated murder. After arguments by both counsel regarding the quantum of punishment, the members sentenced Schwarz to forfeiture of all pay and allowances, to be discharged from the Marine Corps with a dishonorable discharge, and confinement for life.*

At his later general court-martial, with a different trial team and a different military jury, the patrol leader was acquitted of all charges. It was not Nuremberg, but it was two of many valiant efforts to live up to the examples set there.

REGINA V. FINTA

[1994] 1 S.C. R. 701

Introduction. *During World War II, Captain Imre Finta commanded the Royal Hungarian Gendarmerie in Nazi-occupied Szeged, Hungary. During his command, 8,617 Jews were arrested and deported to various concentration camps from Budapest, an area in Finta's charge. The authority for Finta's Gendarmerie to arrest and deport the victims was the so-called "Baky Order," a decree issued by the Hungarian Ministry of the Interior. Following the war, Finta was tried in absentia in a Hungarian court and found guilty of "crimes against the people." In 1948, before his Hungarian trial, Finta had immigrated to Toronto, Canada, where he became a citizen in 1956. In 1987, Canada charged Finta with manslaughter, kidnapping, robbery, and unlawful confinement, all charges arising from his command of the police units that forced the wartime Jewish deportations. His defense? He was only following orders. There was no suggestion of a gun held to his head or other direct physical coercion. The orders he argued that he followed were those in the Baky Order. After a six-month jury trial, Finta was acquitted of all charges. His acquittal was upheld by Canada's Court of Appeals and by the Supreme Court.*

From the opinion of Canada's Supreme Court:

The defense of obedience to superior orders and the peace officer defense are available to members of the military or police forces in prosecutions for war crimes and crimes against humanity. Those defenses are subject to the manifest illegality test: the defenses are not available where the orders in question were manifestly unlawful. Even where the orders were manifestly unlawful, the defense of obedience to superior orders and the police officers' defense will be available in those circumstances where the accused had no moral choice as to whether to follow the orders. There can be no moral choice where there was such an air of compulsion and threat to the accused that he or she had no alternative but to obey the orders.

Conclusion. *What is your opinion of the Canadian court's view of "moral choice"? In your opinion, does it comport with the "moral choice" holding of the Nuremberg IMT? What is your standard of comparison?*

PROSECUTOR V. ERDEMOVIĆ

IT-96–22 Indictment (May 22, 1996) Footnotes omitted.

Introduction. *Forty-eight years after the Ohlendorf judgment, and twenty-five years after the Schwarz court-martial, the ICTY was still trying cases in which the defense of obedience was raised to the commission of war crimes. The Erdemović decisions illustrate the complexities that can arise in responding to a seemingly simple defense.*

2. On or about 6 July 1995, the Bosnian Serb army commenced an attack on the U.N. "safe area" of Srebrenica. This attack continued through until 11 July 1995, when the first units of the Bosnian army entered Srebrenica.

8. Between 13 July 1995 and approximately 22 July 1995, thousands of Bosnian Muslim men were summarily executed by members of the Bosnian Serb army and Bosnian Serb police at divers locations. . . .

11. On or about 16 July 1995, buses containing Bosnian Muslim men arrived at the collective farm in Pilica. Each bus was full of Bosnian Muslim men, ranging from approximately 17–60 years of age. After each bus arrived at the farm, the Bosnian Muslim men were removed in groups of about 10, escorted by members of the 10th Sabotage Detachment to a field adjacent to farm buildings and lined up in a row with their backs facing Drazen Erdemović and members of his unit.

12. . . . Erdemović, did shoot and kill and did participate with other members of his unit and soldiers from another brigade in the shooting and killing of unarmed Bosnian Muslim men at the Pilica collective farm. These summary executions resulted in the deaths of hundreds of Bosnian Muslim male civilians.

IT-96–22-T bis (5 March 1998)

On review of Erdemović's trial, the Appeals Chamber found the guilty plea to be voluntary but also found that it was not informed. The Trial Chamber did not make clear to Erdemović, held the Appeals Chamber, that crimes against humanity was a more serious charge than violation of laws and customs of war. On that thin basis the Appeals Chamber ordered a second trial. The record of Erdemović's second trial, quoting from his various prior appearances before the ICTY, describes the circumstances of the events that were the basis of the charges against him:

14. .... Your Honour, I had to do this. If I had refused, I would have been killed together with the victims. When I refused, they told me: "If you are sorry for them, stand up, line up with them and we will kill you too". I am not sorry for myself but for my family my wife and son who then had nine months, and I could not refuse because they would have killed me. . . .

Q.   What happened to those civilians?
A.   We were given orders to fire at those civilians, that is, to execute them.

Q.   Did you follow that order?
A.   Yes, but at first I resisted and Brano Gojkovic told me if I was sorry for those people that I should line up with them; and I knew that this was not just a mere threat but that it could happen, because in our unit the situation had become such that the Commander of the group has the right to execute on the spot any individual if he threatens the security of the group or if in any other way he opposes the Commander of the group appointed by the Commander Milorad Pelemis. . . .

. . . I said immediately that I did not want to take part in that and I said, "Are you normal? Do you know what you are doing?" But nobody listened to me.. . .

It was . . . I was under orders. If I had not done that, my family would have been hurt and nothing would have been changed.

Q.   Did you know at the time of anyone who was shot for having disobeyed orders?
A.   You know, I will tell you, I am sure that I would have been killed had I refused to obey because I remember that Pelemis had already ordered one man to slaughter another man and I am familiar with some other orders, I mean, what a Commander was entitled to do if he was disobeyed; he could order this person's liquidation immediately. I had seen quite a bit of that over those few days and it was quite clear to me what it was all about.

. . . . I was not afraid for myself at that point, not that much. If I were alone, I would have run away, I would have tried to do something, just as they tried to flee into the forest, or whatever. But what would happen to my child and to my wife? So there was this enormous burden falling on my shoulders. On the one hand I knew that I would be killing people, that I could not hide this, that this would be burning at my conscience.

. . . I was not afraid for myself at that point, not that much. If I were alone, I would have run away, I would have tried to do something, just as they tried to flee into the forest, or whatever. But what would happen to my child and to my wife? So there was this enormous burden falling on my shoulders. On the one hand I knew that I would be killing people, that I could not hide this, that this would be burning at my conscience.

IT-96–22-T (29 November 1996)

With the circumstance of Erdemović's charges before them, the Trial Chamber of his first trial considered his plea of guilty and ruled:

15. The defence of obedience to superior orders has been addressed expressly in Article 7(4) of the [ICTY's] Statute. This defence does not relieve the accused of criminal responsibility. The [U.N.] Secretary-General's report which proposed the Statute … clearly stated in respect of this provision that, at most, obedience to superior orders may justify a reduced penalty "should the International Tribunal determine that justice so requires".

16. In respect to the physical and moral duress accompanied by the order from a military superior (sometimes referred to as "extreme necessity"), which has been argued in this case, the Statute provides no guidance. …

17. A review by the United Nations War Crime Commission of the post-World War Two international military case law … considered the issue of duress as constituting a complete defence. After an analysis of some 2,000 decisions by these military tribunals, the United Nations Commission cited three features which were always present and which it laid down as essential conditions for duress to be accepted as a defense for a violation of international humanitarian law (IHL).

(i) the act charged was done to avoid an immediate danger both serious and irreparable;
(ii) there was no adequate means of escape;
(iii) the remedy was not disproportionate to the evil. …

18. … The absence of moral choice was recognized on several occasions as one of the essential components for considering duress as a complete defence. A soldier may be considered as being deprived of his moral choice in the face of imminent physical danger. This physical threat, understood in the case-law as a danger of death or serious bodily harm, must in some sense also meet the following conditions: it must be *"clear and present"* or else be *"imminent, real, and inevitable."*

These tribunals also took into account the issue of voluntary participation in an enterprise that leaves no doubt as to its end results in order to determine the individual responsibility of the accused members of the armed forces or paramilitary groups. The rank held by the soldier giving the order and by the one receiving it has also been taken into account in assessing the duress a soldier may be subject to when forced to execute a manifestly illegal order.

Although the accused did not challenge the manifestly illegal order he was allegedly given, the Trial Chamber would point out that according to the case-law referred to, in such an instance, the duty was to disobey rather than to obey. This duty to disobey could only recede in the face of the most extreme duress.

19. Accordingly, while the complete defence based on moral duress and/or a state of necessity stemming from superior orders is not ruled out absolutely, its conditions of application are particularly strict. …

20. On the basis of the case-by-case approach and in light of all the elements before it, the Trial Chamber is of the view that proof of the specific circumstances which would fully exonerate the accused of his responsibility has not been provided. Thus, the defence of duress accompanying the superior order will … be taken into account at the same time as other factors in the consideration of mitigating circumstances. …

48. Since the International Tribunal is confronted for the first time with a guilty plea accompanied by an application seeking leniency by virtue of mitigating circumstances based on superior orders which are likely to have limited the accused's freedom of choice at the time the crime was committed, the Trial Chamber believes it necessary to ascertain

in the relevant case-law whether such a defence has indeed permitted the mitigation of sentences handed down.. ...

51. However, the Trial Chamber considers that the rejection by the Nuremberg Tribunal of the defence of superior orders [in the cases of Field Marshals Keitel and Jodl], raised in order to obtain a reduction of the penalty imposed on the accused, is explained by their position of superior authority and that, consequently, the precedent setting value of the judgment in this respect is diminished for low ranking accused.

52. As regards other tribunals which have ruled on cases involving accused of various ranks, the Trial Chamber notes that superior orders, whether or not initial resistance on the part of the accused was present, have been admitted as mitigating circumstances or have led to considerably mitigated sentences. This was the case in the following decisions. ...

53. ... The Trial Chamber emphasises, however, that a subordinate defending himself on the grounds of superior orders may be subject to a less severe sentence only in cases where the order of the superior effectively reduces the degree of his guilt. If the order had no influence on the unlawful behavior because the accused was already prepared to carry it out, no such mitigating circumstances can be said to exist. ...

89. In accordance with the principles the Trial Chamber has established ... it identified a certain number of questions ... :

- could the accused have avoided the situation in which he found himself?
- was the accused confronted with an insurmountable order which he had no way to circumvent?
- was the accused, or one of his immediate family members, placed in danger of immediate death or death shortly afterwards?
- did the accused possess the moral freedom to oppose the orders he had received? Had he possessed that freedom, would he have attempted to oppose the orders?

91. The Trial Chamber would point out, however, that as regards the acts in which the accused is personally implicated and which, if sufficiently proved, would constitute grounds for granting mitigating circumstances, the Defence has produced no testimony, evaluation or any other elements to corroborate what the accused has said. For this reason, the Judges deem that they are unable to accept the plea of extreme necessity.

In accordance with Erdemović's continuing plea of guilty, the Trial Chamber, with its odd finding (paragraph 18) that the accused had not challenged his illegal order, sentenced him to ten years' confinement. Erdemović appealed the sentence.

IT-96–22-A (7 October 1997)

19. ... The majority of the Appeals Chamber finds that duress does not afford a complete defence to a soldier charged with a crime against humanity and/or a war crime involving the killing of innocent human beings. Consequently, the majority of the Appeals Chamber finds that the guilty plea of the Appellant was not equivocal. ...

20. However, the Appeals Chamber ... finds that the guilty plea of the Appellant was not informed and accordingly remits the case to a Trial Chamber other than the one which sentenced the Appellant in order that he be given an opportunity to replead. ...

21. Consequently, the Appellant's application for the Appeals Chamber to revise his sentence is rejected by the majority. The Appeals Chamber also unanimously rejects the Appellant's application for acquittal.

IT-96–22-T bis (5 March 1998)

... at Erdemović's retrial:

13. ... The parties agreed on the facts. In particular, the accused agreed that the events alleged in the indictment were true, and the Prosecutor agreed that the accused's claim to have committed the acts in question pursuant to superior orders and under threat of death was correct.[152]

15. *Aggravating factors*

The Trial Chamber accepts that hundreds of Bosnian Muslim civilian men between the ages of 17 and 60 were murdered by the execution squad of which the accused was part. The Prosecution has estimated that the accused alone, who says that he fired individual shots using a Kalashnikov automatic rifle, might have killed up to a hundred (100) people. This approximately matches his own estimate of seventy (70) persons. No matter how reluctant his initial decision to participate was, he continued to kill for most of the day. The Trial Chamber considers that the magnitude of the crime and the scale of the accused's role in it are aggravating circumstances to be taken into account. ...

17. *Duress*

The Trial Chamber has applied the ruling of the Appeals Chamber that *"duress does not afford a complete defence to a soldier charged with a crime against humanity and/or a war crime involving the killing of innocent human beings."* It may be taken into account only by way of mitigation [of the sentence]. ...

[There has been testimony of] the Accused's vulnerable position as a Bosnian Croat in the BSA [Bosnian Serb Army] and his history of disagreements with his commander, Milorad Pelemis, and subsequent demotion. ...

The evidence reveals the extremity of the situation faced by the accused. The Trial Chamber finds that there was a real risk that the accused would have been killed had he disobeyed the order. He voiced his feelings, but realised that he had no choice in the matter: he had to kill or be killed.

Conclusion. *A plea bargain accepted by the Trial Chamber called for Erdemović to plead guilty to certain charges, which he did, in return for which the Prosecution recommended a sentence of seven years' imprisonment. The Trial Chamber sentenced Erdemović to five years confinement "for the violation of the laws or customs of war," with credit for his time in pretrial confinement, which was three weeks short of two years.*

Do you think the ICTY Trial Chamber's opinion was consistent with the judgment in Nuremberg's Ohlendorf case? Is consistency with Nuremberg a concern?

There has been criticism that the Erdemović case and sentence were overly harsh, given the circumstances of his crime.[153] *There are also opinions that the sentence was*

---

[152] A significant concession by the prosecution, made pursuant to a plea bargain agreement.

[153] Aaron Fichtelberg, "Liberal Values in International Criminal Law: A Critique of Erdemović," 6–1 *J. of Int'l Crim. Justice* (March 2008), 3, 18: "The court made an inappropriate decision ... In essence, they undermined the moral and theoretical core of international humanitarian law. ... Of course, the Tribunal's decision was influenced by a number of 'extra-legal' considerations." And, Illan Rua Wall,

inappropriately light,[154] *and still other opinions that the Trial Chamber's opinion created new legal norms,*[155] *or that it was simply badly decided.*[156]

As a matter of law, Article 31.1(d) of the ICC Statute breaks with the ICTY's Erdemović majority:[157]

1 ... [A] person shall not be criminally responsible if, at the time of that person's conduct: (d) The conduct which is alleged to constitute a crime ... has been caused by duress resulting from a threat of imminent death or of continuing or imminent serious bodily harm against that person or another person, and the person acts necessarily and reasonably to avoid this threat, provided that the person does not intend to cause a greater harm than the one sought to be avoided. ...

Had Erdemović been tried by the ICC he likely would have been found not guilty.

UNITED STATES V. STAFF SERGEANT RAYMOND L. GIROUARD

General Court-Martial, Fort Campbell, Kentucky (March 2007)

Introduction. *A U.S. Army case that arose near Tikrit, Iraq, in May 2006, illustrates the reticence of young junior soldiers to inform superiors of war crimes committed by other soldiers. As often occurs, the failure to report war crimes involved soldiers who were themselves involved in the wrongdoing, surely no encouragement to exposure.*

The incident involved a squad from the 101st Airborne Division which was sent on a patrol to a remote and dangerous area near a former chemical plant, now a suspected insurgent training camp. Before departing, the squad was allegedly told by a senior officer, the brigade commander, to "kill all military-age men" they encountered. "[A later] investigation ultimately concluded that [Colonel Michael D.] Steele [the brigade commander] had led his soldiers to believe that distinguishing combatants from noncombatants – a main tenet of the military's rules of engagement – wasn't necessary during the mission."[158] *During the mission, after a brief firefight three Iraqi men were captured and blindfolded,*

"Duress, International Criminal Law and Literature," 4–4 J. of Int'l Crim. Justice (Sept. 2006), 724, at 724: "Erdemović should never have stood trial." At 727–8: "The dissenting opinion of Judge Cassese provides a rich source of jurisprudence, as well as ethical and philosophical knowledge. ... He argues that the majority decision is founded on the idea that the subject of duress 'ought rather die himself than kill an innocent'. 'However, where an accused cannot save the life of the victim, no matter what he does, the rationale for the common law exception ... disappears.'" Footnotes omitted.

[154] Yoram Dinstein, *The Conduct of Hostilities under the Law of International Armed Conflict* (New York: Cambridge, 2004), 247–8: "The correct approach is that an accused cannot be exonerated on the ground of duress if the war crime consisted of murder. This proposition is founded on the simple rationale that neither ethically nor legally can the life of the accused be regarded as more valuable than that of another human being (let alone a number of human beings). ... At that critical moment, the accused is not allowed to play God."

[155] Schabas, *UN International Criminal Tribunals*, supra, note 141, at 120.

[156] Antonio Cassese, *International Criminal Law* (New York: Oxford University Press, 2003), 34. "It may be respectfully noted that the Court not only failed to indicate on what national laws it had relied but also omitted to specify whether it had taken into account ... national laws on war crimes. ... It would therefore seem that the legal proposition set out by the Court does not carry the weight it could have, had it been supported by convincing legal reasoning."

[157] Kriangsak Kittichaisaree, *International Criminal Law* (New York: Oxford University Press, 2001), 264.

[158] David Cloud and Greg Jaffe, *The Fourth Star: Four Generals and the Epic Struggle for the Future of the United States Army* (New York: Crown, 2009), 236.

and their hands were bound with plastic "zip ties." While reporting the encounter by radio, the squad leader, Staff Sergeant (SSgt.) Girouard, was allegedly told by a senior non-commissioned officer that the prisoners should have been killed.

Pursuant to a quickly hatched conspiracy, it was agreed between several squad members that the detainees' zip ties would be cut and they would be told to run. They would be shot and killed as they ran. To make a later account of escaping prisoners plausible, SSgt. Girouard would punch in the face one member of the squad and inflict a knife cut on the arm of another. The visible wounds would substantiate a false account of a struggle with the escaping detainees.

The following extracts are from a written, sworn statement provided by one of the members of the patrol to an Army investigator.[159] It was the soldier's second statement, after an initial statement disclaiming all knowledge of any wrongdoing. This second statement was later admitted in evidence at the court-martial of SSgt. Girouard.

A.   ... As we all stood there, SSgt. Girouard said to bring it in close. In a low toned voice he said, "We are going to change the zip-ties. ..." and glanced at the detainees, who were outside. He mentioned that 1st Sgt. ____ transmitted over the radio that the detainees should have been killed. ... [Girouard's] hands and his body language was as to say that the detainees were going to get roughed up. I didn't like the idea so I walked towards the door. He looked around at everyone and asked if anyone else had an issue or a problem. Nobody said anything. ... [Outside] I told Sergeant ____ that I was smoked. ... Right there, I heard "Oh shit" and saw 2 detainees running away. They all got shot and fell. ... I made my way to the house only to see 3 bodies, which were the detainees, and SSgt. Girouard. I asked him what happened. But he couldn't answer. ... A week later, while we sat at combat outpost 2, in Samarra, I overheard all the talk about what had really happened. ... PFC C____ mentioned to people in his truck that SSgt. Girouard had punched [him] pretty hard. ... I heard about a kitchen knife being used to cut Specialist H____. Specialist G____ did not say who did the cutting. ...

Q.   While in the house did you specifically hear Girouard state that he was going to cut the detainees' zip-ties and shoot them?

A.   After he pulled us in close, yes he did.

Q.   Did he specify who was going to do the shooting?

A.   Not while I was in the room. ...

Q.   While in the room, did Girouard state that he or someone else will cut H____ and punch C____?

A.   No, not while I was in the room. ...

Q.   Did you witness anyone shoot the detainees?

A.   No, I could not see rifles pointed or firing.

Q.   Why did you tell A____ [in your first sworn statement] the detainees were shot inside the house?

---

[159] On file with author.

A.   I told him 1 person was shot inside the house when we first assaulted the objective. Not a detainee. The first K.I.A. [enemy killed in action] was shot through the window from the outside of the house when we ran to the house. . . .

Q.   Besides yourself, C____, H____, Girouard, M____, and G____, who else knows about the conspiracy to shoot the detainees and subsequently killed them? Who else knows the circumstances of how they were killed?

A.   Only myself, Corporal S____, and Sergeant A____. No one else to my knowledge. . . .

Q.   Is all the detail you provided in your previous sworn statement on 29 May 06, from when you heard "Oh shit" and saw 2 detainees get shot, to when you arrived back to the house and saw the bodies and H____, Girouard and C____, correct to the best of your knowledge?

A.   Yes.

Q.   Why didn't you attempt to stop Girouard, H____, and C____ from killing the detainees?

A.   Afraid of being called a pussy.

Q.   Why didn't you immediately inform your platoon leader or anyone else, on the radio?

A.   Peer pressure and I have to be loyal to the squad.

Q.   Do you feel what Girouard, H____, and C____ did was wrong?
A.   Yes, it was wrong.

Q.   Do you know what they did is a violation and is punishable under the UCMJ [Uniform Code of Military Justice]?

A.   Yes.

Q.   Do you know that you are obligated as a soldier to report any crime you witness?
A.   Yes.
A.   Do you know by withholding that information, you have violated the UCMJ?
A.   Yes. . . .

Q.   What was C____'s demeanor while Girouard was talking about the plan?
A.   His reaction was normal. It was later on that I took notice how he was feeling. 3 days later he told me he couldn't stop thinking about it. As if it bothered him. He then asked me about my previous deployment [in Iraq] and how I dealt with seeing dead bodies and shooting the enemy. I told him it was alright that he felt like that. He was really stressed because when he slept the few hours he did, he dreamed about it over and over. . . .

Q.   Has Girouard ever threatened you or anyone else's lives if they spoke of the circumstances of how the detainees were killed?

A.   When we were at the Combat Out Post #2 we talked it over briefly. SSgt. Girouard, Specialist H____, Private First Class M____, Private First Class C____ and Specialist G____ were all there. He said to be loyal and not to go bragging or spreading rumors about the objective. He said to act like grown men and be quiet professionals. After that he said if he found out who told anyone anything about it he would find that person after he got out of jail and kill him or her. I laughed about it and most of the squad smiled and blew it off. . . .

Q.   Is there anything you want to add to this statement?
A.   No.

Conclusion. *At trial, SSgt. Girouard was acquitted of the premeditated murder of three Iraqi detainees, and acquitted of conspiracy to commit murder. He was convicted of negligent homicide, obstruction of justice, and conspiracy to obstruct justice. He was sentenced to a reduction in rank to private, the loss of all pay and allowances, ten years confinement, and a dishonorable discharge. At separate general courts-martial, two co-accused who actually shot the victims were convicted and sentenced to eighteen years confinement and dishonorable discharges. (Their sentences had been reduced from confinement for life, in return for their testimony against Girouard.) A fourth coaccused, who was not so deeply involved, was convicted of lesser charges and sentenced to nine months confinement and a bad conduct discharge.*

The soldier who provided the foregoing statement testified in the trials of the others. Pursuant to a grant of immunity, charges against him were dropped.

In late 2009, Girouard was paroled after having served two and-a-half years confinement. In April, 2011, his conviction for negligent homicide was set aside by the U.S. Court of Appeals for the Armed Forces because of the court-martial judge's sentencing error at Girouard's court-martial.[160] In January 2012, at Fort Campbell, Kentucky, Girouard was re-sentenced by a new court-martial panel (jury). Efforts to discover the new sentence have been unsuccessful. Having been paroled years before his negligent homicide conviction was set aside, however, Girouard would not have been returned to confinement. The issue would be whether or not his dishonorable discharge would be reduced to a less prejudicial discharge characterization.

[160]   70 MJ 5 (CAAF, April 2011).

10 Command Responsibility and *Respondeat Superior*

10.0 Introduction

Command responsibility, also referred to as "superior responsibility," is the other side of the obedience to orders coin. The soldier who obeys a manifestly unlawful order is culpable for any violation of the law of armed conflict (LOAC) resulting. The superior who gave the unlawful order is equally culpable for the subordinate's violation by reason of having given the unlawful order. In the past, it was viewed as a form of the crime of aiding and abetting.[1] No longer. Today, most authorities accept that "[command responsibility] does not mean ... that the superior shares the same responsibility as the subordinate who commits the crime ... but that the superior bears responsibility for his own omission in failing to act."[2] The superior is not responsible as an aider and abettor, but is responsible for his neglect of duty in regard to crimes that he knew were committed by his subordinates. "The superior's criminal responsibility flows from the neglect of a specific duty to take the measures that are necessary and reasonable in the given circumstances."[3]

Respondeat superior, "let the master answer," is a broader legal concept than command responsibility. In case law and in most LOAC/international humanitarian law (IHL) texts there is no distinction between command responsibility and *respondeat superior*, and the distinction is thematic rather than doctrinal. Command responsibility, as the term suggests, indicates the criminal liability a commander bears for illegal orders that he or she issues. *Respondeat superior* is the same concept applied when the commander is criminally responsible, but did not actually order the wrongful act done. *Respondeat superior* liability is based on accomplice theory; although there was no order, the commander is responsible because in one way or another he/she initiated or acquiesced in the wrongdoing, or took no corrective action upon learning of it. Prosecutors rarely make a command responsibility/*respondeat superior* distinction. In practice, *respondeat superior* versus command responsibility is a differentiation more pedagogical in nature than substantive.

---

[1] "Aiding means giving assistance to someone, whereas abetting involves facilitating the commission of an act by being sympathetic thereto, including providing mere exhortation or encouragement." Kriangsak Kittichaisaree, *International Criminal Law* (Oxford: Oxford University Press, 2001), 241, citing *Prosecutor v. Akayesu*, ICTR-96–4-T (Sept. 2, 1998), para. 484; and *Prosecutor v. Furundžija*, IT-95–17/1-T (Dec. 10 1998), para. 231.

[2] *Prosecutor v. Orić*, IT-03–68-T (June 30, 2006), para. 293.

[3] Chantal Meloni, "Command Responsibility," 5–3 *J. of Int'l Crim. Justice* (July 2007), 619, 628.

In militarily themed movies and television dramas, a subordinate often asks a superior, "Is that a direct order?" There are no *direct* orders or *indirect* orders. There are only orders: written or oral directives from a senior to a subordinate to do, or refrain from doing, some act related to a military duty. Although some directives can be communicated indirectly, or even in silence, such orders are not favored as bases for punitive action because of obvious problems of proof.

Both *respondeat superior* and superior orders have long histories as bases for, and defenses to, alleged violations of LOAC.

10.1 Command Responsibility and *Respondeat Superior*: A Brief History

"As early as 1439, Charles VII of Orleans . . . promulgated an Ordinance providing . . . the King orders that each captain or lieutenant be held responsible for the abuses, ills and offenses committed by members of his company. . . . If, because of his negligence or otherwise, the offender escapes and thus evades punishment, the captain shall be deemed responsible for the offense as if he had committed it himself."[4]

In the seventeenth century, Grotius wrote, "A community or its rulers may be held responsible for the crime of a subject if they knew of it and did not prevent it when they could and should prevent it."[5] Geoffrey Best points out, "If servicemen are to be brought to trial for carrying out unlawful and atrocious orders, do not logic and equity demand that their superiors must be brought to trial for issuing the same?"[6]

In 1779, during the American Revolution, the British lieutenant governor of Quebec, Henry Hamilton, was captured and tried for depredations committed by American Indians allied with the British. "It is noteworthy that the language of the indictment held that the acts of the Indians were the acts of Hamilton. He was considered personally liable for the acts of subordinates."[7]

In American military practice, Professor Best's thought, that logic demands that those issuing unlawful orders should also be held responsible for their execution, is reflected in the 1886 writings of the U.S. legal historian Colonel William Winthrop: "In the case of an act done [by an enlisted soldier] under an order admitting of question as to its legality or authority, the inferior who executed it will be more readily justified than the superior who originated the order."[8]

After the American Civil War, Major Henry Wirz was charged with thirteen counts of murder and conspiracy to maltreat prisoners. Despite his plea of superior orders, he was convicted and hanged. Wirz was convicted of murder for acts he had ordered – *respondeat superior* – as well as for acts he personally committed – direct responsibility.

After World War I, Article 227 of the Treaty of Versailles, ending the war, called for the prosecution of the most senior German officer, the former German emperor, William II, "for a supreme offense against international morality and the sanctity of treaties. A special

---

[4] Leslie C. Green, *Essays on the Modern Law of War*, 2d ed. (Ardsley, NY: Transnational, 1999), 283.

[5] Hugo Grotius, 2 *De Jure Belli ac Pacis Libri Tres* [*The Law of War and Peace*], bk. II, ch. XXI, sec. ii, Francis W. Kelsey trans. (1925), 138.

[6] Geoffrey Best, *War and Law since 1945* (Oxford: Oxford University Press, 1994), 190.

[7] George L. Coil, "War Crimes in the American Revolution," 82 *Mil. L. Rev.* (1978), 171, 197.

[8] Col. William Winthrop, *Military Law and Precedents*, 2d ed. (Washington, DC: GPO, 1920), 297, fn. 2. (Case citations omitted.)

tribunal will be constituted to try the accused."[9] Offenses against "international morality and the sanctity of treaties" are not war crimes and, although Kaiser Bill was granted sanctuary in Holland, beyond the jurisdictional reach of Allied tribunals, his case is one of the international community's earliest efforts to hold the superior responsible for, in this case, initiating war.

The post–World War I case against the German general Karl Stenger had a similarly unsatisfactory outcome. Tried at Leipzig before the German Supreme Court of the Reich, contrary to the evidence of involved subordinates, he was acquitted of ordering his soldiers to give no quarter and to shoot all prisoners of war.[10] "There can be no logical explanation for Stenger's acquittal"[11] (Chapter 3, Cases and Materials).

Shortly before World War II ended, the Japanese general Tomoyuki Yamashita surrendered to U.S. forces. In October 1945, in Manila, he was tried by a U.S. military commission of five general officers. Upon the October 1944 American invasion, in Manila, Japanese defenders murdered an estimated eight thousand civilians and raped nearly five hundred. Yamashita was charged with having "unlawfully disregarded and failed to discharge his duty as a commander to control the operations of ... his command, permitting them to commit brutal atrocities and other high crimes."[12] Yamashita's charges did not allege that he ordered, or even knew of, the crimes described in his charge sheet. It was a charge for which there was no precedent in U.S. military law.

On December 7, 1945, the military commission convicted Yamashita and sentenced him to hang. In its opinion, the commission wrote:

> The crimes were so extensive and widespread, both as to time and area, that they must either have been willfully permitted by the Accused, or secretly ordered by the Accused. ... Where murder and rape and vicious, revengeful actions are widespread offenses, and there is no effective attempt by a commander to discover and control the criminal acts, such a commander may be held ... criminally liable, for the lawless acts of his troops. ... The Commission concludes: ... that during the period in question you failed to provide effective control of your troops as was required by the circumstances.[13]

Yamashita stood convicted not of having committed war crimes. That would be a simple case of command responsibility. He was convicted on the basis of *respondeat superior*, of being responsible for the acts of his troops – not by ordering them, but through his failure to control their actions or stop their crimes; he *must* have known of their acts.

Lawyers and scholars will long argue about the quality of justice received by Yamashita. While much of the evidence admitted in his trial by military commission would not have been admissible in an American courtroom, Yamashita's was not a trial like that enjoyed by an accused in a U.S. civilian criminal trial. "Although the procedures used in the trial ... were deplorable and worthy of condemnation, there were sufficient facts

[9] 14 *AJIL* (1920) (Supp), 95.

[10] Claude Mullins, *The Leipzig Trials* (London: H. F. & G. Witherby, 1921), 151; George G. Battle, "The Trials before the Leipzig Supreme Court of Germans Accused of War Crimes," 8 *Va. L. Rev.* (1921), 1, 11.

[11] Col. Howard S. Levie, "Command Responsibility," 8 *USAF Academy J. of Legal Studies* (1997–8), 1, 3.

[12] Maj. Bruce D. Landrum, "The Yamashita War Crimes Trial: Command Responsibility Then and Now," 149 *Military L. Rev.* (1995), 293, 295.

[13] Maj. William H. Parks, "Command Responsibility for War Crimes," 62 *Military L. Rev.* (1973), 1, 30, quoting the military commission's written opinion. Also, Lt.Cmdr. Weston D. Burnett, "Command Responsibility and a Case Study of the Criminal Responsibility of Israeli Military Commanders for the Pogrom at Shatila and Sabra," 107 *Mil. L. Rev.* (1985), 71, 88.

given to enable the board which reviewed the record of trial to conclude [Yamashita was guilty] on the issue of command responsibility."[14]

Was Yamashita convicted on the basis of strict liability – convicted merely because of his status as commander, without a showing of fault on his part? If that were true, the prosecutor would not have to prove his guilt to gain a conviction, nor could the accused avoid conviction by showing that there was no culpability on his part. No, in Yamashita's case the prosecution argued and convinced the tribunal that he knew, or must have known, of the numerous and widespread atrocities committed by men under his command. Judging by the tribunal's opinion, he was not convicted simply because he was in command when the crimes occurred. For all the procedural and evidentiary questions the Yamashita case raises, and there are several, "Yamashita was no virtuous innocent wrongly convicted."[15]

Yamashita was hanged four months after his military commission first convened. His case turned on the <u>question of knowledge</u>. Did he know, or must he have known, of the crimes of soldiers and sailors under his command? The commission answered that he did know, or must have known, of his subordinates' crimes and took no action to stop or later punish them. This is *respondeat superior*. Hays Parks writes:

> Acceptance of command clearly imposes upon the commander a duty to supervise and control the conduct of his subordinates. . . . Equally clear, a commander who orders or directs the commission of war crimes shares the guilt of the actual perpetrators of the offense. This is true whether the order originates with that commander or is an order patently illegal passed from a higher command through the accused commander to his subordinates. . . . No less clear is the responsibility of the commander who incites others to act.[16]

The World War II Japanese general Masaharu Homma was also tried by a U.S. military commission. Homma was the commander in the Philippines at the time of the Bataan Death March.[17] During that infamous sixty-five-mile forced march, approximately two thousand American and eight thousand Filipino prisoners of war either were executed or died. Like Yamashita, Homma was found guilty of permitting members of his command to commit "brutal atrocities and other high crimes."[18] In his posttrial review of the Homma trial, General MacArthur wrote, "Isolated cases of rapine may well be exceptional but widespread and continuing abuse can only be a fixed responsibility of highest field authority. . . . To hold otherwise would prevaricate the fundamental nature of the command function. This imposes no new hazard on a commander. . . . He has always, and properly, been subject to due process of law . . . he still remains responsible before the bar of universal justice."[19] Although Homma's verdict was predicated on *respondeat superior*, MacArthur's review suggests that MacArthur applied a strict liability standard.

---

[14] Capt. Jordan J. Paust, "My Lai and Vietnam: Norms, Myths and Leader Responsibility," 57 *Military L. Rev.* (1972), 99, 181.

[15] Colonel Frederick Bernays Wiener, "Comment, *The Years of MacArthur.* Vol. III. MacArthur Unjustifiably Accused of Meting Out 'Victor's Justice' in War Crimes Cases," 113 *Military L. Rev.* (1986), 203, 206.

[16] Parks, "Command Responsibility," supra, note 13, at 77.

[17] Theater Staff Judge Advocate's Review of the Record of Trial by Military Commission of Gen. Masaharu Homma, March 5, 1946, at 1. On file with author.

[18] Id.   [19] Gen. of the Army Douglas MacArthur, *Reminiscences* (New York: McGraw-Hill, 1964), 298.

The significant difference between the two is that evidence in support of a finding of *respondeat superior* may be rebutted; a finding of strict liability cannot be rebutted.

There were many other post–World War II trials relating to a commander's responsibility. The Nazi general Kurt Meyer was convicted by a Canadian military commission of "inciting and counseling" soldiers under his command to murder prisoners of war, a case of *respondeat superior*.[20] The Nazi captain Erich Heyer instructed a prisoner escort of three prisoners of war not to interfere should the townspeople attempt to molest the prisoners. The townspeople subsequently beat to death the prisoners while the escort stood by. Heyer was sentenced to death for inciting the murders, a case of command responsibility.[21] The Japanese major general Shigeru Sawada was tried in Shanghai by a U.S. military commission for permitting the illegal trial and execution of three U.S. airmen. Although the trial occurred in Sawada's absence, he endorsed and forwarded the record. As the commander, he had ratified the illegal acts of subordinates and therefore was responsible for them – *respondeat superior*.[22]

These World War II era cases emphasize the commander's responsibility: Knowledge, actual or constructive, is required for a conviction based on either command responsibility or *respondeat superior*. The fact that the commander had no hand in the actual crime is immaterial. If she ordered the crime, incited the crime, acquiesced in the crime, ignored her own knowledge of the crime, closed her eyes to an awareness of the crime, passed on a patently unlawful order, or failed to control her troops who were committing war crimes, she may herself be found guilty of those crimes. This is a broad range of situations allowing a finding that a commander is guilty of LOAC/IHL violations committed by subordinates.

> **SIDEBAR.** On June 27, 1943, General George S. Patton spoke to the assembled officers and men of his 45th Infantry Division, just prior to their invasion of Sicily. In his remarks he said, "Attack rapidly, ruthlessly, viciously and without rest, and kill even civilians who have the stupidity to fight us."[23] According to court-martial defense lawyers and the court-martial testimony of numerous witnesses, including at least one colonel,[24] and confirmed by Major General (later General) Troy Middleton,[25] Patton also told his soldiers, "if the enemy resisted until we got to within 200 yards, he had forfeited his right to live."[26] In heavy fighting near Biscari, Italy, a few days later, Captain John C. Compton, of the 45th Infantry Division, formed "a firing party of about two dozen men,"[27] lined up forty-three captured Germans and Italians, and directed their execution. At roughly the same time, a sergeant of the 45th Infantry Division, Horace T. West,

---

[20] *Trial of S.S. Brigadeführer Kurt Meyer* ("The Abbaye Ardenne Case"), 1945. IV L.R.T.W.C. (London: HMSO, 1947), 97.

[21] *Trial of Erich Heyer, et al.* ("The Essen Lynching Case"), 1945. I L.R.T.W.C., 88.

[22] *Trial of Lieutenant-General Shigeru Sawada and Three Others*, 1946. V L.R.T.W.C., 1.

[23] Aubrey M. Daniel III, "The Defense of Superior Orders," 7–3 *U. Rich. L. Rev.* (Spring 1973), 477, 498–9.

[24] Review of Board of Review, *United States v. Sgt. Horace T. West* (Oct. 25, 1943), at 7. On file with author. Under World War II practice, a board of review was the final legal authority to pass on the legal sufficiency of a court-martial's findings and sentence.

[25] Frank J. Price, *Troy H. Middleton: A Biography* (Baton Rouge: Louisiana State University, 1974), 168–71.

[26] Ladislas Farago, *Patton: Ordeal and Triumph* (New York: Obolensky, 1964), 415.

[27] James J. Weingartner, "Massacre at Biscari: Patton and an American War Crime," LII(1), *Historian* (Nov. 1989), 24, 29.

> murdered by submachine gun fire thirty-seven German prisoners he was escorting to the rear. At their courts-martial, convened by General Patton, both Compton and West raised as their defense the "orders" issued by Patton in his June 27 speech.[28] The sergeant was convicted and sentenced to imprisonment for life; the captain was acquitted. A subsequent three-officer Washington-initiated inquiry into Patton's remarks exonerated the general.[29] (In a letter to his wife, General Patton wrote, "Some fair-haired boys are trying to say that I killed too many prisoners. . . . Well, the more I killed, the fewer men I lost, but they don't think of that.")[30] As General Eisenhower said of General Patton, "His emotional range was very great and he lived at either one end or the other of it."[31] The trials of Patton's two subordinates illustrate that it was not only postwar Nazi accused who exercised the defense of superior orders.

There were other postwar cases, however, that reveal a subtle legal distinction in the standard of "must have known."

Article 47 of the 1872 German Military Penal Code, in effect throughout World War II, reads, "If through the execution of an order pertaining to the service, a penal law is violated, then the superior giving the order is alone responsible. However, the obeying subordinate shall be punished as accomplice: (1) if he went beyond the order given, or (2) if he knew that the order of the superior concerned an act which aimed at a general or military crime or offense."[32] The Nazis, then, were well acquainted with the concept of command responsibility. Perhaps the most significant "subsequent proceeding" was that of "the High Command Case." In its 1948 judgment of the Nazi field marshals Wilhelm von Leeb, Georg von Kuechler, Hugo Sperrle, and ten other senior officers, the tribunal held that for criminal culpability to attach to a commander for the war crimes of subordinates, "it is not considered . . . that criminal responsibility attaches to him merely on the theory of subordination and over-all command. He must be shown both to have knowledge and to have been connected with such criminal acts, either by way of participation or criminal acquiescence."[33] There would be no assertions by the victorious Allies of strict liability. "It is also urged [by the prosecution] that the defendant must have known of the neglect of prisoners of war from seeing them upon the roads. This is a broad assumption."[34] The American prosecutors were urging the Yamashita "must have known" standard to find criminal responsibility in the Nazi commanders. But although the tribunal balked at imputing knowledge on the part of a commander merely on the basis that emaciated prisoners were visible on the roads, in another tribunal, "the Hostage Case,"[35] involving Field Marshal Wilhelm List, the judges made clear that neither can a commander plead ignorance of that which he is tasked with knowing:

[28] L. C. Green, *Superior Orders in National and International Law* (Leyden: Sijthoff, 1976), 131.
[29] Farago, *Patton*, supra, note 26, at 415–6.
[30] Martin Blumenson, *Patton Papers, 1940–1945* (Boston: Houghton Mifflin, 1972), 431.
[31] Dwight D. Eisenhower, *Crusade in Europe* (New York: Doubleday, 1948), 225.
[32] *U.S. v. von Leeb, et al.*, "The High Command Case" XI *T.W.C. Before the Nurnberg Military Tribunals under Control Council Law No. 10* (Washington, DC: GPO, 1950), 509.
[33] Id., 555.   [34] Id., 559.
[35] *U.S. v. List, et al.* ("The Hostage Case") XI *T.W.C. before the Nurnberg Military Tribunals under Control Council Law No. 10* (Washington, DC: GPO, 1950).

We have been confronted repeatedly with contentions that reports and orders sent to the defendants did not come to their attention. ... The German *Wermacht* was a well equipped, well trained, and well disciplined army. Its efficiency was demonstrated on repeated occasions throughout the war. ... They not only received their own information promptly but they appear to have secured that of the enemy as well. We are convinced that military information was received by these high ranking officers promptly. ... An army commander will not ordinarily be permitted to deny knowledge of reports received at his headquarters, they being sent there for his special benefit. Neither will he be ordinarily permitted to deny knowledge of happenings within the area of his command while he is present therein.[36]

Nevertheless, the von Leeb judges were willing to give commanders the benefit of the doubt on the issue of knowledge. "Noting that modern warfare is highly decentralized, this court held that a commander *cannot know* everything that happens within the command, so the prosecution must prove knowledge."[37]

In the cases of Field Marshals von Leeb and List, then, we see a distinction that separates the standard required for a commander's *respondeat superior* culpability for the acts of his subordinates. The concept was refined from a "must have known" standard (Yamashita) to a "should have known" standard (von Leeb and List). Nor was it a distinction without a difference. After von Leeb and List, a commander's knowledge of widespread atrocities constituting guilt under *respondeat superior* was rebuttably presumed (von Leeb and List) rather than irrebuttably presumed (Yamashita).

Did the von Leeb and List tribunals knowingly shade the standard articulated in the Yamashita case? History does not tell, but there is no reason to believe they did. Regardless, it is the shaded standard that the Western world has long followed. The 1956 U.S. Army Field Manual, *The Law of Land Warfare*, notes, "The commander is also responsible if he has actual knowledge, or should have knowledge, through reports received by him or through other means, that troops ... subject to his control are about to commit or have committed a war crime and he fails to take the necessary and reasonable steps to insure compliance with the law of war or to punish violators thereof."[38] Great Britain's standard for commanders is the same.[39]

10.1.1 My Lai and *Respondeat Superior*

How, then, to account for the acquittal of Captain Ernest L. Medina, U.S. Army, Lieutenant William L. Calley Jr.'s company commander at My Lai? According to the testimony of twenty-five members of Calley's platoon, on March 15, 1968, the day before

---

[36] Id., 1259–60.

[37] Landrum, "Yamashita War Crimes Trial," supra, note 12, at 299. Emphasis in original. The *von Leeb* judgment reads, "Modern war such as the last war entails a large measure of decentralization. A high commander cannot keep completely informed of the details of military operations of subordinates. ... He has the right to assume that details entrusted to responsible subordinates will be legally executed. ... There must be a personal dereliction." "High Command Case," supra, note 32, at 543.

[38] Dept. of the Army, FM 27–10, *The Law of Land Warfare* (Washington, DC: GPO, 1956), para. 501, at 178.

[39] U.K. Ministry of Defense, *The Manual of the Law of Armed Conflict* (Oxford: Oxford University Press, 2004), para. 16.36. "A commander will be criminally responsible if he participates in the commission of a war crime himself ... particularly if he orders its commission. However, he also becomes criminally responsible if he knew or, owing to the circumstances at the time, should have known that war crimes were being or were about to be committed."

the massacre at My Lai, Captain Medina briefed the company on the next day's operation. "He is quoted as having told his company to leave nothing living behind them and to take no prisoners."[40] (Not all who were present agreed that Medina made such an incriminating statement.) The next morning, 136-strong, Company C of the American Division's Task Force Barker was air-lifted to My Lai, anticipating a fight with a Viet Cong force. Instead, only civilians were there. The soldiers took no incoming fire all day. Poorly trained, weakly led, and ill disciplined, they began killing the unresisting noncombatants, raping and maiming many as they murdered approximately 350 Vietnamese. A precise number has never been fixed.

There being evidence that Medina had either ordered or incited the crimes at My Lai, or known of them and taken no subsequent action, he was tried before a general court-martial. Calley had already been convicted of murdering twenty-two civilians, far fewer than he actually killed.[41] (See Cases and Materials, Chapter 9, for an extract from Calley's appellate opinion.) At Medina's trial there was ambiguous evidence that Medina gave the inciting briefing and clear evidence that he was in fields adjacent to My Lai while his subordinates' heavy firing was going on. The prosecution urged that Medina knew, or should have known, of the massacre, but, in addition to inciting it, he took no action either to stop it or subsequently to bring to justice those who committed crimes. "Even if he did not personally commit any crimes in My Lai, Medina clearly failed to maintain control over men under his command who were committing scores of them."[42] Despite apparently meeting the von Leeb–List standard – knew or should have known – and, for that matter, the Yamashita standard – must have known – Medina was acquitted.[43] One civilian nonlawyer who viewed the trial found the case poorly prosecuted.[44] Another calls it "a striking example of the extent to which a domestic ... tribunal will devise a restricted formulation of the superior responsibility doctrine in order to avoid the prosecution of its own nationals."[45] But that ascribes a sinister motive to the court-martial that did not exist.

Captain Medina's acquittal notwithstanding, LOAC/IHL standard for a commander's responsibility has not changed. The problem of proof for Medina's prosecutors lies in the government's choice of Uniform Code of Military Justice (UCMJ) charges. Medina did not personally commit the war crime of murder in My Lai. However, in the *Manual for Courts-Martial*, which implements the UCMJ, there is no charge for negligence in the exercise of command, a charging route for commanders in some European military codes. Medina was charged as a principal – an aider and abettor to the murders committed by his subordinates.

---

[40] Michael Walzer, *Just and Unjust Wars*, 3d ed. (New York: Basic Books, 2000), 310.

[41] *U.S. v. Calley*, 48 CMR 19 (USCMA, 1973).

[42] Michael R. Belknap, *The Vietnam War on Trial* (Lawrence: University of Kansas Press), 2002, 68.

[43] *U.S. v. Medina*, C.M. 427162 (ACMR, 1971). Unreported acquittal.

[44] Mary McCarthy, *Medina* (New York: Harcourt Brace Jovanovich, 1972), 6–7: "It was the third of the My Lai 4 cases [the two judge advocates] had prosecuted, and the third they were going to lose, quite evidently. ... They appeared poorly prepared and were repeatedly taken by surprise by their own witnesses;" 58–9: "Why was [Medina] not tried for dereliction, misconduct, and misprision of a felony, as well as war crimes ... especially after he checked in at the [Col. Orin] Henderson court-martial and freely testified to having lied to Henderson, the Peers Panel, and the Army Inspector General's office."

[45] Emily Langston, "The Superior Responsibility Doctrine in International Law: Historical Continuities, Innovation and Criminality: Can East Timor's Special Panels Bring Militia Leaders to Justice?" 4–2 *Int'l Crim. L. Rev.* (2004), 141, 157.

Under the *Manual for Courts-Martial* in effect in 1969, for conviction as an aider and abettor the prosecution must prove the accused intended to aid or encourage the persons who committed the crime. "The aider and abettor must share the criminal intent or purpose of the perpetrator."[46] Newer editions of the *Manual for Courts-Martial* have not altered this requirement, which is a difficult standard for a prosecution to meet. Proving intent is often a vexing problem for prosecutors, civilian or military.

Compounding the prosecution's burden was the judge's instruction to the members (military jury). The prosecution asked that the members be instructed that proof of Medina's <u>actual</u> knowledge of Calley's acts was required for conviction. "Or should have known" was not included in the prosecution's requested instruction. Actual knowledge was not, and is not, an element of proof for aiding and abetting required by either the UCMJ or the *Manual for Courts-Martial*. Nor is it included in the military judge's guide to jury instructions, the *Benchbook*.[47] The prosecution's requested instruction was apparently based on the provision in *The Law of Land Warfare* that repeats the now-traditional von Leeb–List standard,[48] "The commander is also responsible if he has *actual* knowledge, or should have knowledge."[49] Needless to say, Medina's defense counsel, the prominent civilian lawyer F. Lee Bailey, did not object to the prosecution's proposed instruction. The members in Medina's case were instructed by Colonel Kenneth A. Howard, the military judge, in accordance with the prosecution's proposed instruction:

> As a general principle of military law and custom a military superior in command is responsible for and required, in the performance of his command duties, to make certain the proper performance by his subordinates of their duties as assigned by him. ... Furthermore, a commander is also responsible if he has *actual knowledge* that troops or other persons subject to his control are in the process of committing or are about to commit a war crime and he wrongfully fails to take the necessary and reasonable steps to insure compliance with the law of war. ... These legal requirements placed upon a commander require actual knowledge plus a wrongful failure to act. Thus mere presence at the scene will not suffice. That is, the commander-subordinate relationship alone will not allow an inference of knowledge.[50]

"Critics could argue that Howard's charge [to the jury] violated the army's own *Law of Land Warfare*, which authorized consideration of should have known logic."[51] Actual knowledge beyond a reasonable doubt was a high bar for the prosecutors to surmount, certainly more difficult than "knew or should have known." Although it is difficult to understand how an officer present at the location while the law of war breach is being

---

[46] *Manual for Courts-Martial United States*, 1969 (revised ed.), para. 156. Article 77 – Principals, at 28–4. In the discussion of Art. 77 applicable at the time of Medina's trial, the *Manual* notes that certain individuals, under some circumstances, have an affirmative duty to act if they witness a crime. Would not Medina have been such an individual?

[47] Dept. of the Army Pamphlet 27–9, *Military Judge's Benchbook* (Sept. 30, 1996), 151.

[48] Col. William G. Eckhardt, "Command Criminal Responsibility: A Plea for a Workable Standard," 97 *Military L. Rev.* (1982), 10, 18.

[49] FM 27–10, *Law of Land Warfare*, supra, note 38. Emphasis supplied.

[50] Judge's instructions, *U.S. v. Medina* (1971), Appellate Exhibit XCIII, quoted in: L. C. Green, *Essays on the Law of War*, 2d ed., supra, note 2, at 301. Emphasis supplied. Excerpts from the instructions are also found at Eckhardt, "Command Criminal Responsibility," supra, note 48, at 15.

[51] Richard L. Lael, *The Yamashita Precedent* (Wilmington, DE: Scholarly Resources, 1982), 132.

committed to the accompaniment of large volumes of semiautomatic and automatic weapons fire over a matter of hours would not know of the breach, actual knowledge proved an insurmountable bar. Medina was acquitted, an outcome that has rightly drawn considerable criticism.[52]

Medina was not acquitted because the commander's standard had changed, however. Because of the constraining language of the UCMJ – "must share the criminal intent or purpose" – and the prosecution-requested "actual knowledge" instruction, the von Leeb–List standard was not applied. Even if it had been, Medina might have been acquitted. "A panel may well have concluded that there was insufficient evidence to establish that Captain Medina 'knew or should have known' of the atrocities of My Lai."[53] The precedential value of the Medina case should be minimal, yet the same result could be obtained again because the UCMJ provision requiring that aiders and abettors share the "criminal intent or purpose" remains in today's *Manual for Courts-Martial*. That requirement is sufficient in straightforward obedience to orders cases in which a senior orders a subordinate to commit an offense, but the requirement is deficient in *respondeat superior* cases, in which the superior instead fails to control his troops, or fails to take action regarding war crimes of which he knows or should know.

The army's investigation of My Lai resulted in cover-up charges against eleven officers and war crime charges against four officers and nine enlisted soldiers.[54] Two officers, Captain Eugene Kotouc and 1st Lieutenant Thomas Willingham, were in both categories. None of the eleven cover-up cases involved obedience of unlawful orders or *respondeat superior*.

10.2 Recent Command Responsibility and *Respondeat Superior* Cases

The law of command responsibility and *respondeat superior* did not end with World War II, or with Vietnam's Medina acquittal.

In the 1990s, a reunited Germany struggled with the issue of command responsibility (and obedience to orders) through a series of more than three hundred divisive cases involving former East German military border guards who, on the orders of their military and civilian superiors, shot and killed Germans attempting to escape to West Germany over the Berlin Wall, in the 1970s and 1980s. In 1992, two junior border guards were convicted of killing two East Germans fleeing to the West. (An estimated six hundred were killed attempting to flee.) Told by the German court that "they had a duty to disobey the Communist government's . . . shoot-to-kill policy along the wall,"[55] they were

---

[52] E.g., R. S. Clark, "Medina: An Essay on the Principles of Criminal Liability for Homicide," 5 *Rutgers-Camden L. J.* (1975), 59, 72.

[53] Maj. Michael L. Smidt, "Yamashita, Medina, and Beyond: Command Responsibility in Contemporary Military Operations," 164 *Military L. Rev.* (June 2000), 155, 199.

[54] Lt.Gen. W. R. Peers, *The My Lai Inquiry* (New York: Norton, 1979), 214, 227. Of the twenty-two individuals charged, only six were court-martialed: Calley, Medina, Col. Oran Henderson, Capt. Eugene Kotouc, Sgt. David Mitchell, and Sgt. Charles Hutto. All were acquitted except Calley. Because of sentence reductions by senior officers and political appointees in President Nixon's administration, Calley spent four and a half months in confinement and two years and eleven months under house arrest in his on-base officers' quarters.

[55] Marc Fisher, "German Court Finds Guards Guilty of Death at Berlin Wall," *Int'l Herald Tribune*, Jan. 21, 1992.

sentenced to three and a half years and two years, respectively. The trials of more than fifty other border guards followed.

Then, former East German colonels and generals were tried and convicted. "The court held for the first time that … officers who issue an order to shoot must be held responsible for any resulting deaths. They will be judged the same as the perpetrator, not merely as the instigator."[56] The officers' sentences to years of imprisonment "contrasted with the greater leniency that has been shown toward many low-ranking border guards."[57]

Finally, senior political leaders were tried. Erich Honecker, the unrepentant eighty-year-old former leader of Communist East Germany for three decades, was tried for manslaughter. His prosecution ended in midtrial because he suffered from terminal cancer. He went into exile in Chile,[58] where he died sixteen months later. Other political leaders were tried, including Egon Krenz, East Germany's former security chief, who was sentenced to six and a half years' confinement for his role in issuing manifestly unlawful shoot-to-kill orders. In a 2001 judgment, the European Court of Human Rights unanimously held that the prosecutions of the leaders of the German Democratic Republic were not a violation of the principle of *nullum crimen sine lege*.[59] The border guard cases did not involve orders given and obeyed in armed conflict, but they illustrate the continuing international concern with obedience to orders and *respondeat superior*.

In 1997, in France, Maurice Papon, eighty-seven years old and the senior French authority in occupied France during World War II, was tried for orders he issued regarding the wartime deportation of French Jews. He was convicted and sentenced to ten years' confinement. In a 2001 case, in Rio de Janeiro a Brazilian police commander was sentenced to 638 years' confinement for ordering the shooting of prisoners, some of whom had surrendered, during a prison riot.[60] The trials of commanders continue today.

10.3 A Commander's Seven Routes to Trial

By the end of World War II and its war crimes trials, the outlines of command responsibility and *respondeat superior* and their variations were clear. Although some versions of command responsibility overlap somewhat with others, seven variations may be identified.

1 . First, **a commander is liable for LOAC/IHL violations that he personally commits**. Command and subordinate status plays no role in such cases. In Bosnia in 1993, Vladimir Santic was the commander of a Croatian military police company and commander of "the Jokers," a particularly brutal "special unit" of the Croatian military police. Among his numerous crimes, Santic personally participated in the murder of a Muslim non-combatant and the burning of his house. The International Criminal Tribunal for the Former Yugoslavia (ICTY) trial chamber found that Santic's "presence on the scene of the attack also served as an encouragement for your subordinates to abide by the

---

[56] A.P. "Ex-East German Retried, Held Guilty in Wall Death," *Int'l Herald Tribune*, March 6, 1996.

[57] Alan Cowell, "Germans Sentence Six Generals in Border Killings," *Int'l Herald Tribune*, Sept. 11, 1996.

[58] "The Honecker Bungle," *Wash. Post*, Feb. 1, 1993, A18.

[59] *Streletz, Kessler and Krenz v. Germany*, App. Nos. 34044/96, 35532/97, and 44801/98.49 ILM 811 (2001), reported at 95–4 *AJIL* (Oct. 2001), 904, 910.

[60] Anthony Faiola, "Brazilian Official Guilty in Massacre," *NY Times*, July 1, 2001, A17.

[manifestly illegal] orders they had received."[61] Found guilty of murder and multiple crimes against humanity, Santic was sentenced to twenty-five years' imprisonment.

A later ICTY case, *Lukić*, found an accused commander guilty of personally committing a variety of offenses, including sexual crimes, and murder, sentencing him to imprisonment for life.[62]

Lieutenant Calley was convicted by an army court-martial of the premeditated murder of twenty-two unarmed, unresisting South Vietnamese women, children, and old men in the village of My Lai-4. These murders were aside from the hundreds of similar murders committed by soldiers under Calley's command. For his personal acts at My Lai, Lieutenant Calley was sentenced by the military jury to dismissal from the army and confinement at hard labor for life.[63]

2. Second, on the basis of command responsibility, **a commander is responsible for LOAC/IHL violations that he orders a subordinate to commit**. In South Korea, in 1952, a Korean noncombatant caught inside a U.S. Air Force base without authorization was critically wounded during his apprehension by an enlisted air policeman. In deciding what action to take regarding the unconscious civilian prisoner, the lieutenant in charge directed the airman who had injured the Korean to "take him to the bomb dump and shoot him." "Is that an order?" the airman asked. "That's an order," the lieutenant replied. The airman murdered the injured Korean. In separate courts-martial, both the airman and the lieutenant were convicted of murder.[64] The lieutenant was sentenced to dismissal from the air force and confinement for life for the unlawful order he gave a subordinate.[65]

In 2007, the ICTY sentenced Dragomir Milošević, the chief of staff of the Sarajevo Romanija Corps of the Bosnian Serb Army, to thirty-three years' confinement for planning and ordering the shelling and sniping of civilians in Sarajevo with the intent to spread terror among the population, unlawful orders he gave to subordinates.[66]

3. Third, **a commander is responsible for disregarding LOAC/IHL violations of which he is aware, or should be aware, or for knowing of them and taking no action to punish those involved**. There must be information available to the commander that puts him or her on notice that there have been LOAC/IHL violations by a subordinate. "[The] reason to know standard does not require that actual knowledge, either explicit or circumstantial, be established. Nor does it require that the [ICTR Trial] Chamber be satisfied that the accused had 'some general information in his possession, which would put him on notice of possible unlawful acts by his subordinates.'"[67] That is the "should have known" standard.

In 1946, at a U.S. military commission held at Yokahama, Japan, it was charged that Yuicki Sakamoto "at prisoner-of-war camp Fukuoka 1, Fukuoka, Kyushu, Japan . . . failed to discharge his duty as Commanding Officer in that he permitted members of his command to commit cruel and brutal atrocities."[68] Found guilty, Sakamoto was sentenced to life imprisonment for the violations of which he was aware but took no action.

---

[61] *Prosecutor v. Kupreškić*, IT-95–16-T (Jan. 14, 2000), para. 827.

[62] *Prosecutor v. Milan Lukić and Sredoje Lukić*, IT-98-32/1-T (July 20, 2009), para. 907.

[63] U.S. *v. Calley*, supra, note 41.   [64] U.S. *v. Kinder*, 14 C.M.R. 742 (AFBR, 1954).

[65] U.S. *v. Schreiber*, 18 C.M.R. 226 (CMA, 1955).

[66] *Prosecutor v. Milošević*, IT-98–29/1-T (Dec. 12, 2007), para. 966.

[67] *Prosecutor v. Bagilishema*, ICTR-95–1A-A, Judgment (July 3, 2002), para. 28.

[68] Cited in: *Trial of General Tomoyuki Yamashita*, U.S. Military Commission, Manila, IV *LRTWC* 1 (London: U.N. War Crimes Commission, 1947), at 86.

In June 2008, in relation to the deaths of twenty-four Iraqi noncombatants at Haditha, Iraq, a U.S. Marine Corps lieutenant colonel and battalion commander was charged with having "willfully failed to direct a thorough investigation into [a] possible, suspected, or alleged violation of the law of war."[69] Because of perceived unlawful command influence, the charges, based on his failure to take action, were dismissed and the lieutenant colonel's case did not go to trial.

In late 2008, the ICTY convicted the commander of the main staff of the army of Bosnia-Herzegovina, Colonel Rasim Delić, of, inter alia, failure to take measures to punish subordinates known by him to have committed crimes against Serb prisoners. "[A] superior," the trial chamber held, "is bound to take active steps to ensure that the perpetrators of the crimes in question are brought to justice."[70]

In ICTY jurisprudence, the legal standard for a superior's "being aware," or "knowing," and justifying the superior's further inquiry was "sufficiently alarming information putting a superior on notice of the risk that crimes might subsequently be carried out by his subordinates and justifying further inquiry."[71]

In clarifying the standard, the tribunal's use of the word "superior" is significant because that term includes civilians who have command or control of military or paramilitary units. Thus, in 2010, the Belgrade Higher Court's War Crimes Department convicted two civilians, the mayor of Zvormik, Bosnia, and Herzegovina, and the local defense chief, of the imprisonment, inhumane treatment, and death of "around 700 Muslims," sentencing them to six and fifteen years' confinement, respectively.[72]

In ICTY jurisprudence, at least, if a commander fails to impose appropriate punitive action, in the form of either disciplinary action or a criminal proceeding such as a court-martial, or if the action is clearly not proportionate to the offense committed, the commander may be held responsible.[73] (See *Prosecutor v. Hadžihasanović*, Cases and Materials, this chapter.)

4. Fourth, **a commander is responsible for LOAC violations that he incites**. In late 1944, in Essen-West, Germany, the police handed three captured British airmen to the Nazi captain Eric Heyer. In front of a crowd of angry Germans, Heyer instructed his men to walk the prisoners to a nearby Luftwaffe interrogation unit, thus informing the crowd of the time and route of the prisoners. Heyer told his soldiers not to interfere with the crowd, should they molest the prisoners. On the route through town the crowd grew increasingly unruly. Stones were thrown at the fliers, and they were beaten with sticks. Finally, they were seized and thrown off a bridge, killing one of them. The other two were then beaten and shot to death by the crowd. The prosecutor argued that

> Heyer "lit the match." ... From the moment they left those barracks, the men were doomed and the crowd knew they were doomed and every person in that crowd who struck a blow was both morally and criminally responsible for the deaths of the three

[69] *U.S. v. Lt.Col. Jeffrey Chessani* (Camp Pendleton, CA, 2008). Unreported. See *Marine Corps Times*, June 30, 2008, 12; and http://www.usmc.mil/lapa/Iraq/Haditha/Haditha-Preferred-Charges-061221.htm

[70] *Prosecutor v. Delić*, IT-04-85-T (Sept. 15, 2008), para. 552. Delić's sentence to three years' confinement was affirmed by the appeals chamber.

[71] *Prosecutor v. Pavle Strugar*, IT-01-42-A, Appeals Judgment (July 17, 2008), para. 304.

[72] ICRC, "National Implementation of International Humanitarian Law," 93–181 *Int'l Rev. of the Red Cross* 227 (March 2011), 235.

[73] *Prosecutor v. Hadžihasanović*, IT-01-47-T (March 15, 2006), paras. 1770–80.

men. Hauptmann Heyer admittedly never struck any physical blow … [but] an instigator may be regarded as a principal. … Although the person who incited was not present when the crime was committed, he was triable and punishable as a principal. [74]

Heyer was convicted and sentenced to hang.

5.   Fifth, **a commander is responsible for violations committed by his troops whom he fails to control**. This was the charge of which General Yamashita was convicted in 1945. The theater judge advocate reviewing Yamashita's record of trial, citing Article 1.1 of 1907 Hague Regulation IV ("To be commanded by a person responsible for his subordinates"), wrote, "The doctrine that it is the duty of a commander to control his troops is as old as military organization itself and the failure to discharge such duty has long been regarded as a violation of the Laws of War."[75]

6.   Sixth, **a commander is responsible for the violations committed by his subordinates that he permits or acquiesces in**. In 1942, Major General Shigeru Sawada was the commanding general of the Japanese Imperial 13th Expeditionary Army in China. Eight Doolittle raiders were captured by his troops after their thirty seconds over Tokyo (and, in some cases, Nagoya, Kobe, and Osaka). While Sawada was visiting the front, three hundred miles from his Shanghai headquarters, the eight U.S. Army fliers were court-martialed. In a two-hour "trial," the Americans were not allowed to enter a plea, and there were no defense counsel, no witnesses, and no evidence offered. All eight were found guilty and sentenced to death. Tokyo confirmed three of the death sentences and, without explanation, ordered that five be commuted to life imprisonment. Three weeks after the court-martial, General Sawada returned to his headquarters, where he was given the record of the trial to review. Sawada put his chop on the record, then went to Nanking, where he protested to the commanding general of China Forces that the death sentences were too severe. Imperial headquarters trumped officers in the field, however, and the three Americans were executed. At a 1946 U.S. military commission, General Sawada was convicted of "knowingly, unlawfully and willfully and by his official acts cause eight named members of the United States forces to be denied the status of Prisoners of War and to be tried and sentenced … in violation of the laws and customs of war … thereby causing the unlawful death of four of the fliers."[76] General Sawada was sentenced to be confined for five years.

In the 1948 Hostages Trial, a subsequent proceeding at Nuremberg, a U.S. tribunal tried twelve senior Nazi officers, including two field marshals. The tribunal's judgment held, "We agree that … commanders are responsible for ordering the commission of criminal acts. But the superior commander is also responsible if he orders, permits, or acquiesces in such criminal conduct."[77]

In 1991, in the dissolution of the former Yugoslavia, the prosecution was unable to prove that the Yugoslav lieutenant general Pavle Strugar ordered the bombing of the

---

[74] *Trial of Erich Heyer and Six Others*, "The Essen Lynching Case," British Military Court (Dec. 1945), I *LRTWC* 88, 89–90.

[75] "Review of the Record of Trial by a Military Commission of Tomoyuki Yamashita, General, Imperial Japanese Army," Dec. 26, 1945, n.p. On file with author.

[76] U.N. War Crimes Commission, *Law Reports of Trials of War Criminals*. Vol. V. *Trial of Lieutenant-General Sawada and Three Others*, supra, note 22, at 1.

[77] *U.S. v. List* ("The Hostage Case"), supra, note 35, at 1298.

Croatian port of Dubrovnik, in which a number of noncombatants were killed and wounded and civilian cultural objects were destroyed. It did prove that he failed to stop it when he could have done so. He was convicted on the basis of command responsibility and sentenced to eight years' imprisonment.[78]

7. Seventh, **an officer may be responsible for violations committed by subordinates pursuant to manifestly illegal orders that he passes on to those subordinates**. The least clear and least exercised route to criminal liability, it is nevertheless a long-observed basis of command responsibility. "When subordinates are confronted with potentially illegitimate orders from their superiors ... judgments of responsibility become complex, both for subordinates themselves and for outside observers."[79] In the 1945 *Jaluit Atoll* case, Rear Admiral Nisuke Masuda issued an order to execute summarily three captured American aviators who were in the custody of the Japanese navy lieutenant Yoshimura. The prisoners were handed over to their executioners by Ensign Tasaki, who repeated the admiral's order. Lieutenant Yoshimura and three warrant officers carried out the unlawful order by shooting and stabbing to death the aviators. Yoshimura and the warrant officers were convicted of murder by a U.S. military commission and sentenced to death by hanging. Ensign Tasaki, who did not participate in the executions but passed on the admiral's patently unlawful order, was sentenced to ten years' confinement, his punishment lighter than the others because of his "brief, passive and mechanical participation."[80]

In the *Hostage* case, the tribunal was reluctant to hold Generalmajor Kurt von Geitner, a chief of staff of major Nazi units throughout the war, criminally liable for numerous illegal orders he passed on because he had no command authority. He was acquitted although, by standards that are clearer today than in 1948, there was a basis for his conviction.[81] At the Tokyo International Military Tribunal, Lieutenant General Akira Mutō, chief of staff to General Yamashita, who also had no direct command authority, was held liable on the basis of command responsibility.[82]

Liability for passing on unlawful orders expands the concept of *respondeat superior* to staff officers and other subordinate officers in the chain of command who, as in Ensign Tasaki's case, are between the commander who issues the unlawful order and the subordinate who carries it out, for example, staff officers, in the case of a battalion operations officer who is told to contact all company commanders in the battalion and advise them that rations are critically short and all prisoners must be "disposed of" so the battalion will have sufficient rations to carry on with the mission. In passing that unlawful order down the chain, the operations officer becomes a principal to the crime of the commander who issued it.

There are limits to liability on the basis of passing on unlawful orders. The tribunal noted in the High Command case:

> Orders are the basis upon which any army operates. It is basic to the discipline of an army that orders are issued to be carried out. Its discipline is built upon this principle.

---

[78] *Prosecutor v. Strugar*, IT-01–42-T, trial judgment (Jan. 31, 2005).

[79] Herbert C. Kelman and V. Lee Hamilton, *Crimes of Obedience* (New Haven, CT: Yale University Press, 1989), 209.

[80] *Trial of Rear-Admiral Nisuke Masuda and Four Others of the Imperial Japanese Navy* ("The Jaluit Atoll Case"), U.S. Military Commission, Kwajalein Island, Marshall Islands (Dec. 1945), I *LRTWC* 71–80, at 76.

[81] *U.S. v. List* ("The Hostage Case"), supra, note 35, at 1319.

[82] Neil Boister and Robert Cryer, *The Tokyo International Military Tribunal: A Reappraisal* (New York: Oxford University Press, 2008), 304.

Without it, no army can be effective and it is certainly not incumbent upon a soldier in a subordinate position to screen the orders of superiors for questionable points of legality. Within certain limitations, he has the right to assume that the orders of his superiors and the state which he serves and which are issued to him are in conformity with international law.[83]

Does the totality of these "routes to trial" mean that a commander is responsible for all that happens or fails to happen on her watch? If a soldier attached to a U.N. peacekeeping mission kidnaps, rapes, and murders an eleven-year-old girl, is his lieutenant responsible? No. The lieutenant did not know and, absent a preact announcement by the soldier, had no way of knowing the criminal intent of his subordinate. The lieutenant could not have reasonably foreseen the criminal act intended and could not be expected to have acted to prevent the subordinate's unforeseeable criminal acts. In such a case, the soldier, alone, is criminally liable for his misconduct. *Respondeat superior* is a broad concept, but its reach is not unreasonable. "It must be accentuated that command responsibility is all about dereliction of duty. The commander is held accountable for his own act (of omission), rather than incurring 'vicarious liability' for the acts ... of the subordinates."[84]

During the United States–Vietnam War, the My Lai killings and many other grave breaches were perpetrated during General William Westmoreland's watch. He was the four-star commander of the Military Assistance Command, Vietnam, with authority over all U.S. military personnel in South Vietnam. Could he have been charged with being a war criminal because of the grave breaches committed while he was in command, similarly to General Yamashita? By no means. General Westmoreland went to great lengths to see that orders were regularly published forbidding acts constituting war crimes. His written orders were republished on a regular basis, reminding members of all the armed forces under his command not to become involved in war crimes and that it was an offense not to report such crimes, known or suspected. When he learned of violations, they were prosecuted at court-martial. That is not to say that all Vietnam War crimes were discovered, or were in some cases adequately punished. But General Westmoreland did all that could be done within his authority to prevent, suppress, and punish war crimes. LOAC asks no more of a commander.

"This principle [of command responsibility] is also applicable to civilian non-military commanders.... International instruments and case law do not restrict its application to military commanders only but extend it to cover political leaders and other civilian superiors in positions of authority."[85] The International Criminal Tribunal for Rwanda (ICTR) has held, "The crucial question ... was not the civilian status of the accused, but the degree of authority he exercised over his subordinates. Accordingly, the Chamber accepts the submission made by the Prosecution that a civilian in a position of authority may be liable under the doctrine of command responsibility."[86]

---

[83] *U.S. v. von Leeb*, "High Command Case," supra, note 32, at 510–1.

[84] Yoram Dinstein, *The Conduct of Hostilities under the Law of International Armed Conflict* (Cambridge: Cambridge University Press, 2004), 238.

[85] Kittichaisaree, *International Criminal Law*, supra, note 1, at 251.

[86] *Prosecutor v. Kayishema & Ruzindana*, ICTR-95-1-T (May 21, 1999), para. 216. To the same effect, several ICTY cases, including *Prosecutor v. Aleksovski*, IT-95-14/1-A (March 24, 2000), paras. 118–9, 133–7.

Commanders, be they military or civilian, trained and experienced as they are, rarely need worry about the consequences of their orders because rarely are they of questionable lawfulness. When manifestly unlawful orders are issued, however, the leader risking his career and honor for a perceived *jus in bello* gain will discover the breadth of LOAC/IHL's road to trial.

10.4 When Officers Disobey

Officers are no less subject to the requirements of LOAC/IHL obedience – and penalties for disobedience – than are enlisted service members. In his classic work *The Soldier and the State*, Samuel Huntington notes that obedience to lawful orders is the soldier's paramount duty. "For the profession to perform its function, each level within it must be able to command the instantaneous and loyal obedience of subordinate levels."[87] What if a military officer receives an order that he or she believes to be unlawful but is expected to lead in executing? Just as an enlisted soldier, he or she must approach the issuing officer for clarification and, if remaining convinced of its unlawfulness, refuse to obey or to require subordinates to obey, and report the unlawful order to a senior officer. Particularly for officers, problems occasionally arise if the order is not manifestly unlawful on its face, but the officer believes it clearly to be an immoral but not necessarily unlawful order.

During World War II, in August 1944, nine months before Germany's surrender ended the war in Europe, Henri Salmide, a German navy petty officer and explosives expert, was ordered to destroy the extensive port facilities and docks of Bordeaux, France. "I could not accept that the port of Bordeaux be wantonly destroyed when the war was clearly lost."[88] Instead, he blew up the bunker where thousands of pounds of explosive ordnance, intended for Bordeaux's port facilities, were stored.

Sixty years later, in 2005, a major in Germany's Bundeswehr, the Federal Armed Forces, refused to participate in a military software project that he believed would be used in support of U.S. combat operations in Iraq. He based his refusal on his belief that the conflict was itself illegal. Because he was the commander of the information technology project, his disobedience was significant. Months before his refusal he had contacted an army chaplain and his superior officer about his moral reservations about the project, the conflict, and Germany's involvement. Without assurances that his project would not be used in the war, the major would not continue working on it. Assurances were not given, and he was relieved and charged with disobedience. At court-martial, the major was convicted of insubordination and demoted to the grade of captain. On appeal, however, the civilian Federal Administrative Court of Germany (FCA) reversed the military court and upheld the major's position that he did not act unlawfully in refusing to obey the order.

The FCA found it a fundamental right under Germany's Basic Law to disobey certain orders. Using the case as a platform to examine the larger issue of the legality of the United States–Iraq conflict, the FCA made an assessment of the conflict in terms of

---

[87] Samuel P. Huntington, *The Soldier and the State* (Cambridge, MA: Belknap Press of Harvard University, 1957), 73.

[88] Maïa de la Baume, "Henri Salmide, 90, Dies; German's Defiance Saved a French Port," *NY Times*, March 7, 2010, A31.

German military law, domestic law, and the U.N. charter. It "concluded that the soldier was right in his considerable doubts about the legality of the war against Iraq."[89] The German major's case notwithstanding, American officers, at least, are well advised not to "try this at home."

Given a similar case, the American court-martial system, even with its five-civilian-member appellate Court of Appeals of the Armed Forces (CAAF), is unlikely to reach a similar result. In September 1994, a U.S. Army captain, Lawrence P. Rockwood, a Tibetan Buddhist, was deployed to Haiti as part of a U.N. multinational force. He became increasingly disturbed by intelligence reports that, he believed, reflected deplorable conditions in the Haitian National Penitentiary, in Port au Prince. After unsuccessful efforts to engage his unit in efforts to inspect the prison, and after repeated confrontations with his commanding officer about the matter, including orders by the commander directing him to take no action, Captain Rockwood acted on his own. He went to the prison and, with a loaded M-16 rifle, demanded to be allowed to inspect the building. Put off until U.S. authorities could arrive and take him into custody, Captain Rockwood was court-martialed. Contrary to his pleas of not guilty, he was convicted at court-martial of a variety of offenses, including disobedience and conduct unbecoming an officer. On appeal, CAAF, the highest appellate court in the military system, exhibited little sympathy. "Appellant cites us to no legal authority – international or domestic, military or civil – that suggests he had a 'duty' to abandon his post ... and strike out on his own to 'inspect' the penitentiary. Neither does he suggest any provision of any treaty, charter, or resolution as authority for the proposition."[90] CAAF affirmed Captain Rockwood's sentence of dismissal from the army and forfeiture of fifteen hundred dollars pay per month for two months.

Over the years, the Israeli Defense Force has seen many refusals of officers and enlisted personnel to obey orders on the basis of conscience. In 2007, twelve Israeli officers and enlisted men refused to evacuate by force Jewish settlers who had moved to the West Bank city of Hebron without permission. The soldiers were court-martialed.[91] In 2005, hundreds of Israeli soldiers signed declarations that on religious grounds they would refuse to serve if ordered to dismantle Israeli settlements in the Gaza Strip and the West Bank.[92] Many were court-martialed. In 2003, twenty-seven Israeli Air Force pilots, including a brigadier general who had participated in the 1981 Osirak raid (Cases and Materials, Chapter 5), signed a petition vowing that they would not take part in "illegal and immoral" air strikes in Palestinian areas of the West Bank and Gaza Strip. Their commanding officer said, "An officer who decides which mission he will perform and which he will not is in my view an officer morally unfit to command."[93] In 1982, a colonel commanding an armored brigade demanded to be relieved because of his moral objections to the Israeli campaign in West Beirut.[94]

---

[89] Ilja Baudisch, "International Decisions," 100–4 AJIL (Oct. 2006), 911, 913, discussing *Germany v. N*, Decision No. 2 WD 12.04., Bundesverwaltungsgericht (German Federal Administrative Court), June 21, 2005, http://www.bverwg.de

[90] *U.S. v. Rockwood*, 52 MJ 98, 112 (CAAF, Sept. 1999).

[91] Ilene R. Prusher, "Soldiers' Refusal to Heed West Bank Evacuation Orders Roils Israel," *Christian Science Monitor*, Aug. 8, 2007, 1.

[92] Haim Watzman, "At War with Themselves," *NY Times*, May 20, 2005, A25.

[93] Greg Myre, "27 Israeli Reserve Pilots Say They Refuse to Bomb Civilians, *NY Times*, Sept. 25, 2003, A12.

[94] Kelman and Hamilton, *Crimes of Obedience*, supra, note 79, at 75fn.

In the 2014 Israeli-Hamas conflict in the Gaza Strip, twenty-one hundred Palestinians, most of them civilians, were reportedly killed. In 2015, "more than 60 enlisted men and officers who served in Gaza during Operation Protective Edge ... called the rules of engagement in the offensive ... an 'ethical failure ... from the top of the chain of command.'"[95] The group's 240-page report included anonymous testimony that could not be independently verified.

The Israeli Defense Force has consistently responded to refusals of orders by officers with courts-martial.

On the other hand, one wonders why so many World War II enemy officers did obey. A few senior German officers, including Field Marshals Erwin Rommel and Georg von Kuechler, refused to obey Hitler's commando order directing the summary execution of captured Allied soldiers.[96] Generalleutnant Karl-Wilhelm von Schlieben reportedly disobeyed Hitler's 1944 order to destroy the French port of Cherbourg.[97] "There is reason to suspect that officially recorded history has captured only a small subset of all such incidents [of disobedience],"[98] yet the great preponderance of Nazi officers did obey multiple manifestly unlawful orders.

Guenter Lewy writes, "The principle of unconditional obedience and of complete freedom from responsibility for superior orders has all but disappeared today."[99] All but disappeared, perhaps, but not disappeared completely, and certainly not for officers. In the case of manifestly unlawful orders an officer's duty is clear. Moral issues raised by superior orders are a murkier topic. An objecting officer "must not be obstinate, must give way in marginal controversies, and persist in his case only where his conscientious conviction is fundamentally involved."[100] Even "conscientious conviction" is highly risky. Officers, as well as enlisted personnel, must be wary of looking behind superior orders and hesitant to conclude that a commander's order is manifestly unlawful because it is contrary to a particular subordinate's moral holding. Personal morality and personal political viewpoints can be misread as something more, leading to serious results. Article 90 of the UCMJ prohibits disobeying a superior commissioned officer. The *Manual for Courts-Martial*, in its discussion of Article 90 and the lawfulness of orders, counsels, "An order ... may be inferred to be lawful and it is disobeyed at the peril of the subordinate."[101] This admonition applies to officers as well as enlisted personnel.

---

[95] William Booth, "Israeli Soldiers Allege 'Ethical Failure' in Gaza," NY *Times*, May 5, 2015, A7.

[96] Paul Christopher, *The Ethics of War and Peace*, 2d ed. (Upper Saddle River, NJ: Prentice Hall, 1999), 143. In his memoirs, Rommel wrote, "We had continually to circumvent orders from the Fuehrer or Duce in order to save the army from destruction." Erwin Rommel, B. H. Liddell Hart, ed., *The Rommel Papers* (London: Collins, 1953), 321. Rommel was forced to commit suicide for his involvement with anti-Hitler officers. After the war, Von Kuechler was sentenced to twenty years' imprisonment by a U.S. tribunal at Nuremberg.

[97] Martin van Creveld, *The Transformation of War* (New York: Free Press, 1991), 89.

[98] Mark J. Osiel, *Obeying Orders* (New Brunswick, NJ: Transaction, 1999), 313.

[99] Guenter Lewy, "Superior Orders, Nuclear Warfare, and Conscience," in Richard Wasserstrom, ed., *War and Morality* (Belmont, CA: Wadsworth Publishing, 1970), 124.

[100] Nico Keïjzer, *Military Obedience* (The Netherlands: Sijthoff & Noordhoff, 1978), 279.

[101] *Manual for Courts-Martial, United States* (2008 Edition), at IV-19.

10.5 Command Responsibility and *Respondeat Superior* Today

Today, command responsibility and *respondeat superior* have a wider scope than sixty years ago when the concepts were articulated in the *Yamashita* tribunal decision. As much of LOAC/IHL does, the "knew or should have known" standard continues to evolve. Today, for those countries that have ratified it, it is reflected in Additional Protocol I, which addresses *respondeat superior*: Article 86.1 covers LOAC breaches resulting from a commander's inaction following breaches, and Article 86.2 addresses the responsibility of commanders who do not take measures to prevent foreseeable violations or take action regarding violations already committed by subordinates:

> The fact that a breach of the Conventions or this Protocol was committed by a subordinate does not absolve his superiors from penal or disciplinary responsibility ... if they knew, or had information which should have enabled them to conclude in the circumstances at that time, that he was committing or was going to commit such a breach and if they did not take all feasible measures within their power to prevent or repress the breach.[102]

Article 86.2 deals with a commander's *failure* to act. "The responsibility of those who have refrained from taking the requisite measures to prevent or repress [war crimes], has been dealt with explicitly only since the end of the First World War."[103] Although the article speaks only of "breaches," the term encompasses grave breaches, as well.[104] To establish a commander's legal responsibility it must be established that the commander or civilian superior knew or had reason to know there was, or was about to be, a violation, he failed to act when he had a duty to do so, and there was a direct link between the superior and the offending subordinate. "Only that superior is normally in the position of having information enabling him to conclude in the circumstances at the time that the subordinate has committed or is going to commit a breach."[105] A difficulty with "this provision perhaps consists in the difficulty of establishing intent (*mens rea*) in case of a failure to act, particularly in the case of negligence."[106] "Every case of negligence, however, is not necessarily criminal. It appears that the drafters of the Additional Protocol intended a *mens rea* that approached recklessness or willful blindness, rather than mere negligence. The drafters wanted to ensure that a superior who 'deliberately wishes to remain ignorant' would not avoid criminal liability."[107] Deliberate ignorance is a continuing concern in *respondeat superior* cases.

> What is the position if the superior concerned persists in maintaining that he was not aware of the breaches committed or of information enabling him to conclude that they had been committed or were going to be committed, and if no proof can be furnished to the contrary? It is not possible to answer this question in the abstract. ... It is not impossible for a superior actually to be ignorant of breaches committed by his subordinates because he deliberately wishes to remain ignorant.[108]

---

[102] 1977 Additional Protocol I, Art. 86.2.

[103] Yves Sandoz, Christophe Swinarski, and Bruno Zimmerman, eds., *Commentary on the Additional Protocols* (Geneva: ICRC/Martinus Nijhoff, 1987), para. 3530, at 1007.

[104] Id., para. 3541, at 1010–11.		[105] Id., para. 3544, at 1013.		[106] Id., para. 3530, at 1007.

[107] Arthur T. O'Reilly, "Command Responsibility: A Call to Realign Doctrine with Principles," 20–1 *Am. U. Int'l L. Rev.* (2004), 71, 80.

[108] Sandoz, Swinarski, and Zimmerman, *Commentary on the Additional Protocols*, supra, note 103, para. 3546, at 1014.

In such cases it becomes a matter of proof for the prosecution, involving the particular circumstances, the location of the commander, his statements to others or their lack, the state of his communications, whether the subordinate was a member of the commander's unit or of an attached unit, the repetitive or singular nature of the breach, and so forth. These are essentially the issues of fact employed by the *Yamashita* tribunal prosecutors. Article 82, requiring legal advisers on the staffs of military commanders to advise them on the application of LOAC, makes it even more difficult for commanders to plead ignorance or oversight.

Article 87.1 of Protocol I is the reciprocal of Article 86.2, and the two provisions should be read together. Article 87.1 addresses the commander's duty to *take* action: "The High Contracting Parties and the Parties to the conflict shall require military commanders, with respect to members of the armed forces under their command ... to prevent and, where necessary, to suppress and report ... breaches of the Conventions and of this Protocol."

Who is a "commander"? For purposes of this article, "commander" is intended "to refer to all those persons who had command responsibility, from commanders at the highest level to leaders with only a few men under their command'. This is quite clear. ... As there is no part of the army which is not subordinated to a military commander at whatever level, this responsibility applies from the highest to the lowest level of the hierarchy, from the Commander-in-Chief down to the common soldier."[109] The article enumerates several duties: to prevent breaches, to suppress or minimize them when they have been committed, and to report violations.

In identical terms, Article 7.3 of the statute of the ICTY and Article 6.3 of the ICTR recite the von Leeb–List standard: "Individual Criminal Responsibility: The fact that any of the acts referred to in ... the present Statute was committed by a subordinate does not relieve his or her superior of criminal responsibility if he or she knew or had reason to know that the subordinate was about to commit such acts or had done so and the superior failed to take the necessary and reasonable measures to prevent such acts or to punish the perpetrators thereof."[110]

The command responsibility provision of the statute of the International Criminal Court (ICC), Article 28, although generally maintaining the von Leeb–List standard, is more detailed than the ICTY and ICTR provisions, reducing the vagaries of judicial interpretation. For the first time, in ICC practice command responsibility is applicable to civilian superiors (the "person effectively acting as a military commander"), as well as military commanders, and the rules for the two are slightly different.

> In order to incur liability, a ~~military commander~~ must know or "should have known", whilst a civilian superior must either have known or "consciously disregarded information which clearly indicated" that subordinates were committing or about to commit crimes. The military commander can be prosecuted for what amounts to negligence ("should have known"). Guilt of a civilian superior ... however, must

---

[109] Id., at 1019.

[110] *Prosecutor v. Nahimana, et al.*, ICTR-99–52-A (Nov. 28, 2007), para. 625, taking a minority view, suggests otherwise. It holds that, while de jure authority implies the ability to prevent or punish, de jure authority "is neither necessary nor sufficient to prove effective control."

meet a higher standard. It is necessary to establish that the civilian superior had actual or "constructive" knowledge of the crimes being committed.[111]

To establish the civilian superior's requisite *mens rea* it must be shown not only that he or she had information regarding the unlawful acts of subordinates, but that the civilian superior consciously disregarded that information.[112] This is a somewhat higher standard than is required for military superiors.

The ICC military commander's standard is more confining than that of Protocol I. Protocol I, Article 86.2, enables the charging of commanders "if they knew, or had information which would have enabled them to conclude" that a violation was committed. The ICC's Article 28 (a)(i), in contrast, enables charging if the commander "knew or, owing to the circumstances at the time, should have known" of violations. The ICC formulation, "owing to the circumstances," is broader than "or had information." A military commander might argue that she did not objectively "know" of violations, the protocol term, but she might be unable to argue convincingly that "owing to circumstances," the ICC term, she was unaware. Future cases will reveal whether conviction or acquittal will turn on such a fine point.

What is clear are the three conditions that customary international law requires to be proven for a conviction based on command or superior responsibility based upon an Additional Protocol, Article 86, failure to act.[113] The necessary conditions are established in ICTY jurisprudence and will likely be followed in ICC litigation. They are, first, the existence of a superior–subordinate relationship between the commander (military) or superior (civilian) and the accused individuals;[114] second, that the commander or superior knew or had reason to know that the subordinate had committed a violation or was about to do so;[115] and third, that the superior failed to take necessary and reasonable steps to prevent the violation or to punish the offender.[116] Absence of proof of any one condition is sufficient for acquittal.[117]

Mixed tribunals ("internationalized domestic tribunals"), established by the U.N. in East Timor and Sierra Leone, also have jurisdiction over war crimes. Their regulations contain provisions allowing for prosecution on the basis of command responsibility/*respondeat superior* doctrine that mirrors the traditional von Leeb–List standard.[118]

---

[111] William A. Schabas, *An Introduction to the International Criminal Court* (Cambridge: Cambridge University Press, 2001), 85.

[112] ICRC, "National Implementation of International Humanitarian Law," supra, note 72, is such a case. Branko Grujic, the mayor of Zvornik, Bosnia and Herzegovina, knew of the murder, by others, of 352 Muslim prisoners and failed to act to prevent their deaths. Although Grujic had no part in their killing, he was sentenced to six years' confinement for his conscious disregard of the information.

[113] Sandoz, Swinarski, and Zimmerman, *Commentary on the Additional Protocols*, supra, note 103, para. 3543, at 1012–13, specifies these three requirements.

[114] *Prosecutor v Delalić* (aka *Mucić/* aka "Čelebici"), IT-96–21-A (Feb. 20, 2001), paras. 189–98, 225–6, 238–9, 256, and 263; *Prosecutor v. Aleksovski*, supra, note 86, at paras. 72, 76.

[115] *Delalić*, id., at paras. 196–7.

[116] Id., at para. 226; *Prosecutor v. Krnojelac*, IT-97–25-T (March 15, 2002), para. 95.

[117] For an excellent review of ICTY case law on the three conditions, see Guénaël Mettraux, *International Crimes and the Ad Hoc Tribunals* (Oxford: Oxford University Press, 2005), 298–310.

[118] Suzannah Linton, "New Approaches to International Justice in Cambodia and East Timor," 845 *Int'l Rev. of the Red Cross* (2002), 93–119.

Various states have also enacted domestic versions of command responsibility/*respondeat superior* laws, most of them more or less approximating the traditional standard.[119] Civil cases in domestic U.S. courts have been decided on the basis of command responsibility, as well.[120]

10.5.1 *Recent Evolutionary Changes*

In command responsibility and *respondeat superior* cases, the most troublesome issue has always been the commander's state of mind – his <u>mens rea,</u> or guilty mind, or its absence. Did the commander know of his troops' violations, or was he unaware? Was he willfully unaware, or did he honestly not know of his subordinates' bad acts? After World War II, there was criticism that some tribunals, particularly the *Yamashita* tribunal, employed an overly broad interpretation of mens rea to find a former enemy commander criminally liable. No less a personage than Brigadier General Telford Taylor, Nuremburg International Military Tribunal chief prosecutor, compared war crime prosecutions in the European theater, with their inconsistent results, to prosecutions in the Pacific. Taylor wrote:

> American Regular Army attitudes toward their defeated German compeers were remarkably inconsistent. Clarity was by no means served by the fact that ... in the Philippines, five Regular Army U.S. generals, at the behest of General Douglas MacArthur, were trying General Tomoyuki Yamashita for failing to prevent his troops from massacring numerous Filipino civilians. There was no specific allegation that Yamashita had ordered these atrocities, or even that he knew at the time that they were in process, or that he could have stopped them had he known. On such a record, the indictment of a German general, much less the conviction and execution imposed on Yamashita, would have been highly unlikely. Apparently, in old-line military circles yellow generals did not rank as high in the scale of virtue as Nordic white ones.[121]

That may be granting Yamashita's conviction too great a moral significance, but it is representative of opinion in some military circles. In many World War II cases the required mens rea could be presumed from the circumstances of the accused officers' case. Times change; law evolves.

"The ICTY first [in 1998], and then also the ICTR [in 2003[122]] opted for a more careful approach to this element of command responsibility. In *Delalić*, the ICTY concluded that the 'knew or had reason to know' standard set in Article 7(3) of the [ICTY] Statute must be interpreted as requiring the commander: (i) to have 'actual knowledge, established through direct or circumstantial evidence, that his subordinates were committing or about to commit crimes ... ' or (ii) to have 'in his possession information of a nature,

---

[119] Germany's domestic law, for example, divides the commander's conduct into three categories of liability, two relating to violations of duty to supervise subordinates, the third to failures to report violations. Antonio Cassese, *International Criminal Law* (Oxford: Oxford University Press, 2003), 206–7.

[120] E.g., *Kadic v. Karadzic*, 70 F. 3d 232 (2nd Cir., 1995); and, *Ford v. Garcia*, 289 F. 3d 1283 (11th Cir., 2002).

[121] Telford Taylor, *The Anatomy of the Nuremberg Trials* (New York: Alfred Knopf, 1992), 239.

[122] *Prosecutor v. Kajelijeli*, ICTR-98–44A-T (Dec. 1, 2003), para. 776. "While an individual's hierarchical position may be a significant *indicium* that he or she knew or had reason to know about subordinates' criminal acts, knowledge will not be presumed from status alone."

which at least, would put him on notice of the risk of such offenses'"[123] *but Delalić* was a short-lived shift.[124] On appeal, the appeals chamber clarified:

> 237 ... The [commander's] duty is limited by the terms of [Additional Protocol] Article 87(3) to circumstances where the commander "is aware" that his subordinates are going to commit or have committed such breaches. ...
>
> 238. Contrary to the Prosecution's submission, the Trial Chamber did not hold that a superior needs to have information on subordinate offences in his actual possession for the purpose of ascribing criminal liability under the principle of command responsibility. A showing that a superior had some general information in his possession, which would put him on notice of possible unlawful acts by his subordinates would be sufficient to prove that he "had reason to know". The ICRC Commentary (Additional Protocol I) refers to "reports addressed to (the superior), ... the tactical situation, the level of training and instruction of subordinate officers and their troops, and their character traits" as potentially constituting the information referred to in Article 86(2) of Additional Protocol I. As to the form of the information available to him, it may be written or oral, and does not need to have the form of specific reports submitted pursuant to a monitoring system. This information does not need to provide specific information about unlawful acts committed or about to be committed. For instance, a military commander who has received information that some of the soldiers under his command have a violent or unstable character, or have been drinking prior to being sent on a mission, may be considered as having the required knowledge.
>
> 239. Finally, the relevant information only needs to have been provided or available to the superior, or in the Trial Chamber's words, "in the possession of." ... It is not required that he actually acquainted himself with the information. Command responsibility is not a form of strict liability. A superior may only be held liable for the acts of his subordinates if it is shown that he "knew or had reason to know" about them.

The ICTY and ICTR also have revisited the issue of the superior–subordinate relationship. In virtually all cases prior to the 1993 formation of the ICTY, the hierarchical military positions of the individuals – captain to lieutenant, major to sergeant, and so forth – allowed an inference that the superior had authority and command of the subordinate. The ICTY and ICTR reassessed that formal assessment, instead looking for effective control of a subordinate.

> [A] position of command is indeed a necessary precondition for the imposition of command responsibility. However, this statement must be qualified by the recognition that the existence of such a position cannot be determined by reference to formal status alone. Instead, the factor that determines liability for this type of criminal responsibility is the actual possession, or non-possession, of powers of control over the actions of subordinates. Accordingly, formal designation as a commander should not be considered to be a necessary prerequisite for command responsibility to attach.[125]

---

[123] Beatrice I. Bonafé, "Finding a Proper Role for Command Responsibility," 5–3 *J. of Int'l Crim. Justice* (July 2007), 599, 606.

[124] *Prosecutor v. Delalić* (aka *Mucić/* aka "Čelebici"), IT-96-21-T (16 Nov. 1998), para. 386; " [Regarding the standard of actual knowledge] in the absence of direct evidence of the superior's knowledge of the offenses committed by his subordinates, such knowledge cannot be presumed, but must be established by way of circumstantial evidence." The *Blašić* Trial Chamber disagreed with *Delalić* regarding the commander's required knowledge, a disagreement reversed by the appeals chamber. *Prosecutor v. Blašić*, IT-95-14-A (July 29, 2004), para. 62.

[125] Id., *Delalić*, at para. 370.

"The accused has to be, by virtue of his position, senior in some sort of formal or informal hierarchy to the perpetrator. [Effective control will] almost invariably not be satisfied unless such a relationship of subordination exists."[126]

To be considered the superior of an offending subordinate, the superior must be proved by the prosecution to have exercised effective control over the accused individual. In ICTY jurisprudence, effective control is indicated by an ability to prevent or punish. "According to the Appeals Chamber, the ability to initiate criminal investigations against the perpetrators may be an indicator of effective control."[127]

There are indeed unusual situations in which seniority in military rank or grade is not determinative of effective control. Imagine an intelligence specialist of the rank of staff sergeant who is attached to a patrol led by a sergeant. Although senior in rank, the intelligence specialist is not an infantryman and may not be trained to lead patrols, so he would not be the patrol's leader. While on patrol, if the patrol leader directs the intelligence specialist to commit a war crime, such as burning a dead enemy body, and the intelligence specialist does so, the patrol leader may be held criminally liable as the superior, despite his junior rank vis-a-vis the intelligence specialist. (The specialist, too, will be disciplined for obeying the manifestly unlawful order.) This change in approach focuses on the conduct of the accused, rather than on his relationship with the perpetrator.

The effect of the *Delalić* opinion in U.S. military courtrooms was nil. First, there rarely is a trial of a U.S. commander for command responsibility-based charges. Beyond that, ICTY opinions are persuasive but not binding in U.S. courts. However, as seen in the *Medina* trial, the elements of proof required for a conviction of a commander as an aider or abettor effectively incorporate the requirement of *Delalić*. The "knew or should have known" standard for command responsibility remains unchanged.

10.6 Summary

Commanders are liable for the unlawful battlefield acts of which they know or should know of their subordinates. The commander's liability is not that of an aider and abettor. Instead, it is grounded in his own negligence in acting or not acting in regard to the subordinate's criminal acts; the commander either failed to anticipate the criminality when she possessed specific facts that should have led her to act; or failed to prevent criminal acts of which she knew or, under the circumstances, should have known; or she failed to take corrective action as to crimes already committed. Today, the traditional formulation, reached through a series of trials of commanders starting after World War II, with the *Yamashita* tribunal, is customary law. It is a standard that is enforceable even if it was not codified.

Every military leader knows that authority entails responsibility. The ambit of command responsibility and *respondeat superior* is particularly broad. It reaches commanders who personally violate LOAC; who order it violated; who fail to suppress – punish – past violations; who incite violations; who fail to control troops who commit violations; who acquiesce in the violations of subordinates; and who knowingly pass on illegal orders to

---

[126] *Prosecutor v. Halilović*, IT-01–48-A (Oct. 16, 2007), para. 59.
[127] Helen Brady and Barbara Goy, "Current Developments in the Ad Hoc International Criminal Tribunals," 6–3 *J. of Int'l. Crim. Justice* (1998), 569, 576, citing *Halilović*, id., at para. 182.

subordinates. Of course, subordinates who execute manifestly illegal orders also remain liable for their unlawful actions in carrying out manifestly unlawful orders.

In most jurisdictions, a conviction of a military commander or a civilian superior requires proof of three elements: a superior–subordinate relationship, that the commander/superior knew or had reason to know that the subordinate had committed a crime or was about to, and that the commander/superior failed to take necessary and reasonable steps to prevent the crime or, if already committed, to punish the violator. No commander will be tried for subordinates' criminal acts of which he had no knowledge, actual or constructive, although the issue of knowledge may always be contested.

In U.S. military practice, the standard for command responsibility continues to be "knew or should have known." As important as command responsibility/ *respondeat superior* is in LOAC/IHL, it is "one of the forms of liability that is least likely to lead to successful convictions. ... Of the 99 accused who have faced trial before the ICTY and the ICTR [as of 2007], only 54 were prosecuted on a theory of command responsibility and only 10 have been convicted."[128] Those convictions occurred in cases involving traditional military superior–subordinate contexts.

CASES AND MATERIALS

YAMASHITA V. STYER

327 U.S. 1; 66 S. Ct. 340 (Feb. 4, 1946). Footnotes omitted.

Introduction. *Upon his conviction by military tribunal in Manila, the Philippines, General Tomoyuki Yamashita petitioned the Supreme Court of the United States for writs of habeas corpus and prohibition. The Court did not review either the facts or the military tribunal's conclusions of law. The Court denied the petitions.*

In discussions of the Yamashita case, the dissent of Justice William Francis (Frank) Murphy is often cited. Murphy was no stranger to high-profile contested cases or to the Philippines. Early in his legal career, Justice Murphy had been an assistant U.S. attorney. In the 1930s he was governor-general of the Philippines, then U.S. high commissioner of the Philippines. Just prior to his appointment to the Supreme Court bench, Murphy was the attorney general of the United States. Although much of his dissent relates to other matters, given his background, Justice Murphy's comments, including those relating to command responsibility, bear strong consideration.

The significance of the issue facing the Court today cannot be overemphasized. ... The failure of the military commission to obey the dictates of the due process requirements of the Fifth Amendment is apparent in this case. ... No military necessity or other emergency demanded the suspension of the safeguards of due process. Yet petitioner

---

[128] Bonafé, "Finding a Proper Role for Command Responsibility," supra, note 123, at 602.

was rushed to trial under an improper charge, given insufficient time to prepare an adequate defense, deprived of the benefits of some of the most elementary rules of evidence, and summarily sentenced to be hanged. In all this needless and unseemly haste there was no serious attempt to charge or to prove that he committed a recognized violation of the laws of war. He was not charged with personally participating in the acts of atrocity or with ordering or condoning their commission. Not even knowledge of these crimes was attributed to him. It was simply alleged that he unlawfully disregarded and failed to discharge his duty as commander to control the operations of the members of his command, permitting them to commit the acts of atrocity. The recorded annals of warfare and the established principles of international law afford not the slightest precedent for such a charge. This indictment in effect permitted the military commission to make the crime whatever it willed. . . .

That there were brutal atrocities inflicted upon the helpless Filipino people, to whom tyranny is no stranger, by Japanese armed forces under the petitioner's command is undeniable. Starvation, execution or massacre without trial, torture, rape, murder, and wanton destruction of property were foremost among the outright violations of the laws of war and of the conscience of a civilized world. That just punishment should be meted out to all those responsible for criminal acts of this nature are also beyond dispute. But these factors do not answer the problem in this case. They do not justify the abandonment of our devotion to justice in dealing with a fallen enemy commander. To conclude otherwise is to admit that the enemy has lost the battle but has destroyed our ideals. . . .

If we are ever to develop an orderly international community based upon a recognition of human dignity it is of the utmost importance that the necessary punishment of those guilty of atrocities be as free as possible from the ugly stigma of revenge and vindictiveness. Justice must be tempered by compassion rather than by vengeance. . . . Otherwise stark retribution will be free to masquerade in a cloak of false legalism. . . .

Read against the background of military events in the Philippines . . . these charges amount to this: "We, the victorious American forces, have done everything possible to destroy and disorganize your lines of communication, your effective control of your personnel, your ability to wage war. In those respects we have succeeded. We have defeated and crushed your forces. And now we charge and condemn you for having been inefficient in maintaining control of your troops during the period when we were so effectively besieging and eliminating your forces and blocking your ability to maintain effective control. Many terrible atrocities were committed by your disorganized troops. Because these atrocities were so widespread we will not bother to charge or prove that you committed, ordered or condoned any of them. We will assume that they must have resulted from your inefficiency and negligence as a commander. In short, we charge you with the crime of inefficiency in controlling your troops. We will judge the discharge of your duties by the disorganization which we ourselves created in large part. . . .

But it is urged that the charge does not allege that petitioner has either committed or directed the commission of such acts, and consequently that no violation is charged as against him. But this overlooks the fact that the gist of the charge is an unlawful breach of duty by petitioner as an army commander to control the operations of the members of his command by "permitting them to commit" the extensive and widespread atrocities specified. The question then is whether the law of war imposes on an army commander a duty to take such appropriate measures as are within his power to control the troops under his command for the prevention of the specified acts which are violations of the law of war ... and whether he may be charged with personal responsibility for his failure to take such measures when violations result. ...

The law of war presupposes that its violation is to be avoided through the control of the operations of war by commanders who are to some extent responsible for their subordinates.

This is recognized by the Annex to Fourth Hague Convention of 1907, respecting the laws and customs of war on land. Article I lays down as a condition which an armed force must fulfill in order to be accorded the rights of lawful belligerents, that it must be "commanded by a person responsible for his subordinates." ...

These provisions plainly imposed on petitioner ... an affirmative duty to take such measures as were within his power and appropriate in the circumstances to protect prisoners of war and the civilian population. ...

... There is no contention that the present charge, thus read, is without the support of evidence, or that the commission held petitioner responsible for failing to take measures which were beyond his control ... in the circumstances.

Conclusion. *In reading Justice Murphy's dissent, one should remember that it was a dissent in a 6–2 decision. The majority included Hugo Black, Felix Frankfurter, and William O. Douglas, as experienced and learned jurists as Justice Murphy. (Justice Robert Jackson, on a year's leave from the Court while acting as Chief Prosecutor of the Nuremberg International Military Tribunal, took no part in the decision.)*

Justice Murphy's first paragraph is in error when he asserts that there is no precedent for charging General Yamashita. This chapter has related several such precedents, although none are precisely on point in that they do not find guilt for a failure to control subordinate troops. In that regard, Yamashita was indeed the groundbreaking case that established a principle sometimes encountered even today.

Is it unreasonable to hold a commander responsible for the widespread misconduct of his or her subordinates? If not the commander, who should answer for an epidemic of war crimes in which specific actors are unidentified and unknowable? Should no one except the actual perpetrators be held accountable for gross indiscipline in such circumstances? Would that approach result in no charges, at all? Is a commander responsible for the conduct of his troops, or is he not? If a unit excels, who is awarded the medal – each stellar subordinate or the commander? If a unit fails in combat, are the troops responsible, or is the commander accountable? How far up – or down – the chain of command should one look?

THEATER JUDGE ADVOCATE'S REVIEW: THE UNITED STATES V. GENERAL TOMOYUKI YAMASHITA[129]

Introduction. *A viewpoint different from Justice Murphy's is found in the U.S. Army's review of the Yamashita trial proceedings. Under World War II legal procedure, the senior military lawyer for the commander who initiated a court-martial or military tribunal, in this case the theater judge advocate, was required to review the verbatim record of the proceedings to confirm the legality of the trial and the propriety of the findings. That review*

---

[129] On file with author. Citations and references to transcript pages omitted.

*would be approved or disapproved by the officer who ordered the trial held, in this case
General Douglas MacArthur.*

*In this extract from the review, the charge-by-charge review of the evidence is deleted, to
focus on the reviewing officer's legal assessment of the accused's command responsibility:*

GENERAL HEADQUARTERS
UNITED STATES ARMY FORCES, PACIFC
OFFICE OF THE THEATER JUDGE ADVOCATE
JA 201-Yamashita, Tomoyuki
A.P.O. 500,
General, Imperial Japanese Army
26 December 1945
SUBJECT: Review of the Record of Trial by a Military Commission of Tomoyuki
Yamashita, General, Imperial Japanese Army.
TO: The Commander-in-Chief, United States Army Forces, Pacific, APO 500.

3.a. ... The prosecution introduced the following evidence on the issue of the direct
responsibility of accused as distinguished from that incident to mere command. Accused
testified that he had ordered the suppression or "mopping up" of guerrillas. About the
middle of December 1944, Colonel Nishiharu, the Judge Advocate and police officer of
the 14th Army Group, told Yamashita that there was a large number of guerrillas in
custody and there was not sufficient time to try them and said that the Kempei Tai would
"punish those who were to be punished." To this Yamashita merely nodded in apparent
approval. Under this summary procedure over 600 persons were executed as "guerrillas"
in Manila. ... In that same month, by a written order, Yamashita commended the ...
Kempei Tai garrison for their fine work in "suppressing guerrilla activities." The captured
diary of a Japanese warrant officer assigned to a unit operating in the Manila area
contained an entry dated 1 December 1944, "Received orders, on the mopping up of
guerrillas last night ... it seems that all the men are to be killed. ... Our object is to
wound and kill the men, to get information and to kill the women who run away."

Throughout the record, evidence was presented in the form of captured documents
and statements of Japanese made in connection with the commission of atrocities,
referring to instructions to kill civilians. ...

The witness Galang testified that he was present and overheard a conversation
between Yamashita and Ricarte, in December 1944. The conversation was interpreted
by Ricarte's 12 year old grandson, Yamashita speaking Japanese which the witness did not
understand and the interpreter translating into Tagalog which the witness did understand. When asked by Ricarte to revoke his order to kill all the Filipinos, Yamashita
became angry and spoke in Japanese. ... "The order is my order. And because of that it
should not be broken or disobeyed. ... " (Note: The defense introduced Bislummo
Romero, the 13 year old grandson of Ricarte, who said he had never interpreted between
his grandfather and Yamashita, and specifically denied interpreting the conversation
testified to by Galang.)

... Under this directive [Instruction on Rules of Evidence for Military Commissions, promulgated by General MacArthur's headquarters], the commission accepted
hearsay testimony, ex parte affidavits, reports of investigation, official motion pictures
and documents which ordinarily could not have been received by a court-martial but

which, in the mind of the commission, had probative value. This method of procedure is assigned as error but this contention is without merit. It has long been
recognized that military commissions are not bound by ordinary rules of evidence
but ... may prescribe their own rules so long as they adhere to the elementary
principles of fairness inherent in Anglo-Saxon procedure. ... The procedure in the
instant case is in the main the same as that followed in the celebrated Saboteur Case
(Ex parte Quirin 317 US 1), the legality of the trial in which was upheld by the
Supreme Court. ...

... The evidence of the atrocities alleged in the ninety different specifications on
which proof was adduced is clear, complete, convincing and, for the most part, uncon-
tradicted by the defense. ...

The only real question in the case concerns accused's responsibility for the atrocities
shown to have been committed by members of his command. Upon this issue a careful
reading of all the evidence impels the conclusion that it demonstrates this responsibility.
In the first place the atrocities were so numerous, involved so many people, and were so
widespread that accused's professed ignorance is incredible. Then too, their manner of
commission reveals a striking similarity of pattern throughout. ... Almost uniformly the
atrocities were committed under the supervision of officers or noncommissioned officers
and in several instances there was direct proof of statements by the Japanese participants
that they were acting pursuant to orders of higher authorities, in a few cases Yamashita
himself being mentioned as the source of the order. ... All this leads to the inevitable
conclusion that the atrocities were not the sporadic acts of soldiers out of control but were
carried out pursuant to a deliberate plan of mass extermination which must have
emanated from higher authority or at least had its approval. Evidence in the form of
captured diaries and documents also indicates that the executions of civilians were
ordered by higher command. For example, captured notes and instructions by Colonel
Fujishigo, one of accused's subordinates, contained the following: "Kill American troops
cruelly. Do not kill them with one stroke. Shoot guerrillas. Kill all who oppose the
Emperor, even women and children." ... This group was commanded by a major
general and the source of the order therefore comes high in the chain of command,
close to the accused himself. ... The conclusion is inevitable that the accused knew
about them and either gave his tacit approval to them or at least failed to do anything
either to prevent them or to punish their perpetrators. ...

RECOMMENDATIONS: It is accordingly recommended that the sentence be confirmed and ordered executed under the supervision of and at a time and place to be
designated by the Commanding General, United States Army Forces Western Pacific.

Conclusion. *Do you find the review of the record of trial legally persuasive? It is admittedly
unfair to form a responsible opinion from a brief and selective extract, but it provides the
flavor of the Yamashita review. How do you view the standard of admissibility of hearsay
evidence, which is not unlike the standard initially employed in proceedings against
Guantánamo Bay detainees in the "war on terrorism"? What of a twelve-year-old "interpreter" whose hearsay account is later denied by its maker? Should direct evidence of guilt
be required for conviction? Should one consider the theater judge advocate's conclusionary
statements as reflecting evidence admitted at trial or as opinion?*

*From a reading of these selective review extracts one suspects that firm direct evidence of
Yamashita's guilt was thin. Yet, should a commander of troops who committed so many
atrocities over a lengthy period be permitted simply to say, "I didn't know"? Military*

commissions have historically been summary in their procedure and permissive in terms of admissible evidence. Were this not the first command responsibility case involving specific crimes by specific units commanded by a particular officer there would be little question of a guilty verdict. In this first such case in modern times, however, the prosecution was necessarily finding its way. Would that justify a conviction based on questionable evidence?

In 1945, the international community had little time for such questions. The accused were only Nazis and Japanese, and everyone knew their record of wartime conduct. Who cared about legal niceties, as long as they were hammered? It is a different world today. When ongoing combat is televised in real time, and nongovernmental organizations watch courts-martial on CNN, or in person, military commissions, with their relaxed evidentiary standards and ultrastreamlined procedure, may no longer be satisfactory prosecutorial vehicles.

The U.S. Army captain Frank Reel, a Boston labor lawyer until the war began, was assigned to Yamashita's defense team. Until his death in 2000, he remained convinced of Yamashita's wrongful conviction. Captain Reel wrote, "We have been unjust, hypocritical, and vindictive. We have defeated our enemies on the battlefield, but we have let their spirit triumph in our hearts."[130]

Another informed commentator, Professor Allan Ryan, writes of Yamashita's conviction, "And how can there be any law when its enforcement is so capricious? The vanquished cannot punish the victor's crimes, and the victors only rarely punish their own, and certainly never their generals and their political leaders. Is not all enforcement of the laws of war merely victors' justice, which is to say no justice?"[131]

Allied veterans of the Pacific war, and Filipino survivors of the Japanese occupation of Manila, might see General Yamashita's conviction differently than did Captain Reel and Professor Ryan. But a victim's passion does not translate to lawful execution of the laws and customs of war, and not all war crime cases are as morally clear as we would wish.

PROSECUTOR V. HALILOVIĆ

IT-01–48-T (November 16, 2005). Footnotes omitted.

Introduction. *The Halilović judgment articulates the legal basis, under the ICTY statute, of a commander's culpability – negligent performance of duty, rather than as an aider and abettor of the criminal actor. Although individuals not before the court are not bound by an ICTY judgment, there is little basis for disagreeing with it.*

54. The Trial Chamber finds that under Article 7(3) command responsibility is responsibility for an omission. The commander is responsible for the failure to perform an act required by international law. This omission is culpable because international law imposes an affirmative duty on superiors to prevent and punish crimes committed by their subordinates. Thus "for the acts of his subordinates" as generally referred to in the jurisprudence of the Tribunal does not mean that the commander shares the same responsibility as the subordinates who committed the crimes, but rather that because of the crimes committed by his subordinates, the commander should bear responsibility for

[130] A. Frank Reel, *The Case of General Yamashita* (New York: Octagon Books, 1971), 247.
[131] Allan P. Ryan, *Yamashita's Ghost: War Crimes, MacArthur's Justice, and Command Accountability* (Lawrence: University Press of Kansas, 2012), 334.

his failure to act. The imposition of responsibility upon a commander for breach of his duty is to be weighted against the crimes of his subordinates; a commander is responsible not as though he had committed the crime himself, but his responsibility is considered in proportion to the gravity of the offenses committed. ...

"THE ĈELEBIĆI CASE," PROSECUTOR V. DELALIĆ, ET AL.

IT-96–21-T (November 16, 1998). Footnotes omitted. All italics as in original.

Introduction. *In this extract from the* Delalić *opinion, the trial chamber holds that Article 86 of the ICTY's statute did not intend that a commander's negligence be an entirely objective standard. That approach, the trial chamber writes, rejected "knew or should have known" language. Accordingly, the prosecution must prove that the accused possessed specific information putting him/her on notice of the violations of subordinates.*

385. The Commentary to the Additional Protocols, on which the Prosecution relies, also cites the *High Command* case and the judgment of the Tokyo Tribunal, neither of which, however, make a clear ruling on the existence of any such general rule or presumption. While, in the *High Command* case, the tribunal held in relation to the accused von Kuechier that the numerous reports of illegal executions which were made to his headquarters "must be presumed" to have been brought to his attention, this case offers no support for the existence of a more general rule of presumption such as that proposed by the Prosecution. In contrast, the tribunal in that case explicitly rejected the argument that, in view of the extent of the atrocities and the communications available to them, it could be held that all the accused must have knowledge of the illegal activities carried out in their areas of command. The tribunal declared that no such general presumption could be made and held that the question of the knowledge of the commanders had to be determined on the basis of the evidence pertaining to each individual defendant.

386. It is, accordingly, the Trial Chamber's view that, in the absence of direct evidence of the superior's knowledge of the offenses committed by his subordinates, such knowledge cannot be presumed, but must be established by way of circumstantial evidence. In determining whether a superior, despite pleas to the contrary, in fact must have possessed the requisite knowledge, the Trial Chamber may consider, *inter alia*, the following indicia. ...

   (a)   The number of illegal acts;
   (b)   The type of illegal acts;
   (c)   The scope of illegal acts;
   (d)   The time during which the illegal acts occurred;
   (e)   The number and type of troops involved;
   (f)   The logistics involved, if any;
   (g)   The geographical location of the acts;
   (h)   The widespread occurrence of the acts;
   (i)   The tactical tempo of operations;
   (j)   The modus operandi of similar illegal acts;
   (k)   The officers and staff involved;
   (l)   The location of the commander at the time.

B. "Had Reason to Know"

387. Regarding the mental standard of "had reason to know", the Trial Chamber takes as its point of departure the principle that a superior is not permitted to remain wilfully blind to the acts of his subordinates. There can be no doubt that a superior who simply ignores information within his actual possession compelling the conclusion that criminal offenses are being committed, or are about to be committed, by his subordinates commits a most serious dereliction of duty for which he may be held criminally responsible under the doctrine of superior responsibility. Instead, uncertainty arises in relation to situations where the superior lacks such information by virtue of his failure to properly supervise his subordinates.

388. In this respect, it is to be noted that the jurisprudence from the period immediately following the Second World War affirmed the existence of a duty of commanders to remain informed about the activities of their subordinates. Indeed, from a study of these decisions, the principle can be obtained that the absence of knowledge should not be considered a defense if, in the words of the Tokyo judgment, the superior was "at fault in having failed to acquire such knowledge".

389. For example, in the *Hostage* case the tribunal held that a commander of occupied territory is

> charged with notice of occurrences taking place within that territory. He may require adequate reports of all occurrences that come within the scope of his power and, if such reports are incomplete or otherwise inadequate, he is obliged to require supplementary reports to apprise him of all the pertinent facts. *If he fails to require and obtain complete information, the dereliction of duty rests upon him and he is in no position to plead his own dereliction as a defense.*

Likewise, in the trial against Admiral Toyoda, the tribunal declared that the principle of command responsibility applies to the commander who *"knew, or should have known, by use of reasonable diligence"* of the commission of atrocities by his subordinates. Similarly, the tribunal in the *Pohl* case, describing Mummenthey's position as one of an "assumed or *criminal* naivete", held that the latter's assertions that he did not know what was happening in the labour camps and enterprises under his jurisdiction did not exonerate him, adding that *"it was his duty to know"*. Again, in the *Roechling* case, the court, under the heading of "The defence of lack of knowledge", declared that:

> no superior may prefer this defence indefinitely; for it is his duty to know what occurs in his organization, and lack of knowledge, therefore, can only be the result of criminal negligence.

393. An interpretation of the terms of this provision in accordance with their ordinary meaning thus leads to the conclusion ... that a superior can be held criminally responsible only if some specific information was in fact available to him which would provide notice of offences committed by his subordinates. This information need not be such that it by itself was sufficient to compel the conclusion of the existence of such crimes. It is sufficient that the superior was put on further inquiry by the information, or, in other words, that it indicated the need for additional investigation in order to ascertain whether offences were being committed or about to be committed by his subordinates ... The Trial Chamber thus makes no finding as to the present content of customary law on this

point. It may be noted, however, that the provision on responsibility of military commanders in the Rome Statute of the International Criminal Court provides that a commander may be held criminally responsible for failure to act in situations where he knew or should have known of offences committed, or about to be committed, by forces under his effective command and control, or effective authority and control.

(D) Necessary and Reasonable Measures

394. The legal duty which rests upon all individuals in positions of superior authority requires them to take all necessary and reasonable measures to prevent the commission of offenses by their subordinates or, if such crimes have been committed, to punish the perpetrators thereof. It is the view of the Trial Chamber that any evaluation of the action taken by a superior to determine whether this duty has been met is so inextricably linked to the facts of each particular situation that any attempt to formulate a general standard *in abstracto* would not be meaningful.

395. It must, however, be recognized that international law cannot oblige a superior to perform the impossible. Hence, a superior may only be held criminally responsible for failing to take such measures that are within his powers. The question then arises of what actions are to be considered to be within the superior's powers in this sense. ... We conclude that a superior should be held responsible for failing to take such measures that are within his material possibility. ...

Conclusion. *The exact contours of the information required to put a commander on notice are not specified in the opinion and probably could not be. As the Trial Chamber says in paragraph 394, regarding evaluating the actions taken by a commander, the information requirement is inextricably linked to the facts of each particular situation.*

Given the factors listed in paragraph 386 that would put a commander on notice, would they indicate guilt or innocence, if applied in General Yamashita's case? In Captain Medina's case?

PROSECUTOR V. BLAŠKIĆ

IT-95–14-T (March 3, 2000). Footnotes omitted.

Introduction. *In 1992, in central Bosnia, the accused, General Tihomir Blaškić, commanded the HVO – the Croatian Defence Council – which consisted of eleven regular brigades. Among other grave breaches, he was charged with knowing that his subordinates were planning war crimes, including the murder of Muslim noncombatants and, without military necessity, the destruction of noncombatant property, including Muslim churches and homes, and not taking steps to prevent such acts. The Trial Chamber's opinion is instructive in addressing who a "superior" is, the commander's duty to know, what constitutes measures to prevent or punish war crimes, and what is meant by the term "prevent or punish."*

Significantly, however, the Blaškić judgment disagrees with the Delalić judgment with regard to the scope of the commander's knowledge requirement.[132] Drawing on post–World

---

[132] See Jenny S. Martinez, "Understanding Mens Rea in Command Responsibility, 5–3 *J. of Int'l Criminal Justice* (July 2007), 638–57, for a full discussion of this distinction.

War II case law, Blaškić imposes an affirmative duty on commanders to investigate the
conduct of subordinates, regardless of whether they have information arousing suspicion.
Compare paragraph 322 with Delalić paragraph 393, which requires "specific information"
for a commander's liability to attach.

322. From this analysis of jurisprudence, the Trial Chamber concludes that after
World War II, a standard was established according to which a commander may be
liable for crimes by his subordinates if "he failed to exercise the means available to him to
learn of the offence and, under the circumstances, he should have known and such
failure to know constitutes criminal dereliction.

331. Lastly, the Trial Chamber considers that the findings of the Israeli Commission of
Inquiry responsible for investigating the atrocities perpetrated in the Shatila and Sabra
refugee camps in Beirut in 1982 constitute further evidence of the state of customary
international law. With respect to the responsibility of the Chief of Staff of the Israel
Defence Forces, the Commission held that his knowledge of the feelings of hatred of the
particular forces involved towards the Palestinians did not justify the conclusion that the
entry of those forces into the camps posed no danger. Accordingly,

> the absence of a warning from experts cannot serve as an explanation for ignoring the
> danger of a massacre. The Chief of Staff should have known and foreseen – by virtue of
> common knowledge, as well as the special information at his disposal – that there was a
> possibility of harm to the population in the camps at the hands of the Phalangists. Even
> if the experts did not fulfil their obligation, this does not absolve the Chief of Staff of
> responsibility.

The Commission clearly held that the applicable standard for imputing responsibility is
negligence.

If the Chief of Staff did not imagine at all that the entry of the Phalangists into the
camps posed a danger to the civilian population, his thinking on this matter constitutes a
disregard of important considerations that he should have taken into account. ... We
determine that the Chief of Staff's inaction ... constitute[s] a breach of duty and
dereliction of the duty incumbent upon the Chief of Staff.

332. In conclusion, the Trial Chamber finds that if a commander has exercised due
diligence in the fulfilment of his duties yet lacks knowledge that crimes are about to be or
have been committed, such lack of knowledge cannot be held against him. However,
taking into account his particular position of command and the circumstances prevailing
at the time, such ignorance cannot be a defence where the absence of knowledge is the
result of negligence in the discharge of his duties: this commander had reason to know. ...

D) Necessary and Reasonable Measures to Prevent or Punish

I) Arguments of the Parties

333. The Prosecution put forth several measures which a commander can take in
order to discharge his obligation to prevent offences from being committed. Accordingly, the exercise of effective command and control through the proper and diligent
application of discipline is a common thread. The duty to punish entails the obligation
to establish the facts, to put an end to the offences and to punish. "Necessary measures"
are those required to discharge the obligation to prevent or punish, in the

circumstances prevailing at the time. "Reasonable" measures are those which the commander was in a position to take in the circumstances prevailing at the time. The lack of formal legal jurisdiction does not necessarily relieve the superior of his criminal responsibility. If subordinates act pursuant to criminal orders passed down from higher up in the chain of command the commander remains under an obligation to take all measures within his power. ...

Ii) Discussion and Conclusions

335. The Trial Chamber has already characterized a "superior" as a person exercising "effective control" over his subordinates. In other words, the Trial Chamber holds that where a person has the material ability to prevent or punish crimes committed by others, that person must be considered a superior. Accordingly, it is a commander's degree of effective control, his material ability, which will guide the Trial Chamber in determining whether he reasonably took the measures required either to prevent the crime or to punish the perpetrator. ... This implies that, under some circumstances, a commander may discharge his obligation to prevent or punish by reporting the matter to the competent authorities.

336. Lastly, the Trial Chamber stresses that the obligation to "prevent or punish" does not provide the accused with two alternative and equally satisfying options. Obviously, where the accused knew or had reason to know that subordinates were about to commit crimes and failed to prevent them, he cannot make up for the failure to act by punishing the subordinates afterwards.

Conclusion. *General Blaškić was convicted of nineteen various charges and sentenced to forty-five years' confinement, reduced on appeal to nine years' confinement.*[133]

Must a commander comply with the "failure to investigate" liability standard of the Blaškić *judgment or with the* Delalić *judgment's "only if you have specific information" standard of culpability? The question so far remains unresolved in the ICTY, suggesting that the prudent commander should comply with the higher "failure to investigate" standard.*

PROSECUTOR V. HADŽIHASANOVIĆ

IT-01–47-T (March 15, 2006). Footnotes omitted.

Introduction. *During the armed conflicts in the former Yugoslavia (1991–2001), in 1993, Brigadier General Enver Hadžihasanović was appointed to the Joint Command of the Army of the Federation of Bosnia and Herzegovina (ABiH). In this extract from the ICTY trial chamber's judgment, the chamber differentiates between war crimes "disciplinary" measures – administrative punishments such as negative service record entries, poor efficiency reports, or other nonjudicial measures that might be taken by a local commander – and "criminal" measures – prosecution at a court-martial or civilian criminal trial. Here, the trial chamber is considering the accused's response to reports of beatings and the murder of a prisoner at an ABiH confinement facility known as "the Furniture Salon."*

---

[133] *Prosecutor v. Blaškić*, IT-95–14-A (July 29, 2004).

1770. In response to his report of 18 August 1993, Fehim Muratović spoke with the Accused Hadžihasanović about how two soldiers beat six prisoners of war at the Furniture Salon and, on that occasion, the Accused Hadžihasanović informed him that he was satisfied with the measures taken against those two 307th Brigade soldiers.

1772. . . . [A]fter the alleged incidents there was no investigation or criminal prosecution of the perpetrators of those crimes.

1773. Sead Zerić, Travnik District Military Prosecutor . . . stated that he never received a criminal complaint alleging that ABiH soldiers killed or mistreated prisoners of war or civilian detainees in his zone of responsibility. . . .

1776. On the basis of the evidence, the Chamber is convinced beyond a reasonable doubt that following the mistreatment of six prisoners of war at the Furniture Salon, and the murder of one of them, Mladen Havranek, the 3rd Corps initiated no investigation or criminal proceedings against the perpetrators of those acts. The Chamber is, however, convinced beyond a reasonable doubt that the 307th Brigade took disciplinary measures against them and that the Accused Hadžihasanović was aware of those measures. . . . The measures taken after the alleged incidents were disciplinary in nature.

1777. The Chamber considers that the exercise of disciplinary power to punish the crimes of murder and mistreatment of prisoners of war is not sufficient punishment of the perpetrators of those crimes. The Chamber cannot overemphasize that in international law, a commander has a duty to take the necessary and reasonable measures to punish those who violate the laws or customs of war. Faced with the crimes of murder and mistreatment committed in a detention location controlled by his troops . . . the Accused Hadžihasanović could not consider as acceptable punishment the disciplinary sanction of a period of detention not exceeding 60 days. He had the duty to take specific measures to ensure that the perpetrators were prosecuted. . . . Although he knew that his subordinates had committed the crimes of murder and mistreatment against six prisoners of war at the Furniture Salon, the Accused Hadžihasanović failed in his duty to take the appropriate and necessary measures to punish the perpetrators.

1778. The basis of a commander's duty to punish is to create and maintain an environment of discipline and respect for the law among those under his command. By failing to take the appropriate measures to punish the most serious crimes, a commander adopts a pattern of conduct which may in fact encourage his subordinates to commit further acts of mistreatment and, as a result, may entail his responsibility.

1779. In this case, by failing to punish appropriately the members of the 307th Brigade who committed the crimes of mistreatment and murder at the Furniture Salon, the Accused Hadžihasanović created a situation which encouraged repeated commission of similar criminal acts, not only at the Furniture Salon but also in all of the other detention locations controlled by the members of the 307th Brigade. . . .

1780. Consequently, the Chamber is of the opinion that the Accused Hadžihasanović must be held criminally responsible . . . for the cruel treatment of six prisoners of war committed at the Furniture Salon on 5 August 1993, for the murder of Mladen Havranek on 5 August 1993, and for the mistreatment committed after 18 August 1993.

Conclusion. *The trial chamber sentenced Hadžihasanović to imprisonment for five years. On appeal, the appeals chamber, although not disagreeing with the law or facts asserted by the trial chamber, found portions of the trial chamber's judgment unsupported by the* *evidence. With regard to the failure of General Hadžihasanović to punish the soldiers who allegedly abused and murdered prisoners adequately, the appeals chamber held*[134]:

33. ... The assessment of whether a superior fulfilled his duty to prevent or punish ... has to be made on a case-by-case basis, so as to take into account the "circumstances surrounding each particular situation." ... It cannot be excluded that, in the circumstances of a case, the use of disciplinary measures will be sufficient to discharge a superior of his duty to punish crimes. ... In other words, whether the measures taken were solely of a disciplinary nature, criminal, or a combination of both, cannot in itself be determinative of whether a superior discharged his duty to prevent or punish. ...

320. The Appeals Chamber recalls that a position of authority does not in and of itself attract a harsher sentence. ... Rather, it is the superior's abuse of that level of authority which could be taken into consideration at sentencing. ...

Conclusion. *The appeals chamber overturned several findings of guilt and reduced General Hadžihasanović's sentence to imprisonment for three years and six months.*

The assessment of whether a commander fulfilled his duty to prevent or punish war crimes and grave breaches committed by subordinates must be made on a case-by-case basis. As leaders in all wars have, U.S. commanders in the conflicts in Iraq and Afghanistan have confronted that issue and, particularly early in the conflicts, sometimes made questionable decisions regarding their duty to charge. In August 2004, the army sergeant James P. Boland was charged with assaulting an Afghan detainee killed while in U.S. custody in Bagram. The victim was one of two Iraqis found dead in the same cell, hanging "in a standing position with hands suspended above shoulder level for a prolonged period of time."[135] *Both detainees had been beaten to death, according to their military death certificates. In June 2005, the sergeant received a letter of reprimand and was honorably discharged without trial.*

Lieutenant P — —, an American Marine, was charged with the 2004 premeditated murder of two Iraqis apprehended at the scene of insurgent activity. At Lieutenant P — —'s pretrial investigation ("the legal bullshit," he called it) the lieutenant reportedly testified that he feared that the two victims were about to attack him, so he shot them, up to fifty times, having to reload to do so. The commanding officer agreed with the investigating officer's recommendation that charges not be preferred, and the case did not go to trial.

In 2006, the army investigated a Special Operations unit that, continuously for seven days, reportedly kept detainees "in cells so small that they could neither stand nor lie down, while interrogators played loud music" so they could not sleep.[136] *Some detainees were stripped, soaked, and then interrogated in air-conditioned rooms. One detainee died from such treatment, the investigation found. The report recommended no disciplinary action, saying what was done was wrong but not deliberate abuse. The commanding officer agreed, and no one was charged with any offense.*

These are isolated cases among hundreds that have resulted in courts-martial. They nevertheless raise LOAC/IHL concerns.

---

[134] *Prosecutor v. Hadžihasanović*, IT-01–47-A (April 22, 2008).
[135] Tim Golden, "Years After 2 Afghans Died, Abuse Case Falters," *NY Times*, Feb. 13, 2006, A1.
[136] Eric Schmitt, "Pentagon Study Describes Abuse by Special Units," *NY Times*, June 17, 2006, A1.

PROSECUTOR V. KRISTIĆ

IT-98–33-T (Aug. 2, 2001). Footnotes omitted.

Introduction. *General Radislav Kristić was the commanding general of the Drina Corps of the Bosnian Serb Army when, at Srebrenica, in July 1995, approximately eighty-one hundred men and boys were murdered. In his capacity as commander of the troops involved in the massacre, Kristić was charged with genocide. This charge was not based on the actions of his subordinates, but on General Kristić's own actions.*

608. The evidence establishes that General Kristić, along with others, played a significant role in the organisation of the transportation of the civilians from Potocari. Specifically, the Trial Chamber has concluded that, on 12 July, General Kristić ordered the procurement of buses and their subsequent departure carrying the civilians from Potocari. At some later stage, he personally inquired about the number of buses already en route. The Trial Chamber has also found that General Kristić ordered the securing of the road from Luke to Kladanj up to the tunnel where the people on the buses were to disembark. It has further been established that General Kristić knew that this was a forcible, not a voluntary transfer.

609. The Trial Chamber has similarly concluded that General Kristić was fully aware of the ongoing humanitarian crisis at Potocari as a result of his presence at the hotel Fontana meeting ... where General Mladić and Colonel Karremans of Dutchbat discussed the urgency of the situation, and, at the meeting on 12 July, when General Mladić decided that the VRS [Bosnian Serb Army] would organize the evacuation of the Bosnian Muslim women, children and elderly. Following this meeting, General Kristić was present himself at Potocari, for one to two hours, thus he could not help but be aware of the piteous conditions of the civilians and their mistreatment by VRS soldiers on that day.

610. In light of these facts, the Trial Chamber is of the view that the issue of General Kristić's criminal responsibility for the crimes against the civilian population of Srebrenica occurring at Potocari is most appropriately determined ... by considering whether he participated, along with General Mladić and key members of the VRS Main Staff and the Drina Corps, in a joint criminal enterprise to forcibly "cleanse" the Srebrenica enclave of its Muslim population and to ensure that they left the territory otherwise occupied by Serbian forces.

617. In sum, the Trial Chamber finds General Kristić guilty as a member of a joint criminal enterprise whose objective was to forcibly transfer the Bosnian Muslim women, children and elderly from Potocari on 12 and 13 July and to create a humanitarian crisis in support of this endeavour by causing the Srebrenica residents to flee to Potocari where a total lack of food, shelter and necessary services would accelerate their fear and panic and ultimately their willingness to leave the territory. General Kristić thus incurs liability also for the incidental murders, rapes, beatings and abuses committed in the execution of this criminal enterprise at Potocari.

618. Finally, General Kristić knew that these crimes were related to a widespread or systematic attack directed against the Bosnian Muslim civilian population of Srebrenica; his participation in them is undeniable evidence of his intent to discriminate against the Bosnian Muslims. General Kristić is therefore liable of inhumane acts and persecution as crimes against humanity.

631. The Trial Chamber concludes that ... General Kristić exercised "effective control" over Drina Corps troops and assets throughout the territory on which the detentions, executions and burials were taking place. The Trial Chamber finds furthermore that from that time onwards, General Kristić participated in the full scope of the criminal plan to kill the Bosnian Muslim men originated earlier by General Mladić and other VRS officers. ...

633. ... General Kristić may not have devised the killing plan, or participated in the initial decision to escalate the objective of the criminal enterprise from forcible transfer to destruction of Srebrenica's Bosnian Muslim military-aged male community, but there can be no doubt that, from the point he learned of the widespread and systematic killings and became clearly involved in their perpetration, he shared the genocidal intent to kill the men. This cannot be gainsaid given his informed participation in the executions through the use of Drina Corps assets.

644. ... General Kristić did not conceive the plan to kill the men, nor did he kill them personally. However, he fulfilled a key coordinating role in the implementation of the killing campaign. In particular, at a stage when his participation was clearly indispensable, General Kristić exerted his authority as Drina Corps Commander and arranged for men under his command to commit killings. He thus was an essential participant in the genocidal killings in the aftermath of the fall of Srebrenica. In sum ... General Kristić must be considered a principal perpetrator of these crimes.

Conclusion. *General Kristić, a commander who passed on manifestly unlawful orders, who issued manifestly unlawful orders, who acquiesced in his subordinates' violations, and who disregarded grave breaches of which he was aware, was the first accused individual convicted of genocide by the ICTY. At one point in his trial, Kristić argued that it was impossible to refuse the orders of his superior, General Mladić, to kill the Muslims in his control. The prosecutor asked Kristić, "What should a general do who received those orders?" General Kristić replied, "He should refuse the order."[137]*

Kristić was sentenced to forty-five years' imprisonment. On appeal, his conviction of genocide was overturned, reduced to aiding and abetting genocide, and his sentence was reduced to thirty-five years.[138]

[137] Marlise Simons, "Trial Reopens Pain of 1995 Bosnian Massacre," *NY Times*, Nov. 7, 2000, A3.
[138] *Prosecutor v. Kristić*, IT-98–33-A (April 19, 2004).

11 Ruses and Perfidy

11.0 Introduction

Treaties addressing modern weapons aside, there is little that is new in the law of armed conflict (LOAC). Discussions of "new paradigms" in warfare usually illustrate the speaker's lack of awareness of history – allusions to the treachery of terrorists, for instance.

In the twelfth or thirteenth century B.C., in the Trojan War, the Greeks employed the legendary Trojan horse to defeat Troy. In the seventh century, the Islamic caliph Abu Bakr ordered his forces, "Let there be no perfidy, no falsehood in treaties with the enemy, be faithful to all things, proving yourselves upright and noble and maintaining your word and promises truly."[1] The Lieber Code holds that "military necessity ... admits of deception, but disclaims acts of perfidy,"[2] yet perfidy persists.

In 1882, near El Obeid, Egypt, the Egyptian government had grown weary of Muhammad Ahmad, a young Muslim who proclaimed himself the Mahdi, the Awaited One. Ahmad initiated a surprisingly effective rebellion against the government, and Cairo finally sent an army to capture or kill the Mahdi. The force was led by a retired British Indian army officer, General William Hicks. "To Cairo's horrified astonishment, Hicks and most of his force was slaughtered at Shaykan. ... The Mahdi's sharpshooters had feigned retreat, luring inward Hick's army of 7,000 infantry, 1,000 cavalry, and 5,000 camels, together with its precious cannons and a horde of camp followers."[3]

Does LOAC/IHL allow an armed force to "feign retreat" and then kill the pursuing enemy? May armed forces professing to comply with LOAC and IHL engage in such trickery? Yes, they may. This was an example of what is, in common Article 2 armed conflicts, a ruse. A ruse is not a LOAC violation.

11.1 Perfidy

Perfidy is a violation of LOAC and, according to Additional Protocol I, Article 85.3(f), in certain cases, a grave breach. It is described in Article 37 of Additional Protocol I as an act inviting the confidence of an adversary, leading him to believe he is protected under the

---

[1] C. AD 634, Alib Hasan al Muttaqui, *Book of Kanzul'ummal*, Vol. 4 (1979), 472, cited in Leslie C. Green, *The Contemporary Law of Armed Conflict*, 2d ed. (Manchester: Manchester University Press, 2000), 22.

[2] Instructions for the Government of Armies of the United States in the Field (Army General Orders 100 of 24 April 1863) (the Lieber Code), Art. 16.

[3] Karl E. Meyer and Sharen B. Brysac, *Kingmakers: The Invention of the Modern Middle East* (New York: W. W. Norton, 2008), 39.

rules of armed conflict,[4] with an intent to betray that confidence, resulting in the killing, injuring, or capturing of the adversary.[5] Perfidy, in other words, is **any attempt to gain the enemy's confidence by assuring his protection under the law of war, while intending to kill, wound, or capture him**. There is "a modicum of mutual trust which must exist even between enemies, if [LOAC] is to be fully complied with."[6] Perfidy, which is prohibited in both international and noninternational armed conflicts,[7] is punishable under several provisions of the Rome Statute of the International Criminal Court. Those provisions include improper use of a flag of truce or the uniform of the enemy (resulting in death or serious injury) and killing or wounding treacherously in international or noninternational conflicts, usually interpreted as prohibiting assassination for hire.[8]

As the *Commentary* points out, the essential element of perfidy is the deliberate claim to legal protection for hostile purposes.[9] It is a narrow crime, the definition of which is based on three elements: inviting the confidence of an enemy, a subjective intent to betray that confidence, and an actual betrayal involving the protection afforded by LOAC.[10] "It should be underscored that the betrayal of confidence does not constitute an offence by itself: it only becomes so when it is linked to the act of killing, injuring or capturing the adversary."[11] If there is no intent to kill, wound, or capture the enemy, the act does not constitute perfidy. "The essential concept of perfidy is not difficult to grasp: a broken word, dishonesty, unfaithful breaking of promises, deliberate deception."[12] Perfidy is prohibited to prevent the abuse, and consequent undermining, of the protection afforded by LOAC.[13] The prohibition of perfidy covers attempted and unsuccessful acts.[14] Perfidy is sometimes said to apply in noninternational armed conflicts, as well.[15] No LOAC treaty, however, adopts a prohibition of perfidy applicable in noninternational armed conflicts. A commentator points out that the ICRC's customary law study "concludes that the prohibition applies in both international and non-international armed conflicts.[16] ... [The study's] analysis of state practice, however, may not sufficiently support that conclusion."[17] The commentator suggests that the ICRC study's assertion

---

[4] Pietro Verri, *Dictionary of the International Law of Armed Conflict* (Geneva: ICRC, 1992), 84.

[5] 1977 Protocol I, Additional to the Geneva Conventions of August 12, 1949, Art. 37. Hereafter: Additional Protocol I.

[6] Yoram Dinstein, *The Conduct of Hostilities under the Law of International Armed Conflict* (New York: Cambridge University Press, 2004), 198

[7] United Kingdom Ministry of Defense (MOD), *The Manual of the Law of Armed Conflict* (Oxford: Oxford University Press, 2004), para. 15.12.1. Also see *Prosecutor v. Tadić*, IJ-94–1. Decision Interlocutory Appeal on Jurisdiction (oct. 2, 1993), para. 125.

[8] The statute articles referred to are Articles 8(2)(b)(vii), 8(2)(b)(xi), and 8(2)(e)(ix), respectively. An intent to capture is not included in the statute's articles.

[9] Yves Sandoz, Christophe Swinarski, and Bruno Zimmermann, eds., *Commentary on the Additional Protocols* (Geneva: ICRC, 1987), para. 1500, at 435.

[10] Id.

[11] Frits Kalshoven, *Constraints on the Waging of War* (Dordrecht, The Netherlands: ICRC/Martinus Nijhoff, 1987), 82.

[12] Id., at 434.

[13] United Kingdom MOD, *Manual of the Law of Armed Conflict*, supra, note 7, at para. 5.9.3.

[14] Sandoz, *Commentary on the Additional Protocols*, supra, note 9, para. 1524, at 444.

[15] United Kingdom MOD, *Manual of the Law of Armed Conflict*, supra, note 7, at para. 15.12.1.

[16] Jean-Marie Henckaerts and Louise Doswald-Beck, eds., *Customary International Humanitarian Law*. Vol. I. *Rules* (Cambridge: Cambridge University Press, 2005), Rule 65, 222–3.

[17] Major John C. Dehn, "Permissible Perfidy?" 6–4 *J. of Int'l Crim. Justice* (Sept. 2008), 627, 635.

that the prohibition applies in common Article 3 conflicts is "quite tenuous."[18] There is reason to conclude that perfidy's prohibition is not customary international law and its prohibition is inapplicable to noninternational armed conflicts. "A lengthy debate took place during the 1974–7 Diplomatic Conference [regarding the additional protocols] as to the applicability of the prohibition on perfidy to non-international armed conflict. It was said ... that if the Protocol set out that 'killing by resort to perfidy was prohibited, it might be deduced *a contrario* that killing without such methods was allowable."[19]

The terms "perfidy" and "the somewhat old-fashioned word"[20] "treachery" are often used interchangeably. There is a difference in the two terms, although so slight as not to bear extended consideration here. "The difference between perfidy and treachery is the difference between wrongful deception and betrayal. ... In international law, treachery and perfidy are used interchangeably."[21] The 1907 Hague Regulation IV, Article 23, for example, reads, "it is especially forbidden ... to kill or wound treacherously individuals belonging to the hostile nation or army. ... "[22] This provision is construed as prohibiting assassination of an enemy.[23] Ultimately, however, the term "treachery" was considered too narrow, replaced in law of war discussions by "perfidy,"[24] illustrating the close relationship of the two terms.

Examples of perfidy are feigning an intent to negotiate under a flag of truce or surrender; feigning incapacitation by wounds or sickness to kill an enemy when his back is turned;[25] feigning civilian, noncombatant status; or feigning protected status by use of signs, emblems, or uniforms of the U.N. or another neutral body.[26]

In July 2008, Colombian soldiers, disguised as members of a nongovernmental international aid group, made a daring jungle rescue of fifteen hostages held by the Colombian rebel group the Fuerzas Armadas Revolucionarias de Colombia (FARC). During this common Article 3 event, one of the rescuers wore a bib over his Kevlar vest with a large red cross on it.[27] In a common Article 2 conflict, presuming the disguised soldiers intended to kill, wound, or capture one or more of the FARC captors, that would have been an act of perfidy in violation of Additional Protocol I, Articles 37.1(d) and 38.1,[28] as well as being a grave breach under Article 85.3(f). (Two of the FARC captors were taken aboard the helicopter, along with the soon-to-be-freed captives, and the FARC captors were themselves made captives of the Colombian armed forces.) Because the rescue

---

[18] Id., at 637.

[19] Sandesh Sivakumaran, *The Law of Non-International Armed Conflict* (Oxford: Oxford University Press, 2012), 70.

[20] Geoffrey Best, *War and Law since 1945* (New York: Oxford University Press, 1994), 288.

[21] Roy Gutman and David Rieff, eds., *Crimes of War* (New York: Norton, 1999), 271.

[22] 1907 Hague Regulation IV, Art. 23(b).

[23] Dept. of the Army, FM 27–10, *The Law of Land Warfare* (Washington, DC: GPO, 1956), at para. 31.

[24] Sandoz, *Commentary on the Additional Protocols*, supra, note 9, at 432.

[25] Ibid., 438. Feigning death simply to save one's life is not an act of perfidy because the purpose is not to raise and betray the confidence of the enemy.

[26] Additional Protocol I, Art. 39. It would not automatically be perfidy to use the U.N. uniform or symbol, however, where U.N. members intervene as combatants in an armed conflict.

[27] "Colombia: ICRC Underlines Importance of Respect for Red Cross Emblem," http://www.icrc.org/web/eng/siteengo.nsf/htmlall/columbia-news-160708?opendocument.

[28] Additional Protocol I, Art. 38: "It is prohibited to make improper use of the distinctive emblem of the red cross, red crescent or red lion and sun or of other emblems, signs or signals provided for by the Conventions or by this Protocol."

occurred in the course of a common Article 3 conflict, Additional Protocol I, relating to international armed conflicts, was not applicable. Additional Protocol II, applicable in noninternational conflicts, in Article 12, makes the improper use of the emblem a violation, if not a grave breach, as does Article 6 of Additional Protocol III.[29] At the time of the incident, Colombia had ratified Additional Protocol II but not Additional Protocol III. (The International Committee for the Red Cross [ICRC] study of customary law concludes that the perfidy prohibition applies in both international and noninternational armed conflicts, but its analysis of state practice does not strongly support that conclusion.)[30] "Ultimately, the Colombian rescue operation might be argued to represent an exceedingly rare circumstance – one where a minor violation of IHL remedies a criminal violation."[31] Sagely, perhaps, the ICRC chose to simply consider the humanitarian object of the act and look the other way as to the misuse of the emblem.

In May 1982, in the Falkland Islands, the United Kingdom was wresting the Falkland Islands, a British possession, from Argentine forces that had invaded and seized the islands the month before. At times the armed conflict between Britain and Argentina was fierce, nowhere more so than at Goose Green, a spit of land that controlled the Falklands' main airfield. The Argentines were fighting off hard-fought assaults on their positions near the airfield by 2 Para, of the British Parachute Regiment. Then the Brits saw a white flag at the enemy position. As the British lieutenant Jim Barry moved forward to parley and accept the apparent Argentine surrender he was shot dead. "The infuriated paras unleashed 66mm rockets, Carl Gustav [84 mm antitank recoilless rifle] rounds and machine-gun fire into the building. It was quickly ablaze. No enemy survivors emerged."[32]

It is perfidy to fight in the enemy's uniform.[33] It is perfidious to mark a historic building or monument falsely to indicate protected status,[34] or to indicate that it is the property of a neutral state not a party to the conflict.[35] It is perfidy to use a booby trap[36] in the form of an apparently harmless portable object, or to booby-trap wounded or dead bodies, children's toys, or religious objects.[37] It is perfidy for a *parlementaire* (one under a white flag who relays, for example, a surrender demand) to use the white flag as cover for the

---

[29] *Protocol Additional to the Geneva Conventions of 12 August 1949, and Relating to the Adoption of an Additional Distinctive Emblem.* Art. 6.1: "In particular, the High Contracting Parties shall take measures necessary for the prevention and repression, at all times, of any misuse of the distinctive emblems."

[30] Henckaerts and Doswald-Beck, *Customary International Humanitarian Law,* supra, note 16, at Rule 65, 221–3. Also see Vol. II. *Practice,* 1369–77.

[31] Dehn, "Permissible Perfidy," supra, note 17, at 651.

[32] Max Hastings and Simon Jenkins, *The Battle for the Falklands* (New York: Norton, 1983), 247. There is evidence that Lt. Barry may have been killed by enemy troops who were unaware of their own white flag. Note that a white flag is a sign of a desire to communicate with the enemy. It does not necessarily indicate surrender, although that is often the outcome. See: 1907 Hague Regulation IV, Annex Regulations Respecting the Laws and Customs of War on Land, Article 32; and: Yves Sandoz, *Commentary on the Additional Protocols,* supra, note 9, at 457.

[33] Case No. 56, U.S. Military Court in Germany, *Trial of Otto Skorzeny and Others,* IX LRTWC (1947).

[34] 1923 Hague Draft Rules of Aerial Warfare, Arts. 25 and 26(6).   [35] Additional Protocol I, Art. 37.

[36] A booby trap is "any device or material which is designed, constructed, or adapted to kill or injure and which functions unexpectedly when a person disturbs or approaches an apparently harmless object or performs an apparently safe act." Sandoz, *Commentary on the Additional Protocols,* supra, note 9, at 442.

[37] 1980 U.N. Convention on Prohibitions or Restrictions on the Use of Certain Conventional Weapons Which May Be Deemed to Be Excessively Injurious or to Have Indiscriminate Effects, 1980 Optional Protocol II, Art. 6.1.

collection of information, or for the sole purpose of moving troops without interference.[38] It is perfidious to feign a cease-fire.[39] It would be perfidy for an aircraft to employ a false identification by use of a transponder[40] or to employ false markings indicating that it is a medical aircraft.[41] At sea, it is perfidious to launch an attack after sending distress signals or feigning distress by the crew's taking to life rafts.[42]

The wearing of the ubiquitous camouflage field uniform is not perfidy. Although the camouflaged soldier hopes to kill, wound, or capture the enemy, his wearing of camouflage does not involve any assurance of protection under LOAC. A soldier may attempt to become invisible in the landscape, but not in a crowd.

In the fall of 1939, Russia invaded its small neighbor, Finland, an act for which Russia was later expelled from the League of Nations. Russia, with hundreds of thousands of soldiers and thousands of tanks, anticipated a quick and easy victory over an opponent with no armor, no antitank guns, and a twelve-aircraft air force. They overlooked the Finnish soldier's tenacity, the lack of roads suitable for tracked vehicles, and the dense forests that broke large formations into small groups suitable for ambush. There was another thing: As the Finns retreated, they burned everything to the ground to deny its use to the invader, and they booby-trapped whatever remained. "Booby traps had been placed with such cunning and imagination that Pravda was moved to complain about the Finns' 'barbaric and filthy tricks.' Everything that moved seemed attached to a detonator; mines were left in haystacks, under outhouse seats, attached to cupboard doors and kitchen utensils, underneath dead chickens and abandoned sleds."[43]

A booby trap is any device or material designed, constructed, or adapted to kill or injure and that functions unexpectedly when a person disturbs or approaches an apparently harmless object or performs an apparently safe act.[44] With restrictions, the use of booby traps was lawful in 1939, and their use remains lawful today.[45]

In World War II, the Nazi SS Obergruppenführer (lieutenant general) Reinhard Heydrich was Heinrich Himmler's deputy, and a leading proponent of the Final Solution. In 1942, he was based in Prague, and his title was deputy reichsprotektor of Bohemia and Moravia. Czechoslovakians simply referred to him as the Butcher of Prague. So broad were his powers and so wide his malevolent influence (and so effective his antiespionage program), the British government decided that, despite the harsh Nazi retribution that was sure to follow, Heydrich had to be killed. Eight British-trained Free Czech agents were parachuted into Bohemia. On May 27, two of them, disguised as civilian workmen, intercepted Heydrich on his way to his office in an open Mercedes

---

[38] Green, *Contemporary Law of Armed Conflict*, supra, note 1, at 92–3.

[39] Sandoz, *Commentary on the Additional Protocols*, supra, note 9, at 436 fn. 31.

[40] Dieter Fleck, ed., *The Handbook of Humanitarian Law in Armed Conflicts* (Oxford: Oxford University Press, 1995), para. 1019.

[41] Leslie C. Green, *Essays on the Modern Law of War*, 2d ed. (New York: Transnational, 1999), 589; and Additional Protocol I, Art. 18.

[42] 1994 *San Remo Manual on International Law Applicable to Armed Conflicts at Sea*, para. 111(b).

[43] William R. Trotter, *The Winter War: The Russo-Finnish War of 1939–40* (London: Aurum, 1991), 68.

[44] Pietro Verri, *Dictionary of the International Law of Armed Conflict* (Geneva: ICRC, 1992), 27.

[45] See Article 7, Protocol II (as amended on May 3, 1996), Convention on Prohibitions or Restrictions on the Use of Certain Conventional Weapons Which May Be Deemed to Be Excessively Injurious or to Have Indiscriminate Effects. Prohibitions include booby-trapping the wounded or dead, children's toys, religious objects, or animals or employing booby traps in cities, towns, or villages where fighting is not taking place. See Article 7 for the full range of booby trap prohibitions and allowances.

staff car and wounded him with a hand grenade. Eight days later, Heydrich died of septicemia that originated in his wound. As a result, the village of Lidiče was razed, 198 male villagers murdered, 184 women sent to a death camp, and 98 children abducted and given to Nazi families. There were other reprisals, as well. The two Czech agents, and five others who assisted them, were betrayed to the Nazis by the eighth Czech agent. Four of the betrayed Czechs committed suicide just before capture, and three others died resisting capture.[46]

As unlawful and terrible as the outcome was, the action of the Free Czech agents was perfidious. They attacked Heydrich, a uniformed combatant, while they wore civilian clothing and passed themselves off as noncombatants. Through their disguises as noncombatants they relied on being undiscovered and being protected by the law of war while intending to kill Heydrich. Despite the moral justness of targeting a monstrous enemy individual, the civilian disguises in which the Czechs fought constituted perfidy.

Other examples of perfidy are deliberately lying or misleading conduct involving a breach of faith where there is a moral obligation to speak the truth. It may initially seem odd that one may not lie to the enemy, but it is not lying that is prohibited, but lying or misleading the enemy with an intended breach of faith so as to cause the enemy to rely on the law of war to his detriment – his death, wounding, or capture. For example, it is perfidious to feign surrender so as to gain an advantage over the enemy, or to broadcast to the enemy that an armistice has been agreed. "On the other hand, it is a perfectly proper ruse to summon a force to surrender on the ground that it is surrounded and thereby induce such surrender with a small force. Treacherous or perfidious conduct in war is forbidden because it destroys the basis for a restoration of peace."[47]

In contrast, feigning being wounded with the intent of surrendering when the enemy's successful attack subsides is neither perfidy nor a ruse. It is not perfidy because it involves no intent to kill, wound, or capture, and it is not a ruse because, as we will see, it is not done in the interest of military operations for the purpose of misleading the enemy. "It is simply an expedient, used to ... withdraw from combat definitively."[48]

During the first Gulf War (1991–2), Iraqi troops reportedly dressed in civilian clothes and appeared to welcome approaching U.S. troops, then ambushed them.[49] Near the end of the war, in January 1992, at the opening of a mechanized battle, "Iraqi tanks entered Ras Al-Khafji with their turrets reversed, turning their guns forward only at the moment action began between Iraqi and Coalition forces. While there was some media speculation that this was an act of perfidy, it was not; a reversed turret is not a recognized indication of surrender per se."[50] Still, if not perfidy, it was an effort to deceive, which is no LOAC or IHL violation. It is a ruse.

---

[46] Callum MacDonald, *The Killing of SS Obergruppenführer Reinhard Heydrich* (New York: Free Press, 1989); and: Charles Wighton, *Hitler's Most Evil Henchman* (London: Odhams Press, 1962). At war's end, the traitorous agent, Karel Čurda, was captured and tried by a Czech "revolutionary tribunal." He was convicted and hanged.

[47] FM 27–10, *Law of Land Warfare*, supra, note 23, at para. 50.

[48] Sandoz, *Commentary on the Additional Protocols*, supra, note 9, at 436.

[49] Gen. Sir Peter de la Billière, *Storm Command* (New York: Harper Collins, 1993), 250.

[50] Dept. of Defense, *Conduct of the Persian Gulf War* (Washington, DC: GPO, 1992), appendix O, at 621.

11.1.1 *The Trial of Captain Jack*

On April 11, 1873, a group of four U.S. "peace commissioners," appointed by the secretary of the interior and led by the army brigadier general Edward R. S. Canby, met under a flag of truce with a group of six Modoc Indians near Tule Lake, California. Their purpose was to arrange terms by which hostilities between the United States and the Modoc band, consisting of only thirty-nine men, sixty-four women, and sixty children, might end.

The parley reached an impasse. The Modoc leader, Kientpoos, or "Captain Jack," gave a signal, and hidden Modocs opened fire, killing one of the civilian peace commissioners and wounding the other two civilians. Captain Jack shot General Canby in the face, killing him.

On June 4, U.S. troops captured Captain Jack and the other Indians involved in the shootings. On July 4, at Fort Klamath, Oregon, the Indians, Captain Jack, Black Jim, John Schonchin, Boston Charley, Brancho, and Slolux, were tried before a military commission. The charges: The six Modoc Indians, "in wanton violation of the sacred character of the flag of truce under the laws of war, willfully, feloniously, and with malice aforethought, [did] murder Brig. Gen. Canby" and the Reverend Dr. Eleasar Thomas, and assault with intent to kill Alfred B. Meacham and L. D. Dyar. Four days later, the six Modocs, who had no defense counsel, were found guilty and sentenced to death by hanging. On September 10, President Ulysses S. Grant approved the death sentences of four, including Captain Jack, and remitted the sentences of Brancho and Slolux to imprisonment for life. He also ordered that the remainder of Captain Jack's band be held as prisoners of war, and they were sent to the Quaw Paw Agency in Indian Territory (Oklahoma). On October 3, Captain Jack and the three others convicted were hanged at Fort Klamath.[51]

The Captain Jack trial is a diverting historical case, but it is more than that in terms of LOAC. One hundred thirty years ago, the United States effectively accorded a small band of rebellious Modoc Indians what amounted to statehood and belligerent status. The record of the military commission indicates that the United States considered Modoc fighters to be combatants who enjoyed the combatant's privilege, lawfully entitled to kill opposing U.S. soldiers in lawful combat. That view was necessary to the commission's jurisdiction for, even in 1873, military commissions had jurisdiction only over enemies charged with violations of the laws and customs of war. The captured followers of Captain Jack, moreover, were nominated "prisoners of war" by order of President Grant, who was well familiar with that period's laws of war. Nor was Captain Jack's case a one-off, as indicated by the 1891 federal trial of the Sioux Indian Plenty Horses (Chapter 1, Cases and Materials).

---

[51] This account is from: Col. Fred L. Borch and Robert F. Dorr, "Ambush in Oregon," *Army Times*, Oct. 8, 2007, 45; "The Canby Murderers," *NY Times*, June 10, 1873; and Don C. Fisher and John E. Doerr, "Outline of Events in the History of the Modoc War," *Crater Lake Nat'l Park Nature Notes* (Aug. 1937), http://www.nps.gov/archive/crla/notes/vol10–3e.htm. For a comprehensive history of American Indian trials, see: Carol Chomsky, "The United States–Dakota War Trials: A Study in Military Justice," 43 *Stanford L. Rev.* (1990), 13.

It is also of interest that Captain Jack and his five codefendants were convicted of murder while in violation of "the sacred character of the flag of truce." This was one of the first American trials that charged an enemy with an act of perfidy.

11.2 Ruses

Perfidy is not the same as ruses of war, which are allowed.[52] As the Lieber Code notes, "Deception in war is admitted as a just and necessary means of hostility ... consistent with honorable warfare."[53] Sometimes a ruse is the only course open to a weak combatant. The distinction between legitimate ruses and forbidden acts of perfidy is sometimes indistinct. "What primarily distinguishes perfidy from ordinary ruses of war is ... [that in perfidy there is] the exploitation of deliberately induced trust on the part of the adversary in order to injure, kill, or capture him. There must be a deliberate attempt to instill confidence with an 'intent to betray'."[54] **A ruse, in contrast, is a "deceit employed in the interest of military operations for the purpose of misleading the enemy."**[55] Ruses are intended to confuse the enemy, to induce him to act recklessly – to make a mistake or to act imprudently. Ruses are permitted in both international and noninternational armed conflicts.[56]

British Major General Anthony Rogers nicely illustrates the difference between perfidy and ruses:

> (a) the camouflaging of a tank so that the enemy pass by unaware of its existance and are then fired on at short and lethal range (a ruse) and (b) the soldier who feigns wounds so that he can fire at short and lethal range on an enemy soldier who comes to his assistance (perfidy). In the first case the tank crew do not feign protected status at all; in the second, the soldier lures the adversary into danger by pretending to have the protected status of someone *hors de combat*.[57]

Ruses such as camouflage; decoys; dummy artillery pieces, aircraft, or tanks; ambushes; mock operations; feigned attacks or retreats; communicating with nonexistent units; simulating the noise of an advancing column; using small units to simulate large forces; allowing the enemy to intercept false documents; altering landmarks and road signs; and misinformation are not perfidious because they invite no confidence with respect to the protections of the law of war.[58] Victor Hugo, in his novel *Les Misérables*, recounts how English troops, before the battle, pruned trees and bushes to create fields of fire – small windows through which they could fire on unsuspecting enemy soldiers who would soon advance into the British ambush. It was "an entirely legitimate stratagem of war," Hugo

---

[52] 1907 Hague Regulation IV, Art. 24. "Ruses of war and the employment of measures necessary for obtaining information about the enemy ... are considered permissible." Also, 1977 Additional Protocol I, Art. 37.2. "Ruses of war are not prohibited."

[53] Lieber Code, supra, note 2, Art. 101.

[54] Fleck, *Handbook of Humanitarian Law*, supra, note 40, at para. 472.

[55] Lassa Oppenheim and Hersch Lauterpacht, *International Law*. Vol. II. Disputes, War and Neutrality (London: Longmans, Green, 1944) para. 163.

[56] Henckaerts and Doswald-Beck, *Customary International Humanitarian Law*, supra, note 16, Rule 57, at 204. The ICRC study is somewhat more conservative, saying that "no [State] practice was found suggesting ruses were prohibited in either type of conflict."

[57] A. V. P. Rogers, *Law on the Battlefield*, 2d ed. (Manchester: Juris, 2004), 37.

[58] Additional Protocol I, Art. 37.

correctly notes.[59] Similarly, in 1944, Field Marshal Erwin Rommel directed ruses, all of which were lawful, to confuse the Allies' upcoming invasion of continental Europe: "Amongst the deceptions were, naturally, dummy minefields ... dummy [artillery] batteries which, in fact, were later heavily bombed. ... Infantry and artillery commanders were ordered to be ready to light fires on dummy batteries and on dummy emplacements and entrenchments ... to distract enemy gunfire from the beaches."[60]

SIDEBAR. A World War II ruse involved General George S. Patton's command of the First U.S. Army Group (FUSAG). Code named Fortitude South, FUSAG was based in England, across the English Channel from France's Pas de Calais. In early 1944, the Pas de Calais was the obvious invasion route to Germany and to Nazi V-1 and V-2 rocket launch sites. The Germans discovered Patton's presence in England and, acting on intercepted FUSAG radio traffic, stationed forces to oppose his anticipated landing at the Pas de Calais. "By April 1944 the secret decrypts of German message traffic, collectively known as Ultra, clearly showed that the Germans were convinced that the Allies fully intended to employ their best combat general to lead *Armeegruppe Patton*."[61] FUSAG never existed, however. It was created, with bogus radio messages and vehicle traffic, solely to pin enemy forces to the area far north of the actual landing beaches at Normandy. General Eisenhower said that the enemy "was convinced that we intended to launch an amphibious attack against that fortress stronghold [at Calais] and as a result stubbornly refused to use those forces to reinforce the Normandy garrison. We employed every possible ruse to confirm him in his misconception."[62] Even after the Allied landings on June 6, 1944, Nazi forces remained immobilized at the Pas de Calais to repel the "real" landings by Patton's FUSAG. It was a classic lawful ruse.

"Operation Bertram" was a World War II ruse in North Africa. In 1942, prior to the battle of El Alamein, the entire British X Corps moved to a new position, allowing their movement to be observed by Nazi elements. "Over the next four nights ... X Corps moved north again in secret, leaving behind canvas replicas of virtually every vehicle in the Corps, 400 tanks and 4,000 trucks, along with ... fake supply dumps, and even a dummy pipeline 20 miles long."[63] Bogus radio traffic completed the ruse. The Nazi enemy believed, to their great loss, that the El Alamein attack would occur in an entirely different sector, weeks later than it did.

Captured enemy equipment – tanks and aircraft, for example – may be used by the opposing side as long as their identification markings are replaced with the capturing state's markings before using them in combat. In international armed conflicts, 1977 Additional Protocol I, Art. 39.2, prohibits the "use of the flags or military emblems, insignia or uniforms of adverse Parties while engaging in attacks or in order to shield, favor, protect or impede military operations." This is a change from pre-1977 rules, which permitted

[59] Victor Hugo, *Les Misérables*, Norman Denny, trans. (London: Penguin Classics, 1982), 292.

[60] Brig. Desmond Young, *Rommel, the Desert Fox* (New York: Harper & Brothers, 1950), 175.

[61] Carlo D'Este, *Patton: A Genius for War* (New York: Harper Collins, 1995), 593.

[62] General of the Army Dwight D. Eisenhower, *Crusade in Europe* (New York: Doubleday, 1948), 288.

[63] Robert M. Citino, *Death of the Wehrmacht* (Lawrence: University Press of Kansas, 2007), 275.

the use of the enemy's uniform, provided it was not worn in actual combat.[64] The last phrase of Article 39.2, while offering very narrow circumstances in which the enemy uniform might be worn, remains sufficiently restrictive that it essentially bans completely the wearing of enemy uniforms. Additional Protocol II, relating to noninternational armed conflicts, makes no mention of uniforms. POWs should not volunteer false statements, but they are justified in giving false answers to questions that they are not obliged to answer correctly.[65] These examples do not exhaust the many opportunities to deceive the enemy lawfully.

Traditionally "it has been considered lawful to advance under the enemy flag or wearing enemy or even neutral uniform, so long as the correct insignia is worn during attack."[66] In the same vein, one could traditionally proceed under a false flag but not fight under it. But 1977 Additional Protocol I, Article 39.2, ends the lawfulness of wearing the enemy's uniform and using false flags for states that have ratified Protocol I. In fact, the protocol's restriction goes beyond simply forbidding the wearing of the enemy uniform in attacks: "It is prohibited to make use of the flags or military emblems, insignia or uniforms of adverse Parties while engaging in attacks or in order to shield, favour, protect or impede military operations."[67] The *Commentary* on the protocols explains:

> Traditionally the use of emblems of nationality of the enemy in combat was strictly prohibited by the laws of war. Lieber's code leaves no room for doubt. ... However, Article 23(f) of the Hague Regulations of 1907 merely prohibited their "improper use," which left ample room for controversy. The famous Skorzeny case could only further stir up feelings about this issue. ... The experts themselves were divided on this question. Some preferred a pure and simple prohibition, believing the Hague formula had given rise to excessive misuse. ... The final wording is a compromise between those two positions.[68]

The plain meaning of Protocol I's restriction evidences little compromise, however, and seems to impose a complete restriction on the wearing of the enemy uniform, and the use of false flags, in all situations directly related to military operations. For those states that have ratified Protocol I, one can think of few situations other than training exercises outside the combat zone, and escaping POWs, that would not be covered by its restrictions.

SIDEBAR. Ruses are not a relic of long-past wars. "During December 1990 the eyes of the world and the attention of its leaders focused on the Persian Gulf and Arabian Peninsula. For months, the United States had been building a strong naval and military presence throughout the region in response to Saddam Hussein's 2 August 1990 attack upon and occupation of Kuwait."[69] Rear Admiral John B. LaPlante commanded the

---

[64] The 1863 Lieber Code, supra, note 2, Art. 64, was even looser in allowing wearing of the enemy uniform: "If American troops capture a train containing uniforms of the enemy, and the commander considers it advisable to distribute them for use among his men, some striking mark or sign must be adopted to distinguish the American soldier from the enemy."

[65] Morris Greenspan, *The Modern Law of Land Warfare* (Berkeley: University of California Press, 1959), 320.

[66] Green, *Contemporary Law of Armed Conflict*, supra, note 1, at 146.   [67] Additional Protocol I, Art. 39.2.

[68] Sandoz, *Commentary on the Additional Protocols*, supra, note 9, at 466, citations omitted.

[69] Col. Gary J. Ohls, "Eastern Exit: Rescue 'From the Sea'," 61–4 *Naval War College Rev.* (Autumn 2008), 125, 127–8.

thirty-one-ship amphibious task force, and the marine major General Harry W. Jenkins commanded a landing force of two Marine Expeditionary Brigades. General Norman Schwarzkopf, commander in chief of Central Command, was the overall commander. He decided upon a ruse to pin down Iraqi forces that would otherwise be available to counterattack his planned "left hook" attack that he hoped would flank Iraqi lines.

Schwarzkopf directed LaPlante and Jenkins to prepare for a contested landing on the Kuwaiti coastline. Central Command provided opportunities to the American news media to observe and report on landing preparations. Their accounts were featured on television newscasts shortly before the Desert Storm ground attack was launched. The deception tied down five or six enemy divisions along the coastline. Only the highest level of command was aware that the amphibious landing was actually a ruse. Not even General Jenkins, the Marine commander, was told. Ultimately, there was no landing, but "as a deception, their operations constituted the most successful undertaking since the Second World War."[70]

Additional Protocol I provides special protections for journalists, including identity cards.[71] In the conflict against the Irish Republican Army, British forces dressed in civilian clothes, with false identity cards, passed themselves off as journalists. This unwise practice, the kind of abuse spoken of in the *Commentary*, was soon discovered and stopped. It was considered to constitute perfidious conduct that endangered true journalists and their civilian status.[72]

11.3 Perfidy Problems

The British professor Geoffrey Best notes that "the distinction between perfidy and *ruses de guerre* is . . . as important as it is in some respects delicate, and misjudgments of it are easily made."[73]

If a force raises a white flag, indicating a desire to parley, but the real purpose is to delay an enemy attack, has the force committed an act of perfidy? No, because the intent of raising the flag was not to kill, injure, or capture the enemy. It is a violation of Hague Regulation IV, Article 23(f), but it is not perfidy. "On the other hand, [after such an incident] people will be killed, injured or captured in the course of combat. It will be no easy matter to establish a causal relation between the perfidious act that has taken place and the consequences of combat. . . . This grey area forms a subject of permanent controversy in practice as well as in theory."[74]

If the enemy loads ammunition in an ambulance marked with a red cross and transports the ammunition to frontline distribution points, has the enemy engaged in perfidy? The ammunition clearly is intended for the purpose of killing or wounding, but is the act of loading the ammo in the ambulance and moving it forward in itself perfidious? Is the ultimate deadly purpose of the ammunition divorced from the acts of

---

[70] Id., at 128.   [71] Additional Protocol I, Art. 79.

[72] Green, *Essays on the Modern Law of War*, supra, note 41, at 239.

[73] Best, *War and Law since 1945*, supra, note 20, at 291.

[74] Sandoz, *Commentary on the Additional Protocols*, supra, note 9, at 433.

loading and transporting? Clearly, putting ammunition in an ambulance is a LOAC violation,[75] but is it perfidy?

Spies and others engaged in espionage who do not lead the enemy to act in the belief that they are protected by the law of war may nevertheless falsely pass themselves off as part of the enemy force. Although such acts are considered lawful[76] and do not involve perfidy, with equal legality spies may be tried and executed, if captured. If spying is not unlawful and it is not considered perfidy, how can spies be convicted and executed? Spies, although engaging in acts not considered unlawful, are considered unlawful combatants – civilians taking a direct part in hostilities, although being an unlawful combatant is not itself an LOAC violation.

> The question is what will be the gravamen of the penal prosecution of espionage. It is indisputable that espionage does not constitute a violation of [LOAC] on the part of the State engaging in it. But what is the status of the person perpetrating the act of espionage ... ? A spy ... is an unlawful combatant, and as such he is deprived of the status of prisoner of war. ... He may be prosecuted and punished, but only on the basis of the national criminal legislation of the belligerent State against whose interests he acted. As a rule, the charge will be espionage. ... But if the spy owes allegiance ... to the prosecuting State, he is liable to be indicted for treason.[77]

In naval warfare, as in land and aerial warfare, until 1977 Additional Protocol I, false flags were not considered contrary to LOAC. With regard to armed conflict at sea, despite Article 39.2's prohibition of the use of flags of adverse parties and Article 37's prohibition of perfidy, naval vessels are exempted.[78] "The rules of international humanitarian law applicable in warfare on land and those applicable in warfare at sea are not always identical."[79] Also, warships "have traditionally been conceded the right to disguise themselves – *inter alia*, by flying false neutral colours – except when going into action."[80] Before opening fire, the vessel's true flag must be displayed.[81]

In 1914, during World War I, the German cruiser *Emden*, a successful German raider plying the Indian Ocean, entered the port of Penang while flying the false flag of Japan. Just before attacking the Russian cruiser *Shemtshug*, the *Emden* ran up its German navy colors and opened fire, sinking the *Shemtshug*. During World War II, under true colors, the Allies successfully employed "Q ships" and the Germans used "raiders." These ships were heavily gunned, disguised to appear as merchant ships and easy prey for enemy

---

[75] E.g., 1907 Hague Regulation IV, Art. 23(f); 1949 Geneva Convention I, Art. 44.

[76] 1907 Hague Regulation IV, Art. 31, by implication.

[77] Dinstein, *The Conduct of Hostilities*, supra, note 6, at 210–11. Footnotes omitted.

[78] Sandoz, *Commentary on the Additional Protocols*, supra, note 9, at 470. "The final text [of Article 37] ... removed espionage and the conduct of armed conflict at sea from the field of application of Article 37 (*Prohibition of perfidy*), paragraph 1(d)."

[79] Knut Dörmann, *Elements of War Crimes* (Cambridge: ICRC/Cambridge University Press, 2003), 16.

[80] Dept. of the Navy, *U.S. Commander's Handbook on the Law of Naval Operations* (NWP 1–14M) (Washington, DC: GPO, 1995), at 12–1. "Naval surface and subsurface forces may fly enemy colors and display enemy markings to deceive the enemy. Warships must, however, display their true colors prior to an actual armed engagement." Also see: Dinstein, *Conduct of Hostilities*, supra, note 6, at 206, citing A. R. Thomas and J. C. Duncan, eds., *Annotated Supplement to the Commander's Handbook on the Law of Naval Operations* (Newport, RI: U.S. Naval War College, 1999), 511.

[81] Fleck, *Handbook of Humanitarian Law*, supra, note 40, at para. 1018.

combatant ships and submarines. On contact, the Q ship's false sidings would be dropped to provide fields of fire for the now-revealed deck guns. This action was not considered perfidy.

During the war in Bosnia, in the former Yugoslavia, Srebrenica was a U.N. "safe haven" protected by 750 lightly armed Dutch peacekeepers. In July 1995, Bosnian Serb soldiers, wearing stolen U.N. uniforms and driving stolen U.N. vehicles, told a long column of Bosnian Muslim fighters and their families that they were U.N. peacekeepers there to monitor the Muslims' surrender, guaranteeing no harm would come to them. Without a shot, the Dutch peacekeepers ceded to the Serbs the southern half of the safe haven they were meant to defend and acquiesced as Serbs arrested and led away the people in their charge. One Dutch lieutenant helped the Serbs control their captives.[82] At the order of General Ratko Mladić, orders were given to Serb units to kill all the Muslim men and older children. These orders were passed by oral instructions that avoided use of radios or cell phones.[83] In the worst atrocity committed in Europe since World War II, over a period of four days at least seven thousand Muslim men and boys taken in by the Serbs' perfidy were murdered by Serb firing squads.[84] The bodies were buried in mass graves. This was classic perfidy – gaining the opponent's confidence by assuring the protection of the law of war, then killing him.

After the conflict, in 2002, Momir Nikolić, a captain first class, Army of the Serbian Republic, during the Srebrenicia massacre, was arrested and tried before the ICTY for offenses associated with Srebrenica. He was sentenced to twenty-seven years' confinement for crimes against humanity.[85]

11.4 Summary

Ruses of war have been practiced since armies were first formed and, sometimes, have played vital roles in defeating the enemy. Unfortunately, perfidy also has a long, if less valorous, history. Although the two are easily defined, sometimes the line separating them can be indistinct, particularly in the confusion of combat. At other times unscrupulous commanders have knowingly stepped over the line. "Honest writing about IHL can never pretend that it is ever observed perfectly, even where circumstances are most favourable to its being so, and must always admit that the usual levels of observance range between the indifferent and the lamentable. . . . Yet the enterprise is not abandoned. The self-respect of civilization dares not let it be."[86]

---

[82] John Grimond, "How Bosnian Serbs Executed 7,000 Muslims under the Eyes of the U.N. and the World," *NY Times*, Book Review, May 11, 1997, n.p. (reviewing David Rohde, *Endgame: The Betrayal and Fall of Srebrenica* [1997]).

[83] Marlise Simons, "Officers Say Bosnian Massacre Was Deliberate," *NY Times*, Oct. 12, 2003, A10.

[84] Nicholas Wood, "Bosnian Serbs Admit Responsibility for the Massacre of 7,000," *NY Times*, June 12, 2004, A2.

[85] *Prosecutor v. Momir Nikolić*, IT-02-60/1-T (Dec. 2, 2003), para. 183. A coactor, Dragan Obrenović, IT-02-60-T Dec. 10, 2003), para. 156, was sentenced to seventeen years' confinement for associated crimes. Vidoje Blagojević, IT-02-60-T (Jan. 17, 2005), para. 861, was sentenced to eighteen years' confinement, and his coaccused, Dragan Jokić, para. 862, to nine years'.

[86] Best, *War and Law since 1945*, supra, note 20, at 290–1.

CASES AND MATERIALS

TRIAL OF OTTO SKORZENY AND OTHERS

General Military Government Court of the U.S. Zone of Germany
August 18 to September 9, 1947

Introduction. *The commonly cited case involving perfidy, and there are few cases, is Skorzeny. (His trial by U.S. military commission is briefly described in Chapter 6, Section 6.6.1.) In World War II, during the 1944 Ardennes Offensive, often referred to as the Battle of the Bulge, SS Obersturmbannführer (Lieutenant Colonel) Otto Skorzeny led an understrength Nazi brigade in operations behind U.S. lines. While planning the operation, "Skorzeny had been worried that any of his men captured while wearing U.S. uniforms might be treated as spies, but [he was advised] that the practice was within the rules as long as the men did not actually participate in combat."[87] When his mission failed and some of his men were captured, eighteen who were captured in American uniforms were indeed executed as spies. Skorzeny escaped, but was arrested and brought to trial after the war, in 1947, along with nine coaccused. Today, much of the Skorzeny holding has been rendered moot by Additional Protocol I, Article 39.2, which restricts the wearing of the enemy's uniform in virtually any circumstance.*

A. Notes on the Case

1 *The Use of Enemy Uniforms, Insignia, Etc.*

It is a generally recognized rule that the belligerents are allowed to employ ruses of war or stratagems during battles. A ruse of war is defined by Oppenheim-Lauterpacht (*International Law*, Vol. II, paragraph 163) as a "deceit employed in the interests of military operations for the purpose of misleading the enemy". When contemplating whether the wearing of enemy uniforms is or is not a legal ruse of war, one must distinguish between the use of enemy uniforms in actual fighting and such use during operations other than actual fighting.

On the use of enemy uniforms during actual fighting the law is clear. Lauterpacht says: "As regards the use of the national flag, the military insignia and the uniforms of the enemy, theory and practice are unanimous in prohibiting such use during actual attack and defence since the principle is considered inviolable that during actual fighting belligerent forces ought to be certain of who is friend and who is foe". The Defence, quoting Lauterpacht, pleaded that the 150th Brigade [Skorzeny's unit] had instructions to reach their objectives under cover of darkness and in enemy uniforms, but as soon as they were detected, they were to discard their American uniforms and fight under their true colours.

On the use of enemy uniforms other than in actual fighting, the law is uncertain. Some writers hold the view that until the actual fighting starts the combatants may use

---

[87] Donald M. Goldstein, Katherine V. Dillon, and J. Michael Wenger, *Nuts!: The Battle of the Bulge* (Washington, DC: Brassey's, 1994), 85.

enemy uniforms as a legitimate ruse of war, others think that the use of enemy uniforms is illegal even before the actual attack.

Lawrence (*International Law*, p. 445) says that the rule is generally accepted that "troops may be clothed in the uniform of the enemy in order to creep unrecognized or unmolested into his position, but during the actual conflict they must wear some distinctive badge to mark them off from the soldiers they assault."

J. A. Hall (*Treatise on International Law*, eighth edition, p. 537) holds it to be "perfectly legitimate to use the distinctive emblem of an enemy in order to escape from him or draw his forces into action".

Spaight (*War Rights on Land*, 1911, p. 105) disagrees with the views expressed above. He argues that there is little virtue in discarding the disguise after it has served its purpose, i.e. to deceive the enemy. "If it is improper to wear the enemy's uniform in a pitched battle it must surely be equally improper to deceive him by wearing it up to the first shot or clash of arms".

Lauterpacht observes (*International Law*, Vol. II, p. 335, note 1) that before the second World War "the number of writers who considered it illegal to make use of the enemy flag, ensigns and uniforms, even before the actual attack, was becoming larger."

Article 23 of the Annex of the Hague Convention, No. IV, 1907, says: "in addition to the prohibitions provided by special conventions it is especially forbidden ... (f) to make improper use of a flag of truce, of the national flag, or of the military insignia or uniform of the enemy, as well as the distinctive badges of the Geneva Convention". This does not carry the law on the point any further since it does not generally prohibit the use of enemy uniforms, but only the improper use, and as Professor Lauterpacht points out, it leaves the question what uses are proper and what are improper, open. ...

Paragraph 43 of the Field Manual published by the War Department, United States Army, on 1st October, 1940, under the title "Rules of Land Warfare", says: "National flags, insignias and uniforms as a ruse – in practice it has been authorised to make use of these as a ruse. The foregoing rule (Article 23 [of 1907 Hague Regulation IV]) does not prohibit such use, but does prohibit their improper use. It is certainly forbidden to make use of them during a combat. Before opening fire upon the enemy, they must be discarded". The American *Soldiers' Handbook*, which was quoted by Defence Counsel, says: "The use of the enemy flag, insignia and uniform is permitted under some circumstances. They are not to be used during actual fighting, and if used in order to approach the enemy without drawing fire, should be thrown away or removed as soon as fighting begins."

The procedure applicable in this case did not require that the Court make findings other than those of guilty or not guilty. Consequently no safe conclusion can be drawn from the acquittal of all accused, but if the two above-mentioned American publications contain correct statements of international law, as it stands today, they dispose of the whole case for the Prosecution, apart from the two instances of use of American uniforms during actual fighting.

Conclusion. *The military commission's (and Geneva's) expectation that soldiers, at the moment of combat, will initiate a sudden Clark Kent–like change from the enemy's uniform to their own has always seemed unrealistic; wardrobe is not on one's mind at such times. Nevertheless, until Article 39.2 of Additional Protocol I, that was the expectation. Now, Article 39.2 renders the Skorzeny case of mere historical interest. Today, if a combatant is captured in an enemy uniform with no showing that he engaged in combat* *while so dressed, it probably would be a violation of Additional Protocol I, and a minor LOAC violation. If captured while directly participating in hostilities in enemy uniform, however, the wearer has committed a war crime and forfeited POW status.*[88]

What of states that have not ratified Additional Protocol I? They are, of course, not bound by Article 39.2's prohibition and may apply the traditional rule articulated in Skorzeny: Wear the enemy uniform until the moment of combat, then revert to the combatant's true uniform.

MEDAL OF HONOR CITATION

Thomas R. Norris

Introduction. *Those familiar with the United States–Vietnam War may recognize Lieutenant Norris as the hero of events portrayed in the book and motion picture* Bat-21. *In reading the Medal of Honor citation, note Lieutenant Norris's disguise and consider its LOAC significance.*

> **Rank and organization:** Lieutenant, U.S. Navy, SEAL Advisor, Strategic Technical Directorate Assistance Team, Headquarters, U.S. Military Assistance Command.
> **Place and date:** Quang Tri Province, Republic of Vietnam, 10 to 13 April 1972.
> **Entered service at:** Silver Spring, Md.
> **Born:** 14 January 1944, Jacksonville, Fla.

Citation: Lt. Norris completed an unprecedented ground rescue of two downed pilots deep within heavily controlled enemy territory in Quang Tri Province. Lt. Norris, on the night of 10 April, led a five-man patrol through 2,000 meters of heavily controlled enemy territory, located one of the downed pilots at daybreak, and returned to the Forward Operating Base (FOB). On 11 April, after a devastating mortar and rocket attack on the small FOB, Lt. Norris led a three-man team on two unsuccessful rescue attempts for the second pilot. On the afternoon of the 12th, a forward air controller located the pilot and notified Lt. Norris. Dressed in fisherman disguises and using a sampan, Lt. Norris and one Vietnamese traveled throughout that night and found the injured pilot at dawn. Covering the pilot with bamboo and vegetation, they began the return journey, successfully evading a North Vietnamese patrol. Approaching the FOB, they came under heavy machinegun fire. Lt. Norris called in an air strike which provided suppression fire and a smokescreen, allowing the rescue party to reach the FOB. By his outstanding display of decisive leadership, undaunted courage, and selfless dedication in the face of extreme danger, Lt. Norris enhanced the finest traditions of the U.S. Naval Service.

Conclusion. *Did Lieutenant Norris's wearing of civilian clothing while behind enemy lines constitute either a ruse or perfidy?*

It was not perfidy because the wearing of noncombatant clothing by Lieutenant Norris was not an attempt to gain the enemy's confidence by assuring the enemy's protection

---

[88] W. Hays Parks, "'Special Forces' Wear of Non-Standard Uniforms," 4–2 *Chicago J. of Int'l L.* 545–6 (Fall, 2003). As Colonel Parks notes, however, "state practice in international armed conflicts has tended *not* to treat wear of civilian attire, non-standard uniforms, and/or enemy uniforms by regular military forces as a war crime." Emphasis supplied.

under the law of war. Lieutenant Norris hoped to avoid the enemy completely, with no issue of confidence arising. Nor did he intend to kill, wound, or capture the enemy; to the contrary, he hoped to go undetected.

His civilian disguise was a lawful ruse, a deceit employed in the interest of military operations for the purpose of misleading the enemy. One doubts that the enemy would have seen it that way, had he been captured, however.

(Six months after this incident, Lieutenant Norris, on another rescue mission behind enemy lines, was badly wounded and, at first, left for dead as his patrol retreated to the sea. Another SEAL, Petty Officer Michael E. Thornton, noted that Norris was missing. Thornton returned to the still heavily contested scene of Norris's wounding and, under heavy fire, found Norris, threw him onto his shoulder, and carried him to the shoreline. For two hours, Thornton towed Lieutenant Norris out to sea until they were picked up by Navy surface craft searching for them. Petty Officer Thornton was awarded the Medal of Honor, the only such award for the rescue of another Medal of Honor holder.)

12 Rules of Engagement

12.0 Introduction

At Bunker Hill, in 1775, William Prescott (or was it Israel Putnam?) is said to have ordered his Continental rebels, "Don't shoot until you see the whites of their eyes." Because the order specified the circumstances in which deadly force could be employed by infantry forces it could be considered an early rule of engagement (except that it is too clear and too brief to qualify).

Rules of engagement (ROE) are *not* law of armed conflict (LOAC) or international humanitarian law (IHL). They are not mentioned in the Geneva Conventions or additional protocols, and they are not the subject of a multinational treaty bearing on armed conflict. Nor are they are domestic law. They are military directives, heavy with acronyms. ROE are examined here because they play a significant role in executing the state's LOAC/IHL obligations and because they are frequently cited when LOAC/IHL violations are alleged. Most states' armed forces have some version of ROE to guide their combatants. (The record of U.N. peacekeeping forces and their ROE implementation has been troubled,[1] making a "strong [U.N.] response to provocation close to impossible.")[2] Although not LOAC/IHL, ROE violations are typically punished through the state's military code. In U.S. practice, violations are prosecuted as violations of a lawful general order, a common Uniform Code of Military Justice offense.[3]

ROE are often misunderstood, even by junior military personnel who are tasked with executing them. Say "rules of engagement" to a naval officer, and she will think, freedom

---

[1] Lt.Gen. Roméo Dallaire, *Shake Hands with the Devil* (New York: Carroll & Graff, 2003), 99, 229, 233, 264. Gen. Dallaire describes his continued difficulties in gaining approval of his U.N. peacekeeping force's ROE, and the interference of U.N. officials in the ROE, to the detriment of the Rwandans he was assigned to protect.

[2] Gen. Tony Zinni, in Tom Clancy with Gen. Tony Zinni, *Battle Ready* (New York: G. P. Putnam's Sons, 2004), 251.

[3] *U.S. v. John Winnick*. In 2008, Sgt. Winnick was charged with two specifications (counts) of involuntary manslaughter and one specification of failure to obey a lawful order, in that he failed to adhere to the rules of engagement by firing without reasonable certainty that his targets were hostile. After a pretrial investigation, the investigating officer recommended a general court-martial on lesser charges. The convening authority, however, dismissed all charges "in light of the circumstances." There are several earlier cases, for example, from the U.S. invasion of Panama, *U.S. v. McMonagle*, 34 M.J. 825 (ACMR, 1992), and *U.S. v. Finsel*, 33 M.J. 739 (ACMR, 1991); and from the peacekeeping mission to Somalia, *U.S. v. Conde* (USMC SpCM, Mogadishu, 1993), among six other ROE-related courts-martial.

[handwritten annotation: ROE can be interpreted in many different ways]

of navigation. Say "ROE" to an air force officer, and he will think, targeting constraints. Say "ROE" to an infantry officer, and he will think, use of deadly force. These viewpoints are variations on a common theme but with different applications, which can make a common understanding of ROE difficult. Say "rules of engagement" to an infantry squad leader, and he will think, "Damn lawyers!"

Each combatant sees this elephant differently, a distinction that can lead to battle-field confusion. The marine colonel Hays Parks goes so far as to write, "Overly restrictive ROEs are a key factor in the loss of confidence by company-grade officers and enlisted soldiers and Marines in their senior leaders and in the exodus of good men and women from the military."[4] That comment applies not to ROE as a concept, but to their use, and the restrictions they impose. There is no doctrinal cure for bad judgment, and as long as there are ROE there will be occasional ill-considered ROE formulations.[5]

Unless one is an experienced field grade officer – a midlevel leader, major or colonel, lieutenant commander or commander – ROE can be a mystery, as they are to the public and the media.[6] A Navy SEAL (sea, air, and land) veteran of Afghan combat, awarded the Navy Cross for a patrol in which his patrol leader, the Navy Lieutenant Michael Murphy, was posthumously awarded the Medal of Honor, writes:

> Each of the six of us in that aircraft en route to Afghanistan had constantly in the back of our minds the ever-intrusive rules of engagement. These are drawn up for us to follow by some politician sitting in some distant committee room in Washington, D.C. .... And those ROE are very specific: we may not open fire until we are fired upon or have positively identified our enemy and have proof of his intentions. Now, that's all very gallant. But how about a group of U.S. soldiers who have been on patrol for several days; have been fired upon; have dodged rocket-propelled grenades and homemade bombs; have sustained casualties; and who are very nearly exhausted and maybe slightly scared? How about when a bunch of guys ... brandishing AK-47s come charging over the horizon straight toward you? Do you wait for them to start killing your team, or do you mow the bastards down before they get a chance to do so? That situation might look simple in Washington, where the human rights of terrorists are often given high priority. ... However, from the standpoint of the U.S. combat soldier, Ranger, SEAL, Green Beret, or whatever, those ROE represent a very serious conundrum. ... They represent a danger to us; they undermine our confidence on the battlefield in the fight against world terror. Worse yet, they make us concerned, disheartened, and sometimes hesitant.[7]

[handwritten margin note: soldier's perspective]

A half-century of experience indicates, however, that, for combat operations involving large units, ROE are probably necessary on the modern battlefield, even given misunderstandings like those in the SEAL's complaint.

---

[4] W. Hays Parks, "Deadly Force *Is* Authorized," U.S. Naval Institute *Proceedings* (Jan. 2001), 33.

[5] For example, some ROE include the oxymoronic "use minimum deadly force"; also, "shoot to wound," and "fire no more rounds than necessary." Such provisions are not reassuring to war fighters.

[6] For example, Kenneth P. Werrell, "Across the Yalu: Rules of Engagement and the Communist Air Sanctuary during the Korean War," 72-2 *J. of Military History* (April 2008), 451, 458. The author frequently refers to Korean War era JCS policy and directives as ROE, misunderstanding their operational and legal distinctions.

[7] Marcus Luttrell, *Lone Survivor* (New York: Little, Brown, 2007), 37–8.

12.1 A Brief History of ROE

In the United States, the law of war developed along two lines, the law of the sea and the law of land armies. The two did not merge until the 1950 implementation of the Uniform Code of Military Justice, which finally blended the army and air force Articles of War and the navy's Articles for the Government of the Navy. In American practice, the development of ROE has been similar. They first were restrictions on use of force in the air force. "Although not yet referred to as such, modern rules of engagement first appeared during the air campaign over North Korea in 1950, when General Douglas MacArthur received orders from Washington that American bomber aircraft were neither to enter Chinese airspace nor destroy the Suiho Dam on the North Korean side of the Yalu River."[8] General MacArthur was eventually relieved of his duties because, among other reasons, he violated those ROE. Nor is he the only officer relieved of duty for doing so.[9]

In November 1954, the Joint Chiefs of Staff issued "Intercept and Engagement Instructions" to the air force, which were soon referred to as "rules of engagement." The term was officially adopted by the Joint Chiefs of Staff in 1958. The United States–Vietnam War hastened further development of air combat ROE, which became highly detailed and restrictive, with unprecedented domestic political involvement in day-to-day tactical operations of the air force. In the late 1960s, even before the end of the war in Vietnam,

> ROE were in a state of disorganization only slightly short of anarchy. In 1979, the Chief of Naval Operations, Admiral Thomas B. Hayward, directed a study to standardize the worldwide peacetime maritime rules of engagement ... to bring together in a single document these various references while also providing a list of supplemental measures from which a force commander could select when he felt it necessary to clarify force authority beyond basic self-defense statements. The Worldwide Peacetime Rules of Engagement for Seaborne forces ... were approved by the JCS in 1981. ... They were a clear statement of national views on self-defense in peacetime that also could smooth the transition to hostilities.[10]

Today's ROE are historically related to the navy's service-specific first-strike directive in Admiral Hayward's 1981 rules. That is, must U.S. combatant naval vessels take the first blow before initiating offensive measures? The navy standardized ships' captain's guidance, reversing prior instructions that they could fire only if fired upon. That new guidance, allowing for an accelerated sequence up the scale of force, was approved for naval use by the secretary of defense in June 1986. Meanwhile, as Admiral Hayward's

---

[8] Major Mark S. Martins, "Rules of Engagement for Land Forces: A Matter of Training, Not Lawyering," 143 *Military L. Rev.* (Winter 1994), 3, 35.

[9] The U.S. Air Force captain Dolph Overton studied radar records of enemy MIG fighters landing inside China. Armed with this information, over the course of four days in 1952, contrary to orders, he flew his F-86 fighter across the Yalu into China, joined groups of landing enemy planes, and shot down five, making him an ace. Called before his commanding officer, he admitted his actions. Overton was grounded, sent home, and denied medals for which he had been submitted, and no announcement of his ace status was made for a year. Overton resigned from the air force. Twenty-five years later, he was given his medals. Other pilots who violated the ROE in similar fashion, including the Korean War's leading U.S. ace, Capt. Joseph McConnell, also were grounded and/or sent home. Werrell, "Across the Yalu," supra, note 5, at 468–70.

[10] W. Hays Parks, "Righting the Rules of Engagement," U.S. Naval Institute *Proceedings* (May 1989), 83, 84.

[handwritten annotation: ROE = political rather than a realistic measure.]

study progressed, ROE applied by ground and air forces in Vietnam underwent their own development, which was not met with universal appreciation.

The 1968 My Lai massacre intensified ROE familiarization efforts. A panel of senior officers was convened to inquire into the My Lai events' causes. The panel discussed the two ROE-related pocket cards that all U.S. combatants in South Vietnam were required always to carry, "Nine Rules" and "The Enemy in Your Hands." Officers were required to carry a third card, "Guidance for Commanders in Vietnam." Lieutenant General William Peers, the senior My Lai investigating officer, wrote, "Some panel members thought the MACV [Military Advisory Command, Vietnam] policy of requiring soldiers to carry a variety of cards was nothing short of ludicrous."[11] Too often the cards were considered a substitute for training.

General Peers was not alone in his low opinion of Vietnam era ROE pocket cards, for "the resulting thicket of rules and cards did not effectively transmit to the individual soldier what was expected of him."[12] Senator James Webb, holder of the Navy Cross for combat valor in Vietnam, said of his 1969 arrival in Vietnam, when he was a U.S. Marine Corps lieutenant, "[I] was told to read and sign a copy of the rules of engagement. The document ran seven pages. Some of it made sense, but a lot of it seemed an exercise in politics, micromanagement, and preventive ass covering, a script for fighting a war without pissing anybody off."[13] Enlisted personnel disparaged the Vietnam era ROE, as well. "Grunts had little respect for rules of engagement that prohibited them from burning down a village that had been used as an ambush site with white phosphorus grenades but allowed a jet to do the same thing with bombs dropped from the sky."[14] A few years after the war, Hays Parks wrote, "Since the Vietnam War a sense of frustration, confusion, and distrust has seethed within the operational community with respect to rules of engagement."[15]

[handwritten annotation: Q on Lavelle demotion ?]

During the Vietnam conflict, there was opposition to ROE sufficient to cause General John D. "Jack" Lavelle, commander of the 7th Air Force, to disregard them and order twenty-eight raids on North Vietnamese targets that were prohibited by his ROE. When his apostasy was discovered, in March 1972, General Lavelle was relieved of command, demoted to major general, and forced to retire. The Army General Bruce Palmer confirmed, "The purpose of the U.S. restraints on the employment of U.S. airpower was, of course, a political one."[16] As General Creighton Abrams said, however, in testimony before Congress about the Lavelle case, "The rules [of engagement] have been forever . . . a source of frustration to many commanders. And they have had to live with them. And they have had to do their job with them."[17] General Lavelle's relief and demotion were a reminder to combatants that, like it or not, political considerations are always one basis of ROE.

In 1988, the Joint Chiefs of Staff issued a set of standing rules called the Peacetime ROE, applicable to all military operations short of actual war or prolonged conflict. The

[11] Lt.Gen. W. R. Peers, *The My Lai Inquiry* (New York: Norton, 1979), 230, fn. 1.
[12] Martins, "Rules of Engagement for Land Forces," supra, note 8, at 49, fn. 158.
[13] Robert Timberg, *The Nightingale's Song* (New York: Simon & Schuster, 1995), 152.
[14] Michal R. Belknap, *The Vietnam War on Trial* (Lawrence: University Press of Kansas, 2002), 49.
[15] Parks, "Righting the Rules of Engagement," supra, note 10, at 83.
[16] Gen. Bruce Palmer Jr., *The 25 Year War* (New York: DaCapo Press, 1984), 125.
[17] Lewis Sorley, *Thunderbolt* (Washington, DC: Brassey's, 1998), 341.

Peacetime ROE could be modified by the commanders in chief of unified commands (i.e., major multiservice, or "unified commands," led by full generals or admirals, of which there are nine worldwide) to meet contingencies of a given mission. "In turn, each subordinate commander is free to issue ROE specific to his unit, provided that they are neither less restrictive nor otherwise inconsistent with the ROE from higher headquarters. The individual soldier typically learns of the ROE in a briefing from his immediate commander. ... Later, the soldier may consult a pocket-sized card that purports to summarize the most important and relevant ROE."[18] In cases of war or prolonged armed conflict, the Peacetime ROE would be replaced by separately formulated ROE approved by the Joint Chiefs of Staff.

In 1994, the Peacetime ROE were redesignated the Standing Rules of Engagement (SROE), although little changed but the name. Significant portions of the SROE were, and remain, classified "secret." They were revised in January 2000 to give individual self-defense increased emphasis. The current SROE went into effect in June 200, and now include Standing Rules for the Use of Force (SRUF).

12.1.1 *Standing Rules of Force (SRUF)*

SRUF apply in domestic civil support missions and land defense missions within U.S. territory.[19] For example, SRUF would have applied, had they existed at the time, to military personnel present at the February 1993 siege and attack at the Waco, Texas, Branch Davidian Compound, where eighty-one Davidians and four Bureau of Alcohol, Tax and Firearms agents died. No military personnel were directly involved in that domestic attack, but soldiers were present to advise law enforcement personnel. Although new and untested, the SRUF applied throughout the army's and the national guard's Hurricane Katrina peacekeeping assignments in August and September 2005. The Military Sealift Command has SRUF that are applicable to its civilian seamen and-women.[20] One could argue that these varying concerns merely create a distinction without a difference. Whether RUF or ROE, we are still referring to what type of force [U.S. combatants] can use, under which circumstances, and when.

ROE military concerns generally involve the tactical and operational implications of performing missions in situations in which host-nation law enforcement and civil authorities are nonexistent, nonfunctional, or resistant to a U.S. military presence. In contrast, RUF military concerns generally presuppose a permissive military environment with a functional civil government capable of enforcing the law and maintaining order.[21]

An important distinction between SRUF and SROE is the different legal regimes that undergird the two. "ROE are generally shaped by international legal obligations, such as the United Nations Charter, international treaties, and customary international law. RUF are generally shaped by domestic or host-nation legal obligations."[22]

---

[18] Martins, "Rules of Engagement for Land Forces," supra, note 8, at 24. Footnote omitted.
[19] Chairman of the Joint Chiefs of Staff Instruction (CJCSI) 3121.01B (5 July 2007), "Standing Rules of Engagement/Standing Rules for the Use of Force for US Forces," appendix A, para. 1.e.
[20] ALMSC 017/06, "Standing Rules for the Use of Force (SRUF) by MSC [Military Sealift Command] Personnel," (July 10, 2006).
[21] Center for Law and Military Operations (CLAMO), "ROE v. RUF" *Marine Corps Gazette* (March 2006), "website exclusive," available at: http://www.mca-marines.org/gazette/2006/06clamo.html
[22] Id.

Although SRUF are domestically oriented and based on U.S. constitutional law, the current SRUF also contain concepts usually associated with ROE, such as "hostile act," "hostile intent," and "escalation of force." Incorporation of these ROE concepts introduces international law concepts to domestic law–based SRUF, and the possibility of confusion.[23]

12.2 What Are "Rules of Engagement"?

Joint Publication 1–02, *Dictionary of Military and Associated Terms*, defines ROE as "directives issued by competent military authority that delineate the circumstances and limitations under which U.S. [naval, ground, and air] forces will initiate and/or continue combat engagement with other forces encountered."

ROE are the primary means of regulating the use of force in armed conflict, and in situations short of armed conflict. They are akin to a tether, with which senior commanders control the use of force by individual combatants. They are the commander's rules for employing armed force, arrived at with the help of military lawyers and implemented by those who execute the military mission. ROE are "based upon three pillars – national policy, operational requirements and law."[24] The foundations of ROE are customary law and LOAC/IHL, along with considerations of political objectives and the military mission. Limitations contained in ROE guard against the escalation of situations involving armed force. They may regulate a commander's action by granting or denying use of particular weapons – artillery or tear gas, for example. In 1994–5's Operation Uphold Democracy, in Haiti, the ROE specified that only brigade commanders and higher-level officers could authorize the use of riot control agents – tear gas.

ROE *never* limit the right and obligation of combatants to exercise self-defense. Nor may ROE authorize a violation of LOAC/IHL. Their provisions may be more restrictive than those of LOAC/IHL, however. For example, they may direct that soldiers not fire at specified targets, or that they use ammunition of no greater than a specified caliber, even though those targets or that ammunition is not prohibited by LOAC/IHL. Also, they may direct that enemy aircraft not be engaged by friendly aircraft without permission of the area air defense commander. In the U.S.–Vietnamese conflict (1965–72), air force pilots flying Operation Rolling Thunder missions were restricted from attacking North Vietnamese dikes. During Operation Just Cause, the 1989 U.S. invasion of Panama, the Joint Task Force commanding general, General Carl Steiner, U.S. Army, required that an officer of the grade of at least lieutenant colonel approve all artillery fire that impacted any populated area.

ROE are not tactical in nature; they do not instruct soldiers or Marines, sailors or airmen, in how a mission is to be executed. Tactics and ROE are complementary, not synonymous. "ROE are designed to provide boundaries and guidance on the use of force that are neither tactical control measures nor substitutes for the exercise of the commander's military judgment."[25] To say that soldiers charged with committing a LOAC/IHL violation were only following their ROE is often an incorrect use of the term.

cant use the defence "just following orders w/ ROE

[23] For an examination of SRUF: Maj. Daniel J. Sennott, "Interpreting Recent Changes to the Standing Rules for the Use of Force," *Army Lawyer*, Nov. 2007, 52.

[24] Richard J. Grunawalt, "The JCS Standing Rules of Engagement: A Judge Advocate's Primer," *Air Force L. Rev.* (1997), 245, 247.

[25] Maj. Marie Anderson and Emily Zukauskas, eds., *Operational Law Handbook*, 2008 (Charlottesville, VA: Judge Advocate General's Legal Center and School, 2008), 79.

how is this a thing?

In times past, senior politicians have inserted their wishes into the ROE process, with dangerous results for U.S. combatants. During the 1980 Iranian rescue mission, the Carter administration sought to require an impractical shoot-to-wound directive. During the 1982 U.S. involvement in Beirut, Reagan administration officials amended the ROE at several levels, with the result that Marine sentries carried empty weapons on the morning they were attacked by a truck bomb (see the SIDEBAR). Later in the Reagan administration, the National Security Council initially directed that U.S. advisers in El Salvador, who often engaged in firefights with insurgents, carry only personal weapons – 9mm pistols but no rifles.[26]

In 1986, the commanding officer of the army's 75th Ranger Regiment was ordered to deploy a Ranger battalion to an exercise in Honduras, across a major guerrilla infiltration route. The colonel refused to accept the tasking until the ROE were changed from "no live ammunition authorized" to one magazine of live ammunition in a taped-shut ammo pouch, to live ammunition authorized in the weapon but no round in the chamber, to (finally) live ammunition with a chambered round. This time, the risk to U.S. Rangers that an empty weapon represented had been imposed by *military* seniors. Although he could have been relieved of his duties for his intransigence at any point, the Ranger commander's insistence was not career ending.[27]

That was not an isolated instance of ill-considered ROE dictated by military superiors. In October 2000, al Qaeda's suicide bombing of the USS *Cole* in the port of Aden, Yemen, killed seventeen U.S. sailors and nearly sank the ship. The sailors' "'rules of engagement' would have prevented them from firing without first obtaining permission from the *Cole*'s captain or another officer, the crew members said."[28] This was "because of orders issued not by the ship's captain, but from the Navy's Fifth Fleet. ... That directive was based on diplomatic concerns about repercussions should American sailors fire weapons – even as warnings – in the port of an Arab country."[29] The military has no corner on ill-considered ROE decisions, however.

> Higher authorities in the United States on occasion have imposed restrictions on lawful weapons because of political sensitivities. ... At the time of the 1983 Grenada rescue operation, a request was forwarded ... for permission to employ riot control agents. ... However, realizing a key vote on modernization of the U.S. chemical weapon deterrence capability was scheduled in the Senate that week, a response to the request was delayed lest the anticipated reaction to the use of riot control agents on Grenada undermine the Senate vote.[30]

Although extraneous pressures bearing on ROE content are always possible, judge advocates usually take the lead in ROE formulation. Orders issued by each of the U.S. Armed Services task judge advocates with training members of their branches in ROE, as well as law of war matters, generally.[31]

---

[26] Parks, "Deadly Force *Is* Authorized," supra, note 4, at 34.   [27] Id., at 37.

[28] Thomas E. Ricks and Steve Vogel, "USS *Cole* Guards Told Not to Fire First Shot," *Wash. Post*, Nov. 14, 2000, A1.

[29] Steven Lee Myers, "Inquiry Faults the *Cole*'s Captain and Crew," *NY Times*, Dec. 9, 2000, A6.

[30] Parks, "Righting the Rules of Engagement," supra, note 10, at 92–3.

[31] For example, Marine Corps Order 3300.4A, "Marine Corps Law of War Program," (Jan. 9, 2014), contains detailed lists of LOAC subject matter that U.S. Marine Corps judge advocates are required to study and be familiar with, including ROE and RUF, and be able to brief their commanders on, before they deploy.

> **SIDEBAR.** In June 1982, Israel invaded Lebanon in an effort to end attacks on Israel that were emanating from there. That fall, in an effort to restore calm to the area, the United States participated in a multinational stability effort. U.S. Army Special Forces initiated the training of pro-Western Lebanese forces, and Marines were assigned to protect the Beirut airport. To keep their footprint to a minimum, the Marine component of the Multinational Force, Battalion Landing Team 1/8, of the 24th Marine Amphibious Unit, was billeted almost entirely in the four-story Beirut Airport terminal building.
>
> At 0622 on October 23, 1983, Lance Corporal Eddie DiFranco was in sandbagged sentry Post 7, between a parking lot and the terminal building. He watched a yellow Mercedes truck circle the parking lot, as lost trucks occasionally did, then suddenly accelerate and burst through the barbed-wire barrier between the parking lot and the terminal, heading for the front of the terminal building.[32] Following the ROE, DiFranco had a loaded magazine in his weapon but no round chambered.[33] Lance Corporal DiFranco jerked the charging handle of his M-16 to the rear and let it slam forward, chambering a round, but before he could flick off the safety and raise the weapon to his shoulder, the truck was past him. It roared directly into the lobby of the terminal building – the Battalion Landing Team headquarters – where it detonated its load of an estimated twelve thousand pounds of explosives. Two hundred forty-one Marines and sailors died in the blast.
>
> A later investigation of the bombing reported, "The Commission concludes that the ... ROE contributed to a mind-set that detracted from the readiness of the [Marines] to respond to the terrorist threat which materialized on 23 October 1983."[34]

Today, most U.S. operations are joint operations, often involving a unified geographic commander, such as Southern Command, Central Command, European Command, or Southern Command, or Joint Forces Command, whose forces operate with other countries' armed forces. "The standing ROE (SROE) provide that U.S. forces assigned to be OPCON [under operational control, or command] or TACON [under tactical control, or command] to a multinational force will follow the ROE of the multinational force if authorized by the SECDEF [the secretary of defense]."[35] In such cases every

---

The navy's order, SECNAVINST 3300.1C, "Department of the Navy Law of War Program" (May 28, 2009), is far less specific, simply advising that judge advocates are "responsible for advising operational commanders shall have sufficient understanding of the law of war to advise and assist those commanders independently and expeditiously." The air force order, Air Force Policy Directive 51–4, "Compliance with the Law of Armed Conflict" (Aug. 4, 2011), does not refer to ROE at all.

[32] Eric Hammel, *The Root* (New York: Harcourt Brace Jovanovich, 1985), 292–4.

[33] Some sources, for example, Martins, "Rules of Engagement for Land Forces," supra, note 8, at 11, disagree with Hammel, saying that the sentries, including DiFranco, did not have loaded magazines inserted in their weapons. The first two points of the ten-point ROE in effect on the day of the bombing read: "1. When on post, mobile or foot patrol, keep loaded magazine in weapon, bolt closed, weapon on safe, no round in the chamber. 2. Do not chamber a round unless told to do so by a commissioned officer unless you must act in immediate self-defense where deadly force is authorized." Id., Hammel, at 427. If the sentries did not have a loaded magazine in their weapons, they were in violation of their ROE.

[34] Dept. of Defense, *Report of the Commission on Beirut International Airport Terrorist Act* (Dec. 20, 1983), 135.

[35] Anderson and Zukauskas, *Operational Law Handbook*, 2008), supra, note 24, at 594.

effort is made to arrive at a common ROE or, if possible, have common ROE in place before operations begin.[36] If that proves impractical, U.S. forces will employ their own ROE, after discussing the differences in ROE with the allied forces and informing subordinate units of the differences they may encounter. The United States does have standing combined ROE with a number of other states. Those standing combined ROE ease joint operations planning.

However, if an American unit is under the *operational control* of a multinational force that employs a different ROE, as opposed to the American unit's merely *operating with* a multinational force with a different ROE, the guidance is different. In such cases, unless directed otherwise, the U.S. unit will follow the ROE of the multinational force.[37] (There are occasions when U.S. units are directed otherwise.)

12.3 When SROE/ROE Apply[38]

To understand ROE, one must understand the SROE. Although complementary, the two are quite different. If U.S. forces engage in an unanticipated armed conflict, it is the SROE that apply by default. The SROE apply to all military operations and contingencies outside U.S. territory. Inside U.S. territory, the SROE apply only to air and seaborne homeland defense missions.

"The SROE establish fundamental policies and procedures governing the actions of U.S. force commanders."[39] SROE apply in common Article 2 and common Article 3 armed conflicts and in peacekeeping missions, peace-enforcing missions, and antiterrorist missions. They also apply in military operations other than war – what the military used to refer to as "OOTW," pronounced "OUGHT-wah." The term is not as frequently employed as in pre-9/11 years. SROE do not apply, however, in *posse comitatus* situations – when soldiers are deployed on land within the United States to assist federal or local civilian authority in time of disaster or civil disturbance. That is when the SRUF come into play.

The SROE are always present, applicable to all U.S. armed forces, standing by in the "military supermarket" that is managed by the Pentagon's Joint Staff.[40] It is the Joint Staff that is responsible for developing and maintaining the SROE.[41] The SROE are like a catalog of provisions from which a military "tactical shopper," with the agreement of the Joint Staff, selects precisely the items that will fit into his military mission shopping

---

[36] See Cmdr. Mike Spence, "Lessons for Combined Rules of Engagement," U.S. Naval Institute *Proceedings* (Oct. 2000), 56–60, for a discussion of issues in formulating combined ROE.

[37] Appendix A, *Joint Chiefs of Staff Standing Rules of Engagement*; supra, note 19, at para. 1.c.(1).

[38] This section is largely based on Anderson and Zukauskas, *Operational Law Handbook*, 2008, supra, note 24, chapter 5.

[39] Army Field Manual 3–24 and Marine Corps Warfighting Publication 3–33.5, *U.S. Army–Marine Corps Counterinsurgency Field Manual* (Chicago: University of Chicago Press, 2007), D-9, at 350.

[40] Chairman of the Joint Chiefs of Staff Instruction (CJCSI) 5810.01d, "Implementation of the DOD Law of War Program," (April 30, 2010), para. 6.b.(2): "Ensure that the Joint Operations Planning and Execution System includes appropriate guidance to ensure review of plans and rules of engagement for compliance with the law of war."

[41] The Joint Staff supports the chairman of the Joint Chiefs of Staff, who, among other duties, directs the staff. The Joint Staff is "purple," that is, staffed by a roughly equal number of select senior U.S. Army, Navy, Air Force, and Marine Corps officers. It is the J-3, the Joint Operations Division of the Joint Staff, that develops and maintains the SROE.

MEU = marine expeditionary Unit.

basket. In other words, when a specific military task is contemplated, the SROE are the basis for the formation of mission-specific ROE that will apply to that military task alone; the SROE are mined to make up mission-specific ROE.

Throughout the ROE formulation process and the implementation phase, mission-specific ROE are the commander's responsibility, not her judge advocate's. Responsibility for the content of ROE, and for combatants observing the ROE, resides in the commander. Rarely, commanders and their staffs have defaulted in this responsibility, leaving ROE formation to their military lawyer alone, sometimes leading to ROE that put their men and women at risk.[42] Even more rarely, commanders have used their judge advocate's interpretation of the ROE as an excuse for acting or not acting in a tactical situation.[43] Although judge advocates have a major voice in ROE planning and implementation, they can only recommend. It is the commanding officer who decides.

They rarely give up this authority!

The basic requirements for employment of SROE, and mission-specific ROE that are developed from them, are <u>military necessity</u> and <u>proportionality.</u> Before armed force may be employed, there must be a military necessity to do so; that is, whether in a common Article 2 or 3 situation, lawful force must be indispensable for securing the submission of the enemy. Also when armed force is employed, that force must be proportional to the threat faced; the loss of civilian life and damage to civilian property must not be excessive in relation to the direct military advantage to be gained. Unit commanders have the obligation to ensure that individuals within their units understand and are trained in when and how to use force in self-defense and in accomplishing the mission.[44]

12.4 Formulating Mission-Specific ROE

No two tactical cases are alike, and no ROE formula applies across the board. In considering how mission-specific ROE come about, however, a typical case might be a noncombatant evacuation order.

The ROE process begins when a deployment order is issued to, for example, a Marine Expeditionary Unit (MEU) afloat off the European coast. The order is to carry out a noncombatant evacuation order in a small country where civil war has erupted. The lives of Americans in the country are at risk, and they must be quickly evacuated: "Execute in 48 hours" may be the order that the Joint Chiefs of Staff initially send to the unified commander – the four-star general located in Florida, in this case, who directs the

---

[42] Parks, "Deadly Force *Is* Authorized," supra, note 4.

[43] An example of a judge advocate unfairly blamed for a superior's tactical decision occurred during an early stage of the conflict in Afghanistan. In October 2001, a Taliban convoy suspected to include the Taliban leader, Mullah Omar, was sighted. Expedited permission for an armed Predator to fire on the convoy was denied by Central Command's commanding general, Tommy Franks. His reported reply to the request to fire was "My JAG doesn't like this, so we're not going to fire." Thereafter, General Frank's "JAG," a Navy judge advocate captain who had voiced her qualms about noncombatants who might be in the convoy, was heavily criticized in the unknowing media, sometimes by name; e.g., Seymour M. Hersh, "King's Ransom: How Vulnerable Are the Saudi Royals," *New Yorker*, Sept. 22, 2001, 36; Thomas E. Ricks, "Target Approval Delays Cost Air Force Key Hits," *Wash. Post*, (Nov. 18, 2001, A1 (a circumspect depiction of the event); Rebecca Grant, "An Air War like No Other," *Air Force*, Nov. 2002, 31, 34; and, on television, *Face the Nation*, Bob Schieffer and Colin Powell, Oct. 21, 2001.

[44] Field Manual 3–24, *Counterinsurgency Field Manual*, supra, note 39, D-10, at 351.

European MEU's operations. The unified commander passes on the Joint Chiefs' order to the MEU commander afloat off the European coast. "The SROE are in effect," the unified commander's order to the MEU might read, recognizing that the SROE are always in effect until mission-specific ROE can be formulated and approved. The unified commander's order continues, "Request ROE supplemental measures that you desire": that is, begin to formulate your mission-specific ROE in coordination with the Pentagon's Joint Staff.

If the time to mission execution is short, the MEU may not have an opportunity to formulate mission-specific ROE and will have to conduct the noncombatant evacuation order with the SROE. In this case there is enough time, so, aboard ship, the MEU commander and his staff, who will execute the noncombatant evacuation order, quickly formulate a plan for the operation. The Marine commander and his staff, including the MEU's judge advocate, review the SROE notebook, including its enclosures and annexes, which are key to forming mission-specific ROE.

The SROE's Enclosure A contains unclassified general-purpose SROEs. Enclosures B–H of the SROE are classified enclosures that provide guidance for various types of operations, such as maritime operations, land operations, antidrug operations, and non-combatant evacuation operations. Embarked aboard navy shipping that is cruising off the European coast, the Marine MEU commander will use the noncombatant evacuation order guidance as his template, to which he will add supplemental measures to arrive at mission-specific ROE for his unit's assignment.

SROE Enclosure J is unclassified and provides administrative guidelines for incorporating ROE development in the mission-planning process.

Enclosure K contains theater-specific ROE that apply in various geographic areas where combatant units may be called upon to fight. Enclosure L is an unclassified assemblage of ROE previously employed by combatant commanders in their particular areas of responsibility – "Here's what the last commander in your location did."

Returning to the noncombatant evacuation-planning example, typically the unit commander, assisted by his military lawyer and other staff officers, decides what supplemental measures to request for the mission. Will an opposing force be declared hostile prior to landing? Can riot control agents be employed? Can international boundaries be crossed if considered necessary? Can artillery fire be preplanned? May the commander detain civilians? Possible supplemental measures are many. Each requested supplemental measure will go through the Joint Staff in the Pentagon, and on to the Joint Chiefs of Staff for approval.

The unit commander turns to SROE Enclosure I, which contains hundreds of numbered ROE "supplemental measures," most of them classified. Some of Enclosure I's supplemental measures are left blank, for unique situations that require formulation of one-time supplemental measures. There are three levels of supplemental measures available. At the lowest level, the on-scene commander, the MEU commanding officer afloat off the European coast in this case, may approve some supplemental measures. The unified commander in Florida can approve a higher level of supplemental measures. At the highest level, only the National Command Authority, the president, and the secretary of defense may approve the most sensitive supplemental measures.

Using secure communications, there are back-and-forth discussions throughout the rapid ROE formulation process between the MEU commander at sea and the Joint Staff at the Pentagon. Within hours, standard and supplemental ROE measures are agreed upon and approved by the Joint Chiefs of Staff; at that point, the MEU has mission-specific ROE. Aboard ship, the ROE are written into the MEU's operation order in an annex that may be twenty pages in length, or more. All of the MEU's component units – the infantry companies, the artillery battery, the helicopter squadron, and so forth – receive a much-condensed version of the ROE. The commanders of the subunits brief their individual Marines on the ROE in even briefer fashion. If time permits, the mission-specific ROE may be summarized on a single card. To the individual Marine, then, the ROE are a card in his pocket, rather than the twenty-page document arrived at through the harried efforts of planners and commanders aboard his ship, at unified command headquarters in Florida, at the Pentagon, and perhaps at the White House.

Sometimes, formulation of the ROE can be unhurried. An example was the planning stage of the 2003 invasion of Iraq, when, among many U.S. Army, Navy, and Air Force units, as well as allied British, Polish, and Danish forces, a Marine Expeditionary Force (MEF) prepared for the coming common Article 2 armed conflict. In their Kuwait staging area, the MEF staff had a lengthy period in which to fine craft mission-specific ROE in coordination with the Pentagon's Joint Staff.

> The MEF's legal office spent the months before the war working up the ROE and then preparing and disseminating presentations for the major subordinate commands. ... [The Marine commander, Major General James Mattis] issued written, detailed guidance on the law of war on at least two occasions. ... In one prewar memorandum he ... went on to outline eleven commonsense law of war "principles." ... To drive the message home, General Mattis had his staff judge advocate ... deliver classes on the law of war and rules of engagement to Division units both before and during the deployment.[45]

On March 20, when the Marines finally crossed into Iraq to confront the enemy, each Marine carried an ROE card. ROE pocket cards are the barest summary of the mission-specific ROE, intended as a concise and unclassified distillation to serve as training aid and memory tool. Upon reading an ROE card, one is impressed with its effort also to be a mini-LOAC/IHL primer. Confronted with a crisis in the field, soldiers and Marines will not be able to consult a pocket card, but must rely upon the principles of the ROE they have internalized during training. Along with that training, ROE cards may be a useful tool. Many military officers view them with disfavor, however, because they are sometimes thought of as substitutes for training and supervision on battlefield conduct.

After mission-specific ROE are published, they are not immutable. Commanders at any level may, and often do, request additional or modified ROE in response to new circumstances on the ground. ROE are routinely amended, sometimes as frequently as week to week, while a lengthy operation plays out.[46] Adjacent units on a single battlefield may have differing ROE, reflecting the different units' differing missions. All units, however, have ROE of some nature.

---

[45] Col. Nicholas E. Reynolds, *Basrah, Baghdad, and Beyond* (Annapolis, MD: Naval Institute Press, 2005), 157–8.

[46] C. J. Chivers, "Perfect Killing Method, but Clear Targets Are Few," NY *Times*, Nov. 22, 2006, A1. "The military has also tightened rules of engagement [in Iraq] as the war has progressed, toughening the requirements before a [U.S.] sniper may shoot an Iraqi. Potential targets must be engaged in a hostile act, or show clear hostile intent."

12.5 ROE Content

When mission-specific ROE are formulated, what are their contents? Most ROE are similar, but, because every military mission is unique, no two are exactly the same. All will have one or more common elements and a common philosophic outlook: SROE and ROE are usually permissive in nature.[47] That is, in the beginning of the combat operation they allow "commanders the authority and obligation to use all necessary means to defend their units and, for the most part, allows commanders to use any lawful weapon or tactic for mission accomplishment unless specifically restricted from doing so by higher authority. This permissive framework affords commanders wide latitude in shaping ROE unique to their mission."[48] For example, early in the conflict in Iraq, if there was a "troops in contact" situation, if U.S. forces were actually engaging enemy combatants, in keeping with the ROE some requirements for approving supporting fires were ignored; houses could be bombed, aviation assets could be called in, artillery was available, all on a squad leader's say-so.[49] As the conflict progressed, the mission-specific ROE often became more restrictive.

All ROE contain a clear statement of the right to self-defense. Occasionally, ROE also describe escalation-of-force measures. Most contain other common elements addressing enemy hostile acts, enemy hostile intent, dealing with enemy forces declared hostile, and a positive identification requirement.

12.5.1 *The Right to Self-Defense*

The SROE stress the right of self-defense. To an even greater extent than previous versions, the "new" January 15, 2000, SROE emphasize that right:

> Unit Self-Defense. A unit commander has the authority and obligation to use all necessary means available and to take all appropriate action to defend the unit, including elements and personnel thereof, or other US forces in the vicinity, against a hostile act or hostile intent. In defending against a hostile act or hostile intent under these SROE, unit commanders should use only that degree of force necessary to decisively counter the hostile intent and to ensure the continued safety of US forces.[50]

When employing self-defense, as long as the opposing force remains a threat, it may be pursued and engaged. Unless the ROE specify otherwise, there is no requirement that a self-defense engagement be terminated when the opposing force attempts to break off contact.

---

[47] Center for Law and Military Operations (CLAMO), "Rules of Engagement: What Are They and Where Do They Come From?" *Marine Corps Gazette*, April 2002, 59, 60.

[48] CLAMO, "'ROE' Rhymes with 'We'," *Marine Corps Gazette*, Sept. 2002, 78.

[49] A "troops in contact" ROE provision in use in Iraq in 2009: "TROOPS IN CONTACT (TIC). While friendly forces are in contact with enemy forces, either in self-defense (in response to hostile act/intent) or in reaction to a positively identified declared hostile force, the OSC [on-site commander] has approval authority for all counter battery and reactive fire, including all organic and non-organic weapon systems. The OSC is responsible for establishing PID [positive identification] minimizing collateral damage and responding in a proportional manner."

[50] Appendix A, *Joint Chiefs of Staff Standing Rules of Engagement*; supra, note 19, para. 7.c.

Unit self-defense and individual self-defense trump all other ROE provisions. In 2003, immediately before the U.S.–Iraqi common Article 2 conflict began, Major General James Mattis, the commanding general of the 1st MEF, went from unit to unit, addressing his Marines. One junior officer recalls, "The theme was rules of engagement, and he wanted to make [several points] very clear. First, commanders had an inherent obligation – not merely a right, but a legal and ethical obligation – to defend their Marines."[51] If civilians were killed in the process, "a commander would be held responsible not for the facts as they emerged from an investigation, but for the facts as they appeared to him in good faith at the time – at night, in a sandstorm, with bullets in the air."[52]

In October 1993, in Mogadishu, Somalia, Army Rangers and Delta Force soldiers of Task Force Ranger were on a mission to capture two lieutenants of the Somali warlord Mohammed Farah Aidid. When the mission went awry, the U.S. force was engaged in a furious fifteen-hour firefight in which eighteen U.S. soldiers were killed and seventy-three wounded, many seriously. Somalia, a failed state, had no army, but it did have an abundance of heavily armed civilian fighters, none with uniform or distinguishing sign. Thousands of them were attacking a group of heavily outnumbered American soldiers who were conducting a fighting retreat.

> Moving in from more distant parts were vehicles overflowing with armed men. ... Somalis approached in groups of a dozen or more from around corners several blocks up, and others, closer, darted in and out of alleys taking shots at them. ... The Rangers were bound by strict rules of engagement. They were to shoot only at someone who pointed a weapon at them, but already this was unrealistic. It was clear they were being shot at, and down the street they could see Somalis with guns. But those with guns were intermingled with the unarmed, including women and children. ... Rangers peering down their sights silently begged the gawkers to get the hell out of the way.[53]

Soon, the Rangers were firing on the Somali shooters in the approaching crowds. They knew that, no matter how well aimed their fire, women and children would fall victim to their shooting. Proportionality and collateral damage were subsumed by the onslaught of Somali fighters surrounding them. Unit self-defense does not negate the requirements of proportionality, but self-defense trumps other ROE provisions.

12.5.1.1 A Legal Fine Point: Self-Defense in Human Rights Law and in LOAC/IHL

It is argued by the International Committee of the Red Cross and human rights activists that human rights law has a greater role in LOAC/IHL than the United States acknowledges. As discussed elsewhere (Chapter 1, Section 1.4.2.), the argument that the two have a coequal status on the battlefield is resisted by the United States, which sees LOAC/IHL as distinct from human rights law. The United States believes that human rights law was not intended to be, and should not be, controlling in *jus in bello* situations.

The influence of human rights law is illustrated, however, in the issue of self-defense as contained in ROE. It is common to describe returning enemy fire as firing in "self-defense," but be wary of casual use of the legal term of art, "self-defense." Imagine a British patrol in Iraq during the common Article 2 phase of the conflict, before the

---

[51] Nathaniel Fick, *One Bullet Away* (New York: Houghton Mifflin, 2006), 182.   [52] Id.

[53] Mark Bowden, *Black Hawk Down* (New York: Atlantic Monthly Press, 1999), 18.

Saddam Hussein regime fell. The patrol fires on and kills an Iraqi civilian as he fires an automatic weapon at the patrol. In layman's terms, the killing of the civilian was self-defense, but was it? The British colonel Charles Garraway, warns:

> This [self-defense characterization] is classic human rights law. But the incident was taking place during an international armed conflict. Under the law of armed conflict, the right to use lethal force would depend on whether or not the Iraqi was a legitimate target. If he was a combatant, or a civilian taking an active part in hostilities, he was, as such, a legitimate target and there was no need to justify the soldiers' actions by reliance on self-defense, or the defense of anyone else.[54]

In time of armed conflict, whether international or noninternational, when a lawful or unlawful combatant takes up arms against an opponent combatant, he becomes a lawful target. To fire on the lawful or unlawful combatant is simply a lawful use of force and an exercise of the combatant's privilege. Self-defense, as that term is used in domestic law, with its potentially contentious human rights issues, is not an issue. "When evaluating the lawfulness of the Soldier's use of force under international law, reference should be made to [international] humanitarian law alone."[55]

It is unrealistic to expect that the term "self-defense" not be used colloquially in instances when one combatant returns the fire of another, but Colonel Garraway's point should be kept in mind.

12.5.2 *Escalation of Force*

Escalation of force is not a part of ROE, but in Iraq it became a significant related factor. "Escalation of force" indicates that combatants should use lower levels of force when it is possible to do so without endangering themselves or others.[56] If tactical circumstances permit, soldiers are expected to not to resort to deadly force immediately. For example, "the proper configuration of a Traffic Control Point will allow Soldiers to identify approaching vehicles sooner, thus providing Soldiers more time to apply warnings (visual signs, loudspeakers, barricades, tire strips, laser pointers, laser dazzlers, warning shots, etc.)."[57] The "time to apply warnings" refers to the escalation of force: If it comes to firing his weapon, a soldier is trained to "apply warnings" by first firing at the approaching vehicle's tires. If the vehicle continues, again warn, this time by firing at the engine block. If the vehicle still continues, the time for warnings is past; fire at the driver. Easier said than done, this is all considered and accomplished in a matter of seconds, perhaps at night in poor visibility, as the car hurtles toward the soldier's position.

Escalation of force is sometimes taught through the phrase "Shout, show, shove, shoot." A soldier confronted by individuals approaching on foot should "shout" at them

---

54 Charles Garraway, "The 'War on Terror': Do the Rules Need Changing?" 3 *Chatham House* (2006), http://www.chathamhouse.org.uk/pdf/research/il/BPwaronterror.pdf

55 Maj. Michelle A. Hansen, "Preventing the Emasculation of Warfare: Halting the Expansion of Human Rights Law into Armed Conflict," 194 *Military L. Rev.* (Winter 2007), 1, 47.

56 In European military practice, the seminal "use of force" case is the European Court of Human Rights' *McCann and Others v. the United Kingdom*, 18984/91 (1995). *McCann* holds that not only must the use of force be proportionate, but that military (and law enforcement) operations, even against suspected terrorists, must be planned so as to minimize possible recourse to deadly force.

57 Anderson and Zukauskas, *Operational Law Handbook*, 2008, supra, note 25, 81.

to stop, ideally in the local language. If the individuals continue, the soldier should "show" (i.e., brandish) his weapon. If the individuals still continue to advance, they should be "shoved" (i.e., be physically restrained, at which point, in practice, it would be far too late to avert an armed enemy). Finally, if they still advance, they may be fired upon.[58]

ROE are interpreted in a reasonable way. In exercising self-defense, a soldier is not necessarily required to employ each option before escalating to the next higher force level,[59] and when circumstances dictate, the soldier may go immediately to deadly force. In Iraq, during the 2003 dash to Baghdad by tank-mounted U.S. forces:

> Gruneisen ordered Peterson to speed through the [traffic] circle. He wanted to just plow through the circle, past the [enemy] trucks and soldiers. ... As they rolled into the circle, Hernandez saw a yellow pickup truck speeding toward them with two men in the front seat. There wasn't time for a warning shot – no time to determine whether these were wayward civilians or militiamen trying to ram them. Hernandez got off a burst from the M-240 machine gun]. He saw a spray of blood stain the windshield and watched the passengers go down.[60]

The circumstances of each case determine whether immediate deadly force is, or is not, the best response. Meanwhile, there are four terms that often appear in ROE, knowledge of which will help in understanding ROE.

12.5.3 *Hostile Act*

Appendix A of the SROE defines a number of SROE/ROE/SRUF terms, including "hostile act": "**An attack or other use of force by a foreign force or terrorist unit (organization or individual) against the United States, US forces, and in certain circumstances, US citizens, their property, US commercial assets. ... It is also force used directly to preclude or impede the mission and/or duties of US forces, including the recovery of US personnel and US government property. When a hostile act is in progress, the right exists to use proportional force, including armed force, in self-defense by all necessary means available.**"[61] A hostile act is "simply the actual use of armed force – attacking."[62]

When a hostile act is involved, immediate firing on the opposing force or individual is permitted because of the opponent's *conduct*, rather than his *status*. That is, regardless of the individual's status – civilian, combatant, or protected person – his conduct in firing on you, or otherwise conducting a hostile act, renders him a legitimate target without the

---

[58] A "use of force" ROE provision in use in Iraq in 2009: "**GRADUATED FORCE**. If individuals pose a threat to Coalition Forces by committing a hostile act or demonstrating hostile intent, US Forces may use force, up to and including deadly force, to eliminate the threat. When time and circumstances permit, use the following graduated measures of force when responding to hostile act or hostile intent: Shout verbal warnings to halt; Show your weapon and demonstrate intent to use it; Physically restrain, block access, or detain; Fire a warning shot (if authorized); Shoot to eliminate the threat."

[59] This is in keeping with U.S. Supreme Court jurisprudence relating to civilian law enforcement use of deadly force. *Illinois v. Lafayette*, 462 U.S. 640 (1983).

[60] David Zucchino, *Thunder Run* (New York: Grove Press, 2004), 43.

[61] Appendix A, *Joint Chiefs of Staff Standing Rules of Engagement*, supra, note 19, at "Definitions, para. 5.e. Emphasis supplied.

[62] Capt. Ashley Roach, "Rules of Engagement," *Naval War College Rev.* (Jan.–Feb., 1983), 50.

necessity of determining his status. As the U.S. Supreme Court has written, "Detached reflection cannot be demanded in the presence of an uplifted knife."[63]

In late 2005, in the town of Haditha, where seventeen Iraqis, most of them noncombatants, were killed by a squad of Marines, the squad leader fired on four dismounted and unarmed Iraqi taxi passengers and the driver, killing all five. "[The squad leader] has said he shot the five men, but only after they ran away, which he believed constituted a hostile act that allowed him to use deadly force."[64] This is evidence of the squad leader's unfamiliarity with the ROE. Even in Iraq in 2005, the ROE did not allow firing on unarmed individuals not involved in a combat incident only because they were fleeing. If the squad leader was aware of other factors, that could change the calculus.

A hostile act is usually clear: Someone is firing at you. A hostile act can be something less than weapons fire, however. Under certain circumstances, it could be considered a hostile act if an individual initiates a cell phone call from a rooftop location as you approach a vehicle choke point. The ICRC's report on direct participation in hostilities makes this point (Chapters 6.4.1 and 15.6.2). Hostile acts are such whether occurring in a common Article 2 or 3 conflict or a peacekeeping or peace-enforcing mission. Upon the occurrence of a hostile act by an opposing force or individual, one may immediately exercise self-defense, including deadly force.

Whereas hostile acts are usually self-evident, determining what constitutes "hostile intent" is more difficult.

12.5.4 *Hostile Intent*

There can be no bright-line test for what constitutes hostile intent. To be overly cautious in assessing intent may lead to the death of fellow combatants. Yet, being too quick to presume hostile intent may result in the death of innocent noncombatants. The circumstances of combat, in which a decision to fire or not fire sometimes must be made virtually instantly, only complicate the decision. The SROE define hostile intent as **"the threat of imminent use of force by a foreign force or terrorist unit (organization or individual) against the United States, U.S. forces, and in certain circumstances, U.S. citizens ... , their property, US commercial assets. ... When hostile intent is present, the right exists to use proportional force, in self-defense by all necessary means available to deter or neutralize the potential attacker."**[65] This definition is broad and gives considerable discretion to the individual perceiving the actions of others. "Many countries do not share the aggressive American [hostile intent] stance, woven into the fabric of the Standing ROE. Nonetheless, that stance is the one carried in the pockets of American troops everywhere."[66] The interpretation of hostile intent can indeed be aggressive. The Marine sergeant major Brad Kasal, awarded the Navy Cross for his heroism in the 2004 second battle of Fallujah, writes:

> Keyholing [attacking a house by employing two rockets, the first to punch a hole in the wall, and a second thermobaric rocket through the same hole to collapse the house] was

---

[63] *Brown v. United States*, 41 S. Ct. 501, 502 (1921).

[64] Paul von Zielbauer, "At Marine's Hearing, Testament to Violence," NY *Times*, Sept. 1, 2007, A4.

[65] Appendix A, *Joint Chiefs of Staff Standing Rules of Engagement*, supra, note 19, "Definitions," para. 5.f.

[66] Lt.Col. W. A. Stafford, "How to Keep Military Personnel from Going to Jail for Doing the Right Thing: Jurisdiction, ROE & the Rules of Deadly Force," *Army Lawyer* (Nov. 2000), 1, 5.

not exactly what higher headquarters had in mind when it promulgated the ROE for Fallujah. ... According to its tenets someone inside a building had to display hostile intent before the Marines could engage him. When the rules were followed precisely they often put the young Marines taking the risks at a significant disadvantage, so they were quietly ignored.[67]

As Sergeant Major Kassel suggests, "hostile intent" is sometimes given an elastic definition by troops in contact with the enemy. If so, military necessity and proportionality had best be given consideration, as well. Today, in Iraq and Afghanistan, terrorists' disregard of the distinction requirement "means that their enemy is barely able to discriminate between combatants and non-combatants. The only criteria left are those of 'hostile intent' and of the 'hostile act,' as defined in the rules of engagement. While these concepts have been defined by NATO, the somewhat theoretical sounding definitions can quickly become unclear in practice. ... And this is certainly true in situations where events are taking place in quick succession."[68]

Explaining what constitutes hostile intent can be challenging, akin to a divine epiphany for soldiers who must make a decision in seconds while on patrol in the mean streets of an Afghan village. "The key in determining whether or not the use of force in self-defense is authorized against a demonstration of hostile intent is a keen awareness of what constitutes a threat. Soldiers must be able to recognize indicators of both hostile intent and existing capabilities to accomplish what is intended."[69] Harsh experience and a steep learning curve may be the best, if most harsh, teacher. "Determining the existence of a hostile act or demonstration of hostile intent is a function of the professional military judgment of the on-scene commander."[70] Sometimes the on-scene commander is a nineteen-year-old squad leader.

12.5.5 *Declared Hostile*

Only high-level commanders, the National Command Authority, the Joint Chiefs of Staff, or regional commanders may declare an enemy force hostile. Doing so reflects issues of national self-defense as much as, or more than, concern for U.S. combatant forces.

"Once a force is declared hostile by appropriate authority, U.S. units need not observe a hostile act or a demonstration of hostile intent before engaging that force. The responsibility for exercising the right and obligation of national self-defense and declaring a force hostile is a matter of the utmost importance demanding considerable judgment of command."[71]

Being declared hostile "clears the decks" for units to shoot on sight opposing forces or individuals. In Iraq, "'declared hostile' meant there were no rules of engagement. It meant shoot first and ask questions later."[72] During the 2003 armored thrust to Baghdad

[67] Nathaniel R. Helms, *My Men Are My Heroes* (Des Moines, IA: Meredith Books, 2007), 184.

[68] Th. A. van Baarda and D. E. M. Verweij, *Military Ethics: A Dutch Approach* (Leiden: Martinus Nijhoff, 2006), 85.

[69] Maj. Steven A. Gariepy, "On Self-Defense" (2008) (Unpublished paper in partial fulfillment of master of laws degree, Judge Advocate General's Legal Center and School) (on file with author).

[70] Grunawalt, "JCS Standing Rules of Engagement," supra, note 24, at 252.

[71] Appendix A, *Joint Chiefs of Staff Standing Rules of Engagement*, supra, note 19, at "Definitions," para. 6.

[72] Fick, *One Bullet Away*, supra, note 50, 237.

by U.S. forces, a tank commander unexpectedly sighted a group of uniformed enemy soldiers through his tank's gun sight:

> A dozen Iraqi soldiers in green uniforms were leaning against a building, chatting, drinking tea, their weapons propped against a wall. They were only a few hundred meters away, but they seemed oblivious to the grinding and clanking of the approaching armored column. "Sir, can I shoot at these guys?" LaRocque asked. The rules of engagement said anyone in a military uniform or brandishing a weapon was a legitimate target. "Uh, yeah, they're enemy," Ball replied. ... Through the tank's magnified sights, Ball could see their eyes, their mustaches, their steaming cups of tea. LaRocque mowed them down methodically, left to right.[73]

No hostile intent or hostile act was required. When an opposing force is declared hostile, as Iraqi army forces were at the time of the U.S. invasion, they may be engaged on sight. The basis for engagement is shifted from conduct to status;[74] the target does not have to do anything (*conduct*), such as fire on friendly forces or show some cloudy hostile intent. As soon as they are positively identified (*status*) they may be engaged with deadly force. The ROE requirement of "military necessity" is considered met.

A "declared hostile" ROE provision in use in Iraq in 2009:

> DECLARED HOSTILE FORCES. CRD, CENTCOM [Commander-in-Chief, Central Command] has designated certain Iraqi military and paramilitary forces (former regime security forces, conventional and/or unconventional air, ground, and naval forces) as declared hostile forces. Since the end of major combat operations, these forces have transitioned from overt conventional resistance to insurgent methods of resistance. This declaration continues to apply to Former Iraqi Military and Paramilitary personnel who are operating as insurgent individuals or groups that continue hostilities against the Iraqi Government and MNF [Multi-National Forces]. These individuals and/or groups may be engaged and destroyed. Hostile armaments, munitions, and equipment are also included in this category. All pre-planned kinetic strikes against these targets must be executed in accordance with the collateral damage considerations required by the CDEM [Collateral Damage Estimation Methodology] and these ROE.

There follows a list of ten Iraqi groups, members of which are declared hostile: Special Republican Guard, Special Security Organization, Directorate of General Security, Iraqi Intelligence Service/Directorate of General Intelligence, Directorate of Military Intelligence, Ba'ath Party Militia, Mojahedin E-Khalk, Fedayeen Saddam, Al Quds, and Mahdi Army and armed supporters of Muqtada Al-Sadr.

12.5.6 Positive Identification

Before a U.S. combatant can fire on an individual or group, even those declared hostile, or those committing hostile acts, many ROE require that the targeted individual or group be positively identified.

Positive identification (PID) is undefined in the SROE, leaving it to combatants to apply the plain meaning of the phrase. PID concerns recognizing hostile intent and

---

[73] Zucchino, *Thunder Run*, supra, note 60, at 10.
[74] The Judge Advocate General's Legal Center & School, *Operational Law Handbook*, 2006 (Charlottesville, VA: JAGC&S, 2006), 92.

hostile acts. If a soldier is returning enemy fire, the ROE only requires that he do so on a target he has positively identified; he cannot "spray and pray" that he hits an enemy combatant rather than a civilian child.

What if a soldier believes he has positively identified his enemy target, but he is in error, and instead he fires and kills a civilian? An investigation always follows. If prosecution is considered, what legal standard should be applied to his act? The international criminal law general intent standard of honest and reasonable belief applies. "The mistake of fact must be honestly, and reasonably, made on the basis of the conditions prevailing at the time of the commission of the unlawful act."[75] As the military tribunal said in its 1948 judgment in the case of the Nazi Generaloberst Lothar Rendulic, "We are obliged to judge the situation as it appeared to the defendant at the time. If the facts were such as would justify the action by the exercise of judgment, after giving consideration to all the factors and existing possibilities, even though the conclusion reached may have been faulty, it cannot be said to be criminal."[76] The U.S. Supreme Court has enunciated a similar standard for domestic law enforcement officers.[77]

In 1994, over Iraq, a failure of PID had tragic results. During Operation Provide Comfort, a U.S. Air Force E-3 Airborne Warning and Control System (AWACS) aircraft was controlling other U.S. aircraft patrolling Iraq's no-fly zone. The E-3 alerted two Air Force F-15 fighters to the presence of two enemy helicopters that were, in fact, friendly. There had been prior erroneous alerts to "enemy" aircraft. "AWACS aircraft incorrectly have cleared Navy fighter aircraft to engage civilian airliners and U.S. Air Force C-5 aircraft misidentified as Iraqi fighters. Navy pilots' insistence on positive visual identification prevented other tragedies."[78] In this case, several other operational failures followed the E-3's misidentification, including the F-15 pilots' own misidentification of the targets. The F-15s shot down two U.S. Army UH-60 Black Hawk helicopters, killing twenty-six passengers and crew. "This was not an 'accidental' shoot down. Two Air Force pilots failed to follow their rules of engagement and caused the deaths of 26 persons."[79]

Other LOAC/IHL considerations may be applicable even when there is positive identification. Pilots, for example, cannot always engage ground targets that have been PIDed as hostile.

> "Those insurgents are wily," said ... the commanding officer of [a fighter squadron aboard a deployed aircraft carrier, the USS] Roosevelt. ... "They will meld themselves within the population. They will fire from areas that they know that if we put a bomb in there, it's going to look bad. ... If it was positively identified hostile in Iraq, you took it out. ... Here [in Afghanistan], just because it's positively identified as hostile, you've still got to mitigate the other things around."[80]

[75] Kriangsak Kittichaisaree, *International Criminal Law* (Oxford: Oxford University Press, 2001), 264.

[76] *U.S. v. List*, "The Hostage Case," XI TWC (Wahington, DC: GPO, 1950), 1113, 1296.

[77] *Graham v. Connor*, 490 U.S. 386 (1989), 396. "The 'reasonableness' of a particular use of force must be judged from the perspective of a reasonable officer on the scene, rather than with the 20/20 vision of hindsight."

[78] Hays Parks, *Friendly Fire: The Accidental Shootdown of U.S. Black Hawks over Northern Iraq* (book review), U.S. Naval Institute's *Proceedings* (Aug. 1999), 83, 84.

[79] Id. Also see Maj. Dawn R. Eflein, "A Case Study of Rules of Engagement in Joint Operations: The Air Force Shootdown of Army Helicopters in Operation Provide Comfort," *Air Force L. Rev.* (1998), 33.

[80] Elisabeth Bumiller, "From A Carrier, Another View of America's Air War in Afghanistan," NY *Times*, Feb. 24, 2009, A6.

If the pilot fires a missile, is it likely to kill civilians as well as insurgents? One civilian? Ten? How many insurgents are likely to be killed? One insurgent? Ten? Is the target the head of al Qaeda in Afghanistan? Or is he a Taliban messenger? Does the pilot, *can* the pilot, know which? In seconds, despite PID, the pilot must consider issues of distinction, military necessity, and proportionality.

In Afghan ground combat, what if Corporal A is watching a group of individuals approach a friendly position on his right flank. Suddenly he sees two men in the group thrust up two rocket propelled grenades (RPGs) from the midst of the group, then lower them back into invisibility. Corporal A quickly radios Sergeant B at his position on the right flank, "The guys coming up on your position are enemy – I just saw their RPGs!" "Are you sure?" the sergeant responds. "I'm positive!" Corporal A answers. May Sergeant B, who has the group in sight, but has seen nothing suspicious, open fire on the group on the basis of Corporal A's PID? The answer is not found in any ROE but, yes, PID is "transferable," and Sergeant B may act on Corporal A's PID.

A "positive identification" ROE provision in use in Iraq ground combat in early 2009: **"Positive Identification (PID) of all targets is required prior to engagement. PID is a reasonable certainty that the individual or object of attack is a legitimate military target in accordance with these ROE."**

12.6 ROE Issues

In March 2003, Delta Company, 1st Light Armored Reconnaissance Battalion, 1st Marine Division, was preparing for the invasion of Iraq from their position across the Iraqi border, in Kuwait. Predeployment training included a procession of exercises, practices, and classes. The company commander attended one of his company's ROE classes:

> Capt Portiss taught a class for the company on the standing rules of engagement, and soon every Marine seemed to be asking a situational question. ... Portiss patiently answered each question until I finally stepped in. ... I paraphrased what General Wilhelm had said when he was the commanding general. "If the enemy initiates contact with you, the question is proportionality of your return fires. If you initiate contact with the enemy, the question is what collateral damage you may cause. ... Marines, this is the important thing. If you perceive yourselves to be in danger, then you either return fire or initiate fire on the enemy. Period." I thought it was a simple matter, but it had been legally complicated over the previous ten years or more.[81]

A continuing ROE problem is troop compliance. Lax enforcement of ROE restrictions are quickly sensed by junior combatants, leading to battlefield excesses, as happened in the Vietnam conflict. In contrast, overly restrictive ROE, and frequent prosecutions for violations, may make troops hesitant to take action when immediate force is necessary.

In Somalia's Operation Restore Hope (1992–3), the ROE prevented U.S. soldiers from using armed force to stop massive looting and theft.[82] Worse, when six soldiers were court-martialed for violating the ROE, "soldiers ... perceived that prosecution would follow every decision to fire."[83] Soon, soldiers hesitated to fire even when fired upon.

---

[81] Maj. Seth W. B. Folsom, *The Highway War* (Washington, DC: Potomac Books, 2006), 56.

[82] Col. Frederick M. Lorenz, "Law and Anarchy in Somalia," 23 *Parameters* (1993–4), 39.

[83] Martins, "Rules of Engagement for Land Forces," supra, note 8, at 64.

In 2004, in Mahmudiyah, Iraq, a Marine lieutenant complained, "We had become an 'ineffective occupier' and not because of the [insufficient] number of troops ... but because of our overly restrictive Rules of Engagement and our discomfort with killing the guys that needed to be killed."[84]

> **SIDEBAR.** In February 1993, during a platoon-size sweep of a Somali village for weapons and munitions reported to be there, Army Specialist James Mowris saw a Somali run from the approaching platoon. Mowris chased the man and fired, he said, a warning shot into the ground to make him stop. The shot killed the running Somali. "Specialist Mowris' platoon did not understand and had not received training on the written ROE."[85] A general court-martial convicted Mowris of negligent homicide.[86] An Army colonel in Somalia commented that "because of this case, soldiers in some cases were reluctant to fire even when fired upon for fear of legal action. It took weeks to work through this."[87] The court-martial convening authority set aside Mowris's conviction, perhaps as a result of the hesitation to fire that Mowris's court-martial quickly generated in his unit.

Troop compliance is not the only issue in interpreting ROE. In the U.S. conflict in Afghanistan, the American concern with the death and wounding of civilians not involved in the fighting, other than as victims, led U.S. armed forces to take extraordinary measures to minimize collateral damage. In Afghanistan in 2009, the four-star general Stanley McChrystal took command of the allied International Security Assistance Forces (ISAF). McChrystal had a lengthy record of outstanding combat command. Upon taking command of ISAF he quickly addressed the issue of collateral damage. His solution was strictly circumscribing the circumstances under which requests by engaged troops for artillery and air support could be granted. ROE across the combat zone were changed. The new parameters were widely and deeply disliked by troops in the field. The tree-star lieutenant general Daniel Bolger, the senior U.S. adviser to the Afghan army, wrote, "Soldiers often groused about overly restrictive rules of engagement supposedly written by overly sissified military lawyers, but they missed a key fact. The actual rules of engagement are written by operations officers, checked by lawyers, and approved by commanders. The ROE remained rather permissive throughout the war, with little change since 2001. The real screws got applied in tactical directives."[88] General Bolger was harshly critical of General McChrystal's tightening of ROE requirements for fire support (and thus reducing distinction and proportionality errors) in a July 2009, tactical directive:

> Maybe all of those years with the Rangers and Special Forces convinced [McChrystal] that you could be purely precise with armed force and kill only those who merited killing. In any event, the general believed his conventional forces must become significantly more discriminating. He spoke of the value of "courageous restraint," the willingness to take ISAF casualties to protect the Afghan people. ... The ISAF commander then got down to specifics, no doubt helped immensely by clever

[84] Capt. Ilario Pantano, *Warlord* (New York: Threshold Editions, 2006), 315.
[85] Martins, "Rules of Engagement for Land Forces," supra, note 8, at 18.
[86] *U.S. v. Mowris* (GCM, Fort Carson, Colorado, July 1993).
[87] Martins, "Rules of Engagement for Land Forces," supra, note 8, at 66.
[88] Daniel P. Bolger, *Why We Lost* (New York: Eamon Dolan/Houghton Mifflin Harcourt, 2014), 294.

military lawyers. ... "The use of air-to-ground munitions and indirect fire [artillery and mortars] against residential compounds," the directive stated, "is only authorized under very limited and prescribed conditions." That amounted to hardly ever.[89]

Two months after General McChrystal's directive, on 8 September 2009, in Afghanistan's Ganjigal valley, Marine Corps Sergeant Dakota Meyer and 105 other U.S. and Afghan combatants, under the command of Army Captain William Swensen, were ambushed by sixty Taliban fighters and were taking heavy fire from three sides. Captain Swensen, through Sergeant Kaplan, a radioman on a nearby hillside, called for fire support seven times, through Shadow 4, a radio relay of Army scouts on a nearby ridge. The Army tactical operations center (TOC) that controlled supporting fires and air support, received the requests but was not responding.[90]

Shadow 4 kept assuring Kaplan that the fire missions were getting through, but ... "The TOC won't clear the missions," Kaplan radioed to Swensen. "The bastards won't shoot the arty." ... Swensen radioed to Kaplan, "It's on me! Give them my initials. I'm making the decision, not them!" ... By sending his initials, Swensen was taking full responsibility. If anything went wrong – if a friendly soldier or a civilian were hit – the burden rested squarely on Swensen, not with the TOC in the rear. The TOC responded ... by asking again for information impossible to provide. Where were all the friendly troops? What was the forward line of trace of friendly units? Was everyone accounted for? Were any civilians endangered?... The TOC denied Shadow's fire mission. Furious, Sergeant Summers at Shadow pressed back against the TOC. "The main element is being hit from the north, east, and south," he said. "All elements are engaged. I repeat, all elements are heavily engaged. We need fire missions now." ... Yet it seemed to Sergeant Summers that every time he relayed a fire mission, the TOC asked him "twenty questions."[91]

Swensen and his men were fighting for their lives. Meanwhile, a small "command group" of Swensen's column was pinned down by enemy fire in a house in a nearby small village. They were "taking fire from three sides. ... Lieutenant Johnson came back on the [radio] net, again requesting smoke 'to conceal their movement [to safety].' I heard him give the grid," Sergeant Meyer wrote, "exactly where he wanted the shells to land. ... Shadow, the Army outpost on the southern ridge, replied that the TOC ... said the fire mission was too close to the village. 'Too close to the village?' Lieutenant Johnson said. 'If you don't give me those rounds right now, I'm gonna die!' 'Try your best,' Shadow replied, knowing the TOC wouldn't fire. *Try your best?*' ... He was on the verge of complete rage. He wanted to strangle the officers in the TOC."[92]

Before the column was finally extracted, many of them through Sergeant Dakota Meyer's heroic efforts, and no thanks to the TOC, fifteen of Captain Swensen's men were killed by Taliban fire.

Two years later, in the White House, the president presented Sergeant Dakota L. Meyer with the Medal of Honor. Later still, the president also presented the Medal of Honor to Captain William D. Swensen.

The officers manning the TOC believed that by requiring detailed information from a unit requesting artillery support they were minimizing the potential death and wounding

---

[89] Id., at 304–5.
[90] Dakota Meyer and Bing West, *Into the Fire* (New York: Random House, 2012), 99–101.
[91] Id., at 99–102.   [92] Id., at 115.

of innocent civilians – General McChrystal's tactical directive for greater concern for distinction and proportionality executed to a fault.

Was General McChrystal's concern for distinction and proportionality misplaced? Or was his ROE-changing directive ill conceived? Was good intent poorly communicated and blindly executed? Or was it a case of LOAC/IHL being observed as it should be: to the protection of the victims of war, innocent civilians?

There is no prescribed solution to lax enforcement/strict enforcement issues. A commander can only provide strong ROE training, be aware of the potential problem, and have faith that his/her subordinate officers and noncommissioned officers will do the right thing.

There will always be problems interpreting ROE. After the U.S. invasion of Iraq, in early 2003, soldiers of the army's 3rd Infantry Division were pushing toward Baghdad. One night, an infantry company was guarding a small town on the division's route of advance. "Not appreciating the night vision capability of the U.S. forces, [the insurgents] had shut off the electricity to provide themselves with a cover of darkness. Uncertain as to whether the ROE allowed them to shoot the Iraqis as they retrieved arms from the battlefield, the U.S. soldiers withheld their fire."[93] Seeking tactical direction from a document never meant to serve that purpose, soldiers were intimidated into not firing on the enemy because that tactical situation was not covered in their ROE.

Lieutenant General Ricardo Sanchez relates an event in Kosovo, in 2000, when he commanded Multi-National Brigade East, as a brigadier general. While on a routine patrol, a military police platoon commander found his route cut off by a dead-end valley and, blocking his exit, a mob of hostile Serbs. From adjacent surrounding mountains, a group of Serbs began rolling rocks, boulders, even tree trunks, down on the patrol. As the patrol slowly retreated from the valley and attempted to detour around the Serb blocking force, Sanchez flew to the scene in a helicopter. He recalled:

> I could clearly see the Serbs attacking the soldiers. So I got on the radio and spoke directly with the MP commander. "Sir, we're taking all kinds of injuries," he said. . . . "You've got to fight back," I said. "But, sir, I can't fire into the mob. There are some women and children up front." "Well, you're going to have to make a decision on the ground . . . but if you are taking this level of casualties, I recommend that you shoot to drive them back." After a couple of hours, the MPs finally withdrew. . . . During the after-action review, I asked the commander why he had not opened fire. "Sir, I just didn't know if the rules of engagement allowed me to do that," he said. "I was afraid there might be an investigation if we had killed someone." "First of all, the rules of engagement do allow you to open fire in a situation like that," I said. "Second, you should never, ever allow the fear of an investigation to hinder your decision-making process when engaged with the enemy. . . . Always use your best judgment based on what you know at the time. . . . " But what happened in Kosovo was a significant learning experience for both of us. I realized that training for rules of engagement had to be conducted by warfighters and not by lawyers."[94]

In that account, General Sanchez relates that a lieutenant of his command, in combat, lacked an understanding of his ROE and failed to take appropriate self-defense measures when his soldiers were being killed and wounded, but General Sanchez blames

---

[93] Michael R. Gordon and Lt.Gen. Bernard E. Trainor, *Cobra II* (New York: Pantheon Books, 2006), 226.
[94] Lt.Gen. Ricardo Sanchez, *Wiser in Battle* (New York: Harper Collins, 2008), 125.

"lawyers." Does that indicate a lack of appreciation for the responsibilities of command and a misunderstanding of whose responsibility ROE *always* are? Because of their specialized training and experience, judge advocates play a role in the formulation of ROE and, by service regulation, are responsible for training personnel in the ROE. But it is always the commander and the commander alone who is responsible for the content of his/her ROE and for ensuring that subordinates are trained in, and understand, those ROE.

12.7 Summary

ROE are relatively new to U.S. Armed Forces. They reflect the commander's need to control the use of force by subordinate combatants, and ROE are the means of doing that. In a day when "the strategic corporal" can, either through the wise use of firepower or its disastrous use, virtually decide battles, commanders need such a tool.

ROE also are a tool occasionally misused by efforts of senior commanders or political agents to micromanage tactical engagements, by tying combatants' hands through overly restrictive provisions, or by paying scant attention to ROE training until it goes wrong. Subordinates may inadvertently misuse ROE by failing to understand their intent and their limits or by consciously evading their mandates.

The value of ROE is not found in a card in a corporal's pocket. It is in the guidance and authority that mission-specific ROE provide a commander in executing the mission. Beyond that, LOAC/IHL training, combined with leadership at all levels, is the real guarantor of battlefield conduct that accords with LOAC/IHL.

CASES AND MATERIALS

THE DEATH OF MR. ESEQUIEL HERNANDEZ

Introduction. *On May 20, 1997, at a crossing of the Rio Grande River near Redford, Texas, four marines, led by Corporal B_____, were temporarily assigned to Joint Task Force-6 (JTF-6). The marines' mission was to observe the river crossing and report suspected undocumented aliens and narcotics traffic they might observe to U.S. domestic law enforcement authorities located at the nearby Presidio Border Patrol Station. On May 20, the four-man team was on its first mission. The marines were authorized by the SROE (version of October 1, 1994) to use force. Congress had specifically authorized use of military forces for such interdiction missions as an exception to the prohibition of using the Armed Forces in a* posse comitatus *role.*

Military personnel assigned to JTF-6 were trained in the JTF's ROE during mission planning and training phases from February 22 to April 8, and April 1–22, and April 23–5, although how much of the training pertained specifically to ROE could not be determined. There is no evidence that Corporal B_____'s team received training in domestic use-of-force standards.

Early in the evening, the team saw a goat herder and, near the river, a man on horseback. The marines had been briefed that drugs were often transported on horseback, with armed individuals accompanying them as scouts. Corporal B_____ radioed his sightings to the Tactical Operations Center. Soon after he radioed the center, the goat herder, later identified as Esequiel Hernandez, at a range of approximately 120 meters fired two shots at the marine team from his .22 rifle. Corporal B_____ ordered his team to chamber a round in their M16 rifles, and they moved to higher ground. (The marines did not know that Mr. Hernandez was an eighteen-year-old high school student who lived 500 meters from the marines' position. Neither did they know that he had reportedly also fired on law enforcement officers three months before.) B_____ radioed the Tactical Operations Center, "As soon as he readies that rifle back downrange" (i.e., aims at the team again), "we're taking him." A lance corporal manning the center's radio responded, "Roger, fire back." Corporal B_____ reported that Mr. Hernandez was "ducking down" and hiding while looking for the team. Now a sergeant on the Tactical Operation Center's radio instructed B_____, "You're to follow the ROE."

While maneuvering his team across the high ground, Corporal B_____ saw Hernandez raise his rifle and aim at another team member, Lance Corporal B, at a range of approximately 130 meters. Before Hernandez fired, B_____ fired one round, killing Mr. Hernandez.

JTF-6 immediately conducted a formal investigation and concluded that Corporal B_____'s actions were consistent with the ROE. Two Texas grand juries and a federal grand jury also investigated. All three declined to indict the corporal.

Prodded by a media and public outcry over the killing of Mr. Hernandez, the Marine Corps appointed a major general to yet again investigate the shooting. The general, in turn, requested the marine colonel W. Hays Parks to provide his expert opinion to determine if the shooting was in accord with the SROE. At the time, Parks was retired from the Marine Corps and was employed as the Special Assistant for Law of War Matters to the judge advocate general of the U.S. Army.

The following are extracts from Colonel Parks's report:[95]

4. Questions. ... I [Parks] share the reticence expressed by the JTF-6 commander to reach conclusions inconsistent with or beyond those made in the JTF-6 investigation, due to his (and my) "inability to place myself into the shoes of the Marines on the ground and to fully understand and appreciate their thought processes while they moved from the point where they were initially fired upon to the point where the fatal shot occurred." Any decision as to the actions of Corporal B_____ necessarily must be based upon the information reasonably available to him at the time, and not what became known after the incident.

Military forces operating within the United States are subject to U.S. domestic law standards regarding the use of deadly force, not rules of engagement for armed conflict. ... In articulating a standard [for domestic law enforcement officers], the [Supreme] court has stated that the decision to resort to deadly force is one of "objective reasonableness ... at the moment" that decision is taken. Continuing, the court [in *Graham v. Connor*, 490 U.S. 386 (1989)] has stated that, "the question is whether the

---

[95] Col. W. H. Parks report to Maj.Gen. J. T. Coyne; Subj.: "Request for Expert Opinion Concerning Compliance with Rules of Engagement" (Nov. 15, 1997). On file with author. Footnotes omitted.

officers' actions are 'objectively reasonable' in light of the facts and circumstances confronting them, without regard to their underlying intent or motivation." The calculus of reasonableness "must embody allowance for the fact that police officers are often forced to make split-second judgments – in circumstances that are tense, uncertain, and rapidly evolving – about the amount of force that is necessary in a particular situation." The court has acknowledged [*Graham v. Connor*, 396] that "the test of *reasonableness* is not capable of precise definition or mechanical application." But if a police officer – or a military member discharging his or her duties within the United States – "reasonably believes that an individual poses a threat of serious physical harm . . . to the officer or others," resort to deadly force is authorized. [*Tennessee v. Garner*, 471 U.S. 1, 11 (1985).] This standard is set forth in relevant Department of Defense and Marine Corps directives. [DOD Directive 5210.56, (25 February 1992), Subject: Use of Deadly Force and the Carrying of Firearms by DOD Personnel Engaged in Law Enforcement and Security Duties; and Marine Corps Order 5500.6F over POS, (20 July 1995), Subject: Arming of Security and Law Enforcement Personnel and the Use of Force.]

Based upon my review of the materials provided me, I see no reason to disagree with the conclusion reached by the JTF-6 investigating officer that "The Joint Chiefs of Staff . . . Standing Rules of Engagement . . . , which were in effect for this mission, were followed." . . .

. . . Recent decisions are particularly relevant. . . . The Ninth Circuit stated [*Scott v. Henrich*, 978 F.2d 481 (9th Cir. 1992), withdrawn and reissued, 34 F. 3d 1498 (2 November 1994).] that "the appropriate inquiry is whether the officers acted reasonably, not whether they had less intrusive alternatives available to them." Continuing, the court stated:

> Requiring officers to find and choose the least intrusive alternative would require them to exercise superhuman judgment. In the heat of battle with lives potentially in the balance, an officer would not be able to rely on training and common sense to decide what would best accomplish his mission. Instead, he would need to ascertain the least intrusive alternative (an inherently subjective determination) and choose that option and that option only. Imposing such a requirement would inevitably induce tentativeness by officers, and thus deter police from protecting the public and themselves. It would also entangle the courts in endless second-guessing of police decisions made under stress and subject to the exigencies of the moment.

. . . There are perhaps a dozen lawful ways in which the situation might have been handled, including the use of deadly force when Mr. Hernandez fired the first time. . . . The issue is whether the decisions taken by Corporal B_____ were those of a reasonable man, and whether it was reasonable for Corporal B_____ to believe that Esequiel Hernandez, who previously had fired at the Marines and now was pointing his rifle at Lance Corporal B, posed an imminent threat of serious bodily harm. . . . I believe the decisions taken by Corporal B_____ on 20 May 1997, including the decision to resort to deadly force, were those of a reasonable man under the circumstances.

5. a. Rules of engagement. The basic ROE reference document for the mission . . . may be legally correct for the purposes for which it was intended, but it is an inappropriate set of terms of reference for military support to domestic law enforcement operations for the following reasons.

Colonel Parks goes on to illustrate the deficiencies of the 1994 SROE for domestic use. Those SROE were revised in 2000, and those were, in turn, replaced by the 2005 SROE discussed in this chapter. The 2005 SROE were accompanied by implementation of the SRUF, for use in domestic civil support missions and land defense missions within U.S. territory. (See Chapter 13, Section 13.1.1.) The SRUF are intended to address situations like this case. Parks's report concludes:

5.d. ROE cards. There is a certain popularity for ROE cards, highly-abbreviated summaries of larger ROE principles. The ROE card issued JTF-6 personnel, including [Corporal B_____'s team], is representative.

ROE cards and similar aspects of ROE training represent a military tendency to reduce each aspect of training to the "bare bones." However, there is no substitute for effective training and learning. ROE cards seldom are able to provide adequate information to properly reinforce previous training, and it is unlikely that a soldier, sailor, airman or Marine will have time to refer to his or her ROE card when the occasion presents itself to make decisions based upon the ROE training previously received. ...

ROE cards also are prone to poor drafting and inconsistency. The JTF-6 ROE card ... is not an accurate statement of U.S. domestic law relating to the use of deadly force. An ROE card that promulgates improper information is contrary to the leadership principle of clarity of orders, and may cause confusion for those who must live or die by them.

Recommend the JCS and military services conduct an assessment as to the continued value of ROE cards.

Conclusion. *Colonel Parks's report illustrates the distinction between SROE and today's SRUF. It also lays out the standard to be employed when exercising deadly force. Although the cases he cites relate to domestic law enforcement, the guidelines they provide are equally applicable to the use of deadly military force in armed conflicts. He also forcefully notes the dangers of ROE cards, a concern that, more than a decade after Parks's report, many military officers continue to share.*

In 1998, the U.S. government paid the family of Mr. Hernandez $1,900,000 in settlement of their wrongful death suit.

ROE CARDS

Introduction. *MNC-I, Multi-National Corps – Iraq, "stood up" on May 15, 2004, to replace the former U.S. headquarters in Iraq, CJTF [Combined Joint Task Force] 7. The MNC-I ROE card, double-sided and 2 ¾ inches by 4 ½ inches in size, as most ROE cards are, was employed by MNC-I in late 2005 into 2006. Emphasis and underlining are as in the original card. On the actual card, very small type was necessarily used. The face of the card read:*

MNC-I ROE Card

Nothing on this card prevents you from using necessary and proportional force to defend yourself

1. You may engage the following individuals based on their conduct:
   a. Persons who are committing hostile acts against CF [Corps forces].
   b. Persons who are exhibiting hostile intent towards CG.

2. These persons may be engaged subject to the following instructions:
    a. Positive Identification (PID) is required prior to engagement.
        PID is a reasonable certainty that the proposed target is a legitimate military target. If no PID, contact your next higher commander for decision.
    b. **Use Graduated Measures of Force**. When time and circumstances permit, use the following degrees of graduated force when responding to hostile act/intent: (1) shout verbal warnings to halt; (2) show your weapon and demonstrate intent to use it; (3) Block access or detain; (4) fire a warning shot; (5) shoot to eliminate threat.
    c. **Do not target or strike** anyone who has surrendered or is out of combat due to sickness or wounds.
    d. **Do not target or strike** hospitals, mosques, churches, shrines, schools, museums, national monuments, and any other historical and cultural sites, civilian populated areas or buildings **UNLESS** the enemy is using them for military purposes or if necessary for your self-defense.
    e. **Do not target or strike** Iraqi Infrastructure (public works, commercial communication facilities, dams), Lines of Communication (roads, highways, tunnels, bridges, railways) and Economic Objects (commercial storage facilities, pipelines) **UNLESS** necessary for self-defense or if ordered by your commander. If you must fire on these objects, fire to disable and disrupt rather than destroy.
    f. ALWAYS minimize incidental injury, loss of life, and collateral damage.

The obverse of the same card read:

3. The use of force, including deadly force, is authorized to protect the following:
    - Yourself, your unit, and other friendly forces
    - Detainees
    - Civilians from crimes that are likely to cause death or serious bodily harm, such as murder or rape
    - Personnel or property **designated by the OSC** when such actions are necessary to restore order and security
3. In general, WARNING SHOTS are authorized ONLY when the use of deadly force would be authorized in that particular situation.
4. **Treat all civilians and their property with respect and dignity**. Do not seize civilian property, including vehicles, unless the property presents a security threat. When possible give a receipt to the property's owner.
5. **You may DETAIN civilians based upon a reasonable belief that the person:** (1) must be detained for purposes of self-defense; (2) is interfering with CF mission accomplishment; (3) is on a list of persons wanted for questioning, arrest or detention; (4) is or was engaged in criminal activity; or (5) must be detained for imperative reasons of security. **Anyone you detain MUST be protected**. Force, up to and including deadly force, is authorized to protect detainees in your custody. You MUST fill out a detainee apprehension card for EVERY person you detain.
6. **MNC-I General Order No. 1 is in effect**. Looting and the taking of war trophies are prohibited.
7. **ALL personnel MUST report any suspected violations of the Law of War committed by any US, friendly or enemy force**. Notify your chain of command, Judge Advocate, IG [Inspector General], Chaplain, or appropriate service-related investigative branch (e.g. CID, NCIS).

Conclusion. After reading the MNC–I ROE card, would you agree or disagree with Colonel Parks's statement in his Hernandez case report that "ROE cards . . . represent a military tendency to reduce each aspect of training to the 'bare bones' . . . ROE cards seldom are able to provide adequate information to properly reinforce previous training, and it is unlikely that a soldier, sailor, airman or Marine will have time to refer to his or her ROE card when the occasion presents itself to make decisions based upon the ROE training"?

DESERT STORM ROE

Eleven years before the MNC-I ROE card was issued in Iraq, in the Persian Gulf War U.S. forces were issued this ROE card for Operation Desert Storm (January 16–21, 1991). Desert Storm was the combat phase of the UN-authorized mission to eject invading Iraqi forces from Kuwait. They are "a good example of rules of engagement issued by many states when contemplating a straightforward international armed conflict between the armed forces of different states. They are, in effect, a distillation of the Geneva Conventions and related treaties, or of customary international law."[96] *Like the MNC-I ROE card just examined, this Desert Storm card was slightly smaller than a playing card, with print on both sides. This ROE card, based on 1988 ROE, is in many respects similar to that issued to MNC-I troops, based on the 2000 SROE, but is less sophisticated and easier to understand:*

ALL Enemy Military Personnel and Vehicles Transporting the Enemy or Their Supplies May Be Engaged Subject to the Following Restrictions:

A. Do not engage anyone who has surrendered, is out of battle due to sickness or wounds, is shipwrecked, or is an aircrew member descending by parachute from a disabled aircraft.

B. Avoid harming civilians unless necessary to save U.S. lives. Do not fire into civilian populated areas or buildings which are not defended or being used for military purposes.

C. Hospitals, churches, shrines, schools, museums, national monuments, and other historical or cultural sites will not be engaged except in self-defense.

D. Hospitals will be given special protection. Do not engage hospitals unless the enemy uses the hospital to commit acts harmful to U.S. forces, and then only after giving a warning and allowing a reasonable time to expire before engaging, if the tactical situation permits.

E. Booby traps may be used to protect friendly positions or to impede the progress of enemy forces. They may not be used on civilian personal property. They will be recovered and destroyed when the military necessity for their use no longer exists.

F. Looting and the taking of war trophies are prohibited.

G. Avoid harming civilian property unless necessary to save U.S. lives. Do not attack traditional civilian objects, such as houses, unless they are being used by the enemy for military purposes and neutralization assists in mission accomplishment.

---

[96] Peter Rowe, "The Rules of Engagement in Occupied Territory: Should They Be Published?" 8–2 *Melbourne J. of Int'l L.* (2007), 327, 331.

H. Treat all civilians and their property with respect and dignity. Before using privately
    owned property, check to see if publicly owned property can substitute. No
    requisitioning of civilian property, including vehicles, without permission of a
    company level commander and without giving a receipt. If an ordering officer
    can contract the property, then do not requisition it.
I. Treat all prisoners humanely and with respect and dignity.
J. ROE annex to the OPLAN provides more detail. Conflicts between this card and
    the OPLAN should be resolved in favor of the OPLAN.

Remember

1. FIGHT ONLY COMBATANTS.
2. ATTACK ONLY MILITARY TARGETS.
3. SPARE CIVILIAN PERSONS AND OBJECTS.
4. RESTRICT DESTRUCTION TO WHAT YOUR MISSION REQUIRES.

*Conclusion. Is it better to have a more detailed ROE card? Do greater specificity and
smaller type merely increase chances that the card will be unread? Is it immaterial, as the
cards will be unread by many troops no matter how specific or how general?*

13 Targeting Objects

13.0 Introduction

In this chapter we examine what *objects* may be lawfully targeted in armed conflict. The law of armed conflict/international humanitarian law (LOAC/IHL) pertaining to the targeting of objects differs from that pertaining to targeting of combatants – human beings – which is discussed in a following chapter. When "targeting" is described throughout this chapter, it is the targeting of objects – not combatants or unprivileged civilian belligerents – that is being described. That is not to suggest that human beings cannot be military objectives, cannot be targets. They can be, just as military pack animals and working dogs, in certain circumstances, are valid targets.

The targeting of objects involves all of LOAC's four core principles – distinction, military necessity, unnecessary suffering, and proportionality – but it particularly involves distinction and proportionality. Distinction, the cardinal principle of LOAC/IHL, is at the heart of lawful targeting. Proportionality is always a primary consideration for an attacking force and its targeting planning. Proportionality may dictate the timing of an attack to minimize damage collateral to that inflicted on the military personnel on the target; proportionality may dictate that a lawful military object not be targeted at all. A lack of military necessity should also scratch a legitimate target from an air tasking order or fire support plan. Unnecessary suffering may decide that certain lawful weapons should not be employed against enemy combatants, white phosphorus or napalm, for example. Command responsibility also is a possible targeting issue, as is its counterpoint, obedience to orders; the lawfulness of a commander's targeting decisions, and their execution by subordinates, may raise issues of LOAC/IHL lawfulness. Every targeting issue, however, implicates distinction and proportionality.

Targeting issues have become ever more important, particularly in urban settings, such as cities, and in more austere situations, villages.

13.1 Defining a Lawful Objective

"Targeting" is the process of selecting enemy objects to be attacked, assigning priorities to the selected objects, and matching appropriate weapons to those objects to assure their destruction.

Through the nineteenth and early twentieth centuries, states generally agreed that only military objects should be targeted, but there was no definition of what a "military objective" was. "During the Second World War ... each belligerent determined what should be understood by such objectives as it pleased. ... Their ideas often differed, depending on whether the territory concerned was their own, or was enemy territory, or territory of an ally occupied by enemy forces."[1] Not until 1977 Additional Protocol I was an authoritative definition codified in a binding multinational document.

Article 52.2: **"Attacks shall be limited strictly to military objectives. Insofar as objects are concerned, military objectives are limited to those objects which by their nature, location, purpose or use make an effective contribution to military action and whose total or partial destruction, capture or neutralization ... offers a definite military advantage."** This definition requires that an object meet two criteria to be a lawful military target or objective: First, it must make an effective contribution to military action, and, second, its total or partial destruction, capture, or neutralization must offer a definite military advantage.

Complementing Article 52.2, Article 48 reads: **"The Parties to the conflict shall at all times distinguish between the civilian population and combatants and between civilian objects and military objectives."** The requirements of Articles 52.2 and 48 are customary law.[2] (The terms "objects" and "objectives" are distinct, with different meanings. As will be discussed, using one when the other is meant may generate confusion.)

Protocol I, Article 57.2 (a) goes on to require that those planning an attack "do everything feasible to verify that the objectives to be attacked are neither civilians nor civilian objects." The International Criminal Tribunal for the Former Yugoslavia (ICTY) has noted that "the determination whether civilians were targeted is a case-by-case analysis based on a variety of factors, including the means and method used during the attack, the distance between victims and the source of fire, ongoing combat activity at the time and location of the incident, the presence of military activities or facilities in the vicinity of the incident ... and the nature of the crimes committed in the course of the attack."[3]

Although Article 52.2 is customary law, its rather vague wording can lend itself to different interpretations. There are targets that are clearly military objects, but Article 52.2. does little to clarify the term in cases when it is not obvious. "What constitutes an 'effective contribution' to military action? What is a 'definite' military advantage? What is the difference, if any, between an 'indefinite' and a 'definite' military advantage?"[4] No protocol article, no law or rule, can resolve all definitional questions, but those surrounding Article 57.2 have proved vexing.

An exception to Article 52's abstraction is the definition of an "attack." An attack is an act of violence, whether offensive or defensive, against the enemy.[5] A massive air

---

[1] Yves Sandoz, Christophe Swinarski, and Bruno Zimmerman, eds., *Commentary on the Additional Protocols* (Geneva: ICRC/Martinus Nijhoff, 1987), 631.

[2] Jean-Marie Henckaerts and Louise Doswald-Beck, eds., *Customary International Humanitarian Law*. Vol. I. *Rules* (Cambridge: Cambridge University Press, 2005), rules 7 and 8, at 25 and 29, respectively. Also see: Committee Established to Review the NATO Bombing Campaign against the Federal Republic of Yugoslavia, Final Report, § 365.

[3] Katharina Margetts and Patrick Hayden, "Current Developments at the Ad Hoc International Criminal Tribunals," 8–2 *J. of Int'l Crim. Justice* (May, 2010), 249, 250, citing *Prosecutor v. Milošević*, IT-98-29/1-A (Nov. 12, 2009).

[4] Michael Bothe, "Targeting," in Andru E. Wall, ed., *International Law Studies*. Vol. 78. *Legal and Ethical Lessons of NATO's Kosovo Campaign* (Newport, RI: Naval War College, 2002), 173, 177.

[5] 1977 Protocol Additional to the Geneva Conventions of 12 August 1949, and Relating to the Protection of Victims of International Armed Conflicts (hereafter, 1977 Additional Protocol I), Art. 49.1.

bombardment or a sniper firing a single round may both be an attack. Beyond that, a closer examination of remaining definitional terms is needed.

13.2 Interpreting "Military Objective"

The term "military objective" first appeared in relation to the law of war in the 1923 Hague Draft Rules of Aerial Warfare, Article 24.1: "An air bombardment is legitimate only when directed against a military objective, i.e. an objective whereof the total or partial destruction would constitute an obvious military advantage for the belligerent." Several major powers objected to aspects of the 1923 rules, and they were never adopted,[6] but the 1923 Hague definition remains a broad but useful description of a military objective.

A military objective must have certain characteristics. The destruction of the target or objective must offer "a concrete and perceptible military advantage rather than a hypothetical and speculative one."[7] It would be impermissible for a targeting team to muse, "If we take out the electrical grid it might cut power to the air defense system" and act on that musing; the military nature of the power grid is speculative, lacking the clear military advantage required of a lawful military objective. Additionally, the required military advantage may not be purely political, for example, to force a change in the enemy's negotiating stance.

> The notion of "military advantage" is not singularly helpful. Surely, military advantage is not restricted to tactical gains. The spectrum is necessarily wide. . . . The key problem is that the outlook of the attacking party is unlikely to match that of the party under attack in evaluating the long-term military benefits of any action contemplated. Moreover . . . assessment of the military advantage can be made in light of "an attack as a whole," as distinct from "isolated or specific parts of the attack." The attacking party may thus argue, e.g., that an air raid of no perceptible military advantage in itself is justified by having misled the enemy to shift its strategic gaze to the wrong sector of the front.[8]

In this regard, Colonel Hays Parks cites the 1942 morale-boosting Doolittle raid (launched from a U.S. aircraft carrier against targets on the Japanese mainland) and the 1971 heavy bombing of targets in the Hanoi–Haiphong area of North Vietnam, which are widely believed to have forced the North Vietnamese to negotiate a conclusion to the U.S.–North Vietnamese conflict, and the 1986 bombing of Libyan targets in response to Libyan-supported terrorist attacks that demonstrated U.S. resolve. "In each of the preceding cases," Parks writes, "the United States would have been hard pressed to state that there was a 'definite military advantage' resulting from the operations described, or that

---

[6] Although the 1923 rules were never adopted, "at the time of their conclusion they were regarded as an authoritative attempt to clarify and formulate rules of air warfare, and largely corresponded to customary rules." Adam Roberts and Richard Guelff, eds., *Documents on the Laws of War*, 3d ed. (Oxford: Oxford University Press, 2000), 139. The term is subsequently used in 1949 Geneva Convention I, Art. 19, and Convention IV, Art. 18.

[7] Waldemar Solf, "Article 52," in Michael Bothe, Karl Partsch, and Waldemar Solf, eds., *New Rules for Victims of Armed Conflict: Commentary on the Two 1977 Protocols Additional to the Geneva Conventions of 1949* (The Hague: Martinus Nijhoff, 1982), 326.

[8] Yoram Dinstein, "Legitimate Military Objectives under the Current *Jus In Bello*," in Wall, *Legal and Ethical Lessons, supra*, note 4, at 144–5. Footnotes omitted.

? = does objective just differ from object in that it can be destroyed?

The Law of Armed Conflict

the gain was not 'potential' or 'indeterminate'; the result sought in each was speculative, as are most actions in war, and more psychological than military, although each had military effects."[9]

Merely denying the use of an object (e.g., a highway or railway bridge) to the enemy may constitute a military advantage. In World War II, the military significance to the American army of the Rhine River's Remagen Bridge was great: In 1945, its intact capture opened the way into Germany for tanks, towed artillery, and other wheeled and tracked weapons that would have had difficulty fording the Rhine without a secure bridge. Had the German army succeeded in destroying the bridge and denying its use to the Allies the tactical disadvantage would have been great. General Dwight Eisenhower called the capture of that single bridge "one of those bright opportunities of war which . . . produce incalculable effect on future operations."[10] Another example is the Arnhem bridge over the Lower Rhine. In September 1944 it was key to the British field marshal Bernard Montgomery's plan to end the war in three months.[11] After furious fighting, it proved "a bridge too far," however. German forces denied the bridge to Allied forces, and the war went on for another fourteen months. The Remagen and Arnhem bridges were of great military advantage to one side or the other.

The breadth of the term "military advantage" is not without limits, however. One cannot target at will, suggesting that the effect of destruction of this or that object bears on the war as a whole. Each attack must provide a concrete and perceptible military advantage. Furthermore, not every military *object* is necessarily a military *objective* to be targeted. "I would suggest that the USS *Constitution* in Boston Harbor is a military object, but not necessarily a military objective. Similarly, a civilian house, which may not be being used by the military in any way but may be interrupting a tank advance, can by its location be a military objective [that can be destroyed]."[12] However, if military necessity dictates that a civilian house be seized or destroyed to clear a field of fire or block an enemy avenue of approach, for example, the house ceases to be a civilian object and may be considered a military object.[13]

The presence of civilians at or near a military objective does not automatically make that objective immune from attack. "This is the case, for example, of civilians working in a munitions factory. . . . Such persons share the risk of attacks on that military objective but are not themselves combatants. . . . Such attacks are still subject to the principle of proportionality."[14]

Economic targets, including multiple economic targets, are legitimate military objectives as long as they effectively support military operations, and if attacking them provides a definite military advantage.[15] Economic targets are traditional targets such as oil production facilities – pipelines, pumping stations, refineries, and cracking plants – as

[9] W. Hays Parks, "Air War and the Law of War," 32–1 *Air Force L. Rev.* (1990), 1, 143.

[10] Gen. Dwight D. Eisenhower, *Crusade in Europe* (New York: Doubleday, 1948), 378.

[11] Cornelius Ryan, *A Bridge Too Far* (New York: Simon & Schuster, 1974), 90.

[12] Col. Charles Garraway, "Discussion: Reasonable Military Commanders and Reasonable Civilians," in Wall, *Legal and Ethical Lessons*, supra, note 4, at 215. To same effect: Parks, "Air War and the Law of War," supra, note 9, at 146–7.

[13] Maj. Marie Anderson and Emily Zukauskas, eds., *Operational Law Handbook*, 2008 (Charlottesville, VA: Judge Advocate General's Legal Center and School, 2008), 20.

[14] Henckaerts and Doswald-Beck, *Customary International Humanitarian Law*, supra, note 2, at 31–2.

[15] Id., at 32.

well as natural gas facilities and steel plants. These resources are of great economic value and are also vital to sustain the conflict. Without them the state's capability to carry on the conflict would wither, if not die. Once again, there are limits on what may be considered a legitimate economic target:

> If a country relies almost entirely on, say, the export of coffee beans or bananas for its income and even if this income is used to great extent to support its war effort ... it would not be legitimate to attack banana or coffee bean plantations or warehouses. The reason for this is that such plants would not make an *effective* contribution to *military* action nor would their destruction offer a *definite* military advantage. The definition of military objectives thus excludes the general industrial and agricultural potential of the enemy.[16]

A frequently cited example of an economic target is the Confederate cotton crop during the American Civil War. The South's cotton crop was a war-sustaining product, providing the Confederacy with almost its total means to prosecute the war – to import arms, provision its army, and finance the conflict. In 1870, a U.S. court reportedly recognized that the cotton crop constituted a war-sustaining character, making an effective contribution to military action and legitimizing its targeting.[17] Even though the United States takes an expansive view of what constitutes a lawful military objective, that court's conclusion is contrary to today's LOAC/IHL. "Objects such as raw cotton or, to take a more contemporary example, oil, only under exceptional preconditions and circumstances are subject to military measures, i.e., only if they are used for military purposes."[18] Of course, oil usually *is* used for military purposes. Professor Yoram Dinstein writes:

> The raw cotton illustration (which may be substituted today by the instance of a country relying almost entirely on the export of coffee beans or bananas) displays the danger of introducing the slippery-slope concept of "war-sustaining capability." The connection between military action and exports, required to finance the war effort, is "too remote." Had raw cotton been acknowledged as a valid military objective, almost every civilian activity might be construed by the enemy as indirectly sustaining the war effort.[19]

Nor is enemy morale a valid targeting objective.[20] "Air attacks have a definite impact on the morale of the entire population and, thus, on political and military decision-makers. ... [But] this type of 'advantage' is political, not military. The morale of the

---

[16] Maj.Gen. A. V. P. Rogers, *Law on the Battlefield*, 2d ed. (Manchester: Juris, 2004), 70–1. Emphasis in original.

[17] Id., at 59, citing U.S. Dept. of the Air Force, *Commander's Handbook on the Law of Armed Conflict* (AFP 110–34) 1980, p. 2–1. The case has not been located, however.

[18] Wolff H. von Heinegg, "Commentary," in Wall, *Legal and Ethical Lessons*, supra, note 4, at 204.

[19] Yoram Dinstein, "Legitimate Military Objectives under the Current *Jus In Bello*," in Wall, *Legal and Ethical Lessons*, supra, note 4, at 146. Footnotes omitted.

[20] Brig.Gen. Charles Dunlap, a former senior U.S. Air Force judge advocate, disagrees. In a controversial article he writes, "We need a new paradigm when using force against societies with malevolent propensities. We must hold at risk the very way of life that sustains their depredations, and we must threaten to destroy the world as they know it if they persist. This means the air weapon should be unleashed against entirely new categories of property." Brig.Gen. Charles J. Dunlap, "The End of Innocence: Rethinking Noncombatancy in the Post-Kosovo Era," *Strategic Rev.* (Summer 2000), 14.

population and of political decision-makers is not a contribution to 'military action.'
Thus [it] cannot be used as a legitimation for any targeting decision."[21] Weakening
enemy morale was one purported goal of World War II "area bombing," although Parks
suggests that "this may well have been an afterthought to explain away the inherent
inaccuracy of [World War II] bombing."[22] In any event, today area bombing is considered a clear example of indiscriminate targeting and a LOAC/IHL violation.[23] The
psychological effect of destroying a particular military object or objective may be a
legitimate targeting consideration, if the object is an otherwise lawful target. Like morale,
however, psychological effect alone is not a valid military objective.

Other prohibited targets include cultural property (Chapter 18), objects indispensable
to the survival of the civilian population (Additional Protocol I, Article 54), undefended
places (1907 Hague Regulation IV, Article 25), and, not surprisingly, medical units and
establishments (Geneva Convention I, Article 19).

Military objectives are not addressed in 1977 Additional Protocol II, in reference to
noninternational armed conflicts. A definition of military objects is included, however, in
Amended Protocols II and III of the 1980 *Convention on Prohibitions on the Use of
Certain Conventional Weapons*, both of those protocols being applicable in noninternational conflicts (Chapter 16).

non-international!

13.3 Targets by Virtue of Nature, Location, Purpose, or Use

Military targets are commonly defined in terms of the two criteria of Article 52.2. First,
military targets are objects that by their nature, location, purpose, or use make an
effective contribution to military action. Second, military targets are objects whose
destruction offers a concrete and perceptible military advantage. Those four criteria –
nature, location, purpose, and use – are by no means the sole considerations involved in
targeting decisions, but they are key considerations. If a targeting cell correctly determines that a proposed target meets the two criteria of Article 52.2, it is a lawful target and
military objective.

Notice the intertwining of nature, location, purpose, and use. Often, a military object
will be included in more than one of those descriptive categories.

13.3.1 Military Objectives Are Limited to Objects Which, by Their *Nature* . . .

The intended target's "nature" refers to the type of object it is. Does the proposed target
make an effective contribution to enemy military action? The military nature of some
targets is clear: defense- or weapons-related industrial plants, major highways, military

---

[21] Michael Bothe, "Targeting," in Wall, *Legal and Ethical Lessons*, supra, note 4, at 180. Also, Yoram
      Dinstein, *The Conduct of Hostilities under the Law of International Armed Conflict* (Cambridge:
      Cambridge University Press, 2004), 116.

[22] Parks, "Air War and the Law of War," supra, note 9, at 55.

[23] 1977 Additional Protocol I, Art. 51.4: "Indiscriminate attacks are prohibited. Indiscriminate attacks are:
      (a) those which are not directed at a specific military objective." Art. 51.5 (b): "An attack which may be
      expected to cause incidental loss of civilian life, injury to civilians, damage to civilian objects, or a
      combination thereof, which would be excessive in relation to the concrete and direct military advantage
      anticipated."

laboratories, navigable rivers, shipping ports, power plants that serve the military, rail lines, equipment marshalling yards, and command centers such as the Pentagon. On a tactical level, enemy ships and boats, military barracks, fortifications, armored vehicles, artillery, aircraft, and tactical positions, all meet the "nature" criteria for military objects. The military *nature* of other objects becomes apparent only when the intended *use* of the object becomes clear. For example, a glassworks facility that produces eyeglass lenses and binocular lenses for hunters is not an inherently military object. If, upon the outbreak of armed conflict, the facility switches to the manufacture of optical sights for tactical rifles, the facility's *nature* has changed, and its new *use* makes it a military object and lawful target.

13.3.2 Military Objectives Are Limited to Objects Which, by Their *Location* . . .

"Location" includes areas that are militarily important because they must be captured or denied the enemy. When flying into or out of civilian airports, one sometimes observes military aircraft parked in a remote portion of the airfield – tactical helicopters, gray-painted transport aircraft, or jet fighters. That civilian airport is home to a military reserve or air national guard unit. Were there an international armed conflict in progress, civilian passenger aircraft landing or departing from that airport would be "located" at a military objective. If the civilian aircraft were strafed and destroyed by an attacking enemy as collateral damage to a lawful attack on the military portion of the airfield, the civilian passengers would perish with the satisfaction of knowing that they had not been unlawfully purposely targeted.

"The notion underlying the reference to location is that a specific land area can be regarded as a military objective."[24] If there is an inherently civilian object within a clearly military objective, for instance, a marked infirmary within an ammunition depot, or an elementary school on a naval base, the ammunition depot and naval base retain their character as military objectives. Logic and experience dictate that the damage or destruction of the civilian object placed close to or within a military objective must be accepted.

13.3.3 Military Objectives Are Limited to Objects Which, by Their *Purpose* . . .

"Purpose" means the intended future use, or possible use. "The criterion of purpose is concerned with the intended future use of an object, while that of use is concerned with its present function. Most civilian objects can become useful objects to the armed forces. Thus, for example, a school or a hotel is a civilian object, but if they are used to accommodate troops . . . they become military objectives."[25]

The purpose of a recently launched cruise ship is to serve as a civilian luxury liner, but it may become a military object, quickly transformed into a troop transport, as was often done in World War II and the Korean conflict. As late as the 1982 U.K.–Argentine Falklands conflict, the P&O Cruise Line's forty-five-thousand-ton *Canberra* was

---

[24] Dinstein, "Legitimate Military Objectives under the Current *Jus in Bello*," in Wall, *Legal and Ethical Lessons*, supra, note 8, at 150.

[25] Sandoz, Swinarski, and Zimmerman, *Commentary on the Additional Protocols*, supra, note 1, at 636.

requisitioned by the British Ministry of Defense, hastily converted to troop use, and used to transport two thousand combatants to the Falklands.[26] *Purpose* may be superseded by later *use*.

During the U.S. invasion of Iraq, was Saddam Hussein's lavish 360-foot, 7,359-ton presidential yacht, *al Mansur* (*The Victor*), a military object? In March 2003, after reports that military communications were emanating from the yacht, a U.S. Navy S-3B Viking aircraft from the aircraft carrier USS *Constellation* (CV-64) fired a missile into the ship, setting it afire. Days later, after additional strikes, the *al Mansur* finally settled on its side in Basra's Shatt al Arab waterway, to become a longtime navigation hazard. "It seems a safe conclusion, albeit with incomplete information, that targeting the yacht intended either (or perhaps both) to create a powerful symbol of the [Saddam] regime's demise ... or to prevent her use as a regime sanctuary or headquarters. On the other hand, three factors suggest the *al Mansur* was simply a maritime target of opportunity."[27] The three factors were the unlikelihood that the yacht was designated a priority target, the novel use of a missile-firing S-3B in an overland strike, and the practice at the time of expending unused munitions on targets of opportunity rather than returning to the aircraft carrier with armed weapons.

Was the possible *use* of the *al Mansur* as a command and control vessel, with its Republican Guard crew, sufficient to overcome the yacht's *purpose* and render it a military objective? Did its destruction offer a definite military advantage? A U.S. Navy intelligence analyst who was involved in the targeting writes, "Considering the cost, labor, risk ... and the arguably minimal effect achieved, perhaps it does not serve as a case of how to use naval air power."[28]

13.3.4 Military Objectives Are Limited to Objects Which, by Their *Use* ...

Like purpose, "use" does not depend on the object's original or intended utilization. A location inhabited by civilians, if defended by military personnel – a defended place – is a lawful target by virtue of its use.[29] The environment illustrates how use may influence targeting decisions. In the U.S.–Vietnamese conflict, bamboo was widely used in making sharpened punji stakes that were embedded in camouflaged holes to impale the feet of passing U.S. soldiers. Bamboo groves did not therefore become military objects and lawful targets because of the use to which they were often put. Their destruction would neither make an effective contribution to military action nor offer a definite military advantage. In any event, the natural environment is protected with debatable effectiveness by the 1976 Environmental Modification Convention,[30] and by 1977 Additional

---

[26] Max Hastings and Simon Jenkins, *The Battle for the Falklands* (New York: Norton, 1983), 88.

[27] Cmdr. John Patch, "Taking Out Saddam's Floating Pleasure Palace," U.S. Naval Institute's *Proceedings* (Sept. 2008), 33.

[28] Id., at 36.

[29] 1907 Hague Regulation IV, Art. 25; 1977 Additional Protocol I, Art. 59 (2); International Criminal Court Statute, Art. 8 (2)(b)(v).

[30] U.N. Convention on the Prohibition of Military or Any Other Hostile Use of Environmental Modification Techniques (1976), Art. I.1: "Each State Party to this Convention undertakes not to engage in military or any other hostile use of environmental modification techniques having widespread, long-lasting or severe effects."

Protocol I, Articles 35.3 and 55.1: "Care shall be taken in warfare to protect the natural environment against widespread, long-term, and severe damage."[31] Environmental attacks are prohibited only when the damage is anticipated to be all three – widespread, long term, and severe. Proportionality is a consideration when the environment may be collaterally damaged. The International Court of Justice warns, "States must take environmental considerations into account when assessing what is necessary and proportionate in the pursuit of legitimate military objectives."[32]

"Taking care" and "environmental considerations," however, are not the same as excluding all targeting that may effect the environment. "These provisions do not automatically prevent certain types of military objectives such as nuclear submarines or super tankers from being legitimate targets nor do they automatically prevent the use of certain means of warfare such as herbicides and chemical agents. The effects of attacking these targets or using these means *must be considered*."[33] Despite noble intentions, Articles 35 and 55 are not customary law. A thousand-year-old grove of redwood trees or a supertanker, whose loss or sinking would cause untold environmental damage, could be targeted if *used* for enemy military purposes, as long as military necessity and proportionality considerations were satisfied.

Schools, hospitals, and mosques, among other civilian objects, are protected and may not be targeted.[34] During the common Article 2 phase of Operation Iraqi Freedom, in March 2003, units of the U.S. Army's 82nd Airborne Division were advancing toward the city of As Samawah against heavy enemy resistance. "The paratroopers quickly learned that the Iraqis in As Samawah were using schools, mosques, and hospitals as headquarters and logistics sites."[35] The objects being used in violation of LOAC lost their protected status and became lawful military objectives.[36]

---

[31] Protocol I, Art. 35.3 similarly reads, "It is prohibited to employ methods or means of warfare which are intended, or may be expected, to cause widespread, long-term and severe damage to the natural environment." Still, "belligerents can continue to wage 'conventional warfare' (including artillery bombardment with its attendant disturbance of the ecosystem) without fear of violating the principle of protection of the natural environment. Such fear they need to harbour solely when they have recourse to rather less conventional modes of warfare, such as the use of herbicides or other methods or means specifically designed to damage the environment; even then, the protection afforded to the environment remains restricted to really serious forms of large-scale damage, meeting the requirements of being 'widespread, long-term and severe.'" Frits Kalshoven, *Reflections on the Law of War* (Leiden: Martinus Nijhoff, 2007), 232–3.

[32] International Court of Justice (ICJ), *The Legality of the Threat or Use of Nuclear Weapons* (Nuclear Weapons Advisory Opinion), (1996), para. 30. Footnotes omitted.

[33] United Kingdom Ministry of Defence, *The Manual of the Law of Armed Conflict* (Oxford: Oxford University Press, 2004), para. 5.29.3, at 76. Emphasis supplied.

[34] 1907 Hague Regulation IV, Art. 27; 1949 Geneva Convention IV, Art. 18; and 1977 Additional Protocol I, Art. 52.3.

[35] COL Gregory Fontenot, LTC E. J. Degen and LTC David Tohn, *On Point: The United States Army in Operation Iraqi Freedom* (Fort Leavenworth, KS: Combat Studies Institute Press, 2004), 214.

[36] Loss of protected status is addressed in 1907 Hague Regulation IV, Art. 27; 1949 Geneva Convention IV, Art. 19; 1977 Additional Protocol I, Arts. 13.1, 52.3; and Additional Protocol II, Art. 11.2. Also, Dinstein, "Legitimate Military Objectives under the Current *Jus in Bello*," in Wall, *Legal and Ethical Lessons*, supra, note 4, at 150: "If ... the minaret of a mosque is used as a sniper's nest, the presumption [of Art. 52(3) protection] is rebutted and the enemy is entitled to treat it as a military objective."

SIDEBAR. Can a civilian passenger airliner be a military object and a lawful target?[37] At 0846, on September 11, 2001, al Qaeda hijackers flew American Airlines Flight 11 into the North Tower of New York City's World Trade Center. At 0903, other hijackers flew United Airlines Flight 175 into the South Tower. President George W. Bush was visiting an elementary school in Sarasota, Florida. In Washington, D.C., Secret Service agents hustled Vice President Richard Cheney into a shelter deep under the East Wing of the White House. American Airlines Flight 77 and United Airlines Flight 93 were known to be still speeding in the direction of Washington, D.C. Sometime between 1010 and 1015, a military aide asked the vice president a question regarding Flight 77, with sixty-four passengers and crew aboard, and closing on Washington, D.C. "The jetliner was presumed hostile, but packed with innocents. Should the Air Force shoot it down? Cheney paused. . . . Then he answered: Yes."[38]

Although there are questions surrounding the vice president's order – what LOAC/ IHL applied at the moment of his order and whether he had authority to issue the order since the vice president is not in the military chain of command – the status of the target was apparent: The civilian aircraft had become a military object and lawful target by virtue of its use. Had air force interceptors shot down Flight 77, the sixty-four innocent passengers aboard would have been (one hesitates to use the words, with their horrific implications) collateral damage.

13.4 Dangerous Forces

In international armed conflict, three types of targets, referred to as "dangerous forces," are exempt from attack despite being military objectives. "Works or installations containing dangerous forces, namely dams, dykes and nuclear generating stations, shall not be made the object of attack, even when these objects are military objectives, if such attack may cause the release of dangerous forces and consequent severe losses among the civilian population."[39] Additional Protocol II, Article 15, applies the same prohibition to noninternational armed conflicts. The term "severe losses" must be judged in good faith on the basis of objective elements, such as the existence of heavily populated civilian areas that might be affected by the release of dangerous forces.[40]

The exemption of dangerous forces was not always the case. In World War II, on the night of May 16–17, 1943, sixteen British Lancaster heavy bombers, flying in darkness at an altitude of only sixty feet, each armed with a single 9,250-pound bomb especially designed for the mission, attacked and breached the Möhne and Eder dams, deep in western Germany. Eight of the sixteen bombers were shot down, but millions of gallons of water from the breached dams cascaded down the Ruhr valley. "Buildings standing on

---

[37] The targeting of civilian aircraft, generally, is addressed in the 1929 Hague Rules of Air Warfare, Arts. 33 and 34.

[38] Barton Gellman, *Angler* (New York: Penguin Press, 2008), 119.

[39] 1977 Additional Protocol I, Art. 56.1. The article concludes, "Other military objectives located at or in the vicinity of these works or installations shall not be made the object of attack if such attack may cause the release of dangerous forces from the works or installations and consequent severe losses among the civilian population."

[40] Sandoz, Swinarski, and Zimmerman, *Commentary on the Additional Protocols*, supra, note 1, at 1463.

the floor of the valley were destroyed up to a distance of 65km from the dam; so were bridges 50km away. . . . Destruction in the valley was undoubtedly severe, with water and electricity supplies seriously affected."[41] Vital German military industries were deprived, at least temporarily, of the power needed to function. "A week later the waters reached Holland and Belgium more than 100 miles away, sweeping away countless bridges and embankments en route."[42] German civilians also paid a heavy price. "The village of Günne had been virtually washed away, [and] most of the town of Neheim-Hüsten."[43] Indeed, 1,300 noncombatants, including Allied prisoners of war were killed in the raid.[44] Air Marshal Harris reported, "Staggering destruction had been inflicted throughout the Ruhr."[45] The leader of the bombing raid, Wing Commander Guy Gibson, was awarded the Victoria Cross, England's highest award for combat valor. Books and movies heralded "the Dambusters raid." Could the acts for which the Victoria Cross was awarded in 1943 earn a court-martial today?

Professor L. C. Green writes of today's dangerous forces targeting exemption. "It is nearly inconceivable that massive risks to the civilian population could ever be outweighed by military considerations so as to justify an attack on such installations *used purely for civilian purposes*. The attack is accordingly strictly prohibited and cannot be justified by any claim of military necessity, except under the exception of paragraph 2 of Article 56 [Additional Protocol I]"[46] (emphasis supplied). Professor Dinstein, in contrast, considers the exemption "extraordinary." He writes: "The exemption attaches to them not only where they are civilian objects, but even when they glaringly constitute military objectives."[47] Still, the exception Professor Green mentioned is significant:

The special protection against attack . . . shall cease:

(a) for a dam or dyke only if it is used for other than its normal function and in regular, significant and direct support of military operations and if such attack is the only feasible way to terminate such support.

(b) for a nuclear electrical generating station only if it provides electric power in regular, significant and direct support of military operations and if such attack is the only feasible way to terminate such support.

(c) for other military objectives located at or in the vicinity of these works or installations only if they are used in regular, significant and direct support of such support.

A disapproving Frits Kalshoven writes:

Evidently, the "special protection" afforded under [Article 56] paragraph I . . . does not amount to unconditional immunity from attack. Rather, the protection remains dependent on whether the attack *"may cause"* the release of dangerous forces and consequent *severe* losses among the civilian population. . . . The test seems to be whether, in light of all the information available at the time, these effects could objectively have been foreseen.[48]

---

[41] John Sweetman, *The Dambusters Raid* (London: Arms and Armour, 1990), 153.

[42] Alan Cooper, *The Dambusters Squadron* (London: Arms and Armour, 1993), 29.   [43] Id., at 101.

[44] Sandoz, Swinarski, and Zimmerman, *Commentary on the Additional Protocols*, supra, note 1, at 667.

[45] Henry Probert, *Bomber Harris: His Life and Times* (London: Greenhill Books, 2001), 254.

[46] Leslie C. Green, *The Contemporary Law of Armed Conflict*, 2d ed. (Manchester: Manchester University Press, 2000), 158.

[47] Dinstein, *Conduct of Hostilities*, supra, note 21, at 173.

[48] Kalshoven, *Reflections on the Law of War*, supra, note 31, at 235. Emphasis in original.

One may reasonably argue that if exceptions may be made on the grounds of military necessity, subjective and elastic as that concept is, that leaves military commanders considerable discretion to employ the exception rather than observe the rule. Another issue is that defensive weapons, such as antiair or antimissile weapons, may be installed to defend installations containing dangerous forces. "This gives rise to quite complicated considerations for military commanders. They have to be able to distinguish defensive weapons from other military objectives and they have to be able to distinguish offensive from defensive uses of those weapons."[49] The International Committee of the Red Cross (ICRC) responds, "It should be stressed ... that in such cases where the highest human interests are at stake, the decision to deprive them of protection can only be taken at a high military level."[50] To a lieutenant, however, a colonel is a "high military level."

The ICRC study of customary international law indicates that the exemption of dams, dykes, and nuclear generating stations is customary law.[51] The study's supporting text is tentative and somewhat unconvincing, however. Dinstein's disagreement that it is customary law seems well founded.[52] What remains clear is that, despite Article 56, there remains considerable room for attacks on installations containing dangerous forces, particularly if they have even slight military use.

13.5 Making Targeting Decisions

Military forces employ strict protocols in making targeting decisions. Those protocols improve and mature, change to meet conflict circumstances, and seldom remain static for long. The target selection process, for military objects to be attacked by air forces, at least, can be described in general terms.

In aviation usage, targets can be "planned" or "immediate." "Planned targets are those known to exist in the operational area and are attacked in accordance with an air tasking order (ATO), mission-type order, or fire support plan. ... Immediate targets are not identified (or selected for attack) soon enough to be included in the normal targeting process. ... As a general matter, planned targets are more conducive to precision attack than unplanned."[53] In Operation Desert Storm (1991), "the ATO did not respond as rapidly when air operations progressed and emphasis shifted to more mobile targets."[54]

---

[49] United Kingdom Ministry of Defence, *Manual of the Law of Armed Conflict*, supra, note 33, at para. 5.30.10, at 79. Indeed, Kalshoven writes, "Article 56 ... undoubtedly contains one of the most peculiar and complex sets of rules in the Protocol." Kalshoven, *Reflections on the Law of War*, supra, note 31, at 234. Professor Kalshoven, a retired Dutch naval officer turned scholar, ascribes at least part of the hidden complexity of Art. 56 to its author: "The quoted words were written by a lawyer who has never in his life been a member of the armed forces: [American] Mr. George Aldrich, Rapporteur of Committee III [which was responsible for the Article]." Id., at 236.

[50] Sandoz, Swinarski, and Zimmerman, *Commentary on the Additional Protocols*, supra, note 1, at 670.

[51] Henckaerts and Doswald-Beck, *Customary International Humanitarian Law*, Vol. I, supra, note 2, Rule 42, at 139.

[52] Dinstein, *Conduct of Hostilities*, supra, note 21, at 173: "This is an innovative stricture, which cannot be viewed as part of customary international law (unless excessive collateral damage to civilians is anticipated). It is definitely inconsistent with previous practice."

[53] Michael N. Schmitt, "Precision Attack and International Humanitarian Law," 859 *Int'l Rev. of the Red Cross* (Sept. 2005), 445, 450–1.

[54] Dept. of Defense, *Conduct of the Persian Gulf War* (Washington, DC: GPO, 1992), 103.

In other words, an ATO is not suited to targets of opportunity. Here, we examine the targeting of planned targets, rather than targets of opportunity.

Professor Michael Schmitt, a former U.S. Air Force targeting officer, has described the targeting process as a six-phased exercise. His description is not immutable, and other targeting experts may offer varying descriptions. Phases may overlap to greater or lesser degrees – the targeting process is not always a distinct series of isolated decisions and actions. Also, Schmitt's depiction may differ from major U.S. command to major U.S. command, but he provides a useful outline of the targeting process, a process throughout which judge advocates are involved:

> The legal advisor's role/responsibility ... is to offer well-reasoned advice. ... This requires knowing the law, awareness of other restrictions, understanding of the military and political objectives, familiarity with the methods of achieving those objectives and, finally, the ability to synthesize and make a recommendation on a target or set of targets. ... Legal advisors provide recommendations on whether the proposed use of force abides by the law of war and do this by offering advice on both restraint and the right to use force. ... However, the final decision will always be the commander's. Legal advisors do not ... approve or disapprove targets.[55]

In Schmitt's six-phase targeting model, first, the force commander establishes campaign objectives, thereby setting the targeting process in motion. Schmitt writes, "During this phase, the enemy's military, political and economic systems ... are studied. The value of potential targets is analyzed to determine the relative need to strike them, and international humanitarian law and rules of engagement factors are considered."[56] In Operation Desert Storm, for instance, twelve strategic "target sets" were formulated to assist in achieving the coalition's five military objectives. "The method for producing the daily attack plan involved synthesizing many inputs – battle damage assessment (BDA) from previous attacks, CINCCENT [commander in chief, Central Command] guidance, weather, target set priorities, new targets, intelligence, and the air campaign objectives. The target sets were interrelated and were not targeted individually."[57] The vast majority of targets are approved in-theater – the location in which the conflict occurs. Targets that are sensitive s a result of their location or nature, such as electric power grids, infrastructure objects, and targets in built-up areas, may require approval by the Pentagon's Joint Staff and the Joint Chiefs of Staff. Occasionally, secretary of defense approval is sought. Given the lengthy Operation Desert Storm buildup period before the Iraqis were attacked and ejected from Kuwait, planners had the unusual luxury of detailed and well-considered target planning.

> To help strike planners, CENTCOM [Central Command] target intelligence analysts, in close coordination with the national intelligence agencies and the State Department,

---

[55] Col. Tony Montgomery, "Legal Perspective from the EUCOM Targeting Cell," in Wall, *Legal and Ethical Lessons*, supra, note 4, at 189–90.

[56] Dept. of Defense, *Conduct of the Persian Gulf War*, supra, note 54, at 452.

[57] Id., at 95. The twelve target sets were Leadership Command Facilities; Electricity Production Facilities; Telecommunications and Command, Control, and Communications Nodes; Strategic Integrated Air Defense System; Air Forces and Airfields; Nuclear, Biological and Chemical Weapons Research, Production, and Storage Facilities; Scud Missiles, Launchers, and Production and Storage Facilities; Naval Forces and Port Facilities; Oil Refining and Distribution Facilities; Railroads and Bridges; Iraqi Army Units Including Republican Guard Forces; and Military Storage and Production Sites.

produced a joint no-fire target list. This list was a compilation of historical, archaeological, economic, religious and politically sensitive installations in Iraq and Kuwait that could not be targeted. Additionally, target intelligence analysts were tasked to look in a six-mile area around each master attack list target for schools, hospitals, and mosques to identify targets where extreme care was required in planning. ... When targeting officers calculated the probability of collateral damage was too high, the target was not attacked.[58]

Planners are not often able to devote such time and effort to targeting decisions. There were still many friendly fire incidents involving both aircraft and ground combatants. Any targeting plan, no matter how meticulously formulated, is subject to the vagaries of combat. Weather, visibility, smoke, and enemy defenses all degrade the accuracy sought by planners and mandated by Protocol I's Articles 48 through 60.

In Schmitt's second phase, target development, the enemy's military, political, and economic systems are studied. Their relative values and their interrelationships help to decide targeting priorities.

In the third phase, weaponeering, force application is decided. This decision involves consideration of the best-suited weapons available, the degree of damage desired, and issues of potential collateral damage. "During Operation Iraqi Freedom, US forces engaged in computer modeling to 'determine the weapon, fuse, attack, angle, and time of day that will ensure maximum effect on the target with minimum civilian casualties.' When the model estimate exceeded 30 civilian casualties, Secretary of Defense approval was required for the mission."[59] "The intense concern over the issue of collateral damage ... meant that only a certain type of munitions could be used or the target could only be attacked at certain times of day. Thus, something as simple as a change in munitions could raise the level of collateral damage above what had been approved and, thus, remove a target from the 'approved for strike' category."[60]

The fourth targeting phase is the force application phase: What aerial weapons system is best suited to achieve the best result for the particular target? What available aircraft is the best delivery platform for the selected weapon? Is an F-117 stealth ground attack aircraft more likely to penetrate enemy defenses? Will the F-117's limited bomb capacity be sufficient to achieve the desired degree of target damage? Do its stealth characteristics offer a better chance of evading enemy defenses, or is a flight of B-52 heavy bombers with its immense weapons capacity better suited to the mission?

Fifth, in the execution planning and force execution phase the actual mission is designed: how the target will be identified and tactics decided – target approach and egress routes, altitudes, air-to-air refueling points, radio frequencies – tactical issues vital to pilots and controllers.

In the final phase, combat assessment, the execution and effectiveness of the completed mission are evaluated to determine whether another attack is required or if the mission was successful.[61] Finally, "just as each level of command has its own operators and intelligence officers, so too do they have their own legal advisor. The legal advisors

---

[58] Id., at 100.   [59] Id., at 458. Footnote omitted.
[60] Montgomery, "Legal Perspective from the EUCOM Targeting Cell," in Wall, *Legal and Ethical Lessons*, supra, note 55, at 195.
[61] Schmitt, "Precision Attack and International Humanitarian Law," supra, note 53, at 453.

were in constant contact discussing both the broad impact of changes in guidance, as well as specific issues on individual targets."[62]

SIDEBAR. The Gulf War (1990–1) involved Iraq's invasion and annexation of Kuwait. A United States–led coalition of thirty-four states responded. General Colin Powell, then-chairman of the Joint Chiefs of Staff, relates the target selection process : "Lawyers got into the act. We could not complete a list of air targets until the Pentagon general council's office approved. In one preliminary list we had targeted a triumphal arch celebrating Iraq's proclaimed victory over Iran ... and a huge statue of Saddam, both in Baghdad. Colonel Fred Green, my legal advisor, came to see me with a battery of lawyers. They had gone over the list and approved everything except the arch and the statue. "Sorry, General," Fred said, "you can't touch them." "Why not?" I asked, puzzled. "You'd be bombing cultural landmarks of no military significance." "Cultural landmarks! Gimme a break. I want to show his people Saddam's not out of bounds." "Can't do it, General," Green said. "It would be like someone bombing the Lincoln Memorial or the Washington Monument. It contravenes international laws governing the conduct of war." The arch and the statue were crossed off the target list. When I explained what happened to [Secretary of Defense Richard] Cheney, he shook his head and muttered, "Lawyers running a war?"[63]

Collateral damage is a primary targeting concern. For example, Operation Allied Force, March to June 1999, was NATO's bombing attack on Serbian civilian and military infrastructure to force a Serbian retreat from Kosovo. For targets that were not approved in-theater because of their sensitivity, the operation's American elements employed a complex analysis of collateral damage. Proposed targets involving the potential of significant civilian casualties were forwarded to the Pentagon. The Joint Staff's intelligence division made an independent assessment of the target. Using slides, the intelligence division briefed the Joint Chiefs of Staff, and, if considered necessary, the secretary of defense. Rarely, the president was briefed. "The contents of the slides showed the objective. ... Was it command and control, was it integrated air defense, was it industrial-military, and what was the collateral damage estimate? ... The slide would also have a casualty estimate which would include sometimes both the combatants and the noncombatants."[64] Attempting to quantify military necessity and proportionality, the Joint Staff created a matrix rating the military significance of the target and rating collateral damage as high, medium, or low. The matrix also included consideration of outliers, "the potential for a bomb or missile to miss its target. ... This assessment [of outliers] was particularly important where ... there was a heavily built-up area with large urban structures around the target. There was a greater risk of outliers in those situations."[65] Judge advocates then conducted a legal assessment of the target to ensure that, by its nature, location, purpose, or use, the targeted object made an effective contribution to the military action and that its damage or destruction offered a definite military

---

[62] Montgomery, "Legal Perspective from the EUCOM Targeting Cell," in Wall, *Legal and Ethical Lessons,* supra, note 55, at 196.

[63] Colin L. Powell, *A Soldier's Way: An Autobiography* (London: Hutchinson/Random House, 1995), 496.

[64] Harvey Dalton, "Commentary," in Wall, *Legal and Ethical Lessons,* supra, note 4, at 200.   [65] Id.

advantage. Finally, the target was approved or disapproved by the Joint Chiefs, the secretary of defense, or the president. NATO allies have systems that are similarly stringent in their efforts to minimize collateral damage.

The targeting processes described are already two decades old. Today, more detailed targeting models are in place for aviation-delivered ordnance, using more sophisticated computer-based graphics, modeling, and algorithms.

Targeting decisions are not limited to aerial munitions, of course. Ground artillery units are integral to all large ground units. Artillery in support of infantry forces relies on trained spotters, or the infantrymen themselves, to locate and identify suitable targets. Shared map references, continuous radio contact, and Fire Direction Center personnel place ordnance on the target.

Differing missions may call for differing targeting methods. The targeting decision process varies, depending on the tactical goal and the particular mission. What all decision processes share are the requirements of distinction, military necessity, and proportionality.

Despite best efforts, combat zone targeting will always result in collateral damage and injury or death from friendly fire. "Protocol I prescribes that efforts have to be made in order to ascertain the military character of an objective. On the other hand, the targeting decision is certainly one which has to be taken in a context of uncertainty."[66] Advances in tactics and technology continue to reduce the number of such incidents. Precision-guided munitions (PGMs) – global position satellites (GPS) – and laser-guided munitions – result in impressive reductions in civilian injuries and deaths, as well as fewer damaged or destroyed civilian objects. During 1991's Operation Desert Storm, 8.8 percent of U.S. aerial attacks employed PGMs. Operation Allied Force, the 1999 NATO air strikes on President Milosevic's military and security structure in Kosovo, saw a rise to roughly 33 percent of aerial attacks that employed PGMs. In 2001's Operation Enduring Freedom, in Afghanistan, 65 percent and in Operation Iraqi Freedom, in 2003, 68 percent of U.S. air strikes involved PGMs.

Given the greater accuracy of PGMs, one may ask why their use is not mandatory. The reason is that PGMs remain sufficiently expensive that they are beyond the economic reach and technological capabilities of most states.[67] A delegate to 1977 Additional Protocol I said of Article 48, which mandates that combatants distinguish between civilian and military targets, "this article will apply within the capability and practical possibility of each party to the conflict. As the capability of the parties to distinguish will depend upon the means and methods available to each party generally at a particular moment, this article does not require a party to do something which is not within its means or its capacity."[68]

13.6 Precautions in the Attack

The principle of precautions in attack was first set out in 1907 Hague Convention IX, Article 2(3). In international armed conflicts, attackers must take certain precautions

---

[66] Bothe, "Targeting," in Wall, *Legal and Ethical Lessons*, supra, note 4, at 183.

[67] John F. Murphy, "Some Legal (and a Few Ethical) Dimensions of the Collateral Damage Resulting from NATO's Kosovo Campaign," 31 *Israel Yearbook on Human Rights* (2001), 51, 63.

[68] Sandoz, Swinarski, and Zimmerman, *Commentary on the Additional Protocols*, supra, note 1, at 599.

whenever they initiate an attack. Additional Protocol I, Article 57(1) requires that "[in] the conduct of military operations, constant care shall be taken to spare the civilian population, civilians and civilian objects." This requirement is most probably customary international law. "Yet, the obligation imposed on Belligerent Parties is 'essentially relative in nature, as situations may arise where civilians simply cannot be spared.'"[69]

Article 57(2)(a) specifies the active precautions that must be taken by parties who plan or execute an attack:

(i)   Do everything feasible to verify that objectives constitute military objectives.
(ii) Take all feasible precautions in choosing the means and methods of attack, with a view to avoiding, or minimizing, collateral damage to civilians and civilian objects.
(iii) Refrain from launching attacks expected to be in breach of the principle of proportionality.

"Feasible precautions" are difficult to define. Article 3(4) of the 1980 Convention on Conventional Weapons describes them as "those precautions which are practicable or practically possible taking into account all circumstances ruling at the time, including humanitarian and military considerations."
In regard to noninternational armed conflicts,

> The requirement to take precautions in attack was included in the draft of Additional Protocol II but was dropped at the last moment as part of a package aimed at the adoption of a simplified text. As a result, Additional Protocol II does not explicitly require such precautions. Article 13(1), however, requires that "the civilian population and individual civilians shall enjoy general protections against the dangers arising from military operations," and it would be difficult to comply with this requirement without taking precautions in attack. More recent treaty law applicable in non-international armed conflicts ... does spell out the requirement of precautions in attack.[70]

Precautions in attack are sufficiently important that many commentators consider them a core LOAC/IHL principle.

13.7 Dual-Use Targets

Like the term "unlawful combatant," the term "dual-use target" does not appear in the Geneva Conventions or additional protocols. The term "has arisen out of an apparent need to describe the class of objects that do not appear to fit neatly within Additional Protocol I, Article 52(3), i.e. 'normally dedicated' to civilian purposes, such that the presumption that they are civilian cannot be readily applied."[71] A dual-use target is one with both military and civilian functions, such as an airfield from which both civilian and military aircraft fly. Examples also include electric power grids, oil-refining facilities, and radio and television broadcasting sites. Even highways, bridges, ports, and railways can be

[69] Yoram Dinstein, *The Conduct of Hostilities under the Law of International Armed Conflict*, 2d ed. (Cambridge: Cambridge University Press, 2010), 138, citing, Kalshoven, *Reflections on the Law of War*, supra, note 31, at 546.

[70] Henckaerts and Doswald-Beck, *Customary International Humanitarian Law*, supra, note 2, Rule 15, at 52.

[71] Marco Sassòli and Lindsey Cameron, "The Protection of Civilian Objects – Current State of the Law and Issues *de Lege Ferenda*," in Natalino Ronzitti and Gabriella Venturini, eds., *The Law of Air Warfare* (Utrecht, the Netherlands: Eleven International, 2006), 35, 57.

considered dual-use. They all serve needs of both the civilian community and the armed forces. In industrialized, urbanized states in which such potential military objects are intermingled, "it is difficult to neutralize the military effectiveness of those targets without simultaneously harming the civilian population."[72] Yes, the destruction of the enemy capital city's electrical power grid will degrade or eliminate the country's military radar system and communications link, but it will also cut off power to the city's hospitals, domestic water supply system, and central sewage plant. Is a dam that produces hydro-electric power for armament plants and acts as a reservoir for drinking water a military object, or is it a civilian facility with the potential to flood the countryside? Is a television broadcasting facility a civilian object providing civil defense information to civilians, or, because it may be used to broadcast instructions to military forces and disseminate propaganda, is it a lawful target? Proportionality and military necessity, the yin and yang of military operations, become difficult assessments.[73]

In Gulf War I (1990), the Al Furdos bunker in central Baghdad was an important command and control center, military communications hub, and secret police head-quarters. Clearly a military object, it was bombed by U.S. aircraft late at night, when the fewest military personnel would be inside. (See Chapter 7, Section 7.1.1.) Unknown to the United States, at night the bunker also sheltered families of military personnel assigned to the bunker, and 204 individuals, most of them civilians, were killed in the attack. Had the dual use of the bunker been known, would the bombing have been lawful or not? Viewed solely as a military object, the bunker was obviously a lawful target. Given the information available at the time to U.S. targeting personnel, and in light of the satellite reconnaissance and human intelligence that appeared to support that infor-mation, targeting the bunker was reasonable. Nevertheless, after the Al Furdos incident, American planners effectively put central Baghdad targets off limits to bombing. Would the result have been different had CNN not televised the bodies of women and children being removed from the ruined bunker? Would it have made a difference if 20 non-combatants had been killed, rather than 200?

Dual-use targeting decisions are sometimes easier. Electric power grids have been mentioned. Major-General A. V. P. Rogers, former director of legal services of the British army, writes of Gulf War I:

> The modern military machine relies very heavily on electrical power, especially for command, control, communications and air defence systems. Take away that power and the enemy is severely handicapped and may be rendered blind and leaderless and vulnerable to air attack. The suggestion by [writers in disagreement] that repeated attacks are not necessary where a war is going to be short is unrealistic ... and the allies were fully entitled to take no risks in that respect. In these circumstances, power sources become military objectives. ... The writer would reject the allegation that repeated bombing of previously disabled electrical facilities served no military purpose. The purpose obviously is to prevent repair and keep the facility out of action.[74]

---

[72] Rogers, *Law on the Battlefield*, supra, note 16, at 71.

[73] Sandoz, Swinarski, and Zimmerman, *Commentary on the Additional Protocols*, supra, note 1, at 636: "In such situations the time and place of the attack should be taken into consideration, together with, on the one hand, the military advantage anticipated, and on the other hand, the loss of human life which must be expected among the civilian population and the damage which would be caused to civilian objects."

[74] Rogers, *Law on the Battlefield*, supra, note 16, at 75–6.

NATO bombers dropped munitions that deployed tinfoillike streamers to drape over power lines and short them out, requiring days to repair. The power grid remained largely intact, however, without requiring total rebuilding. General Rogers stresses the importance of proportionality in all cases. Professor Dinstein, in agreement, writes, "From a legal viewpoint, a 'dual use' of Iraq's electric grid did not alter its singular and unequivocal status as a military objective."[75] Just as there were factors other than LOAC/IHL that made the Al Furdos bunker exempt from further bombing, there could be factors exempting an electric power grid from attack. Every case has distinctive features.

During Operation Allied Force, the 1999 NATO bombing of Serbian targets, including some in the Yugoslav capital, the Serbian state television and radio station, RTS, in Belgrade, was bombed. Are television facilities, such as studios and transmission towers, lawful targets? "To answer that question, we need to decide whether the television tower was a military objective or a civilian object. It is impossible to say *a priori* whether a television tower is a legitimate military objective, as this depends not on the nature of the building or object, but on the use actually made of it. The broadcasting facilities may have served civilian purposes or military ones such as transmission of commands and war propaganda."[76] This attack, which resulted in the deaths of ten to seventeen noncombatants (a firm number was never established), along with other air attacks, caused numerous formal complaints from nongovernmental organizations to be lodged with the ICTY's chief prosecutor. In accordance with Article 18 of the ICTY Statute, she established a committee of experts to assess all of the complaints and charges, including the bombing of the radio and television station. In its final report, the committee said:

> NATO stressed the dual-use to which such communications systems were put, describing civilian television as "heavily dependent on the military command and control system and military traffic is also routed through the civilian system." ... NATO claimed that the RTS facilities were being used "as radio relay stations and transmitters to support the activities of the FRY [Federal Republic of Yugoslavia] military and special police forces, and therefore they represent legitimate military targets. ... More controversially, however, the bombing was also justified on the basis of the propaganda purpose to which it [RTS] was employed.[77]

With the proviso that an attack based solely on RTS's role in Serbian propaganda dissemination would be questionable, the committee of experts recommended there be no formal investigation. (See Cases and Materials, this chapter.) Targeting radio and television facilities remains controversial, nevertheless. The U.S. position is that, generally, such dual-use facilities are military objectives. That position is supported by the 1954 Hague Cultural Property Convention, which refers to broadcasting stations as military objectives.

---

[75] Yoram Dinstein, "Discussion: Reasonable Military Commanders and Reasonable Civilians," in Wall, *Legal and Ethical Lessons*, supra, note 4, at 219.

[76] Daniel Thürer, *International Humanitarian Law: Theory, Practice, Context* (The Hague: Hague Academy of International Law, 2011), 370.

[77] *Final Report to the Prosecutor by the Committee Established to Review the NATO Bombing Campaign against the Federal Republic of Yugoslavia* (June 13, 2000), paras. 72–4. Available online.

Some Europe-based commentators, disagree.[78] "Many in the humanitarian law community," as well, "believe the attack was unlawful under the circumstances."[79]

A reasonable guideline: "Attacks on a media station may be permissible ... subject to the rule of proportionality, if it helps the enemy in its military operations, for example, if it is integrated into the military communications system ... but not if it merely broadcasts news."[80] A similar guideline may be applied to other dual-use objects.

13.8 Indiscriminate Attacks

"Attacks against civilian objects are banned not only when they are direct and deliberate, but also when they are indiscriminate."[81] The basic rule of Protocol I, Article 48, requiring that only military objectives be targeted, is complemented by the rule that attackers must also observe distinction – must discriminate – in their attacks. The prohibition on indiscriminate attacks, first raised in the 1923 Hague Rules of Air Warfare, Article 24(3), are repeated in 1977 Additional Protocol I, Article 51.4:

Indiscriminate attacks are prohibited. Indiscriminate attacks are:

(a) those which are not directed at a specific military objective;
(b) those which employ a method or means of combat which cannot be directed at a specific military objective; or
(c) those which employ a method or means of combat the effects of which cannot be limited as required by this Protocol; and consequently, in each such case, are of a nature to strike military objectives and civilians or civilian objects without distinction.

Parts (a) and (b) of Article 51.4 restate the core concept of distinction, and part (c) restates the proportionality concept in saying that any attack that violates proportionality is an indiscriminate attack, and, if a civilian population or civilian objects are knowingly affected in an international armed conflict, such an attack constitutes a grave breach.[82] Additional Protocol II does not contain a similar prohibition, but it is considered customary international law, applicable in any armed conflict. Accordingly, in all armed conflicts, "the area bombing attacks of World War II would now be illegal. This does not mean, however, that merely because a built-up area exists the larger area is no longer a military objective."[83] This despite Additional Protocol I, Article 51,(5)(a) prohibiting bombing "by any methods or means which treats as a single objective a number of clearly separated and distinct military objectives located in a city, town, village or other area containing a similar concentration of civilians or civilian objects."

---

[78] Not all European experts disagree: "Concentrating on the broadcasting station ... we must admit that under the laws of war, enemy means of communication have always been and always will be considered legitimate military objectives." Wolff H. von Heinegg, "Commentary," in Wall, *Legal and Ethical Lessons*, supra, note 4, at 205.

[79] Michael N. Schmitt, "Targeting and Humanitarian Law: Current Issues," 33 *Israel Yearbook on Human Rights* (2003), 59, 69.

[80] Rogers, *Law on the Battlefield*, supra, note 16, at 83.

[81] Dinstein, *Conduct of Hostilities*, supra, note 21, at 116.   [82] 1977 Additional Protocol I, Art. 85 (3)(b).

[83] Green, *The Contemporary Law of Armed Conflict*, supra, note 46, at 160.

The ICRC *Commentary* discreetly notes, "This provision [Article 51.4] . . . confirms the unlawful character of certain regrettable practices during the Second World War. . . . Far too often the purpose of attacks was to destroy all life in a particular area or to raze a town to the ground without . . . substantial military advantages."[84] The comment refers to indiscriminate "area bombing," practiced by the Japanese in 1932 in prewar Shanghai; by the Germans at Guernica, Spain, in 1937, as well as Weiluń, Poland (1939), Rotterdam, the Netherlands, and Elverum, Norway (1940); then London and Coventry, later in the war.[85] "The German bombardments of . . . English coast towns ignored the spirit of the [1907 Hague] Convention, for those raids had no military purpose whatever, unless it is a legitimate military purpose to attempt to frighten and terrorise the civil population of the enemy."[86] The Allies in turn attacked Berlin, Hamburg, Dresden, and other German cities, and U.S. bombers attacked sixty-eight Japanese cities,[87] leveling at least seven,[88] including Tokyo, which, on the night of March 9–10, 1945, was firebombed, leaving between ninety and one hundred thousand dead.[89] It has been charged, unfairly, one suspects, that Air Marshall Arthur Harris, the air officer commander in chief of the Royal Air Force's Bomber Command in the latter part of World War II, believed "railroads and oil – as well as ball bearings, chemicals, and U-boat pens – were nothing but 'panacea' targets that diverted him from his area bombing campaign against German cities."[90] Area bombing was not and is not a lawful aspect of modern warfare. The rule against indiscriminate attacks has become customary law, applicable in noninternational armed conflicts as well as international conflicts.[91]

In an indiscriminate attack, whether by aerial bombing, artillery, or missile, the attacker does not seek to harm civilians; he simply is not concerned whether they are injured. World War II Nazi "buzz bombs" and V-1 and V-2 rockets aimed at London – no specific target, just London – and Iraqi SCUD missiles fired at Israel and Saudi Arabia during Gulf War I are examples of indiscriminate attacks and indiscriminate targeting. Those weapons are by their nature indiscriminate. "If the military objective consists of scattered enemy tank formations in an unpopulated desert, it would be permissible to use weapons having a wider area of effect than would be possible if the target were a single communications site in the middle of a heavily populated area. Military objectives dispersed about populated areas have to be attacked separately."[92] As one writer caustically puts it, "the line must . . . be drawn somewhere, and on the plainly illegal other side of it henceforth lie the kind of attacks which sacrifice any number of civilians for even

---

[84] Sandoz, Swinarski, and Zimmerman, *Commentary on the Additional Protocols*, supra, note 1, at 619.

[85] Thilo Marauhn and Stefan Kirchner, "Target Area Bombing," in Ronzitti and Venturini, *Law of Air Warfare*, supra, note 71, at 87, 88–9.

[86] L. Oppenheim, *International Law: A Treatise*. Vol. II. *Disputes, War and Neutrality*, 7th ed., H. Lauterpacht, ed. (London: Longman, 1952), para. 213, at 513–14.

[87] Stephen L. McFarland, *America's Pursuit of Precision Bombing, 1910–1945* (Washington, DC: Smithsonian Institution Press, 1995), 204.

[88] Kenneth P. Werrell, *Blankets of Fire* (Washington, DC: Smithsonian Institution Press, 1996), photos p. 2.

[89] Conrad C. Crane, *Bombs, Cities, and Civilians* (Lawrence: University of Kansas Press, 1993), 132. Parks, "Air War and the Law of War," supra, note 9, at 154, fn. 459, places the number killed at 83,793.

[90] Phillip S. Meilinger, 74–2 *J. of Military History* 631 (April 2010) (reviewing Robert S. Ehlers Jr., *Targeting the Third Reich: Air Intelligence and the Allied Bombing Campaign* [2009]).

[91] Henckaerts and Doswald-Beck, *Customary International Humanitarian Law*. Vol. I. *Rules*, supra, note 2, Rule 11, at 37.

[92] UK Ministry of Defence, *Manual of the Law of Armed Conflict*, supra, note 33, para. 5.23.3, at 69.

small and dubious military advantages, and which . . . are likely to signify the restlessness of materially well-endowed belligerents given to believing that (to use the too familiar phrase) 'anything is permissible which saves the life of one of our men.'"[93]

"Basically, the commander will have to ask himself three questions before he proceeds with the attack: 1, Is the target a military objective? 2, Is the attack indiscriminate? 3, Is the rule of proportionality likely to be offended?"[94] "Applying the law of armed conflict is not like using a calculator to solve a mathematical equation."[95] Charges of indiscriminate targeting will turn on the attacker's state of mind, given the circumstances and the facts known to the commander, after a conscientious gathering of such facts as were available to him at the time. Like attacks on dangerous forces, attacks on civilian areas are not flatly prohibited, but they must meet the requirements of military necessity and proportionality.

13.9 Summary

Military objectives – targets –are restricted to objects that by their nature, location, purpose, or use make an effective contribution to military action; their destruction or neutralization offers a definite military advantage. How difficult it is to apply that Additional Protocol I rule in armed conflict. Professor Peter Rowe writes of targeting restrictions in NATO's 1999 Kosovo bombing campaign, "The Protocol is, when it comes to the test, very weak in determining what may or may not be attacked."[96] Commanders, he says, in good faith overestimate the military advantage to be gained from a planned mission while underestimating collateral damage. That is why, out of the public eye, targeting decisions have become the complex multifaceted, multilayered process required by modern armed forces. Today, distinction is more than an abstract principle; it is a defining feature of targeting.

As with much of LOAC/IHL, the application of targeting rules depends on the good faith of the states that have accepted and ratified its precepts. Prohibitions on targeting dangerous forces, dual-use objects, and indiscriminate targets each have undefined "work arounds" potentially subject to abuse. We necessarily accept that "the text [of Article 52] adopted by the Diplomatic Conference largely relies on the judgment of soldiers who will have to apply these provisions."[97]

Targeted killing, a frequent tactic of choice in fighting terrorists, raises complex targeting issues. What constitutes "direct participation in hostilities" and "continuous combat function"? How broadly may, or should, the terms be interpreted?

Despite its difficult issues, targeting still largely concerns distinction and proportionality. Extensive and painstaking efforts are made by most armed forces to meet their requirements.

---

[93] Geoffrey Best, *War and Law since 1945* (Oxford: Oxford University Press, 1994), 281.

[94] Rogers, *Law on the Battlefield*, supra, note 16, at 27.

[95] Col. Frederic L. Borch, "Targeting after Kosovo: Has the Law Changed for Strike Planners?" Vol. LVI-2 *Naval War College Rev.* (Spring 2003), 64.

[96] Peter Rowe, "Kosovo 1999: The Air Campaign – Have the Provisions of Additional Protocol I Withstood the Test?" 837 *Int'l Rev. of the Red Cross* (2000), 147.

[97] Sandoz, Swinarski, and Zimmerman, *Commentary on the Additional Protocols*, supra, note 1, at 638.

CASES AND MATERIALS

"THE EINSATZGRUPPEN CASE," THE UNITED STATES V. OTTO OHLENDORF, ET AL.[98]

Introduction. One of the twelve Subsequent Proceedings held in Nuremberg during and after the Nuremberg International Military Tribunal was the Einsatzgruppen case, in which Otto Ohlendorf, head of the Interior Division of the Sicherheitsdienst (SD Security Service), a sister organization of the SS, was tried by a U.S. military commission for his role in the murder of Jews during the war. A portion of the trial is instructive as historical comment on targeting. Evidence at Ohlendorf's trial indicated that, under his leadership, at least ninety thousand people, and doubtless many more, mostly Jews, were executed.[99] Twenty-three coaccused were tried with Ohlendorf. This extract from the judgment casts light on the thinking of American judges regarding area bombing, which in World War II had not yet been specifically prohibited as indiscriminate attacks.

Then it was submitted that the defendants must be exonerated from the charge of killing civilian populations since every Allied nation brought about the death of noncombatants through the instrumentality of bombing. Any person, who, without cause, strikes another may not later complain if the other in repelling the attack uses sufficient force to overcome the original adversary. That is fundamental law between nations as well.

... Germany, under its Nazi rulers started an aggressive war. The bombing of Berlin, Dresden, Hamburg, Cologne, and other German cities followed the bombing of London, Coventry, Rotterdam, Warsaw, and other Allied cities; the bombing of German cities succeeded, in point of time, the acts discussed here. But even if it were assumed for the purpose of illustration that the Allies bombed German cities without Germans having bombed Allied cities, there still is no parallelism between an act of legitimate warfare, namely the bombing of a city, with a concomitant loss of civilian life, and the premeditated killing of all members of certain categories of the civilian population in occupied territory.

A city is bombed for tactical purposes; communications are to be destroyed, railroads wrecked, ammunition plants demolished, factories razed, all for the purpose of impeding the military. In these operations it inevitably happens that nonmilitary persons are killed. This is an incident, a grave incident to be sure, but an unavoidable corollary of battle action. The civilians are not individualized. The bomb falls, it is aimed at the railroad yards, houses along the tracks are hit and many of their occupants killed. But that is entirely different, both in fact and in law, from an armed force marching up to these same railroad tracks, entering those houses abutting thereon, dragging out the men, women and children and shooting them.

It was argued in behalf of the defendants that there was no normal distinction between shooting civilians with rifles and killing them by means of atomic bombs. There is no doubt that the invention of the atomic bomb, when used, was not aimed at

---

[98] U.S. v. Ohlendorf ("The Einsatzgruppen Case"), *Trials of War Criminals before the Nuremberg Military Tribunals*, Vol. IV (Washington, DC: GPO, 1950), 1, 466.

[99] Id., at 511.

noncombatants. Like any other aerial bomb employed during the war, it was dropped to overcome military resistance.

Thus, as grave a military action as an air bombardment, whether with the usual bombs or by atomic bomb, the one and only purpose of the bombing is to affect the surrender of the bombed nation. The people of that nation, through their representatives, may surrender and, with the surrender, the bombing ceases, the killing is ended.

Conclusion. *Ohlendorf, who practiced law before the war, raised the defense of obedience of orders. As did accused in several other Subsequent Proceedings, he argued that his acts and those of his subordinates were no worse than those of Americans who had dropped the atomic bombs on Japan. The chief prosecutor, Brigadier General Telford Taylor, responded in his closing argument:*

> *The common denominator of all these expressions [in defense] is the same. It is the doctrine that total war means total lawlessness. The doctrine is logically indefensible and is based upon wanton indifference to facts and the order in which certain events took place. As to the atom bomb ... the laws of war have never attempted to prohibit such developments. ... The atomic bomb, therefore, is neither more nor less legal than ordinary bombs; under the laws of war, the question is not as to the character or explosive capacity of the bomb, but how it is used.*[100]

> *Ohlendorf was convicted of having committed crimes against humanity, war crimes, and being a member of a criminal organization, and was hanged.*

> *The military commission, made up of three American civilian jurists and an alternate (a North Carolina superior court judge, a Navy Reserve rear admiral, a Pennsylvania common pleas court judge, and a lawyer from Alabama) seem to have had a view of proportionality without shades of gray. Would you agree with the commission's judgment regarding the atom bomb? How persuasive is General Taylor's argument?*

FINAL REPORT TO THE PROSECUTOR BY THE COMMITTEE ESTABLISHED TO REVIEW THE NATO BOMBING CAMPAIGN AGAINST THE FEDERAL REPUBLIC OF YUGOSLAVIA[101]

Introduction. *When may a dual-use target be considered a military objective? The 2000 report of a committee of experts assembled by the ICTY provides guidelines and limits. Is it feasible to apply the same or similar guidelines to other dual-use targets, such as electrical grids, oil-refining facilities or railway bridges? Would you recommend other parameters?*

I. Background and Mandate

1. The North Atlantic Treaty Organization (NATO) conducted a bombing campaign against the Federal Republic of Yugoslavia (FRY) from 24 March 1999 to 9 June 1999. During and since that period, the [ICTY] Prosecutor has received numerous requests that she investigate allegations that senior political and military figures from NATO countries committed serious violations of international humanitarian law during the campaign, and that she prepare indictments pursuant to ... the [ICTY] Statute.

---

[100] Id., at 380–1.   [101] June 13, 2000. Footnotes and references omitted. Available online.

2. On 14 May 99 the then Prosecutor established a committee to assess the allegations . . .
    and advise . . . whether or not there is a sufficient basis to proceed with an investigation
    into some or all the allegations . . . related to the NATO bombing.

Ii. Review Criteria

28. In brief, in combat military commanders are required: a) to direct their operations
against military objectives, and b) when directing their operations against military
objectives, to ensure that the losses to the civilian population and the damage to civilian
property are not disproportionate to the concrete and direct military advantage anticipated. Attacks which are not directed against military objectives (particularly attacks
directed against the civilian population) and attacks which cause disproportionate civilian casualties or civilian property damage may constitute the *actus reus* for the offense of
unlawful attack under . . . the ICTY Statute. The *mens rea* for the offence is intention or
recklessness, not simple negligence. In determining whether or not the *mens rea* requirement has been met, it should be borne in mind that commanders deciding on an attack
have duties:

a) to do everything practicable to verify that the objectives to be attacked are military
    objectives,
b) to take all practicable precautions in the choice of methods and means of warfare
    with a view to avoiding or, in any event to minimizing incidental civilian casualties
    or civilian property damage, and
c) to refrain from launching attacks which may be expected to cause disproportionate
    civilian casualties or civilian property damage.

IV. Assessment

B. *Specific Incidents*

iii) The Bombing of the RTS (Serbian TV and Radio Station) in Belgrade on 23/4/99

71. On 23 April 1999, at 0220, NATO intentionally bombed the central studio of the
RTS (state-owned) broadcasting corporation . . . in the center of Belgrade. . . . While
there is some doubt over exact casualty figures, between 10 and 17 people are estimated to
have been killed.

72. The bombing of the TV studio was part of a planned attack aimed at disrupting and
degrading the C3 (Command, Control and Communications) network. In
co-coordinated attacks, on the same night, radio relay buildings and towers were hit
along with electrical power transformer stations. At a press conference . . . NATO officials
justified this attack in terms of the dual military and civilian use to which the FRY
communication system was routinely put, describing this as a:

> very hardened command and control communications system [which . . .] uses
> commercial telephone, . . . military cable, . . . fibre optic cable, . . . high frequency
> radio communication, . . . microwave communication and everything can be
> interconnected. There are literally dozens, more than 100 radio relay sites around the

country, and ... everything is wired in through dual use. Most of the commercial system serves the military and the military system can be put to use for the commercial system.

Accordingly, NATO stressed the dual-use to which such communications systems were put, describing civilian television as "heavily dependent on the military command and control system and military traffic is also routed through the civilian system." ...

73. ... NATO claimed that the RTS facilities were being used "as radio relay stations and transmitters to support the activities of the FRY military and special police forces, and therefore they represent legitimate military targets."

74. ... More controversially, however, the bombing was also justified on the basis of the propaganda purpose to which [RTS] was employed:

> [We need to] directly strike at the very central nerve system of Milosovic's regime. This of course are those assets which are used to plan and direct and to create the political environment of tolerance in Yugoslavia in which these brutalities can not only be accepted but even condoned. ... Strikes against TV transmitters and broadcast facilities are part of our campaign to dismantle the FRY propaganda machinery which is a vital part of President Milosovic's control mechanism.

. . . .

75. NATO intentionally bombed the radio and TV station and the persons killed or injured were civilians. The questions are: was the station a legitimate objective and; if it was, were the civilian casualties disproportionate to the military advantage gained by the attack? ... The 1956 ICRC list of military objectives, drafted before the Additional Protocols, included the installations of broadcasting and television stations of fundamental military importance as military objectives. ... As indicated in paras. 72 and 73 above, the attack appears to have been justified by NATO as part of a more general attack aimed at disrupting the FRY Command, Control and Communications network, the nerve centre and apparatus that keeps Milosevic in power, and also as an attempt to dismantle the FRY propaganda machinery. Insofar as the attack actually was aimed at disrupting the communications network, it was legally acceptable.

76. If, however, the attack was made because equal time was not provided for Western news broadcasts, that is, because the station was part of the propaganda machinery, the legal basis was more debatable. Disrupting government propaganda may help to undermine the morale of the population and the armed forces, but justifying an attack on a civilian facility on such grounds alone may not meet the "effective contribution to military action" and "definite military advantage" criteria required by the Additional Protocols. The ICRC Commentary on the Additional Protocols interprets the expression "definite military advantage anticipated" to exclude "an attack which only offers potential or indeterminant advantages" and interprets the expression "concrete and direct" as intended to show that the advantage concerned should be substantial and relatively close rather than hardly perceptible and likely to appear only in the long term (ICRC Commentary ... para. 2209). While stopping such propaganda may serve to demoralize the Yugoslav population and undermine the government's political support, it is unlikely that either of these purposes would offer the "concrete and direct" military advantage necessary to make them a legitimate military objective. NATO believed that Yugoslav broadcast facilities were "used entirely to incite hatred and propaganda" and alleged that the Yugoslav government had put all private TV and radio stations in Serbia under military control ... However, it was not

claimed that they were being used to incite violence akin to *Radio Milles Collines* during the Rwandan genocide, which might have justified their destruction. . . . At worst, the Yugoslav government was using the broadcasting networks to issue propaganda supportive of its war effort: a circumstance which does not, in and of itself, amount to a war crime . . . The committee finds that if the attack on the RTS was justified by reference to its propaganda purpose alone, its legality might well be questioned by some experts in the field of international humanitarian law. It appears, however, that NATO's targeting of the RTS building for propaganda purposes was an incidental . . . aim of its primary goal of disabling the Serbian military command and control system and to destroy the nerve system and apparatus that keeps Milosevic in power. . . .

77. Assuming the station was a legitimate objective, the civilian casualties were unfortunately high but do not appear to be clearly disproportionate. . . .

78. . . . The radio relay and transmitting station near Novi Sad was also an important link in the air defence command and control communications network. Not only were these targets central to the Federal Republic of Yugoslavia's governing apparatus, but formed, from a military point of view, an integral part of the strategic communications network which enabled both the military and national command authorities to direct the repression and atrocities taking place in Kosovo.

79. On the basis of the above analysis . . . the committee recommends that the OTP [Office of the ICTY Prosecutor] not commence an investigation related to the bombing of the Serbian TV and radio station.

Conclusion. Unless the sole motive for targeting a television broadcasting station is to stop transmission of enemy propaganda, the committee finds it to be a military object. Will that caveat ever be a bar to targeting a broadcasting station?

PROSECUTOR V. KORDIĆ AND ČERKEZ

It-95–14/2-T (February 26, 2001), footnotes omitted.

Introduction. During the conflict in the former Yugoslavia, Dario Kordić was a Bosnian local politician who allied himself with Croatian military forces. Mario Čerkez was a Croatian brigade commander. Because of the military and political relationship of the two throughout the period that the charged offenses occurred, 1992–1993, both were charged with committing various crimes in connection with the conflict, including crimes against humanity, inhumane treatment, ethnic cleansing, and the wanton destruction of property not justified by military necessity.

In this extract from the Judgment, the trial chamber discusses what constitutes the unlawful destruction of property. It does not refer to targeting or mention Additional Protocol I. Under Geneva Convention IV (and the ICTY Statute), the extent of the unlawful destruction is nevertheless found to constitute the grave breach of extensive destruction of property not justified by military necessity, sounding in unlawful targeting.

328. In short, prohibited attacks are those launched deliberately against civilians or civilian objects in the course of an armed conflict and are not justified by military necessity. They must have caused deaths and/or serious bodily injuries within the civilian population or extensive damage to civilian objects. . . .

335. Article 147 of Geneva Convention IV sets out the crime of extensive destruction as a grave breach. The ICRC Commentary thereto states, in relation to the crime of extensive destruction:

Furthermore, the Occupying Power may not destroy in occupied territory real or personal property except where such destruction is rendered absolutely necessary by military operations. On the other hand, the destruction of property on enemy territory is not covered by the provision. In other words, if an air force bombs factories in an enemy country, such destruction is not covered either by Article 53 or by Article 147. On the other hand, if the enemy Power occupies the territory where the factories are situated, it may not destroy them unless military operations make it absolutely necessary.

336. Several provisions of the Geneva Conventions identify particular types of property accorded general protection thereunder. For example, Article 18 of Geneva Convention IV provides that "civilian hospitals organized to give care to the wounded and sick, the infirm and maternity cases, may in no circumstances be the object of an attack, but shall at all times be respected and protected by the Parties to the conflict." While property thus protected is presumptively immune from attack, the Conventions identify certain highly exceptional circumstances where the protection afforded to such property will cease.

337. Article 53 of Geneva Convention IV sets forth a general prohibition on the destruction of property in occupied territory:

Any destruction by the Occupying Power of real or personal property belonging individually or collectively to private persons, or to the state, or to other public authorities, or to social or cooperative organizations, is prohibited, except where such destruction is rendered absolutely necessary by military operations.

While the protective scope of this provision encompasses all real and personal property, other than property accorded general protection under the Geneva Conventions, it only applies in occupied territories. . . .

340. In *Blaškić*, the only case to date before the International Tribunal to have provided a definition of this crime [extensive destruction of property], the Trial Chamber found that

[a]n Occupying Power is prohibited from destroying movable and non-movable property except where such destruction is made absolutely necessary by military operations. To constitute a grave breach, the destruction unjustified by military necessity must be extensive, unlawful and wanton. The notion of "extensive" is evaluated according to the facts of the case – a single act, such as the destruction of a hospital, may suffice to characterize an offense under this count.

341. In view of the foregoing, the Trial Chamber finds that the crime of extensive destruction of property as a grave breach comprises the following elements, either:

 (i) Where the property destroyed is of a type accorded general protection under the Geneva Convention of 1949, regardless of whether or not it is situated in occupied territory; and the perpetrator acted with the intent to destroy the property in question or in reckless disregard of the likelihood of its destruction; or

(ii) Where the property destroyed is accorded protection under the Geneva Conventions, on account of its location in occupied territory; and the destruction occurs on a large scale; and

(iii) the destruction is not justified by military necessity; and the perpetrator acted with the intent to destroy the property in question or in reckless disregard of the likelihood of its destruction.

Conclusion. Convicted of committing a variety of crimes under the ICTY Statute, including multiple counts of wanton destruction of private property not justified by military necessity, Kordić was sentenced to twenty-five years' confinement, affirmed on appeal.[102] Čerkez, the military commander, was similarly convicted and sentenced to fifteen years' confinement. On appeal, his sentence was reduced to six years.[103]

WIRED FOR WAR

Excerpted from an Amaud de Borchgrave book review of Peter W. Singer's boo, Wired for War: The Robotics Revolution and Conflict in the 21st Century *(Penguin Press, 2009).*

Introduction. *This review, bearing on targeted killing, illustrates how quickly warfare is changing. Is LOAC keeping pace? Issues of distinction and proportionality are raised by the pilots' decisions and actions – issues that infantrymen will have to deal with, should errors be made.*

From their cockpit at Creech Air Force Base in Nevada, the pilot and co-pilot are flying a pilotless Predator on a bombing mission over Afghanistan, 8,000 miles away. Ordnance aboard includes four Hellfire missiles and two 500-pound bombs. A forward air controller in another unmanned drone spots the target and the Predator bomber takes off under local control from Kandahar in Afghanistan. Minutes later, control of the bomber is handed over to satellite control in the cockpit at Creech.

Two hours later, the crew sees on the cockpit screen two suburban vehicles stop in front of the targeted mud-baked house. Half a dozen men hurry into the dwelling that intelligence has spotted as a Taliban command post. The ultra-sensitive cameras in the aircraft's nose showed a door latch and a chicken inside. Seconds later, the bombardier in Nevada squeezed the trigger and a 500-pound bomb flattened the Taliban dwelling with a direct hit.

Watching the action on identical screens are CIA operators at Langley, Va., who can call in last-minute course corrections.

Their-eight-hour mission over, pilot and co-pilot, both experienced combat pilots, climb into their vehicles and drive home. Thirty minutes later, they are playing with their children. War by remote control is here. ... There are already some 5,000 unmanned drones of one kind or another in Iraq and Afghanistan and a shortage of experienced pilots. Those unfit to fly conventional fighter bombers, either over age or for medical reasons, can extend their flying careers in unmanned bombers. But drones now in combat will soon look like Model T Fords.

---

[102] *Prosecutor v. Kordić and Čerkez,* IT-95–14/2-A (Dec. 17, 2004), para. 1067.   [103] Id., at para. 1092.

Science fiction is already reality on the battlefield, not just how wars are fought, but also the geopolitics of war. At the end of Gulf War I, Air Force Chief of Staff Merrill "Tony" McPeak forecast that by 2010 the fighter pilot will have been taken out of the cockpit. The Air Force isn't there yet, though the next phase in robotic flying will be fighter aircraft, now on the drawing board at a fraction of the cost of today's state-of-the-art fighters and bombers.

The cost of Lockheed Martin's 5th generation stealth fighter aircraft is now just under $140 million per copy for 187 F-22 Raptors, whose development costs are in the $70 billion range. The most expensive U.S. Air Force aircraft is the B-2 bomber. Twenty Northrop Grumman B-2s were deployed at a cost of $2.2 billion per aircraft (one crashed in Guam last year).

The British designed Taranis drone is expected to fly in 2010 and its designers forecast even fighter pilots may get excited. . . .

The U.S. military invaded Iraq with a handful of drones in the air and zero unmanned systems on the ground. Today, there are some 12,000 with a lethal armory of missiles, rockets and grenades.

Deadly mistakes are, of course, unavoidable, such as the man who was a dead ringer for Osama bin Laden, though an innocent civilian. He lost his life to digitized warfare. . . .

But potential enemies like Hezbollah in Lebanon have already picked up or stolen the rudiments of pilotless machines. They used them for reconnaissance over Israeli lines in the 2006 war. . . .

Today, a general can already see at the very same moment what a war fighter sees through the bull's eye of his rifle sights – and take over the decision to shoot or not. . . .

Moving humans off the battlefield . . . will make wars easier to start, but more complex to fight.

14 Autonomous Weapons, Drones, and Targeted Killing

14.0 Introduction

Autonomous weapons will have a significant effect on future international and non-international armed conflicts. Drones armed with autonomous weapons have created major changes in targeting strategies and tactics to counter armed opposition groups. Drones and autonomous weapons have also raised calls for their restriction or outright ban, based largely on philosophical and moral grounds.[1] Some urge that autonomous weapons should not even be categorized as weapons.[2] Others, including Dr. Jakob Kellenberger, former president of the International Committee of the Red Cross (ICRC), question whether "autonomous technologies will be technically capable of conforming to existing [international humanitarian law]."[3]

An outright ban of either autonomous weapon systems or drones, practically speaking, "is insupportable as a matter of law, policy, and operational good sense."[4] Neither of them is going away.

It is often pointed out that there already are numerous "autonomous weapons" in use. The ground-based Samsung SGR-A1 surveillance and security guard robot, for example, that reportedly can deliver lethal force without human decision making, is installed on the border of North/South Korea. Unmanned ground vehicles (UGVs) are being used "for tasks ranging from reconnaissance to bomb disposals to defending borders. Today's generation of UGVs, which enjoy only limited autonomy, are capable of the 'persistent stare' required for long-term surveillance, as well as collaboration with other UGVs."[5] "U.S. forces have operated two 'human supervised' autonomous systems for many years – the

---

[1] Human Rights Watch, "Losing Humanity: The Case against Killer Robots" (2012), 46: "States should preemptively ban fully autonomous weapons because of the thereat these kinds of robots would pose to civilians during times of war." Nick Cumming-Bruce, "U.N. Expert Calls for Halt on Robots for Military," *NY Times*, May 31, 2013, A-9; John Markoff, "Fearing Bombs That Can Pick Whom to Kill," *NY Times*, Nov. 12, 2014, A-1.

[2] Hin-Yan Liu, "Categorization and Legality of Autonomous and Remote Weapons Systems," 94/886 *Int'l Rev. of the Red Cross* (Summer, 2012), 627, 628: at 629.

[3] Peter Asaro, "On Banning Autonomous Weapon Systems: Human Rights, Automation, and the Dehumanization of Lethal Decision-Making," 94/886 *Int'l Rev. of the Red Cross* (Summer 2012), 687, 691.

[4] Michael N. Schmitt and Jeffrey S. Thurnher, "'Out of the Loop'": Autonomous Weapons Systems and the Law of Armed Conflict," 4–2 *Harvard National Security Journal* (2013), 231, 233. Schmitt and Thurner make this statement only as to autonomous weapons.

[5] Dan Saxon, "Introduction," in Dan Saxon, ed., *International Humanitarian Law and the Changing Technology of War* (Boston: Martinus Nijhoff, 2013), 1, 4.

Aegis at sea and the Patriot on land – both designed to defend against short-notice missile attacks. Another human-supervised autonomous weapon system [is] Israel's Iron Dome [anti-missile] system."[6] Many more autonomous weapon systems are on the horizon. "Unmanned systems have proven they can enhance situational awareness, reduce human workload, improve mission performance, and minimize overall risk to both civilian and military personnel, and all at a reduced cost."[7] Unmanned systems include drones, of course. "The robot can delay the use of force until the last, most appropriate moment, when it has been established that the target and the attack are legitimate. Certainly there may be technical failures, but all those who drive cars and every traffic policeman knows that most accidents are not due to technical, but human, failures."[8]

Before looking at drones, the law of armed conflict (LOAC) involving the autonomous weapon systems they sometimes carry should be considered.

14.1 Defining "Autonomous"

A definition of "autonomous" is among the least agreed upon in LOAC, as there are almost as many definitions as there are proponents and opponents of autonomous weapons . A definition employed by the ICRC is, weapon systems "that can learn or adapt [their] functioning in response to changing circumstances in the environment in which [they are] deployed."[9] Another, fuller, definition is that of the U.S. Department of Defense (DoD): "**A weapon system that, once activated, can select and engage targets without further intervention by a human operator. This includes human-supervised autonomous weapon systems that are designed to allow human operators to override operation of the weapon system, but can select and engage targets without further human input after activation.**"[10] Note that this DoD definition links "autonomous" with "human-supervised."

Upon hearing the word "autonomous," most of us visualize a weapon that, on its own, can seek out an enemy target, decide whether or not to fire, and then, on its own initiative, may fire and kill or destroy the target it selects. DoD's Defense Science Board points out that this is a misconception: "Unfortunately, the word 'autonomy' often conjures images in the press and the minds of some military leaders of computers making independent decisions and taking uncontrolled action."[11] The board continues: "It should be made clear that all autonomous systems are supervised by human operators at some level, and autonomous systems' software embodies the designed limits on the actions and decisions delegated to the computer."[12] Autonomy is better thought of as

---

[6] Schmitt and Thurnher, "'Out of the Loop,'" supra, note 4, at 235–6.

[7] U.S. Dept. of Defense Directive 3000.09, *Autonomy in Weapon Systems* ("Unmanned Systems Integrated Roadmap, FY 2013–2038") (Nov. 21, 2012), para. 3.1, at 20.

[8] Marco Sassóli, "Autonomous Weapons and International Law: Advantages, Open Technical Questions and Legal Issues to Be Clarified," in U.S. Naval War College's *Int'l L. Studies*, Vol. 90 (Newport RI: USNWC, 2014) 308, 310–11.

[9] ICRC, *International Humanitarian Law and the Challenges of Contemporary Armed Conflict: Report Prepared for the 31st International Conference of the Red Cross and Red Crescent* (2011), 39.

[10] DoD Directive 3000.09, *Autonomy in Weapon Systems*, supra, note 7, at glossary, part II. Definitions.

[11] Dept. of Defense, Defense Science Board, "Task Force Report: The Role of Autonomy in DoD Systems" (July 2012), 1.

[12] Id.

"a capability (or set of capabilities) that enables a particular action of a system to be automatic or, within programmed boundaries, 'self-governing.'"[13]

Automated operation should not be confused with autonomous operation. A human always makes or approves or overrides the fire/don't fire decision made by an "autonomous weapon system." "A truly autonomous system would have artificial intelligence that would have to be capable of implementing IHL. Such systems have not yet been weaponized although there is considerable interest … and considerable funding of relevant research. The deployment of such systems would reflect a paradigm shift and a major qualitative change in the conduct of hostilities."[14] But it is slow going.

> Little headway has been made in "cognition," the higher-level humanlike processes required for robot planning and true autonomy. … There has been a re-emphasis on the idea of human-machine partnerships …. "Without the person, these machines could hardly do anything at all." In fact, the steep challenge in making progress toward mobile robots that can mimic human capabilities is causing robotics researchers worldwide to rethink their goals.[15]

The United States does not field any *fully* autonomous weapon systems.

There sometimes are said to be four levels of weapon system "autonomy": human operated,[2] human delegated,[3] human supervised, and[4] fully autonomous.[16] Describing autonomy in terms of "levels," however, is discouraged in U.S. military circles because levels "focus too much attention on the computer rather than on the collaboration between the computer and its operator/supervisor. … Further, these taxonomies imply that there are discrete levels of intelligence and autonomous systems."[17] U.S. combatant forces speak reassuringly of human control of autonomous weapon systems: "Semi-autonomous weapon systems that are onboard or integrated with unmanned platforms must be designed such that, in the event of degraded or lost communications, the system does not autonomously select and engage individual targets or specific target groups that have not been previously selected by an authorized human operator."[18] The same source adds, "It is DoD policy that … autonomous and semi-autonomous weapon systems shall be designed to allow commanders and operators to exercise appropriate levels of human judgment over the use of force."[19]

Even in reputedly fully autonomous weapon systems, as those systems function today, a human always makes, approves, or overrides a fire/don't-fire decision. "Of course, a fully autonomous system is never entirely human-free. Either the system designer or an operator would at least have to program it to specified parameters, and an operator would have to decide to employ it in a particular battlespace."[20]

> Autonomy is not a binary feature – that is, one that either exists or does not. Robots can act autonomously or not along many axes, and the same robot can perform some

---

[13] Id.

[14] ICRC, *International Humanitarian Law and the Challenges of Contemporary Armed Conflict*, supra, note 9, at 39.

[15] John Markoff, "A Reality Check for A.I.," *NY Times*, May 26, 2015, D2.

[16] Capt. George Galdorisi, US Navy (Ret.), "Keeping Humans in the Loop," U.S. Naval Institute *Proceedings* (Feb. 2015), 36, 38.

[17] DoD, Defense Science Board, "Task Force Report," supra, note 11, at 4.

[18] Dept. of Defense Directive 3000.09, supra, note 10, para. 4.c.(1) (Policy).   [19] Id., at para. 4.a.

[20] Schmitt and Thurnher, "'Out of the Loop,'" supra, note 4, at 235.

functions on its own and reserve others for human control. For example, a robot might navigate, avoid enemy fire, and feed surveillance video back to humans all on its own but rely on humans for targeting and firing instructions. At least for now, people seem committed to keeping humans "in the loop" when it comes to the use of lethal force. That said, increased robot autonomy seems inevitable. Having one person control one robot is just too inefficient; as technology improves, robots will be able to accomplish some functions better without human involvement; and communications between people and devices will sometimes break down, necessitating that robots make their own decisions.[21]

For now, however, no state, including the United States, fields a truly autonomous weapon system; nor is one foreseeable in the near-future. Professor Michael Schmitt notes, however, "Operational realities will likely drive the United States to discard its practice of keeping a human in the loop for lethal targeting decisions. First, requiring a human in the loop can be personnel intensive. ... It can take scores of people, from · pilots and weapon systems operators to technicians and intelligence analysts, to operate a single tethered unmanned aircraft. As a rule, the more autonomous the system, the fewer personnel needed to operate it."[22]

14.2 Testing Autonomous Weapon Systems

When a fully autonomous weapon system actually arises it will have to comply with Additional Protocol I, Article 36, which requires that all new weapons and weapon systems be tested for compliance with LOAC and "any other rule of international law applicable."[23]

Some new weapons are tested only when adopted by a state's armed forces. A pistol, rifle, or knife, for instance: in its development phase it may rightfully be considered a weapon intended for civilians rather than combatants, even if the manufacturer plans to market the finished item primarily to the military. If not eventually adopted by the state's armed forces, the pistol, rifle, or knife is simply "redirected" to a civilian market. An autonomous weapon system, however, from its conception has no application other than military. Article 36 calls for determinations of a new weapon's LOAC compliance in the study, development, and acquisition phases of its production. "For a State producing weapons ... reviews should take place at the stage of the conception/design of the weapon, and thereafter at the stages of its technological development (development of prototypes and testing), and ... before entering into the production contract."[24] This reflects U.S. policy, which requires at least two legal reviews: one before taking the decision to begin formal development of the system, and another before the autonomous weapon system is fielded.[25] For an autonomous weapon system, with its myriad subsystems and sensors, each of them with algorithm-laden programs, Article 36 testing will require a continuous and even more rigorous test process. Testing will be lengthy,

---

[21] Benjamin Wittes and Gabriella Blum, *The Future of Violence: Robots and Germs, Hackers and Drones* (New York: Basic Books, 2015), 32.

[22] Id., at 237. Footnote omitted.   [23] 1977 Additional Protocol I, Article 36.

[24] Int'l Committee of the Red Cross, *A Guide to the Legal Review of New Weapons, Means and Methods of Warfare* (Geneva: ICRC, 2006), 23.

[25] DoD Directive 3000.09, supra, note 10, encl. 3, paras. 1.a (5) and 1.b. (6).

complex, and on-going for any autonomous system. The greater the system's autonomy, the more rigorous its testing will be.

14.3 Autonomous Weapon Systems and Core LOAC/IHL Principles

Ongoing Article 36 testing aside, autonomous weapons, whether semi- or fully autonomous, are bound by the familiar four core armed conflict constraints of distinction, military necessity, unnecessary suffering, and proportionality, just as every artillery fire mission plan, or cyber warfare tactic, or close air support mission, is bound.

14.3.1 *Distinction*

In any targeting issue, the critical considerations are always distinction and proportionality. How is distinction applied to an autonomous weapon system, either through a drone's sensors or through the weapon system's own targeting system?[26] First, "the same issues that present themselves with regard to other weapon systems appear in the case of autonomous weapon systems. For instance, the exception to the prohibition on attacking civilians that exists for those who directly participate in hostilities also applies to the use of autonomous weapon systems against them." But in a noninternational armed conflict can any weapon system *autonomously* distinguish between a civilian and an enemy fighter with a continuous combat function? Not yet. "A major IHL issue is that autonomous armed robot systems cannot discriminate between combatants and non-combatants or . . . combatants that are wounded, [or] have surrendered . . . in a way that would satisfy the principle of distinction."[27] Soon, perhaps, but not yet. "Weapon systems that would be able to assess civilian status . . . as part of their own independent targeting decisions . . . do not exist today and research toward such capabilities currently remains in the realm of theory."[28] For now, distinguishing between non-targetable civilians and lawfully targetable civilians – those directly participating in hostilities, or members of a *levée en masse* – remains an issue for on-board sensors that can recognize weapons by their shape and heat signature, and high-resolution cameras that show the system's operators the combatant-like activities of the individual in real time.

Of course, it is possible to employ autonomous weapon systems in locations where civilians are not present, such as against enemy objectives located in deserts, mountainous areas, and, particularly, most of the open sea.

Distinguishing civilian objects from military objectives can be considerably easier than distinguishing civilians from combatants.

There is . . . established technology which enables sensors to detect and recognize predetermined categories of military equipment, such as artillery pieces, tanks, armoured personnel carriers, anti-aircraft batteries, and so on. The technology uses algorithms,

---

[26] 1977 Additional Protocol I, Art. 48: "Parties to the conflict shall at all times distinguish between the civilian population and combatants and between civilian objects and military objectives." Articles 51.1 and 51.2 also apply.

[27] Noel E. Sharkey, "The Evitability of Autonomous Robot Warfare," 94–886 *Int'l Rev. of the Red Cross* (Summer 2012), 787, 788.

[28] Kenneth Anderson, Daniel Reisner, and Matthew Waxman, "Adapting the Law of Armed Conflict to Autonomous Weapon Systems," in Naval War College's *Int'l L. Studies*, supra, note 8, at 386, 389.

such that the sensors on the attacking [weapon system] detect features in the target object which accord with data pre-programmed into the fire control system. When sufficient points of recognition have been achieved to a given level of probability, the unmanned [weapon system] will, depending on the instructions programmed into the system in advance of the mission, characterize the observed object as a target and may then commence attack procedures.[29]

Still, given the chances of error, for now distinction remains a process most commanders will want to determine for themselves.

14.3.2 *Proportionality*

Proportionality also presents difficult issues for fully autonomous weapon systems. Articles 51(5)(b) and 57(2)(a)(iii) of Additional Protocol I prohibit attacks "which may be expected to cause incidental loss of civilian life, injury to civilians, damage to civilian objects, or a combination thereof, which would be excessive in relation to the concrete and direct military advantage anticipated." This calls for a subjective assessment of complex and fluid battlefield situations.

> Even for the best military minds, proportionality is extremely difficult to apply. ... On one side of the proportionality scale is the assessment of the anticipated military advantage to be gained. ... Assigning military value depends on a matrix of interrelated issues heavily reliant upon the subjective view of the military commander. ... On the other side of the proportionality scale is the assessment of the expected civilian harm. The rule offers no guidance on how civilian harm should be calculated. Finally, an attack will be deemed proportionate only if the expected civilian harm was not *excessive* in relation to the anticipated military value. The excessive standard is particularly dependent on the perspective of the evaluator.[30]

A system for gauging the likely level of collateral damage already exists. The U.S. military's Collateral Damage Estimate Methodology (CDEM), for example, allows a commander to make such a pre-attack judgment by considering the precision of the weapon to be employed, the planned attack tactics, the probability of the presence of civilians in buildings near the target, and the composition of the structure, to estimate civilian casualties.

Gauging the military advantage to be gained would be challenging, if not impossible, for an autonomous weapon system because military advantage determinations are always contextual and unique.[31]

> The greatest difficulty an autonomous weapon system will have in applying the proportionality principle is ... the evaluation of the military advantage anticipated. ... The concrete and direct military advantage anticipated from an attack on a legitimate target constantly changes according to the plans of the commander and the development of military operations on both sides. ... [A] machine, even if perfectly

---

[29] Bill Boothby, "How Far Will the Law Allow Unmanned Targeting to Go?" in Dan Saxon, ed., *International Humanitarian Law and the Changing Technology of War* (Leiden: Martinus Nijhoff, 2013) 45, 55.

[30] Id., David Akerson, "The Illegality of Offensive Lethal Autonomy," at 65, 83–4.

[31] Schmitt and Thurnher, "'Out of the Loop,'" supra, note 4, at 255.

programmed, could, therefore, not be left to apply the proportionality principle unless constantly updated about military operations and plans."[32]

Again, it is possible to employ autonomous weapon systems in locations where proportionality would not be an issue because civilians are not present. Moreover, there are tactics besides CDEM available to minimize collateral damage.

> By constraining loiter or search times, the period when collateral risks would be minimized can be selected. ... These human judgments at the mission planning stage may, in certain circumstances, ensure that an autonomous attack only takes place when the collateral damage that is expected would be clearly outweighed by the military advantage in attacking the sorts of target to which the algorithms relate. ... There is, however, currently no known software capable of mechanizing qualitative decision-making. The process that is implicit in the application of the proportionality test is one that only a human brain can properly undertake. At first glance, that would appear conclusively to exclude any idea that autonomous [weapon system] can be used in attack. ... There may nevertheless be ... circumstances in which the use of such systems would be legitimate. ... In short, a man need not be 'in the loop' in all circumstances.[33]

The future will amaze, no doubt. Presently, however, there are no tools that allow autonomous weapon systems to meet the critical LOAC/IHL requirements of distinction or, especially, proportionality. This explains why, so far, the military mandates that there be a human in the operational loop of "autonomous" weapon systems.

14.3.3 *Military Necessity and Unnecessary Suffering*

Military necessity is a relatively low standard for commanders and operators of autonomous weapon systems to satisfy. Most attacks, regardless of the weapon involved, may be interpreted as leading to the complete or partial submission of the enemy at the earliest possible moment. In other words, autonomous weapon systems "would not be unlawful *per se* because there are clearly situations in which they are valuable militarily."[34]

Additional Protocol I's Article 35.2 prohibition of weapons, projectiles, and materials and methods of warfare of a nature to cause superfluous injury or unnecessary suffering, a prohibition applicable to enemy combatants and fighters, as well as to friendly combatants, is a similarly relatively low threshold for autonomous weapon systems to overcome; it is most unlikely that an autonomous weapon system would employ a weapon or munition that was per se unlawful.

14.4 Other LOAC Issues

Those calling for a ban on autonomous weapons raise other issues meant to illustrate the weapon system's inability to distinguish human emotion and intent. Objectors argue, "Distinguishing between a fearful civilian and a threatening enemy combatant requires a soldier to understand the emotions behind a human's actions, something a robot

---

[32] Sassóli, "Autonomous Weapons and International Law," supra, note 8, at 332.
[33] Boothby, "How Far Will the Law Allow?" in Saxon, *International Humanitarian Law*, supra, note 29, at 57.
[34] Schmitt and Thurnher, "'Out of the Loop,'" supra, note 4, at 258.

cannot do."[35] But human combatants are not required to divine another person's intent any more than robots are. If a combatant sees a civilian pointing a rifle at her, she is not expected to know whether that civilian's action is a result of fear or of an intent to fire on her. The combatant cannot then be faulted if she fires on the civilian, regardless of the civilian's subjective intent.

Objectors ask, what if "a frightened mother may run after her two children and yell at them to stop playing with toy guns near a soldier. . . . A human soldier could identify with the mother's fear and the children's game and thus recognize their [innocent] intentions."[36] An autonomous weapon system could not. Professor Marco Sassóli responds:

> First, I am not so sure that in some of today's fighting environments, where there are child soldiers, fanaticized mothers, and differences in language and culture between soldiers and local populations, a human soldier would always be able to easily identify what was happening in such a situation. Second, what the soldier must determine is not the intent of the children (becoming a kind of child psychologist), but the objective risk to him, his comrades and his mission, based upon objective indicators. Even if the mother was inciting the children to hate and the children were crying out in hate and subjectively willing to kill the soldier, the latter could not fire if it was apparent that the pistols were toy guns.[37]

Opponents of autonomous weapon systems point to human emotion as a positive factor on the battlefield, saying, "Robots would not be restrained by emotions and the capacity for compassion, which can provide an important check on the killing of civilians."[38] That argument cuts both ways. "Although emotions can restrain humans, it is equally true that they can unleash the basest of instincts. From Rawanda and the Balkans to Darfur and Afghanistan, history is replete with tragic examples of unchecked emotions leading to horrendous suffering."[39]

Article 57 of Additional Protocol I mandates several precautions that must be considered when attacking enemy objectives – for example, verify targets are not civilians or civilian objects; avoid or minimize collateral death, injury, and damage; cancel attacks discovered to be against unlawful objectives or expected to result in disproportionate death, injury, or damage.[40] These precautions are required "if feasible," or "when a choice is possible." Autonomous weapons, which do not risk the operator's life, may permit a higher degree of precaution than, say, a manned pre-attack reconnaissance aircraft. "Powerful sensors and processing powers . . . can potentially lift the fog of war for human soldiers . . . [and] thus save lives."[41]

Neither weaponized drones nor human combatants are perfect.[42] But we cannot expect more from autonomous weapon systems than we can from a human war fighter.

---

[35] Human Rights Watch, "Losing Humanity," supra, note 1, at 4.   [36] Id., at 5.

[37] Sassóli, "Autonomous Weapons and International Law," supra, note 8, at 333.

[38] Human Rights Watch, "Losing Humanity," supra, note 1, at 4.

[39] Schmitt and Thurnher, "'Out of the Loop,'" supra, note 4, at 249.

[40] Article 57 has additional precautionary requirements. See Section 13.6.

[41] Christof Heyns, Special Rapporteur on Extrajudicial, Summary or Arbitrary Executions, *Report*, U.N. Doc. A/HRC/23/47 (April 9. 2013), para. 69.

[42] E.g., Azam Ahmed, "Afghan Children Reported among Dead in U.S. Strike," NY *Times*, April 8, 2013, A8. Eighteen were killed; on Nov. 16, 2013, a Reaper drone lost control and crashed into a U.S. Navy guided-missile cruiser, the USS *Chancellorsville* (CG 62), injuring two sailors; Ismail Khan, "Drone Strikes a Seminary in Pakistan," NY *Times*, Nov. 22, 2013, A11, killing six, wounding five.

14.5 War Crime Liability and Autonomous Weapons

Any lawful weapon can be employed unlawfully. A hand grenade is a lawful weapon. But if it is armed and thrown into an orphanage crowded with children, it is a lawful weapon used unlawfully. If a drone armed with an autonomous weapon system were to "commit" a grave breach, presuming it was not an accident or software malfunction, who might be tried for that crime?

Who are the possibilities? The commander who ordered the strike, the operator controlling the weapon system at the time of the act, and, further down the causation chain, the software designer? Consider four scenarios:

Did the military commander of the unit controlling the system knowingly and intentionally order an unlawful action be executed by the operator of the system? "Captain, fire into that crowd of civilians who look like they could be about to harass our soldiers – aim for center mass! Do it now!"

Did the civilian Central Intelligence Agency (CIA) agent directing the operation of a drone with an autonomous system aboard order the CIA civilian pilot, "Trigger that bunker-buster laser! Right into that church. No more Father Nice Guy!"

Did the operator of the weapon system, struggling to escape the two air policemen trying to restrain him, manage to fire the system's tactical nuclear round into the presidential palace where peace negotiations were in progress?

Three years ago, did the civilian software designer at Magnum MicroSystems, the developer, secretly bury a line of rogue code in a sensor of the autonomous weapon system software, directing that, on the seventh day of the seventh month of the seventh year from that date, the sensor would cause the system to fire on and incinerate the next village or town the sensors detected?

The likelihood of an autonomous weapon system's being unlawful in and of itself is very remote; it would not meet Article 36 testing requirements and thus would not be put into use. And the foregoing four scenarios involving possible unlawful acts by operators or manufacturers are so unlikely, so phantasmagorical, that they are easily lampooned. Yet, military personnel have, with some frequency, used military weapons on military bases to murder, or kill through misadventure or negligence, civilians[43] and fellow service members.[44] Additionally, the U.S.-Israeli insertion of rogue code into Iranian centrifuge computers associated with Iran's nuclear program is well known.[45] While acts such as those described in the four scenarios are unlikely, they are possible.

Individual criminal responsibility for breaches of the law of war has been in place since the 1946 Nuremberg International Military Tribunal. "Crimes against international law

---

[43] On July 3, 1988, the USS *Vincennes* fired two guided missiles, shooting down an Iranian civilian airliner, killing 290 civilian passengers. The correct targeting data related to the semiautonomous weapon system had been misinterpreted. See Cases and Materials, this chapter.

[44] At Fort Hood, Texas, on Nov. 5, 2009, a U.S. Army major, Nidal Hasan, without provocation, shot and killed thirteen soldiers and civilians and wounded thirty-two others. A court-martial later convicted him and sentenced him to death. On May 11, 2009, at Camp Liberty, near Baghdad, Iraq, Sergeant John Russell, U.S. Army, shot and killed four soldiers and a navy officer. There are numerous other such incidents.

[45] Stuxnet was one of three computer viruses that were part of the U.S. Operation Olympic. The three viruses attacked Iran's centrifuges with destructive computer code, critical to that state's uranium enrichment program, in 2009 and 2010. See Chapter 17, Cases and Materials.

are committed by men, not by abstract entities, and only by punishing individuals who commit such crimes can the provisions of international law be enforced."[46] The law of command responsibility has ancient roots dating at least to the thirteenth century. The 1977 Additional Protocol I, in Articles 86 and 87, generally recognized as customary law, specifies the duty of military commanders to ensure compliance with LOAC. The commander who issues an unlawful command, the civilian CIA officer (an unprivileged belligerent) who issues an unlawful direction, and the enlisted airman acting unlawfully on his own are all criminally liable for their unlawful acts. The case of the civilian software designer is a more difficult legal issue.

14.5.1 *Criminal Liability of Autonomous Component Developers*

Professor Marco Sassóli writes, "I reject the idea that IHL is inadequate to regulate autonomous weapons. . . . However far we go into the future and no matter how artificial intelligence will work, there will always be a human being at the starting point . . . an autonomous weapon system will always operate within the limits of its software; software designed by humans. . . . This human being is bound by the law."[47] This comports with DoD policy: "Autonomous and semi-autonomous weapon systems shall be designed to allow commanders and operators to exercise appropriate levels of human judgment over the use of force."[48]

"The mere fact that a human might not be in control of a particular engagement does not mean that no human is responsible for the actions of the autonomous weapon system. A human must decide how to program the system, and when to launch it. Self-evidently, that individual would be accountable for programming the weapon system to engage in actions that amounted to war crimes."[49]

As criminal trial lawyers know, however, the critical question is not whether the accused committed the charged offense, but whether the prosecutor can prove it. Problems of proof make the prosecution of a weapon system developer problematic.

"'Developers,' . . . refer broadly to people who play some significant role in defining the behavior of an autonomous weapon system, as opposed to 'operators,' which refer to those responsible for utilizing the system in some situation during armed conflict."[50] Software written by developers is, of course, critical to the control systems of any autonomous weapon system:

> [A] weapons system . . . is an inanimate object; its existence and its capacity to cause harm result from the efforts of weapon developers . . . a highly autonomous weapons system has the potential to partially or fully displace combat personnel from the role they have traditionally occupied, so that accountability for prescribed acts committed via such systems may not be easily ascribed to those personnel or to their commanders. Rather, developers will exert greater control over . . . the specific actions

---

[46] International Military Tribunal for the Trial of German Major War Criminals (Nuremberg, Sept. 30–Oct. 1, 1946), 41.

[47] Sassóli, "Autonomous Weapons and International Law," supra, note 8, at 323.

[48] DoD Directive 3000.09, supra, note 10, paras. 4.a., and 4.c.(1).

[49] Schmitt and Thurnher, "'Out of the Loop,'" supra, note 4, at 277.

[50] Tim McFarland and Tim McCormack, "Mind the Gap: Can Developers of Autonomous Weapons Systems Be Liable for War Crimes?" in Naval War College's *Int'l L. Studies*, supra, note 8, at 361, 363.

that [the weapon system] in fact performs after being deployed. Accordingly, the question of developer accountability becomes pertinent.[51]

Developer criminal responsibility could arise anytime the weapon system's autonomous operation relates to an action subject to legal regulation, such as crossing an international border or firing a weapon. Criminal responsibility might arise when "the degree of control over the regulated action exercised by the system itself – and by extension by its developers – has increased to the point where it is not reasonable to say that a human operator alone exercises effective control; that is, the individual who would normally decide to 'pull the trigger' is no longer solely responsible for that decision."[52]

Today's semiautonomous weapon systems do not approach that level of autonomy, although their range of action will surely expand in the future. But prosecutors will have other difficult issues to overcome, as well.

Presume a highly unlikely event: a developer knowingly conspires with other code writers/developers to implant unauthorized computer code in a sub-system of the autonomous weapon system. The rogue code assures that the corrupted subsystem will, first, evade discovery during testing and, second, will commit a grave breach of the law of war and, third, will block any operator effort to stop or override the unlawful process.

The first requirement for the prosecution of a war crime is that it be committed in the course of an international or noninternational armed conflict.[53] (See Chapter 8.1.) Given the lengthy design, development, and testing period an autonomous system undergoes, it is likely that the developers will have completed their unlawful contribution to the autonomous weapon system *before* the armed conflict began. Their unlawful act was completed before an armed conflict was in progress and a court's subject matter jurisdiction is defeated.[54]

Additionally, the coding of weapon system computers is carried out by teams of developers – often teams of considerable size. The Stuxnet virus was reportedly developed by a team of thirty individuals writing the computer code for six months. There commonly are teams of teams cooperating to write the totality of a weapon system's subsystems. Even if the weapon system developer's unlawful code writing *was* completed while the armed conflict was in progress, and even if the unlawful code *could* be discovered and isolated for identification after its unlawful work was done, it would be challenging for prosecutors to pinpoint the few rogue code writers among the greater number of innocent code writers who contributed to the weapon system's corrupted subsystem. "Highly sophisticated autonomous weapons systems would be – and are being – developed by organizations and by groups of organizations ... hundreds or thousands of subsystems constructed by large networks of organizations: military and governmental bodies. ... Attribution of individual responsibility for a flaw, whether deliberate or accidental, would likely be exceedingly difficult."[55]

14.6 Drones

"Advances in precision weapons, especially drones, became a significant part of the new counter-terrorism [after 9/11]. ... It is hard to imagine this move in counter-terrorism

---

[51] Id., at 366.   [52] Id., at 370.   [53] *Prosecutor v. Haradinaj, et al.*, IT-04–84-T (April 3, 2008), para. 36.
[54] McFarland and McCormack, "Mind the Gap," supra, note 50, at 374.   [55] Id., at 381.

gaining the traction it has without technologies that enable precise attacks."[56] Semi-autonomous weapon systems and their aerial transportation system, the armed drone, have become major factors in antiterrorist conflicts.

Autonomous weapons systems cannot be discussed without also considering the aerial vehicles to which they are often mated: remotely piloted aircraft, often referred to as unmanned aerial vehicles or remotely piloted vehicles, or, most commonly, "drones."

The U.S. Department of Defense *Dictionary of Military and Associated Terms* defines neither "drone" nor "autonomous weapon system," but both are essentially self-defining. Drones are remotely piloted unmanned aerial vehicles that mount integral sensor systems and may be armed with semiautonomous weapon systems.

In 1916, Elmer Sperry, of gyroscope fame, designed and built a "flying bomb," which he tested on more than a hundred flights in Curtis seaplanes with automatic controls and a "safety pilot" aboard. Direction was set by his gyroscope; distance gauged by a propeller-revolution-counter, which, when the estimated distance was reached, stopped the engine, ideally diving the plane into the target. Both direction and distance elements proved unsatisfactory. By the 1920s, planes were controlled by radio, rather than by propeller revolution. Further "advances" came with further wars.

> **SIDEBAR.** During World War II, in 1944, the U.S. Army Air Corps launched Operation Aphrodite. Remotely controlled B-17 bombers were to be crashed into Nazi targets that had proven difficult for conventional bombers. Upon crashing, ten tons of explosives would detonate. Three attempts failed, however. U.S. Navy Operation Anvil followed. Its first mission was to destroy large-caliber guns the Nazis were building into chalk cliffs near Mimoyecques, France, to bombard England. The navy would use remotely piloted B-24 Liberator bombers loaded with twelve tons of Torpex explosive. An-board pilot and engineer were required to get the B-24s airborne and into radio contact with the mother ship, after which the two would bail out while still over England. The mother ship would then fly the B-24 drone into the target via radio control. On August 12 the B-24, *Zootsuit Black*, took off from Suffolk, England. Minutes later, before the pilot and engineer bailed out, the B-24 inexplicably exploded, killing the engineer, Lt. Wilford Willy, and the pilot, Lt. Joseph P. Kennedy Jr., elder brother of John F. Kennedy, the future president of the United States.[57]

In World War II, Nazi Germany used two types of missiles, precursors of drones, primarily against England. Despite military interest, there was little developmental progress until after World War II, when, in 1948, terrain-following radar became available and early U.S. cruise missile programs flourished, despite many failed programs.

---

[56] David P. Fidler, "The Path to Less Lethal and Destructive War? Technological and Doctrinal Developments and International Humanitarian Law after Iraq and Afghanistan," in Saxon, *International Humanitarian Law and the Changing Technology*, supra, note 29, at 315, 335.

[57] Konstantin Kakaes, "From Orville Wright to September 11: What the History of Drone Technology Says about Its Future," in Peter L. Bergen and Daniel Rothenberg, eds., *Drone Wars: Transforming Conflict, Law, and Policy* (New York: Cambridge University Press, 2015), 359; and Richard Whittle, *Predator: The Secret Origins of the Drone Revolution* (New York: Henry Holt, 2014), 20–1.

During the U.S. – Vietnam War (1965–73) unarmed drones flew more than thirty-four hundred reconnaissance flights. By the war's end, some drones were equipped with Maverick air-to-ground missiles. In the 1970s and 1980s, Israel's military used drones in the 1973 Yom Kippur War and 1982 invasion of Lebanon, proving their utility. "This is the moment when drones came into their own. This is when the machines that what we understand today as 'drones' became a transformative military technology."[58]

In the 1991 Gulf War, a group of Iraqi soldiers waved a white flag to a Predator drone flying over Faylaka Island. That was the first time combatants are known to have attempted to surrender to a drone.

In 1993, when the former Yugoslavia was beginning to implode, both the CIA and the DoD were developing an advanced version of the Gnat 750–45 drone. It was called the Predator. Its deployment in the mid-1990s marked the first operational use of the new Global Positioning System, which solved drone navigation issues. Early Predators were equipped with radios that allowed their remotely located pilots to talk to local air traffic controllers, crucial to sharing airspace with manned aircraft. The loss of at least twenty-one drones over Kosovo suggests the high operational tempo of drones in that conflict.[59]

"Each year since 2009, the U.S. Air Force has trained more drone pilots than pilots to fly fighter or bomber aircraft."[60] In 2009, Air Force MQ-9 Reapers, an upgrade of the MQ-1 Predator, were first deployed to Iraq. The Global Hawk, which, unlike other drones, can take off and land autonomously, can cruise at an elevation of eleven miles for up to thirty-two hours. So far, the Global Hawk is not armed. In 2013, the U.S. Navy's stealth-designed, bat-winged X-47 drone passed aircraft carrier acceptance tests, landing and taking off semiautonomously. In 2015, the secretary of the navy announced that naval aviation is going to stop using manned aircraft and move to unmanned aerial vehicles: "Unmanned systems, particularly autonomous ones, have to be the new normal in ever-increasing areas. For example ... the F-35 [the navy's newest manned fighter aircraft] should be, and almost certainly will be, the last manned strike fighter aircraft the Department of the Navy will ever buy or fly."[61]

Drones are sometimes said to be less expensive to produce than manned counterparts. That is true only in terms of initial acquisition costs. If one includes maintenance and personnel costs, specialized ground crew equipment, austere-base operating costs, and, particularly, "higher costs for personnel needed to monitor and analyze data streams that do not exist on manned platforms, as well as the costs for hardware and software that go into sensor packages,"[62] drones are no less expensive than many manned aircraft.

Most drones are not weaponized. In 2014, less than 1 per cent of approximately eight thousand DoD-operated drones carried operational weapon systems at any given time. Drones should not be equated solely with targeted killing.[63] Nevertheless, in the future the lethal capabilities of drones will only increase.

---

[58] Id., Kakaes, at 359, 375.   [59] This history of drones is closely based on Kakaes, id., at 362–79.

[60] Walter Pincus, "Air Force Training More Pilots for Drones than for Manned Planes," *Wash. Post*, Aug. 11, 2009, A11.

[61] Sam LeGrone, "Mabus: F-35 Will Be 'Last Manned Strike Fighter' the Navy, Marines 'Will Ever Buy or Fly,'" *USNI News* (online) (April 15, 2015).

[62] Stimson Center, *Recommendations and Report of the Task Force on US Drone Policy* (Washington, DC: Stimson Center, 2014), 23.

[63] Id., at 22.

drone programs are limited to active battlefields. when conducted by U.S. armed forces

CIA drone programs target enemies NOT in active battlefields.

14.7 A Critical Legal Difference

America fields two combat drone programs. One is conducted by U.S. armed forces, privileged combatants with targeting parameters that have been in place on battlefields for many years. Whether in international or noninternational armed conflicts, the military armed drone program is limited, by and large, to active battlefields, such as Afghanistan, where traditional enemy objects (i.e., targets) are encountered.

The CIA conducts a second and separate armed drone program manned by civilians, many of whom are not permanent CIA personnel but civilian contract employees. Paramilitary activities are as old as the CIA itself, but never to the breadth and depth of their paramilitary activities in the recent Iraq and Afghanistan conflicts.[64] CIA targeting parameters are not transparent and are different from those of the armed forces. The CIA drone program predominantly targets enemy persons and objects outside the active battlefield, as in Pakistan and Yemen. The CIA reportedly joins forces with the U.S. military – Joint Special Operations Command – to conduct drone attacks in Yemen.

"During an armed conflict, there is no prohibition in international humanitarian law on operations being conducted by intelligence or security agencies. However ... they do not enjoy belligerent immunity from prosecution for actions in which they engage."[65] Because CIA personnel and their contractors are civilians, they are unprivileged belligerents who lack the combatant's privilege (Chapter 2.3.1). If captured in an international armed conflict, they would not be entitled to prisoner of war status.[66] Lacking the combatant's privilege, such persons are subject to prosecution for any death or injury to persons, and any destruction or damage to objects, that they might cause on an active battlefield or elsewhere, be it an international armed conflict or noninternational. Prosecution would vest in the state in which the unlawful act was committed, and/or where the unlawful result obtained. *In rem* jurisdiction would be in the domestic courts or military commission of the same states.

This does not suggest that CIA personnel are outlaws, or that they do not provide essential service in protecting the lives of Americans, their allies, and their interests. LOAC is clear, however, in declaring the individual status of civilians who directly participate in armed conflicts, and the American public should be aware of the legal status of those who apply deadly force in foreign states in their name.

More tangible issues are involved, as well. In 2010, the United Nations Special Rapporteur on Extrajudicial, Summary or Arbitrary Executions said, "With the Defense Department you've got maybe not perfect but quite abundant accountability [for their armed drone activities]. ... The whole process that follows is very open. Whereas if the C.I.A. is doing it, by definition they are not going to answer questions, not provide any information."[67] "Parallel CIA and military UAV [unpiloted aerial vehicle] programs are, at best, duplicative and inefficient. At worst, the existence of parallel programs makes oversight more difficult and increases the risk of error and arbitrariness, since the CIA

---

[64] Tim Weiner, *Legacy of Ashes: The History of the CIA* (New York: Doubleday, 2007), 24, 45.

[65] Michael N. Schmitt, "Extraterritorial Lethal Targeting: Deconstructing the Logic of International Law," 52–1 *Columbia JTL* (2013), 77, 99.

[66] 1977 Additional Protocol I, Art. 50.1 defines who are civilians. Art. 43.2 defines who are combatants. Art. 51.2 and Additional Protocol II, Art. 13.3 describe, but do not define, unprivileged belligerency.

[67] Charlie Savage, "U.N. Official Wants American Drone Strikes in Hands of Military, Not C.I.A.," NY *Times*, May 28, 2010, A8.

and military may have different standards for evaluating intelligence and identifying appropriate targets."[68] In 2010 the Obama administration planned to move authority to conduct targeted killings by drones from the CIA, activities of which fall under Title 50 of the United States Code, to the Department of Defense alone, whose activities fall under Title 10 of the U.S. Code – a far different and more restrictive series of laws with differing oversight requirements. "This fragmented oversight system is particularly problematic given that in practice, the military and CIA generally work together quite closely when planning and executing targeted UAV strikes [outside active battlefields]: few strikes are 'all military' or 'all CIA.'"[69] "Generally" works together is a correct description; the CIA is unlikely to share its target acquisition methods and information with military drone operators.

The president's plan to move all armed drone operational authority to the military was blocked by the Senate.[70] The shift from the CIA to the Department of Defense has nevertheless progressed by informal means. John Brennan was appointed director of the CIA in March 2013.

> Brennan is trying to shift the C.I.A.'s focus back toward traditional spying and strategic analysis. ... It could take years for a spy agency that has evolved into a paramilitary service to rebalance its activities. ... Administration officials said this week that some drone operations would shift to the Pentagon, particularly those in Yemen, where the Pentagon's Joint Special Operations Command is already running a parallel drone program. And, they said, the "preference" for the future is for all drone operations to be run by the Department of Defense, rather than the C.I.A.[71]

Time will tell whether a reported internal CIA redirection can achieve what the president, thanks to an intransigent and dysfunctional Congress, could not. Meanwhile, the CIA's drone program continues to enjoy strong political support. Congressional leaders "defend it vigorously and ... authorize its sizable budget each year. ... The program is under fire like never before, but the White House continues to champion it."[72]

SIDEBAR. Sometimes, CIA paramilitary activities have been examined by foreign courts, although accountability, per se, has been rare. On April 7, 2015, a justice of Pakistan's high court directed that criminal charges be filed against the CIA's former acting general council and the former Islamabad CIA station chief. Both John Rizzo, the lawyer who oversaw the CIA drone program until his 2010 retirement, and Jonathan Bank, the station chief, were charged with murder, conspiracy, terrorism, and waging war against Pakistan, an outgrowth of a 2009 drone strike that killed two Pakistani citizens said to be Taliban leaders. It was one of roughly four hundred drone targeted killings conducted by the United States in Pakistan since 2004. The Pakistani justice's order may be refused by the Pakistani federal police force and may be appealed by the government of Pakistan itself, more concerned with U.S. diplomatic relations than is the

---

[68] Stimson Center, *Task Force on US Drone Policy*, supra, note 62, at 43.   [69] Id., at 13–14.

[70] Greg Miller, "Lawmakers Seek to Stymie Plan to Shift Control of Drone Campaign from CIA to Pentagon," *Wash. Post*, Jan. 15, 2014, A1.

[71] Mark Mazzetti, "New Terror Strategy Shifts C.I.A. Focus Back to Spying," *NY Times*, May 23, 2013, A1.

[72] Mark Mazzetti and Matt Apuzzo, "Deep Support in Washington for C.I.A.'s Drone Missions," *NY Times* (April 26, 2015), A1.

high court justice. Even were the charges to be filed, without U.S. cooperation, which is certain to be refused, any case against the CIA officers is unlikely to go to trial – although Italy has convicted CIA officers in absentia for agency activities in Italy during early years of the "war on terror."

In February 2003, Italian military intelligence personnel, at the direction of the CIA's Special Activities Division, abducted a radical Egyptian cleric known as Abu Omar, from a Milan street. Omar was secretly "rendered" to Egypt, where he was questioned, beaten, and tortured. Four years later, he was unceremoniously released. Italian extradition requests having been quashed by the Italian government, in November 2009, twenty-two CIA employees, including the Milan station chief, and a U.S. Air Force lieutenant colonel, were convicted in absentia by Italian courts of kidnapping, receiving sentences varying from eight to five years' confinement.[73] In 2012, the convictions were upheld on appeal.[74] In the United States, all of the convicted CIA personnel, and the lieutenant colonel, remain free.

14.8 The Lawfulness of Drones in LOAC

The testing of new weapons and weapon systems has been discussed in relation to autonomous weapon systems (Chapter 14.3). The same comments apply generally to drones. A drone is an airframe with sensors. Both are common fare for Additional Protocol I, Article 36, testing. As manufactured, a drone has no weapons that are part of the aircraft structure itself. That may change with new drone variants; a means of defense against attacking enemy aircraft is a significant weakness of current drones. Today's drones are not built to survive in contested airspace. ("According to Lieutenant General David Deptula, former Air Force deputy chief of staff for intelligence, 'Some of the [drones] that we have today, you put in a high-threat environment, and they'll start falling from the sky like rain.'")[75] If the drone is armed, any integrated weapons would have been tested for compliance with LOAC. A weaponized drone is simply one tested weapon system combined with another tested means of warfare.

Drones are superior to manned aircraft, or artillery, in several ways. Drones can gather photographic intelligence from geographic areas too dangerous for manned aircraft. Drones carry no risk of friendly personnel death or capture. Drones have an operational reach greater than that of other aircraft, allowing them to project force from afar in environments otherwise inaccessible to manned aircraft. Drones have a loiter time over targets far in excess of that of manned aircraft.[76] The accuracy of drone-fired munitions is greater than that of most manned aircraft, and that accuracy allows them to employ munitions with a kinetic energy far less than artillery or close air support require, thus reducing collateral damage

---

[73] John Hooper, "Italian Court Finds CIA Agents Guilty of Kidnapping Terrorism Suspect," *Guardian*, Nov. 4, 2009.

[74] Ian Shapira, "Italy's High Court Upholds Convictions of 23 Americans in Abu Omar Rendition," *Wash. Post*, Sept. 19, 2012.

[75] Micah Zenko, *Reforming U.S. Drone Strike Policies* (New York: Council on Foreign Relations, 2013), 7.

[76] The Global Hawk drone can take off and land fully autonomously and cruise at an elevation of eleven miles for thirty-two hours. So far, the Global Hawk is not armed.

On the other hand, manned aircraft offer land-bound commanders a wider range of platforms with a broader variety of mission capabilities. Manned aircraft carry more and heavier munitions. Manned aircraft have far greater speed, maneuverability, and defensive capabilities. Manned aircraft have a human's field of view while drones are limited to the view of their sensors.[77] Comparisons to other aircraft aside, combat drones and their weapon systems are lawful weapons.

14.8.1 *Distinction and Drones* — *pass distinction component*

Through their technological capabilities, armed drones have a unique ability to "distinguish between the civilian population and combatants and between civilian objects and military objectives."[78] Their sensors are ideally suited to meet the distinction requirement.

> The Multi-Spectral Targeting System ("MTS-B") ... integrates an infrared sensor, a color/monochrome video camera, an image-intensified video camera, a laser designator, and a laser illuminator to maximize precision. The laser-guided AGM-114 Hellfire missiles employed in these drones further ensure the accuracy of targeting with minimum collateral damage. ... Although these drones are not entirely fail-safe, they are far more discriminate than the vast majority of aerial or artillery bombardments, let alone ground soldiers acting hastily in life-threatening situations.[79]

Although missiles are a munition, rather than an autonomous weapon system, their laser aiming capability provides missiles with similar targeting precision, although targeting accuracy is not the same as distinction. Even with sophisticated sensors, one suspects that commanders will want their judge advocate legal adviser to assess a drone's distinction decisions, if they do not make that call themselves.

14.8.2 *Proportionality and Drones* — *pass*

The same features that assist drones in meeting distinction's requirements assist them in meeting proportionality requirements. In past conflicts, the relative crudeness of aerial gun sights and bombsights often gave rise to proportionality and distinction issues. Target identification from aircraft could be "detrimentally affected by poor visibility as a result of inclement weather, effective air defense systems, failure of electronic devices ... sophisticated camouflage, etc."[80] The sensors, high-definition cameras, and heat-signature recognition capabilities of drones address many targeting issues of the past. Today, proportionality violations are most often the result of operator misjudgment, rather than an inadequacy of equipment. The stakes involved in proportionality decisions, as in distinction decisions, nevertheless remain high, and technology cannot supplant combat-experienced human judgment. Commanders will continue in their

---

[77] Jacquelyn Schneider and Julia MacDonald, "Are Manned or Unmanned Aircraft Better on the Battlefield?" *Cicero Magazine*, June 16, 2014, 1.

[78] 1977 Additional Protocol I, Art. 48.

[79] Heeyong Daniel Jang, "The Lawfulness of and Case for Combat Drones in the Fight against Terrorism," 2–1 *Nat'l Security L. J.* (2013), 1, 12.

[80] Yoram Dinstein, *The Conduct of Hostilities under the Law of International Armed Conflict*, 2d ed. (London: Cambridge University Press, 2010), 118.

traditional role of making proportionality decisions for themselves, even when aided by drone-mounted sensors and legal advisers.

14.8.3 Military Necessity, Unnecessary Suffering, and Drones

The same military necessity and unnecessary suffering issues considered in regard to autonomous weapon systems are applicable to drones. As with autonomous weapon systems, those two core principles of armed conflict are unlikely to often pose issues to impede combat drone operations.

14.9 Objections to Drones and Semiautonomous Weapon Systems

The employment of armed drones in the U.S.-Afghan armed conflict, especially CIA-controlled drones operating beyond the active battlefield, was strongly criticized by human rights groups, the media, and large segments of the American public.

One objection is that drone strikes are enemy recruiting tools. "Among those testifying before a [Senate] subcommittee . . . was a young Yemeni activist who argued passionately that American drone strikes in Yemen are emboldening the country's al-Qaeda franchise, embittering Yemenis against the United States and delegitimizing the government in Sanaa."[81] Conversely, the former *New York Times* reporter David Rohde, wrote, "I was kidnapped by the Haqqani Network and held captive for seven months . . . in North and South Waziristan. My guards absolutely feared drones."[82] Rohde goes on to describe his guards' terrified reactions to merely hearing a drone, and the precautions drones caused them to take.

The secrecy surrounding drone strikes is the basis for objections. "A former legal advisor to the State Department [Harold H. Koh] has sharply criticized the secrecy surrounding . . . use of drones for the targeted killing of terrorism suspects, saying it is unnecessary and has backfired. . . . The result is 'a growing perception that the program is not lawful and necessary, but illegal, unnecessary and out of control.'"[83] The authoritative 2014 Stimson Center Report agrees: "As a general principle, the United States should acknowledge the use of lethal force in foreign countries both to Congress and to the American public. While secrecy may be required before and during each strike, strikes should generally be acknowledged by the United States after the fact."[84] The CIA does not discuss targeted killing methods or numbers. One commentator writes, "Of course, there are good reasons for not having in the case of targeted killings the sort of investigations we routinely conduct into domestic cases of self-defense. Intelligence sources might be compromised; the procedures would obstruct military and counter-terrorist activity, and so on. . . . The lack of any prospect of investigations analogous to those we conduct in criminal law is therefore understandable."[85]

---

[81] Ernesto Londoño, "Drones Instill Hatred of U.S., Senate Panel Is Told," *Wash. Post*, April 24, 2013, A8.

[82] David Rohde, "My Guards Absolutely Feared Drones: Reflections on Being Held Captive for Seven Months by the Taliban," in Peter L. Bergen and Daniel Rothenberg, *Drone Wars*, supra, note 57, at 9.

[83] Scott Shane, "Ex-Lawyer in State Department Criticizes Drone Secrecy," *NY Times*, May 9, 2013, A11.

[84] Stimson Center, *Task Force on US Drone Policy*, note 62, supra, at 42.

[85] Jeremy Waldron, "Justifying Targeted Killing with a Neutral Principle?" in Claire Finkelstein, Jens David Ohlin, and Andrew Altman, eds., *Targeted Killings: Law and Morality in an Asymmetrical World* (Oxford: Oxford University Press, 2012), 112, 121.

Should those considerations be applicable, however, in a context of a geographically wide use of lethal force in a lengthy armed conflict?

Military, as opposed to CIA, drone strikes and targeting parameters are not announced, but neither are they secret; the armed forces are bound by LOAC/IHL-based targeting regulations, virtually all of which are available from open-source materials. (See Chapter 13.5.) Collateral civilian casualties due to military action are required to be investigated, even if only by the unit involved. Reports of military commanders relieved or disciplined for excessive or unnecessary civilian casualties are not unusual. Still, secrecy, even perceived secrecy, breeds suspicion. Targeting U.S. citizens outside the active battlefield, a CIA initiative, has not been a military mission. For the armed forces, however, the citizenship of enemy fighters on an active battlefield is irrelevant; when meeting the enemy in combat an exchange of passports is not required. Unlike the CIA, the armed forces have not had to deal with the question of whether a targeted victim actually *was* an enemy fighter.

Moral objections to drones have been raised. In a *New York Times* opinion piece, a philosophy professor wrote, "Drones point to a new and terrible kind of cruelty – violence far removed from the perpetrator, and easier to inflict in that regard. ... We can be less vigilant about the darker tendencies of our leaders, the unintended consequences of their actions. ... Drones represent the new normal, and an easy invitation to enter into and wage war – indefinitely."[86] In rebuttal, a Brookings Institution fellow (a civilian) asked, "Is it ethical to *decline* to use drones if a drone strike promises fewer civilian casualties than any other comparably-effective military option in a given situation? Is it ethical to *decline* to use drones if a drone strike promises to better protect military personnel for which a command structure has responsibility?"[87]

Some moral objections appear based on the observer's mistaken views of armed conflict: "Drone warfare takes away the traditions of battle, which by nature is limited and allows for reciprocity. ... With drones, the ethics of warrior culture have been superseded, and the warriors have turned into invulnerable, cold-hearted executioners."[88] Romantic and unrealistic views of modern warfare that echo the fourteenth century's cursing of the crossbow.

An associated issue has been referred to as the drone crew's "PlayStation mentality." "Young military personnel raised on a diet of video games now kill real people remotely using joysticks. Far removed from the human consequences of their actions, how will this generation of fighters value the right to life?"[89] Army artillerymen, navy cruise missile technicians, air force bomber crews and navy submariners never see the effects of their weapons targeting. Do they have a PlayStation mentality devaluing the right to life? This is an objection by individuals unfamiliar with military service.

It is civilian casualties, however, that have been the most serious, persistent, and understandable objection to drones.

civilian casualties = most cause for objection to drones

[86] Firmin DeBrabander, "Drones and the Democracy Disconnect," *NY Times*, Sept. 15, 2014.

[87] Ben Wittes, "Drones and Democracy: A Response to Firmin DeBrabander," *Lawfare*, http://www.lawfareblog.com/2014/09/drones-and-democracy-a-response-to-firmin-debrabander/. Emphasis in original.

[88] Karen J. Greenberg, *The Cost of Drone Warfare: Higher than We Knew*, Wash. *Post* Book World, March 22, 2015, B6 (reviewing Grégoire Chamayou, *A Theory of the Drone* [2015]).

[89] Philip Alston and Hina Shamsi, "A Killer above the Law?" *Guardian*, Feb. 8, 2010.

Civilian casualties, even if relatively few, can anger whole communities, increase anti-US sentiment and become a potent recruiting tool for terrorist organizations. Even strikes that kill only terrorist operatives can cause great resentment, particularly in contexts in which terrorist recruiting efforts rely on tribal loyalties. ... UAV strikes by the United States have also generated a backlash in states not directly affected by the strikes, in part due to the perception that such strikes cause excessive civilian deaths, and in part due to concerns about sovereignty, transparency, [and] accountability.[90]

There are widely differing estimates of civilian deaths resulting from drone strikes: low estimates from government sources, high estimates from human rights-oriented groups. What is clear is that, unlike prior targeting systems, drones have the ability to spend hours, even days, observing and monitoring potential targets. From high altitudes their sensors can even transmit images of faces to distant operators. Combatants, fighters, and civilians often can be differentiated more effectively than by any past means. A drone's air-to-surface missiles are more accurate than any prior weapon. "While you can make mistakes with drones, you can make bigger mistakes with big bombers, which can take out whole neighborhoods. A B-2 [manned bomber] pilot has no idea who he is hitting; a drone pilot should know exactly who he is targeting."[91]

It cannot be denied that "incidental civilian casualties caused by U.S. attacks [in Iraq] threaten the legitimacy of these military operations on a fundamental level, especially when humanitarian motives are invoked as a basis for U.S. intervention. By making such casualties more avoidable and thus even less politically acceptable, virtual technologies are helping to redefine success in warfare."[92] Or failure.

Objections related to collateral damage and calls for investigations of drones will continue. Meanwhile, the deaths of innocent civilians, including American and Allied hostages,[93] continue to highlight the need for the military and the CIA to constantly make every effort to prevent noncombatant death and wounding by armed drones.

14.10 Targeted Killing

In mid-2013, the *New York Times* asserted a disturbing U.S. policy on targeted killing:

> [Targeted killing] is shaped by several factors: the availability of a weapon that does not risk American casualties; the resistance of authorities in Pakistan and Yemen to even brief incursions by American troops; and the decreasing urgency of interrogation at a time when the terrorist threat has diminished and the United States has deep intelligence on its enemies. Though no official will publicly acknowledge it, the bottom line is clear: killing is more convenient than capture for both the United States and the foreign countries where the strikes occur.[94]

Whether or not that assertion may fairly be attributed to the CIA's foreign countries drone program, it is not "the bottom line" of the U.S. military drone practice.

[90] Stimson Center, *Task Force on US Drone Policy*, supra, note 62, at 10–11.
[91] David E. Sanger, *Confront and Conceal: Obama's Secret Wars and Surprising Use of American Power* (New York: Crown, 2012, 257.
[92] Jack M. Beard, "Law and War in the Virtual Era," 103–3 AJIL (July 2009), 409, 423.
[93] Peter Baker, "Obama Apologizes after Drone Kills American and Italian Held by Al Qaeda" NY *Times*, April 23, 2015, A1. This was a CIA strike.
[94] Scott Shane, "Targeted Killing Comes to Define War on Terror," NY *Times*, April 8, 2013, A1.

Targeted killings are carried out by a variety of means –cruise missile, some other precision guided munition, a special operations team, or a single sniper – but it is armed drones that come to mind when targeted killing is mentioned. How does LOAC/IHL apply to the use of drones for the purpose of targeted killings? Much the same as it would apply to a human combatant in any combat-related killing.

Although they were cut back sharply in the final two years of President Obama's administration, 2014–15, targeted killing has become a common antiterrorism tactic.[95] There is no generally accepted definition of "targeted killing," and government publications dealing with the subject have a variety of definitions. A definition that encompasses applicable LOAC/IHL elements is, **the intentional killing of a specific enemy combatant or civilian enemy fighter, who cannot reasonably be apprehended, who is taking a direct part in hostilities, the targeting done at the direction of the state, in the context of an international or noninternational armed conflict.**[96]

When a combatant squeezes the trigger on his rifle, the weapon fires and two hundred meters away an enemy combatant falls dead. Although the shooter "targeted" the enemy he killed in the sense of consciously selecting an individual target, that is *not* what is meant by the term "targeted killing."

If rebellious citizens shoot and kill their state's political leader as he watches a parade of the nation's military forces, *that* is not targeted killing. It is assassination and the domestic crime of murder.

"In November 2002, Israel was the first State to openly acknowledge that it operated a policy of targeted killing in its confrontation with Palestinian militants."[97] The United States first admitted engaging in targeted killing in 2002.[98] On November 3, 2002, over the desert near Sana, Yemen, a CIA-controlled Predator drone tracked an SUV automobile containing six men. One of the six, Qaed Salim Sinan al-Harethi, was believed to be a senior al Qaeda lieutenant who played a major role in the 2000 bombing of the American destroyer USS *Cole*. He "was on a list of 'high-value' targets whose elimination, by capture or death, had been called for by President George W. Bush."[99] The United States and Yemen had tracked al-Harethi's movements for months. Now, away from any inhabited area, and with the permission of the government of Yemen,

---

[95] Predator UAVs deployed to the Balkans in 1995. Since then their offensive capabilities have greatly increased. Many carry a daylight television nose camera, a forward-looking infrared camera for low-light and night operations, a laser designator, and more. Cruising at eighty-five miles per hour at twenty-five thousand feet, Predators can loiter for forty hours. The first armed Predator mission in Afghanistan was flown on October 7, 2001.

[96] There are other definitions. An ICRC legal adviser defines targeted killing as "the use of lethal force attributable to a subject of international law with the intent, premeditation and deliberation to kill individually selected persons who are not in the physical custody of those targeting them." Nils Melzer, *Targeted Killing in International Law* (Oxford: Oxford University Press, 2008), 5. Another is "premeditated killing of an individual by a government or its agents," in William C. Banks and Peter Raven-Hansen, "Targeted Killing and Assassination: The U.S. Legal Framework," 37 *U. Richmond L. Rev.* (2002–3), 667, 671.

[97] Id., Melzer, *Targeted Killing*, at xi.

[98] It can be argued that the United States–Vietnam War's Phoenix Program constituted targeted killing, or Operation Eldorado Canyon, the 1986 bombing attack on the Libyan leader Muammar Qadhafi, or the 1998 attacks on Osama Bin Laden, when he was linked to the bombing of U.S. embassies in Dar es Salaam and Nairobi. Those attacks may also be argued to be assassinations and attempted assassinations, with political rather than tactical motives.

[99] Seymour M. Hersh, "Manhunt," *New Yorker*, Dec. 23 and 30, 2002, 66.

the Predator fired a Hellfire missile at the vehicle. Its occupants, including al-Harethi, who was a U.S. citizen, were killed.[100]

Legal justification for targeted killing rests in the assertion of national self-defense. "It is the prime duty of a democratic state to effectively defend its citizens against any danger posed to their lives and well-being by acts or activities of terror."[101] In the United States, the preamble of the Constitution includes the words "in order to ... provide for the common defense." Arguing against a state's assertion of self-defense as justification is that "this type of practice is incompatible with international law, which categorically prohibits extra-judicial executions."[102] Some human rights organizations hold that "suspected terrorists should be detained and put on trial before they can lawfully be punished for their actions. ... To kill under these circumstances is simply execution – but carried out without any trial or proof of guilt."[103] The ICRC says "any order of liquidation is prohibited, whether it concerns ... irregular troops or so-called irregular troops ... or other cases."[104] These arguments do not address targeted killing in the course of armed conflict, however.

Some objections presume the employment of a law enforcement model in combating terrorists. "The problem with the law-enforcement model in the context of transnational terror is that one of its fundamental premises is invalid: that the suspected perpetrator is within the jurisdiction of the law-enforcement authorities in the victim state, so that an arrest can be affected."[105]

Israel has openly engaged in targeted killing since September 2000 and the second *intifadah*.[106] Before that admission, in 1996 a Hamas bomb maker known as "The Engineer," Yehiya Ayash, was killed when he answered an Israeli-booby-trapped cell phone.[107] In 2000, helicopter-fired missiles killed a Palestinian Fatah leader and Arafat deputy.[108] In 2001, Israeli helicopters fired missiles into the West Bank offices of Hamas, killing eight.[109] Later, in 2002, in Gaza, Salah Shehade, the civilian founder and leader of Hamas's military wing and an individual said by the Israelis to be responsible for hundreds of noncombatant deaths, was targeted. In predawn hours an Israeli F-16 fighter jet dropped a one-ton bomb on the three-story apartment building where Shehade was sleeping. He was killed, along with fourteen others asleep in the building, including nine children. One hundred and seventy were reportedly wounded. Other casualties were the core concepts distinction and proportionality. These Israeli actions were not

---

[100] "No Holds Barred," *Economist*, Nov. 9, 2002, 49.

[101] Asa Kasher and Amos Yadlin, "Assassination and Preventive Killing," XXV, no. 1, *SAIS Rev. of Int'l Affairs* (Winter-Spring 2005), 41, 45.

[102] Vincent Joël Proulx, "If the Hat Fits, Wear It, If the Turban Fits, Run for Your Life: Reflections on the Indefinite Detention and Targeted Killing of Suspected Terrorists," 56 *Hastings L. J.* (2004–5), 801, 873.

[103] Anthony Dworkin, "The Killing of Sheikh Yassin: Murder or Lawful Act of War?" Crimes of War Project (March 30, 2004), www.crimesofwar.org/onnews/news-yassin.html

[104] Yves Sandoz, Christophe Swinarski, and Bruno Zimmerman, eds., *Commentary on the Additional Protocols* (Geneva: ICRC/Martinus Nijhoff, 1987), para. 1595, at 476.

[105] David Kretzmer, "Targeted Killing of Suspected Terrorists: Extra-Judicial Executions or Legitimate Means of Defence?" 16–2 *European J. of Int'l L.* (2005), 171, 179.

[106] O. Ben-Naftali and K. R. Michaeli, "We Must Not Make a Scarecrow of the Law: A Legal Analysis of the Israeli Policy of Targeted Killings," 36 *Cornell Int'l L. J.* (2003), 233, 239.

[107] Keith B. Richburg and Lee Hockstader, "Israelis Kill Arab Militia Official," *Wash. Post*, Nov. 10, 2000, A1.

[108] Deborah Sontag, "Israelis Track Down and Kill a Fatah Commander," *NY Times*, Nov. 10, 2000, A1.

[109] Clyde Haberman, "Israeli Raid Kills 8 at Hamas Office; 2 Are Young Boys," *NY Times*, Aug. 1, 2001, A1.

taken in a vacuum, of course. Israeli civilians have been victims of countless terrorist attacks over a period of many years.

Once an anathema to America,[110] after 9/11 targeted killing became tolerated,[111] and then embraced.[112] Under a series of classified presidential findings, President George W. Bush broadened the number of named terrorists who could be killed if their capture was impractical.[113] In June 2006 the targeted killing of Abu Musab al-Zarqawi, leader of al Qaeda in Iraq, was celebrated as an American strategic and political victory. The roster of victims lengthened and attacks by armed drones in Afghanistan and the border regions of Pakistan became routine, as did complaints of proportionality violations. Given the successful targeted killing of so many senior Taliban and al Qaeda fighters by CIA-operated drones, it was clear that there would be no turning back for the United States. The Obama administration expanded the use of targeted killing in Afghanistan, Pakistan, Yemen, and Somalia. Even considering their inevitable collateral damage, the effectiveness of armed drones, combined with their zero exposure of friendly personnel, assured their continued use.

In an April 2012 speech, John Brennan, then the assistant to the president for homeland security and counterterrorism, addressed the U.S. view of targeted killing and provided a roadmap to U.S. targeted killing policy and practices in armed conflicts:

> As a matter of international law, the United States is in an armed conflict . . . in response to the 9/11 attacks. The Constitution empowers the president to protect the nation from any imminent threat of attack . . . [and] we may also use force consistent with our inherent right of national self-defense. There is nothing in international law that bans the use of remotely piloted aircraft for this purpose or that prohibits us from using lethal force against our enemies outside of an active battlefield, at least when the country involved consents or is unable or unwilling to take action against the threat. . . . Second, targeted strikes are ethical. . . . Targeted strikes conform to the principle of necessity. . . . Targeted strikes conform to the principles of distinction. . . . Targeted strikes conform to the principle of proportionality. . . . Targeted strikes conform to the principle of humanity which requires us to use weapons that will not inflict unnecessary suffering. . . . First and foremost, the individual must be a legitimate target under the law. . . . We conduct targeted strikes because they are necessary to mitigate an actual ongoing threat, to stop plots, prevent future attacks, and to save American lives. And what do we mean when we say significant threat? . . . A significant threat might be posed by an individual who is an operational leader of al-Qaida . . . or is himself an operative in the midst of actually training for or planning to carry

[110] "Self-Licensed to kill," *Economist*, Aug. 4, 2001, 12; and, "Assassination Ill Befits Israel," *NY Times*, Oct. 7, 1997, A24.

[111] In 1989, Abraham D. Sofaer, then the U.S. State Department legal adviser, equivocated, "While the U.S. regards attacks on terrorists being protected in the sovereign territory of other States as potentially justifiable when undertaken in self-defense, a State's ability to establish the legality of such an action depends on its willingness openly to accept responsibility for the attack, to explain the basis for its action, and to demonstrate that reasonable efforts were made prior to the attack to convince the State whose territorial sovereignty was violated to prevent the offender's unlawful activities from occurring." Abraham D. Sofaer, "Terrorism, the Law, and the National Defense." 126 *Military L. Rev.* (1989), 89, 121.

[112] Craig R. Whitney, "War on Terror Alters U.S. Qualms about Assassination," *Int'l Herald Tribune*, March 29, 2004, 2.

[113] James Risen and David Johnston, "Bush Has Widened Authority of C.I.A. to Kill Terrorists," *NY Times*, Dec. 15, 2002, A1.

out attacks. ... Or perhaps the individual possesses unique operational skills. ... In addition ... capturing the individual is not feasible.[114]

State practice has moved toward the legitimization of targeted killing. "Today, targeted killing is in the process of escaping the shadowy realm of half-legality and non-accountability, and [is] gradually gaining legitimacy as a method of counter-terrorism and 'surgical' warfare. Several Governments have expressly or implicitly acknowledged that they have resorted to targeted killings in their respective efforts to curb insurgent or terrorist activities."[115] In the years since that statement (2008), the use of armed drones has outpaced their predicted use.

14.10.1 *Characteristics of Targeted Killing*

There is no announced U.S. policy directive regarding targeted killing, although there was a 2013 presidential speech on the subject.[116] Assassination is addressed in Executive Order 12333, which does not prohibit killing absolutely, but only without presidential approval. But assassination and targeted killing are legally different acts. Given that there is no official protocol, one looks to LOAC/IHL principles for targeted killing guidelines.

Recall the five characteristics or requirements of targeted killing. First, an international or noninternational armed conflict must be in progress. Without an ongoing armed conflict the targeted killing of an individual, including a terrorist, would be homicide and a domestic crime. It is armed conflict that raises the right of lawful combatants to kill an enemy. In a common Article 3 noninternational conflict, the basis of the targeted killing must rest upon domestic law provisions, rather than LOAC/IHL since, in a noninternational conflict LOAC/IHL, other than common Article 3, is inapplicable.

Second, the targeted individual must be a specific individual. This is a significant requirement. If the targeted person is not known in advance of the drone's employment, it is not a targeted killing; it is simply a mission in search of a target of opportunity to be attacked. That an individual enemy fighter or group of enemy fighters are killed by a drone-launched missile does not necessarily make it a targeted killing.

To constitute a targeted killing, the individual must be targeted by reason of his or her confirmed activities in relation to the armed conflict. If the targeted individual is a lawful combatant, uniformed and openly armed, as in an international armed conflict, he is an opposing combatant's lawful target with no further discussion necessary. It is not always required that the target's identity be known because, in an international armed conflict, he is targetable on the basis of his combatant status alone. If not a combatant but a civilian, as in a noninternational armed conflict, identification of the targeted individual should be positive. That requires military intelligence of a high caliber, a quality not always available in armed conflict. It is clear that civilians who are not directly

---

[114] John O. Brennan, "The Ethics and Efficacy of the President's Counterterrorism Strategy," address at the Woodrow Wilson International Center for Scholars, Washington, D.C. (April 30, 2012); reported at, John R. Crook, ed., "Contemporary Practice of the United States Relating to International Law," 106–3 *AJIL* (July 2012), 643, 670.

[115] Melzer, *Targeted Killing in International Law*, supra, note 96, at 9–10.

[116] President Barack Obama, Address at the National Defense University, Washington, D.C. (May 23, 2013).

participating in the hostilities at the time of their targeting, and who do not have a continuous combat function, may not be lawfully targeted.[117]

As Additional Protocol I points out, in an international armed conflict, "civilians shall enjoy the protection afforded by this Section [General Protection Against Effects of Hostilities], unless and for such time as they take a direct part in hostilities."[118] That provision is mirrored in Article 13 of Additional Protocol II, in relation to noninternational armed conflicts. A civilian who injects himself directly into ongoing hostilities violates the basic concept of distinction and becomes an unprivileged belligerent, often called an unlawful combatant, who lacks the combatant's privilege to kill, wound, or destroy property without penalty of law. By their unlawful acts, they forfeit their civilian immunity and become lawful targets. "For instance, a driver delivering ammunition to combatants and a person who gathers military intelligence in enemy-controlled territory are commonly acknowledged to be actively taking part in hostilities. . . . A person cannot (and is not allowed to) be both a combatant and a civilian at the same time, nor can he constantly shift from one status to the other."[119]

3. Third, the individual who has engaged directly in hostilities must have no reasonable possibility of arrest – not a LOAC/IHL principle, but an important human rights concern. The United States has no extraterritorial arrest authority, and rarely would an allied state in a noninternational armed conflict be in a position to make an arrest. If capture is reasonably possible, however, that option must be exercised.

> The policy of the United States is not to use lethal force when it is feasible to capture a terrorist suspect, because capturing a terrorist offers the best opportunity to gather meaningful intelligence and to mitigate and disrupt terrorist plots. Capture operations are conducted only against suspects who may lawfully be captured or otherwise taken into custody by the United States and only when the operation can be conducted in accordance with all applicable law and consistent with our obligations to other sovereign states.[120]

4. Fourth, only a senior military commander representing the targeting state may authorize a targeted killing. The authorizing individual may be the president, or a senior domestic government official to whom the president has delegated targeting authority, such as the secretary of defense or the director of the Central Intelligence Agency. "As commander in chief, the President has the constitutional authority to command the use of deadly force by troops in war, whether it has been declared by Congress or thrust upon us by enemy attack or invasion."[121] Authority to command implies authority to delegate. What level of military commander may authorize a targeted killing? The required military position or required rank is not publicly announced and probably varies from case to

---

[117] 1907 Hague Regulation IV, Art. 25, and 1977 Additional Protocol I, Arts. 3 (1)(a) and (d). Also, "it is a generally recognized rule of international law that civilians must not be made the object of attack directed exclusively against them" in United Kingdom, MOD, *The Law of War on Land: Part III of the Manual of Military Law* (London: HMSO, 1958), para. 13.

[118] Id., Additional Protocol I, Art. 51.3.

[119] Yoram Dinstein, *The Conduct of Hostilities under the Law of International Armed Conflict*, 1st ed. (Cambridge: Cambridge University Press, 2004), 27–8.

[120] The White House, "Fact Sheet: U.S. Policy Standards and Procedures for the Use of Force in Counterterrorism Operations outside the United States and Areas of Active Hostilities" (May 23, 2013).

[121] Banks and Raven-Hansen, "Targeted Killing and Assassination," supra, note 96, at 677, citing *The Prize Cases*, 67 U.S. (2 Black) 635, 668 (1862)

case. Nor does the CIA reveal which of its officers have drone strike approval authority, although the director of its Counter-Terrorism Center reportedly has such authority.[122]

When distinction has been previously satisfied through positive identification of the targeted individual, the military commander's initial consideration is military necessity. Is the planned action indispensable for securing the submission of the enemy? The death of no one person will end terrorism, but would the killing of this particular individual constitute a substantial injury or loss to the terrorist cause, or disrupt terrorist plans? It is not a high hurdle to surmount.

Collateral damage, that is, proportionality, must always be at the top of an authorizing commander's considerations. Prospective collateral damage assessments are a difficult issue, allowing for lenient judgments and moral assessments. In 2002, the Israeli chief of military intelligence, haunted by civilian deaths in killings he oversaw, asked a mathematician to write a mathematical formula to determine the number of acceptable civilian casualties per dead terrorist. Unsurprisingly, the effort was unsuccessful.[123] Each proposed targeted killing raises its own unique moral dilemmas.

14.10.2 *Signature Strikes*

"In summer 2008, senior officials at the CTC [the CIA's Counter-Terrorism Center] . . . persuaded the president [George W. Bush] to authorize a major expansion that would allow the CIA to target groups of suspected militants believed to be associated with terrorism without necessarily knowing their identity. These 'signature strikes,' a form of targeted killing, were based on monitoring patterns of activity to identify signatures."[124] Their use was also urged by the chief of the CIA's Counter-Terrorism Center. "His push for permission to begin launching . . . 'signature strikes' . . . led to a lethal surge that peaked in 2010 when the CIA carried out 117 strikes in Pakistan."[125] The tribal areas of Pakistan were a haven for Taliban and al Qaeda, who were heavily targeted for signature strikes.[126] "President Obama extended and expanded this practice into Yemen."[127] The number of CIA signature targeted killings is not known, but they are said to be numerous. "The available evidence indicates that the vast majority of drone strikes conducted by the CIA have been signature strikes, as opposed to 'personality' strikes – those in which the CIA has a 'high degree of confidence' that it knows the precise identity of the target."[128]

---

[122] Greg Miller, "Counterterrorism Center's Chief Is Out," *Wash. Post*, March 26, 2015, A6; and Mary Ellen O'Connell, "Unlawful Killing with Combat Drones," Notre Dame Law School, Legal Studies Research Paper No. 09–43 (Draft: Nov. 2009), at 7: "All decisions to actually fire a missile are made by the CIA at their headquarters at Langley, Virginia."

[123] Id., Miller article.

[124] Megan Braun, "Predator Effect," in Bergen and Rothenberg, *Drone Wars*, supra, note 57, at 253, 267, citing Greg Miller, "Increased U.S. Drone Strikes in Pakistan Killing Few High-Value Militants," *Wash. Post*, Feb. 21, 2011.

[125] Miller, "Counterterrorism Center's Chief Is Out," supra, note 122.

[126] Scott Shane, "C.I.A. Expanding Drone Assaults inside Pakistan," NY *Times*, Dec. 3, 2009, A1.

[127] Zenko, *Reforming U.S. Drone Strike Policies*, supra, note 75, at 12.

[128] Kevin Jon Heller, "'One Hell of a Killing Machine': Signature Strikes and International Law," 11–1 *J. of Int'l Crim. Justice* (2013), 89–90.

Presuming the validity of that account, a corner had been turned. Targeted killing, previously limited to "personality strikes" against specific known and named individuals (personalities) who were al Qaeda or Taliban trainers, leaders, and commanders known to have continuous combat functions, now ventured onto untested legal ground, treading close to the outer edge of distinction.

> Signature strikes are generally directed at persons "who bear certain signatures, or defining characteristics associated with terrorist activity, but whose identities aren't known." Those who exhibit certain "signatures", such as being involved in planning and executing attacks, are clearly targetable as direct participants in hostilities. The more difficult cases involve individuals who exhibit signatures that do not clearly indicate membership in an organized armed group or direct participation in hostilities.[129]

Neither the CIA nor the U.S. government has disclosed what conduct or what actions qualify one for targeting by signature strike. No reports of military signature strike targeting have been located.

"Drone operators have little way of knowing if those they have killed [through signature strikes] were actually combatants, especially where there are few trustworthy local contacts, limited ground-based intelligence, and no conventional troops or related forces able to investigate and corroborate the accuracy of the targeting process."[130] Professor Robert Kolb notes, "The [targeting] criteria used for signature strikes is inherently imprecise."[131]

When invoking the state's targeted killing apparatus to kill a human target whose name is unknown, without signals intelligence or human intelligence to independently confirm the target's status as an enemy fighter before he is killed, or the ability to make on-the-ground after-action assessments, or confirm the reliability of the signature targeting process, the basic requirement of distinction cannot be satisfied.

14.11 Summary

Today, and for the foreseeable future, autonomous weapons systems are not and will not actually be autonomous in the literal sense of that term. Human beings will remain "in the loop," ensuring that the design and programming of weapon systems conform to LOAC/IHL, and human beings will make final "shoot/don't shoot" decisions, always with a finger near an "abort" button. True autonomous weapons systems may be on the way, but they remain years, perhaps decades, away. For now, land-, air-, and sea-based *semiautonomous* weapons are already integrated into ground positions, ships, and aerial vehicles. These semiautonomous systems have been Article 36 tested for conformance with LOAC. Since humans, for now, remain the ultimate decision makers, existing LOAC strictures are sufficient to control their use; new laws of war regarding their use are

---

[129] Michael N. Schmitt and Eric W. Widmar, "'On Target': Precision and Balance in the Contemporary Law of Targeting," 7 *J. of Nat'l Security & Policy* (2014), 379, 390–1.

[130] Sarah Holewinski, "Just Trust Us," in Bergen and Rothenberg, *Drone Wars*, supra, note 57, at 42, 46–7.

[131] Robert Kolb, *Advanced Introduction to International Humanitarian Law* (Cheltenham, UK: Edward Elgar, 2014), 150–1.

not a requirement. This does not suggest that drones cannot be used in unlawful ways. That is true of any weapon, and unlawful use should not be blamed on the weapon, but on the operator.

Decisions relating to the core principles of distinction and proportionality may be made by autonomous weapons systems but not, one suspects, with a degree of consistency and reliability that would presently allow commanders to step back and allow combat robots to take over those high-stake aspects of command responsibility – particularly where proportionality judgments are concerned.

Individual criminal responsibility is fully applicable for grave breaches perpetrated by drones and semiautonomous weapons systems. That criminal liability will be in a criminally negligent or criminally <u>acting operator</u>, or the criminally negligent or criminally acting <u>commander</u>, or a criminally negligent or criminally <u>acting software programmer or system designer.</u> Difficult, perhaps unresolvable, issues of proof will make developers and manufacturers difficult to convict, but criminal cases implicating either will be rare in the first place.

There are two American drone programs: the military's and the CIA's. Military drones that employ relatively transparent targeting parameters are largely limited to targets on active battlefields. CIA drones employing unrevealed targeting matrixes function outside active battlefields, for the most part. As noted (Chapter 14.7), there appears to be a self-imposed CIA movement away from the use of drones, although that remains to be verified.

There are many objections to drones and their semiautonomous weapons systems, the most vocal being related to proportionality. Critics are not mollified that drones are far more accurate than the weapons and tactics they supplant, such as cruise missiles, aerial bombing, artillery, and close air support, or that drones kill far fewer innocent civilians than their alternatives.

In noninternational armed conflicts, targeted killing, usually carried out by armed drone, is intended to result in the death of specifically targeted civilian enemy fighters. When an innocent civilian death results from a targeted killing, or other combat action, such "collateral damage," as long as it is not excessive in relation to the concrete and direct military advantage anticipated, is not a LOAC/IHL violation. Civilian targets killed on the basis of signature strikes, on the other hand, appear to violate the principle of distinction and, arguably, are unlawful.

Today, the United States leads the world in drone technology and battlefield utility.[132] At least seventy other states now possess drone technology, with more states regularly added to that number. Most other states do not yet have the advanced weapon systems and sensor capabilities of the United States – but some soon will. Today, we are deeply concerned with collateral damage and seemingly unrestricted targeting parameters. Tomorrow, drones of other states may attack American combatants and civilians and have similar problems.[133]

---

[132] China's version of the Predator, the *Wing Loong*, or, Pterodactyl, can carry two laser-guided missiles.

[133] On Feb. 25, 2009, American fighter aircraft shot down an unarmed Iranian Ababil 3 drone with an integral video camera. The Iranian drone was eighty miles inside Iraq and sixty miles northeast of Baghdad. Rod Nordland and Alissa J. Rubin, "U.S. Military Says It Shot Down an Iranian Drone over Iraq," *NY Times*, March 17, 2009, A12.

CASES AND MATERIALS

THE SHOOTING DOWN OF IRAN AIR FLIGHT 655 BY THE USS VINCENNES

From The American Journal of International Law: *It was a tense time in the Persian Gulf in early July 1988. Iraq was conducting air strikes against Iranian oil facilities and ships, Iranian F-14s (sold by the United States to the Shah of Iran a decade earlier) had retaliated, and small boats launched from Iran were challenging ships approaching the Strait of Hormuz. Every American ship captain in the Gulf Remembered the episode a year earlier when an Iraqi missile had – by mistake, it was said – blown a hole in the frigate U.S.S. Stark, with the loss of 37 lives.*

On Sunday, July 3, 1988, the U.S.S. Vincennes (CG-49), already involved in an exchange of fire with a group of Iranian naval craft (Swedish-built Boghammar boats) in the international waters of the Persian Gulf, shot down an unidentified aircraft that had just departed from the joint military-civilian airfield at Bandar Abbas, Iran. After repeated unsuccessful efforts by the Vincennes to establish contact with the unidentified aircraft, the ship's captain, believing his vessel might be attacked within minutes by an Iranian military aircraft sent to assist the gunboats engaged in the surface exchange, ordered the still unidentified aircraft to be fired upon. The aircraft was shot down, and only afterwards was it identified as a civilian airliner, Iran Air Flight 655, an Airbus 300, with 290 persons from six nations on board. It was shot down by two surface-to-air missiles launched from the Vincennes, a guided missile cruiser on duty with the United States Persian Gulf/Middle East Task Force. The first reports from Washington were that the Vincennes had acted in self-defense against a hostile Iranian aircraft. Twelve hours later the Pentagon admitted that the Vincennes had made a mistake, the aircraft it saw approaching on its radar was a wide-bodied airliner on a regularly scheduled flight, not an Iranian F-14 Tomcat with hostile intent and capability. The shooting down of Iran Air Flight 65 was clearly a tragic error.[134]

The foregoing account does not address the Vincennes' semi-autonomous Aegis Combat System and its unique capabilities. The Aegis integrated weapons system used computers and radars to track multiple targets and guide defensive weapons to attack and destroy them. The system was composed of the Aegis anti-aircraft weapon system itself, plus the Phalanx Close-In Weapon System, and a Vertical Launch System that employed add-itional missiles, all of which were semi-autonomous. Different U.S. combatant ships carried different variants of the Aegis weapon system.

The weapon system was not at fault in the shooting down of Flight 655. Subsequent investigation determined that it was functioning properly. The Flight 655 shoot-down illustrates that even when there is a "man in the loop" or, in the case of the Vincennes, many specially-trained and experienced men in the loop, autonomous weapons systems cannot prevent human error in interpreting correct data that the weapon system provides system operators.

---

[134] The foregoing account is a combination of two articles, footnotes omitted: "Agora: The Downing of Iran Air Flight 655, an Introduction," and, Marian Nash Leich, "Denial of Liability: *Ex Gratia* Compensation on a Humanitarian Basis," both in 83–2 *AJIL* at 318 and 319, respectively (April 1989).

The following abbreviated and paraphrased account, written by a retired Marine Corps officer-turned newspaper reporter, was published in Proceedings, *a semi-official magazine published by the United States Naval Institute. The account places the human error squarely on the* Vincennes' *captain, Commander William C. Rogers III, who oversaw the sailors and officers in the* Vincennes' *combat information center (CIC) throughout the event:*

At 0947, Iran Air flight 655 took off from Bandar Abbas international airport, bound for Dubai, twenty-seven minutes away, and began its climb-out toward cruising altitude. At the same time, the Vincennes, commanded by Captain Will Rogers, was proceeding at full speed toward Iranian gunboats he later said were threats to his ship's helicopter, which had been observing nearby Iranian ship and boat traffic. The USS *Sides* (FFG-14), a guided-missile frigate commanded by Captain David Carlson, was also on the scene. Large-screen displays in the *Sides'* CIC saw the same images and heard the same radio traffic as did the *Vincennes'* CIC.

"The *Sides'* air search radar was bouncing off the [Iranian] plane. 'I glanced at it' said Captain Carlson, 'It was around 3,000 feet, 350 knots. Nothing remarkable . . . I evaluated track 4131 [the Airbus's radar tracking designation in the *Sides'* CIC] as not a threat. . . . He's climbing. He's slow. I don't see any radar emissions. He's in the middle of our missile envelope, and there is no precedent for any kind of an attack by an [Iranian] F-14 against surface ships. So, non-threat."[135]

At about 0940, the *Vincennes* crossed the 12-mile line into Iranian waters. In response to his request to his higher command to fire on Iranian boats, Joint Task Force Middle East, "Captain Rogers was given permission to open fire. Note, he was now inside Iranian territorial waters and ready to engage boats that had not fired on him. . . . At about 0943, the Vincennes' forward five-inch gun mount commenced to lob shells at the Iranian gunboats. . . .

On board the *Sides* moments later, the tactical action officer (TAO) informed Captain Carlson, 'Captain, we have a contact. *Vincennes* designated this contact as an [Iranian] F-14 coming out of Bandar Abbas.'

As Captain Carlson and his tactical action officer were evaluating an Iranian P-3's activities on the radar scope they overheard Captain Rogers' transmission announcing to higher headquarters his intention to shoot down track 4131 at 20 miles [distance from the Vincennes]. Captain Carlson was thunderstruck. . . . My guys in the back [in the *Sides'* CIC] had evaluated the IFF [electronic identification friend or foe transponder] and had determined that it was a commercial aircraft. They were horrified. In his book [*Storm Center*], Captain Rogers said that at 0953, just before he authorized missile firing, he again requested verification of the IFF code being broadcast by track 4131 as that of an Iranian military aircraft. 'This was reaffirmed,' he wrote. . . . [A subsequent] investigation accepts the testimony of console operators in the *Vincennes'* combat information center who said the supposed F-14 was diving. However, one officer, Lieutenant William Montford, who was standing right behind Captain Rogers, testified that he never saw

---

[135] Lt. Col. David Evans, USMC (Ret.), "Vincennes: A Case Study," U.S. Naval Institute's *Proceedings* (Aug. 1993), footnotes omitted. All quotes in this portion of the account are from Evans's story. The order of some of the quotes is changed to provide a clearer timeline of events.

indications that the aircraft was descending. At about 0951, Lieutenant Montford warned Captain Rogers that the contact was 'possible COMAIR' [commercial aircraft].

Captain Rezaian [the pilot of Flight 655] could not have guessed that by now his lumbering A300 Airbus had been evaluated in the *Vincennes* as a diving Iranian F-14 – the spearhead of a 'coordinated attack' from the air and from gunboats on the surface. ..."

The information on the transponder emissions is unambiguous, however.... TN 4131 was on a normal commercial air flight plan profile, squawking Mode III 6760, on a continuous ascent in altitude from take-off at Bandar Abbas to shoot down. The number in the 6760 series indicated it was a commercial aircraft. The Aegis data tapes agree with this view."[136]

At Captain Rogers's order, the Vincennes *fired two Standard SM-2 surface-to-air missiles, one of which destroyed Flight 655. Two hundred, ninety civilians were killed.*

Why was no punitive action taken? How were basic target identification mistakes jointly made by numerous well-trained and experienced weapons system operators, their mistakes confirmed and repeated by the ship's commanding officer?

There was a U.S. Navy investigation of the incident, of course. In his Report of Investigation, Rear Admiral William M. Fogarty weakly opined that the conflicting statements in the Vincennes' *CIC regarding Flight 655's flight path, and the resulting firing of Aegis weapon system missiles, were due to "scenario fulfillment" caused by "an unconscious attempt to make available evidence fit a preconceived scenario."*

Admiral Fogarty's full investigation has never been released. Part I of the investigation was released in 1988, Part II in 1993. The critical portions of a navy report of investigation, however, are contained in Part III, Opinions, and Part IV, Recommendations. The unavailability of those two parts strongly suggests damning content regarding Rogers's performance of duty.

Why were there no courts-martial? The Proceedings *article by David Evans answers that "a court-martial might have raised many ugly questions about crew training. ... Add, too, questions about command selection. And ... bedrock questions about professional ethics. ... Instead, an incomplete investigation was blessed."[137]*

Why was there little domestic political interest in finding answers to questions related to the shooting down of a civilian airliner? Eleven days after Flight 655 was shot down, on July 11, in a speech before the United Nations, Vice President George H. W. Bush said, "One thing is clear, and that is that the USS Vincennes *acted in self-defense." Bush, vice president to Ronald Reagan, was four months away from nomination as his party's candidate for the presidency of the United States. At such a time, political interest was not to be focused on 290 dead civilians.*

In 1989, Iran instituted proceedings against the United States in the International Court of Justice. In 1996 the I.C.J. dismissed the case at the parties' request,[138] following settlement and reparations involving U.S. agreement to payment of $61.8 million U.S. dollars to the Islamic Republic of Iran, for distribution to survivors of the victims.

An irritant to members of U.S. Armed Forces who recall the Vincennes *incident is that, upon the ship's end of its overseas tour of duty and return to its San Diego homeport, the officers and crew were awarded the Combat Action Ribbon for their involvement in the July*

---

[136] Id.   [137] Id., at 6.   [138] *Islamic Republic of Iran v. United States of America* (22 Feb. 1996).

3 *action. Particularly dismaying, in 1990 Captain Rogers was awarded the Legion of Merit medal for his tour of duty as commanding officer of the Vincennes.*

The USS Vincennes was decommissioned on June 29, 2005. Upgraded Aegis semiautonomous weapons systems continue in use in the U.S. Navy, and the navies of allied states.

PROSECUTOR V. BLAŠKIĆ

IT-95-14-T, Judgment (March 3, 2000) Footnotes omitted

Who is responsible for grave breaches "committed" by drone-mounted semiautonomous weapons systems? Until a truly autonomous system is designed and made operational, there will always be a human being somewhere in the chain to whom prosecutors will look: either an operator who pulled the trigger, or the operator's military commander or civilian superior who ordered the trigger pulled, or, in rare instances, an individual in the system developer's chain – a criminally minded computer code writer, programmer, or installer or, at the far end of the developer's chain, a system designer. The text of the following extract from the Blaškić judgment discusses problems of proof, should an individual in the developer's chain be charged.

In addition to the issue of whether the charged crime was committed during the existence of an associated armed conflict, a problem would be proving "the mens rea requirements of the most plausible ground of developer liability ... aiding and abetting. The ex ante nature of developers' activities is also likely to present a significant barrier to establishing the mental element required for criminal responsibility."[139] If the charged crime was allegedly done without knowledge, prediction, or foresight of subsequent events, can the charge be proven? The ICTY's Blaškić case discusses the issues of proof involved not only in aiding and abetting, but in the various other forms of participation in criminality.

278. The Trial Chamber holds that proof is required that whoever planned, instigated or ordered the commission of a crime possessed the criminal intent, that is, that he directly or indirectly intended that the crime in question be committed. However, in general, a person other than the person who planned, instigated or ordered is the one who perpetrated the *actus reus* of the offense. In so doing he must have acted in furtherance of a plan or order. In the case of instigating, as appears in the definition below, proof is required of a causal connection between the instigation and the fulfillment of the *actus reus* of the crime. In defining each of the forms of participation, the Trial Chamber concurs with the relevant findings of the Trial Chamber in the _Akayesu_ case.

279. Accordingly, planning implies that "one or several persons contemplate designing the commission of a crime at both the preparatory and execution phases. The Trial Chamber is of the view that circumstantial evidence may provide sufficient proof of the existence of a plan.

280. Instigating entails "prompting another to commit an offense." The wording is sufficiently broad to allow for the inference that both acts and omissions may constitute instigating and that this notion covers both express and implied conduct. The ordinary

---

[139] McFarland and McCormack, "Mind the Gap," supra, note 50, at 378.

meaning of instigating, namely, "bring about" the commission of an act by someone, corroborates the opinion that a causal relationship between the instigation and the physical perpetrator of the crime is an element requiring proof.

281. The _Akayesu_ Trial Chamber was of the opinion that ordering

> implies a superior-subordinate relationship between the person giving the order and the one executing it. In other words, the person in a position of authority used it to convince another to commit an offense.

It is not necessary that an order be given in writing or in any particular form. It can be explicit or implicit. The fact that an order was given can be proved through circumstantial evidence.

282. The Trial Chamber agrees that an order does not need to be given by the superior directly to the person(s) who perform(s) the _actus reus_ of the offense. Furthermore, what is important is the commander's _mens rea,_ not that of the subordinate executing the order. Therefore, it is irrelevant whether the illegality of the order was apparent on its face.

ii) Aiding and abetting

283. As a starting point, the Trial Chamber concurs with the opinion of the Trial Chamber in the _Furundžija_ case, which states that

> the legal ingredients of aiding and abetting in international criminal law to be the following: the _actus reus_ consists of practical assistance, encouragement, or moral support which has a substantial effect on the perpetration of the crime. The mens rea required is the knowledge that these acts assist the commission of the offense.

284. The Trial Chamber holds that the _actus reus_ of aiding and abetting may be perpetrated through an omission, provided this failure to act had a decisive effect on the commission of the crime and that it was coupled with the requisite _mens rea_. In this respect, the mere presence at the crime scene of a person with superior authority, such as a military commander, is a probative indication for determining whether that person encouraged or supported the perpetrators of the crime.

285. Proof that the conduct of the aider and abettor had a causal effect on the act of the principle perpetrator is not required. Furthermore, participation may occur before, during or after the act is committed and be geographically separated therefrom.

286. As to the _mens rea_ requirement for aiding and abetting, a distinction is to be made between "knowledge" and "intent." As held earlier in this Judgment, the mens rea required for establishing the responsibility of an accused for one of the crimes in Articles 2, 3 and 5 of the [ICTY's] Statute is "willingness," comprising both direct and indirect intent. In the case of aiding and abetting, the Prosecution relies on _inter alia_ the _Furundžija_ Judgment and argues that the _mens rea_ applicable to the aider and abettor in "knowledge" that his acts assist the commission of the offense. In the submission of the Defense, however, Article 7(1) of the Statute requires proof of the specific intent on the part of the accused to commit the deliberate act to facilitate the commission of a crime. The Trial Chamber is of the view that in addition to the knowledge that his acts assist the commission of the crime, the aider and abettor needs to have intended to provide assistance, or as a minimum, accepted that such assistance would be a possible and foreseeable consequence of his conduct.

287. Finally, the Trial Chamber concurs with the following finding in the *Furundžija* Judgment:

> [It] is not necessary that the aider and abettor should know the precise crime that was intended and which in the event was committed. If he was aware that one of a number of crimes will probably b e committed, and one of those crimes is in fact committed, he has intended to facilitate the commission of that crime, and is guilty as an aider and abettor.

288. The Trial Chamber deems it appropriate to point out that a distinction is to be made between aiding and abetting and participation in pursuance of a purpose or common design to commit a crime. In the case in point, it notes that the only question raised is the question of aiding and abetting.

This excerpt highlights the problem prosecutors will have in prosecuting developers or manufacturers of drones or autonomous weapons systems on the most likely charge, aiding and abetting. While paragraphs 285 and 287 seem to ease the prosecutorial burden, paragraph 286 sets a high bar. While future cases regarding drone developers will be few, their prosecution may break new international criminal law ground.

15 Human Targeting and Cross-Border Counterattacks

15.0 Introduction

In armed conflicts combatants and civilians are killed, some by mistake, or as collateral damage; some by friendly fire, or mistaken distinction determinations. Most are killed because they were specifically targeted by a member of an opposing armed force, armed opposition group, or revolutionary band.

What is the applicable law of war for such killings? When may human beings, combatants, enemy fighters, or civilians lawfully be killed and when may they not?

15.1 Two Predicate Requirements

For a use of force to fall under LOAC/IHL it must, first, take place in the course of an armed conflict. Second, the use of force must have a nexus with the armed conflict.[1] The core principles of distinction, military necessity, unnecessary suffering, and proportionality remain applicable in any application of military force.

Imagine widespread rioting and looting in a Blueland city, with units of Blueland's armed forces called in to maintain order. Civilian looters are captured and, in some cases, shot and killed by Blueland soldiers. In such a scenario LOAC/IHL is not implicated because there is no armed conflict involving an opposing armed group or unit. Instead, customary international law, domestic law, and human rights law would be applicable. Allegations of unlawful use of force by Blueland soldiers would be tried either by court-martial or by domestic courts.[2]

Now consider a Blueland military unit allied with Redland in Redland's noninternational armed conflict against a nonstate armed opposition group inside Redland. Well-armed narco-criminals have kidnapped the Redland president's family. The Redland president entreats Blueland to intercept the narco-criminals as they cross through Blueland's tactical area of responsibility. Blueland does so and a firefight ensues, with casualties among Blueland troops and the narcos. The first family is rescued. In this

---

[1] Gloria Gaggioli, ed., *The Use of Armed Force in Armed Conflicts: Interplay between the Conduct of Hostilities and Law Enforcement Paradigms* (Geneva: ICRC, 2013), 5.

[2] Military and civilian jurisdiction would be concurrent. In such cases military and civilian authorities meet and decide who will exercise jurisdiction in which cases.

case, unlikely in reality as it is, the fighting takes place while an armed conflict is in progress but it has no nexus with the armed conflict. Domestic law and human rights law prevail.

15.2 Lawful Combatant Human Targets

Recall that there are only two individual statuses on the battlefield: civilians and combatants. There are numerous subcategories of both. Subcategories of combatant, for example, include prisoner of war, detainee, retained person, and spy. Subcategories of civilian include detainee, protected person, member of a *levée en masse*, unprivileged belligerent (often referred to as "unlawful combatant" or "enemy fighter"), and spy.

As discussed in Chapter 6, combatants are **members of the armed forces of a party to the conflict (other than medical personnel and chaplains)**.[3] This definition includes members of the armed forces' reserves, and militias forming part of the armed forces, as well as volunteer corps who fulfill the familiar four conditions enumerated in Geneva Convention III, Article 4.A.(2).[4]

In an international armed conflict, subject to proportionality rules, combatants may be lawfully targeted and killed solely on the basis of their status as combatants; they are "status-based" targets. If a combatant can identify an individual as a member of the opposing armed force, the combatant may target him at any time or place he is identified, simply on the basis of his status as an enemy combatant.

It makes no difference whether a member of the state's armed forces is a clerk, cook, or infantryman. All members of a state's armed forces, except medical personnel and chaplains, are combatants and all are targetable, just as all combatants have the right to target opposing combatants.

In a noninternational armed conflict, if members of the state's armed forces are engaged in, for example, an antiterrorist operation, they may *not* lawfully be killed by a terrorist fighter, because terrorists lack the combatant's privilege to kill, wound, or destroy objects, without penalty of law (Chapter 2.3.1). A terrorist's killing of an opposing combatant or police officer, even in a firefight, constitutes the domestic crime of murder, prosecutable in the state wherein the act occurred, or by a military commission of the victim's state.[5]

15.2.1 *Once a Combatant, Always a Combatant*

A combatant remains a combatant, even when out of uniform, even when away from any battlefield. That can lead to harsh outcomes.

---

[3] 1977 Additional Protocol I, Art. 43.2. It will be remembered that medical personnel and chaplains are retainees. (See Chapter 6.2.1.) Also, members of a *levée en masse*, who are always civilians, are viewed as combatants for so long as the *levée* remains a lawful grouping. Geneva Convention III, Art. 4.A.(6). Today, a *levee en masse* is a rare occurrence.

[4] (a) That of being commanded by a person responsible for his/her subordinates; (b) that of having a fixed distinctive sign recognizable at a distance; (c) that of carrying arms openly; (d) that of conducting their operations in accordance with the laws and customs of war. 1977 Additional Protocol I, Art. 44.3 relaxes the application of (b) and (c) for those states that have ratified Protocol I.

[5] Yves Sandoz, Christophe Swinarski, and Bruno Zimmermann, eds., *Commentary on the Additional Protocols* (Geneva: ICRC/Martinus Nijhoff, 1987), para. 1670, at 510; and, Ex Parte *Quirin*, 317 US 1, 31 (1942).

In the course of an international armed conflict, if a night patrol of Blueland combatants comes across an enemy Redland encampment and the enemy combatants are sleeping, can the Blueland combatants shoot them as they sleep? Yes, they can lawfully target and kill the sleeping Redland soldiers because, sleeping or awake, in uniform or in pajamas, the Redland soldiers remain enemy combatants, and, by virtue of their status alone, combatants of either side are *always* lawful targets of the opposing side.

Some believe the principle of humanity dictates that, whenever possible, a defenceless enemy combatant must be captured, rather than killed. That is not a LOAC/IHL rule or law, however; it is a law enforcement standard based on human rights law.[6] Enemy combatants may be attacked with deadly force any time and any place they are identified. Moreover, "a combatant is not *hors de combat* merely due to being no longer capable of offering effective resistance."[7] For example, "even an unarmed combatant can be attacked until he or she surrenders."[8] Nor is a combatant legally obliged to offer an enemy the chance to surrender. "Whether there should be a legal obligation to offer an opportunity to surrender was expressly considered during the drafting of AP I but is not expressed as a requirement in any article of AP I."[9] When an individual has become a lawful target, there is no obligation in the law of war to minimize harm to that combatant individual. (See this Chapter 15.6.2.1.) Capture may be a sensible policy in terms of gaining possible intelligence, but there is no legal obligation to do so. (Many combatants would nevertheless give a sleeping enemy the chance to surrender out of a sense of chivalry and fair play, rather than a sense of legal obligation.)

The author Sebastian Junger states it starkly: "It sounds dishonorable only if you imagine that modern war is about honor; it's not. It's about winning, which means killing the enemy on the most unequal terms possible. Anything less simply results in the loss of more of your own men"[10] "The kill-or-be-killed nature of combat tends to dull fine perceptions of right and wrong,"[11] as General Colin Powell has written. A military aphorism says, "If you find yourself in a fair fight, you haven't planned your mission well."

There are rules related to the targeting of combatants, too:

> Once it is determined that an individual may lawfully be targeted, the impact of the attack on civilians and civilian property must be assessed and minimized. International humanitarian law requires attackers to take precautions designed to limit collateral damage. This obligation includes: doing everything feasible to verify the target; choosing available weapons or tactics that will minimize collateral damage without sacrificing military advantage; and selecting targets so as to minimize collateral damage. Of particular note is the weapon selection requirement. ... Despite their occasional condemnation, in many cases this will be a drone.[12]

---

[6] ICRC, 31st International Conference of the Red Cross and Red Crescent: *International Humanitarian Law and the Challenges of Contemporary Armed Conflicts* (Geneva: ICRC, Oct. 2011), 21. In accord, Sandesh Sivakumaran, *The Law of Non-International Armed Conflict* (Oxford: Oxford University Press, 2013), 370.

[7] Ian Henderson, *The Contemporary Law of Targeting* (Leiden: Martinus Nijhoff, 2009), 85.

[8] Terry D. Gill and Dieter Fleck, eds., *The Handbook of the International Law of Military Operations* (Oxford: Oxford University Press, 2010), para. 16.10 at 268.

[9] Henderson, *Contemporary Law of Targeting*, supra, at 88. The exception contained in Additional Protocol I, Art. 42.2., will be discussed shortly.

[10] Sebastian Junger, *War* (New York: Hachette Book Group, 2010), 140.

[11] Colin L. Powell, *A Soldier's Way: An Autobiography* (London: Hutchinson/Random House, 1995), 144.

[12] Michael N. Schmitt, "Extraterritorial Lethal Targeting: Deconstructing the Logic of International Law," 52–1 *Columbia JTL* (2013), 77, 107.

Imagine a Redland soldier on leave from his military unit, hundreds of miles from the international armed conflict battlefield. He is in his hometown, wearing civilian clothes, walking to a theater. If a uniformed enemy Blueland combatant could somehow work his way to the Redland soldier's hometown, and could somehow identify the individual as an opposing Redland combatant, the Blueland combatant could lawfully target and kill his opposing combatant. By virtue of his or her continuing status, a combatant remains a combatant regardless of where he is or what he is doing. An opposing lawful enemy combatant, enjoying the combatant's privilege, may lawfully kill him.[13] It is a fantasy scenario, of course, but it accurately reflects LOAC/IHL.

An individual can shed combatant status by retirement from the armed forces or by demobilization – leaving active duty upon the expiration of one's obligated service. It is not precisely accurate, then, to say that once one becomes a combatant, one will *always* be a combatant. But one does remain a combatant for so long as one remains an active member of the armed forces – even if no armed conflict is in progress.

In noninternational armed conflicts, only common Article 3 of the 1949 Geneva Conventions and customary international law are applicable; 1977 Additional Protocol I is not applicable in a noninternational armed conflict, other than its articles that are customary international law. (See Chapter 3.8.6.1.)

Accordingly, in noninternational armed conflicts, there are no "combatants," per se, because combatants are a construct of Additional Protocol I, Article 43.2. – which relates to *international* armed conflicts. Instead, in noninternational armed conflicts there are "government forces" on one side of the conflict who oppose "enemy fighters" on the other side of the conflict.[14] The government forces may be the state's police, or its military units; enemy fighters may be insurgents, rebels, insurrectionists, or terrorists, but enemy fighters are not combatants because they are not members of the armed forces of a state – the definition of a combatant – and, critically, they do not enjoy the combatant's privilege.

When discussing noninternational armed conflicts, it is nevertheless common to use the term "combatants," when referring to government forces, even though that is technically incorrect. It is used because the term "combatant" entails an immediate understanding of who and what government forces are, and what they may and may not lawfully do.

> [Common Article 3] provides a set of basic guarantees that are absolutely fundamental in nature, but [it] does not provide anywhere near sufficient guidance ... in conflicts not of an international character. ... A legally binding source of additional rules applicable in non-international armed conflicts ... is, of course, customary international humanitarian law. ... When both sources of law are combined – the [1949 Geneva] treaty and customary law rules – a far stronger regime of obligations of the parties emerges.[15]

---

[13] The infiltrating enemy combatant must be uniformed or by killing the enemy he would be engaging in perfidy – inviting the confidence of his adversary (by wearing civilian clothing) to lead him to believe he, the shooter, is entitled to protection as a civilian under the rules of international law applicable in armed conflict. 1977 Additional Protocol I, Art. 37.1.

[14] There is no internationally agreed upon descriptive term or name for members of armed opposition groups who oppose government forces in a noninternational armed conflict.

[15] Jelena Pejic, "The Protective Scope of Common Article 3: More than Meets the Eye," 93–881 *Int'l Rev. of the Red Cross* (March 2011), 189, 205–6.

In unusual cases, 1977 Additional Protocol II, which essentially complements common Article 3, may also apply.

In noninternational armed conflicts, use of force rules look to human rights law for guidance. Even when the armed forces are involved, "they are still expected to conduct themselves as *ersatz* policemen: using force as a last resort, in keeping with the law enforcement paradigm."[16] Accordingly, should government forces come upon an encampment of sleeping enemy fighters in a noninternational armed conflict, they *cannot* lawfully kill the sleeping enemy, but must give them an opportunity to surrender before undertaking a use of armed force, if required, for example, if the enemy fighters awake and decide to make a fight of it.

In practice, the noninternational armed conflict requirement that combatants apply human rights standards for the use of force is not a substantial barrier to use of deadly force. Either the lawful combatants are fired on first by the enemy fighters, in which case the combatants may return fire in self-defense, or, upon encountering enemy fighters a two-way fire fight ensues and self-defense is again applicable. Chapter 15.6.3

15.3 Exceptions to Lawful Combatant Targets

There are exceptions – combatants who may *not* be lawfully targeted even though recognized as enemy combatants. The most prominent exceptions are combatants who are *hors de combat* (out of the fight). They may not be attacked. The expression "*hors de combat*" does not apply to civilians since civilians may not lawfully be engaged in an armed conflict fight in the first place; only combatants can become *hors de combat*.[17] A combatant " is *hors de combat* if:

a. 'he is in the power of an adverse Party',
b. 'he clearly expresses an intention to surrender'; or
c. 'he has been rendered unconscious or is otherwise incapacitated by wounds or sickness, and therefore incapable of defending himself';

'provided that in any of these cases he abstains from any hostile act and does not attempt to escape'."[18]

15.3.1 *A Combatant "In the Power of an Adverse Party"*

Combatants in the power of an adverse party include prisoners of war (POWs), of course. The general rule is that POWs may never lawfully be killed. "Camps may be fenced to prevent escape. However, weapons may not be used against prisoners of war, even if attempting to escape, except as a last resort and after prior warning."[19] The International Committee of the Red Cross (ICRC) explains:

---

[16] Yoram Dinstein, *Non-International Armed Conflicts in International Law* (Cambridge: Cambridge University Press, 2014), 22.

[17] Yoram Dinstein, *The Conduct of Hostilities under the Law of International Armed Conflict*, 2d ed. (Cambridge: Cambridge University Press, 2010), 34.

[18] UK Ministry of Defence, *The Manual of the Law of Armed Conflict* (Oxford: Oxford University Press, 2004), para. 5.6, at 57–8, citing Additional Protocol I, Arts. 44(1) and 41(1) and (2).

[19] Id., para. 8.40, at 159.

Captivity is based on force, and ... it is recognized in international customary law that the Detaining Power has the right to resort to force in order to keep prisoners captive. At the same time, this consideration also limits the use of weapons against prisoners. Whether in the case of attempted escape or any other demonstration (e.g. mutiny or revolt), the use of weapons "shall constitute an extreme measure, which shall always be preceded by warnings. ... "An extreme measure" means that fire may be opened only when there is no other means of putting an immediate stop to the attempt.[20]

In international armed conflicts, captured combatants are POWs from the moment of capture. In noninternational armed conflicts, captured enemy fighters are prisoners, or detainees, not only because POWs are a construct of Convention IV, which does not directly apply in noninternational armed conflicts, but because enemy fighters belonging to an armed opposition group very rarely meet the four preconditions for POW status.[21]

Sometimes, during commando or special operations missions, POWs or detainees, depending on the conflict status, are captured while the capturing force is itself behind enemy lines and cannot hand off its captives to the military police, as it normally would. What should the capturing commander do with captives when far from friendly lines and without the manpower to guard and adequately care for them?

A commander may not put his prisoners to death because their presence retards his movements or diminishes his power of resistance by necessitating a large guard, or by reason of their consuming supplies. ... It is likewise unlawful for a commander to kill his prisoners on grounds of self-preservation, even in the case of airborne or commando operations, although the circumstances of the operation may make necessary rigorous supervision of and restraint upon the movement of prisoners of war.[22]

Not even grounds of self-preservation will excuse the killing – murder – of POWs or detainees. "If ... it is not possible to evacuate prisoners of war, they are to be released and all feasible precautions taken to ensure their safety. ... This principle admits of no exceptions."[23] The release of POWs or prisoners may include requirements for the detaining power's provision of food and water, map and compass, even protective clothing, if chemical attack is a possibility.

SIDEBAR. During World War II, in March 1944, a Nazi submarine, the *U-852*, sank the Greek civilian steamer *Peleus*. After the war, at their British military court, five accused German submariners from the *Peleus*, including the captain, claimed there had been an operational necessity to ensure their boat would not later be identified by

---

[20] Jean de Preux, *Commentary, III Geneva Convention: Relative to the Treatment of Prisoners of War* (Geneva: ICRC, 1960), 246.

[21] In "The Hostage Case" (*United States v. Wilhelm List, et al.*), one of the twelve Nuremberg "Subsequent Trials," the tribunal's judgment speaks of "convincing evidence in the record that certain band units in both Yugoslavia and Greece complied with the requirements of international law entitling them to the status of a lawful belligerent [and POW status, if captured]." The judgment provides no specifics, however. *Trials of War Criminals before the Nuernberg Military Tribunals*, Vol. XI (Washington, DC: GPO, 1950), 1244.

[22] U.S. Dept. of the Army Field Manual FM 27-10, *The Law of Land Warfare* (Washington, DC: GPO, 1956), para. 85, at 35.

[23] United Kingdom, *Manual of the Law of Armed Conflict*, supra, para. 8.32.1, at 156, repeating 1977 Additional Protocol I, Art. 41.3; see also, *UK Manual*, para. 5.8.1, at 59.

survivors of the sinking as being in the area. For their own self-preservation, the accused said, the survivors of the sinking who were still in the water were killed by grenades and machine-gun fire from the sub. There were only three survivors of that attack. The sub's commander, *Kapitänleutnant* Heinz Eck, plus his second-in-command, and the ship's medical officer, and two crewmen, were convicted of the murders of the *hor de combat Peleus* survivors: the captain for unlawfully ordering them fired on, the others for carrying out the captain's patently unlawful order. Upon conviction and after legal review of the proceedings, the three officers were executed by a firing squad. The two enlisted men received lengthy sentences of imprisonment.[24]

15.3.2 *A Combatant Showing "an Intention to Surrender"*

As previously noted, combatants are not *hors de combat* merely because they are no longer capable of offering effective resistance. For example, if a military unit that is outnumbered and about to be overcome by a superior enemy force throws down their weapons and begins to run from the field of battle in disarray, they are no longer capable of offering effective resistance. But neither are they *hors de combat*. The principle of humanity notwithstanding, they may lawfully be targeted, shot in the back as they run away. The fleeing enemy, if allowed to escape, may later reform, rearm, and reappear to fight again.

The outgunned enemy's options are three: continue to engage their enemy, or make a clear indication of surrender,[25] or risk their lives by fleeing under enemy fire. "Surrender is not inferred for the mere fact of defencelessness."[26] The nongovernmental organization, Human Rights Watch, confirms that, "international humanitarian law does not prohibit soldiers from killing enemy combatants – even if the opposing fighters are in retreat – so long as they are not wounded, captured or otherwise out of combat (*hors de combat*)."[27]

However, in either international or noninternational armed conflicts, if at any point a clear indication of surrender is made, the attacking force must cease fire and respect the surrender. "In land warfare, surrender is not bound by strict formalities."[28] "[A] clear indication to surrender is generally shown by laying down one's weapons and raising one's hands. Other indications, such as emerging from one's position displaying a white flag, are mentioned in many military manuals."[29] An unconditional surrender may not be refused,[30] and upon surrender, the enemy fighter or enemy combatant is no longer a lawful target, of course.

Surrender also illustrates how quickly one's individual status may change: One minute a combatant is firing her weapon at the enemy; the next minute she is wounded by

---

[24] United Nations War Crimes Commission, *Law Reports of Trials of War Criminals*, Vol. I (London: UNWCC, 1947; William Hein reprint, 1997), 1–21.

[25] 1977 Additional Protocol I, Art. 41.2.(b).

[26] Henderson, *Contemporary Law of Targeting*, supra, note 7, at 85.

[27] Human Rights Watch, *Legal Issues Arising from the War in Afghanistan and Related Anti-Terrorism Efforts* (Oct. 2001), at 3.

[28] Sandoz, Swinarski, and Zimmermann, *Commentary on the Additional Protocols*, supra, note 5, para. 1618, at 486.

[29] Jean-Marie Henckaerts and Louise Doswald-Beck, *Customary International Humanitarian Law*. Vol. I. *Rules* (Cambridge: Cambridge University Press, 2005), Rule 47, at 168.

[30] Sandoz, Swinarski, and Zimmermann, *Commentary on the Additional Protocols*, supra, note 5, para. 1619, at 487.

enemy fire and is forced to surrender, becoming both *hors de combat* and, in an international armed conflict, a prisoner of war, a substatus of combatant. In a noninternational armed conflict, surrendering enemy fighters or government forces become detainees and protected persons.

15.3.3 A Combatant "Incapable of Defending Himself"

A wounded combatant, or wounded enemy fighter, even if grievously wounded, is not always incapacitated and *hors de combat*. Numerous posthumous Victoria Cross and Medal of Honor citations recount the valorous actions of dying war fighters who continued the fight to their last breaths. A dying enemy may kill an opponent as readily as one who is unscathed. Veteran combatants will counsel caution when approaching a wounded but still-living enemy. Such caution is wise, but killing the wounded out of a misguided impulse to "take no chances" would be a grave breach of LOAC/IHL (Chapter 8.5.10). Equally unlawful is delivering a *coup de grâce* shot because the shooter had heard that dying enemy fighters sometimes detonate explosives as an opponent approaches to render aid. Eugene Sledge, a World War II Marine, wrote that during the battle for Okinawa, corpsmen (medics, in U.S. Army units) "learned to be extremely wary of treating wounded Japanese, who 'invariably exploded grenades when approached ... killing their enemies along with themselves.'"[31] If one approaches a fatally wounded enemy fighter, however, and he reaches for a grenade or other weapon, the wounded enemy may lawfully be immediately killed in self-defense.

In combat, how is a infantryman to know what the movement of a wounded enemy portends? Is he reaching for a weapon, or is it the twitching muscle of a dying man? If the soldier shoots and kills a wounded enemy who upon inspection turns out to be unarmed, and a wrongful use of force investigation results, by what standard will the soldier be judged?

In U.S. practice, guidelines for wrongful use of force investigators are found in military orders such as the Standing Rules of Engagement, and in established military practice. U.S. "military members may exercise individual self-defense in response to a hostile act or demonstrated hostile intent."[32] (A hostile act is an "attack or other use of force against ... US forces."[33] Hostile intent is the "threat of imminent use of force.")[34] "All necessary means available and all appropriate actions may be used in self-defense."[35] Finally, the "use of force in self-defense should be sufficient to respond decisively to hostile acts or demonstrations of hostile intent. Such use of force may exceed the means and intensity of the hostile act or hostile intent, but the nature, duration and scope of force used should not exceed what is required."[36]

The mental element, or *mens rea*, required to condemn a use of force is not included in the Standing Rules of Engagement but has been determined through military practice. The standard an investigator should employ is derived from U.S. Supreme Court opinions involving use of force by police officers:

---

[31] Eugene B. Sledge, *With the Old Breed: At Peleliu and Okinawa* (Oxford: Oxford University Press, 1990), 118.

[32] Chairman of the Joint Chiefs of Staff Instruction 3121.01B, "Standing Rules of Engagement/Standing Rules For the Use of Force for US Forces," (June 13, 2005), Enclosure A, para. 3.a.

[33] Id., para. 3.e.   [34] Id., para. 3.f.   [35] Id., para. 4.a.   [36] Id., at para. 4.a.(3).

The decision to resort to deadly force is one of "objective reasonableness ... at the moment"[37] that decision is taken. "The question is whether the officer's actions are 'objectively reasonable' in light of the facts and circumstances confronting them, without regard to their underlying intent or motivation."[38] The calculus of reasonableness "must embody allowance for the fact that police officers are often forced to make split-second judgments – in circumstances that are tense, uncertain, and rapidly evolving – about the amount of force that is necessary in a particular situation."[39] If a police officer "reasonably believes that an individual poses a threat of serious physical harm ... to the officer or others," resort to deadly force is reasonable.[40]

When the young infantryman used deadly force, did he honestly and reasonably believe that the individual was a threat to him or his fellow combatants? If so, the second determination is whether it was reasonable for the shooter to have held that belief.

15.4 "Mercy Killings"

Two other combatant targeting situations, mercy killings and parachutists, follow, not because they frequently arise (they do not) but because they can be confusing and they are legally interesting.

There is no such thing as a lawful "mercy killing," whether on the streets of one's hometown in peacetime or on the battlefield. If a fellow combatant, or an enemy fighter, is incapacitated by wounds and is incapable of defending himself, and is in great pain, to "put him out of his misery" is a violation of the laws and customs of war, a grave breach if the victim is an enemy, and a violation of the military codes of most states. The 1863 Lieber Code warns, "Whoever intentionally inflicts additional wounds on an enemy already wholly disabled, or kills such an enemy, or who orders or encourages soldiers to do so, shall suffer death, if duly convicted, whether he belongs to the Army of the United States, or is an enemy captured after having committed his misdeed."[41]

Nevertheless, so-called mercy killings are not unknown on battlefields. Nearly a century ago, after the First World War, the British colonel Thomas E. Lawrence, also known as Lawrence of Arabia, wrote, "The Turks did not take Arab prisoners. Indeed, they used to kill them horribly; so in mercy, we were finishing those of our badly wounded who would have to be left helpless on abandoned ground."[42] A century ago a commander might have admitted to killing a subordinate without consequences, as Colonel Lawrence did. Today, a court-martial conviction would be the likely result of a purported mercy killing, as they were in the recent U.S. conflict in Afghanistan.[43] Although there have been calls to permit battlefield mercy killings of both friendly and

---

[37] *Graham v. Connor*, 490 U.S. 386, 397 (1989). This language is repeated in Chapter 12, Cases and Materials, "The Death of Mr. Esequiel Hernandez."

[38] Id.   [39] Id., at 397–8.   [40] *Tennessee v. Garner*, 471 U.S. 1, 11 (1985).

[41] *Instructions for the Government of Armies of the United States in the Field* (April 24, 1863), "the Lieber Code," Art. 71.

[42] T. E. Lawrence, *Seven Pillars of Wisdom: A Triumph* (New York: Anchor Books, 1991), 373.

[43] E.g., *United States v. Captain Rogelio Maynulet* 68 MJ 374 (CAAF, 2010); and Canadian soldier Michael Friscolanti, "Capt. Robert Semrau Dismissed from the Forces," *Maclean's* magazine (Canada), Oct. 5, 2010; and *U.S. v. SSgt. John L. Horne, Jr.* Unreported; pet. for rev. den., CAAF Daily Journal (Nov. 29, 2012).

enemy fighters,[44] the dangers of allowing untrained combatants the unreviewable power of deciding which of the wounded are likely to die or to live, particularly if decided in the heat of battle, are obvious.

Besides being contrary to military and domestic criminal codes, a mercy killing involving an enemy victim is a grave breach of Geneva Convention I, Article 12, and, for those states that have ratified it, a violation of Additional Protocol I, Article 41.1.[45] If involving a victim of one's own armed services, it constitutes the crime of murder.

15.5 Parachutists

There is another exception to the generalization that combatants may always be targeted. Since World War II it is an exception rarely encountered. It is also an exception to the rule that there is no legal obligation to give an enemy combatant an opportunity to surrender.

Persons parachuting from an aircraft in distress are parachutists, not to be confused with paratroopers, or airborne troops. Airborne troops are armed combatants entering a combat zone by parachute in order to close with the enemy. Airborne troops are targetable combatants from the moment they are recognized by the enemy on the ground and they may be fired upon while they are still descending,[46] just as the paratroopers, while still descending, may fire on enemy combatants and enemy fighters.

If airborne troops over contested battle space jump from an aircraft, the paratroopers are lawful targets as they descend and, of course, after they have landed. After the airborne troops have exited their aircraft, if the enemy shoots down the aircraft and its crew is forced to abandon the aircraft and parachute to safety, the crew are parachutists and they may *not* lawfully be targeted.[47] The parachutists can only hope that, in the heat of the moment, their enemy on the ground recalls the difference between paratroopers and parachutists.

If recognized as a parachutist, "upon reaching the ground in territory controlled by an adverse Party, a person who has parachuted from an aircraft in distress shall be given an opportunity to surrender before being made the object of attack, unless it is apparent that he is engaging in a hostile act."[48]

Parachutists are considered to be *hors de combat*.[49] Paratroopers are not. There is no other situation in which enemy combatants are required to pause before firing and give an opponent combatant an opportunity to surrender.

If the pilot of a fighter aircraft or an attack helicopter is shot down and parachutes from the aircraft, she is not a paratrooper but, like the crew of a transport aircraft, she is a parachutist, even though pilots in combat are customarily armed with a pistol. As she

---

[44] Colonel (Dr.) Steven Swann, "Euthanasia on the Battlefield," 152(11) *Military Medicine* (1987), 546; Dr. David L. Perry, "Battlefield Euthanasia: Should Mercy-Killings Be Allowed?" 44–4 *Parameters* (Winter 2014–15), 119.

[45] Geneva Convention I, Art. 12 is customary law applicable in NIACs. The United States does not consider AP I, Art. 41 to be customary law.

[46] 1977 Additional Protocol I, Art. 42.3.   [47] Id., Art. 42.1.   [48] Id., Art. 42.2

[49] Sandoz, Swinarski, and Zimmermann, *Commentary on the Additional Protocols*, supra, note 5, para. 1635, at 494. Henderson refers to it as "a qualified form of *hors de combat*." Henderson, *Contemporary Law of Targeting*, supra, note 7, at 85.

descends, if she is seen by the enemy to reach for her sidearm, that may be interpreted as "engaging in a hostile act" and she may be lawfully targeted.

How does a downed parachutist indicate surrender? The same way as an infantryman: by making a clear indication of surrender, such as raised hands or a white flag or cloth. There are no strict formalities. Such an indication can be made even before the parachutist has landed.

15.6 Lawful Civilian Human Targets

The general rule is that civilians may never be lawfully targeted (Additional Protocol I, Article 51.2; Additional Protocol II, Article 13.2.). But there are limited circumstances in which civilians may lose their protected status, particularly in noninternational armed conflicts. Combatants may defend themselves from civilians who are firing at them, and may target civilians who are directly participating in hostilities at the time they are targeted, and may fire on positively identified civilians who have a continuous combat function.

In an oft-quoted definition, "civilian" is defined in the negative. "A civilian is any person who does not belong to one of the categories of persons referred to in Article 4A (1); (2), (3) and (6) of the Third Convention." The article referred to describes combatants who, if captured, are entitled to POW status. If an individual is not eligible for POW status, and is not a combatant, he is a civilian. A more simple definition is used in International Criminal Tribunal for the Former Yugoslavia (ICTY) case law: **Civilians are "Persons who are not, or no longer, members of the armed forces."**[50]

"While the term non-combatant is not a defined term, it does have a popular meaning . . . [and] the term is now used to mean *any person* who is not a combatant."[51]

15.6.1 *Lawful Civilian Targets in Self-Defense*

In an international or noninternational armed conflict, if a civilian with a weapon approaches a combatant and suddenly points it at the combatant, it is understood that a combatant thus confronted may lawfully defend him- or herself, and fire on the civilian.

Combatants may always exercise self-defense, that is, employ defensive deadly force in response to a hostile act (an attack or other use of force) or upon a showing of hostile intent (the *threat* of an imminent use of force). The response may include all necessary means available.

In a noninternational armed conflict, a U.S. convoy of armored troop carriers, plus lightly armored wheeled vehicles, each filled with infantrymen, approaches a small town that is the mission's objective. On the way, the convoy passes through a village close to the target town. As the convoy speeds through the village the convoy commander sees a civilian on a rooftop. In the few seconds he is in view, the civilian points at the convoy while talking on a cell phone. The commander immediately knows the civilian is calling someone in the target town to inform them of the approaching convoy and its makeup. The civilian is helping to organize an ambush and the commander has seen it happen before.

---

[50] *Prosecutor v. Blaškić*, IT-95-14-T, Judgment (March 3, 2000), para. 180.
[51] Henderson, *Contemporary Law of Targeting*, supra, note 7, at 91.

May the convoy commander direct fire on the civilian in self-defense? No, because while experience tells him what the civilian may be doing, he cannot objectively "know" whom the civilian is calling or what he is saying. "Probably" cannot justify the use of deadly force. In terms of an investigator's standard, the convoy commander honestly believes it is a case of self-defense but, under the circumstances, it is not a legally reasonable belief.

In the same noninternational armed conflict, as German combatants patrol an Afghan town on foot they come under small-arms fire from ambush. They take cover and fire back . A team from the German patrol flanks the enemy position and engages them. As quickly as it started, the ambush ends and the enemy fighters dart away and escape.

This illustrates combatants killing civilian enemy fighters who are unprivileged belligerents, in self-defense. The rules of engagement of every state's armed forces permit combatants to defend themselves when under enemy fire, without regard to the individual status of those firing on them.

SIDEBAR. In Iraq, U.S. Lieutenant General Daniel Bolger commanded the 1_{st} Cavalry Division. He relates the difficulties of distinction in noninternational armed conflict: "Even face-to-face encounters had moments when separating friend from foe got very tricky. A foot patrol ... in pursuit of a Taliban shooter, halted to allow the passage of women and children. Two of the 'women' lifted their head-to-toe burqas, produced AK-47s, and clipped [shot] two American soldiers. The Americans killed the disguised opponents. The Taliban, of course, put out the word that the infidels had slaughtered a pair of women. Guerrilla warfare thrives on such incidents."[52]

Were the two women shot in self-defense, or were they killed while directly participating in hostilities? (Does the distinction really matter?)

15.6.2 Lawful Civilian Targets Directly Participating in Hostilities

The civilian fighters in the preceding incident permitted a lawful responsive use of deadly force in self-defense. The civilian fighters *also* were unprivileged belligerents directly participating in hostilities.[53]

Professor Dinstein writes, "When persons belonging to one of the categories selected for special protection – for instance, women and children – take an active part in hostilities, no immunity from an ordinary attack can be invoked."[54] As Additional Protocol I specifies, civilians are not lawful targets "unless and for such time as they take a direct part in hostilities."[55] The lawfulness of their killing, then, turns on interpretation of the phrase "direct participation in hostilities." It is usually agreed that a civilian driver delivering ammunition to combatants, and a civilian gathering military intelligence in enemy-controlled territory, are both actively participating in hostilities. Is a civilian POW camp guard directly participating in hostilities? A civil defense worker who directs military traffic through his town? Is a civilian, seated in the Pentagon, controlling an armed drone over an international armed conflict battlefield directly participating in

---

[52] Daniel P. Bolger, *Why We Lost* (New York: Houghton Mifflin Harcourt, 2014), 313.
[53] Additional Protocol II, Art. 13.3; Additional Protocol I, Art. 51.3.
[54] Dinstein, *Conduct of Hostilities*, supra, at 150.   [55] 1977 Additional Protocol I, Art. 51.3.

hostilities?[*] The United States authorizes the arming of civilian defense contractors in combat zones, and they "may be authorized to provide security services."[56] Are they directly participating?

Civilians are protected unless and *for such time* as they take a direct part in hostilities. Civilians who take a direct part in hostilities "do not have the right to prisoner-of-war status."[57] By virtue of their positions, civilians who lead terrorist armed opposition groups seldom, if ever, literally pick up arms. In essence, however, commanders never lay down their arms. That is the position of the ICRC's interpretive guidance.[58] General Kenneth Watkin, former Judge Advocate general of Canada's armed forces, rightly says, "It is not just the fighters with weapons in their hands that pose a threat."[59]

Was Yehiya Ayash, a civilian and the chief bomb maker of Hamas, known as "The Engineer," who constructed bombs but led no combatants, who gave no orders, who acted only as a fabricator of tools of the anti-Israeli insurgency, a lawful target only when he was actually constructing a bomb? Two hundred years ago, Vattel wrote, "Assassins and incendiaries by profession, are not only guilty in respect of the particular victims of their violences, but likewise of the state to which they are declared enemies. All nations have a right to join in punishing, suppressing, and even exterminating these savages."[60] Contrary to Vattel, the ICRC, in its *Interpretive Guidance on the Notion of Direct Participation in Hostilities*, opines that "the assembly and storing of an improvised explosive device (IED) ... unlike the planting and detonation of that device, do not cause" the direct harm required to constitute direct participation in hostilities.[61] That assessment is disagreed with by combatant commanders and many LOAC commentators.

Is mere membership in al Qaeda sufficient to make one a target, wherever the member may be found? Given traditional LOAC/IHL targeting predicates, and the ICRC's interpretive guidance, unless the individual has a continuous combat function, which goes beyond mere membership, the answer is no. Is there a common Article 3 armed conflict in progress? If so, whether the al Qaeda member is directly participating in the conflict with a continuous combat function or as a spontaneous act, he may be targeted in self-defense. His direct participation is the key. (Although "direct participation" is a construct raised in Additional Protocol I relating to international conflicts, it remains instructive in noninternational contexts by analogy.)[62]

---

[*] In April 2007, the U.S. Department of Defense and the air force reportedly decided that UAV pilots could qualify for award of the Distinguished Flying Cross. Joel Garreau, "Bots on the Ground," *Wash. Post*, May 6, 2007, D1.

[56] Dept. of Defense Instruction 3020.41 (Dec. 20, 2011), "Operational Contract Support," Enclosure 2, para. 4.e. (2) (a).

[57] Henckaerts and Doswald-Beck, *Customary International Humanitarian Law*. Vol. I. *Rules*, supra, note 29, Rule 106, at 384.

[58] ICRC, "Interpretive Guidance on the Notion of Direct Participation in Hostilities under International Humanitarian Law," 90/872 *Int'l Rev. of the Red Cross* (Dec. 2008), 991, 1043.

[59] Brig.Gen. Kenneth Watkin, "Humans in the Cross-Hairs: Targeting and Assassination in Contemporary Armed Conflict," in David Wippman and Matthew Evangelista, eds., *New Wars, New Laws? Applying the Laws of War in 21st Century Conflicts* (Ardsley, NY: Transnational, 2005), 137, 147.

[60] Vattel, *The Law of Nations, or, Principles of the Law of Nature* (Northampton, MA: Thomas M. Pomroy for S. & E. Butler, 1805), 327. Spelling rendered contemporary.

[61] ICRC, "Interpretive Guidance," supra, note 58, at 1022.

[62] "The application of IHL to noninternational conflicts, and the conflict with Al Qaeda in particular, is often an exercise in analogical or deductive reasoning. One reason to examine the rules that apply in international conflict is their use as an analogy." Ryan Goodman, "Editorial Comment: The Detention of

In a noninternational armed conflict, three civilians are seen burying an improvised explosive device on a road leading to a military headquarters. By their actions they are directly participating in hostilities. The three requirements for direct participation are satisfied: Their act will likely kill, wound, or cause destruction of objects; there is a direct causal link between their act and the harm likely to result; and their act is designed to directly cause that required threshold of harm.[63] Opposing lawful combatants may target the three civilians as they dig.

During a noninternational armed conflict, a civilian works in a defense factory in the enemy state. The civilian is the lead technician on a highly effective new sniper rifle scope. May that civilian lawfully be targeted and killed because his expertise in producing a critical weapons system constitutes direct participation in hostilities? Are his actions instrumental in manufacturing a sniper scope that is likely to kill, wound, or cause destruction of objects? Is there a direct causal link between his uniquely skilled actions and the harm that is likely to result? Are his actions specifically designed to cause the required threshold of harm in support of the enemy state and to the detriment of your state? Is he therefore a lawful civilian target?[64]

Finally, in a world where the enemy also has missiles, "the United States and countries that follow its [continuous combat function targeting] example must be prepared to accept the exploitation of the new policy by adversaries who will not abide by the standards of proof or evidential certainty adhered to by Western democracies."[65]

15.6.2.1 A Legal Duty to Wound, Rather than Kill, Capture Rather than Wound?

As to civilians who are directly participating in hostilities, there is no duty to capture rather than wound, or to wound rather than kill. Some will disagree. Indeed, after six years of meetings of forty international experts who laid the groundwork for the ICRC's *Interpretive Guidance on the Notion of Direct Participation in Hostilities*, disagreement on this issue caused some ICRC experts to disavow the *Guidance*.[66] "This discussion ...

   Civilians in Armed Conflict," 103–1 *AJIL* (Jan. 2009), 48, 50. Concurring: LTC William Johnson, ed., *Operational Law Handbook, 2014* (Charlottesville VA: The Judge Advocate General's Center & School, 2014), 73.

[63] ICRC/Nils Melzer, *Interpretive Guidance on the Notion of Direct Participation in Hostilities under International Humanitarian Law* (Geneva: ICRC, 2009), 46. The factors mentioned are the ICRC's three criteria for direct participation in hostilities.

[64] The arguable answer: no. The individual is not a member of an armed opposition group, so he is unlikely to have a continuous combat function. If, through his work on the scope's optical system, he is directly participating in hostilities, he may be targeted and killed for so long as he is actually doing that work. His work, however, appears too attenuated from the armed conflict to constitute direct participation. "For a specific act to qualify as 'direct' ... participation in hostilities there must be a sufficiently close causal relation between the act and the resulting harm. ... Examples of indirect participation include scientific research and design, as well as production and transport of weapons and equipment." ICRC, "Interpretive Guidance," supra, note 58, at 1021–2.

[65] Kristen Eichensehr, "On the Offensive: Assassination Policy under International Law," 25(3) *Harvard Int'l Rev.* (Fall 2003), 1149.

[66] Papers by two American ICRC experts detailing their several disagreements with the final version of the *Guidance* are: Michael N. Schmitt, "The Interpretive Guidance on the Notion of Direct Participation in Hostilities: A Critical Analysis," 1 *Harvard Nat'l Security J.* (May 2010), 5; and, W. Hays Parks, "Part IX of the ICRC 'Direct Participation in Hostilities' Study: No Mandate, No Expertise, and Legally Incorrect," 42 *N.Y.U. J. Int'l L. & Pol.* (2010), 769.

highlighted the difference of opinion between those who believe and those who do not believe the general principles of humanity and military necessity require – as a matter of law – restraint in the kind and degree of force permissible when attacking civilians who are directly participating in hostilities."[67]

In the *Guidance*, the ICRC asserts, as do others, that, "the ... force which is permissible against persons [directly participating in hostilities] must not exceed what is actually necessary to accomplish a legitimate military purpose."[68] That is, combatants must employ the least amount of force necessary to force the persons to cease their direct participation.

That position is not in accord with LOAC/IHL. There is no legal obligation in LOAC/IHL to capture rather than kill, or to give an opportunity to surrender before an attack, or to employ the *Guidance*'s law enforcement paradigm.[69] To the contrary.

> Conventional and customary IHL does not expressly restrict the kind and degree of force that can be applied against an individualized target so long as the attack is otherwise lawful under IHL. ... The Geneva Conventions of 1949, the Additional Protocols of 1977, and customary international law [all] expressly remove the protections against attack from civilians who directly participate in hostilities. In law of war terms, these civilians become legitimate military objectives.[70]

As the basis for its restrictive capture-wound-kill position, the *Guidance* asserts that "in the absence of express regulation, the kind and degree of force permissible in attacks against legitimate military targets should be determined, first of all, based on the fundamental principles of military necessity and humanity, which underlie and inform the entire framework of IHL."[71] That assertion is flawed because "before turning to the general principles underlying IHL to inform the law, the written law must lack clarity. In other words, there must be a genuine need to interpret the law, such as an unforeseen case or vagueness in the law ... not merely a desire to do so."[72] There is no vagueness or lack of clarity in the law of war regarding the lethal targeting of civilians who are directly participating in hostilities.

The ICRC's own customary law study, in Rule 6, concludes that "State practice establishes ... as a norm of customary international law applicable in both international and non-international armed conflicts [that] civilians are protected against attack unless and for such time as they take direct part in hostilities."[73] When civilians directly participate, they "become legitimate military targets."[74]

---

[67] Major Richard S. Taylor, "The Capture versus Kill Debate: Is the Principle of Humanity Now Part of the Targeting Analysis When Attacking Civilians Who Are Directly Participating in Hostilities?" *Army Lawyer* (June 2010), 103.

[68] ICRC/Melzer, *Interpretive Guidance on the Notion of Direct Participation in Hostilities*, supra, note 58, at 77. This view follows ICRC authority Jean Pictet's statement that a combatant "capture[s] rather than wounds, and wounds rather than death." Pictet, *Humanitarian Law and the Protection of War Victims* (Leyden, Netherlands: Henry Dunant Institute, 1975), 32.

[69] Taylor, "Capture versus Kill Debate," supra. Additional Protocol I, Art. 42.2 does require that parachutists be given an opportunity to surrender before they may be fired upon, the sole such exception in LOAC/IHL.

[70] Id., at 105.

[71] ICRC/Melzer, *Interpretive Guidance on the Notion of Direct Participation*, supra, note 58, at 78.

[72] Taylor, "Capture versus Kill Debate," supra, note 69, at 107.

[73] Henckaerts and Doswald-Beck, *Customary International Humanitarian Law*, supra, note 29, Rule 6, at 19–20.

[74] Id., at 19.

In agreement, the ICRC's *Commentary on the Additional Protocols* says that a civilian who takes a direct part in hostilities "becomes a legitimate target, though only for so long as he takes part in hostilities."[75] The *Commentary* on Article 13.3 of Protocol II repeats that statement.[76] The law of war and customary law are in agreement, and they are clear: There is no limitation on the kind or degree of force applicable when attacking civilians who are directly participating in hostilities; they may be targeted and killed just as other opposing unlawful combatants may be.

"By taking the position that the principle of humanity now mandates consideration of the kind and degree of force used in an attack as part of the traditional targeting analysis, the ICRC is in effect attempting to legislate in an area in which states have not consented to be encumbered by additional restraints."[77]

15.6.3 *Lawful Civilian Targets Who Have a Continuous Combat Function*

As detailed earlier (Chapter 6.4.3), the term "continuous combat function" was coined in 2008, having arisen in multiyear (2003–8) meetings of LOAC/IHL experts convened by the ICRC. (Cases and Materials, this chapter) The concept of unprivileged belligerents' having a continuous combat function was seen as a reasonable solution to the issue of the "revolving door" individual status raised by Additional Protocol I's Article 51.3: Civilians who directly participate in hostilities may be targeted and killed only *for so long as* they are directly participating. "For so long as" created a revolving door that allowed unlawful civilian fighters temporarily to cease their direct participation and, upon ceasing, again become protected civilians; then, when convenient, they again take up arms and directly participate in hostilities in a repetitive revolving-door-like fashion. Instead, organized armed groups and their constituent members constitute the armed forces of a non-state party to a noninternational armed conflict. The decisive criterion for individual membership in an organized armed group is whether a person performs a continuous function for the group involving his or her direct participation in hostilities.[78] (Continuous combat function differentiates the civilian who takes a fleeting one-time direct part in hostilities from the civilian whose full-time employment, as it were, is armed conflict. It is a significant evolution in interpreting LOAC.)

"Continuous combat function requires lasting integration into an organized armed group acting as the armed forces of a non-State party to an armed conflict. Thus, individuals whose continuous function involves the preparation, execution, or command of acts or operations amounting to direct participation in hostilities are assuming a continuous combat function."[79]

For an act to constitute direct participation in hostilities it must satisfy three cumulative criteria. First, it must be likely to adversely affect the military operations or military capacity of a party to an armed conflict or, alternatively, inflict death, injury or destruction on persons or objects protected against direct attack. (i.e., the act must meet a threshold of harm.)

---

[75] Sandoz, Swinarski, and Zimmermann, *Commentary on the Additional Protocols*, supra, note 5, para. 1942, at 618.

[76] Id., para. 4787, at 1453.   [77] Taylor, "Capture versus Kill Debate," supra, note 67, at 111.

[78] Jelena Pejic, "Extraterritorial targeting by means of armed drones: Some legal implications," 96/893 *Int'l Rev. of the Red Cross* 67, 89-90 (Spring 2014).

[79] ICRC/Melzer, *Interpretive Guidance on the Notion of Direct Participation*, supra, note 58, at 34.

Second, there must be a direct causal link between the act and the harm likely to result either from that act, or from a coordinated military operation of which that act constitutes an integral part. (i.e., direct causation is required.) Third, the act must be specifically designed to directly cause the required threshold of harm in support of a party to the conflict and to the detriment of another. (i.e., there must be a belligerent nexus.)

Two scenarios: In a noninternational armed conflict, the commander of the local Taliban is positively identified through an intercepted GPS-located cell phone call. As the commander of the enemy armed opposition group, by his status alone, he has a continuous combat function.[80] Presuming no proportionality issue, he may lawfully be killed through attack by kinetic weapons or by ground units. If tactically reasonable to do so, he may be captured for interrogation.

In the same conflict, at a U.S. Army checkpoint, all cars are stopped and their occupants briefly questioned. An army sergeant takes a close look at one car's occupant. The occupant is secretly the operational leader of the district's al Qaeda network and the planner of numerous actions that have cost the lives of American combatants. He has long been considered to have a continuous combat function. He is on a Central Intelligence Agency (CIA) targeting list. Can the sergeant seize the individual?

Yes, he could be seized *if* the sergeant knew the individual had a continuous combat function. But he does not know that, and there is no practical way he could know. The soldier on the ground and in the daily fight has no way of knowing who does and who does not have a continuous combat function. That knowledge is held by a higher headquarters that has the authority to initiate nighttime raids and armed drone strikes against civilians confirmed to be enemy commanders, operational specialists and planners, all of whom have a continuous combat function.[81] But for lower-ranking U.S. combatants, designating a civilian enemy fighter as having continuing combat function has little relevance because the soldier on the street is unaware of the designation.

Note that the concept of continuous combat function does not enjoy either universal state practice or universal acceptance. "The creation of CCF category is, de facto, a status determination that is questionable given the specific treaty language that limits direct participation to 'for such time' as opposed to 'all the time'."[82] Several experts involved in the ICRC's formulation of the concept disagree with portions of it, believing it does not go far enough. They reasonably urge "that all members of organized armed groups (except for medical and religious personnel) are targetable at all times. Function in the group is irrelevant."[83]

> While there is widespread consensus that members of an organized armed group with a continuous combat function are susceptible to direct attack at any time, many experts ... take a broader approach by which all of the group's members may be targeted irrespective of their function. They argue that limiting attacks to members with a continuous combat function would create disequilibrium in the law because

---

[80] Id.

[81] Id., "Individuals whose continuous function involves the preparation, execution, or command of acts or operations amounting to direct participation in hostilities are assuming a continuous combat function."

[82] Philip Alston, Special Rapporteur on extrajudicial, summary or arbitrary executions *Study on Targeted Killings*, Addendum, Report to the Human Rights Council, U.N. Document A/HRC/14/24/Add.6, May 28, 2010, para. 65.

[83] Schmitt, "Extraterritorial Lethal Targeting," supra, note 12, at 102.

members of the armed forces and other lawful combatants are targetable regardless of the role they play in the unit.[84]

Whether it goes far enough or not, the concept of a continuous combat function has utility and helps resolve the "revolving door" of direct participation in hostilities . Because of its ICTY provenance and sponsorship, the concept appears destined to become an accepted targeting criterion among states with the technological ability to implement it, and whose armed forces are engaged in conflicts against transnational nonstate terrorist groups. The United States and United Kingdom, among others, act on the basis of continuous combat function status, indicating their acceptance of the status. Eventually, state practice will speak for itself.

Civilians targeted as having a continuous combat function, or for directly participating in hostilities, or in self-defense, overlap, of course: When an enemy fighter who has a continuous combat function is directly participating in hostilities he will be fired on in self-defense. There is a degree of artificiality in addressing them as distinct categories. One should not be concerned if each group does not have the sharply defined edges that lawyers prefer. This is similar to domestic criminal law's speeding, shading into recklessness, shading into manslaughter.

15.6.4 *Collateral Damage*

In his 1863 code, Francis Lieber wrote, "Military necessity admits of all direct destruction of life or limb of *armed* enemies, and of other persons whose destruction is incidentally *unavoidable* in the armed contests of the war."[85] The ICRC customary law study recognizes collateral damage in its Rule 17.[86] Unintended deaths are recognized as inevitable in any armed conflict and not subject to sanction, as long as they are proportional to the immediate military advantage gained. Note that proportionality assessments of collateral damage are made in regard to the *anticipated* military advantage to be gained, not as to military advantage *actually* gained when examined after the engagement concludes. "The actual collateral damage caused and the military advantage that actually results are relevant to evaluating the reasonableness of the attacker's pre-attack proportionality assessment but are not dispositive of whether the attacker has satisfied the rule of proportionality."[87]

No treaty can numerically define acceptable collateral damage, but it is clear that, as long as it is not so excessive as to amount to a significant imbalance, its incidents are not LOAC/IHL violations.[88] The core principle of proportionality, as well as the prohibition of indiscriminate attacks, are "complemented by the principle of precaution in attack, which aims to prevent erroneous targeting and to avoid or, at least, minimize incidental harm to civilians."[89]

---

[84] Michael N. Schmitt and Eric W. Widmar, "'On Target': Precision and Balance in the Contemporary Law of Targeting," 7 no. 379 *J. of Nat'l Security L. & Pol.* (2014), 379, 387.

[85] Lieber Code, supra, note 41, at Art. 15. Emphases in original.

[86] Henckaerts and Doswald-Beck, *Customary International Humanitarian Law*, supra, note 29, at 56: "Each party to the conflict must take all feasible precautions in the choice of means and methods of warfare with a view to avoiding, and in any event to minimizing, incidental loss of civilian life."

[87] Michael N. Schmitt, "The Law of Cyber Targeting," 68–2 *Naval War College Review* (Spring 2015), 11, 26.

[88] Judge Advocate General's School, *Operational Law Handbook*, 2014, supra, note 62, at 13.

[89] Nils Melzer, *Targeted Killing in International Law* (Oxford: Oxford University Press, 2008), 363–4.

The rule [of proportionality] discussed here sets no absolute limits to the acceptable level of damage.... Under Article 51, para. 5 [(b)], AP I, the greatest permissible potential losses among the civilian population ... are measured in proportion to the extent of the anticipated military advantage. The greater the advantage, the greater the acceptable level of acceptable civilian casualties. ... Although the rule is silent on this point, it must be assumed that there is an upper limit to the extent of acceptable damage to the civilian sector.[90]

15.7 Civilian Heads of State

Different heads of state have differing levels of authority over the state's armed forces. Their authority is the distinguishing factor determining the lawfulness of their targeting.

Some states' political leaders are also the state's military leaders. Saddam Hussein, the deposed and deceased former Iraqi head of state, also commanded its armed forces. He often wore a military uniform and was armed with a sidearm. He decided strategic military issues and directed the deployment of the state's armed forces. In an armed conflict the lawfulness of the enemy's targeting this type of head of state is clear. Such heads of state are considered combatants and, in an international armed conflict, are lawful targets of opposing combatants.

Other states' political leaders are ceremonial commanders in chief. "Wearing military uniforms, carrying weapons, or using military rank suggest combatant status, but are not dispositive. The Queen of England wears a uniform and carries a ceremonial dagger during the 'trooping of the colours', but is hardly a combatant by virtue of doing so."[91] The queen (or king) makes no decisions regarding the United Kingdom's armed forces, leaving such matters to the prime minister and Parliament. "In practice, there is little concern about the ceremonial commanders-in-chief, as it is realized that they do not exercise military authority."[92] In international armed conflicts, civilian heads of state who exercise only ceremonial duties vis-à-vis the armed force are not lawful targets.

Another type of head of state are "the political leaders who are not members of the armed forces, who do not wear uniform, etc, but who do have substantive roles in the conduct of an armed conflict. ... These people are taking a direct part in hostilities by controlling and directing the use of the armed forces."[93] The president of the United States, for example, is the commander in chief of the U.S. Armed Forces and, by law, is advised on military matters by the chairman of the Joint Chiefs of Staff. The president appoints military officers to all positions of high military responsibility and, on occasion, dismisses them, as well. During armed conflicts, the U.S. president may set military strategy. Human Rights Watch agrees that "political leaders who are effectively commanders of a state's forces would be legitimate targets."[94] During an international armed conflict, the civilian president of the United States is a lawful target for an opposing combatant. He would not be a lawful target in a noninternational armed conflict because

---

[90] Dieter Fleck, ed., *The Handbook of International Humanitarian Law*, 2d ed. (Oxford: Oxford University Press, 2008), para. 509.11, at 250–1.

[91] Michael N. Schmitt, "Targeting and Humanitarian Law: Current Issues," 34 *Israel Yearbook on Human Rights*, (2004), 59, 74.

[92] Henderson, *Contemporary Law of Targeting*, supra, note 7, at 110.   [93] Id., at 111.

[94] Human Rights Watch, *Legal Issues Arising from the War in Afghanistan*, supra, note 27, at 7–8.

an opposing enemy fighter would not be a lawful combatant with the combatant's privilege.

Historically, "in international armed conflicts, attacks against heads of state who also serve as commanders-in-chief have been limited 'as a matter of comity'."[95]

SIDEBAR. First Lieutenant Dwight D. Eisenhower, United States Army, became a lawful target of German combatants on April 6, 1917, when the United States entered the First World War against Germany. On November 11, 1918, that war ended. Major Eisenhower, although still a combatant because he remained in the army, was no longer a lawful target because there no longer was an armed conflict to which the United States was a party.

The United States declared war on Japan the day after the Pearl Harbor attack, December 8, and declared war on Nazi Germany on December 11, 1941. On those dates Lieutenant Colonel Eisenhower became a lawful target of Japanese and German combatants. On May 8 and August 15, 1945, the wars against German and Japan, respectively, ended. Four-star General Eisenhower, still a combatant, was no longer a lawful target.

On January 20, 1953, civilian Eisenhower became president of the United States and the lawful target of North Korean combatants, because the United States was a party to the Korean armed conflict, in progress since June 1950. With the signing of an armistice six months later, on July 27, 1953, President Eisenhower no longer was a lawful target.

On August 10, 1964, the Gulf of Tonkin Resolution effectively put the United States in the Vietnam War. Was five-star General of the Army (Retired) Dwight D. Eisenhower again a lawful target, this time of North Vietnamese combatants?[96]

15.8 The Geographic Limits of Civilian Targets

The "battlefield" is not defined in U.S. joint service doctrine. Nor is there an agreed upon international definition. Although not all commentators concur,[97] most agree that in international armed conflicts "international humanitarian law continues to apply in the whole territory of the warring States or, in the case of internal [non-international] armed conflicts, the whole territory under the control of a party, whether or not actual combat takes place there."[98] In other words, in any armed conflict, presuming the government controls the entire state, the battlefield *is* the entire state in which the conflict is occurring, whether or not there is actual fighting in the area being considered, *and* the entire state of each of the parties to the conflict.[99] "There is

---

[95] Sivakumaran, *Law of Non-International Armed Conflict*, supra, note 6, at 366, citing Dept. of the Army, Memorandum of Law, Executive Order 12333 and Assassination (Nov. 2, 1989), at fn. 12.

[96] He was not. Having retired from active service, he was a civilian, no longer an active member of the state's armed forces.

[97] Sivakumaran, *Law of Non-International Armed Conflict*, supra, note 6, at 250.

[98] Gaggioli, *Use of Armed Force in Armed Conflicts*, supra, note 1, at 5, citing *Prosecutor v. Tadić*, IT-94-1-AR72, Defense Motion for Interlocutory Appeal on Jurisdiction, para. 70 (2 Oct. 1995).

[99] Under this view, all of the United States is "the battlefield" when the United States is a party to an armed conflict.

no necessary correlation between the area where the actual fighting takes place and the geographical reach of the laws of war."[100]

During the noninternational armed conflict involving the United States in Afghanistan, enemy fighters affiliated with al Qaeda and the Taliban often attacked U.S. and allied combatants inside the borders of Afghanistan – the active battlefield – then retreated across the nearby Pakistan border – *not* the battlefield, because Pakistan was not a party to the armed conflict against the Taliban. Could pursuing U.S. combatants in Afghanistan lawfully follow the al Qaeda and Taliban enemy fighters who fired on them into their areas of shelter in Pakistan, away from the active battlefield? Or were they legally bound to stop at the border like a posse in a western movie? "Sorry, boys, that's the Rio Grande river and the other side of it ain't in our jurisdiction."

15.9 Justification for Transgressing a State's Borders to Engage the Enemy

In international law, what are lawful justifications for a state's disregarding another state's sovereignty and crossing its borders? There are at least four justifications: authorization from the United Nations Security Council, consent of the trespassed state, self-defense, and collective self-defense.

Why does legal justification for crossing a state's border matter? Because in noninternational armed conflicts involving transnational nonstate armed opposition groups, who usually are terrorists, often it is only by crossing an adjoining state's border that an attacked state can pursue and engage the unprivileged belligerents who first attacked them, thus defending the attacked state from future cross-border attacks.

15.9.1 *Authorization from the U.N. Security Council*

The United Nations may authorize a state to take action that includes crossing the border of another state. The existence of an ongoing armed conflict is not required for the United Nations to act.

> [If] the Security Council determines pursuant to Article 39 that a breach of the peace, act of aggression, or threat to the peace exists ... [it] may authorize the use of force to maintain or restore international peace and security pursuant to Article 42. ... In the eyes of the Security Council, international terrorism qualifies as a threat to international peace and security. It made exactly that finding the very day after the attacks of September 11th ... [i]n Resolution 1368. ... It did so again on 28 September in Resolution 1373.[101]

Twenty-nine days after al Qaeda's 9/11 attacks on America, on October 7, 2001, pursuant to Security Council Resolution 1368, the United States crossed Afghanistan's borders, initiating an international armed conflict.

---

[100] *Prosecutor v. Kunarac*, IT-96-23/1-A, Judgment, paras. 56–7 (June 12, 2002).
[101] Michael N. Schmitt, "Responding to Transnational Terrorism under the Jus ad Bellum: A Normative Framework," in Michael Schmitt and Jelena Pejic, eds. *International Law and Armed Conflict: Exploring the Faultlines* (Leiden: Martinus Nijhoff, 2007), 157, 159–60.

15.9.2 *Authorization by Consent of the Trespassed State*

A second justification for combatants' crossing a neighboring border is the consent of the trespassed state. Professor Antonio Cassesse sets five rules for consent:

> The principle *volenti non fit injuria* (an illegal act is no longer such if the party whose rights have been infringed previously consented thereto), [is] enshrined in State law, [and] is also acknowledged as valid by the international community in the area of armed force. ... First, the consent must be freely given. ... Second, it must be given by the lawful government. ... Third, it may not be given as a blanket authorization for the future.... Fourth, it may not validly legitimize the use of force against the territorial integrity or political independence of the consenting or requesting State. ... Fifth, consent cannot run counter to other principles of *jus cogens*.[102]

The Draft Articles on State Responsibility affirm that "valid consent by a State to the commission of a given act by another State precludes the wrongfulness of that act in relation to the former State to the extent that the act remains within the limits of that consent."[103] The lawfulness of a state's allowing other states to use force on their territory "was explicitly acknowledged by the International Court of Justice in the *Armed Activities* Case."[104]

"In some cases, the territorial state may, for domestic or international political reasons, wish to publicly distance itself from operations to which it has in fact consented."[105] For example, it is clear that the government of Pakistan, despite repeated public objections, secretly consented to future U.S. drone strikes and targeted killings within its borders from 2007 through 2011.[106] Since that secret but no less valid consent was given, there have been regime changes in Pakistan. It is doubtful that a similar agreement granting foreign armed forces border-crossing rights exists today.

15.9.3 *On Grounds of Collective Self-Defense*

Justification for a state's combatants to cross a neighboring state's border may rest on grounds of collective self-defense, a legal concept about which there is considerable international disagreement. "It is well known that there is comparatively little [state] practice on the use of force in collective self-defence; states have generally avoided direct and open military participation by their armed forces in conflicts between other states."[107] In addition to satisfaction of self-defense requirements, collective self-defense requires a prior treaty, agreement, or express request between the states proposing to join in future collective self-defense.[108] The prior treaty may relate to future attacks or specify an

---

[102] Antonio Cassese, *International Law*, 2d ed. (Oxford: Oxford University Press, 2005), 370–1.

[103] Draft Articles on Responsibility of States for Intentionally Wrongful Acts; Report of the International Law Commission, 53rd session (2001), Article 20.

[104] Yoram Dinstein, *War Aggression and Self-Defence*, 5th ed. (Cambridge: Cambridge University Press, 2011), 120–1, citing *Case Concerning Armed Activities on the Territory of the Congo* (Congo v. Uganda), [2005] *ICJ Rep.*168, 198–9.

[105] Schmitt, "Extraterritorial Lethal Targeting," supra, note 12, at 83.

[106] Greg Miller and Bob Woodward, "Secret Memos Reveal Explicit Nature of U.S., Pakistan Agreement on Drones," *Wash. Post.*, Oct. 24, 2013, A1.

[107] Christine Gray, *International Law and the Use of Force* (Oxford: Oxford University Press, 2000), 120.

[108] Cassese, *International Law*, supra, note 102, at 365–6.

imminent attack against a party to the agreement. A collective self-defense treaty or agreement, or request of one state to another to join in collective self-defense, must be made public, often by communicating the agreement to the United Nations.

Past instances of collective self-defense include those of the United States and Jordan, in 1958; the United Kingdom and Jordan in 1958; the United States and South Vietnam, 1961–75; the Soviet Union and Czechoslovakia, 1969; and France and Chad, 1983–4.[109]

A recent example of collective self-defense involved a September 20, 2014, letter from Iraq to the president of the United Nations Security Council, informing the council of an armed attack against it by the Islamic State in Syria, often referred to as "ISIS" or "ISIL," and requesting assistance. Three days later, the United States sent a letter to the Security Council, basing its imminent use of force against ISIS – in Syria – primarily on the right of collective self-defense to the benefit of Iraq. "The collective self-defense claim is construed as follows: The US and its allies use force in Syria at the request of Iraq to defend that State against the non-State armed attack carried out by the Islamic State against Iraq from Syrian soil."[110] The description of this exercise of collective self-defense, convoluted as it is, suggests its murky standing in international law and LOAC. That is because this 2014 collective self-defense (which did come to pass) involved the United States' defending Iraq through the use of force not in Iraq but in Syria. Instances of collective self-defense are not usually as conceptually complex. The legal outlines of the Iraqi-U.S. arrangement were not universally agreed upon, but, properly initiated, collective self-defense is generally seen as a valid basis for the use of force.

15.9.4 *On Grounds of Self-Defense*

A remaining justification for following enemy fighters – human targets – from an active battlefield into an adjoining state is self-defense.

Self-defense is authorized by United Nations Charter Article 51, which "has to be read in conjunction with Article 2(4) [which] promulgates the general obligation to refrain from the use of inter-State force. Article 51 introduces an exception to this norm by allowing Member States to employ force in self-defence in the event of an armed attack."[111] According to some states and commentators, particularly in the West, this includes armed attacks by nonstate actors, as well as attacks by states.[112]

"The essence of self-defence is self-help: under certain conditions set by international law, a State acting unilaterally . . . may respond with lawful force to unlawful force (or, according to some, to the imminent threat of unlawful force). The reliance on self-help, as a remedy available to States when their rights are violated, is and always has been one of the hallmarks of international law."[113]

---

[109] Gray, *International Law and the Use of Force*, supra, note 7, at 120.

[110] Claus Kreß, "The Fine Line between Collective Self-Defense and Intervention by Invitation: Reflections on the Use of Force against 'IS' in Syria," Just Security blog (17 Feb. 2015), justsecurity.org/ 20118/class-kreb-force-isil-syria/

[111] Id., at 189.

[112] The argument that, for purposes of self-defense, attacks can only be mounted by states, is now largely viewed by states and commentators as fallacious. See Ashley S. Deeks, "'Unwilling or Unable': Toward a Normative Framework for Extra-territorial Self-Defense, 52-3 *Virginia J. Int'l L.* 483, 492-93 (2012).

[113] Dinstein, *War Aggression and Self-Defence*, supra, at 187. In accord, Pejic, "Extraterritorial targeting," supra, note 104, at 71.

"States do not today challenge the view that actions by irregulars can constitute armed attack."[114] It is the U.S. view that a terrorist ambush of government combatants in Blueland, leading to the terrorists' subsequent retreat into nearby Grayland, is an armed attack. An armed attack, even if by a nonstate armed opposition group, need not be a large military operation; simply sending armed bands into the territory of another state may constitute an armed attack, the International Court of Justice has held.[115]

> The usual pattern would consist of an organized armed group or terrorists locating themselves in [Grayland] – without conniving with the [Grayland] Government ... emerging when the opportunity presents itself, for cross-border hit-and-run attacks against [Blueland] and then returning to [Grayland] for shelter. ... [Grayland] may actually be a dysfunctional "failed State". ... In any event, if self-defence is to be exercised by [Blueland] against the terrorists or the organized armed group, any forcible measures will have to take place "in the territory of a state where the attackers are headquartered or have taken refuge", i.e. [Grayland].[116]

The core principles of military necessity and proportionality apply to any exercise of self-defense.[117] For purposes of self-defense, necessity requires the invoking state establish that the armed attack was launched by a particular state, terrorist organization, or armed opposition group, and that it was an intentional event, not an accident or mistake. The proportionality standard of reasonableness applies, as well. A further requirement of immediacy mandates that there be no undue delay between the initial attack and the responsive self-defense.

If the state in which the retreating terrorists have taken refuge denies entry to pursuing government forces, or interposes armed forces to block entry, the exercise of self-defense becomes problematic. That is because "if the authorities of one State are required by international law to take appropriate acts in order to protect the interests of another State, and – while they have the means at their disposal to do so – completely fail to comply with their obligations, the inactive State bears international responsibility towards the other State. This is incontrovertible."[118] May Blueland, the state seeking to exercise its right of self-defense, do so in the face of armed confrontation with Grayland, the state in which the terrorists have sheltered? Only if the seeking state is willing to initiate an international armed conflict with the sheltering state.

With that thought, may ambushed Blueland combatants cross the border into Grayland to pursue and engage terrorist enemy fighters? Keep in mind that international debate and disagreement regarding this question are continuing. "Controversy surrounds cases of intrusion into other states in self-defense outside the context of an international conflict. ... The crux of the border crossing issue is whether the law of self-defense

---

[114] Gray, *International Law and the Use of Force*, supra, note 107, at 97. As suggested above, fn. 111, this widely-held view is not universally accepted. Also, what constitutes "imminence" continues to be argued by scholars and commentators.

[115] *Case Concerning Military and Paramilitary Activities in and against Nicaragua* (Merits) (*Nicaragua v. United States*), [1986] *ICJ Rep*. 14, at 103. In accord, *Advisory Opinion on the Legal Consequences on the Construction of a Wall in the Occupied Palestinian Territory*, [2004] ICJ Rep. 215 (Higgins, J., Separate Opinion).

[116] Dinstein, *War Aggression and Self-Defence*, supra, note 104, at 225–6.

[117] *Case Concerning Oil Platforms* (Iran v. United States) [2003] *ICJ Rep*., at 198.

[118] Dinstein, *War Aggression and Self-Defence*, supra, note 104, at 226–7.

extends to attacks by non-state groups that are not under a state's control."[119] Today, as previously mentioned, despite two International Court of Justice (ICJ) opinions,[120] the view that counterattacks may be launched only if the initial attack was launched by a state is largely dismissed. "[A] majority of scholars accept that a strict insistence on State imputability is no longer tenable."[121] Another commentator writes, "the [ICJ's] restrictive approach is increasingly out of touch with state practice."[122] A third adds, "State practice in the aftermath of the 9/11 attacks provides firm support for the existence of a right of self-defense against non-State actors, even if [they are] unrelated to any State."[123]

There is no *opino juris* to guide a response to the issue of self-defense against nonstate actors. But "international law must always be interpreted in light of the context to which it is being applied and with sensitivity to the underlying norm in question. In particular, as a form of self-help, self-defense has to be construed in a way that renders it meaningful; self-help must help."[124]

The state practice that does exist, as well as the international law concept of self-defense itself, suggests lawful bases for the exercise of self-defense, including crossing the border into Grayland to pursue nonstate enemy fighters wherever they may shelter in Grayland. "The essential feature of self-defense is its purpose of ending the illegal situation posed by the armed attack. A State may use the necessary counter-force to achieve that end, but no more than necessary under the circumstances."[125]

15.10 "Cross-Border" Counterattacks in Noninternational Armed Conflicts

During the armed conflict in Afghanistan, U.S. and allied forces crossing the borders of adjacent states to target nonstate transnational armed opposition groups and individual members of those groups assumed major legal significance; particularly with the rise of U.S. targeted killings by armed drones in Pakistan. The Taliban tactic of retreating from the Afghan battlefield into the rugged and uncontrolled Federally Administered Tribal Areas of Pakistan was sometimes met with pursuit by U.S. ground forces, if retreating Taliban fighters were close to the border. If the enemy was inside the tribal areas, drone strikes were the means of attack.

Common Article 3, in its first sentence, says, "In the case of armed conflict not of an international character occurring in the territory of one of the High Contracting Parties." That preamble indicates that a noninternational armed conflict must take place within the borders of a single state. As previously noted (Chapter 5.1.3), the plain meaning of the Article 3 phrase "occurring in the territory of one" state has come to be disregarded in

---

[119] Schmitt, "Extraterritorial Lethal Targeting," supra, note 103, at 85.
[120] ICJ, Wall Advisory Opinion, supra, at 136, para. 139; and: ICJ, *Democratic Republic of the Congo v. Uganda*, supra, note 104, at 116–220, paras. 132, 146, 147.
[121] Tom Ruys, *"Armed Attack" and Article 51 of the UN Charter* (Cambridge: Cambridge University Press, 2010), 487.
[122] Theresa Reinold, "State Weakness, Irregular Warfare, and the Right to Self-Defense Post 9/11" 105–2 *AJIL* (April 2011), 244, 261.
[123] Laurie R. Blank, "International Law and Cyber Threats from Non-State Actors," U.S. Naval War College, 89 *Int'l L. Studies* (2013), 406, 413.
[124] Schmitt, "Responding to Transnational Terrorism," supra, note 101, at 158, 174.
[125] Terry D. Gill, "The Temporal Dimension of Self-Defense: Anticipation, Pre-Emption, Prevention and Immediacy," in Schmitt and Pejic, *International Law and Armed Conflict*, supra, note 101, at 113, 124.

state practice. "In view of the recognition by the ICJ that the provisions of Article 3 emanate from general principles of law, namely 'elementary considerations of humanity', the territorial requirement of Article 3 can be regarded as obsolete."[126] The ICRC agrees: "Common Article 3 may nowadays be evolutively interpreted as a matter of treaty law to apply not only to non-international armed conflicts occurring wholly within the territory of a state but also to armed conflicts involving state and non-state parties initially *arising* in the territory of a state. . . . [A] NIAC will be governed by Common Article 3 as long as there is a 'hook' to a national territory."[127] Professor Schmitt adds, "It is not apparent why, for example, it should be lawful to target a Danish soldier in Copenhagen based on status alone, but not a member of the Taliban who had found his way to, say, a remote area of Turkmenistan."[128]

Since the 1977 additional protocols became effective, and particularly since 9/11, LOAC/IHL state practice has evolved, and a changed *opino juris* is developing: Today, there is more than one type of common Article 3 noninternational armed conflict. One of those types, **the "cross-border" variety of noninternational armed conflict, recognizes that "hostilities with a non-state party operating from the territory of a neighboring host state without that state's control or support" may edge into the territory of states adjoining an active battlefield.**[129] An example was the United States–al Qaeda/Taliban conflict in Afghanistan, which often crossed the border into neighboring Pakistan.

> There is but one conflict that is fought in two places. . . . In such a situation, what needs to be established is whether Al-Qaeda in its various locations – Afghanistan, the Arabian Peninsula, and the like – constitute different groups or whether they are parts of the same group. If it is the same group, then it is submitted that a single conflict exists, albeit the actor is located in different states, as there is a nexus between the violence in the different places.[130]

It may be argued that the United States–al Qaeda/Taliban conflict illustrated another variety of noninternational armed conflict, one closely related to the cross-border noninternational armed conflict: a "spillover" conflict. "Certain [noninternational armed conflicts] originating within the territory of a single state between government armed forces and one or more organized armed groups . . . 'spill over' into the territory of neighboring states."[131]

---

[126] Andreas Paulus and Mindia Vashakmadze, "Asymmetrical War and the Notion of Armed Conflict – a Tentative Conceptualization," 91/873 *Int'l Rev. of the Red Cross* (March 2009), 95, 17, citing *Prosecutor v. Tadić*, Decision on Interlocutory Appeal, supra, note 98, at paras. 67 and 70; and, *Dem. Rep. Congo v. Uganda*, supra, note 104, Separate Opinion of Judge Sima, para. 23.

[127] Pejic, "The Protective Scope of Common Article 3, supra, note 15, at 204–5. Emphasis in original. In accord: Sivakumaran, *Law of Non-International Armed Conflict*, supra, note 6, at 229, citing the drafting history of common Art. 3.

[128] Michael N. Schmitt, "Charting the Legal Geography of Non-International Armed Conflict," 90 *Int'l L. Studies*, 1, U.S. Naval War College, 1, 11 (2014).

[129] Id., at 195. Emphasis added. Pejic, senior legal adviser in the ICRC's Geneva Legal Division, describes seven varieties of common Article 3 armed conflicts. In accord, ICRC, 31st International Conference: *International Humanitarian Law*, supra, note 6, at 9–10.

[130] Sivakumaran, *Law of Non-International Armed Conflict*, supra, note 6, at 233.

[131] Pejic, "Protective Scope of Common Article 3," supra, note 15, at 194.

The approach by which borders bound IHL has lost favor among States, scholars, and practitioners. In particular, there is a growing acceptance of the proposition that IHL applies to 'spillover' conflicts in which government armed forces penetrate the territory of a neighboring State in order to engage organized armed opposition groups operating in border areas. Indeed, the jurisdiction of the International Criminal Tribunal for Rwanda extends to "serious violations of international humanitarian law committed in the territory of Rwanda and Rwandan citizens responsible for such violations committed *in the territory of neighboring States.*"[132]

"While common Article 3 does not expressly provide for this scenario, there seems to be increasing acknowledgment by States and scholarly opinion that the applicability of IHL between the parties may be extended to the territory of an adjacent non-belligerent State."[133] This comports with Pictet's assessment that common Article 3 "should be applied as widely as possible."[134]

The narrow difference between a cross-border conflict and a spillover conflict seems to be that in a cross-border conflict the state in which the armed opposition group shelters, the "host" state, does not control or necessarily support the armed opposition group. In a spillover conflict, the sheltering state *does* control or support.

In both cases the result is the same: the conflict crosses over, or spills over, into the neighboring state and the armed forces initially attacked by nonstate fighters on an active battlefield pursue and attack the nonstate fighters in the neighboring state.

In both cases, this is a dangerous LOAC tactic. In a spillover or cross-border armed conflict, when the armed forces pursue and attack nonstate actors sheltering in a neighboring state, an international armed conflict may be the result on two bases. First, the pursuing armed force will be perilously close to employing armed force between itself and the state in which it is operating. Secondly, if the sheltering state is in overall control of the nonstate armed opposition group, an attack on the latter will be considered an attack on the former, resulting in a state versus state conflict.

Cross-border and spillover conflicts are far from universally accepted concepts in LOAC/IHL communities; nor are they a tactic that has risen to customary law status. "Both the application and the precise threshold for the lawful use of force in self-defence remain uncertain. ... It is arguably the case that a state that uses an armed drone in a cross-border operation, which has not been consented to by the state on whose territory the 'terrorist' is located, may only legitimately claim it was acting in self-defence if the threat or use of force against it amounts to an armed attack."[135]

On the other hand, both cross-border and spillover conflicts are apparently accepted by the ICRC. Recent history indicates that, besides being a logical LOAC approach to a difficult modern battlefield dilemma, they are the state practice of the United States and several of its allies, who are specially affected states. "The practice of specially affected states is especially important in developing international law because the extent and

---

[132] Schmitt, "Charting the Legal Geography of Non-International Armed Conflict," supra, note 128, at 11, citing Art. 1 of the ICTR Statute. (Emphasis supplied).

[133] Pejic, "Extraterritorial Targeting," supra, note 78, at 80.

[134] Jean Pictet, ed., *Commentary, I Geneva Convention* (Geneva: ICRC, 1952), Art. 3, p. 50.

[135] Stuart Casey-Maslen, "Pandora's Box? Drone Strikes under *Jus ad Bellum, Jus in Bello,* and International Human Rights Law," 94–886 *Int'l Rev. of the Red Cross* (Summer 2012), 597, 605.

depth of their experience provides a useful background against which to evaluate possible new rules."[136] (Additional discussion of cross-border attacks is in Chapter 5.2.1.)

15.10.1 *How Far over the Border Is Not the Issue*

Except for those adhering to the formerly traditional circumscribed definition of non-international armed conflicts (i.e., occurring in the territory of one state), a cross-border conflict may be a lawful basis for crossing a neighboring state's border in pursuit of enemy fighters as a lawful exercise of self-defense, if the state crossed into has failed to "fulfill its international obligation of 'vigilance', and fails 'in its specific duty not to tolerate the preparation in its territory of actions which are directed against a foreign government or might endanger the latter's security'."[137]

Presuming the lawfulness of a cross-border or spillover noninternational armed conflict, if pursuing combatants advance into a neighboring state that is not a party to the armed conflict, how far may they advance in pursuit of terrorist groups that have attacked them? A mile? Ten miles? As far as they wish? Or, under those circumstances does *any* advance into a neighboring state's territory, however slight, constitute an unlawful violation of sovereign territory? That question is debated but unanswered.

Abbottabad, Pakistan, where, in May 2011, U.S. Navy SEALs killed Osama Bin Laden, presumably without the knowledge or consent of the Pakistan government, is 120 miles inside Pakistan. LOAC justification offered by the United States was that "Bin Laden was the head of al Qaeda, the organization that conducted the attacks of September 11, 2001. And al Qaeda and bin Laden himself had continued to plot attacks against the United States.."[138] The U.S. Department of State's Legal Adviser added that "existence of an armed conflict between the United States and al Qaeda justified the use of force by the United States in the exercise of its inherent right to self-defense."[139] The location of the use of force within Pakistan went unmentioned.

As one academic frames the issue, "The law of non-international armed conflict extends to fighters who are located in the border regions of another state despite not being present in the territory in which the conflict is taking place. The applicable law does not suddenly cease when it reaches a territorial frontier, nor is it transformed into the law of international armed conflict when it crosses the border."[140]

15.10.2. *"Either Cannot or Will Not"*

Could Osama Bin Laden have been killed by Navy SEALs had he been identified while sitting at a sidewalk cafe in Paris, drinking espresso? Clearly, no. France has effective governmental processes of arrest, trial, and extradition, which the United States would request the French to employ. If the French captured him and refused a subsequent U.S.

---

[136] John B. Bellinger III and Vijay M. Padmanabhan, "Detention Operations in Contemporary Conflicts: Four Challenges For the Geneva Conventions and Other Existing Law," 105–2 *AJIL* (April 2011), 201, 243.

[137] Dinstein, *War Aggression and Self-Defence*, supra, note 104, at 227, citing R. Ago, "Fourth Report on State Responsibility," (1972) II *ILC Ybk* 71, at 120.

[138] White House Press Release, Press Briefing by Press Secretary Jay Carney (May 4, 2011), 105–3 *AJIL* (July 2011), 603–4.

[139] Id., at 604.   [140] Sivakumaran, *Law of Non-International Armed Conflict*, supra, note 6, at 251.

request to extradite him, unlikely as that would be, the United States could only abide by the French decision and allow France's governmental processes to work.

What if Bin Laden had been located and identified in Mogadishu, Somalia? In mid-2011, Somalia arguably had no *effective* state processes to capture or kill, try or extradite, Bin Laden. "An attacked State...should also evaluate whether the host State [in which the attacker shelters] is 'unwilling or unable' to deal with the non-State actor threat emanating from its territory. If that is the case, the use of force in self-defence would be lawful, provided the other criteria, such as proportionality, are satisfied."[141] Presuming that Somalia could not, or would not, control Bin Laden's unlawful activities, it is submitted that the United States could have lawfully sought to capture or kill him within Somalia as an exercise of national self-defense. In considering the issue, the question would be, had Somalia failed in its specific duty not to tolerate the preparation in its territory of terrorist actions that were directed against a foreign government or that might endanger a foreign government's security?

Did Pakistan, where Bin Laden was killed, have effective governmental processes to capture or kill, or try or extradite him? Pakistan did, but past experience indicated that its military and government authorities were highly unreliable partners in antiterrorist efforts.[142] Pakistan *could* have but, arguably, *would* not have controled the preparation in its territory of terrorist actions directed against a foreign government – the United States – or that presented an imminent threat to the foreign government's security.

The 1956 U.S. field manual *The Law of Land Warfare* reads, "Should the neutral State be unable, or fail for any reason, to prevent violations of its neutrality by the troops of one belligerent entering or passing through its territory, the other belligerent may be justified in attacking the enemy forces on this territory."[143] This is not settled law, however.

> This rule can be traced to, among others, the decision of the Greco-German Mixed Arbitral Tribunal [circa 1920] after the First World War, which had to deal with the German bombardment of Salonika. ... The Tribunal concluded that ... the occupation of Salonika was, as regards Germany, an illicit act which authorized her [Germany] to take, even on Greek territory, any acts of war for her defense. ... [In a similar incident] British naval vessels entered then neutral Norway's territorial waters in 1940 to liberate British prisoners on the *Altmark*, a German auxiliary vessel. ... As far back as the 18th century, Vattel had this to say: On the other hand, it is certain that if my neighbor offers a retreat to my enemies, when they have been defeated and are too weak to escape me, and allows them time to recover and to watch for an opportunity of making a fresh attack upon my territory ... (this is) inconsistent with neutrality. ... [These precedents]show general recognition of the need to provide a lawful and effective remedy to a belligerent harmed by its enemy's violations of a neutral's rights. ... [The UN Charter] changed the situation by imposing new and important limitations on the use of armed force. However, they are surely authority for the proposition that ... a belligerent may take action on a neutral's territory to prevent

---

[141] Pejic, "Extraterritorial targeting," supra, note 78, at 73, citing Deeks, "'Unwilling or Unable'," supra, at 495.

[142] Miller and Woodward, "Secret Memos Reveal Explicit Nature of U.S., Pakistan Agreement on Drones," supra: "Files describe tense meetings in which senior U.S. officials, including then–Secretary of State Hillary Rodham Clinton, confront their Pakistani counterparts with U.S. intelligence purporting to show Pakistan's ties to militant groups involved in attacks on American forces."

[143] Army Field Manual FM 27–10, *Law of Land Warfare*, supra, note 22, para. 520, at 185.

violation of another belligerent of the neutral's neutrality which the neutral cannot or will not prevent, provided such action is required in self-defense.[144]

In U.S. practice, the "cannot or will not" concept predates the U.S.–Vietnamese conflict (1965–73) and the concept retains vitality, though it is far from customary law. "Failure to comply with the obligation to police its territory opens the door for another Belligerent State's forces to cross into the Neutral State for the express and limited purpose of putting an end to its enemy's breach of neutrality. . . . It is irrelevant whether the Neutral State fails to fulfill its duty because it is unwilling to do so or simply incapable of taking the appropriate measures."[145] "If a host country permits the use of its territory as a staging area for terrorist attacks when it could shut those operations down, and refuses requests to take action, the host government cannot expect to insulate its territory against measures of self-defense."[146] Professor Yoram Dinstein refers to noninternational conflict cross-border attacks in self-defense as "extra-territorial law enforcement" (Chapter 5.2.1). Referring to the two involved states as "Arcadia" and "Utopia," Dinstein writes:

> Although acting beyond the limits of Arcadian consent Utopia – in taking these exceptional measures [of extraterritorial law enforcement] – does what Arcadia itself should have done, "had it possessed the means and disposition to perform its duty". The fundamental point to keep in mind is that the non-State actors confronted by Utopia cannot be regarded as Arcadian organs. Hence, in the relations between Utopia and Arcadia there is no armed conflict.[147]

Accepting the "cannot or will not" paradigm does not suggest a literal *global* war on terrorism, or suggest that the battlefield follows the terrorist fighter wherever he may go. To the contrary, it limits the use of force beyond states engaged in an armed conflict to those few nations where armed opposition groups, or their leaders, shelter and the sheltering state cannot or will not take action to stop their unlawful activities that threaten the security of other states. Even under human rights standards, lethal force is allowed if it is necessary to protect persons against the imminent threat of death or serious injury or to prevent the perpetration of a particularly serious crime involving grave threat to life.[148] Still, "cannot/will not" lacks *opino juris* or broad international support.

In 2011, these issues arose regarding Yemen, twenty-eight hundred miles away from the active Afghan battlefield, and certainly not a neighboring state of Afghanistan, where Anwar Al-Aulaqi was killed by a U.S. drone-fired missile.

15.11 Killing Anwar Al-Aulaqi

The targeted killing in Yemen, of the American citizen Anwar Al-Aulaqi, overlaid LOAC/IHL issues of self-defense and cross-border attacks with concerns involving U.S.

---

[144] John R. Stevenson (then–Legal Advisor, U.S. Dept. of State), "United States Military Action in Cambodia: Questions of International Law," in Richard A. Falk, ed., *The Vietnam War and International Law*, Vol. 3 (Princeton NJ: Princeton University Press, 1972) 23, 29–30.

[145] Schmitt, "Extraterritorial Lethal Targeting," supra, note 12, at 82.

[146] Ruth Wedgwood, "Responding to Terrorism: The Strikes against Bin Laden," 24 *Yale JIL* (1999), 559, 565.

[147] Dinstein, *War Aggression and Self-Defence*, supra, note 104, at 270, quoting C. C. Hyde, *International Law Chiefly as Interpreted and Applied by the United States*, 2d ed. (Boston: Little Brown, 1947), 240

[148] ICCPR, Article 6, Basic Principles on the Use of Force and Firearms by Law Enforcement Officials, adopted by the Eighth Congress on the Prevention of Crime and the Treatment of Offenders; Havana, Cuba (7 Sept. 1990), at Principle 9.

citizenship. On what basis was the use of deadly force exercised by the United States in a foreign state with which the U.S. was not at war, what was the legal basis of Al Aulaqi's killing, and what constitutional rights does a U.S. citizen who may be an enemy fighter have before being killed by U.S. combatants or CIA personnel?

"There is also a wide range of views and significant disagreement among lawyers, scholars and others regarding the applicability of IHL to the territory of a non-belligerent [and non-neighboring] State...Can...a person be targeted by a third State in the non-belligerent's territory?

> From a policy perspective, humanitarian law was never designed to prevent armed conflicts or to confine them territorially but, rather, to regulate them whenever and wherever they occur. From a legal perspective, the prevention and territorial confinement of armed conflicts are not a matter for humanitarian law, but for the UN Charter and the law of neutrality. ...What is decisive is not where hostile acts occur but whether, by their nexus to an armed conflict, they actually do represent "acts of war".[149]

The general U.S. rule is that the death of a soldier in a foreign uniform, on a battlefield, killed by a U.S. combatant does not raise due process concerns, even if the enemy killed was a U.S. citizen, since such a killing would not constitute government conduct that shocks the conscience,[150] and the use of force used against a U.S. citizen who engages in combat against U.S. forces is constitutionally permissible.[151]

In September 2011, Al-Aulaqi, a dual U.S.-Yemeni citizen born in New Mexico, was in Yemen in a vehicle with Samir Khan, also a U.S. citizen, when a U.S. missile hit their vehicle, killing both. Al-Aulaqi's father brought suit against the director of the CIA, claiming, *inter alia*, that the director and other officials had violated al-Aulaqi's Fifth Amendment rights by authorizing the drone strike that killed him.

From a LOAC/IHL standpoint there were two issues: Was Al-Aulaqi a legitimate target and was he targeted in a location in which the targeting of individuals was permitted by U.S. domestic law and the law of armed conflict? (As illustrated by Al-Aulaqi's case, it is the U.S. position that an individual's targetability turns on his status, not his location.)

Prior to the lawsuit, in a response to a senator's inquiry about the killing of Al Aulaqi, the U.S. attorney general wrote a letter outlining a series of plots against the United States that Al-Aulaqi had allegedly been involved in as instigator, accomplice, or co-conspirator.[152] Those actions, the attorney general wrote, gave Al-Aulaqi "an increasingly operational role"[153] in the terrorist armed opposition group Al Qaeda in the Arabian Peninsula. "It was al-Aulaqi's actions – and, in particular, his direct personal involvement in the continued planning and execution of terrorist attacks against the U.S. homeland – that ... led the United States to take action. ... Based on this information, high level

---

[149] Nils Melzer, *Human Rights Implications of the Usage of Drones and Unmanned Robots in Warfare*, Study, European Parliament, Directorate-General for External Policies, Policy Dept., May 2013, at 21. Available on line.

[150] *Sacramento v. Lewis*, 523 U.S. 833, 847 (1998).

[151] *Hamdi v. Rumsfeld*, 542 U.S. 507, 518 (2004) (plurality).

[152] Letter from Eric H. Holder, Jr., Attorney General of the United States, to Patrick J. Leahy, Senator (May 22, 2013). Available online.

[153] *Nasser Al-Aulaqi v. Leon C. Panetta, et al.*, Civil Action No. 12–1192 (RMC), U.S. Dist. Ct. for DC (4 April 2014), 6, available online.

officials appropriately concluded that al-Aulaqi posed a continuing and imminent threat of violent attack to the United States."[154]

Not included in the letter was that, in 2010, U.S. Joint Special Operations Command placed Al-Aulaqi on a "kill list" and attempted to kill him, and that the Department of the Treasury had designated him a specially designated global terrorist, finding him to be a key leader of AQAP.[155]

Accepting the accuracy of the information provided to the senator by the attorney general, does an individual's role as an operational leader of an enemy armed opposition group, involving participation in the planning and execution of actions likely to affect adversely the military operations of a party to the conflict, with a direct causal link between those acts and the harm likely to result, and those actions specifically designed to cause the required threshold of harm to another directly, make the individual a legitimate target? On the letter's facts, Al-Aulaqi fit the parameters of a leader of enemy fighters with a continuous combat function. For those states that have adopted the ICRC's concept, as the United States has, Al-Aulaqi was a lawful LOAC target.

The attorney general's letter did not mention continuous combat function but informed the senator that the United States had other targeting protocols it had followed:

> Such considerations allow for the use of lethal force in a foreign country against a U.S. citizen who is a senior operational leader of al-Qa'ida or its associated forces, and who is actively engaged in planning to kill Americans, in the following circumstances: (1) the U.S. government has determined, after a thorough and careful review, that the individual poses an imminent threat of violent attack against the United States; (2) capture is not feasible; and (3) the operation would be conducted in a manner consistent with applicable law of war principles.[156]

The attorney general's letter to the senator was dated one day prior to the announcement of U.S. policy standards regarding the use of force in counterterrorism operations outside the United States. They read, in pertinent part:

> Lethal force will be used only to prevent or stop attacks against U.S. persons and even then, only when capture is not feasible and no other reasonable alternatives exist to address the threat effectively. In particular, lethal force will be used outside areas of active hostilities only when [specified] preconditions are met. ... If the United States considers an operation against a terrorist identified as a U.S. person, the Department of Justice will conduct an additional legal analysis to ensure that such action may be conducted against the individual consistent with the Constitution and laws of the United States.[157]

In an April 2014 opinion, the Court of Appeals rejected Al-Aulaqi's father's charges. The Court's opinion recites a number of events indicating Al-Aulaqi was a terrorist who had directed or influenced a number of attacks, failed and successful, against America on behalf of AQAP. The attacks described included planning and supervising the failed

---

[154] Id., at 10.

[155] Dana Priest, "U.S. U.S. Military Teams, Intelligence Deeply Involved in Aiding Yemen on Strikes," *Wash. Post*, Jan. 27, 2010, A-1; and Id., *Al-Aulaqi v. Panetta*, at 5.

[156] *Al-Aulaqi v. Panetta*, supra, note 153, at fn. 13.

[157] The White House, "Fact Sheet: U.S. Policy Standards and Procedures for the Use of Force in Counterterrorism Operations outside the United States and Areas of Active Hostilities" (May 23, 2013).

attack of Umar Farouk Abdulmutallab, the 2009 Christmas Day "underwear bomber"; influencing the U.S. Army major Nidal Hasan, who, at Fort Hood, Texas, in 2009, murdered thirteen and wounded thirty; and in 2010, being involved in planning the flight of disguised explosive devices in two U.S.-bound cargo planes.

The Court found Al Aulaqi's Fourth and Fifth Amendment constitutional rights had not been violated. The case also raised issues of separation of powers, national security, and interference with military decisions. Citing Supreme Court holdings, the court held that the "Constitution contemplated that the Legislative Branch has plenary control over rights, duties, and responsibilities in the framework of the military establishment,"[158] and "courts "have traditionally been reluctant to intrude upon the authority of the Executive in military and national security affairs."[159] In answer to the second LOAC issue, the location of the targeting, the Court's opinion continued:

> Congress enacted the AUMF [2001 Authorization for Use of Military Force], authorizing the Executive to use necessary and appropriate military force against al-Qa'ida *and affiliated forces.* ... Further, the AUMF does not contain geographical limits. ... Thus, the fact that Anwar Al-Aulaqi was targeted in Yemen does not undermine the AUMF as the source of authority for the use of force against him. Further, the record is replete with evidence that Anwar Al Aulaqi was an AQAP leader. ... Anwar Al Aulaqi was an active and exceedingly dangerous enemy of the United States, irrespective of his distance, location, and citizenship. As evidenced by his participation in the Christmas Day attack, Anwar Al Aulaqi was able to persuade, direct, and wage war against the United States from his location in Yemen. ... Anwar Al Aulaqi's classification as a key AQAP leader to target by a drone strike raises fundamental questions regarding the conduct of armed conflict. The Constitution commits decision-making in this area to the President, as Commander in Chief, and to Congress.[160]

In April 2014, with that endorsement of targeted killing regardless of U.S. citizenship and in states not parties to the conflict, the U.S. Court of Appeals for the District of Columbia dismissed the complaint. It is unknown at this writing whether an appeal is contemplated. For now, the door to the targeted killing of enemy fighters of any citizenship, in states that cannot or will not meet their international obligation to not tolerate the preparation of terrorist actions directed against a foreign government, appears to be open with the imprimatur of a federal appellate court.

A year before the Court of Appeals case, President Obama said:

> We act against terrorists who pose a continuing and imminent threat to the American people, and when there are no other governments capable of effectively addressing the threat. ... But when a U.S. citizen goes abroad to wage war against America and is actively plotting to kill U.S. citizens, and when neither the United States nor our partners are in a position to capture him before he carries out a plot, his citizenship should no more serve as a shield than a sniper shooting down on an innocent crowd should be protected from a SWAT team.[161]

---

[158] *Chappell v. Wallace*, 462 U.S. 296, 301 (1983).   [159] *Dept. of the Navy v. Egan*, 484 U.S. 518, 530 (1988).
[160] *Al-Aulaqi v. Panetta*, supra, note 153, at 34–6. Emphasis in original.
[161] President Barack Obama, Address at the National Defense University, Washington D.C.: untitled (May 23, 2013). Available online.

The president uses the word "imminent," as did the attorney general Professor Yoram Dinstein has written of the term:

> Perhaps the most widely adduced adjective about an armed attack is that it has to be "imminent". .... However, imminence may mean different things to different people: either too little or too much. Hence, its usefulness is doubtful. There is no authoritative definition of imminence in the context of an armed attack. Yet it is noteworthy that, in its 1997 *Gabčikovo-Nagymaros Project* Judgment, the International Court of Justice addressed the issue of imminence ... [saying]: "'imminent' is synonymous with 'immediacy' or 'proximate' and goes far beyond the concept of 'possibility'. ... That does not exclude, in the view of the Court, that a 'peril' appearing in the long term might be held to be 'imminent' as soon as it is established ... that the realization of that peril, however far off it might be, is not thereby any less certain and inevitable."[162]

One should not confuse imminence with immediacy. Dinstein continues, "Surely, a far off peril cannot be deemed to be 'imminent'. Still, if an act is 'certain and inevitable', there is no doubt that it qualifies."[163]

A 2015 coda to the targeted killing of Al Aulaqi was the case of another American citizen, Mohanad Mahmoud al Farekh. Born in Texas, al Farekh was charged with conspiracy to provide material support for terrorism, a discredited military commission charge but a valid U.S. domestic charge (Chapter 21.7.4). According to the complaint and affidavit,[164] al Farekh, inspired in part by online lectures of Anwar Al-Aulaqi, traveled from the United States, through Karachi, to the Tribal Areas of Pakistan, where he received military training. Upon returning to Karachi, al Farekh was arrested by Pakistani security forces acting on U.S. intelligence information. After being held in Pakistan for several months he was transferred to the United States. In April 2015, in the federal Eastern District of New York, he was charged with conspiracy to provide material support for terrorism.

According to the *New York Times*, the Department of Defense and the CIA had urged al Farekh's targeted killing in Pakistan, but at the Department of Justice (DOJ) the attorney general was sceptical of the intelligence in his case. "Because he was an American citizen, we needed more information," said a former senior official. "Post-Awlaki, there was a lot of nervousness about this."[165] Indeed, the DOJ affidavit supporting the warrant application for al Farekh's arrest makes no assertion of a leadership position, or involvement in operational planning. Those differences from Al Aulaqi's involvement may have precluded the targeted killing of al Farekh and confirmed the targeting parameters employed in Al Aulaqi's case.

Al Farekh's arrest in Pakistan also supports the argument that the arrest of terrorist suspects abroad is sometimes possible without endangering U.S. combatants or civilians. The outcome of Al Farekh's trial remains to be seen.

---

[162] Dinstein, *War Aggression and Self-Defence*, supra, note 104, at 205, citing, *Case Concerning Gabčikovo-Nagymaros Project* (Hungry/Slovakia), Judgment, Merits, ICJ GL No 92, [1997]; ICJ Rep 7, [1997].

[163] Id.

[164] *United States v. Muhanad Al Farekh*, "Complaint and Affidavit in Support of Application for Arrest Warrant," U.S. Dist. Ct., EDNY, 8 Jan. 2015, available on-line.

[165] Mark Mazzetti and Eric Schmitt, "U.S. Considered Killing a Citizen Now Facing Trial," NY *Times*, April 13, 2015, A1.

15.12 Summary

All lawful human targets have not been discussed, but those most frequently encountered in armed conflicts have been outlined.

The two individual statuses encountered in international armed conflicts are "combatant" and "civilian." There are numerous subcategories of both statuses. Combatants (except retained personnel – doctors and clerics) are always lawful targets of opposing lawful combatants, an example of status-based targeting.

Since members of armed opposition groups, terrorists, and other unprivileged belligerents (so-called unlawful combatants) are civilians and not lawful combatants, they may not lawfully target opposing lawful combatants..

In noninternational armed conflicts, the two primary individual statuses are "government forces" (police forces and military units) and "enemy fighter." Enemy fighter is not a universal designation, and there are several synonyms, "unprivileged belligerent" and "unlawful combatant" among them. What matters is an understanding of their place in LOAC/IHL. When discussing noninternational armed conflicts, although "government forces" and "enemy fighters" are correct designations of the parties, international armed conflict terminology is often imported and employed because it is familiar and fairly indicates, even in noninternational armed conflicts, the rights and duties of the individuals being considered.

Combatants who are *not* targetable are those who become *hors de combat* (out of the fight) through disabling wounds or surrender. Being wounded does not necessarily render one *hors de combat*; being disabled by wounds does. Nor may surrender be presumed; to surrender an individual must make a clear indication of an intent to do so, unless so seriously wounded as to be unable to indicate surrender.

If a fatally wounded enemy, before dying, reaches for a weapon, the dying enemy may lawfully immediately be killed by an opposing lawful combatant. Should there be a question of the lawfulness of such a killing, the standard applied to the act is, did the shooter honestly and reasonably believe the victim represented a threat to the shooter or his fellow combatants?

Killing a badly wounded enemy fighter (or fellow combatant), no matter how grievous his wounds, and calling it a "mercy killing" will not legally excuse the act, which may be prosecuted as murder. As in domestic jurisdictions, combatants may not decide who is going to recover and who is going to die.

The basic rule remains that civilians may never purposely be targeted. Civilians directly participating in hostilities may lawfully be killed, however. In a noninternational armed conflict, for instance, combatants who come under fire from opposing enemy fighters – unprivileged belligerents – may return fire in self-defense. In U.S. practice, civilians having a continuous combat function, a status not yet accepted by all states, may be targeted as well, just as any other combatant.

In a noninternational armed conflict, if enemy fighters attack combatants of an opposing state, then retreat across a nearby state's border to escape and shelter, many if not most commentators agree that the attacked state's combatants may pursue and target the enemy fighters, and their fellow armed opposition group members, in the sheltering state in at least four circumstances: if the U.N. Security Council authorizes it, if the state in which the enemy fighters are sheltering consents to the attacked state's entry, and in the cases of self-defense and collective self-defense.

Noninternational armed conflicts no longer confine themselves to the territory of a single high contracting party, as described in the first sentence of common Article 3. Recognizing the realities of today's battlefields, several types of common Article 3 armed conflicts are currently recognized – not by all states or by all commentators, but apparently by the ICRC and many states that have fought nonstate terrorist groups since 9/11. One such type employed in the exercise of self-defense is the "cross-border" noninternational armed conflict, which recognizes that armed conflict with a nonstate party, often terrorists, may edge into the territory of states adjoining the active battlefield. Cross-border noninternational conflicts arguably provide a lawful basis for combatants of an attacked state to cross into a neighboring state to combat transnational nonstate terrorist groups who retreat and shelter in the neighboring state that cannot or will not control the unlawful activities of the terrorist group. This was frequently seen in the U.S. armed conflict in Afghanistan in opposition to Taliban and al Qaeda forces.

Another type is the similar "spillover" noninternational armed conflict, in which the government of the state in which the armed opposition group shelters, controls or supports the armed opposition group. The targeted killing of Osama Ben Laden was an incident in either a cross-border or spillover noninternational armed conflict in Pakistan, depending on whether one believes Pakistan did (spillover) or did not (cross-border) materially support al Qaeda fighters.

As all legal systems do, LOAC/IHL evolves to meet the realities of real-world events. As repeatedly mentioned, several of the concepts discussed in this chapter are not universally accepted and cannot even be said to represent widespread state practice. Students of LOAC/IHL should not be dismayed by this uncertainty in the law. Important changes in any system of laws are subject to debate and disagreement, which are healthy and necessary for LOAC, particularly, to evolve and remain vital and effective.

CASES AND MATERIALS

THE PUBLIC COMMITTEE AGAINST TORTURE IN ISRAEL V. THE GOVERNMENT OF ISRAEL

The Supreme Court Sitting as the High Court of Justice
[December 11, 2005]

Introduction: *In late 2005, Israel released a long-awaited opinion on targeted killing. In the wide-ranging opinion written by Judge Aharon Barak, the Israeli court wrestled with the same issues the ICRC's panel of experts would contend with in producing the 2009 Interpretive Guidance on the Notion of Direct Participation in Hostilities. Upon reading the Israeli court's opinion one is struck by the number of its views that are adopted in modified form by the ICRC's Interpretive Guidance. The Israeli court's effort to find a workable solution to the problem of civilian direct participation in hostilities, and the restricting language of Additional Protocol I, Article 51.3, are evident.*

Judgment (excerpted)

The Government of Israel employs a policy of preventative strikes which cause the death of terrorists in Judea, Samaria, or the Gaza Strip. It fatally strikes these terrorists, who plan, launch, or commit terrorist acts. . . . Strikes at times also harm innocent civilians. Does the State thus act illegally? That is the question posed before us.

2. The Petitioners' Arguments

5. Alternatively, petitioners claim that the targeted killings policy violates the rules of international laws applicable to the armed conflict between Israel and the Palestinians are the laws of war. These laws recognize only two statuses of people: combatants and civilians. Combatants are legitimate targets, but they also enjoy the rights granted in international law to combatants, including immunity from trial and the right to the status of prisoner of war. Civilians enjoy the protections and rights granted in international law to civilians during war. *Inter alia*, they are not a legitimate target for attack. . . .

6. Petitioners note that a civilian participating in combat might lose part of the protections granted to civilians at a time of combat; but that is so only when such a person takes a direct part in combat, and only for such time as that direct participation continues. . . .

8. Petitioners' stance is that the targeted killings policy, as employed in practice, violates the proportionality requirements which are part of Israeli law and customary international law. . . .

3. The Respondents' Response

10. . . . Respondents' stance is that the argument that Israel is permitted to defend herself only by means of law enforcement is to be rejected. It is no longer controversial that a state permitted to respond with military force to a terrorist attack against it. That is pursuant to the right of self-defense. . . . That is especially the case when dealing with wide scale acts of terrorism which continue for a long period of time. . . .

12. Alternatively, respondents position is that the targeted killings policy is legal even if the Court should reject the argument that terrorist organization members are combatants and party to the armed conflict, and even if they are seen as having the status of civilians. . . . However, a "civilian" who takes a direct paer in hostilities loses his immunity, and can be harmed. Thus, it is permissible to harm civilians in order to frustrate the intent to commit planned or future hostilities. Every person who takes a direct part in committing, planning, or launching hostilities directed against civilian or military targets is a legitimate target for attack. . . . Respondents' stance is that the simultaneity requirement determined in article 51(3) of *The First Protocol*, pursuant to which a civilian who takes a direct part in hostilities can be harmed only during such time that he is taking that direct part, does not obligate Israel, as it does not reflect a rule of customary international law. On this point respondents note that Israel, like other states, has not joined *The First Protocol*. Thus, harming civilians who take a direct part in hostilities is permitted even when they are not participating in the hostilities. . . . Thus, the term "hostilities" is to be interpreted as including acts such as the planning of terrorist attacks, launching of terrorists, and command of a terrorist ring. . . . In

addition, the term "direct part" should be given a wide interpretation, so that a person who plans, launches, or commits a terrorist attack is considered to be taking a direct part in hostilities. Finally, even the simultaneity condition should be interpreted widely, so that it is possible to strike at a terrorist at any time that he is systematically involved in terrorist acts. . . . It appears from the stance of petitioners . . . that terrorists are granted immunity from harm for the entire time that they plan terrorist attacks, and that this immunity is removed for only a most short time, at the time of the actual execution of the terrorist attack. After the execution of the terrorist attack the immunity once again applies to the terrorists, even if it is clearly known that they are returning to their homes to plan and execute the next terrorist attack. This interpretation allows those who take an active part in hostilities to "change their hat" at will, between the hat of a combatant and the hat of a civilian. That result is unacceptable. . . .

5. The General Normative Framework

25. The terrorists and their organizations, with which the State of Israel has an armed conflict of international character, do not fall into the category of combatants. They do not belong to the armed forces, and they do not belong to units to which international law grants status similar to that of combatants. Indeed, the terrorists and the organizations which send them to carry out attacks are unlawful combatants. They do not enjoy the status of prisoners of war. They can be tried for their participation in hostilities. . . .

26. Customary international law regarding armed conflicts protects "civilians" from harm as a result of the hostilities. . . . From that follows also the duty to do everything possible to minimize collateral damage to the civilian population during the attacks on "combatants". . . . The approach of customary international law is that "civilians" are those who are not "combatants". . . . It defines the concept of "civilian" as the opposite of "combatant". It thus views unlawful combatants – who, as we have seen, are not "combatants" – as civilians. Does that mean that the unlawful combatants are entitled to the same protection to which civilians who are not unlawful combatants are entitled? The answer is, no. Customary international law regarding armed conflicts determines that a civilian taking a direct part in hostilities does not, at such time, enjoy the protection granted to a civilian who is not taking a direct part in the hostilities. The result is that an unlawful combatant is not a combatant, rather a "civilian". However, he is a civilian who is not protected from attack as long as he is taking a direct part in hostilities. . . . Civilians who are unlawful combatants are legitimate targets for attack . . . provided that they are taking a direct part in hostilities at such time. Nor, as we have seen, do they enjoy the rights granted to combatants. Thus, for example, the law of prisoners of war does not apply to them.

27. The State asked us to recognize a third category of persons, that of unlawful combatants. . . .

28. . . . In our opinion, as far as existing law goes, the data before us are not sufficient to recognize this third category. The is the case according to the current state of international law, both international treaty law and customary international law. . . .

6. Civilians Who Are Unlawful Combatants

33. Civilians lose the protection of customary international law dealing with hostilities of international character if they "take . . . part in hostilities." What is the meaning of that

provision? The accepted view is that "hostilities" are acts which by nature and objective are intended to cause damage to the army. Thus determines *Commentary on the Additional Protocols* ... : "Hostile acts should be understood to be acts which by their nature and purpose are intended to cause actual harm to the personnel and equipment of the armed forces" (Y. Sandoz et al. *Commentary on the Additional Protocols* 618 (1987)). ... It seems that acts which by nature and objective are intended to cause damage to civilians should be added to that definition. According to the accepted definition, a civilian is taking part in hostilities when using weapons in an armed conflict, while gathering intelligence, or while preparing himself for the hostilities. Regarding taking part in hostilities, there is no condition that the civilian use his weapon, nor is there a condition that he bear arms (openly or concealed). It is possible to take part in hostilities without using weapons at all. *Commentary on the Additional Protocols* discussed that issue: "It seems that the word 'hostilities' covers not only the time that the civilian actually makes use of a weapon, but also, for example, the time that he is carrying it, as well as situations in which he undertakes hostile acts without using a weapon" (p. 618–9). ...

34. ... It seems accepted in the international literature that an agreed upon definition of the term "direct" in the context under discussion does not exist. On this issue, the following passage from *Commentary on the Additional Protocols* is worth quoting: "Undoubtedly there is some room here for some margin of judgment: to restrict this concept to combat and active military operations would be too narrow, while extending it to the entire war effort would be too broad, as in modern warfare the whole population participates in the war effort to some extent, albeit indirectly." (p. 516) Indeed, a civilian bearing arms (openly or concealed) who is on his way to the place where he will use them against the army, at such place, or on his way back from it, is a civilian taking "an active part" in the hostilities. ...

35. ... The following cases should also be included in the definition of taking a "direct part" in hostilities: a person who collects intelligence on the army ... a person who transports unlawful combatants to or from the place where the hostilities are taking place; a person who operates weapons which unlawful combatants use, or supervises their operation, or provides service to them, be the distance from the battlefield as it may. All those persons are performing the function of combatants. The function determines the directness of the part taken in hostilities. ... However, a person who sells food or medicine to an unlawful combatant is not taking a direct part. ... The same is the case regarding a person who aids the unlawful combatants by general strategic analysis, and grants them logistical, general support, including monetary aid. The same is the case regarding a person who distributes propaganda supporting those unlawful combatants. ...

36. What is the law regarding civilians serving as a "human shield" for terrorists taking a direct part in hostilities? Certainly, if they are doing so because they were forced to do so by terrorists, those innocent civilians are not to be seen as taking a direct part in hostilities ... However, if they do so of their own free will, out of support for the terrorist organization, they should be seen as persons taking a direct part in hostilities. ...

37. Is there a difference between his [a civilian taking a direct part in hostilities] direct commanders and those responsible for them? Is the "direct" part taken only by the last terrorist in the chain of command, or by the entire chain? In our opinion, the "direct"

character of the part taken should not be narrowed merely to the person committing the physical act of attack. Those who have sent him, as well, take "a direct part". The same goes for the person who decided upon the act, and the person who planned it. ...

39. With no consensus regarding the interpretation of the wording "for such time", there is no choice but to proceed from case to case. ... On the one hand, a civilian taking a direct part in hostilities one single time, or sporadically, who later detaches himself from that activity, is a civilian who, starting from the time he detached himself from that activity, is entitled to protection from attack. He is not to be attacked for the hostilities which he committed in the past. On the other hand, a civilian who has joined a terrorist organization which has become his "home", and in the framework of his role in that organization he commits a chain of hostilities, with short periods of rest between them, loses his immunity from attack "for such time" as he is committing the chain of acts. Indeed, regarding such a civilian, the rest between hostilities is nothing other than preparation for the next hostility. ...

40. These examples point out the dilemma which the "for such time" requirement presents before us. ... In the wide area between those two possibilities [sporadic or one-time direct participation and "revolving door" direct participation] one finds the "gray" cases, about which customary international law has not yet crystallized. There is thus no escaping examination of each and every case. ... The burden of proof on the attacking army is heavy. ... In the case of doubt, careful verification is needed before an attack is made. Henckaerts & Doswald-Beck [in the ICRC Customary Law study] made this point: "When there is a situation of doubt, a careful assessment has to be made under the conditions and restraints governing a particular situation as to whether there are sufficient indications to warrant an attack. One cannot automatically attack anyone who might appear dubious" (p. 24). Second, a civilian taking a direct part in hostilities cannot be attacked at such time as he is doing so, if a less harmful means can be employed. In our domestic law, that rule is called for by the principle of proportionality. ... Thus, if a terrorist taking a direct part in hostilities can be arrested, interrogated, and tried, those are the means which should be employed. ... Trial is preferable to use of force. ... Arrest, investigation, and trial are not means which can always be used. At times the possibility does not exist whatsoever; at times it involves a risk so great to the lives of the soldiers, that it is not required. ... Third, after an attack on a civilian suspected of taking an active part, at such time, in hostilities, a thorough investigation regarding the precision of the identification of the target and the circumstances of the attack upon him is to be performed (retroactively). That investigation must be independent. ... In appropriate cases it is appropriate to pay compensation as a result of harm caused to an innocent civilian. ...

7. Proportionality

45. The proportionality test determines that attack upon innocent civilians is not permitted if the collateral damage caused to them is not proportionate to the military advantage (in protecting combatants and civilians). ... That is a values based test. It is based upon a balancing between conflicting values and interests. ... As we have seen, this requirement of proportionality is employed in customary international law regarding protection of civilians. ...

46. That aspect of proportionality is not required regarding harm to a combatant, or to a civilian taking a direct part in hostilities. ... That killing is permitted. However, that proportionality is required in any case in which an innocent civilian is harmed. ...

Conclusion

63. The question is not whether it is possible to defend ourselves against terrorism. Of course it is possible to do so, and at times it is even a duty to do so. The question is how we respond. On that issue, a balance is needed between security needs and individual rights. That balancing casts a heavy load upon those whose job is to provide security. Not every efficient means is also legal. The ends do not justify the means. ...
Let it be so.

Conclusion: Is the Israeli court's decision persuasive? Agree or disagree, it is a laudable effort to thread the legal needle of direct participation in hostilities. Compare the court's views with the following ICRC Interpretive Guidance on the same subject, adopted by the Assembly of the International Committee of the Red Cross on February 26, 2009. Read the excerpts from the ICRC Guidance that follow and see whether you think the ICRC reaches the same destination the Israeli court sought to reach:

INTERPRETIVE GUIDANCE ON THE NOTION OF DIRECT PARTICIPATION IN HOSTILITIES UNDER INTERNATIONAL HUMANITARIAN LAW[166]

ICRC/Nils Melzer, Legal Adviser, ICRC

Introduction. It is ironic that the ICRC, dedicated to the protection of the victims of armed conflict, including civilians, has formulated a category of civilian who may be killed in either international or noninternational armed conflicts. The ICRC says, "[The Interpretive Guidance] represents the views of the ICRC as a neutral and independent humanitarian organization that has been mandated by States to promote IHL and work for a better understanding of the law. ... While the Interpretive Guidance is not legally binding, the ICRC hopes that it will be persuasive to States, non-State actors, practitioners and academics alike and that, ultimately, it will help better protect the civilian population from the dangers of warfare."[167]
From the Interpretive Guidance:

Foreword

... The Interpretive Guidance provides a legal reading of the notion of "direct participation in hostilities" with a view to strengthening the implementation of the principle of distinction. ...

First ... the positions enunciated are the ICRC's alone. Second, while reflecting the ICRC's views, the Interpretive Guidance is not and cannot be a text of a legally binding

---

[166] ICRC/Melzer, *Interpretive Guidance*, supra, note 58.
[167] ICRC Resource Center, "Direct Participation in Hostilities: Questions and Answers" (02-06-2009 FAC).

nature. ... Third, the Guidance does not purport to change the law, but provides an interpretation of the notion of direct participation in hostilities within existing parameters. ...

Today, more than ever, it is of utmost importance that all feasible measures be taken to prevent the exposure of the civilian population to erroneous or arbitrary targeting based, among other things, reliable guidance as to how the principle of distinction should be implemented.

A. The Concept of Civilian

I. The Concept of Civilian in International Armed Conflict

2. Armed Forces

a) Basic Concept
... While all members of irregular armed forces failing to fulfill the four requirements [for recognition as an armed force, and for POW status] may not be entitled to combatant privilege and prisoner-of-war status after capture, it does not follow that any such person must necessarily be excluded from the category of armed forces and regarded as a civilian for the purposes of the conduct of hostilities. On the contrary. ... Therefore ... all armed actors showing a sufficient degree of military organization and belonging to a party to the conflict must be regarded as part of the armed forces of that party. ...

b) Meaning and Significance of "Belonging to" a Party to the Conflict
In order for organized armed groups to qualify as armed forces under IHL, they must belong to a party to the conflict. ... This relationship may be officially declared, but may also be expressed through tacit agreement or conclusive behavior that makes clear for which party the group is fighting. ... In practice, in order for an organized armed group to belong to a party to the conflict, it appears essential that it conduct hostilities on behalf and with the agreement of that party. ...

c) Determination of Membership
For the regular armed forces of States, individual membership is generally regulated by domestic law and expressed through formal integration into permanent units distinguishable by uniforms, insignia, and equipment. ... Membership in irregular armed forces, such as militias, volunteer corps, or resistance movements belonging to a party to the conflict, generally is not regulated by domestic law and can only be reliably determined on the basis of functional criteria, such as those applying to organized armed groups in non-international armed conflict.

3. Organized Armed Groups

II. The Concept of Civilian in Non-International Armed Conflict

3. Organized Armed Groups

a) Basic Concept
Organized armed groups belonging to a non-State party to an armed conflict include both dissident armed forces and other armed groups. Dissident armed forces essentially

constitute part of a State's armed forces that have turned against the government. Other organized armed groups recruit their members primarily from the civilian population but develop a sufficient degree of military organization to conduct hostilities on behalf of a party to the conflict, albeit not always with the same means, intensity and level of sophistication as State armed forces. . . .

. . . The term organized armed group . . . refers exclusively to the armed or military wing of a non-State party: its armed forces in a functional sense. This distinction has important consequences for the determination of membership in an organized armed group as opposed to other forms of affiliation with, or support for, a non-State party to the conflict.

Other Organized Armed Groups: More difficult is the concept of membership in organized armed groups. . . . Membership in these irregularly constituted groups has no basis in domestic law. It is rarely formalized through an act of integration other than taking up a certain function for the group; and it is not consistently expressed through uniforms, fixed distinctive signs, or identification cards. In view of the wide variety of cultural, political, and military contexts in which organized armed groups operate, there may be various degrees of affiliation with such groups that do not necessarily amount to "membership" within the meaning of IHL . . . In practice, the informal and clandestine structures of most organized armed groups and the elastic nature of membership render it particularly difficult to distinguish between a non-State party to the conflict and its armed forces.

. . . Instead, membership must depend on whether the continuous function assumed by an individual corresponds to that collectively exercised by the group as a whole, namely the conduct of hostilities on behalf of a non-State party to the conflict. Consequently, under IHL, the decisive criterion for individual membership in an organized armed group is whether a person assumes a continuous function for the group involving his or her direct participation in hostilities (hereafter: "continuous combat function"). Continuous combat function does not imply *de jure* entitlement to combatant privilege. Rather, it distinguishes members of the organized fighting forces of a non-State party from civilians who directly participate in hostilities on a merely spontaneous, sporadic, or unorganized basis, or who assume exclusively political, administrative or other non-combat functions.

Continuous combat function requires lasting integration into an organized armed group acting as the armed forces of a non-State party to an armed conflict. Thus, individuals whose continuous function involves the preparation, execution, or command of acts or operations amounting to direct participation in hostilities are assuming a continuous combat function. An individual recruited, trained and equipped by such a group to continuously and directly participate in hostilities on its behalf can be considered to assume a continuous combat function even before he or she first carries out a hostile act. . . . Individuals who continuously accompany or support an organized armed group, but whose function does not involve direct participation in hostilities, are not members of that group within the meaning of IHL. Instead, they remain civilians assuming support functions, similar to private contractors and civilian employees accompanying State armed forces. Thus recruiters, trainers, financiers and propagandists may continuously contribute to the general war effort of a non-State party, but they are not members of an organized armed group belonging to that party. . . . The same applies to individuals whose function is limited to the purchasing, smuggling, manufacturing and maintaining of weapons and other equipment outside specific military operations or to the collection of intelligence other than of a tactical nature. Although such persons may accompany organized armed groups and provide substantial support to a party to the conflict, they do not assume continuous combat function and, for the purposes of the principle of distinction, cannot be regarded as members of an organized armed group.

Conclusion: *Upon comparison with Israel's "targeted killing" high court opinion, the ICRC's use of several of that opinion's constructs is apparent. One might view the ICRC's* Interpretive Guidance *as a how- to directive to targeting and killing armed opposition group and terrorist leaders, planners and fighters. Or, more charitably, as an attempt to deal with the difficult problem of the "revolving door" terrorist phenomenon. Although it is already accepted by states involved in Afghan armed conflict, including the United States, time will indicate the acceptance or rejection of the ICRC Guidance through state practice, or its lack.*

Finally, combatants on the ground may not be able to distinguish enemy fighters with continuous combat function, but their combatant commanders, with the ability to tap enemy radio traffic and cell phone calls, and to designate armed drone strike targets, can.

PROSECUTOR V. GALIĆ

IT-98-29-A (November 30, 2006) Citations omitted

Introduction: *During the armed conflict in the former Yugoslavia, Major General Stanislav Galić commanded the Sarajevo Romanija Corps ("SRK"), of the Bosnian-Serb Army, from September 1992 to August 1994 – the height of the three-and-a-half-year siege of Sarajevo. During the period of Galić's command, the SRK conducted a protracted campaign of sniping and shelling of civilians and civilian objects. The International Criminal Tribunal for the Former Yugoslavia (ICTY) charged Galić with being personally and criminally liable for the acts of the unit he commanded. He was charged, inter alia, with attacks on civilians, murder, and inhumane acts.*

This brief extract from the ICTY appeals chamber opinion confirms Galić's trial chamber guilty findings and his sentence to twenty years' confinement. The extract summarizes the detailed considerations of the trial chamber in determining whether or not, through the doctrine of command responsibility, Galić knew or should have known that the many civilian deaths that occurred on his watch, and at the hands of his subordinates, were not "collateral" to lawful combat activities. The civilians killed in the siege of Sarajevo, the court found, were not lawful deaths involving damage collateral to the lawful targeting of military objectives.

A. Assessment of the Legality of the Attacks

190. One of the fundamental principles of international humanitarian law is that civilians and civilian objects shall be spared as much as possible from the effects of hostilities. This principle stems from the principles of distinction and the principle of protection of the civilian population, "the cardinal principles contained in the text constituting the fabric of humanitarian law", constituting "intransgressible principles of international customary law." According to the principle of distinction, warring parties

must at all timed distinguish between the civilian population and combatants, between civilian and military objectives, and accordingly direct attacks only against military objectives. These principles establish an absolute prohibition on the targeting of civilians in customary international law but do not exclude the possibility of legitimate civilian casualties incidental to the conduct of military operations. However, those casualties must not be disproportionate to the concrete and direct military advantage anticipated before the attack (the principle of proportionality).

191. In Part II of the Trial Judgement (Applicable Law), the Trial Chamber considered that Article 51(2) of Additional Protocol I "states in a clear language that civilians and the civilian population as such should not be the object of attack", that this principle "does not mention any exceptions", and in particular that it "does not contemplate derogating from this rule by invoking military necessity."It then held that [Additional Protocol I] Article 51(2) "explicitly confirms the customary rule that civilians must enjoy general protection against the danger arising from hostilities" and "stems from a fundamental principle of international humanitarian law, the principle of distinction, which obliges warring parties to distinguish *at all times* between the civilian population and combatants and between civilian objects and military objectives and accordingly to direct their operations only against military objectives." The Trial Chamber also considered that:

> once the military character of a target has been ascertained, commanders must consider whether striking this target is "expected to cause incidental loss of life, injury to civilians, damage to civilian objectives or a combination thereof, which would be excessive in relation to the concrete and direct military advantage anticipated."

192. The Appeals Chamber is satisfied that the Trial Chamber correctly assessed the legality of the incidents.

B. Assessment of Evidence in Relation to Those Attacks

193. The Trial Chamber clearly explained the methodology it used to assess the legality of the attacks for the scheduled incidents and more generally. It held:

> The Trial Chamber gave particular attention to questions of distance between the victim and the most probable source of fire; distance between the location where the victim was hit and the confrontation line; combat activity going on at the time and the location of the incident, as well as relevant nearby presence of military activities or facilities; appearance of the victim as to age, gender, clothing; the activity the victim could appear to be engaged in; visibility of the victim due to weather, unobstructed line of sight or daylight. The Trial Chamber was hence in a position to assess in each case, in accordance with the law set out in Part II of this Judgment and in fairness to the Accused, whether a scheduled incident is beyond reasonable doubt representative of the alleged campaign of sniping and shelling or whether it is reasonable to believe that the victim was hit by ABiH [Army of the Republic of Bosnia and Herzegovina] forces, by a stray bullet, or taken for a combatant.

The Appeals Chamber finds that the approach of the Trial Chamber is indeed in accordance with its enunciation of the applicable law. Galić does not point to any specific finding of the Trial Chamber in which it departed from a correct application of the law applicable to the assessment of the legality of the attacks. To the contrary, for example, the Trial Chamber determined with regard to the attacks at Grbavica that there was no military activity in the vicinity. For Scheduled Sniping Incident number 24, the attack of a tram near the Holiday Inn Hotel, the Trial Chamber determined that the tram "could not have been confused for a military objective," and that there was neither military activity nor military objectives in the area; it thus concluded that "a civilian vehicle was deliberately targeted from SRK-controlled territory."

194. With regard to Galić's arguments that the Trial Chamber ignored the issue of "dual use" objects, the Appeals Chamber notes that, for the attack on the front-end loader collecting garbage on Brace Ribara Street (Scheduled Sniping Incident 15), for example, the Trial Chamber considered the arguments of the Defence that this vehicle could have been used for a military purpose but rejected them based on the circumstances of the incident. With respect to Galić's argument that the Trial Chamber failed to assess the possibility of artillery errors, the principles of protection, distinction and proportionality apply, and Galić does not point to any part of the Trial Judgment in which the Trial Chamber erred in applying those principles. With regard to his argument that the question of the use of civilians as "human shields" was not considered by the Trial Chamber, the Appeals Chamber underlines that the Trial Chamber noted the following:

> As suggested by the Defence, the parties to a conflict are under an obligation to remove civilians, to the maximum extent feasible from the vicinity of military objectives and to avoid locating military objectives within or near densely populated areas [but] the failure of a party to abide by this obligation does not relieve the attacking side of its duty to abide by the principles of distinction and proportionality when launching an attack.

Galić's argument is therefore without merit. With regard to his arguments pertaining to the alleged failure of the Trial Chamber to define the confrontation line and its depth, the Appeals Chamber notes that those arguments are merely repetitive of those made in his fourteenth ground of appeal and will accordingly be dealt with under that ground.

195. For the foregoing reasons, Galić's twelfth ground of appeal is dismissed.

Conclusion: *The conviction of Galić was one of several that resulted from the unlawful targeting of civilians in Sarajevo. Both the trial and appeals chamber opinions demonstrate that any unlawful targeting of civilians asserted to be "collateral damage" is subject to the objective investigation and determination of judicial bodies. In addition, the Sarajevo trials confirm the lead of the post–World War II Nuremberg International Military Tribunal in holding military commanders personally and criminally responsible for the law of war offenses of their subordinates that they knew, or should have known of, and about which they either made no effort to stop, or took no action to punish.*

16 Torture

16.0 Introduction

The law of armed conflict (LOAC) and international humanitarian law (IHL) are clear in their positions regarding torture: It may never be engaged in, under any circumstances. U.S. military law, as does the military law of all states, forbids torture. No exceptions are provided for. Torture nevertheless happens because, as the Harvard law professor Alan Dershowitz points out, "the tragic reality is that torture sometimes works, much though many people wish it did not."[1] Of course, asserting that torture sometimes works tells us nothing of its legal dimensions.

After the 9/11 attacks, a change in attitude overtook a portion of the American public, including members of the armed forces: In some circles torture became acceptable. A 2005 Associated Press–Ipsos survey of one thousand Americans found that, where terrorism is involved, 61 percent of Americans do not rule out torture. Eleven percent responded that torture could be used often, 27 percent said sometimes, and 23 percent said rarely; 36 percent said it could never be justified.[2] It is dismaying that even the editor of *Armed Forces Journal*, a respected Washington publication, expressed support for torture in terrorism cases.[3] Richard A. Posner, the influential U.S. Court of Appeals judge for the Seventh Circuit, declared that in extreme circumstances the president can authorize torture to prevent catastrophic attack.[4] In 2004, Senator Trent Lott, when asked about his vocal defense of interrogation techniques used at Iraq's Abu Ghraib prison, replied, "Interrogation is not a Sunday-school class. You don't get information that will save American lives by withholding pancakes. [Interviewer]: But unleashing killer dogs on naked Iraqis is not the same as withholding pancakes. [Lott]: I was amazed that people reacted like that. Did the dogs bite them? Did the dogs assault them? How are you going to get people to give information that will lead to the saving of lives?"[5] In 2006, President George W. Bush said, in a televised speech to the nation, "In some cases, we determine

---

[1] Alan M. Dershowitz, *Why Terrorism Works* (New Haven, CT: Yale University Press, 2002), 137.

[2] Will Lester, "Poll Finds Support for Use of Torture In War on Terror," *Wash. Times*, Dec. 7, 2005, 14. Majorities in Great Britain, France, and South Korea responded similarly. In Italy and Spain majorities opposed torture under any circumstances.

[3] John G. Roos, "Editorial: Torture and Terrorists," *Armed Forces J.* May 2005, 4.

[4] Richard A. Posner, *Not a Suicide Pact: The Constitution in a Time of National Emergency* (New York: Oxford University Press, 2006), 38.

[5] Deborah Solomon, "Questions for Trent Lott: All's Fair," *NY Times Sunday Magazine*, June 20, 2004, 15.

that individuals we have captured pose a significant threat, or may have intelligence that we and our allies need . . . and they withhold information that could save American lives. In these cases, it has been necessary to move these individuals to an environment where they can be held secretly, questioned by experts. . . . And so the CIA used an alternative set of procedures."[6] Those "alternative procedures," of course, were the infamous "enhanced interrogation techniques."

Professor Dershowitz has suggested "an alternative set of procedures" for interrogating captured terrorist suspects:

> Say, a sterilized needle inserted under the fingernails to produce unbearable pain without any threat to health or life, or . . . a dental drill through an unanesthetized tooth. The simple cost-benefit analysis for employing such nonlethal torture seems overwhelming: it is surely better to inflict nonlethal pain on one guilty terrorist who is illegally withholding information needed to prevent an act of terrorism than to permit a large number of innocent victims to die.[7]

"American abhorrence to torture now appears to have extraordinarily shallow roots."[8] Is *kriegsraison* resurrected in America? Where terrorism is involved are any limits recognized? What is the worth of laws against torture, in practice? Should states honor treaties they have ratified, such as the Geneva Conventions and the Convention against Torture, or should they not? Are the post–World War II convictions of Nazis for torture no more than victor's justice? Shall state governments ask their combatants to risk court-martial for extracting questionable intelligence from prisoners through torture? Proponents of torture ask, "What is torture and who defines it?" Shall military personnel shelter behind such sophistic hair splitting to commit breaches of law and duty?

During the "war on terrorism," standards previously taken for granted have been questioned or ignored. "Just as worrisome is the subtler numbing effect on American society when the idea of torture begins to seem acceptable, even normal; when it becomes euphemized as 'extreme duress' or 'coercive' interrogation."[9]

If a government orders or condones torture, is anyone other than the actual perpetrator responsible for the domestic and international law violations committed? In LOAC/IHL, principles of command responsibility and superior responsibility apply in an armed conflict, but how far up the chain of command does one go in finding culpability? To commanding generals? To theater commanders? Even higher?[10] In 2009, Peru's

---

[6] The White House, "President Discusses Creation of Military Commissions to Try Suspected Terrorists" (Sept. 6, 2006), available online. Also see 100–4 *AJIL* (Oct. 2006), 936.

[7] Dershowitz, *Why Terrorism Works*, supra, note 1, at 144.

[8] David Luban, "Liberalism, Torture, and the Ticking Bomb," 91 *Va. L. Rev.* (2005), 1425, 1426.

[9] Pamela Constable, "Torture's Echoes," *Wash. Post*, July 17, 2005, B3.

[10] Dan Eggen, "Bush Approved Meetings on Interrogation Techniques," *Wash. Post*, April 12, 2008, A3: "President Bush said Friday that he was aware his top national security advisors had discussed the details of harsh interrogation tactics to be used on detainees. Bush also said . . . that he approved of the meetings, which were held as the CIA began to prepare for a secret interrogation program that included waterboarding, or simulated drowning, and other coercive techniques. . . . Bush said . . . 'And yes, I'm aware our national security team met on this issue. And I approved.'" Also, Sheryl G. Stolberg, "Bush Defends Interrogations, Saying Methods Aren't Torture," *NY Times*, Oct. 6, 2007, A1: "'I have put this program in place for a reason, and that is to protect the American people,' the president said." Also, Joby Warrick, "Top Officials Knew in 2002 of Harsh Interrogations," *Wash. Post*, Sept. 25, 2008, A7:

Supreme Court convicted the former president of Peru, Alberto K. Fujimori, of ordering kidnappings and of the murder of twenty-five individuals in the early 1990s, during an internal armed conflict with Maoist Shining Path and Tupac Amaru guerrillas. Fujimori was sentenced to twenty-five years' confinement.[11] In 2012, however, the U.S. District Court for the District of Columbia ruled that the president of Sri Lanka was immune from suit under the Torture Victim Protection Act (TVPA) while in office.[12] The court found that, under federal common law, the act does not override the immunity of heads of state while they are in office. The month before, the U.S. Supreme Court unanimously affirmed dismissal of a suit against the Palestinian Authority by relatives of a U.S. citizen allegedly tortured and killed by agents of the Palestinian Authority and the Palestine Liberation Organization "... [T]he Court held that the TVPA authorizes only suits against natural persons, not against organizations."[13] The concepts of civilian superior responsibility and military command responsibility are more well settled in LOAC/IHL jurisprudence.[14] The Yale professor W. Michael Reisman writes:

> The national debate as to whether the president, as commander in chief in wartime, has an inherent "constitutional" power to order subordinates to torture in self-defense is irrelevant to an international inquiry. ... Violations of international law by any organ or agency of a state will engage that state's responsibility; insofar as international law provides for individual responsibility, that responsibility now tracks up and down the chain of command that has ordered a violation of international law. Contrary national legal commands do not provide a defense.[15]

The potential responsibility of senior officers in the military chain of command for LOAC/IHL violations is clear:

> Superiors, by virtue of their elevated positions in the [military] hierarchy, have an affirmative duty to ensure that IHL is duly respected and that breaches are appropriately repressed. Their failure to do so can be interpreted as acquiescence in the unlawful acts of their subordinates, thereby encouraging further breaches and developing a culture of impunity. ... The consequences of a person's acts are

---

"According to ... the office of Secretary of State Condoleezza Rice ... details of the controversial program were discussed in multiple meetings inside the White House over a two-year period. ... The written accounts specifically name former attorney general John D. Ashcroft and former defense secretary Donald H. Rumsfeld as participants. ... The committee's questionnaire did not specifically ask whether President Bush or Vice President Cheney attended the meetings." Also, Joby Warrick, "CIA Tactics Endorsed in Secret Memos," *Wash. Post*, Oct. 15, 2008 A1: "Rice last month became the first Cabinet-level official to publicly confirm the White House's awareness of the program in its earliest stages."

[11] For head of state immunity issues, see: Sarah Williams and Lena Sherif, "The Arrest Warrant for President Al-Bashir: Immunities of Incumbent Heads of States," 14–1 *J. of Conflict & Security L.* (Spring 2009), 71–92. Spain considered initiating prosecutions for torture against former-president Bush, Alberto R. Gonzales, John C. Yoo, Jay Bybee, William J. Haynes, David S. Addington, and Douglas J. Feith. Marlise Simons, "Spanish Court Weighs Criminal Inquiry on Torture for 6 Bush-Era Officials, *NY Times*, March 29, 2009, A6. The matter was quickly dropped after a preliminary review.

[12] *Manoharan v. Rajapaksa*, 845 F.Supp. 2d 260 (D.D.C. 2012).

[13] John R. Crook, ed., "Contemporary Practice of the United States Relating to International Law," 106–3 *AJIL* (July 2012), 643, 668, citing *Mohamad v. Palestinian Authority*, 132 S.Ct. 1720 (2012).

[14] For example, *Prosecutor v. Delalić*, IT-96–21-T (Nov. 16, 1998), paras. 377–8; and *Prosecutor v. Delalić*, IT-96–21-A (Feb. 20, 2001), paras. 200–9.

[15] W. Michael Reisman, "Editorial Comment: Holding the Center of the Law of Armed Conflict," 100–4 *AJIL* (Oct. 2006), 852, 854.

necessarily more serious if he is at the apex of a military or political hierarchy and uses his position to commit crimes. Because he is a leader, his conduct is that much more reprehensible.[16]

Superior responsibility aside, a response to the assertion that torture is never permissible is that such an absolutist approach will cost American lives. Possibly it will, as do infantry attacks on enemy positions, air strikes on enemy facilities, or assaults on enemy-held coastlines. In wars, including the fight against terrorism, lives are lost, even the lives of civilians who have not enlisted in the fight. As British, Timorese, Irish, Spanish, and other civilian communities found in their conflicts with terrorists, Americans found on 9/11 that in some armed conflicts there are no exempt individuals, military or civilian. If a nation is prepared to fight for principles, must not that nation be prepared to sacrifice, even die, for the same principles?

The Israeli high court writes, "A democracy must sometimes fight with one hand tied behind its back. Even so, a democracy has the upper hand. The rule of law and the liberty of an individual constitute important components in its understanding of security. At the end of the day, they strengthen its spirit and this strength allows it to overcome its difficulties."[17]

During its war in Algeria, the French army tortured Algerian terrorist prisoners. "This was to become a growing canker for France, leaving behind a poison that would linger in the French system long after the war itself had ended."[18] For seventeen years, during the Pinochet regime, Chile was a state of torture, murder, and disappearances. In their conflicts with terrorists, Israel, France, and Chile paid high prices for torturing.

In discussing torture it is difficult to separate the subject from societal values and imperatives that underlie its prohibition. In examining LOAC/IHL concerns relating to torture, this chapter includes issues that are not matters of law, but may influence a combatant's decisions regarding torture.

16.1 Torture Background

Ancient Greek law provided for the torture of foreigners and slaves to extract confessions. Freemen were exempted. Prior to the thirteenth century, trial by ordeal was conducted by the church, as it was around 1250, during the Inquisition. "Pope Innocent IV authorized the use of torture against heretics. Heresy, essentially 'treason against God,' was treated just like a serious crime before the civil courts."[19] What the law refers to as "proof" developed in the thirteenth century in the city–states of Italy, and the concept of proof spread across the Continent. In early Roman law, circumstantial evidence alone, no matter how strong, was insufficient proof for conviction. Without two eyewitnesses, an

---

[16] Jamie Allan Williamson, "Some Considerations on Command Responsibility and Criminal Liability," 870 *Int'l Rev. of the Red Cross* (June 2008), 303, 312–13. This is emphasized in an ICTR case: "This Chamber finds as an aggravating circumstance that Kayishema as *Prefect*, held a position of authority. This Chamber finds that Kayishema was a leader ... and this abuse of power and betrayal of his office constitutes the most significant aggravating circumstance." *Prosecutor v. Kayishema and Ruzindana*, ICTR-95-1-T (Sentence, May 21, 1999), para. 15.

[17] H.C. 5100/94, *Public Committee against Torture in Israel v. The State of Israel* (Sept. 6, 1999), at para. 39.

[18] Alistair Horne, *A Savage War of Peace* (New York: New York Review of Books, 1977), 195.

[19] James Ross, "A History of Torture," in Kenneth Roth, Minky Worden, and Amy Bernstein, eds., *Torture* (New York: New Press, 2005), 10.

accused could be convicted only if he confessed, and confessions were encouraged by torture. "Torture was permitted only when a so-called half proof had been established against the suspect. That meant either one eyewitness, or circumstantial evidence that satisfied elaborate requirements of gravity."[20] Unlike earlier Greek and Roman law, which allowed torture on the basis of the status of the accused, the European justice system folded torture into general legal practice.[21]

Cases arose, however, in which the actual criminal was found out after an innocent accused had confessed under torture. By the mid-eighteenth century, after five hundred years of practice, judicial torture was abolished.

In 1863, the Lieber Code, in Article 16, addressed torture in a military context. "Military necessity does not admit of cruelty – that is, the infliction of suffering for the sake of suffering or for revenge . . . nor of torture to extort confessions." Today, torture is a grave breach of the 1949 Geneva Conventions. The 1993 Statutes of the International Criminal Tribunals for the Former Yugoslavia and for Rwanda (ICTY, ICTR) charge it as a grave breach, and it is a crime against humanity under the Rome Statute of the International Criminal Court (ICC).

In international law, the 1984 U.N. Convention against Torture (CAT),[22] and its Optional Protocol,[23] prohibit torture, as does the Universal Declaration of Human Rights.[24] The CAT is a human rights convention, not a LOAC treaty. The United States ratified the CAT in 1994.[25] Torture is a *jus cogens* offense – a peremptory norm in international law; a state may not "opt out" of the criminality of torture or of the enforcement of international legal provisions against it. "Perpetrators may be held criminally responsible notwithstanding national or even international authorization by legislative or judicial bodies to apply torture."[26]

A U.S. effort in the U.N. to set aside a 2002 optional protocol to the CAT establishing a system of worldwide inspections of prisons and detention centers was defeated in U.N. committee.[27] The United States has not signed the protocol.[28]

---

[20] John H. Langbein, "The Legal History of Torture," in Sanford Levinson, ed., *Torture: A Collection* (New York: Oxford University Press, 2004), 93–103, 95.

[21] Ross, "History of Torture," supra, note 19, at 8.

[22] Convention against Torture and Other Cruel, Inhuman or Degrading Treatment or Punishment. Annex, 39 U.N. GAOR Supp. (No. 51) at 197, U.N. Doc. A/39/51 (1984).

[23] The CAT's Optional Protocol entered into force in June 2006. It establishes a Sub-Committee for the Prevention of Torture with authority to visit places of detention, such as police stations, prisons, military facilities, refugee camps, and immigration facilities, to assess their conditions and compliance with the CAT. State parties are required to enact complementary domestic preventive mechanisms. See Alice Edwards, "The Optional Protocol to the Convention against Torture and the Detention of Refugees," 57–4 *Int'l and Comp. L. Quarterly* (2008), 789–825.

[24] Universal Declaration of Human Rights, Dec. 10, 1948, G.A. Res. 217A (III), UN Doc. A/810 (1948), Art. 5. "No one shall be subjected to torture or to cruel, inhuman or degrading treatment or punishment."

[25] At ratification, the United States attached a reservation interpreting cruel, inhuman, and degrading treatment to mean treatment that violates the U.S. Constitution's Fifth, Eighth, and Fourteenth Amendments.

[26] Christoph Burchard, "Torture in the Jurisprudence of the Ad Hoc Tribunals," in 6–2 *J. of Int'l Crim. Justice* (May 2008), 159–82, at 162.

[27] Barbara Crossette, "U.S. Fails in Effort to Block Vote on U.N. Convention on Torture," *NY Times*, July 25, 2002, A5.

[28] Optional Protocol, U.N.G.A. Res. A/RES/57/199 (Dec. 18, 2002). At the time of writing, seventy-eight states have ratified the protocol, in force since June 2006.

In U.S. domestic law implementing the CAT's prohibitions, torture is a felony under 28 U.S. Code §§ 1350, 2340(1) and 2340A, the latter section often referred to as the "Extraterritorial Torture Statute."* U.S. domestic law outlaws torture, but does not ban cruel, inhuman, or degrading treatment. The effectiveness of U.S. antitorture laws has not yet been demonstrated. Efforts of former Guantánamo detainees to bring torture charges against government officials encounter legal barriers that, so far, have closed courthouse doors to allegations of torture by U.S. officials.[29]

The CIA was aware that the "enhanced interrogation methods" it employed were unlawful. When an agent at a "black site" sent a message to CIA headquarters evincing concern for the legality of the interrogation methods he was employing, the chief of the Counter-Terrorism Center replied, "Strongly urge that any speculative language as to the legality of given activities or, more precisely, judgment calls as to their legality vis-à-vis operational guidelines for this activity agreed upon and vetted at the most senior levels of the agency, be refrained from in written traffic (email or cable traffic). Such language is not helpful."[30]

In military law, torture may be prosecuted under several provisions of the Uniform Code of Military Justice, including Article 128, assault and aggravated assault; Article 124, maiming; plus articles relating to the maltreatment of prisoners, dereliction of duty, and conduct unbecoming an officer or conduct prejudicial to good order and discipline. There are numerous military orders, directives, and instructions that may give rise to court-martial prosecution for violation of lawful general orders that prohibit torture.

16.2 Defining Torture

Wrenching fingernails from a prisoner's fingers is easily recognized as torture. Wiring a detainee's genitalia to an electrical source and applying current is torture. Hammering a captive's toes with a blunt instrument is torture. Tying the arms of a prisoner of war

---

* In 2008, in Miami, Florida, Charles Taylor, the Boston-born son of the former Liberian president Charles Taylor, was convicted of torturing prisoners, conspiring to torture, and using a firearm in a violent crime, in Liberia's 1999–2003 common Article 3 armed conflict. The charges included allegations of electrically shocking various body parts of prisoners, and ordering the cutting of genitals of prisoners. Indictment, *U.S. v. Roy M. Belfast* (a.k.a. Chuckie Taylor, a.k.a. Charles M. Emmanuel) No. 06–20758 (S.D. Fla.), 2008. It was the first trial in the history of the 1994 "Extraterritorial Torture Act." John R. Crook, ed., "Contemporary Practice of the United States Relating to International Law," 103–1 *AJIL* (Jan. 2009), 132, 166. In January 2009, having been convicted of torture, conspiracy to torture seven victims, and use of a firearm in a violent crime, Taylor was sentenced to ninety-seven years' confinement.

[29] *Shafiq Rasul et al. v. General Richard Meyers, et al.*, 512 F3d 644 (C.A.D.C., Jan. 11, 2008). The federal appeals court held, at 661, "It was foreseeable that conduct that would ordinarily be indisputably 'seriously criminal' would be implemented by military officials responsible for detaining and interrogating suspected enemy combatants." Besides the court's surprising assertion of foreseeability of military misconduct in Guantánamo interrogations, the court went on to find that the former detainees possessed no constitutional rights and ruled against them on all claims, even after assuming their allegations of torture and unlawful detention to be true. "The Court's ruling has the peculiar effect of validating the superior orders defence that has been criticized since Nuremburg. According to the Court, US military officials are immune for any action taken pursuant to superior orders, because such actions would be within the scope of employment." Jaykumar A. Menon, "Guantánamo Torture Litigation," 6–2 *J. of Int'l Crim. Justice* (May 2008), 323, 42. In Dec. 2008 the Supreme Court instructed the *Rasul* court to reconsider its opinion. An earlier federal appeals court decision, *Leon v. Wainwright*, 734 F.2d 770 (C.A. 11 (Fla.), 1984), was similarly unsympathetic to a plaintiff's action after Leon was tortured by Miami police officers to reveal a kidnap victim's location.

[30] Senate Select Committee on Intelligence, *The Senate Intelligence Committee Report on Torture* (Brooklyn, NY: Melville House, 2014), 53. Footnotes omitted.

(POW) behind his back until his elbows touch, then raising him off the floor by his bound arms via an overhead rope until his shoulders dislocate, is torture.[31]

Some mistreatment so clearly constitutes torture that it requires no definitional validation, but mistreatment meeting legal definitions of torture can be less clear. Is it torture to force a captive to stand for five hours? It depends. Is the captive a healthy twenty-four-year-old military pilot or a seventy-year-old grandmother with diabetes, asthma, and a heart condition?

"The basic formula [prohibiting the ill-treatment of prisoners], 'torture or cruel, inhuman or degrading treatment or punishment', is that of Article 5 of the Universal Declaration of Human Rights. All the human rights treaties that contain the prohibition effectively reproduce this formula. ... This approach, of dividing the formula into its component parts, was started by the European Commission of Human Rights."[32] Early cases attempting to differentiate between what constitutes torture and what is "merely" cruel, inhuman, and degrading treatment include the 1969 *Greek* case[33] and the 1978 *Five Techniques* case.[34]

Article 1 of the CAT provides a frequently cited human rights–oriented definition of torture:

> For the purposes of this Convention, the term "torture" means **any act by which severe pain or suffering, whether physical or mental, is intentionally inflicted on a person for such purposes as obtaining from him or a third person information or a confession, punishing him for an act he or a third person has committed or is suspected of having committed, or intimidating or coercing him or a third person, or for any reason based on discrimination of any kind, when such pain or suffering is inflicted by or at the instigation of or with the consent or acquiescence of a public official or other person acting in an official capacity.** It does not include pain or suffering arising only from, inherent in or incidental to lawful sanctions.

The CAT's definition is altered by the ICTY's *Kunarac* decision, in that the involvement of a public official is not required.[35] (See the ICTY's *Brdanin* decision, Cases and Materials, this chapter.) Although not bound by ICTY decisions, it is likely that a U.S. war crime prosecution for torture would apply the *Kunarac* amendment.

CAT Article 2.2. notes, "No exceptional circumstances whatsoever, whether a state of war or a threat of war, internal political instability or any other public emergency, may be invoked as a justification of torture."

Definitions of torture contained in U.S. domestic law incorporate the central focus of the CAT's lumbering definition: severe pain or suffering, whether physical or mental. Under customary law, "the enumerated purposes [for torturing] do not constitute an exhaustive list, and there is no requirement that the conduct must be solely for a

---

[31] Such torture is described in VAdm. James B. Stockdale and Sybil Stockdale, *In Love and War* (Annapolis, MD: Naval Institute Press, 1990), 170–2; and, Lt.Cmdr. John M. McGrath, *Prisoner of War: Six Years in Hanoi* (Annapolis, MD: Naval Institute Press, 1975), 78–9.

[32] Nigel S. Rodley, *The Treatment of Prisoners under International Law*, 2d ed. (Oxford: Oxford University Press, 1999), 75.

[33] *Askoy v. Turkey* (1996) 23 EHRR 533.

[34] *Ireland v. U.K.* (1978) 2 EHRR 25, ECtHR. The "five techniques" employed by British forces in interrogating IRA suspects were wall standing, hooding, subjection to noise, deprivation of sleep, and deprivation of food and drink.

[35] *Prosecutor v. Kunarac, et al.*, IT-96-23 & 23/1-A-T (Feb. 22, 2001), at paras. 482–9.

prohibited purpose. It suffices that the prohibited purpose is part of the motivation behind the conduct."[36]

Conventions and definitions do not, however, pin down what actually constitutes torture. No document could. Torture, like "reasonableness," is a moving target. It cannot be defined with exactness. "Besides, it is always dangerous to try to go into too much detail – especially in this domain. However great the care taken in drawing up a list of all the various forms of infliction, it would never be possible to catch up with the imagination of future torturers who wished to satisfy their bestial instincts; and the more specific and complete a list tries to be, the more restrictive it becomes."[37] Torture to one person might be merely bothersome to another. Torture is individual and situational.

Nor is torture always physical in nature. "Psychological torture is a very real thing. It should not be minimized under the pretext that pain and suffering must be physical in order to be real."[38] Particularly in cases involving female prisoners, mental torture suggesting sexual assault may occur even where actual rape or assault does not follow.

The American Psychological Association prohibits members from involvement in what it considers torture: waterboarding, mock execution, forced nakedness, induced hypothermia, stress positions, extended sleep deprivation, exposure to extreme heat or cold, and the use of psychotropic drugs,[39] among other restrictions sounding not only in torture but so-called torture lite – acts that may constitute cruel, inhuman, or degrading treatment short of torture. The Geneva Conventions do not distinguish between torture and "torture lite" but simply ban the mistreatment of prisoners.

From the description of torture found in the CAT, in the Statute of the ICC, and in domestic laws, three categories of torture may be distinguished: torture as a crime against humanity under international criminal law as applied by international criminal legal bodies such as the ICTY; torture as a crime under customary international law, relating particularly to the CAT, as prosecuted most often in domestic courts; and torture as a war crime.[40] We concentrate here on torture, including cruel, inhuman, and degrading treatment, as a war crime. Although torture is everywhere denied,

> implicit justifications of torture and inhuman treatment reappear even in democratic societies when they consider themselves under threat. Blunt denial of ... torture or inhuman treatment is replaced by legalistic interpretations of what constitutes torture, as opposed to "only" cruel, inhuman or degrading treatment, or by considerations as to which measures should be allowed in so-called "highly coercive", "enhanced" or "in-depth" interrogation. A narrow interpretation of torture would render

---

[36] Kriangsak Kittichaisaree, *International Criminal Law* (Oxford: Oxford University Press, 2001), 111.

[37] Jean S. Pictet, ed., *Commentary, IV Geneva Convention* (Geneva: ICRC, 1958), 39.

[38] Hernán Reyes, "The Worst Scars Are in the Mind: Psychological Torture," 867 *Int'l Rev. of the Red Cross* (Sept. 2007), 591, 615.

[39] APA Press Release (Aug. 20, 2007), "American Psychological Association Calls on U.S. Government to Prohibit the Use of Unethical Interrogation Techniques," http://www.apa.org/releases/councilres0807 .html. In Sept. 2008, the association membership voted to prohibit any consultation in the interrogation of detainees at Guantánamoo, and at any CIA-operated "black site." Later, it was revealed that CIA "Office of Medical Services" psychologists had nevertheless routinely been significant participants in the torture of detainees in secret CIA prisons. Memorandum for John A. Rizzo, Senior Deputy General Counsel, Central Intelligence Agency; From: U.S. Department of Justice, Office of Legal Counsel; Re: Application of United States Obligations under Article 16 of the Convention against Torture (May 30, 2005), at 8.

[40] Burchard, "Torture in the Jurisprudence of the Ad Hoc Tribunals," supra, note 26, at 161.

its prohibition virtually meaningless. An absurd interpretation of that kind culminated in an infamous memorandum.[41]

The "infamous memorandum" referred to is the 2002 Bybee memo, named for its signatory, Assistant Attorney General Jay S. Bybee. Written largely by John Yoo in the Office of Legal Counsel (OLC) of the U.S. Department of Justice (DOJ), the Bybee memo defined torture so narrowly that no executive branch officer or employee, Central Intelligence Agency (CIA) agents, for example, could be convicted of torture in a U.S. domestic court. According to the U.S. Senate Armed Services Report on Torture, the Bybee memo "distorted the meaning and intent of anti-torture laws, rationalized the abuse of detainees ... and influenced Department of Defense determinations as to what interrogation techniques were legal."[42] Addressing the "specific intent" aspect of the crime, for example, the memo held that, "the infliction of such pain must be the defendant's precise objective. ... If the defendant acted knowing that severe pain or suffering was reasonably likely to result ... he would have acted only with general intent. ... [A] defendant is guilty of torture only if he acts with the express purpose of inflicting severe pain or suffering "[43] What constitutes "severe pain"? The memo answered, "the level [of pain] that would ordinarily be associated with a sufficiently serious physical condition or injury such as death, organ failure, or serious impairment of body functions."[44] Apropos to interrogations conducted by military personnel, the memo ascribed surprisingly broad powers to the president: "As Commander-in-Chief, the President has the constitutional authority to order interrogations of enemy combatants to gain intelligence information. ... Any effort to apply Section 2340A [a U.S. federal law criminalizing torture] in a manner that interferes with the President's direction of such core war matters as the detention and interrogation of enemy combatants thus would be unconstitutional."[45] The Bybee memo also asserted the availability of defenses understood in most courtrooms to be inapplicable for alleged acts of torture.

A subsequent head of the Justice Department's OLC wrote, "How could OLC have written opinions that, when revealed to the world ... made it seem as though the administration was giving official sanction to torture, and brought such dishonor to the United States ... ? How could its opinions reflect such bad judgment, be so poorly reasoned, and have such a terrible tone?"[46] John Yoo, reportedly the Bybee memo's principal author, argued:

> Classified memos prepared by OLC ... were handed to the press. After administration opponents had finished scouring them for juicy passages for popular consumption, the charges that the Bush administration had sought to undermine or evade the law flew fast and furious. ... But would limiting a captured terrorist to six hours sleep, isolating him, interrogating him for several hours, or requiring him to exercise constitute "severe physical or mental pain or suffering"?[47]

[41] Toni Pfanner, "Editorial," 867 *Int'l Rev. of the Red Cross* (Sept. 2007), 502.
[42] "Executive Summary: Senate Armed Services Report on Torture" (Dec. 12, 2008), 15, available online.
[43] Memorandum for Alberto Gonzales; from Department of Justice, Office of Legal Counsel; *Re: Standards of Conduct for Interrogation under 18 U.S.C. §§ 2340–2340A* (Aug. 1, 2002), reprinted in Karen J. Greenberg and Joshua L. Dratel, *The Torture Papers* (New York: Cambridge University Press, 2005).
[44] Id.   [45] Id.   [46] Jack Goldsmith, *The Terror Presidency* (New York: Norton, 2007), 165.
[47] John Yoo, *War by Other Means* (New York: Atlantic Monthly Press, 2006), 169, 171–2.

The Bybee memo covered much more than that, however. Because it was directed to federal law enforcement interrogations, the memo was not applied by the military. In 2003, however, another Yoo-authored memo that *was* applicable to military interrogators was delivered by OLC to the Pentagon's general counsel. The eighty-one-page memo asserted "that federal laws prohibiting assault, maiming and other crimes did not apply to military interrogators who questioned al-Qaeda captives because the president's ultimate authority as commander in chief overrode such statutes."[48] Nine months later, in December 2003, that memo was withdrawn by a new head of the OLC, who considered it badly reasoned and legally defective. In June 2004, the Bybee memo itself was withdrawn, two years after it was issued. It was replaced by a December 2004 memo that retained some of the core Bybee elements.[49]

In March 2003, Jay S. Bybee left the Justice Department to become a judge on the U.S. Ninth Circuit Court of Appeals. That might give pause to those who suggest court-issued "torture warrants."[50]

Professor Ruth Wedgwood and James Woolsey, a former director of the CIA, wrote of the OLC memos:

> Interrogation methods for combatants and detainees must be framed in light of the applicable law, even in the war against al Qaeda, and a president needs to know where the red lines are. ... Yet the recently released memos delivered by the Justice Department's Office of Legal Counsel to the White House ... do not give an adequate account of the law. ... The president's need for wise counsel is not well served by arguments that bend and twist to avoid any legal restrictions. ... This diminished definition of the crime of torture will be quoted back at the United States for the next several decades.[51]

Army Lieutenant General Ricardo Sanchez was commander of coalition ground forces in Iraq from June 2003 to June 2004. He placed partial responsibility on Washington's political leadership for torture committed by military personnel under his command. Citing a presidential memorandum that, he incorrectly says, stated that the Geneva Conventions did not apply to the Taliban or al Qaeda,[52] General Sanchez writes:

---

[48] Dan Eggen and Josh White, "Memo: Laws Didn't Apply to Interrogators," *Wash. Post*, April 2, 2008, A1; and, Mark Mazzetti, "'03 U.S. Memo Approved Harsh Interrogations," *NY Times*, April 2, 2008, A1. The two accounts refer to Working Group Report on Detainee Interrogations in the Global War on Terrorism: Assessment of Legal, Historical, Policy, and Operational Considerations (April 4, 2003). Reprinted in Greenberg and Dratel, *Torture Papers*, supra, note 43, at 286.

[49] John R. Crook, ed., "Contemporary Practice of the United States Relating to International Law," 99–2 *AJIL* (April 2005), 479.

[50] For example, Dershowitz, *Why Terrorism Works*, supra, note 1, at 158. Torture warrants would be violations of international law.

[51] Ruth Wedgwood and R. James Woolsey, "Law and Torture," *Wall Street Journal* June 28, 2004, 10.

[52] White House memorandum (Feb. 7, 2002), For the Vice President, Secretary of State, Attorney General, Chief of Staff to the President, Director of Central Intelligence, Assistant to the President for National Security Affairs, and the Chairman of the Joint Chiefs of Staff; Subject: Humane Treatment of al Qaeda and Taliban Detainees. "2. Pursuant to my authority as Commander-in-Chief ... I hereby determine as follows: a. ... None of the provisions of Geneva apply to our conflict with al Qaeda in Afghanistan or elsewhere throughout the world. ... b. ... I determine that the provisions of Geneva will apply to our present conflict with the Taliban [in Afghanistan]." The memo goes on to say that common Article 3 does not apply to either the Taliban or al Qaeda, and that neither group qualifies for POW status. Reprinted in Greenberg and Dratel, *Torture Papers*, supra, note 43, at 134.

During the last few months of 2002 ... there is irrefutable evidence that America was torturing and killing prisoners in Afghanistan. ... In essence, the administration had eliminated the [U.S. military's] entire doctrinal, training, and procedural foundations that existed for the conduct of interrogations. It was now left to individual interrogators to make the crucial decisions of what techniques could be utilized. ... In retrospect, the Bush administration's new policy triggered a sequence of events that led to harsh interrogation tactics against not only al-Qaeda prisoners, but also eventually prisoners in Iraq.[53]

General Sanchez would draw a straight line from the White House to military interrogators in the field, but there are multiple layers of command authority between the two.[54] Regardless of the wisdom of the president's initially denying Geneva coverage to prisoners, there were Department of Defense (DoD) Instructions, Department of the Army Directives, plus theater, corps, division, and battalion orders prohibiting torture and detailing permissible interrogation methods. Still, a confusing presidential directive that "detainees be treated humanely and, to the extent appropriate and consistent with military necessity, in a manner consistent with the principles of Geneva"[55] gives military commanders chilling guidance: If you consider that military necessity requires it, disregard Geneva. Humanitarian protections were only a matter of policy, and the CIA was not included even as a matter of policy.

Does a threat to inflict pain constitute torture? In the well-known *Daschner* case, such a threat was a central issue.[56] In 2002, the Frankfurt Police vice-president Wolfgang Daschner questioned the prisoner Magnus Gaefgen, a law student who had kidnapped the eleven-year-old son of a German bank executive. Gaefgen was captured by Frankfurt police as he picked up the ransom money, and, at first, he resisted interrogation. At Daschner's order, a subordinate officer told Gaefgen that the police were prepared to inflict pain on him that "he would never forget" and that a police specialist in such matters was flying to Frankfurt for that purpose. Gaefgen promptly revealed that he had accidentally killed the child during the initial kidnapping and gave police the body's location. Gaefgen was unharmed by the police, although a specially trained officer apparently had in fact been dispatched to Frankfurt. Gaefgen was convicted of murder and sentenced to life imprisonment. Daschner and the subordinate officer were also tried, giving rise to international debate heavily weighted in support of the policemen.

The German court trying the policemen dodged the legal issue of threatening to torture. It is a simplification of the court's judgment to relate that Daschner's written report admitting his order was ruled inadmissible. However, the court found he had

---

[53] Lt.Gen. Ricardo Sanchez, *Wiser in Battle* (New York: Harper Collins, 2008), 150.

[54] General Sanchez did not approach the issue with clean hands. See "Executive Summary: Senate Armed Services Report on Torture," supra, note 39, at 12, 17: "On September 14, 2003 ... Lieutenant General Ricardo Sanchez issued the first CJTF-7 interrogation SOP [Standard Operating Procedure]. That SOP authorized interrogators in Iraq to use stress positions, environmental manipulation, sleep management, and military working dogs in interrogations. Lieutenant General Sanchez issued the ... policy with the knowledge that there were ongoing discussions about the legality of some of the approved techniques. ... Conclusion 17: Interrogation policies approved by Lieutenant General Sanchez ... were a direct cause of detainee abuse in Iraq."

[55] White House memorandum (Feb. 7, 2002), For the Vice-President ... and the Chairman of the Joint Chiefs of Staff, supra, note 52. Reprinted in Greenberg and Dratel, *Torture Papers*, supra, note 43, at 135.

[56] No court opinion in English has been located. The case is discussed at length in, Florian Jessberger, "Bad Torture – Good Torture?" 3–5 *J. of Int'l Crim. Justice* (Nov. 2005), 1059; and (no author cited) "Respect for Human Dignity in Today's Germany," 4–4 *J. of Int'l Crim. Justice* (Sept. 2006), 862.

committed coercion and had ordered coercion, both of which are violations of the German Criminal Code. The subordinate officer was also found to have committed coercion. In German practice, however, court findings of "having committed" offenses are not the same as *convictions* of those offenses. The sympathetic court, invoking a rarely used rule, reprimanded both policemen, rather than convicting them. Daschner was fined 10,800 Euros, the subordinate 3,600 Euros. In 2010, Gaefgen's appeals of his conviction and sentencing were denied by the European Court of Human Rights.[57]

To constitute a violation the CAT, Article 1 requires the actual *"infliction* of torture." Apropos to the Daschner case, however, the European Court of Human Rights, in a 1982 decision, held that a threat to torture that is "sufficiently real and immediate" itself constitutes torture.[58] No military case involving a threat to torture has been located.

16.2.1 *Defining Torture as a LOAC Violation*

Torture is prohibited by 1907 Hague Regulation IV, Article 4 (by implication); by 1949 Geneva Convention common Article 3, and common Article 50/51/130/147; by 1977 Additional Protocol I, Article 75.2 (ii); Additional Protocol II, Article 4.2.(a); and by the Statutes of the ICTY and ICTR. "State practice establishes this rule [against torture] as a norm of customary international law applicable in both international and non-international armed conflicts."[59] LOAC/IHL similarly prohibits cruel, inhuman, and degrading treatment.[60] The prohibitions against torture – international, domestic, military, and civilian – are universal and comprehensive, yet torture appears to be more common today than in any recent time.

As mentioned, ICTY case law has modified the CAT's definition of torture. Initially, the ICTY's definition retained the CAT's requirement that the torture must be committed by a public official,[61] but the ICTY eventually abandoned that element.[62] The ICTY also finds torture without involvement of a public official in noninternational armed conflicts, where it can also be committed by nonstate actors.[63]

The Rome Statute of the ICC, Article 8(2) (a) (ii)-1, lists the war crime of torture committed in an international armed conflict.[64] That war crime has six elements, akin to a definition of torture:

---

[57] *Gäfgen v. Germany*, (2011) 52 E.E.H.R. 1 (Grand Chamber), available online. Also see, David J. Bederman, ed., "International Decisions," 105–2 *AJIL* (April 2011), 313.

[58] *Campbell and Cosans v. U.K.* (Feb. 1982) 4 EHRR 293, para. 26.

[59] Jean-Marie Henckaerts and Louise Doswald-Beck, eds., *Customary International Humanitarian Law.* Vol. I. *Rules* (Cambridge: Cambridge University Press, 2005), Rule 90, at 315.

[60] Id.   [61] *Prosecutor v. Furundžija*, IT-95–17/1 (Dec. 10, 1998), para. 162.

[62] *Prosecutor v. Kunarac*, supra, note 35, at, paras. 491, 493. See Cases and Materials, this chapter.

[63] Cordula Droege, "'In Truth the Leitmotiv': The Prohibition of Torture and Other Forms of Ill-Treatment in International Humanitarian Law," 867 *Int'l Rev. of the Red Cross* (Sept. 2007), 515, 525–6. The 2006 Military Commissions Act, at 10 USC § 950v (b)(12), listed two definitions of cruel and inhuman treatment, one applying to mistreatment occurring before enactment of the act, the other, more stringent definition, applying to acts after its enactment. The two definitions were an effort to immunize CIA personnel who engaged in torture early in the war on terrorism.

[64] ICC Article 8 (2) (c) (i)-4 is the war crime of torture in *noninternational* armed conflict, the elements of which are much the same as in 8(2) (a) (ii)-1. Article 7 (1) (f) is the crime against humanity of torture, involving conduct "committed as part of a widespread or systematic attack directed against a civilian population."

1. The perpetrator inflicted severe physical or mental pain or suffering upon one or more persons.[65]
2. The perpetrator inflicted the pain or suffering for such purposes as obtaining information or a confession, punishment, intimidation, or coercion or for any reason based on discrimination of any kind.
3. Such person or persons were protected under one or more of the Geneva Conventions of 1949.
4. The perpetrator was aware of the actual circumstances that established that protected status.
5. The conduct took place in the context of and was associated with an international armed conflict.[66]
6. The perpetrator was aware of factual circumstances that established the existence of an armed conflict.

"The war crime of torture is significantly different from that of torture as a crime against humanity, in that it requires proof of purpose. For this reason, it has been described as a crime of specific intent."[67]

Definitions and discussions of what constitutes cruel, inhuman, and degrading treatment, as opposed to torture, are the subject of articles and books. "There is no difference in meaning between cruel and inhuman treatment. Also, the lines between degrading treatment, cruel or inhuman treatment and torture are fluid."[68] Cruel treatment does constitute a violation of common Article 3[69] and of Article 4(2)(a) of Additional Protocol II, which, reminiscent of common Article 3, describes it as "torture, mutilation or any form of corporal punishment." Taking its guidance from Protocol II, one ICTY trial chamber concluded that "these instances of cruel treatment [specified in ICTY Statute Article 4(2)(a)], and the inclusion of 'any form of corporal punishment' demonstrate that no narrow or special meaning is here being given to the phrase 'cruel treatment'."[70]

---

[65] What level of pain or suffering is required? "It is difficult to establish precisely the threshold of suffering or pain required. ... Mental anguish alone may constitute torture provided that the resulting suffering is sufficiently serious. ... The 'severity' of the pain or suffering is, 'in the nature of things, relative; it depends on all the circumstances of the case, such as the duration of the treatment, its physical or mental effects and, in some cases, the sex, age and state of health of the victim, etc:'" Knut Dörmann, *Elements of War Crimes under the Rome Statute of the International Criminal Court* (Cambridge: Cambridge University Press, 2003), Art. 8(2) (a) (ii), at 51, citing ECtHR, *Selmouni v. France*, Judgment of July 28, 1999, Reports of Judgments and Decisions, 1999-V, para. 100.

[66] With respect to both the fifth and sixth elements, it is not required that the accused make a legal evaluation as to the existence of an armed conflict or its character; and there is no requirement the accused be aware of the facts that established the character of the conflict. The requirement is that the accused be aware of facts establishing the existence of an armed conflict. Id., Dörmann, at 15.

[67] William A. Schabas, *The International Criminal Court: A Commentary on the Rome Statute* (Oxford: Oxford University Press, 2010), 215.

[68] Droege, "'In Truth the *Leitmotiv*'," supra, note 63, at 519.

[69] In an unreported Oct. 2005 case, *LJN: AU4373*, *Rechtbank's-Gravenhage*, 09/751005–04, and 09/750006–05, on the basis of common Article 3, the Hague District Court convicted two Afghan asylum seekers of torturing civilians and of other war crimes in the 1978–92 Afghan War. The two former members of the Afghan military intelligence service were sentenced to twelve and nine years' confinement, respectively. Guénaël Mettraux, "Dutch Courts' Universal Jurisdiction over Violations of Common Article 3 qua War Crimes," 4–2 *J. of Int'l Crim. Justice* (May 2006), 362; and Ward Ferdinandusse, "On the Question of Dutch Courts' Universal Jurisdiction," 4–4 *J. of Int'l Crim. Justice* (Sept. 2006), 881.

[70] *Prosecutor v. Tadić*, IT-94-1-T, Judgment (May 7, 1997), para. 725.

In ICTY jurisprudence, cruel treatment has been charged in cases of beatings[71] and inhumane living conditions in detention centers.[72]

In the ICC's view there is no difference between "cruel treatment" and "inhuman treatment."[73] ICTY case law similarly defines both cruel treatment and inhuman treatment as "treatment which causes serious mental or physical suffering or constitutes a serious attack upon human dignity, which is equivalent to the offence of inhuman treatment in the framework of the grave breaches provisions of the Geneva Conventions."[74] "Cruel treatment, inhuman treatment, and inhumane acts basically require proof of the same elements, though the terminology may vary slightly between the three of them. All three prohibitions function … as residual clauses capturing all serious charges not otherwise enumerated."[75]

What constitutes LOAC/IHL grave breach of torture is reasonably clear. Although cruel, inhuman, and degrading treatment are LOAC/IHL violations in both international and noninternational armed conflicts, they are not as well defined. What can be said is that torture and cruel treatment are differentiated by the degree of seriousness required for the two offenses, and by the requirement of a prohibited purpose for the offense of torture.[76]

16.3 Why Torture?

Why engage in torture? The ethicist Professor David Luban posits that a person tortures with one of five aims, or purposes.[77] First, as a form of victor's pleasure – the military victor captures his enemy and tortures him to demonstrate his mastery and to humiliate the loser. Second, to instill terror – dictators from Hitler to Saddam Hussein tortured political prisoners to terrorize their subjects into submission. Third, punishment – criminal punishment to deter opposition and demonstrate the power of the government, or the ruler, was employed until the last two centuries. Fourth, extracting confessions – as mentioned, premodern legal rules required eyewitnesses or confessions for criminal convictions, perversely resulting in judicial torture. Other confessions related to "true faith" – the Inquisition and the Salem witchcraft trials, for instance. The torturer was merely the instrument of justice of the Almighty. Fifth, intelligence gathering – torture to extract information from prisoners who will not willingly talk. We are concerned with Professor Luban's last purpose, torture applied in times of armed conflict: its reasons, justifications, results, ands LOAC/IHL issues.

---

[71] *Prosecutor v. Jelisić*, IT-95-10-T (Dec. 14, 1999), paras. 42–5; and *Prosecutor v. Krnojelac*, IT-97-25-T (March 15, 2002), para. 176.

[72] Id., *Krnojelac*, para. 128; and *Prosecutor v. Delalić*, supra, note 14, at, paras. 554–8.

[73] Dörmann, *Elements of War Crimes*, supra, note 65, Art. 8(2) (c) (i) – 3, at 398.

[74] *Prosecutor v. Delalić*, supra, note 14, at para. 551.

[75] Guénaël Mettraux, *International Crimes and the Ad Hoc Tribunals* (Oxford: Oxford University Press, 2005), 116. Footnote omitted. *Prosecutor v Delalić*, supra, note 14, does specify elements required to prove cruel treatment, at para. 424. *Prosecutor v. Vasiljević*, IT-98-32-T (Nov. 29, 2002), paras. 234–7, specifies elements necessary to prove inhumane acts, in this case, attempted murders.

[76] Mettraux, id., at 117. The prohibited purposes necessary to commit the LOAC/IHL violation of torture, per the CAT, are obtaining information or a confession; punishing, intimidating, or coercing the victim or a third person; and discriminating on any ground against the victim or a third person.

[77] Luban, "Liberalism, Torture, and the Ticking Bomb," supra, note 8, at 1429.

Torture related to LOAC/IHL differs from torture related to law enforcement. "The nature and objectives of police interrogations differ significantly from those in military or intelligence contexts. In essence, most LE interrogations seek to obtain a confession from a suspect, rather than to gather accurate, useful intelligence."[78] What little empirical study has been conducted regarding interrogation relates to law enforcement scenarios. Still, there are instructive parallels between torture for military intelligence and torture for police confessions.

16.3.1 Torture Does Not Produce Actionable Intelligence

In the summer of 1969, in the United States–Vietnam conflict, the 1st Battalion of the 7th Marines was in continuous combat. In a single August engagement, the battalion commander was killed, along with eighteen other Marines and two navy corpsmen.

After one of that summer's firefights, a North Vietnamese Army (NVA) soldier with a slight buttock wound was captured. "The NVA had a battle dressing placed on his buttocks and tied around his leg, and he was stiff, frightened, and in a lot of pain. Two Vietnamese scouts crouched beside him and began firing off questions. The NVA gritted his teeth in a grimace of pain, and shook his head no, no, no. One of the scouts slid his knife up the prisoner's anus, then twisted. The man's eyes almost popped from his head. He talked."[79]

Talked of what, one wonders? Did he reveal weapons caches or tactical plans? Tactical interrogation of low-level suspected terrorists is unlikely to yield significant intelligence, according to reports from Iraq.

Military interrogation experts confirm that torture is unproductive. Major General Geoffrey Miller, past commander of Guantánamo's detention center, reported that on a monthly basis as much as 50 percent more actionable intelligence was obtained from prisoners after coercive practices such as hooding, stripping, and sleep deprivation were banned and a system encouraging rapport between prisoner and interrogator was initiated. Miller said, "In my opinion, a rapport-based interrogation that recognizes respect and dignity, and having well-trained interrogators, is the basis by which you develop intelligence rapidly and increase the validity of that intelligence."[80] At a 2007 reunion of World War II interrogators, the interrogator of Hitler's deputy, Rudolf Hess, commented, "We got more information out of a German general with a game of chess ... than they do today with their torture."[81] The history professor Philip Zelikow notes, "in World War II, the United States and Britain had special programs for 'high value' captives. Thousands of lives were at stake. Yet, even in a horrifyingly brutal war, neither government found it necessary to use methods like the ones in this C.I.A. program. [The World War II army chief of staff General] George Marshall would not have needed a lawyer to tell him whether such methods were O.K."[82]

---

[78] Randy Borum, "Approaching Truth: Behavioral Science Lessons on Educing Information from Human Sources," in *Educing Information: Interrogation: Science and Art* (Washington, DC: Nat'l Defense Intelligence College, 2006), 17, 18.

[79] Keith William Nolan, *Death Valley* (Novato, CA: Presidio Press, 1987), 60.

[80] Dexter Filkins, "General Says Less Coercion of Captives Yields Better Data," NY *Times*, Sept. 7, 2004, A12.

[81] Petula Dvorak, "Fort Hunt's Quiet Men Break Silence on WW II," *Wash. Post*, Oct. 6, 2007, A1.

[82] Philip Zelikow, "A Dubious C.I.A. Shortcut," NY *Times*, April 24, 2009, A23.

The Federal Bureau of Investigation (FBI) agent George L. Piro, a professional interrogator, interviewed the captured Saddam Hussein and gained valuable intelligence. "'The interviews were designed to develop a rapport between him and me,' Piro says. . . . Piro established trust with Saddam. He interviewed him every day. . . . He spent five to seven hours a day with him. Piro took no holidays or days off."[83] After an initial period during which the United States concedes using harsh tactics, including waterboarding, the same rapport building was reportedly employed in the interrogation of Khalid Sheikh Mohammed.[84] The actionable intelligence that led to the 2006 targeted killing of Abu Musab al-Zarqawi, the savage Jordanian leader of Al Qaeda in Iraq, was teased, bit by bit, day by day, from prisoners held by experienced Air Force, Army, and Navy interrogators of Task Force 145 – not through violence or pressure, but by calculated patient conversation and noncoercive questioning.[85]

The objection is sometimes raised that in interrogating a suspected terrorist, there is no time to develop a relationship of rapport. In response, the need for instant actionable intelligence is not often the case. Even presuming that it is, Major Matthew Alexander, leader of the Task Force 145 team that gained the information that led to al-Zarqawi's killing, responds, "A trained, experienced interrogator with a Koran can get more information from a subject in ten minutes than a heavy hand can extract in three days."[86] "Rapport" does not imply a deep personal relationship of enduring trust; a modest level of rapport can be established quickly, as demonstrated in "good cop–bad cop" civilian interrogations.

There is a case in which actionable intelligence reportedly was gained through torture. In Manila, in January 1995, a week before Pope John Paul II was to visit the Philippine capital, Abdul Hakim Murad, a Pakistani citizen, accidentally started a small fire in his apartment. Responding police found extensive bomb-making materials. They set about learning what their prisoner might know. "For weeks, agents hit him with a chair and a long piece of wood. . . . His captors were surprised that he survived."[87]

> His interrogators reportedly beat him so badly that most of his ribs were broken; they extinguished cigarettes on his genitals; they made him sit on ice cubes; they forced water down his throat so that he nearly drowned. This went on for several weeks. In the end, he provided names, dates and places behind an al Qaeda plan to blow up 11 commercial airliners and fly another one into the headquarters of the Central Intelligence Agency. He also confessed to a plot to assassinate the pope. . . . Murad may have nearly died, but he didn't crack until a new team of interrogators told him falsely that they were from the Mossad and would be taking him to Israel.[88]

Torture worked and critical intelligence was obtained; therefore, the end justified the means? Professor Luban points out, "And they tortured him for weeks, during which time

---

[83] Ronald Kessler, *The Terrorist Watch* (New York: Crown Forum, 2007), 147, 148.

[84] Scott Shane, "Inside the Interrogation of a 9/11 Mastermind," *NY Times*, June 22, 2008, A1.

[85] Mark Bowden, "The Ploy," *Atlantic*, May, 2007, 54–68.

[86] Maj. Matthew Alexander, USAF, "Interrogating Terrorists," Address to student body, Command & Staff College, Marine Corps University; Quantico, Virginia, Jan. 23, 2009.

[87] Marites D. Vitug and Glenda M. Gloria, *Under the Crescent Moon: Rebellion in Mindanao* (Quezon City, PI: Institute for Popular Democracy, 2000), 223. Murad was tortured for sixty-seven days.

[88] Peter Maas, "If a Terror Suspect Won't Talk, Should He Be Made To?" *NY Times*, March 9, 2003, wk4. Also, Dershowitz, *Why Terrorism Works*, supra, note 1, at 137.

they didn't know about any specific al Qaeda plot. What if he too didn't know? Or what if there had been no al Qaeda plot? Then they would have tortured him ... for nothing. ... You cannot use the argument that preventing the al Qaeda attack justified the decision to torture, because at the moment that decision [to torture] was made no one knew about the al Qaeda attack."[89]

Thanks to an iconic motion picture, many military officers know of the battle for Algiers, fought during the French battle against Algerian nationalists. The French army engaged in torture to win that battle, but "What did torture achieve in the Battle of Algiers? Putting aside any consideration of morality, was it even effective?"[90] Military historians agree that the French commander, General Jacques Massu, could not have won the battle without the use of torture. "This is certainly true of the short term, but in the longer term – as the Nazis in the Second World War, and as almost every other power that has ever adopted torture as an instrument of policy, have discovered – it is a double-edged weapon."[91]

> In January 1989, the CIA informed the [Senate Intelligence] Committee that "inhumane physical or psychological techniques are counterproductive because they do not produce intelligence and will probably result in false answers."[92] Testimony of the CIA deputy director of operations in 1988 denounced coercive interrogation techniques, stating, "[p]hysical abuse or other degrading treatment was rejected not only because it is wrong but because it has historically proven to be ineffective."[93]

Those CIA comments were made before the 9/11 attacks on America; before the CIA employed extraordinary renditions, black sites, enhanced interrogation techniques, waterboarding, and "rectal rehydration."

In 2006, the U.S. Army published a new interrogation manual. At a briefing for reporters, the army's deputy chief of staff for intelligence was asked whether torture was useful in gaining military intelligence. He replied:

> No good intelligence is going to come from abusive practices. ... I think the empirical evidence of the last five years, hard years, tells us that. And moreover, any piece of intelligence which is obtained under duress, through the use of abusive techniques, would be of questionable credibility, and additionally it would do more harm than good when it inevitably became known that abusive practices were used. ... Some of our most significant successes on the battlefield have been – in fact, I would say all of them, almost categorically all of them, have accrued from expert interrogators using mixtures of authorized humane interrogation practices.[94]

It would be foolish to suggest that torture never succeeds; that torture does not sometimes produce actionable information. "If official and unofficial government reports are to be believed, the methods work. In report after report hard-core terrorist leaders are said to be either cooperating or, at the very least, providing some information – not just vague statements but detailed, verifiable, useful intelligence."[95] No doubt torture has elicited valuable intelligence in some cases. Repeated exaggerated or false assertions of valuable

---

[89] Luban, "Liberalism, Torture, and the Ticking Bomb," supra, note 8, at 1442.
[90] Horne, *A Savage War of Peace*, supra, note 18, at 204.   [91] Id., at 205.
[92] *Senate Intelligence Committee Report on Torture*, supra, note 30, at 32. Footnotes omitted.   [93] Id.
[94] George Packer, "The Talk of the Town; Comment: Prisoners," *New Yorker*, Sept. 18, 2006, 26.
[95] Mark Bowden, "The Dark Art of Interrogation," *Atlantic Monthly*, Oct. 2003.

lifesaving information gained through "enhanced interrogation" methods have led, however, to a jaded disbelief that is not always warranted. Hidden behind the impenetrable screen of "national security," it is impossible either to verify or to discredit every assertion of success or failure of abusive interrogation. It can only be said that history, research, and international experience make clear that positive results from torture are, at best, unusual.

"CIA records indicate that the first CIA briefing for the president [George W. Bush] on the CIA's enhanced interrogation techniques occurred on April 8, 2006. CIA records state that when the president was briefed, he expressed discomfort with the 'image of a detainee, chained to the ceiling, clothed in a diaper, and force to go to the bathroom on himself.'"[96] Two years later, in March 2008, the president, apparently having overcome his discomfort, "vetoed a bill [an amendment to the 1978 Foreign Intelligence Surveillance Act] that would have explicitly prohibited the [Central Intelligence] agency from using interrogation methods like waterboarding."[97] In a national radio address regarding the veto the president said, "This program [that includes enhanced interrogation methods] has produced critical intelligence that has helped us prevent a number of attacks. The program helped us stop a plot to strike a U.S. Marine camp in Djibouti, a planned attack on the U.S. consulate in Karachi, a plot to hijack a passenger plane and fly it into Library Tower in Los Angeles, and a plot to crash passenger planes into Heathrow Airport or buildings in downtown London."[98]

Senator John D. Rockefeller IV responded,

> As Chairman of the Senate Intelligence Committee, I have heard nothing to suggest that information obtained from enhanced interrogation techniques has prevented an imminent terrorist attack. And I have heard nothing that makes me think the information obtained from these techniques could not have been obtained through traditional interrogation methods used by military and law enforcement interrogators. On the other hand, I do know that coercive interrogation can lead detainees to provide false information in order to make the interrogation stop.[99]

In a 2008 interview, "F.B.I. director since 2001, Robert S. Mueller III, was asked whether any attacks had been disrupted because of intelligence obtained through the coercive methods. 'I don't believe that has been the case,' Mr. Mueller answered."[100]

An August 2002 message quoted by the Senate Intelligence Committee related the agency's Alice in Wonderland-logic: "The interrogation team later deemed the use of the CIA's enhanced interrogation techniques a success, not because it resulted in

---

[96] *Senate Intelligence Committee Report on Torture*, supra, note 30, at 51. Footnotes omitted.

[97] Steven Lee Myers, "Bush Vetoes Bill on C.I.A. Tactics, Affirming Legacy," NY *Times*, March 9, 2008, A1. Also see John R. Crook, "Contemporary Practice of the United States Relating to International Law: President Vetoes Legislation to Limit CIA Interrogation Methods," 102–3 *AJIL* (July 2008), 650.

[98] President's Radio Address (March 8, 2008), http://www.whitehouse.gov/news/releases/2008/03/print/20080308.html.

[99] Dan Froomkin, "A Legacy of Torture," *Wash. Post*, March 10, 2008, n.p.

[100] Scott Shane, "Interrogations' Effectiveness May Prove Elusive," NY *Times*, April 23, 2009, A14. Director Mueller's assessment is in sharp contrast to assertions by four former CIA directors. Still, FBI refusal to participate in interrogations it viewed as unlawful caused them to withdraw from all CIA interrogations. An FBI supervisory special agent initially involved in the CIA interrogations said, "The message came through from . . . an F.B.I. assistant director, that 'we don't do that'." Ali Soufan, "My Tortured Decision," NY *Times*, April 23, 2009, A25.

critical threat information, but because it provided further evidence that [detainee] Abu Zubaydah had not been withholding the aforementioned information from the interrogators."[101] The ends justify the means, and so do the nonends.

16.3.2 *Intelligence Gained through Torture Is Unreliable*

In October 1967, at the height of the U.S.–North Vietnamese conflict, a U.S. Navy pilot flying an A-4 Skyhawk off the aircraft carrier *Oriskany* was shot down while on a bombing run over Hanoi, North Vietnam. In ejecting, both of his arms and his right knee were broken. Immediately captured upon landing, he was beaten, questioned, and given little medical care. A few weeks later, when medical complications set in, the pilot was left to die in his cell. Fate intervened when the North Vietnamese learned that the prisoner's father was commander in chief of U.S. naval forces in Europe. Lieutenant John S. McCain was taken to a hospital in time to save his leg. McCain writes, "Once my condition had stabilized, my interrogators resumed their work. Demands for military information were accompanied by threats to terminate my medical treatment if I did not cooperate. Eventually, I gave them my ship's name and squadron number. . . . Pressed for more useful information, I gave the names of the Green Bay Packers' offensive line, and said they were members of my squadron."[102]

Vice Admiral James B. Stockdale, awarded the Medal of Honor for heroism as a prisoner of the North Vietnamese for seven and a half years, was shot down in September 1965. When captured, he realized that, as a navy commander, he was the senior American military captive in the war. While recovering from his initial interrogations under torture he considered his duty as the senior captured officer. "I put a lot of thought into what my first orders should be. They would be orders that could be obeyed, not a 'cover your ass' move of reiterating some U.S. government policy like 'name, rank, serial number and date of birth,' which we had no chance of standing up to in the torture room."[103] He recounts instances when he and other American military prisoners provided false information under torture. "Some of my accounts matched reality and some did not."[104] Admiral Stockdale's statement that "the more the degradation, the more the pain, the more the humiliation, the more the human spirit was challenged, the better it performed"[105] was demonstrated by American prisoners' continued resistance to North Vietnamese torture. Torture increased resistance and often resulted in the giving of false information. That torture results in unreliable information is supported by research:

> Fear may motivate an enemy source to "talk," but not necessarily to provide accurate intelligence. . . . Psychological theory . . . and related research suggests that coercion or pressure can actually *increase* a source's resistance and determination not to comply. Although pain is commonly assumed to facilitate compliance, there is no available

---

[101] *Senate Intelligence Committee Report on Torture*, supra, note 30, at 49. Footnote omitted.

[102] John McCain, *Faith of My Fathers* (New York: Random House, 1999), 193–4.

[103] VAdm. James B. Stockdale, *Stockdale on Stoicism II: Master of My Fate* (Annapolis, MD: United States Naval Academy, Center for the Study of Professional Military Ethics, n.d.), 9.

[104] Stockdale and Stockdale, *In Love and War*, supra, note 31, at 260.

[105] James Bond Stockdale, "Leadership in Times of Crisis," in *Thoughts of a Philosophical Fighter Pilot* (Stanford, CA: Hoover Institution Press, 1995), 41.

scientific or systematic research to suggest that coercion can, will, or has provided accurate useful information from otherwise uncooperative sources.[106]

The unreliability of military information obtained through coercion is also documented in law enforcement–oriented research. Many of the same interrogation techniques are employed in both arenas. Gisli Gudjonsson, a psychologist expert on law enforcement interrogation techniques, documents cases of false confessions – innocent suspects, influenced by interrogators without the use of physical force, who make detailed false confessions to serious crimes. Gudjonsson writes:

> No police interrogation is completely free of coercion, nor will it ever be. Furthermore, a certain amount of persuasion is often needed for effective interrogation. The real issue [is] about the extent and nature of the manipulation and persuasion used. . . . Innocent suspects may be manipulated to confess falsely, and in view of the subtlety of the techniques utilized innocent suspects may actually come to believe that they are guilty.[107]

For military personnel, the significance of Gudjonsson's research, and his compilation of cases of false confessions, is in documenting the unreliability of information obtained through interrogation. In the law enforcement realm, false confessions commonly lead to innocent suspects' being imprisoned. The media frequently report individuals released from prison, exonerated through DNA evidence. A 2007 report noted, "In about a quarter of the 201 wrongful convictions that have been overturned with the use of DNA evidence, people had confessed or admitted to crimes they did not commit."[108] In 1997, for example, three U.S. Navy sailors confessed to rape and murder, each of their separately given accounts including specific lurid details of the rape–murder of a fellow sailor's wife. All three were convicted and sentenced to life imprisonment, only to be exonerated through DNA evidence eight years later.[109] Individually, each of the three, without physical coercion, swore to committing heinous crimes of which he actually had no knowledge or involvement.

Add torture to the mix, and the reliability of military intelligence obtained only becomes more doubtful. "A suspect who wants to avoid the unkindness of having his teeth extracted with a set of dirty pliers may say whatever he thinks his torturers want to hear."[110] A tortured prisoner will admit any act, confess any crime, or offer any intelligence to end the pain. During the Korean War (1950–3) the U.S. Air Force colonel Harold E. Fischer was shot down and captured. A captain then, he was held for more than two years in Manchuria, where he was tortured and finally confessed to germ warfare. "I was grilled day and night, over and over, week in and week out, and, in the end, to get Chong and his gang off my back, I confessed. . . . The charges, of course, were ridiculous. . . . It was not really me . . . who signed that paper. It was a mentality reduced to putty."[111]

---

[106] Borum, "Approaching Truth," in *Educing Information*, supra, note 78, 17, 35. Emphasis in original.

[107] Gisli H. Gudjonsson, *The Psychology of Interrogations and Confessions* (West Sussex, UK: Wiley, 2003), 37.

[108] Tina Kelley, "DNA Clears Inmate of New Jersey Child Murders," *NY Times*, May 16, 2007, A18.

[109] Brian Bennett, "True Confessions?" *Time*, Dec. 12, 2005, 45–6; and Alan Berlow, "What Happened In Norfolk?" *NY Times Magazine*, Aug. 19, 2007, 36.

[110] Maas, "If a Terror Suspect Won't Talk, Should He Be Made To?" supra, note 88.

[111] Dennis Hevesi, "Harold E. Fischer Jr., 83, American Flier Tortured in a Chinese Prison, Is Dead," *NY Times*, May 8, 2009, B10.

"From a purely intelligence point of view, experience teaches that more often than not the collating services are overwhelmed by a mountain of false information extorted from victims desperate to save themselves further agony."[112]

The [Senate Intelligence] Committee reviewed 20 of the most frequent and prominent examples of purported counterterrorism successes that the CIA has attributed to the use of its enhanced interrogation techniques, and found them to be wrong in fundamental respects. In some cases, there was no relationship between the cited counterterrorism success and the information provided by detainees. ... In the remaining cases, the CIA inaccurately claimed that specific, otherwise unavailable information was acquired from a CIA detainee "as a result" of the CIA's enhanced interrogation techniques.[113]

16.3.3 *Torture Can Accompany and Promote Other Battlefield Misconduct*

A military unit that tortures prisoners may be undisciplined in other ways, as well. Michael Walzer writes, "The best soldiers, the best fighting men, do not loot and rape. Similarly, the best soldiers do not wantonly kill civilians."[114]

During the U.S.–Vietnamese conflict, the army lieutenant William Calley's 1st Platoon of C Company was attached to Task Force Barker. At My Lai, in March 1968, in a single horrific incident, the 1st Platoon committed hundreds of murders, many rapes and sexual mutilations, and other grave breaches. It was a prototypical undisciplined and poorly led military unit. C Company was commanded by Captain Ernest Medina. Even before My Lai, a deterioration in C Company's performance was noted.

Whereas Medina had once been a strong disciplinarian ... he now began to let slide misdemeanors he would have previously pounced on. ... The battalion commander ... saw Medina's troops behaving sloppily. Their appearance was not up to scratch and he found them drinking alcohol in the field. ... The troops' physical condition and general behavior had deteriorated ... there was virtually no discipline, leadership, or respect for those in command. ... Calley continued to be particularly detested by his men. [115]

Even before My Lai, Calley "was so detested by his men ... that they put a bounty on his head. That was only one indication of the total deterioration of discipline within Charlie Company."[116] Lieutenant General William Peers, who led the army's investigation of the My Lai incident, considered "that at all levels, from division down to platoon, leadership or the lack of it was perhaps the principle causative factor in the tragic events."[117] Military officers recognize that units like C Company are candidates for battlefield excesses, candidates even for a My Lai massacre.

In early 2004, Lieutenant Colonel Nathan Sassaman, a nineteen-year army veteran, was one of the most highly regarded battalion commanders in Iraq. His battalion was assigned to Balad, a difficult and deadly area. As time wore on, however, disciplinary problems appeared in the battalion. Lieutenant Colonel Sassaman recalled that

[112] Horne, *Savage War of Peace*, supra, note 18, at 205.
[113] *Senate Intelligence Committee Report on Torture*, supra, note 30, at 4.
[114] Michael Walzer, *Arguing about War* (New Haven, CT: Yale University Press, 2004), 26.
[115] Michael Bilton and Kevin Sim, *Four Hours in My Lai* (New York: Viking, 1992), 196–7.
[116] Michal R. Belknap, *The Vietnam War on Trial* (Lawrence: University of Kansas Press, 2002), 88.
[117] Lt.General W.R. Peers, *The My Lai Inquiry* (New York: Norton, 1979), 232.

"a degree of cynicism had infiltrated the ranks."[118] A group of his soldiers went to the house of a suspected truck hijacker. Sassaman was not there, but, according to the *New York Times*, his soldiers gave the absent man's family fifteen minutes to pull furniture from the house before they destroyed it with four antitank missiles, as they did. Elsewhere, Sassaman's soldiers threw a wounded prisoner into a cell and threatened to withhold treatment "unless he told them everything he knew."[119] One of the battalion's sergeants said, "People don't exactly get beaten up. . . . They got slapped around, roughed up, usually after they were detained. It was gratuitous. Sassaman didn't do it, but he definitely knew about it."[120]

The indiscipline culminated when one of Lieutenant Colonel Sassaman's officers, First Lieutenant Jack Saville, ordered five of his men to throw two Iraqis caught out after curfew into the Tigris River. One of the five soldiers refused the order. The other four carried out the drowning of one of the Iraqis, who was nineteen years old. His body was never found.

When the incident was investigated, Lieutenant Colonel Sassaman admittedly directed a subordinate to conceal evidence ("'Don't say anything about the water' [into which the Iraqis had been thrown], I instructed.")[121] and he withheld portions of the incident from investigators. At court-martial, Lieutenant Saville pleaded guilty to reduced charges of two specifications (counts) of assault, obstruction of justice, and dereliction of duty. He was sentenced to forfeit two thousand dollars' pay per month for six months, and confinement for forty-five days.[122] Sassaman and two others received written reprimands for impeding the investigation. His career over, an outspokenly disrespectful and embittered Lieutenant Colonel Sassaman retired from the army, a victim of his own indiscipline and the indiscipline of his command.[123] "The real product of his aggressive leadership was a more emboldened insurgency and a more undisciplined unit."[124]

The ICTY, while trying individuals for 1993 war crimes committed in Sarajevo, in the former Yugoslavia, heard testimony that "there were units where there was talk of indiscipline and insubordination. . . . According to Dževad Tirak, the 6th Corps chief of staff . . . two brigades had the worst reputation in terms of discipline and [war crimes] incidents."[125] Indiscipline, insubordination, and incidents in the same brigades caused dishonor of the army as a whole.

The best-led military units rarely commit LOAC violations.

---

[118] Lt.Col. Nathan Sassaman, *Warrior King* (New York: St. Martin's Press, 2008), 207.

[119] Dexter Filkins, "The Fall of the Warrior King," NY *Times Magazine*, Oct. 23, 2005, 52, 59.

[120] Id., at 66.   [121] Sassaman, *Warrior King*, supra, note 118, at 245.

[122] *U.S. v. Saville* (Fort Hood, TX, 2005). Because the punishment adjudged by the court-martial, a fine, and confinement for forty-five days was below (*well* below) that required by UCMJ Art. 66 for appellate review, the case was reviewed by no appellate body and no appellate opinion was generated. For a criticism of this and similar court-martial outcomes see Lt.Col. Gary Solis, "Military Justice?" U.S. Naval Institute *Proceedings* (Oct. 2006), 24–7.

[123] Sassaman, *Warrior King*, supra, note 118, at 267. Lieutenant Colonel Sassaman writes of his reprimand by the commanding general Major General Raymond Odierno, "I did not trust my commanding officers. I didn't trust my brigade commander at all. And General Odierno? He lived in the palace in Tikrit. He was in the same room Saddam used to be in."

[124] Major Jeffrey S. Dietz, Book Review, *Army Lawyer* (Aug. 2010), 60, 61 (reviewing Lieutenant Colonel Nathan Sassaman, *Warrior King: The Triumph and Betrayal of an American Commander in Iraq* (2008).

[125] *Prosecutor v. Halilavić*, IT-01-48-T (Nov. 16, 2005), para. 122.

16.3.4 *Torture Is Counterproductive on an International Level*

History demonstrates that, ultimately, torture is ineffective in achieving a state's larger goals, while diminishing the state in the eyes of the world. The executive director of the 9/11 Commission writes, "There is another variable in the intelligence equation: the help you lose because your friends start keeping their distance. ... Some of America's best European allies found it increasingly difficult to assist us in counter-terrorism because they feared becoming complicit in a program their governments abhorred."[126]

In 1987, the government of Israel appointed a commission of inquiry headed by a former Israeli Supreme Court president, Moshe Landau. The Landau Commission examined the General Security Service's (GSS, roughly equivalent to the American CIA) methods of questioning suspected terrorists and formulated guidelines regarding interrogation methods. The guidelines allowed use of a "moderate degree of physical pressure" to obtain information when dealing with terrorists who represented a grave threat to the state and its citizens. In a still-secret section of its report, the commission specified permissible forms of pressure.[127] In 1997, a *New York Times* editorial scolded, "The character of a country is determined in some measure by how it treats its enemies and prisoners. Israel harms its international stature by torturing its foes."[128]

After objections regarding prisoner treatment were raised, an Israeli investigation confirmed "systematic abuses while interrogating prisoners during the Palestinian uprising and that its agents had lied about their actions in court."[129] The Committee against Torture, an enforcement body required by Article 17 of the CAT, also assessed the methods used by the GSS in a 1997 report:

> Although these combined [interrogation] methods were fairly similar to those applied by British security forces in *Northern Ireland* and found ... to violate Article 3 ECHR [European Convention on Human Rights] (restraining in very painful conditions, hooding under special conditions, sounding of loud music for prolonged periods, sleep deprivation, threats, including death threats, violent shaking and using cold air to chill), the Israeli Government maintained that they had not crossed the threshold of either Article 1 or 16 [of the] CAT as they did not cause suffering. The Committee strongly rejected this position and concluded that the interrogation methods ... constitute torture as defined in Article 1 of the Convention [Against Torture].[130]

Israel contested the committee's judgment, but, in 1999, the Israeli Supreme Court held that GSS interrogation methods involving physical force, and those of the GSS's successor, the Israel Security Agency, were indeed illegal and violated suspects' constitutional protections to a right to dignity. The Court specifically rejected hooding,

---

[126] Zelikow, "A Dubious C.I.A. Shortcut," supra, note 82.

[127] The account of the Israeli experience is from Manfred Nowak and Elizabeth McArthur, *The United Nations Convention against Torture: A Commentary* (New York: Oxford University Press, 2008), at 55–8.

[128] "Using Torture in Israel," *NY Times*, May 9, 1997, n.p.

[129] Joel Greenberg, "Israel Reports Abuses in Past Interrogations of Palestinians," *NY Times*, Feb. 10, 2000, A-3.

[130] Nowak and McArthur, *United Nations Convention against Torture*, supra, note 127, at 56. Footnotes omitted. The British case referred to in the text as, "*Northern Ireland*," is: *A and others v. Secretary of State for the Home Department* [2005] UKHL 71.

shaking, forced crouching on toes, painful handcuffing, seating suspects on low and inclined stools, sleep deprivation, and prolonged extremely loud music. The judgment was based on Israeli domestic law, rather than the CAT.[131]

Moderate physical pressure was initially authorized only in special cases, but Israeli security services soon saw every case involving suspected terrorists as a special case. The exception became the norm until, in 1999, the abused norm was declared illegal.

Israel is hardly alone among democratic states in committing torture. During the "Algerian independence war" (1954–62), the conduct of France's military forces in Algeria, including their use of torture, generated international condemnation of France and "absolutely voided the capability of the military force."[132]

The Algerian armed conflict pitted French settlers, *colons*, against Algerian nationalists, most of whom were Muslims. In 1954, encouraged by the French defeat at Dien Bien Phu, the Algerian nationalists began planning to evict the French in a bid for national independence. The nationalists' political arm was the *Front de Libération Nationale* (FLN). The FLN became a classic insurgent force. Beginning in 1954, from bases in neighboring Tunisia they launched strikes on public buildings, communications centers, and police and military posts. Ultimately, 415,000 French troops were stationed in Algeria to fight them. At first, the FLN limited their kidnappings, murders, and mutilations to *colons* and captured soldiers, but eventually they expanded their victims to include nonsupportive civilians. schools, shops, and cafes became FLN bombing targets.

In response, the French army initiated stern "counterterrorist" measures. Under a concept of collective responsibility, remote villages were attacked and the inhabitants killed. Although there were dissenting voices,[133] the French raised arguments that would later be heard in the conflict against al Qaeda and the Taliban. "[T]e soldiers . . . saw themselves as unencumbered by traditional norms of military justice. One note from [he French army commander] General Massu finished . . . 'Our current laws are unsuited to dealing with terrorism for the simple reason that this form of aggression was never envisioned.'"[134]

In the 1956 battle of Algiers, General Jacques Massu's 10th Colonial Parachute division, employing torture and murder, achieved impressive results. Within three months, French forces prevailed. Massu's intelligence chief was Colonel Paul Aussaresses. In his postwar account of the war (after a 1968 French amnesty was declared for crimes committed during the war), Aussaresses freely admitted to torture, disappearances, and murder. Describing a "ticking bomb" scenario, he wrote:

> Just think for a moment that you are personally opposed to torture as a matter of principle and that you have arrested a suspect who is clearly involved in preparing

---

[131] *Israel v. The State of Israel* (HCJ 5100/94), 1999, supra, note 17.

[132] General Rupert Smith, *The Utility of Force* (New York: Alfred Knopf, 2007), 246.

[133] General Jacques de Bollardière objected in writing to Massu that his orders were "in absolute opposition to the respect for man that constituted the very foundation of my life and I refuse to take responsibility for them." General de Bollardière then ordered his troops not to engage in torture. He soon resigned his command, telling his longtime friend Massu, "I despise your action." Alon Harel and Assaf Sharon, "What Is Really Wrong with Torture?" 6–2 *J. of Int'l Crim. Justice* (May 2008), 241, 241–1.

[134] Marie-Monique Robin, "Counterinsurgency and Torture," in Roth, Worden, and Bernstein, *Torture*, supra, note 19, at 48.

a violent attack. The suspect refuses to talk. You choose not to insist. The attack takes place and it's extremely bloody. What explanation will you give to the victim's parents, the parents of a child, for instance, whose body was torn to pieces by the bomb, to justify the fact that you didn't use every method available to force the suspect into talking? ... Torture a suspected terrorist or tell the parents of the victims that it's better to let scores of innocent people be killed rather than make a single accomplice suffer.[135]

Aussaresses later describes his interrogation technique. "[F]or 'extreme' interrogations: first, a beating, which in most cases was enough; then other means, such as electric shocks, known as the famous '*gégène*'; and finally water. Torture by electric shock was made possible by generators used to power field radio transmitters. ... Electrodes were attached to the prisoner's ears or testicles, then electric charges of varying intensity were turned on."[136] How did General Massu's intelligence chief, a career army officer and holder of the Légion d'Honneur who retired as a brigadier general, handle hardcore FLN? "The diehards, those who were ready to start all over again the next day ... how should we handle them once they had been questioned and had told us everything they knew? I picked a few groups of NCOs and ordered them to shoot the prisoners. ... They didn't have any qualms."[137]

When Aussaresses's book was published in France in 2001, it "brought cries of outrage,"[138] but "Aussaresses wasn't telling the French something that they could claim had been kept from them. Yet his very brazenness forced the French public to confront some uncomfortable truths about their *mission civilisatrice* in Algeria."[139]

In Algiers the FLN, at great cost to both sides, had demonstrated its ability to strike French power bases in Algeria, but its leadership had been killed or compromised and military defeat was near. In France, however, public opinion grew weary of conscripted service to continue the fight and, internationally, France's major allies deserted, repelled by French tactics.

In 1959, the French president, Charles De Gaulle, a former general and World War II leader, recognized Algeria's right to self-determination and withdrew French forces from the country. Shockingly, in 1960 and 1961, armed French army revolts and assassination attempts against De Gaulle were unsuccessfully mounted. The army was years in recovering its reputation and French popular trust.

In 1962, Algeria gained independence. Deaths in the conflict totaled twenty-four thousand French and an estimated half-million Algerians. The army's torture, disappearances, and murders had not forestalled the outcome and, as the tactics became known to the French public, played a role in achieving the FLN's ultimate goal.

Today, some see the United States as tarred with the brush that marred the national reputations of Israel and France. An American commentator referred to a 2006 presidential speech that cited a need for harsh interrogation tactics:[140]

The president of the United States. Interrogation by torture. This just can't be happening. ... It is not possible for our elected representatives to hold any sort of

---

[135] BGeneral Paul Aussaresses, *The Battle of the Casbah* (New York: Enigma Books, 2002), 17.

[136] Id., at 20.   [137] Id., at 50–1.

[138] Keith B. Richburg, "France Faces Its Demons for Algerian War Brutality," *Wash. Post*, May 10, 2001, A26.

[139] Adam Shatz, "The Torture of Algiers," *New York Review of Books*, Nov. 21, 2002, 53, 54.

[140] White House. "President Discusses Creation of Military Commissions," supra, note 6.

honorable "debate" over torture. . . . Civilized nations do not debate slavery or genocide, and they don't debate torture, either. . . . There is one ray of encouragement: the crystal clear evidence that the men and women of our armed forces want no part of torturing anybody. . . . But we shouldn't have to talk about the practicalities of torture, because the real question is moral: What kind of a nation are we? What kind of people are we?[141]

A former commandant of the Marine Corps and a former commanding general of Central Command in 2007 urged:

These assertions that "torture works" may reassure a fearful public, but it is a false security . . . and any "flexibility" about torture at the top drops down the chain of command like a stone. . . . The rules must be firm and absolute; if torture is broached as a possibility, it will become a reality. . . . If we forfeit our values by signaling that they are negotiable in situations of grave or imminent danger, we drive those undecideds into the arms of the enemy. This way lies defeat, and we are well down the road to it.[142]

The U.N.'s special rapporteur on torture noted that nations charged with torture point to the United States as their example. "We're not doing something different than what the United States is doing."[143] A 2008 Canadian manual for diplomats listed the United States among the countries that potentially torture prisoners.[144] A retired U.S. Army colonel and Vietnam era special forces officer commented:

At this moment in Iraq, we are turning to the lessons of the French – and we will make exactly the same mistakes the French made in Algeria and the Americans made in Vietnam. In the name of gathering information, we will use torture, which is not only immoral but ineffective, since information obtained under torture is absolutely not reliable. Torture is an expression of shortsighted policy . . . because it is the best recruiter for the terrorists it claims to fight.[145]

Alberto J. Mora, former general counsel of the U.S. Navy, who, in 2006, retired in protest of government interrogation policies, and John Shattuck, a former assistant secretary of state, note that "cruelty diminishes the international standing of the United States. . . . The damage to our national security may be even worse. Our ability to build and maintain the broad alliance needed to efficiently fight the war on terrorism has been crippled."[146]

An army general adds, "If anyone believes that the information gained through torture has been worth the price to our national honor and capacity to persuade other nations to follow our lead, it's time for them to produce hard evidence of torture's superior worth. Our torture policy has been disastrously counterproductive."[147]

---

[141] Eugene Robinson, "Torture Is Torture," *Wash. Post*, Sept. 19, 2006, A21.

[142] Generals Charles C. Krulak and Joseph P. Hoar, "It's Our Cage, Too," *Wash. Post*, May 17, 2007, A17.

[143] Nick Wadhams, "U.N. Says Human Rights Violators Cite U.S.," *Wash. Post*, Oct. 24, 2006, A4.

[144] Ian Austen, "Canadian Manual Has U.S. on Torture List," *NY Times*, Jan. 18, 2008, A10. When the diplomatic training manual became public, the Canadian government removed the United States from the list. "Canada to Remove U.S., Israel from List of Nations That Torture," *Wash. Post*, Jan. 20, 2008, A21.

[145] Robin, "Counterinsurgency and Torture," supra, note 134, at 65.

[146] Alberto Mora and Jack Shattuck, "Self-Inflicted Wounds," *Wash. Post*, Nov. 6, 2007, A19.

[147] BGen. (Ret.) David R. Irvine, "Rationalizing Torture," *Wash. Times*, Nov. 2, 2005, 17.

SIDEBAR. Does the "frequent flier program" constitute torture? Canada's Department of Foreign Affairs reported that Omar Khadr, held at Guantánamo since he was sixteen years old (his detention continued beyond his twenty-first birthday), was charged with killing an American soldier in Afghanistan. The report says that, in 2004, to make him "'more amenable and willing to talk' Khadr was moved to a new cell every three hours for three weeks, 'thus denying him uninterrupted sleep.' ... This practice, [is] referred to as the 'frequent flier program'."[148] According to Guantánamo confinement facility records, in 2004, another prisoner, Mohammed Jawad, "was moved repeatedly from one detention cell to another in quick intervals and usually at night, a program designed to deprive detainees of sleep. ... Prison logs show that [Jawad] was moved 112 times in 14 days ... for no apparent reason."[149] The air force lieutenant general Randall M. Schmidt, who investigated the practice,[150] said it was banned in March 2004. "I did not term the frequent flier program as torture," but it "was considered abusive if it was not properly done."[151] The general did not detail the proper method. In September 2012, after pleading guilty to several offenses, Kadhr was sent to Canada, pursuant to a pretrial agreement allowing him to serve the final three years of his sentence there. He was freed in May 2015.

Frequent forced movement from location to location is nowhere specifically described as torture or cruel, inhuman, or degrading treatment. But methods and techniques of torture are nowhere exhaustively specified. Applying the basic elements of most definitions of torture, does the frequent flier program cause severe physical or mental pain or suffering? Is the frequent flier program merely an aggressive and permissible preinterrogation technique, or is it torture?

16.3.5 Torture Endangers War Fighters

If the United States is perceived as torturing prisoners, it can be anticipated that similar tactics will be employed against future U.S. prisoners. In the Vietnam conflict, Senator John McCain was a prisoner for five years and five months. He says, "Mistreatment of enemy prisoners endangers our own troops who might someday be held captive. While some enemies, and Al Qaeda surely, will never be bound by the principle of

[148] Ian Austen, "Citing New Report, Lawyers for Canadian Detainee Denounce Abuse," NY Times, July 11, 2008, A9. A copy of the brief Canadian report, p. 9 of a U.S. Air Force interrogation report, is available at http://media.miamiherald.com/smedia/2008/07/10/08/khadrdocs.source.prod_affiliate.56.pdf

[149] Josh White, "Detainee's Attorney Seeks Dismissal over Abuse," Wash. Post, June 8, 2008, A4.

[150] See Army Regulation 15–6: Final Report; Investigation into FBI Allegations of Detainee Abuse at Guantánamo Bay, Cuba Detention Facility (April 1, 2005, amended June 9, 2005), http://www.defenselink.mil/news/Jul2005/d20050714report.pdf As well as confirming the "frequent flier program," the Final Report documents a female interrogator's wiping fake menstrual blood on a detainee, frequent use of loud music, use of extremes of heat and cold, sleep deprivation, a use of duct tape to cover a detainee's mouth and head, chaining detainees to the floor in a fetal position, use of a military dog to threaten a detainee, female interrogators' "lap dancing" on restrained detainees, forcing a "high-value" detainee to wear a bra and a thong over his head, leading him by a leash, and forcing him to perform dog tricks and to stand naked before female interrogators.

[151] Id.

reciprocity, we should have concern for those Americans captured by more traditional enemies, if not in this war then in the next."[152]

The lead air force interrogator of Task Force 145, which gleaned intelligence leading to the 2006 killing of Abu Musab al-Zarqawi without using harsh techniques, states:

> Torture and abuse cost American lives. I learned in Iraq that the No. 1 reason foreign fighters flocked there to fight were the abuses carried out at Abu Ghraib and Guantánamo. Our policy of torture was directly and swiftly recruiting fighters for al-Qaeda in Iraq. ... It's no exaggeration to say that at least half of our losses and casualties in that country have come at the hands of foreigners who joined the fray because of our program of detainee abuse. ... How anyone can say that torture keeps Americans safe is beyond me.[153]

16.4 Waterboarding Is Torture

The American debate about waterboarding – it is torture/ it is not torture – calls to mind the 1957 television play, and later Broadway production and motion picture, *Judgment at Nuremberg*. Near the drama's end, the central character, the American judge Dan Haywood, says,

> This trial has shown that under the stress of a national crisis, ordinary men, even able and extraordinary men, can delude themselves into the commission of crimes and atrocities. ... There are those in our country today, too, who speak of the protection of the country. Of survival. The answer to that is: survival as what? A country isn't a rock. And it isn't an extension of one's self. It's what it stands for, when standing for something is the most difficult.[154]

There is a certain attraction to waterboarding as an "enhanced interrogation technique." It leaves no mark, and within an hour, or less, the victim can be alert and on his feet. "Waterboarding" and its variations, "water torture," "water rag," "wet bag," *"chiffon,"* *"submarino,"* and the "water cure," are, by any name, torture. Applying the basic elements of most definitions of torture, does waterboarding cause severe physical or mental pain or suffering? One account of water torture from the French-Algerian conflict, a half-century ago, suggests the answer:

> Then there were the various forms of water torture: heads thrust repeatedly into water troughs until the victim was half-drowned; bellies and lungs filled with cold water from a hose placed in the mouth, with the nose stopped up. "'I couldn't hold on for more than a few moments,' says Alleg [an Algerian prisoner of the French]; 'I had the impression of drowning, and a terrible agony, that of death itself, took possession of me.'"[155]

In the U.S.–Philippine war (1899–1902), the water cure was commonly inflicted on prisoners of the United States. George Kennan, a well-known American explorer and

---

[152] John McCain, "Torture's Terrible Toll," *Newsweek*, Nov. 21, 2005, 34.
[153] Matthew Alexander, "Torture's the Wrong Answer. There's a Smarter Way," *Wash. Post*, Nov. 30, 2008, B1.
[154] Abby Mann, *Judgment at Nuremberg* (London: Cassell, 1961), 170–1.
[155] Horne, *Savage War of Peace*, supra, note 18, at 200.

writer of the day, and second cousin to the later U.S. diplomat George F. Kennan, was commissioned to investigate charges of cruelty by U.S. military forces. He reported:

> That we have inspired a considerable part of the Philippine population with a feeling of intense hostility toward us, and given them reason for deep-seated and implacable resentment, there can be no doubt. . . . We hold fifteen hundred or two thousand of them in prison . . . and we are now resorting directly or indirectly to the old Spanish inquisition methods such as the "water cure" in order to compel their silent prisoners to speak. [156]

What was the water cure? "The most notorious method of interrogation was the 'water cure,' described by one witness thus: 'The victim is laid flat on his back and held down by his tormentors. Then a bamboo tube is thrust into his mouth and some dirty water, the filthier the better, is poured down his unwilling throat.'"[157]

In U.S. "war on terrorism" practice, waterboarding is a more clinical event, described by the Department of Justice in workmanlike clinical detail:

> The individual is bound securely to an inclined bench, which is approximately four feet by seven feet. The individual's feet are generally elevated. A cloth is placed over the forehead and eyes. Water is then applied to the cloth in a controlled manner. . . . The cloth is lowered until it covers both the nose and the mouth. Once the cloth is saturated and completely covers the mouth and nose, air flow is slightly restricted for 20 to 40 seconds. . . . This causes an increase in carbon dioxide level in the individual's blood. . . . The cloth produces the perception of "suffocation and incipient panic," i.e., the perception of drowning. . . . During those 20 to 40 seconds, water is continuously applied from a height of twelve to twenty-four inches. After this period, the cloth is lifted, and the individual is allowed to breath unimpeded for three or four breaths. . . . The procedure may then be repeated. . . . The waterboard, which inflicts no pain or actual harm whatsoever, does not, in our view inflict "severe pain or suffering." . . . The waterboard is simply a controlled acute episode, lacking the connotation of a protracted period of time generally given to suffering.[158]

"No actual harm whatsoever." Three prisoners were waterboarded by the CIA in 2002 and 2003, the United States has admitted.[159] One of the three was waterboarded 183 times, another 83 times.[160] The third, twice.[161]

---

[156] Charles F. Adams, Carl Schurz, Edwin B. Smith, and Herbert Welsh, *Secretary Root's Record: "Marked Severities" in Philippine Warfare* (Boston: Geo. H. Ellis Co., 1902), 60.

[157] Brian McAllister Linn, *The Philippine War* (Lawrence: University of Kansas Press, 2000), 223.

[158] Memorandum for John Rizzo, Acting General Counsel of the Central Intelligence Agency; from U.S. Department of Justice, Office of Legal Counsel (August 1, 2002), 3–4, 11. This was one of four "Top Secret" DOJ memos released on April 16, 2009. The memo later addresses severe *mental* pain or suffering, declaring, at 15, "We find that the use of the waterboard constitutes a threat of imminent death," finding, at 18, "we conclude . . . the use of these methods separately or [as] a course of conduct would not violate Section 2340A [of Title 18, U.S. Code]."

[159] Memorandum for John A. Rizzo, Senior Deputy General Counsel, Central Intelligence Agency; from: U.S. Department of Justice, Office of Legal Counsel (May 30, 2005), at 6. The three who were waterboarded were Khalid Shaikh Mohammed, the alleged 9/11 master planner who reportedly went through "about 100" waterboardings; Abd al-Rahim al-Nashiri, a Saudi who allegedly planned the 2000 bombing of the USS *Cole*; and Abu Zubaydah, allegedly al Qaeda's logistics specialist, who reportedly broke "after 35 seconds" of waterboarding. Scott Shane, "Inside a 9/11 Mastermind's Interrogation," *NY Times*, June 22, 2008, A1.

[160] Scott Shane, "Memo Says Prisoner Got Waterboarded 183 Times," *NY Times*, April 20, 2009, A8.

[161] Memorandum for John Rizzo; from: Department of Justice (May 30, 2005), supra, note 158, at 8.

Some object that waterboarding cannot be torture because the United States subjects its own soldiers, pilots, civilian contractors, and DoD civilians to Survival, Evasion, Resistance and Escape (SERE) training that includes waterboarding. SERE school provides training on how to survive and resist the enemy in the event of capture. Waterboarding is indeed in the syllabus of several SERE schools. A former chief of training at the U.S. Navy's San Diego SERE school (who was himself waterboarded) writes, "Waterboarding is called 'simulated drowning,' but that's a misnomer. It does not simulate drowning, as the lungs are actually filling with water. There is no way to simulate that. The victim *is* drowning."[162] SERE interrogation methods have been used against U.S. detainees in Iraq, as well.[163]

To confuse waterboarding in training with waterboarding by an enemy captor misunderstands the crux of what constitutes torture. No formalized training, with supervisors standing by and medical personnel present, can replicate an actual torture victim's utter dependency on the torturer for mercy and surcease, for life itself.[164] SERE school introduces the student to the horror that may await, but it cannot *be* the horror.

In the U.S.–Philippine war (1898–1902), two U.S. Army officers were convicted by courts-martial for torturing prisoners by application of the "water cure." A particularly barbarous officer, Major Edwin F. Glenn, was convicted in 1902.[165] (See Chapter 2, Cases and Materials, for an extract from Glenn's record of trial.) The other officer convicted by court-martial was First Lieutenant Julien Gaujot.[166] Two other lieutenants were tried for imposing the water cure and acquitted.[167] Another officer, Captain Cornelius Brownell, escaped court-martial for the murder of a local priest he water cured because Brownell was discharged from the Army before his act was discovered.[168]

After World War II, it was the enemy who was tried for waterboardlike war crimes. The Supreme Court of Norway convicted a Nazi, Karl-Hans Klinge, of, inter alia, beating a Norwegian prisoner, stripping the bound victim, and placing him in a bath of ice-cold water, where his head was repeatedly forced underwater, after which he died.[169] Klinge was sentenced to death.

---

[162] Malcolm Nance, "Waterboarding Is Torture ... Period," *Small Wars Journal Blog*, Oct. 31, 2007, http://smallwarsjournal.com/blog/2007/10/waterboarding-is-torture-perio/ Emphasis in original.

[163] Erik Holmes, "Interrogator: SERE Tactics Used in Iraq," *Marine Corps Times*, Oct. 13, 2008, 32.

[164] "Executive Summary: Senate Armed Services Report on Torture," supra, note 42, at 8: "There are fundamental differences between a SERE school exercise and a real world interrogation. At SERE school, students are subject to an extensive medical and psychological pre-screening prior to being subjected to physical and psychological pressures. The schools impose strict limits on the frequency, duration, and/or intensity of certain techniques. Psychologists are present throughout SERE training to intervene should the need arise and to help students cope with associated stress. And SERE school is voluntary; students are even given a special phrase they can use to immediately stop the techniques from being used against them."

[165] *U.S. v Maj. Edwin F. Glenn*, Samar, P.I. (1902). Glenn eventually retired from the army with the grade of brigadier general.

[166] Lieutenant Gaujot's sentence, reflecting the court-martial's dismissive view of the water cure, was suspension from command for three months and forfeiture of fifty dollars' pay each month for three months.

[167] Major Mynda G. Ohman, "Integrating Title 18 War Crimes into Title 10: A Proposal to Amend the Uniform Code of Military Justice," 57 *Air Force L. R.* (2005), 1, fn. 78.

[168] Id., at fn. 79.

[169] *Trial of Kriminalassistent Karl-Hans Hermann Klinge*, S. Ct. of Norway (Dec. 8, 1945 and Feb. 27, 1946), in, *LRTWC*, Vol. III (London: U.N. War Crimes Commission, 1948), 1.

American judge Evan Wallach cites four other post–World War II U.S. military commission convictions for water torture.[170] *U.S. v. Shigeru Sawada*[171] involved the water torture of a U.S. Army Air Corps captain, Chase Nielsen, one of Lieutenant Colonel James Doolittle's 1942 raiders, who, after his thirty seconds over Tokyo, ditched near China and was captured and tortured.[172] In another case, the Japanese sergeant-major Chinsaku Yuki was sentenced to life imprisonment for torture and murder, including the water torture of a suspected Philippine guerrilla.[173] In *U.S. v. Nakamura et al.* and an associated case,[174] two Japanese soldiers, Lieutenant Seitara Hata and Master Sergeant Takeo Kita, the civilian interpreter Yukio Asano, and the civilian camp guard Yagoheiji Iwata were convicted of the water torture of Americans held in POW camps in Japan.[175] The Japanese soldiers were sentenced to twenty-five and fifteen years' confinement, respectively; the two civilians, to fifteen and twenty years'.

In World War II, a British lieutenant, Eric Lomax, was captured and held by the Japanese for three and a half years and forced to help construct the Burma–Siam railway described in Pierre Boulle's book *The Bridge over the River Kwai*. Discovered with a radio he had made, Lomax was repeatedly tortured.

> The NCO suddenly stopped hitting me. He went off to the side and I saw him coming back holding a hosepipe dribbling with water. . . . He directed the full flow of the now gushing pipe on to my nostrils and mouth at a distance of only a few inches. Water poured down my windpipe and throat and filled my lungs and stomach. The torrent was unimaginably choking. This is the sensation of drowning, on dry land, on a hot dry afternoon. Your humanity bursts from within you as you gag and choke. I tried very hard to will unconsciousness, but no relief came. . . . When I was choking uncontrollably, the NCO took the hose away. . . . I had nothing to say; I was beyond invention. So they turned on the tap again, and again.[176]

After World War II, the Far East International Military Tribunal called the water treatment "torture."[177] In the U.S.–Vietnamese conflict, a 1970 *Washington Post* front-page photo of an American soldier pouring water onto a rag held over a prisoner's mouth and nose while the prisoner was held down by South Vietnamese soldiers led to the

---

[170] Evan Wallach, "Drop by Drop: Forgetting the History of Water Torture in U.S. Courts," 45–2 *Columbia J. of Transnational L.* (2007), 468, fns. 59, 66, 71 and 85 (2007).

[171] Cited by Judge Wallach at fn. 59 as *U.S. v. Sawada*, 5 LRTWC 1 (1948), Judge Advocate General's Office File No. 119–19–5 (1946), at 1, available at National Archives. (The correct year of trial is 1946.)

[172] General James H. Doolittle, *I Could Never Be So Lucky Again* (New York: Bantam, 1991), 549.

[173] Cited by Judge Wallach at fn. 66 as *U.S. v. Yuki*, Philippines Trials, March 21, 1947, SCAP Prosecution Section File 142, available at National Archives, NND 775011, Record Group 331: Allied Operational and Occupation Headquarters, World War II, Entry 1321; SCAP; Legal Section; Prosecution Division, *U.S. v. Japanese War Criminals Case File*, 1945–9, Box 1586.

[174] Cited by Judge Wallach at fn. 85 as *U.S. v. Mineno*, Military Commission Case Docket No. 47 Tried at Yokohama June 25–8, 1946. NARA NND 735027 Record Group 153, Office of the Judge Advocate General (Army), Entry 143: War Crimes Branch; Case Files, 1944–9, Box 1025, File No. 36–449 – Vol. I.

[175] Cited by Judge Wallach at fn. 71 as *U.S. v. Nakamura, Asano, Hata and Kita*, U.S. Military Commission, Yokohama, 1947, available at National Archives, NND 735027, Record Group 153; Office of the Judge Advocate General (Army), Entry 143: War Crimes Branch; Case Files, 1944–9, Box 1025, File No. 36–219 – Vol. I.

[176] Eric Lomax, *The Railway Man* (London: Jonathan Cape, 1995), 143.

[177] Judgment of the International Military Tribunal at Tokyo (1948), para. 663, at 49.

criminal investigation of Staff Sergeant David Carmon. Army records indicate unspecified disciplinary action, but no court-martial is recorded.[178]

South Africa's Truth and Reconciliation Commission found that the "wet bag" was a standard torture method. A wet cloth or bag "placed over the victim's heads took them to the brink of asphyxiation, over and over again."[179]

U.S. domestic courts have punished domestic government authorities for waterboard-inglike acts, one case involving a Texas sheriff abetted by three deputies,[180] the other involving Philippine government agents who inflicted water torture in the course of interrogations.[181] The sheriff of San Jacinto County, Texas, handcuffed prisoners to chairs. In the words of the court, "This generally included the placement of a towel over the nose and mouth of the prisoner and the pouring of water in the towel until the prisoner began to move, jerk, or otherwise indicate that he was suffocating and/or drowning."[182]

Domestic laws notwithstanding, it is well known that the CIA employed waterboarding on Abu Zubaydah, Abd al-Rahim al-Nashiri, and Khalid Shaikh Mohammed, and several others. According to the U.S. Senate Intelligence Committee, the waterboarding gained little or no actionable intelligence, but their waterboarding does imperil their prosecutions because their cases rest, in part, on information gained through torture, inadmissible evidence in either military commissions or domestic federal trials. The Senate Intelligence Committee related Abu Zubaydah's waterboarding as described in a series of CIA messages:

> At times Abu Zubaydah was described as "hysterical" and "distressed to the level that he was unable to effectively communicate." Waterboarding sessions "resulted in immediate fluid intake and involuntary leg, chest and arm spasms" and "hysterical pleas." In at least one waterboarding session, Abu Zubaydah "became completely unresponsive, with bubbles rising through his open, full mouth." According to CIA records, Abu Zubaydah remained unresponsive until medical intervention, when he regained consciousness and expelled "copious amounts of liquid."[183]

In 2003, Chile's president established a National Commission of Political Imprisonment and Torture to identify those who had undergone state-administered political imprisonment and torture during the rule of General Augusto Pinochet. Waterboarding was among the interrogation tortures reported by the commission.

> [It was] aimed at causing physical and psychological suffering by confronting them with the possibility of death. Asphyxiation was usually caused by submerging the detainee's head into water several times, producing a near-death experience. . . . Usually the water used was contaminated or filled with debris. Other alternatives included . . . forcing with high pressure great amounts of water through hoses into the detainee's mouth or nose.[184]

---

[178] Author's 2008 inquiry of Washington D.C. Army Judge Advocate General's Corps records.

[179] Suzanne Daley, "Apartheid Torturer Testifies, as Evil Shows Its Banal Face," NY Times, Nov. 9, 1997, A1.

[180] U.S. v. Lee, 744 F.2d 1124 (5th Cir. 1984).

[181] In Re Estate of Ferdinand E. Marcos, Human Rights Litigation, 910 F. Supp. 1460, 1463 (1995).

[182] U.S. v. Lee, supra, note 180, at appeal record (May 31, 1984), Brief for U.S., at 3. Plaintiffs were awarded $766 million in damages.

[183] Senate Intelligence Committee Report on Torture, supra, note 30, at 54. Footnotes omitted.

[184] Cristián Correa, "Waterboarding Prisoners and Justifying Torture: Lessons for the U.S. from the Chilean Experience," 14–2 Human Rights Brief (Winter 2007), 21, Washington, DC: Cntr. for Human Rts. & Humanitarian Law, American University, Washington College of Law, 21.

The commission report describes one victim's water torture at the hands of military captors: "They tied my hands and legs and submerged me in a 250-liter tank that had ammonia, urine, excrement, and sea water. They submerged me until I could not breathe anymore. They repeated it over and over, while beating me and asking me questions. That is what they call the submarine."[185]

In 2008, the U.N. high commissioner for human rights specified waterboarding as torture and called for prosecutions on the basis of universal jurisdiction.[186] The U.N. special rapporteur on torture called waterboarding unjustifiable and "absolutely unacceptable."[187] In 2008, the retired admiral Mike McConnell, then the U.S. director of national intelligence, ventured that waterboarding "would be torture" if used against him, or if someone under interrogation was taking water into his lungs.[188] Tom Ridge, the first secretary of homeland security, said, "There's just no doubt in my mind, under any set of rules, waterboarding is torture."[189] A former CIA officer involved in the interrogation of Zayn abu Zubaida, whom the United States admitted waterboarding, said he "now regards the tactic as torture."[190] A former chief prosecutor at Guantánamo, the air force colonel Morris Davis, writes, "After . . . simulating the drowning of detainees to persuade them to talk, we can no longer say we 'don't do stuff like that' – and we do not have to look far to see the damage."[191]

Waterboarding is torture. In Algeria, the French believed it to be so and employed it as such. A body of U.S. military commission and court-martial convictions from 1899 to 1947 confirms that it is torture. U.S. domestic case law finds it to be torture. International and American domestic antiterrorism officers say it is torture. No judicial body has found it not to be torture.

The CAT, international and domestic U.S. case law, expert testimony and commentary, and U.S. and foreign experience in armed conflicts all clearly demonstrate that waterboarding constitutes severe physical or mental pain or suffering, the essentials of torture.

16.5 The Ticking Time Bomb

Opponents of torture are sometimes challenged with a familiar scenario: A powerful time bomb has been planted in a heavily populated area. Military (or civilian) authorities have captured a suspected terrorist, who, the authorities are confident, knows where the bomb is located, but the prisoner will not reveal the location. When it detonates it will kill hundreds, perhaps thousands, of innocent civilians. "We cannot afford to be squeamish in the midst of a war on terrorism. Because the United States has been spared further attacks at home . . . moralists may delude ourselves into thinking that we can once again afford the luxury of pure principle and uncompromised civil liberties."[192]

---

[185] Id., at 22.　　[186] "Tactic Called Torture," NY Times, Feb. 9, 2008, A8.

[187] Dan Eggen, "White House Pushes Waterboarding Rationale," Wash. Post, Feb. 13, 2008, A3.

[188] "Intelligence Chief Couches Reference to Waterboarding as 'Torture.'" Wash. Post, Jan. 13, 2008, A6.

[189] "National Briefing," NY Times, Jan. 19, 2008, A12.

[190] Joby Warrick and Dan Eggen, "Waterboarding Recounted," Wash. Post, Dec. 11, 2007, A1.

[191] Morris Davis, "Unforgivable Behavior, Inadmissible Evidence," NY Times, Feb. 17, 2008, WK 12.

[192] Fred Hiatt, "The Consequences of Torture," Wash. Post, June 14, 2004, A17. Contrary to the tone of this quote, the writer's point is that torture should never be permitted.

What should be done with the recalcitrant prisoner? The U.S. Supreme Court associate justice Antonin Scalia suggests that "some physical interrogation techniques could be used on a suspect in the event of an imminent threat, such as a hidden bomb about to blow up. 'It would be absurd to say you couldn't do that,' Scalia says."[193] The columnist Charles Krauthammer agrees with Justice Scalia:

> A terrorist has planted a nuclear bomb. . . . It will go off in one hour. A million people will die. You capture the terrorist. He knows where it is. He's not talking. . . . On this issue there can be no uncertainty: Not only is it permissible to hang this miscreant by his thumbs. It is a moral duty. . . . The conclusion – yes, in this case even torture is permissible – is telling because it establishes the principle: Torture is not always impermissible.[194]

"Absurd" not to torture? "A moral duty" to torture? The sociologist and philosopher Slavoj Žižek, writes:

> Some don't find [torture] troubling. The counterargument goes: The war on terrorism *is* dirty, one is put in situations where the lives of thousands may depend on information we can get from our prisoners, and one must take extreme steps. . . . And when torture becomes just another in the list of counterterrorism techniques, all sense of horror is lost. . . . One does not need to argue against rape: it is "dogmatically" clear to everyone that rape is wrong. If someone were to advocate the legitimacy of rape, he would appear so ridiculous as to disqualify himself from any further consideration. And the same should hold for torture. . . . Are we aware that the last time such things were part of the public discourse was back in the late Middle Ages, when torture was still a public spectacle . . . ? Do we really want to return to this kind of primitive warrior ethics?[195]

European human rights courts (no authorities, for Justice Scalia) are clear in their rulings on public emergency cases: "The [1950 Convention on Human Rights] prohibits in absolute terms torture and inhuman or degrading treatment or punishment, irrespective of the victim's conduct . . . there can be no derogation therefrom even in the event of a public emergency threatening the life of the nation."[196]

The ticking time bomb scenario, transforming the torturer from criminal to public savior, means to force torture opponents to concede that, if 100,000 lives were at stake, torture would be acceptable. The opponent of torture, in making that concession, would concede his "no torture" principle. If torture is acceptable to save 100,000 lives, how about 10,000 lives? How about 100? When the principle is breached, all that is left is haggling over price. "Once you accept that only the numbers count, then anything, no matter how gruesome, becomes possible."[197]

The ticking time bomb scenario is an intellectual fraud. It presumes there actually is a hidden bomb. It presumes the authorities know the bomb has been planted in a public place. It presumes the authorities have seized the correct individual, the person who

---

[193] Eggen, "White House Pushes Waterboarding Rationale," supra, note 187.

[194] Charles Krauthammer, "Case Study: Terrorist Hides Bomb. Terrorist Is Captured, but Won't Speak. Is Torture O.K.?" *NY Times*, Dec. 11, 2005, n.p.

[195] Slavoj Žižek, "Knight of the Living Dead," *NY Times*, March 24, 2007, A27.

[196] *Case of Ireland v. United Kingdom*, App. no. 5310/71, Judgment (Jan. 1978), para. 163. To the same effect, *Tomasi v. France*, Series A, No. 241-A, App. No. 12850/87, 15 EHRR 1, at para. 115 (1992); and *Chahal v. United Kingdom*, App. No. 22414/93, Judgment (Nov. 1996), at paras. 79–80.

[197] Luban, "Liberalism, Torture, and the Ticking Bomb," supra, note 8, at 1444.

planted the bomb or knows its details. It presumes the authorities know they have the correct bomb-planting individual, or individual who knows of the bomb planting. The possibility of those conjoined circumstances is slim.

The ticking time bomb is nevertheless the argument of first resort for those who believe that, in some cases, good people must resort to torture. No actual case of a ticking time bomb scenario has been found in U.S. or Israeli experience.[198]

16.6 Torture: Never, Sometimes, or Maybe?

Deontology is the science of duty or moral obligation. Deontologists, as have students of LOAC/IHL, have long studied torture. They suggest there are two camps with regard to torture: "absolutists," who contend that torture is never justified, no matter the seriousness of the circumstances or the human consequences of not acting, and "consequentialists," who argue that torture may be necessary in extreme circumstances – when its perceived benefits exceed its costs: "Torture may be permissible or even mandatory as an immediate response to urgent circumstances."[199]

Consequentialists can speak of torture as "a means for fulfilling one's duty," and of torture's being "morally commendable,"[200] designating such acts "preventive (administrative) torture,"[201] when employed in extreme cases – in a ticking time bomb case, for example, when the torturer argues the criminal law defense of necessity.[202] Two consequentialists write:

> It is not surprising that the absolutist view is unpopular even among committed deontologists. The idea that the possible death of a great number of innocent people cannot warrant the torture of a single terrorist seems unreasonable. Judge Richard Posner gives this sentiment sharp expression when he says: "no one who doubts that [if the stakes are high enough, torture is permissible] should be in a position of responsibility." Indeed, the absolutist interpretation of deontology seems like a form of moral fundamentalism.[203]

In the view of LOAC/IHL antitorture absolutists, there is a problem with the utilitarian consequentialist position that transcends torture's illegality and moral repugnance:

> The utilitarian argument for justifiability (that ill-treatment is justified in order to elicit information that may save others) has been advanced in a number of cases. ... Those who argue in the language of utilitarian reasoning, when seeking to rebut the utilitarian

---

[198] There are anecdotal reports of captured bombers in Israel who, under interrogation, revealed planned bombings in public places, leading to evacuations and discovery of bombs of deadly but nonapocalyptic size.

[199] Harel and Sharon, "What Is Really Wrong with Torture?" supra, note 133, at 243.

[200] Id., at 254 and 250, respectively.

[201] Kai Ambos, "May a State Torture Suspects to Save the Life of Innocents?" 6–2 *J. of Int'l Crim. Justice* (May 2008), 261, 264, 286.

[202] Jens David Ohlin, "The Bounds of Necessity," 6–2 *J. of Int'l Crim. Justice* (May 2008), 289. In the context of criminal law, rather than war crimes, the author interestingly examines the defense of necessity as legal excuse, and as legal justification. He contends that if necessity is viewed as a legal justification, it negates the unlawfulness of the act; if viewed as a legal excuse, it only negates the culpability of the actor while the criminal act remains unlawful.

[203] Harel and Sharon, "What Is Really Wrong with Torture?" supra, note 133, at 245–6. Brackets in original. Footnotes omitted.

challenge, tend to point to the impossibility of confining the facts to the classic example of the lesser evil for the greater good. How many broken wills to save a government? Will torture create more terrorists? It is a version of the "slippery slope" argument: once torture is permitted on grounds of necessity, nothing can stop it from being used on grounds of expediency.[204]

David Luban adds that the consequentialist position "assumes a single, ad hoc, decision about whether to torture, by officials who ordinarily would do no such thing except in a desperate emergency. But in the real world of interrogations, decisions are not made one-off. The real world is a world of policies, guidelines, and directives. It is a world of practices, not of ad hoc emergency measures."[205] Michael Reisman agrees that "torture, by its nature, once sanctioned and however contingent and restrictive in intent the authorization for its application may be, metastasizes quickly, infecting the whole process of interrogation."[206]

Still, there are consequentialist civilians and soldiers, who believe that in exceptional circumstances torture is acceptable, even a civic duty. They usually agree that torture, by whatever definition, must always be unlawful, but there must be those who, in exceptional circumstances, such as ticking bombs, are willing to violate the law for the greater good and face later punishment.[207] One academic, in a display of ignorance that also is a towering insult to America's armed forces, has no problem with torture as a concept, and he suggests who should do the job. "Torturers should . . . be drawn, not from the general [American military] enlisted population, but rather from special forces like Delta Force, Green Berets, or Navy SEALs. These special forces are trained in relevant ways, including interrogation and interrogation resistance. . . . In other words, these units know what a hostile interrogation looks like, so they would not be starting from scratch if imported into such settings."[208]

Absolutists who oppose torture under any circumstance are seen by consequentialists as romantics, willing to trade innocent lives for airy idealism. Despite military and civilian laws, judicial opinion, and historical experience, the two viewpoints are unlikely to be reconciled while terrorists are at large, as they always will be. In the armed forces, however, actions, if not viewpoints, can be imposed.

16.7 U.S. Military Practice

Torture has always been prohibited, absolutely, by the armed services of most states.[209] *The Law of Land Warfare*, the 1956 U.S. war fighting field manual, forbids torture,[210] as do its predecessor manuals, as did Article 16 of the 1863 Lieber Code. Torture of a prisoner is a violation of the Uniform Code of Military Justice.[211]

---

[204] Rodley, *Treatment of Prisoners under International Law*, supra, note 32, at 80.

[205] Luban, "Liberalism, Torture, and the Ticking Bomb," supra, note 8, at 1445.

[206] Reisman, "Holding the Center of the Law of Armed Conflict," supra, note 15, at 855–6.

[207] Bowden, "The Dark Art of Interrogation," supra, note 95, is a persuasive example of this position.

[208] Fritz Allhoff, *Terrorism, Ticking Time-Bombs, and Torture* (Chicago: University of Chicago Press, 2012), 151.

[209] Jean-Marie Henckaerts and Louise Doswald-Beck, eds., *Customary International Humanitarian Law.* Vol. II. *Practice* (Cambridge: Cambridge University Press, 2005), §§ 1039–1215, at 2112–34, specifying the military manuals, handbooks, regulations, rules, instructions, guides, and codes of the armed forces of forty-one states, along with domestic legislation relating to the conduct of the armed forces of ninety states.

[210] Dept. of the Army, *The Law of Land Warfare* (Washington, DC: GPO, 1956), at para. 271.

[211] UCMJ, Art. 93, Cruelty and maltreatment.

An objective view of recent history makes evident that, in the "war on terrorism," the United States, including its armed forces, has engaged in torture – not in isolated cases involving a few criminally inclined individuals, but as a matter of policy. It is not a definitional issue or a matter of fine legal distinctions.

When an army lieutenant general, formerly commanding all ground forces in Iraq, writes, "There is irrefutable evidence that America was torturing and killing prisoners in Afghanistan," torture is indicated.[212] When the convening authority for Guantánamo military commissions declines to refer a detainee's case to trial because the prisoner was tortured, torture is indicated.[213] When the International Committee of the Red Cross (ICRC), in a confidential report to a U.S. government agency, writes of "high value detainees," that "ill-treatment to which they were subjected ... constituted torture," torture is indicated.[214] When the military death certificates of two Bagram detainees state that both were beaten to death, torture is indicated.[215]

The full U.S. Senate Armed Services Report on Torture remains classified and unavailable. Its Executive Summary is public, however:

> The abuse of detainees in U.S. custody cannot simply be attributed to the actions of "a few bad apples" acting on their own. The fact is that senior officials in the United States government solicited information on how to use aggressive techniques, redefined the law to create the appearance of their legality, and authorized their use against detainees. Those efforts damaged our ability to collect accurate intelligence that could save lives, strengthened the hand of our enemies, and compromised our moral authority. ... The decision to replace well established military doctrine, i.e., legal compliance with the Geneva Conventions, with a policy subject to interpretation, impacted the treatment of detainees. ... In early November 2002 ... the military services identified serious legal concerns about the techniques and called for additional analysis.[216]

In April 2009, four formerly top secret Department of Justice memoranda regarding CIA interrogation techniques were made public.

"Arguments for torture, regardless of how they are framed, suffer from the same defect. We deny terrorists the right to be free from torture, but we are not willing to forego this right for ourselves. ... If we can use torture to prevent armed attacks, then our enemies can use torture against us as well."[217] Torture becomes nothing more than business as usual.

After 9/11, U.S. military civilian leadership initiated changes in the long-standing absolute military torture prohibition. In November 2002, the DoD general counsel, William J. Haynes, advised Secretary of Defense Donald Rumsfeld that it was acceptable

---

[212] Sanchez, *Wiser in Battle*, supra, note 53, at 210.

[213] Bob Woodward, "Detainee Tortured, Says U.S. Official," *Wash. Post*, Jan. 14, 2009, A1.

[214] ICRC Report to Acting General Counsel, Central Intelligence Agency (Feb. 14, 2007), 26.

[215] Solis, "Military Justice?" supra, note 122, at 24. The incident was one of eleven 2005 Bagram detainee abuse cases that resulted in eleven courts-martial referrals, three of which were dropped before trial. Two others ended in acquittal. An army private first class, Willie Brand, accused of beating one of the two shackled detainees to death, was convicted of assault, maiming, and maltreatment. He was merely sentenced to a reduction in rank to private.

[216] Executive Summary: "Senate Armed Services Report on Torture," supra, note 42, at 1–2.

[217] George P. Fletcher and Jens David Ohlin, *Defending Humanity: When Force Is Justified and Why* (Oxford: Oxford University Press, 2008), 170.

to subject Guantánamo detainees to two categories of interrogation techniques that, it has been argued, constituted cruel treatment, if not torture.[218] What the general counsel referred to as "category II interrogation techniques" included use of stress positions for up to four hours, isolation for up to thirty days, sound and light deprivation, twenty-hour questioning sessions, and forced nudity. Category III "advanced counter-resistance strategies" included exposure to cold weather or water, convincing "the detainee that death or severely painful consequences are imminent," and "use of a wet towel to induce the misperception of suffocation."[219] Secretary of Defense Rumsfeld approved use of all these, and other, interrogation techniques. The staff judge advocates general of all the U.S. Armed Services[220] strongly objected, however, and in January 2003, authority to employ category III techniques was withdrawn.[221]

A year later, in 2004, Major General Antonio M. Taguba of the U.S. Army was directed to investigate detainee abuses by military personnel that had been revealed at Iraq's Abu Ghraib prison. His report documented many interrogations that exceeded the approved category II techniques and revealed misconduct and derelictions of duty from the most junior soldier to generals.[222] General Taguba said, "The fact is that we violated the laws of land warfare in Abu Ghraib. We violated the tenets of the Geneva Convention. We violated our own principles and we violated the core of our military values. The stress of combat is not an excuse, and I believe, even today, that those civilian and military leaders responsible should be held accountable."[223]

Public disclosure of events at Abu Ghraib, along with revelation of approval of category II and III interrogation techniques, led to congressional amendment of the Detainee Treatment Act (DTA).[224] The DTA amendment, bearing the *sub silentio* endorsements of the Judge Advocates General of all the armed services, was passed by Congress over presidential objection. The amendment prohibited use of cruel, inhuman, or degrading treatment by U.S. government personnel anywhere in the world and prohibited U.S. military interrogators from using any interrogation technique not included in the army's *Field Manual on Intelligence Interrogation*.[225] Upon signing the amended DTA into law, President Bush issued a "signing statement" indicating that his authority as commander

---

[218] Action Memo for: Secretary of Defense; from: William J. Haynes II, General Counsel; Subject: Counter-Resistance Techniques (Nov. 27, 2002). Reprinted in Greenberg and Dratel, *Torture Papers*, supra, note 43, at 237.

[219] Memorandum for Commander, Joint Task Force 170; from LTC Diane E. Beaver, Staff Judge Advocate, JTF 170, Guantánamo Bay; Subject: Legal Brief on Proposed Counter-Resistance Strategies; dtd. Oct. 11, 2002. Reprinted in Greenberg and Dratel, *Torture Papers*, supra, note 43, at 229.

[220] Including the Marine Corps' staff judge advocate to the commandant of the Marine Corps (SJA to the CMC). The Marines have no judge advocate general. They look to the navy's JAG for those few acts that statutorily must be accomplished by a judge advocate general. Otherwise, the Marines' SJA to the CMC functions as do the other U.S. service JAGs.

[221] James Ross, "Black Letter Abuse: The Legal Response to Torture since 9/11," 867 *Int'l Rev. of the Red Cross* 561, 573(Sept. 2007). Footnotes omitted.

[222] "Article 15-6 Investigation of the 800th Military Police Brigade (2004), http://www.npr.org/iraq/2004/prison_abuse_report.pdf

[223] Seymour M. Hersh, "The General's Report," *New Yorker*, June 25, 2007, 69. General Taguba believes the frank truthfulness of his investigation report led to his forced early retirement from the army. David S. Cloud, "General Says Prison Inquiry Led to His Forced Retirement," *NY Times*, June 17, 2007, A10.

[224] Detainee Treatment Act of 2005, Pub. L. No. 109–148, §§ 1001–1006 (2005).

[225] DTA, http://thomas.loc.gov/cgi-bin/cpquery/T?&report=hr359&dbname=109&. See § 1002.A.

in chief trumped the Act's restrictions.[226] "For good measure, he reserved the power to violate the torture bill itself if he thought it necessary for the purposes of national security."[227]

In September 2006, the army, the lead authority for POW and detainee matters for all U.S. Armed Forces, issued *Human Intelligence Collection Operations*, to replace the *Manual on Intelligence Interrogation*. The new manual reads: "In accordance with the Detainee Treatment Act of 2005, the only interrogation approaches and techniques that are authorized for use against any detainee, regardless of status or characterization, are those authorized and listed in this Field Manual."[228] The manual directs:

> Any inhumane treatment – including abusive practices, torture, or cruel, inhuman, or degrading treatment or punishment . . . is prohibited and all instances of such treatment will be reported immediately. . . . Beyond being impermissible, these unlawful and unauthorized forms of treatment are unproductive because they may yield unreliable results, damage subsequent collection efforts, and result in extremely negative consequences at national and international levels.[229]

The manual prohibits military working dogs in interrogations and requires non-DoD agencies that interrogate military prisoners, such as the CIA, to adhere to the manual's standards.[230] It also prohibits hooding, forced nakedness, hypothermia or heat injury, mock executions, electric shocks, burns, "or other forms of physical pain," specifically including waterboarding.[231] With this 2006 manual, the armed forces reaffirmed their absolutist position against torture.

No law will deter the lawless, however. Inevitably, instances of torture by military personnel will come to light. The Uniform Code of Military Justice, written orders, and field manual mandates provide the military's requirements and prohibitions, and, when violations become known, the means of charging, trial, and punishment.

The potential ineffectiveness of such prohibitions was highlighted in a 2006 anonymous survey of 1,767 soldiers and Marines of the Multi-National Force–Iraq, conducted by a mental health advisory team from the Office of the Army Surgeon General.[232] Thirty-six percent of soldiers surveyed and 39 percent of Marines responded that, in Iraq, torture should be allowed to gather important information about insurgents. Additionally, if torture will save the life of a soldier or Marine it should be allowed, responded 41 percent of soldiers and 44 percent of Marines surveyed. Only 46 percent of soldiers and 32 percent of Marines would report a unit member who mistreated a noncombatant.[233] Those surveyed were junior enlisted combatants, and youthful bravado may have influenced responses. Also, there sometimes is a gap between a

---

[226] President's Statement on Signing of HR 2836 (Dec. 30, 2005), Available on-line. "The executive branch shall construe . . . the Act, relating to detainees, in a manner consistent with the constitutional authority of the President . . . as Commander in Chief and consistent with . . . achieving the shared objective of the Congress and the President . . . of protecting the American people from further terrorist attacks."

[227] Jonathan Mahler, "After the Imperial Presidency," NY *Times Sunday Magazine*, Nov. 9, 2008, 49.

[228] Dept. of the Army, FM 2–22.3, *Human Intelligence Collection Operations* (Washington, DC: GPO, 2006), vi.

[229] Id., at appendix M-5.   [230] Id.   [231] Id., para. 5–75, at 5–21.

[232] Mental Health Advisory Team (MHAT) IV; Operation Iraqi Freedom 05–07; Final Report, Nov. 17, 2006, available online.

[233] Id., Figures 16 and 18, respectively.

soldier's or Marine's talk and his behavior. No matter how viewed, however, the survey results were more than a disappointment.

After release of the survey, General David H. Petraeus, then the commander of U.S. forces in Iraq, cautioned against torture in a letter to all members of his command. He wrote:

> I was concerned by the results of a recently released survey ... that revealed an apparent unwillingness on the part of some US personnel to report illegal actions taken by fellow members of their units. ... Seeing a fellow trooper killed by a barbaric enemy can spark frustration, anger, and a desire for immediate revenge. ... We must not let these emotions lead us – or our comrades in arms – to commit hasty, illegal actions. In the event that we witness or hear of such actions, we must not let our bonds prevent us from speaking up. Some may argue that we would be more effective if we sanctioned torture ... to obtain information from the enemy. They would be wrong. Beyond the basic fact that such actions are illegal, history shows that they are also frequently neither useful nor necessary. Certainly, extreme physical action can make someone "talk"; however, what the individual says may be of questionable value. ... Leaders, in particular, need to discuss these issues with their troops. – and, as always, they need to set the right example and strive to ensure proper conduct.[234]

West Point's Colonel David Wallace succinctly summarizes the U.S. military's position: "The best way to approach the torture and ill-treatment question is simply through a principle-oriented approach. The appropriate guidance for any soldier participating in the current conflict (or any conflict for that matter) is: 'no torture, no ill-treatment, no exceptions'."[235]

16.8 Summary

Torture "works," says Professor Dershowitz. No doubt it does sometimes "work." Even if torture gained actionable intelligence in the preponderance of cases, and the evidence is that it does not, the greater issue is not whether torture works or does not work. If results were all that mattered, should the military torture every captive? Of course not.

It is unusual for torture to result in actionable intelligence. Information gained through torture is seldom reliable. Torture may accompany other military indiscipline. Torture damages the nation's image in international eyes and diminishes the armed forces in the domestic view. Torture endangers one's own soldiers who are subsequently captured. Torture is illegal under domestic, international, and customary law. Finally, naive as it may sound, torture is simply wrong.

More than a hundred and fifty years ago, Clausewitz, using the term "intelligence" as a mental attribute, wrote, "If, then, civilized nations do not put their prisoners to death or devastate cities and countries, it is because intelligence plays a larger part in their methods of warfare and has taught them more effective ways of using force than the crude expression of instinct."[236]

---

[234] Commanding General David H. Petraeus's Letter about Values (May 10, 2007). Available on-line.
[235] Col. David A. Wallace, "Torture v. the Basic Principles of the US Military," 6–2 *J. of Int'l Criminal Justice* (May 2008), 309, 316.
[236] Carl von Clausewitz, *On War* (Michael Howard and Peter Paret, eds. and trans., New York: Knopf, Everyman's Library, 1993), 85.

The U.S. military counterinsurgency manual puts it clearly: "No exceptional circumstances permit the use of torture. ... Prohibitions against mistreatment may sometimes ... place leaders in difficult situations, where they must choose between obedience to the law and the lives of their Soldiers and Marines. U.S. law and professional values compel commanders to forbid mistreatment of noncombatants, including captured enemies."[237]

The veteran military interrogator Major Matthew Alexander led the interrogation team that painstakingly located and made possible the 2006 targeted killing of Abu Musab al-Zarqawi, leader of Al Qaeda in Iraq. Alexander says, "*Coerce* information and the subject will tell you the location of a safe house. *Convince* the subject to give you the information and he'll tell you it's booby-trapped."[238]

Yet, one fears that, should there be another terrorist attack inside America's borders, the percentage of Americans, military and civilian, favoring torture will be higher than ever.

CASES AND MATERIALS

PROSECUTOR V. VASILJEVIC

IT-98–32-T (November 29, 2002), footnotes omitted.

Introduction. *This ICTY opinion defines, for purposes of ICTY jurisprudence, at least, what constitutes an "inhumane act."*

Xi. Inhumane Acts

A. *The Law*

234. The Accused is charged ... with inhumane acts as a crime against humanity pursuant to Article 5(i) of the [ICTY] Statute. The crime of inhumane acts, like inhumane treatment under Article 3, and cruel treatment under Article 2, functions as a residual category for serious charges which are not otherwise enumerated under Article 5. All of these offenses require proof of the same elements. The elements to be proved are:

(i) the occurrence of an act or omission of similar seriousness to the other enumerated acts under the Article;

(ii) the act or omission caused serious mental or physical suffering or injury or constituted a serious attack on human dignity; and

---

[237] *The U.S. Army–Marine Corps Counterinsurgency Field Manual* (Chicago: University of Chicago Press, 2007), paras. 7–42 and – 43, at 251.

[238] Maj. Matthew Alexander, USAF, address at United States Military Academy's Rule of Law Conference, on "The Future of International Criminal Justice," West Point, NY (April 17, 2009).

(iii) the act or omission was performed deliberately by the accused or a person or persons for whose acts and omissions he bears criminal responsibility.

235. To assess the seriousness of an act, consideration must be given to all the factual circumstances. These circumstances may include the nature of the act or omission, the context in which it occurred, the personal circumstances of the victim including age, sex and health, as well as the physical, mental and moral effects of the act upon the victim. While there is no requirement that the suffering imposed by the act have long term effects on the victim, the fact that an act has had long term effects may be relevant to the determination of the seriousness of the act.

Conclusion. Do you agree with the elements specified by the trial chamber's definition? Does it substitute a new series of undefined terms for the original undefined term? Is it reasonable to expect any better definitional effort?

"THE ĈELEBIĆI CASE," PROSECUTOR V. DELALIĆ, ET AL.

IT-96–21-T, Trial Judgment (November 16, 1998), footnotes omitted.

Introduction. Delalić does not provide a definition of torture, but it does specify examples of what has been found to constitute torture. It also gathers authorities and confirms that, in LOAC, rape constitutes the grave breach of torture. Most of the examples arise from human rights courts, rather than war crime trials, but they would likely be considered torture in any judicial forum. The judgment confirms that the prohibition of torture is customary law and a nonderogable jus cogens norm. When the opinion refers to the "Torture Convention," it is referring to the CAT. The Delalić judgment is also notable for applying the prohibition of torture to nonstate actors in IHL situations.

(Iii) Discussion

1. A. *The Definition of Torture under Customary International Law*

452. There can be no doubt that torture is prohibited by both conventional and customary international law.

452. There can be no doubt that torture is prohibited by both conventional and customary international law. In addition to the proscriptions of international humanitarian law ... there are also a number of international human rights instruments that express the prohibition. ...

453. In addition, there are two international instruments that are solely concerned with the prohibition of torture, the most significant of which is the Torture Convention. This Convention was adopted by the General Assembly ... and has been ratified or acceded to by 109 States ... representing more than half of the membership of the United Nations. It was preceded by the Declaration on the Protection from Torture, which was adopted by the United Nations General Assembly on ... 1975 without a vote.

454. Based on the foregoing, it can be said that the prohibition on torture is a norm of customary law. It further constitutes a norm of *jus cogens*, as has been confirmed by the United Nations Special Rapporteur for Torture. It should additionally be noted that the

prohibition contained in the aforementioned international instruments is absolute and non-derogable in any circumstances.

455. Despite the clear international consensus that the infliction of acts of torture is prohibited conduct, few attempts have been made to articulate a legal definition of torture. In fact, of the instruments prohibiting torture, only three provide any definition. The first such instrument is the Declaration on torture, article 1. . . .

456. This definition was used as the basis for the one subsequently articulated in the Torture Convention, which states, in article 1 that,

> the term "torture" means any act by which severe pain or suffering, whether physical or mental, is intentionally inflicted on a person for such purposes as obtaining from him or third person information or a confession, punishing him for an act he or a third person has committed or is suspected of having committed, or intimidating or coercing him or a third person, or for any reason based on discrimination of any kind, when such pain or suffering is inflicted by or at the instigation of or with the consent or acquiescence of a public official or other person acting in an official capacity.

458. The third such instrument, the Inter-American Convention ... definition of torture contained in Article 2 thereof incorporates, but is arguably broader than, that contained in the Torture Convention, as it refrains from specifying a threshold level of pain or suffering which is necessary for ill treatment to constitute torture.

B. *Severity of Pain or Suffering*

461. Although the Human Rights Committee, a body established by the ICCPR [1966 International Covenant on Civil and Political Rights] to monitor its implementation, has had occasion to consider the nature of ill-treatment prohibited under article 7 of the ICCPR, the Committee's decisions have generally not drawn a distinction between the various prohibited forms of ill-treatment. However, in certain cases, the Committee has made a specific finding of torture, based upon the following conduct: beating, electric shocks and mock executions, *plantones*, beatings and lack of food; being held incommunicado for more than three months whilst being kept blindfolded with hands tied together, resulting in limb paralysis, leg injuries, substantial weight loss and eye infection.

467. Finally, it should also be noted that the Special Rapporteur on Torture ... provided a detailed, although not exhaustive, catalogue of those acts which involve the infliction of suffering severe enough to constitute the offense of torture, including: beating; extraction of nails, teeth, etc.; burns; electric shocks; suspension; suffocation; exposure to excessive light or noise; sexual aggression; administration of drugs in detention or psychiatric institutions; prolonged denial of rest or sleep; prolonged denial of food; prolonged denial of sufficient hygiene; prolonged denial of medical assistance; total isolation and sensory deprivation being kept in constant uncertainty in terms of space and time; threats to torture or kill relatives; total abandonment; and simulated executions.

469. As evidenced by the jurisprudence set forth above, it is difficult to articulate with any degree of precision the threshold level of suffering at which other forms of mistreatment become torture. However, the existence of such a grey area should not be seen as an invitation to create an exhaustive list of acts constituting torture, in order to neatly categorise the prohibition. As stated by [Nigel S.] Rodley [when he was the U.N.'s special

rapporteur on torture], "a judicial definition cannot depend upon a catalogue of horrific practices; for it to do so would simply provide a challenge to the ingenuity of the torturers, not a viable legal prohibition."

471. A fundamental distinction regarding the purpose for which torture is inflicted is that between a "prohibited purpose" and one which is purely private. The rationale behind this distinction is the prohibition on torture is not concerned with private conduct, which is ordinarily sanctioned under national law. In particular, rape and other sexual assaults have often been labeled as "private", thus precluding them from being punished under national or international law. However, such conduct could meet the purposive requirements of torture as, during armed conflicts, the purposive elements of intimidation, coercion, punishment or discrimination can often be integral components of behaviour, thus bringing the relevant conduct within the definition. Accordingly,

> only in exceptional cases should it therefore be possible to conclude that the infliction of severe pain or suffering by a public official would not constitute torture ... on the ground that he acted for purely private reasons.

472. ... The Defence argues that an act can only constitute torture if it is committed for a limited set of purposes, enumerated in the Commentary to article 147 of the Fourth Geneva Convention. This proposition does not reflect the position at customary law ... which clearly envisages prohibited purposes additional to those suggested by the Commentary.

D. *Official Sanction*

473. Traditionally, an act of torture must be committed by, or at the instigation of, or with the consent or acquiescence of, a public official or person acting in an official capacity. In the context of international humanitarian law, this requirement must be interpreted to include officials of non-State parties to a conflict, in order for the prohibition to retain significance in situations of internal armed conflicts or international conflicts involving some non-State entities.

474. The incorporation of this element into the definition of torture contained in the Torture Convention again follows the Declaration on Torture and develops it further by adding the phrases "or with the consent or acquiescence of" and "or other person acting in an official capacity". It is thus stated in very broad terms and extends to officials who take a passive attitude or turn a blind eye to torture, most obviously by failing to prevent or punish torture under national penal or military law, when it occurs.

(IV) Rape as Torture

475. The crime of rape is not itself expressly mentioned in the provisions of the Geneva Conventions relating to grave breaches, nor in common article 3, and hence its classification [in the ICTY Statute] as torture and cruel treatment. ...

476. There can be no doubt that rape and other forms of sexual assault are expressly prohibited under international humanitarian law. ...

477. There is on the basis of these provisions alone [Geneva Convention IV, Article 27; Additional Protocol I, Article 76 (1); Additional Protocol II, Articles 4 (1) and (2);

implicitly in 1907 Hague Regulation IV, Article 46; the Nuremberg IMT Charter, Article 6(c); and the ICTY Statute, Article 5] a clear prohibition of rape and sexual assault under international humanitarian law. However the relevant provisions do not define rape. Thus, the task of the Trial Chamber is to determine the definition of rape in this context.

486. ... First, in considering whether rape gives rise to pain and suffering, one must not only look at the physical consequences, but also at the psychological and social consequences of the rape. Secondly, in its definition of the requisite elements of torture, the Inter-American Commission did not refer to the customary law requirement that the physical and psychological pain and suffering be severe. However, this level of suffering may be implied from the Inter-American Commission's finding that the rape, in the instant case, was "an act of violence" occasioning physical and psychological pain and suffering that caused the victim: a state of shock; a fear of public ostracism; feelings of humiliation; fear of how her husband would react; a feeling that family integrity was at stake and an apprehension that her children might feel humiliated if they knew what had happened to their mother.

489. By stating that it would have found a breach of article 3 [of the European Convention] even if each of the grounds had been considered separately, the European Court ... specifically affirmed the view that rape involves the infliction of suffering as a requisite level of severity to place it in the category of torture. ...

490. In addition, the Akayesu Judgment [*Prosecutor v. Akayesu*, ICTR-96–4-T (2 Sept. 1998), para. 597] expresses a view on the issue of rape as torture most emphatically, in the following terms:

> Like torture rape is used for such purposes as intimidation, degradation, humiliation, discrimination, punishment control or destruction of a person. Like torture rape is a violation of personal dignity, and rape in fact constitutes torture when inflicted by or at the instigation of or with the consent or acquiescence of a public official or other person acting in an official capacity.

Conclusion. In the foregoing quote, note the ICTR trial chamber's language, reflecting the long-accepted view of the ICTY and other IHL and human rights courts, and based on the CAT definition of torture, that to constitute the war crime of torture, rape must be committed by a public official. Indeed, the opinion itself reflects that requirement. That long-accepted requirement is rejected in the following ICTY case.

PROSECUTOR V. KUNARAC, ET AL.

IT-96-23 & 23/1-A-T (February 22, 2001), footnotes omitted[239]

Introduction. The Kunarac trial judgment announces a shift in the definition of the war crime of torture. The trial chamber also provides an instructive tutorial on the similarities and differences between the mandates of human rights law versus the legal requirements of IHL. It also discusses distinctions between human rights law and international criminal law.

---

[239] The inconsistent capitalizing of the word "State" and the hyphenating of terms is as in the original.

466. Torture is prohibited under both conventional and customary international law and it is prohibited both in times of peace and during armed conflict. The prohibition can be said to constitute a norm of *jus cogens*. However, relatively few attempts have been made at defining the offence of torture. . . . All [past definitional attempts have been contained in] human rights instruments.

467. Because of the paucity of precedent in the field of international humanitarian law, the Tribunal has, on many occasions, had recourse to instruments and practices developed in the field of human rights law. Because of their resemblance, in terms of goals, values and terminology, such recourse is generally welcome and needed assistance to determine the content of customary international law in the field of humanitarian law. With regard to certain of its aspects, international humanitarian law can be said to have fused with human rights law.

469. . . . The absence of an express definition of torture under international humanitarian law does not mean that this body of law should be ignored altogether. The definition of an offence is largely a function of the environment in which it develops. Although it may not provide its own explicit definition of torture, international humanitarian law does provide some important definitional aspects of this offence.

470. In attempting to define an offence under international humanitarian law, the Trial Chamber must be mindful of the specificity of this body of law. In particular, when referring to definitions which have been given in the context of human rights law, the Trial Chamber will have to consider two crucial structural differences between these two bodies of law:

> (i) Firstly, the role and position of the state as an actor is completely different in both regimes. Human rights law is essentially born out of the abuses of the state over its citizens and out of the need to protect the latter from state-organised or state-sponsored violence. Humanitarian law aims at placing restraints on the conduct of warfare so as to diminish its effects on the victims of the hostilities.

In the human rights context, the state is the ultimate guarantor of the rights protected and has both duties and a responsibility for the observance of those rights. In the event that the state violates those rights or fails in its responsibility to protect the rights, it can be called to account and asked to take appropriate measures to put an end to the infringements.

In the field of international humanitarian law, and in particular in the context of international prosecutions, the role of the state is, when it comes to accountability, peripheral. Individual criminal responsibility for violation of international humanitarian law does not depend on the participation of the state and, conversely, its participation in the commission of the offence is no defence to the perpetrator. Moreover, international humanitarian law purports to apply equally to and expressly bind all parties to the armed conflict whereas, in contrast, human rights law generally applies to only one party, namely the state involved, and its agents.

This distinction can be illustrated by two recent American decisions of the Court of Appeals for the Second Circuit rendered under the Alien Torts Claims Act. The Act gives jurisdiction to American district courts for any civil action by an alien for a tort committed in violation of the law of nations or a treaty of the United States. In the first decision, *In re Filártiga*, the Court of Appeals of the Second Circuit held that "deliberate torture perpetrated under colour of official authority violates universally accepted norms of the international law of human rights, regardless of the nationality of the parties". This decision was only concerned with the situation of an individual *vis-à-vis* a state, either his national state or a foreign state. In a later decision in *Kadic v Karadžic*, the same court made it clear that the body of law which it applied in the *Filártiga* case was customary international law of *human rights* and that, according to the Court of Appeals, in the human rights context torture is proscribed by international law only when committed by state officials or under the colour of law. The court added, however, that atrocities including torture are actionable under the Alien Tort Claims Act regardless of state participation to the extent that the criminal acts were committed in pursuit of genocide or war crimes.

> (ii) Secondly, that part of international criminal law applied by the Tribunal [i.e., the ICTY] is a penal law regime. It sets one party, the prosecutor, against another, the defendant. In the field of international human rights, the respondent is the state. Structurally, this has been expressed by the fact that human rights law establishes lists of protected rights whereas international criminal law establishes lists of offences.

482. . . . In view of the international instruments and jurisprudence reviewed above [the 1948 Universal Declaration of Human Rights, the 1950 European Convention for the Protection of Human Rights and Fundamental Freedoms ("European Convention"), European Court of Human Rights torture decisions, the 1966 International Covenant on Civil and Political Rights, and the ICTY's own *Furundžija* decision, the Trial Chamber is of the view that the definition of torture contained in the Torture Convention [the CAT] cannot be regarded as the definition of torture under customary international law which is binding regardless of the context in which it is applied. The definition of the Torture Convention was meant to apply at an inter-state level and was, for that reason, directed at the states' obligations. The definition was also meant to apply only in the context of that Convention, and only to the extent that other international instruments or national laws did not give the individual a broader or better protection. The Trial Chamber, therefore, holds that the definition of torture contained in Article 1 of the Torture Convention can only serve, for present purposes, as an interpretational aid.

483. Three elements of the definition of torture contained in the torture Convention are, however, uncontentious and are accepted as representing the status of customary international law on the subject:

  (i) Torture consists of the infliction, by act or omission, of severe pain or suffering, whether physical or mental.
 (ii) This act or omission must be intentional.
(iii) The act must be instrumental to another purpose, in the sense that the infliction of pain must be aimed at reaching a certain goal.

484. On the other hand, three elements remain contentious:

  (i) The list of purposes the pursuit of which could be regarded as illegitimate and coming within the realm of the definition of torture.
 (ii) The necessity, if any, for the act to be committed in connection with an armed conflict.
(iii) The requirement, if any, that the act be inflicted by or at the instigation of or with the consent or acquiescence of a public official or other person acting in an official capacity.

485. The Trial Chamber is satisfied that the following purposes have become part of customary international law: (a) obtaining information or a confession, (b) punishing, intimidating or coercing the victim or a third person. There are some doubts as to whether other purposes have come to be recognized under customary international law. The issue does not need to be resolved here, because the conduct of the accused is appropriately subsumable under the above-mentioned purposes.

486. There is no requirement under customary international law that the conduct must be solely perpetrated for one of the prohibited purposes. As was stated by the Trial Chamber in the *Delalić* case, the prohibited purpose must simply be part of the motivation behind the conduct and need not be the predominating or sole purpose.

487. Secondly, the nature of the relationship between the underlying offence – torture – and the armed conflict depends, under the [ICTY's] Statute, on the qualification of the offence, as a grave breach, a war crime or a crime against humanity. If, for example, torture is charged as a violation of the laws or customs of war under ... the Statute, the Trial Chamber will have to be satisfied that the act was closely related to the hostilities. If, on the other hand, torture is charged as a crime against humanity ... the Trial Chamber will have to be convinced beyond reasonable doubt that there existed an armed conflict at the relevant time and place.

488. Thirdly, the Torture Convention requires that the pain or suffering be inflicted by or at the instigation of or with the consent or acquiescence of a public official or other person acting in an official capacity. As was already mentioned, the Trial Chamber must consider each element of the definition "from the specific viewpoint of international criminal law relating to armed conflicts." In practice, this means that the Trial Chamber must identify those elements of the definition of torture under human rights law which are extraneous to international criminal law as well as those which are present in the latter body of law but possibly absent from the human rights regime.

489. The Trial Chamber draws a clear distinction between those provisions which are addressed to individuals. Violations of the former provisions result exclusively in the responsibility of the state to take the necessary steps to redress or make reparation for the negative consequences of the criminal actions of its agents. On the other hand, violations of the second set of provisions may provide for individual criminal responsibility, regardless of an individual's official status. While human rights norms are almost exclusively of the first sort, humanitarian provisions can be of both or sometimes of mixed nature. This has been pointed out by the Trial Chamber in the *Furundžija* case:

> Under current international humanitarian law, in addition to individual criminal liability, State responsibility may ensue as a result of State officials engaging in torture or failing to prevent torture or to prevent torturers. If carried out as an extensive practice of State officials, torture amounts to a serious breach on a widespread scale of an international obligation of essential importance for safeguarding the human being, thus constituting a particularly wrongful act generating State responsibility.

490. Several humanitarian law provisions fall within the first category of legal norms, expressly providing for the possibility of state responsibility for the acts of its agents: thus, Article 75 ("Fundamental Guarantees") of Additional Protocol I provides that acts of violence to the life, health or physical or mental well-being of persons such as murder, torture, corporal punishment and mutilation, outrages upon personal dignity, the taking of hostages, collective punishments and threats to commit any of those acts when

committed by civilian or by military agents of the state could engage the state's responsibility. The requirement that the acts be committed by an agent of the state applies equally to any of the offences provided under paragraph 2 of Article 75 and in particular, but no differently, to the crime of torture.

491. This provision should be contrasted with Article 4 ("Fundamental Guarantees") of Additional Protocol II. The latter provision provides for a list of offences broadly similar to that contained in Article 75 of Additional Protocol I but does not contain any reference to agents of the state. The offences provided for in this Article can, therefore, be committed by any individual, regardless of his official status, although, if the perpetrator is an agent of the state he could additionally engage the responsibility of the state. The Commentary to Additional Protocol II dealing specifically with the offences mentioned in Article 4 (2)(a) namely, violence to the life, health, or physical or mental well being of persons in particular murder and cruel treatment such as torture, states:

> The most widespread form of torture is practiced by public officials for the purpose of obtaining confessions, but torture is not only condemned as a judicial institution; *the act of torture is reprehensible in itself, regardless of its perpetrator,* and cannot be justified in any circumstances.

493. A violation of one of the relevant articles of the Statute will engage the perpetrator's individual criminal responsibility. In this context, the participation of the state becomes secondary and, generally, peripheral. With or without the involvement of the state, the crime committed remains of the same nature and bears the same consequences. ...

494. Likewise, the doctrine of "act of State", by which an individual would be shielded from criminal responsibility for an act he or she committed in the name of or as an agent of a state, is no defence under international criminal law. This has been the case since the Second World War, if not before. ... Neither can obedience to orders be relied upon as a defence playing a mitigating role only at the sentencing stage. In short, there is no privilege under international criminal law which would shield state representatives or agents from the reach of individual criminal responsibility. On the contrary, acting in an official capacity could constitute an aggravating circumstance when it comes to sentencing, because the official illegitimately used and abused a power which was conferred upon him or her for legitimate purposes.

495. The Trial Chamber also points out that those conventions, in particular the human rights conventions, consider torture *per se* while the Tribunal's Statute criminalises it as a form of war crime, crime against humanity or grave breach. The characteristic trait of the offence in this context is to be found in the nature of the act committed rather than in the status of the person who committed it.

496. The Trial Chamber concludes that the definition of torture under international humanitarian law does not comprise the same elements as the definition of torture generally applied under human rights law. In particular, the Trial Chamber is of the view that the presence of a state official or of any other authority-wielding person in the torture process is not necessary for the offence to be regarded as torture under international humanitarian law.

497. On the basis of what has been said, the Trial Chamber holds that, in the field of international humanitarian law, the elements of the offence of torture, under customary international law are as follows:

(i) The infliction, by act or omission, of severe pain or suffering, whether physical or mental.

(ii) The act or omission must be intentional.

(iii) The act or omission must aim at obtaining information or a confession, or at punishing, intimidating or coercing the victim or a third person, or at discriminating, on any ground, against the victim or a third person.

Conclusion. *The definition of the war crime of torture enunciated by the* Kunarac *trial chamber is followed in subsequent ICTY torture trials.*

Does the trial chamber's discussion in paragraphs 488–94, regarding the responsibility of state officials for torture, suggest possible liability as to authors of policies regarding the interrogation of detainees in the Iraq and Afghanistan conflicts?

PROSECUTOR V. BRDANIN

IT-99-36-T (September 1, 2004), footnotes omitted

Introduction. *The* Brdanin *trial judgment summarizes and clarifies the definition of torture in ICTY jurisprudence. Though ICTY judgments are binding only on the parties before the court, such judgments are "persuasive" in other forums.*

481. Both this Tribunal and the ICTR have adopted a definition of the crime of torture along the lines of that contained in the Convention Against Torture ("CAT"), which comprises the following constitutive elements:

1. the infliction, by act or omission, of severe pain or suffering, whether physical or mental;

2. the act or omission must be intentional; and

3. the act or omission must have occurred in order to obtain information or a confession, or to punish, intimidate or coerce the victim or a third person, or to discriminate, on any ground, against the victim or a third person.

482. The definition of "torture" remains the same regardless of the Article of the Statute [of the ICTY] under which the Accused has been charged. The *mens rea* as set out above [in element 2.] is not controversial in the jurisprudence of the Tribunal. However, a number of issues regarding the *actus reus* may usefully be addressed.

(a) Severity of Pain or Suffering

483. The seriousness of the pain or suffering sets torture apart from other forms of mistreatment. The jurisprudence of this Tribunal and of the ICTR has not specifically set the threshold level of suffering or pain required for the crime of torture, and it consequently depends on the individual circumstances of each case.

484. In assessing the seriousness of any mistreatment, the objective severity of the harm inflicted must be considered, including the nature, purpose and consistency of the acts committed. Subjective criteria, such as the physical or mental condition of the victim, the effect of the treatment and, in some cases, factors such as the victim's age, sex, state of health and position of inferiority will also be relevant in assessing the gravity of the harm.

Permanent injury is not a requirement for torture; evidence of the suffering need not even be visible after the commission of the crime.

485. The criteria mentioned in the previous paragraph will be used by this Trial Chamber in assessing whether the treatment alleged by the Prosecution ... amounts to severe pain or suffering. Some acts, like rape, appear by definition to meet the severity threshold. Like torture, rape is a violation of personal dignity and is used for such purposes as intimidation, degradation, humiliation and discrimination, punishment, control or destruction of a person. Severe pain or suffering, as required by the definition of the crime of torture, can be said to be established once rape has been proved, since the act of rape necessarily implies such pain or suffering.

(b) Prohibited Purpose

486. Acts of torture aim, through the infliction of severe mental or physical pain, to attain a certain result or purpose. Thus, in the absence of such a purpose or goal, even a very severe infliction of pain would not qualify for torture for the purposes of Article 2 and Article 5 of the [ICTY] Statute.

487. The prohibited purposes mentioned above do not constitute an exhaustive list, and there is no requirement that the conduct must *solely* serve a prohibited purpose. If one prohibited purpose is fulfilled by the conduct, the fact that such conduct was also intended to achieve a non-listed purpose is immaterial.

c. Official Sanction Not Required

488. Even though the CAT envisages that torture be committed "with the consent or acquiescence of a public official or other person acting in an official capacity, the jurisprudence of this Tribunal does not require that the perpetrator of the crime of torture be a public official, nor does the torture need to have been committed in the presence of such an official.

489. In this context, the Trial Chamber notes that the definition of the CAT relies on the notion of human rights, which is largely built on the premises that human rights are violated by States or Governments. For the purposes of international criminal law, which deals with the criminal responsibility of an individual, this Trial Chamber agrees with and follows the approach of the *Kunarac* Trial Chamber that "the characteristic trait of the offence [under the Tribunal's jurisdiction] is to be found in the nature of the act committed rather than in the status of the person who committed it."

Conclusion. Besides clearly stating the elements of torture for ICTY cases, the opinion continues the streamlined definition of torture initiated in Kunarac *and, in a sentence, cogently explains why it is the legally correct track to follow.*

THE LIEUTENANT COLONEL AND THE MOCK EXECUTION

Lieutenant Colonel Allen B. West, with nineteen years of army service, commanded an artillery battalion in the 4th Infantry Division, near Saba al Boor, in "the Sunni Triangle" of northern Iraq. Lieutenant Colonel West had been in Iraq for four months.

In August 2003, in conversation with an army intelligence officer, Lieutenant Colonel West was told that there was an Iraqi plot to kill him. Such a plot could also kill or wound soldiers accompanying him. An Iraqi policeman who sometimes worked for the Americans, Yehiya Kadoori Hamoodi, was reported to be involved in the plot. After a week or so, during which a patrol he was supposed to be with was fired upon, Lieutenant Colonel West directed several of his soldiers to go to the nearby village, seize Hamoodi, and take him to the U.S. base. They did so, depositing him in an on-base interrogation room, blindfolded and in handcuffs. Roughly questioned, Hamoodi denied knowledge of any ambush.

"Hamoodi said he felt relieved to hear the colonel was expected. He considered Colonel West to be 'calm, quiet, clever and sociable.'"[240] Lieutenant Colonel West recalled, "I asked for soldiers to accompany me and told them we had to gather information and that it could get ugly."[241] According to a newspaper interview of West, as the lieutenant colonel entered the interrogation room he drew his 9-millimeter pistol, cocked it, sat down and placed it in his lap, in view of Hamoodi. After briefly questioning him further, other soldiers in the room began to shove and punch Hamoodi. Lieutenant Colonel West, an artillery officer who had never before questioned a prisoner, said that he would have stopped the punching of the handcuffed prisoner, "had it become too excessive."[242] Instead, according to an army pretrial investigator's report, West said to Hamoodi, "I came here for one of two reasons, to get the information I need, or to kill you."[243] Such a dramatic approach seems unsupported by the level of combat experienced by Lieutenant Colonel West, who had but one of his soldiers wounded and none killed during his tour of duty in Iraq. Even the wounded soldier returned to duty with the unit.[244]

The lieutenant colonel and his soldiers moved Hamoodi outside and threatened to kill him. West fired a pistol shot in the air, and then directed his soldiers to force Hamoodi's head into a sand-filled metal barrel used to ensure soldiers' weapons were clear before entering office spaces. Pointing his pistol at Hamoodi's head, Lieutenant Colonel West began to count down from five. When Hamoodi failed to respond, West fired a round into the sand-filled barrel, angling his pistol away from Hamoodi's head. Hamoodi promptly admitted a planned attack and provided the names of involved Iraqis. Interviewed later, Hamoodi said he gave false information out of fear.

One of the Iraqis named by Hamoodi was arrested and his home searched. No ambush plans or weapons were found. Hamoodi was held for forty-five days, after which he was released without charges.

"The abusive interrogation might never have come to light if a sergeant in another battalion had not subsequently written a letter of complaint about the 'command climate' under Colonel West's immediate superior officer, the artillery brigade commander. In that letter, the sergeant mentioned ... that Colonel West had interrogated a detainee using a pistol."[245] A general court-martial was initiated by Lieutenant Colonel West's division commander. West was relieved of command, transferred to another unit, and charged with aggravated assault and communicating a threat. If convicted,

[240] Deborah Sontag, "How Colonel Risked His Career by Menacing Detainee and Lost," NY Times, May 27, 2004, A1.

[241] Rowan Scarborough, "Army Files Charges in Combat Tactic," Wash. Times, Oct. 29, 2003, A1.

[242] Sontag, "How Colonel Risked His Career," supra, note 240, A1.

[243] Richard Berry, A Missing Link in Leadership (Bloomington, IN: Author House, 2008), 27.

[244] Id., at 59.   [245] Sontag, "How Colonel Risked His Career," supra, note 240, at A1.

Lieutenant Colonel West faced dismissal from the army and possible imprisonment for eight years. At a November 2003 pretrial investigation held in Tikrit, Lieutenant Colonel West testified that he would "go through hell with a gas can" to protect the lives of his soldiers.

Some within the U.S. Army, and many American civilians, considered criminal charges against Lieutenant Colonel West to be an injustice. One congressman urged that West should be "commended for his actions and interrogation."[246] Other lawmakers wrote to the secretary of the army to protest West's charges. Not everyone took so sympathetic a view, however. "Even more disturbing than West's decision to fire his pistol near the head of the Iraqi detainee, [an un-named army] official said, was West's admission during the preliminary hearing that, before firing his pistol, he watched as his soldiers beat the Iraqi in an attempt to get him to talk."[247] The retired general Barry McCaffrey agreed, saying, "You can't physically maltreat prisoners, and we can't have our officer corps tolerating that."[248]

Attempting to turn official condemnation into heroism, Lieutenant Colonel West "said his actions might have caused the end of his career, but they saved lives."[249] The army disagreed: "According to the evidence, the organization and its decision-makers did not believe there was an extraordinary threat to LTC West or his unit."[250]

Shortly after his pretrial investigation, which recommended administrative punishment rather than a court-martial, Lieutenant Colonel West's commanding general, Major General Raymond Odierno, accepted the investigating officer's recommendation and fined West twenty-five hundred dollrs' pay per month for two months. Lieutenant Colonel West, who consistently confused friendship with subordinates with leadership of subordinates, and who never saw the inherent conflict between mission accomplishment and force security,[251] was allowed to retire, as he had requested just before his pretrial investigation.[252]

Conclusion. *Did Lieutenant Colonel West torture the detainee? There are other, more compelling, cases in which younger officers, their soldiers killed by a duplicitous enemy in their midst, gave in to anger and carried out mock executions.[253] Do you agree with*

---

[246] Vernon Loeb, "Army Officer's Actions Raise Ethical Issues," *Wash. Post*, Sept. 30, 2003, A24.

[247] Id.   [248] Id.

[249] Emily Tower, "Retired Officer Discusses Ethics with Upperclassmen," *Pointer View*, newspaper of the West Point campus, Oct. 23, 2008, 5.

[250] Berry, *Missing Link in Leadership*, supra, note 247, at 23, referring to Lieutenant Colonel West's pretrial Article 32 investigating officer's report.

[251] Id., at 59. Lieutenant Colonel West: "My mission was security and stability in my designated area in Iraq and the return of my men to their loved ones." Every commander wishes for minimal casualties and, whenever possible, acts to ensure that end. Mission accomplishment is always primary, however. Most troop leaders recognize the hard truth that in combat there can be no assurance that men and women in their charge will not be killed or wounded. The enemy always has a vote in that outcome. A commander's mission cannot at the same time be mission accomplishment and the assured return home of subordinates. A commander's concern for subordinates' welfare is never an excuse to abuse prisoners in violation of military law and LOAC.

[252] Vernon Loeb, "Army Fines Officer for Firing Pistol Near Iraqi Detainee," *Wash. Post*, Dec. 13, 2003, A18.

[253] P. J. Tobia, "The Other Front," *Wash. Post*, Dec. 14, 2008, B1, an account of the pretrial investigation of a 101st Airborne Division company commander, his second in command, his first sergeant, and several of his soldiers, some of whom allegedly beat bound captives, after which the company commander admittedly carried out a mock execution. An enlisted accused said, "If it was us, they'd cut our heads off, videotape it and put it on al-Jazeera for our families to see."

Lieutenant Colonel West's commanding general's decision? What would you have done, in Colonel West's place, if told there was a plot to kill you?

Does a mock execution constitute torture in violation of LOAC? It is not among the ICC Statute's Article 8 war crimes. The ICTR, however, has held "that the following acts committed by the Accused or by others in the presence of the Accused, at his instigation or with his consent or acquiescence, constitute torture: (i) the interrogation of Victim U, under threat to her life, by the Accused."[254] The U.N. Human Rights Committee and the Inter-American Commission on Human Rights consider mock executions torture.[255]

The U.S. Army's interrogation manual (which did not take effect until September 2006, three years after Lieutenant Colonel West's interrogation) specifically prohibits mock executions.[256] That manual also notes, "Compliance with laws and regulations, including proper treatment of detainees, is a matter of command responsibility. Commanders have an affirmative duty to ensure their subordinates are not mistreating detainees."[257]

FROM A "TOP SECRET" CIA TORTURE MEMORANDUM

Introduction. *This memo, classified "Top Secret" until released on April 16, 2009, pursuant to a litigation-generated Freedom of Information request, describes and discusses each of the "enhanced interrogation techniques" employed by the CIA and indicates why, according to the DOJ's Office of Legal Counsel, none of them, alone or in combination, necessarily constitutes severe physical or mental pain or suffering. The memo also takes the reader through a "typical" thirty-day interrogation cycle. Only that portion of the memo is extracted here. The many quotation marks in the extract indicate quotes from an internal CIA document provided to the Justice Department for use in determining the lawfulness of CIA interrogation techniques. That document is entitled,* Background Paper on CIA's Combined Use of Interrogation Techniques. *The bracketed term "[detainee]" appears frequently in the original. Any material elided here is minimal; nothing is taken out of context:*

May 10, 2005

Memorandum for John A. Rizzo, Senior Deputy General Counsel, Central Intelligence Agency

From: U.S. Department of Justice, Office of Legal Counsel

Re: Application of 18 U.S.C. 2340–2340A to the Combined Use of Certain Techniques in the Interrogation of High Value al Qaeda Detainees

... Phases of the Interrogation Process

The first phase of the interrogation process, "Initial Conditions," does not involve interrogation techniques. ... The "Initial Conditions" nonetheless set the stage for use of the interrogation techniques, which come later.

---

[254] *Prosecutor v. Akayesu*, ICTR-96-4-T (Sept. 2, 1998), para. 682.

[255] Dörmann, *Elements of War Crimes*, supra, note 65, at 54, citing *Muteba v. Zaire* and *Gilboa v. Uruguay*, Report of the Human Rights Committee, Communication No. 124/1982, UN Doc. A/39/40, pp. 182 ff; 79 ILR 253; and Communication No. 147/1983, UN Doc. A/41/40, pp. 128 ff., respectively.

[256] FM 2–22.3, *Human Intelligence Collection Operations*, supra, note 228, at para. 5–75.

[257] Id., at para. 5–54.

Before being flown to the site of interrogation, a detainee is given a medical examination. He then is "securely shackled and is deprived of sight and sound through the use of blindfolds, earmuffs, and hoods" during the flight. ... Upon arrival at the site, the detainee "finds himself in complete control of Americans" and is subjected to "precise, quiet, and almost clinical" procedures designed to underscore "the enormity and suddenness of the change in environment, the uncertainty about what will happen next, and the potential dread [a detainee] may have of US custody." His head and face are shaved, his physical condition is documented through photographs taken while he is nude; and he is given medical and psychological interviews to assess his condition and to make sure there are no contraindications to the use of any particular interrogation techniques.

The detainee then enters the next phase, the "Transition to Interrogation." The interrogators conduct an initial interview, "in a relatively benign environment," to ascertain whether the detainee is willing to cooperate. The detainee is "normally clothed but seated and shackled for security purposes." The interrogators take "an open, non-threatening approach," but the detainee "would have to provide information on actionable threats and location information on High-Value Targets at large – not lower-level information – for interrogators to continue with [this] neutral approach." If the detainee does not meet this "very high" standard, the interrogators submit a detailed interrogation plan to CIA headquarters for approval. If the medical and psychological assessments find no contraindications ... the interrogation moves to the next phase.

Three interrogation techniques are typically used to bring the detainee to "a baseline, dependent state," "demonstrat[ing] to the [detainee] that he has no control over basic human needs" and helping to make him "perceive and values his personal welfare, comfort, and immediate needs more than the information he is protecting." The three techniques used to establish this "baseline" are nudity, sleep deprivation (with shackling and, at least at times, with use of a diaper), and dietary manipulation. ...

Other techniques, which "require physical interaction between the interrogator and detainee," are characterized as "corrective" and "are used principally to correct, startle, or achieve another enabling objective with the detainee." These techniques "are not used simultaneously but are often used interchangeably during an individual interrogation session." The insult slap is used "periodically throughout the interrogation process when the interrogator needs to immediately correct the detainee or provide a consequence to a detainee's response or non-response." The insult slap "can be used in combination with water dousing of kneeling stress positions" – techniques that are not characterized as "coercive." Another corrective technique, the abdominal slap "is similar to the insult slap in application and desired result" and "provides the variation necessary to keep a high level of unpredictability in the interrogation process." The abdominal slap may be simultaneously combined with water dousing, stress positions, and wall standing. A third corrective technique, the facial hold, "is used sparingly throughout interrogation." It is not painful, but "demonstrates the interrogator's control over the [detainee]." It too may be simultaneously combined with water dousing, stress positions, and wall standing. Finally, the attention grasp "may be used several times in the same interrogation" and may be simultaneously combined with water dousing or kneeling stress positions.

Some techniques are characterized as "coercive." These techniques "place the detainee in more physical and psychological stress." Coercive techniques "are typically not used in combination, although some combined use is possible." Walling "is one of the most effective interrogation techniques because it wears down the [detainee] physically, heightens uncertainty in the detainee about what the interrogator may do to him, and creates a sense of dread when the [detainee] knows he is about to be walled again." A detainee "may be walled one time (one impact with the wall) to make a point or twenty to thirty times consecutively when the interrogator requires a more significant response to a question," and "will be walled multiple times" during a session designed to be intense. . . .

Water temperature and other considerations of safety established by OMS [the CIA Office of Medical Services] limit the use of another coercive technique, water dousing. The technique "may be used frequently within those guidelines." As suggested above, the interrogators may combine water dousing with other techniques, such as stress positions, wall standing, the insult slap, or the abdominal slap.

The use of stress positions is "usually self-limiting in that temporary muscle fatigue usually leads to the [detainee's] being unable to maintain the stress position after a period of time." Depending on the particular position, stress positions may be combined with water dousing, the insult slap, the facial hold, and the attention grasp. Another coercive technique, wall standing, is "usually self-limiting" in the same way as stress positions. It may be combined with water dousing and the abdominal slap. OMS guidelines limit the technique of cramped confinement to no more than eight hours at a time and 18 hours a day, and confinement in the "small box" is limited to two hours. . . .

We understand that the CIA's use of all these interrogation techniques is subject to ongoing monitoring by interrogation team members who will direct that techniques be discontinued if there is a deviation from prescribed procedures and by medical and psychological personnel from OMS who will direct that any or all techniques be discontinued if in their professional judgment the detainee may otherwise suffer severe physical or mental pain or suffering.

A Prototypical Interrogation

In a "prototypical interrogation," the detainee begins his first interrogation session stripped of his clothes, shackled, and hooded, with the walling collar over his head and around his neck. The interrogators remove the hood and explain that the detainee can improve his situation by cooperating and may say that the interrogator "will do what it takes to get important information." As soon as the detainee does anything inconsistent with the interrogators' instructions, the interrogators use an insult slap or abdominal slap. They employ walling if it becomes clear that the detainee is not cooperating in the interrogation. This sequence "may continue for several more iterations as the interrogators continue to measure the [detainee's] resistance posture and apply a negative consequence to [his] resistance efforts." The interrogators and security officers then put the detainee into position for standing sleep deprivation, begin dietary manipulation through a liquid diet, and keep the detainee nude (except for a diaper). The first interrogation session, which could have lasted from 30 minutes to several hours, would then be at an end.

If the interrogation team determines there is a need to continue, and if the medical and psychological personnel advise that there are no contraindications, a second session may begin. The interval between sessions could be as short as an hour or as long as 24 hours. At the start of the second session, the detainee is released from the position for standing sleep deprivation, is hooded, and is positioned against the walling wall. . . .

Even before removing the hood, the interrogators use the attention grasp to startle the detainee. The interrogators take off the hood and begin questioning. If the detainee does not give appropriate answers to the first questions, the interrogators use an insult slap or abdominal slap. They employ walling if they determine that the detainee "is intent on maintaining his resistance posture." This sequence "may continue for multiple iterations as the interrogators continue to measure the [detainee's] resistance posture. The interrogators then increase the pressure on the detainee by using a hose to douse the detainee with water for several minutes. They stop and start the dousing as they continue the interrogation. They then end the session by placing the detainee in the same circumstances as at the end of the first session: the detainee is in the standing position for sleep deprivation, is nude (except for a diaper), and is subjected to dietary manipulation. Once again, the session could have lasted from 30 minutes to several hours.

... [A] third session may follow. The session begins with the detainee positioned as at the beginning of the second. If the detainee continues to resist, the interrogators continue to use walling and water dousing. The corrective techniques – the insult slap, the abdominal slap, the facial hold, the attention grasp – "may be used several times during this session based on the responses and actions of the [detainee]. The interrogators integrate stress positions and wall standing into this session. Furthermore, "intense questioning and walling would be repeated multiple times." Interrogators "use one technique to support another." For example, they threaten the use of walling unless the detainee holds a stress position, thus inducing the detainee to remain in the position longer than he otherwise would. At the end of the session, the interrogators and security personnel place the detainee into the same circumstances as at the end of the first two sessions, with the detainee subject to sleep deprivation, nudity, and dietary manipulation.

In later sessions, the interrogators use those techniques that are proving most effective and drop the others. Sleep deprivation "may continue to the 70 to 120 hour range, or possibly beyond that for the hardest resisters, but in no case exceed the 180-hour time limit. If the medical or psychological personnel find contraindications, sleep deprivation will end earlier. While continuing the use of sleep deprivation, nudity, and dietary manipulation, the interrogators may add cramped confinement. As the detainee begins to cooperate, the interrogators "begin gradually to decrease the use of interrogation techniques." They may permit the detainee to sit, supply clothes, and provide more appetizing food.

The entire process in this "prototypical interrogation" may last 30 days. If additional time is required and a new approval is obtained from headquarters, interrogation may go longer than 30 days. Nevertheless, "on average, the actual use of interrogation techniques covers a period of three to seven days, but can vary upward to fifteen days based on the resilience of the [detainee]."

Conclusion. A country is what it stands for, when standing for something is the most difficult. *One can only wonder what the Supreme Court Justice Robert Jackson, chief prosecutor of the Nuremberg International Military Tribunal (and former attorney general of the United States), would say upon reading this document, his wrath at the perversion of American justice and ideals. What would he have responded to the tired argument that it was all for the protection of Americans?*

Telford Taylor, Justice Jackson's successor as Nuremberg chief prosecutor, and later Nash Professor of Law at Columbia University's School of Law, wrote of Nazi documents admitted as trial evidence at Nuremberg, "even the most damning memoranda of this sort can be minimized by clever explanation and excuse. "[258]

The April 2009 release of this document, signed by Steven G. Bradbury, principal deputy assistant attorney general of the Department of Justice, along with three other "torture memos," was controversial.[259] Mr. Karl Rove, deputy chief of staff to President George W. Bush for seven years, on a televised talk show encouraged Americans to read the memos, saying, "You'll be reassured about what your government was doing." Mr. Rove continued, "All of these techniques have now been ruined."[260]

One can only hope.

---

[258] BGen. Telford Taylor, *Final Report to the Secretary of the Army on the Nuernberg War Crimes Trials Under Control Council Law No. 10* (Washington, DC/Buffalo, NY: Hein reprint, 1949/1997), 67.

[259] R. Jeffrey Smith, Michael D. Shear, and Walter Pincus, "In Obama's Inner Circle, Debate over Memos' Release Was Intense," *Washington Post*, April 24, 2009, A1.

[260] *The O'Reilly Factor* (Fox television broadcast April 18, 2009), available at: http://realclearpolitics.com/video/2009/04/17/oreilly_is_america_a_torture_nation.html

17 Cyber Warfare

17.0 Introduction

This discussion is out of date. Cyber warfare policy and strategies evolve so rapidly that it is difficult to stay current. A snapshot of the topic must suffice.

Much has been made of the revolution in the law of armed conflict (LOAC) necessitated by the advent of cyber warfare. But, "this is by no means the first time in the history of [LOAC] that the introduction of a new weapon has created the misleading impression that great legal transmutations are afoot . . . *viz.*, the submarine."[1] Hannibal's elephants probably elicited a similar impression. Actually, cyber warfare issues may be resolved in terms of traditional law of war concepts, although there is scant demonstration of its application because, so far, instances of actual cyber warfare have been unusual. Although cyber questions are many, the law of war offers as many answers.

A threshold question: Does existing LOAC apply to cyber issues? Yes, it does. The International Court of Justice (ICJ), in its 1996 *Nuclear Weapons* Advisory Opinion, notes that LOAC applies to "any use of force, regardless of the weapons employed."[2] Whether a five-hundred-pound bomb or a computer is used to effect death and destruction, a weapon remains a weapon. The U.S. position is made clear in its 2011 *International Strategy for Operating in Cyberspace*: "The development of norms for State conduct in cyberspace does not require a reinvention of customary international law, nor does it render existing international norms obsolete. Long-standing international norms guiding State behavior – in times of peace and conflict – also apply in cyberspace."[3] Article 36 of 1977 Additional Protocol I, requiring testing of new weapons and weapons systems for conformance with LOAC, illustrates that the law of war and international humanitarian law (IHL) rules apply to new technologies.

Defining many aspects of cyber warfare is problematic because there is no multinational treaty directly dealing with cyber warfare. That is because, so far, many aspects of cyber war are not agreed upon. The law of war, as well as customary international law, lacks cyber-specific norms, and state practice interpreting applicable norms is slow to

---

[1] Yoram Dinstein, "Cyber War and International Law: Concluding Remarks at the 2012 Naval War College International Law Conference," in 89 *International Law Studies: Cyber War and International Law* (Newport, RI: Naval War College, 2013), 276, 286.

[2] ICJ, *Legality of the Threat or Use of Nuclear Weapons*, Advisory Opinion (July 8, 1995), ICJ Rep 226–67, para. 39.

[3] White House, *International Strategy for Cyberspace: Prosperity, Security, and Openness in a Networked World* (May 2011), at 9. Available online.

evolve. There is not even agreement as to whether "cyber attack" is one word or two. What can be said is that the *jus ad bellum* and *jus in bello* apply to cyber operations and it seems safe to follow existing LOAC/IHL.

What is cyber warfare? It is not cyber crime – the use of computers in violation of domestic law for criminal purposes. In the United States, the Computer Fraud and Abuse Act defines Internet criminal acts.[4] European Union members of the NATO alliance have domestic laws implementing the 1995 E.U. Privacy Directive. On an international level, cyber crime is addressed by the Council of Europe's 2001 Convention on Cybercrime, currently the only multinational treaty addressing the criminal cyber problem. But cyber warfare and cyber crime should not be confused.

The word "cyber" is not found in the Geneva Conventions or 1977 Additional Protocols. In common usage, "cyber" relates to computers and computer networks, not only the Internet but all computer networks in the world, including everything they connect with and control. **Cyber warfare may be defined as "warfare waged in space, including *defending* information and computer networks, *deterring* information attacks, as well as denying an adversary's ability to do the same. It can include *offensive* information operations mounted against an adversary."[5]** Cyber warfare, then, includes offense, defense, and deterrence.

Cyber warfare may be engaged in by states, agents of states, and nonstate actors and groups. It does not necessarily constitute terrorism, but it may, depending on one's definition of terrorism. The U.S. Federal Emergency Management Agency defines cyber terrorism as "unlawful attacks and threats of attack against computers, networks, and the information stored therein when done to intimidate or coerce a government or its people in furtherance of political or social objectives."[6] Cyber terrorism is a relatively minor threat today, but its potential is obvious.

17.1 The Internet as Battlefield

The importance of the Internet to military, government, commercial, and private interests requires no discussion. We daily read and hear of cyber breaches and cyber incidents involving our critical national infrastructure. China and Russia are identified as primary actors in those breaches.

China is particularly aggressive in its cyber intrusions and cyber theft of intellectual property.[7] China's cyber operations in U.S. systems have been so frequent and serious that they have been the subject of repeated diplomatic, even presidential, entreaties and complaints.

---

[4] 10 US Code § 1030.

[5] Steven A. Hildreth, *Cyberwarfare* (Washington, DC: Congressional Research Service), June 19, 2001), 16. Emphasis in original. Another definition is offered by the ICRC: "Means and methods of warfare that consist of cyber operations amounting to or conducted in the context of an armed conflict within the meaning of IHL." Cordula Droege, "Get Off My Cloud: Cyber Warfare, International Humanitarian Law, and the Protection of Civilians," 94/886 *Int'l. Rev. of the Red Cross* (Summer 2012), 533, 538. There is no definition of cyber warfare in Joint Publication 1–02, *Department of Defense Dictionary of Military and Associated Terms* (amended through Oct. 15, 2013).

[6] Clay Wilson, "*Botnets, Cybercrime, and Cyberterrorism: Vulnerabilities and Policy Issues for Congress,*" Washington, DC: Congressional Research Service (Jan. 29, 2008), 3. Footnotes omitted.

[7] Li Zhang, "A Chinese Perspective on Cyber War," 94/886 *Int'l Rev. of the Red Cross* (Summer 2012), 801, offers a different, far milder viewpoint.

Pursuant to a 1998 agreement with Cuba, China has two network monitoring stations there, one located in the northernmost Cuban city of Benjucal to monitor U.S. Internet traffic, the other northeast of Santiago de Cuba to monitor U.S. Department of Defense (DoD) traffic.[8] Such penetrations are not particularly challenging, in part because China is so familiar with U.S. Internet routers; many routers are brands of the U.S. firm Cisco and all brands of Cisco routers are made in China.

The Chinese People's Liberation Army's strategic cyber command is located in the 3rd General Staff Department, whose estimated 130,000 personnel focus on signals intelligence and defense information systems. Unit 61398 of the 2nd Bureau conducts the 3rd General Staff Department's cyber operations against America out of its Shanghai head-quarters.[9] In recent years Unit 61398 has been busy. "Because they broke the law and to deter China from conducting future cyber espionage, the [U.S.] Justice Department indicted five members of the People's Liberation Army for stealing U.S. intellectual property to directly benefit Chinese companies."[10]

"Night Dragon" involved China's cyber theft of hundreds of terabytes of secret aspects of the then-new U.S. F-35 fighter from Lockheed Martin's data storage system. That theft began in 2007 and continued undiscovered through 2009.[11]

In September 2011, a virus of unknown (or undisclosed) origin infected classified U.S. Air Force drone control stations at Creech Air Force Base, in Nevada. The virus was repeatedly wiped off and, just as often, promptly returned. It exhibited no immediate effects and Predator and Reaper missions in Afghanistan and Iraq continued uninter-rupted. The air force said, "We think it's benign. But we just don't know."[12]

In 2010, the vice-chairman of the Joint Chiefs of Staff noted that "penetrations of Pentagon systems were efforts to map out U.S. government networks and learn how to cripple America's command-and-control systems as part of a future attack."[13]

SIDEBAR. Many DoD computer systems in the Pentagon that involve classified material are safeguarded from intrusion by security devices referred to as "tokens." Access to Pentagon computers requires the user's password and a random number provided by the user's token. The token is a small key-shaped thumb-drive-like object manufactured by several civilian information security companies. The token generates a new random six-digit number every sixty seconds. To unlock classified network com-puters, users insert their token into their computer's USB port and enter the number

---

[8] Richard A. Clarke and Robert K. Knake, *Cyber War* (New York: Ecco, 2010), 58.
[9] Mandiant Intelligence Center Report: "Advanced Persistent Threat 1: Exposing One of China's Cyber Espionage Units" (Washington, DC: Mandiant, Jan. 2013), widely available online.
[10] *The Department of Defense: Cyber Security, April 2015*, at 12. Available online.
[11] Clarke and Knake, supra, note 8, at 233; and Jason Healey, "A Brief History of US Cyber Conflict," in Jason Healey, ed., *A Fierce Domain: Conflict in Cyberspace, 1986 to 2012* (Vienna, VA: Cyber Conflict Studies Association, 2013), 14, 68.
[12] Wired, Oct. 7, 2011, http://www.wired.com/dangerroom and "Virus Hits Networks Used for Drone Flights," *Wash. Post*, Oct. 9, 2011, A7.
[13] J. P. London, "Made in China," US Naval Institute *Proceedings* (April 2011), 54, 56. The then-vice-chairman was General James Cartwright.

then showing in a small window on the token. In March 2011, "an extremely sophisti-cated"[14] cyber attack by "a foreign intelligence service"[15] hacked the computer system of RSA Security, a major civilian information security company, and gained data pertain-ing to the manufacture and the capabilities of the tokens that RSA Security supplies the Pentagon. "RSA has tens of millions of dollars worth of contracts across the federal government. Agencies with large contracts include ... the Defense Department and its service branches."[16]

Rather than attacking DoD computers directly, the March 2011 cyber attack targeted the firm that provided cyber security for DoD computers. Three months later, "con-firming the fears of security experts about the safety of the ... tokens,"[17] hackers using the stolen RSA token data attacked Lockheed Martin, maker of fighter aircraft and satellites. (This is not the same Lockheed Martin attack mentioned previously.) Soon thereafter, DoD admitted that the March 2011 cyber attack was "one of its worst digital attacks in history [losing] 24,000 Pentagon files during a single intrusion."[18] A deputy secretary of defense confirmed "that over the years crucial files stolen ... have included plans for missile tracking systems, satellite navigation devices, surveillance drones and top-of-the-line jet fighters."[19] "Bad as it was to lose secrets, that wasn't the worst threat from government hacking. Once a system has been compromised, the attacker can choose its fate; he can keep the system alive and milk it for its secrets; or he can kill it – shut it down for as long as he likes."[20]

China is hardly alone it its cyber boldness. Shortly after midnight on September 6, 2007, seventy-five miles inside Syria, at least four Israeli F-15 Eagle and F-16 Falcon fighter bombers attacked and destroyed their Syrian target. The U.S. government had known the attack was planned and did not oppose it.[21] Although there were no casualties, it "was, by almost any definition, an act of war. But ... nothing was heard from the government of Israel. ... It was not until October 1st that Syrian President Bashar Assad ... acknowledged that the Israeli warplanes had hit their target, which he described as an 'unused military building'."[22] In fact, the Israelis had bombed into rubble a partially completed gas-cooled, graphite-moderated nuclear reactor, designed and built with years of assistance from North Korea. A month after the attack, Benjamin Netanyahu, then the Israeli government's opposition leader, admitted the strike.[23] Postattack photographs of

[14] Ellen Nakashima, "Agencies Probe Breach at Information Security Firm," *Wash. Post*, March 24, 2011, A2.
[15] Thom Shaker and Elisabeth Bumiller, "After Suffering Damaging Cyberattack, the Pentagon Takes Defensive Action," *NY Times*, July15, 2011, A-6.
[16] Nakashima, "Agencies Probe Breach," supra, note 14.
[17] Christopher Drew, "Stolen Data Is Tracked to Hacking at Lockheed," *NY Times*, June 4, 2011, B-1.
[18] Shaker and Bumiller, "After Suffering Damaging Cyberattack," supra, note 19. Other sources say the attack was on a defense contractor's computer system, e.g., Ellen Nakashima, "U.S. Cyber Approach 'Too Predictable,'" *Wash. Post*, July 15, 2011, A2.
[19] Id., Shaker and Bumiller.
[20] Stewart Baker, *Skating on Stilts: Why We Aren't Stopping Tomorrow's Terrorism* (Stanford, CA: Hoover Institution Press, 2010), 20.
[21] George W. Bush, *Decision Points* (New York: Crown, 2010), 420–2; and much more revealing, Robert M. Gates, *Duty: Memoirs of a Secretary at War* (New York: Alfred Knopf, 2014), 171–7.
[22] Seymour M. Hersh, "A Strike in the Dark," *New Yorker*, Feb. 11 and 18, 2008, 58.
[23] Steven Lee Myers and Steven Erlanger, "Bush Declines to Lift Veil of Secrecy over Israeli Airstrike in Syria," *NY Times*, Sept. 21, 2007, A12.

the target site showed mangled control rods and what appear to be elements of the reactor's cooling system.[24] Unaddressed by press reports of the bombing was how Israeli warplanes managed to penetrate Syrian airspace, conduct an attack, and escape without a shot fired at them by Syria's modern air defense system. The answer, related by Richard Clarke, former U.S. national coordinator for security, infrastructure protection, and counterterrorism, is an example of a cyber attack that prepped a battlefield:

> Israel had "owned" Damascus's pricey air defense network the night [of the attack]. What appeared on [Syrian] radar screens was what the Israeli Air Force had put there, an image of nothing. ... Syrian air defense missiles could not have been fired because there had been no targets in the system for them to seek out. Syrian air defense fighters could not have scrambled ... because their Russian-built systems required them to be vectored toward the target aircraft by ground-based controllers. The Syrian ... controllers had seen no targets.[25]

Israel screened its kinetic attack with a cyber attack that cloaked Syrian air defense radar screens with a false image of a clear sky. Clarke continues, "Whatever method the Israelis used to trick the Syrian air defense network, it was probably taken from a playbook they borrowed from the U.S."[26]

In 2015 it was reported that the United States has embedded surveillance and sabotage malware in Chinese, Russian, and Iranian computers so deeply that it infects the computer firmware that prepares computer hardware before the operating system boots up. This enables an attacker to hide from antivirus programs and, even if the operating system is wiped and a new hard drive and software is installed, perpetually reinfect the computer.[27]

These examples did not involve armed conflict in a traditional sense. They nevertheless illustrate the danger cyber warfare poses for national defense and the degradation of military command and control systems that could result in the death or wounding of combatant victims of a cyber attack.

17.2 *Jus ad Bellum* and *Jus in Bello* in Cyber Warfare

This text is focused on the *jus in bello*, the corpus of the laws and customs of war applicable once a state resorts to the use of force. In considering cyber warfare, however, one must also be aware of the *jus ad bellum*, the law applicable to a state's initial resort to armed force, before considering the application of the *jus in bello*. That is because cyber attacks may occur when no armed conflict is in progress between the victim state and attacking state, or its proxies. Whether a cyber attack is state initiated, state sponsored, or conducted by independent nonstate actors, an initial question is not the applicable LOAC (the *jus in bello*), but whether it is lawful to initiate an armed response (the *jus ad bellum*) in the first place.

Jus ad bellum, sometimes thought of as "just war theory," has a long and often disreputable history.

---

[24] David E. Sanger, "Bush Administration Releases Images to Bolster Its Claim about Syrian Reactor," *NY Times*, April 25, 2008, A5.
[25] Clarke and Knake, *Cyber War*, supra, note 8, at 5.   [26] Id., at 8.
[27] Nicole Perlroth and David E. Sanger, "U.S. Embedded Spyware, Report Says," *NY Times*, Feb. 17, 2015.

Attempts to place war within a legal framework date back to the earliest articulation of the theory of "just war", by virtue of which war was considered a "just" response to illegal aggression. Ultimately, it was a means to restore the rights offended by the aggressor as well as a means of punishment. By relying on the validity of the cause for war, this doctrine brought into place a legal regime that reflected "the belligerent's right to resort to force".[28]

In the fifth century B.C., China "recognized rules stipulating that no war should begin without just cause."[29] Xenophon, in *Cyropaedia* (fourth century B.C.), wrote about when to wage war, as did the Roman Cicero in his first century B.C. work *De Republica*. Early Christians, notably Saints Ambrose and Constantine, developed just war doctrine. "The central notion here is that the use of force requires justification – the presumption is always against violence – but violence may be permitted to protect other values."[30] Thomas Aquinas and Francisco de Vitoria took just war doctrine from the Roman Empire into the Dark Ages.

Hugo Grotius, looking to natural law, provided a sharp focus to just war theory in his 1625 work *On the Law of War and Peace*. "Modern Just War theory recognizes as many as eight conditions that are necessary to justify a nation's resorting to arms. Grotius ... accepts only six."[31] In Grotius's teaching, there first must be a just cause prior to resorting to arms; this forbids wars of anticipation. Second, the positive aims of going to war must be proportional to the evil that the war itself will cause. Next, there must be a reasonable chance of success, thus rejecting futile or suicidal armed resistance. Fourth, wars must be publicly declared, allowing public debate of the wisdom of going to war. Only a legitimate authority may declare war; rogue commanders may not take a state to war. Finally, war must always be the last resort, undertaken only if the other five preconditions have been met and no other solution remains. These preconditions may be debated, but, basically, they encompass classic just war theory, traditionally termed *jus ad bellum* – the circumstances in which states may rightfully resort to armed force.

Today, just war theory has been overtaken by the United Nations Charter, which provides international legislation, as it were, mandating when states may lawfully resort to force.

"The reason for adopting a rigorous distinction between *jus ad bellum* and *jus in bello* is the need for a bright-line cleavage that is workable in the field of battle. Soldiers do not have to think about who started the war. They know that, regardless of who started the conflict, certain means of warfare are clearly illegal."[32] *Jus ad bellum* theory provides the background for deciding how to respond to attacks, including cyber attacks, and how they may lawfully be countered.

---

[28] Jasmine Moussa, "Can *Jus ad Bellum* Override *Jus in Bello*? Reaffirming the Separation of the Two Bodies of Law," 872 *Int'l Rev. of the Red Cross* (Dec. 2008), 963, 966.

[29] Paul Christopher, *The Ethics of War and Peace*, 2d ed. (Saddle River NJ: Prentice Hall, 1994), 8.

[30] Id., at 23.

[31] Id., at 82. Some theorists add a seventh requirement, one rejected by Grotius, that a war must be waged only for the ends of peace.

[32] George P. Fletcher and Jens David Ohlin, *Defending Humanity: When Force Is Justified and Why* (Oxford: Oxford University Press, 2008), 21–2. There is a view that if the war is itself unlawful, any offensive act by a soldier of the offending state is similarly unlawful and the actor-soldier therefore is a criminal. See, e.g., Thomas Nagel, "War and Massacre," 1 *Phil. & Public Affairs* (1972), 123, discussing U.S. soldiers in the Vietnam conflict. This position is clearly a minority view.

17.3 What Constitutes a Cyber Attack?

The United States initiates offensive cyber warfare operations, of course.[33] "DoD officials reportedly stated that the U.S. could confuse enemies by using cyber attack to open floodgates, control traffic lights, or scramble the banking systems in other countries."[34] (Such a self-confident statement calls to mind the military tactical adage that when the enemy is in range, so are you.) Actually, all of the examples cited would not constitute cyber attacks.

Some civilian and government computer networks are so essential to a nation's well-being that the state will protect them at almost any cost. In the United States, military and civilian computer networks relating to communications, transportation, power, water, and electrical systems; gas and oil storage; as well as banking and finance systems, are referred to as "critical national infrastructure."[35] Because they are vital to the functioning of the state, computer network attacks (CNAs) against the critical national infrastructure are considered more serious than those against many military objectives.

In May 2007, Estonia suffered massive cyber intrusions in the form of rolling CNAs, widely believed to have been initiated by Russian actors using as many as a million bots rented from scores of nations as distant as the United States.[36] Estonia's critical national infrastructure was taken to a standstill, apparently by Russian civilian hackers encouraged and/or coordinated by their government.[37] There were no armed groups involved in the cyber attack, however, and the law of war was not implicated.

Then, in August 2008, the first cyber attack that coincided with an armed conflict occurred when, shortly before attacking Georgia by kinetic means, Russia overwhelmed Georgian government Web sites with distributed-denial-of-service attacks. The next year, in mid-2009, there was another cyber event when the American-Israeli Stuxnet worm appeared, eventually attacking and destroying a third of Iran's centrifuges, crucial to its nuclear enrichment program – a U.S. cyber attack. (See Cases and Materials, this chapter.)

An attack by frontal assault, naval gunfire, or aerial bombing makes clear that a kinetic attack (one using "traditional" explosive weapons) is under way. Cyber warfare sometimes allows room to question whether an attack is even occurring and therefore, whether LOAC/IHL applies. If a college student hacks a Blueland military command computer network, how is the network's command duty officer to know the intrusion is not the precursor of an all-out Redland kinetic attack? Further complicating the CDO's calculation is her inability to know immediately who mounted the intrusion, or where it originated.

---

[33] William Matthews, "Pentagon Expanding Domestic Cyber Role," *Marine Corps Times*, Nov. 1, 2010, 12, reporting an agreement between the Department of Homeland Security and the Department of Defense to share DoD's electronic spying experience and expertise.

[34] Wilson, "Botnets, Cybercrime, and Cyberterrorism," supra, note 6, at 18.

[35] Executive Order 13010 (July 17, 1996) describes critical national infrastructure as including "telecommunications, electrical power systems, gas and oil storage and transportation, banking and finance, transportation, water supply systems, emergency services ... and continuity of government."

[36] A "bot," also called a "zombie," is a computer in which malware has been entrenched and, akin to a human "sleeper agent," lies inactive until triggered by the attacker. A network of bots constitutes a "botnet."

[37] Healey, "A Brief History of US Cyber Conflict," supra, note 11, at 68.

The distinction between "cyber intrusions" and "cyber attacks" is meaningful: In LOAC/IHL, a cyber *attack* may raise a lawful right to respond with armed force. A cyber *intrusion*, or any other cyber operation short of an armed attack, probably does not. "However, whether cyber operations not qualifying as attacks under IHL may initiate an armed conflict remains unsettled. ... As noted by the [ICRC], 'it would appear that the answer to these questions will probably be determined in a definite manner only through future State practice.'"[38]

Keeping in mind that there is no international agreement on cyber terminology, what constitutes a cyber "attack"? Additional Protocol I, Article 49.1 tells us, "'Attacks' means acts of violence against the adversary, whether in offense or in defense." Additional Protocol I's *Commentary* notes, "It is quite clear that the meaning given [the word "attack" in Article 49.1] is not exactly the same as the usual meaning of the word. In the larger dictionaries the idea of instigating the combat and striking the first blow is predominant. ... Closest to the meaning of the term as used in the Protocol [is], 'to set upon with hostile action.'"[39]

Further defining "attack," the *Commentary* asks whether the laying of land mines would constitute an attack: "The general feeling [of the Protocol Drafting Committee] was that there is an attack whenever a person is directly endangered by a mine laid. ... An attack is unrelated to the concept of aggression or the first use of armed force; it refers simply to the use of armed force to carry out a military operation."[40] For cyber warfare, this indicates that when an individual is "directly endangered" it constitutes an attack. "An 'armed attack'," adds a European writer, "can be committed by means of conventional weapons ... but also by unconventional means. ... Arguably, the same would be true in the hypothetical case of a so-called 'computer network attack' (CNA) were it to cause fatalities or large-scale property destruction."[41]

Reference to fatalities and property destruction suggests an objective guide for determining when a cyber operation constitutes a cyber attack:

> Some States, including the US, have adopted a "results test" as a way of determining whether IO [cyber information operations] constitute a use of force or an armed attack. Such a test attempts to adapt traditional State-centric kinetic concepts of the use of force in assessing whether the deliberate actions of an aggressor cause injury, death, damage, and destruction to the military forces, citizens, and property of a State, such that those actions are likely to be judged by applying traditional jus ad bellum and jus in bello principles.[42]

Several definitions of "cyber attack" are available in scholarly and military writings. "The term 'cyber attack' is regularly used in the mass media to denote an extremely wide range of cyber conduct, much of which falls below the threshold of an 'armed attack' as understood in the *jus ad bellum*, or an attack as defined in LOAC."[43]

---

[38] Michael N. Schmitt, "The Law of Cyber Targeting," 68–2 *Naval War College Review* (Spring, 2015), 11, 14.

[39] Yves Sandoz, Christophe Swinarski, and Bruno Zimmerman, eds., *Commentary on the Additional Protocols – 1977* (Geneva: ICRC/Martinus Nijhoff, 1987), para. 1879, at 603.

[40] Id., paras. 1881–2, at 603.

[41] Tom Ruys, *"Armed Attack" and Article 51 of the UN Charter* (Cambridge: Cambridge University Press, 2010), 176.

[42] Terry D. Gill and Dieter Fleck, *The Handbook of the International Law of Military Operations* (Oxford: Oxford University Press, 2010), para. 4.01.3, at 52–3.

[43] Laurie R. Blank, "International Law and Cyber Threats from Non-State Actors," in Naval War College, *Int'l L. Studies* , Vol. 89, supra, note 1, at 406, 437.

For both international and noninternational armed conflicts, an excellent definition of a *cyber attack* **is a cyber operation, whether offensive or defensive, that is reasonably expected to cause injury or death to persons, or damage or destruction to objects.**[44]

What extent of death, injury, damage, or destruction is required to constitute a cyber attack? The LOAC does not specify, although they clearly must be greater than de minimis. An indication is that cyber theft, cyber intelligence gathering, and cyber intrusions that involve brief or periodic interruption of nonessential cyber services clearly do not qualify as cyber attacks.[45]

> [The definition of cyber attack] should not be understood as excluding cyber operations against data (non-physical entities, of course) from the ambit of the term attack. Whenever an attack on data results in the injury or death of individuals or damage or destruction of physical objects, those individuals or objects constitute the "object of attack" and the operation therefore qualifies as an attack.[46]
>
> [As long as] data is treated as an object, any operation that manipulates civilian data would qualify as "damage" to (alteration of data) or "destruction" of (deletion of data) a "civilian object" and thus would be unlawful. ... [This includes] "loss of functionality" in the concept of damage. ... On this view, a cyber operation that affects the functionality of cyber infrastructure ... in a manner that necessitates repair qualifies as an attack even if no physical damage results.[47]

Although there is no internationally agreed-upon definition, cyber intrusions are cyber operations that do not rise to the level of attacks. Cyber intrusions may be described as covert actions employing small-scale operations against a specific computer, computer system, or user, whose individual compromise would have significant value, such as a government's nuclear command and control system.[48] The difference is that cyber intrusions do not cause death, wounding, or significant destruction or physical damage.

What if there have been a series of minor cyber intrusions from a common source, none of them individually rising to the threshold of an attack? Can they, in the aggregate, rise to an armed attack? Only if the related incidents, taken together, rise to the requisite scale and effect.

What about that Blueland command duty officer whose military computer network was hacked by a college student? The resulting damage, if any, will likely have been inflicted by the time, or before, she became aware of the hack; at the moment of awareness of the intrusion (or attack), all she knows is that there has been a cyber

---

[44] Michael N. Schmitt, *Tallinn Manual on the International Law Applicable to Cyber Warfare* (Cambridge: Cambridge University Press, 2013), Rule 30, at 106. A transborder element is added by Rule 13, at 54. In agreement, Droege, "Get Off My Cloud: Cyber Warfare, International Humanitarian Law," supra, note 5, at 546. Also, Michael N. Schmitt, "Wired Warfare: Computer Network Attack and *Jus in Bello*," 846 *Int'l Rev. of the Red Cross* (June 2002), 365, 373. The first staff judge advocate of the U.S. Cyber Command offers a more conservative definition: "The unsatisfactory answer to 'what is a cyber attack?' is: exactly what we decide is a cyber attack at a given time under given circumstances that cannot be determined in advance. As accurate as this answer is, it is completely unhelpful, of course." Gary D. Brown, "The Wrong Questions about Cyberspace," 217 *Military L. Rev.* (Fall 2013), 214, 221.

[45] Id., Schmitt, *Tallinn Manual*, at 55.   [46] Id., Rule 30.6, at 107–8.

[47] Schmitt, "The Law of Cyber Targeting," supra, note 38, at 17.

[48] Robert D. Williams, "(Spy) Game Change: Cyber Networks, Intelligence Collection and Covert Action," 79–4 *George Washington L. Rev.* (June 2011), 1162, 1185, citing Nat'l Research Council, *Technology, Policy, Law, and Ethics Regarding U.S. Acquisition and Use of Cyberattack Capabilities* §4.2.1, at 194 (William A. Owens, et al., eds., 2009).

operation involving penetration of the network. She will alert her superiors that the system may have been breached, although she would not know how, by whom, from where, or to what extent. This illustrates that, absent specific knowledge, sometimes one cannot know whether an attack has even been executed.

17.4 Cyber Attacks Are a Use of Force

Nowhere is the term "use of force" clearly defined. U.N. Charter Article 2(4) provides that "all members [of the U.N.] shall refrain in their international relations from the threat or use of force against the territorial integrity or political independence of any State." Exceptions are use of force authorized by the Security Council and self-defense pursuant to Article 51. Customary international law also applies the use of force prohibition to non-U.N. members, although *not* to nonstate actors or organized armed groups.

Whether a cyber attack constitutes a use of force matters because U.N. Charter Article 51 requires that an armed counterattack be a response not only to a use of force, but to a use of *armed* force. The initial question, then, is whether cyber attacks constitute a use of force and, if so, the second question follows: Are they a use of *armed* force?

"Ultimately, it is the victim state that determines whether . . . an act was use of force and what response it will take; however, these decisions are always subject to judgment by the international community."[49] Professor Michael Schmitt notes that "since the advent of cyber operations, States and scholars have struggled to define the threshold at which an act becomes a 'use of force.' The interpretive dilemma lies in the application of the norm to cyber operations that . . . produce severe non-physical consequences."[50] While the required degree of injury or damage remains unresolved, a cyber *intrusion* (a cyber operation short of an attack) into a state's cyber systems would not constitute a use of force; nor would it violate international law.[51] The ICJ, rejecting a narrow interpretation of "use of force," held in the *Nicaragua* case that "scale and effects" are to be considered in determining whether particular actions amount to an attack.[52] "In other words, 'scale and effects' is a shorthand term that captures the quantitative and qualitative factors to be analyzed in determining whether a cyber operation qualifies as a use of force."[53] In regard to the required threshold of harm:

> Any cyber operation causing greater than *de minimis* damage or injury suffices. . . . In particular, operations that non-destructively target critical infrastructure may come to be viewed by States as presumptive use of force. The same approach might be applied to military targets or State systems designed to provide cyber security. Another possibility is that States will begin to treat data destruction as the functional equivalent of physical

---

[49] Lt. Cmdr. Brian Evans and Rick Lanchantin, "Lifting the Fog on Cyber Strategy," U.S. Naval Institute *Proceedings*, 66, 68 (Oct. 2013).

[50] Michael N. Schmitt, "The Law of Cyber Warfare: *Quo Vadis?*" 25–2 *Stanford L. & Pol. Rev.* (June 2014), 269, 279.

[51] Schmitt, *Tallinn Manual*, supra, note 44, Rule 10.8, at 44.

[52] *Case Concerning Military and Paramilitary Activities in and against Nicaragua* (Merits), 1986 ICJ Rpt. 14, Judgment (June 27), para. 195.

[53] Schmitt, *Tallinn Manual*, supra, note 44, Rule 11.1, at 46.

destruction for use of force characterization purposes whenever the destruction of the data severely disrupts societal, economic or governmental functions.[54]

A cyber attack, as opposed to a cyber intrusion, constitutes a "use of force" if undertaken by a state's armed forces or intelligence services, or by a private contractor whose conduct is attributable to the state, and whose scale and effects are comparable to those of noncyber operations that rise to a level of a use of force.[55]

A use of force alone, however, does not allow a victim state to respond in self-defense. The attack must be serious enough to amount to an "armed attack."

17.5 Cyber Attacks Are Armed Attacks

Having determined that a cyber attack constitutes a use of force, then the second question follows. U.N. Charter Article 51 and customary law specify that only an *armed* attack justifies armed response in self-defense. If the attacker's use of force does not amount to an armed attack, the victim state may bring the matter before the Security Council, or it may employ nonforcible countermeasures. "But it cannot use counterforce in self-defense."[56]

An attack mounted without actual physical force of arms may nevertheless give rise to lawful self-defense by a victim state, whether the attack be kinetic or electronic. It is "unreasonable to argue that because a [computer network attack] does not physically destroy the object of attack in the traditional sense, it can never amount to a use of force or an armed attack."[57] Moreover, "the choice of arms by the attacking State is immaterial."[58] "The use of any device, or number of devices, which results in considerable loss of life and/or extensive destruction of property must therefore be deemed to fulfill the conditions of an 'armed attack'."[59] Cyber attacks are singular in their ability to kill and wound, and to destroy or damage civilian and military objects without the use of traditional kinetic weapons. That includes attacks on the critical national infrastructure.

> The mere manipulation of a banking system or other manipulation of critical infrastructure, even if it leads to serious economic loss, would probably stretch the concept of armed force. ... But the disruption of such vital infrastructure as electricity or water supply systems, which would inevitably lead to severe hardship for the population if it lasted over a certain period, even if not to death or injury, might well have to be considered as armed force. ... They are precisely the kind of severe consequences from which IHL seeks to protect the civilian population.[60]

---

[54] Schmitt, "Law of Cyber Warfare, *Quo Vadis?*" supra, note 50, at 10–11. Professor Schmitt's statement includes attacks on the critical national infrastructure as constituting a use of armed force.

[55] For a (brief) contrary view, see, Evans and Lanchantin, "Lifting the Fog on Cyber Strategy," supra, note 49, at 68.

[56] Dinstein, "Cyber War and International Law," supra, note 1, at 276, 278.

[57] Eric Talbot Jensen, "Computer Attacks on Critical National Infrastructure: A Use of Force Invoking the Right of Self-Defense," 38 *Stanford J. Int'l L.* (2002), 207, 222.

[58] Yoram Dinstein, *War, Aggression and Self-Defence*, 4th ed. (Cambridge: Cambridge University Press, 2005), 196.

[59] Marco Roscini, *Cyber Operations and the Use of Force in International Law* (Oxford: Oxford University Press, 2014), 71.

[60] Droege, "Get of My Cloud: Cyber Warfare, International Humanitarian Law," supra, note 5, at 548. U.S., Executive Order 13010, supra, note 35, specifically includes banking and finance systems in its definition of critical infrastructure. See fn. 37, supra.

"The right of self-defence may be triggered by an armed attack or a clear threat of an impending attack," Professor Yoram Dinstein notes. "Whenever a lethal result to human beings – or serious destruction to property – is engendered by an illegal use of force by State A against State B, that use of force will qualify as an armed attack. The right to employ counter-force in self-defense against State A can then be invoked by State B."[61] Dinstein continues, "From a legal perspective, there is no reason to differentiate between kinetic and electronic means of attack. A premeditated destructive [CNA] can qualify as an armed attack just as much as a kinetic attack bringing about the same ... results. The crux of the matter is not the medium at hand (a computer server in lieu of, say, an artillery battery), but the violent consequences of the action taken."[62]

A traditional physical assault by force of arms is not required for an act to constitute an armed attack. For example, during a period of peace, a surprise attack employing biological or chemical weapons would be viewed as an armed attack and could initiate an armed conflict. The 9/11 attacks on the United States by al Qaeda initiated an armed conflict, even though a traditional armed enemy force was not involved. A cyber attack that substantially kills, wounds, or destroys constitutes an armed attack, just as kinetic weapons causing the same results would be considered an armed attack.

17.6 Cyber Attacks and the Initiation of Armed Conflict

The ICTY has held that "an armed conflict exists whenever there is a resort to armed force between States, or protracted armed violence between governmental authorities and organized armed groups."[63] Cyber attacks may accordingly initiate either inter-national or non-international armed conflicts.

> [International] humanitarian law principles apply whenever computer network attacks can be ascribed to a State ... and are either intended to cause injury, death, damage or destruction ... or such consequences are foreseeable. ... By this standard, a computer network attack on a large airport's traffic control system by agents of another State would implicate humanitarian law. So too would an attack intended to destroy oil pipelines by surging oil through them after taking control of computers governing flow ... or using computers to trigger a release of toxic chemicals from production and storage facilities.[64]

Most commentators agree that attacks no longer need be ascribed to a state for IHL and LOAC to apply; nonstate actors' actions suffice to invoke LOAC/IHL, if they rise to noninternational armed conflict status. (This Chapter 17.7.) *De minimis* damage or destruction probably does not meet the threshold of destruction required to initiate an armed conflict.

---

[61] Yoram Dinstein, "Computer Network Attacks and Self-Defense," in Michael N. Schmitt and Brian T. O'Donnell, eds., *International Law Studies.* Vol. 76. *Computer Network Attack and International Law* (Newport, RI: Naval War College, 2002), at 99, 100.

[62] Id., at 103.

[63] *Prosecutor v. Tadić*, IT-94-1-A, Decision on Defense Motion for Interlocutory Appeal on Jurisdiction (Oct. 12, 1995), para. 70.

[64] Sean Watts, "Combatant Status and Computer Network Attack," 50–2 *Virginia J. of Int'l L.* (2010), 391, 394. Emphasis in original. Also see, Schmitt, *Tallinn Manual*, supra, note 44, Rule 30, at 106–7: "The crux of the notion lies in the effects that are caused. ... For instance, a cyber operation that alters the running of a SCADA [supervisory control and data acquisition] system controlling an electrical grid and results in a fire qualifies. Since the consequences are destructive, the operation is an attack."

Can a CNA trigger an international armed conflict in the absence of an accompany-ing kinetic use of force? The International Committee of the Red Cross responds, "The answer depends on whether a computer network attack is (1) attributable to the state and (2) amounts to a resort to armed force – a term that is not defined under [international humanitarian law]."[65] As the ICRC response suggests, a CNA initiated by nonaffiliated nonstate actors cannot initiate an *international* armed conflict. A state-initiated CNA, however, even without a kinetic element may initiate an international armed conflict.

17.7 Cyber Attacks and Nonstate Actors

Cyberspace affords individuals the same ability to deliver harmful cyber effects as a state. If a cyber attack is attributable to an individual whose actions are not state affiliated, however, the act is illegal but not an act of war. LOAC/IHL is not applicable because the acts of an individual cannot satisfy the requirements for a noninternational armed conflict. Attacks by a state's armed forces are, of course, within the purview of U.N. Charter Article 51 relating to self-defense. That is also true if similar acts by nonstate actors are attributable to a sponsoring state, although attribution is a difficult cyber issue, in part because "geography is irrelevant to the issue of attribution. Non-State actors may, and likely often will, launch a cyber operation from outside territory controlled by the State to which the conduct is attributable."[66]

A question raised by recent ICJ opinions is whether nonstate cyber actors, or an armed opposition group acting *without* state sponsorship or control, can initiate a cyber attack that raises a victim state's right to armed self-defense. Although nothing in Article 51 limits self-defense to armed attacks by a state or by state-sponsored groups, the ICJ twice ruled that self-defense is limited to instances of states attacked by other states. In its 2004 *Palestinian Wall* advisory opinion, self-defense against other than an attacking state is dismissed by the court in a single paragraph:

> Article 51 . . . recognizes the existence of an inherent right of self-defense in the case of armed attack by one State against another State. However, Israel does not claim that the attacks against it [emanating from the Occupied Palestinian Territories] are imputable to a foreign State . . . and therefore Israel could not in any case invoke those [post-9/11 U.N. Security Council] resolutions in support of its claim to be exercising a right of self-defense.[67]

A year later, the ICJ again rejected self-defense in response to attacks by nonstate actors[68] and reaffirmed the restrictive state-centric approach enunciated in its pre-Taliban, pre-al Qaeda, 1984 *Nicaragua* opinion (Chapter 5, Cases and Materials). The two opinions,

---

[65] Droege, "Get Off My Cloud: Cyber Warfare, International Humanitarian Law," supra, note 5, at 543.

[66] Michael N. Schmitt, "Below the 'Threshold' Cyber Operations: The Countermeasures Response Option and International Law," 54–3 *Va. J. of Int'l L.* (2014), 697, 713.

[67] ICJ, *Legal Consequences of the Construction of a Wall in the Occupied Palestine Territory* (The Wall Advisory Opinion), [July 9, 2004] ICJ Rep. 136, para. 139.

[68] ICJ, *Case Concerning Armed Activities on the Territory of the Congo (Democratic Republic of the Congo v. Uganda)* [Dec. 19, 2005] ICJ Rep. 116–220, paras. 132, 146, 147.

although criticized,[69] hold that the self-defense provisions of Charter Article 51 are of "no relevance" to attacks by nonstate actors because that provision applies only "in the case of armed attack by one State against another State."[70]

Both holdings were soon questioned, however. "[A] majority of scholars accept that a strict insistence on State imputability is no longer tenable."[71] Another commentator declares, "The Court's restrictive approach is increasingly out of touch with state practice."[72] Another adds, "State practice in the aftermath of the 9/11 attacks provides firm support for the existence of a right of self-defense against non-State actors, even if unrelated to any State."[73] Today, the court's view is essentially disregarded.

During a time of armed conflict, what if attacking nonstate actors who are not state sponsored – civilians, taking a direct part in hostilities – attack a party to the conflict? What if a single unaffiliated actor initiates a cyber attack? "Some examples of cyber acts that could constitute direct participation in hostilities include writing and executing malicious code, launching distributed denial of service attacks, providing malware or other cyber tools to a party to the conflict."[74]

Both the attacking group and the individual lack the necessary organizational character to constitute an armed opposition group. The attacking nonstate actors lack a "headquarters, designated zones of operation, and the ability to procure, transport, and distribute arms"[75] – or, in the case of cyber attackers, the ability to formulate and distribute electronic instructions and orders, or control the electronic means of attack. What if the attackers are an unorganized aggregate, affiliated only in philosophy, united only in their determination to cripple or destroy government institutions? Lacking the organization to constitute an armed opposition group they could not be a party to a conflict and there could be no armed conflict in the sense of common Article 2 or 3. "Cyber operations conducted by individuals or by unorganized groups of 'hackers,' no matter how intense ... cannot qualify as a non-international armed conflict."[76] The attackers would be criminals to be captured and prosecuted under the domestic law of the state wherein their attack originated, or the state where it was aimed.

17.8 Cyber Intrusions and Cyber Attacks

Some cyber intrusions, such as those initiated for purposes of cyber theft, intelligence gathering, espionage, or periodic disruptions or denials of nonessential cyber services,[77] may be mistakenly viewed as attacks.

---

[69] e.g., Sean D. Murphy, "Self-Defense and the Israeli *Wall* Advisory Opinion: An *Ipse Dixit* from the ICJ?" 99–1 *AJIL* (Jan. 2005), 62. At 64:"First, nothing in ... Article 51 ... requires the exercise of self-defense to turn on whether an armed attack was committed directly by, or can be imputed to, another state ... [and] the Security Council has repeatedly found that the conduct of nonstate actors can be a threat to international peace and security."

[70] ICJ, *Consequences of the Construction of a Wall*, supra, note 67, at para. 139.

[71] Ruys, *'Armed Attack' and Article 51*, supra, note 41, at 487.

[72] Theresa Reinold, "State Weakness, Irregular Warfare, and the Right to Self-Defense Post 9/11" 105–2 *AJIL* (April 2011), 244, 261.

[73] Blank, "International law and Cyber Threats," supra, note 43, at 413.   [74] Id., at 430.

[75] *Prosecutor v. Limaj, et al.*, IT-03-66-T (Nov. 30, 2005), para. 90.

[76] Schmitt, "Law of Cyber Warfare, *Quo Vadis*?" supra, note 38, at 19.   [77] Id., at 11.

Absent a conventional attack component, manipulation or intrusion by itself does not automatically indicate hostile intent. A[n] intrusion into the communications network could be just an intelligence probe for future operations. ... In the case of a CNA with only network effects, the consequences, although degrading a particular computer network, may not place [a military] force in imminent danger or be evidence of an impending attack. ... This situation would be analogous to tolerating an aircraft tracking radar, but not a locked on fire control radar.[78]

Espionage – using spies to collect information about what another government is doing or plans to do – is not a LOAC violation.[79] Covert actions against a state *in time of peace* are generally considered domestic law violations.[80] "The utilization of cyber networks in carrying out collection activities likely entails a measure of conceptual overlap with covert action."[81] But, as the word "likely" suggests, when considering peacetime cyber operations, the status of covert acts remains unclear in LOAC and in international law.

17.8.1 *Cyber Attacks on the Critical National Infrastructure*

"[T]he first known use of malicious software designed to produce material damage to physical property by attacking the ... national critical infrastructure is Stuxnet"[82] (Cases and Materials, this chapter). Was Stuxnet a cyber attack? On critical national infrastructure?

The principle of distinction prohibits attacks on civilians and civilian objects, which include civilian computers. A cyber operation targeting, say, the U.S. civilian aviation air control computer system, which the United States considers an element of its critical national infrastructure,[83] would be a cyber attack. Such an intrusion by another state would likely result in the death of a substantial number of civilians in crashing aircraft and the substantial destruction of aviation-related objects, meeting the U.S. definition of a cyber attack justifying acts in armed self-defense, even though the target was a civilian computer system.

What if the intrusion were an Estonia-type series of intrusions that shut down America's banking system, closed Wall Street financial markets, silenced cell phone towers, and seriously disrupted interstate communications? Professor Schmitt may be correct when he writes:

Given the pervasive importance of cyber activities, an interpretation that limits the notion of attacks to acts generating physical effects cannot possibly survive. ... Perhaps the likeliest prospect is eventual expansion of the notion of attack to include

---

[78] VAdm. James H. Doyle Jr., U.S. Navy, "Computer Networks, Proportionality, and Military Operations," in Schmitt and O'Donnell, *International Law Studies*. Vol. 76. *Computer Network Attack*, supra, note 61, at 147, 152, 153–4.

[79] 1907 Hague Regulation IV, Art. 24. No customary law or treaty forbids the practice, although the domestic laws of all nations criminalize espionage, e.g., in American law, 18 U.S. Code §§ 793, 794.

[80] See, e.g., 50 U.S. Code § 413b(e). The Computer Fraud and Abuse Act, 18 U.S. Code § 1030(a)(5)(A) (1), is also on point. Neither law explicitly criminalizes covert acts, however.

[81] Williams, "(Spy) Game Change, supra, note 48, at 1166–7.

[82] Roscini, *Cyber Operations and the Use of Force*, supra, note 59, at 53.

[83] Executive Order 13010, supra, note 35, describes critical national infrastructure as including "telecommunications, electrical power systems, gas and oil storage and transportation, banking and finance, transportation, water supply systems, emergency services ... and continuity of government."

interference with essential civilian functions. The difficulty with such an approach is that the notion of attack does not currently contain a severity of consequences component other than the exclusion of *de minimus* damage or injury. Rather, it focuses on the nature of the harm – damage, destruction, injury, or death. ... A more plausible prospect is that States will simply begin to treat operations against essential civilian services and data as attacks ... creating the State practice upon which the evolution in meaning can be based. ... Some activities, like banking and operation of critical civilian infrastructure, are self-evidently essential. Beyond that ... only State practice will definitively pinpoint those civilian activities and data that qualify as essential.[84]

If no one is killed or injured, however; if property is not physically destroyed or materially damaged, LOAC is uncertain on the subject and the question is left open, to be determined by state practice and *opinio juris*. Still, "the pervasive use of civilian cyber infrastructure for military purposes has transformed much of it into the character of valid [dual use] military objectives."[85]

In U.S. practice the direction Schmitt suggests is already indicated in U.S. government documents relating to national cyber security. In the 2011 *Department of Defense Strategy for Operating in Cyberspace* the United States warns, "The Department will ... oppose those who would seek to disrupt networks and systems, dissuade and deter malicious actors, and reserves the right to defend these vital national assets as necessary and appropriate."[86] An executive order issued a month after the 9/11 attacks also suggests counterforce, should the critical national infrastructure be attacked: "It is the policy of the United States to protect against disruption of the operation of information systems for critical infrastructure and thereby help to protect the people, economy, essential human and government services, and national security."[87] Presidential Policy Directive 20, of October 2012, states that "the United States Government shall retain DCEO [Defensive Cyber Effects Operations], including anticipatory action against imminent threats [to critical national infrastructure] ... as an option to protect such infrastructure."[88] If one were to put key terms from those documents in a single sentence, it is U.S. "policy," to "oppose" through "Defensive Cyber ... Operations," attacks on the critical national infrastructure. That would seem to support a view that a decision to defend the critical national infrastructure, largely involving civilian computer systems, as well as military objectives, has already been made.

What has to be emphasized again is that ... not all cyber operations amounting to a use of force, not even those resulting in physical damage to property or persons, will automatically amount to an 'armed attack': the destruction or disruption must be extensive enough to constitute a "more serious use of force" giving rise to the right of self-defence. With regard to cyber attacks affecting the infrastructure functionality but not resulting in material damage, only coordinated cyber attacks seriously

---

[84] Schmitt, "Law of Cyber Warfare, *Quo Vadis?*" supra, note 50, at 215.

[85] Schmitt, "Law of Cyber Targeting," supra, note 38, at 17.

[86] *International Strategy for Cyberspace*, supra, note 3.

[87] Executive Order 13231, "Critical Infrastructure Protection in the Information Age," (Oct. 6, 2001). Available online.

[88] Presidential Policy Directive/PPD-20, "U.S. Cyber Operations Policy," at 8 (Oct. 2012).

disrupting several or all national critical infrastructures of a heavily digitized state for a prolonged time will be likely to meet the high scale and effects threshold of an armed attack.[89]

17.9 Cyber War Conflict Classification

Conflict classification, the first step in a LOAC analysis of any armed conflict, can be complex when a cyber attack is involved. Customary factors to determine conflict classification apply in cyber warfare.

An international armed conflict must by definition be "armed" and must be "international." The "armed" criterion has been discussed (Chapter 17.5). In considering the "international" aspect of a common Article 2 conflict, if a cyber attack were launched from Blueland against Redland by an individual, or a group of individuals acting on their own initiative, should a resulting conflict be viewed as "international"? Only if Blueland exercised overall control of the individual or group,[90] or otherwise endorsed or encouraged the attack. Otherwise, the attack would be the unlawful act of individuals subject to domestic law enforcement of the state from which the attack was launched. "States are required to take all necessary measures to ensure that their territories are not used by other States or non-State actors for purposes of armed activities, including planning, threatening, perpetrating or providing material support for armed attacks against other States and their interests."[91]

Might the same attack, launched by the same state-unaffiliated individuals, be considered a noninternational conflict? As previously discussed, a cyber-initiated noninternational conflict would require the participation of an organized armed group, or individuals, and protracted armed violence of a certain level of intensity.[92] Organization would require that the group act in a coordinated manner, with a headquarters; command structure; issuance of orders, including disciplinary orders; and ability to enforce LOAC compliance.[93] An individual cyber attacker cannot meet such criteria; nor can most groups, particularly those who "organize" online without physical connections among members. These inabilities "would preclude virtually organized armed groups for the purpose of classifying a conflict as non-international."[94] Nor would cyber attacks initiated by an individual or group of individuals be likely to meet the noninternational armed conflict criterion of intensity of violence.

In combination, these impediments raise a high bar that would prevent cyber operations launched by individuals or groups from rising to noninternational armed conflict status. Instead, their acts would be left to domestic law enforcement agencies, guided by human rights norms.

---

[89] Roscini, *Cyber Operations and the Use of Force*, supra, note 59, at 75.

[90] *Prosecutor v. Tadić*, IT-94-1-A (July 15, 1999), para. 145

[91] Rep. of the Secretary-General, "Developments in the Field of Information and Telecommunications in the Context of International Security," UN Doc. A/66/152 (July 20, 2010), at 19.

[92] *Prosecutor v. Haradinaj*, IT-04-84 T, Judgment, (April 3, 2008), para. 49.

[93] *Prosecutor v. Limaj*, supra, note 75, at paras. 90, 94–129; and *Prosecutor v. Boškoski*, IT-04-82-T (July 10, 2008), paras. 190, 196–7, and 199–203.

[94] Michael N. Schmitt, "Classification of Cyber Conflict," 17 *J. of Conflict & Security L.* (2012), 245, 248.

The resolution of conflict status classification issues, many of which remain un-agreed-upon in LOAC/IHL, will continue to evolve through state practice.

17.10 Cyber Self-Defense

"Clearly, cyber will be an element of almost any crisis we're going to see in the future," the incoming commander of Cyber Command and the National Security Agency told the Senate Armed Services Committee, in March 2014.[95] Cyber has become one more military weapon to be employed as a matter of course in defense of the nation. "When exercised against a cyber armed attack, self-defense need not be circumscribed to 'cyber-on-cyber' warfare. Once a State is at war ... it can use all the military assets available to it ... whether they are kinetic or cyber."[96]

Presume that, during a time of peace, a state being cyber attacked knows it is being attacked – not always a safe presumption. "In fact, in most cases, the attack will already be over and the damage done by the time it is identified."[97] Once aware of an attack, however, a possible response is armed counterattack. Counterstrikes raise difficult LOAC issues, such as "the problems of identifying the perpetrators, determining their intent, affixing responsibility, and applying appropriate sanctions."[98] Those calculations involve painstaking investigation, making an immediate counterattack impractical, if not impossible.[99]

✳   The principle of distinction remains applicable in cyber counterattacks, of course. "Not only are civilians and the civilian population protected from direct attack, but [measures] ... must also be taken to reduce as much as possible the incidental effects on civilians and civilian property of attacks."[100] An immediate counterattack against a presumed source, without prior trace-back efforts or requests for investigative assistance from the state where the attack originated, would likely violate the principle of distinction.

To escape identification – attribution – and frustrate distinction, cyber attackers route their strikes through zombies, botnets, and networks, masked by multiple routers and hosts, making immediate identification of the state from which the attack was mounted, let alone attributing the attack to a group or individual, most difficult.

> Attribution is one of the most difficult issues in cyberattacks. Rarely is it possible ... to determine who launched a given attack. The reasons for this are both legal and

---

[95] David E. Sanger, "N.S.A. Nominee Promotes Cyberwar Units," NY *Times*, March 12, 2014, A18.

[96] Dinstein, "Cyber War and International Law," supra, note 1, at 280.

[97] Maj. Jeffrey K. Souder, "Information Operations in Homeland Computer-Network Defense" *J. of Electronic Def.*, Oct. 1, 2001.

[98] Jensen, "Computer Attacks," supra, note 57, at 213. Footnotes omitted.

[99] A group of individuals, angered by PayPal's decision no longer to process donations for WikiLeaks, orchestrated a series of denial of service attacks on PayPal's computer system, for example. All involved were United States–based, used their own personal computers, and employed no "foreign" routers, networks, or hosts to disguise their cyber tracks. Some did not bother to obscure their Internet Protocol addresses. Law enforcement officials took weeks to identify and apprehend those involved. Somini Sengupta, "For Suspected Hackers, a Sense of Social Protest," NY *Times*, July 26, 2011, B-1. A foreign-based CNA would be a harder nut to crack.

[100] United Kingdom MOD, *The Manual of the Law of Armed Conflict* (Oxford: Oxford University Press, 2004), para. 5.20.1, at 66.

technical. Virtually every nation has statutes that forbid the unauthorized access into personal computers and internet service providers' servers, actions that would be necessary to trace-back (hack back) the attack to its origins. The process to seek judicial authorization is time consuming and burdensome; by the time it is granted the evidence is gone. And this presumes that this action is even possible.[101]

Often, with or without the cooperation of the state from which the attack originated, sophisticated computer-driven trace-back techniques can zero in on an attacker's computer.[102]

> But eventually you will probably get to a server that does not cooperate. You could, at that point, file a diplomatic note requesting that the law enforcement authorities in the country get a warrant, go around to the server, and pull its records as part of international cooperation in investigating a crime. That could take days, and the records might be destroyed by then. Or the country in question may not want to help you. When trace-back stops working, you do have the option of "hack back," breaking into the server and checking its records. Of course, that is illegal for U.S. citizens to do, unless they are U.S. intelligence officers.[103]

"This appears to be potentially the most serious problem, i.e., aiming accurately at what the intended target is and, even if one manages to strike it with precision, not at the same time creating a host of unforeseen and unforeseeable effects."[104] If, one *can* aim accurately, however, a counterattacker will have a target-rich environment because, "in cyber warfare . . . the physical infrastructure through which the cyber weapons (malicious codes) travel <u>qualify as military objectives</u>. . . . Disabling the major cables, nodes, routers, or satellites that these systems rely on will almost always be justifiable by the fact that these routes are used to transmit military information and therefor qualify as military objectives."[105] Indeed, at some point in cyber warfare, the principle of distinction could become almost meaningless in protecting civilian cyber infrastructure.

✱ <u>Military necessity</u> justifies measures that are not forbidden by international law and that are indispensable for defeating the enemy. In observing military necessity, a state attacked during a time of peace must first make good faith efforts to determine whether the state from which the attack was launched (presuming the state itself was not involved) will take action to identify and apprehend the attacker. Military "necessity addresses whether there are adequate non-forceful options to deter or defeat the attack, such as diplomatic avenues, defensive measures to halt any further attacks, or reparations for

---

[101] Richard Pregent, "Cyber Defense and Counterintelligence," NATO *Legal Gazette*, Issue 26, 13, 16 (Sept. 19, 2011). Mr. Pregent is NATO Headquarters' legal adviser for Allied Command Counterintelligence.

[102] Adnan Aijaz, Syed Raza Mohsin, and Mof Assir-ul-Haque, "IP Trace Back Techniques to Ferret Out Denial of Service Attack Sources," paper submitted at 6th World Scientific & Engineering Academy & Society Int'l Conf. on Information Security and Privacy, Tenerife, Spain, Dec. 14–16, 2007. This brief paper by students of Pakistan's Military College of Signals outlines the three most common trace-back techniques. On file with author and available on Internet.

[103] Clarke and Knake, *Cyber War*, supra, note 8, at 214.

[104] Doswald-Beck, "Thoughts on Computer Network Attack," in Schmitt and O'Donnell, *Computer Network Attack*, supra, note 61, at 169.

[105] Droege, "Get Off My Cloud: Cyber Warfare, International Humanitarian Law," supra, note 5, at 564.

injuries caused."[106] Should those efforts fail, the need to assure the safety of the attacked armed forces and the critical national infrastructure from further attack is apparent. A counterattack, for example, to disable an attacking computer network could be considered a military necessity – the defeat of the enemy by lawful means.[107]

✳ A final precounterattack hurdle, whether in time of peace or during an ongoing armed conflict, is proportionality – whether the military advantage gained by the envisioned counterforce is proportionate to the estimated civilian death and damage, and the need to repel or deter further attacks. Proportionality does not require a counterstrike to be equivalent in force or effect to that of the attack. The counterstrike may be significantly greater in force than that of the attack and still be proportional.

Once distinction, military necessity, and proportionality issues are sorted out, the specifics of a counterattack may be considered. Satisfying these core requirements narrows a victim state's options, especially if the attack occurred during a time of peace. Can a counterattack oriented on an attacker's reverse azimuth, routed through civilian computer networks, servers, and routers, avoid catastrophic damage to a civilian computer network, raising potential violations of distinction and proportionality? If a counterattack is not considered politically feasible or militarily possible, a means other than a cyber counterattack may be required.

17.11 A Possible Response to Cyber Attacks in International Armed Conflicts

Should there be an attack on the United States, including a cyber attack, U.S. Standing Rules of Engagement allow a military response.[108] If an attack were conducted in the course of an *ongoing* armed conflict, it would be a lawful military action and an armed response would be lawful, as it would be were it a kinetic attack.

If a cyber attack is a surprise attack in a time of peace, however – an unlawful Pearl Harbor-like event – the victim state must decide several points: Are the consequences of the unlawful cyber sneak attack sufficiently serious to justify initiating a common Article 2 international armed conflict? Are traditional *jus ad bellum* requirements satisfied? Are Grotius's six just war conditions met? The initial attack without warning would seem to constitute just cause to respond with force of arms; there would be a reasonable chance of eventual success in ending the conflict; the initiation of armed conflict would presumably be publicly announced; and the public announcement would be made by a legitimate state authority. Two of Grotius's conditions might give reason to hesitate, however: Are the positive aims of going to war *proportional* to the evil that the armed conflict itself will cause, and is armed conflict the *last resort*, in the particular case? Professor Dinstein has written, "There are many reasons for the contemporary reluctance to indulge in a declaration of war."[109]

Are the destruction and damage to the initial unlawful attack's target so great as to justify taking the country to war? Did the attack cause extensive death and wounding, or

---

[106] Blank, "International Law and Cyber Threats," supra, note 43, at 418.

[107] *United States v. Wilhelm List, et al.* ("The Hostage Case"), (1948), XI TWC 1253–54. Also, Jensen, "Computer Attacks on Critical National Infrastructure," supra, note 57, at 218.

[108] Chairman, Joint Chiefs of Staff Instruction 3121.01B, *Standing Rules of Engagement for U.S. Forces* (June 13, 2005), para. 3.

[109] Yoram Dinstein, *War, Aggression and Self-Defense*, 5th ed. (Cambridge: Cambridge University Press, 2012), 32.

were casualties minimal? Were critical systems completely destroyed, badly harmed, or merely damaged? What if they were not? Is the victim state then bound simply to turn the other cheek? There is an option short of war but responsive to the seriousness of an unlawful armed attack.

A responsive option to an unlawful cyber attack – one carried out as a surprise attack that initiates hostilities – is a defensive belligerent reprisal. **A reprisal is a specific violation of the law of armed conflict, undertaken in the course of an armed conflict, to encourage an enemy who has violated the law of armed conflict, to refrain from continuing their unlawful conduct.**[110] (If the cyber attack was lawful, a reprisal would be an unlawful response.) Reprisals are limited to international armed conflicts.[111] "Reprisal amounts to an argument that crimes are justifiable as a proportionate response to criminal acts committed by the other party. In a sense, it is the most ancient means of enforcement of the law."[112] There are four requirements for a reprisal:[113]

1. It must be a response to a prior violation of international law that is imputable to the state against which the reprisal is directed;
2. It must be reasonably proportionate;
3. It must be undertaken for the purpose of putting an end to the enemy's unlawful conduct and preventing further illegalities and not for mere revenge; and
4. Since reprisals are a subsidiary means of redress, no other effective means of redress must be available.

"Reprisals must be based on reasonable notice ... , must be publicized (presumably to facilitate their deterrent effects), authorized only 'at the highest level of government (presumably to exclude emotive acts of personal revenge), and must be discontinued after the enemy eschews [its] egregious conduct."[114]

Professor Dinstein writes, "On the whole, the most effective modality of self-defense against an armed attack in the shape of a CNA is recourse to defensive armed reprisals, to wit, forcible counter-measures undertaken at a different time and place."[115] Judge George Aldrich, head of the U.S. delegation to the Geneva conferences that produced the 1977 protocols, adds, "Despite the 'limitations, risks, and unfairness of reprisals,' they may be the only remedial measure the victim State can take to coerce the enemy into respecting the law."[116]

[110] Pictet, *Commentary, I Geneva Convention 1949* (Geneva: ICRC, 1952), 341–2.

[111] Jean-Marie Henckaerts and Louise Doswald-Beck, *Customary Humanitarian Law.* Vol. I. *Rules* (Cambridge: Cambridge University Press, 2005), Rule 148, at 526.

[112] William A. Schabas, *The International Criminal Court: A Commentary on the Rome Statute* (Oxford: Oxford University Press, 2010), 496.

[113] Christopher Greenwood, *The Twilight of Belligerent Reprisals* (London: Cameron May, 2006), 299.

[114] Michael A. Newton, "Reconsidering Reprisals," 20 *Duke J. of Comparative & Int'l L.* (2010), 361, 375, citing: United Kingdom MOD, *Manual of the Law of Armed Conflict,* supra, note 100, § 16.17, at 419.

[115] Dinstein, "Computer Network Attack," in Schmitt and O'Donnell, *Computer Network Attack,* supra, note 61, at 107. A reprisal is not the same as self-defense. "The main difference between them is that in case of self-defense force is used to directly rebut an attack or counter some other form of prejudicial conduct, while reprisals are designed to force the adversary to change its conduct." Sandoz, *Commentary on the Additional Protocols,* supra, note 39, para. 3431, at 983.

[116] Theodor Meron, *The Humanization of International Law* (Leiden: Martinus Nijhoff, 2006), 12–13, citing George Aldrich, "Compliance with International Humanitarian Law," *Int'l Rev. Red Cross* (May–June 1991), 282, 301.

A reprisal need not be immediate, giving a victim state time to identify the attacker positively and minimize issues of distinction, and it can be calibrated to meet proportionality requirements.[117] While the period between an attack and a reprisal may not be excessive, it may be sufficiently lengthy to seek the assistance of the state from which the attack originated. Although an unfriendly state is unlikely to meet its obligations to assist in identifying and apprehending cyber attackers within its borders, perhaps because the state was itself involved, an attempt to gain cooperation must be made.[118]

Belligerent reprisals, that is, reprisals taken by belligerents in the course of an armed conflict, as opposed to peacetime reprisals,[119] have a long and disreputable history. Their widespread abuse in World War II, when they were permitted by the law of war, led to their prohibition in many circumstances. Today, reprisals against prisoners of war, civilians, civilian objects, cultural objects, medical and religious personnel, places of worship, works containing dangerous forces, and the natural environment, among other target categories, are prohibited.[120] (The United States does not consider Additional Protocol I's prohibition on reprisals against civilians to be customary law, viewing it as binding only on states ratifying that protocol.) Belligerent reprisals are considered unlawful in peacetime.[121] Some view them as unlawful even in time of armed conflict. Although the line is often faint, "[a] reprisal is not revenge or retribution, but an act of compliance with the law of war."[122] An ICTY opinion suggests that reprisal may be a violation of customary law,[123] a view that itself does not reflect customary law.[124] The ICRC suggests that ad hoc tribunals are an adequate substitute for reprisals, rendering reprisals unlawful. A trial by tribunal, however, cannot be assured and is a questionable deterrent to cyber violations.[125]

The guiding statutes of the ICTY, the International Criminal Tribunal for Rwanda, and the Rome Statute for the International Criminal Court do not criminalize reprisals; they do not mention them at all. The ICRC's *Customary International Law Study* concludes that "it is difficult to conclude that there has yet crystallized a customary rule specifically prohibiting reprisals during the conduct of hostilities."[126] The ICRC *Study*

---

[117] Philip Sutter, "The Continuing Role for Belligerent Reprisals," 13–1 *J. Conflict & Security L.* (Spring 2008), 93, 100–1. Sutter notes two theories of proportionality in reprisals. The predominant view is that reprisals must be proportionate to the initial violation. The second theory, that reprisals may be disproportionate in order to achieve the desired goal, the enforcement of LOAC, is generally rejected.

[118] See 1977 Additional Protocol I, Art. 85.1 and .2.

[119] A post–Additional Protocol I nonbelligerent reprisal was, for example, European Community Regulation 1901/98 (Sept. 7, 1998), prohibiting Yugoslavian airline flights between the Federal Republic of Yugoslavia and European Community nations. The financial reprisal was in response to continued Yugoslav *jus cogens* violations.

[120] See 1949 Geneva Convention I, Art. 46; Convention II, Art. 47; Convention III, Art. 13; Convention IV, Art. 33; 1977 Additional Protocol I, Arts. 20, 51.6, 52.1, 53(c), 54.4, 55.2, and 56.4.

[121] ICJ, *Threat or Use of Nuclear Weapons*, supra, note 2, at para. 39.

[122] Schabas, *The International Criminal Court*, supra, note 112, at 95.

[123] *Prosecutor v. Kupreškić*, IT-95-16-T, Judgment (Jan. 14, 2000), paras. 527–36.

[124] See, e.g., Theodor Meron, "The Humanization of Humanitarian Law," 94–2 *AJIL* (April 2000), 239, 250; and, Frits Kalshoven, "Reprisals and the Protection of Civilians: Two Recent Decisions of the Yugoslavia Tribunal," in Lal C. Vohrah, et al., eds., *Man's Inhumanity to Man: Essays in Honour of Antonio Cassese* (The Hague, Kluwer Law International (2003), 481, 510; and MOD, *Manual of the Law of Armed Conflict*, supra, note 100, para. 16.19.2 fn. 62, at 421: "The assertion that there is prohibition [against reprisals] in customary law flies in the face of most of the state practice that exists."

[125] Sutter, "Continuing Role for Belligerent Reprisals," supra, note 117, at 119.

[126] Henckaerts and Doswald-Beck, *Customary Humanitarian Law*, Vol. I. supra, note 111, at 523.

also finds that there is "insufficient evidence that the very concept of lawful reprisal in *non*-international armed conflict has ever materialized in international law."[127]

In international armed conflicts, the law of neutrality would be a complex issue in conducting a belligerent reprisal, because "neutral states must refrain from allowing their territory to be used by belligerent states for the purposes of military operations."[128] Military aircraft, for example, may not lawfully enter the airspace of another state without that state's permission.[129] A belligerent electronic reprisal routed through the cyberspace of another state on its way to its ultimate target in a third state would require the permission of the traversed state. A neutral state that knowingly permitted another state's reprisal access to its cyber network would be allowing a violation of its noninvolvement in the conflict, potentially drawing the neutral state into the armed conflict on the side of the reprising state.

Although not all commentators agree,[130] in international armed conflicts, reprisal appears a viable response to cyber attack. Frits Kalshoven, author of the leading text on reprisals, writes, "Belligerent reprisals, though by now [the year 2005] prohibited in important fields of the law of war, have not so far come under a total prohibition."[131] Lawful reprisal targets would be unlawful and lawful belligerents on the battlefield, and command and control elements of a violating combatant force. It is fairly clear that "in some circumstances a defense of 'reprisal' will be allowed if the violation [i.e., the reprisal] was a proportionate response to a violation committed by the opposing side."[132] And "exact equivalence between the target of the attack and the response has never been a requirement of belligerent reprisals."[133] Their precise form, and how they might be delivered, would be dictated by the political and tactical situations at the time.

Belligerent reprisal is a possible response to an *unlawful* cyber attack only in the course of an international armed conflict. If a state were cyber attacked by an opposing state in an ongoing international armed conflict, reprisal would not be a lawful option because the initial cyber attack would simply be another form of attack in the course of the armed conflict. But in some circumstances, it appears a lawful response to cyber attack.

17.11.1 A Possible Response to Cyber Intrusions in International Armed Conflicts

If belligerent reprisal is a possible response to a cyber attack, how might a state lawfully respond to a peacetime cyber intrusion not rising to an attack? The ICJ holds that uses of force short of armed attacks entitle a victim state only to respond with nonforcible and

---

[127] Id., at 527. Emphasis supplied.

[128] United Kingdom MOD, *Manual of the Law of Armed Conflict*, supra, note 100, para. 1.43, at 20.

[129] Dept. of the Army Field Manual, FM 27–10, *The Law of Land Warfare* (Washington, DC: GPO, 1956), para. 520: "Should the neutral State ... fail for any reason, to prevent violations of its neutrality by the troops of one belligerent entering or passing through its territory, the other belligerent may be justified in attacking the enemy forces on this territory."

[130] Richard B. Lillich, "Forcible Self-Help under International Law," in John Norton Moore and Robert F. Turner, *National Security Law*, 2d ed. (Durham NC: Carolina Academic Press, 2005), 113, 114.

[131] Frits Kalshoven, *Belligerent Reprisals*, republished ed. (Leiden: Martinus Nijhoff, 2005), 375. (Neither the cover nor the title page indicates that it is, in fact, a republication of the original 1971 edition.)

[132] Sean D. Murphy, "Progress and Jurisprudence of the International Criminal Tribunal for the Former Yugoslavia," 93–1 *AJIL* (Jan. 1999), 57, 89.

[133] Judith Gardam, *Necessity, Proportionality and the Use of Force by States* (Cambridge: Cambridge University Press, 2004), 79.

proportionate countermeasures.[134] A category of possible responses offering lawful options is "countermeasures." In the early twentieth century, countermeasures were referred to as "peacetime reprisals." Essentially, they are reprisals without the use or threat of force. Possible countermeasures are varied, each being tailored to the situation giving rise to its use.

The authoritative but nonbinding Articles of State Responsibility describe counter-measures as "**state actions, or omissions, directed at another State that would other-wise violate an obligation owed to that State and that are conducted by the former in order to compel or convince the latter to desist in its own internationally wrongful acts or omissions.**"[135] Moreover, "in light of the imminent advent of 'cyber terrorism' a State's obligation to control cyber activities taking place on its territory looms especially large."[136] Like reprisals, countermeasures may be unlawful acts or omissions undertaken by a victim state in response to an internationally wrongful act committed by or attribut-able to another state. They may be taken solely to induce, convince, or compel the other state to restore a situation to lawfulness. "They must be 'commensurate with the injury suffered' and may not affect certain fundamental rules such as the prohibition on the use of force, human rights and humanitarian law obligations, and *jus cogens*."[137]

For instance, if wrongful Redland cyber operations are ongoing against Blueland's banking system, Blueland may respond with cyber countermeasures blocking Redland's access to its own state bank accounts, a limited pinpoint intrusion into the offending state's banking system that would not constitute a cyber attack. Blocking access to all Redland bank accounts, however, would affect nonstate accounts and be a violation of distinction.

Countermeasures, like reprisals, must be preceded by a request that the responsible state remedy its wrongful act. Like reprisals, they may only be taken to induce compli-ance with international law after an earlier international wrong attributable to a state, they must be proportionate,[138] and they must be ended when the responsible state resumes compliance with its obligations. Like reprisals, countermeasures to internation-ally wrongful cyber activity may be cyber or noncyber in character, and they may not involve the threat or use of force.

Because countermeasures involve acts that are otherwise unlawful, they differ from acts in retorsion, a term that "refers to the taking of measures that are lawful, but 'unfriendly.' A State may, for example, block certain cyber transactions emanating from another State because the former enjoys sovereignty over cyber infrastructure on its territory."[139]

---

[134] *Military and Paramilitary Activities against Nicaragua* (Merits), Judgment, supra, note 52, at para. 249.

[135] Schmitt, "Below the "Threshold" Cyber Operations," supra, note 66, at 700. Emphasis supplied. Schmitt notes that the articles of *Responsibility of States for Internationally Wrongful Acts*, including Article 22, are not a treaty and therefore are nonbinding. They nevertheless are authoritative, having been developed by the International Law Commission and commended to governments by the U.N. General Assembly in 2001. They are generally, although not universally, accepted as customary international law. Countermeasures are discussed in part 3, chapter II of the Draft Articles. See, generally, Omar Yousif Elagab, *The Legality on Non-Forcible Counter-Measures in International Law* (London: Clarendon Press, 1988).

[136] Id., Schmitt, at 706.

[137] Pierre-Hugues Verdier and Erik Voeten, "Precedent, Compliance, and Change in Customary International Law: An Explanatory Theory," 108–3 AJIL (July 2014), 389, 396–7.

[138] Countermeasure proportionality differs from the more familiar proportionality in LOAC/IHL. In gauging countermeasures proportionality the focus is on the injury suffered by the victim state, rather than limiting defensive measures to those required to defeat the armed attack of another state.

[139] Schmitt, "'Below the Threshold' Cyber Operations," supra, note 66, at 701.

SIDEBAR. In September 1998, Electronic Disturbance Theater (EDT), a small group of individuals located in California, launched a preannounced distributed denial of service program against a Pentagon Web site. EDT referred to its cyber program as a virtual sit-in, and as "performance art." EDT's denial of service program, called Flood-Net, entered and searched the Pentagon Web site's search engine every nine seconds, effectively shutting it down. Having been forewarned, the Defense Information Systems Agency (DISA, now colocated and associated with CyberComm, at Fort Meade, Maryland) responded with a denial of service intrusion of its own and crashed the browsers being used by EDT.[140]

Was EDT's denial of service a cyber attack, a cyber intrusion, or an unlawful hack? There was no death, injury, destruction, or damage; nor was it transborder; thus it was not an attack. It was small scale and targeted a specific computer system whose penetration was of some value: a characterization that describes a cyber intrusion. Taking place within the borders of the United States, it also was unlawful as a violation of the federal Computer Fraud and Abuse Act.[141] Was DISA's hack-back a countermeasure, or a retorsion? It was neither, because another state was not involved and there was no apparent violation by EDT of international law. What was DISA's countermeasure, then?

17.11.2 Cyber Attacks and Intrusions in Noninternational Armed Conflicts

Reprisals and belligerent countermeasures are limited to employment by states engaged in international armed conflicts. Cyber attacks and intrusions initiated by nonstate actors and armed opposition groups not attributable to a state are criminal acts to be prosecuted and punished by domestic authorities of the state where the event emanated. Such cyber intrusions occur thousands of times every day, but they do not implicate LOAC.

17.12 U.S. Cyber Practice

The United States was aware of cyber warfare's threat before the last century ended but took few defensive measures until well into the twenty-first century. In 2008, the president signed National Security Presidential Directive 54, Comprehensive National Cybersecurity Initiative.[142] NSPD-54 discusses U.S. cyber security goals, which, at the time, were rudimentary and predictable. NSPD-54's notable result, one with lasting effect, was the construction of America's principal cyber data collection center at Bluffdale, Utah, near Salt Lake City.[143]

---

[140] Winn Schwartau, "Cyber-Civil Disobedience," *Network World*, Jan. 11, 1999.

[141] 18 USC § 1030 (a)(3).

[142] National Security Presidential Directive 54 (Jan. 8, 2008), "The Comprehensive National Cybersecurity Initiative."

[143] Completed in late 2013, the $1.5 billion Community Comprehensive National Cybersecurity Initiative Data Center was the Pentagon's largest construction project in the United States to date. Operated by NSA, the data collection center can intercept, capture, and store exabytes of a wide variety of electronic data, including foreign signals intelligence and U.S. domestic telephone, Internet, credit card usage data, and parking receipts. James Bamford, "The NSA Is Building the Country's Biggest Spy Center (Watch What You Say)," *Wired Magazine*, March 15, 2012; Henry Kenyon, "New NSA Data Center Breaks Ground on Construction," *Defense Systems*, Jan. 7, 2011.

In March 2015, before a Senate committee, the commander of U.S. Cyber Command testified that the United States needed to increase its ability to conduct cyber attacks as a deterrent to countries that might attack it, and erecting ever-higher digital fences was not enough. "Because in the end, a purely defensive reactive strategy will be both late [and] incredibly resource-intense."[144] A month later, those views were national strategy.

The 2015 *Department of Defense Cyber Strategy (DoD Strategy)* notes in its introduction that "our reliance on the confidentiality, availability, and integrity of data stands in stark contrast to the inadequacy of our cybersecurity."[145] In an unusually public way, the *DoD Strategy* names the countries presenting the most serious cyber threats to the United States: China, Russia, Iran, and North Korea.[146] It also establishes a hierarchy of cyber attacks: "routine" attacks that should be met by civilian companies and corporations; more complex cyber attacks that are the responsibility of the Department of Homeland Security; "about 2 percent of attacks on American systems, officials say, may rise to the level of prompting a national response – led by the Pentagon and through the military's Cyber Command."[147]

The 2015 *Strategy* explains that U.S. military cyber strategy centers on a five-point program that calls for the cooperation of the entire defense establishment, including civilian defense corporations, agencies, and individuals. The *DoD Strategy* also lays out its five "strategic initiatives": Build and maintain ready forces and capabilities to conduct cyberspace operations; defend the DoD information network, secure DoD data, and mitigate risks to DoD missions; be prepared to defend the U.S. homeland and U.S. vital interests from cyberattacks of significant consequence; build viable cyber options and plan to use those options to control conflict escalation and to shape the conflict environment; and, finally, build international alliances to deter shared threats.

The *DoD Strategy* also lists three "Primary Missions": Defend DoD's own networks, defend the U.S. and its interests against cyberattacks, and provide cyber capabilities to support military operations. Notably, the third mission indicates that "there may be times when the President or the Secretary of Defense may determine that it would be appropriate for the U.S. military to conduct cyber operations to disrupt an adversary's military-related networks or infrastructure so that the U.S. military can protect U.S. interests in an area of operations."[148] That suggests a broad range of possible DoD cyber activity, including preemptive attacks against an enemy's military and civilian networks, as well as an enemy's military objectives *and* critical national infrastructure.

The 2015 *Strategy* briefly discusses a still-building Cyber Mission Force that will include sixty-two hundred military, civilian, and contractor support personnel from all military branches and DoD components. "The Cyber Mission Force will be composed of cyber operators organized into 133 teams. ... Cyber Protection Forces will augment traditional defensive measures and defend priority DoD networks and systems against priority threats; National Mission Forces ... will defend the United States and its interests against cyberattacks of significant consequence; and Combat Mission Forces ... will support combatant commands."[149] Although the *DoD Strategy* understandably says

---

[144] David E. Sanger, "U.S. Must Step Up Capacity for Cyberattacks, Chief Argues," NY *Times*, March 20, 2015, A4.

[145] *DoD: Cyber Security, April 2015*, supra, note 10, at 1.   [146] Id., at 9.

[147] David E. Sanger, "Pentagon Announces New Strategy for Cyberwarfare," NY *Times*, April 24, 2015, A3.

[148] Id., at 5.   [149] Id., at 6.

nothing about anticipated activities of the Cyber Mission Force, the outline of its missions suggests an active effort to meet threats and prepare offensive strategies.

The *Strategy* requires DoD to act with other government departments and agencies, and the private (i.e., defense contractor) sector, to generate an overarching cybersecurity. Note that the *Strategy* is intended to protect DoD cyber operations and networks, not the United States as a whole, although through its second primary mission civilian organizations and corporations supplying defense technologies and weapons are no doubt encompassed.

The former secretary of defense Robert Gates has written, "There was a deep division within the government – in both the executive branch and Congress – over who should be in charge of our domestic cyber defense: government or business, the Defense Department's National Security Agency, the Department of Homeland Security, or some other entity. ... The result was paralysis."[150] The paralysis of past years was soon cured.

Executive Order 13231, *Critical Infrastructure Protection in the Information Age* (October 16, 2001), issued only a month after the 9/11 attacks, clearly intimates retaliation, should the critical national infrastructure be attacked: "It is the policy of the United States to protect against disruption of the operation of information systems for critical infrastructure and thereby help to protect the people, economy, essential human and government services, and national security." Any covert cyber act initiated by the DoD and, presumably, the Central Intelligence Agency requires a presidential finding and notification of both the House and Senate intelligence committees.

Dual use doctrine qualifies much of any enemy's critical national infrastructure as lawful military objectives, in any case. "To take a simple example, many air-traffic control and airspace management systems serve both civilian and military aircraft [and therefore] they are military objectives irrespective of the extent of civilian reliance on them."[151]

In May 2011, the United States published its *International Strategy for Operating in Cyberspace*. Surprisingly, the *Operating Strategy* is more direct than the *DoD Strategy* in asserting America's response to cyber attack: "When warranted, the United States will respond to hostile acts in cyberspace as we would to any other threat to our country. All states possess an inherent right to self-defense. ... We reserve the right to use all necessary means – diplomatic, informational, military, and economic – as appropriate and consistent with applicable international law, in order to defend our Nation, our allies, our partners, and our interests."[152]

U.S. Cyber Command ("CyberCom") was established in May 2010. It is a subordinate unit of U.S. Strategic Command. CyberCom is colocated with a major National Security Agency (NSA) facility, NSA's Threat Operations Center, at Fort Meade, Maryland. CyberCom and NSA are commanded by the same four-star general. Colocating Cyber Command and NSA allows each to take advantage of the expertise of the other, "obviating the need for reinventing many wheels."[153] CyberCom includes all armed service elements, intermixed with civilian cyber experts. Its mission is to plan, coordinate, integrate, and conduct activities to direct the operations and defense of DoD information networks; and to prepare and conduct military cyberspace operations; and to deny adversaries freedom of action in cyberspace.[154] This includes offensive, as well as

[150] Gates, *Duty*, supra, note 21, at 449.   [151] Schmitt, "The Law of Cyber Targeting," supra, note 38, at 19.
[152] *International Strategy for Cyberspace*, supra, note 3, at 14.
[153] Clarke and Knake, *Cyber War*, supra, note 8, at 39.
[154] U.S. Cyber Command Fact Sheet, http://www.stratcom.mil/factsheets/cyber_command/

defensive, cyber operations. Indeed, as early as 2010, the United States deployed an expeditionary cyber-support element to the Afghanistan combat zone.[155]

Both the 2008 *Comprehensive National Cybersecurity Initiative* and the 2011 *International Strategy for Operating in Cyberspace* are vague in regard to a U.S. response to cyber attacks.

> Neither defines a hostile act in cyberspace, nor is there language explicitly stating when, how, and to what extent the United States will respond to such acts. ... The United States is better served in the long run by not establishing such thresholds. ... If red lines are established, we will be compelled to respond to each threat that crosses the line, which is unrealistic. ... Not doing so allows government leaders the latitude to tailor response options. ... [R]ed lines that automatically result in a response could escalate an already volatile situation.[156]

Since the establishment of CyberCom, however, the United States has been anything but vague in announcing its intended cyber practice. In 2013, CyberCom's commander revealed the establishment of forty cyber teams, thirteen of them programming teams to formulate and execute offensive cyber counterattacks in response to cyber attacks on the United States. "I would like to be clear that this team, this defend-the-nation team, is not a defensive team," the general testified at a House Armed Services Committee hearing (apparently missing the irony of testifying that the "defend-the-nation team" is not defensive). He continued, "This is an offensive team ... to defend the nation if it were attacked in cyberspace. Thirteen of the teams that we're creating are for that mission alone."[157] The other twenty-seven teams, he said, focus on training and surveillance. In September 2013, CyberCom activated a "Cyber Mission Force," composed of 133 National Mission Teams, Combat Mission Teams, and Cyber Protection Teams.[158] Although the teams' missions are unannounced, their titles indicate their direction.

In 2011, the *New York Times* reported:

> The Pentagon has developed a list of cyber-weapons and-tools, including viruses that can sabotage an adversary's critical networks. ... The military needs presidential authorization to penetrate a foreign computer network and leave a cyber-virus that can be activated later. The military does not need such approval, however, to penetrate foreign networks for a variety of other activities. These include studying the cyber-capabilities of adversaries or examining how power plants or other networks operate. Military cyber-warriors can also, without presidential authorization, leave beacons to mark spots for later targeting by viruses. ... The United States need not respond to a cyberattack in kind but may use traditional force instead as long as it is proportional. ... The use of any cyber-weapon outside an area of hostility or when the United States is not at war ... requires presidential approval.[159]

---

[155] General Keith B. Alexander, commanding general designate, U.S. Cyber Command, testimony before House Armed Services Subcommittee, Washington, D.C. (September 23, 2010).

[156] Lt.Cmdr. John A. Mowchan, "Don't Draw the (Red) Line," U.S. Naval Institute *Proceedings* (Oct. 2011), 10, 19–20.

[157] Mark Mazzetti and David E. Sanger, "Security Chief Says Cyberattacks Will Meet with Retaliation," NY *Times*, March 13, 2013, A4.

[158] Admiral James Stavridis and David Weinstein, "Time for a U.S. Cyber Force," U.S. Naval Institute's *Proceedings* (Jan. 2014), 40, 41.

[159] Ellen Nakashima, "Defense Dept. Develops List of Cyber-Weapons," *Washington Post*, June 1, 2011, A3.

In November 2012, President Obama signed Presidential Policy Directive 20 (PPD-20), *U.S. Cyber Operations Policy*, detailing U.S. cyber policies and initiatives. PPD-20 directs that the U.S. government shall conduct neither offensive nor defensive cyber operations "that are intended or likely to produce cyber effects within the United States unless approved by the President."[160] A less sanguine section of PPD-20 directs that

> the United States Government ... shall make all reasonable efforts ... to identify the adversary and the ownership and geographic location of the targets and related infrastructure where DCEO [defensive cyber effects operations] or OCEO [offensive cyber effects operations] will be conducted or cyber effects are expected to occur, and to identify the people and entities, including U.S. persons, that could be affected by proposed DCEO or OCEO.[161]

Another section discusses the critical national infrastructure, saying, "The United States Government shall retain DCEO, including anticipatory action taken against imminent threats ... as an option to protect such infrastructure."[162] While specifying a governmental protective interest in the critical infrastructure, the PPD does not announce how it will be defended *before* an attack, other than to say its protection shall be coordinated with the Department of Homeland Security.[163] PPD-20 authorizes the secretary of defense to conduct "Emergency Cyber Actions necessary to mitigate an imminent threat or ongoing attack using DCEO if circumstances at the time do not permit obtaining prior Presidential approval."[164] PPD-20 suggests a strong U.S. offensive capability, along with an awareness of need for that capability's high-level control. It also illustrates that, for cyber defense and responsive actions to be effective, they must be predetermined and coordinated with armed service cyber security units, civilian law enforcement agencies, the Department of State, and international police agencies.

Additionally, a 2015 Executive Order authorizes financial and travel sanctions against anyone involved in cyber attacks on the United States that originate outside U.S. borders and pose "a significant threat to the national security, foreign policy or economic health or financial stability of the United States."[165]

Is there any *law* regarding cyber operations, any codified regulation of cyber warfare activity? Although domestic laws and multistate treaties are sure to come, the publicly known guidance comprises the 2001 executive order protecting critical infrastructure, the 2008 presidential directive on national cyber security, a 2011 executive-issued international strategy, the 2012 presidential policy directive on cyber operations, and the 2015 DoD strategy guidance: an order, two directives, and two strategies. They may not be legislated law, but they authorize a broad range of U.S. defensive and offensive cyber warfare practices.

Meanwhile, the thrust-and-parry of cyber warfare, with its cycles of intrusion, detection and counter, continue. At the same time, diplomatic and political efforts to achieve an international *modus vivendi* lurch from effort to effort. In 2015, a United Nations "consensus document" offered promising recommendations to guide state activity in cyberspace.[166] In the document, the U.S. succeeded in having its preferred norms

---

[160] PPD-20, *Cyber Operations Policy*, supra, note 88, at 6.   [161] Id., at 7.   [162] Id., at 8.   [163] Id.
[164] Id., at 10.
[165] Executive Order (unnumbered) – "Blocking the Property of Certain Persons Engaging in Significant Malicious Cyber-Enabled Activities," (April 1, 2015).
[166] UN General Assembly A/70/72, "Developments in the Field of Information and Telecommunications in the Context of International Security (July 22, 2015).

regarding the protection of critical national infrastructure included, while China prevailed with language urging states to substantiate public accusations of state-sponsored cyber intrusions. The document also recommended that states respond to requests for assistance by another state whose critical infrastructure was subject to malicious attack. At the same time, the U.S. warned that substantial sanctions against Chinese hackers were being prepared, and "the combination of intellectual property theft and espionage on an unprecedented scale…cannot go unanswered."[167]

Soon thereafter, during a 2015 state visit to the White House, China's President Xi Jinping and President Obama, surprisingly, "embraced"[168] the then-recent U.N. consensus document, and reached a "common understanding" that Chinese cyber intrusions against the U.S. must stop and that Chinese hackers would be sought out and punished. Although short of a written pact, the two leaders agreed to "what could become the first arms control accord for cyberspace…a commitment by each country that it will not be the first to use cyberweapons to cripple the other's critical infrastructure during peacetime."[169]

It remains to be seen if words become deeds. Every state has its own definition of "critical national infrastructure," and the U.S.-China agreement addresses neither theft of intellectual property nor state-sponsored cyber intrusions. But the agreement may be a notable possible first step.

17.13 Summary

If there is a circumstance in armed conflict that was unforeseen (and unforeseeable) by the 1949 Geneva Conventions, it is cyber warfare. Still, cyber warfare can be dealt with using traditional law of war tools, recognizing that today's *jus ad bellum* cyber war questions can instantly ripen into *jus in bello* issues. Cyber attacks are not per se LOAC violations. They are another strategy or tactic of warfare, like psychological operations and artillery barrages. When considering their effect or use, they may be thought of as being similar to kinetic weapons.

How does one distinguish a hacker's cyber intrusion from an enemy state's cyber attack? The United States employs a results test. If the cyber intrusion results in the death or wounding of civilian or military individuals, or the significant destruction or damage of military or civilian objects, including data, an attack may be presumed, just as if the event involved kinetic weapons. Death, wounding, or destruction may be neither presumed nor potential; they must be actual. In U.S. policy, an attack apparently may be presumed if a CNA targets an element of the critical national infrastructure, or a civilian computer network associated with the military so as to constitute a dual use network, such as that of a major defense contractor's classified network – as long as death, wounding, or physical destruction follows or might reasonably be anticipated. Although there is no formal international agreement to the U.S. position, such consequences, the

[167] David E. Sanger, "Cyberthreat Posed by China and Iran Confounds White House," *NYTimes* (Sept. 16, 2015), A6.

[168] Julie Hirschfeld Davis and David E. Sanger, "U.S. and China Agree to Rein In State-Sponsored Computer Thefts," *NYTimes* (Sept. 26, 2015), A11.

[169] David E. Sanger, "U.S. and China Seek Arms Deal For Cyberspace," *NYTimes* (Sept. 20, 2015).

United States considers, may be considered an attack with armed force, giving rise to self-defense under U.N. Charter Article 51. Whether a CNA or a bombing attack, an attackers' choice of arms is immaterial.

Nonstate armed opposition groups, such as al Qaeda and its offshoots, are not known to have engaged in cyber attacks, yet. If past is prelude, a cyber attack will be initiated by another state or an individual or group whose actions are attributable to a state: that is, an international armed conflict in which the 1949 Geneva Conventions, in their entirety, and Additional Protocol I will apply, along with customary international law. Should a nonstate armed opposition group without state sponsorship mount an attack, the circumstances would be examined to determine whether it was an effort to initiate an armed conflict or "merely" a criminal act. In either case, the attack should be a matter for domestic law enforcement authorities.

Responding to a confirmed cyber attack during a time of peace raises difficult issues. Immediate counterattacks would likely consist of preprogrammed automated cyber operations. "Such 'hack-backs' simply target the computers from which the intrusion originates."[170] But, to whom, or to what entity, should the attack be attributed? How can the requirement for distinction be satisfied by a counterattacker at each stop on the attacker's electronic back-trail? How may a counterstrike be made proportional? In an international armed conflict a possible answer is belligerent reprisal. Because a reprisal need not be immediate, there can be a reasonable period to calibrate a response and assure the identity and lawfulness of the target. Reprisals are not problem free; nor are they universally agreed upon as a tactic. They are, however, a possible means of responding to a cyber attack that can avoid the most obvious pitfalls associated with an immediate response, electronic or kinetic.

Numerous attacks against U.S. networks involve computer hardware compromised at point of manufacture. "Software is most of the problem. We have to find a way to write software which has many fewer errors and which is more secure. . . . Hackers get in where they don't belong, most often because they have obtained 'root' or administrator status, through a glitch they have discovered in the software."[171] Threats from within, personnel with legitimate access to secrets, government workers willing to provide information to a nation's enemies, will always be a major threat to cyber secrets.

Yet, so far, no one is known to have died from a cyber attack anywhere in the world. A longtime cyber expert in the military and civilian communities writes:

> The most meaningful cyber conflicts rarely occur at the "speed of light" or "network speed." . . . [Cyber] conflicts are typically campaigns that encompass weeks, months, or years of hostile contact between adversaries, just as in traditional warfare. . . . While some attacks are technically difficult to attribute, it is usually a straightforward matter to determine the nation responsible, since the conflict takes place during an on-going geo-political crisis. . . . Despite early fears that nations would strike at each other using surprise . . . there is no evidence that such conflicts have occurred. Nations seem to be willing to launch significant cyber assaults during larger crises, but not out of the blue.[172]

---

[170] Droege, "Get Off My Cloud: Cyber Warfare, International Humanitarian Law," supra, note 5, at 574.

[171] Clarke and Knake, *Cyber War*, supra, note 8, at 173.

[172] Healey, "A Brief History of US Cyber Conflict," supra, note 11, at 21–3.

Reassuring words. There need be but one cyber Pearl Harbor to prove them wrong, however. In any event, much will have occurred since this writing that will change the terrain of cyber warfare.

CASES AND MATERIALS

UNITED STATES V. JEANSON J. ANCHETA

U.S. District Court, Central District of California (March 2006)[173]

The first prosecution under the U.S. domestic Computer Fraud and Abuse Act (Chapter 19.0) was concluded in May 2006, in Los Angeles, California. Twenty-one-year-old Jeanson Ancheta, a U.S. citizen, pleaded guilty to violating the act, conspiring to violate the CNA-SPAM Act, causing damage to federal computers used in national defense, and accessing protected computers to commit fraud.

Among those domestic crimes, which included the insertion of ads on thousands of personal computers, for which he was well paid, Ancheta created zombies on the hacked computers to extend his criminal reach into additional computers. Pertinent to LOAC/IHL, he hacked into computer systems of the Weapons Division of the U.S. Naval Air Warfare Center, at China Lake, California, and the Defense Information Systems Agency, whose national defense networks were intentionally damaged through Ancheta's insertion of malicious code. Ancheta was sentenced to fifty-seven months' imprisonment and ordered to pay fifteen thousand dollars in restitution to the government.

Since *Ancheta*, federal prosecutions under the Computer Fraud and Abuse Act have become common, often resulting in lengthy sentences to confinement.[174]

WHAT CONSTITUTES AN ATTACK? THE 1980 U.S. HOSTAGE RESCUE

In late 1979, the United States–supported shah of Iran left Tehran to seek cancer treatment in America, but it was too late to arrest the cancer. The shah, generally despised in Iran for the brutality of his regime, left the United States for Egypt and died ten months later. Meanwhile, in November 1979, an armed group of militant Islamic students stormed the American Embassy in Tehran, taking it over, making sixty-six Americans captive. (Eventually, fourteen women and African Americans and two ill captives were released.) Although an earlier 1979 embassy break-in had resulted in the

---

[173] U.S. Dept. of Justice press release (May 8, 2006), https://www2.fbi.gov/page2/may06/botnet050806.htm.

[174] E.g., *US v. Jeremy Hammond*, Case 1:12-cr-00185 (LAP), S.D.N.Y. (Nov. 15, 2013). Hammond was sentenced to ten years' confinement for hacking into, inter alia, U.S. government agency networks.

death of an Iranian employee and the wounding of two Marine guards, no one was killed or wounded in the November seizure.

In April 1980, fearing for the continued safety of the hostages, a U.S. military rescue of the hostages was attempted. "Operation Eagle Claw" was a complex plan involving multiple military commanders sometimes operating at cross-purposes, and civilian political inter-meddlers.[175] The rescue effort involved 120 Army Ranger, Green Beret, and Delta soldiers; six Air Force C-130 transport aircraft; and eight Navy RH-53 Sea Stallion helicopters initially flown from the aircraft carrier *Nimitz* (CVN-68). Most of the helicopters were piloted by Marines. Contrary to LOAC/IHL, the helicopters carried large aircraft nationality identifi-cation symbols from various Middle Eastern countries that, when the helicopters were landed, could quickly be applied over their U.S. markings.[176]

On April 24–5, the various U.S. units landed and assembled at a remote Iranian location code-named "Desert One," from which the soldiers were to drive vehicles carried by the C-130s into Tehran to rescue the hostages. Instead, in blowing sand raised by idling aircraft prop engines, a helicopter crashed into a parked C-130, exploding the transport, which carried fuel for the return flights. Five men died aboard the transport, three aboard the chopper, and four more were seriously burned. The rescue attempt was abandoned and the fifty-two hostages were held for 444 days before being released on January 20, 1981.

Did the armed students' seizure of the embassy and the American hostages constitute an attack? Could the attack be described as having involved armed force even though no one was shot? Would an armed American counterattack have been in accord with LOAC/IHL? Was the rescue attempt itself in accord with LOAC/IHL?

Although cyber attacks had no role in the seizure of the embassy, issues pertinent to cyber warfare were present: Applying the definition of "attack" from Additional Protocol I, Article 49.1, and in the *Commentary*, the takeover was an act of violence by Iranian civilians against an adversary. Persons were set upon with hostile action and were endangered, making the seizure an attack. The attackers were Iranian civilian citizens whose actions were arguably attributable to the Iranian state.[177] The students, during the time of the takeover, appear to have lacked the organizational and structural character necessary to constitute a "party" to a conflict. (Immediately after the takeover, with the encouragement of the Ayatollah Khomeini–led Iranian government and Revolutionary Guards reinforcements, the students sufficiently organized themselves to allow attribu-tion of their acts to the Iranian government.) Although two states were involved, the attack did not rise to armed conflict status, either international or noninternational.[178] Nor does common Article 3 apply in internal instances of riot or disorder, such as the embassy takeover (Chapter 3.8.6.1). If neither common Article 2 nor 3 applied, what law applied? Iranian domestic law and a variety of multinational treaties to which Iran was a party. Because the attack involved diplomatic personnel, archives, and premises, the 1963 Vienna Convention on Consular Relations applied.[179] Although Iran has not

---

[175] Paul B. Ryan, *The Iranian Rescue Mission* (Annapolis, MD: United States Naval Institute, 1985), 86.

[176] After-action briefing attended by author, who was then the staff judge advocate of Headquarters, Fleet Marine Forces, Atlantic, located in Norfolk, Virginia (June 1980).

[177] The International Court of Justice found that the students' actions initially were not attributable to the state. *Case Concerning United States Diplomatic and Consular Staff in Tehran* ("The Tehran Case"), 64 ICJ Reports (May 24, 1980), para. 58.

[178] *Prosecutor v. Tadić*, supra, note 63.   [179] "The Tehran Case," supra, note 177.

ratified the 1961 Vienna Convention on Diplomatic Relations, a 1980 ICJ Judgment found Iran to have been in violation of its terms. The International Convention against the Taking of Hostages did not enter into force until June 1983.

How should the aborted hostage rescue attempt, conducted by combatants not involved in an armed conflict, be viewed? The embassy takeover was the subject of a 1980 ICJ judgment. Because the rescue attempt did not involve cyber warfare (and because the rescue attempt was not a matter before the court), we merely note that the ICJ held, significantly for cyber warfare study, that the embassy takeover constituted an "armed attack."[180] "The Judgment registered the American plea that the [hostage rescue] operation had been carried out in exercise of the right of self-defense, with a view to extricating the victims of an armed attack against the US Embassy. In his later dissenting opinion in the *Nicaragua* case, [ICJ] Judge Schwebel called that American plea 'a sound legal evaluation of the rescue attempt'."[181]

THE STUXNET VIRUS[182]

Enriched uranium is critical to the manufacture of nuclear weapons. Uranium is enriched in high-speed centrifuges. Centrifuges depend on computerized operating directions and controls. Few companies have the technical ability to build such complex machines or their controlling electronic systems. Centrifuges, and millions of other mechanical devices that play vital roles in everyday life, are essentially controlled by small plastic boxes the size of a cigarette pack called programmable-logic controllers. "These controllers, or P.L.C.s, perform the critical scut work of modern life. They open and shut valves in water pipes, speed and slow the spinning of uranium centrifuges, mete out the dollop of cream in each Oreo cookie, and time the change of traffic lights from red to green."[183]

On June 17, 2010, a computer in Iran would not stop rebooting. Within a few days, a virus was found to be infecting the computer's Microsoft Windows operating system. The virus was a worm that replicated through infected e-mail, or when an infected flash drive was plugged into the computer. Leaving no sign of its presence, the virus uploaded two files: a "rootkit dropper," giving the worm administrator status in the computer's operating system, and a payload injector of encrypted malicious code. "The most unsettling thing about the virus was that its components hid themselves as soon as they got into the host."[184] Later, it was determined that the first Stuxnet infection occurred in June 2009.[185]

Within a few days, a German security analyst decrypted most of the infected payload and discovered that its target was P.L.C.s, specifically, P.L.C.s in certain gas centrifuge models made by the German engineering conglomerate Siemens.[186] On July 16, 2009, Microsoft issued the first of a series of patches, defenses against the virus, which had been found in only a few American and European sites. Thousands of infections were reported

---

[180] Id., at para. 57.
[181] Dinstein, *War, Aggression and Self-Defence*, 5th ed., supra, note 109, at 215. Footnote omitted.
[182] Except where indicated, this material is based on Michael Joseph Gross, "A Declaration of Cyber-War," *Vanity Fair* , April 2011, available online.
[183] Id., p. 1 of Internet version.   [184] Id., at 2.
[185] John Markoff, "Malware Aimed at Iran Hit Five Sites, Report Says," NY *Times*, Feb. 13, 2011, A12.
[186] Other sources cite another target: frequency converters, which apparently are P.L.C.-based power sources that control the speed of motors by changing the frequency converter's output frequency.

in India, Indonesia, and Iran. A Microsoft researcher named the virus "Stuxnet," for an anagram of letters from two sections of its code.

The digital code that allowed Stuxnet to pass from computer to computer was quickly revoked, but a new Stuxnet version, with a new digital pass code, immediately appeared, and the worm continued to spread the virus. When it too was revoked, a third version appeared. When the third code was revoked no new digital pass code version arose, but the virus continued to spread from computers already infected.

It was apparent to researchers that a national government must have written the complex and lengthy (said to be a half-megabyte)[187] virus that exploited Windows' source code. Symantec became a major analyst of Stuxnet and "[a] Symantec strategist estimated that as many as 30 different people helped write it . . . [taking] at least six months."[188] Nor were the writers ordinary hackers.

When Stuxnet entered a host computer, it attempted to spread to all computers on that network, specifically searching for Siemens software. When found, the virus determined whether the host computer was connected to a P.L.C. If so, the virus searched for a particular model of Siemens machine that the P.L.C. controlled and inquired whether the machine was operating under a specific range of conditions. If it was running within that range, Stuxnet injected the rogue code into the P.L.C. to vary the machine's operation. The variation radically varied the speed of the centrifuge's rotors, causing them to destroy themselves.[189] "In a spooky flourish . . . the worm ends the attack with a command to restore the current to the perfect operating frequency for the centrifuges."[190] "Even as it sabotages its target system, it fools the machine's digital safety system into reading as if everything were normal. . . . Stuxnet is like a self-directed stealth drone: the first known virus that, released into the wild, can seek out a specific target, sabotage it, and hide both its existence and its effects until after the damage is done."[191] This is the course taken by Stuxnet in three waves of attacks on Iran's centrifuges at Natanz, the desert site of Iran's nuclear enrichment facility, where the Bushehr nuclear power plant is located.[192] The first attack was in late 2009, the other two in 2010.[193]

What damage did Stuxnet inflict on Iran's centrifuges, and its nuclear program? Reports vary, some reports being suspect. The *New York Times* wrote that Stuxnet involved Siemens' initial cooperation with the United States (almost surely incorrect) and that Stuxnet "appears to have wiped out roughly a fifth of Iran's nuclear centrifuges."[194] That would be as many as a thousand centrifuges. A *Times* security analyst source said, "The attackers took great care to make sure that only their designated targets were hit. . . . It was a marksman's job."[195] Such care suggests someone concerned

---

[187] Richard A. Falkenrath, "From Bullets to Megabytes," *NY Times*, Jan. 27, 2011, A27.

[188] Gross, "A Declaration of Cyber-War," supra, note 182, at 4.

[189] William J. Broad and David E. Sanger, "Worm in Iran Was Perfect for Sabotaging Nuclear Centrifuges," *NY Times*, Nov. 19, 2010, A1.

[190] Id.   [191] Gross, "A Declaration of Cyber-War," supra, note 182, at 5.

[192] Markoff, "Malware Aimed at Iran," supra, note 185. Other sources assert there were two waves.

[193] Joby Warrick, "Iran Recovered Swiftly in Wake of Cyberattack," *Wash. Post*, Feb. 16, 2011, A1.

[194] William J. Broad, John Markoff, and David E. Sanger, "Israel Tests Called Crucial In Iran Nuclear Setback," *NY Times*, Jan. 16, 2011, A1.

[195] Id.

with distinction and proportionality.[196] "No independent hacker or criminal would bother with such niceties."[197]

> Stuxnet's code telegraphs the inherent caution of its makers in yet another way: it has a "fail-safe" feature to limit its propagation. The USB-spreading code, for instance, limits the number of devices that each infected device can itself infect. (The limit is three, enough to create a moderate chain reaction, but not so many that its effects would rage out of control.) Most dramatically, on June 24, 2012, the worm will self-destruct altogether; erase itself from every infected machine and simply disappear.[198]

In November 2010, Mahmoud Ahmadinejad, Iran's president, announced that a cyber attack had caused "minor problems with some of our centrifuges,"[199] and the U.N. International Atomic Energy Agency reported that nearly one thousand of Iran's Natanz centrifuges had been shut down for as long as a week. That is a period consistent with replacing all forty-eight hundred centrifuges' operating software.[200] Despite the widespread damage, the Iranian enrichment process recovered in remarkably quick time, and "the net impact was relatively minor."[201]

To whom may the Stuxnet cyber attack be attributed? Most accounts credit it as a joint U.S.-Israeli project.[202] Although there is no proof of origin, media sources provide confirming details,[203] for example, details that Stuxnet was designed by a small programmer cell, the Office of Tailored Access Operations, at the Fort Meade, Maryland, headquarters of the National Security Agency, with improvements and new versions from Israel's NSA equivalent, Unit 8200.[204] Also, "[the retired air force general] Michael D. Hayden, the former chief of the CIA, [said], ... 'This is the first attack of a major nature in which a cyberattack was used to effect physical destruction. ... You can't help but describe it as an attack on critical infrastructure."[205] American and Israeli authorities have denied neither their role, nor reports that Stuxnet was part of what is called "Operation Olympic." Another virus, Duqu, was an earlier reconnaissance tool for Stuxnet that copied blueprints of Iran's

---

[196] One source, Markoff, "Malware Aimed at Iran," supra, note 185, notes that, based on a Symantec analysis, Stuxnet infected twelve thousand computers. Unless those computers were part of a network associated with Siemens centrifuges, however, the impact of the infections likely was imperceptible. The 2010 repeated rebooting of the computer that brought Stuxnet to light apparently was a one-off.

[197] Brown, "The Wrong Questions about Cyberspace," supra, note 44, at 218.

[198] Gross, "A Declaration of Cyber-War," supra, note 182, at 7.

[199] Broad, Markoff, and Sanger, "Israel Tests," supra, note 194.

[200] Glenn Kessler, "Centrifuges in Iran Were Shut Down, IAEA Report Says," Wash. Post, Nov. 24, 2010. Other reports indicate nine thousand centrifuges, e.g., Warrick, "Iran Recovered Swiftly, supra, note 193.

[201] Id., Warrick, "Iran Recovered Swiftly." To the same effect, Gross, "Declaration of Cyber-War," supra, note 182, at 10.

[202] Kessler, "Centrifuges in Iran," supra, note 200.

[203] David E. Sanger, "Obama Order Sped Up Wave of Cyberattacks against Iran," NY Times, June 1, 2012, A1. A few months later, Sanger expanded on his detailed information in, Confront and Conceal (New York: Crown, 2012), iv-xiii; 188–209; and, Ellen Nakishima, "Flame Virus Has Infected Computers, Iran Says," Wash. Post, May 30, 2012, A3.

[204] Id., Sanger, Confront and Conceal, at 197. The Office of Tailored Access Operations (TAO) has additional units in San Antonio, Texas; Wahiawa, Hawaii; Fort Gordon, Georgia; Buckley Air Force Base, near Denver, Colorado; and a European liaison office in Darmstadt, Germany. TAO's mission reportedly is "breaking into, manipulating and exploiting computer networks, making them hackers and civil servants in one." Spiegel Online, "Inside TAO: Documents Reveal Top NSA Hacking Unit," Dec. 29, 2013.

[205] Sanger, Confront and Conceal, supra, note 203, at 200.

nuclear program.[206] A third Operation Olympic virus is Flame, a data-mining virus confirmed by Iran to have stolen information from its computers.[207]

"One big question is why its creators let the software spread widely, giving up so many of its secrets in the process."[208] The answer, according to one writer, is that Stuxnet was aimed only at Natanz's centrifuges, but a careless Iranian scientist "plugged his laptop into the [centrifuge] computer controllers and the worm had hopped aboard. When he later connected the same laptop to the Internet, the worm broke free and began replicating itself, a step its designers never anticipated."[209] Although it should have been foreseen, it was not intended that Stuxnet should spread beyond the targeted machines.

Was Stuxnet a cyber attack? Is attribution satisfied? General Michael Hayden, former head of the NSA, and before that the CIA, says it was an attack on Iran by America. It resulted in the destruction of military or civilian objects. If similar results resulted from a kinetic strike, would it be an attack? Would self-defense have been justified under IHL? "Stuxnet was the first time a cyber activity could indisputably be labeled a cyber attack."[210] The United States will find it difficult to complain, should another state mounts a similar attack against similar American targets.

"One big question is why its creators let the software spread widely, giving up so many of its secrets in the process."[211] The question is significant because "Stuxnet is now a model code for all to copy and modify to attack other industrial facilities."[212]

"In the end, the most important thing now publicly known about Stuxnet is that Stuxnet is now publicly Known."[213]

---

[206] Nicole Perlroth, "Researchers Find Clues in Malware," NY *Times*, May 31, 2012, B1.

[207] Id.; and, Thomas Erdbrink, "Iran Confirms Attack by Virus That Collects Information," NY *Times*, May 30, 2012, A4; Hayley Tsukayama, "Malware is linked to Stuxnet, Flame," *Wash. Post*, Aug. 10, 2012, A3. Flame, first encountered in December 2007, first reported on in May 2012, reportedly can steal computer screen images, record e-mail and chats, monitor keystrokes, remotely turn on microphones, and take screen shots.

[208] John Markoff, "A Silent Attack, but Not a Subtle One," NY *Times*, Sept. 27, 2010, A6.

[209] Sanger, *Confront and Conceal*, supra, note 203, at xii.

[210] Brown, "Wrong Questions about Cyberspace," supra, note 44, at 218.

[211] Markoff, "Silent Attack," supra, note 208.

[212] Warrick, "Iran Recovered Swiftly," supra, note 193. In late 2011 a "new program [to steal digital information] was written by programmers who must have had access to Stuxnet's source code, the original programming instructions." John Markoff, "New Worm by Creators of Stuxnet Is Suspected," NY *Times*, Oct. 19, 2011, B6.

[213] Gross, "Declaration of Cyber-War," supra, note 182, at 11.

18 Attacks on Cultural Property

18.0 Introduction

We have discussed how law of armed conflict/international humanitarian law (LOAC/IHL) consists, at least, of 1907 Hague Regulation IV, the 1949 Geneva Conventions, the 1977 Additional Protocols, customary international law, case law, and multinational treaties. In fact, there are scores of treaties, conventions, declarations, compacts, and resolutions that bear on LOAC/IHL in one way or another.

Six multinational treaties are particularly significant to LOAC/IHL: the 1925 Gas Protocol Prohibiting the Use in War of Asphyxiating, Poisonous or Other Gases; the 1954 Hague Convention for the Protection of Cultural Property; the 1971 Convention on the Prohibition of Development, Production and Stockpiling of Biological and Toxin Weapons; the 1997 Ottawa Treaty Banning the Use, Stockpiling, Production and Transfer of Anti-Personnel Land Mines; the 1980 Convention on Certain Conventional Weapons; and the 1993 Convention on the Prohibition of Development, Production, Stockpiling and Use of Chemical Weapons. The 1976 Convention on Environmental Modification might reasonably be added to that list.

Of these, the 1980 Conventional Weapons and 1993 Chemical Weapons Conventions, particularly, have potential impact on war fighters. Violations of either could lead to war crime charges against combatants in the field or, at the least, intensely negative international scrutiny.[1] In this chapter, the 1954 Hague Convention for the Protection of Cultural Property in the Event of Armed Conflict and its two protocols, also receive attention. It is essentially a treaty about targeting.

> Looting the enemy's cultural treasures and religious shrines has been a regular feature of aggressive and imperial war time out of mind; it was still so for the war-lords of Germany in the Second World War. Bombarders devoted to cracking enemy civilian morale may believe, almost certainly mistakenly, that wrecking his treasures and shrines is a good way to go about it. One of the first things the Germans did on seizing Warsaw at the end of September 1939 was to destroy the Poles' most beloved national monument, the one to Chopin. ... The Dresden climax of [British] Bomber Command's offensive has acquired its peculiarly bad reputation because, in addition to being of little military

---

[1] See, e.g., William Bogdanos, *Thieves of Baghdad* (New York: Bloomsbury, 2005) 110–11, in which U.S. forces, during the U.S.–Iraqi conflict, received international condemnation, not all deserved, for failure to prevent the looting of Iraq's National Museum, just as common Art. 2 fighting was ending.

importance, it was uniquely destructive of cultural treasures. By the time of the Second World War, however, the countervailing tendency was well in evidence.[2]

That countervailing tendency is found nine years after the war's end in the United Nations Educational Scientific and Cultural Organization (UNESCO)–sponsored Hague Cultural Property Convention.

18.1 Background: 1954 Hague Convention for the Protection of Cultural Property

In the eighteenth century, the Swiss jurist Vattel wrote, "For whatever cause a country is ravaged, we ought to spare those edifices which do honour to human society, and do not contribute to increase the enemy's strength . . . such as temples, tombs, public buildings, and all works of remarkable beauty. What advantage is obtained by destroying them?"[3] Indeed, LOAC has long provided for the protection of cultural objects. Article 35 of the 1863 Lieber Code provides: "Classical works of art, libraries, scientific collections, or precious instruments, such as astronomical telescopes . . . must be secured against all avoidable injury, even when they are contained in fortified places" (alas, in Article 36 Lieber also wrote, "If such works of art, libraries, collections, or instruments belonging to a hostile nation or government can be removed without injury, the ruler of the conquering state or nation may order them to be seized and removed for the benefit of the said nation. The ultimate ownership is to be settled by the ensuing treaty of peace"). Article 27, 1907 Hague Regulation IV, established a quite different and more lasting rule: "All necessary steps must be taken to spare, as far as possible, buildings dedicated to religion, art, science, or charitable purposes, historic monuments." Hague Regulation IV, Article 56, further provides, "All seizure, destruction or wilful damage done to institutions of this character, historic monuments, works of art and science, is forbidden, and should be made the subject of legal proceedings." Professor Geoffrey Best adds, "Typical of that generation's optimism about international law was the unguarded assumption that victor no less than loser would, if charged, go to court and, if found guilty, pay up."[4] The World War I free-for-all on cultural property supports Best's negative view.

Article 58 of the 1940 edition of Field Manual (FM) 27–10, *Rules of Land Warfare*, repeats the Lieber Code's prohibition,[5] of which Oppenheim, no less cynical than Best, wrote, "No bombardment takes place without the sufferers accusing the attacking forces of neglecting the rule that such places must be spared. In practice, whenever one belligerent accuses the other of having intentionally bombarded a hospital, church, or similar building, the charge is always either denied with indignation or justified by the

---

[2] Geoffrey Best, *War and Law since 1945* (Oxford: Oxford University Press, 1994), 285.

[3] Cited in Sharon A. Williams, *The International and National Protection of Movable Cultural Property: A Comparative Study* (Dobbs Ferry, NY: Oceana, 1978), 5–6.

[4] Best, *War and Law since 1945*, supra, note 2, at 284.

[5] Dept. of the Army, FM27–10, *Rules of Land Warfare* (Washington, DC: GPO, 1956), para. 58, at 14. "In sieges and bombardments all necessary steps must be taken to spare, as far as possible, buildings dedicated to religion, art, science, or charitable purposes, historic monuments, hospitals, and places where the sick and wounded are collected, provided that they are not being used at the time for military purposes."

assertion that these sacred buildings have been used improperly by the accuser."[6] Major-General A. V. P. Rogers more charitably suggests, "It is more likely, though, that such destruction is caused in the main incidental to attacks on military objectives, caused by mistake."[7] Whether foreseeing incidental or purposeful damage, in World War II, the United States and United Kingdom went to considerable lengths to spare and protect cultural property "so far as war allows."[8] Today, under customary international law, the Statute of the International Criminal Tribunal for the Former Yugoslavia (ICTY), and the Rome Statute of the International Criminal Court, attacking protected cultural objects in both international and noninternational armed conflicts constitutes war crimes, although the scope of protection under customary law is ambiguous.[9]

The protection of cultural property and places of worship receives special emphasis in the 1954 Hague Cultural Property Convention – protection from attack as well as protection from use for military purposes so an attack is not necessary or justifiable.

SIDEBAR. Throughout World War II, the area bombing of European targets by both the Allies and the Axis resulted in the loss on both sides of cathedrals, museums, historic churches, centuries-old monuments, and other irreplaceable cultural objects.

In April 1945, Soviet army troops were approaching German-occupied central Vienna. A white flag was hoisted by Austrian resistance fighters in the south tower of the twelfth-century St. Stephan's Cathedral in an effort to save the historic landmark, one of Austria's most significant cultural treasures. Upon seeing the white flag, the senior Nazi officer in the city ordered Captain Gerhard Klinkicht, the commander of a German artillery battery, to fire one hundred rounds directly into the cathedral, to foil the efforts of the resistance and assure the cathedral's destruction. Captain Klinkicht quickly determined that the cathedral was "out of range" of his guns and he would not order his battery to fire.

Long after the war, in April 1997, Klinkicht, by then eighty-seven years old, was present when Archbishop Christoph Schönborn unveiled a plaque at the base of the south tower of St. Stephan's Cathedral, honoring Klinkicht for his refusal to obey the unlawful order to destroy one of Austria's most significant cultural objects.[10]

After World War II there were military tribunal convictions based on 1907 Hague Regulation IV for the destruction of cultural objects.[11] In the judgment of the Nuremberg

---

[6] L. Oppenheim, *International Law: A Treatise.* Vol. II. *Disputes, War and Neutrality,* 7th ed., H. Lauterpacht, ed. (London: Longman, 1952), para. 158, at 421.

[7] Maj-Gen. A. V. P. Rogers, *Law on the Battlefield,* 2d ed. (Manchester: Juris Publishing, 2004), 136.

[8] Roger O'Keefe, *The Protection of Cultural Property in Armed Conflict* (Cambridge: Cambridge University Press, 2006), 74.

[9] Statute of the International Criminal Tribunal for the former Yugoslavia, Art. 8(2) (b) (ix) – Intentionally directing attacks against buildings dedicated to religion, education, art, science or charitable purposes, historic monuments, hospitals and places where the sick and wounded are collected, provided they are not military objectives; and Art. 8(2) (e) (iv), employing the same title.

[10] One account of the wartime event is available at: http://www.vienna.cc/english/stephansdom.htm

[11] For example, *Trial of Karl Lingenfelder,* French Permanent Military Tribunal at Metz (March 11, 1947), U.N. War Crimes Commission, *Law Reports of Trials of War Criminals,* Vol. IX (London: H. M. Stationery Office, 1949), 67–8. In occupied France, the accused, acting on the order of a German official, used four horses to pull down a city's monument to local World War I dead and destroyed marble

International Military Tribunal, the tribunal held, in regard to Alfred Rosenberg, the Nazi Party's ideologist, that "Rosenberg is responsible for a system of organized plunder ... throughout the invaded countries of Europe. ... He organized and directed the '*Einsatzstab* Rosenberg,' which plundered museums and libraries, confiscated art treasures and collections."[12] Rosenberg was sentenced to death for having plundered on a grand scale, particularly art objects.

In 1949, with the recent war's well-publicized Nazi theft of European public and private art and cultural objects, an initiative that had first been advanced by the Netherlands prior to the war led to the United Nations' drafting preliminary articles that were considered by fifty-six states. "The main advantage of having special rules for cultural property is in making attacking commanders more aware of the existence of cultural property."[13] Today the 1954 Hague Cultural Convention, written before the 1949 Geneva Conventions and before the 1977 Additional Protocols, has been ratified by most of the world's states, with new ratifiers of the basic convention continually being added. The United States ratified the basic convention in September 2008.

18.2 The 1954 Hague Convention for Protection of Cultural Property

"The Convention is the first comprehensive international agreement for the protection of cultural property."[14] It consists of the convention itself, with forty articles. There also are Regulations for the Execution of the Convention appended to the convention. Also part of the convention are the 1954 First Protocol (fifteen articles) and 1999 Second Protocol (forty-four articles).

The 1954 Hague Convention's definition of cultural property, in Article 1.(a), is admirably broad, "yet so vague that it is clear some measures of dissemination to inform the military ... will be absolutely vital."[15]:

> Movable or immovable property of great importance to the cultural heritage of every people, such as monuments of architecture, art or history, whether religious or secular, archaeological sites; groups of buildings which, as a whole, are of historical or artistic interest; works of art; manuscripts, books and other objects of artistic, historical or archaeological interest; as well as scientific collections and important collections of books or archives or of reproductions of the property defined above.

No code or convention can anticipate every eventuality, but vague words and terms like "important," "great importance," and "artistic" are not the 1954 Hague Convention's only terms in need of clarification for those who are expected to apply it. In fact, two

---

tablets bearing their names. The tribunal admitted evidence of extenuating circumstances and sentenced him to one year's confinement.

[12] Judgment, Trial of the Major War Criminals before the International Military Tribunal (1945–1946), in Leon Friedman, ed., *The Law of War: A Documentary History*, Vol. II (New York: Random House, 1972), 922, 981.

[13] United Kingdom Ministry of Defence, *The Manual of the Law of Armed Conflict* (Oxford: Oxford University Press, 2004), para. 5.23.3, at 71.

[14] Adam Roberts and Richard Guelff, *Documents on the Laws of War*, 3d ed. (Oxford: Oxford University Press, 2000), 371.

[15] Leslie C. Green, *Essays on the Modern Law of War*, 2d ed. (New York: Transnational, 1999), 235.

somewhat repetitive provisions, Articles 7[16] and 25,[17] address the required dissemination to the armed forces of the convention's protections.

The 1954 Hague Convention for Protection of Cultural Property, which originally applied only in international armed conflicts, does not include in its coverage charitable or educational institutions that are not themselves of historical interest. Nor does it protect items of geographic "natural heritage," as it does manmade landmarks. Unless a church is of historical or special cultural significance, it is not protected by the convention. There is no provision addressing incidental damage, indicating that incidental damage to protected objects does not constitute a breach. The 1954 convention does prohibit reprisals against protected objects. Unsurprisingly, any protected object that abuses its protected status loses that status.[18] The convention also applies in periods of belligerent occupation. Notably for targeting purposes, in requiring that protected cultural objects be separated from "any important military objective" the convention includes broadcasting stations, along with airports and seaports, as military objectives (Article 8.1. (a)).

A controversial issue was the convention's use of the terms "imperative military necessity" (Article 4.2) and "unavoidable military necessity" (Article 11.2). The convention's basic protection of cultural property can be waived, that is, ignored, "in cases where military necessity imperatively requires."[19] No description or definition of imperative military necessity is offered, however. The convention's *special* protection, described in Article 8.1, can be waived in "exceptional cases of unavoidable military necessity."[20] Again, no description or definition of the term "unavoidable military necessity" is offered.

"The inclusion of the notion of military necessity was the result of fierce negotiations at the Diplomatic Conference that drew up the 1954 Convention."[21] The undefined conditions for invoking military necessity, so often the offending military commander's rote defense, made the scope for invoking the waiver very large and left its definition to the state applying the waiver. At the diplomatic conference, some state representatives wanted to exclude military necessity altogether, arguing that its inclusion lessens protections and invites abuse. Others insisted it remain as a commander's protection in the

---

[16] Art. 7. "The High Contracting Parties undertake to introduce in time of peace into their military regulations or instructions such provisions as may ensure observance of the present Convention, and to foster in the members of their armed forces a spirit for the culture and cultural property of all peoples. The High Contracting Parties undertake to plan or establish in peacetime, within their armed forces, services or specialist personnel whose purposes will be to secure respect for cultural property and to co-operate with civilian authorities responsible for safeguarding it."

[17] Art. 25. "The High Contracting Parties undertake, in time of peace as in time of armed conflict, to disseminate the text of the present Convention and the Regulations for its execution as widely as possible in their respective countries. They undertake, in particular, to include the study thereof in their programs of military and, if possible, civilian training."

[18] Arts. 8.1. (b), and 11; First Protocol Arts. 8.1 (b), and 11; and Second Protocol, Art. 13.

[19] Art. 4.2. "The obligations mentioned in paragraph 1 of the present Article [respect for cultural property] may be waived only in cases where military necessity imperatively requires such a waiver."

[20] Art. 11.2. "Apart from the case provided for in paragraph 1 of the present Article, immunity shall be withdrawn from cultural property under special protection only in exceptional cases of unavoidable military necessity, and only for such time as that necessity continues. Such necessity can be established only by the officer commanding a force the equivalent of a division in size or larger. Whenever circumstances permit, the opposing Party shall be notified, a reasonable time in advance, of the decision to withdraw immunity."

[21] Jan Hladík, "The 1954 Hague Convention for the Protection of Cultural Property in the Event of Armed Conflict and the Notion of Military Necessity," 835 *Int'l Rev. of the Red Cross* (Sept. 1999), 621.

event of militarily unavoidable consequences. The issue was finally addressed, if not resolved, to the satisfaction of all parties, in the 1999 Second Protocol. In two articles, 6 and 13, the Second Protocol specifies criteria for the invocation of military necessity. The need for workable criteria was emphasized in 1991, in the Bosnia-Herzegovina conflict in the former Yugoslavia. In Dubrovnik and Mostar, cultural objects that reflected the area's rich cultural and religious heritage were destroyed or damaged, purposely targeted as an aspect of ethnic cleansing. Military necessity was the rationalization. "If imperative requirements of military necessity can trump the protection of cultural property, no real progress has been achieved since the days of the 'as far as possible' exhortation, since the attacking force is prone to regard almost any military necessity as 'imperative'."[22] Several ICTY cases demonstrate, however, that the prohibition against attacking cultural objects has real teeth. (See Cases and Materials, this chapter.)

"The [1954 convention] affords two levels of protection – general protection and special protection. General protection applies to all cultural property while special protection applies to a subset thereof."[23] The convention calls for ratifying states to prepare in peacetime for Article 8's "special protection" of cultural property that will be, or has already been, deposited in designated places of refuge in time of armed conflict, be it international or noninternational, and in periods of belligerent occupation. There are three categories of specially protected objects: first, refuges that shelter cultural property, such as the Alt-Aussee refuge – an unused salt mine near Steinberg, Upper Austria;[24] second, centers containing monuments, such as Vatican City, the sole registered center of the second category; and third, immovable cultural property of great importance is protected. No such property has been registered.

Prior to an armed conflict, immovable protected cultural property (e.g., cathedrals, palaces, mosques, national libraries) is to be marked with a distinctive emblem – a five-sided shieldlike figure with alternating blue and white segments.[25] The placement of the emblem and its visibility are left to the convention's state parties. In the 1991 armed conflict in Croatia, the emblem was painted on boards approximately two meters high that were placed on hundreds of protected monuments and institutions. More often, the emblem is several inches high, placed in prominent positions on protected buildings and other immovables. Special protection may be granted immovable cultural property and places of refuge and, in limited numbers, movable cultural property that is distanced from vulnerable military objects, such as airports and arms-manufacturing plants. To secure this special protection, a cultural object must be described and entered in the International Register of Cultural Property under Special Protection. Entries may be

---

[22] Yoram Dinstein, *The Conduct of Hostilities under the Law of International Armed Conflict*, 1st ed. (Cambridge: Cambridge University Press, 2004), 158. Professor Dinstein provides excellent coverage of the convention and its protocols at 157–66 of the first edition of his book, and 170–85 of the second edition, as does General Rogers in, *Law on the Battlefield*, supra, note 7, at 139–56.

[23] Sandesh Sivakumaran, *The Law of Non-International Armed Conflict* (Oxford: Oxford University Press, 2012), 377.

[24] The International Register of Cultural Property under Special Protection, available online.

[25] Art. 16 of the convention describes the distinctive emblem in terms that make a mental image difficult to capture: "[A] shield, pointed below, per saltire blue and white (a shield consisting of a royal-blue square, one of the angles of which forms the point of the shield, and of a royal-blue triangle above the square, the space on either side being taken up by a white triangle)."

made during an armed conflict and during belligerent occupation, as well. Misuse of protection will subject the object to attack.

Entry in the International Register initiates the convention's special protection. The public announcement of an object's registration is thought to reduce the probability of accidental damage or destruction of the object. Less trusting individuals suggest that registration may increase the risk of deliberate destruction.

The legal significance of special protection registration is debatable, for it adds little to the protection of cultural objects already afforded by customary international law. Professor Dinstein, with the military necessity exception in mind, writes: "The stark fact is that the status of special protection does not guarantee to any cultural property – not even of the greatest importance – genuine immunity from attack and destruction. ... It must be acknowledged that the construct of special protection is only marginally more satisfactory than that of general protection."[26] That viewpoint may account for the few registrations that have been made. Several ratifying States have registered several individual refuge sites and objects; only the Vatican has registered a center containing monuments.

The Register of Cultural Property is prepared and maintained by the sponsor of the 1954 Hague Convention, the director general of UNESCO, who accepts and records applications for special protection under the convention. "Of course, effective protection of cultural property involves much more than compliance with the treaty obligations. It requires comprehensive listing of property, coordination between ministries, local government and the armed forces, plans for protection of cultural property in peacetime including establishing refuges, duplicating important archives and the protection of electronic data."[27] Such comprehensive preparation has not yet generally occurred.

Why is UNESCO the sponsoring agency, and not the International Committee of the Red Cross (ICRC)? Because the ICRC deals with the protection of the *victims* of armed conflict. Objects, including cultural objects, are outside the ICRC's mandate.

The United States initially did not ratify the 1954 convention because it objected to the special protection scheme. The United States feared that an enemy could make too liberal use of special protection, limiting legitimate targeting options. Even with this fear, the United States "regards its provisions as relevant to the targeting process: 'United States policy and the conduct of operations are entirely consistent with the Convention's provisions. In large measure, the practices required by the Convention to protect cultural property were based upon the practices of US military forces during World War II.'"[28] In the 1991 Gulf War, the United States was at pains to comply with the tenets of the 1954 Hague Convention:

> Planners were aware ... that Iraq has a rich cultural and religious heritage dating back several thousand years. Within its borders are sacred religious areas and literally thousands of archaeological sites that trace the evolution of modern civilization.

---

[26] Dinstein, *Conduct of Hostilities under the Law of International Armed Conflict*, 1st ed., supra, note 22, at 160. Footnote omitted.

[27] Rogers, *Law on the Battlefield*, supra, note 7, at 146–7.

[28] Maj. Marie Anderson and Emily Zukauskas, eds., *Operational Law Handbook*, 2008 (Charlottesville, VA: Judge Advocate General's Legal Center and School, 2008), 15, citing a message from the president of the United States transmitting the convention's First Protocol to the 106th Congress for advice and consent, Jan. 6, 1999.

Targeting policies, therefore, scrupulously avoided damage to mosques, religious shrines, and archaeological sites. ... Target intelligence analysts ... produced a joint no-fire target list. This list was a compilation of historical, archaeological, economic, religious and politically sensitive installations in Iraq and Kuwait that could not be targeted.[29]

The initial 1958 U.S. decision not to ratify has been reversed, perhaps in light of the disturbing deliberate targeting of cultural property in the former Yugoslavia.[30] The 1954 convention was ratified by the United States in 2009. American armed forces needed an awareness of the convention if for no other reason than that many European NATO allies are state parties. The United States has concluded agreements with at least fourteen foreign states party to the 1970 UNESCO Convention on the Means of Prohibiting and Preventing the Illicit Import, Export and Transfer of Ownership of Cultural Property. The agreements combat the smuggling of archaeological and ethnological materials that are illegally taken from their countries of origin.[31]

The issues with which the 1954 convention is concerned are repeated, in part, in 1977 Additional Protocol I, Article 53, and in Additional Protocol II, Article 16. (This Chapter 18.3.)

18.2.1 First Protocol to the 1954 Cultural Property Convention

The First Protocol is unusual in that its subject is not the destruction of objects, but their preservation. It relates to the ancient practice of occupying armies' carrying away the cultural objects of occupied territory. Examples range from Sweden's 1655–60 occupation of the Polish-Lithuanian Commonwealth, which left the commonwealth in ruins; to Napoleon's captured campaign spoils taken to Paris; to World War II Nazi looting of territories occupied by the Wehrmacht.

During the formation of the basic convention, conferees could not agree on issues concerning the possible export and sale of cultural property from occupied territory during periods of armed conflict. The 1954 First Protocol, which was adopted on the same date as the basic convention, addresses these issues. It "sets forth in some detail provisions on the prevention of the export of cultural property from occupied territory, and the safeguarding and return of any such property which has been exported. In addition, in cases where cultural property has been deposited in third states to protect it from the dangers of an armed conflict, the Protocol provides for the return of such property."[32] A weakness of the protocol is that it maintains the basic convention's military necessity escape provision. Article 53:

Without prejudice to the provisions of the [1954 convention], and of other relevant international instruments, it is prohibited:

---

[29] Dept. of Defense, *Conduct of the Persian Gulf War* (Washington, DC: GPO, 1992), 100.

[30] Theodor Meron, "The Time Has Come for the United States to Ratify Geneva Protocol I," in *War Crimes Law Comes of Age: Essays* (Oxford: Oxford University Press, 1998), 184. Also see: Aryeh Neier, *War Crimes* (New York: Times Books, 1998), 157–61, regarding the intentional targeting of cultural objects in the former Yugoslavia.

[31] John R. Crook, ed., "Contemporary Practice of the United States Relating to International Law," 106–2 *AJIL* (April 2012), 360, 386.

[32] Roberts and Guelff, *Documents on the Laws of War*, supra, note 14, at 396.

(a) to commit any acts of hostility directed against the historic monuments, works of art or places of worship which constitute the cultural or spiritual heritage of peoples;

(b) to use such objects in support of the military effort.

The phrase "without prejudice to" confirms the protocol's adherence, and the basic convention's continued adherence, to the inclusion of military necessity.

To date, more than a hundred states have ratified the First Protocol. The United States has neither signed nor ratified, fearing that the protocol could be interpreted to impose upon peacekeeping forces an obligation to prevent the unlawful export of cultural property from occupied territory. Peacekeeping forces, which often involve U.S. military units, lack the resources of an occupying force that might be used to prevent such exports. The Department of Defense has nevertheless recommended ratification of the First Protocol.

18.2.2 *Second Protocol to the 1954 Cultural Property Convention*

The 1999 Second Protocol is a result of the failure of the basic convention to protect cultural property effectively in practice, particularly during the 1980–8 Iran–Iraq armed conflict. "Iran requested a review of UNESCO's role in ensuring proper application of the 1954 Convention. The upshot was a series of studies, expert meetings, and eventually the 1999 diplomatic conference that adopted the Second Protocol."[33] The protocol, only five operational articles in length, is intended to clarify the basic convention's meaning of the term "military necessity" and to align the protection of cultural objects with similar protections in the 1977 Additional Protocols.

The Second Protocol also clarifies that the convention and protocols are applicable in non-international, as well as international armed conflicts. As did the earlier 1949 Geneva Conventions, Article 15.2 of the Second Protocol requires ratifying parties to establish criminal punishments in their domestic law for five specific violations listed in Article 15.1. Three of the five violations are grave breaches of either the Geneva Conventions or Additional Protocol I; the other two are war crimes under the Rome Statute of the International Criminal Court.[34]

The Second Protocol creates a new category of protection, "**enhanced protection**," which is in addition to the basic Convention's "special protection." Three conditions must be met for enhanced protection:

(a) it [the protected object] is cultural heritage of the greatest importance for humanity;

(b) it is protected by adequate domestic legal and administrative measures recognizing its exceptional cultural and historic value and ensuring the highest level of protection;

---

[33] Ronald J. Bettauer, *Book Review* (reviewing Roger O'Keefe, The Protection of Cultural Property in Armed Conflict (Cambridge: Cambridge University Press, 2006)), 102–1 AJIL 220,223.

[34] The "serious violations" listed in Art. 15.1 are (1) making cultural property under enhanced protection the object of attack; (2) using cultural property under enhanced protection or its immediate surroundings in support of military action; (3) extensive destruction or appropriation of protected cultural property; (4) making protected cultural property the object of attack; and (5) theft, pillage or misappropriation of, or acts of vandalism directed against protected cultural property.

(c) it is not used for military purposes or to shield military sites and a declaration has been made by the Party which has control over the cultural property, confirming that it will not be so used.[35]

Confusingly, eligible property may be eligible for both special and enhanced protection. In such cases, only the provisions of enhanced protection apply.

Second Protocol Article 6 again allows for the waiver of enhanced protection of cultural objects in limited conditions that involve "imperative military necessity," the term from the basic convention. The conditions for waiver, that is, for allowing the attack or targeting of a protected object, are that the object or property has been made into a military objective, that there is no feasible alternative to obtaining a military advantage regarding the object or property other than a hostile act, and that the decision to waive the protection must be made, unless circumstances dictate otherwise, by the commander of a battalion or larger unit, and an effective advance warning must be given if circumstances permit. (There is no warning requirement in the basic convention.) The room for interpretation of the Second Protocol's waiver is apparent, yet it is probably as detailed an effort to narrow military necessity as can be expected.

An example of the Second Protocol's waiver of enhanced protection that would permit destruction or military use of cultural property would be an old and historic bridge that is the sole river crossing for an approaching military force.[36] Despite its being a recognized cultural object, if it is used to block an enemy crossing – perhaps with gun emplacements at each end of the bridge – and there is no alternate crossing site within a feasible distance, it is being used for military purposes, it loses its protection, and it may be attacked. Another exception might be a centuries-old monastery overlooking a broad valley through which an attacking army is approaching. There is no other reasonably available avenue of advance for a unit of that size. Enemy artillery spotters, with a commanding overview of the approaching force, are wrongfully situated throughout the monastery. Radio and air-dropped-leaflet warnings to the enemy spotters to withdraw have been ignored. The cultural property has been made a military objective and there is no feasible alternative to removing the threat to the advancing army other than attacking the monastery. In accordance with the Second Convention's terms, warning has been given, and we will presume that the situation constitutes an imperative military necessity, in which case the commander of the advancing army may order the bombing of the monastery. The lawful destruction of the priceless religious cultural object follows. This description, of course, is the World War II Monte Cassino case, except that the intelligence reports relied upon by Lieutenant-General Freyberg, who ordered the attack, were mistaken. There were no enemy personnel in or close to the abbey.

> This rule [provision for waiver of protection] should not be confused with the prohibition on attacking cultural property contained in Article 53 (1) of Additional Protocol I and Article 16 of Additional Protocol II, which do not provide for a waiver in case of imperative military necessity. ... These articles were meant to cover only a limited amount of very important cultural property ... while the scope of the Hague Convention is broader and covers property which forms part of the cultural heritage of

---

[35] 1999 Second Protocol to the Hague Convention of 1954, Art. 10.
[36] Rogers, *Law on the Battlefield*, supra, note 7, at 145.

"every people". The property covered by the Additional Protocols must be of such importance that it will be recognized by everyone, even without being marked.[37]

Such protected but unmarked objects would be the pyramids, the Eiffel Tower, the Washington Monument, and similarly significant and universally recognized objects.

So far, the Second Protocol is ratified by far fewer than a hundred states. The United States has neither signed nor ratified.

18.3 Protected Cultural Property in the 1977 Additional Protocols

Going beyond the 1954 Hague Convention, Articles 50–53 of 1977 Additional Protocol I are a significant advance in the protection of cultural property. They codify that only military objectives may be attacked, they define military objects and civilian objects, they address proportionality, and they prohibit reprisals against cultural property.

Article 53(a) forbids "acts of hostility" directed against cultural objects and places of worship, a range of protection initially appearing to be narrower than that of the 1954 Hague Convention. But Article 53(a)'s protected cultural objects include "historic monuments, works of art or places of worship which constitute the cultural or spiritual heritage of peoples." The *Commentary* confirms, "Despite this difference in terminology, the basic idea is the same,"[38] explaining that "cultural" applies to historic monuments and works of art, and "spiritual" also applies to places of worship.

As in the 1954 Hague Convention, not all places of worship are protected; those having "only a local renown or sanctity which does not extend to the whole nation"[39] are outside the protection of both the convention and the protocol. That language does not suggest that modest neighborhood places of worship are without protection: In addition to Additional Protocol I, Articles 53 and 85, 1907 Hague Regulation IV, Article 27 continues to protect "buildings dedicated to religion," as well as those dedicated to "art, science, or charitable purposes, historic monuments, [and] hospitals." The 1954 convention simply means to add an expanded layer of protections to churches of cultural significance. The *Commentary* further points out that "the article prohibits not only substantial detrimental effect, but all acts directed against the protected objects. For a violation of the article to take place it is therefore not necessary for there to be any damage."[40] Notably, unlike in the 1954 convention, there is no provision for waiver of protection in Article 53, and no provision for derogation for reason of military necessity. Of course, should the enemy make improper use of the protected cultural object, it loses its protection.

In a single difficult-to-follow sentence, Additional Protocol I, Article 85.4(d) complements Article 53(a). It makes "clearly-recognized historic monuments, works of art or places of worship which constitute the cultural or spiritual heritage of peoples and to which special protection has been given ... for example, within the framework of a competent international organization, the object of attack, causing as a result extensive destruction thereof" a war crime and a grave breach. The article's reference to "a competent international organization" presumably refers to the UNESCO trustees

---

[37] Jean-Marie Henckaerts and Louise Doswald-Beck, eds., *Customary International Humanitarian Law.* Vol. I. *Rules* (Cambridge: Cambridge University Press, 2005), Rule 38, at 130.

[38] Yves Sandoz, Christophe Swinarski, and Bruno Zimmermann, eds., *Commentary on the Additional Protocols* (Geneva: ICRC, 1987), para. 2064, at 646.

[39] Id., para. 2067, at 647.   [40] Id.

of the 1954 convention. To constitute a grave breach, an attack on a protected object must be committed willfully, the object must not have been used in the military effort, the object must not have been located in the immediate vicinity of a military objective, and the attack must cause extensive destruction of the object. Additionally, the object must have been given special protection within the framework of a competent international organization (i.e., UNESCO, or the 1972 Convention Concerning the Protection of the World Cultural and Natural Heritage).[41]

Whereas the prohibition on attacking places of worship is customary international law, the 1977 Additional Protocols are not in their entirety customary law – although "the United States will consider itself legally bound by the rules contained in Protocol I . . . to the extent that they reflect customary international law, either now or as it may develop in the future."[42]

Article 85.4(d), difficult to follow as it may be, is clearly intended to link with the provisions of Article 53 and lend specific elements of behavior to Article 53's general wording, but "despite the undoubtedly good intentions of the drafters . . . one cannot but ask oneself whether it [Article 85.4] really adds much of substance to the grave breach consisting of 'the extensive destruction and appropriation of protected property . . . ' as covered by Article 147 [of 1949 Geneva Convention IV]."[43]

As in Article 53(a), there is no provision for waiver of protection, no provision for derogation for reason of military necessity, in Article 85.4.

For noninternational armed conflicts, Additional Protocol II, Article 16, repeats verbatim the substantive wording of Additional Protocol I's Article 53.

18.4 Summary

The inviolate nature of cultural property in armed conflict has been recognized for centuries. Today, the seriousness of the combatant's obligations in relation to cultural objects is illustrated not only by its specification in 1907 Hague Regulation IV, the 1954 Hague Cultural Property Convention, and 1977 Additional Protocols I and II, but by its inclusion as a war crime in international and noninternational armed conflicts in the Rome Statute of the International Criminal Court. A review of ICTY's prosecutions for the destruction of cultural property provides further evidence of the proscription. The 1954 Cultural Property Convention is not itself customary law, but the obligation of states both to protect cultural objects by not attacking them and not to endanger them by making military use of them clearly is customary law.[44]

The widely ratified 1954 Hague Cultural Convention continues to add state parties but, despite its numerous ratifications, its provisions have not been widely embraced. The

---

[41] The 1972 Convention Concerning the Protection of World Cultural and Natural Heritage is a second UNESCO treaty by which 878 properties and objects located in 145 states are protected. The convention has 186 state parties, including the United States.

[42] Mike Matheson, "Additional Protocol I as Expression of Customary International Law," 2–2 *Am. U. J. Int'l L. & Policy* (Fall 1987), 415, 425.

[43] Julian J. E. Schutte, "The System of Repression of Breaches of Additional Protocol I," in, Astrid J. M. Delissen and Gerard J. Tanja, eds., *Humanitarian Law of Armed Conflict Challenges Ahead* (Dordrecht: Martinus Nijhoff, 1991), 177, 195.

[44] Henckaerts and Doswald-Beck, *Customary International Humanitarian Law*, supra, note 37, Rule 38, at 129.

convention is burdened with vague terms and military necessity escape clauses. One could question whether it really adds significant protections to those already applicable in customary law. "State adherence to the marking requirement has been limited. U.S. practice has been to rely on its intelligence collection to identify such objects in order to avoid attacking or damaging them."[45] Recall, however, that marking is not "a precondition for the protection of cultural property. It is a method of implementing that protection."[46] The convention remains a valuable step toward the protection of those buildings and objects that constitute the culture and history of territories in which conflicts are fought (not necessarily for the specifics of the convention). The awareness of cultural property that the convention raises and the conduct it seeks to require and prohibit are valuable. Its reinforcement by Additional Protocol I should make combatants, particularly commanders, carefully consider targeting choices.

After the conflict in the former Yugoslavia, and subsequent ICTY prosecutions for targeting cultural property, it is reasonable to anticipate a greater awareness of the protections that such objects are provided. Violations that might have been overlooked in past conflicts, especially if committed by officers of the losing side, are ever more likely to result in war crime charges.

Although UNESCO is the Convention's Sponsor and overseeing body, the protection of cultural property is the concern of all war fighters. "Clearly ... although the protection of cultural objects for obvious reasons will never become a core activity of the Red Cross and Red Crescent world, it has not lost sight of either."[47]

CASES AND MATERIALS

PROPERTY VERSUS COMBATANT LIVES

Soldiers or property? Mosques or Marines? Every combat commander has two concerns foremost in her mind: her mission and her subordinates. Successful completion of the assigned mission is always the leader's first duty, the first consideration. The well-being and protection of subordinates are always the commander's next concern. Is it reasonable to expect war fighters to give consideration to cultural objects when their consideration in combat might put their men's lives at risk? Is Professor L. C. Green correct when he says, "Cynics might be excused if they regard such provisions [requiring combatants to protect cultural property] as somewhat idealist and completely out of tune with the realities of active warfare"?[48]

---

[45] Anderson and Zukauskas, eds., *Operational Law Handbook*, 2008, supra, note 28, at 22.

[46] ICRC, *Protection of Cultural Property in the Event of Armed Conflict: Report on the Meeting of Experts* (Geneva: ICRC, 2002), 126.

[47] Frits Kalshoven, *Reflections on the Law of War: Collected Essays* (Leiden: Martinus Nijhoff, 2007), 429.

[48] Green, *Essays on the Modern Law of War*, supra, note 15, at 237.

The historian T. R. Fehrenbach, who served as an army infantry officer in both World War II and Korea, describes U.S. Marines fighting their way through Korean villages in September 1950, early in the U.S.–Korean conflict:

> The American way of street and town fighting did not resemble that of other armies. To Americans, flesh and blood and lives have always been more precious than sticks and stones, however assembled. An American commander, faced with taking the Louvre from a defending enemy, unquestionably would blow it apart or burn it down without hesitation if such would save the life of one of his men. And he would be acting with complete accord with American ideals and ethics in doing so. Already, in the Korean War, American units were proceeding to destroy utterly enemy-held towns and villages rather than engage in the costly business of reducing them block by block with men and bayonets, as did European armies. If bombing and artillery would save lives, even though they destroyed sites of beauty and history, saving lives obviously had preference. And already foreign observers with the United States Army ... were beginning to criticize such tactics.[49]

In contrast to Fehrenbach's dark account of American military practice fifty years ago, is that of Sir Harold Nicholson, a noted World War II British author and politician:

> I am not among those who feel that religious sites are as such, of more importance than human lives, since religion is not concerned with material or temporal things; nor should I hesitate, were I a military commander, to reduce some purely historical building to rubble if I felt that by doing so I could gain a tactical advantage or diminish the danger to which my men were exposed. Works of major artistic value fall, however, into a completely different category. It is to my mind absolutely desirable that such works should be preserved from destruction, even if their preservation entails the sacrifice of human lives. I should assuredly be prepared to be shot against a wall if I were certain that by such a sacrifice I could preserve the Giotto frescoes; nor should I hesitate for an instant (were such a decision ever open to me) to save St. Mark's even if I were aware that by so doing I should bring death to my sons. I should know that in a hundred years from now it would matter not at all if I or my children had survived; whereas it would matter seriously and permanently if the Piazza at Venice had been reduced to dust and ashes. ... The irreplaceable is more important than the replaceable, and the loss of even the most valued human life is ultimately less disastrous than the loss of something which in no circumstances can ever be created again.[50]

Although Sir Harold might have found describing his own execution, or that of a son, more tolerable than the reality, these two excerpts illustrate the varied views of cultural property and its significance in armed conflict. Is it reasonable to expect combatants to risk – or lose – their lives for the sake of a cultural object. For the sake of property? Few commanders would respond affirmatively.

"Property or lives" is a false choice, however. If the enemy makes military use of cultural property, it loses its protection, just as any other protected property does. Upon encountering militarized cultural property, the commander must consider military necessity (a more attractive option to combatants under fire than critics of the convention might have appreciated) and proportionality in deciding whether the property should be

---

[49] T. R. Fehrenbach, *This Kind of War* (New York: MacMillan, 1963), 223–4.
[50] Cited in John Henry Merryman and Albert E. Law Elsen, *Ethics and the Visual Arts* (London: Kluwer Law International, 2002), 80–1.

attacked or, if tactically feasible, whether it should be bypassed and dealt with later, perhaps by means other than kinetic force.

If the tactical situation is different (say advancing troops unexpectedly come under fire from the enemy's state museum), there is no question that troops in contact with the enemy may lawfully exercise proportional self-defense. No convention expects a combatant to sacrifice himself unthinkingly just because an enemy threat emanates from a cathedral rather than a bunker. Combatants are expected to avoid targeting cathedrals, however, because an enemy threat *could* emanate from there.

PROSECUTOR V. JOKIĆ

IT-01–42-T (March 18, 2004), footnotes omitted

Introduction. *In late 1991, during the armed conflict in the former Yugoslavia, Vice-Admiral Miodrag Jokić, of the Yugoslav navy, commanded the Ninth Naval Sector. The charges against him involving the destruction of cultural objects stem from his exercise of that command. The following is extracted from the trial chamber's opinion following his plea of guilty, pursuant to a pretrial agreement.*

As a criminal trial forum with its own code of offenses, the ICTY looks to its statute when charging crimes. In this extract, the indictment's references to "Articles" are to the ICTY's statute.

21. According to the Parties, from 8 October 1991 through 31 December 1991, Miodrag Jokić, acting individually or in concert with others, conducted a military campaign, launched on 1 October 1991 and directed at the territory of the then Municipality of Dubrovnik ("Dubrovnik").

22. In the same period, during military operations directed at Srd Hill and the wider Dubrovnik Region, Yugoslav forces (JNA) under the command of Miodrag Jokić fired hundreds of shells which struck the Old Town of Dubrovnik (the "Old Town").

23. Miodrag Jokić was aware of the Old Town's status, in its entirety, as a United Nations Educational, Scientific and Cultural Organization ("UNESCO") World Cultural Heritage site pursuant to the 1972 Convention for the Protection of the World Cultural and Natural Heritage ("UNESCO World Heritage Convention"). He was further aware that a number of buildings in the Old Town and the towers of the Old Town's walls were marked with the symbols mandated by the 1954 Hague Convention on the Protection of Cultural Property in the Event of Armed Conflict ("1954 Hague Convention"). He was also aware of the presence of a substantial number of civilians in the Old Town on 6 December 1991.

24. The shelling of 6 December 1991 was preceded by military operations around the Old Town of Dubrovnik which had led to approximately three months of occupation of the areas surrounding the city. There was no investigation initiated by the JNA following the shelling of the Old Town in October and November 1991, nor were any disciplinary measures taken, to punish the violation of the standing JNA order to protect the Old Town of Dubrovnik.

26. On 6 December 1991, JNA forces under the command of, among others, Miodrag Jokić unlawfully shelled the Old Town. Notwithstanding the fact that the forces shelling the Old Town were under the *de jere* control of Miodrag Jokić, the Prosecution's expressed position is that the unlawful attack was "not ordered by Admiral Jokić". Miodrag Jokić told the Trial Chamber: "I was aware of my command responsibility for

the acts of my subordinates in combat and for the failings and mistakes in the exercise of command over troops."

27. As a result of the shelling, two civilians were killed ... and three civilians were wounded. ... Six buildings in the Old Town were destroyed in their entirety and many more buildings suffered damage. Institutions dedicated to religion, charity, education, and the arts and sciences, and historic monuments and works of art and science were damaged or destroyed.

42. Three of the crimes to which Miodrag Jokić has pleaded guilty entail violations of the duty incumbent upon soldiers to direct their operations only against military object-ives. In order to comply with this duty, the military must distinguish civilians from combatants and refrain from targeting the former. The other three crimes [charged against Jokić] entail violations of the duty to distinguish civilian objects from military objectives and not to protect protected objects.

45. Two crimes among those to which Miodrag Jokić has pleaded guilty – devastation not justified by military necessity and unlawful attack on civilian objects – are, in the present case, very serious crimes in view of the destruction that one day of shelling ravaged upon the Old Town and its long-lasting consequences. According to the Plea Agreement, six buildings in the Old Town were destroyed, and many more buildings suffered damage. "Hundreds, perhaps up to a thousand projectiles" hit the Old Town on 6 December 1991. ...

46. Another crime to which Miodrag Jokić pleaded guilty is the crime of destruction or wilful damage done to institutions dedicated to religion, charity, education, and the arts and sciences, and to historic monuments and works of art and science. This crime represents a violation of values especially protected by the international community.

47. Codification prohibiting the destruction of institutions of this type dates back to the beginning of the last century, with the Regulations annexed to the Hague Convention Respecting the Laws and Customs of War on Land (the "Hague Regulations") and the Hague Convention Concerning Bombardment by Naval Forces in Time of War of 18 October 1907.

48. The 1954 Hague Convention provides a more stringent protection for "cultural property", as defined in Article 1 of the Convention. The protection comprises duties of safeguard and respect of cultural property under "general protection."

49. The preamble to the UNESCO World Heritage Convention provides "that deterioration or disappearance of any item of the cultural or natural heritage *constitutes a harmful impoverishment of the heritage of all the nations of the world.*" The Old Town of Dubrovnik was put on the World Heritage List in 1975.

50. Additional Protocols I (Art. 53) and II (Art. 16) of 1977 to the Geneva Conventions of 1949 reiterate the obligation to protect cultural property and expand the scope of the prohibition by, *inter alia*, outlawing "any acts of hostility directed against the historic monuments, works of art or places of worship which constitute the cultural or spiritual heritage of peoples." According to the Additional Protocols, therefore, it is prohibited to direct attacks against this kind of protected property, whether or not the attacks result in actual damage. This immunity is clearly *additional* to the protection attached to civilian objects.

51. The whole of the Old Town of Dubrovnik was considered, at the time of the events contained in the indictment, an especially important part of the world cultural heritage. It was, among other things, an outstanding architectural ensemble illustrating a significant

stage in human history. The shelling attack on the Old Town was an attack not only against the history and heritage of the region, but also against the cultural heritage of humankind. Moreover, the Old Town was a "living city" . . . and the existence of its population was intimately intertwined with its ancient heritage. Residential buildings within the city also formed part of the World Cultural Heritage site, and were thus protected.

52. Restoration of buildings of this kind, when possible, can never return the buildings to their state prior to the attack because a certain amount of original, historically authentic, material will have been destroyed, thus affecting the inherent value of the buildings.

53. The Trial Chamber finds that, since it is a serious violation of international humanitarian law to attack civilian buildings, it is a crime of even greater seriousness to direct an attack on an especially protected site, such as the Old Town, constituted of civilian buildings and resulting in extensive destruction within the site. Moreover, the attack on the Old Town was particularly destructive. Damage was caused to more than 100 buildings, including various segments of the Old Town's walls, ranging from complete destruction to damage to non-structural parts. The unlawful attack on the Old Town must therefore be viewed as especially wrongful conduct.

55. The gravity of the crimes committed by the convicted person also stems from the degree of his participation in the crimes. Both parties have acknowledged Miodrag Jokić's awareness of the circumstances surrounding the offences, as well as his knowledge of the conduct of his subordinates from the early morning of 6 December 1991. The parties have agreed that Miodrag Jokić was aware of the protected status of the whole of the Old Town as a UNESCO World Cultural Heritage site.

56. Individual criminal responsibility attaches to persons who, in the terms of Article 7 (1) of the Statute, "planned, instigated, ordered, committed or otherwise aided and abetted in the planning, preparation or execution of a crime referred to in articles 2 to 5 of the present Statute." Moreover, according to Article 7 (3) of the [ICTY] Statute, "The fact that any of the acts referred to in articles 2 to 5 of the present Statute was committed by a subordinate does not relieve his superior of criminal responsibility if he knew or had reason to know that the subordinate was about to commit such acts or had done so and the superior failed to take the necessary and reasonable measures to prevent such acts or to punish the perpetrators thereof" ("superior responsibility").

Conclusion. *In deciding a sentence, the trial chamber takes into account the tribunal's considerations on sentencing but is also careful to consider the significance of the offenses in light of 1907 Hague Regulation IV (para. 47), the 1954 Convention on Cultural Property (para. 48), the UNESCO World Heritage Convention (paras. 49, 51, 55), and 1977 Additional Protocol I (para. 50).*

Vice Admiral Jokić was sentenced to seven years' confinement. That sentence was affirmed on appeal.

PROSECUTOR V. PRLIĆ, ET AL.

IT-04–74-T Second Amended Indictment (June 11, 2008)

Introduction. *The Prlić case, initiated in 2004, dragged on for years and still continues! The case was delayed by numerous motions by defense counsel for Prlić and his five coaccused. Prlić surrendered to the tribunal and made an initial court appearance in April 2004. The* *trial chamber's judgment for the six accused was not handed down until May 2013. Prlić was sentenced to twenty-five years' confinement. Three c-accused were sentenced to twenty years', one was sentenced to sixteen years', another to ten years' confinement. Their case is on appeal and the tribunal's appeals chamber decision is "expected" in June 2017*

The accused Prlić was a professor at Mostar University until appointed to various political positions in the Socialist Republic of Bosnia and Herzegovina (SRBiH). At the time of the events charged, 1993, he was the prime minister of the Croatian Republic of Herceg-Bosnia, the most powerful civilian official in that short-lived secessionist government.

The internationally unrecognized Croatian Republic of Herceg-Bosnia was formed in November 1991 by extremist secessionist elements of the Croatian Democratic Union of Bosnia and Herzegovina (HDZ-BiH). Its capital was Western Mostar. During its brief existence, Herceg-Bosnia engaged in ethnic cleansing, eventually leading to ICTY charges of war crimes and crimes against humanity. In January 1994, Herceg-Bosnia was declared illegal by the Constitutional Court of Bosnia-Herzegovina.

The accused Stojić was the civilian head of the Ministry of Defence. Praljak was a major general in the Croatian Army and assistant minister of defence of the Republic of Croatia. Petković was a Croatian army lieutenant colonel and chief of the Croatian Defence Council Main Staff.

From the ICTY's Second Amended Indictment:

17.1. (u) JADRANKO PRLIĆ facilitated supported, encouraged and participated in the joint crime enterprise and crimes charged in this indictment in planning, approving, preparing, supporting, ordering, and/or directing military operations and actions during and as part of which cultural and religious property such as mosques were destroyed, and private property of Bosnian Muslims was looted, burned or destroyed, without justification or military necessity, and failing to prevent, stop, punish or redress such destruction and looting.

17.2. (m) BRUNO STOJIĆ [indicted on the same charges and in the same terms as co-accused Prlić].

17.3. (k) SLOBODAN PRALJAK [indicted on the same charges and in the same terms as co-accused Prlić and Stojić].

17.4. (h) MILIVOJ PETKOVIĆ [indicted on the same charges and in the same terms as co-accused Prlić, Stojić and Praljak].

25. By a decision dated 8 April 1992, leaders and members of the joint criminal enterprise ... established the Croatian Defence Council (the "HVO"), as Herceg-Bosna's "supreme defence body," "to defend the sovereignty of the territories of the Croatian Community of Herceg-Bosna." On 15 May 1992, the HVO was likewise declared Herceg-Bosna's "supreme executive and administrative body," combining political, governmental and military powers. While the self-proclaimed political entity and its territory were referred to as "Herceg-Bosna," the government and armed forces of Herceg-Bosna were called the "Croatian Defence Council" or "HVO." The governmental and political leadership and administrative authorities of Herceg-Bosna and the HVO ... were in charge of, and worked closely with the Herceg-Bosna/HVO armed forces, special units, military and civilian police, security and intelligence services, paramilitaries, local defence forces and other persons acting under the supervision of or in coordination or association with such armed forces, police and other elements. ... While not every member of the HVO or the

HDZ-BiH was part of the joint criminal enterprise, Herceg-Bosna, the HVO and the HDZ-BiH were essential structures and instruments of the joint criminal enterprise.

39. (c) Appropriation and Destruction of Property: Herceg-Bosna/HVO authorities and soldiers forced Bosnian Muslims to abandon their homes and sign them over to the HVO. Money, cars and personal property were often taken or looted. Muslim dwellings and other buildings, including public buildings and services, were appropriated, destroyed or severely damaged, together with Muslim buildings, sites and institutions dedicated to religion or education, including mosques. Much of this destruction was meant to ensure that Muslims could not, or would not, return to their homes and communities. . . .

97. On or about 9 May 1993, Herceg-Bosna/HVO forces blew up the Baba Besir Mosque (also known as the Balinovac Mosque) in the Balinovac district, in West Mostar. On or about 11 May 1993, Herceg-Bosna/HVO forces dynamited the Hadži Ali-Beg Lafo Mosque (sometimes known as the Hadji Ali-Bey Lafa Mosque) at Pijesak, also in West Mostar.

116. As part of and in the course of the East Mostar siege, the Herceg-Bosna/HVO forces deliberately destroyed or significantly damaged the following mosques or religious properties in East Mostar: Sultan Selim Javuz Mosque (also known as the Mesdjid Sultan Selimov Javuza Mosque), Hadži Mehmed-Beg Karadjoz Mosque, Koski Mehmed-Paša Mosque, Nesuh Aga Vučjaković Mosque, Ćejvan Ćehaja Mosque, Hadži Ahmed Aga Lakišić Mosque, Roznamedžija Ibrahim Efendija Mosque, Ćosa Jahja Hodža Mosque (also known as the Džamiha Ćose Jahja Hodžina Mosque), the Hadži Kurto or Tabačica Mosque, and the Hadži Memija Cernica Mosque. On 9 November 1993, the Herceg-Bosna/HVO forces destroyed the Stari Most ("Old Bridge"), an international landmark that crossed the Neretva River between East and West Mostar.

Conclusion. *The charge of destroying the sixteenth-century Old Bridge, a world-known cultural object, is notable. It was destroyed on November 9, 1993, by the Croation Defence Council, allegedly at the order of Major General Slobadan Praljak. Until Prlić, there has been no prosecution for that international offense. The bridge was rebuilt and reopened in July 2004.*

The ICTY has transferred to domestic courts or concluded all but a few of its prosecutions. It remains to be seen how this long-delayed trial, and its appeal, will be resolved. Given the periods of pretrial and prejudgment confinement already served, releases on the basis of time served are a possibility for at least two of the co-accused.

PROSECUTOR V. STRUGAR

IT-01–42-T (January 31, 2005), footnotes omitted

Introduction. *The Strugar case interprets the requirements of the 1954 cultural property convention in terms of the ICTY statute, Article 3(d), which prohibits destruction or willful damage of cultural property. In this extract from the decision, the trial chamber compares provisions of the 1977 Additional Protocols with provisions of the 1954 Hague Convention in regard to breadth of protections and briefly discusses the nature of the protection enjoyed by cultural property and the convention's waiver provisions.*

2. Law on Destruction or Wilful Damage of Cultural Property (Count 6)

298. Count 6 of the Indictment charges the Accused with destruction or wilful damage done to institutions dedicated to religion, charity and education, the arts and sciences, historic monuments and works of art and science, punishable under Article 3 (d) of the Statute.

299. Article 3 (d) of the Statute reads:

The International Tribunal shall have the power to prosecute persons violating the laws or customs of war. Such violations shall include, but not be limited to:

. . .

(d) seizure of, destruction or wilful damage done to institutions dedicated to religion, charity and education, the arts and sciences, historic monuments and works of art and science;

300. This provision has been interpreted in several cases before the Tribunal to date. The *Blašić* Trial Chamber adopted the following definition:

The damage or destruction must have been committed intentionally to institutions which may clearly be identified as dedicated to religion or education and which were not being used for military purposes at the time of the acts. In addition, the institutions must not have been in the immediate vicinity of military objectives.

302. Further, the *Kordić* Trial Judgment held that while this offence overlaps to a certain extent with the offence of unlawful attacks on civilian objects, when the acts in question are directed against cultural heritage, the provisions of Article 3 (d) is *lex specialis*.

307. The Hague Convention of 1954 protects property "of great importance to the cultural heritage of every people." The Additional Protocols refer to "historic monuments, works of art or places of worship which constitute the cultural or spiritual heritage of peoples. The *Kordić* Appeals Judgment … stated that despite this difference in terminology, the basic idea [underlying the two provisions] is the same. Whether there may be precise differences is not an issue raised by the facts of this case. The Chamber will limit its discussion to property protected by the above instruments (hereinafter "cultural property").

309. The Hague Regulations of 1907 make the protection of cultural property dependent on whether such property was used for military purposes. The Hague Convention of 1954 provides for an obligation to respect cultural property. This obligation has two explicit limbs, *viz.* to refrain "from any use of the property and its immediate surroundings … for purposes which are likely to expose it to destruction or damage in the event of armed conflict", and, to refrain "from any act of hostility directed against such property." The Convention provides for a waiver of these obligations, however, but only when "military necessity imperatively requires such a waiver." The Additional Protocols prohibit the use of cultural property in support of military efforts, but make no explicit provision for the consequences of such a use, *i.e.* whether it affords a justification for acts of hostility against such property. Further, the Additional Protocols prohibit acts of hostility against cultural property, without any explicit reference to military necessity. However, the relevant provisions of both Additional Protocols are expressed to be "[w]ithout prejudice to" the provisions of the Hague Convention of

1954. This suggests that in these respects, the Additional Protocols may not have affected the waiver provision of the Hague Convention of 1954 in cases where military necessity imperatively requires waiver. In this present case, no military necessity arises on the facts in respect of the shelling of the Old Town, so that this question need not be further considered. For the same reason, no consideration is necessary to the question of what distinction is intended (if any) by the word "imperatively" in the context of military necessity in Article 4, paragraph 2 of the Hague Convention of 1954.

310. Nevertheless, the established jurisprudence of the Tribunal confirming the "military purposes" exception which is consistent with the exceptions recognised by the Hague Regulations of 1907 and the Additional Protocols, persuades the Chamber that the protection accorded to cultural property is lost where such property is used for military purposes. Further, with regard to the differences between the *Blaškić* and *Naletilić* Trial Judgments noted above (regarding the use of the immediate surroundings of cultural property for military purposes), and leaving aside any implication of the issue of imperative military necessity, the preferable view appears to be that it is the use of cultural property and not its location that determines whether and when the cultural property would lose its protection. Therefore ... the Chamber considers that the special protection awarded to cultural property itself may not be lost simply because of military activities or military installations in the immediate vicinity of the cultural property. In such a case, however, the practical result may be that it cannot be established that the acts which caused destruction of or damage to cultural property were "directed against" that cultural property, rather than the military installation or use in its immediate vicinity.

320. The Chamber also observes that among those buildings which were damaged in the [6 December 1991 JNA Dubrovnik] attack, were monasteries, churches, a mosque, a synagogue and palaces. Among other buildings affected were residential blocks, public places and shops; damage to these alone would have entailed grave consequences for the residents or the owners, *i.e.* their homes and businesses suffered substantial damage.

326. ... The Chamber finds that the Old Town sustained damage on a large scale as a result of the 6 December 1991 JNA attack. In this regard, the Chamber has considered the following factors: that 52 individually identifiable buildings and structures were destroyed or damaged; that the damaged or destroyed buildings and structures were located throughout the Old Town ... and finally, that overall the damage varied from totally destroyed, i.e. burned out, buildings to more minor damage to parts of buildings and structures.

327. ... Military necessity can, in certain cases, be a justification for damaging or destroying property. In this respect, the Chamber affirms that in its findings there were no military objectives in the immediate vicinity of the 52 buildings and structures which the Chamber has found to have been damaged on 6 December 1991, or in the Old Town or in its immediate vicinity. In the Chamber's finding, the destruction or damage of property in the Old Town on 6 December 1991 was not justified by military necessity.

329. As to the *mens rea* element ... the Chamber makes the following observations. ... The Chamber infers the direct perpetrators' intent to destroy or damage property from the findings that the attack on the Old Town was deliberate, and that the direct perpetrators were aware of the civilian character of the Old Town. Similarly ... the direct perpetrators' intent to deliberately destroy cultural property is inferred by the Chamber from the evidence of the deliberate attack on the Old Town, the unique

cultural and historical character of which was a matter of renown, as was the Old Town's status as a UNESCO World Heritage site. As a further evidentiary issue regarding this last factor, the Chamber accepts the evidence that protective UNESCO emblems were visible, from the JNA positions at Žarkovica and elsewhere, above the Old Town on 6 December 1991.

330. . . . The Chamber finds that all elements of the offense of devastation not justified by military necessity . . . and destruction or wilful damage of cultural property . . . are established.

Conclusion. *Strugar was convicted and sentenced to eight years' confinement. Upon finding certain errors of law, that sentence was reduced by the appeals chamber to seven and a half years.*[51]

---

[51] *Prosecutor v. Strugar*, IT-01–42-A (July 17, 2008), para. 393.

19 The 1980 Certain Conventional Weapons Convention

19.0 Introduction

Two multinational treaties, particularly, have a potential impact on combatants. Violation of either the 1954 Hague Convention for the Protection of Cultural Property (Chapter 18) or the 1980 Convention on Certain Conventional Weapons (CCW) could lead to war crimes charges against combatants in the field. This chapter examines the CCW, the full title of which is the "Convention on Prohibitions or Restrictions on the Use of Certain Conventional Weapons Which May Be Deemed to Be Excessively Injurious or to Have Indiscriminate Effects." In the maze of law of armed conflict/international humanitarian law (LOAC/IHL) acronyms, do not confuse the CCW, the Certain Conventional Weapons treaty, with the CWC, the Chemical Weapons Convention (Chapter 20).

Antipersonnel land mines, white phosphorus munitions, laser weapons, flamethrowers, cluster bombs, improvised explosive devices (IEDs) – these weapons and munitions are all subjects of, or are implicated by, the CCW, which seeks to define their lawful and unlawful uses and limitations.

Restrictions on weapons are hardly a modern conception. "The epic poem *Mahabharatha*, [200 B.C.–200 A.D.] forbids the use of 'hyper-destructive' weapons: 'Arjuna, observing the laws of war, refrained from using the *pasupathastra* ... because when the fight was restricted to ordinary conventional weapons, the use of extraordinary or unconventional types was not even moral, let alone in conformity with religion or the recognized rules of warfare."[1] We twenty-first-century mortals may not know what the *pasupathastra* was, but we do know that, out of humanitarian concerns, it was unused in combat.[2] The Lateran Council of 1132 attempted to outlaw the crossbow and arbalest – a crossbow with a special drawing mechanism allowing it to fire bolts and stones, by declaring them "unchristian" weapons.[3] In his 1625 masterwork, *De Jure Belli ac Pacis*,

---

[1] Leslie C. Green, *Essays on the Modern Law of War*, 2d ed. (Ardsley, NY: Transnational, 1999), 330, citing Nagendra Singh, "The Distinguishable Characteristics of the Concept of the Law as It Developed in Ancient India," in *Liber Amicorum for Lord Wilberforce* (1987), 93.

[2] The *pasupathastra*, also spelled *pashupatastra*, was Siva's mythological personal weapon, capable of destroying all beings and creation itself.

[3] G. I. A. D. Draper, "The Interaction of Christianity and Chivalry in the Historical Development of the Law of War," 5 *Int'l Rev. of the Red Cross* (1965), 3, 19. W. Hays Parks, "Conventional Weapons and Weapons Reviews," in 8 *Yearbook of IHL* (2005), 55, 61: "The author could buy a meal in a fine restaurant were he given one euro for every time he has heard a lecture on the law of war related to weapons begin with reference to the condemnation and banning of the crossbow by the second Lateran Council in 1139. Seldom does the lecturer acknowledge it was an arms control failure, or explain why."

Grotius writes, "Different in a degree from poisoning [of an enemy] ... is the poisoning of javelins. This is a doubling of the causes of death. ... But this is also contrary to the law of nations."[4] The 1868 St. Petersburg Declaration Renouncing the Use in War of Certain Explosive Projectiles banned the use of explosive rounds against individuals, and dumdum bullets are prohibited by Declaration IV.3 of the 1899 Hague Peace Conference.[5] In a similar vein, the League of Nations sponsored a 1932–4 Disarmament Conference.

> There were efforts at regulating or prohibiting weapons or weapons systems in the post–World War I era, including military aircraft, submarines, machineguns, chemical and bacteriological weapons and incendiary weapons. Each endeavour proved either unsuccessful or of limited success, either because each weapon or weapon system had proven military value and/or due to government and popular skepticism of arms control agreements.[6]

After World War II, the influence of the International Committee of the Red Cross (ICRC) increased. The ICRC proposed draft rules that would limit or ban weapons it perceived as being particularly dangerous to civilian populations, or having indiscriminate effect, weapons such as incendiaries, chemical weapons, and land mines.[7] The U.S.–Vietnamese conflict, in which American use of napalm, flechettes, cluster bombs, and exotic weapons was widely publicized, initiated the weapons debate anew.

With a weapons treaty in mind, the ICRC hosted weapons limitation conferences in 1974, 1976, and 1977, but the ICRC was concerned that involvement in a weapons-related treaty would detract from its humanitarian role and, furthermore, that its participation might force an acknowledgment of LOAC/IHL core concept of military necessity, which the ICRC has long avoided. As the conferences ended, the participants resolved that further negotiations be conducted under the auspices of the United Nations (U.N.). Those U.N.-sponsored negotiations did continue, in 1979 and 1980. Throughout the many conferences, "governments were not prepared to conclude that pre-existing weapons caused superfluous injury or adopt new rules that prohibited employment of historically lawful weapons against combatants. Last-minute resolution of difficult issues, particularly relating to incendiary weapons, resulted in the adoption of a foundation treaty and three protocols on 10 October 1980."[8] As the title indicates, the 1980 convention applies only to conventional weapons. Chemical, biological, and nuclear weapons are outside its scope.

19.1 The 1980 U.N. Certain Conventional Weapons Convention

The CCW and its five protocols (two further protocols have been added to the original three and more will likely be added in the future) rests on three fundamental principles

[4] Hugo Grotius, *De Jure Belli Ac Pacis*, Vol. 2, Francis W. Kelsey, trans. (Buffalo, NY: William Hein reprint, 1995), book III, chapter IV, XVI.I, 652–3.
[5] "The contracting Parties agree to abstain from the use of bullets which expand or flatten easily in the human body, such as bullets with a hard envelope which does not entirely cover the core or is pierced with incisions." There were twenty-four original signatories. Today, the prohibition is considered customary law.
[6] Parks, "Conventional Weapons and Weapons Reviews," supra, note 3, at 67–8.
[7] Robert J. Mathews, "The 1980 Convention on Certain Conventional Weapons: A Useful Framework despite Earlier Disappointments," 844 *Int'l Rev. of the Red Cross* (2001), 991, 992.
[8] Parks, "Conventional Weapons and Weapons Reviews," supra, note 3, at 76.

of customary international law; The right of a belligerent to adopt means of warfare is not unlimited, belligerents must always distinguish between civilians and combatants, and weapons calculated to cause unnecessary suffering are prohibited.

Exploding bullets and bayonets with serrated edges are examples of weapons and munitions that cause unnecessary suffering. They increase suffering without increasing military advantage. "[A] weapon is not banned on the ground of 'superfluous injury or unnecessary suffering' merely because it causes 'great' or even 'horrendous' suffering or injury."[9] The distinction is between injury and suffering that is preventable and that which is unavoidable; that which achieves a military advantage and that which does not.

The 1980 CCW's brief foundational, or framework, treaty, eleven articles in length, is merely a preamble and introduction to the protocols that follow, restating accepted and noncontroversial basics of LOAC/IHL: Every state has the duty to refrain from the threat or use of force against other states; the right of parties to an armed conflict to choose methods or means of warfare is not unlimited; and, in cases not covered by the convention or other agreements, civilians and combatants remain protected by international law principles derived from established custom, principles of humanity, and the dictates of public conscience – the Martens Clause (Chapter 2.7.1).

Initially, the foundation treaty specified that the CCW and its three protocols applied only in common Article 2 international armed conflict "situations," including 1977 Additional Protocol I "CARs" conflicts (Chapter 4.2.1.3.1). In December 2001, the application of the convention's protocols was amended to include common Article 3 noninternational armed conflict situations (CCW Article 1.2). The foundational treaty, as the 1949 Geneva Conventions do, specifies that, should one party to an armed conflict not be bound by the CCW or one of its protocols, other parties to the conflict who have ratified the treaty and that protocol remain bound (CCW Article 7.1).

To become a party to the CCW, states must ratify the foundation treaty *and* any two or more of the three protocols (Article 4.3). As of this writing there are five protocols. Ratification of any two of them remains the requirement for accession. The foundation treaty provides for amendment of the convention (Article 8.1) and for "additional protocols relating to other categories of conventional weapons not covered" by existing protocols (Article 8.2). In future years, additional protocols will no doubt be added.

The convention's foundation treaty has been ratified by well more than a hundred states, with state accessions continually added at a modest rate. The United States ratified the foundation treaty in 1995.

In its original form, the CCW fell short of hopes of states that wanted to ban or restrict a range of conventional weapons. Ratifications by African states were (and continue to be) slow. Lacking compliance-monitoring provisions or sanctions for violations, the CCW was initially "a major disappointment for its proponents, who felt that military considerations had been given much greater priority than humanitarian concerns."[10] The provisions for amendment and added protocols were created to meet those initial disappointments.

In 1996, Protocol II was amended to broaden the CCW's application to noninternational armed conflicts, a material advance over the original version. Further international review conferences led to new CCW additions. In 1995, a fourth protocol on blinding

---

[9] Yoram Dinstein, *The Conduct of Hostilities under the Law of International Armed Conflict* 1st ed. (Cambridge: Cambridge University Press, 2004), 59. Footnote omitted.

[10] Mathews, "1980 Convention on Certain Conventional Weapons," supra, note 7, at 996.

lasers was adopted, and in 2003 a fifth protocol, on explosive remnants of war, was added. Proponents continue to press for further restrictions and bans on a variety of weapons and munitions – antivehicle land mines, naval mines, fuel-air explosives, flechettes, and depleted-uranium munitions, for example.

SIDEBAR. Hays Parks, the U.S. representative to several ICRC conferences on weapons, relates an instructive account illustrating the need for judge advocates and other combatants to be aware of weapons-related legal issues.

> In January 2006 a US Army sniper in Iraq went to an ammunition supply point to draw ammunition for his rifle. The ammunition is the 7.62 … open-tip M118LR (for "Long Range") cartridge in use by snipers in each of the four U.S. military services. It contains a tiny aperture at its nose for external ballistics, i.e., enhanced long range accuracy. The aperture is not a "hollow point" as that term has been associated with the 1899 Hague Declaration Concerning Expanding Bullets. It contains no skiving or other characteristics that would cause it to "expand or flatten easily," as prohibited by the [Hague Declaration]. Legal reviews supported by wound ballistic tests have confirmed the legality of open-tip designs.[11]

Open-tip rifle ammunition is in the inventory and has been employed by snipers in the military services of several nations because of its superior long-range accuracy.

> An individual unaware of the legal review of the M118LR [bullet] opened one of the boxes the sniper was receiving, incorrectly identified the ammunition as a "hollow point" and refused to issue the ammunition to the sniper. The issue was brought to the attention of the staff judge advocate of the sniper's command. … A copy of the legal review [of M118LR ammunition] was forwarded electronically to the staff judge advocate … reconfirming its legality, coordinated with and concurred in by the Offices of the Judge Advocates General of the Army, Navy and Air Force, and the Office of the Staff Judge Advocate to the Commandant of the Marine Corps. The issue was resolved quickly because legal reviews had been conducted.[12]

Had the staff judge advocate been aware of the legal review (written by Hays Parks, of course), she could have prevented an issue that drew negative international press coverage of purported U.S. use of "hollow point" ammunition, as well as harming the career of the sniper, who (until the issue was resolved) was relieved of duty for alleged use of unlawful ammunition.[13]

19.1.1 CCW Protocol I, Concerning Nondetectable Fragments

CCW Protocol I, along with Protocols II and III, took force in 1980, at the same time as the foundation treaty. Protocol I reads in its entirety, "It is prohibited to use any weapon the primary effect of which is to injure by fragments which in the human body escape detection by X-rays."

---

[11] "Memorandum for Commander, United States Army Special Operations Command; Subject: Sniper Use of Open-Tip Ammunition" (Sept. 23, 1985), 86 *Army Lawyer* (Feb. 1991).

[12] Parks, "Conventional Weapons and Weapons Reviews," supra, note 3, at 106–7. Footnotes omitted.

[13] Bill Gertz and Rowan Scarbourough, "Sniper Rounds," *Wash. Times*, Jan. 20, 2006.

CCW framers feared the production and use of glass bullets, and the difficulty in treating wounds involving them, for which X-rays would be useless. There was almost no evidence of any effort to develop such bullets, but the framers were also concerned about munitions that possibly could cause injury by nondetectable plastic or wood fragments that could impede medical treatment and increase unnecessary suffering. In the United States–Vietnam conflict, there had been criticism of U.S. cluster bomb submunitions that employed plastic pieces in the arming mechanism. On detonation, small plastic shards could remain undetected in X-rays of enemy fighters and other civilians wounded by them. (The text of Protocol I specifies that it is concerned with weapons *whose primary effect* is to injure by fragments. The primary effect of cluster bombs surely is not to injure by fragments.)

Protocol I banned a weapon that did not exist, and "[i]t was adopted without any controversy."[14] Indeed, when the CCW opened for signature, no weapon using non-detectable fragments as a wounding or lethal agent was even under development. "It is tempting to observe that this was the main reason for the virtually instantaneous and unanimous consent to Protocol I."[15]

So far, CCW Protocol I has been ratified by more than a hundred states, including, in 1995, the United States. One or two additional states usually ratify each year.

19.1.2 *CCW Protocol II, Concerning Mines and Booby-Traps*

Protocol II's full title is "Protocol in Prohibitions or Restrictions on the Use of Mines, Booby-Traps and Other Devices."[16] Much as Protocol I did, Protocol II pushed on an open door. "Protocol II . . . does not prohibit their use per se, but does prohibit use which is indiscriminate or directed against civilians."[17] The drafting of the protocol was relatively straightforward and noncontentious, perhaps because it follows generally accepted military doctrine for the employment of antipersonnel land mines.[18]

Land mines were first used in significant numbers by Confederates in the U.S. Civil War, when they were known as "torpedoes."From that time until the late twentieth century, their use in armed conflicts grew exponentially. Protocol II does not apply to all land mines, but to antipersonnel mines and, apparently, antivehicle mines. Antiship mines, whether at sea or in inland waterways, are expressly excluded from coverage. Nor are Claymore mines –aboveground, tripwire, or command-detonated antipersonnel mines – covered.[19]

---

[14] Jean-Marie Henckaerts and Louise Doswald-Beck, eds., *Customary International Humanitarian Law*, Vol. I. *Rules* (Cambridge: Cambridge University Press, 2005), Rule 79, at 275.

[15] David Turns, "Weapons in the ICRC Study on Customary International Humanitarian Law," 11–2 *J. of Conflict & Security L.* (Summer, 2006), 201, 227.

[16] When Protocol II is quoted here, the reference is to CCW Protocol II as amended on May 3, 1996. See this chapter, 19.1.2.1.

[17] Adam Roberts and Richard Guelff, *Documents on the Laws of War*, 3d ed. (Oxford: Oxford University Press, 2000), 517.

[18] Parks, "Conventional Weapons and Weapons Reviews," supra, note 3, at 77.

[19] A command-detonated munition is remotely detonated by an individual observing the kill zone. Protocol II, Art. 5.6, is the Claymore exception. It describes Claymore-like mines, saying they are exempt from the restrictions on marked minefields (Art. 5.2.(a)) if they are emplaced for no longer than seventy-two hours and remain in proximity to the unit using them, and civilians are kept clear – all characteristic of Claymores.

An antipersonnel "mine" is a munition placed under, on, or near the ground; "primarily designed to be exploded" by pressure, proximity, or contact with a person or vehicle; and designed to injure or kill people (CCW Articles 2.1, 2.3). This definition would include antitank and antivehicle mines, as well as antipersonnel mines. "Thus, where reference is made throughout the treaty to 'mines' it is understood that such reference applies to both anti-personnel and anti-vehicle mines."[20] The definitional phrase "primarily designed" was added to clarify that antitank mines with antihandling elements are not included in the definition of antipersonnel mines – a critical issue in U.S. Senate advice and consent debates. U.S. Army mine doctrine was to lay antipersonnel and antitank minefields together, to hinder enemy personnel from detecting and removing antitank mines. Now, individual antitank mines must be equipped with antihandling features.[21]

A booby trap, in contrast, is any apparently harmless object designed, constructed, or adapted to kill or injure, which detonates when a person disturbs or approaches it (Article 2.4). A pair of binoculars, for instance, that has been filled with explosives that detonate when the binoculars are picked up is a booby trap. Booby traps commonly alert friendly troops to the presence of hostile soldiers, hamper mine-removal efforts, and delay an enemy advance. "In the opinion of a number of experts, the use of booby-traps for some of those purposes was militarily essential."[22] Often, however, the intent is simply to kill or wound. During the World War II Nazi siege of Leningrad (1941–3), "the Germans began to try some tricks. ... They dropped booby traps, sometimes in the form of children's toys, fountain pens and cigarette lighters."[23] Even when used in ways conforming to the protocol, booby traps remain subject to the principle of distinction.

"Other devices" include "improvised explosive devices designed to kill, injure or damage and which are actuated manually, by remote control or automatically after a lapse of time" (Article 2.5). IEDs became notorious in the United States–Iraq war. The CCW is one of their earliest references. "Other devices" also include the command-detonated Claymore antipersonnel mine.

When, or in what form, is use of antipersonnel mines, booby traps, or IEDs prohibited by Protocol II? They may not be designed to detonate upon contact with a mine detector (CCW Article 3.5), they may not be undetectable (Article 4),[24] they may not be employed against a civilian population or civilian objects (Article 3.7), and they may not be deployed indiscriminately (Article 3.8). Civilian objects that may not be booby-trapped include medical supplies, gravesites, and cultural or religious property.[25] "All feasible precautions shall be taken to protect civilians from the effects of weapons to which this Article [3] applies." These are among the more significant of the numerous Protocol II restrictions on the use of antipersonnel mines.

---

[20] Maj. Michael Lacey, "Passage of Amended Protocol II," *Army Lawyer* (March 2000), 7–8.   [21] Id., at 9.

[22] *Conference of Government Experts on the Use of Certain Conventional Weapons* (Geneva: ICRC, 1975), 68.

[23] Harrison E. Salisbury, *The 900 Days: The Siege of Leningrad* (Cambridge MA: DeCappo Press, 1969), 302.

[24] Protocol II's 1980 version did not prohibit nondetectable mines, leading several enterprising states to produce nondetectable antipersonnel mines encased in plastic. A nonbinding technical annex to Amended Protocol II requires all antipersonnel mines to have at least eight grams of iron in a single mass to ensure they register on mine detectors.

[25] Henckaerts and Doswald-Beck, *Customary International Humanitarian Law*, supra, note 14, Rule 80, at 278.

Booby traps, those aboveground apparently harmless objects, are addressed in CCW Article 7. Booby-trapping of the wounded or dead is prohibited, as is booby-trapping of children's toys or other objects specially designed for children's feeding, health, hygiene, clothing, or education. Religious objects may not be booby-trapped; nor may historic monuments or places of worship or cultural objects.

A confusing prohibition (Article 7.2) forbids booby-trapping "apparently harmless portable objects . . . specifically designed and constructed to contain explosive material." "In other words, 'a belligerent may booby-trap a camera, but it may not manufacture booby-traps which appear to be cameras'."[26] You may booby-trap as many cameras as you can find, but you may not employ factory-made exploding cameras.

Protocol II also addresses the required recording and marking of minefields, and their removal after hostilities (Article 3.2). It addresses remotely delivered antipersonnel mines – those delivered by air or artillery – with slightly fewer restrictions than those on manually emplaced mines. American forces rely heavily on remotely delivered mines, so this provision is significant to the United States. In a provision urged by the United States, Protocol II requires that remotely delivered mines contain self-destructing or self-deactivating mechanisms (Article 6.3). The 1992 amendment to Protocol II, besides making it applicable to common Article 3 armed conflicts, in addition to common Article 2 international armed conflicts, requires states party to provide for penal sanctions for persons who willfully kill or seriously injure civilians through misuse of antipersonnel mines or booby traps (Article 14.2).

Although Protocol II is not customary law,[27] it is significant because it affirms the lawfulness of the use of mines, booby traps, and other devices against combatants, "i.e., that their injury, often severe, frequently fatal, does not constitute superfluous injury."[28] The United States ratified Protocol II, with reservations, in 1995. More than one hundred other states have also ratified, with new accessions each year.

19.1.2.1 CCW Amended Mines Protocol II

After the CCW took effect, it slowly gathered ratifications, but there was dissatisfaction with some provisions, particularly those relating to Protocol II antipersonnel land mines. After more than ten years, further negotiations led to Amended Protocol II, which strengthens and clarifies many of the initial Protocol II provisions. The United States has ratified the 1996 Amended Mines Protocol II. As of this writing, ninety-one other states have also ratified it. Negotiations on some changes were hard-fought, reflecting the disappointment of several states in the original protocol and their desire to strengthen and tighten its provisions. Other states, satisfied with the original terms, argued to maintain the flexibility that the provisions represented.

The Amended Protocol extends the original protocol's scope of application to non-international armed conflicts (CCW Article 1). Internal armed conflicts, particularly African conflicts, see the greatest use of antipersonnel mines and the highest number of civilian casualties. The Amended Protocol defines mines with greater detail and

---

[26] Dinstein, *Conduct of Hostilities*, supra, note 9, at 65. Citation omitted.

[27] Henckaerts and Doswald-Beck, *Customary International Humanitarian Law*, supra, note 14, Rule 81, at 282.

[28] Parks, "Conventional Weapons and Weapons Reviews," supra, note 3, at 77.

applies more stringent rules regarding their use (Articles 2–7). It also introduces prohibitions and limits on the transfer of antipersonnel mines (Article 8) and requires ratifying states to implement domestic law to deal with protocol violations (Article 14). "Amended Protocol II, while representing an advance ... has also been criticized. ... [It] "still fails to prohibit mines that do not self-destruct within a given period, and [does not ban] remotely-delivered mines. It also still lacks substantive verification or compliance mechanisms."[29]

19.1.2.2 The 1997 Ottawa Convention

CCW Protocol II should not be confused with the 1997 Ottawa Convention, which applies only to antipersonnel land mines.[30] Under Ottawa's stricter terms, states party undertake "never under any circumstances" to use antipersonnel land mines or to develop, produce, transfer, or acquire them. It also requires parties to destroy existing stocks of antipersonnel mines. With more than one hundred and fifty states party, and more added each year, the Ottawa Convention, it may be argued, is approaching customary status (except for states that have been persistent objectors, including the United States). The United States has previously indicated a belief that the Ottawa Convention fails to balance legitimate military requirements with humanitarian concerns.[31] That position is softening, however. In December 2009, although not a party to the convention, the United States sent an observer delegation to the Second Review Conference of the Ottawa Convention and announced that the United States was undertaking a review of its policy on land mines. The delegation said the United States had ended the use of all nondetectable land mines, both antipersonnel and antivehicle. It also announced that the United States would end all use of antipersonnel and antivehicle persistent mines by the end of 2010.[32] Later, in May 2010, sixty-eight U.S. senators, in a letter to President Obama, supported the administration's decision to review U.S. antipersonnel land mine policy, concluding that, through the review, the United States can identify obstacles to joining the Ottawa Convention by accession.[33]

Even in light of Ottawa, the CCW's Protocol II, as amended in 1996, still has vitality. It specifies limitations on the use of antitank mines, booby traps, and other devices that are not addressed by the Ottawa Convention. As a result of Amended Protocol II and the Ottawa Convention, "there is every reason to believe that the prohibition of antipersonnel mines will gradually be endorsed by customary international law."[34]

---

[29] Roberts and Guelff, *Documents on the Laws of War*, supra, note 17, at 518, quoting a publication of the U.N. Department of Public Information.

[30] Formal title: 1997 Ottawa Convention on the Prohibition of the Use, Stockpiling, Production and Transfer of Anti-Personnel Mines and on Their Destruction.

[31] John R. Crook, ed., "Contemporary Practice of the United States Relating to International Law," 102–1 *AJIL* (Jan. 2008), 190.

[32] John R. Crook, ed., "Contemporary Practice of the United States Relating to International Law," 104–2 *AJIL* (April 2010), 271, 299–300.

[33] John R. Crook, ed., "Contemporary Practice of the United States Relating to International Law," 104–3 *AJIL* (July 2010), 489, 524.

[34] Dinstein, *Conduct of Hostilities*, supra, note 9, at 69.

> **SIDEBAR.** The Ottawa Convention has a unique history that points the way to future modifications of LOAC – to the surprise of major military powers. In 1992, disappointed with the outcome of Amended Mines Protocol II, Ms. Jody Williams, a Los Angeles–based peace activist working from her kitchen table, formed the International Campaign to Ban Landmines (ICBL), which was no more than a loose coalition of similar-minded small nongovernmental organizations (NGOs) around the world. With no NGO experience, the ICBL pressed for national, then regional, then international measures to ban antipersonnel land mines altogether. In 1996, Canada hosted an ICBL meeting in Ottawa. The Canadian foreign minister, Lloyd Axworthy, challenged the group to write a simple, unambiguous ban treaty within one year, and, surprisingly enough, the ICBL did. NGO groups from small and midsized states, working outside normal diplomatic channels, and not subject to the military objections of major war fighting states, combined to produce the Ottawa Treaty, which, so far, has been ratified by 161 states. In 1997, Ms. Williams shared the Nobel Prize in peace with the group she founded, the ICBL.[35] The Ottawa model could be a route to future modifications of the law of war. Similar negotiating tactics were used in arriving at the 2008 Dublin Convention on Cluster Munitions.

19.1.2.3 U.S. Antipersonnel Land Mine Policy

U.S. antipersonnel land mine policy has been convoluted and burdened by domestic politics. In 1992, the United States banned the export of antipersonnel land mines and committed to employing no "persistent" (i.e., without self-destructing or self-deactivating mechanisms) land mines after 2010[36] and "ended use of all non-detectable anti-personnel and anti-vehicle landmines in 2005."[37] That was followed, in 2004, by an announcement committing the United States "not to use any persistent landmines – neither anti-personnel nor anti-vehicle – anywhere after 2010."[38] In 1996, President Clinton announced that the United States would no longer employ non-self-destructing antipersonnel mines, except for training purposes, and on the Korean Peninsula to defend the Demilitarized Zone.[39] In 1998, President Clinton also pledged to join the Ottawa Convention by 2006, if the Department of Defense could by then develop a suitable substitute for land mines. In 2004, the Bush administration rejected the Clinton pledge. In fact, the United States has not produced land mines since 1997, yet in 2014 the chairman of the Joint Chiefs of Staff testified that land mines are "an important tool in the arsenal of the United States."[40]

In June 2014, at the Third Review Conference for the Ottawa Anti-personnel Land-mines Treaty, the United States again altered its policy, making it still closer to Ottawa Convention guidelines: "The United States will not produce or otherwise acquire any anti-personnel munitions that are not compliant with the Ottawa Convention in the

---

[35] http://nobelprize.org/nobel_prizes/peace/articles/williams/index.html
[36] Crook, "Contemporary Practice of the United States Relating to International Law," supra, note 31.
[37] Id., at 190.   [38] U.S. Dept. of State,"U.S. Landmine Policy," Feb. 27, 2004, available on line.
[39] Statement by President Clinton, "U.S. Announces Anti-Personnel Landmine Policy," May 16, 1996, available online.
[40] Testimony of Gen. Martin Dempsey, Defense Dept. Fiscal Year 2015 Budget Request, Hearing before the H. Armed Services Comm., 113th Congress (March 6, 2014).

future, including [replacing] such munitions as they expire in coming years. Meanwhile, we are diligently exploring other solutions that would be compliant with the Convention and that would allow us to accede to the Convention."[41] Three months later, the Department of State announced that the United States pledged not to use land mines outside the Korean Peninsula and asserted that it would "diligently undertake to destroy stockpiles of ... landmines that are not required for the defense of the Republic of Korea."[42]

U.S. land mine policy has been amended several times and will be again. The trend toward the United States' becoming a party to the Ottawa Convention could be reversed by a future political administration, but the drawdown of the U.S. antipersonnel land mine inventory seems sufficiently executed that a reversal is improbable.[43]

Advances toward U.S. accession to the Ottawa Convention aside, the controlling U.S. *law* (as opposed to U.S. *policy*) on antipersonnel land mines remains the U.S.-ratified 1980 CCW Amended Mines Protocol II.

19.1.3 CCW Protocol III, Concerning Incendiary Weapons

It is prohibited in all circumstances to make any military objective located within a concentration of civilians the object of attack by air-delivered incendiary weapons. Using napalm against military targets located within concentrations of civilians, such as towns and villages, is also prohibited (Article 2). This "prohibits the type of attacks on cities that were common during the Second World War."[44]

Protocol III, entitled "Protocol on Prohibitions or Restrictions on the Use of Incendiary Weapons," as with Protocol II on antipersonnel land mines, does not prohibit entirely the use of incendiary weapons. Again, history was a driving force in the protocol's creation.

> The US Air Force's use of napalm bombs in Vietnam had reinforced international concern about incendiary weapons. While some states at the 1970–80 weapons conference demanded a complete ban on such weapons, this was opposed by others. ... Arguments in favour of such weapons included their utility in 'close air support' ... without causing disastrous collateral damage that would be caused by explosives.[45]

Protocol III's definition of "incendiary weapon," contained in Article 1.1, is broad:

> "Incendiary weapon" means any weapon or munition which is primarily designed to set fire to objects or to cause burn injury to persons through the action of flame, heat, or combustion thereof, produced by a chemical action. ...

---

[41] John R. Crook, ed., "Contemporary Practice of the United States Relating to International Law," 108–4 *AJIL* (Oct. 2014), 783, 836.

[42] Id., at 837.

[43] The Ottawa Convention bans reservations. The U.S. statement regarding continuation of land mine use on the Korean Peninsula is, in effect, a reservation that would preclude U.S. accession to the convention.

[44] United Kingdom Ministry of Defence, *The Manual of the Law of Armed Conflict* (Oxford: Oxford University Press, 2004), para. 6.12, fn. 41, at 110.

[45] Roberts and Guelff, *Documents on the Laws of War*, supra, note 17, at 517.

(a) Incendiary weapons can take the form of, for example, flame throwers ... shells, rockets, grenades, mines, bombs. ...

(b) Incendiary weapons do not include:

    (i) munitions which may have incidental incendiary effects, such as illuminants, tracers, smoke or signaling systems;

    (ii) munitions designed to combine penetration, blast or fragmentation effect, such as armour-piercing projectiles, fragmentation shells, explosive bombs and similar combined-effects munitions in which the incendiary effect is not specifically designed to cause burn injury to persons.

One might question Protocol III's utility, given the gaps in its application. It does not ban napalm or flamethrowers, both clearly incendiaries. and, under the protocol, both remain lawful weapons. "It is of interest to note that the experts the ICRC had brought together [in 1974, before negotiations were moved to the U.N.] were hopelessly divided on the question of whether the use of napalm was permissible or not."[46] "The formulation of the Protocol reflects a compromise between those that were in favor of a complete prohibition on the use of incendiary weapons and those who were against a complete prohibition."[47]

A response is that any lawful weapon can be used in an unlawful way. Recognizing that there are legitimate instances of military necessity justifying the use of incendiaries, Protocol III defines the ways in which incendiaries may *not* be used. They may not be used directly against civilians or concentrations of civilians, or directly against civilian objects. Incendiary attacks on plant cover, such as forests, are prohibited unless the plant cover is used to cover or conceal combatants or military objects (Article 2.4).[48] The United States has indicated that it will "reserve the right to use incendiaries against military targets located in concentrations of civilians where it is judged that such use would cause fewer casualties and less collateral damage than alternative weapons."[49]

Combatants are not protected by the protocol. "Use of weapons such as napalm and flamethrowers against combatant personnel [is] governed by the unnecessary suffering principle so that they should not be used directly against personnel but against armoured vehicles, bunkers, and built-up emplacements, even though personnel inside may be burnt."[50] There is a difference, of course, between "should not" and "may not."

"Protocol III contributed little from a practical standpoint inasmuch as its rules generally paraphrase pre-existing rules for all weapons. This was no surprise, given centuries of state practice of employment of fire as an anti-materiel and anti-personnel weapon."[51] Still, its reiteration of civilian protection is valuable. Protocol III has been ratified by more than one hundred states, so far. The United States ratified in 2009.

---

[46] Frits Kalshoven, *Reflections on the Law of War* (Leiden: Martinus Nijhoff, 2007), 381.

[47] Sandesh Sivakumaran, *The Law of Non-International Armed Conflict* (Oxford: Oxford University Press, 2012), 398.

[48] 1980 CCW, Art. 2.4. This limited restriction is perhaps compensated for by the more rigorous provisions of the 1976 Convention on the Prohibition of Military or Any Other Hostile Use of Environmental Modification Techniques (ENMOD Convention), although only seventy-three states, including the United States, have ratified the ENMOD convention.

[49] Message from the President of the United States Transmitting Protocols to the 1980 Convention, reproduced in 1 *YIHL* 566, 569 (1998).

[50] United Kingdom Ministry of Defence, *Manual of the Law of Armed Conflict*, supra, note 44, para. 6.12.6, at 112.

[51] Parks, "Conventional Weapons and Weapons Reviews," supra, note 3, at 78.

19.1.4 CCW Protocol IV, Concerning Blinding Laser Weapons

Protocol IV, adopted in October 1995, prohibits the use and the transfer of weapons that cause permanent blindness. Concern had been building for some years over advances in laser-based weaponry, with human-rights groups calling for its ban.[52] Weapons that blind are not new.

> One of the most enduring images of the first World War was a painting by John Sargent of a line of blinded soldiers being led from the battlefield after being exposed to phosgene gas. The inhumanity and cruelty ... presented by the photo helped produce an outcry of world public opinion [against weapons that blind]. ... Recent developments in laser technology have made the proliferation of these weapons – many as small as a rifle – a real possibility.[53]

Lasers offer the malignant possibility of blinding without the difficulties of storing dangerous chemical agents or the hazards to friendly troops presented by changes in wind direction. Their moral issues aside,

> the possibility of laser weapons capable of producing sudden and irreversible blindness in large numbers of battlefield personnel presents difficult, if not catastrophic, consequences, both for the individuals themselves and the societies to which they will return. ... Of all the various battlefield injuries, blindness of combatants would be by far the most serious, both to the soldier and to his or her country.[54]

Protocol negotiations were complicated by the emergence of missile-disabling lasers, as well as target-marking and range-finding lasers, militarily necessary for many precision-guided munitions that reduced collateral damage to new lows. "Therefore, from a humanitarian as well as military point of view, complete elimination of all lasers from military operations was not practical or even desirable."[55] In 1986, when battlefield lasers were still viewed as science fiction, their complete elimination was proposed in a draft resolution submitted to the ICRC by Sweden and Switzerland.[56] Meetings of experts followed, discussing whether lasers were in the category of weapons causing unnecessary suffering, negating the need for a new protocol. Initially, the United States was of that camp. "The fact that lasers are not indiscriminate in nature and that the blinding lasers in question would not inflict death created a particular difficulty" among the experts.[57]

Spurred by Chinese and American commercially produced laser weapons about to be marketed to their armed forces, and laser weapons research being conducted by at least six other states,[58] a campaign was mounted by the ICRC, joined by NGOs (and several prominent American politicians), to adopt a new treaty. Protocol IV is the result, ratified by nearly a hundred states, so far, with new states accessioning each year. Despite

---

[52] A.P., "Laser Beams That Could Blind Soldiers Draw Vitriol of Human-Rights Groups," *Wash. Times*, May 22, 1995, A6.

[53] Lane Evans, "Laser Warfare's Blinding Effect," *Christian Science Monitor*, Aug. 15, 1995, 20.

[54] Dr. R. DeVour, "Possible Psychological and Societal Effects of Sudden Permanent Blindness of Military Personnel Caused by Battlefield Use of Laser Weapons," in Louise Doswald-Beck, ed., *Blinding Weapons: Reports of the Meetings of Experts Convened by the International Committee of the Red Cross on Battlefield Laser Weapons 1989–1991* (Geneva: ICRC, 1993), 46, 51.

[55] Roberts and Guelff, *Documents on the Laws of War*, supra, note 17, at 517.

[56] Louise Doswald-Beck, "New Protocol on Blinding Laser Weapons," 312 *Int'l Rev. of the Red Cross* (May–June 1996), 272.

[57] Id.   [58] Turns, "Weapons in the ICRC Study," supra, note 15, at 233.

occasional allegations of lasers' being used as unlawful weapons,[59] "there are no known instances of blinding laser weapons being developed, deployed or used by any State."[60]

There are legitimate military uses for lasers besides target designators for precision-guided munitions. There are two laser target designator systems and five "dazzler" laser systems in the U.S. military inventory, to be used when deadly force is not required. They are employed to "dazzle" or disorient individuals or groups of enemy combatants, and drivers of vehicles approaching checkpoints, by glare or flash blindness, akin to a strong photographic flash or a vehicle's high-beam headlights. All of the five dazzler systems "are green laser devices that deliver a limited amount of force, at a distance, without causing injury ... and can be hand-carried or mounted on individual – and crew-served weapons."[61] They have a range of 200 meters in daylight and 370 meters in darkness. If used improperly, for example, at short ranges of less than 20 meters, dazzlers may cause lasting injury, but "these lasers, under standard conditions of use would not cause eye injury."[62] Like all weapons, dazzler lasers were reviewed and found in compliance with the 1980 CCW and other applicable LOAC/IHL treaties before entering the military inventory.

Laser systems may be employed against military objectives, such as military optical equipment – the sights on antiaircraft or other guns, and laser range-finders, for instance – even though this may produce an incidental effect, such as blindness, for users of that equipment.[63]

The 2015 headline read, "The U.S. Military Has a Laser Gun."[64] The article describes a telescope-like ship-mounted laser weapon:

> They sizzle rather than go boom, providing pin-point accuracy that ... can prevent the kind of collateral damage that is unavoidable with missiles or bombs. ... [Today, a] 30-kilowatt laser [is] mounted on the deck of the USS *Ponce* in the Persian Gulf. ... As long as there is power, lasers can also keep firing with an "unlimited magazine" that never needs to be reloaded. ... "This isn't something in a Buck Rogers comic book. It's being deployed now." ... Amnesty International said lasers should be "very strictly regulated and controlled so that it is never used against a human target where there is a risk of eye damage."[65]

Laser weapons have already been tested in operational circumstances, and, ironically, human targets may be killed by them, but not blinded by them.

The scope of Protocol IV's application, noninternational conflicts as well as international, is unspecified in the protocol. The framers clearly intended that it apply in both. The ICRC study on customary law determines the ban applicable in both,[66] although most commentators believe that insufficient time has passed to determine

---

[59] Bill Gertz, "Trial Aims to Tie Russia to Laser Attack," *Wash. Times*, Oct. 7, 2002, 8.   [60] Id.

[61] Richard B. Jackson, "Lasers Are Lawful as Non-Lethal Weapons," *Army Lawyer*, Aug. 2006, 15. This comprehensive article specifies U.S. lasers and their characteristics, capabilities, and effects, as well as their testing regime.

[62] Id., at 16.

[63] Art. 3. "Blinding as an incidental or collateral effect of the legitimate military employment of laser systems, including laser systems used against optical equipment, is not covered by the prohibition of this Protocol."

[64] Christian Davenport, "The U.S. Military Has a Laser Gun," *Wash. Post*, Jan. 7, 2015, A12.   [65] Id.

[66] Henckaerts and Doswald-Beck, *Customary International Humanitarian Law*, supra, note 14, rule 86, at 292.

whether the ban on blinding lasers has become customary law.[67] An ICRC lawyer writes, "There can be no doubt that Protocol IV represents a major achievement. It is the first time since 1868 that a weapon has been prohibited before it has been used on the battlefield. ... This Protocol represents a victory of civilization over barbarity."[68] The United States ratified the CCW's Protocol IV in 2009.

19.1.5 CCW Protocol V, Concerning Explosive Remnants of War

Explosive remnants of war are munitions fired or dropped during armed conflict that fail to explode, or that are abandoned on the battlefield – the deadly detritus of modern war. One regularly reads of unexploded bombs from wars long past, discovered in a European city during sewer repairs, or a cluster bomb submunition found on a children's soccer pitch. In 2004, thirty years after the United States–Vietnam War ended, the United States increased the amount of aid from $1.4 million to $2.5 million to Laos for removal of unexploded American ordnance dropped on that country during the war.[69] The United States has spent more than $2 billion in recent years to help other countries to remove land mines and assist victims. "Protocol V establishes new rules that require the parties to a conflict to clear explosive remnants of war, to take measures to protect civilians from the effects of these weapons and to assist the efforts of international and non-governmental organizations (NGOs) working in these areas."[70] Protocol V does not ban the production, use, or stockpiling of any weapon, however.

In 2000, the ICRC and a British NGO, Landmine Action, met to discuss the possibility of adding unexploded and abandoned land mines to the next CCW review conference agenda. A subsequent meeting noted that cluster bombs created explosive remnants, as well. At the 2001 review conference, delegates established a Group of Government Experts. An unusual feature of the experts' meetings and states partys' negotiations was that NGOs fully participated, "bringing their expertise and field-based experience to bear on the discussions."[71] In 2003 the CCW state parties adopted Protocol V, consisting of eleven articles and a technical annex.

Throughout the protocol, reference is made to obligations of the "High Contracting Party and party." "And party" refers to nonstate actors – armed opposition groups – rather than to states that have not ratified. Use of the term is an effort to clarify the protocol's application to such groups.[72]

The protocol applies in both international and noninternational armed conflicts (Article 1.3) that arise *after* the protocol's implementation (Article 1.4). Under Article 3, high contracting parties and parties are responsible for the clearance of explosive remnants from territory they control and are bound to minimize risks associated with remnants until they

---

[67] For example, Parks, "Conventional Weapons and Weapons Reviews," supra, note 3, at 85, fn. 118; and Turns, "Weapons in the ICRC Study," supra, note 15, at 233.

[68] Doswald-Beck, "New Protocol," supra, note 55, at 272. Footnote omitted. In mentioning 1868, Doswald-Beck refers to the 1868 St. Petersburg Declaration that banned explosive projectiles under 400 g in weight.

[69] Frederic J. Frommer, "U.S. Boosts Aid for Bomb Removal in Laos," *Wash. Post*, Dec. 27, 2004, A7.

[70] Louis Maresca, "A New Protocol on Explosive Remnants of War: The History and Negotiation of Protocol V to the 1980 Convention on Certain Conventional Weapons," 856 *Int'l Rev. of the Red Cross* (Dec. 2004), 815.

[71] Id., at 834.   [72] Id., at 829.

can be cleared. Risk minimization involves, inter alia, surveys and marking of dangerous areas. If a party's explosive remnants are in an area the party does not control, that party is nevertheless obligated to assist, where feasible, in marking and clearing those remnants. Assistance may be in technical, material, financial, or personnel form.

Article 4.1 requires that information on abandoned explosive ordnance be recorded and retained, "to the maximum extent possible and as far as practicable," to be shared with other parties after the end of hostilities. Article 5 mandates "all feasible" precautions to protect civilians and civilian objects from the effects of explosive remnants.

Reaching agreement on Article 7 was difficult. It gives parties "the right" to seek and receive assistance from other parties "in dealing with the problems posed by existing explosive remnants of war" and requires parties "in a position to do so" to provide assistance. Article 8 specifies such assistance to include marking, clearing, removal, and destruction of explosive remnants; assisting in the care, rehabilitation, and social and economic reintegration of victims; contributing to U.N. trust funds to facilitate assistance; and exchanging equipment and scientific and technological information. Those rights are significant and broad, and they entail potentially heavy technical and financial burdens for those called upon to provide assistance. Some parties, envisioning the possibility of making future requests for assistance to former enemy states, wanted the obligation requiring assistance to apply to *all* explosive remnants. Other parties, foreseeing the possibility of receiving such requests from past foes, were concerned that the protocol's language called on them to provide assistance regarding explosive ordnance from conflicts predating the protocol. Article 7's elastic language, "where appropriate," "[if] in a position to do so," and "as necessary and feasible," represents compromise between the potential seekers and potential providers. "The qualifications in this article ... show that it was intended to be a flexible provision and was not meant to be absolutely binding for the parties to earlier conflicts."[73] (If a provision is "not absolutely binding," is it binding at all?)

Protocol V was adopted in 2003, only moments ago in terms of international law, and almost ninety states have already ratified – the United States in 2009. Proponents of greater regulation were disappointed that Protocol V contained no language regarding acceptable munitions failure ("dud") rates or requirements to destroy aging stockpiles. Nevertheless, the protocol is a step forward in protections for civilians. Only a few of the protocol's provisions are mentioned here, some of them potential problem areas. The several inexact and ambiguous terms that were purposely inserted in contentious articles for the sake of consensus could prove to be escape hatches that will render those articles hollow. As with compliance with most LOAC/IHL agreements, Protocol V relies on the good faith and honest effort of ratifying states. Jaded cynicism might be forgiven, where non-state-organized armed groups – high contracting parties *and parties* – are addressed by the protocol. Time will reveal the effectiveness of the protocol's admirable high intentions.

19.2 Cluster Munitions

Cluster bombs, a type of cluster munition, are not banned weapons. Cluster bomb units (CBUs) do not fall under any of the five CCW protocols. "Although the effects of unexploded cluster bomblets are in some respects analogous to the effects of anti-personnel

---

[73] Id., at 830.

mines, they do not fall within the [Protocol II] definition of anti-personnel mine."[74] Some CBU variants are incendiaries that fall under Protocol III, and unexploded CBU submunitions were a primary factor in Protocol V's adoption. Despite these close affinities to other protocols, CBUs are "conventional" weapons not addressed by the CCW.

Opponents of CBUs point to the CCW foundation treaty's classic language "that the right of the parties to an armed conflict to choose methods or means of warfare is not unlimited" as an argument for their ban. Opponents' concern centers on the high ratio of unexploded CBU submunitions, or bomblets, left on former battlefields to maim and kill civilians years after the conflict ends. NGOs disappointed by Protocol V's outcome shifted their sights and joined forces with cluster bomb opponents, hoping that humanitarian impact could trump military utility.

"Employment of anti-personnel bomblets was not new. During World War I, the German Air Force employed the *Splitterbombe*, its 1kg ... *Ifl-Mäuse* or *Ilf-Bomben*, for attack of enemy ground forces."[75] In World War II, although the term "cluster bomb" had not been coined, the German Luftwaffe dropped "butterfly bomb" submunitions on the British port city of Grimsby. The United States used hundreds of thousands of four-pound M-50 incendiary bomblets similar to later incendiary CBUs to set fire to lightly constructed Japanese cities.[76] Approximately 330,000 Japanese civilians were killed, another 476,000 injured in those bombings.[77] By the time of the U.S.–Vietnamese conflict, cluster bombs had been "perfected." They have been used in major conflicts since, including Gulf War I (1990–1), and in the former Yugoslavia. During the 2006 Israeli incursion into Lebanon against Hezbollah, Israel employed an estimated four million CBU submunitions.[78] Their use in the united States–Iran and United States–Afghanistan conflicts was limited out of concern about their lack of distinction, collateral damage, and dud persistence.

CBUs can be bombs or artillery or mortar rounds that, when dropped or fired, spin while in flight, opening at a predetermined, preset, height and rate of spin. Each opened spinning bomb canister disperses many, sometimes hundreds of, smaller submunitions, or bomblets, over a long and wide area of the ground. Dispersed like sand tossed onto a beach, each bomblet results in a relatively small but deadly and destructive detonation. CBUs used as area-denial weapons are particularly effective against enemy infantry in the open, such as an attacking force of soldiers. There are incendiary CBUs, antipersonnel CBUs, antiarmor CBUs, runway-cratering CBUs, mine-laying CBUs, antielectrical CBUs, leaflet CBUs, and combined-effects CBUs;[79] they can be delivered by artillery, missile, or aircraft – low-flying fighters or high-altitude bombers, via high-speed delivery or toss delivery. They employ contact fuses to explode on impact, air-burst fuses, or delayed-action fuses. Their military advantages are many.

---

[74] Stuart Maslen, *Explosive Remnants of War* (Geneva: ICRC, 2000), 35.

[75] Parks, "Conventional Weapons and Weapons Reviews," supra, note 3, at 76, fn. 81.

[76] Kenneth P. Werrell, *Blankets of Fire* (Washington, DC: Smithsonian, 1996), 48.

[77] *The United States Strategic Bombing Surveys* (Maxwell AFB, AL: Air University Press Reprint, 1987), 92.

[78] Handicap International, "Fatal Footprint: The Global Human Impact of Cluster Munitions, Preliminary Report," (Nov. 2006), 35, available online.

[79] "The CBU-87B 'Combined Effects Munition' contains 202 BLU-97 bomblets in each canister. ... The BLU-97 has three destructive capabilities. ... The primary charge is a shaped metal cone that, upon detonation of the bomblet, is converted into a molten slug to penetrate armoured vehicles or tanks. ... The body of the BLU-97 fragments into scores of metal shards to kill or maim personnel or disable trucks over a radius of tens of meters. The third destructive element is an incendiary ring made of metal zirconium, which can start fires if petrol or diesel are located in the vicinity." Maslen, *Explosive Remnants of War*, supra, note 73, at 7.

A single thousand-pound CBU may contain 202 bomblets; the bomblets are often described in appearance and size as soft-drink cans or, in some models, hockey pucks or tennis balls. Bomblets are sometimes brightly colored to facilitate the location of duds; however, children are attracted to the colored objects, as well. The shape and size of the impact area are determined by the preset spin rate of the dispenser, resulting in an elliptical impact footprint measuring as much as sixteen hundred by eleven hundred feet – a target footprint roughly five football fields long and three football fields wide.[80]

The problem with CBUs is their "dud" rate, the number of submunitions in each bomb, missile, or artillery round that do not detonate because of fuse or detonator failure. According to a manufacturer, the dud rate of one of the more widely used antipersonnel CBUs, the CBU-87 Combined Effects Munition, is about 5 percent. Some field reports, however, put the rate as high as 23 percent.[81] Given the high number of CBUs used in Gulf War I, for example, NGO estimates of as many as two million unexploded bomblets are credible.[82] Even though CBUs were never purposely used in or near populated areas, many dud bomblets were inevitably left on Kuwaiti and Iraqi battlefields. These explosives presented obvious problems of distinction and proportionality.[83] Hundreds of civilians were reportedly killed or maimed long after the conflicts.

For years, NGOs, human rights groups, and the media protested the continued use of CBUs and called for their ban. The United States and Israel, only two of many states employing them, were most often the targets of protests.[84] In 2008 the concerns of protesters had effect – in Dublin.

19.2.1 2008 Convention on Cluster Munitions

In 2008, in Dublin, Ireland, the issue of CBUs was addressed by the Convention on Cluster Munitions, sometimes referred to as "the Dublin Convention," a multinational treaty that bans cluster munitions.

The movement for a cluster bomb ban began in earnest in 2003, when the CCW's Protocol V failed to restrict or ban them. "Widespread international disappointment at the weak outcome ... contributed to emergence of a free-standing negotiation, the so-called 'Ottawa Process', outside the United Nations system and orthodox negotiating rules ... very different from the technically oriented CCW in which big military powers were predominant."[85] Loosely following the template of the International Campaign to

---

[80] Virgil Wiebe, "Footprints of Death: Cluster Bombs as Indiscriminate Weapons under International Humanitarian Law," 22 *Mich. J. Int'l L.* 85, 89 (2000). Other reports of coverage are more conservative.

[81] Thomas M. McDonnell, "Cluster Bombs over Kosovo: A Violation of International Law?" 44 *Ariz. L. Rev.* (2002), 31, 51, 61.

[82] *Ticking Time Bombs: NATO's Use of Cluster Munitions in Yugoslavia*, Human Rights Watch Report 11–6 (D), (June 1999), available online.

[83] Harvard Human Rights Clinic and Human Rights Watch, "Cluster Munitions and the Proportionality Test, Memorandum to the Delegates of the Convention on Conventional Weapons (May 19, 2008)," available online.

[84] For example, William M. Arkin, "America Cluster Bombs Iraq," *Wash. Post*, Feb. 26, 2001; Thom Shanker, "Rights Group Faults U.S. Over Cluster Bombs," *NY Times*, Dec. 12, 2003, A12; Isabel Kershner, "Israel Won't Prosecute for Use of Cluster Bombs in Lebanon," *NY Times*, Dec. 25, 2007, A4; "Cluster Bombs, Made in America," *NY Times*, June 1, 2008, Wk 11.

[85] John Borrie, "The 'Long Year': Emerging International Efforts to Address the Humanitarian Impacts of Cluster Munitions, 2006–2007," in Timothy L. H. McCormack, ed., *YIHL*, Vol. 10, 2007 (The Hague: Asser Press, 2009), 251, 256.

Ban Landmines' anti-land mine process, cluster munition treaty negotiations commenced in Oslo in 2007; the final step was the Dublin Diplomatic Conference, in May 2008. More than one hundred states and numerous NGOs attended. The United States, Israel, and China were not represented. The Convention on Cluster Munitions, consisting of twenty-three articles, was agreed upon by 110 states. It is modeled on the Ottawa Convention on antipersonnel landmines, sometimes using the same language.

Under the Dublin Convention's Article 1, parties agree never to use, produce, acquire, transfer, or stockpile cluster munitions. Excepted from the definition of cluster munitions are munitions that have fewer than ten submunitions, all having electronic self-destruction and self-deactivating mechanisms (Article 2.2 (c)). Article 3 requires parties to destroy their CBU stockpiles not later than eight years after the convention takes effect, although a four-year extension may be requested. A "limited number" of CBUs and submunitions may be retained for training purposes (Article 2.6). Echoing CCW Protocol V, parties to the convention are required to clear and destroy cluster munition remnants in areas under their control within ten years of the convention's entry into force (Article 4.1), with renewable five-year extensions available (Article 4.5). Article 5.1 is a novel provision, not included even in the Ottawa Convention on land mines, which requires state parties to provide assistance, including medical care, rehabilitation, psychological support, and "social and economic inclusion," to victims of cluster munitions. States party in a position to do so shall provide technical and financial assistance in implementing convention obligations to other state parties that are affected by cluster munitions (Article 6.2). Article 9 requires parties to impose domestic penal sanctions for activities prohibited by the convention. Article 21 is unique in that it encourages cooperation between states even if one of the states cooperated with is not a party to the convention.

The Dublin convention took force in August 2010, after ratification by the thirtieth state. As of this writing, nearly one hundred states have ratified, with additional ratifications every year. Ratifying states include the United Kingdom, France, Germany, Italy, and Canada. States having the majority of cluster munitions have, so far, avoided the convention, choosing instead to address the humanitarian impact of their weapons through the CCW. For the major powers, without a substitute weapon, CBUs are considered too effective to consider giving up entirely. For those major states, questions of cluster munitions' compliance or violation of distinction and proportionality will continue to be an issue, and NGOs, human rights groups, and media will continue to question their use and, when they are used, their lawfulness.

Judging from state practice, their continued use seems probable. During the 2011 Libyan civil war, in the city of Misurata, Muammar Qaddafi's military forces employed Spanish-made 120-millimeter mortar cluster bombs, each mortar round scattering twenty-one high-explosive bomblets on the civilian areas that were targeted.[86] Cluster bombs were employed dozens of times in Syria's long-running civil war, as well, and at least a dozen times by both the Ukrainian army and Russian-sponsored rebels in the 2014–15 rebellion in the Ukraine, according to the NGO Human Rights Watch.[87] (Libya, Syria, the Ukraine, and Russia are not parties to the Convention on Cluster Munitions.)

For states retaining cluster munitions, the issue of submunition failure rates must be addressed. CBUs *can* be manufactured with near-zero dud rates, but the cost of a

---

[86] C. J. Chivers, "Qaddafi Is Using Cluster Bombs in Civilian Area," NY *Times*, April 16, 2011, A1.
[87] Rick Gladstone, "Report Says Syrian Forces Have Used Cluster Bombs," NY *Times*, Sept. 5, 2013, A12; Andrew Roth, "Ukrainian Forces Used Cluster Bombs, Evidence Indicates," NY *Times*, Oct. 21, 2014, A9.

near-perfect weapon is considerably greater. Meanwhile, cluster munitions continue to be employed in, so far, smaller noninternational armed conflicts.

19.2.2 U.S. Cluster Munitions Policy

The United States has consistently opposed calls to ban cluster munitions. "At the same time, the United States has pressed for international measures to increase the reliability of cluster munitions, to lessen the likelihood of postconflict casualties caused by unexploded submunitions."[88] (The United States is one of the few states able to afford the high cost of manufacturing cluster munitions with the elevated standard of reliability it urges.)

In 2008, the secretary of defense announced a new U.S. policy on cluster munitions. After reciting the considerable combat benefits that cluster munitions provide, the statement noted, "Blanket elimination of cluster munitions is therefore unacceptable." The announcement continued:

> The DoD policy establishes a new U.S. technical norm for cluster munitions, requiring that by the end of 2018, DoD will no longer use cluster munitions which, after arming, result in more than one percent unexploded ordnance. ... Additionally, cluster munitions sold or transferred by DoD after 2018 must meet this standard. ... As soon as possible, military departments will initiate removal from active inventory cluster munitions that exceed operational planning requirements. ... These excess munitions will be demilitarized as soon as practical. ... Through 2018, any U.S. use of cluster munitions that do not meet the one percent unexploded ordnance standard must be approved by the applicable combatant commander.[89]

The statement concluded:

> The new policy is viewed as a viable alternative to a complete ban proposal generated by the Oslo Process in Dublin. ... The new policy serves as the basis for the U.S. position in negotiations toward an international agreement at the U.N. Convention of Conventional Weapons. ... The United States has called for the completion of a new cluster munitions protocol. ... The CCW, unlike the Oslo process, includes all of the nations that produce and use cluster munitions, making any agreement reached there much more practically effective.[90]

The United States–sponsored protocol to the convention was widely criticized and its adoption was blocked, raising a brief response: "In the wake of this outcome, the United States will continue to implement its own voluntary policy to prohibit by 2018 the use of cluster munitions with more than a one percent unexploded ordnance rate, and we encourage other countries to take similar steps."[91]

For those states that have not ratified the Dublin Convention, cluster munitions, employed with care and with a low submunitions failure rate, are as lawful as artillery or high-explosive bombs. Although some weapons are per se unlawful – poisons,

---

[88] John R. Crook, ed., "Contemporary Practice of the United States Relating to International Law," 102–4 AJIL (Oct. 2008), 889.

[89] U.S. Dept. of Defense News Release, "Cluster Munitions Policy Revised (July 9, 2008), available online.

[90] Id.

[91] U.S. Mission to the U.N. in Geneva Press Release, reported at John R. Crook, ed., "Contemporary Practice of the United States Relating to International Law," 106–2 AJIL (April 2012), 388–90.

dum-dum bullets, serrated edged weapons – most often it is a weapon's *use* that determines its lawfulness. Such is the case of cluster munitions, for nonratifying states.

19.3 A Legal Review of Weapons

The 1980 CCW requires that state parties not field weapons containing nondetectable fragments and that laser weapons not cause permanent blindness. Customary international law mandates that ammunition not have certain characteristics – bullets with a tendency to yaw excessively in flight so as to wound with unnecessary suffering. Other weapons raise other questions. Are depleted uranium antiarmor rounds prohibited because the trace amounts of toxic uranium residue, left where rounds have impacted, may cause cancers and organ failures? Are combat shotguns unlawful because they create multiple wounds, or because the shot they fire flattens too easily in the human body, creating unnecessary suffering? How is a state to determine the answer to such questions? How can a commander know that the weapons issued to his soldiers, perhaps new weapons untested in combat, comply with the Geneva Conventions, the CCW, and other LOAC/IHL treaties?

He knows they comply because his government has a weapons legal review program in place. According to 1977 Additional Protocol I, Article 36: "In the study, development, acquisition or adoption of a new weapon, means or method of warfare, a High Contracting Party is under an obligation to determine whether its employment would, in some or all circumstances, be prohibited by the Protocol or by any other rule of international law applicable." The legal testing obligation of Article 36 applies not only to states that manufacture weapons but to states that purchase them. In addition, "the purchaser should not blindly depend on the attitude of the seller or the manufacturer, but should proceed itself to evaluate the use of the weapon in question."[92] Article 36 "implies the obligation to establish internal procedures for the purpose of elucidating the issue of legality [of new weapons]."[93] All countries with modern armies have a process in place for the legal review of new methods of warfare and new weapons.[94] "No single model for compliance with Article 36 exists. It is not a situation in which 'one size fits all', nor one in which one government's weapons review programme would be suitable for another government."[95]

Although not a party to Additional Protocol I, a U.S. weapons legal review process for land-based weapons is carried out by the army. Naval weapons are reviewed by the navy, aerial weapons by the air force. The pertinent army regulation for land-based weapons directs that the judge advocate general of the army "reviews weapons or weapon systems in accordance with DOD Instruction . . . to determine whether the weapons or weapon systems or their intended use in combat are consistent with the obligations assumed by the United States Government under all applicable treaties and with customary international law."[96] Other armed forces branches review their branch-specific weapons under similar instructions.

---

[92] Yves Sandoz, Christophe Swinarski, and Bruno Zimmerman, eds., *Commentary on the Additional Protocols* (Geneva: ICRC/Martinus Nijhoff, 1987), 426.

[93] Id., at 424.

[94] "Means and methods of warfare" is a nebulous phrase with no agreed-upon meaning. Parks includes in the term destruction of crops, blockade, and an artillery projectile that kills or injures in a new way. Parks, "Conventional Weapons and Weapons Reviews," supra, note 3, at 119.

[95] Id., at 107.

[96] Army Regulation 27–53, *Review of Legality of Weapons under International Law* (Jan. 1, 1979), para. 5.e. (1)., available online.

The arduous U.S. weapons review process results in a written published report indicating the weapon's conformance or nonconformance with LOAC/IHL.[97] Although the assessment of a new weapon's characteristics and probable effects inevitably leaves room for subjective interpretation, the review process is impressively comprehensive.

19.4 Summary

It bears repeating that any weapon can be used in an unlawful way. Few weapons are unlawful in and of themselves. "It follows that in determining the lawfulness or otherwise of existing or new weapons, the main function of the [CCW's] principles may lie in their capacity to be used as guidelines."[98] Ironically, "neither the Convention nor its annexed protocols specifically deemed any weapons to be excessively injurious or to have indiscriminate effects."[99]

Theodor Meron writes, "The tremendous progress in the humanization of the law of war brings into sharp relief the stark contrast between promises made in treaties and declarations ... on the one hand, and the harsh, often barbaric practices actually employed on the battlefield."[100] The 1980 CCW is an effort to control those "harsh practices actually employed" and limit the suffering of combatants and civilians. Its loosely worded requirements, as in Protocol V, warn, however, against overoptimism. Cluster bombs, for example, remain in frequent use despite the international effort to ban them. "Another source of possible concern is the extent to which the protocol [and the CCW itself] can be implemented by non-State actors involved in the hostilities. ... Securing implementation and compliance among organized armed groups will be a major challenge."[101]

CASES AND MATERIALS

PROSECUTOR V. MARTIĆ

IT-95–11-T (June 12, 2007), footnotes omitted.

Introduction. From January 1991 to August 1995, Milan Martić, a civilian, held various positions within the Serbian Autonomous Region of Krajina and the Republic of Serbian Krajina. He serially was the chief of police of Knin and, in the Serbian Region of Krajina,

---

[97] Parks, "Conventional Weapons and Weapons Reviews," supra, note 3. Colonel Parks, a longtime U.S. representative to international armaments conferences, describes in detail the review process at 107–42.

[98] Kalshoven, *Reflections on the Law of War*, supra, note 46, at 395.

[99] William Fenrick, "The Conventional Weapons Convention: A Modest but Useful Treaty," 279 *Int'l Rev. of the Red Cross* (1990), 498, 499.

[100] Theodor Meron, *The Humanization of International Law* (Leiden: Martinus Nijhoff, 2006), 85.

[101] Maresca, "New Protocol on Explosive Remnants of War" supra, note 70, at 835.

the secretary for internal affairs, the minister of defence, the deputy commander of the territorial defence, and the minister of the interior. He was eventually the president of the short-lived Republic of Serbian Krajina. His trial touches not only on the criminal use of cluster bombs, but on indiscriminate targeting and its corollaries, violations of distinction, and the targeting of cultural objects.

235. ... Škabrnja [in south-western Croatia] had about 2,000 inhabitants and was almost exclusively Croat. There were three churches in and around Škabrnja, the church of the Assumption of the Virgin in the center of Škabrnja, St. Mary's Church in the hamlet of Ambar, and St. Luke's Church to the west of the centre of Škabrnja. In 1991, Nadin was located in the Benkovac municipality and was approximately three kilometers south-east of Škabrnja. Nadin, which was also almost exclusively Croat, had between 300 and 660 inhabitants, living in approximately 120 to 150 houses. ...

(b) Situation in Škabrnja, Nadin and Surroundings Prior to 18 November 1991

236. In August 1991, running water and electricity to Nadin had been switched off. ... In September 1991, Škabrnja and Nadin were shelled and subjected to aerial bombings, including cluster bombs. ...

(g) Destruction in Škabrnja and Nadin

263. As noted above, during the attack on 18 and 19 November 1991 cluster bombs were dropped on Škabrnja with resulting damage to buildings. ... Marko Miljanić testified that by 19 November 1991, 30 to 40% of the houses in Škabrnja had been "destroyed" and that also the church of the Assumption of the Virgin and the school had been "destroyed." ...

264. ... By 1994 about 90 to 95% of Škabrnja was destroyed and the church of St. Mary in Ambar and church of St. Luke near the centre of Škabrnja were badly damaged. By October or November 1995, all the houses in Škabrnja and the church of the Assumption of the Virgin had been destroyed.

310. ... Ivan Markulin, a bomb disposal technician and police officer, died when the bomblet he was trying to deactivate exploded outside Klaićeve Street Children's Hospital.

311. The Trial Chamber heard evidence from some of those who were injured on 3 May 1995. ... Shortly after midday, 18 people, including Božica Lisak, were injured when bombs fell through the glass roof of the Croatian National Theater. Božica Lisak was severely injured by 27 pieces of shrapnel. Milan Smoljan was injured in his knee by bomblets. ...

460. In light of the totality of the evidence, the Trial Chamber finds beyond reasonable doubt that Milan Martić ordered the shelling of Zagreb on 2 and 3 May 1995.

(b) Military Targets in Zagreb and the Nature of the M/87 Orkan

461. ... The Trial Chamber notes the report of 2 May 1995 from the SVK [Army of the Republic of Srpska] Main Staff to the VJ [Army of the Federal Republic of Yugoslavia] General Staff, which provides that the following targets in Zagreb were fired at by Orkan

rockets on that day: the Ministry of Defence, the Presidential Palace and Zagreb/Plešo airport. The Trial Chamber notes that of these targets, the only one that was hit was the Zagreb/Plešo airport, where one bomblet landed in the parking lot. .... However, as will be shown below, the presence or otherwise of military targets in Zagreb is irrelevant in light of the nature of the M-87 Orkan.

462. The M-87 Orkan is a non-guided projectile, the primary military use of which is to target soldiers and armoured vehicles. Each rocket may contain either a cluster warhead with 288 so-called bomblets or 24 anti-tank shells. The evidence shows that rockets with cluster warheads containing bomblets were launched in the attacks on Zagreb on 2 and 3 May 1995. Each bomblet contains 420 pellets of 3mm in diameter. The bomblets are ejected from the rocket at a height of 800–1,000m above the targeted area and explode upon impact, releasing the pellets. The maximum firing range of the M-87 Orkan is 50 kilometers. The dispersion error of the rocket at 800–1,000m in the air increases with the firing range. Fired from the maximum range, this error is about 1,000m in any direction. The area of dispersion of the bomblets on the ground is about two hectares. Each pellet has a lethal range of ten meters.

463. The evidence shows that the M-87 Orkan was fired on 2 and 3 May 1995 from the Vojnić area, near the Slavsko Polje, between 47 and 51 kilometers from Zagreb. However, the Trial Chamber notes the characteristics of the weapon, it being a non-guided high dispersion weapon. The Trial Chamber therefore concludes that the M-87 Orkan, by virtue of its characteristics and the firing range in this specific instance, was incapable of hitting specific targets. For these reasons, the Trial Chamber also finds that the M-87 is an indiscriminate weapon, the use of which in densely populated civilian areas, such as Zagreb, will result in the infliction of severe casualties. By 2 May 1995, the effects of firing the M-87 Orkan on Zagreb were known to those involved. Furthermore, before the decision was made to once again use this weapon on Zagreb on 3 May 1995, the full impact of using such an indiscriminate weapon was known beyond doubt as a result of the extensive media coverage on 2 May 1995 of the effects of the attack on Zagreb.

472. In examining the responsibility of Milan Martić for the crime of attacks on civilians under Article 3 [of the ICTY Statute], the Trial Chamber recalls that a direct attack on civilians may be inferred from the indiscriminate character of the weapon used. The Trial Chamber has previously found that the M-87 Orkan was incapable of hitting specific targets. The Trial Chamber has also found that these attacks resulted in the death and serious injury to the civilian population. Having regard in particular to the nature of the M-87 Orkan and the finding that Milan Martić knew of the effects of this weapon, the Trial Chamber finds that Milan Martić wilfully made the civilian population of Zagreb the object of this attack. Milan Martić therefore incurs individual criminal responsibility [for the] attacks in civilians under Article 3 [of the ICTY Statute].

519. The Trial Chamber sentences Milan Martić to a single sentence of thirty-five (35) years of imprisonment.

Conclusion. Although cluster munitions used by most Western European and U.S. forces are delivered by guided weapon systems, countless nonguided rockets like the Orkan, which are easier and cheaper to produce, store, and maintain, are in the inventories of less advanced armed forces and some nonstate armed opposition groups.

WHITE PHOSPHORUS MUNITIONS

White phosphorus (WP) is a yellowish translucent, waxlike substance that spontaneously ignites upon exposure to oxygen, producing a yellow flame and a dense, bright white smoke. Although it has many industrial uses, from soft drinks to toothpaste, WP is most often noted because it can be weaponized as an artillery round, bomb, mortar round, or hand grenade. Upon ignition, WP burns until deprived of oxygen, producing highly effective smoke screens, as well as deep and painful second- and third-degree burns on human tissue.[102]

On November 8, 2004, Italian public television aired a documentary film in which the United States was charged with using artillery-delivered WP against enemy human targets in the November 2004 battle for Fallujah, Iraq, in violation of international law.[103] Four days later, the U.S. Department of State issued a denial of wrongful use, while confirming that WP had been sparingly used in Fallujah for illumination purposes.[104] Three months later, a report on the battle for Fallujah, written by U.S. Army artillery personnel, appeared in *Field Artillery* magazine. The authors wrote that WP "proved to be an effective and versatile munition. We used it for screening missions . . . [and] as a potent psychological weapon against the insurgents in the trench lines and spider holes when we could not get effects on them with HE [high explosive rounds]. We fired 'shake and bake' missions at the insurgents, using WP to flush them out and HE to take them out."[105] An embarrassed Department of State retracted its prior denial, emphasizing that WP remains a lawful weapon. Of course, "the U.S. retraction fueled the controversy started by the allegations made in the Italian documentary about the illegal use of WP."[106]

The initial question is whether WP is a chemical weapon, banned by the 1925 Geneva Protocol on the use of poisonous gases, or by the Gas Protocol's successor treaty, the 1993 CWC. Is it banned by the 1980 CCW, Protocol III, relating to incendiary weapons? "It is not altogether clear exactly what type of weapon WP constitutes: its principal component is a chemical, but the effect it produces on contact with human skin is to burn . . . which suggests that it is more in the nature of an incendiary weapon."[107]

As virtually all weapons do, WP contains chemicals, but chemical content does not make it a chemical weapon. To be a chemical weapon not only must it be chemical in nature, but its military uses must also be proscribed by the CWC. The primary military uses of WP munitions are to create smoke screens, provide illumination, and serve incendiary purposes. These uses are permitted by the CWC as "military purposes not connected with the use of chemical weapons and not dependent on the use of the toxic

---

[102] Agency for Toxic Substances and Disease Registry, "ToxFAQs for White Phosphorus," (Sept. 1997), http://www.atsdr.cdc.gov/tfacts103.html

[103] Sigfrido Ranucci and Maurizio Torrealta, "Fallujah: The Hidden Massacre."

[104] U.S. Dept. of State, "Did the U.S. Use Illegal Weapons in Fallujah?" (27 Jan. 2005) available online: "The United States categorically denies the use of chemical weapons at anytime in Iraq, which includes the ongoing Fallujah operation." The Nov. 12, 2004, Dept. of State press release has been removed from the agency's Web site.

[105] Capt. James T. Cobb, 1st Lt. Christopher A. LaCour, and SFC William H. Hight, "TF 2–2 in FSE AAR: Indirect Fires in the Battle of Fallujah," *Field Artillery* (March–April 2005), 23, 26.

[106] David P. Fidler, "The Use of White Phosphorus Munitions by U.S. Military Forces in Iraq," *ASIL Insights* (Dec. 6, 2005), http://www.asil.org/insights051206.cfm This is a fine, brief legal analysis of the issue.

[107] Turns, "Weapons in the ICRC Study," supra, note 15, at 222–3.

properties of chemicals as a method of warfare" (CWC, Article 11.9 (c)). In other words, a weapon's primary military uses, not the weapon's collateral effects, determine its character. A detonating antitank mine may kill nearby infantrymen. That fact does not make it an anti-personnel mine.

> The argument that the use of WP munitions in Fallujah constituted a prohibited use of a chemical weapon is difficult to sustain because WP munitions can [lawfully] be used as incendiary weapons against enemy military targets. ... The "shake and bake" uses of WP munitions appear to have used the incendiary capacities of these munitions to dislodge insurgents from entrenched positions. The use does not reflect intent to kill or incapacitate insurgents specifically by exposing them to the toxic chemicals produced in the fire and smoke generated by detonations of WP munitions.[108]

By its nature WP is in large part a chemical, but it is not a chemical weapon.[109]

Is WP a toxic weapon? "In sum, there are a number of negative effects on human and animal physiology that occur, through various routes of exposure, as a direct result of WP chemical interactions. As a result ... and using the definition of Article II (2) [of the Chemical Weapons Convention], WP could be classified as a 'toxic chemical' and thus it has the potential to be classed as a chemical weapon under Article II (1)(a)."[110] Again, however, WP's usual uses as a smoke screen do not rely on its toxic properties, meaning it is not a prohibited toxic weapon.

Was the use of WP in Fallujah in violation of CCW Protocol III, which restricts, but does not ban, the use of incendiary munitions? Because the United States was not a party to Protocol III during the time of the battle for Fallujah, the protocol did not then bind the United States. Was the use of incendiary munitions against enemy personnel unlawful as a matter of customary international law? The ICRC Study of Customary IHL clearly suggests that, as to combatants, it is not.[111] Even if the United States had been a party to CCW Protocol III, the "use of such munitions for marking, illuminating, screening, and (in certain circumstances) incendiary weapons against enemy targets has long been recognized as legitimate with full knowledge of its potential effects on the human body."[112] Once more, WP's usual uses do not rely on its incidental incendiary effect, and it is not a prohibited weapon for that reason.

There may be international public relations issues involved that militate against the use of WP, but there is no prohibition, customary or treaty-based, that makes the use of WP munitions, even when employed directly against combatants, a violation of LOAC/IHL.[113] Without a showing that it was used directly against civilians, its use in Fallujah was lawful.

---

[108] Fidler, "Use of White Phosphorus Munitions," supra, note 106.

[109] 1993 Chemical Weapons Convention, Art. II (1)(a).

[110] I. J. MacLeod and A. P. V. Rogers, "The Use of White Phosphorous and the Law of War," in Timothy L. H. McCormack, ed., *YIHL* (The Hague: Asser Press, 2009), 75, 90.

[111] Henckaerts and Doswald-Beck, *Customary International Humanitarian Law*, Vol. I, supra, note 14, Rule 85, at 290–1: "It can be concluded from this practice that incendiary weapons may not be used against combatants if such use would cause unnecessary suffering, i.e., if it is feasible to use a less harmful weapon to render a combatant *hors de combat*." This quotation suggests the ICRC's agreement that, if a less harmful weapon is not available, WP may lawfully be used directly against enemy personnel.

[112] Fidler, "The Use of White Phosphorus Munitions by U.S. Military Forces in Iraq," supra, note 106.

[113] MacLeod and A. P. V. Rogers, "Use of White Phosphorus," supra, note 110, at 110.

20 Gas, Biological, and Chemical Weapons Treaties

20.0 Introduction

At Strasbourg, in 1675, a Franco-German accord prohibited the use of poisoned bullets for the duration of the war between the two parties. Article 16 of Lieber's 1863 Code reads, "Military necessity ... does not admit of the use of poison in any way." In 1901, twenty-three of twenty-eight states attending the 1899 Hague Peace Conference ratified Declaration (IV, 2) Concerning Asphyxiating Gases. By 1907, four more states had either ratified or signed adhesions[1] to the declaration. (The United States was the sole nation not to sign.) "The contracting Powers," the 1899 declaration reads, "agree to abstain from the use of projectiles the sole object of which is the diffusion of asphyxiating or deleterious gases." According to 1907 Hague Regulation IV, Article 23, "It is especially forbidden – (a) To employ poison or poisoned weapons."

> In late 1914, however, amid the futile slaughter of [World War I] trench warfare, the traditional legal and moral restraints on the use of poison gas began to erode under the pressure of military necessity. ... The German High Command had interpreted the Hague gas-projectile declaration as banning only the release of lethal gases from shells specifically designed for that purpose. ... [The chemist Fritz Haber, winner of the 1918 Nobel Prize in chemistry] proposed instead that chlorine be released directly from pressurized gas cylinders, allowing the wind to carry the poisonous cloud over the enemy's trenches. This tactic offered a number of potential advantages: chlorine released directly from cylinders would blanket a far larger area than could be achieved with projectiles, and the gas would dissipate rapidly, allowing the affected areas to be occupied by friendly troops.[2]

By that point in 1914, both Germany and France had already fired thousands of artillery rounds of tear gas, but lethal gases had not been used. Now, General Erich von Falkenhayn, chief of the German General Staff, selected Ypres, Belgium, for first use of the chlorine gas against the enemy, intending to reduce a nine-mile bulge of Allied trench line into the German lines. Informed of the pending use of poison gas, the local commander, General Bertthold von Deimling, was at first resistant. But, illustrating the elasticity of military necessity as it was interpreted in that day, the general was persuaded: "The commission for poisoning the enemy ... was repulsive to me. If, however, the

---

[1] The entrance of a state into an existing treaty with respect to only such parts of the treaty as are agreed to specifically. Compare accession, by which a joining state accepts and is bound by the entire treaty.

[2] Jonathan B. Tucker, *War of Nerves* (New York: Pantheon, 2006), 11–12.

poison gas were to result in the fall of Ypres, we would win a victory that might decide the entire campaign. In view of this worthy goal, all personal reservations had to be silent."[3]

Lethal poison gas made its combat debut on April 22, 1915, in the Second Battle of Ypres. "More than six hundred French and Algerian troops lay blinded and dying in the wake of the poisonous cloud. ... Drowning on dry land as their lungs filled with fluid, [they] gasped painfully for air and coughed up a greenish froth flecked with blood. Gradually their faces changed from pallid white to grayish yellow, and their eyes assumed the glassy stare of death."[4] The poison gas allowed Germans to reduce the salient but, after heavy losses on both sides, the British Second Army stemmed further German advances.

Within months, the British and French armies formed special gas companies, and gas warfare became an established weapon of the war. When the Americans arrived in Europe in 1917, "gas held special horrors for the Doughboys."[5] General Pershing of the U.S. Army ordered the formation of the First Gas Regiment to defend against, and to employ, gas. The Chemical Warfare Service was formed. There were setbacks, of course. At the 1915 battle at Loos, Belgium, a British force attacked German lines after releasing a chlorine gas attack. An unanticipated wind shift blew the gas back on the attackers, resulting in more British than German casualties.[6]

More potent gases were introduced – initially phosgene and mustard gases. By the war's end, thirty-nine different toxic agents had been employed, resulting in roughly one million casualties, of which an estimated ninety thousand were fatal. Many survivors were left blinded or chronically disabled.[7] In an odd juxtaposition, both Lance Corporal Adolf Hitler and Colonel Douglas MacArthur were gassed and survived.[8]

20.1 The 1925 Geneva Protocol for the Prohibition of Poisonous Gases and Bacteriological Methods of Warfare

The 1919 Versailles Treaty, and the other treaties ending World War I, all incorporated articles referring to the prohibition of poisonous gases in warfare. In 1925, in Geneva, the Council of the League of Nations convened a Conference for the Supervision of the International Trade in Arms and Ammunition and Implements of War, but "attention was focused on the use of asphyxiating and other gases ... the horrifying effects of which had been amply demonstrated during the First World War. ... This resulted in the adoption of the Geneva Protocol of 1925."[9] It is "the watershed instrument on gas warfare."[10]

The one-page 1925 Protocol for the Prohibition of Poisonous Gases and Bacteriological Methods of Warfare is an arms control agreement, rather than a law of war document. As the title indicates, it extends beyond the banning of poisonous gases.

---

[3] Id., at 13, citing Berthold von Deimling, *Aus der alten in die neue Zeit* (Berlin, 1930), 201.   [4] Id., at 15.

[5] Frank E. Vandiver, *Black Jack*, Vol. II (College Station: Texas A & M University Press, 1977), 885.

[6] Obituary: Albert Marshall, *Economist*, May 28, 2005, 87. Marshall was the last surviving British cavalryman of World War I.

[7] Tucker, *War of Nerves*, supra, note 2, at 20.

[8] William Manchester, *American Caesar* (Boston: Little, Brown, 1978), 89.

[9] Frits Kalshoven, *Reflections on the Laws of War* (Leiden: Martinus Nijhoff, 2007), 342.

[10] Yoram Dinstein, *The Conduct of Hostilities under the Law of International Armed Conflict*, 1st ed. (Cambridge: Cambridge University Press, 2004), 74.

"The Gas Protocol reinforced the earlier prohibition in the Hague Declaration Respecting Asphyxiating Gases of 1899. The Protocol of 1925 both consolidated that prohibition and extended it to 'bacteriological methods of warfare.'"[11] The 1925 protocol reads:

> Whereas the prohibition of such use [in war of asphyxiating, poisonous or other gases] has been declared in Treaties to which the majority of Powers of the world are Parties; and to the end that this prohibition shall be universally accepted as part of International Law ... declare: That the High Contracting Parties, so far as they are not already Parties to Treaties prohibiting such use, accept this prohibition, agree to extend this prohibition to the use of bacteriological methods of warfare and agree to be bound as between themselves.

Within five years, 28 states had ratified the protocol. Today, there are 137 state parties, and the protocol's prohibitions are customary law with regard to both international and noninternational armed conflicts.[12] Similar to the 1925 protocol, employing asphyxiating, poisonous, or other gases or all analogous liquids, materials, or devices is a war crime pursuant to Article 8 (b)(2)(xviii) of the Rome Statute of the International Criminal Court.

20.1.1 *Parsing the 1925 Gas Protocol*

The 1925 protocol, "having regard to the many reservations, [amounts] to a prohibition of the first use of chemical and biological methods of warfare."[13] The protocol, less than a page in length, does not ban the acquisition, development, production, or stockpiling of poisonous gas or bacteriological agents – only their first use. Nor does it define that which it prohibits. "When this prohibition was introduced ... the meaning of the word 'poison' was apparently so clear that there was no debate about it."[14] A 1969 U.N. resolution, adopted without dissent, remedies the 1925 protocol's lack of definition. It interprets the protocol as prohibiting the use of

(a) Any chemical agents of warfare – chemical substances, whether gaseous, liquid or solid – which might be employed because of their direct toxic effects on man, animals or plants;

(b) Any biological agents of warfare – living organisms, whatever their nature, or infective material derived from them – which are intended to cause disease or death in man, animals or plants, and which depend for their effects on their ability to multiply in the person, animal or plant attacked.[15]

The protocol does not provide an investigative mechanism to verify alleged violations. That, too, has been addressed, at least provisionally, by U.N. resolution.[16]

---

[11] Col. G. I. A. D. Draper, "The Development of International Humanitarian Law," in Michael A. Meyer and Hilaire McCoubrey, eds., *Reflections on Law and Armed Conflicts* (The Hague: Kluwer Law International, 1998), 69, 75.

[12] Jean-Marie Henckaerts and Louise Doswald-Beck, eds., *Customary International Humanitarian Law.* Vol. I. *Rules* (Cambridge: Cambridge University Press, 2005), Rule 72, at 251.

[13] United Kingdom Ministry of Defence, *The Manual of the Law of Armed Conflict* (Oxford: Oxford University Press, 2004), para. 1.2.7., at 11.

[14] Antonio Cassese, Paola Gaeta, and John R. W. D. Jones, eds., *The Rome Statute of the International Criminal Court: A Commentary*, Vol. I (Oxford: Oxford University Press, 2002), 406.

[15] U.N. General Assembly Resolution 2603A (XXIV) (Dec. 16, 1969).

[16] U.N. General Assembly Resolution 37/98 (D) (Dec. 13, 1982): "4. Requests the Secretary-General to investigate, with the assistance of qualified experts, information that may be brought to his attention by any Member

During World War II, many states maintained poison gas stocks, and several planned for their possible use or actually used them. Just prior to the war, "Italy used gas in 1935–6 during its invasion of Ethiopia. . . . The most important exception was the Japanese use of gas and experimentation with biological weapons in China between 1937 and 1945."[17] For the most part, however, nations refrained from use of poison gases, one reason for which was the fear of retaliation.

President Franklin D. Roosevelt publicly proclaimed America's policy of not engaging in gas warfare and was personally opposed to its use.[18] Late in the war, however, the United States had plans to employ gas in the invasion of the Japanese home islands. In June 1945, the army's Chemical Warfare Service submitted a plan to the chief of staff, General George C. Marshall, that called for artillery and aerial bombing of Japan, using phosgene, hydrogen cyanide, cyanogen chloride, and mustard gases. Army planners "had chosen 50 'profitable urban and industrial targets,' with 25 cities listed as 'especially suitable for gas attacks.'"[19] Of course, many military plans are discussed, some of them formulated, but few are executed.

> [The U.S. Army chief of staff, General George C.] Marshall had earlier asked his Operations Division to consider the use of disabling gases . . . enough incapacitating gas to drive defenders from their bunkers or to keep the Japanese in gas masks for a week. That would leave them so weakened that the battle [for the Japanese home islands] would be a walkover, Marshall suggested. Marshall's willingness to consider the use of noxious gases, a violation of the Geneva Convention, was a reflection of his concern about the cost of ultimate victory. . . . Nonetheless, the "character of the weapon was no less humane than phosphorus and flame throwers." British protests shelved the plan. . . . "They were afraid that this would be the signal for the Germans to use gas against England," Marshall explained later.[20]

> **SIDEBAR.** In 1943, President Roosevelt approved the shipment of chemical munitions to the Mediterranean theater of war. On November 29, the American ship SS *John Harvey* arrived in the bustling port of Bari, Italy, which had been captured by the Allies only months earlier. The *John Harvey*'s secret cargo included 1,350 tons of mustard gas bombs. General Dwight Eisenhower wrote, "One of the ships was loaded with a quantity of mustard gas, which we were always forced to carry with us because of uncertainty of German intentions in the use of this weapon. . . . We manufactured

State concerning activities that may constitute a violation of the Protocol . . . to ascertain thereby the facts of the matter, and promptly to report the results of any such investigation to all Member States."

[17] Adam Roberts and Richard Guelff, *Documents on the Laws of War*, 3d ed. (Oxford: Oxford University Press, 2000), 156. As to Italy's use of gas in Ethiopia, see Lassa Oppenheim, *International Law*. Vol. II. *Disputes, War and Neutrality*, 7th ed., H. Lauterpacht, ed. (London: Longman, 1952), 344, fn. 1.

[18] Barton J. Bernstein, "Why We Didn't Use Poison Gas in World War II," 36–5 *American Heritage* (Aug./Sept. 1985), 40, 42.

[19] Norman Polmar and Thomas B. Allen, "The Most Deadly Plan," *U.S. Naval Institute Proceedings* (Jan. 1998), 79.

[20] Ed Cray, *General of the Army: George C. Marshall, Soldier and Statesman* (New York: W. W. Norton, 1990), 534–5. Gases, noxious or poisonous, are not mentioned in the two 1929 Geneva Conventions, nor in the 1949 conventions. Their use *would* have been a violation of the 1925 Geneva Gas Protocol, but the United States had not ratified that protocol in 1945.

and carried this material only for reprisal purposes."[21] Moored in the stream with fourteen other ships close by, the *John Harvey* awaited a berth at a pier where it could be unloaded. On the evening of December 2, "several thousand Allied servicemen and Italian spectators sat in the oval Bambino Stadium near Bari's train station as a baseball scrimmage between two quartermaster squads entered the late innings under the lights."[22] At about 1930, a score of German bombers attacked Bari – and the ships in its harbor. As port buildings and surrounding houses and businesses went up in flames, the *Joseph Wheeler* was among the first of the ships to be hit. The *John Bascom* followed. Set afire and adrift, the *Bascom* collided with the *John L. Motley*, whose cargo of ammunition exploded. On shore, Italian civilians were killed in the rush to reach already full air raid shelters. In the harbor, other ships were hit, including the *John Harvey*, which soon exploded, scattering its cargo of mustard gas throughout the harbor, as well as contaminating the seawater in which survivors swam.

"By dawn, the [hospital] wards were full of men unable to open their eyes, 'all in pain and requiring urgent treatment.' Surgeons were mystified to also find themselves operating with streaming eyes. ... The first skin blisters appeared Friday morning. ... The first mustard death occurred eighteen hours after the attack."[23] More than 1,000 Allied military personnel were killed or missing. Eventually, 617 were confirmed killed from exposure to mustard gas, including 83 Allied servicemen.[24]

News of the raid, the only case of deaths from chemical weapons in World War II, was censored.

The United States signed the 1925 protocol in June 1925 and "every peacetime President from Warren G. Harding to Franklin D. Roosevelt had defined gas as immoral and pledged to abide by the agreement."[25] Still, the United States only ratified the protocol in 1975, half a century after signing.

One of the main problems arising out of this [Gas Protocol] text has been whether it includes teargas and other so-called "riot control agents" (RCAs). For most countries, it does; but the United States has always maintained grave objections against this interpretation. Its underlying concern ... was that the text when given this broad meaning would not only exclude the use of such substances in war, against an enemy, but also, by implication, would throw doubt on the legality of their use by the police as riot control agents.[26]

Given the possible divergent interpretations of the protocol's RCA prohibition, states other than the United States have had the same concern. As early as 1930, efforts were

---

[21] Gen. Dwight D. Eisenhower, *Crusade in Europe* (Garden City, NY: Doubleday, 1948), 204. General Eisenhower, writing shortly after the war, chooses not to reveal the casualties caused by the *Harvey's* sinking: "Fortunately the wind was offshore and the escaping gases caused no casualties. Had the wind been in the opposite direction, however, great disaster could well have resulted. It would have been indeed difficult to explain" (p. 204.) The then–major general Jimmy Doolittle, whose headquarters were in Bari, and who was present during the raid, describes it in some detail but omits any mention of gas. Gen. James H. Doolittle, *I Could Never Be So Lucky Again* (New York: Bantam, 1991), 368–9.

[22] Rick Atkinson, *The Day of Battle* (New York: Henry Holt, 2007), 272.   [23] Id., 275–6.

[24] Id.; and Albert J. Mauroni, *Chemical and Biological Warfare: A Reference Handbook*, 2d ed. (Oxford: ABC-Clio, 2006), 102.

[25] Bernstein, "Why We Didn't Use Poison Gas in World War II," supra, note 18, at 41.

[26] Kalshoven, *Reflections on the Laws of War*, supra, note 9, at 139.

made by the International Committee of the Red Cross's (ICRC's) Preparatory Commission to clarify the prohibition's meaning. In commission meetings the United States asserted that "it would be inconsistent to prohibit the use in warfare of gases which could still continue to be used within states in peacetime for police purposes."[27] Finally, in 1975, the United States ratified the 1925 protocol with an understanding, much like that of the United Kingdom, that the protocol did not extend to RCAs or to chemical herbicides, but, as a matter of policy, the use of such substances would be restricted. The protocol applies only in time of armed conflict, so it has no bearing on peacetime riot control situations. Upon ratification the United States also entered a reservation similar to one entered by several other major powers: "The said Protocol shall cease to be binding on the Government of the United States ... in regard to an enemy state if such state or any of its allies fails to respect the prohibitions laid down in the Protocol."

Since World War II, protocol violations have been alleged. In 1982, the Soviet Union was accused by the United States of using chemical and toxic weapons in Laos, Cambodia, and Afghanistan. In the Iran–Iraq War (1980–8), chemical weapons were in fact repeatedly used, including the first battlefield use of nerve gas.[28] In Oregon, in a 1984 biological incident involving civilians, rather than combatants, the Bhagwan Shree Rajneesh cult sickened 751 people with *Salmonella enteritidis* grown in a home laboratory and placed in restaurants in doctored salad dressing. In Japan, in 1995, in another civilian-instigated noncombat incident, members of a religious cult employed a form of nerve gas in Tokyo's subway system, killing twelve.[29] In March 1991, during the first Gulf War, approximately 110,000 U.S. troops were exposed to low levels of an unspecified nerve gas when Iraqi munitions and rockets found at the Khamisiyah weapons depot were destroyed by the U.S. Army.[30]

The most notorious recent use of gas was Iraq's use of poison gases in the town of Halabja. During the Iran–Iraq War, in 1988, Kurdish rebels, accompanied by Iranian army elements, captured and occupied the Iraqi town of Halabja, just south of the Iranian border and 150 miles northeast of Baghdad. Saddam Hussein, seeking to repel the Iranian force and, at the same time, deliver a psychological blow to his own rebellious Kurdish *peshmerga*, authorized a poison gas attack. A day later, on March 16, eleven Soviet-made Sukhoy bombers of the Iraqi Air Force bombed Halabja from a low altitude. An Iranian officer reported, "'The sound of the explosions was unlike that of conventional bombs, more like a 'tap.' The smoke went up, then down to the ground.' ... The chemical strikes continued intermittently until the next morning,' he said."[31] More than five thousand Iraqi Kurds were estimated killed by the Iraqi bombing barrage of mustard gas, sarin, tabun, and VX.[32]

---

[27] Roberts and Guelff, *Documents on the Laws of War*, supra, note 17, at 155–6.

[28] Joost R. Hiltermann, *A Poisonous Affair* (Cambridge: Cambridge University Press, 2007), 34; and Dept. of Defense, *Conduct of the Persian Gulf War* (Washington, DC: GPO, 1992), 15.

[29] AP, "Two Sentenced to Death for 1995 Gas Attack on Tokyo Subways," *NY Times*, July 18, 2000, A10; "Japan: Death Sentence for Nerve Gas Attack," *NY Times*, Oct. 12, 2002, A7: Seiichi Endo, leader of the Aum Shinrikyo cult, admitted to producing the sarin gas used in the attack.

[30] Pauline Jelinek, "Figures on Gulf War Gas Exposure Revised," *NY Times*, Oct. 28, 2000, A4.

[31] Hiltermann, *Poisonous Affair*, supra, note 28, at 121.

[32] Donna Miles, "Halabja Revisited after 16 Years," U.S. Dept. of Defense, *News Articles* (March 16, 2004), available online.

"The [1925] Geneva Gas Protocol was the principal basis for asserting the illegality of the use of chemical weapons in the Iran-Iraq conflict 1980–8."[33] More recently, in Syria's long-running civil war that began in 2011, the United Nations confirmed that, in 2013, President Bashar al-Assad employed rocket-delivered sarin gas in attacks on civilian neighborhoods of Damascus,[34] killing as many as fifteen hundred civilians.[35] The U.N. secretary general commented, "The findings are beyond doubt and beyond the pale. This is a war crime."[36] In 2014, and again in 2015, after Syria agreed to give up its chemical weapons for destruction, al-Assad's forces continued to drop jury-rigged chlorine barrel bombs from helicopters onto civilian villages in northern Syria.[37] Syria has, so far, suffered no sanction for its confirmed and continued use of chemical weapons.

Despite its age, the 1925 Gas Protocol continues to gain new state parties into the twenty-first century. By now, however, its prohibitions on biological and chemical weapons have been supplemented and overtaken by two other treaties – the 1972 Biological Weapons Convention and the 1993 Chemical Weapons Convention. The 1925 Gas Protocol nevertheless remains enforceable, even if superseded. In 2009, a Dutch chemicals trader was charged with aiding and abetting genocide and prosecuted for violation of the 1925 Gas Protocol for supplying the Iraqi regime of Saddam Hussein with large quantities of raw materials for the production of mustard gas, from 1985 to 1988. Mustard gas was used by Saddam Hussein in the attacks on Kurdish villages in Iraq and in Iran, including the infamous attack on Halabja, Iraq. The Dutch trader was acquitted of the original charge but convicted of being an accessory to violations of the laws and customs of war. He was sentenced to fifteen years' confinement.

On appeal, his conviction was affirmed but his sentence was increased to seventeen years. On further appeal to the Dutch Supreme Court, his conviction and sentence were confirmed but, because of court delays in processing the appeal, his confinement was reduced to sixteen and a half years.[38]

Commentators argue that the 1925 Geneva Gas Protocol, by its terms, applies to international armed conflicts. "Arguably," the commentators write, "the use of chemical weapons in non-international armed conflicts was already prohibited under customary international law [when the attacks in Iraq occurred]. However, it is difficult to determine if this rule ... was already established back in the 1980s [when the attack within Iraq occurred]."[39] Other commentators disagree, believing that, as a result of a 1970 U.N. Resolution adopted by the General Assembly,[40] the 1925 protocol became applicable to noninternational armed conflicts, as well as international conflicts, mooting the question

---

[33] UK MOD, *Manual of the Law of Armed Conflict*, supra, note 13, para. 1.27.3, at 12.

[34] Rick Gladstone and C. J. Chivers, "U.N. Implicates Syria in Using Chemical Arms," *NY Times*, Sept. 17, 2013, A1; and, William J. Broad, "Rockets Carried Large Payload of Gas, Experts Say," *NY Times*, Sept. 5, 2013, A12.

[35] Steve Erlanger, "A Weapon Seen as Too Horrible, Even in War," *NY Times*, Sept. 7, 2013, A1.

[36] Gladstone and Chivers, "U.N. Implicates Syria," supra, note 34.

[37] Nick Cumming-Bruce, "Chlorine Used as Weapon In Syria War, Group Says," *NY Times*, Sept. 11, 2014, A8; Anne Barnard and Somini Sengupta, "Syria Is Again Using Chemical Weapons, Relief Workers Say," *NY Times*, May 7, 2015, A12.

[38] *Prosecutor v. Frans van Anraat*. Case No. 07/10742. 2009 Nederlandse Jurisprudentie 481, reported at 104–1 *AJIL* 86 (Jan. 2010).

[39] Marten Zwanenburg and Guido den Dekker, "Supreme Court of the Netherlands," in David J. Bederman, ed., "International Decisions," 104–1 *AJIL* (Jan. 2010), 66, 91–3.

[40] GA Res 2677, (XXIV) (1970).

of customary law applicability in 1980.[41] It is clear that, today, the 1925 Gas Protocol is customary law in both international and noninternational armed conflicts.[42]

20.2 The 1972 U.N. Convention on the Prohibition of the Development, Production and Stockpiling of Bacteriological (Biological) and Toxin Weapons and on Their Destruction

"In 1971 a historic attempt to create the world's first international legal regime banning the development and possession of an entire class of weapons of mass destruction ... culminated in the conclusion of the Biological Weapons Convention (BWC)."[43]

Biological warfare is older even than gas warfare. In 590 B.C., the Athenian ruler Solon is said to have used hellebore root to contaminate the drinking water of the besieged Greek city of Kirrha. During the French and Indian War, the British used smallpox against the Delaware Indians. In World War I, in addition to poison gas, the Germans employed anthrax and glanders against horses and mules of the U.S. Army. In World War II, the Japanese used typhoid against attacking Russians as well as Chinese civilians.[44]

The simultaneous prohibition of chemical and biological weapons had been discussed and debated before the 1925 Gas Protocol. The gas protocol, as its title indicates, attempted twin bans on gas, a present danger, and bacteriological weapons, which were perceived as an emerging future danger. In 1969, the United Nations reported on the problems raised by chemical and biological warfare,[45] and the World Health Organization issued reports detailing the unpredictability of such weapons and their extraordinary threat to both civilians and combatants.[46]

In the late 1960s, the U.N. Committee on Disarmament decided to attack the chemical weapon/biological weapon issue serially. It proposed a concentrated effort at banning biological weapons alone, leaving the issue of chemical weapons for another day and unlinking biological weapons from gas warfare. Although the use of biological weapons is not addressed in the 1972 convention, they were already proscribed, however ineffectually, in the 1925 Gas Protocol.

"A factor which facilitated this development was the unilateral renunciation of biological weapons by the United States, announced in November 1969, and the decision by the US government to destroy its stockpile of these weapons, irrespective of a possible future international agreement."[47] In February 1970, the United States also renounced the production, stockpiling, and use of toxins for purposes of war, confining military

---

[41] Sandesh Sivakumaran, *The Law of Non-International Armed Conflict* (Oxford: Oxford University Press, 2012), 393.

[42] Henckaerts and Doswald-Beck, *Customary International Humanitarian Law*, supra, note 12, rule 24, at 259.

[43] Jack M. Beard, "The Shortcomings of Indeterminacy in Armed Control Regimes: The Case of the Biological Weapons Convention," 101–2 *AJIL* (April 2007), 271.

[44] Col. (Dr.) Jim A. Davis, USAF, "The Looming Biological Warfare Storm," *Air & Space Power J.* (Spring 2003), 57, 58, footnotes omitted.

[45] United Nations, *Chemical and Bacteriological (Biological) Weapons and the Effects of Their Possible Use* (New York: United Nations, 1969).

[46] World Health Organization, *Health Aspects of the Use of Chemical and Biological Weapons* (Geneva: WHO, 1970).

[47] Jozef Goldblat, "The Biological Weapons Convention – an Overview," 318 *Int'l Rev. of the Red Cross* 251 (June 1997). The account of the BWC given here is based on the Goldblat article.

programs to research and development for defensive purposes. There were both ulterior and altruistic motives behind the U.S. moves. President Richard Nixon saw the cost of biological weapon programs ballooning, and the announcement would also deflect, at least temporarily, growing protests against the Vietnam conflict.[48] Regardless of motive, the U.S. announcements generated renewed negotiations that in less than two years resulted in the 1972 BWC. "The question of chemical weapons in their totality was laid to rest."[49] Problems of enforcement remained, however.

20.2.1 *Parsing the 1972 BWC*

The BWC, continuing and expanding the prohibitions of the 1925 Gas Protocol, bans the development, production, stockpiling, acquisition, or retention of microbial or other biological agents or toxins, and their delivery systems. Although the convention, like the Gas Protocol, does not define what it prohibits, World Health Organization definitions relating to biological weapons are often consulted: "***Biological agents*** **include those that depend for their effects on multiplication within the target organism, and are intended for use in war to cause disease or death in man, animals or plants.**"[50] **"Toxins are poisonous products of organisms; unlike biological agents, they are inanimate and not capable of reproducing themselves.** The Convention applies to all natural or artificially created toxins 'whatever their origin or method of production'. . . . Since toxins are chemicals by nature, their inclusion in the BWC was a step towards the projected ban on chemical weapons."[51] The key to the definition is in BWC Article II: A chemical weapon is one that is toxic; "its chemical action on life processes can cause death, temporary incapacitation or permanent harm to humans or animals."

Another striking feature of the BWC is found in Article II. "Each State Party ... undertakes to destroy, or to divert to peaceful purposes, as soon as possible but not later than nine months after the entry into force of the Convention, all agents, toxins, weapons, equipment and means of delivery ... which are in its possession or under its jurisdiction or control." This disarmament provision, as mentioned, is the first treaty providing for the abolition of an entire category of arms. The United States soon announced that its biological and toxin agents, other than small amounts for defensive research purposes, had been destroyed. It would be some time later that U.S. chemical weapons would be destroyed.[52] The Soviet Union stated that it had no biological or toxin agents, a statement that would later prove false.

---

[48] Richard Nixon, "Remarks Announcing Decisions on Chemical and Biological Defense Policies and Programs" (Nov. 25, 1969), available online: "First, in the field of chemical warfare, I hereby reaffirm that the United States will never be the first country to use chemical weapons to kill. ... I am asking the United States Senate for its advice and consent in ratification of the Geneva [Gas] Protocol of 1925. ... Second, biological warfare ... I have decided that the United States of America will renounce the use of any form of deadly biological weapons."

[49] Dinstein, *Conduct of Hostilities, supra*, note 9, at 75.

[50] World Health Organization, *Health Aspects of Chemical and Biological Weapons, supra*, note 46, at Chapter 4, at 12.

[51] Goldblat, "Biological Weapons Convention," *supra*, note 47, citing the W.H.O. and Art. I of the convention.

[52] Jeffrey Gettleman, "Army Begins Burning Biological Weapons in Alabama Town," *NY Times*, Aug. 10, 2003, A12.

The BWC's prohibitions are not absolute. They apply "only to types and quantities that have no justification for prophylactic, protective or other peaceful purposes. Retention, production or acquisition ... of certain quantities of biological agents and toxins may thus continue, and there may be testing in laboratories and even in the field."[53] States may continue to use biological agents for medical purposes such as therapy, diagnosis, and immunization, as well as in the development of protective masks, clothing, and detection, warning, and decontamination systems. There are no standards, no parameters, however, for quantities of agents or toxins that may be retained. These permitted uses and undefined limits offer clear opportunities to circumvent the prohibitions, so the convention is widely seen as porous, at best.

The convention itself raises issues of construction. Article III, for instance, requires state parties "not to transfer to any recipient whatsoever, directly or indirectly, and not in any way to assist, encourage, or induce any State ... to manufacture or otherwise acquire any of the agents, toxins ... or means of delivery specified" in the convention. Yet, Article X commits state parties "to facilitate ... the fullest possible exchange of equipment, materials and scientific and technological information for the use of bacteriological (biological) agents and toxins for peaceful purposes." These seemingly inconsistent provisions are an inviting portal for a state wishing to evade the convention's prohibitions.

The BWC and the 1925 Gas Protocol overlap in significant particulars. Article VIII of the BWC clarifies that, for parties to both the convention and the 1925 protocol, nothing in the convention limits or detracts from the obligations assumed by a state under the 1925 protocol to ban the use of poisonous gases. This overlap could raise a problem, however, if a state's reservation to the 1925 Gas Protocol allows it to use poison gas in retaliation against another state using gas against it. Such retaliatory use, permissible under the Gas Protocol reservation, would be a violation of the BWC's Article I, banning use "in any circumstances." Because a number of parties to the 1925 Gas Protocol entered just such a reservation, the conflict has been addressed by many states by withdrawing their Gas Protocol reservations. "They have thereby recognized that since the retention and production of biological weapons are banned, so must, by implication, be their use, because use presupposes possession."[54]

SIDEBAR. Georgi Markov was a popular Bulgarian novelist and playwright. Becoming disenchanted with the authoritarian Communist government of Bulgaria, Markov defected in 1969, eventually residing in London. Working as a broadcaster for the British Broadcasting Corporation (BBC) World Service, he also made anti-Communist broadcasts to his homeland for Radio Free Europe. Given his continuing popularity in Bulgaria, his anti-Soviet programs were a continuing thorn in the Russian bear's paw. One morning in 1989, on London's Waterloo Bridge, as Markov waited for a bus to his BBC office, he felt a sharp pain in his leg. Turning, he saw a man, who apologized as he picked up the umbrella he had dropped. The man had a foreign accent, Markov said, as he lay ill, that evening. Markov died three days later, at age forty-nine. An autopsy found a small metal pellet embedded in his leg. It was coated with a substance that melted at body temperature, releasing from a tiny cavity within the pellet 0.2 milligram of ricin, a

---

[53] Id.   [54] Id.

highly toxic biological agent derived from the castor plant.[55] An Italian suspect was identified in a newspaper account, but Markov's killer was never arrested or tried. Markov's murder was not a war crime. Was it a violation of the 1972 BWC?

In November 2006, Alexander V. Litvinenko, a former Russian K.G.B. officer and a fierce critic of President Vladimir Putin, drank a cup of tea in a London hotel. Three weeks later he died a lingering, painful death. The teapot from which he drank was later found to have a high concentration of polonium 210, a rare radioactive isotope. U.K. officials said they knew who poisoned Litvinenko and sought the extradition of Andrei Lugovoi, a former K.G.B. officer. Russia refused the extradition request and no further action has been taken.

The British professor Geoffrey Best, always pithy, has written, "Legal prohibitions of weapons . . . are mere plowings of the sand unless they are accompanied by convincing measures of verification."[56] The BWC contains no compliance or verification provisions, although they have long been sought.[57] Given advances in biological production capabilities, the absence is significant. It is not difficult to mask weapons research as defensive measures.[58] "The effort to bolt some monitoring provisions on to the BWC got a big push after Russia . . . admitted in the early 1990s that the Soviet Union had built up a huge biological-weapons programme."[59] Alarmed by the 1979 Sverdlovsk incident,[60] and by Iraq's apparent biological arsenal, revealed in the Iraq–Kuwait conflict (1990–1), a six-year international effort was mounted to create an enforcement protocol.[61] It failed when the United States withdrew from the effort in 2001, largely for reasons stated in the American announcement of nonsupport: "The protocol could (1) allow foreign governments to harass U.S. government laboratories working on vaccines . . . to defend against the possibility of biological attacks, (2) cause U.S. companies to lose industrial secrets, and (3) undermine U.S. regulations designed to stem the export of technology used in

---

[55] Lt.Col. Terry N. Mayer, USAF, "The Biological Weapon: A Poor Nation's Weapon of Mass Destruction," in Berry R. Schneider and Lawrence E. Grinter, eds., *Battlefield of the Future: 21st Century Warfare Issues* (Maxwell Air Force Base, AL: Air Warfare College, Sept. 1995); and, CNN.com, "Ricin and the Umbrella Murder (Oct. 23, 2003), available online.

[56] Geoffrey Best, *War and Law since 1945* (Oxford: Oxford University Press, 1994), 308.

[57] Elizabeth Olson, "Talks Inching Ahead on Monitoring'72 Germ Warfare Pact," NY *Times*, May 14, 2001, A6; Elizabeth Olson, "U.S. Rejects New Accord Covering Germ Warfare," NY *Times*, July 26, 2001, A5; and, Michael R. Gordon, "Germ Warfare Talks Open in London; U.S. Is the Pariah," NY *Times*, July 24, 2001, A7: "European nations and other major powers today urged the completion of a draft agreement to enforce the 1972 ban on biological weapons, a move that puts them at odds with the Bush administration. . . . The European endorsement . . . has left the Bush administration increasingly isolated."

[58] Judith Miller, Stephen Engelberg, and William J. Broad, "U.S. Germ Warfare Research Pushes Treaty Limits," NY *Times*, Sept. 1, 2001, A1; and Judith Miller, "When Is a Bomb Not a Bomb? Germ Experts Confront U.S.," NY *Times*, Sept. 5, 2001, A5.

[59] "Bugs in the System," *Economist*, June 16, 2001, 47; and Tim Weiner, "Soviet Defector Warns of Biological Weapons," NY *Times*, Feb. 25, 1998, A1.

[60] In April 1979, anthrax in aerosol form was released from a Russian military bioweapons manufacturing facility near Sverdlovsk. Livestock and at least sixty-four humans were killed. See Ken Alibek, *Biohazard* (New York: Arrow Books, 2000), 70–86.

[61] For a full account of the contentious and unsuccessful protocol process, see, Onno Kervers, "Strengthening Compliance with the Biological Weapons Convention: The Protocol Negotiations," 7–2 *J. of Conflict & Security L.* (Oct. 2002), 275.

biological weapons."[62] The proposed enforcement protocol raised the possibility of commercial espionage. It is unfortunate that there still is no enforcement mechanism, leaving the convention largely toothless.

What the convention does provide is that state parties may not transfer or assist another state to manufacture or acquire any prohibited agent, toxin, weapon, or means of delivery (Article III). Article VI allows that "any State Party ... which finds that any other State Party is acting in breach of obligations deriving from ... the Convention may lodge a complaint with the Security Council of the United Nations. Such a complaint should include all possible evidence ... as well as a request for its consideration by the Security Council." This is a thin reed upon which to base compliance expectations because, international politics aside, few states have the ability to gather evidence of breach in other states, and the U.N. Security Council is not empowered by the charter to investigate compliance with arms control agreements.

There have nevertheless been formal complaints. In 1980, the United States accused the Soviet Union of maintaining an offensive biological weapons program. The complaint was based on a suspected 1979 airborne release of anthrax spores from a biological facility that caused an anthrax outbreak near Sverdlovsk. Although it was attributed at the time to contaminated meat, in 1992 the Soviet government admitted to the breach and agreed to convert all previously secret military research centers to civilian use, in compliance with the BWC. In 1981, on the basis of chemical analyses and eyewitness accounts of aircraft spraying, the United States accused the Soviet Union of the production and use of mycotoxins in Laos, Kampuchea, and Afghanistan. The eyewitness reports were eventually discredited, and medical analyses were unable to corroborate the allegations. In 2001, the United States accused North Korea, Iraq, Iran, Syria, and Libya of violating the convention, as well. The accusations came to nothing.

20.2.2 Negotiating the BWC

Although there are significant weaknesses in the BWC, its negotiation proved quick, even with continuing disagreements over CS gas (discussed later). The unpredictability of biological weapon effects, and their resulting limited combat value, combined with long-standing international repugnance toward biological weapons, allowed rapid treaty formation. (The same cannot be said with regard to chemical weapons, covered by the 1993 CWC.) Close to 175 states have ratified the 1972 BWC. The United States ratified in 1975.

> The aim of the BW Convention was not so much to remove an immediate peril, as to eliminate the possibility that scientific and technological advances, modifying the conditions of production, storage or use of biological weapons, would make these weapons militarily attractive. ... The Convention is comprehensive enough to cover all relevant scientific and technological developments, including biological agents and toxins that could result from genetic engineering processes.[63]

---

[62] Sean D. Murphy, ed., "Contemporary Practice of the United States Relating to International Law," 95–4 AJIL 873, 901 (Oct. 2001), citing U.S. Dept. of State Daily Press Briefing, Philip T. Reeker, Dept. Spokesman (July 25, 2001), available online.

[63] Goldblat, "Biological Weapons Convention – an Overview," supra, note 47.

Biological agents are difficult to weaponize, but their threat remains real. Although there has been vast improvement in bioweapon defenses, past exercises simulating biological attacks on civilian targets reveal a general American unpreparedness.[64] Anthrax, plague, smallpox, glanders, tularemia, foot-and-mouth disease, swine fever – all deadly – are within the reach of the trained terrorist. "Recently developed techniques permit the manipulation of key biological processes with a precision and power not dreamed of 20 years ago. ... It is becoming possible to synthesize biological agents to military specifications. Thus, the world lies on the threshold of a dangerous era of designer bugs as well as designer drugs."[65]

The weaknesses of the BWC are summarized by a former Department of Defense deputy general counsel:

> Although the BWC purports to outlaw the development and possession of all biological weapons, deadlier and more sophisticated biological weapons than were imaginable in 1972 can now be and have been produced, as evidenced in October 2001 by two letters sent to the Capitol Hill offices of [two U.S.] Senators. ... These letters reportedly contained ... a dangerous and sophisticated form of "weapons-grade" anthrax spores. ... In addition to the empirical evidence of new "super" biological weapons, the failings of the BWC are further manifested by the growing significance that countries like the United States attach to the BW threat ... and contentious review conferences of the BWC states parties that have been unable to resolve cheating and compliance concerns. Furthermore, a significant number of states have not yet joined the BWC ... prompting statements of concern about its lack of universality. [66]

The same writer cites the indeterminate language of key BWC provisions as a primary cause for what he sees as the convention's failure. Whatever the basis of the BWC's problems, the lack of effective international inspection and compliance regimes is a continuing problem for all states and for their armed forces who may be targeted.

20.3 The 1993 Convention on the Prohibition of the Development, Production, Stockpiling and Use of Chemical Weapons

President Bill Clinton correctly said in his letter of transmittal to the Senate urging this treaty's ratification, "The Chemical Weapons Convention is unprecedented in its scope."[67] The roots of the 1993 CWC were in the 1899 and 1907 Hague peace conferences; 1899 Declaration IV, 2, Concerning Asphyxiating Gases, was ratified by twenty-five states. Article 23 of 1907 (and 1899) Hague Regulation IV forbade use of "poison or poisoned weapons."

By 1971, the international community realized that initial optimism regarding the banning of chemical and biological weapons was not justified, and the two were given separate consideration, the BWC resulting in 1972, the CWC in 1993. As of this writing,

---

[64] Lt.Col. Raymond S. Shelton, "No Democracy Can Feel Secure," U.S. Naval Institute *Proceedings* (Aug. 1998), 39, 44; and, "America the Unready," *Economist*, Jan. 22, 2000, 34.

[65] Cmdr. Stephen Rose, "The Coming Explosion of Silent Weapons," 42 *Naval War College Rev.* (Summer 1989), 6.

[66] Beard, "Shortcomings of Indeterminacy," supra, note 43, at 271–2.

[67] Letter of transmittal, 1993 CWC (Nov. 23, 1993), cited in 88–2 *AJIL* (April 1994), 323.

the CWC has been ratified by virtually all of the world's states. The United States ratified in 1997, with numerous declarations.

The overlap of chemical, gas, and biological weapons is now clearly seen. For instance, the 1995 release of sarin gas in a Tokyo subway, in which twelve commuters were killed, was a chemical attack perpetrated through a gaslike aerosol delivery system. The delivery method involved a gas, whereas the poisonous substance was a chemical. In June 1990, the Liberation Tigers of Tamil Eelam, the "Tamil Tigers" of Sri Lanka, assaulted and overran a Sri Lankan army special forces camp in Sri Lanka's Batticaloa district using a chemical-based chlorine gas. Such incidents underscore the value of the interlocking gas, biological, and chemical treaties.

20.3.1 *Parsing the 1993 CWC*

The lengthy CWC consists of twenty-four articles and three annexes that cover chemical warfare agents, implementation and verification, and the protection of confidential information. The CWC obliges that state parties "never under any circumstances" use, develop, produce, acquire, stockpile, retain, or transfer chemical weapons; not encourage or assist anyone to do so; destroy any chemical weapons they own or possesses; and destroy any chemical weapons production facilities they own or possess. Retaliatory use of chemical weapons is also prohibited. (U.S. ratification of the CWC made moot its reservation to the 1925 Gas Protocol, which preserved the right of retaliation to an enemy's gas attack.)

The internationally contentious argument that CS gas is a riot control agent rather than a weapon of war is not settled by the CWC. Article I.5 reads, "Each State Party undertakes not to use riot control agents as a method of warfare."[68] That language is short of a prohibition. In fact, RCAs for law enforcement purposes are specifically exempted in Article II.9(d). Some hold that in noninternational armed conflicts Additional Protocol II controls the use of RCAs:

> Additional Protocol II [of 1977] is a relevant source of applicable rules that should inform interpretation of Article II.9(d). Military action taken against insurgents who exercise control over part of a State's territory and carry out sustained and concerted military operations constitutes armed conflict rather than law enforcement, and thus falls outside Article II.9(d). The CWC's prohibition of the use of chemical weapons "under any circumstance" encompasses civil conflict as well as international conflict. This reasoning also suggests that use of RCAs in counter-insurgency operations would be a method of warfare prohibited by Article I.5 of the CWC. The State practice of military forces in Iraq to date supports this interpretation, because such forces have not used RCAs.[69]

Moving beyond RCAs, chemical weapons are broadly defined in CWC Article II:

(a) Toxic chemicals and their precursors, except where intended for purposes not prohibited under this Convention;

---

[68] A "riot control agent" is described in Article II.7 as "any chemical ... which can produce rapidly in humans sensory irritation or disabling physical effects which disappear within a short time."

[69] David P. Fidler, "The Meaning of Moscow: 'Non-Lethal' Weapons and International Law in the Early 21st Century," 859 *Int'l Rev. of the Red Cross* (Sept. 2005), 525, 547. Footnote omitted.

(b) Munitions and devices, specifically designed to cause death or other harm through the toxic properties of those toxic chemicals ... which would be released as a result of the employment of such munitions and devices;

(c) Any equipment specifically designed for use directly in connection with the employment of munitions and devices specified [above].

Article III requires a state party to provide a number of declarations: to declare whether it owns or possesses chemical weapons and specify their location with an inventory of their quantity and to declare chemical weapons transferred or received since 1946, specifying the weapons. Production facilities require similar declarations, including present or past existence, transfers of production equipment since 1946, and the "general plan" for destruction or conversion to nonweapon use of production facilities.

The United States complies with its agreement to destroy its thirty-one thousand metric tons of assorted chemical weapons through a network of destruction facilities;[70] VX, for instance, was destroyed at the army's Newport Chemical Depot, in Indiana; bulk mustard agent was destroyed at Maryland's Aberdeen Proving Ground; chemical weapons previously deployed to European and Pacific military bases were destroyed at the Johnston Atoll Chemical Agent Disposal System, in the mid-Pacific.

Multinational treaty compliance and verification are always troublesome issues. In the case of the CWC, "the foundation [of the convention] is a verification program so rigorous that potential disputes may be preempted even before they emerge."[71] State parties agree that stored or destroyed chemical weapons shall be subject to systematic verification "through on-site inspection and monitoring with on-site instruments," and annual declarations are to be submitted regarding destruction plans.

There are compliance exemptions. State parties may "develop, produce, otherwise acquire, retain, transfer and use toxic chemicals ... for purposes not prohibited" by the convention (Article VI). "Making the matter more complex, there is the unavoidable dual use of the technologies that create medicines and vaccines as well as biological toxins. The tricky task of distinguishing between the use of enriched uranium for energy and for nuclear weapons is child's play compared to the difficulty of maintaining a distinction between research for bioweapons and research for biotreatments."[72]

Cyanide and phosgene, for example, are dual-use chemicals (i.e., potential chemical weapons as well as innocent industrial agents) that are critical for innocent uses in the chemical industry. Malathion and parathion also have valuable agricultural uses, and mustard agents are used in cancer chemotherapy. Five million tons of ricin toxin, the chemical that killed Georgi Markov, is produced annually as waste mash in processing castor beans.[73] Refined ricin is also used in the treatment of severe glaucoma. Other purposes not prohibited by the CWC include "the right of any State Party to conduct research into, develop, produce, acquire, transfer or use means of protection against chemical weapons" (Article X.2).

---

[70] John R. Crook, ed., "Contemporary Practice of the United States Relating to International Law," 100–3 *AJIL* (July 2006), 690, 720. Tucker, *War of Nerves*, supra, note 2, at 356, puts the amount at 31,000 tons.

[71] David A. Koplow, 94–1 *AJIL* (Jan. 2000), 221, 222 (reviewing Michael Bothe, Natalino Ronzitti, and Allan Rosas, eds., *New Chemical Weapons Convention* [2000]).

[72] Philip Bobbitt, *Terror and Consent* (London: Penguin Books, 2009), 104.

[73] Sherman McCall, M.D., "A Higher Form of Killing," U.S. Naval Institute *Proceedings* (Feb. 1995), 38, 43.

CWC Article VIII establishes the Organization for the Prohibition of Chemical Weapons. Located in the Hague, the organization's executive council, forty-one representatives elected from the state parties, handles the organization's day-to-day business. The Conference of State Parties meets annually to hear verification challenges and plan routine inspections (Article VIII.B), among other duties.

Monetary issues have strained the organization's agenda.[74] For several years the United States refused to pay its organization dues because of its Brazilian director, whom the United States (and a large majority of the executive council) considered overreaching and focused on personal salary issues rather than organization business.[75]

Any state party may request a "challenge inspection" to resolve any question in relation to another state's CWC compliance (Article IX.2 and 8). In a challenge inspection, inspected state parties are obligated to make reasonable efforts to demonstrate compliance, although the inspected state may invoke "managed access" to protect sensitive installations and confidential information unrelated to the CWC (Article IX.11.(c)). The CWC has unique confidentiality provisions aimed at protecting private industries that use chemical agents and thus may be subjects of challenge inspections. For example, a challenged state might believe a challenge regarding alleged wrongful activity in, say, a civilian medical corporation's facility is actually aimed at the challenger's learning proprietary secrets of the medical corporation's breakthrough in medical devices. The challenged state may assert a right to managed access to protect proprietary secrets. "The treaty's Confidentiality Annex spells out in elaborate detail how the inspectors will operate, what procedural protections will be in place for the acquired information, and how the balance will be struck between the international community's 'need to know' about suspicious or problematic activities, and the facility's need to protect itself against unwarranted snooping."[76]

Article XII details sanctions for noncompliance with the CWC. They range from suspending a party's rights under the convention to "in cases of particular gravity," asking the issue to the U.N. General Assembly and Security Council. As with the 1972 BWC, the CWC does not provide for individual criminal responsibility for violators. Instead, both the BWC and the CWC "do this indirectly through the obligation for state parties to adopt measures to ensure that no activities prohibited ... take place. ... However, the ability to prosecute a violator depends on the quality of the national implementation legislation (if adopted at all) and the presence of relevant provisions in the national penal code."[77]

Neither the articles nor annexes of the CWC are subject to reservations "incompatible with its object and purpose" (Article XXII). U.S. implementation of the CWC was initially accomplished by executive order and codification as federal law.[78]

---

[74] Marlise Simons, "Money Short for Battle on Chemicals Used in War," NY Times, Oct. 5, 2001, A5: "The group, the Organization for the Prohibition of Chemical Weapons, has managed to make less than half the inspections scheduled for this year ... because the United States and several other countries have been late in paying their dues."

[75] Amy E. Smithson, "The Failing Inspector," NY Times, April 8, 2002, A23.

[76] Koplow, reviewing Bothe, Ronzitti, and Rosas, New Chemical Weapons Convention, supra, note 71, at 222.

[77] Jean Pascal Zanders, "International Norms against Chemical and Biological Warfare: An Ambiguous Legacy," 8–2 J. of Conflict & Security L. (Oct. 2003), 391, 397.

[78] Executive Order 13128, "Chemical Weapons Convention Implementation Act of 1998" (June 25, 1999); 22 U.S. Code, §§ 6701–6771.

Binary weapons, not addressed in the CWC, remain a concern.[79] A binary chemical weapon is one in which the toxic agent remains physically separate from the munition, or *in* the munition, in the form of two nontoxic chemical precursors. When the munition is fired (or just before firing, if the nontoxic precursors are physically separate) the precursor chemicals combine to form a prohibited chemical weapon. The discovery of binary weapons is difficult, because the precursor chemicals are harmless until combined.

The ICRC study on customary law asserts that the prohibition of use of chemical weapons is a norm of customary law in both international and noninternational armed conflicts.[80] It also finds the prohibitions of use of biological weapons[81] and RCAs as a method of warfare to be norms of customary law.[82] A commentator writes, as to chemical weapons, "This, it is submitted, is a quite astonishing exercise in extrapolation of a detailed rule from very little hard evidence."[83] (See, however, Cases and Materials, this chapter, *Prosecutor v. Tadić.*) The same commentator makes a similar objection to the ICRC study's finding regarding biological weapons.[84] The question is not whether use of chemical or biological weapons in warfare is lawful; it surely is not. The question is whether their use in warfare is contrary to customary international law.

Like the BWC, the CWC is not without critics. "Deterrence must also be maintained by producing retaliatory quantities of binary nerve agent. . . . The military advantages and allure of surreptitious chemical weapons guarantee that the new treaty will be violated. The experience of arms control says that deterrence is the only real hope of preventing their use."[85] The former U.S. secretary of state James Baker replies, "The United States does not need chemical weapons as a deterrent . . . with our overwhelming conventional force and vast nuclear arsenal. Each is more than sufficient to deter a chemical attack."[86] Although Secretary Baker's 1977 response was made before the day of nonstate actors and their resilience in the face of conventional armed forces, his conclusion probably remains accurate.

20.4 CS Gas

CS gas is not "tear" gas. As a matter of fact, CS is not a gas. Although tear gas and CS are often thought of as the same agent with different military designations, and although they have much the same effects, they are quite different.

Tear gas, first used in 1914 in World War I, is a chemical substance that produces tears, a runny nose, even temporary blindness, by irritating the mucous membranes of the eyes and nose through a process that is still not well understood.

CS, in contrast, was discovered in 1928 by Ben Corson and Roger Stoughton, at Middlebury College, Vermont. Its name, "CS," is the initials of the last names of its discoverers. CS is not a gas, but a solid form of an active chemical that has several

---

[79] "Binary" is mentioned in Arts. 2.3, 2.4, and 8.(a)(ii) in defining other terms. The term is not used in any prohibitory form.

[80] Henckaerts and Doswald-Beck, *Customary International Humanitarian Law*. Vol. I. *Rule* , supra, note 12, rule 74, at 259.

[81] Id., rule 73, at 256.   [82] Id., rule 75, at 263.

[83] David Turns, "Weapons in the ICRC Study on Customary International Humanitarian Law," 11–2 *J. of Conflict & Security L.* (Summer 2006), 202, 225.

[84] Id., at 221.   [85] McCall, "Higher Form of Killing," supra, note 73, at 44.

[86] James A. Baker III, "Our Best Defense," *NY Times*, Feb. 16, 1997.

varieties, ground extremely fine (particles one micrometer in size – 1/25,000 inch) and dispersed as a vapor. "gas" was first used in 1961 by British forces on Cyprus. Depending on its chemical makeup and concentration, its effects range from those of tear gas, to immediate vomiting, to prostration. Because mild CS formulations in common use cause the same tearing as tear gas, it is commonly referred to as tear gas. Neither CS, nor tear gas, nor other RCAs are mentioned in the BWC.

The U.S. Army designated CS its standard riot control agent in 1959 and employed it against enemy bunkers in the U.S.–Vietnamese conflict. In thickened form, it was used as a terrain denial agent; there its lingering effects closed trails, tunnels, and perimeters for days or, absent wind or precipitation, weeks. "One of the major uses of CS gas in Vietnam is to flush enemy soldiers out of bunkers preceding high explosive [artillery] fire or infantry assault."[87] Adding liquid silicone to CS made it weatherproof, and dyeing thickened CS green made it less visible in vegetated terrain.[88]

In conflicts against terrorists, however, CS is not to be found on U.S. supply manifests. In U.S. military practice, the use of CS is controlled by Executive Order 11850.[89] "The United States renounces, as a matter of national policy, first use of . . . riot control agents in war except in defensive military modes to save lives." The order's exceptions are to control U.S. prisoners of war, situations in which civilians are used to screen attacks, rescue missions of downed aircrew, and protection of convoys in noncombat areas. "The Secretary of Defense shall take all necessary measures to ensure that the use by the Armed Forces . . . is prohibited unless such use has Presidential approval, in advance." Executive Order 11850, first issued by President Gerald R. Ford, has not been modified since it was issued, and it remains in effect.[90] In periods of armed conflict, presidential approval authority has doubtless been delegated to combatant commanders, if not to division commanders. Approval of use of CS in combat zones, however, remains tightly controlled.

20.5 Summary

The obvious dangers of gas, chemical, and biological weapons extend beyond the effects of the weapons themselves. The acquisition of such weapons of mass destruction by an irresponsible state, or a nonstate armed opposition group, can be the basis for armed intervention, "not just reactively but preventively and before a latent threat becomes imminent."[91]

Although the 1925 Gas Protocol has been all but superseded by the 1993 CWC, issues of verification, clandestine production, and weapons destruction remain. The same issues are more significant in the 1972 BWC. The 1993 CWC goes far in providing credible verification procedures, but even the challenge inspection provisions of that pact

---

[87] Matthew S. Meselson, "Chemical and Biological Weapons," 222–5 *Scientific American* (May 1970), 3.

[88] Lt.Col. Rufus T. Brinn, "U.S. Policy and the Uncertain State of Military Usage of Riot Control Agents" (U.S. Army War College, Carlisle Barracks, PA, Strategic Research Project, 1998), 12–15.

[89] Executive Order 11850, "Renunciation of Certain Uses in War of Chemical Herbicides and Riot Control Agents," 40 *Fed. Reg.* 16187 (April 8, 1975), available online.

[90] Statement of Joseph Benkert, Principal Deputy Asst. Secretary of Defense for Int'l Security Policy, before the Senate Committee of Armed Services, Subcommittee on Readiness and Management Support (Sept. 27, 2006).

[91] "A More Secure World: Our Shared Responsibility," Report of the U.N. Secretary-General's High-level Panel on Threats, Challenges and Change (Dec. 2, 2004), para. 194, at 64. Available online.

depend on self-declaration, which has proven porous.[92] The CWC's destruction require-ment has encountered technical problems and delays, as well.

Yet, despite gaps, and less than complete compliance, the good faith efforts of many state parties have reduced the potential for employment of these weapons.

CASES AND MATERIALS

THE UNITED KINGDOM'S MANUAL OF THE LAW OF ARMED CONFLICT[93]

Introduction. *The United Kingdom's 2004 Manual of the Law of Armed Conflict provides a brief but thoughtful essay on basic issues involved in drafting weapons treaties. In doing so, the manual mentions issues of military necessity and proportionality that are considered in treaty formation, illustrating the interplay of those core concepts in all considerations of LOAC/IHL.*

Although use of weapons is an integral feature of armed conflict, there have been several attempts over the centuries to ban certain weapons or to restrict their use. More recent international treaties on the use of weapons have been formulated in one of two ways. The first approach is an absolute ban on the use of a specific weapon or projectile. This has the advantage of precision, simplifying compliance and verification. On the other hand, the ban may be easily circumvented by equipping forces with another weapon that achieves the same result but is not caught by the precise terms of the prohibition. The second approach takes a more general form by referring to the effects of weapon use. But here there may be room for argument about whether the weapon use has that effect. An example of the first approach is the Hague Declaration 2 Concerning Asphyxiating Gases 1899 in which the parties agreed to abstain from "the use of projectiles the sole object of which is the diffusion of asphyxiating or deleterious gases". The use of canisters to release gas carried by the wind in the direction of the enemy lines was not caught by this treaty. An example of the second approach is the prohibition in Article 23(e) of the Hague Regulations [IV] of the employment of "arms, projectiles, or material calculated to cause unnecessary suffering". Arguments continue to this day about whether certain weapons that have undoubted military utility cause unnecessary suffering.

The current practice is to combine the two approaches by regarding the "unnecessary suffering" provision as a guiding principle upon which specific prohibitions or restric-tions can be built.

---

[92] Barbara Crossette, "Countries Admit Use of Poisons in Weapons," *NY Times*, Aug. 17, 1997; Judith Miller, "Libya Discloses Production of 23 Tons of Mustard Gas," *NY Times*, March 6, 2004, A5.

[93] United Kingdom MOD, *Manual of the Law of Armed Conflict*, supra, note 13, at 103–4, footnotes omitted.

Application of the Guiding Principle

The correct criterion is whether the use of a weapon is of a nature to cause injury or suffering greater than that required for its military purpose.

In deciding the legality of use of a specific weapon, therefore, it is necessary to assess:

a. its effects in battle;
b. the military task it is required to perform; and
c. the proportionality between factors (a) and (b).

However, even if the use of a weapon is considered under this test to be generally lawful, its use in certain ways, or in certain circumstances, may still be unlawful.

Conclusion. With these guidelines in mind, what is a lawful weapon that may be used in unlawful ways? We know that all lawful weapons may be used in unlawful ways. White phosphorus comes to mind, lawful for use against fortified enemy emplacements, unlawful if used directly against civilians. (There is no treaty outlawing the use of white phosphorus against combatants – even directly against them.) A most basic implement of warfare, a bullet, becomes unlawful if its tip is scored, making it a "dum-dum," or expanding, bullet. The dum-dum's military necessity is zero and its use causes unnecessary suffering.

The British Manual's guidelines are a template for the legal review of new weapons required by 1977 Additional Protocol I, Article 36.

PROSECUTOR V. TADIĆ

(IT-94–1-A) Decision on Defense Motion for Interlocutory Appeal on Jurisdiction
(Oct. 2, 1995)

Introduction. The several trial and appeal chamber opinions in the ICTY's Tadić case provide guidance in several LOAC/IHL areas. In this portion of the trial chamber's decision regarding a pretrial motion by the accused, the chamber determines the applicability of weapons restrictions to noninternational armed conflicts, using the Iraqi chemical attack on Halabja as the case in point. (The Iraq–Iran War predated the 1993 CWC, so the trial chamber refers to the 1925 Gas Protocol, which earlier banned chemical weapons in warfare.) Brackets are as in the original.

119. . . . We shall now briefly show how the gradual extension to internal armed conflict of rules and principles concerning international wars has also occurred as regards means and methods of warfare. [A] general principle has evolved limiting the right of the parties to conflicts "to adopt means of injuring the enemy." The same holds true for a more general principle, laid down in the so-called Turku Declaration of Minimum Humanitarian Standards of 1990, and revised in 1994 . . . whereby "[w]eapons or other material or methods prohibited in international armed conflicts must not be employed in any circumstances.. . ."

Indeed, elementary considerations of humanity and common sense make it preposterous that the use by States of weapons prohibited in armed conflicts between themselves be allowed when States try to put down rebellion by their own nationals on their own territory. What is inhumane, and consequently proscribed, in international wars, cannot but be inhumane and inadmissible in civil strife.

120. . . . By way of illustration, we will mention chemical weapons. Recently a number of States have stated that the use of chemical weapons by the central authorities of a State against its own population is contrary to international law. On 7 September 1988 the [then] twelve Member States of the European Community made a declaration whereby:

"The Twelve are greatly concerned at reports of the alleged use of chemical weapons against the Kurds [by Iraqi authorities]. They confirm their previous positions, condemning any use of these weapons. They call for respect of international humanitarian law, including the Geneva Protocol of 1925, and Resolutions 612 and 620 of the United Nations Security Council [concerning the use of chemical weapons in the Iraq-Iran war]." . . .

121. A firm position to the same effect was taken by the British authorities: in 1988 the Foreign Office stated that the Iraqi use of chemical weapons against the civilian population of the town of Halabja represented "a serious and grave violation of the 1925 Geneva Protocol and international humanitarian law. The U.K. condemns unreservedly this and all other uses of chemical weapons. . . . " A similar stand was taken by the German authorities. . . .

122. A clear position on the matter was also taken by the United States Government. In a "press guidance" statement issued by the State Department on 9 September 1988 it was stated that:

Questions have been raised as to whether the prohibition in the 1925 Geneva Protocol against [chemical weapon] use "in war" applies to [chemical weapon] use in internal conflicts. However, it is clear that such use against the civilian population would be contrary to the customary international law that is applicable to internal armed conflicts, as well as other international agreements." (United States, Department of State, Press Guidance (9 September 1988).)

On 13 September 1988, Secretary of State George Schultz, in a hearing before the United States Senate Judiciary Committee strongly condemned as "completely unacceptable" the use of chemical weapons by Iraq . . .

123. It is interesting to note that, reportedly, the Iraqi Government "flatly denied the poison gas charges." (New York Times, 16 September 1988, at A11.) Furthermore, it agreed to respect and abide by the relevant international norms on chemical weapons. . . .

It should also be stressed that a number of countries (Turkey, Saudi Arabia, Egypt, Jordan, Bahrain, Kuwait) as well as the Arab League . . . strongly disagreed with the United States' assertions that Iraq had used chemical weapons against its Kurdish nationals. However, this disagreement did not turn on the legality of the use of chemical weapons. . . .

124. It is therefore clear that, whether or not Iraq really used chemical weapons against its own Kurdish nationals – a matter on which this Chamber obviously cannot and does not express any opinion – there undisputedly emerged a general consensus in the international community on the principle that the use of those weapons is also prohibited in internal armed conflicts.

Conclusion. *In the years since the trial chamber's opinion, clear proof of the Iraqi attack emerged. Was the Iraqi attack on Halabja, a city in Iraq, inhabited largely by Iraqis, albeit Kurdish Iraqis, an incident of an international armed conflict?*

THE MOSCOW THEATER HOSTAGE CRISIS AND THE CHEMICAL WEAPONS CONVENTION[94]

On the evening of October 23, 2002, forty to fifty armed Chechen separatists, females among them, entered Moscow's Nord-Est theater during an opera performance. They took 850 to 900 civilian theatergoers and performers hostage. Some 90 civilians escaped. Russian secrecy at the time and afterward makes precise numbers impossible to obtain. The Chechens, several of whom wore explosive vests, wired the building with explosives.[95] They demanded that Russia withdraw its military forces from Chechnya, or hostages would be executed. Over the following two days, the Chechens released about 150 to 200 children, pregnant women, Muslims, and ill captives. Another 54 hostages were released for various reasons.

At 0505 on the morning of October 26, Russian military forces and security police pumped an unknown gas into the theater through the ventilation system. Visible to the naked eye, the gas quickly incapacitated most of the Chechens in the theater, as well as many hostages. Simultaneously, Russian Special Forces stormed the building from adjacent structures, from basement theater entrances and through the theater's main doors. In the assault several Russian soldiers were overcome by the gas.

Many of the Chechens were also killed by the gas. Those not killed by the gas or in the brief firefight when Russian forces stormed the theater were summarily executed as they lay unconscious or incapacitated by the gas. Roughly twelve Chechens were apparently captured alive.

Numbers vary from report to report, but at least 127 civilian hostages were killed by the gas, another 2 by gunfire. Some hostages who reached medical workers were unconscious but still alive, but soon died from effects of the gas because Russian authorities would not identify and to this day have not identified the gas they used, precluding administration of an effective antidote.[96] The percentage of those killed by the gas was "a fatality rate of 16%, more than twice the fatality rate of 'lethal' chemical weapons used on World War I battlefields."[97]

The usual preliminary questions regarding an armed conflict incident, conflict status, and individual status are of little relevance in this case. They are mooted by the treaty involved, the 1993 CWC, which applies in times of peace, as well as war.

What gas was used by the Russian forces, and did its use constitute a violation of the 1993 CWC? Most reports suggest that the gas probably was fentanyl, "a well-known drug with many medical applications, as a human incapacitant ... used for treating chronic pain. ... 'It's like heroin times 1,000'. ..."[98] If it was indeed fentanyl, it was employed in a situation and manner in which neither dosage nor exposure could be controlled.

---

[94] Reprinted with the kind permission of Dr. Maria Granovsky, who, besides a law degree, holds a doctorate in chemistry, "When the Right Action Is Illegal: Russian Use of Toxic Chemicals to End the Theater Hostage Crisis in October 2002" (May 13, 2003), unpublished seminar research paper, Georgetown University Law Center (on file with author).

[95] Peter Baker and Susan B. Glasser, "Rebels Hold Hundreds Hostage in Moscow," *Wash. Post*, Oct. 24, 2002, A1.

[96] Michael Wines, "Hostage Drama in Moscow: The Aftermath," *NY Times*, Oct. 28, 2002, A1.

[97] Fidler, "Meaning of Moscow" supra, note 69, at 525, 532–3.

[98] Judith Miller and William J. Broad, "U.S. Suspects Opiate in Gas in Russia Raid," *NY Times*, Oct. 29, 2002, A1.

Symptoms exhibited by the freed hostages, as well as analyses of fluid samples taken from some of the hostages, were [also] consistent with inhalation of halothane, a halogenated gas used for surgical anesthesia. Halothane has the advantage of being a gas ... but it also has an extremely narrow range of safe dosing. ... [A] chemist who previously worked in the Soviet weapons program stated that the grey-purple colour of the gas suggests that the mixture contained a combination of halothane and Substance 78. Substance 78, which was developed by the Soviet chemical weapons program, is a hallucinogen. ... His suspicions are shared by American physicians.

In determining whether Russia violated the CWC, does the agent they employed make a difference if state parties are obligated "never under any circumstances" to use, produce, acquire, or retain chemical weapons? In listing "Purposes Not Prohibited under the Convention," 1993 CWC Article II.9 (d) provides "law enforcement including domestic riot control purposes." That exemption would seem to cover the chemical-based agents apparently used by Russian forces.

For those advocating the law enforcement exemption, the Moscow theater incident demonstrated that "the law enforcement provision offered room to develop the potential of incapacitating chemicals and demonstrate their utility for both law enforcement purposes and missions that the military would face in twenty-first-century armed conflict."[99] (The 127 dead hostages suggest a questionable utility.)

Most experts consider the Russian use, however inexpert, of either fentanyl or halothane/Substance 78 no violation of the CWC,[100] but "the use of chemical incapacitants in paramilitary operations is dangerous because it blurs the line between law enforcement and warfare ... that makes the battlefield use of chemical weapons more likely."[101]

---

[99] Fidler, "Meaning of Moscow," supra, note 69, at 535.
[100] Mark Wheelis, "Will the New Biology Lead to New Weapons," *Arms Control Today*, July/Aug. 2004.
[101] Tucker, *War of Nerves*, supra, note 2, at 384.

Dealing with Violations of Customs and Usages of Warfare

21 Military Commissions

21.0 Introduction

Today, "military commission" is a term often spoken with derision, associated with indefinite detention without charges, torture, and star chamber trials. It was not always so and it need not be so tomorrow. In democratic societies there remains a legitimate need for military commissions during and after armed conflicts and, as long as there are armed conflicts there likely will be military commissions in one form or another. Their misuse, however, negates both their moral legitimacy and their legal utility.

"Military tribunal" is the unifying term for all military proceedings of a judicial nature. Courts-martial, employed in all states' military legal systems, are a form of military tribunal. So, too, are courts of inquiry, which investigate serious military incidents such as the loss of ships at sea. Provost courts, another form of military tribunal in U.S. practice, convene in occupied territory to try offenses alleged against civilians. Military government courts and provisional courts are other forms of American military tribunal, both now disused. Military commissions are a type of military tribunal.

In 1780, after a congressional resolution directing his military trial, Joshua Hett Smith, a civilian, was tried by court-martial for aiding and abetting General Benedict Arnold's treason. In 1815, a civilian, Louis Louaillier, was similarly tried as a spy by a court-martial convened in New Orleans by General Andrew Jackson. Two British civilians, Alexander Arbuthnot and Robert Ambrister, were tried by court-martial in 1818 for inciting Creek Indians to war against the United State. These courts-martial are often erroneously referred to as America's first military commissions. "Though foreshadowed in some respects by earlier tribunals like the Board of General Officers that General Washington convened to try British Major John André for spying during the Revolutionary War, the [military] commission 'as such' was inaugurated in 1847 [by General Winfield Scott]."[1]

Nor should military commissions be confused with their military tribunal brethren, courts-martial. Courts-martial try offenses committed by members of the armed forces against the state's military criminal code. Today, the courts-martial of most states employ rigorous procedural rules and evidentiary standards. On the other hand, **military commissions are wartime tribunals, appointed by the executive, for the trial of enemies**

---

[1] *Salim Ahmed Hamdan v. Rumsfeld, et al.*, 548 U.S. 557, 590 (plurality opinion) (June 29, 2006). This case is often referred to as "Hamdan I," as opposed to the later U.S. Court of Appeals (D.C. Circuit, 2012) case, often referred to as "Hamdan II." In agreement, David Glazier, "Kangaroo Court or Competent Tribunal?: Judging the 21st Century Military Commission," 89 *Virginia L. Rev.* (2003), 2005, 2027.

accused of violating the laws and customs of war.[2] In keeping with their utilitarian, in-the-field nature, military commissions historically employed less stringent rules of procedure and evidence than did domestic civilian courts or courts-martial. A state of armed conflict is not necessary for military commission jurisdiction to attach.[3]

21.1 Legal Background and Composition

In 1896, Colonel William Winthrop, an early U.S. Army judge advocate and military historian, wrote of American military commissions, "The [military] commission is simply an instrumentality for the more efficient execution of the war powers vested in Congress and the power vested in the President as Commander-in-Chief."[4] Article I, §8, clause 14, of the Constitution grants Congress the power "to define and punish ... Offenses against the Law of Nations" and "[t]o make Rules for the ... Regulation of the land and naval forces." "But the power to create them lies at a constitutional crossroad. Both Congress and the President have authority in this area ... the President's authority to establish military commissions based upon ... Article II, clause 1. ... The President's power to appoint a military commission without an express grant of that authority from Congress is inherent to his role as the Commander in Chief of the armed forces."[5] The president's authority, absent congressional action to the contrary, to establish military commissions without an express grant from Congress is confirmed in *Madsen v. Kinsella*.[6]

Today, the U.S. *Manual for Courts-Martial* also specifically provides for military commissions.[7] Article 18 grants courts-martial the authority to try those charged with violations of the law of war. Article 21 expresses Congress's intent not to interfere with the jurisdiction of military commissions over war crimes.

Military commissions have no standing rules – no continually applicable directive relating to their procedure or evidence, and no normative charges. That is because military commissions may, within authority granted by higher authority, lawfully be created by different senior commanders at differing times and locations. Unless POWs are to be tried, each iteration of military commission writes its own evidentiary and procedural rules, and charges. Today, when prisoners of war are to be tried by military commission, lowered trial standards are prohibited by Geneva Convention III, Article 102, about which more will be said (Chapter 21, Section 21.5).

In keeping with their similarity to court-martials, military commissions are historically made up of military officers. Their members (whom civilians refer to as "jurors") may be of any military grade, any military background. The number of members is indeterminate. Because there is no law fixing the number, a single-member commission would

---

[2] *Index and Legislative History: Uniform Code of Military Justice* (Washington, DC: GPO, 1950), 975. Emphasis added.

[3] Jean S. Pictet, *Commentary: III Geneva Convention Relative to the Treatment of Prisoners of War* (Geneva: ICRC, 1960), 408, discussing Art. 85.

[4] Col. William Winthrop, *Military Law and Precedents*, 2d ed. (Washington, DC: GPO, 1920), 831.

[5] Major Timothy C MacDonnell, "Military Commissions and Court-Martial: A Brief Discussion of the Constitutional and Jurisdictional Distinctions Between the Two Courts," *Army Lawyer* (Jan. 2015), 6, 7.

[6] 343 U.S. 341, 348 (1952).

[7] See Part I, ¶ 2(b)(2), and Rule of Court-Martial 201(f)(1)(B), *Manual for Courts-Martial* (2012), and UCMJ Art. 21. UCMJ Art. 18, pertaining to general courts-martial jurisdiction, is not applicable to terrorists. With some exceptions, civilians, including civilian terrorists, are not generally subject to UCMJ jurisdiction.

presumably be lawful. An American general court-martial, however, requires a minimum of five members, twelve if the case is sent to court with a sentence to death provided for specifically. Lesser numbers would not be expected in a modern military commission.

The 1945 military commission trial of the Japanese general Tomoyuki Yamashita was composed of five U.S. Army general officers (none of whom had legal training). Although he had a team of six U.S. Army defense counsels, all experienced lawyers, the trail procedure employed in Yamashita's tribunal clearly would be found legally deficient today. Also, he was a prisoner of war, unlike, say, the detainees of Guantánamo Bay, Cuba. The POW/detainee distinction is significant today because of the requirements mandated by Geneva Convention III, Article 102.

The "war on terrorism" produced a new version of U.S. military commission. Past commissions generally hewed to court-martial rules, procedures, and charges, whereas the Guantánamo version of military commission differed in material ways.

21.2 A Beginning

Military commissions were born of military necessity.[8] They were first employed in 1847, during the occupation phase of the United States' War with Mexico (1846–8). While encamped at Tampico the American commander, General Winfield Scott, was faced with lawlessness among his own troops and volunteers, and among the Mexican populace. His American troops were sometimes intoxicated or disobedient, and Mexican civilians often stole supplies and committed minor assaults. America's 1806 Articles of War were 101 articles in length, but none addressed the "simple crime" offenses that vexed General Scott.[9] With no charging vehicle, Scott was left without a means of disciplining his own soldiers or, of course, Mexican nationals. Before he became a soldier Scott was a well-respected lawyer. His lawyerlike solution to his disciplinary problem was to make up, out of whole cloth, what he called "military commissions" and "councils of war." The latter, eventually totaling a mere three cases, tried Mexicans for offenses that were otherwise outside military jurisdiction. Scott's military commissions, however, tried some four hundred American soldiers for criminal offenses that would have been sent to domestic courts had they occurred within the continental United States. Some of the military commissions involved offenses committed by American troops against Mexican combatant-prisoners and against civilians. "Without anyone quite understanding what was happening – without even using the phrase – Winfield Scott and the U.S. Armies in Mexico had given life to the idea of the war crime."[10] Perhaps so. Upon departing Mexico, Scott's councils of war quickly fell into disuse. His military commissions, however, were about to come into their own. It was during America's Civil War (1861–5), fourteen years after their initial formation in Mexico, that military commissions took the shape we recognize today.[11]

---

[8] *Hamdan v. Rumsfeld*, supra, note 1, at 590.

[9] Early American Articles of War primarily addressed order and discipline within the army. Criminal acts were not provided for; they were left for charging and prosecution in domestic civilian courts.

[10] John Fabian Witt, *Lincoln's Code: The Laws of War in American History* (New York: Free Press, 2012), 130.

[11] An excellent history of Civil War military commissions is Gideon M. Hart, "Military Commissions and the Lieber Code: Toward a New Understanding of the Jurisdictional Foundations of Military Commissions," 203 *Military Law Review* (Spring 2010), 1–69.

21.3 Military Commissions Transformed

The military commission was transformed by the U.S. Civil War era Lieber Code, adopted in 1863, in the midst of that war as Union Army General Order 100 (Chapter 2.1 to 2.4, this volume). The code was the first compilation of the rules and customs of war provided for soldiers in the field. It was written by Professor Francis Lieber, but also fathered in small but critical part by the Union Army general Henry W. Halleck. Halleck recognized General Scott's military commissions as a potential vehicle by which Confederate soldiers and their civilian sympathizers who took a direct part in the hostilities could be prosecuted for violations of the laws of war, *and* for civilian anti-Union activities, as well. Seeking a route to the trial of rebel *civilians* by a military tribunal, Halleck urged Lieber to include provisions in his code for the prosecution of civilian Confederate collaborators, whom Halleck termed "war traitors."

Halleck wanted captured civilians who took active roles on behalf of the Confederacy tried by the military, rather than civilian courts, which might be sympathetic to the rebel cause, of which there were many in Union-controlled states. Such activities were not always offenses against the laws and customs of war. But, absent martial law, civilians were not subject to military jurisdiction while the civilian courts were open. Halleck correctly foresaw, however, that military commissions would look to the military-oriented Lieber Code for guidance in trying civilians if jurisdiction over them *were* available, for example, during periods of martial law. For that reason Halleck was eager to have war traitors included in the code and urged its author to include them.

Lieber did so. He wrote, "A traitor under the law of war, or a war-traitor, is a person in a place or district under martial law who ... gives information of any kind to the enemy, or holds intercourse with him. ... If his offense consists in betraying to the enemy anything concerning the condition, safety, operations, or plans of the troops holding or occupying the place or district, his punishment is death."[12] With these provisions, the door was opened for a military commission metamorphosis from a simple disciplinary tribunal of Union soldiers to an expanded forum for the prosecution of enemy law of war violators, military or civilian, and, significantly, for civilians ("war traitors") who committed non–war crime offenses detrimental to the Union cause. The U.S. Supreme Court would later refer to such trials as "the hybrid military commissions of the Civil War."[13]

In September 1863, five months after the Lieber Code was adopted, President Lincoln, with congressional concurrence, declared martial law in areas where hostilities were ongoing, including the Union-controlled states. Halleck, now general-in-chief of the Union Armies, seized the opportunity to urge his commanders to bring before military commissions civilians charged with anti-Union acts, as opposed to war crimes. Military commissions flourished. Their procedure and evidentiary rules loosely followed those of courts-martial of the day.

Military commissions have a lengthy statutory history. They were first recognized as lawful courts in section 30 of the Act of March 3, 1863, c. 75. The Supreme Court

---

[12] Articles 90–91, "Instructions for the Government of the Armies of the United States in the Field," General Orders 100 (April 24, 1863).

[13] *Hamdan v. Rumsfeld*, supra, note 1, at 608.

acknowledged their validity in 1864's Ex Parte *Vallandigham* case.[14] The 1874 Articles of War, section 1343, provided for military commissions, as did the first U.S. *Manual for Courts-Martial* in Article 15 of the 1917 Articles of War. A January 1862 army general order, in effect into the twentieth century, kept a restraining hand on military commissions and other tribunals: "They needed to be 'ordered by the same authority' as courts-martial and 'be constituted in a similar manner and their proceedings conducted according to the same general rules as courts-martial. . .'"[15]

In *Vallandigham*, the Supreme Court ruled that it did not have appellate jurisdiction over military commission convictions.[16] That decision made commissions answerable only to their appointed military reviewing authority – if any. Although there were infrequent appellate opinions in disagreement with aspects of military commissions, their transformation was soon complete.[17] Military commissions became the accepted venue for the trial of enemies, civilian or military, charged with violation of the laws and customs of war *and*, when authorized, ordinary crimes.

Throughout the Civil War more than two thousand military commissions were convened, including the 1865 commission that tried eight conspirators for the assassination of President Lincoln.[18] After the war and after the Reconstruction Acts, 1,435 trials by military commission took place.[19] Nor were they kangaroo courts. By 1864, military commission convictions were reviewed by the newly formed Army Bureau of Military Justice. "The rate at which judgments and sentences were reversed or mitigated increased in 1865 [when 1864's high tide of commission convictions was reviewed]. Of the 341 files [cases] reviewed, forty-eight were reversed entirely, and 169 sentences were mitigated to some lesser punishment (rates of about fifteen and fifty percent respectively)."[20]

Thirty-five years later, the U.S.-Philippine War (1900–1) saw 769 Philippine nationals tried by military commission, although the provenance of the evidence in many of those proceedings was suspect. As in the Civil War, the Philippine military commissions generally employed court-martial rules and procedures.

---

[14] Ex parte *Vallandigham*, 68 US 243 (Wall.) (1864).

[15] Louis Fisher, *Military Tribunals and Presidential Power: American Revolution to the War on Terrorism* (Lawrence: University Press of Kansas, 2005), 48–9.

[16] *Vallandingham*, supra, note 14, at 251: "In other words, the petition [of *certiorari* for review of a military commission conviction] before us we think not to be within the letter or spirit of the grants of appellate jurisdiction to the Supreme Court."

[17] *Ex parte Milligan*, 71 U.S. 2 (1866), confirmed that military courts lacked jurisdiction over civilians where civil courts remained open. In later years, however, *Milligan* has often been disregarded by the Supreme Court and is suspect as a modern precedent. See, e.g., in regard to rent and price controls: *Block v. Hirsh*, 256 U.S. 135 (1921), *Chastleton Corp. v. Sinclair*, 264 U.S. 543 (1924), *Yakus v. U.S.*, 321 U.S. 414 (1944), *Bowles v. Willingham*, 321 U.S. 503 (1944), and *Woods v. Cloyd Miller Co.*, 333 U.S. 138 (1948); in regard to renegotiation of contracts: *Lichter v. U.S.*, 334 U.S. 742 (1948); re wartime prohibitions: *Hamilton v. Kentucky Distilleries & Warehouse Co.*, 251 U.S. 146 (1919), and *Ruppert v. Caffey*, 251 U.S. 264 (1920); re seizure of enemy property: *Miller v. U.S.*, 78 U.S. (11 Wall.) 268 (1870), *Stoehr v. Wallace*, 255 U.S. 239 (1921), *Central Union Trust Co. v. Garvan*, 254 U.S. 554 (1921), and *Silesian American Corp. v. Clark*, 332 U.S. 469 (1947); re suppression of brothels: *McKinley v. U.S.* 397 (1919), and *Keller v. U.S.*, 213 U.S. 138 (1909). In *Korematsu v. U.S.*, 323 U.S. 214 (1944), the court famously ignored the limits on the government's emergency powers suggested in *Milligan*.

[18] Winthrop, *Military Law and Precedents*, supra, note 4, at 834.

[19] Mark E. Neely Jr., *The Fate of Liberty: Abraham Lincoln and Civil Liberties* (New York: Oxford University Press, 1991), 46–69.

[20] Hart, "Military Commissions and the Lieber Code," supra, note 11, at 60.

21.4 World War II

By World War II (1939–45), in U.S. practice military commissions were a congressionally enacted Article I trial forum, validated by long use and appellate approval.[21] They exist only in time of armed conflict; their subject matter jurisdiction extends only to violations of the laws and customs of war, unless the trial of ordinary crimes is also authorized; and their personal jurisdiction may reach civilians, as well as enemy combatants or fighters. A historian of World War II tribunals judiciously wrote, "As a general rule the procedure employed in hearings before military tribunals was fair and resulted in adequate presentation of both sides of the case, although such hearings were usually conducted expeditiously and without regard to technicalities. . . . Occasionally, however, there were slight slips."[22] Many LOAC commentators consider the World War II Nazi saboteurs' military commission to be such a legal slip.

On June 12, 1942, eight Nazi saboteurs (two of whom were American citizens) landed by submarine, four men on Long Island, New York, four others at Ponte Verde, Florida. Within a week all eight were in U.S. custody, the F.B.I. having been alerted by one of the saboteurs themselves. On July 2, President Roosevelt issued Proclamation 2561, creating a military commission to try the eight enemy combatants. The trial was held in secret from July 8 to August 1 before seven army general officers, one of whom was the judge advocate general of the army. Despite language in the proclamation prohibiting the involvement of any civil court,[23] on July 23 the accuseds' military defense counsel personally delivered a writ of habeas corpus to the Supreme Court associate justice Owen Roberts at the justice's home. Nervy. Six days later, the defense counsel's audacious act having succeeded, the Court heard argument on the writ. One day after that, 30 July 30, in a *per curium* order, the Court discharged (dismissed) the application. A written opinion revealing the Court's reasoning would have to wait, however. The eight saboteurs were found guilty on August 1. On August 8, fifty-seven days after they landed by submarine, six of the eight were executed by electrocution. The death sentences of two who had assisted in apprehending the others were commuted to imprisonment for thirty years, and for life. In 1948, their sentences were again commuted and they were released and deported to Germany.

On October 29, 1942, the Supreme Court finally issued its opinion denying the July writ of habeas corpus. History suggests the Court had difficulty reconciling the procedures applied in the saboteurs' trial with the law, and with the president's actions.[24] The Court was in a bind: The case was already concluded and six of the petitioners had been executed. Any result other than affirming their denial of habeas corpus and affirming the government's case would cast a harshly negative light on the Supreme Court. The Court

---

[21] An Article I court is one raised by Congress under its authority in Article I, §8, of the Constitution, as opposed to courts authorized under Article III of the Constitution. Interestingly, the military commissions raised immediately after the 9/11 attacks were Art. II courts raised on the authority of the president. With Congress's passage of the Military Commissions Act of 2006 they became Art. I courts.

[22] John Alan Applelman, *Military Tribunals and International Crimes* (Indianapolis, IN: Bobbs-Merrill, 1954), 322. This excellent history was written near the time of the events described by Appleman, a lawyer trained in international law.

[23] "Such persons shall not be privileged to seek any remedy or maintain any proceeding directly or indirectly, or to have any such remedy or proceeding sought on their behalf, in the courts of the United States, or of its States, territories, and possessions."

[24] E.g., Fisher, *Military Tribunals*, supra, note 15, at 114–19.

affirmed all. The highest court had spoken, but had justice been done? In 1942, in a besieged America, with U.S. soldiers in combat with Nazi forces, few critics arose. As the Supreme Court justice Antonin Scalia later wrote, "[Quirin] was not this Court's finest hour"[25] – although it did settle the status of unlawful combatants, more correctly referred to as "unprivileged belligerents":

> By universal agreement and practice, the law of war draws a distinction between the armed forces and the peaceful populations of belligerent nations and also between those who are lawful and unlawful combatants. Lawful combatants are subject to capture and detention as prisoners of war by opposing military forces. Unlawful combatants are likewise subject to capture and detention, but in addition they are subject to trial and punishment by military tribunals for acts which render their belligerency unlawful.[26]

Note that unprivileged belligerents are not subject to trial for their being unprivileged belligerents but, lacking the combatant's privilege, for their acts that render their belligerence unlawful, such as murder or wounding, or the destruction of property.

Late in World War II, in November 1944, two more Nazi agents (one of them an American citizen) landed by submarine on Maine's Crabtree Point. As their predecessors had, one quickly surrendered, leading to the other's capture. Also as with Quirin and company, both were tried by military commission. This time, cooler political heads prevailed and their commission's procedures and evidentiary rules approximated those of courts-martial of that day. Both were convicted and sentenced to hang.[27]

The four years following World War II, 1945 to 1949, were the apogee of commission proceedings. After Germany's surrender, the Nuremberg International Military Tribunal convened, followed by Nuremberg's twelve "subsequent trials," conducted under Control Council Law #10, all twelve subsequent trials military commissions. Individual military commissions were also conducted by most of the World War II Allies. Great Britain, Australia, France, the Netherlands, Poland, Norway, Canada, China, and Greece conducted a combined 1,166. The number of Russian commissions has never been released, but it was clearly large. The United States conducted about 500 military commissions in the European theater of operations and another 450 in the Pacific theater.[28] The acquittal rate in Pacific theater commissions was typical for U.S. commissions, about 10 percent.

For some, the lasting impression of World War II military commissions is the searing dissent of the Supreme Court justice William F. Murphy in the appeal of the Japanese general Yamashita: "Petitioner was rushed to trial under an improper charge," Murphy wrote, "given insufficient time to prepare an adequate defense, deprived of the benefits of some of the most elementary rules of evidence and summarily sentenced to be hanged."[29] It is true that Yamashita's trial was uncomfortably summary in nature, with rules and procedures allowed that were not permitted even in courts-martial of that day.

---

[25] *Hamdi v. Rumsfeld*, 542 U.S. 507, 569 (2000) (Scalia, J., dissenting).

[26] *Ex parte Quirin*, 317 U.S. 1 (1942), 30–1.

[27] President Harry Truman commuted their sentences to confinement for life. Erich Gimple was deported to Germany in 1955, Curtis Colepaugh, the U.S. citizen, was paroled in 1960, moved to Pennsylvania, and, in 2005, died there. *Colepaugh v. Looney*, 235 F.2d 429 (10th Cir. 1956), cert. den. 352 U.S. 1014 (1957), concerns the District Court's discharge of Colepaugh's writ for habeas corpus.

[28] Appleman, *Military Tribunals and International Crimes*, supra, note 22, at x.

[29] *Yamashita v. Styer*, 327 U.S. 1, 27–8 (1946).

Still, it seems hyperbolic to write, as one critic of Yamashita's military commission has, that "the doctrine [of command responsibility] was not only created in the Yamashita case; it was created specifically *for* Yamashita. And it was created in order to convict him."[30]

An arguably more accurate valedictory for World War II era military commissions is the opening statement of the Supreme Court justice Robert H. Jackson, the American chief prosecutor, at the Nuremberg IMT:

> The wrongs which we seek to condemn and punish have been so calculated, so malignant and so devastating, that civilization cannot tolerate their being ignored, because it cannot survive their being repeated. That four great nations, flushed with victory and stung with injury, stay the hands of vengeance and voluntarily submit their captive enemies to the judgment of the law, is one of the most significant tributes that Power has ever paid to Reason.[31]

By 1946, military commissions were recognized by all nations and employed by many of them. The broad customary use of military commissions after World War II ensured there would be no repetition of post–World War I Leipzig-like trials (Chapter 3.2.1). In those unsatisfactory 1921 proceedings the Allies charged 895 former enemy individuals with war crimes but allowed the defeated Germans to try their own citizens at Leipzig. Twelve were actually tried, six of those acquitted, the other six receiving notably light sentences. Military commissions had come into their own.

The Supreme Court wrote in 2006, "The military commission was not born of a desire to dispense a more summary form of justice than is afforded by courts-martial; it developed, rather, as a tribunal of necessity to be employed when courts-martial lacked jurisdiction over either the accused or the subject matter. ... Exigency lent the commission its legitimacy, but did not further justify the wholesale jettisoning of procedural protections."[32]

Exigency – military necessity – is another reason why military commissions survive. Domestic courts, with finely balanced rules of procedure and evidence, are not always equipped to deal with every aspect of enemy battlefield misconduct. In combat, evidence of war crimes might be collected, if at all, in an ammunition box or body bag that is heaved into a momentarily grounded med-evac helicopter under enemy fire, perhaps to be off-loaded at a tactical refueling point, perhaps damaged or lost at stops between the scene of the offense and a judge advocate's office. Soldiers in contact with the enemy lack the legal luxury of a chain of custody for seized evidence. Marines in a defensive perimeter cannot take witness statements. Military commissions admit some hearsay evidence because sometimes the maker of the statement is captured, wounded, or dead. There are valid reasons of military necessity why a military commission judge may find that "evidence having probative value to a reasonable person is admissible."[33]

There are no defensible reasons, however, to adopt unreasonably biased rules of procedure, or charge offenses not generally recognized as violations of the laws and customs of war.

---

[30] Allan A. Ryan, *Yamashita's Ghost* (Lawrence: University Press of Kansas, 2012), 339. Ryan makes a persuasive case for Yamashita's legal innocence while also detailing the troubling deficiencies in his trial.

[31] *Trial of German Major War Criminals: Opening Speeches of the Chief Prosecutors* (William S. Hein reprint of London: H. M. Stationary Office, 1946), 3.

[32] *Hamdan v. Rumsfeld*, supra, note 1, at 624.

[33] *Manual for Military Commissions – United States* (2010 ed.), Part III, Section IV, Rule 402.

21.4.1 *The Three Bases of Military Commission Jurisdiction*

By the end of World War II, state practice made clear that the jurisdictional basis of military commissions extended beyond the trial of grave breaches and other violations of the laws and customs of war. Two distinct additional jurisdictional bases were discernable: first, military government military commissions, martial law military commissions, and, second, the more familiar law of war military commissions.[34]

Military government commissions, as the name implies, "may try ordinary crimes – e.g., manslaughter or robbery – and violations of military orders committed by soldiers or civilians in territories under … military government."[35] They are established either outside the United States or in areas within the United States in a state of rebellion. Military government courts were the basis of the military commissions devised and employed in Mexico by General Winfield Scott in 1847 (although unrecognized by that name, of course) and employed by the Allied forces, the United States, the United Kingdom, France, and the Soviet Union, in occupied Germany after World War II when German domestic courts were not functioning. Military government commissions may try offenses committed even before the military government was imposed, an in the two French tribunal cases described in Chapter 8.2.

Martial law military commissions "may try ordinary crimes and violations of military orders committed by soldiers and civilians in territory under martial law – as much of our country was during the [American] Civil War."[36] The distinction between this narrow variety of military commission and military government military commissions is that the latter calls for a *military government* to be in place while the former calls for *martial law* to be in effect.

"Third, and 'utterly different' from the first two categories, military commissions may try offenses against the law of war."[37] This is the jurisdictional version of military commission legislatively raised by the Military Commissions Acts of 2006 and 2009 and employed at Guantánamo Bay, Cuba. This jurisdictional category of military commission is limited to the trial of international war crimes and no other offenses.

21.5 Postwar Developments

After World War II, the international community was concerned that legal regimes for military commissions be strengthened and, to an extent, harmonized. An innovation effecting military commissions was 1949 Geneva Convention common Article 3. Of the 429 articles in the four 1949 conventions common Article 3 is the sole article applicable to internal armed conflicts – uprisings, sustained insurrections, civil wars, and insurgencies – the predominant type of armed conflict since World War II. Common Article 3 broadly defines principles of humane treatment for those taking no part in the conflict and those who are hors de combat. It also means to ensure that captured rebels not be subjected to summary justice, but be tried by regularly constituted courts. Today, common Article 3 is considered customary law, applicable in all armed conflicts,

---

[34] *Hamdan v. Rumsfeld*, supra, note 1, at 595–8. At 597–8, the Court also repeats Colonel. Winthrop's preconditions for military commission jurisdiction.

[35] *Ali Hamza Ahmad Suliman al Bahlul v. United States*, 367 F.3d 1 (D.C. Cir., 2014).

[36] Id., citing Winthrop, *Military Law and Precedents*, supra, note 4, at 832–4.

[37] Id., citing *Hamdan*, supra, note 1, at 596.

regardless of their characterization. In 2006, it was common Article 3 that the U.S. Supreme Court looked to in determining the legitimacy of American military commissions convened at Guantánamo Bay, Cuba, to try alleged terrorists.

Article 102 of 1949 POW Convention III portends significant change to trials of future POWs charged with precapture war crimes. Article 102 mandates that, in international armed conflicts, POWs may validly be tried only if their sentences are pronounced by the same courts, and after trial by the same procedures, as applicable to members of the armed forces of the capturing state. Thus, if there were American-held POWs in the "war on terrorism," Article 102 would require those enemy captives be tried just as U.S. military personnel would be tried: by a court-martial-like proceeding, subject to charges and rules of procedure and evidence required by the U.S. *Manual for Courts-Martial* and the Uniform Code of Military Justice. Military commissions like those after World War II, with their "relaxed" rules of procedure and rules of evidence, are now prohibited for POWs.[38] The high standard of Article 102, however, provides little incentive to designate captured enemy fighters as POWs because, in many cases, pretrial detention and interrogation techniques, the admissibility of incriminating pretrial statements, and other trial issues would be ripe for attack by defense lawyers employing well-settled military case law.

Many issues applicable in military commissions – interrogations, voluntariness of pretrial statements, admissible evidence, even the trials themselves – are essentially human rights–related issues reflecting a law enforcement paradigm, rather than a law of war paradigm. Such issues are indicative of the direction in which the law of armed conflict (LOAC) has moved in the last half-century: the direction of human rights.

International human rights law burgeoned after World War II and its numerous atrocities. The growth of international human rights law is evidenced in the 1948 Universal Declaration of Human Rights, the 1950 European Convention for the Protection of Human Rights, the 1966 International Covenant on Civil and Political Rights, and the 1969 American Convention on Human Rights, human rights treaties all. Contrary to the European position, since the late twentieth century the United States has asserted that, on the battlefield, human rights law is applicable only in the infrequent gaps in LOAC.

> The United States ... has advanced a categorical and contrarian position that the obligations contained in the relevant human rights instruments have no extraterritorial application. This unqualified position is increasingly out-of-step with the established jurisprudence and with arguments being advance – and conceded – by our coalition partners and other allies.[39]

Despite the frequently enunciated American position, human rights law has assumed increasing relevance in combat zones involving U.S. combatants. In Afghanistan, U.S. combatants routinely photographed evidence of enemy bomb-making and other violations of LOAC. Soldiers initiated formal evidentiary chains of custody and took written

---

[38] Major Timothy MacDonnell, in his seminal article, "Military Commissions and Courts-Martial," supra, note 5, at 17, disagrees with this reading of Art. 102. He posits that its meaning is that the United States may employ "military commissions to try prisoners of war when they are used to try U.S. military personnel. Because the [United States] does not currently use commissions to try its military personnel, it could not use them to try prisoners of war."

[39] Beth Van Schaack, "The United States' Position on Extraterritorial Application of Human Rights Obligations: Now Is the Time for Change" 90 *Int'l L. Stud.* (2014), 20, 22–3. Footnotes omitted.

statements for use at trial, all human rights–related procedures. The infusion of human rights concepts emphasized the changed nature of military commissions from informal field tribunals to more traditional criminal trials by another name; combatants often became like policemen collecting evidence for the prosecution.

The two 1977 additional protocols to the 1949 Geneva Conventions are also significant, of course. Although not ratified by the United States, both Protocols contain numerous provisions now considered customary law. Article 75 of Additional Protocol I, "Fundamental Guarantees," for example, provides a long list of prisoners' rights sounding in human rights law. These due process provisions have altered the way U.S. war fighters treat captured enemy fighters in both noninternational and international conflicts. Procedures specified for the prosecution of precapture offenses have reshaped military commission evidentiary rules and evidence-gathering procedures. No conflict prior to Iraq and Afghanistan, early in the twenty-first century, had seen such concern for the legal niceties of later prosecutions. These concerns, plus emergent human rights treaties, combined with a greater international willingness to enforce LOAC, and altered how prisoners are tried by military commissions.

21.5.1 9/11 and Post–World War II Developments Applied

There were no military commissions after the Korean and Vietnam conflicts. In Korea, the U.S. Army's War Crime Division identified 936 North Korean and Chinese prisoners of war for war crime trials, but the repatriation of POWs at war's end, combined with an August 1953 United Nations Command blanket amnesty for suspected war criminals, ended any thought of prosecutions.[40] At the close of the Vietnam conflict, although enemy individuals had again been identified for war crime charges, the United States did not press for their custody lest doing so endanger the pending release of American POWs. Results of the juxtaposition of military commissions and post–World War II human rights changes had to wait for the later conflicts in Iraq and Afghanistan.

In 2001, five days after the 9/11 armed attacks on American soil, the Authorization for Use of Military Force became U.S. law.[41] Shortly thereafter, the first military commissions in half a century were authorized.

21.6 The 2001 Authorization for Use of Military Force

The Authorization for Use of Military Force (AUMF) in Afghanistan, upon which a broad range of armed actions have been taken, is so brief – sixty words – that it may be quoted in full:

> That the President is authorized to use all necessary and appropriate force against those nations, organizations, or persons he determines planned, authorized, committed, or aided the terrorist attacks that occurred on September 11, 2001, or harbored such organizations or persons, in order to prevent any future acts of international terrorism against the United States by such nations, organizations or persons.[42]

---

[40] Allan R. Millett, *Their War for Korea: American, Asian, and European Combatants and Civilians, 1945–1953* (Dulles, VA: Potomac Books, 2004), 230–1.
[41] Authorization for Use of Military Force, Pub.L. 107–40, Sept. 18, 2001, 115 Stat. 224, 50 USCA § 1541.
[42] S.J. Res. 23, 107th Cong. (2001).

The 2001 Afghanistan AUMF was conceived on the afternoon of September 12, the day after the 9/11 terrorist attacks on the United States, and passed by the U.S. Senate on the morning of September 14. For a law granting the executive branch such broad powers it was a strikingly brief time for debate and deliberation. In practice, the 2001 AUMF has been interpreted to grant the executive branch a maximum of operational and detention flexibility, but more than thirteen years later (and counting) there is no consensus regarding the scope of the AUMF's authority.

The 2001 AUMF is nebulous regarding what it authorizes. With judicial acquiescence, it has been cited as authorizing targeted killing in every combat zone with which the United States is associated, including drone strikes in states with which the United States is not at war,[43] as legal authority for the detention of detainees, and for Guantánamo-based military commissions.

There is no temporal limit in the 2001 AUMF. Does the passage of time vitiate Congress's authorization of the use of force? It has not appeared to do so. At some point, however, the nations, organizations, or persons involved in the 9/11 attacks will have new or different governments, virtually all Taliban and al Qaeda fighters will have died or been killed, and 9/11 associated terrorist groups will have disbanded or no longer exist as a result of combat losses.

There is no geographic element in the 2001 AUMF. Presumably it is not an authorization for the use of force within U.S. borders, but that is unstated in the document. Is it an authorization for the use of force worldwide? One cannot know from reading the AUMF.

It says nothing regarding the authority to detain, although its authority to kill presumably subsumes authority to detain. The former U.S. Department of State legal counsel John Bellinger writes that "the [2001 AUMF] does not specify who may be detained, for how long or what review procedures may be used,"[44] and, "we're relying on the AUMF as our legal justification to detain members of al-Qaeda and the Taliban, essentially indefinitely."[45] While the right to hold enemy combatants and fighters in the course of an armed conflict is clear, even without codified authority,[46] the United States claims jurisdiction, based on the AUMF, to hold and to prosecute at military commissions,[47] not only those involved in the 9/11 attacks, but those who substantially support Taliban or al Qaeda forces, or *associated forces*, a vague grouping.

Nor does the 2001 AUMF state with specificity who may be targeted. The United States has emphasized the phrase "associated forces," to justify the targeting of individual terrorists and to expand the AUMF's geographic reach, although the words "associated forces" do not appear in the authorization. But how far can "associated forces" be pushed? John Bellinger noted in 2011, "our military is being forced to carry out counter-terrorism operations against individuals and groups who don't have an

---

43 Charlie Savage, "Obama Sees Iraq Resolution as a Legal Basis for Airstrikes, Official Says," *NY Times*, Sept. 13, 2014, A8, referring to bombing ISIS fighters in Iraq and Syria.

44 John B. Bellinger III, "An Outdated Terrorism Law," *Wash. Post*, Nov. 26, 2010, A21.

45 John B. Bellinger III, "Revisiting a Stale Counterterrorism Law," Council on Foreign Relations interview (Sept. 1, 2011).

46 *Hamdi v. Rumsfeld*, supra, note 25, at 518.

47 *Hamdan v. Rumsfeld*, supra, note 1, at 594–5: "Together, the UCMJ [Uniform Code of Military Justice], the AUMF, and the DTA [Detainee Treatment Act] at most acknowledge a general Presidential authority to convene military commissions . . . "

association with the groups who carried out 9/11. The 2001 AUMF is getting increasingly thin to rely on."[48] One federal court has noted, "'Associated forces' do not include terrorist organizations who merely share an abstract philosophy or even a common purpose with al Qaeda," and, "there must be an actual association in the current conflict with al Qaeda or the Taliban."[49] There have been terrorist armed opposition groups (AOGs) with which the United States has been in armed combat that arguably do not fall within the ambit of the AUMF, either because their formation postdates the 9/11 attacks, or their relationship to al Qaeda is remote or nonexistent – the Pakistani Taliban, al Qaeda in the Arabian Peninsula, and Jemaah Islamiyah in Indonesia, for example. Al Qaeda does not control all Islamic terrorist AOGs, or individual terrorists everywhere, and the AUMF is clear that Congress did not authorize "military action against terrorists generally."[50] What if the United States were to detain an individual who clearly was a lone actor, not affiliated with al Qaeda or *any* AOG?[51] Invoking the AUMF as authority would be baseless, yet there is no other authority.

During much of the war on terrorism, despite abortive efforts to replace the 2001 AUMF,[52] and its analogue, the 2002 Authorization for the Use of Military Force in Iraq, America's Congress has been too dysfunctional to craft a new or revised AUMF addressing the original version's infirmities. The executive branch, lacking explicit authority for the use of force against newly risen AOGs or "established" AOGs in newly infiltrated states, and without congressional authority for detentions reaching past the 9/11 al Qaeda–Taliban axis, must raise ever more tenuous rationales the use of force under the only authority it has, the inadequate AUMFs. Rewriting or revising them is "not just an issue of legal and academic curiosity, but a matter of vital domestic and international concern."[53]

21.7 Guantánamo Bay Military Commissions

Trial by military commission was provided for by President George W. Bush's Military Order of November 13, 2001.[54] However, "in formulating the [military] order the administration sought little help from the JAG offices in the services, where considerable experience about military trials resides."[55] A civilian judge on the U.S. Court of

---

[48] Bellinger, "Revisiting a Stale Counterterrorism Law," supranote 45..

[49] *Hamlily v. Obama*, 616 F.Supp.2d 63, 75, n.17 (D.D.C. 2009).

[50] Richard F. Grimmett, "Authorization for Use of Military Force in Response to the 9/11 Attacks (P.L. 107–40): Legislative History" (Washington, DC: Congressional Research Serv., updated Jan. 16, 2007), 3.

[51] The Obama administration defined an associated force as "(1) an organized armed group that has entered the fight alongside al Qaeda, and (2) is a co-belligerent with al Qaeda in hostilities against the United States or its coalition partners . . . . Thus, an 'associated force' is not any terrorist group in the world that merely embraces the al Qaeda ideology." Jeh C. Johnson, then-General Counsel, U.S. Dept. of Defense, speech at Yale Law School (Feb. 22, 2012).

[52] Pete Baker and Ashley Parker, "Congress Shows a Lack of Enthusiasm for Giving War Powers to Obama," *Wash. Post*, Feb. 13, 2015, A18.

[53] Beau D. Barnes, "Reauthorizing the 'War on Terror': The Legal and Policy Implications of the AUMF's Coming Obsolescence," 211 *Military L. Rev.* (Spring 2012), 57, 59.

[54] Military Order: Detention, Treatment, and Trial of Certain Non-Citizens in the War against Terrorism, 66 Fed. Reg. 57, (Nov. 16, 2001), 833.

[55] Harold H. Bruff, *Bad Advice: Bush's Lawyers in the War on Terror* (Lawrence: University Press of Kansas, 2009), 217.

Appeals for the Armed Forces wrote of the military order, "Numerous issues were left unanswered, suggesting fairly or unfairly that the proposal was half-baked and ill-advised. Nor could the experts in those omitted areas field the questions, for they were not included [in the Order's preparatory meetings]. ... The initial order was drafted by a handful of lawyers without the input of military lawyers or even the national security advisor."[56] The Military Commissions Act of 2006, while an improvement on the Military Order, introduced new issues of its own.

Guantánamo military commissions were at a legal disadvantage from their inception. They raised offenses never before tried in U.S. military trial forums and divided responsibility for trial decisions between uniformed judge advocates and Department of Justice lawyers. To oversee the process, add a divisive civilian political appointee who was unequal to the task, and the table was set for failure.

The Guantánamo commissions were a unique legal regime, subject to the teething problems and legal objections of any new legal system. "No one involved in issuing the President's November 2001 order had any idea how difficult it would be to, in effect, build a brand new court system from scratch."[57] Legal objections to many aspects of the new system were immediate. The system raised by the 2001 AUMF and the 2001 military order included new charges not found in U.S. courts-martial.

Guantánamo was selected as the prison for suspected terrorists in large part so they would be beyond the jurisdiction of American domestic, and international, courts – a legal black hole. Then-president Bush wrote that "holding captured terrorists on American soil could activate constitutional protections they would not otherwise receive. ... The Justice Department advised me that prisoners brought there had no right of access to the U.S. criminal justice system."[58]

The first prisoners, referred to as "detainees," arrived at Guantánamo Bay in January 2002, shortly after the international armed conflict phase of the U.S.-Afghan conflict concluded and its occupation phase began. At about the same time, several individuals designated "illegal enemy combatants" were arrested and held in U.S. military confinement facilities on the U.S. mainland. The first commanding officer of the Guantánamo detention facility, Marine Corps Major General Michael Lehnert, later said of those early detainees, "I think we did a poor job in the beginning of determining who we needed to go to Guantánamo. ... We relied pretty heavily on the Afghans to tell us who they were. ... A good chunk of them probably were of no value and should never have been there."[59]

In November 2005, shortly before Salim Hamdan's military commission was to convene at Guantánamo, the Supreme Court granted Hamdan's petition for *certiorari*

---

[56] James E. Baker, *In the Common Defense: National Security Law for Perilous Times* (New York: Cambridge University Press, 2007), 25.

[57] Jack Goldsmith, *The Terror Presidency: Law and Judgment inside the Bush Administration* (New York: W.W. Norton, 2007), 121.

[58] George W. Bush, *Decision Points* (New York: Crown, 2010), 166.

[59] Carol Rosenberg, "First Guantánamo Prison Camps Commander Says It's Time for Them to Close," *Miami Herald*, Jan. 12, 2014. "While ... [then-Secretary of Defense] Donald Rumsfeld famously described the Guantánamo prisoners as 'the worst of the worst,' the Pentagon ... has disclosed that only five percent of the detainees were apprehended by U.S. forces and only four percent were ever alleged to have actually been involved in fighting." Michael P. Scharf and Gwen Gillespie, "Foreword: Security Detention," 40–3 *Case Western Reserve J. of Int'l L.*, 315, 320.

to decide military commission jurisdiction and Geneva Convention applicability to military commission proceedings. The Court found that Guantánamo military commissions indeed lacked jurisdiction in Hamdan's case and noted that the 1949 conventions apply, in part, in the "war on terrorism":

> There is at least one provision of the Geneva Conventions that applies here even if the relevant conflict is not one between [State] signatories. Article 3, often referred to as Common Article 3 ... prohibits "the passing of sentences and the carrying out of executions without previous judgment pronounced by a regularly constituted court affording all the judicial guarantees which are recognized as indispensable by civilized peoples."[60]

"For practitioners and scholars versed in the law of war, this aspect of the opinion was perhaps the most profound. For the first time in our nation's history, the Supreme Court analyzed the applicability of Common Article 3 to an ongoing armed conflict ... and endorsed the broad application of the principle of humane treatment."[61] The Court further found that the military commissions established by the Bush administration's 2001 AUMF and Military Order were inconsistent with their asserted legal basis, the Uniform Code of Military Justice, and were in violation of Geneva Convention common Article 3, in that they were not "regularly constituted courts."

With the *Hamdan* decision, it was clear that the Geneva Conventions would continue to have an impact not only on individuals seeking their protections but on contemporary law of war, as well. Other significant matters were decided in the *Hamdan* decision, but the applicability of common Article 3 to military commissions involving nonstate accuseds was itself a landmark ruling.

21.7.1 *The Military Commissions Act of 2006*

The initial military order's version of military commissions having been found unlawful in *Hamdan*, the president and Congress moved to cure the deficiencies specified by the Supreme Court in that case. The 2006 Military Commissions Act (MCA),[62] enacted three months after the *Hamdan* decision, was a new legislative blueprint for U.S. military commissions. "The MCA generally requires that the rules for military commissions mirror the rules for courts-martial. Departure from this general requirement is permitted only if explicitly provided for in the MCA or if military or intelligence operations require otherwise."[63] Those departures were sometimes substantial, however. As Jack Goldsmith, the newly appointed head of the Department of Justice's Office of Legal Counsel in 2003 and 2004, wrote:

> The Military Commissions Act of 2006 explicitly authorized many aspects of the military commission regime that the Supreme Court had invalidated three months earlier. And it gave the President much more, including a broadened definition of

---

[60] *Hamdan v. Rumsfeld* ("Hamdan I"), supra, note 1, at 629–30.
[61] Geoffrey S. Corn, "*Hamdan*, Fundamental Fairness, and the Significance of Additional Protocol II," *The Army Lawyer*, Aug. 2006, 1, 2.
[62] Pub. L. No. 109–366, 120 Stat. 2600 (2006).
[63] *United States v. David Hicks*, Court of Military Commissions Review 13–004 (Feb. 18, 2015), (Krauss, J., concurring), at 10.

"unlawful enemy combatant"; ... immunity from prosecution for those who participated in past interrogations that crossed the prohibited line; narrowing interpretations of the Geneva Conventions ... that minimized the impact of the Supreme Court's [Hamdan] decision ... and a prohibition on the judicial use of the Geneva Conventions to measure the legality of the Guantánamo detentions.[64]

Administratively, the 2006 MCA directed that appeals of Guantánamo commissions would be heard by a newly created United States Court of Military Commission Review. Appeals from that court would be heard by the United States Court of Appeals for the District of Columbia, with possible further appeal to the Supreme Court of the United States.

Under the MCA, no court, justice, or judge had jurisdiction to hear Guantánamo detainee habeas corpus applications. (As to habeas applications already filed and pending resolution, the Supreme Court sidestepped the MCA's jurisdictional roadblock in its *Boumediene v. Bush* opinion.[65] Subsequent requirements imposed by the Court of Appeals for the District of Columbia made the Supreme Court's habeas ruling virtually unworkable, however.) Critics of the 2006 MCA pointed out that it had no speedy trial requirement. Also, conspiracy, without reference to an underlying criminal act, and material support of terrorism, were new offenses, both of them questionable charges. Classified "sources, methods, or activities" were protected from inquiry, a blow to defenders, although evidence derived from them would be admissible, a gift to prosecutors. Evidence obtained through cruel, inhuman, or degrading treatment was admissible if found to be probative and reliable – another boon for prosecutors. The MCA directed that no court, justice, or judge had jurisdiction to hear any action against the United States relating to any aspect of the detention or treatment of a detainee. Also, the president could interpret the meaning and application of nongrave breach violations of the Geneva Conventions, effectively allowing the executive branch to define away such violations, *including* common Article 3 breaches.

One commentator charged that the 2006 MCA contradicted the law of war by having lowered the legal standard for the trial and treatment of detainees, redefined combatancy, created new law of war offenses, and conflated the law governing international and noninternational armed conflicts.[66] A United Nations special rapporteur "directed scathing criticism at the [2006] Military Commissions Act, concluding that the military commission process 'utterly fail[s] to meet basic due process standards.'"[67] Critics notwithstanding, Guantánamo military commissions were soon convened.

21.7.2 *Guantánamo's Trials*

U.S. federal courts beat the military to the prosecution punch. From the outset there was confusion as to whether the war on terrorism should follow the military model or the law enforcement model. In prosecuting law of war violations both models were pursued;

---

[64] Goldsmith, *Terror Presidency*, supra, note 57, at 138.   [65] *Boumediene v. Bush*, 553 U.S. 723 (2008).

[66] Jack M. Beard, "The Geneva Boomerang: The Military Commissions Act of 2006 and U.S. Counterterror Operations," 101-1 *AJIL* (Jan. 2007), 56–64.

[67] Philip Alston, *Report of the Special Rapporteur on Extrajudicial, Summary or Arbitrary Executions, Mission to the United States of America*, Addendum, UN doc. A/HRC/11/2/Add.5 (May 28, 2009).

prisoners held within U.S. borders would be tried in domestic federal courts, while detainees held at Guantánamo would be tried by military commission.

John Walker Lindh, the "American Taliban," was captured in Afghan combat but tried in a civilian U.S. federal court. In a 2002 plea agreement, Lindh pleaded guilty to supplying services to the Taliban and carrying explosives during the commission of a felony, both federal crimes. He was sentenced to twenty years' confinement.[68] The trials of others accused of aiding or being terrorists followed. Yaser Hamdi, a dual citizen of Saudi Arabia and the United States, was captured in Afghanistan and transferred to a succession of military brigs, where he was designated an "illegal enemy combatant" and held in solitary confinement, without charges, for three years. After the Supreme Court ruled he must be allowed a trial, in 2004 Hamdi was simply released and returned to Saudi Arabia.[69] In 2006, Zacarias Moussaoui, arrested in Minnesota in 2001, pleaded guilty to terrorism-related charges in a civilian trial and was sentenced to six life terms without possibility of parole.[70] José Padilla was arrested in Chicago in 2002 and held incommunicado in military brigs for more than four years. In 2007, in a federal courtroom, Padilla was convicted of conspiracy to murder, kidnap, and maim and sentenced to seventeen years and four months' confinement.[71] (Seven years later, after government appeals, Padilla's sentence was vacated, reconsidered by the sentencing judge, and increased to twenty-one years.)[72] Other civilian federal court terrorism cases followed, only one involving Guantánamo detainees, all others involving individuals arrested in the United States.

Meanwhile, at Guantánamo in 2007, after Hamdi and Moussaoui had been tried and sentenced by *civilian* courts, Australian detainee David Hicks, with a plea agreement in hand, pleaded guilty to material support of terrorism. His was the first completed American military commission since World War II commissions had concluded. Captured in Afghanistan in 2001, Hicks was sentenced by a military commission jury to seven years' confinement, all but seven months suspended by virtue of the pretrial agreement. He was released to serve his brief post-conviction confinement in Australia.

Salim Hamdan, whose earlier Supreme Court case established the applicability of common Article 3 at military commissions, was recharged in 2008 and tried again under the 2006 MCA. Convicted of material support of terrorism, he was sentenced to five and a half years' confinement. The military judge granted Hamdan credit for sixty-one months of pretrial confinement, in keeping with U.S. court-martial practice. Hamdan was transferred to his native Yemen to serve his brief remaining confinement. Military commission rules were quickly changed to preclude sentencing credit for time served, in future cases.

A series of Guantánamo military commissions followed, if slowly: Ali al-Bahlul stood mute throughout his trial and, in 2008, was convicted and sentenced to imprisonment for life;[73] in 2010, Ibrahim al-Qosi, entered a guilty plea and was sentenced to fourteen years,

---

[68] *U.S. v. John Walker Lindh*, 212 F. Supp. 2d 541 (E.D. Va., 2002).   [69] *Hamdi v. Rumsfeld*, supra, note 25.

[70] *U.S. v. Zacarias Moussaoui*, (Criminal # 01–455-A, E.D.Va., 2006).

[71] *U.S. v. Jose Adham Amin Hassoun* [aka Padilla], *and Kifah Wael Jayyousi* (Case No. 04–60001, S.D. Fl., 2007). Padilla, a lawful permanent resident of the United States, was not subject to military commission jurisdiction under the Military Order of 2001, or the 2006 MCA.

[72] AP, "Florida: New, Longer Sentence in Terrorism Case, "*NY Times*, Sept. 10, 2014, A20.

[73] In 2009, Ahmed Khalfan Ghailani became the sole Guantánamo detainee to be transferred to the U.S. mainland for trial by a domestic court. Acquitted of 284 counts of murder and conspiracy, he was convicted

with a pre-trial agreement calling for considerably less confinement and repatriation to Sudan; Omar Khadr also entered a 2010 guilty plea, with a pretrial agreement for eight years, seven to be served in his native Canada. In 2011, Noor Uthman Mohammed also entered a plea bargain and pleaded guilty to providing material support for terrorism, an offense codified by Congress *after* the dates of his alleged wrongful acts. In a secret plea bargain, his sentencing was postponed after he agreed to testify in other cases, as was Majid Khan's sentencing, with a similar plea bargain. Pursuant to his plea bargain, Mohammed was released in late 2013 and returned to his native Sudan. In January 2015, however, Mohammed's conviction was dismissed by the Convening Authority for Military Commissions on the basis that his conviction rested upon a charge found by a civilian appellate court to not constitute a violation of the laws and customs of war.[74] In February 2014, Ahmed Mohammed Haza al-Darbi pleaded guilty pursuant to a plea agreement to participating in the bombing of a civilian tanker off the coast of Yemen. He was sentenced to nine to fifteen years' confinement, most of it to be served in his native Saudi Arabia.[75]

At this writing, several other military commissions have been convened but not gone to trial. Khalid Sheikh Mohammed, the alleged "mastermind" of the 9/11 attacks, and four coaccused, were arraigned in May 2012. A trial date was set for thirty-two months later, January 2015, a date that came and went without substantive proceedings. Such modest movement to trial leads one to wonder whether the military commissions of the arraigned accused will ever be completed.

In 2011, President Obama reversed his 2009 order that had halted any new charges against Guantánamo detainees.[76] (Charges against the indicted 9/11 accused were initiated before the 2011 presidential order.) Stymied by domestic political opposition from either closing Guantánamo or moving detainees to the U.S. mainland for trial in federal courts, the president directed resumption of Guantánamo military commissions, the only American forum remaining available.[77]

21.7.3 *The Military Commissions Act of 2009*

In October 2009, Congress revised the 2006 MCA[78] and "somewhat enhanced defendants' rights before military commissions."[79] The new act prohibited the use of statements made under torture, or cruel, inhuman, or degrading treatment. The circumstances under which hearsay evidence was admissible were more closely defined. Revisions also

---

of 1 count of conspiracy to destroy government buildings and property (two U.S. embassies). He was sentenced by the court to confinement for life. *U.S. v. Ghailani*, 733 F.3d 29, 54 (2d Cir., 2013).

[74] Carol Rosenberg, "Pentagon Throws Out Foot Soldier's Guantánamo War Court Conviction," *Miami Herald*, Jan. 9, 2015; and, Digest, "General Overturns Terrorism Conviction," *Washington Post*, Jan. 11, 2015, A3.

[75] Charlie Savage, "Guantánamo Detainee Pleads Guilty in 2002 Attack on Tanker off Yemen," NY *Times*, Feb. 20, 2014, A1.

[76] Statement of President Barack Obama on Military Commissions (May 15, 2009), available online.

[77] White House Fact Sheet, "New Actions on Guantánamo and Detainee Policy" (March 7, 2011), available online.

[78] Enactment was part of the 2010 National Defense Authorization Act: Pub. L. No. 111–84, 123 Stat. 2190 (2009).

[79] John R. Crook, "Contemporary Practice of the United States Relating to International Law," 104–1 *AJIL* (Jan. 2010), 100, 117.

provided that no accused could invoke the Geneva Conventions as a basis for a private right of action. The 2009 MCA was not the major course correction that the 2006 MCA was. Neither was it as contentious. It made military commissions a step closer to U.S. court-martial procedures, while retaining questionable 2006 MCA charges.

21.7.4 *International War Crimes That Are Not*

The 2009 MCA purports to take a traditional view of war crimes tribunals, saying, "The provisions of this subchapter codify offenses that have traditionally been triable by military commission. This chapter does not establish new crimes that did not exist before the date of the enactment."[80] Actually, it did.

The jurisdictional basis of military commissions authorized by the 2009 MCA was "the third type: a law-of-war military commission."[81] There would be no trials of ordinary crimes, no military order violations charged, no martial law involvement, only prosecutions for violation of international war crimes. "An initial problem is that most common acts of terrorism, although crimes under domestic law, are not war crimes."[82]

Providing material support for terrorism, for example, was one of the Guantánamo military commission charges most frequently brought against detainees. But was it a commonly recognized international violation of the laws and customs of war? In reversing the 2008 military commission conviction of Salim Hamdan, the United States Court of Appeals for the District of Columbia wrote in 2012, "the issue here is whether material support for terrorism is an international-law war crime. The answer is no."[83] A 2014 opinion in another Guantánamo case from the same court added, "The Government offers little domestic precedent to support the notion that material support or a sufficiently analogous offense has historically been triable by military commission."[84]

Congress does have the constitutional authority in Article I, section 8, to make material support for terrorism a law of war offense. However, while there is no universal definition of what a triable war crime is, it is commonly agreed that such offenses must be recognized by the international community as being triable war crimes. Some European states have made material support for terrorism a *domestic* crime.[85] But prior to the MCA, no American military tribunal had ever prosecuted such a charge. It is unmentioned in 1907 Hague Regulation IV, in any U.S. field manual, in the Statutes of the International Criminal Court and the International Criminal Tribunal for the Former Yugoslavia. The Congressional Research Service noted that, "defining as a war crime the 'material support for terrorism' does not appear to be supported by historical precedent."[86]

---

[80] 10 USC, § 950p.(d). Oct. 16, 2012.   [81] *al Bahlul v. United States*, supra, note 35, at 6.

[82] Gabor Rona and Raha Wala, "In Defense of Federal Criminal Courts for Terrorism Cases in the United States, in Fionnuala Ní Aoláin and Oren Gross, eds., *Guantánamo and Beyond* (New York: Cambridge University Press, 2013), 137, 142.

[83] *Salim Hamdan v. United States*, 696 F.3d 1238 at 1250 (U.S. Ct. of Appeals, D.C. Cir., 2012). This case is often referred to as *"Hamdan* II."

[84] *al Buhlul v. United States*, supra, note 35, at 45.

[85] Erling Johannes Husabø and Ingvild Bruce, *Fighting Terrorism through Multilevel Criminal Legislation* (Leiden: Martinus Nijhoff, 2009), Chapter 5, 97–192, and 381.

[86] Jennifer K. Elsea, "The Military Commissions Act of 2006: Analysis of Procedural Rules and Comparison with Previous DoD Rules and the Uniform Code of Military Justice," (Washington, DC: Congressional Research Service, Sept. 27, 2007), 16.

Military commissions are not a forum for the prosecution of domestic crimes unless so provided in their establishing statute.

Congress can make loitering a law of war offense, if it chooses. But it may only prosecute the "war crime" of loitering in U.S. Article I and Article III courts over which it has constitutional authority. Congress may not make up its own international law of war, and it cannot validly unilaterally declare battlefield acts to be violations of the laws and customs of war. Saying something is a war crime, even if Congress says it, does not make it so. As the Supreme Court wrote in 1887, "Whether the offense as defined is an offense against the law of nations depends on the thing done, not on any declaration to that effect by Congress."[87]

Congress did declare material support for terrorism a war crime in the Military Commissions Act of 2006. Hamdan was charged with committing the offense on the basis of his actions from 1996 to 2001, but that was *before enactment of the Military Commissions Act.* The Court of Appeals for the D.C. Circuit continued, "At the time of Hamdan's conduct, the extant federal statute authorized and limited military commissions to try violations of 'the law of war.'" The court concluded, "Because we read the Military Commissions Act not to retroactively punish new crimes, and because material support for terrorism was not a pre-existing war crime under 10 U.S.C. § 821 [the UCMJ's jurisdictional article], Hamdan's conviction … cannot stand."[88] In Hamdan's case, not only was the charge against him not a war crime, it was an *ex post facto* bogus charge, as well.

Another frequent Guantánamo military commission charge was conspiracy. Hamdan was convicted of that offense, as well.

> The charge against Hamdan is not that Hamdan, [Osama] bin Laden, and others entered into an agreement to commit terrorist acts, but rather that Hamdan, as bin Laden's driver, "joined an existing conspiracy." … Even if we knew precisely what membership meant, American lawyers would properly have qualms about punishing the passive status of just being there and being counted. … Membership does not threaten anyone. It cannot be a criminal wrong. … Neither conspiracy nor membership in a terrorist organization meets the standards of an international crime acceptable to the leading legal systems of the world.[89]

Professor George Fletcher, the Cardozo Professor of Jurisprudence at Columbia University School of Law, continues, "Some legal systems recognize conspiracy and others do not. Americans do. Others do not. When only some countries accept a particular doctrine, it cannot become part of customary international law."[90]

In 2006, the U.S. Supreme Court wrote in the *Hamdan* plurality opinion, "The most serious defect of this charge [of conspiracy]: The offense it alleges is not triable by law-of-war military commission. … The crime of 'conspiracy' has rarely if ever been tried as such in this country by any law-of-war military commission … and does not appear in either the Geneva Conventions or the Hague Conventions."[91] The Court continued, "Finally, international sources confirm that the crime charged here is not a recognized

[87] *U.S. v. Arjona*, 120 U.S. 479 (1887).   [88] *Hamdan v. United States* , supra, note 83, at 1240 and 1241.

[89] George P. Fletcher, "*Hamdan* Confronts the Military Commissions Act of 2006," 45–2 *Columbia J. of Transnat'l L.* 427, 445–6.

[90] Id., at 449.   [91] *Hamdan v. Rumsfeld*, ("*Hamdan* I"), supra, note 1, at 600, 603–4.

violation of the law of war. ... None of the major treaties governing the law of war identifies conspiracy as a violation thereof. ... The International Military Tribunal at Nuremberg ... pointedly refused to recognize as a violation of the law of war conspiracy to commit war crimes."[92]

A third, less frequent Guantánamo charge, was murder in violation of the law of war. Omar Ahmed Khadr was a fifteen-year-old Canadian citizen. In 2002, at the urging of his father, Khadr moved to Afghanistan to wage jihad against America. He was one of three individuals in an Afghan compound constructing improvised explosive devices for use by al Qaeda agents against U.S. forces. The compound was surrounded by a U.S. Army Special Forces unit. The occupants refused an order to surrender and a firefight commenced, followed by the bombing of the compound. Firing by both sides continued as the U.S. force then entered the compound. Khadr, badly wounded, blindly threw a hand grenade toward approaching soldiers, killing an American combatant. Khadr was captured, interrogated, medically treated, and eventually confined at Guantánamo Bay. He could have been tried in a U.S. federal court for murder in violation of federal law but, instead, was charged under several sections of the Military Commissions Act. At his August 2010 military commission, eight years after his capture, the first of many charges against Khadr was that he threw a grenade that killed an American soldier. It was, the charge sheet read, a "murder violation of the law of war." But an unprivileged belligerent cannot be prosecuted for a "war crime" whose underlying act would not have been a war crime if committed by a privileged combatant.[93] How can the same act logically be a war crime for fighters on one side and not for fighters on the other side?

In *Hamdan*, the Supreme Court unambiguously wrote of the charge of murder in violation of the laws and customs of war, "It is not a stand-alone offense against the law of war."[94] Other writers add, "In fact, the laws of war contain no such prohibition. What they do prohibit is the targeting of civilians and the use of perfidious means to target even legitimate military objectives."[95]

If a Guantánamo detainee were charged with the murder of a protected person in his custody or control, *that* would be a murder in violation of the law of war. So far, no such scenario has been charged at Guantánamo. For an unprivileged belligerent, lacking the combatant's privilege, to return fire and kill an attacking privileged combatant would be murder under the domestic law of the state in which the event occurred, but not a war crime. "The U.S. approach ... asserts U.S. combatants had the right to shoot Khadr on sight ... yet criminally prosecute him for fighting back."[96]

---

[92] Id., at 610–11. In a 2014 opinion, the Court of Appeals for the District of Columbia found that conspiracy had *not* been settled by *Hamdan*. "In Hamdan," the *en banc* D.C. Court of Appeals held, "seven justices ... debated the question at length. Four justices concluded that conspiracy is not triable by military commission. ... Three justices opined that it is. ... The case was resolved on other grounds and the eighth vote – one justice was recused – left the conspiracy question for another day, noting that the Congress may 'provide further guidance in this area.'" *al Bahlul v. U.S.*, supra, note 35, at 36. Thus, a final disposition of the validity of conspiracy as a law of war offense has not been decided as of this writing.

[93] Kevin Jon Heller, "The Non-Existent War Crime of 'Murder in Violation of the Law of War,'" *Opino Juris Blog* (Aug. 8, 2008), 1.

[94] *Hamdan v. Rumsfeld*, supra, note 1, at 608.

[95] Rona and Wala, "In Defense of Federal Criminal Courts for Terrorism Cases," supra, note 82, at 137, 143. Footnote omitted.

[96] David Glazier, "A Court without Jurisdiction: A Critical Assessment of the Military Commission Charges against Omar Khadr," at 14 (unpublished paper, on file with author).

A fourth Guantánamo military commission charge held not to be an international war crime was solicitation to commit war crimes – although a valid *domestic* charge in U.S. courts. About the military commission charge of solicitation, the Court of Appeals for the D.C. Circuit held:

> We also conclude that solicitation of others to commit war crimes is plainly not an offense traditionally triable by military commission. The Government concedes that it is not an international law-of-war offense. . . . The Government contends that solicitation "possesses a venerable lineage as an offense triable by military commission," but it cites only two Civil War-era field orders involving three defendants in support thereof.[97]

With that holding, four of Guantánamo's thirty-two charges, two of them the most frequently charged Guantánamo offenses, were found by U.S. federal appellate courts to fall short of being international war crimes within the jurisdiction of the military commissions.

The Supreme Court ruled in the first *Hamdan* case that, to constitute an offense under the laws and customs of war, "the precedent must be plain and unambiguous. To demand any less would be to risk concentrating in military hands a degree of adjudicative and punitive power in excess of that contemplated either by statute or the Constitution."[98]

The government's response to the courts' rejections of material support for terrorism and conspiracy has been to appeal the rulings and continue charging the same offenses. Should another Guantánamo case arise that alleges murder in violation of the law of war, presumably the United States will carry on with that charge, as well. "Attorney General Eric Holder decided to press forward. . . . Mr. Holder overruled the recommendation of the solicitor general . . . who had wanted to drop the [conspiracy] case."[99] Also overruled was Guantánamo's respected and highly regarded chief prosecutor, Army Brigadier General Mark S. Martins.

> He [General Martins] has engaged in an increasingly public dispute with the administration centered on an uncomfortable question he is refusing to drop: is it valid for the United States to use tribunals to charge idiosyncratic American offenses like "conspiracy," even though they are not recognized as war crimes under international law? . . . General Martins pushed to abandon [Salim Hamdan's case] and scale back the charges that are triable in a military commission, contending that pressing forward with failed arguments would delegitimize the system. . . . But Attorney General Eric H. Holder Jr. decided to go forward with defending . . . the validity of conspiracy as a tribunal charge, and the schism opened.
>
> General Martins refused to sign the Justice Department brief [charging conspiracy] in [Hamdan's second] case. . . . But the Pentagon official who oversees tribunals refused to withdraw the conspiracy charge, citing the Justice Department. General Martins responded that his prosecutors would not argue against a defense motion asking a judge to scuttle it.[100]

The ultimate disposition of the rejected charges awaits further appellate review. Many observers anticipate further, and presumably final, rejection of the government's positions.

---

[97] *al Buhlul v. United States*, supra, note 35, at 51.

[98] *Hamdan v. Rumsfeld*, supra, note 1, at 601–2. Footnote omitted.

[99] Charlie Savage, "U.S. to Press Fight of Detainee's Appeal," NY *Times*, Jan. 10, 2013, A14.

[100] Charlie Savage, "Who Decides the Laws of War?" NY *Times*, Jan. 28, 2013, at SR5.

SIDEBAR. In 2009, Attorney General Eric Holder announced that the 9/11 "mastermind," Khalid Sheikh Mohammed, would be tried in a New York City federal court, rather than at Guantánamo. The outcry from both major political parties was sharp and immediate. Many said it would put the New York City at risk of terrorist attack. Others objected that terrorists should not benefit from the trial rights afforded American citizens. Holder's plan was quickly abandoned. Yet, in thirteen years, Hamdan and al-Bahlul are the only contested Guantánamo military commission trials that went to verdict. And their convictions were vacated by the Supreme Court and a U.S. court of appeals. In roughly the same period that all eight of the contested and uncontested military commissions were completed, at least 509 terror-related cases were adjudicated in civilian courts, with an 89 percent conviction rate.[101] At least sixty federal district courts in thirty-seven U.S. states have successfully and safely convicted terrorists since 9/11.[102] Guantánamo is restricted to prosecuting violations of the laws and customs of war, while federal courts may try terrorists accused of violating *any* federal offense. So far, no one confined after conviction of a terrorism-related offense in a civilian court has ever escaped. Senator Lindsay Graham said of a terrorist suspect convicted in a New York City federal court, "He was a treasure trove of potential information, and we blew it."[103] But, in thirteen years, has any actionable intelligence been gleaned from a Guantánamo proceeding? No such treasure trove has been publicly announced.

21.7.5 *Legal Ethics*

As a trial forum, civilian court proceedings have a greater legitimacy, in the eyes of many, than do Guantánamo's military commissions. U.S. practice demonstrates that civilian courts are equal to complex terrorism trials while military commissions are seen by some to be ill-conceived vehicles dispensing second-tier justice. Early in the process, ethical issues within Guantánamo's military commissions were raised by military lawyers – "JAGs" – some of whom paid a price for voicing concerns.[104]

In 2005, "two Air Force prosecutors … requested that they be reassigned rather than participate in the proceedings, having charged that their fellow prosecutors were ignoring torture allegations, failing to protect exculpatory evidence, and withholding information from superiors."[105] In 2007, a defense counsel, formerly the Marines' chief defense counsel for the western United States, called the commissions "disgraceful," and "a sham."

---

[101] Clyde Haberman, "Vexed by Terrorism, Trials and Guantánamo, and Bearing Witness," NY *Times*, May 20, 2013, A1. The period referred to in the article is Sept. 11, 2001, to May 2013. The number of domestic court convictions varies, however, according to the source consulted.

[102] Human Rights First, "Trying Terror Suspects in Federal Courts, Fact Sheet" (July 2012).

[103] Benjamin Weiser, "Terror Trial Proves Civilian Courts Are Safe, Holder Says in Visit to Manhattan," NY *Times*, April 2, 2014, A22.

[104] Marine major Michael Mori, who vigorously defended the Australian detainee David Hicks, was given the Australian Lawyers Alliance's civil justice award. Mori was twice passed over for promotion to lieutenant colonel. Mori reportedly sued the Marine Corps and, while suit was pending, was selected for promotion. Several years later, he was again passed over for promotion, this time to colonel. Mori retired from active service. Navy lieutenant commander Charles Swift, a Naval Academy graduate, later selected one of America's top 100 lawyers, took the first *Hamdan* case to the Supreme Court and won, after which he was passed over for promotion to commander. Swift retired from active service.

[105] Laura A. Dickinson, "Military Lawyers on the Battlefield: An Empirical Account of International Law Compliance," 104–1 *AJIL* (Jan. 2010), 1, 27.

An Army lieutenant colonel resigned as a prosecutor in 2008, citing ethical concerns over failures to turn over exculpatory material to defense attorneys.[106] Also in 2008, Guantánamo's chief prosecutor, an Air Force colonel, resigned his office and testified for the defense in the *Hamdan* case, charging "that Pentagon officials interfered with prosecutors, exerted political pressure and approved the use of evidence obtained by torture."[107] Later, the judge in the *Hamdan* case, a Navy judge advocate captain, disqualified the military commission's legal adviser to the convening authority from acting in the case, ruling that the legal adviser, an Air Force brigadier general, had exerted improper influence over military prosecutors.[108] In 2008, the military judge in the *Mohammed Jawad* case excluded the defendant's confession because it was extracted under torture.[109] In 2009, Guantánamo's convening authority, civilian Susan Crawford, a retired judge on the U.S. Court of Appeals for the Armed Forces, refused to refer to trial the case of Mohammed al-Qahtani. "'We tortured Qahtani,' said Crawford. '. . . Crawford said detainee interrogation practices are a blot on the reputation of the United States and its military judicial system."[110] In 2012, another Guantánamo prosecutor, a major, resigned from the Army, charging on National Public Radio that at Guantánamo the U.S. government was crafting a "show trial."[111]

In 2013, in regard to the forced feeding of detainees, the American Medical Association notified the Department of Defense that "any doctor who participated in forcing a prisoner to eat against his will was violating 'core ethical values of the medical profession..'"[112] Yet, a year later, when a male Navy lieutenant nurse refused to continue participating in the force feeding of detainees, he was sent to an administrative discharge board.[113] In 2014, the American Psychological Association opened a review into whether A.P.A. members "colluded with the Bush administration to support torture during the war on terror."[114]

Denunciations of Guantánamo military commission practices by judge advocates, civilian lawyers, medical officials, and military commission officials, diminished the perception of Guantánamo military commissions, as well as their utility in future conflicts.

21.8 Summary

Military commissions, created in the fertile imagination of General Winfield Scott to deal with criminal conduct on the battlefield, have come a great legal distance. They are recognized as meeting a continuing military necessity. All states employing military commissions are obliged, through their ratification of the 1949 Geneva Conventions, to conduct prosecutions of POWs as they would if trying one of their own combatants; the relaxed trial procedures and evidentiary standards of the past are no longer permissible. A similar approach to the trial of detainees in noninternational armed conflicts would seem wise.

[106] Peter Finn, "Guantánamo Prosecutor Quits, Says Evidence Was Withheld," *Wash. Post*, Sept. 25, 2008, A6.

[107] William Glaberson, "Ex-Guantánamo Prosecutor to Testify for Detainee," *NY Times*, Feb. 28, 2008, A14.

[108] John R. Crook, "Contemporary Practice of the United States Relating to International Law," 103–1 *AJIL* (Jan. 2009), 132, 159.

[109] Id., at 160.   [110] Bob Woodward, "Detainee Tortured, Says U.S. Official," *Wash. Post*, Jan. 14, 2009, A1.

[111] NPR Staff, "Guantánamo Defense Lawyer Resigns, Says U.S. Case Is 'Stacked,'" Aug. 31, 2012.

[112] Charlie Savage, "Obama Renews Effort to Close Prison in Cuba," *NY Times*, May 1, 2013, A1.

[113] Carol Rosenberg, "Navy Nurse Who Refused to Force-Feed Still Working at Guantánamo" *Miami Herald*, Aug. 8, 2014; and, Rosenberg, "No Court-Martial for Nurse Who Refused to Give Force-Feeding at Guantánamo," *Miami Herald*, Sept. 15, 2014. The board ultimately allowed him to remain in the navy.

[114] American Psychological Association, "Statement of APA Board of Directors: Outside Counsel to Conduct Independent Review of Risen Allegation" (Nov. 12, 2014); and, James Risen, "Psychologists to Review Role in Interrogations," *NY Times*, Nov. 14, 2014, A 8.

Although military commissions may also be established with jurisdiction to try domestic offenses, in U.S. practice their historical application has been to try enemies, military or civilian, charged with the violation of internationally recognized laws and customs of war. After World War II, most Allied states employed military commissions in one form or another, and they were generally seen as successful in dealing with the enemy excesses of that war.

Recent U.S. military commissions were not as successful and made the future of such bodies, no matter how well-executed, questionable. Although a few Guantánamo cases continue on the military commission's docket, it becomes apparent that they will not be prosecuted to verdict.

The first twenty detainees arrived at Guantánamo Bay on January 11, 2002. Fourteen years later, eight detainees had gone to trial and been convicted. Six of the eight convictions (Hicks, al Qosi, Khadr, Noor Uthman Mohammed, Khan, and al-Darbi) resulted from pretrial agreements to plead guilty in exchange for sentencing leniency.

Two of the eight convictions, those of Noor Uthman Mohammed[115] and David Hicks,[116] were eventually dismissed by appellate courts because the trials were based on charges found not to be violations of the laws and customs of war. The only two contested military commissions that went to verdict (Hamdan and al-Bahlul), were also dismissed on appeal. Initially, al-Bahlul's case was not a complete dismissal. Two of the three charges of which he was convicted, material support and solicitation, were vacated (dismissed) by the U.S. Court of Appeals for the District of Columbia. His third charge, conspiracy, was remanded to a panel of the court of appeals for resolution, and the case was further remanded to the Court of Military Commission Review for reconsideration of sentencing.[117]

Ultimately, al-Bahlul's conspiracy charge was also vacated, the court of appeals panel finding that conspiracy was not an international war crime. The dismissal also mooted sentence reconsideration since all charges against him had then been dismissed. In a concurring opinion, one panel judge wrote, "The government can always fall back on the apparatus it has used to try federal crimes for more than two centuries: the federal courts. . . . Federal courts hand down thousands of conspiracy convictions each year, on everything from gunrunning to financial fraud to, most important here, terrorism."[118]

In early 2016, more than ninety detainees remained confined at Guantánamo Bay at a reported cost of $800,000 per prisoner per year.[119] Many of them, found by a federal panel not to constitute a danger to the United States, have for years been recommended for release and transfer to other states. Forty-eight other detainees are reportedly designated for eventual security detention even if tried and found not guilty.[120] (An official figure for potential security detainees has not been released.)

---

[115] U.S. Department of Defense, News Release No. NR-013–15 (Jan. 8, 2015) announcing that the Convening Authority for Military Commissions had disapproved the findings and sentence.

[116] *United States v. David Hicks*, Court of Military Commissions Review 13–004 (Feb. 18, 2015).

[117] *Al-Bahlul v. U.S.*, supra.note 35.

[118] Charlie Savage, "Guantánamo Detainee's Conviction Is Thrown Out on Appeal," NY *Times*, June 13, 2015, A12.

[119] Helene Cooper, "127 Prisoners Remain at Guantánamo as U.S. Sends 5 to Kazakhstan," NY *Times*, Jan. 1, 2015, A10; "By the Numbers," *Miami Herald*, Aug. 12, 2013. Several figures, one (Helene Cooper, "Guantánamo Releases 5, Angering Senators," NY *Times*, Jan. 15, 2015, A-13) as high as $1,000,000 per man per year, are said to reflect the cost of maintaining Guantánamo. None is assured to be accurate.

[120] Peter Finn and Anne E. Kornblut, "Obama Creates Indefinite Detention System for Prisoners at Guantánamo Bay," *Wash. Post*, March 8, 2011. Another number, fifty-nine, is cited in, Charlie Savage, "Board Says Saudi Detainee Should be Repatriated," NY *Times*, Oct. 21, 2014, A18.

"The level of diminished procedural safeguards [in military commissions] is appalling ... the defendant's right to choose a lawyer is limited; hearsay evidence and evidence obtained prior to 2005 through cruel, inhuman, or degrading treatment is admissible; classified and exculpatory evidence can be withheld; and the right of appeal is severely curtailed."[121]

There will always be a military necessity for military commissions. Francis Lieber, the Civil War general Henry Halleck, the Nuremberg prosecutor Telford Taylor, and many others implemented military commissions that were firm yet essentially fair to captured enemies. Whether public and political antipathy to Guantánamo military commissions comes to outweigh their future military necessity is an open question.

Each iteration of military commissions is unique to the armed conflict to which it responds. Guantanamo's problems may be avoided if future military commissions, without domestic political interference, implement Geneva Convention III's Article 102 and prosecute detainees and prisoners of war as U.S. combatants would be prosecuted: under the charges, evidentiary rules, and procedural requirements of the Uniform Code of Military Justice and the U.S. *Manual for Courts-Martial.* Although 1949 Geneva Convention III and Article 102 are applicable to common Article 2 international armed conflicts, it has long been U.S. military policy to "comply with the law of war during all conflicts, however such conflicts are characterized."[122] Military commissions need not be an exception to that policy.

In his 1945 opening statement to the Nuremberg International Military Tribunal, Supreme Court Justice Jackson said, "We must never forget that the record on which we judge these defendants is the record on which history will judge us tomorrow. To pass these defendants a poisoned chalice is to put it to our own lips as well."[123]

CASES AND MATERIALS

FRENCH LAW CONCERNING TRIALS OF WAR CRIMINALS BY MILITARY TRIBUNALS AND BY MILITARY GOVERNMENT COURTS IN THE FRENCH ZONE OF GERMANY [FOLLOWING WORLD WAR II][124]

Introduction. *There is more to military commissions than the Guantánamo experience, of course. After World War II, all of the major Allied powers convened military commissions. As indicated in this chapter's section 21.3, there are three commission jurisdictional bases. All three were employed by one or another Allied power. The authorization for French*

---

[121] Sikander A. Shah, *Daniel Moeckli's Human Rights and Non-Discrimination in the War on Terror*, 103–3 AJIL (July 2009), 635, 638 (book review).

[122] U.S. Dept. of Defense Directive 5100.77, *DoD Law of War Program*, para. 5.3.1. (Dec. 9, 1998. Additionally, Art. 102 is arguably customary law.

[123] Justice Robert H. Jackson, *Trial of German Major War Criminals*, supra, note 31, at 5.

[124] United Nations War Crimes Commission, *Law Reports of Trials of War Criminals*, Vol. III (London: U.N. War Crimes Commission, 1948), annex II, at 93.

military commissions, a part of which is reproduced verbatim here, permitted both military government and military (i.e., law of war) tribunals/commissions, two of the three jurisdictional bases.

I. The Two Types of Tribunal

War crimes trials conducted according to French law have been heard either by permanent military tribunals or by military government tribunals in the French Zone of Germany.

Since the great majority of trials have been held before permanent military tribunals, this annex deals mainly with these courts. Two sections, however, relate to military government tribunals.

II. The Jurisdiction and Legal Basis of French Permanent Military Tribunals for the Trial of War Criminals

The competence of French Military Tribunals to try war criminals, apart from those sitting in the French Zone of Germany, is based on the Ordinance of 28th August, 1944, concerning the suppression of war crimes, which, by virtue of Art. 6 thereof, is applicable not only to Metropolitan France but also to Algeria and the Colonies.

The first paragraph of Art. 1 of the Ordinance runs as follows:

"Enemy nationals or agents of other than French nationality who are serving the enemy administration or interests and who are guilty of crimes or delicts committed since the beginning of hostilities, either in France or in territories under the authority of France, or against a French national, or a person under French protection, or a person serving or having served in the French armed forces, or a stateless person resident in French territory before 17th June, 1940, or a refugee residing in French territory, or against the property of any natural persons enumerated above, and against any French corporate bodies, shall be prosecuted by French military tribunals and shall be tried in accordance with the French laws in force, and according to the provisions set out in the present Ordinance, where such offenses, even if committed at the time or under the pretext of an existing state of war, are not justified by the laws and customs of war."

The Military Tribunals which have heard cases tried under the Ordinance have been Permanent Military Tribunals sitting at Strasbourg, Lyons and a number of other centres.

Art. 124 of the *Code de Justice Militaire* states that: "In time of war, there shall be at least one Permanent Military Tribunal in each military region; the seat of this Military Tribunal shall, in principle, shall be the chief town of the military region. ..."

III. The Composition of a French War Crimes Tribunal

Art. 5 of the Ordinance runs as follows: "For adjudicating on war crimes, the military tribunal shall be constituted in the manner laid down in the *Code de Justice Militaire*. The majority of the military judges shall be selected from among officers, non-commissioned officers and other ranks belonging, or having belonged, to the French Forces of the Interior or a Resistance Group. ...

IV. Persons Subject to the Jurisdiction of French Military Tribunals for the Trial of War Crimes

Art. 1 of the Ordinance states that the persons liable to prosecution thereunder are: "Enemy nationals or agents of other than French nationality who are serving the enemy administration and interests and who are guilty of crimes or delicts committed since the beginning of hostilities; either in France or in territories under the authority of France, or against a French national, or a person under French protection, or a person serving or having served in the French armed forces, or a stateless person resident in French territory before 17th June, 1940, or a refugee residing in French territory, or against the property of any natural persons enumerated above, and against any French corporate bodies." [Editor's note: Although similar to section ii, section IV differs substantially in content.]

Art. 4 lays down that where the subordinate is prosecuted as the actual perpetrator of a war crime, and his superiors cannot be indicted as being equally responsible, they shall be considered as accomplices insofar as they have organized or tolerated the criminal acts of their subordinates. ..."

Art. 59 of the Code states that "The accomplices to a crime or a delict shall be visited with the same punishment as the authors thereof, excepting where the law makes other provisions. ... "

V. Crimes Made Punishable by the Ordinance

The terms "War Crime" and "War Criminal" are left undefined in the Ordinance, but it seems to follow from the wording of Art. 1 that the offenses to be punished are such infractions of French Law as are not made justifiable by the laws and customs of war. ...

"Article 2. The provisions of the *Code Pénal* and of the *Code de Justice Militaire* shall be interpreted as follows:

"(1) The illegal recruitment of armed forces ... shall include all recruitment by the enemy or his agents;

"(2) Criminal association ... shall include within its scope organizations or agencies engaged in systematic terrorism;

"(3) Poisoning ... shall include the exposure of persons in gas chambers, the poisoning of water or foodstuffs, and the depositing, sprinkling, or applying of noxious substances intended to cause death;

"(4) Premeditated murder ... shall include killing as a form of reprisal;

"(5) Illegal restraint ... shall include forced labour of civilians and deportation for any reason whatever of any detained or interned person against whom no sentence which is in accordance with the laws and customs of war has been pronounced.

"(6) Illegal restraint ... shall include the employment on war work of prisoners of war or conscripted civilians;

"(7) Illegal restraint ... shall include the employment of prisoners of war or civilians in order to protect the enemy.

"(8) Pillage ... shall include the imposition of collective fines, excessive or illegal requisitioning, confiscation of spoliation, the removal or export from French territory by whatever means of property of any kind, including movable property and money.

... As this annex states elsewhere, Art. 302 [of the *Code Pénal*] provides the penalty for premeditated murder, patricide and poisoning, and Art. 304 provides the penalty for murder.

Of the remainder, Art. 132 of the *Code Pénal* deals with the counterfeiting and altering of French money and the circulation thereof, Arts. 265 *et seq.*, with conspiracies to prepare or commit crimes against persons or property, 303 with torture and acts of barbarity, 309–317 with voluntary wounding and striking , not regarded as murder, and other voluntary crimes and delicts, 332 and 334 with certain sexual offenses, 379 with theft, 400 with extortion, and 434–459 with arson and other forms of destruction. Art. 214 of the *Code de Justice Militaire* deals with abuse of authority and 216 with offenses against wounded, sick and dead soldiers.

VI. Provisions Regarding the Defense of Superior Orders

Art. 3 of the Ordinance runs as follows: "Laws, decrees or regulations issued by the enemy authorities orders or permits issued by these authorities, or by authorities which are or have been subordinated to them, cannot be pleaded as justification within the meaning of Art. 327 of the *Code Pénal*, but can only, in suitable cases, be pleaded as an extenuating or exculpating circumstance."

Art. 327 of the *Code Pénal* makes the following provision: "No crime or delict is committed when the homicide, wounded or striking was ordered by the law or by legal authority." ...

VII. Penalties Attaching to War Crimes

Art. 1 of the Ordinance states simply that the persons specified therein shall be "prosecuted by French Military Tribunals and shall be judged in accordance with the French laws in force. ..."

These articles provide the possible range of punishment under French Criminal Law; Articles providing against individual offenses supply the relevant penalties. ..."

VIII. The Procedure Followed in French War Crimes Trials

The Ordinance makes no special provisions regarding procedure, but simply makes reference to trial "in accordance with the French laws in force." ... [There follow two pages of trial procedures that were followed in a noted earlier French war crime trial.]

IX. Provisions Regarding Appeals

In time of war, according to the provisions of a Decree of 3rd November 1939, Permanent Military Appeal Tribunals are to be set up, their number, seat, and jurisdiction being fixed by decree. They are to deal only with cases involving persons convicted by Military Tribunals. Art. 135 of the *Code de Justice Militaire* states that such persons shall have twenty-four hours during which they may appeal to such a court. ...

This appeal to a Permanent Military Appeal Tribunal is the only one possible in wartime against a decision of a Permanent Military Tribunal. ... [There follows a page of appellate procedures to be complied with.]

X. The Legal Basis of Military Government Tribunals in the French Zone of Germany

The number of war crime trials held before French Military Government Courts has been relatively small. ... The legal basis of war crimes legislation in the zones of Germany was provided originally by the power of a military commander to act as the legislative and executive authority for territories occupied by him, and later also by the fact that, by the Declaration regarding the defeat of Germany and the assumption of supreme authority with respect to Germany made in Berlin on the 5th June, 1945, the four Allied Powers occupying Germany have assumed supreme authority with respect to Germany including all the powers possessed by the German government and any state, municipal or local government, or authority.

Acting as Supreme Allied Commander before the emergence as separate entities of the four Allied Zones of Germany, General Eisenhower promulgated Ordinance No. 1 (Crimes and Offenses) and Ordinance No. 2 (Military Government Courts). A French High Command in Germany was created on 15th June, 1945, and Ordinance No. 1 of 28th July, 1945, of the French Commander-in-Chief, which was thus enacted after the Berlin Declaration and after the emergence of the four Allied Zones, maintained in force the two Ordinances of the Supreme Allied Commander referred to above. ...

Law No. 10 of the Allied Control Council (*Punishment of Persons Guilty of War Crimes, Crimes Against Peace and Crimes Against Humanity*), reaffirms the right of the Commander-in-Chief of each Zone to establish within his Zone tribunals for the punishment, *inter alia*, of war crimes. ...

Conclusion. In section III of the French law, note the unusually broad pool from which judges may be drawn. In section V, "Crimes Made Punishable," note the references to human shields and to conspiracies.

Those interested in the post–World War II war crimes trials will find section X interesting, with its mention of the division of Germany into American, British, French and Russian control zones (although the four controlling Allied states are unnamed), and Control Council Law # 10, which was the jurisdictional basis for Nuremberg's twelve "subsequent trials."

All of the Allied states promulgated occupation laws generally similar to this French law, each specifying the state's jurisdiction to conduct war crime tribunals.

GUANTÁNAMO ARRAIGNMENT – YOU HAD TO BE THERE (OR NOT?)

Professor David Glazier, Loyola School of Law

Introduction. Non-government organizations (NGOs) are permitted to periodically send representatives to Guantánamo, Cuba as observers of military commissions. Housed in hard-back "tents" (with air-conditioning!), observers must always be escorted by a military officer or non-commissioned officer. The two accounts that follow are representative of the "Gitmo experience." Professor Glazier's 2012 report was initially submitted to his sponsoring NGO, the National Institute of Military Justice. Glazier is a retired U.S. Navy officer, a former combatant ship commander, and now a law professor. Mr. Richter was a 2014 observer for the New York City Bar Association. He is a trial attorney with long experience as a civilian intelligence officer with the Defense Intelligence Agency and the Office of the Director of National Intelligence.

Just getting to Guantánamo gives one perspective on the challenges confronting military commission attorneys, particularly defense attorneys, on a regular basis, including the multi-day lead time for travel approval and the requirement to show up several hours before flight time in classic military "hurry up and wait" style. And there is nothing like flying in 20+ year old aircraft operated by low-budget charter operators you've never heard of to inspire confidence. (U.S. troops deploying overseas also frequently get to travel this way.) And of course, you come and go not when convenient, but when these irregular flights are scheduled.

Next I got to experience the curious realities of military commission security. You must present a passport – the only form of ID accepted – at a checkpoint where you are validated against the pre-approved entry list and undergo a traditional security screening – X-ray of all possessions; metal detector/wand of your person; before being led a short distance to a second location where this entire process is repeated. (Imagine if TSA tried to adopt this approach.) Only then are you allowed to proceed to the courtroom gallery entrance where you show your passport a third time and receive an individual seat assignment. I am tempted to conclude from this passport fetish that these are actually foreign courts. Observers cannot bring any pens, pencils, electronic devices, notebooks, etc. with them – courtroom staff provides loaner writing implements and plain white pads. If this is how U.S. nationals, physically separated from the courtroom by a glass wall, are screened, claims that defendants experience much more rigor, including strip searches, seem entirely credible.

A real value added from traveling to Guantánamo is the ability to see the full courtroom, from before the arrival of the detainees (observers had to start our entry process a full hour before the scheduled start time), until the completion of the trial day. Observers sit in a soundproof glass booth listening to the same 40-second time delay as remote observers, and have video monitors showing the same picture. It is generally less surreal to watch the monitors, so what you hear and see match up. But there is merit to being able to see what is happening throughout the courtroom rather than just the view of the currently speaking participant offered on the monitors.

Watching from the gallery, for example, highlighted the largely dysfunctional attorney-client relationships. The courtroom is arranged with six long defense tables arranged one behind the other. (It was specifically designed for this trial, but former convening authority Susan Crawford, refused to approve charges against alleged twentieth 9/11 hijacker, Mohamed al Kahtani, leaving one extra table). The defendants sit one behind the other at the extreme left end (as viewed from the gallery) of their respective tables. The lead attorneys generally sat near the right end of their respective table, convenient to the center podium from which they were expected to address the court, meaning but what looked to be at least twenty-five feet away from their client with wholly empty table in between. . . . This physical separation highlighted the gulf between these attorneys and clients, and the resulting need for the attorney to stand up and walk over to the defendant [and] made it easy to observe how little actual attorney-client conversation took place. The fact that KSM and bin Attash's lawyers conferred with their clients without use of an interpreter revealed that these defendants' refusal to wear headphones does not mean they weren't following trial events; they can do so in English. . . . It appeared from the gallery that the prosecution outnumbered the five separate defense teams combined. . . .

But perhaps the most significant thing I saw was five defendants sitting quietly in their assigned chairs for the vast majority of the lengthy day, with approximately twenty uniformed guards sitting in a row little more than an arm's length away from them, ready to intervene instantly if called upon. From media reports one might assume this was the Chicago Seven trial [of seven young men charged with crimes while engaged in street-protests at the 1968 Democratic National Convention] redux, with outrageous defendant conduct largely responsible for drawing out the proceedings so long. Other than the extension of the lunch break by continuing prayers which may have been either schedule confusion or deliberate defendant misconduct, by my estimation what we saw otherwise was substantially less than five minutes of activity over the course of a thirteen-hour day that violated traditional courtroom decorum. It could have been limited to mere seconds if the judge had been so inclined. The fact that the judge tolerated even a few minutes' interruption provides concern that this will just prove to be a dry run for future tactics. But I think the commission's inadequate preparation for the session, including lack of contingency planning for technical or translation issues, issuance of a new arraignment script the day before trial unavailable in Arabic for defendant or translator use, last-minute bickering over a pre-trial conference, etc. were actually much more significant issues for concern than defendant [mis]conduct.

Finally, although NGO reps are required to be relatively passive observers, and are not to ask questions at the press conferences or initiate contacts with the media or actual commission participants, I certainly gained a lot from the opportunity to benefit from hearing the views of a number of other participants and observers. I have been a close scholar of both past and present military commissions since President Bush announced their use in November 2001, and have read many thousands of pages of Guantánamo transcripts and documents from every case conducted to date. I still found the opportunity to see the events in person to be a valuable compliment to that experience.

COMEDY AND TERROR IN GUANTÁNAMO BAY

Michael P. Richter, in *The New Jurist* (October 10, 2014)

My mission was clear: go to the US Naval Station at Guantánamo Bay, Cuba on behalf of the New York City Bar Association and observe and report on the pre-trial proceedings against Abd al Rahim Hussayn Muhammad al Nashiri, the alleged mastermind behind the attack on the USS Cole.

. . . I landed in Cuba, and I started to wonder, how, five years after he had been captured, with this much evidence, and a defense that is more fit for a comedy than the serious charges leveled against him, are we not even at trial. . . . [I]t was October 2012! As I attended one hearing after another I watched as simple issues that state and federal courts often resolve in a matter of minutes languished without resolution.

On the morning of the first day, al Nashiri refused to leave his cell. . . . The issue surrounding his absence is what lawyers call KVI – was al Nashiri's waiver of his right to attend these proceedings Knowing, Voluntary and Intelligent. ∴ . . . The debate took hours. Court decisions from multiple jurisdictions were cited. As I told one of the defense attorneys later, this issue would have lasted ten minutes in a civilian court. He politely disagreed: "five minutes." ... Ultimately, the Court ruled that al Nashiri must attend. We adjourned and waited for his arrival.

Finally, he was there. With plenty of time to plan his soliloquy, I was expecting something worth printing – and al Nashiri didn't disappoint: ... "But if you order the guards to bring me a bad chair, when I'm sitting in an uncomfortable place, I have the right to leave this court. You have to provide me with a comfortable chair where I can sit down comfortably." Al Nashiri also didn't like his ride: "I need a more comfortable vehicle to bring me here."

... The Judge had trouble moving things along. "I would like to limit these discussions, as much as I can, which at times I don't feel I can, to the motion before me." Right after that the defense asked if it could say something "briefly."

Judge: Counsel used the term 'briefly.'
Defense: 'Briefly' is a relative term.

Eventually the judge got fed up with the defense, which was hell-bent on wasting everyone's time. ...

The irony of this slow process is that some had the idea that a military tribunal would be faster and tougher. ... But this is slow justice.

Defense: Here we are a year and a half into the case ... because of all the procedural and logistic particulars and all the other Guantánamo-related craziness –
Judge: Let's say 'challenges.'
Defense: Challenges ... We haven't even begun to get to where we would normally be in a less-challenged court within the first two months of representation. ...

After the defense expressed concern that the microphones on their table were listening devices, forcing them to scurry to the corner to whisper, the prosecution invoked the same metaphor: "and I'll note for the record that we have some theatrics going on here as counsel parade, you know, over to the corner of the room."

... In state and federal courts across the country routine disputes are often quickly resolved because there is a history of how to deal with them. The Court in Guantánamo, however, has virtually no history, and that slows things down.

In addition, it became clear to me that the Judge was focused on creating a full record for the appellate court, and likely the Supreme Court, which will probably be the ultimate arbiter of al Nishiri's fate. Indeed, the defense has already telegraphed its intent to appeal. ...What I saw is that the law creating the terror trials is a mess, and the travel back and forth to Cuba has slowed these proceedings to a snail's pace.

... I can't help but think that if this trial were held in a normal federal court we would be further along, and the victim's family members would be closer to getting at least some closure. Before I left I asked one of the victim's family members how he was feeling. This man's brother, not yet old enough to drink, was killed in the attack on the Cole. He wasn't a lawyer or an intelligence officer. "I'm just trying to understand this," he said. Me too.

Conclusion. *As the years progressed, courtroom events continued sometimes to confound. Security measures became more rigorous. Hostile courtroom glares from U.S. military reservist master-at-arms men and women, ever alert for an observer who might surreptitiously chew gum, were more irritating than reassuring.*

The requirement for military escorts was always strictly observed: In the Guantánamo "courthouse" there is a men's room and a ladies' room visible from the trial observers' section, through the large doors to the center of the courthouse. (The courthouse is a refurbished aircraft control tower.) NGO observers, however, were relegated to two "porta-potties" outside the courthouse and across a parking area; only trial participants could use the bathrooms. Since an escort was always required, and because there was but one escort per group of trial observers, if one of the group went somewhere, either all of the group went, or no one went. During a court recess, when a lady in a group of six NGO observers asked to use the ladies' room, the officer escort required that the other five in the group follow her, and him, outside to the portable facility and stand outside the plastic utility, shuffling feet and staring at the sky, until she emerged, grinning broadly and waving a four-foot long toilet paper banner.

22 Security Detention

22.0 Introduction

"Planner of 9/11 Attacks Might Not Face Trial,"[1] the *New York Times* headline read. In March 2003, Khalid Sheik Mohammed ("KSM"), reputed to be the guiding hand behind the 2001 attacks on the United States, was captured in Pakistan by U.S. forces. He was held in secret CIA "black sites" for three and a half years, then was transferred to Guantánamo Bay, Cuba, in September 2006. The *Times* article continued, "Khalid Sheik Mohammed ... will probably remain in military detention without trial for the foreseeable future." The *Times* was almost wrong. Six years after his arrival at Guantánamo, in May 2013, KSM was arraigned, along with four other Guantánamo coaccused, before a military commission. It appeared that he would stand trial, contrary to the *Times*. Because of Guantánamo's dysfunctional military commission process, however, one may question whether KSM's military commission will ever progress to verdict, but the *Times* may be correct about his remaining in detention for the foreseeable future. Whether convicted or acquitted, or even if his case never goes to verdict, he will likely remain detained for years, if not for the rest of his life. He is one of forty-eight Guantánamo detainees reportedly slated for security detention;[2] the government has not released the actual number considered for security detention.

Sex offenders are routinely kept in custody beyond the expiration of their court-imposed sentences.[3] Long-term detention often occurs in the context of immigration law. "All states authorize the detention of the mentally ill under some circumstances. And while the Supreme Court has placed considerable limitations on this practice, it has also repeatedly upheld its constitutionality."[4] The law of armed conflict (LOAC) allows for such detention. It is provided for in international human rights law and U.S. domestic law. Referring to the many Guantánamo prisoners who have been detained without charges or trial for years, two academics write:

---

[1] Peter Finn and Anne E. Kornblut, "Planner of 9/11 Attacks Might Not Face Trial," *NY Times*, Nov. 13, 2010, A1.

[2] Peter Finn and Anne E. Kornblut, "Obama Creates Indefinite Detention System for Prisoners at Guantánamo Bay," *Washington Post*, March 8, 2011. Another number, fifty-nine, is cited in, Charlie Savage, "Board Says Saudi Detainee Should Be Repatriated," *NY Times*, Oct. 21, 2014, A18.

[3] *Kansas v. Hendricks*, 521 U.S. 346 (1997).

[4] Benjamin Wittes, *Law and the Long War: The Future of Justice in the Age of Terror* (New York: Penguin Press, 2008), 34, citing an early example, *Ex rel. Pearson v. Probate Court of Ramsey*, 309 U.S. 270 (1940).

It is something of an article of faith in public and academic discourse that preventive detention runs counter to American values and law. ... It treats the past ... years of extra-criminal detention of terrorism suspects as an extraordinary aberration from a strong American constitutional norm, under which the government locks up citizens pursuant only to criminal punishment, not because of mere fear of their future acts. ... The trouble with such civic mythology is that ... preventive detention is not prohibited by U.S. law or especially frowned upon in tradition or practice. The circumstances in which it arises are not isolated exceptions to a strong rule against it; rather, they are relatively frequent.[5]

Or is it correct that "in many ways the introduction and design of counter-terrorist detention in the 'War on Terror' reflects characteristics of panic-related law-making in which domestic rights protections, including normal political rigor, can become vulnerable to panic and fear"?[6] Oxford University's Sir Adam Roberts writes:

The moral difficulties raised by the holding of security detainees can be summarized quite simply. On the one hand, most societies that have been faced with certain types of serious security threats, especially those involving terrorism, have resorted to one form or another of detention without trial. Yet, on the other hand, the holding of people who may have committed no offence, for an indefinite period, often with little or no international supervision or right of appeal, runs contrary to basic norms of justice, and creates extraordinary opportunities for abuse of power by the detaining authority. It risks being, or being seen as, the "practice of arbitrary imprisonments" that was memorably condemned by Alexander Hamilton as "the favorite and most formidable instrument of tyranny". ... Controversies about detention without trial, and mistreatment of detainees, are all too common in guerrilla and counter-terrorist campaigns. This is not just a U.S. problem.[7]

22.1 Security Detention Defined

Security detention, also referred to as "administrative detention" or "preventive detention," is a form of internment, a long-recognized aspect of armed conflict. In 1886, Colonel William Winthrop, U.S. Army, in his classic treatise on military law, wrote, "a neutral State cannot lend assistance to belligerents, and especially cannot allow them to make use of its territory without compromising its neutrality. Humanity, on the other hand, demands that a neutral State shall not be obliged to repel persons who beg refuge from death or captivity. ... Such neutral does not and cannot make them prisoners, but *interns* them."[8]

The 1907 Hague Convention V, Article 11, requires that "a neutral Power which receives on its territory troops belonging to the belligerent armies shall intern them ...

---

[5] Adam Klein and Benjamin Wittes, "Preventive Detention in American Theory and Practice," 85 *Harvard Nat'l Security J.* 85 (2011).

[6] Fiona de Londras, *Detention in the War on Terror* (Cambridge: Cambridge University Press, 2011), 9.

[7] Adam Roberts, "Detainees: Misfits in Peace and War," in Sibylle Scheipers, ed., *Prisoners in War* (Oxford: Oxford University Press, 2010), 263, 267, citing Hamilton, *The Federalist*, no. 84 (May 28, 1788).

[8] Col. William Winthrop, *Military Law and Precedents* (Washington, DC: Gov't Printing Office,1886), 796. Emphasis in original.

at a distance from the theatre of war. It may keep them in camps and even confine them in fortresses or in places set apart for this purpose."[9] During World War II, the Swiss government interned 1,740 American aircrew and 13,500 other foreign combatants, primarily German and British aircrew who crash-landed in Switzerland after their planes were damaged in combat in German skies. They were not prisoners of war because Switzerland was not at war with the United States or Germany, or any other state. "There was no warm welcome from the Swiss. Surrounded by forces of the Third Reich, the Alpine nation enforced its neutral status with vigor. Inbound aircraft were met by the *Flugwaffe*, Switzerland's small air force, and could be shot down unless clearly in distress or having lowered their undercarriage [landing gear] in surrender."[10] Interned aircrew were held in roughly a hundred camps across Switzerland, all with armed Swiss guards. Guarded at night, the internees were allowed outside their camps during the day, after giving their parole to return at night.[11] In England, the British interned 569 individuals.[12] As is well known, the United States interned roughly 110,000 Japanese Americans during World War II, 62 percent of whom were American citizens.

SIDEBAR. In World War II, early in 1941, the twenty-three-year-old American Roland Wolfe left Nebraska and volunteered to be a pilot for British forces already at war with the Nazis in Europe. Upon qualifying, he was assigned to the Royal Air Force's 133 "Eagle Squadron," made up entirely of American pilots. Since the United States was not then at war, many Eagle Squadron flyers, including Wolfe, were stripped of their U.S. citizenship for joining the armed forces of another state. On a November 30, 1941, flight, the engine of Wolfe's Spitfire malfunctioned and he was forced to bail out over County Donegal, Ireland. Ireland was still a neutral in the war. As required by international law, Wolfe was interned by Ireland, along with forty other RAF pilots and several Nazis. Two weeks after his internment, however, Wolfe walked out of the lightly guarded camp and caught a train back to England. The British government, loath to irritate their neutral but wavering neighbor, arrested Wolfe and returned him to the same Irish internment camp from which he had escaped, where he spent the next two years. Wolfe then escaped again, this time returning to an American aviation unit in England. He joined the U.S. Army Air Force, regained U.S. citizenship, and returned to flight status. After World War II, he continued to serve in the air force, including service in Korea and Vietnam, where he flew more than nine hundred combat missions. He retired as a lieutenant colonel, with the distinction of having been interned twice in the same conflict. Colonel Wolfe died in 1994.[13]

Internment is the noncriminal detention of a person based on the serious threat that his or her activity poses to the security of the detaining authority in relation to an armed

---

[9] Convention (V) Respecting the Rights and Duties of Neutral Powers and Persons in Case of War on Land (Oct. 18, 1907)

[10] Tom Docherty, "Alpine Sanctuary," *FlyPast* magazine, Nov. 2014, 78.

[11] Cathryn J. Prince, *Shot from the Sky: American POWs in Switzerland* (Annapolis, MD: Naval Institute Press, 2003), 21–43 and 140–62.

[12] I. C. B. Dear, ed., *The Oxford Companion to the Second World War* (Oxford: Oxford University Press, 1995), 570.

[13] BBC News Magazine (June 27, 2011), www.bbc.co.uk/news/magazine-13924720

conflict.[14] Assigned residence[15] is a looser form of internment that allows an internee to remain in his own home or another assigned residence, with limited freedom to move about in a closely defined geographic area. Prisoners of war (POWs) are normally interned in POW camps controlled and guarded by the capturing power. Today, 1949 Geneva Convention IV provides for the internment of protected persons in international armed conflicts and details the rights and duties of detainees and the holding state.[16] 1977 Additional Protocol II provides for internment in noninternational armed conflicts but offers no details on its execution.[17] "Internal armed conflicts, since they are principally governed by domestic law, will inevitably lead to an increase in detentions . . . imposed by that [domestic] law for security reasons related to the conflict."[18] In noninternational armed conflicts, common Article 3(1) is applicable but merely requires that internees be treated humanely.

Security detention is a form of internment differing from the internment regimes imposed during armed conflicts. In limited circumstances, LOAC and international humanitarian law (IHL), as well as international human rights law, allow security detention. **Security detention is the deprivation of liberty, without criminal charges, of a protected person, ordered by the executive branch, for security reasons during international or noninternational armed conflicts, or other situations of violence.[19] During periods of armed conflict involving occupation, internment may only be employed for reasons of security related to the armed conflict.[20] In peacetime, it may only be employed for the purpose of protecting the security of the detaining power, or to maintain public order.[21]**

This definition is not entirely satisfying. "Although the Geneva Conventions address the treatment and trials of detainees in noninternational armed conflict, the Conventions do not explicitly authorize detention [in] such conflicts, as they do for wars between States. The drafters expected that the power to detain in such conflicts would be covered by domestic law."[22] Where security detention is involved, it is important that the expectation of regulation by domestic law be fulfilled so that captives and captors each know the legally imposed responsibilities and prohibitions of the other.

The difference between ordinary internment and security detention is twofold. Security detention is initiated by the executive branch of the government, rather than by the judiciary or military authorities, as internment is. Second, internment, including the internment of POWs, ends "without delay after the cessation of active hostilities."[23]

---

[14] ICRC, "Internment in Armed Conflict: Basic Rules and Challenges," Opinion Paper (Nov. 2014), at 3. Available online.

[15] 1949 Geneva Convention IV, Art. 42. An Israeli assigned residence case is: *Kipah Ajuri v. IDF Commander*, HCJ 7015/02 (Sept. 3, 2002).

[16] 1949 Geneva Convention IV, Arts. 41–3, 68, 70, 77–8, and 84.   [17] 1977 Protocol II, Arts. 5 and 6.

[18] United Kingdom Ministry of Defense, *The Manual of the Law of Armed Conflict* (Oxford: Oxford University Press, 2004), para. 15.40.2, at 401.

[19] Jelena Pejic, "Procedural Principles and Safeguards for Internment/Administrative Detention in Armed Conflict and Other Situations of Violence," 87/858 *Int'l Rev. of the Red Cross* (June 2005), 375.

[20] 1949 Geneva Convention IV, Art. 78

[21] Id., Art. 42. Also see, Tyler Davidson and Kathleen Gibson, "Experts Meeting on Security Detention Report," 40–3 *Case Western Reserve J. of Int'l L.* (2009), 323, 327, fn. 1.

[22] Human Rights First, "Detained and Denied in Afghanistan: How to Make U.S. Detention Comply with the Law," (May 2011), 6.

[23] 1949 Geneva Convention IV, Arts. 132–3.

Security detention's unspecified duration beyond cessation of hostilities is its significant distinction from ordinary internment.

The qualified right to intern protected persons in wartime "flows from the practice of armed conflict and the logic of IHL that parties to a conflict may capture persons deemed to pose a serious security threat and that such persons may be interned as long as they continue to pose a threat. Otherwise, the alternatives would be to either release or kill captured persons."[24]

Under what authority are security detainees held beyond the end of hostilities? That question is unaddressed in Geneva Convention IV; the answer must be found in domestic legislation and state practice.

If security detainees may be held beyond the end of hostilities, as modest state practice and the International Committee of the Red Cross (ICRC) suggest, for how long thereafter and under what conditions may they be held? If a detainee's ultimate release is not temporally foreseeable, security detention may become indefinite detention, which is clearly unacceptable. Periodic reviews to determine whether the need for security detention continues are designed to prevent that circumstance.

SIDEBAR. Objects may also be interned, although an infrequent occurrence. In 1940, during World War II, after Nazi forces overwhelmed France, ships of the French navy, stranded in British ports, were interned, along with their crews.[25] In 1914, shortly after the outbreak of World War I, the German steamer *Kamilla Rickmers*, top speed eleven knots, with a three-inch deck gun forward and a six-inch gun aft, was seized by U.S. Customs officials and interned in Manila. (The Philippines were then a U.S. possession.) Taken over by the U.S. Navy when America entered the war in 1917, it was renamed the *Ticonderoga* and resumed its career as a cargo ship, crossing the Atlantic several times until, on September 22, 1918, it was attacked and sunk by the German submarine *U-152*, with the loss of 213 American lives. The *Ticonderoga*'s skipper, the navy lieutenant commander James J. Madison, survived the sinking and was awarded the Medal of Honor for his heroic fighting defense of the once-interned *Ticonderoga*, even as it was sinking.[26]

Security detention is increasingly used in noninternational armed conflicts against terrorism for reasons relating to protection of state security or public order. The United Kingdom,[27] Israel,[28] Turkey,[29] and Canada, among other states, employ forms

---

[24] Chatham House/International Committee of the Red Cross, "Expert Meeting on Procedural Safeguards for Security Detention in Non-International Armed Conflict," 91/876 *Int'l Rev. of the Red Cross* (Dec. 2009), 859, 863. This is a foundational article for anyone interested in internment and security detention.

[25] Dear, *Oxford Companion to the Second World War*, supra, note 12, at 403.

[26] Lt.Cmdr. Thomas J. Cutler, "Exceptionally Heroic Service," U.S. *Naval Institute Proceedings* (Oct. 2013), 92.

[27] See Human Rights Act 1998 (a UK law), available online, incorporating the European Convention on Human Rights, including the government's rights to reservations and derogation. For an overview of the United Kingdom's Control Orders system, see Davidson and Gibson, "Experts Meeting," supra, note 24, at 348–50.

[28] 2002 Incarceration of Unlawful Combatants Law, 576–2002, 1 (Israel). For an overview, again see Davidson and Gibson, "Expert's Meeting," supra, note 24, at 538–62.

[29] See *Turkey v. Askoy* (21987/93) [1966] ECHR 68 (Dec. 18, 1996), often referred to as "the Greek Case."

of security detention.[30] In Europe, security detention is generally permitted only when accompanied by the state's derogation of certain provisions of various human rights instruments, and it is limited to brief periods. Internment, including security detention, however, has no intrinsic temporal limits. In the past, the ICRC has objected that "there is no agreement at the international level on whether administrative detention for security reasons is lawful."[31] Other respected authorities disagree. (Even the ICRC has, in more recent years, seen the need for security detention.)[32]

The lawfulness of security detention in the course of international armed conflicts, including the detention of POWs, is well established. "Under the Fourth Geneva Convention, internment is the severest measure of control that may be taken against a protected person by a party to an international armed conflict."[33] It is no less a severe measure in noninternational armed conflicts, but, because they are noninternational conflicts, the controls of Geneva Convention IV, germane in international armed conflicts, are not directly applicable.[34] By analogy, however, the Fourth Convention's controls are instructive, although not controlling. In noninternational armed conflicts, sources of law for security detention include Geneva Convention common Article 3, which articulates minimum standards for internment of any sort; Additional Protocol I, Article 75, considered customary law; 1977 Additional Protocol II; and customary international law. In 1988 the United Nations adopted the *Body of Principles for the Protection of All Persons under Any Form of Detention or Imprisonment*, which contains a detailed checklist of safeguards.[35] "The Body of [U.N.] Principles does not ... have the force of international law, but [addresses] the two most central questions: the extent to which incommunicado detention is prohibited or restricted and whether there is an unrestricted right to challenge the lawfulness of detention."[36]

In noninternational armed conflicts and other situations of violence, the absence of specific international guidelines for internment, including security detention, requires one to look to domestic law and human rights law for guidance, particularly the 1966 International Covenant on Civil and Political Rights (ICCPR, ratified by the United States in 1992) and, for Europeans, the European Convention on Human Rights.[37] In human rights law, an individual may be deprived

---

[30] For an overview of Canada's Immigration and Refugee Protection Act (2001 S.C. ch. 27, and 2008 revisions, see Davidson and Gibson, "Experts Meeting," supra, note 24, at 362–5.

[31] ICRC, "International Humanitarian Law and the Challenges of Contemporary Armed Conflicts," 867 *Int'l Rev. of the Red Cross* (Sept. 2007), 719, 730.

[32] Most notably so in its well-reasoned 2005 article, Pejic, "Procedural Principles and Safeguards for Internment/ Administrative Detention," supra, note 19.

[33] ICRC, "International Humanitarian Law," supra, note 31, at 729.

[34] 1949 Geneva Convention IV controls on confinement include Arts. 42, 43, and 84. Articles applicable to initial apprehension and eventual release include Arts. 41, 68, 70, 77, 78, and 84.

[35] UNGA Res. 43/173 (Dec. 9, 1988).

[36] Nigel S. Rodley, with Matt Pollard, *The Treatment of Prisoners under International Law*, 3d ed. (Oxford: Oxford University Press, 2009), 451–2. Chapter 11 cites many European cases involving detention.

[37] Doug Cassel, "International Human Rights Law and Security Detention," 40–3 *Case Western Reserve J. of Int'l L.* (2009), 383 provides a description of the impact of human rights law on security detention, particularly in Europe. Although the United States has ratified the ICCPR, it holds that it is not applicable to aliens located beyond U.S. borders.

of liberty only "on such grounds and in accordance with such procedures as are established by law."[38]

The European Court of Human Rights (ECHR) has upheld the imposition of detention without charges during "terrorist campaigns,"[39] providing support for security detention in peacetime. The detention upheld by the ECHR is not the lengthy security detention envisioned by the United States, however. European detention is imposed with a view to eventual criminal charges and trial[40] and is imposed for a few hours or days beyond usual statutory limits,[41] rather than for years without trial, as the United States apparently envisions for Guantánamo security detainees.

22.2 "Other Situations of Violence"

Internment during armed conflict is discussed or mentioned in all four 1949 Geneva Conventions and both 1977 additional protocols. Security detention, by any of its several names, is not. Most often, internment occurs in situations of international armed conflict or occupation, ending at the conclusion of the armed conflict with which it is associated. Security detention, on the other hand, envisions long-term confinement of unspecified duration during *and after* the armed conflict has ended.

Internment, including security detention, is an exceptional measure of control that may be ordered in other situations of violence besides armed conflict. The term "other situations of violence," undefined in LOAC/IHL,[42] refers to situations below the threshold of armed conflict, including internal disturbances or tensions.[43] In considering what constitutes "other situations of violence," the European Court of Human Rights held that the situation in Northern Ireland, circa 1990, constituted a public emergency justifying the British government's invocation of Article 15 of the ECHR, permitting derogation of certain rights in time of war or public emergency.[44]

A similar conclusion would presumably apply during a noninternational armed conflict, and might also apply during a period of sustained and significant terrorist activity when there is no associated armed conflict in progress, but the law is unclear in this regard. A state wishing to exercise security detention absent an armed conflict would likely assert that the sustained terrorist activity itself constituted an "other situation of violence" justifying such detention. The United States, for example, might cite continuing anti-American terrorist activity by al Qaeda affiliates, Taliban-related actors, or other

---

[38] Int'l Covenant on Civil and Political Rights, Article 9 (1). A State Party to the Covenant may derogate from certain of its obligations, including Article 9 (1), in case of a public emergency, such as an ongoing NIAC that threatens the derogating state's existence.

[39] *Ireland v. U.K.*, Application No. 5310/71, Judgment, para. 11 (Jan. 18, 1978), and *Lawless v. Ireland*, Application No. 332/57, Judgment, July 1, 1961, Series A No. 3, "Law" section, paras. 8–15

[40] European Convention on Human Rights, Art. 5, §3: "Everyone arrested or detained in accordance with the provisions of paragraph 1(c) of this Article ... shall be entitled to trial within a reasonable time or to release pending trial."

[41] *Case of Brannigan and McBride*, ECHR, Application 14553/89; 14554/89, Judgment (May 25, 1993), para.15.

[42] ICRC, "Internal Conflicts or Other Situations of Violence – What Is the Difference for Victims?" (ICRC: Interview, Oct. 12, 2012), available online, discusses but never defines or describes the term.

[43] 1977 Additional Protocol II, Art. 1(2) refers to such situations as, "riots, isolated and sporadic acts of violence and other acts of a similar nature."

[44] *Brannigan and McBride v. U.K.*, supra, note 41.

yet-to-be-identified nonstate armed opposition groups, including periodic "lone wolf" attacks, as evidence of an "other situation of violence" justifying security detention. The United States might argue that such activity was a continuation of hostilities covered by the 2001 Authorization for Use of Military Force (AUMF), justifying detention under the law of war beyond the armed conflict that initially justified internment. (See Chapter 21.6.) These possibilities are only that, however – possibilities yet to be debated and tested for acceptance by the international community, by international courts, and, eventually, through state practice.

22.2.1 *"State of Emergency"*

European detention state practice under ECHR Article 15's "state emergency" rubric is scant.

> The notion of a "state of emergency" which allows for derogations is an "eminently indeterminate notion," particularly when applied to armed conflicts. The ICCPR, for example, does not mention "war" or "armed conflict.". ... Not every armed conflict qualifies as an emergency. ... The European Court of Human Rights has qualified a public emergency as "an exceptional situation of crisis or emergency which affects the whole population and constitutes a threat to the organized life of the community of which the State is composed."[45]

Is the "war on terror" an American state of emergency? The United States is not bound by European judicial decisions, but ECHR opinions are instructive, and may be interpreted to support the view that continuing acts and attempted acts of violence against American armed forces, citizens, and interests, domestically or abroad, constitute a state of emergency justifying security detention.[46] As with "other situations of violence," though, these are no more than possibilities yet to be debated and tested for acceptance by the international community.

22.3 What Security Detention Is Not

Security detention is not the same as the deprivation of liberty for purposes of future criminal proceedings, and it may not be employed for that purpose.[47] Nor may it be employed solely for intelligence gathering. Nor should security detention involve prisoners of war, who have an entire convention addressing their rights, duties, and protections. Security detention is not a punitive measure for something that happened in the past, nor a substitute for criminal

---

[45] Gerd Oberleitner, *Human Rights in Armed Conflict: Law, Practice, Policy* (Cambridge: Cambridge University Press, 2015), 171.

[46] See *Brannigan and McBride*, supra, note 41.

[47] Yoram Dinstein, *The International Law of Belligerent Occupation* (Cambridge: Cambridge University Press, 2009), 174: "The two lawful types of detention [security detention and detention on suspicion of criminal activity, prefatory to prosecution] are not hermetically sealed from each other. Detention may initially be undertaken with penal prosecution in mind, yet – upon further reflection – the military government may switch gears and ... opt to have recourse to [security] internment." Also see: *Lawless v. Ireland*, supra, note 39, at 34.

proceedings.[48] In regard to noninternational armed conflicts and other situations of violence, Professor Marco Sassòli and Laura Olson note that "for the individual non-state actor, participation in a conflict constitutes a crime under the domestic law of the state affected by that conflict [and] enemies may also be interned without criminal charge as a preventive security measure."[49]

Finally, security detention should not be confused with the detention of those held by U.S. armed forces during recent conflicts in Afghanistan and Iraq.[50] Those individuals were detained as suspected unprivileged enemy belligerents who directly participated in hostilities. They were, in theory, subject to eventual prosecution by U.S. military or local domestic authorities.

22.4 Security Detention in Israeli Practice

Internment has long been a feature of international armed conflicts,[51] and "administrative detention for security reasons ... [is] clearly a measure that can be taken in noninternational armed conflict, as evidenced by the language of Additional Protocol II, which mentions internment in Articles 5 and 6."[52]

Briefly outlined, in Israel, security detention was initiated by the United Kingdom during the British Mandate, by the Defense (Emergency) Regulations of 1945. Upon attaining statehood in 1948, Israel maintained continued British Mandate rules, supplementing them over the years. In 1979, the Emergency Powers (Detention) Law replaced the Mandate rules. Under this law, by order of the defense minister individuals may be detained for a maximum of six months, with the possibility of six-month extensions. The Israeli High Court of Justice has held that administrative detention is designed to thwart a future danger to the security of the state or public safety. A few detained individuals, convicted of Israeli domestic criminal offenses, have been held beyond the expiration of their sentences, some for as long as ten years.[53] Today in Israel, as opposed to the Occupied Territories, security detention is rarely employed, however.

---

[48] HCJ 369/79, *Ben Zion v. IDF Commander of Judea and Samaria, et al.*, 34 (1) PD 145, 150–1, cited in Dinstein, *International Law of Belligerent Occupation*, id., at 173, an example of an internment case turned criminal prosecution.

[49] Marco Sassòli and Laura M. Olson, "The Relationship between International Humanitarian and Human Rights Law Where It Matters: Admissible Killing and Internment of Fighters in Non-International Armed Conflicts," 90–871 *Int'l Rev. of the Red Cross* (Sept. 2008), 599, 616.

[50] Chatham House/ICRC, "Expert Meeting," supra, note 24, at 860, fn. 3: "In this context it remained unclear whether the 96-hour detention system implemented by ISAF nations in Afghanistan before transfer to Afghan authorities would qualify as internment."

[51] E.g., 1899 Hague Convention Respecting the Laws and Customs of War on Land, Sec. IV ("Hague Regulation IV") Arts. 57–59. Security detention was first imported into international law by the 1874 Draft Convention of the Brussels Conference on the Laws and Customs of War.

[52] Pejic, "Procedural Principles and Safeguards for Internment/Administrative Detention," supra, note 19, at 377. In accord, Sassòli and Olson, "The Relationship between International Humanitarian and Human Rights Law, supra, note 49, at 618.

[53] Davidson and Gibson, "Experts Meeting on Security Detention," supra, note 21, at 356–62, provides an overview of Israel's security detention practice in Israel and in the Occupied Territories.

22.5 Security Detention in U.S. Practice

The United States has long envisioned a need for security detention. In 2009, President Obama said:

> There remains the question of detainees at Guantánamo who cannot be prosecuted yet who pose a clear danger to the American people. . . . Examples of that threat include people who've received extensive explosives training at al Qaeda training camps, or commanded Taliban troops in battle, or expressed their allegiance to Osama bin Laden, or otherwise made it clear that they want to kill Americans. These are people who, in effect, remain at war with the United States. . . . We must recognize that these detention policies cannot be unbounded. . . . We must have a thorough process of periodic review, so that any prolonged detention is carefully evaluated and justified. . . . Our goal is to construct a legitimate legal framework for the remaining Guantánamo detainees that cannot be transferred. . . . If and when we determine that the United States must hold individuals to keep them from carrying out an act of war, we will do so within a system that involves judicial and congressional oversight.[54]

When prosecution is not feasible, as when proof of criminality relies on evidence gained through torture, or when trial options are not available, such as a moribund military commissions system combined with a politically imposed inability to try detainees in domestic courts, the United States will continue "to hold these individuals in lawful military detention."[55] In other words, security detention.

SIDEBAR. Abu Zubaydah was a senior al Qaeda officer, involved in virtually all of the terrorist group's early major operations. In March 2002, in Pakistan, he was captured by CIA operatives and held in a series of foreign CIA "black sites." In July 2002 CIA personnel holding Zubaydah cabled their superiors located at the CIA's ALEC Station in Virginia, saying, "Regardless which [disposition of Zubaydah] we follow however, and especially in light of the planned psychological pressure techniques to be implemented, we need to get reasonable assurances that [Zubaydah] will remain in isolation and incommunicado for the remainder of his life." On July 18, ALEC Station officers replied, "There is a fairly unanimous sentiment within HQS [Headquarters Station ALEC] that [Zubaydah] will never be placed in a situation where he has any significant contact with others and/or has the opportunity to be released. . . . All major players are in concurrence that [Zubaydah] should remain incommunicado for the remainder of his life."[56]

While noninternational armed conflicts in Iraq and Afghanistan continued, in the U.S., the Obama administration claimed authority under the AUMF for the long-term detention of terrorists accused of involvement in the 9/11 attacks. Commentators

---

[54] President Barack Obama, Address at the National Archives, Washington, D.C.: "Remarks on National Security" (May 21, 2009). Available online.

[55] White House, "Fact Sheet: New Actions on Guantánamo and Detainee Policy" (March 7, 2011). Available online.

[56] Senate Select Committee on Intelligence, *The Senate Select Committee Report on Torture* (Brooklyn, NY: Melville House, 2014), 47.

bemoaned administrative detention on that basis and called for legislation authorizing it, instead.[57] The Obama administration was, in fact, formulating domestic legislative authority for security detention independent of the AUMF.

Executive Orders (EOs) have the binding force and effect of legislation, as if passed by Congress. In 2011, President Obama signed Executive Order 13567, "Periodic Review of Individuals Detained at Guantánamo Bay Naval Station."[58] In outline, EO 13567 sets standards for the initial detention and continued detention of Guantánamo detainees, sets requirements for initial and periodic reviews of the continued detention of detainees, and specifies procedures to be followed in the reviews. It lays out a standard for confinement of indefinite duration: "Continued law of war detention is warranted for a detainee ... if it is necessary to protect against a significant threat to the security of the United States." The order's key words are in that sentence: "Continued ... detention is warranted ... if it is necessary to protect against a significant threat to the" United States. The *Washington Post* wrote:

> The executive order applies to at least 48 of the ... detainees who remain at Guantánamo Bay. An inter-agency panel led by Justice Department lawyers determined that this group could not be prosecuted in military commissions or in federal court because of evidentiary problems that would hamper a trial. But intelligence assessments also concluded that these detainees remain a serious threat and could not be safely repatriated or resettled in a third country.[59]

EO 13567 is a domestic legal basis essential to carry out a program of security detention. It applies only to Guantánamo detainees, and only to detention "under the AUMF, as informed by the laws of war."[60] (Chapter 21.6 details AUMF issues.) As far as we know, all of the individuals slated for security detention *are* detained only at Guantánamo and, for the indeterminate future, the AUMF may be the basis for American noninternational armed conflicts with any terrorist armed group. Should EO 13567 not fit future security detention needs, a then-sitting president with views on security detention similar to Obama's can sign another EO curing its deficiencies.[61]

Congressionally crafted domestic legislation for security detention was a provision in the 2012 National Defense Authorization Act (NDAA). Annual NDAAs are federal law enacted by Congress, continuing in effect until revoked, replaced, or modified by subsequent legislation. In 2012, however, a U.S. district court of appeals permanently enjoined enforcement of that portion of the NDAA pertaining to security detention.[62]

---

[57] Jane Harman and Jack Goldsmith, "Taking on Guantanamo's Hard Cases," *Wash. Post*, Feb. 8, 2015, A19: "The legislation needed ... [is] a form of administrative detention akin to civil commitment, one that could apply after the end of the relevant hostilities."

[58] Executive Order 13567, "Periodic Review of Individuals Detained at Guantánamo Bay Naval Station Pursuant to the Authorization for Use of Military Force" (March 7, 2011). Available online.

[59] Peter Finn and Anne E. Kornblut, "Obama Creates Indefinite Detention System," supra, note 1. Charlie Savage, "Board Says Saudi Detainee Should Be Repatriated," *NY Times*, Oct. 21, 2014, A18, cites fifty-nine Guantánamo detainees as being recommended for "continued indefinite detention."

[60] Id.   [61] Executive orders, although having the force of law, may be revoked by subsequent presidents.

[62] *Christopher Hedges, et al. v. Barack Obama, et al.*, USDC, SDNY (Sept. 12, 2012). On July 17, 2013, the district court's permanent injunction was lifted by a three-judge 2nd circuit panel. On Feb. 19, 2013, the plaintiff's application to the U.S. Supreme Court to vacate the 2nd circuit's temporary stay of the permanent injunction was denied.

The following year, the district court's permanent injunction was overturned by the 2nd Circuit Court of Appeals and the Supreme Court declined to review the case.[63]

In 2011, ten months after EO 13567 was signed, the 2012 NDAA became law. With the removal of the district court's permanent injunction there were no further roadblocks. NDAA, Title X, Subtitle D, "Counterterrorism" codifies U.S. indefinite detention authority, essentially repeats the standards announced in EO 13567, and broadens the category of potential detainees to include not only Guantánamo detainees, but anyone who "was a part of or substantially supported" al Qaeda, the Taliban, or associated forces.[64] (See Cases and Materials, this chapter.)

Presuming no subsequent legislation or executive order, Title X, Subtitle D will apparently be the domestic law upon which U.S. security detention will be based. It does not include procedural details of its implementation. Instead, it directs the secretary of defense to formulate and submit those procedural details to Congress within a specified period. Subtitle D does not indicate that a U.S. security detention program is in progress; it simply provides the essential domestic authorization needed to initiate such a program.

22.6 Essential Aspects of Security Detention

Geneva Convention IV tacitly raises three requirements for internment in international armed conflicts: first, a standard for initial detention ("only if the security of the Detaining Power makes it absolutely necessary");[65] second, reconsideration of that initial decision to detain;[66] and third, periodic reviews of continuing detention.[67] These requirements are useful guidelines in relation to noninternational armed conflicts and for detention beyond the conclusion of armed conflict.

22.6.1 *Initiating Security Detention*

Security detention is provided for not only in Geneva Convention IV and Additional Protocols I and II, but in the ICCPR, the American Convention on Human Rights, the European Convention on Human Rights, and the Universal Declaration of Human Rights.[68] It is reasonably well settled that "a person may be deprived of liberty only for reasons ... [and] in accordance with procedures ... that are provided for by domestic and international law."[69] As the ICRC points out, "What has posed a problem more recently, mainly as a result of counter-terrorist operations conducted outside armed conflict, is the

---

[63] Order list: 572 U.S. 13–758, cert. denied (April 28, 2014).

[64] 2012 NDAA, 125 Stat. 1564, Public Law 112–81 – Dec. 31, 2011, Title X, Subtitle D, "Counter-Terrorism," subsections 1021 and 1022.

[65] 1949 Geneva Convention IV, Art. 42.   [66] Id., Art. 43.   [67] Id.

[68] While the ICCPR, ACHR, and UDHR, all human rights instruments, allow for security detention under specified conditions, they also call for prior derogation from human rights instruments on the grounds of a public emergency threatening the life of the state. See ICCPR Art. 4(1), ACHR Art. 27(1), and ECHR Art. 15. For a more detailed discussion of derogation requirements, see Davidson and Gibson, "Experts Meeting on Security Detention," supra, note 21, at 333.

[69] Pejic, "Procedural Principles and Safeguards," supra, note 19, at 383. In agreement, ICCPR, Article 9 (1): Persons may not be deprived of liberty "except on such grounds and in accordance with such procedure as are established by law."

administrative detention, i.e. the detention without criminal charges, of persons suspected of various degrees of involvement in acts of terrorism"[70] – such as the security detention regime raised under authority of Title X, Subtitle D of the 2012 NDAA.

A state party to a noninternational armed conflict, such as the U.S. conflicts in Iraq and Afghanistan, has the inherent power to intern captured persons. Security detention within a state's territory, as noted, must be "absolutely necessary"[71] and, in cases of occupation, for "imperative reasons of security."[72] That does *not* describe Guantánamo detainees because, although they are held during a noninternational armed conflict, they are ostensibly held for trial by military commission. Additionally, there must be a lawful authority for the detention,[73] based upon legally permissible grounds, with a review mechanism initially, and then periodically thereafter, to assess the lawfulness of the detention and the necessity for continued detention.

In noninternational armed conflicts, security detainees must be held in an officially recognized internment location, and an individual registration of each internee "kept in custody for more than two weeks" must be prepared for ICRC use.[74] Unacknowledged detention is prohibited. The 1977 Additional Protocol II has provision for maintaining detainee-family contacts.[75] Medical care is an obvious requirement. These requirements and restrictions would presumably apply to security detainees held beyond the end of armed conflict.

"A fundamental element of these safeguards – and one which has been made particularly vulnerable in counter-terrorist detention in the 'war on terror' – is the capacity to challenge the lawfulness of one's detention."[76] In ongoing international armed conflicts, the criterion for initiating security detention is that it be "absolutely necessary."[77] In cases of occupation, its initiation must be for "imperative reasons of security."[78] There is virtually no jurisprudence defining these terms. The *Commentary* to Geneva Convention IV says, "It did not seem possible to define the expression 'security of the State' in a more concrete fashion. It is left very largely to the Governments to decide the measure of activity prejudicial to the internal or external security of the State which justifies internment."[79]

Although LOAC relating to noninternational armed conflicts offers no explicit legal basis for internment, not even specifying that it be for reasons of security, the security detention of individuals considered a serious security threat has been customary in noninternational conflicts. "Moreover, even IHRL [International Human Rights Law] does not prohibit internment *per se*. What is prohibited

---

[70] ICRC, "International Humanitarian Law and the Challenges," supra, note 31, at 730.

[71] 1949 Geneva Convention IV, Article 42. Geneva Convention IV details one set of rules for security detention within a state party's territory, and another set applicable to security detention in occupied territory.

[72] Id., Article 78.   [73] This corresponds to ICCPR, Article 9 (1), supra, note 69.

[74] 1949 Geneva Convention IV, Arts. 138, 106.

[75] 1977 Additional Protocol I, Art. 5. 2. (b): They [detained persons] shall be allowed to send and receive letters and cards."

[76] deLondras, *Detention in the War on Terror*, supra, note 6, at 56.

[77] 1949 Geneva Convention IV, Art. 42.   [78] Id., Art. 78.

[79] Jean Pictet, ed., *Commentary, IV Geneva Convention* (Geneva: ICRC, 1958), 257.

is the *arbitrary* deprivation of liberty."[80] Detention is only arbitrary when appropriate safeguards are not available to the detainee.

Under Title X, Subtitle D, the basis for security detention is described. "Congress affirms the authority of the President to … detain covered persons … pending disposition under the law of war."[81] "Covered persons" refers to those involved in the 9/11 attacks and those who supported them, or al-Qaeda or the Taliban, or associated forces, as described in succeeding Subtitle D subsections.

22.6.2 *Initial Challenge and Periodic Review of Security Detention*

If, during an armed conflict, the initiation of security detention is justified by "imperative reasons of security," how should that requirement be implemented in practice? Bright-line tests involving inherently imprecise terms are debatable. A 2008 London meeting of government, academic, nongovernmental organizations, and military experts offered guidance in the form of a two-tier test for determining the meaning of "imperative reasons of security": First, on the basis of the individual's past activity, it is "highly likely" or "certain" (the threshold was not agreed upon), that the individual will commit further acts harmful "directly" or "indirectly" (not agreed upon) against the detaining power; second, whether internment is necessary to neutralize the threat posed.[82]

In international armed conflicts and cases of occupation, provisions for challenging the lawfulness of one's detention are specified in Geneva Convention IV.[83] No such provisions are specified for noninternational armed conflicts. Human rights law establishes that "the right to challenge the lawfulness of one's detention before a judicial body must be preserved,"[84] a right that would likely be applicable in noninternational conflicts. An unresolved issue is the evidentiary standard to be applied in the initial challenge to detention. Clear and convincing evidence? A preponderance, or a mere "reason to suspect"? There is no agreed upon standard.

Any protected person who is interned "shall be entitled to have that action reconsidered as soon as possible by an appropriate court or administrative board designated by the Detaining Power for that purpose."[85] Designation of a Guantánamo detainee as a possible security detainee would apparently represent a new status requiring a new initial status consideration. Section 1024 of Title X, Subtitle D, creates a procedure for determining the status of potential security detainees: a hearing conducted before, and decided by, a military judge. Potential security detainees will be represented at such a hearing by military council, if the detainee desires. This procedure for security detainees would address the first of Geneva Convention IV's three requirements for international armed conflict internment, were it applied in that context.

---

[80] Chatham House/ICRC, "Expert Meeting," supra, note 24, at 863. Emphasis in original.

[81] 2012 NDAA, Title X, Subtitle D, supra, note 64, at Sec. 1021(a).

[82] Chatham House/ICRC, "Expert Meeting," supra, note 24, at 865. See article for full discussion of test.

[83] 1949 Geneva Convention IV, Arts. 43 and 78, do not refer specifically to challenges to lawfulness, but to reconsideration and appeal.

[84] Pejic, "Procedural Principles and Safeguards for Internment/Administrative Detention," supra, note 19, at 386.

[85] 1949 Geneva Convention IV, Art. 43. This requirement is repeated in U.S. Army Regulation 190–8, *Enemy Prisoners of War, Retained Personnel, Civilian Internees and Other Detainees* (Oct. 1, 1997), para. 5–1.g.(1). This Regulation pertains to all branches of U.S. Armed Forces.

Meeting Geneva Convention IV's second requirement, if the initial decision to detain the individual as a security detainee is confirmed, the new security detainee may appeal that confirmation by seeking reconsideration of the decision.[86] Title X, Subtitle D, contains no such right to appeal, although one *could* be included in the secretary of defense's procedures for status determinations, required under Section 1024(a).

If the security detainee's appeal for reconsideration fails (presuming he has a right to appeal) and he is confirmed as a security detainee, periodic reviews of his continuing detention are required. A review process is provided for in international armed conflicts but is not addressed in noninternational conflicts.[87] Inasmuch as security detainees are initially anticipated in the context of a noninternational armed conflict and after its conclusion, and recalling that "detention which continues beyond that provided for by law is a violation of the principle of legality and amounts to arbitrary detention,"[88] periodic review is called for in noninternational armed conflicts, despite a lack of formal requirement.

Title X, Subtitle D, also requires "periodic detention review" of Guantanámo detainees, meeting Geneva Convention IV's final requirement for international armed conflict detention. The procedures for security detainee periodic reviews are not described, except to say their purpose is "not to determine the legality of any detainee's law of war detention, but to make discretionary determinations whether or not a detainee represents a continuing threat to the security of the United States."[89]

How often are periodic detention reviews to be made? Title X, Subtitle D does not specify, leaving another blank to be later filled in by the secretary of defense. Geneva Convention IV's frequency of every six months is reasonable in light of past U.S. practice.[90] Although the U.S.-Afghan conflict did not involve security detention, in the later stages of the conflict the initial decision to detain suspected terrorist detainees was required within sixty days of their arrival at the detention facility.[91] If the initial decision to detain was confirmed and detention imposed, six-month reviews were the standard at the U.S. detention facilities in Bagram and their successor Parwan facility.[92]

Provisions for the detention of individuals in noninternational armed conflicts offer no guidance as to whether the detention review body should be a court or an administrative board. Review by either "means that the decision will never be left to one individual. It will be a joint decision, and this," the ICRC writes, "offers the protected person a better guarantee of fair treatment."[93] In U.S. practice, detainees held during the Afghan conflict appeared, along with personal representatives, before six-month administrative continuation boards composed of several officers, one of whom was required to be a judge

---

[86] 1949 Geneva Convention IV, Art. 78.   [87] Id., Art. 43.

[88] Jean-Marie Henckaerts and Louise Doswald-Beck, eds., *Customary International Humanitarian Law*. Vol. I. *Rules* (Cambridge: Cambridge University Press, 2005), rule 99, at 348.

[89] 2012 NDAA, Title X, Subtitle D, supra, note 64, at Sec. 1023.(b)(1).

[90] 1949 Geneva Convention IV, Art. 43 reflects procedure recommended for detainees within the interning state. Art. 78 indicates procedures during a period of occupation. Both articles recommend six-month reviews, as does Army Regulation 190–8, *Enemy Prisoners of War*, supra, note 85, at para. 5–1.g.(2).

[91] Lt.Col. Jeff A. Bovarnick, "Detainee Review Boards in Afghanistan: From Strategic Liability to Legitimacy," *Army Lawyer*, June 2010, 9, 22.

[92] Id., at 19. The last American detention facility in Afghanistan was transferred to the Afghan government on Dec. 11, 2014. Sudarsan Raghavan, "U.S. Closes Last Afghan Detainee Site as Troop Pullout Advances," *NY Times*, Dec. 12, 2014, A12.

[93] Pictet, *Commentary, IV Geneva Convention*, supra, note 79, at 369.

advocate. Title X, Subtitle D, does not specify whether a court or a board will be required to make detention continuation decisions.

Independent of the review process, a right to *habeas corpus* is applicable under human rights law and,[94] arguably, should be available to security detainees. The U.S. Supreme Court has held that "the federal courts have jurisdiction to determine the legality of the Executive's potentially indefinite detention of individuals who claim to be innocent of wrongdoing."[95] Executive Order 13567 grants a right to *habeas corpus* to "Detainees at Guantánamo."[96] Nothing is said about security detainees, per se, although it is apparent that, because security detainees will be held at Guantánamo, they will have a right to *habeas corpus* under the EO.

22.6.3 *Detainee Access to Information and Legal Assistance*

In international armed conflicts, internees have a right to be informed, in a language they understand, of the reasons for their detention, to enable them to challenge its lawfulness.[97] This includes the right to know the grounds for detention, its likely duration, and the ability to inform family or friends of the detention. "Neither the Fourth Geneva Convention nor humanitarian law applicable in noninternational armed conflicts contain explicit provisions on the duty to provide information about the reasons for which a person has been deprived of liberty. [It] is, however, one of the 'Fundamental Guarantees' laid down in Article 75 (3) of Additional Protocol I."[98]

There have been calls from human rights advocates, including the ICRC, to provide legal assistance to detainees who contest their detention.[99] The Statute of the International Criminal Tribunal for the Former Yugoslavia, and that for Rwanda, provide that, if questioned, a suspect is entitled to be assisted by counsel. The Rome Statute of the International Criminal Court requires legal assistance.[100] These are criminal trial forums, however. Neither human rights law nor multinational treaties require such assistance in noncriminal forums and none is mentioned in Title X, Subsection D.

In Afghanistan, United States–held detainees at Bagram/Parwan received basic legal assistance. Upon arrival, detainees were assigned a personal representative (PR), who was required to be "a commissioned officer [not necessarily a judge advocate] familiar with the detainee review procedures and authorized access to all reasonably available information (including classified information) relevant to the determination of whether the detainee meets the criteria for internment and whether the detainee's continued internment is necessary."[101] PRs attended a one-week

---

[94] ICCPR Art. 9; ECHR, Art. 5.

[95] *Rasul v. Bush*, 542 U.S., 485 (2004). Contra: Sassòli and Olson, "Relationship," supra, note 49, at 627. "To give captured fighters the benefit of *habeas corpus* as defined by human rights may be unrealistic and even counterproductive in many conflicts and raises serious conceptual problems when required from armed groups."

[96] Executive Order 13567, "Periodic Review of Individuals Detained at Guantánamo Bay," supra, note 58.

[97] 1977 Additional Protocol I, Art. 75; ICCPR, Art. 9 (4).

[98] Pejic, "Procedural Principles and Safeguards for Internment/Administrative Detention," supra, note 19, at 384. As noted elsewhere, the U.S. chooses to not apply Protocol I's Art. 75 in noninternational conflicts.

[99] Id., at 388.

[100] Jarinde Temminck Tuinstra, "Defending the Defenders," 8–2 *J. of Int'l Crim Justice* (May 2010), 463, 475.

[101] Bovarnick, "Detainee Review Boards in Afghanistan," supra, note 91, at 30.

training course and were required to act "in the best interests of the detainee."[102] Title X, Subtitle D is silent on the subject.

22.6.4 *Release*

A difficult issue for future security detainees will be their release. Customary international law holds that civilian internees must be released as soon as the reasons that necessitated internment no longer exist, and as soon as possible after the close of active hostilities.[103] The United States intends to not release those individuals determined to be security detainees upon the conclusion of active hostilities, however active hostilities may be defined.

An example of internment's requirement for release of POWs at the end of hostilities is found in one of the several treaties ending World War I, a century ago: "In accordance with this general rule, Article 214 of the Treaty of Versailles ... read as follows: 'The repatriation of prisoners of war and interned civilians shall take place as soon as possible ... and shall be carried out with the greatest rapidity.'"[104]

In noninternational armed conflicts, 1977 Protocol II, Article 6.5 requires that "at the end of hostilities, the authorities in power shall endeavor to grant the broadest possible amnesty to persons who have participated in the conflict, or those deprived of their liberty for reasons related to the armed conflict, whether they are interned or detained."

Those guidelines apply in time of armed conflict. While instructive, they do not directly apply to security detention in peacetime. The termination of the global war on terror, should that rather unlikely event arise, will apparently not terminate security detention; a continuing threat – an other situation of violence – may supersede the release of selected Guantánamo detainees upon the ending of hostilities. In 2009, the Department of Defense's general counsel testified before the Senate that, even if tried and acquitted, some terrorists in American custody may not be released.[105] A former director of the Justice Department's Office of Legal Counsel adds, "The government's reliance on detention as a backstop to [federal civilian] trials shows that it [detention] is a foundation for incapacitating high-level terrorists in this war."[106]

22.7 Security Detention beyond the Conclusion of Hostilities?

Title X, Subtitle D, Section 1021(c), reads, "The disposition of a person under the law of war ... may include the following: (1) Detention under the law of war without trial *until the end of the hostilities* authorized by the Authorization for Use of Military Force."[107]

When will the "war on terror" hostilities end and how will we know? When does *any* armed conflict end? "People sometimes speak of peacetime and wartime as sharply

---

[102] Id., at 31, citing deputy assistant secretary of defense "Detainee Review Procedures," dated July 2, 2009.

[103] Henckaerts and Doswald-Beck, *Customary International Humanitarian Law*, Vol. I, supra, note 88, rule 128, at 451; see also,1949 Geneva Convention IV, Art. 132, and 1977 Additional Protocol I, Art. 75 (3)

[104] Jean Pictet, ed., *Commentary, III Geneva Convention* (Geneva: ICRC, 1960), Art. 118, p. 541.

[105] Karen deYoung, "Indefinite Detentions Are Backed," *Wash. Post*, July 8, 2009.

[106] Jack Goldsmith, "Don't Try Terrorists, Lock Them Up," NY *Times*, Oct. 9, 2010, A17. Goldsmith makes the same argument in *The Terror Presidency* (New York: Norton, 2007), 106–7.

[107] Emphasis supplied.

demarcated, their factual foundations and legal consequences being clearly distinct from one another."[108] That is not always so.

Noninternational armed conflicts begin when the well-defined criteria for such conflicts, parties and intensity, are present (Chapter 5.1.3). When, then, must a non-international armed conflict end? "When the fighting declines up until the point that it dissipates entirely, the law of noninternational armed conflict will cease to apply. The exact moment in time at which the law of noninternational armed conflict would cease to operate in such a situation would have to be judged on a case-by-case basis as against the facts on the ground."[109] The question is, who decides? Who decides when the facts on the ground indicate that the fighting has "dissipated entirely"? Admiral Mike Mullin, chairman of the Joint Chiefs of Staff (2007–11), has said, "There isn't going to be a single day when we stand up and say, that's it, it's over, we've won. We will win but we will do so only over time and only after near constant reassessment and adjustment. . . . It will feel a lot less like a knock-out punch and a lot more like recovering from a long illness."[110]

A 2004 Supreme Court opinion referring to captured Taliban and al Qaeda fighters holds that the detention of individuals who fought against the United States in Afghanistan "for the duration of the particular conflict in which they were captured, is so fundamental and accepted an incident to war as to be an exercise of the 'necessary and appropriate force' Congress has authorized the President to use."[111] Fundamental and accepted as such detention may be, security detention of an indeterminate duration *beyond the end of the conflict in which the detainee was captured*, although authorized by U.S. law and executive order, will generate protracted litigation. That litigation will be informed by post–World War II case law.

Kurt Ludecke (1890–1960) was born and raised in Germany. During World War I he briefly served in the German army. In 1924, now an ardent admirer of Hitler, Ludecke moved to the United States to work on the Nazi newspaper the *Voelkischer Beobachter*. An early multitasker, he also founded the Swastika League of America. Denied U.S. citizenship in 1938, he was arrested as an enemy alien on December 8, 1941, the day after America's entry into World War II. Like thousands of Japanese, Italian, and German Americans (but with legal cause, in Ludecke's case) he was interned. In 1947, two years after World War II had ended, Ludecke remained interned. He sued the United States, urging that, because the war was over, his continued internment was unlawful. In a 1948 opinion by Justice Frankfurter, the U.S. Supreme Court disagreed:

> War does not cease with a cease fire order, and power to be exercised by the President . . . is a process which begins when war is declared but is not exhausted when the shooting stops. . . . The state of war may be terminated by treaty or legislation or Presidential proclamation. Whatever the modes, its termination is a political act. . . . It is not for us to question a belief by the President that enemy aliens who were justifiably deemed fit subjects for internment during active hostilities do not lose their potency for mischief during the period of confusion and conflict which is characteristic of a state of war even when the guns are silent and the peace of Peace has not come.

---

[108] Prof. Bobby Chesney, "Law at the End of Conflict," www.lawfareblog.com (Sept. 3, 2014).
[109] Sandesh Sivakumaran, *The Law of Non-International Armed Conflict* (Oxford: Oxford University Press, 2012), 253.
[110] Admiral Mike Mullin, Landon Lecture Address, Kansas State University (March 3, 2010). Available online.
[111] *Hamdi v. Rumsfeld*, 542 U.S. 507, 518 (2004).

These are matters of political judgment for which judges have neither technical competence nor official responsibility. ... Accordingly, we hold that full responsibility for the exercise of this great power may validly be left where the Congress has constitutionally placed it – on the President of the United States.[112]

Another World War II era individual, Kestutis Zadvyda, entered the United States as a displaced person in 1948, later becoming a legal resident alien with Fifth Amendment due process rights. In 1994, he was ordered deported after conviction of possession with intent to distribute cocaine. No other country would accept him, and he remained in indefinite custody, on which basis he sued the United States. The Supreme Court held that Congress had not authorized, nor intended to authorize, indefinite detention. Sidestepping whether indefinite detention is constitutional, the Court established a time limit of six months for cases like Zadvyda's.

Going a step further, the Court held, "we have upheld preventive detention based on dangerousness only when limited to specially dangerous individuals and subject to strong procedural protections. ... .Neither do we consider terrorism or other special circumstances where special arguments might be made for forms of preventive detention and for heightened deference to the judgments of the political branches with respect to matters of national security."[113] A commentator notes, "This dictum in *Zadvydas* leaves the indefinite detention door for suspected alien terrorists decidedly ajar, if not wide open."[114]

Thirteen years after the *Zadvydas* decision and sixty-six years after *Ludecke*, judicial deference to presidential prerogatives is less pronounced and the willingness of the Supreme Court to carve new legal paths is somewhat greater. In 2014, Justice Stephen Breyer considered the case of the Guantánamo detainee Ahmed Hussain. He wrote of Justice O'Connor's decision in a similar prior case:

She concluded that the "detention of individuals falling into the limited category we are considering, for the duration of the particular conflict in which they were captured," is "an exercise of the 'necessary and appropriate force' that Congress authorized under the [Authorization of the Use of Military Force]. ... She explained, however, that the President's power to detain under the AUMF may be different when the "practical circumstances" of the relevant conflict are "entirely unlike those of the conflicts that informed the development of the law of war." ... The Court has not directly addressed whether the AUMF authorizes, and the Constitution permits, detention on the basis that an individual was part of al Qaeda, or part of the Taliban, but was not "engaged in an armed conflict against the United States" in Afghanistan prior to his capture. Nor have we considered whether, assuming detention on these bases is permissible, either the AUMF or the Constitution limits the duration of detention."[115]

These Supreme Court opinions suggest an uphill legal battle for the release of security detainees based on the argument that either the armed conflict in Afghanistan or the war on terror has ended.

---

[112] *Ludecke v. Watkins*, 335 U.S. 160, 162–73 (1948), a 5–4 decision. Footnotes omitted. Although Ludecke was not a POW, and 1949 Geneva Convention III's Article 118, regarding release and repatriation of POWs was not yet in effect, the 1929 Convention on POWs, Art. 75, had similar effect.

[113] *Zadvydas v. U.S.*, 533 U.S. 678, 691, 696 (2001).

[114] Robert H. Wagstaff, *Terror Detentions and the Rule of Law* (New York: Oxford University Press, 2014), 64.

[115] *Abdul al Qader Ahmed v. Obama*. Statement of Breyer J. concurring in respect to denial of certiorari (Detatched Opinion), 572 U.S. ____ (2014).

22.8 Summary

Internment is a legally simple concept that can be difficult in application. In armed conflicts or other situations of violence, captured enemy civilians and enemy fighters – protected persons – may lawfully be deprived of their liberty without criminal charges, if absolutely necessary. The devil is in the details.

As of this writing, forty-eight Guantánamo detainees are reportedly being considered for indefinite security detention.[116] Such detention is authorized by federal law and executive order. While several foreign states employ variations of security detention, few, if any, authorize the long-term security detention envisioned by the United States.

Although reasoned voices warn against it,[117] the United States sees a need for security detention in some cases because critical prosecution evidence gained through torture is inadmissible in the military commissions or domestic trials of those detainees. Indefinite detention is seen as being required because if released, the public is told, those detainees would constitute continuing imminent threats of violence to the nation's security.

Should security detention become reality, resolution of its legal issues will be as contentious as the war on terror itself.

CASES AND MATERIALS

NATIONAL DEFENSE AUTHORIZATION ACT FOR FISCAL YEAR 2012

Pub.L. No. 112–81, 125 Stat. 1298 (31 Dec. 31, 2011)

Introduction. *The National Defense Authorization Act for 2012, in Title X, Subtitle D, Counterterrorism, §§ 1021–1024, specifies Authorization for Use of Military Force, the often-criticized AUMF, as authority and provides for the security detention (referred to here as "law of war detention") of certain individuals ("covered persons"), and details procedures for their initial, and continued, internment.*

SEC. 1021. Affirmation of Authority of the Armed Forces of the United States to Detain Covered Persons Pursuant to the Authorization for Use of Military Force.

(a) In General. – Congress affirms that the authority of the President to use all necessary and appropriate force pursuant to the Authorization for Use of Military Force (Public Law 107–40;

---

[116] Charlie Savage, "Detainee Review Proposal Is Prepared for President," NY *Times*, Dec. 22, 2010, A-1; and, Peter Finn and Anne E. Kornblut, "Obama Creates Indefinite Detention System for Prisoners at Guantánamo Bay," *Wash. Post*, March 8, 2011.

[117] Tom Malinowski, "A Detention Route Obama Should Avoid," *Wash. Post*, Jan. 7, 2011, A-17; Amos N. Guiora and Laurie R. Blank, "Don't Deny Detainees Their Day in Court," *Los Angeles Times*, Jan. 4, 2011).

50 U.S.C. 1541 note) includes the authority for the Armed Forces of the United States to detain covered persons (as defined in sub-section (b)) pending disposition under the law of war.

(b) Covered Persons. – A covered person under this section is any person as follows:

(1) A person who planned, authorized, committed, or aided the terrorist attacks that occurred on September 11, 2001, or harbored those responsible for those attacks.

(2) A person who was a part of or substantially supported al-Qaeda, the Taliban, or associated forces that are engaged in hostilities against the United States or its coalition partners, including any person who has committed a belligerent act or has directly supported such hostilities in aid of such enemy forces.

(c) Disposition under Law of War. – The disposition of a person under the law of war as described in subsection (a) may include the following:

(1) Detention under the law of war without trial until the end of the hostilities authorized by the Authorization for Use of Military Force.

(2) Trial under chapter 47A of title 10, United States Code (as amended by the Military Commissions Act of 2009 (title XVIII of Public Law 111–84)).

(3) Transfer for trial by an alternative court or competent tribunal having lawful jurisdiction.

(4) Transfer to the custody or control of the person's country of origin, any other foreign country, or any other foreign entity.

(d) Construction. – Nothing in this section is intended to limit or expand the authority of the President or the scope of the Authorization for Use of Military Force.

(e) Authorities. – Nothing in this section shall be construed to affect existing law or authorities relating to the detention of United States citizens, lawful resident aliens of the United States, or any other persons who are captured or arrested in the United States.

(f) Requirement for Briefings of Congress. – The Secretary of Defense shall regularly brief Congress regarding the application of the authority described in this section, including the organizations, entities, and individuals considered to be "covered persons" for purposes of subsection (b)(2).

SEC. 1022. Military Custody for Foreign Al-Qaeda Terrorists.

(a) Custody Pending Disposition under Law of War.— (1) in General. – Except as provided in paragraph (4), the Armed Forces of the United States shall hold a person described in paragraph (2) who is captured in the course of hostilities authorized by the Authorization for Use of Military Force (Public Law 107–40) in military custody pending disposition under the law of war.

(b)

(2) Covered Persons. – The requirement in paragraph (1) shall apply to any person whose detention is authorized under section 1021 who is determined –

(A) to be a member of, or part of, al-Qaeda or an associated force that acts in coordination with or pursuant to the direction of al-Qaeda; and

(B) to have participated in the course of planning or carrying out an attack or attempted attack against the United States or its coalition partners.

(3) Disposition under Law of War. – For purposes of this subsection, the disposition of a person under the law of war has the meaning given in section 1021(c), except that no

transfer otherwise described in paragraph (4) of that section shall be made unless consistent with the requirements of section 1028.

(4) Waiver for National Security. – The President may waive the requirement of paragraph (1) if the President submits to Congress a certification in writing that such a waiver is in the national security interests of the United States.

(b) Applicability to United States Citizens and Lawful Resident Aliens

(1) United States Citizens. – The requirement to detain a person in military custody under this section does not extend to citizens of the United States.

(2) Lawful Resident Aliens. – The requirement to detain a person in military custody under this section does not extend to a lawful resident alien of the United States on the basis of conduct taking place within the United States, except to the extent permitted by the Constitution of the United States.

(c) Implementation Procedures. –

(1) In General. – Not later than 60 days after the date of the enactment of this Act, the President shall issue, and submit to Congress, procedures for implementing this section.

(2) Elements. – The procedures for implementing this section shall include, but not be limited to, procedures as follows:

(A) Procedures designating the persons authorized to make determinations under subsection (a)(2) and the process by which such determinations are to be made.

(B) Procedures providing that the requirement for military custody under subsection (a)(1) does not require the interruption of ongoing surveillance or intelligence gathering with regard to persons not already in the custody or control of the United States.

(C) Procedures providing that a determination under subsection (a)(2) is not required to be implemented until after the conclusion of an interrogation which is ongoing at the time the determination is made and does not require the interruption of any such ongoing interrogation.

(D) Procedures providing that the requirement for military custody under subsection (a)(1) does not apply when intelligence, law enforcement, or other Government officials of the United States are granted access to an individual who remains in the custody of a third country.

(E) Procedures providing that a certification of national security interests under subsection (a)(4) may be granted for the purpose of transferring a covered person from a third country if such a transfer is in the interest of the United States and could not otherwise be accomplished.

(d) Authorities. – Nothing in this section shall be construed to affect the existing criminal enforcement and national security authorities of the Federal Bureau of Investigation or any other domestic law enforcement agency with regard to a covered person, regardless whether such covered person is held in military custody.

(e) Effective Date. – This section shall take effect on the date that is 60 days after the date of the enactment of this Act, and shall apply with respect to persons described in subsection (a)(2) who are taken into the custody or brought under the control of the United States on or after that effective date.

SEC. 1023. Procedures for Periodic Detention Review of Individuals Detained at United States Naval Station, Guantánamo Bay, Cuba.

(a) Procedures Required. – Not later than 180 days after the date of the enactment of this Act, the Secretary of Defense shall submit to the appropriate committees of Congress a report setting forth procedures for implementing the periodic review process required by Executive Order No. 13567 for individuals detained at United States Naval Station, Guantánamo Bay, Cuba, pursuant to the Authorization for Use of Military Force (Public Law 107–40; 50 U.S.C. 1541 note).

(b) Covered Matters. – The procedures submitted under sub-section (a) shall, at a minimum –

(1) clarify that the purpose of the periodic review process is not to determine the legality of any detainee's law of war detention, but to make discretionary determinations whether or not a detainee represents a continuing threat to the security of the United States;

(2) clarify that the Secretary of Defense is responsible for any final decision to release or transfer an individual detained in military custody at United States Naval Station, Guantánamo Bay, Cuba, pursuant to the Executive Order referred to in subsection (a), and that in making such a final decision, the Secretary shall consider the recommendation of a periodic review board or review committee established pursuant to such Executive Order, but shall not be bound by any such recommendation;

(3) clarify that the periodic review process applies to any individual who is detained as an unprivileged enemy belligerent at United States Naval Station, Guantánamo Bay, Cuba, at any time; and

(4) ensure that appropriate consideration is given to factors addressing the need for continued detention of the detainee, including –

(A) the likelihood the detainee will resume terrorist activity if transferred or released;

(B) the likelihood the detainee will reestablish ties with al-Qaeda, the Taliban, or associated forces that are engaged in hostilities against the United States or its coalition partners if transferred or released;

(C) the likelihood of family, tribal, or government rehabilitation or support for the detainee if transferred or released;

(D) the likelihood the detainee may be subject to trial by military commission; and

(E) any law enforcement interest in the detainee.

(c) Appropriate Committees of Congress Defined. – In this section, the term "appropriate committees of Congress" means— (1) the Committee on Armed Services and the Select Committee on Intelligence of the Senate; and (2) the Committee on Armed Services and the Permanent Select Committee on Intelligence of the House of Representatives.

SEC. 1024. Procedures for Status Determinations.

(a) In General. – Not later than 90 days after the date of the enactment of this Act, the Secretary of Defense shall submit to the appropriate committees of Congress a report setting forth the procedures for determining the status of persons detained pursuant to the Authorization for Use of Military Force (Public Law 107–40; 50 U.S.C. 1541 note) for purposes of section 1021.

(b) Elements of Procedures. – The procedures required by this section shall provide for the following in the case of any unprivileged enemy belligerent who will be held in long-term detention under the law of war pursuant to the Authorization for Use of Military Force:

(1) A military judge shall preside at proceedings for the determination of status of an unprivileged enemy belligerent.

(2) An unprivileged enemy belligerent may, at the election of the belligerent, be represented by military counsel at proceedings for the determination of status of the belligerent.

(c) Applicability. – The Secretary of Defense is not required to apply the procedures required by this section in the case of a person for whom *habeas corpus* review is available in a Federal court.

(d) Report on Modification of Procedures.– The Secretary of Defense shall submit to the appropriate committees of Congress a report on any modification of the procedures submitted under this section. The report on any such modification shall be so submitted not later than 60 days before the date on which such modification goes into effect.

(e) Appropriate Committees of Congress Defined. – In this section, the term "appropriate committees of Congress" means –

(1) the Committee on Armed Services and the Select Committee on Intelligence of the Senate; and

(2) the Committee on Armed Services and the Permanent Select Committee on Intelligence of the House of Representatives.

Conclusion. *What is the legal effect of a National Defense Authorization Act (NDAA) provision? Such provisions are federal law, passed by Congress and signed by the president, fully as enforceable as provisions of the United States Code. Until changed by Congress they remain federal law. Some NDAA provisions are subsequently incorporated into the U.S. Code, although most are not. Some NDAA provisions contain "sunset" clauses; many do not. The provision quoted here does not.*

BOUMEDIENE, ET AL. V. BUSH

553 U.S. 723 (2008)

Introduction. *Boumediene was one of the earliest cases in which the U.S. Supreme Court began to resist the excesses ushered in by the so-called war on terror. The Guantánamo detainees Lakhdar Boumediene and his copetitioners sought habeas corpus. In opposing Boumediene's petition, the government argued that the Combatant Status Review Tribunals granted every Guantánamo detainee were legally sufficient replacements for habeas corpus. A majority of the Supreme Court disagreed.*

Professor Fiona de Londras, of Durham University's law school in the United Kingdom wrote these well-argued comments on the Court's opinion.[118]

Although the US Supreme Court acknowledged ... that Congress could determine the manner in which a review tribunal would operate in relation to those detained in Guantánamo Bay, it not only found that those detained there could avail themselves of the constitutional right to *habeas corpus* but also laid down what it considered to be a number of essential elements that any review process must contain in order to satisfy constitutional standards. ... Although Kennedy J expressly stated that the elements identified in the judgment were not exhaustive, he outlined the following:

---

[118] de Londras, *Detention in the "War on Terror,"* supra, note 6 at 268–9.

(1) the review process must provide opportunity for the petitioner to make a meaningful case that his detention is unlawful;

(2) the review body must have the capacity to order release although that is not the only remedy that might be provided in the occasion of a successful petition;

(3) where a person is detained on the basis of executive, rather than court order, the review tribunal must be enabled to conduct a thorough and meaningful review in relation to whether due process has been accorded.

In sum, Kennedy J held:

> For the writ of *habeas corpus*, or its substitute, to function as an effective and proper remedy in this context, the court that conducts the habeas proceeding must have the means to correct errors that occurred during the CSRT [Combatant Status Review Tribunal] proceedings. This includes some authority to assess the sufficiency of the Government's evidence against the detainee. It also must have the authority to admit and consider relevant exculpatory evidence that was not introduced during the earlier proceeding. . . .
>
> When the judicial power to issue *habeas corpus* properly is invoked the judicial officer must have adequate authority to make a determination in light of the relevant law and facts and to formulate and issue appropriate orders for relief, including, if necessary, an order directing the prisoner's release.[119]

The processes available to Guantánamo Bay detainees under the applicable statutes . . . did not, the Court held, satisfy these requirements.

Conclusion. *Long-term security detention, if imposed by the United States, as seems probable, is a lightly examined LOAC/IHL tactic with many facets yet to be examined. As with other controversial U.S. antiterrorist strategies, it will receive close and protracted legal scrutiny. The novelty, so to speak, of U.S. security detention will be in its application after the conclusion of hostilities in Afghanistan and Iraq. At what point will U.S. involvement in those hostilities end? Who will make that call? What are the conflict-ending LOAC/IHL markers? Will terrorism writ large become a stand-in for the conflicts in Afghanistan and Iraq, justifying continued security detention? Will lesser conflicts in other states involving new terrorist groups suffice as a basis for its continuation? Are there precedents from which to analogize guidance? Or, will security detention be deferred in favor of deportation to the detainees' home state? Will another alternative, not yet envisioned, arise?*

Answers to the difficult issues raised by postconflict long-term security detention will be arrived at through the discussion, argument, and study of jurists, NGOs, academics, commentators, and interested citizens.

---

[119] *Boumediene v. Bush*, 553 U.S. 723, 786–7 (2008).

References

Books Cited

Adams, Charles F., Carl Schurz, Edwin B. Smith, and Herbert Welsh, *Secretary Root's Record: "Marked Severities" Philippine Warfare* (Boston: Geo. H. Ellis Co., 1902)

Alexandrov, Stanimar A., *Self-Defense Against the Use of Force in International Law* (The Hague: Kluwer, 1996)

Alibek, Ken, *Biohazard* (NY: Arrow Books, 2000)

Allhoff, Fritz, *Terrorism, Ticking Time-Bombs, and Torture* (Chicago: University of Chicago Press, 2012

Ambrose, Stephen E., *Band of Brothers* (NY: Simon & Schuster, 1992)

Andrew, Rod, Jr., *Long Gray Lines: The Southern Military School Tradition, 1839–1915* (Chapel Hill, NC: University of North Carolina Press, 2007)

Aoláin, Fionnuala Ní and Oren Gross, eds., *Guantánamo and Beyond* (NY: Cambridge University Press, 2013)

Appleman, John Alan, *Military Tribunals and International Crimes* (Indianapolis, IN: Bobbs-Merrill, 1954)

Atkinson, Rick, *Crusade* (Boston: Houghton Mifflin, 1993)
    The Day of Battle (NY: Henry Holt, 2007)

Aussaresses, BGen. Paul, *The Battle of the Casbah* (NY: Enigma Books, 2002)

Austin, Jay E. and Carl E. Bruch, eds., *The Environmental Consequences of War: Legal, Economic, and Scientific Perspectives* (NY: Cambridge University Press, 2000)

Bacon, Adm. Sir R.H., *The Life of Lord Fisher of Kilverstone – Admiral of the Fleet*, vol. I (London: Hodder & Stoughton, 1929)

Baker, Gary R., *Cadets in Gray* (Lexington, SC: Palmetto Bookworks, 1990)

Baker, James E., *In the Common Defense: National Security Law for Perilous Times* (NY: Cambridge University Press, 2007)

Baker, Stewart, *Skating on Stilts: Why We Aren't Stopping Tomorrow's Terrorism* (Stanford CA: Hoover Inst. Press, 2010)

Bamford, James, *Body of Secrets* (NY: Doubleday, 2001)

Barnett, Correlli, ed., *Hitler's Generals* (London: Weidenfeld & Nicolson, 1989)

Bassiouni, M. Cherif, *The Legislative History of the International Criminal Court*, vol. 1 (Ardsley, NY: Transnational, 2005)

Belknap, Michael R., *The Vietnam War on Trial* (Lawrence, KS: University of Kansas Press, 2002)

Bergen, Peter L. and Daniel Rothenberg, eds., *Drone Wars: Transforming Conflict, Law, and Policy* (NY: Cambridge University Press, 2015)

Berkowitz, Peter, ed., *Terrorism, the Laws of War, and the Constitution* (Stanford, CA: Hoover Institution Press, 2005)

Berry, Richard, *A Missing Link in Leadership* (Bloomington, IN: Author House, 2008)

Best, Geoffrey, *Humanity in Warfare* (London: Weidenfeld & Nicolson, 1980)

    War and Law Since 1945 (Oxford: Clarendon/Oxford University Press, 1994)

Bicentennial Register of Graduates, 2002 (USMA: AOG, 2002)

Biddle, Tami Davis, *Rhetoric and Reality in Air Warfare* (Princeton NJ: Princeton University Press, 2002)

Bilton, Michael and Kevin Sim, *Four Hours in My Lai* (NY: Viking, 1992)

Bishop, Joseph W., Jr., *Justice Under Fire: A Study of Military Law* (NY: Charterhouse, 1974)

Blair, Clay, Jr., *Silent Victory* (NY: Lippincott, 1987)

Blumenson, Martin, *The Battle of the Generals* (William Morrow & Co., 1993)

    Patton Papers, 1940–1945, (Boston: Houghton Mifflin, 1972)

Bobbitt, Philip, *Terror and Consent* (London: Penguin Books, 2009)

Bogdanos, Col. William, *Thieves of Baghdad* (NY: Bloomsbury, 2005)

Boissier, Pierre, *Henry Dunant* (Geneva: Henry Dunant Institute, 1974)

Boister, Neil and Robert Cryer, *The Tokyo International Military Tribunal: A Reappraisal* (NY: Oxford University Press, 2008)

Bolger, Lt. Gen. Daniel P., *Why We Lost* (NY: Houghton Mifflin, 2014)

Boot, Max, *The Savage Wars of Peace* (NY: Basic Books, 2002)

Borch, Col. Fred L. and Paul S. Wilson, eds., *International Law Studies, vol. 79; International Law and the War on Terror* (Newport, RI: Naval War College, 2003)

Bordwell, Percy, *The Law of War Between Belligerents: A Commentary* (Chicago: Callaghan, 1908)

Borsinger, Nicolas, ed., *125th Anniversary of the 1868 Declaration of St. Petersburg* (Geneva: ICRC, 1994)

Bothe, Michael, Karl Partsch and Waldemar Solf, eds., *New Rules for Victims of Armed Conflict: Commentary on the Two 1977 Protocols Additional to the Geneva Conventions of 1949* (Hague: Martinus Nijhoff, 1982)

Bowden, Mark, *Black Hawk Down* (NY: Atlantic Monthly Press, 1999)

Brace, Ernest C., *A Code to Keep* (NY: St. Martin's Press, 1988)

Bradley, Gen. Omar N., *A Soldier's Story* (NY: Henry Holt, 1951)

Brand, C.E., *Roman Military Law* (Austin: University of Texas, 1968)

Brownlee, R. L. and Gen. Peter J. Schoomaker, *Serving A Nation at War* (Washington: Army Strategic Communications, 2004)

Brownlie, Ian, *International Law and the Use of Force by States* (Oxford: Clarendon Press, 1963)

Bruff, Harold H., *Bad Advice: Bush's Lawyers in the War on Terror* (Lawrence KS: University Press of Kansas, 2009)

Bugnion, François, *The Emblem of the Red Cross: A Brief History* (Geneva: ICRC, 1977)

    The International Committee of the Red Cross and the Protection of War Victims (Oxford: Macmillan/ICRC, 2003)

    Red Cross, Red Crescent, Red Crystal (Geneva: ICRC, 2007)

Bull, Hedley, Benedict Kingsbury, and Adam Roberts, eds., *Hugo Grotius and International Relations* (Oxford: Clarendon Press, 1990)

Bush, George W., *Decision Points* (NY: Crown, 2010)

Byers, Michael, *War Law* (NY: Grove Press, 2005)

Carroll, Peter N., *The Odyssey of the Abraham Lincoln Brigade* (Stanford: Stanford University Press, 1994)

Cassese, Antonio, *International Criminal Law* (Oxford: Oxford University Press, 2003), and 2d ed. (2005)

The Oxford Companion to International Criminal Justice (Oxford: Oxford University Press, 2009)

Violence and Law in the Modern Age, trans. S.J.K. Greenleaves (Princeton, NJ: Princeton University Press, 1988)

with Paola Gaeta and John R.W.D. Jones, eds., *The Rome Statute of the International Criminal Court: A Commentary*, vol. I (Oxford: Oxford University Press, 2002)

Chambers, John W. II, et al., eds., *The Oxford Companion to American Military History* (Oxford: Oxford University Press, 1999)

Christopher, Paul, *The Ethics of War & Peace*, 2nd ed. (Upper Saddle River, NJ: Prentice Hall, 1999)

Citino, Robert M., *Death of the* Wehrmacht (Lawrence KS: University Press of Kansas, 2007)

Claire, Rodger W., *Raid on the Sun* (NY: Broadway Books, 2004)

Clancy, Tom with Gen. Tony Zinni, *Battle Ready* (NY: G.P. Putnam's Sons, 2004)

Clarke, Richard A. and Robert K. Knake, *Cyber War* (NY: Ecco, 2010)

Cloud, David and Greg Jaffe, *The Fourth Star: Four Generals and the Epic Struggle for the Future of the United States Army* (NY: Crown Publishers, 2009)

Coates, A. J., *The Ethics of War* (Manchester: Manchester University Press, 1997)

Conway-Lanz, Sahr, *Collateral Damage* (NY: Routeledge, 2006)

Cooper, Alan, *The Dambusters Squadron* (London: Arms and Armour, 1993)

Corn, Geoffrey, Victor Hansen, Richard B. Jackson, Chris Jenks, Eric Talbot Jensen, and James A. Schoettler, Jr., *The Law of Armed Conflict: An Operational Approach* (NY: Wolter Kluwer, 2012

Cowley, Robert, ed., *No End Save Victory* (NY: Putnam, 2001)

with Michael Howard and Peter Paret, eds. and trans., Carl von Clausewitz, *On War* (New York: Knopf, Everyman's Library, 1993)

Crane, Conrad C., *Bombs, Cities, and Civilians* (Lawrence, KS: University Press of Kansas, 1993)

von Clausewitz, Carl, *On War*, A. Rapoport, ed. (London: Penguin Books, 1982)

Crawford, James, *The International Law Commission's Articles on State Responsibility* (Cambridge: Cambridge University Press, 2002)

Crawley, Aidan, *Escape From Germany* (London: Collins, 1956)

Cray, Ed, *General of the Army: George C. Marshall, Soldier and Statesman* (NY: W.W. Norton, 1990)

Cristol, A. Jay, *The Liberty Incident* (NY; Brassey's, 2002)

Crook, John R., "Contemporary Practice of the United States Relating to International Law," 104–1 *AJIL* 100 (Jan. 2010)

Dallaire, Lt. Gen. Roméo, *Shake Hands With the Devil* (NY: Carroll & Graff, 2003)

Dalton, Harvey, Commentary, in Andru E. Wall, ed., International Law Studies, vol. 78, *Legal and Ethical Lessons of NATO's Campaign* (Newport, RI: Naval War College, 2002)

Davis, Burke, *Sherman's March* (NY: Vintage Books, 1988)

Dear, I.C.B., ed. *The Oxford Companion to the Second World War* (Oxford: Oxford University Press, 1995)

de la Billiere, Gen. Sir Peter, *Storm Command* (NY: Harper Collins, 1993)

Delissen, Astrid J.M., and Gerard J. Tanja, eds., *Humanitarian Law of Armed Conflict Challenges Ahead.* (Dordrecht: Martinus Nijhoff, 1991)

de Londras, Fiona, *Detention in the War on Terror* (Cambridge: Cambridge University Press, 2011)

Denton, Kit, *Closed File* (Adelaide: Rigby Publishers, 1983)

DePeyster, John Watts, *Personal and Military History of Philip Kearny* (NY: Rice & Gage, 1869)

de Preux, Jean, *Commentary: III Geneva Convention Relative to the Treatment of Prisoners of War* (Geneva: ICRC, 1960)

Dershowitz, Alan M., *Shouting Fire* (NY: Little, Brown, 2002)
  Why Terrorism Works (New Haven, CT: Yale University Press, 2002)

D'Este, Carlo, *Patton: A Genius for War* (NY: Harper Collins, 1995)

Detter, Ingrid, *The Law of War*, 2nd ed. (Cambridge: Cambridge University Press, 2000)

deZayas, Alfred M., *The Wehrmacht War Crimes Bureau, 1939–1945* (Lincoln: University of Nebraska Press, 1989)

Dinstein, Yoram, *The Conduct of Hostilities under the Law of International Armed Conflict* (Cambridge: Cambridge University Press, 2004) 1st and 2d ed. (2010)
  ed., *International Law at a Time of Perplexity* (Dordrecht: Nijhoff Publishers, 1989)
  The International Law of Belligerent Occupation (Cambridge: Cambridge University Press, 2009)
  Non-International Armed Conflicts in International Law (Cambridge: Cambridge University Press, 2014)
  War, Aggression and Self-Defence, 4th ed. (Cambridge: Cambridge University Press, 2005), and 5th ed. (2011)

DiSilvestro, Roger L., *In the Shadow of Wounded Knee* (NY: Walker, 2005)

Doenitz, Adm. Karl, *Memoirs: Ten Years and Twenty Days* (NY: DeCapo Press, 1977)

Donald, Mark, *Battle Ready* (NY: St. Martins Press, 2013)

Doolittle, Gen. James H., *I Could Never Be So Lucky Again* (NY: Bantam, 1991)

Dörmann, Knut, *Elements of War Crimes Under the Rome Statute of the International Criminal Court* (Cambridge: ICRC/Cambridge University Press, 2003)

Doswald-Beck, Louise, ed., *San Remo Manual on International Law Applicable to Armed Conflicts at Sea* (Cambridge: Cambridge University Press, 1995)

Duffy, Helen, *The 'War on Terror' and the Framework of International Law* (Cambridge: Cambridge University Press, 2005)

Dunant, Henry, *A Memory of Solferino* (Geneva: ICRC reprint, 1986)

Dyer, Gwynne, *War* (London: Guild Publishing, 1985)

Eby, Cecil D., *Comrades and Commissars: The Lincoln Battalion in the Spanish Civil War* (University Park, PA: Pennsylvania State University Press, 2007)

Edmonds, Col. J.E. and L. Oppenheim, *Land Warfare. An Exposition of the Laws and Usages of War on Land for the Guidance of Officers of His Majesty's Army* (London: H.M.S.O., 1912, ed. of 1929)

Eisenhower, Gen. Dwight D., *Crusade in Europe* (NY: Doubleday, 1948)

Elagab, Omar Yousif, *The Legality of Non-forcible Counter-measures in International Law* (London: Clarendon Press, 1988)

Elsea, Jennifer, *Treatment of "Battlefield Detainees" in the War on Terrorism* (Washington: Congressional Research Service, 13 Jan. 2005)
  and Nina M. Serafino, *Private Security Contractors in Iraq: Background, Legal Status, and Other Issues*, updated (Washington: Congressional Research Service, July 11, 2007)

Eyffinger, Arthur, *The Peace Palace: Residence for Justice – Domicile of Learning* (The Hague: Carnegie Foundation, 1988)

Falk, Richard A., ed., *The Vietnam War and International Law*, vol. 4 (NJ: Princeton University Press, 1976); and vol. 3 (1972)

Farago, Ladislas, *Patton: Ordeal and Triumph* (NY: Obolensky, 1964)

Fehrenbach, T.R., *This Kind of War* (NY: Macmillan, 1963)

Feith, Douglas J., *War and Decision* (NY: Harper, 2008)

Fick, Nathaniel, *One Bullet Away* (NY: Houghton Mifflin, 2006)

Finkelstein, Claire, Jens David Ohlen and Andrew Altman, eds., *Targeted Killings: Law and Morality in an Asymmetrical World* (Oxford: Oxford University Press, 2012)

Fischer, David Hackett, *Washington's Crossing* (Oxford: Oxford University Press, 2004)

Fisher, Louis, *Military Tribunals and Presidential Power: American Revolution to the War on Terrorism* (Lawrence KS: University of Kansas Press, 2005)

Fleck, Dieter, ed., *The Handbook of Humanitarian Law in Armed Conflicts*, 1st and 2nd eds. (Oxford: Oxford University Press, 1995), and (2007)

Fletcher, George P. and Jens David Ohlin, *Defending Humanity: When Force is Justified and Why* (Oxford: Oxford University Press, 2008)

Folsom, Maj. Seth W.B., *The Highway War* (Washington, D.C.: Potomac Books, 2006)

Fontenot, Col. Gregory, LTC E.J. Degen and LTC David Tohn, *On Point: The United States Army in Operation Iraqi Freedom* (Fort Leavenworth, KS: Combat Studies Institute Press, 2004)

Foote, Capt. M.R.D., *SOE in France* (London: HMSO, 1966)

Forsythe, D., *Humanitarian Politics: The ICRC* (Baltimore: Johns Hopkins University Press, 1977)

Fraser, George MacDonald, *Quartered Safe Out Here* (NY: Skyhorse Publishing, 2001)

Friedman, Leon, ed., *The Law of War: A Documentary History*, vols. I and II (NY: Random House, 1972)

Fussell, Paul, *Thank God for the Atom Bomb and Other Essays* (NY: Summit Books, 1988)
Wartime: Understanding and Behavior in the Second World War (NY: Oxford University Press, 1989)
Doing Battle: The Making of A Skeptic (Boston: Little Brown, 1996)

Fyfe, David M., ed., *War Crimes Trials, vol. I – The Peleus Trial* (London: William Hodge, 1948)

Gaggioli, Gloria, ed., *The Use of Armed Force in Conflicts: Interplay Between the Conduct of Hostilities and Law Enforcement Paradigms* (Geneva: ICRC, 2013)

Garcia, Michael John, *The War Crimes Act: Current Issues* (Washington: Congressional Research Service, 15 Sept. 2006)

Gardam, Judith, *Necessity, Proportionality and the Use of Force by States* (Cambridge: Cambridge University Press, 2004)

Gasser, Hans-Peter, *International Humanitarian Law: An Introduction* (Berne: Paul Haupt Publishers, 1993)

Gates, Robert M. , *Duty: Memoirs of a Secretary of War* (NY: Alfred Knopf, 2014)

Gellman, Barton, *Angler* (NY: Penguin Press, 2008)

Generous, William T., Jr., *Swords and Scales* (NY: Kennikat Press, 1973)

George, Peter, *Dr. Strangelove or: How I Learned to Stop Worrying and Love the Bomb* (NY: Barnes & Noble, 1998)

Gill, Terry D. and Dieter Fleck, eds., *The Handbook* of *the International Law of Military Operations*, (Oxford: Oxford University Press, 2010)

Girod, Christophe, DRAFT, *Storm in the Desert: The International Committee of the Red Cross and the Gulf War 1990–1991* (Geneva: ICRC, 2003)

Goldsmith, Jack, *The Terror Presidency* (NY: Norton, 2007)

Goldstein, Donald M., Katherine V. Dillon, and J. Michael Wenger, *Nuts!: The Battle of the Bulge* (Washington: Brassey's, 1994)

Goldstein, Eric, *Wars and Peace Treaties: 1816–1991* (London: Routledge, 1992)

Gong, Gerrit W., *The Standard of "Civilization" in International Society* (Oxford: Clarendon Press, 1984)

Goodman, Ryan, "Editorial Comment: The Detention of Civilians in Armed Conflict," 103-1 48 (Jan. 2009)

Gordon, Michael R. and Lt.Gen. Bernard E. Trainor, *Cobra II* (NY: Pantheon Books, 2006)

Gray, Christine, *International Law and the Use of Force* (Oxford: Oxford University Press, 2000)

Green, Leslie C., *Superior Orders in National and International Law* (Leyden: Sijthoff, 1976)
  Essays on the Modern Law of War, 2nd ed. (Ardsley, NY: Transnational, 1999)
  The Contemporary Law of Armed Conflict, 2nd ed. (Manchester: Juris/Manchester University Press, 2000)

Greenberg, Karen J. and Joshua L. Dratel, *The Torture Papers* (NY: Cambridge University Press, 2005)

Greenspan, Morris, *The Modern Law of Land Warfare* (Berkeley: University of California Press, 1959)

Greenwood, Christopher, *The Twilight of Belligerent Reprisals* (London: Cameron May, 2006)

Grossman, Lt. Col. Dave, *On Killing* (Boston: Little, Brown, 1995)

Grotius, Hugo, *The Law of War and Peace* (Buffalo, NY: Hein reprint of Francis W. Kelsey trans., 1995)

Gudjonsson, Gisli H., *The Psychology of Interrogations and Confessions* (West Sussex, U.K.: Wiley, 2003)

Gutman, Roy and David Rieff, eds., *Crimes of War* (NY: Norton, 1999)

Hammel, Eric, *The Root* (NY: Harcourt Brace Jovanovich, 1985)

Hapgood, David and David Richardson, *Monte Cassino* (NY: Congdon & Weed, 1984)

Hartigan, Richard S., *Lieber's Code and the Law of War* (Chicago: Precedent, 1983)

Hastings, Max and Simon Jenkins, *The Battle for the Falklands* (NY: Norton, 1983)

Healey, Jason, ed., *A Fierce Domain: Conflict in Cyberspace, 1986 to 2012* (Vienna, VA: Cyber Conflict Studies Assn., 2013)

Hearn, Chester, *Sorties into Hell: The Hidden War on Chichi Jima* (Westport, CT: Praeger, 2003)

Heere, Wybo P., ed., *Terrorism and the Military: International Legal Implications* (The Hague: Asser Press, 2003)

Helm, Anthony M., ed., *International Law Studies, Vol. 82, The Law of War in the 21st Century: Weaponry and the Use of Force* (Newport, RI: Naval War College, 2006)

Helms, Nathaniel R., *My Men Are My Heroes* (Des Moines, Iowa: Meredith Books, 2007)

Henckaerts, Jean-Marie and Louise Doswald-Beck, eds., *Customary International Humanitarian Law*, vol. I, *Rules*, and vol. II, *Practice* (Cambridge: Cambridge University Press, 2005)

Henderson, Ian, *The Contemporary Law of Targeting* (Leiden: Martinus Nijhoff, 2009)

Hensel, Howard M., ed., *The Law of Armed Conflict* (Aldershot, UK: Ashgate, 2005)

Higgins, Rosalyn, *Problems & Process* (Oxford: Oxford University Press, 1994)

Hillman, James, *A Terrible Love of War* (NY: Penguin Books, 2004)

Hiltermann, Joost R., *A Poisonous Affair* (Cambridge: Cambridge University Press, 2007)

Holland, Thomas E., *The Laws of War on Land (Written and Unwritten)* (Oxford: Clarendon Press, 1908)

Honig, Jan Willem and Norbert Both, *Srebrenica* (NY: Penguin, 1997)

Horne, Alistair, *A Savage War of Peace* (NY: New York Review of Books, 1977)

Hosoya, C., N. Andō, Y. Ōnuma, and R. Minear, eds., *The Tokyo War Crimes Trial: An International Symposium* (NY: Harper & Row, 1986)

Hough, Lt.Col. Frank O., Maj. Verle E. Ludwig, and Henry I. Shaw, *History of Marine Corps Operations in World War II*, vol. I, *Pearl Harbor to Guadalcanal* (Washington: GPO, 1958)

Howard, Michael, George J. Andreopoulos, and Mark R. Shulman, eds., *The Laws of War* (New Haven: Yale University Press, 1994)

Huang, J.H. trans., *Sun Tzu: The New Translation* (NY: Quill, 1933)

Hughes, Matthew, "War Without Mercy? American Armed Forces and the Deaths of Civilians During the Battle for Saipan, 1944," 75–1 *J. Military History* 93 (Jan. 2011)

Hugo, Victor, *Les Misérables*, Norman Denny, trans. (London: Penguin Classics, 1982)

Huntington, Samuel P., *The Soldier and the State* (Cambridge, MA: Belknap Press of Harvard University, 1957)

Husabø, Erling Johannes and Ingvild Bruce, *Fighting Terrorism Through Multilevel Criminal Legislation* (Leiden: Martinus Nijhoff, 2009)

International Institute of Humanitarian Law, *Terrorism and International Law: Challenges and Responses* (Sanremo, Italy: IIHL, 2002)

The International Military Tribunal Sitting at Nuremberg Germany, *The Trial of German Major War Criminals: Opening Speeches of the Chief Prosecutors* (London: His Majesty's Stationary Office, 1946), reprint: Buffalo NY: William S. Hein, 2001)

James, D. Clayton, *The Years of MacArthur: Triumph and Disaster 1945–1964*, vol. 3 (Wilmington, MA: Houghton Mifflin, 1970)

Jaques, Richard B., ed., *International Law Studies: Issues in International Law and Military Operations*, vol. 80 (Newport, RI: Naval War College, 2006)

Jayaswal, K.P., *Manu and Yâjñavalkya, A Comparison and A Contrast: A Treatise on the Basic Hindu Law* (Calcutta: Butterworth, 1930)

Jørgensen, Nina H.B., *The Responsibility of States for International Crimes* (Oxford: Oxford University Press, 2000)

Junger, Sebastian, *War*, (NY: Hachette Book Group, 2010)

Kalshoven, Frits, *Belligerent Reprisals*, 2nd ed. (Leiden: Martinus Nijhoff, 2005)

 and Liesbeth Zegveld, *Constraints on the Waging of War: An Introduction to International Humanitarian Law* (Geneva: ICRC, 2001)

 Reflections on the Law of War: Collected Essays (Leiden: Martinus Nijhoff, 2007)

Kamiya, Maj. Jason K., *A History of the 24th Mechanized Infantry Division Combat Team During Operation Desert Storm* (Fort Stewart, GA, 1991)

Katzman, Kenneth, *Iraq: Reconciliation and Benchmarks* (Washington: Congressional Research Service, May 12, 2008)

Keegan, John, *The Face of Battle* (London: Barrie & Jenkins, 1988)

 A History of Warfare (NY: Knopf, 1993)

 War and Our World (NY: Vintage Books, 2001)

Keen, M.H., *The Laws of War in the Middle Ages* (London: Routledge & Kegan Paul, 1965)

Keijzer, Nico, *Military Obedience* (The Netherlands: Sijthoff & Noordhoff, 1978)

Kelman, Herbert C. and V. Lee Hamilton, *Crimes of Obedience* (New Haven: Yale University Press, 1989)

Kelsen, Hans, *Peace Through Law* (Chapel Hill, NC: University of North Carolina Press, 1944)

Kennedy, David, *Of War and Law* (Princeton NJ: Princeton University Press, 2006)

Kessler, Ronald, *The Terrorist Watch* (NY: Crown Forum, 2007)

Khadduri, Majid, *War and Peace in the Law of Islam* (Baltimore: Johns Hopkins University Press, 1955)

Kittichaisaree, Kriangsak, *International Criminal Law* (NY: Oxford University Press, 2001)

Kolb, Robert, *Advanced Introduction to International Humanitarian Law* (Cheltenham, UK: Edward Elgar, 2014)

 and Richard Hyde, *An Introduction to the International Law of Armed Conflicts* (Oxford: Hart Publishing, 2008)

Lael, Richard L., *The Yamashita Precedent* (Wilmington, DE: Scholarly Resources, 1982)

La Haye, Eve, *War Crimes in Internal Armed Conflicts* (Cambridge: Cambridge University Press, 2008)

Larsen, Kjetil, Camilla G. Cooper, and Gro Nystuen, *Searchibng for A 'Principle of Humanity,'in International Humanitarian Law* (Cambridge: Cambridge University Press, 2013)

Lauterpacht, H., ed., *Annual Digest and Reports of Public International Law Cases – 1946* (London: Butterworth & Co., 1951)

Lawrence, T.E., *Seven Pillars of Wisdom: A Triumph*, (NY: Anchor Books, 1991)

Lawrence, T.J., *The Society of Nations* (NY: Oxford University Press, 1919)

Lawson, John D., ed., *American State Trials*, vol. VIII (St. Louis: F.H. Thomas Law Book Co., 1916)

Levie, Col. Howard S., *Protection of War Victims: Protocol I to the 1949 Geneva Conventions, Supplement* (NY: Oceana Publications, 1985)

   The Code of International Armed Conflict, vol. 1 (NY: Oceana Publications, 1986)

Levinson, Sanford, ed., *Torture: A Collection* (NY: Oxford University Press, 2004)

Lilly, J. Robert, *Taken by Force: Rape and American GIs in Europe During World War II* (NY: Palgrave Macmillan, 2007)

Linn, Brian M., *The Philippine War: 1899–1902* (Lawrence, KS: University of Kansas Press, 2000)

Lomax, Eric, *The Railway Man* (London: Jonathan Cape, 1995)

Luttrell, Marcus, with Patrick Robinson, *Lone Survivor* (NY: Little, Brown, 2007)

MacArthur, Gen. Douglas, *Reminiscences* (NY: McGraw-Hill, 1964)

MacDonald, Callum, *The Killing of SS Obergruppenführer Reinhard Heydrich* (NY: Free Press, 1989)

MacDonald, Peter Charles B. *United States Army in World War II: The European Theater of Operations; The Siegfried Line Campaign* (Washington: Center of Military History, 2001)

Maguire, Peter, *Law and War: An American Story* (NY: Columbia University Press, 2000)

Manchester, William, *American Caesar* (Boston: Little, Brown, 1978)

Mann, Abby, *Judgment at Nuremberg* (London: Cassell, 1961)

Marsh, Michael A., *Andersonville: The Story Behind the Scenery* (Las Vegas: KC Publications, 2000)

Maslen, Stuart, *Explosive Remnants of War* (Geneva: ICRC, 2000)

Matthews, Lloyd J. and Dale E. Brown, eds., *The Parameters of Military Ethics* (VA: Pergamon-Brassey's, 1989)

Mauroni, Albert J., *Chemical and Biological Warfare: A Reference Handbook*, 2nd ed. (Oxford: ABC-Clio, 2006)

McCain, John, *Faith of My Fathers* (NY: Random House, 1999)

McCarthy, Mary, *Medina* (NY: Harcourt Brace Jovanovich, 1972)

McCormack, Timothy L.H., *Self-Defense in International Law: The Israeli Raid on the Iraqi Nuclear Reactor* (NY: St. Martin's Press, 1996)

   ed., *Yearbook of International Humanitarian Law*, vol. 10, 2007 (The Hague: T.M.C. Asser Press, 2009)

   and Gerry J. Simpson, eds., *The Law of War Crimes: National and International Approaches* (The Hague: Kluwer Law International, 1997)

McCoubrey, Hilaire, *International Humanitarian Law: The Regulation of Armed Conflicts* (Aldershot: Dartmouth Publishing, 1990)

McFarland, Stephen L., *America's Pursuit of Precision Bombing, 1910–1945* (Washington: Smithsonian Institution Press, 1995)

McGrath, Lt.Cmdr. John M., *Prisoner of War: Six Years in Hanoi* (Annapolis, MD: Naval Institute Press, 1975)

Melzer, Nils, *Targeted Killing in International Law* (Oxford: Oxford University Press, 2008)

Meron, Theodor, *Bloody Constraint: War and Chivalry in Shakespeare* (NY: Oxford University Press, 1998)

ed., *Human Rights in International Law* (Oxford: Clarendon Press, 1984)

The Humanization of International Law (Leiden: Martinus Nijhoff, 2006)

Human Rights and Humanitarian Norms as Customary Law (Oxford: Clarendon Press, 1989)

The Making of International Criminal Justice: A View From the Bench (Oxford: Oxford University Press, 2011)

War Crimes Law Comes of Age: Essays (Oxford: Oxford University Press, 1998)

Merryman, John Henry and Albert E. Law Elsen, *Ethics and the Visual Arts* (London: Kluwer Law International, 2002)

Mettraux, Guénaël, *International Crimes and the Ad Hoc Tribunals* (Oxford: Oxford University Press, 2005)

Meyer, Dakota and Bing West, *Into the Fire* (NY: Random House, 2012)

Meyer, Karl E. and Sharen B. Brysac, *Kingmakers: The Invention of the Modern Middle East* (NY: W.W. Norton, 2008)

Meyer, Michael A. and Hilaire McCoubrey, eds., *Reflections on Law and Armed Conflicts* (The Hague: Kluwer Law International, 1998)

Mikesh, Robert C., *Japan's World War II Balloon Bomb Attacks on North America* (Washington: Smithsonian Institution Press, 1972)

Miller, David, *Mercy Ships* (London: Continuum, 2008)

Millett, Allan R., *Their War for Korea: American, Asian, and European Combatants and Civilians, 1945-1953* (Dulles VA: Potomac Books, 2004)

Moir, Lindsay, *The Law of Internal Armed Conflict* (Cambridge: Cambridge University Press, 2002)

Moore, John H., *The Faustball Tunnel* (Annapolis, MD: Naval Institute Press, 1978)

Moore, John Norton, et al., *National Security Law* (Durham, NC: Carolina Academic Press, 1990)

and Robert F. Turner, *National Security Law*, 2d ed. (Durham NC: Carolina Academic Press, 2005)

Moorehead, Caroline, *Dunant's Dream* (NY: Carroll & Graf, 1999)

Morgan, J.H., ed. and trans., *The German War Book* (London: John Murray, 1915)

Morison, Samuel Eliot, *John Paul Jones: A Sailor's Biography* (Boston: Atlantic-Little, Brown, 1959)

History of United States Naval Operations in World War II, vol. V (Boston: Little, Brown, 1966)

de Mulinen, Frederic, *Handbook of the Law of War for Armed Forces* (Geneva: ICRC, 1987)

Mullins, Claud, *The Leipzig Trials* (London: Witherby, 1921)

Murray, Williamson and Allan R. Millett, *A War to Be Won* (Cambridge, MA: Belknap Press of Harvard University Press, 2000)

Nabulsi, Karma, *Traditions of War: Occupation, Resistance, and the Law* (Oxford: Oxford University Press, 1999)

Nagl, John A., *Learning to Eat Soup with a Knife* (Chicago: University of Chicago, 2002)

National Defense Intelligence College, *Educing Information: Interrogation: Science and Art* (Washington: NDIC Press, 2006)

Interrogation: World War II, Vietnam, and Iraq (Washington: NDIC Press, 2008)

Naylor, Sean, *Not A Good Day to Die* (NY: Berkley Books, 2005)

Neely, Mark E., Jr., *The Fate of Liberty: Abraham Lincoln and Civil Liberties* (NY: Oxford University Press 1991)

Neier, Aryeh, *War Crimes* (NY: Times Books, 1998)

Netherlands Committee of the Red Cross, *Protecting Human Dignity in Armed Conflict*, (The Hague: Netherlands Red Cross, 2008)

Nolan, Keith William, *Death Valley* (Novato, CA: Presidio Press, 1987)

Northedge, F.S., *The League of Nations* (Leicester: Leicester University Press, 1986)

Nowak, Manfred and Elizabeth McArthur, *The United Nations Convention Against Torture: A Commentary* (NY: Oxford University Press, 2008)

Oberleitner, Gerd, *Human Rights in Armed Conflict: Law, Practice, Policy* (Cambridge: Cambridge University Press, 2015)

O'Connell, Mary Ellen, *The Power & Purpose of International Law* (NY: Oxford University Press, 2008)

O'Donovan, Oliver, *The Just War Revisited* (Cambridge: Cambridge University Press, 2003)

O'Kane, VAdm. Richard H., *Wahoo* (Novato, Ca: Presidio Press, 1987)

O'Keefe, Roger, *The Protection of Cultural Property in Armed Conflict* (Cambridge: Cambridge University Press, 2006)

Oppenheim, Lassa F.L., *International Law*, vol. II, 1st ed. (London: Longmans Green, 1906)
 ed., *The Collected Papers of John Westlake on Public International Law* (Cambridge: University Press, 1914)
 International Law, vol. II, 6th ed., rev., Hersch Lauterpacht, ed., *Disputes, War and Neutrality* (London: Longmans Green, 1944)
 International Law: A Treatise, vol. II, *Disputes, War and Neutrality*, 7th ed., H. Lauterpacht, ed. (London: Longman, 1952)
 International Law: A Treatise, vol. I, *Peace* (London: Longmans Green, 1967)

Osiel, Mark P., *Obeying Orders* (New Brunswick, NJ: Transaction, 1999)

Palmer, Gen. Bruce, Jr., *The 25 Year War* (NY: DaCapo Press, 1984)

Pantano, Capt. Ilario, *Warlord* (NY: Threshold Editions, 2006)

Paust, Jordan J., *Beyond the Law* (NY: Cambridge University Press, 2007)

Peers, Lt.Gen. William R., *The My Lai Inquiry* (NY: Norton, 1979)

Pictet, Jean S., ed., *Commentary, I Geneva Convention 1949, For the Amelioration of the Condition of the Wounded and Sick in Armed Forces in the Field* (Geneva: ICRC, 1952)
 ed., *Commentary: III Geneva Convention Relative to the Treatment of Prisoners of War* (Geneva: ICRC, 1960)
 ed., *Commentary, IV Geneva Convention 1949, Relative to the Protection of Civilian Persons in Time of War* (Geneva: ICRC, 1958)
 Development and Principles of International Humanitarian Law (Leiden: Kluwer, 1985)
 Humanitarian Law and the Protections of War Victims (Leyden: ICRC, 1975)
 International Humanitarian Law (Geneva: ICRC, 1985)

Pilloud, Claud, et al., eds., *Commentary on the Additional Protocols* (Geneva: ICRC, 1987)

Posner, Richard A., *Not A Suicide Pact: The Constitution in A Time of National Emergency* (NY: Oxford University Press, 2006)

Potter, E.B., *Nimitz* (Annapolis MD: Naval Institute Press, 1976)

Powell, Colin L., *A Soldier's Way: An Autobiography* (London: Hutchinson, 1995)

de Preux, Jean, *Commentary: III Geneva Convention 1949, Relative to the Treatment of Prisoners of War* (Geneva: ICRC, 1960)

Price, Frank J., *Troy H. Middleton: A Biography* (Baton Rouge, LA: Louisiana State University, 1974)

Prince, Cathryn J., *Shot From the Sky: American POWs in Switzerland* (Annapolis: Naval Institute Press, 2003)

Probert, Henry, *Bomber Harris: His Life and Times* (London: Greenhill Books, 2001)

Prugh, Maj.Gen. George S., *Law at War: Vietnam 1964–1973* (Washington: Dept. of the Army, 1975)

Ratner, Steven R. and Jason S. Abrams, *Accountability For Human Rights Atrocities In International Law* (Oxford: Clarendon Press, 1997)

  Accountability for Human Rights Atrocities in International Law: Beyond the Nuremberg Legacy, 2nd ed. (Oxford: Oxford University Press, 2001)

Reel, A. Frank, *The Case of General Yamashita* (NY: Octagon Books, 1971)

Reichberg, Gregory M., Henrik Syse, and Endre Begby, eds., *The Ethics of War* (Malden, MA: Blackwell Publishing, 2006)

Reydams, Luc, *Universal Jurisdiction* (Oxford: Oxford University Press, 2003)

Reynolds, Col. Nicholas E., *Basrah, Baghdad, and Beyond* (Annapolis: Naval Institute Press, 2005)

Ricks, Thomas E., *Fiasco* (NY: Penguin, 2006)

Roberts, Adam and Richard Guelff, *Documents on the Law of War*, 3rd ed. (Oxford: Oxford University Press, 2000)

Rochester, Stuart I. and Frederick Kiley, *Honor Bound* (Washington: Historical Office, Office of the Secretary of Defense, 1998)

Rodley, Nigel S., *The Treatment of Prisoners Under International Law*, 2nd ed. (Oxford: Oxford University Press, 1999).

  with Matt Pollard, *The Treatment of Prisoners Under International Law*, 3d ed. (2009)

Rogers, Maj Gen A.V.P., *Law on the Battlefield*, 2nd ed. (Huntington, NY: Juris/Manchester, 2004), 216.

Rommel, Erwin, B.H. Liddell Hart, ed., *The Rommel Papers* (London: Collins, 1953)

Rona, Gabor and Raha Walla, "In Defense of Federal Criminal Courts for Terrorism Cases in the United States," in Fionnuala Ní Aoláin and Oren Gross, eds., *Guantánamo and Beyond* (NY: Cambridge University Press, 2013)

Roscini, Marco, *Cyber Operations and the Use of Force in International Law* (Oxford: Oxford University Press, 2014)

Rosenne, Shabtai, ed., *The Hague Peace Conference of 1899 and 1907: Reports and Documents* (The Hague, Asser Press, 2001)

Roth, Kenneth, Minky Worden, and Amy Bernstein, eds., *Torture* (NY: The New Press, 2005)

Rowe, Peter, *The Impact of Human Rights Law on Armed Forces* (NY: Cambridge University Press, 2006)

Ruys, Tom, *'Armed Attack' and Article 51 of the UN Charter* (Cambridge: Cambridge University Press, 2010)

Ryan, Allan, *Yamashita's Ghost* (Lawrence KS: University Press of Kansas, 2012)

Ryan, Cornelius, *A Bridge Too Far* (NY: Simon & Schuster, 1974)

Ryan, Paul B., *The Iranian Rescue Mission* (Annapolis MD: Naval Institute Press, 1985)

Safire, William, *Safire's New Political Dictionary* (New York: Random House, 1993)

Salisbury, Harrison E., *The 900 Days: the Seige of Leningrad* (Cambridge MA: De Cappo Press, 1969)

Sanchez, Lt.Gen. Ricardo S., *Wiser in Battle* (NY: Harpers, 2008)

Sandoz, Yves, Christophe Swinarski, and Bruno Zimmermann, eds., *Commentary on the Additional Protocols of 8 June 1977 to the Geneva Conventions of 12 August 1949* (Geneva: ICRC, 1987)

Sanger, David E., *Confront and Conceal: Obama's Secret Wars and Surprising Use of American Power* (NY: Crown Publishers, 2012)

San Remo Manual on International Law Applicable to Armed Conflicts at Sea (San Remo: International Institute of Humanitarian Law, 1994)

Sassaman, Lt.Col. Nathan, *Warrior King* (NY: St. Martin's Press, 2008)

Saxon, Dan, ed., *International Humanitarian Law and the Changing Technology of War*, (Leiden: Martinus Nijhoff, 2013)

Schabas, William A., *The International Criminal Court: A Commentary on the Rome Statute* (Oxford: Oxford University Press, 2010)

 An Introduction to the International Criminal Court (Cambridge: Cambridge University Press, 2001)

 The UN International Criminal Tribunals (NY: Cambridge University Press, 2006)

Sibylle, Scheipers, ed., *Prisoners in War* (Oxford: Oxford University Press, 2010)

Schmitt, Michael N. and Jelena Pejic, eds., *International Law and Armed Conflict: Exploring the Faultlines* (Leiden: Martinus Nijhoff, 2007)

 and Brian T. O'Donnell, eds., *International Law Studies*, vol. 76, *Computer Network Attack and International Law* 99 (Newport RI: Naval War College, 2002)

 Tallin Manual on the International Law Applicable to Cyber Warfare (Cambridge: Cambridge University Press, 2013)

Schneider, Berry R. and Lawrence E. Grinter, eds., *Battlefield of the Future: 21st Century Warfare Issues* (Maxwell Air Force Base, AL: Air Warfare College, Sept. 1995)

Schwarzenberger, Georg, *International Law: As Applied by International Courts and Tribunals*, vol. II, *The Law of Armed Conflict* (London: Stevens & Sons, 1968)

Scott, James Brown, ed., *The Hague Conventions and Declarations of 1899 and 1907* (NY: Oxford University Press, 1918)

 The Proceedings of the Hague Peace Conference (Whitefish, MT: Kessinger Publishing, Reprint, 2007)

Shirer, William L., *The Rise and Fall of the Third Reich* (NY: Simon & Schuster, 1960)

Simmons, Edwin Howard, *The United States Marines: A History*, 4th ed. (Annapolis, MD: Naval Institute Press, 2003)

Sivakumaran, Sandesh, *The Law of Non-International Armed Conflict* (Oxford: Oxford University Press, 2013)

Sledge, Eugene, *With the Old Breed at Peleliu and Okinawa* (Novato, CA: Presidio Press, 1981)

Smith, Gen. Rupert, *The Utility of Force: The Art of War in the Modern World* (NY: Knopf, 2007)

Solis, Lt. Col. Gary D., *Marines and Military Law in Vietnam* (Washington: GPO/USMC, 1989)

Sorley, Lewis, *Thunderbolt* (Washington: Brassey's, 1998)

Spaight, J.M., *Air Power and the Cities* (London: Longmans & Green, 1930)

 Air Power and War Rights, 3rd ed. (London: Longmans & Green, 1947)

Steiner, Henry J. and Philip Alston, *International Human Rights in Context*, 2nd ed. (Oxford: Oxford University Press, 2000)

Stevens, Paul Drew, ed., *The Congressional Medal of Honor: The Names, the Deeds* (Forest Ranch, CA: Sharp & Dunnigan, 1984)

The Stimson Center, "Recommendations and Report of The Task Force on US Drone Policy Washington DC: Stimson Center, 2014)

Stockdale, VAdm. James B., *Stockdale on Stoicism II: Master of My Fate* (Annapolis, MD: United States Naval Academy, Center for the Study of Professional Military Ethics, Occasional Paper Number 2, 1996)

 Thoughts of A Philosophical Fighter Pilot (Stanford: Hoover Institution Press, 1995)

 and Sybil Stockdale, *In Love and War* (Annapolis, MD: Naval Institute Press, 1990)

Storey, Moorfield and Julian Codman, *Secretary Root's Record: "Marked Severities" in Philippine Warfare* (Boston: Ellis Co., 1902)

Stromseth, Jane, David Wippman, and Rosa Brooks, *Can Right Make Rights?* (NY: Cambridge University Press, 2006)

Sweetman, John, *The Dambusters Raid* (London: Arms and Armour, 1990)

Swinarski, Christophe, ed., *Studies and Essays on International Humanitarian Law and Red Cross Principles, in Honour of Jean Pictet* (Geneva: ICRC, 1984)

Taylor, Sean, *Not A Good Day to Die* (NY: Berkley Books, 2005)

Taylor, Telford, *The Anatomy of the Nuermberg Trials* (NY: Knopf, 1992)
   Final Report to the Secretary of the Army on the Nuernberg War Crimes Trials Under Control Council Law No. 10 (Washington D.C. 1949/Buffalo NY: Hein reprint, 1997)
   Nuremberg and Vietnam: An American Tragedy (Chicago: Quadrangle Books, 1970)

Thomas, A.R. and J.C. Duncan, eds., *Annotated Supplement to the Commander's Handbook on the Law of Naval Operations* (Newport, RI: U.S. Naval War College, 1999)

Thomas, Lowell, *With Lawrence In Arabia* (London: Hutchison, 1927)

Thursfield, J.R. *Oxford Manual of Naval War* (Cambridge: Putnam, 1913)

Timberg, Robert, *The Nightingale's Song* (NY: Simon & Schuster, 1995)

Tomuschat, Christian, *Human Rights: Between Idealism and Realism* (Oxford: Oxford University Press, 2003)

Trotter, William R., *The Winter War: The Russo-Finnish War of 1939–40* (London: Aurum, 1991)

Tucker, Jonathan B., *War of Nerves* (NY: Pantheon, 2006)

United Kingdom Ministry of Defense, *The Law of War on Land: Part III of the Manual of Military Law* (London: HMSO, 1958)

Urwin, Gregory J.W., *Facing Fearful Odds* (Lincoln: University of Nebraska Press, 1997)

VanBaarda, Th.A. and D.E.M. Verweij, *Military Ethics: the Dutch Approach* (Leiden: Martinus Nijhoff, 2006)

VanCreveld, Martin, *The Transformation of War* (NY: Free Press, 1991)

Vandiver, Frank E., *Black Jack: The Life and Times of John J. Pershing*, vol. II (College Station, TX: Texas A & M University Press, 1977)

Vattel, Emmerich, *The Law of Nations, or, Principles of the Law of Nature* (Northhampton, MA: Thomas M. Pomroy for S. & E. Butler, 1805)

Verri, Pietro, *Dictionary of the International Law of Armed Conflict* (Geneva: ICRC, 1992)

Vitug, Marites D. and Glenda M. Gloria, *Under the Crescent Moon: Rebellion in Mindanao* (Quezon City, RP.: Institute for Popular Democracy, 2000)

Von Clausewitz, Carl, On War, A. Rappoport, ed. (London: Penguin Books, 1982)
   Michael Howard and Peter Paret, eds. (NY: Knopf, 1993)

Vohrah, Lal C., et al., eds., *Man's Inhumanity to Man: Essays in Honour of Antonio Cassese*, 481 (The Hague: Kluwer Law International, 2003)

Wagstaff, Robert H., *Terror Detentions and the Rule of Law* (NY: Oxford University Press, 2014)

Wall, Andru E., ed., *International Law Studies*, vol. 78, *Legal and Ethical Lessons of NATO's Kosovo Campaign* (Newport, RI: Naval War College, 2002)

Walzer, Michael, *Arguing About War* (New Haven: Yale University Press, 2004)
   Just and Unjust Wars, 3rd ed. (NY: Basic Books, 2000)

Walker, J. Samuel, *Prompt & Utter Destruction: Truman and the Use of Atomic Bombs Against Japan* (Chapel Hill NC: University of North Carolina Press, 1997)

Wasserstrom, Richard, ed., *War and Morality* (Belmont CA: Wadsworth Publishing, 1970)

Watkins, John C., Jr., and John P. Weber, *War Crimes and War Crime Trials: From Leipzig to the ICC and Beyond* (Durham, NC: Carolina Academic Press, 2006)

Weigley, Russell F., *Eisenhower's Lieutenants* (Bloomington: Indiana University Press, 1981)

Weiner, Tim, *Legacy of Ashes: The History of the CIA* (NY: Doubleday, 2007

Weintraub, Stanley, *Silent Night* (NY: Free Press, 2001)

Wells, Donald A., *The Laws of Land Warfare: A Guide to the U.S. Army Manuals* (Westport, CT: Greenwood Press, 1992)

Werrell, Kenneth P., *Blankets of Fire* (Washington: Smithsonian Institution Press, 1996)

West, Bing, *No True Glory* (NY: Bantam, 2006)

Whittle, Richard, *Predator: The Secret Origins of the Drone Revolution* (NY: Henry Holt, 2014)'

Wighton, Charles, *Hitler's Most Evil Henchman* (London: Odhams Press, 1962)

Williams, Sharon A., *The International and National Protection of Movable Cultural Property: A Comparative Study* (Dobbs Ferry, NY: Oceana Publications, 1978)

Wilmshurst, Elizabeth, ed., *International Law and the Classification of Conflicts*, (Oxford: Oxford University Press, 2012)

Wilson, Richard Ashby, ed., *Human Rights in the 'War on Terror'* (NY: Cambridge University Press, 2005)

Winthrop, Col. *William, Military Law and Precedents*, 2nd ed. (Washington: GPO, 1920)

Wippman, David and Matthew Evangelista, eds. *New Wars, New Laws? Applying the Laws of War in 21st Century Conflicts* (Ardsley, NY: Transnational, 2005)

Witt, John Fabian, *Lincoln's Code: The Laws of War in American History* (NY: Free Predd, 2012)

Wittes, Benjamin, *Law and the Long War: The Future of Justice in the Age of Terror* (NY: Penguin Press, 2008)

and Gabriella Blum, *The Future of Violence: Robots and Germs, Hackers and Drones* (NY: Basic Books, 2015)

Woodward, Bob, *State of Denial* (NY: Simon & Schuster, 2006)

Xenophon, *Hellenica*, Books I-V, Carlton L. Brownson trans. (London: William Heinemann, 1918)

Yoo, John, *War By Other Means* (NY: Atlantic Monthly Press, 2006)

Young, Brig. Desmond, *Rommel, The Desert Fox* (NY: Harper & Brothers, 1950)

Zegveld, Liesbeth, *The Accountability of Armed Opposition Groups in International Law* (Cambridge: Cambridge University Press, 2002)

Zenko, Micah, *Reforming U.S. Drone Strike Policies* (NY: Council on Foreign Relations, 2013)

Zucchino, David, *Thunder Run* (NY: Grove Press, 2004)

U.S. Government and UN Publications Cited

Alston, Philip, *Report of the Special Rapporteur on Extrajudicial, Summary or Arbitrary Executions, Mission to the United States of America*, Addendum, UN doc. A/HRC/11/2/Add.5 (May 28, 2009)

Anderson, Maj. Marie and Emily Zukauskas, eds., *Operational Law Handbook*, 2008 (Charlottesville: Judge Advocate General's Legal Center and School, 2008)

Congressional Research Service: Elsea, Jennifer K., "The Military Commissions Act of 2006: Analysis of Procedural Rules and Comparison With Previous DoD Rules and the Uniform Code of Military Justice," (Washington D.C., GPO, Sept. 27, 2007)

Elsea, Jennifer K., Grimmett, Richard F., "Authorization for Use of Military Force in Response to the 9/11 Attacks (P.L. 107-40): Legislative History (updated 16 Jan. 2007)

Elsea, Jennifer K., Hildreth, Steven A., *Cyberwarfare* (19 June 2001)

Elsea, Jennifer K., Wilson, Clay, "Botnets, Cybercrime, and Cyberterrorism: Vulnerabilities and Policy Issues for Congress," 29 Jan. 2008)

Heyns, Christof, Special Rapporteur on Extrajudicial, Summary or Arbitrary Executions, *Report*, U.N. Doc. A/HRC/23/47 (9 April 2013)

Implementation of United Nations General Assembly Resolution 60/251, "Human Rights Council" Report of Commission of Inquiry on Lebanon (15 March 2006)

Index and Legislative History: Uniform Code of Military Justice (Washington DC: GPO, 1950)

Instructions for the Government of Armies of the United States in the Field (Army General Orders 100 of 24 April 1863)

Judge Advocate General's Legal Center & School, *Law of War Workshop Deskbook*, 1997 (Charlottesville, VA: JAGC&S, 1997)

    Operational Law Handbook, 2005, and 2006, and 2014 (Charlottesville, VA (Charlottesville, VA: JAGC&S, 2005); (2006); and (2014)

    International and Operational Law Department, *Law of War Handbook* (Charlottesville, VA: JAG School, 1997)

A *Manual for Courts-Martial, Courts of Inquiry and Other Procedure Under Military Law* (Washington: GPO, 1916)

Manual for Courts-Martial United States, 1969 (Revised edition) (Washington: GPO, 1969)

Manual for Courts-Martial United States (Washington: GPO, 2008)

Manual for Military Commissions – United States (Washington: GPO, 2010)

Owens, William A., et al., eds., National Research Council, *Technology, Policy, Law, and Ethics Regarding U.S. Acquisition and Use of Cyberattack Capabilities* (2009)

Trial of the Major War Criminals before the International Military Tribunal, vol. I (Nuremberg: IMT, 1947)

Trials of War Criminals Before the Nuernberg Military Tribunals, vols. IV, VI, VIII, and XI (Washington: GPO, 1948, 1950, 1951, 1952)

United Kingdom, Ministry of Defense, *The Manual of the Law of Armed Conflict*. (Oxford: Oxford University Press, 2004)

United Nations: "A More Secure World: Our Shared Responsibility," Report of the U.N. Secretary-General's High-level Panel on Threats, Challenges and Change (2 Dec. 2004)

    The Charter and Judgment of the Nurnberg Tribunal: History and Analysis (NY: UNGA, 1949)

    Chemical and Bacteriological (Biological) Weapons and the Effects of Their Possible Use (NY: UN, 1969)

    1968 U. Convention on the Non-Applicability of Statutory Limitations to War Crimes and Crimes Against Humanity, *UN Juridical Y. B.* (1968)

    Historical Survey of the Question of International Criminal Jurisdiction (Lake Success, NY: U.N.G.A., 1949)

    Report of the Secretary-General, "Developments in the Fielf of Information and Telecommunications in the Context of International Security," UN Doc. A/66/152 (20 July 2010)

    Report of the Secretary-General Pursuant to Paragraph 2 of Security Council Resolution 808 (1993) U.N. doc. S/25704 of 3 May 1993

    U.N. War Crimes Commission, *History of the United Nations War Crimes Commission and the Development of the Laws of War* (London: His Majesty's Stationery Office, 1948)

    U.N. War Crimes Commission, *Law Reports of Trials of War Criminals*, vols. I, III, IV, V, XI, XIII, IX, and XI (London: UN, 1947, 1948, 1949, 1950)

    Yearbook of the International Law Commission, 1950, vol. II (Lake Success NY: UNGA, 1952)

U.S. Army Field Manual 3–24 and Marine Corps Warfighting Publication 3–33.5, *U.S. Army-Marine Corps Counterinsurgency Field Manual* (Chicago: University of Chicago Press, 2007)

    Report of the Dept. of the Army Review of the Preliminary Investigation Into the My Lai Incident, vol. 2, book 16 (Pentagon: Dept. of the Army, n.d.)

U.S. Department of the Air Force, *The United States Strategic Bombing Surveys* (Maxwell AFB, AL: Air University Press reprint, 1987)

    Commander's Handbook on the Law of Armed Conflict (AFP 110–34) (1980)

U.S. Department of the Army, *The Army Lawyer: A History of the Judge Advocate General's Corps, 1775–1975* (Washington: GPO, 1975)

Field Manual (FM) 2–22.3, *Human Intelligence Collection Operations* (Washington: GPO, 2006)

FM 3-90.15, Site Exploitation Operations (July 2010)

FM 27–10, *The Law of Land Warfare* (Washington: GPO, 1956)

Office of The Surgeon, Multinational Force – Iraq; and, Office of The Surgeon General, United States Army Medical Command, *Mental Health Advisory Team (MHAT) IV, Operation Iraqi Freedom 05–07, FINAL REPORT* (17 Nov. 2006)

Pamphlet 20–213, *History of Prisoner of War Utilization by the United States Army 1776–1945* (Washington: GPO, 1955)

Pamphlet 27–9, *Military Judge's Benchbook* (30 Sept. 1996)

Pamphlet 27–161-2, *International Law*, vol. II (Washington: GPO, 1962)

Army Regulation 190-8/ OPNAVINST 3461.c/ AFJI 31-304/ MCO 3461.1, "Enemy Prisoners of War, Retained Personnel, Civilian Internees and other Detainees" (1Oct. 1997)

U.S. Department of Defense, *Conduct of the Persian Gulf War: Final Report to Congress* (Washington: GPO, 1992)

Joint Publication 1–02, *Department of Defense Dictionary of Military and Associated Terms* (Washington: GPO, 2001, amended through 17 Oct. 2008)

Joint Publication 3–36, *Detainee Operations*, (6 February 2008)

U.S. Department of the Navy, *U.S. Commander's Handbook on the Law of Naval Operations* (NWP 1–14M), (Washington: GPO, 1995)

U.S. Marine Corps Reference Publication (MCRP) 4–11.8B, *War Crimes* (2005)

U.S. War Department, *Rules of Land Warfare, 1914* (Washington: GPO, 1914)

The Military Laws of the United States, 1915, 5th ed. (Washington: GPO, 1917)

World Health Organization, *Health Aspects of the Use of Chemical and Biological Weapons* (Geneva: WHO, 1970)

24th Mechanized Infantry Division Combat Team, *Historical Reference Book: A Collection of Historical Letters, Briefings, Orders, and Other Miscellaneous Documents Pertaining to the Defense of Saudi Arabia and the Attack to Free Kuwait* (Ft. Stewart, GA, 1991), vol. 1

Articles and blogs Cited

Abi-Saab, Georges, "The Proper Role of Universal Jurisdiction," 1–3 *J. of Int'l Crim. Justice* 596 (Dec. 2003)

Akerson, David, "The Illegality of Offensive Lethal Autonomy," in Dan Saxon, ed., *International Humanitarian Law and the Changing Technology of War*, (Leiden: Martinus Nijhoff, 2013)

Akhavan, Payam, "Reconciling Crimes Against Humanity with the Law of War," 6–1 *J. of Int'l Crim L.* 21 (March 2008)

Aldrich, George H., "Some Reflections on the Origins of the 1977 Geneva Protocols," in Christophe Swinarski, ed., *Studies and Essays on International Humanitarian Law and Red Cross Principles, in Honour of Jean Pictet* (Geneva: ICRC, 1984)

"Prospects for United States Ratification of Additional Protocol I to the 1949 Geneva Conventions," 85 *AJIL* 1 (1991).

"From the St. Petersburg Declaration to the Modern Law of War," in Nicolas Borsinger, ed., *125th Anniversary of the 1868 Declaration of St. Petersburg* (Geneva: ICRC, 1994)

"Comments on the Geneva Protocols," 320 *Int'l Rev. of the Red Cross*, n.p. (31 Oct. 1997)

"Symposium: The Hague Peace Conferences: Introduction," 94–1 *AJIL* 1 (Jan. 2000).

"The Taliban, al Qaeda, and the Determination of Illegal Combatants, 96–4 *AJIL* 891, (Oct. 2002)

review: David Wippman and Matthew Evangelista, eds., *New Wars, New Laws?* 100–2 *AJIL* 496 (April 2006)

Ambos, Kai, "May A State Torture Suspects to Save the Life of Innocents?" 6–2 *J. of Int'l Crim. Justice* 261 (May 2008)

Anderson, Kenneth, Daniel Reisner and Matthew Waxman, "Adapting the Law of Armed Conflict to Autonomous Weapon Systems," *Int'l L. Studies*, vol. 90 (Newport R.I.: Naval War College, 2014)

Arbour, Louise, "Will the ICC Have an Impact on Universal Jurisdiction," 1–3 *J. of Int'l Crim. Justice* 585 (Dec. 2003)

"Legal Professionalism and International Criminal Proceedings," 4–4 *J. of Int'l Crim. Justice* 674 (Sept. 2006).

Asaro, Peter, "On Banning Autonomous Weapon Systems: Human Rights, Automation, and the Dehumanization of Lethat Decision-making," 94/886 *Int'l Rev. of the Red Cross* (Summer, 2012), 687

Askin, Kelly D., "A Decade of the Development of Gender Crimes in International Courts and Tribunals: 1993 to 2003," 11–3 *Human Rights Brief* 16 (American U. Washington College of L., Spring 2004)

Bachelet, Jean-René, "Address by General Jean-René Bachelet," 870 *Int'l Rev. of the Red Cross* 215 (June 2008)

Bamford, James, "The NSA is Building the Country's Biggest Spy Center (Watch What You Say)," *Wired Magazine* (15 March 2012)

Banks, William C. and Peter Raven-Hansen, "Targeted Killing and Assassination: The U.S. Legal Framework," 37 *U. Richmond L. Rev.* 667 (2002–2003)

Barnes, Beau D., "Reauthorizing the 'War on Terror': The Legal and Policy Implications of the AUMF's Coming Obsolescence," 211 *Military L. Rev.* 57 (Spring 2012)

Bassiouni, M. Cherif, "Justice and Peace: The Importance of Choosing Accountability Over Realpolitik," 35–2 *Case Western Reserve J. of Int'l L.* 191, 193 (Spring 2003)

Battle, George G., "The Trials Before the Leipzig Supreme Court of Germans Accused of War Crimes," 8 *Va. L. Rev.*, 1 (1921)

Baxter, Maj. Richard R., "The Municipal and International Law Basis of Jurisdiction Over War Crimes," 28 *BYIL* 382 (1951)

"So-called 'Unprivileged Belligerency': Spies, Guerrillas, and Saboteurs," 28 *BYIL* 323 (1951)

"The First Modern Codification of the Law of War," part I, 25 *Int'l Rev. of the Red Cross* 171, 183 (April 1963); part II, 26 *Int'l Rev. of the Red Cross* 234 (May 1963)

"Modernizing the Law of War," 78 *Military L. R.* 165 (1978)

Beard, Jack M., "The Geneva Boomerang: The Military Commissions Act of 2006 and U.S. Counterterror Operations," 101–1 *AJIL* 56 (Jan. 2007)

"Law and War in the Virtual Era," 103–3 *AJIL* 409 (July 2009)

"The Shortcomings of Indeterminacy in Armed Control Regimes: The Case of the Biological Weapons Convention," 101–2 *AJIL* 271 (April 2007)

Bederman, David J., ed., "International Decisions," 103–1 *AJIL* (Jan. 2009); and 104-1 AJIL 66, 74 (Jan. 2010); and 105-2 *AJIL* 313 (April 2011)

Bellal, Annyssa, Gilles Giacca, and Stuart Casey-Maslen, "International law and armed non-state actors in Afghanistan," 93–881 *Int'l Rev. of the Red Cross* 47 (March 2011)

Bellinger, John B. III and Vijay M. Padmanabhan, "Detention Operations in Contemporary Conflicts: Four Challenges For the Geneva Conventions and Other Existing Law," 105–2 *AJIL* 201 (April 2011) and William J. Haynes II, "A US Government Response to the International Committee of the Red Cross Study Customary International Humanitarian Law," 866 *Int'l Rev. of the Red Cross* 443 (June 2007)

Ben-Naftali, O. and K.R. Michaeli, "We Must Not Make A Scarecrow of the Law: A Legal Analysis of the Israeli Policy of Targeted Killings," 36 *Cornell Int'l L. J.*, 233 (2003)

Bernstein, Barton J., "Why We Didn't Use Poison Gas in World War II," 36–5 *American Heritage* 40 (Aug./Sept. 1985)

Best, Geoffrey, "The Restraint of War in Historical and Philosophic Perspective," in Astrid J.M. Delissen and Gerard J. Tanja, eds., *Humanitarian Law of Armed Conflict Challenges Ahead.* (Dordrecht: Martinus Nijhoff, 1991)

Bettauer, Ronald J., book review of: **Roger O'Keefe**, *The Protection of Cultural Property in Armed Conflict* (Cambridge: Cambridge University Press, 2006), 102–1 *AJIL* 220 (Jan. 2008)

Blank, Laurie R., International Law and Cyber Threats from Non-State Actors," U.S. Naval War College, 89 *Int'l L. Studies* 406 (2013)

Boelaert-Suominen, Sonja, "Grave Breaches, Universal Jurisdiction and Internal Armed Conflict: Is Customary Law Moving Towards A Uniform Enforcement Mechanism for All Armed Conflicts?" 5–1 *J. Conflict & Security L.* 63 (June 2000)

Bonafé, Beatrice I., "Finding a Proper Role for Command Responsibility," 5–3 *J. of Int'l Crim. Justice* 599 (July 2007)

Boothby, Bill, "How Far Will the Law Allow Unmanned Targeting To Go?" in, Dan Saxon, ed., *International Humanitarian Law and the Changing Technology of War*, (Leiden: Martinus Nijhoff, 2013)

Borch, Col. Frederic L., "Targeting After Kosovo: Has the Law Changed for Strike Planners?" vol. LVI–2 *Naval War College Rev.* 64 (Spring 2003)

Borrie, John, "The 'Long Year': Emerging International Efforts to Address the Humanitarian Impacts of Cluster Munitions, 2006–2007," in Timothy L.H. McCormack, ed., *YIHL*, vol. 10, 2007 (The Hague: Asser Press, 2009)

Borum, Randy, "Approaching Truth: Behavioral Science Lessons on Educing Informa-tion from Human Sources," in *Educing Information: Interrogation: Science and Art* (Washington: National Defense Intelligence College, 2006)

Bothe, Michael, "Targeting," in Andru E. Wall, ed., *International Law Studies*, vol. 78, *Legal and Ethical Lessons of NATO's Kosovo Campaign* (Newport, RI: Naval War College, 2002)

Bovarnick, Lt.Col. Jeff A., "Detainee Review Boards in Afghanistan: From Strategic Liability to Legitimacy," *The Army Lawyer* (June 2010)

Bowden, Mark, "The Dark Art of Interrogation," *Atlantic Monthly* (Oct. 2003)
"The Ploy," *The Atlantic* (May 2007)

Brady, Helen and Barbara Goy, "Current Developments in the Ad Hoc International Criminal Tribunals," 6–3 *J. of Int'l. Crim. Justice* 569 (1998)

Brinn, Lt.Col. Rufus T., "U.S. Policy and the Uncertain State of Military Usage of Riot Control Agents" (U.S. Army War College, Carlisle Barracks, PA Strategic Research Project, 1998)

Brown, Gary D., "The Wrong Questions About Cyberspace," 217 *Military L. Rev.* 214 (Fall 2013)

Buergenthal, Thomas, "The Evolving International Human Rights System," 100–4 *AJIL* 783, 785 (Oct. 2006)

Burchard, Christoph, "Torture in the Jurisprudence of the Ad Hoc Tribunals," in 6–2 *J. of Int'l Crim. Justice*, 159 (May 2008)

Burnett, Lt.Cmdr. Weston D., "Command Responsibility and a Case Study of the Criminal Responsibility of Israeli Military Commanders for the Pogrom at Shatila and Sabra," 107 *Mil. L. Rev.* 71 (1985)

Cannizzaro, Enzo, "Contextualizing Proportionality: *jus ad bellum* and *jus in bello* in the Lebanese War," 864 *Int'l Rev. of the Red Cross* 779 (Dec. 2006)

Carnahan, Burris M., "Lincoln, Lieber and the Laws of War: The Origins and Limits of the Principle of Military Necessity," 92–2 *AJIL* 213 (April 1998)

Caron, David D., "War and International Adjudication: Reflections on the 1899 Peace Conference," 94–4 *AJIL* 4 (2000)

Casey-Maslen, Stuart, "Pandora's Box? Drone Strikes under *jus ad bellum, jus in bello*, and international human rights law," 94–886 *Int'l Rev. of the Red Cross* 597 (Summer 2012)

Cassel, Doug, "International Human Rights Law and Security Detention," 40–3 *Case Western Reserve J. Int'l L.* 383 (2009)

Cassese, Antonio, "The Rome Statute of the International Criminal Court: Some Preliminary Reflections," 10–1 *European J. of Int'l L.* 144 (1999)

"Under What Conditions May Belligerents be Acquitted of the Crime of Attacking an Ambulance?" 6–2 *J. of Int'l Crim Justice* 385 (May 2008)

"The Italian Court of Cassation Misapprehends the Notion of War Crimes," 6–3 *J. of Int'l. Crim. Justice* 1077 (Nov. 2008)

Cavaleri, Lt.Col. David P., *"The Law of War: Can 20th-Century Standards Apply to the Global War on Terrorism?"* (Fort Leavenworth, KS: Combat Studies Institute Press, 2005)

Center for Law And Military Operations (CLAMO), "Rules of Engagement: What Are They and Where Do They Come From?" *Marine Corps Gazette* (April 2002)

"'ROE' Rhymes With 'We'," *Marine Corps Gazette* (Sept. 2002)

Chomsky, Carol, "The United States-Dakota War Trials: A Study in Military Justice," 43 *Stanford L. Rev.* 13 (1990)

Clapham, Andrew, "Extending International Criminal Law Beyond the Individual to Corporations and Armed Opposition Groups," 6–5 *J. of Int'l Crim. Justice* 899 (Nov. 2008)

Clark, R.S., "Medina: An Essay on the Principles of Criminal Liability for Homicide," 5 *Rutgers-Camden L. J.* 59 (1975)

Cobb, Capt. James T., 1st Lt. Christopher A. LaCour and SFC William H. Hight, "TF 2–2 in FSE AAR: Indirect Fires in the Battle of Fallujah," *Field Artillery*, 23 (March–April 2005)

Coil, George L., "War Crimes in the American Revolution," 82 *Mil. L. Rev.* 171, 197 (1978)

Commentator, "The Spanish Indictment of High-ranking Rwandan Officials," 6–5 *J. of Int'l Crim. Justice* 1003 (Nov. 2008)

Corn, Maj. Geoffrey, "Hamdan, Fundamental Fairness, and the Significance of Additional Protocol II," *The Army Lawyer* (Aug. 2006)

"International and Operational Law Note," *The Army Lawyer* (July 1998)

"International and Operational Law Note, Principle 2: Distinction," *The Army Lawyer* (Aug. 1998).

"International and Operational Law Note, Principle 4: Preventing Unnecessary Suffering," *The Army Lawyer* (Nov. 1998)

"'Snipers in the Minaret – What Is the Rule?' The Law of War and the Protection of Cultural Property: A Complex Equation," *The Army Lawyer* (July 2005)

Correa, Cristián, "Waterboarding Prisoners and Justifying Torture: Lessons for the U.S. from the Chilean Experience," 14–2 *Human Rights Brief* 21 (Winter 2007), Washington: Center for Human Rights and Humanitarian Law, American University, Washington College of Law (Winter 2007)

Crook, John R., ed., "Contemporary Practice of the United States Relating to International Law," 99–2 *AJIL* (April 2005)

"Contemporary Practice of the United States Relating to International Law: United States Supports Geneva Convention Protocol Authorizing New Emblem," 100–1 *AJIL* 244 (2006)

"Contemporary Practice of the United States Relating to International Law: United States Seeks Limits on Persistent and Non-detectable Landmines," 100–3 *AJIL* 690 (July 2006)

"Contemporary Practice of the United States Relating to International Law: United States Policy Regarding Landmines," 102–1 *AJIL* 190 (Jan. 2008)

"Contemporary Practice of the United States Relating to International Law: President Vetoes Legislation to Limit CIA Interrogation Methods," 102–3 *AJIL* 650 (July 2008)

"Contemporary Practice of the United States Relating to International Law: United States Opposes Ban on Cluster Munitions," 102–4 *AJIL* 889 (Oct. 2008)

"Contemporary Practice of the United States Relating to International Law: United States Responds to ICRC Study on Customary International Law," 101–3 *AJIL* 639 (2009)

Cryer, Robert, "The Boundaries of Liability in International Criminal Law, or 'Selectivity by Stealth'," 6–1 *Conflict & Security L.* 3 (June 2001)

"Of Custom, Treaties, Scholars and the Gavel: The Influence of the International Criminal Tribunals on the ICRC Customary Law Study," 11–2 *J. of Conflict & Security L.* 239 (Summer 2006)

Cutler, Lt.Cmdr. Thomas J., "Exceptionally Heroic Service," U.S. Naval Institute *Proceedings* (Oct. 2013)

D'Amato, Anthony, "Editorial Comment," 84–3 *AJIL* 705 (July 1990)

Danelski, David J., "The Saboteur's Case," vol. 1, *J. of S.Ct. History* (1996)

Daniel, Aubrey M. III, "The Defense of Superior Orders," 7–3 *U. Rich. L. Rev.*, 477 (Spring 1973)

Davidson, Tyler and Kathleen Gibson, "Experts Meeting on Security Detention Report," 40–3 *Case Western Reserve J. Int'l L.* 323 (2009)

Davis, George B., "The Geneva Convention of 1906," 1–2 *AJIL* 409 (April 1907)

Davis, Col. (Dr.) Jim A., USAF, "The Looming Biological Warfare Storm," *Air & Space Power J.*, 57 (Spring 2003)

Davis, Robert S., "Escape from Andersonville: A Study in Isolation and Imprisonment," 67–4 *J. of Military History* 1065 (Oct. 2003)

de Belle, Stéphanie Bouchié, "Chained to Cannons or Wearing Targets on Their T-Shirts," 872 *Int'l Rev. of the Red Cross* 883 (Dec. 2008)

Deeks, Ashley, "'Unwilling or Unable': Toward A Normative Framework for Extra-Territorial Self-Defense," 52–3 *Virginia J. Int'l L.* 483 (2012)

Dehn, Maj. John C., "Permissible Perfidy?" 6–4 *J. of Int'l Crim. Justice* 627 (Sept. 2008)

"Why Article 5 Status Determinations are not 'Required' at Guantanamo," 6–2 *J. of Int'l Crim. Justice*, 371 (May 2008)

Demarest, Geoff, "In Columbia – A Terrorist Sanctuary?" *Military Review*, n.p. (March–April 2002)

Dennis, Michael J., "Current Developments: Newly Adopted Protocols To the Convention on the Rights of the Child," 94–4 *AJIL* 789 (Oct. 2000)

and Andre M. Surena, "Application of the International Covenant on Civil and Political Rights in Times of Armed Conflict and Military Occupation: The Gap Between Legal Theory and State Practice," 6 *European H.R.L. Rev.* 719 (2008)

deVour, R., "Possible Psychological and Societal Effects of Sudden Permanent Blindness of Military Personnel Caused by Battlefield Use of Laser Weapons," in Louise Doswald-Beck, ed., *Blinding Weapons* (Geneva: ICRC, 1993)

Dickinson, Laura A., "Military Lawyers on the Battlefield: An Emperical Account of International Law Compliance," 104–1 *AJIL* 1 (Jan. 2010)

Dietz, Major Jeffrey S., book review of ; LTC Nathan Sassaman, *Warrior King: The Triumph and Betrayal of an American Commander in Iraq* (2008); in *The Army Lawyer* (Aug. 2010)

Dinstein, Yoram, "Comments on Protocol I," 320 *Int'l Rev. of the Red Cross* 515 (Oct. 1997)

"Computer Network Attacks and Self-Defense," in Michael N. Schmitt and Brian T. O'Donnell, eds., *International Law Studies*, vol. 76, *Computer Network Attack and International Law* 99 (Newport RI: Naval War College, 2002)

"Cyber War and International Law: Concluding Remarks at the 2012 Naval War College International Law Conference," 89 *Int'l L. Studies: Cyber War and International Law* (Newport R.I.: U.S. Naval War College, 2013)

"Discussion: Reasonable Military Commanders and Reasonable Civilians," in Andru E. Wall, ed., *International Law Studies*, vol. 78, *Legal and Ethical Lessons of NATO's Kosovo Campaign* (Newport, RI: Naval War College, 2002)

"The Distinction Between Unlawful Combatants and War Criminals," in Yoram Dinstein, ed., *International Law at a Time of Perplexity* (Dordrecht: Nijhoff Publishers, 1989)

"Human Rights in Armed Conflict," in Theodor Meron, ed., *Human Rights in International Law* (Oxford: Clarendon Press, 1984)

"*Ius ad Bellum* Aspects of the 'War on Terrorism,'" in Wybo P. Heere, ed., *Terrorism and the Military* (The Hague: Asser Press, 2003)

"Legitimate Military Objectives Under The Current Jus In Bello," in Andru E. Wall, ed., *International Law Studies*, vol. 78, *Legal and Ethical Lessons of NATO's Kosovo Campaign* (Newport, RI: Naval War College, 2002)

"The Principle of Proportionality," in Kjetil Larsen, Camilla G. Cooper, and Gro Nystuen, *Searchibng for A 'Principle of Humanity,' in International Humanitarian Law* 73 (Cambridge: Cambridge University Press, 2013)

"Unlawful Combatancy," in Fred L. Boch and Paul S. Wilson, eds., *International Law Studies*, vol. 79; *International Law and the War on Terror* (Newport, RI: Naval War College, 2003)

Docherty, Tom, "Alpine Sanctuary," *FlyPast* magazine (Nov. 2014)

Dorf, Michael C., "The Orwellian Military Commissions Act of 2006," 5–1 *J. of Int'l Crim. Justice*, 10 (March 2007)

Dörmann, Knut, "The Legal Situation of 'Unlawful/Unprivileged Combatants,'" 85 *Int'l Rev. of the Red Cross*, 45 (March 2003)

Doswald-Beck, Louise, "New Protocol on Blinding Laser Weapons," 312 *Int'l Rev. of the Red Cross*, 272 (May–June 1996)

"International Humanitarian Law and the Advisory Opinion of the International Court of Justice on the Legality of the Threat or Use of Nuclear Weapons," 316 *Int'l Rev. of the Red Cross* 33 (1997)

and Sylvain Vité, "International Humanitarian Law and Human Rights Law," 293 *Int'l Rev. of the Red Cross* 94 (April 1993)

"Thoughts on Computer Network Attack," in Schmitt and O'Donnell, eds., *International Law Studies*, vol. 76, *Computer Network Attack and International Law* 99 (Newport RI: Naval War College, 2002)

"The *Dover Castle* Case," 16 *Am. J. Int'l L.* 704 (1921)

Downey, William H., "The Law of War and Military Necessity," 47–2 *AJIL* 251 (April 1953)

Doyle, VAdm. James H., Jr., "Computer Networks, Proportionality, and Military Operations," in Schmitt and O'Donnell, eds., *International Law Studies*, vol. 76, *Computer Network Attack and International Law* 99 (Newport RI: Naval War College, 2002)

Draper, G.I.A.D., "The Development of International Humanitarian Law," in Michael A. Meyer and Hilaire McCoubrey, eds., *Reflections on Law and Armed Conflict* (The Hague: Kluwer Law International, 1998)

"Development of the Law of War," in Michael A. Meyer and Hilaire McCoubrey, eds., *Reflections on Law and Armed Conflict* (The Hague: Kluwer Law International, 1998)

"The Historical Background and General Principles of the Geneva Conventions of 1949," in Michael A. Meyer and Hilaire McCoubrey, *Reflections on Law and Armed Conflict* (The Hague: Kluwer Law International, 1998)

"The Interaction of Christianity and Chivalry In the Historical Development of the Laws of War," 5 *Int'l Rev. of the Red Cross* 3 (1965)

"Personnel and Issues of Status," in Michael A. Meyer and Hilaire McCoubrey, eds., *Reflections on Law and Armed Conflicts* (The Hague: Kluwer Law International, 1998)

"Rules Governing the Conduct of Hostilities – the Laws of War and Their Enforcement," in Michael A. Meyer and Hilaire McCoubrey, eds. *Reflections on Law and Armed Conflicts* (The Hague: Kluwer Law, 1998)

"War Criminality," in Michael A. Meyer and Hilaire McCoubrey, eds., *Reflections on Law and Armed Conflicts* (The Hague: Kluwer Law International, 1998)

Droege, Cordula, "Elective Affinities? Human Rights and Humanitarian Law," 871 *Int'l Rev. of the Red Cross* 501 (Sept. 2008)

"Get Off My Cloud: Cyber Warfare, International Humanitarian Law, and the Protection of Civilians," 94–886 *Int'l Rev. of the Rec Cross* 533 (Summer 2012)

"'In Truth the *Leitmotiv*': The Prohibition of Torture and Other Forms of Ill-Treatment in International Humanitarian Law." 867 *Int'l Rev. of the Red Cross* 515 (Sept. 2007)

Dunlap, BGen. Charles, "The End of Innocence: Rethinking Noncombatancy in the Post-Kosovo Era," *Strategic Rev.* 14 (Summer 2000)

Durham, Helen, "International Humanitarian Law and the Gods of War: The Story of Athena Versus Ares," 8–2 *Melbourne J. of Int'l L.* 248 (2007)

Duxbury, Alison, "Drawing Lines in the Sand – Characterising Conflicts For the Purposes of Teaching International Humanitarian Law," 8–2 *Melbourne J. of Int'l L.* 258 (2007)

Eckhardt, Col. William G., "Command Criminal Responsibility: A Plea For A Workable Standard." 97 *Military L. Rev.* 10 (1982)

Edman, Angela J., "Crimes of Sexual Violence in the War Crimes Chamber of the State Court of Bosnia and Herzegovina: Successes and Challenges," 16–1 *Human Rights Brief* 21 American U. Washington College of L. (Spring 2004)

Edwards, Alice, "The Optional Protocol to the Convention Against Torture and the Detention of Refugees," 57–4 *Int'l and Comp. L. Quarterly* 789 (2008)

Eflein, Maj. Dawn R., "A Case Study of Rules of Engagement in Joint Operations," 44 A.F.L. *Rev.* 33 (Jan. 1998)

Eichensehr, Kristen, "On the Offensive: Assassination Policy Under International Law," 25(3) *Harvard Int'l Rev.* (Fall 2003)

Evans, Lt.Cmdr. Brian and Rick Lanchantin, "Lifting the Fog On Cyber Strategy, U.S. Naval Institute *Proceedings* 66 (Oct. 2013)

Evans, Lt.Col. David, "Vincennes: A Case Study," U.S. Naval Institute *Proceedings* (Aug. 1993)

Fenrick, William J., "The Conventional Weapons Convention: A Modest but Useful Treaty," 279 *Int'l Rev. of the Red Cross*, 498 (1990)

"The Rule of Proportionality and Protocol I in Conventional Warfare," 98 *Military L. Rev.* 91 (Fall 1982)

Ferdinandusse, Ward, "On the Question of Dutch Courts' Universal Jurisdiction," 4–4 *J. of Int'l Crim. Justice* 881 (Sept. 2006)

Ferrell, Maj. William H. III, "No Shirt, No Shoes, No Status: Uniforms, Distinction, and Special Operations in International Armed Conflict," 178 *Military L. Rev.* 94 (Winter 2003)

Fichtelberg, Aaron, "Liberal Values in International Criminal Law: A Critique of Erdemović," 6–1 *J. of Int'l Crim. Justice* 3 (March 2008)

Fidler, David P., "The Meaning of Moscow: 'Non-lethal' Weapons and International Law in the Early 21st Century," 859 *Int'l Rev. of the Red Cross* 525 (Sept. 2005)

"The Path to Less Lethal and Destructive War? Technological and Doctrinal Developments and International Humanitarian Law After Iraq and Afghanistan," in Saxon, Dan, ed., *International Humanitarian Law and the Changing Technology of War*, (Leiden: Martinus Nijhoff, 2013)

"The Use of White Phosphorus Munitions by U.S. Military Forces in Iraq, *ASIL Insights* (6 Dec. 2005), at http://www.asil.org/insights051206.cfm

Fischer, Horst, "Television Footage of Prisoners of War: From Violations to War Crimes," *Bofaxe*, No. 244E (24 March 2003)

Fisher, Don C. and John E. Doerr, "Outline of Events in the History of the Modoc War," *Crater Lake Nat'l Park Nature Notes* (Aug. 1937)

Fletcher, George P., "Against Universal Jurisdiction," 1–3 *J. of Int'l Crim. Justice* 580 (Dec. 2003)

"*Hamdan* Confronts the Military Commissions Act of 2006," 45–2 *Columbia J. Transnat'l L.* 427 (2006-2007)

"The Indefinable Concept of Terrorism," 4 *J. of Int'l Criminal Justice* 894 (Nov. 2006)

Fontenot, Col. Gregory, LTC E.J. Degen, and LTC David Tohn, *On Point: The United States Army in Operation Iraqi Freedom* (Fort Leavenworth, KS: Combat Studies Institute Press, 2004)

Franck, Thomas M., "The Taliban, al Qaeda, and the Determination of Illegal Combatants," 96–4 *AJIL* 891 (Oct. 2002)

"On Proportionality of Countermeasures in International Law," 102–4 *AJIL* 715 (Oct. 2008)

Fussnecker, Maj. Jerrod, "The Effects of International Human Rights Law on the Interoperability of Multinational Military Operations," *The Army Lawyer* (May 2014)

Galdorisi, Capt. George, "Keeping Humans in the Loop," *U.S. Naval Institute Proceedings* (Feb. 2015)

Garcia, Michael John, "The War Crimes Act: Current Issues," *Congressional Research Service Report for Congress*, Order Code RS22504 (15 Sept. 2006)

Gardam, Judith Gail, "Proportionality and Force in International Law," 87–3 *AJIL* 391 (July 1993)

Gariepy, Maj. Steven A., "On Self-Defense," (2008) (Unpublished paper in partial fulfillment of Master of Laws degree, Judge Advocate General's Legal Center and School)

Garner, J.W., "Punishment of Offenders Against the Laws and Customs of War," 14 *AJIL*, 70 (1920)

Garraway, Charles H.B., "'Combatants' – Substance or Semantics?," in Michael Schmitt and Jelena Pejic, eds., *International Law and Armed Conflict: Exploring the Faultlines* (Leiden: Martinus Nijhoff, 2007)

"Discussion: Reasonable Military Commanders and Reasonable Civilians," in Andru E. Wall, ed., *International Law Studies*, vol. 78, *Legal and Ethical Lessons of NATO's Kosovo Campaign* (Newport, RI: Naval War College, 2002)

"'England Does Not Love Coalitions.' Does Anything Change?" in Anthony M. Helm, ed., *International Law Studies, Vol. 82, The Law of War in the 21st Century: Weaponry and the Use of Force* (Newport RI: Naval War College, 2006)

"Superior Orders and the International Criminal Court: Justice Delivered or Justice Denied," 836 *Int'l Rev. of the Red Cross*, 785 (Dec. 1999)

"The 'War on Terror': Do the Rules Need Changing?" 3 *Chatham House* (2006)

Gasser, Hans-Peter, "Acts of Terror, 'Terrorism' and International Humanitarian Law," 847 *Int'l Rev. of the Red Cross* 547 (Sept. 2002)

"An Appeal for Ratification by the United States," 81 *AJIL* (Oct. 1987)

Gazzini, Tarcisio, "A Response to Amos Guiora: Pre-Emptive Self-Defence Against Non-State Actors?" 13–1 *J. of Conflict & Security L.* 25 (Spring 2008)

Geiß, Robin, "Asymmetric Conflict Structures," 864 *Int'l Rev. of the Red Cross* 757 (Dec. 2006)

"German War Trials: Judgment in Case of Commander Karl Neumann," 16–4 *AJIL* 704–08 (Oct. 1922)

Gill, Terry D., "The Eleventh of September and the Right of Self-Defense," in Wybo P. Heere, ed., *Terrorism and the Military* (The Hague: Asser Press, 2003)

"The Temporal Dimension of Self-Defense: Anticipation, Pre-emption, Prevention and Immediacy," in Schmitt and Pejic, *International Law and Armed Conflict*: Exploring the Faultlines (Leiden: Martinus Nijhoff, 2007)

Glasser, H.P., "Prohibition of Terrorist Acts in International Humanitarian Law," *Int'l Rev. of the Red Cross* (1986)

Glazier, David, "A Court Without Jurisdiction: A Critical Assessment of the Military Commission Charges Against Omar Khadr," *Social Science Research Network* (31 Aug. 2010)

"Kangaroo Court or Competent Tribunal?: Judging the 21st Century's Military Commission," 89 *Virginia L. Rev.* 2005 (2003)

Goldblat, Jozef, "The Biological Weapons Convention – An Overview," 318 *Int'l Rev. of the Red Cross*, 251 (June 1997)

Goldman, Robert K. and Brian D. Tittemore, "Unprivileged Combatants and the Hostilities in Afghanistan: Their Status and Rights Under International Humanitarian Law and Human Rights Law," ASIL Task Force on Terrorism report (Dec. 2002)

Goldstone, Richard, "The Tension Between Combating Terrorism and Protecting Civil Liberties," in Richard Ashby Wilson, ed., *Human Rights in the 'War on Terror'* (NY: Cambridge University Press, 2005)

Goodman, Ryan, "Editorial Comment: The Detention of Civilians in Armed Conflict," 103–1 *AJIL* 48 (Jan. 2009)

Graham, Col. David E., USA, "The Law of Armed Conflict and the War on Terrorism," in Richard B. Jaques, ed., *International Law Studies: Issues in International Law and Military Operations*, vol. 80 (Newport, RI: Naval War College, 2006)

Granovsky, Maria, "When the Right Action is Illegal: Russian Use of Toxic Chemicals to End the Theater Hostage Crisis in October 2002," unpublished seminar research paper, Georgetown University Law Center (May 2003)

Grant, Rebecca, "An Air War Like No Other," *Air Force* (Nov. 2002)

Green, Leslie C., "Aftermath of Vietnam: War Law and the Soldier," in Richard A. Falk, ed., *The Vietnam War and International Law*, vol. 4 (NJ: Princeton University Press, 1976)

"'Grave Breaches' or Crimes Against Humanity," 8 *J. of Legal Studies* 19 (1997–1998)

Greenwood, Christopher, "Customary Law Status of the 1977 Geneva Protocols," in Astrid J.M. Delissen and Gerard J. Tanja, eds., *Humanitarian Law of Armed Conflict Challenges Ahead.* (Dordrecht: Martinus Nijhoff, 1991)

"Scope of Application of Humanitarian Law," in Dieter Fleck, ed., *The Handbook of Humanitarian Law in Armed Conflict*, 2nd ed. (Oxford: Oxford University Press, 2007)

Grunawalt, Richard J., "The JCS Standing Rules of Engagement: A Judge Advocate's Primer," *Air Force L. Rev.* 245 (1997)

Gross, Michael Joseph, "A Declaration of Cyber-War," *Vanity Fair* (April 2011)

Hampson, Françoise J., "The Relationship Between International Humanitarian Law and Human Rights Law from the Perspective of A Human Rights Treaty Body," 871 *Int'l Rev. of the Red Cross* 549, 550 (Sept. 2008)

Hansen, Maj. Michelle A., "Preventing the Emasculation of Warfare: Halting the Expansion of Human Rights Law into Armed Conflict," 194 *Military L. Rev.* 1 (Winter 2007)

Hanson, Victor Davis, "The Right Man," in Robert Cowley, ed., *No End Save Victory* (NY: Putnam, 2001)

Harel, Alon and Assaf Sharon, "What is Really Wrong With Torture?" 6–2 *J. of Int'l Crim. Justice* 241 (May 2008)

Healey, Jason, "A Brief History of US Cyber Conflict," in Jason Healey, ed., *A Fierce Domain: Conflict in Cyberspace, 1986 to 2012* (Vienna, VA: Cyber Conflict Studies Assn., 2013)

Heller, Jon Heller, "The Non-Existant War Crime of 'Murder in Violation of the Law of War,'" *Opino Juris* blog (2008/08/05)

Henckaerts, Jean-Marie, "The Grave Breaches Regime as Customary International Law," 7–4 *J. Int'l Crim. J.* 683 (Sept. 2009)

Hersh, Seymour M., "A Strike in the Dark," *The New Yorker* (11 and 18 Feb., 2008)
  "The General's Report," *The New Yorker* (25 June 2007)
  "King's Ransom: How Vulnerable Are the Saudi Royals," *New Yorker* (22 Sept. 2001)
  "Manhunt," *The New Yorker* (Dec. 23 & 30, 2002)
  "Overwhelming Force," *The New Yorker* (22 May 2000)

Hershey, Amos S., "History of International Law Since the Peace of Westphalia," 6 *AJIL* 31 (1912)

Hladík, Jan, "The 1954 Hague Convention for the Protection of Cultural Property in the Event of Armed Conflict and the Notion of Military Necessity," 835 *Int'l Rev. of the Red Cross* 621 (Sept. 1999)

Hoffman, Michael H., "Rescuing the Law of War: A Way Forward in an Era of Global Terrorism," *Parameters* (Summer 2005)

Holewinski, Sarah, "Just Trust Us," in Bergen, Peter L. and Daniel Rothenberg, eds., *Drone Wars: Transforming Conflict, Law, and Policy* (NY: Cambridge University Press, 2015)

Hughes, Matthew, "War Without Mercy? American Armed Forces and the Deaths of Civilians During the Battle for Saipan, 1944," 75–1 *J. Military History* 93 (Jan. 2011)

Human Rights First, "Detained and Denied in Afghanistan: How to Make U.S. Detention Comply With the Law" (May 2011)

Human Rights Watch, "Legal Issues Arising From the War In Afghanistan and Related Anti-Terrorism Efforts," (Oct. 2001)
  "Losing Humanity: The Case Against Killer Robots," (2012)
  "Ticking Time Bombs: NATO's Use of Cluster Munitions in Yugoslavia," Human Rights Watch Report 11–6(D), (June 1999)

ICRC, "Interpretive Guidance on the Notion of Direct Participation in Hostilities under International Humanitarian Law," 872 *Int'l Rev. of the Red Cross* (Dec. 2008)

"International Military Tribunal, Nuremberg, Judgment and Sentences," 1946, 41 *AJIL* 172, 248–9 (1947)

Jackson, Richard B., "Lasers Are Lawful as Non-Lethal Weapons," *The Army Lawyer*, 15 (Aug. 2006)

Jacobs, Cmdr. Jan C., "U.S. Naval Aviation and Weapon Development in Review," U.S. Naval Institute *Proceedings* (May 2008)

Jacobsen, Lt.Cmdr. Walter L., "A Juridical Examination of the Israeli Attack on the *U.S.S. Liberty*," 36 *Naval L. Rev.* 1 (Winter 1986)

Jain, Neha, "Forced Marriage as a Crime Against Humanity," 6–5 *J. of Int'l Crim. Justice* 1013 (Nov. 2008)

Jang, Heeyong Daniel, "The Lawfulness Of and Case For Combat Drones in the Fight Against Terrorism," 2–1 *Nat'l Security L. J.* (2013)

Jensen, Eric Talbot, "Computer Attacks on Critical National Infrastructure: A Use of Force Invoking the Right of Self-defense," 38 *Stanford J. Int'l L.*, 207 (2002)

Jescheck, Hans-Heinrich, "The General Principles of International Criminal Law Set Out in Nuremberg, as Mirrored in the ICC Statute," 2–1 *J. of Int'l Crim L.* 38 (March 2004)

Jessberger, Florian, "Bad Torture – Good Torture?" 3–5 *J. of Int'l Crim. Justice* 1059 (Nov. 2005)

Jinks, Derek, "The Applicability of the Geneva Conventions to the 'Global War on Terrorism'," 46–1 *Virginia J. of Int'l L.* 1 (2006)

Jochnick, Chris af and Roger Normand, "The Legitimation of Violence: A Critical History of the Laws of War," 35–1 *Harvard Int'l L. J.* 49 (Winter 1994)

Johansen, Sigred R., "The Occupied and the Occupier: the Case of Norway, in Larsen, Kjetil, Camilla G. Cooper, and Gro Nystuen, *Searchibng for A 'Principle of Humanity,' in International Humanitarian Law* (Cambridge: Cambridge University Press, 2013)

Johnson, Loch K., "On Drawing A Bright Line for Covert Operations," 86–2 *AJIL* 284 (April 1992)

Kalshoven, Frits, "The Conference of Government Experts on the Reaffirmation and Development of International Humanitarian Law Applicable in Armed Conflicts (Second Session), 3 May – 2 June, 1972," in Frits Kalshoven, *Reflections on the Law of War: Collected Essays* (Leiden: Martinus Nijhoff, 2007)

"Reprisals and the Protection of Civilians: Two Recent Decisions of the Yugoslavia Tribunal," in Lal C. Vohrah, et al., eds., *Man's Inhumanity to Man: Essays in Honour of Antonio Cassese*, 481 (The Hague: Kluwer Law International, 2003)

Kakaes, Konstantin, "From Orville Wright to September 11: What the History of Drone Technology Says About Its Future," in Peter L. Bergen and Daniel Rothenberg, eds., *Drone Wars: Transforming Conflict, Law, and Policy* (NY: Cambridge University Press, 2015)

Kasher, Asa and Amos Yadlin, "Assassination and Preventive Killing," XXV no. 1, *SAIS Rev. of Int'l Affairs*, 41 (Winter–Spring 2005)

Kellenberger, Jakob, "Sixty Years of the Geneva Conventions: learning from the past to better face the future, 91–875 *Int'l Rev. of the Red Cross* 613 (Sept. 2009)

Kelsen, Hans, "Collective and Individual Responsibility in International Law With Particular Regard to the Punishment of War Criminals," 31 *Cal. L. Rev.* 530 (1943)

Keller, Kevin Jon, "'One Hell of A Killing Machine': Signature Strikes and International Law," 11-1 *J. of Int'l Crim. Justice* 89 (2013)

Kenton, Henry, "New NSA Data Center Breaks Ground on Construction," *Defense Systems* (Jan. 2011)

Kervers, Onno, "Strengthening Compliance with the Biological Weapons Convention: The Protocol Negotiations," 7–2 *J. of Conflict & Security L.* 275 (Oct. 2002)

Kinacioglu, Muge, "A Response to Amos Guiora: Reassessing the Parameters of Use of Force in the Age of Terrorism," 13–1 *J. of Conflict & Security L.* 33 (Spring 2008)

Kissinger, Henry A., "The Pitfalls of Universal Jurisdiction," *Foreign Affairs* (July/August 2001)

Kleffner, Jann K., "The applicability of International Humanitarian Law to Organized Armed Groups," 93–882 *Int'l Rev. of the Red Cross* 443 (June 2011)

Kline, Adam and Benjamin Wittes, "Preventive Detention in American Theory and Practice," 85 *Harvard Nat'l Security J.* 85 (2011)

Kolb, Robert, "Main Epochs of Modern International Humanitarian Law Since 1864," in Kjetil Larsen, Camilla G. Cooper, and Gro Nystuen, *Searchibng for A 'Principle of Humanity,'* (Cambridge: Cambridge University Press, 2013)

Koplow, David A., Review: Michael Bothe, Natalino Ronzitti, and Allan Rosas, eds., *The New Chemical Weapons Convention* (2000), 94-1 AJIL 221 (Jan. 2000 book review)

Koskenniemi, Martti, "Hersch Lauterpacht and the Development of International Criminal Law," 2–3 *J. of Int'l Crim. Justice* 810 (Sept. 2004)

Kreß, Claus, "The Fine Line Between Collective Self-Defense and Intervention by Invitation: Reflections on the Use of Force Against 'IS' in Syria," *Just Security* blog (17 Feb. 2015)

Kretzmer, David, "Targeted Killing of Suspected Terrorists: Extra-Judicial Executions or Legitimate Means of Defence?" 16–2 *European J. of Int'l L.*, 171 (2005)

Krieger, Heike, "A Conflict of Norms: The Relationship Between Humanitarian Law and Human Rights Law in the ICRC Customary Law Study," 11–2 *J. of Conflict & Security L.*, 265 (Summer 2006)

Lacey, Maj. Michael, "Passage of Amended Protocol II," *The Army Lawyer* (March 2000)

LaFontaine, Fanny, "Canada's Crimes Against Humanity and War Crimes Act on Trial," 8–1 *J. Int'l. Crim. Justice* 269 (March 2010)

Landrum, Maj. Bruce D., "The Yamashita War Crimes Trial: Command Responsibility Then and Now," 149 *Mil. L. Rev.* 293 (1995)

Langbein, John H., "The Legal History of Torture," in Sanford Levinson, ed., *Torture: A Collection* (NY: Oxford University Press, 2004)

Langston, Emily, "The superior responsibility doctrine in international law: Historical continuities, innovation and criminality: Can East Timor's Special Panels bring militia leaders to justice?" 4–2 *Int'l Crim. L. Rev.* 141 (2004)

LaRosa, Anne-Marie and Carolin Wuerzner, "Armed Groups, Sanctions and the Implementation of International Humanitarian Law," 870 *Int'l Rev. of the Red Cross* 327 (June 2008)

Larsen, Kjetil M., "A 'Principle of Humanity' or a 'Principle of Human-rightism'? in Kjetil Larsen, Camilla G. Cooper, and Gro Nystuen, *Searchibng for A 'Principle of Humanity,'in International Humanitarian Law* (Cambridge: Cambridge University Press, 2013)

  and Camilla G. Cooper and Gro Nystuen, "Introduction by the editors," in Kjetil Larsen, Cooper, and Nystuen, *Searchibng for A 'Principle of Humanity,'in International Humanitarian Law* (Cambridge: Cambridge University Press, 2013)

  and Camilla G. Cooper, "Conclusion," in Larsen, Cooper, and Gro Nystuen, *Searchibng for A 'Principle of Humanity,'in International Humanitarian Law* (Cambridge: Cambridge University Press, 2013)

Lauterpacht, Hersch, "The Law of Nations and the Punishment of War Crimes," 21 *British Yearbook of Int'l L.* 58 (1944)

Leich, Marian Nash, "Agora: The Downing of Iran Air Flight 655, An Introduction," 83–2 AJIL 318 (April, 1989)

  "Denial of Liability:"*ex Gratia* Compensation on a Humanitarian Basis," 83–2 AJIL 318 (April, 1989)

Levie, Col. Howard S., "Command Responsibility," 8 *USAF Academy J. of Legal Studies*, 1, 3 (1997–98)

  "The Rise and Fall of an Internationally Codified Denial of the Defense of Superior Orders," 30 *Mil. L. & L. of War Rev.* 204 (1991)

Lewis, Michael W., "The Law of Aerial Bombardment in the 1991 Gulf War," 97–3 AJIL 481 (July 2003)

Lewy, Guenter, "Superior Orders, Nuclear Warfare, and Conscience," in, Richard Wasserstrom, ed., *War and Morality* (Belmont CA: Wadsworth Publishing, 1970)

Liaropoulos, Andrew N., "Revolutions in Warfare: Theoretical Paradigms and Historical Evidence – The Napoleonic and First World War Revolutions in Military Affairs," 70–2 *J. of Military History* 363 (April 2006)

Lijnzaad, Liesbeth, "Developments in International Humanitarian Law Since 1977," in, *Protecting Human Dignity in Armed Conflict* (The Hague: Netherlands Red Cross, 2008)

Lillich, Richard B., "Forcible Self-Help Under International Law," in John Norton Moore and Robert F. Turner, *National Security Law*, 2d ed. (Durham NC: Carolina Academic Press, 2005), 113

Linton, Suzannah, "New approaches to international justice in Cambodia and East Timor," 845 *Int'l Rev. of the Red Cross* 93 (2002)

"The *Llandovery Castle* Case," 16 *Am. J. Int'l L.* 705 (1921)

Lofgren, Stephen J., ed., "Diary of First Lieutenant Sugihara Kinryû: Iwo Jima, January–February 1945" 59 *J. Military History,* 97 (Jan. 1995)

Liu, Hin-Yan, "Categorization and Legality of Autonomous and Remote Weapons Systems, "94/886 *Int'l Rev. of the Red Cross* 627 (Summer, 2012)

London, J.P., "Made in China," U.S. Naval Institute *Proceedings* 54 (April 2011)

Lootsteen, Lt.Col. Yair M., "The Concept of Belligerency in International Law," 166 *Military L. Rev.* 109 (Dec. 2000)

Lorenz, Col. Frederick M., "Law and Anarchy in Somalia," 23 *Parameters* 39 (1993–1994)

Luban, David, "Liberalism, Torture, and the Ticking Bomb," 91 *Va. L. Rev.* 1425 (2005)

MacDonald, Maj. Timothy C., "Military Commissions and Courts-Martial: A Brief Discussion of the Constitutional and Jurisdictional Distinctions Between the Two Courts," *The Army Lawyer* (Jan. 2015)

MacLeod, I.J. and A.P.V. Rogers, "The Use of White Phosphorous and the Law of War," in Timothy L.H. McCormack, ed., *Yearbook of International Humanitarian Law* (The Hague: Asser Press, 2009)

Maged, Adel, "International Legal Cooperation: An Essential Tool in the War Against Terrorism," in Wybo P. Heere, ed., *Terrorism and the Military: International Legal Implications* (The Hague: Asser Press, 2003)

Mallison, W. Thomas, "The Disturbing Questions," 63 *Freedom at Issue* 9 (Nov.–Dec. 1981)

Mandiant Intelligence Center Report, Advanced Persistent Threat 1: Exposing One of China's Cyber Espionage Units (Jan. 2013)

Mann, Christopher, "Combined Operations, the Commandos, and Norway, 1941–1944," 73–2 *J. of Military History* 471 (April 2009)

Maogoto, Jackson N., "The Superior Orders Defense: A Game of Musical Chairs and the Jury is Still Out," 10 *Flinders J. of L. Reform* 1 (2007)

Maresca, Louis, "A New Protocol on Explosive Remnants of War: The History and Negotiation of Protocol V to the 1980 Convention on Certain Conventional Weapons," 86 *Int'l Rev. of the Red Cross* 815 (Dec. 2004)

Margetts, Katharina and Patrick Hayden, "Current Developments at the ad hoc International Criminal Tribunals," 8–2 *J. Int'l. Crim. Justice* 249 (May 2010)

Maridakis, Georges S. (1890–1979), "An Ancient Precedent to Nuremberg," re-published in 4–4 *J. of Int'l Crim. Justice* (Sept. 2006)

Marsh, Maj. J. Jeremy, "Lex Lata or Lex Ferenda? Rule 45 of the ICRC Study on Customary International Humanitarian Law," 198 *Military L. Rev.* 116 (Winter 2008)

Martinez, Jenny S., "Understanding Mens Rea in Command Responsibility, 5–3 *J. of Int'l Crim. Justice,* 638 (July 2007)

Martins, Maj. Mark S., "Rules of Engagement for Land Forces: A Matter of Training, Not Lawyering," 143 *Military L. Rev.* 3 (Winter 1994)

Matheson, Michael J., "Additional Protocol I as Expressions of Customary International Law," 2–2 *Am. U. J. Int'l L. & Policy* 415 (Fall 1987)
    Review: Lindsay Moir, *The Law of Internal Armed Conflict*, 97–2 AJIL 466, 467 (April 2003))

Mathews, Robert J., "The 1980 Convention on Certain Conventional Weapons: A Useful Framework Despite Earlier Disappointments," 844 *Int'l Rev. of the Red Cross*, 991 (2001)
    and Timothy L.H. McCormack, "The Influence of Humanitarian Principles in the Negotiation of Arms Control Treaties," 834 *Int'l Rev. of the Red Cross* 331 (June 1999)

Mayer, Lt.Col. Terry N., USAF, "The Biological Weapon: A Poor Nation's Weapon of Mass Destruction," in Berry R. Schneider and Lawrence E. Grinter, eds., *Battlefield of the Future: 21st Century Warfare Issues* (Maxwell Air Force Base, AL: Air Warfare College, Sept. 1995)

McCall, Sherman, M.D., "A Higher Form of Killing," U.S. Naval Institute *Proceedings* 38 (Feb. 1995)

McCormack, Timothy L. H., "From Sun Tzu to the Sixth Committee: The Evolution of an International Criminal Law Regime," in Timothy McCormack and Gerry J. Simpson, eds., *The Law of War Crimes: National and International Approaches* (The Hague: Kluwer, 1997)

McDonald, Avril, "Terrorism, Counter-terrorism and the *Jus in Bello*," in Int'l Institute of Humanitarian Law, *Terrorism and International Law: Challenges and Responses* (Sanremo Italy: IIHL, 2002)

McDonnell, Thomas M., "Cluster Bombs Over Kosovo: A Violation of International Law?" 44 *Ariz. L. Rev.* 31 (2002)

McFarland, Tim and Tim McCormack, "Mind the Gap: Can Developers of Autonomous Weapons Systems be Liable for War Crimes?" in *Int'l L. Studies*, vol. 90 (Newport R.I., US Naval War College, 2014)

"Means of Warfare: Interview with Terence Taylor," 859 *Int'l Rev. of the Red Cross* 419 (Sept. 2005)

Meilinger, Phillip S., book review of Robert S. Ehlers, Jr., *Targeting the Third Reich: Air Intelligence and the Allied Bombing Campaign*, 74–2 *J. Military History* 631 (April 2010)

Meisels, Tamar, "Combatants – Lawful and Unlawful," 26–1 *L. & Phil.* 31 (2007)

Meloni, Chantal, "Command Responsibility," 5–3 *J. of Int'l Crim. Justice*, 619 (July 2007)

Melzer, Nils, "Human Rights Implications of the Usage of Drones and Unmanned Robots in Warfare," Study, European Parliament, Directorate-General for External Policies, Policy Dept., (May 2013)

"Memorandum for Commander, United States Army Special Operations Command; Subject: Sniper Use of Open-Tip Ammunition", (23 Sept. 1985), 86 *The Army Lawyer* (Feb. 1991)

Menon, Jaykumar A., "Guantánamo Torture Litigation," 6–2 *J. of Int'l Crim. Justice* 323 (May 2008)

Meron, Theodor, "The Geneva Conventions as Customary Law," 81–2 *AJIL* 348 (April 1987)
    "The Humanization of Humanitarian Law," 94 *AJIL* 239 (2000)
    "International Criminalization of Internal Atrocities," 89–3 *AJIL* 554 (July 1995)
    "Leaders, Courtiers and Command Responsibility in Shakespeare," in Michael Schmitt and Jelena Pejic, eds., *International Law and Armed Conflict: Exploring the Faultlines* (Leiden: Martinus Nijhoff, 2007)
    "Rape as a Crime Under International Humanitarian Law," 87–3 *AJIL* 424 (July 1993)
    "Reflections on the Prosecution of War Crimes by International Tribunals," 100–3 *AJIL* 551 (July 2007)

"The Time Has Come for the United States to Ratify Geneva Protocol I," 88 *AJIL* 678 (1994)

Meselson, Matthew S., "Chemical and Biological Weapons," 222–5 *Scientific American*, 3 (May 1970)

Mettraux, Guénaël, "US Courts-Martial and the Armed Conflict in the Philippines (1899–1902): Their Contribution to National Case Law on War Crimes," 1–1 *J. of Int'l Crim. Justice* 134 (April 2003)

"Dutch Courts' Universal Jurisdiction over Violations of Common Article 3 *qua* War Crimes," 4–2 *J. of Int'l Crim. Justice* 362 (May 2006)

"A Little-Known Case From the American Civil War," 8–4 *J. Int'l Crim. J.* 1059 (Sept. 2010)

Meyer, Maj. Richard V., "When a Rose is Not a Rose: Military Commissions v. Courts-Martial," 5–1 *J. of Int'l Crim. Justice*, 48 (March 2007)

Meyrowitz, Henri, "The Principle of Superfluous Injury or Unnecessary Suffering," 299 *Int'l Rev. of the Red Cross* 98 (March–April 1994)

Milanovic, Marko, "Lessons for Human Rights and Humanitarian Law in the War on Terror: Comparing Hamdan and the Israeli Targeted Killing Case," 866 *Int'l Rev. of the Red Cross* 373 (June 2007)

Miles, Col. James R., "Francis Lieber and the Law of War." XXIX-1–2 *Revue de Droit Militaire et de Droit de la Guerre*, 256 (1990)

Moir, Lindsay, "Grave Breaches and Internal Armed Conflicts," 7–4 *J. Int'l Crim. J.* 763 (Sept. 2009)

Montgomery, Col. Tony, "Legal Perspective from the EUCOM Targeting Cell," in Andru E. Wall, ed., *International Law Studies*, vol. 78, *Legal and Ethical Lessons of NATO's Kosovo Campaign* (Newport RI: Naval War College, 2002)

Moussa, Jasmine, "Can *jus ad bellum* Override *jus in bello*? Reaffirming the Separation of the Two Bodies of Law," 827 *Int'l Rev. of the Red Cross* 963 (Dec. 2008)

Mowchan, Lt.Cmdr. John A., "Don't Draw the (Red) Line," U.S. Naval Institute *Proceedings* 10 (Oct. 2011)

Munir, Muhammad, "The *Layha* for the *Mujahideen*: an analysis of the code of conduct for the Taliban fighters under Islamic law," 93–881 *Int'l. Rev. of the Red Cross* 81 (March 2011)

Murphy, John F., "Some Legal (and a Few Ethical) Dimensions of the Collateral Damage Resulting from NATO's Kosovo Campaign," 31 *Israel Yearbook on Human Rights* 51 (2001)

Murphy, Sean D., ed., "Contemporary Practice of the United States Relating to International Law: U.S. Rejection of Protocol to Biological Weapons Convention," 95–4 *AJIL* 899 (Oct. 2001)

"Progress and Jurisprudence of the International Criminal Tribunal for the Former Yugoslavia," 93–1 *AJIL* 57 (Jan. 1999)

"Self-Defense and the Israeli *Wall* Advisory Opinion: An *Ipse Dixit* From the ICJ?" 99–1 *AJIL* 62 (Jan. 2005)

"Terrorism and the Concept of 'Armed Attack' in Article 51 of the U.N. Charter," 43 *Harvard Int'l L. J.* 41 (2002)

Murray, Williamson, "The Meaning of World War II," 8 *Joint Forces Quarterly* 50 (Summer 1995)

Nagel, Thomas, "War and Massacre," 1 *Phil. & Public Affairs* 123 (1972)

Nahlik, Stanislaw E., "A Brief Outline of International Humanitarian Law," in *Int'l Rev. of the Red Cross* (July–August, 1984)

Nash, Marian, "Contemporary Practice of the United States Relating to International Law," 88–2 *AJIL* (April 1994), 312, 323.

Neuborne, Burt, "Spheres of Justice: Who Decides?", 74–5/6 *The George Washington L. R.* 1090 (Aug. 2006)

Newton, Michael A., "Reconsidering Reprisals," 20 *Duke J. Comparative & Int'l L.* 361 (2010)

O'Connell, Mary Ellen, "Unlawful Killing With Combat Drones," *Notre Dame Law School, Legal Studies Research Paper No. 09-43* (Draft: Nov. 2009)

Ohlin, Jens David, "The Bounds of Necessity," 6–2 *J. of Int'l Crim. Justice* 289 (May 2008)

Ohls, Col. Gary J., "Eastern Exit: Rescue 'From the Sea'," 61–4 *Naval War College Rev.* 125 (Autumn 2008)

Ohman, Maj. Mynda G., "Integrating Title 18 War Crimes into Title 10: A Proposal to Amend the Uniform Code of Military Justice," 57 *Air Force L. R.* 1 (2005)

O'Reilly, Arthur T., "Command Responsibility: A Call to Realign Doctrine with Principles," 20–1 *Am. U. Int'l L. Rev.* 71 (2004)

Orie, Alphons M.M., "*Stare decisis* in the ICTY Appeal Sysyem," 10–3 *J. Int'l Crim J.* 635 (July 2012)

Oxman, Bernard H., "International Decisions," 91–3 *AJIL* 518 (July 1997)

Parkerson, John Embry, Jr., "United States Compliance with Humanitarian Law Respecting Civilians During Operation Just Cause," 133 *Mil. L. Rev.* 31 (1991)

Parks, W. Hays, "Air War and the Law of War," 32–1 *Air Force L. Rev.* 1 (1990)

"Command Responsibility for War Crimes," 62 *Military L. Rev.*, 1 (1973)

"Conventional Weapons and Weapons Reviews," in 8 *Yearbook of IHL* (2005)

"Deadly Force *Is* Authorized," *Proceedings* (Jan. 2001)

"Friendly Fire: The Accidental Shootdown of U.S. Black Hawks Over Northern Iraq," (book review) U.S. Naval Institute's *Proceedings* (Aug. 1999)

"Joint Service Combat Shotgun Program," *The Army Lawyer* (Oct. 1997)

"Part IX of the ICRC 'Direct Participation in Hostilities' Study: No Mandate, No Expertise, and Legally Incorrect," 42 *N.Y.U.J. Int'l L. & Pol.* 769 (2010)

"Righting the Rules of Engagement," U.S. Naval Institute *Proceedings* 83 (May 1989)

"'Special Forces' Wear of Non-Standard Uniforms," 4 *Chicago J. of Int'l L.* 519 (2003)

Patch, Cmdr. John, "Taking Out Saddam's Floating Pleasure Palace," U.S. Naval Institute's *Proceedings* (Sept. 2008)

Patton, Maj. George S., Jr., "The Effect of Weapons on War," *Cavalry Journal* (Nov. 1930)

Paulus, Andreas **and** Mindia Vashakmadze, "Asymmetrical war and the notion of armed conflict – a tentative conceptualization," 91/873 *Int'l Rev. of the Red Cross* 95 (March 2009)

Paust, Jordan J., "Detention and Due Process Under International Law," in Wybo P. Heere, ed., *Terrorism and the Military* (The Hague: Asser Press, 2003)

Letter of J.J. Paust, 25 *Naval War College Rev.* (Jan.–Feb 1973)

"My Lai and Vietnam: Norms, Myths and Leader Responsibility," 57 *Military L. Rev.* 99 (1972)

Pejic, Jelena, "Extraterritorial targeting by means of armed drones: Some legal implications," 96/893 *Int'l Rev. of the Red Cross* 67 (Spring 2014)

"Procedural Principles and Safeguards for Internment/Administrative Detention in Armed Conflict and Other Situations of Violence," 876/858 *Int'l Rev. of the Red Cross* 375 (June 2005)

"The Protective Scope of Common Article 3: More Than Meets the Eye," 93–881 *Int'l Rev. of the Red Cross*, 189 (March 2011)

"Terrorist Acts and Groups: A Role for International Law?" 75 *BYIL* 71 (2004)

"'Unlawful/Enemy Combatants:' Interpretations and Consequences," in Michael Schmitt and Jelena Pejic, eds., *International Law and Armed Conflict: Exploring the Faultlines* (Leiden: Martinus Nijhoff, 2007)

Perry, Dr. David L., "Battlefield Euthanasia: Shgould Mercy-Killings Be Allowed? (44–4 *Parameters* 119 (Winter, 2014–15)

Petrig, Anna, "The war dead and their gravesites," 91–874 *Int'l. Rev. of the Rec Cross* 341 (June 2009)

Pinzauti, Giulia, "Protecting Prisoners of War," 8–1 *J. Int'l Crim. J.* 199 (March 2010)

Pfanner, Toni, "Editorial," 859 *Int'l Rev. of the Red Cross* 413 (Sept. 2005)

"Editorial," 867 *Int'l Rev. of the Red Cross* (Sept. 2007)

"Interview with General Sir Rupert Smith," 864 *Int'l Rev. of the Red Cross* 720 (Dec. 2006)

Polmar, Norman and Thomas B. Allen, "The Most Deadly Plan," U.S. Naval Institute *Proceedings* (Jan. 1998)

Pregent, Richard, "Cyber Defense and Counter-Intelligence," 26 NATO *Legal Gazette* 13 (Sept. 2011)

Proulx, Vincent Joël, "If the Hat Fits, Wear It, If the Turban Fits, Run for Your Life: Reflections on the Indefinite Detention and Targeted Killing of Suspected Terrorists," 56 *Hastings L. J.*, 801 (2004–2005)

Prugh, Maj. Gen. George S., "Armed Forces and Development of the Law of War," Armed Forces and the Development of the Law of War (*Recueils de la Société Internationale de Droit Pénal Militaire et de Droit de la Guerre*) (1982)

Pustogarov, Vladimir V., "Fyodor Fyodorovich Martens (1845–1909) – A Humanist of Modern Times," 312 *Int'l Rev. of the Red Cross* 300 (1966)

Quéguiner, Jean-François, "Precautions Under the Law Governing the Conduct of Hostilities," 864 *Int'l Rev. of the Red Cross* 793 (Dec. 2006)

Ratner, Steven R., "Predator and Prey: Seizing and Killing Suspected Terrorists Abroad," 15–3 *J. of Pol. Philosophy* 251 (2007)

Reeves, Jesse S., "The Neutralization of Belgium and the Doctrine of Kriegsraison," XIII, No. 3 *Michigan L. Rev.* 179 (1914–1915)

Reinold, Theresa, "State Weakness, Irregular Warfare, and the Right to Self-Defense Post 9/11," 105–2 *AJIL* 244 (April 2011)

Reisman, W. Michael, "Assessing Claims to Revise the Laws of War," 97–1 *AJIL* 82, 86 (Jan. 2003)

"Editorial Comment: Holding the Center of the Law of Armed Conflict," 100–4 *AJIL* 852 (Oct. 2006)

"Respect for Human Dignity in Today's Germany," 4–4 *J. of Int'l Crim. Justice* 862 (Sept. 2006)

and James Silk, "Which Law Applies To the Afghan Conflict?", 82–3 *AJIL* 459 (July, 1988)

Reydams, Luc, "Belgium Reneges on Universality," 1–3 *J. of Int'l Crim. Justice* (Dec. 2003)

"'A la Guerre Comme à la guerre:' Patterns of Armed Conflict, Humanitarian Law Responses and New Challenges," 864 *Int'l Rev. of the Red Cross*, 729 (Dec. 2006)

Reyes, Hernán, "The Worst Scars Are in the Mind: Psychological Torture," 867 *Int'l Rev. of the Red Cross*, 591 (Sept. 2007)

Reynolds, Maj. Jefferson D., "Collateral Damage on the 21st Century Battlefield: Enemy Exploitation of the Law of Armed Conflict and the Struggle for a Moral High Ground," 56 *Air Force L. Rev.* (Jan. 2005)

Richardson, Brian, "The Use of Vattel in the American Law of Nations," 106–3 *AJIL* 547 (July 2012)

Riggs, Maj. Ronald M., "The Grenada Intervention: A Legal Analysis," 109 *Military L. Rev.* 1 (1985)

Roach, Capt. Ashley, "Rules of Engagement," *Naval War College Rev.* (Jan.–Feb., 1983)

Roberts, Adam, "Detainees: Misfits in Peace and War," in Sibylle Scheipers, ed., *Prisoners in War* (Oxford: Oxford University Press, 2010)

"Environmental Issues in International Armed Conflict: The Experiences of the 1991 Gulf War," 69 *Int'l. L. Studies* 222 (1996)

"The Equal Application of the Laws of War: A Principle under Pressure," 872 *Int'l Rev. of the Red Cross* (Dec. 2008)

"The Laws of War in the War on Terror," in Wybo P. Heere, ed., *Terrorism and the Military: International Legal Implications* (The Hague: Asser Press, 2003)

Roberts, Ken, "The Contribution of the ICTY to the Grave Breaches Regime," 7–4 *J. of Int'l Crim. J.* 743 (Sept. 2009)

Rogers, MGen. A.V.P., "Zero-Casualty Warfare," 837 *Int'l Rev. of the Red Cross* 165 (March 2000)

Röling, Bert V.A., "Are Grotius' Ideas Obsolete in an Expanded World?" in Hedley Bull, Benedict Kingsbury, and Adam Roberts, eds., *Hugo Grotius and International Relations* (Oxford: Clarendon Press, 1990)

Rona, Gabor, "An Appraisal of US Practice Relating to 'Enemy Combatants'," in Timothy L.H. McCormack, ed., *Yearbook of I.H.L.*, Vol. 10, 2007 (The Hague: T.M.C. Asser Press, 2009)

Roos, John G., "Editorial: Torture and Terrorists," *Armed Forces J.* (May 2005)

Rose, Cmdr. Stephen, "The Coming Explosion of Silent Weapons," 42 *Naval War College Rev.* 6 (Summer 1989)

Rosenbaum, Eli M., "An Introduction to the Work of the Office of Special Investigations," 54–1 *United States Attorneys' Bulletin* 1 (Jan. 2006)

Rosenthal, Joel, "New Rules For War?" Vol. LVII, No. 3/4, *Naval War College Rev.* (2004)

Ross, James, "A History of Torture," in Kenneth Roth, Minky Worden, and Amy Bernstein, eds., *Torture* (NY: The New Press, 2005)

"Black Letter Abuse: the Legal Response to Torture Since 9/11," 867 *Int'l Rev. of the Red Cross* 561 (Sept. 2007)

Rowe, Peter, "Kosovo 1999: The Air Campaign – Have the Provisions of Additional Protocol I Withstood the Test?" 837 *Int'l Rev. of the Red Cross* 147 (2000)

"The Rules of Engagement in Occupied Territory: Should They Be Published?" 8–2 *Melbourne J. of Int'l L.* 327 (2007)

Rubin, Uzi, "Hizballah's Rocket Campaign Against Northern Israel: A Preliminary Report," *Jerusalem Center for Public Affairs* (31 Aug. 2006)

Sassòli, Marco, "Autonomous Weapons and International Law: Advantages, Open Technological Questions and Legal Issues To Be Clarified," *Int'l Legal Studies*, vol. 90 (Newport R.I., US Naval War College, 2014)

"The Implementation of International Humanitarian Law: Current and Inherent Challenges," in Timothy L.H. McCormack, ed., *Yearbook of International Humanitarian Law* (The Hague: Asser Press, 2009)

and Lindsey Cameron, "The Protection of Civilian Objects – Current State of the Law and Issues *de lege ferenda*," in, Natalino Ronzitti and Gabriella Venturini, eds., *The Law of Air Warfare* (Utrecht, Netherlands: Eleven International Publishing, 2006)

"Query: Is There a Status of "Unlawful combatant?'," in Richard B. Jaques, ed., *International Law Studies: Issues in International Law and Military Operations*, vol. 80 (Newport, RI: Naval War College, 2006)

and Laura M. Olson, "The Relationship Between International Humanitarian and Human Rights Law Where it Matters: Admissible Killing and Internment of Fighters in Non-International Armed Conflicts," 90–871 *Int'l Rev. of the Red Cross* 599 (Sept. 2008)

"The Status of Persons Held in Guantanamo under International Humanitarian Law," 2–1 *J. of Int'l Crim. Justice* 96 (March 2004)

"Terrorism and War," in 4–5 *J. of Int'l Criminal Justice* 958 (Nov. 2006)

Saxon, Dan, "Introduction," in Dan Saxon, ed., *International Humaniarian Law and the Changing Technology of War* (Boston: Martinus Nijhoff, 2013)

Scharf, Michael P. and Gwen Gillespie, "Foreword: Security Detention," 40–3 *Case Western Reserve J. Int'l L.* 315 (2009)

Schmider, Klaus, "The Last of the First: Veterans of the Jagdwaffe Tell Their Story," 73–1 *J. of Military History* 231 (Jan. 2009)

Schmitt, Michael N., "Below the 'Threshold' Cyber Operations: The Countermeasures Response Option and International Law," 54–2 *Virginia J. Int'l L.* 697 (2014)

"Charting the Legal Geography of Non-International Armed Conflict," 90 *Int'l L. Studies*, 1 U.S. Naval War College 1 (2014)

"Classification of Cyber Conflict," 17 *J. of Conflict & Security L.*, 245 (2012)

"Extraterritorial Lethal Targeting: Deconstructing the Logic of International Law," 52–1 *Columbia J. of Transnational L.* 77 (2013)

"The Interpretive Guidance on the Notion of Direct Participation in Hostilities: A Critical Analysis," 1 *Harvard Nat'l Security J.* 5 (May 2010)

"The Law of Cyber Targeting," 68–2 *Naval War College Rev.* 11,26 (Spring, 2015)

"The Law of Cyber Warfare: Quo Vadis?" 25–2 *Stanford L. & Pol. Rev.* 269 (June 2014)

and Eric W. Widmar, "On Target: Precision and Balance in the Contemporary Law of Targeting," 7 *J. of Nat'l Security & Policy* 379 (2014)

and Jeffrey S. Thurnher, "Out of the Loop: Autonomous Weopens Systems and the Law of Armed Conflict," 4–2 *Harvard National Security Journal* 231, 233 (2013)

"Precision Attack and International Humanitarian Law," 859 *Int'l Rev. of the Red Cross* 445 (Sept. 2005)

"Responding to Transnational Terrorism Under the *Jus ad Bellum*: A Normative Framework," in Michael Schmitt and Jelena Pejic, eds., *International Law and Armed Conflict: Exploring the Faultlines* (Leiden: Martinus Nijhoff, 2007)

"Targeting and Humanitarian Law: Current Issues," 33 *Israel Yearbook on Human Rights* 59 (2003)

"War and the Environment: Fault Lines in the Prescriptive Landscape," in, Jay E. Austin and Carl E. Bruch, eds. (NY: Cambridge University Press, 2000)

"War, Technology and the Law of Armed Conflict," in Anthony M. Helm, ed., *International Law Studies, Vol. 82, The Law of War in the 21st Century: Weaponry and the Use of Force* (Newport RI: Naval War College, 2006)

"Wired Warfare: Computer Network Attack and Jus in Bello," 846 *Int'l Rev. of the Red Cross* 365 (June 2002)

Schomburg, Wolfgang and Ines Peterson, "Genuine Consent to Sexual Violence Under International Criminal Law," 101–1 *AJIL* 121 (Jan. 2007)

Schutte, Julian J.E., "The System of Repression of Breaches of Additional Protocol I," in, Astrid J.M. Delissen and Gerard J. Tanja, eds., *Humanitarian Law of Armed Conflict Challenges Ahead* (Dordrecht: Martinus Nijhoff, 1991)

Schwarzenberger, Georg, "Judgment of Nuremberg," 21 *Tulsa L. Rev.* (1947)

Seaquist, Capt. Larry, USN, "Community War," U.S. Naval Institute *Proceedings* (Aug. 2000)

Sennott, Maj. Daniel J., "Interpreting Recent Changes to the Standing Rules for the Use of Force," *The Army Lawyer* (Nov. 2007)

Shah, Sikander A., *Daniel Moeckli's Human Rights and Non-discrimination in the War on Terror* 103–3 *AJIL* 635 (July 2009 - Book review)

Sharkey, Noel E., "The evitability of autonomous robot warfare," 94/886 *Int'l Rev. of the Red Cross* 787 (Summer 2012)

Shatz, Adam, "The Torture of Algiers," *The New York Review of Books* (21 Nov. 2002)

Shelton, Lt.Col. Raymond S., "No Democracy Can Feel Secure," U.S. Naval Institute *Proceedings* (Aug. 1998)

Simpson, Gerry J., "War Crimes: A Critical Introduction," in Timothy L.H. McCormack and Gerry J. Simpson, eds., *The Law of War Crimes: National and International Approaches* (The Hague: Kluwer Law International, 1997)

Sivakumaran, Sandesh, "Command Responsibility in Irregular Groups," 10–5 *J. Int'l Crim. Justice* 1129 (Dec. 2012)

Smidt, Maj. Michael L., "Yamashita, Medina, and Beyond: Command Responsibility in Contemporary Military Operations," 164 *Military L. Rev.* 155 (June 2000)

Sofaer, Abraham D., "Agora: The Rationale for the United States Decision," 82 *AJIL* 784 (1988)

"Terrorism, the Law, and the National Defense." 126 *Military L. Rev.* 89 (1989)

Solf, Waldemar, "Article 52," in Michael Bothe, Karl Partsch, and Waldemar Solf, eds., *New Rules for Victims of Armed Conflict: Commentary on the Two 1977 Protocols Additional to the Geneva Conventions of 1949* (Hague: Martinus Nijhoff, 1982)

"A Response to Douglas J. Feith's Law in the Service of Terror – The Strange Case of the Additional Protocol," 20 *Akron L. Rev.* 261 (1986)

Solis, Lt.Col. Gary, "Obedience of Orders and the Law of War: Judicial Application in American Forums," 15 *American U. Int'l L.* Rev. 481 (2000)

"Military Justice?" *U.S. Naval Institute Proceedings* (Oct. 2006)

Souder, Maj. Jeffrey K., "Information Operations in Homeland Computer-Network Defense," *J. Electronic Def.* (1 Oct. 2001)

Spataro, Armando, "Why Do People Become Terrorists?" 6–3 *J. of Int'l. Crim. Justice* 507 (July 2008)

Spence, Cmdr. Mike, "Lessons for Combined Rules of Engagement," *U.S. Naval Institute Proceedings* (Oct. 2000)

Stafford, Lt.Col. W.A., "How to Keep Military Personnel from Going to Jail for Doing the Right Thing: Jurisdiction, ROE & the Rules of Deadly Force," *The Army Lawyer* (Nov. 2000)

Stavridis, Admiral James, and David Weinstein, "Time for a U.S. Cyber Force," U.S. Naval Institute *Proceedings* 40 (Jan. 2014)

Stewart, James G., "The Military Commissions Act's Inconsistency with the Geneva Conventions: An Overview, 5–1 *J. of Int'l Crim. Justice* 26 (March 2007)

Stevenson, John R., "United States Military Action in Cambodia: Questions of International Law," in Richard A. Falk, ed., vol. 3, *The Vietnam War and International Law* (Princeton NJ: Princeton University Press, 1972)

Subedi, Suurya P., "The Concept in Hinduism of 'Just War'," 8–2 *J. of Conflict & Security L.* (Oct. 2003)

Sutter, Philip, "The Continuing Role for Belligerent Reprisals," 13–1 *J. of Conflict & Security L.* 93 (Spring 2008)

Swann, Col. (Dr.) Steven, "Euthanasia on the Battlefield," 152(11) *Military Medicine* 546 (1987)

Tafur, Gabriel Chavez, "Using International Law to By-pass Domestic Legal Hurdles," 6–5 *J. of Int'l Crim. Justice* 1060 (Nov. 2008)

Taylor, Maj. Richard S., "The Capture versus Kill Debate: Is the Principle of Humanity Now Part of the Targeting Analysis When Attacking Civilians Who Are Directly Participating in Hostilities? *The Army Lawyer* (June 2010), 103

Thürer, Daniel, "Dunant's Pyramid: Thoughts on the 'Humanitarian Space'," 865 *Int'l Rev. of the Red Cross* 47 (March 2007)

Trainin, I.P., "Questions of Guerrilla Warfare in the Law of War,40–3 *AJIL* 534 (July 1946)

Tremblay, Col. E. Gerald, "Charles Lindbergh Saved My Life," *Marine Corps Gazette* (May 1990)

Tiunstra, Jarinde Temminck, "Defending the Defenders," 8–2 *J. of Int'l Crim Justice* 463 (May 2010)

Turns, David, "Weapons in the ICRC Study on Customary International Humanitarian Law," 11–2 *J. of Conflict & Security L.* 201 (Summer, 2006)

Utley, Robert M., "The Ordeal of Plenty Horses," 26–1 *American Heritage* (Dec. 1974)

van der Wilt, Harmen, "Genocide v. War Crimes in the *Van Anraat* Appeal," 6–3 *J. of Int'l Crim. Justice* 557 (July 2008)

Van Schaack, Beth, "The United States' Position on Extraterritorial Application of Human Rights Obligations: Now is the Time for Change," 90 *Int'l L. Stud.* 20, 22–23 (2014)

Verdier, Pierre-Hugues **and** Eric Voeten, "Precedent, Compliance, and Change in Customary International Law: an Explanatory Theory," 108–3 *AJIL* 389 (July 2014)

Verhaegen, Jaques, "Legal Obstacles to Prosecution of Breaches of Humanitarian Law," 261 *Int'l Rev. of the Red Cross* 607 (Nov.–Dec. 1987)

Villa, Sergio M., "The Philosophy of International Law: Suárez, Grotius and Epigones," 320 *Int'l. R. of the Red Cross* 324 (Oct. 1997)

Von der Groeben, Constantin, "The Conflict in Columbia and the Relationship Between Humanitarian Law and Human Rights Law in Practice," 16–1 *J. of Conflict & Security L.* 141 (Spring 2011)

von Heinegg, Wolff H., "Commentary," in Andru E. Wall, ed., *International Law Studies*, vol. 78, *Legal and Ethical Lessons of NATO's Kosovo Campaign* (Newport, RI: Naval War College, 2002)

Waldron, Jeremy, "Justifying Targeted Killing With A Neutral Principle?" in Claire Finkelstein, Jens David Ohlen and Andrew Altman, eds., *Targeted Killings: Law and Morality in an Asymmetrical World* (Oxford: Oxford University Press, 2012)

Walker, Clive, "Clamping Down on Terrorism in the United Kingdom," 4–5 *J. of Int'l Crim. Justice*, 1137 (Nov. 2006)

Wall, Illan Rua, "Duress, International Criminal Law and Literature," 4–4 *J. of Int'l Crim. Justice* 724 (Sept. 2006)

Wallace, Col. David A., "Torture v. the Basic Principles of the US Military," 6–2 *J. of Int'l Crim. Justice* 309 (May 2008)

Wallach, Evan, "Drop by Drop: Forgetting the History of Water Torture in U.S. Courts," 45–2 *Columbia J. of Transnational L.* 468 (2007)

Walsh, David C., "Friendless Fire," U.S. Naval Institute *Proceedings* (June 2003)

Walzer, Michael, "Two Kinds of Military Responsibility," in Lloyd J. Matthews and Dale E. Brown, eds., *The Parameters of Military Ethics* (VA: Pergamon-Brassey's, 1989)

Watkin, BGen. Kenneth, "Chemical Agents and Expanding Bullets: Limited Law Enforcement Exceptions or Unwarranted Handcuffs?", in Anthony M. Helm, ed., *International Law Studies*, vol. 82, *The Law of War in the 21st Century: Weaponry and the Use of Force* (Newport RI: Naval War College, 2006)

"Controlling the Use of Force: A Role for Human Rights Norms in Contemporary Armed Conflic," 98–1 *AJIL* 1 (Jan. 2004)

"Humans in the Cross-Hairs: Targeting and Assassination in Contemporary Armed Conflict," in David Wippman and Matthew Evangelista, eds. *New Wars, New*

Laws? Applying the Laws of War in 21st Century Conflicts (Ardsley, NY: Transnational, 2005)

"21st Century Conflict and International Humanitarian Law: Status Quo or Change?", in Michael N. Schmitt and Jelena Pejic, eds., *International Law and Armed Conflict: Exploring the Faultlines* (Leiden: Martinus Nijhoff, 2007)

Watts, Sean, "Combatant Status and Computer Network Attack," 50–2 *Virginia J. Int'l L.* 391 (2010)

Wedgwood, Ruth, "Responding to Terrorism: The Strikes Against bin Laden," 24 *Yale J. of Int'l L.* 559 (1999)

Weill, Sharon, "The Targeted Killing of Salah Shehadeh,7–3 *J. of Int'l Crim. Justice* 617 (July 2009)

Weingartner, James J., "Massacre at Biscari: Patton and an American War Crime," vol. LII, No. 1, *The Historian*, 24 (Nov. 1989)

Werrell, Kenneth P., "Across the Yalu: Rules of Engagement and the Communist Air Sanctuary During the Korean War," 72–2 *J. of Military History* 451 (April 2008)

Wheelis, Mark, "Will the New Biology Lead to New Weapons," *Arms Control Today* (July/ Aug. 2004)

White, Maj. Martin N., "Charging War Crimes: A Primer for the Practitioner," *The Army Lawyer* (Feb. 2006)

Whittle, Richard, "A Test, Not a Final Exam," U.S. Naval Institute *Proceedings* (Feb. 2008)

Wiebe, Virgil, "Footprints of Death: Cluster Bombs as Indiscriminate Weapons Under International Humanitarian Law," 22 *Mich. J. Int'l L.* 85 (2000)

Wiener, Col. Frederick Bernays, "Comment, *The Years of MacArthur*, Volume III: MacArthur Unjustifiably Accused of Meting Out 'Victor's Justice' in War Crimes Cases," 113 *Military L. Rev.* 203 (1986)

Williams, Robert D., "(Spy) Game Change: Cyber Networks, Intelligence Collection and Covert Action," 79–4 *George Washington L. Rev.* 1162 (June 2011)

Williams, Sarah and Lena Sherif, "The Arrest Warrant for President Al-Bashir," 14–1 *J. of Conflict & Security L.* 71 (Spring 2009)

Williams, Sharon A., "Laudable Principles Lacking Application: The Prosecution of War Criminals in Canada," in Timothy L.H. McCormack and Gerry J. Simpson, eds., *The Law of War Crimes* (The Hague: Kluwer Law Int'l, 1997)

Williamson, Jamie Allan, "Some Considerations on Command Responsibility and Criminal Liability," 870 *Int'l Rev. of the Red Cross* 303 (June 2008)

Wilmshurst, Elizabeth, "Conclusions," in Wilmshurst, ed., *International Law and the Classification of Conflicts*, 478 (Oxford: Oxford University Press, 2012)

Wilner, Alan M., "Superior Orders As A Defense to Violations of International Criminal Law," 26 *Maryland Law Review* 127 (1966)

Wylie, Neville, "The 1929 Prisoner of War Convention and the Building of the Inter-War Prisoner of War Regime," in Sibylle Scheipers, ed., *Prisoners of War* (Oxford: Oxford University Press, 2010)

Yoo, John, "Enemy Combatants and the Problem of Judicial Competence," in Peter Berkowitz, ed., *Terrorism, the Laws of War, and the Constitution* (Stanford, CA: Hoover Institution Press, 2005)

Yost, Mark J. and Douglas S. Anderson, "The Military Extraterritorial Jurisdiction Act of 2000: Closing the Gap," 95–2 *AJIL* 446, 447 (April 2001)

Zanders, Jean Pascal, "International Norms Against Chemical and Biological Warfare: An Ambiguous Legacy," 8–2 *J. of Conflict & Security L.* 391 (Oct. 2003)

Zhang, Li, "A Chinese Perspective on Cyber War," 94/886 *Int'l Rev. of the Red Cross* 801 (Summer, 2012)

Zwanenburg, Marten, and Guido den Dekker, "Supreme Court of the Netherlands," 104–1
     AJIL 91 (Jan. 2010)

U.S. Government and ICRC Articles/Documents Cited

ALMSC 017/06, Standing Rules for the Use of Force (SRUF) by MSC [Military Sealift
     Command] Personnel, (10 July 2006)
Assembly of the ICRC, Interpretive Guidance on the Notion of Direct Participation in
     Hostilities under International Humanitarian Law, 872 *Int'l Rev. of the Red Cross* 991
     (Dec. 2008)
Chairman of the Joint Chiefs of Staff Instruction 3121.01B, Standing Rules of Engagement/
     Standing Rules for the Use of Force for US Forces (13 June 2005)
     Instruction 5810.01, Implementation of the DOD Law of War Program (12 Aug. 1996)
Department of the Army, Army Regulation 15–6: Final Report; Investigation into FBI
     Allegations of Detainee Abuse at Guantanamo Bay, Cuba Detention Facility (1 April
     2005, amended 9 Jun 2005)
     Army Regulation 27–53, Review of the Legality of Weapons Under International Law (1
     Jan. 1979)
Department of Defense Directive 2310.01E, The Department of Defense Detainee Program
     (5 Sept. 2006)
     Directive 5100.77, DoD Law of War Program (9 Dec. 1998)
     Instruction 5525.11, Criminal Jurisdiction Over Civilians Employed by or Accompanying
     the Armed Forces Outside the United States, Certain Service Members, and Former
     Service Members (3 March 2005)
Department of Defense, Defense Science Board, Task Force Report: The Role of Autonomy
     in DoD Systems (July, 2012)
Executive Order 13440, Interpretation of the Geneva Conventions, Common Article 3 as
     Applied to a Program of Detention and Interrogation Operated by the Central Intelli-
     gence Agency (July 2007), cited at 101–4 *AJIL* 866 (Oct. 2007)
International Committee of the Red Cross," A Guide to the Legal Review of New Weapons,
     Means and Methods of Warfare," (Geneva: ICRC, 2006)
     "Conference of Government Experts on the Use of Certain Conventional Weapons,"
     (Geneva: ICRC, 1975)
     Doswald-Beck, Louise, ed., *Blinding Weapons* (Geneva: ICRC, 1993)
     "Expert Meeting on Procedural Safeguards for Security Detention in Non-international
     Armed Conflict," 91/876 *Int'l Rev. of the Red Cross* 859 (Dec. 2009)
     "ICRC Position on Hostage-Taking," 846 *Int'l Rev. of the Red Cross* 467 (June 2002)
     "International Humanitarian Law and the Challenges of Contemporary Armed Conflicts,"
     867 *Int'l Rev. of the Red Cross* 719 (Sept. 2007)
     "International Humanitarian Law and the Challenges of Contemporary Armed Conflicts,"
     Report Prepared for the 31st Int'l. Conference of the Red Cross and Red Crescent
     (Oct. 2011)
     "Internment in Armed Conflicts: Basic Rules and Challenges," Opinion Paper (Nov. 2014)
     "Interpretive Guidance on the Notion of Direct Participation in Hostilities Under Inter-
     national Humanitarian Law," 90/872 *Int'l Rev. of the Red Cross* 991 (Dec. 2008)
     "National implementation of international humanitarian law," 93–181 *Int'l Rev. of the Red
     Cross* 227 (March 2011
     "Protection of Cultural Property in the Event of Armed Conflict: Report on the Meeting of
     Experts," (Geneva: ICRC, 2002)

International Criminal Tribunal for the Former Yugoslavia, *Final Report to the Prosecutor by the Committee Established to Review the NATO Bombing Campaign Against the Federal Republic of Yugoslavia* (13 June 2000)

Military Advisory Command – Vietnam (MAC-V) Directive 20–5, Inspections and Investigations: Prisoner of War Determinations of Status (17 May 1966)

Senate Select Committee on Intelligence, *The Senate Select Committee Report on Torture* (Brooklyn NY: Melville House, 2014)

U.S. Air Force Policy Directive 51–4, Compliance With the Law of Armed Conflict (4 Aug. 2011)

U.S. Central Command Regulation 27–13, Captured Persons, Determination of Eligibility for Enemy Prisoner of War Status (7 Feb. 1995)

U.S. Marine Corps Order 3300.4A, "Marine Corps Law of War Program," (9 Jan. 2014)

U.S. Navy, SECNAVINST 3300.1B, Law of Armed Conflict (Law of War) Program To Ensure Compliance by the Naval Establishment (28 May, 2009)

Documentary Film

Ranucci, Sigfrido and Maurizio Torrealta, "Fallujah: The Hidden Massacre" (Italy: Radiotelevisione Italiana, 2005)

Index